AMERICAN
CONSTITUTIONAL
LAW

SEVENTH EDITION

AMERICAN CONSTITUTIONAL LAW

Introductory Essays and Selected Cases

ALPHEUS THOMAS MASON

Princeton University

WILLIAM M. BEANEY

University of Denver

DONALD GRIER STEPHENSON, JR.

Franklin and Marshall College

Prentice-Hall, Inc., Englewood Cliffs, N.J. 07632

Library of Congress Cataloging in Publication Data

MASON, ALPHEUS THOMAS
    American constitutional law.

    Bibliography.
    Includes index.
    1. United States—Constitutional law—Cases.
    I. Beaney, William Merritt,   II. Stephenson,
Donald Grier.   III. Title.
KF4549.M3   1983   342.73   82–5240
ISBN 0–13–024695–6   347.302   AACR2

Editorial/production supervision
  and interior design by Joyce Turner
Manufacturing buyer: Edmund W. Leone
Cover design by Edsal Enterprises

Printed in the United States of America

10   9   8   7   6   5   4   3   2

ISBN 0-13-024695-6

Prentice-Hall International, Inc., *London*
Prentice-Hall of Australia Pty. Limited, *Sydney*
Prentice-Hall Canada, Inc. *Toronto*
Prentice-Hall of India Private Limited, *New Delhi*
Prentice-Hall of Japan, Inc., *Tokyo*
Prentice-Hall of Southeast Asia Pte. Ltd., *Singapore*
Whitehall Books Limited, *Wellington, New Zealand*

For
Christine Gibbons Mason
Ellen Walker Stephenson
and
in memory of
Patricia Daniels Beaney

Contents

Three   CONGRESS, THE COURT, AND THE PRESIDENT   78

Four   FEDERALISM   139

Five   COMMERCE POWER AND STATE POWER   184

Six CONGRESSIONAL POWER UNDER THE COMMERCE CLAUSE   225

Seven NATIONAL TAXING AND SPENDING POWER   274

Ten   FIRST AMENDMENT FREEDOMS AND PRIVACY   471

Eleven   EQUAL PROTECTION OF THE LAWS   596

APPENDIX   659

INDEX OF CASES   675

Preface

This edition, following the pattern of earlier versions, is rooted in the conviction that constitutional law is an intricate blend of history and politics. Judicial decisions are but one of its dimensions. Others are the economic and political climate in which these are rendered and the theory that rationalizes both decision and social preference.

The Supreme Court does not function in a vacuum. Besides briefs of counsel, it is influenced by the giants of American constitutional interpretation—Kent, Story, Cooley, Thayer. More perhaps than any other commentator of his time, Edward S. Corwin illustrates his incisive observation: "If judges make law, so do commentators." This book owes a great debt to him.

A distinctive feature is the introductory essay preceding each chapter, which supplies the historical and political context and traces the meandering thread of constitutional doctrine through major decisions. Sparingly selected cases are set in this variegated framework. Although relatively small in number, the cases feature generous excerpts, not snippets.

To a greater extent than earlier editions, this one includes relevant extrajudicial material. The student is thus alerted to illuminating debates, sometimes unstaged, outside the Court room: Alexander Hamilton and Robert Yates's sharply divergent prognoses concerning the possible consequences of judicial review; differences as to the judicial function echoed in the Marshall-Gibson encounter, a refrain that still divides the councils of the judiciary; Jefferson and Madison's drive for a Bill of Rights in the face of Hamilton and James Wilson's vigorous refutation of its necessity; David J. Brewer's fervent advocacy in 1893 of a "strengthened judiciary" and James Bradley Thayer's closely reasoned plea that the Court resist "stepping into the shoes of the lawmaker" lest it lose its "great and stately jurisdiction." Justice Cardozo's unpublished concurring opinion in the Minnesota Moratorium case of 1934 and Justice Frankfurter's letter of 1940 to Justice Stone regarding the first Flag Salute case, reproduced in chapters 8 and 10, respectively, portray an essential ingredient in the decision-making process, judicial bargaining.

In chapter 2, the coupling of Justice Sutherland's dissent from *West Coast Hotel* v. *Parrish* (1937) with the opinions by Justices Roberts and Stone from *United States* v. *Butler* (1936) bring into juxtaposition three theories of judicial review. The separate opinions of Justices Douglas and Marshall from *DeFunis* v. *Odegaard* (1974) and *Regents* v. *Bakke* (1978), respectively, paired in chapter 11, illustrate the constitutional schism on affirmative action.

The goal of this broad approach is better understanding of the present in light of the past and of the past in light of the present. Revealed, among other things, is the Supreme Court as participant in the governing process. The latitude of choice open to the justices is underscored not only by the inclusion of concurring and dissenting opinions but also by Madison's penetrating *Federalist* essays, numbers 37, 47–48, and 51, included in chapter 3. For Madison, constitutional issues are complicated because lines of demarcation between nation and state, and between President, Congress, and Court, to say nothing of the barriers between liberty and authority at all levels, are faint, obscure, and speculative. Definition and interpretation encounter other obstacles: "complexity of the subject," "imperfection of the organs of perception," and "inadequacy of the vehicle of ideas." The result is that under the impact of various pressures, judicial decisions reflect the sometimes capricious selection of hard alternatives rather than the easy dictate of a brooding omnipresence or soulless command of mechanics.

No casebook, however current, can ever be completely abreast of Supreme Court action. This handicap is not insuperable; it can be easily overcome by making available at the outset copies of major cases, say three or four, that have come down since the book went to press. In this way the student is introduced not only to current issues but also to the Court's present membership and its divergent approaches to constitutional interpretation. Thus, interest in the subject is stimulated by catering to students' overweening desire for "relevancy."

Many persons cooperated in shaping the contents and organization of this book. Through the years since publication of the first edition in 1954, users, teachers and students alike, contributed to its betterment. Their suggestions, reflected in both omissions and additions, indicate the measure of our indebtedness.

Typing help in generous portions came from Mrs. Rose Musser and Mrs. Enid Hirsch of the Department of Government at Franklin and Marshall College. Mr. Robert W. Shely (1982) assisted with the index and in other ways as well. Funds for preparation of the manuscript were provided by Franklin and Marshall College.

A.T.M.
D.G.S., Jr.

AMERICAN
CONSTITUTIONAL
LAW

Introduction
to the Seventh Edition

"... [W]e must never forget that it is a *constitution* we are expounding." With this commanding reminder, serviceable to Supreme Court Justices and students of constitutional interpretation, Chief Justice Marshall interrupted a closely reasoned argument in *McCulloch* v. *Maryland.* He did not pause to spell out what he had in mind. His meaning emerges from other passages in the opinion.

The Constitution, more than mere words, is a constituent act, a dictate of the people. The preamble, though no part of the Constitution, sheds significant light on its meaning, indicating goals and purposes. It was designed to form a more perfect union, *union* without *unity,* to provide for the common defense, to establish justice, and to promote the general welfare. The Constitution resulted from "a very great exertion," "not frequently to be repeated." Nor would this be necessary if its provisions received the broad interpretation consistent with the great objectives for which it was established.

Central to the permanency of the Constitution has been the United States Supreme Court, an institution blending contradictions. From John Marshall to Warren Burger, the Justices have been the guardians of particular interests and the promoters of preferred values. Nevertheless, the myth articulated by Chief Justice Marshall endures: "Courts are the mere instruments of the law, and can will nothing," he wrote in *Osborn* v. *Bank of the United States* (9 Wheat. 738: 1824). Accordingly, constitutional interpretation consists in the discovery of meaning clear only to judges. The Supreme Court's version of the Constitution, unlike that of any other organ or agency of government, has the special virtue of never mangling or changing the original instrument. Professor Corwin put it this way: "The *juristic* conception of judicial review invokes a miracle. It supposes a kind of transubstantiation whereby the Court's opinion of the Constitution becomes the very body and blood of the Constitution."

I

America's major contributions to the governing process—judicial review and federalism, inextricably interwoven, both addressed to imponderables—are rooted in the prerevolutionary struggle that led to independence and in the shortcomings of John Locke's imaginary civil society.

John Locke, sometimes identified as the Karl Marx of American constitutionalism, postulated that the legislature, though supreme, would be bound by both the laws of nature and "promulgated established Laws." But Locke provided no organ of government for resolving conflicts between the two levels of law. Confronted with this inescapable clash, the apologist for Britain's Glorious Revolution took refuge in circular reasoning.

> As there can be none (Judge on Earth) between the Legislative and the People, should either
> the Executive or the Legislative, when they have got power in their hands, design, or go about
> to enslave, or destroy them, the People have no other remedy than this, as in other cases when
> they have no Judge on Earth, but to Appeal to Heaven (apparently a euphemism for revolution).

The Constitution's Framers, facing up to Locke's dilemma, provided in the Supreme Court a terrestrial forum for the peaceful resolution of conflicts, thus institutionalizing revolution.

Revolution is America's birthright. "It is," Madison observed, "the only lawful tenure by which the United States hold their existence as a Nation." Since they could not, consistently or gracefully, turn their backs on the right of revolution, it was incumbent on the Framers to attempt accommodation.

John Marshall not only recognized and upheld judicial review prior to ratification of the Constitution, but also suggested judicial review as a peaceful alternative to violent revolution. In the Virginia Ratifying Convention, he said: "What is the service or purpose of a judiciary, but to execute the laws in a peaceful, orderly manner, without shedding

2

blood, or creating a contest, or availing yourselves of force? To what quarter will you look for protection from an infringement of the Constitution, if you will not give power to the judiciary? There is no other body that can afford such protection.''

Since 1789 America has experienced no less than six revolutions, all so designated, all peaceful, except the Civil War. In all these transformations, including the Civil War, the Supreme Court played the role John Marshall had anticipated in the Virginia Ratifying Convention of 1788. The Constitution may fairly be regarded as the completion, or continuation, of the Revolution of 1776.

As to judicial review itself, the fourth Chief Justice was quite specific. In the Virginia Ratifying Convention, he said:

> If Congress makes a law not warranted by any of the powers enumerated, it would be considered by the judges as an infringement of the Constitution which they are to guard. They would not consider such a law coming within their jurisdiction. They would declare it void.

Borrowing from Montesquieu, the Framers built separation of powers into the Constitution. But the American version of Montesquieu's plan meant that separate institutions shared powers and responsibilities. Divided powers thus invited judicial review. But how could the Supreme Court, itself a creation of the Constitution, not only determine the constitutional limits of coequal organs of government but also decide the scope of its own power? The answer is that judicial review, in both theory and practice, carries with it the power to stamp the Constitution with a final interpretation, binding all organs of government with the authority of the document itself.

Robert Yates, Convention delegate from New York, and a nonsigner of the Constitution, probed the realities and predicted that judicial review, which he took for granted, would enable the justices "to mould the government into almost any shape they please. . . . Men placed in this situation will generally soon feel themselves independent of Heaven itself.''

Yates had raised a hard question and made a serious charge. To answer it, Hamilton fused reason and magic. Judicial review, he argued in *Federalist* No. 78, does not suppose "a superiority of the judicial to the legislative power. It only supposes that the power of the people (whose will the Constitution embodies) is superior to both Legislative and Court.'' Thanks to judicial review, the "intentions of the people" would prevail over "the intentions of their agents.'' Hamilton, apparently realizing that such reasoning bordered on magic, went the whole way toward legerdemain: "It may be truly said that the judiciary has neither force nor will, but merely judgment.''

In exercising this high authority the judges claim no supremacy: they claim only to administer the public will. If an act of the legislature is held void, it is not because judges have any control over legislative power but because the act is forbidden by the Constitution and because the will of the people, which is declared supreme, is paramount to that of their representatives. Hence the ideal government of laws and not of men. Hence also the intriguing paradox of judicial review: While wearing the magical habiliments of the law, Supreme Court Justices take sides on vital social and political issues. Although still questioned, one of the oldest tenets in American constitutional jurisprudence is that a judicial decision is equivalent to the Constitution and is, therefore, unchangeable by an ordinary act of Congress. If changed, it must be accomplished by the judges themselves or the amending process.

Like judicial review, federalism also was designed to remedy difficulties encountered before 1776. Patriot John Adams and loyalist Daniel Leonard agreed that *imperium in imperio* was a condition to be avoided at all cost. "Two supreme and independent authorities cannot exist in the same state," Adams wrote, "any more than two supreme beings in one universe." Leonard denounced *imperium in imperio* as the "height of political absurdity," and compared it to "two distinct principles of volition and action in the human body, dissenting, opposing, and destroying each other."

Ironically, this was precisely the situation that the prerevolutionary debate boiled down to. In order to avoid *imperium in imperio*, loyalists argued that the Parliament had to be accorded supreme power. Advocates of independence claimed the same prerogative for the provincial legislatures. No compromise seemed possible. Hence revolution and independence.

The effect was not to solve the problem posed by *imperium in imperio*, but merely to compound it and transfer it to this side of the Atlantic. By declaring that "each state retains its sovereignty, freedom, and independence," the Articles of Confederation created precisely the political absurdity Adams and Leonard deplored. As to the Articles of Confederation, Hamilton commented derisively: "They seem to cherish with blind devotion the political monster of an *imperium in imperio*." Deploring gross inadequacies, John Quincy Adams observed: "The work of the founders of our independence was but half done. For these United States, they had formed no constitution. Instead of resorting to the source of all constituted power (the people) they had wasted their time, their talent, . . . in erecting and roofing and buttressing a frail and temporary shed when they should raise the marble palace to shelter the nation from the storm."

Trying experience under the Articles of Confederation and the new state constitutions made democracy, including its primary tenet, majority rule, suspect. Experience merely confirmed history. "Remember," John Adams warned, "democracy never lasts long. It soon wastes, exhausts, and murders itself. There never was a democracy yet that did not commit suicide."

What the Framers established was not "democracy the most simple" but "the most complicated government on the face of the globe." They called their creation Free Government. More easily described than defined, it involves a complexus of controls designed to temper together into one consistent work the sometimes opposite, sometimes complementary elements of liberty and restraint.

Federalism fits into this pattern. By 1860, it became clear that, as the Framers' most significant creation, it contained within it an inescapable ambiguity, obvious in the blueprint Madison fashioned six weeks before the Philadelphia Convention assembled. Anticipating that "some leading proposition would be expected from Virginia," he wrote Governor Edmund Randolph,

> I hold it for a fundamental point, that an individual independence of the States is utterly irreconcilable with the idea of an aggregate sovereignty. I think, at the same time, that a consolidation of the States into one simple republic is not less unattainable than it would be inexpedient. Let it be tried, then, whether any *middle ground* can be taken, which will at once support a *due supremacy* of the national authority, and leave in force the local authorities so far as they can be *subordinately* useful. (Italics added.)

A carpenter would hesitate to begin construction of a house with drawings so imprecise as Madison carried to the Constitutional Convention. However, the delegates were in Philadelphia not to build a house but to erect a federal system of government—union without unity.

The essence of Madison's blueprint was abandonment of sovereignty as an attribute of either government, state or national. Not unnaturally, the Supreme Court seized the first opportunity to announce the uniqueness of American federalism. As Justice Wilson, a member of the Federal Convention, declared in *Chisholm* v. *Georgia,*

> To the Constitution of the United States the term sovereign is totally unknown. There is but one place where it could have been used with propriety. But, even in that place, it would not, perhaps, have comported with the delicacy of those who ordained and established that constitution. They might have announced themselves ''sovereign'' people of the United States: but serenely conscious of the fact, they avoided the ostentatious declaration.

For Justice Wilson, as for Chief Justice Marshall, the states were merely ''convenient meeting places'' for the people of America in the ratification process. Nevertheless, the states continued to be referred to as ''sovereign.''

Just as years of debate preceding independence proved powerless to resolve the issue of sovereignty between Britain and the colonies, so decades of discussion on the political platform, in Congress, on the hustings, and in the Supreme Court were unable to tame *imperium in imperio.*

In *Federalist,* No. 22, Hamilton had denounced as ''gross heresy'' the notion that ''a party to a *compact* has a right to revoke that *compact.*'' Nullification and secession—state sovereignty asserted in its boldest form—proclaimed the heresy Hamilton had deplored. The constitutional response was the series of Civil War amendments, particularly the Fourteenth. Framed in the most sweeping terms by a radical Republican Congress, the latter was designed, apparently, to clip the wings of state sovereignty once and for all. Directed explicitly to the states, that amendment declares that ''no state shall make or enforce any law which shall abridge the privileges and immunities of citizens of the United States, nor shall any state deprive any person of life, liberty, or property without due process of law, nor deny to any person within its jurisdiction equal protection of the laws.'' The clear intention was to make new restrictions—arguably the first eight amendments—binding on the states and enforceable by Congress and the federal courts.

Yet in its first look at this amendment (The Slaughterhouse Cases), the Supreme Court emasculated its major provisions—''privileges and immunities,'' ''due process,'' ''equal protection.'' For a majority of five, Justice Miller's explanation bordered on apology.

> The argument we admit is not always the most conclusive which is drawn from the consequences urged against the adoption of a particular construction of an instrument. But when, as in the case before us, these consequences are so serious, so far-reaching and pervading, so great a departure from the structure and spirit of our institutions; when the effect is to fetter and degrade the state governments by subjecting them to the control of Congress, in the exercise of powers heretofore universally conceded to them of the most ordinary and fundamental character; when, in fact, it radically changes the whole theory of the relations of the State and Federal governments to each other, and both of these governments to the people; the argument has a force that is irresistible, in the absence of language which expresses such a purpose too clearly to admit of doubt.

Justice Miller's sensitivity to a theory of federal-state relations, presumably established in 1789, is such that, despite the amendment's all-embracing injunctions against state power vis-à-vis individual rights, he shrinks from the belief that the Congress, which framed the Fourteenth Amendment, intended to alter that relationship. Any such change, even by amendment, seemed suspect. In a vehement dissenting opinion, Justice Field charged that the Court's restrictive interpretation reduced the Fourteenth Amendment to a nullity.

Since then, constitutional interpretation has regarded the Fourteenth Amendment as anything but "a vain and idle enactment." The Court has invigorated the Bill of Rights and has applied its strictures to the states. Moreover, the Justices have taken the generalities of the amendment as invitation to enlarge the content of liberty beyond the particulars urged by Madison in the first eight amendments.

When the Civil War was over, the Supreme Court was confronted with a practical question—whether during that conflict Texas was out of the Union. Chief Justice Chase replied in the negative, fashioning a theory of federalism that practically restated the Madisonian formula of 1787.

> The preservation of the States, and the maintenance of their governments, are as much within the design and care of the Constitution as the preservation of the Union and the maintenance of the National government. The Constitution, in all its provisions, looks to an indestructible Union of indestructible States.

By judicial fiat, if not by constitutional amendment, America's "Appeal to Heaven" left federalism virtually intact. A theory of the Union which reason could not establish was won by resort to force. What John Quincy Adams said of the Constitution was equally applicable to the Union. It had to be "extorted from the grinding necessities of a reluctant nation."

II

Judicial review is not merely magic steeped in politics. Like federalism, it is an institution of government. The years since 1968, in several ways among the most remarkable in judicial history, highlight these aspects.

On June 26, 1968, President Lyndon Johnson announced Chief Justice Earl Warren's intention to resign. The next day the President nominated Associate Justice Abe Fortas to succeed the controversial Chief Justice. With the exception of President Washington's recess appointee, John Rutledge, whom the Senate refused to confirm in 1795, only two associate justices had been advanced to the center chair—Edward Douglass White in 1910 and Harlan Fiske Stone in 1941. Accusing President Johnson of "cronyism," opposition formed immediately.

Fortas was charged with various improprieties, including participation in White House strategy conferences on the Vietnam War, and acceptance of high lecture fees raised by wealthy business executives who happened to be clients of Fortas's former law partner, Paul Porter. After four days, the Senate voted 45 to 43 to cut off debate, 14 votes short of the two-thirds necessary to end the anti-Fortas filibuster. Two days later the ill-fated Justice withdrew his name. For the first time, nomination of a Supreme Court Justice had been blocked by a Senate filibuster.

It was a Pyrrhic victory. For the time being, critics of the Warren Court had to reconcile themselves to the continued presence of Chief Justice Warren. "If they don't confirm Abe," the Chief Justice commented cheerfully, while Fortas's fate hung in the balance, "they will have me." So they did for one more year.

When the Senate blocked Fortas's nomination. President Johnson refused to submit another name. L. B. J., a lame duck president, left this high level appointment to President Richard M. Nixon.

Finding himself in precisely the same situation in 1801, President John Adams, much to Thomas Jefferson's chagrin, followed an altogether different course. A few weeks before he left the White House, Adams named Secretary of State John Marshall Chief

Justice of the United States. If Adams had taken President Johnson's route, Chief Justice Ellsworth's successor probably would have been the ardent defender of states' rights, Spencer Roane. In that event, history during the crucial formative years would have been drastically altered, perhaps for the worse.

Appointment of a chief justice is a rare occurrence. There have been 39 presidents, only 15 chief justices. John Marshall sat in the Court's center chair 34 years, from 1801 to 1835. During that time there were six presidents. The contrast is significant substantively as well as statistically, a fact that prompted John Quincy Adams to rate the office of Chief Justice as "more important than that of President."

The most impressive recent illustration of the comparatively greater impact of the Chief Justiceship is the regime of Earl Warren (1953–1969). His Court initiated a revolution. Chief Justice Warren's activism during the quiescent Eisenhower years is measured by Ike's latter-day lament: "The biggest damn fool mistake I ever made."

President Nixon's first step toward fulfilling his 1968 campaign promise to strengthen the "peace forces as against the criminal forces of the country," was the selection of Warren Earl Burger, 61, Chief Judge, U.S. Circuit Court of Appeals, District of Columbia.

Judge Burger's confirmation, June 9, 1969, by a vote of 74 to 3, was hasty—almost pro forma. Earl Warren waited five months for the Senate vote, Burger only 18 days. As a circuit court judge, Burger had commented: "The nature of our system, which seems to have escaped notice occasionally, must make manifest to judges that we are neither gods nor godlike, but judicial officers with narrow and limited authority."

In the spring of 1969, *Life* magazine revealed that Justice Fortas had received a yearly $20,000 fee from the Family Foundation of Louis Wolfson, then serving a prison term for selling unregistered stock. Once again judicial fat was in the political fire. Fortas's resignation, May 16, 1969, opened the way for President Nixon's nomination of Clement F. Haynsworth, Jr., Chief Judge, U.S. Circuit Court of Appeals, Fourth Circuit. As a circuit court judge, Haynsworth had taken a restrictive view of school desegregation and had also been insensitive to proprieties in ways that involved finance and conflict of interest. After weeks of heated debate the Senate, in a surprise vote, rejected the President's nominee 55 to 45.

The Senate's rejection of Haynsworth strengthened President Nixon's determination to "pack" the Court with "strict constructionists." His next nominee, G. Harrold Carswell, had served seven years as a federal district judge in Tallahassee, and six months on the U.S. Court of Appeals, Fifth Circuit. In 1948, he had said: "I yield to no man as a fellow candidate [he was then running for political office] or as a fellow citizen in the firm, vigorous belief in the principles of White Supremacy, and I shall always be so governed."

Quite apart from Judge Carswell's avowed racism (which he now disavowed), critics charged that President Nixon's nominee was in fact mediocre. Accepting the criticism, Nebraska Senator Hruska tried to convert it into an asset: "Even if he is mediocre, there are a lot of mediocre judges and people and lawyers. They are entitled to a little representation, aren't they, and a little chance? We can't have all Brandeises, Cardozos and Frankfurters and stuff like that there."

Judge Carswell was rejected 51 to 45. Even prominent members of the President's own party voted against him. To fill the place vacated by Justice Fortas, President Nixon turned to Chief Justice Burger's longtime Minnesota friend, Judge Harry A. Blackmun of the Court of Appeals for the Eighth Circuit. A product of Harvard College and Harvard Law School and former counsel to the Mayo Clinic, Blackmun aroused little opposition and was promptly confirmed and sworn in on June 9, 1970, too late to participate in any of the term's decisions.

Defenders of Judges Haynsworth and Carswell, piqued by defeat, launched a counteroffensive, calling for the impeachment of libertarian Justice William O. Douglas. When Congressman Gerald Ford, spearhead of the drive, was asked to define "impeachable offense," he replied: "The only honest answer is that an impeachable offense is whatever a majority of the House of Representatives considers it to be at a given moment in history; conviction results from whatever offense or offenses two-thirds of the other body considers to be sufficiently serious to require removal of the accused from office." Ford's definition was not unprecedented. When, with President Jefferson's support, impeachment proceedings were instigated against Justice Samuel Chase, Senator Giles explained:

> A trial and removal of a judge upon impeachment need not imply any criminality or corruption in him . . . [but] was nothing more than a declaration of Congress to this effect: You hold dangerous opinions, and if you are suffered to carry them into effect you will work the destruction of the nation. *We want your offices,* for the purpose of giving them to men who will fill them better.

Applied to Justice Douglas, this open-ended definition failed.

In the fall of 1970, the *New York Times* reported that President Nixon was still determined to appoint a Southerner to the Supreme Court. The most likely spot to be vacated was that occupied by 84-year-old Justice Black. Asked for his reaction to the President's unswerving determination, Justice Black replied: "I think it would be nice to have *another* Southerner up here."

In June 1971, Justice Black selected his law clerks for the 1971–72 term, a sure sign that he intended to carry on. The Justice had moved into third place in length of service. The longevity goal was in sight; fate defeated its realization. In September 1971, Justices Black and Harlan, both ailing, resigned within days of each other. Hugo Black died on September 25, 1971. If Black could have remained on the bench eight months longer, he would have exceeded John Marshall's and Stephen J. Field's record, having served 34 years, 6 months, and 13 days.

In October 1971, Richard Nixon enjoyed an opportunity no president had experienced since 1940—that of simultaneously filling two Supreme Court vacancies. The President nominated Lewis F. Powell, Jr., 64, a distinguished Richmond lawyer, and William H. Rehnquist, 47, law clerk, 1952–53, to the late Justice Robert H. Jackson, and the Nixon administration's assistant attorney general in charge of the Office of Legal Counsel.

Powell, arousing little or no objections, was confirmed, 89 to 1, emphatically disproving Nixon's widely publicized lament of 1969 that the Senate, as then constituted, would not confirm a Southerner. Rehnquist ran into stormy waters. Among other things, critics charged that he had supported curtailment of defendants' rights in criminal cases, use of electronic surveillance, preventive detention, and "no knock" police entry. He had proclaimed practically unlimited war power for the President and sanctioned mass arrest of demonstrators. Confronted with these barbed attacks, Rehnquist told the Judiciary Committee: "My fundamental commitment, if I am confirmed will be to totally disregard my own personal belief." Rehnquist received Senate approval on December 10, 1971, 68 to 26.

With the confirmation of Powell and Rehnquist, the Court had a full complement of Justices—four of them Nixon appointees.

The Court's personnel remained unchanged until November, 1975, when President Ford nominated John Paul Stevens, a 55-year-old Federal Appeals Court judge, seventh circuit, to fill the vacancy created by the retirement of William O. Douglas. The previous New Year's Eve Douglas had suffered a stroke. He had served 36 years on the high bench, surpassing the record long held by John Marshall and Stephen J. Field.

Justice Douglas's reluctance to retire raised again the thorny question of how to remove an incapacitated Supreme Court Justice. The Constitution supplies no answer, but history does. On more than one occasion, the power of persuasion exerted on a faltering justice by the Court itself has proved effective.

In 1869, Associate Justice Field convinced Justice Grier that he was too ill to continue. Later, when Justice Field became incapacitated, Justice Harlan asked his colleague whether he remembered urging Grier to retire. "Yes," Field snapped, "and a dirtier day's work I never did in my life." (Charles Evans Hughes, *The Supreme Court of the United States*, 1928, pp. 75–76.) After Justice McKenna's all too obvious demonstration of mental slowdown, Chief Justice Taft reluctantly persuaded him to retire. Justice Holmes, older than McKenna, then a bystander, was sure he would be "intellectually honest in judging my condition and my product." But the 91-year-old Justice gave up only after Chief Justice Hughes requested him to do so. Ignoring or eluding pressure from whatever source, Justice Douglas reached his own decision, on November 12, 1975, to leave the Court, almost a year after he was stricken. His death came in January 1980.

Douglas's successor, though relatively unknown, seemed eminently qualified. He had established a brilliant academic record. After graduating first in his class at Northwestern University Law School, he served two years as Supreme Court Justice Rutledge's law clerk. The customary labels do not seem to fit. "He's a first-rate lawyer, a first-rate judge, and a first-rate man. What more can you ask?" constitutional law professor Philip Kurland commented. The Senate quickly concurred; on December 19, 1975, Stevens was sworn in.

Ford's successor in the White House was Jimmy Carter, whose one-term administration had mixed impact on the federal judiciary. In one respect, Carter's influence will survive long after his presidency. He was able to make more appointments to the district and appeals courts than any other president in history, thanks in part to a Democratic Congress willing to enlarge both benches substantially. Moreover, while not overlooking the importance of merit, Carter also appointed more females and nonwhites to the federal courts than all of his predecessors combined. In another respect, however, Carter's influence was nil. When his successor took the oath of office on January 20, 1981, Carter became the first president to serve *at least* a full four-year term who did not have the opportunity to fill a single vacancy on the Supreme Court. Even James Garfield, who served less than a year before he was assassinated, was able to appoint Justice Stanley Matthews.

Jimmy Carter's years in the White House did witness an unusual event affecting the Supreme Court: publication in 1979 of *The Brethren*. Authored by newspaper sleuths Bob Woodward and Scott Armstrong, the book purported to reveal the inside scoop on the Court from 1969 to 1976. Controversial in its sources of information and absence of documentation, but unremarkable in its findings, the volume underscored the need for authoritative studies of the Court, drawn largely from material supplied by the Justices themselves.

The judiciary figured in the national campaign of 1980 in a way it did not in 1976 when Jimmy Carter wrested the presidency from Gerald Ford. The Republicans had good reason to be wary of judicial appointments at all levels. Along with everyone else they noted that five years had passed without a Supreme Court vacancy on a bench where more than half the Justices were above seventy years of age. Moreover, the Court only seven years before had injected itself into the most divisive of contemporary moral issues by declaring abortion to be a constitutional right. Three Nixon appointees had voted with the majority, and one of them—Justice Blackmun—had written the majority opinion. This case alone was reminder enough that recent Republican presidents had not been notably adept in picking nominees who accorded with their political views. Warren, Brennan, Blackmun, and Stevens had all proven to be ''surprises'' in various ways. This time, conservative Republicans wanted to be more careful.

The Republican platform therefore called for judges ''who respect traditional family values and the sanctity of innocent human life.'' The second part was a code word for opposition to abortion. Opponents to the Republicans and to candidate Ronald Reagan organized the Committee for an Independent Judiciary and Americans Concerned for the Judiciary. The first warned that a Reagan presidency ''threatens disastrous results.'' The second labeled Reagan as ''a serious threat to the independence and non-partisan nature of our Federal Judiciary.'' There were fears that Reagan, if elected, would be a pawn of The Moral Majority, a political force of the religious right.

Denounced by the National Organization for Women for ''medieval stances on women's issues,'' Reagan confounded the campaign by promising to name a woman to fill one of ''the first Supreme Court vacancies in my administration.''

As if to accommodate, the Justices dropped the notation ''Mr. Justice'' in their orders on November 18, replacing it simply with ''Justice.'' As the most junior member, Justice Stevens relayed the message to the Clerk's Office but declined to discuss with the press the reasons for the change. ''You can probably guess,'' he acknowledged.

Near the close of the 1980–81 term, President Reagan had his chance. But it was not one of the more elderly Justices who provided the opportunity. At age 66, Potter Stewart, appointed by President Eisenhower in 1958 and long regarded as a ''swing vote'' among the Justices, announced his retirement on June 18, 1981. To replace Stewart, Deputy White House Press Secretary Larry Speakes said the President would search for candidates who ''share one key view: the role of the court is to interpret the law and not to enact new law by judicial fiat.''

Reagan's choice for a successor was Judge Sandra Day O'Connor, age 51, of the Arizona Court of Appeals, who had been a law student with Justice Rehnquist at Stanford University (he finished first, she third, in the class of 1952). Not only was Judge O'Connor to be the first woman to sit on the High Court, she was the first since Brennan to have had experience as a state judge. More significantly perhaps, she was the first since Justice Harold Burton, Stewart's predecessor, to have served as a state legislator. State legislative experience has become uncommon in the background of Supreme Court Justices. Of the 45 justices who have gone on the Court in the twentieth century, only four others fall into this category.

''[W]ithout a doubt,'' said President Reagan announcing her nomination, ''the most awesome appointment a President can make is to the United States Supreme Court. Those who sit on the Supreme Court interpret the laws of our land and truly do leave their footprints in the sands of time, long after the policies of Presidents, Senators and Congressmen of a given era may have passed from public memory.'' Criticized by some for injecting gender into justice, Reagan's fulfillment of a campaign pledge placed him squarely in established tradition: other presidents have considered region, religion, and race in making appointments to the Court.

Questions about Judge O'Connor shortly developed—from the right. The Moral Majority and "right-to-life" groups claimed that she was "unsound" on abortion. The debate temporarily split political conservatives. Possessing impeccable conservative credentials, Senator Barry Goldwater of Arizona called on "all good Christians" to kick the leader of The Moral Majority in his posterior. Opponents to the O'Connor nomination were clearly looking beyond her to other opportunities Reagan might have. "I'm not sure we'll defeat her," said Peter Gemma of the National Pro-Life Political Action Committee. "But we want to send the President a clear signal at how much of an insult this is, and how his next appointment had better be pro-life."

Opposition remained more outside than inside the Senate, where she was confirmed 99–0 on September 21. "There is a huge amount of whistling in the graveyard about what kind of Justice Judge O'Connor will be," opined Senator Biden of Delaware. ". . . I believe we should caution the electorate that even if they want us to apply a litmus test, . . . it is not something we can do very well; because once a Justice dons that robe and walks into that sanctum across the way, we have no control, and that is how it should be. . . . They are a separate, independent, and equal branch of Government, and all bets are off." Early assessments—often woefully inaccurate with respect to Supreme Court nominees—considered her at once "flexible" and "tough," with a tendency to be resistant to claims of criminal defendants, to be deferential to legislators and lower court judges, but not to be bound rigidly to a conservative philosophy. As a participant in a symposium on "State Courts and Federalism in the 1980s," held in January of 1981, she was on record as declaring,

> State judges in assuming office take an oath to support the federal as well as the state constitution. State judges do in fact rise to the occasion when given the responsibility and opportunity to do so. It is a step in the right direction to defer to the state courts and give finality to their judgments on federal constitutional questions where a *full* and *fair* adjudication has been given in the state court.
>
> The jurisdiction of state courts to decide federal constitutional questions cannot be removed by congressional action, whereas the federal court jurisdiction can be shaped or removed by Congress. Proposals are sometimes made to restrict federal court jurisdiction over certain types of cases or issues. Among the proposals which have merit from the perspective of a state court judge are the elimination or restriction of federal court diversity jurisdiction, and a requirement of exhaustion of state remedies as a prerequisite to bringing a federal action under section 1983. If we are serious about strengthening our state courts and improving their capacity to deal with federal constitutional issues, then we will not allow a race to the courthouse to determine whether an action will be heard first in the federal or state court. We should allow the state courts to rule first on the constitutionality of state statutes. (Sandra D. O'Connor, "Trends in the Relationship Between the Federal and State Courts from the Perspective of a State Court Judge," 22 *William and Mary Law Review* 801, 814–15: 1981.)

If Judge O'Connor's nomination calmed the fears of those who had used the Court issue to oppose Reagan in the campaign, actions in Congress by fellow Republicans and conservative Democrats did not. Incensed by Warren and Burger Court rulings on school busing, school prayer, and abortion, court-curbing measures surfaced in Congress. These were designed to remove the Court's jurisdiction entirely to consider such matters or, in their most adventuresome form, to attempt to overrule the Court directly. The Court's political vulnerability in the constitutional system again came into sharp focus. Now, perhaps more than at any other time since 1937, the Supreme Court is the "storm center" of politics.

SELECTED READINGS

FUNSTON, RICHARD Y., *Constitutional Counter-Revolution? The Warren Court and the Burger Court: Judicial Policy Making in Modern America.* Cambridge, Mass.: Schenkman, 1977.

MASON, ALPHEUS T., "America's Political Heritage: A Bicentennial Tribute," 91 *Political Science Quarterly* 193 (1976). This is reprinted as chapter 1 in *American Political Institutions in the 1970s, A Political Science Quarterly Reader,* ed. Demetrios Caraley. New York: Columbia University Press, 1976; and as chapter 1 in *Essays on the Constitution of the United States,* ed. M. Judd Harmon. Port Washington, N.Y.: Kennikat Press, 1978.

SHOGAN, ROBERT, *A Question of Judgment; the Fortas Case and the Struggle for the Supreme Court.* Indianapolis: Bobbs-Merrill, 1972.

ONE

Jurisdiction
and Organization
of the Federal Courts

American constitutional law represents a tiny fraction of the entire corpus of the law. Run-of-the-mill litigation between private parties seldom falls into the category of ''cases'' to which the judicial power of the Supreme Court extends. Even cases involving constitutional questions may be sidestepped. The Court decides, as we shall see, only those cases which meet certain prescribed standards. The Supreme Court of the United States is not ''a super legal aid bureau.''

This chapter presents certain rules and procedures guiding the Justices in choosing the cases they will decide and sketches the major steps in the decision-making process. The rules and decisions governing jurisdiction and standing to sue vest in the Justices' considerable discretionary power. They control their workload by selecting the cases that require judicial remedy at the highest level. By perusing these rules one may better understand why a relatively small area of governmental activity is subject to judicial review. In the governing process, the Supreme Court has an important, though circumscribed, role to play. What follows, though somewhat technical, is essential to understanding.

The judicial power granted in Article III, Section 2, Clause 1, includes: cases in law and equity arising under the Constitution, the laws of the United States and treaties made under their authority, cases of admiralty and maritime jurisdiction, controversies between two or more states, controversies between a state and citizens of another state, and controversies to which the United States is a party. Judicial power covers any case in which the United States is a party plaintiff, even where the defendant is a state. But neither an individual nor a state may sue the United States without its consent, and unless the plaintiff brings himself within some permissive act of Congress, no federal court will entertain the suit. Prior to the adoption of the Eleventh Amendment, it was held that under the wording of the judicial article a state could be sued without its consent (*Chisholm* v. *Georgia*). Adoption of the Eleventh Amendment overruled the court's decision. And, though the amendment refers only to suits between a state and citizens of another state or of a foreign country, the principle of immunity prohibits suits against a state by its own citizens (*Hans*

v. *Louisiana,* 134 U.S. 1: 1890). A suit may be brought against a state officer to restrain him from executing an unconstitutional statute, but this is not regarded as a suit against a state (*Osborn* v. *Bank,* 9 Wheat. 738: 1824).*

Controversies between Citizens of Different States.   Federal jurisdiction of disputes between citizens of different states is wholly independent of the nature of the subject matter of such disputes. For jurisdictional purposes, a corporation is treated as a citizen of the state of its incorporation. Corporations organized under a federal statute are not regarded as citizens of any state unless Congress specifically so provides; hence the federal courts have no jurisdiction over them on the basis of diversity of citizenship alone. The doctrine of state immunity from suit applies even where the plaintiff is a foreign state.

The Constitution vests judicial power of the United States in "one Supreme Court and in such inferior courts as the Congress may from time to time ordain and establish" (Art. III, Sec. 1). This provision is not self-executing, and Congress has established the following so-called constitutional courts: (1) courts of appeals for each of the eleven judicial circuits, plus one for the District of Columbia; (2) district courts, of which there are now 91 (89 in the fifty states, plus one in the District of Columbia and one in Puerto Rico); (3) special courts, such as the Court of Claims, established under the power of Congress to pay the debts of the United States, and the Court of Customs and Patent Appeals, to hear appeals from import duty assessment and patent cases.

Under power granted to it by other clauses in the Constitution, Congress has set up so-called legislative courts such as the United States Tax Court, which hears appeals from Treasury tax rulings; the Court of Military Appeals; and "local" courts for the District of Columbia (a trial court called the Superior Court and an appellate court known as the District of Columbia Court of Appeals). Since these courts are "legislative" as opposed to "constitutional," the tenure of the judges rests with statutes passed by Congress. Other legislative courts include the district courts established for the territories (one each in Guam, Northern Mariana Islands, and the Virgin Islands). Even though the judges on the United States District Court in Puerto Rico sit for terms of eight years, as opposed to life tenure, this court is considered "constitutional" rather than "legislative." *American Insurance Co.* v. *Canter* (1 Pet. 511: 1828) remains the leading case on the status of these territorial courts.

Extent of Congressional Power.   The above distinctions are important in determining the power of Congress over the federal courts. Thus a constitutional court is governed by the doctrine of the separation of powers, and no legislative or administrative functions may be given it. In Hayburn's Case (2 Dall. 409: 1792), for example, the Court rejected an attempt by the legislature to impose on federal courts the duty of passing on pension claims. A legislative court, on the other hand, may be given nonjudicial functions, since the doctrine of separation of powers is inapplicable; and Congress has full power over the salary and tenure of its judges.

It does not follow, however, that because a court is a legislative body it may not exercise judicial power. The power exercised by such courts is not, however, that defined and granted by Article III, but a power conferred by Congress in the execution of other provisions of the Constitution.

Jurisdiction of the Supreme Court.   The Supreme Court's original jurisdiction (Art. III, Sec. 2, Cl. 2) can neither be taken away nor added to by Congress; other federal

---

* Case citations indicate where a case may be found. (See the discussion of legal source materials beginning on page 24 *infra.*) Citations appear in the essays for cases referred to, but not reprinted, in the book, and usually only for the initial reference. Citations for reprinted cases appear just above the headnotes.

courts, however, may be given original jurisdiction over the same classes of cases, since the Constitution nowhere provides that the original jurisdiction of the Supreme Court shall be exclusive. The clause relating to the jurisdiction of the Supreme Court does not enlarge the federal judicial power as defined in Article III, Section 2, Clause 1: thus the Supreme Court has no jurisdiction over a suit by a state against its own citizens. Even though a state is a party the judicial power does not extend to such suits.

The Supreme Court has appellate jurisdiction in respect to both law and fact in all other cases, but subject to such exceptions and regulations as Congress may make (Art. III, Sec. 2, Cl. 2). By virtue of this clause and of its power over the jurisdiction of inferior federal courts, Congress has plenary power over the appellate jurisdiction of the Supreme Court. It could thus deprive that court of all such jurisdiction and make final the decisions of the inferior courts. An extreme example occurred in 1869 when Congress, fearing that the Court would invalidate the Reconstruction Acts, hastily withdrew the Court's jurisdiction established under the Habeas Corpus Act of 1867. The Court thus became powerless to pass on a case in which argument had been heard (*Ex parte McCardle*).

Jurisidiction of Courts of Appeals.   Congress has given the courts of appeals jurisdiction in appeals taken from the federal district courts sitting in their respective circuits, from judgments of the Tax Court, and from the rulings of particular administrative and regulatory agencies such as the National Labor Relations Board and the Securities and Exchange Commission. The heaviest responsibility for reviewing decisions of administrative tribunals, however, falls on the Court of Appeals for the District of Columbia Circuit. In addition, some courts of appeals may review cases from the district courts in the territories. (For example, Guam and the Northern Mariana Islands are considered part of the Ninth Circuit.) A small class of appeals may go from a district court directly to the Supreme Court, bypassing the court of appeals, but this procedure is now exceptional (see p. 20, *infra*).

Jurisdiction of District Courts.   The district courts have appellate jurisdiction only with respect to a few classes of cases tried before United States magistrates (formerly United States commissioners). Their original jurisdiction is in part exclusive and in part concurrent with that of the state courts and that of the Supreme Court.

The district courts have jurisdiction over all cases involving more than $10,000 where the parties are citizens of different states, or where the case raises a federal question. Two wholly independent bases of jurisdiction are thus provided. A federal question is raised when it is made to appear on the face of the record that a correct decision necessarily depends upon the construction of the Constitution, a law of the United States, or a treaty; it is not raised by the mere assertion of a right thereunder. The United States District Court for the District of Columbia has a special responsibility in reviewing changes in local electoral practices in certain states by virtue of the Voting Rights Act.

Jurisdiction and Judicial Power.   Congress has been wary of measures designed to curtail judicial power or to influence the manner of its exercise. With rare exceptions, proposals to limit or to destroy judicial review, either of state acts and state decisions or of acts of Congress have failed. On the other hand, Congress has been willing to place in the Court's hands discretionary power to select the cases to be heard (see p. 21). One reason for such Congressional restraint is that the power of judicial review has, on occasion, been regarded as amounting "to little more than the negative power to disregard an unconstitutional enactment, which otherwise would stand in the way of the enforcement of a legal right" (*Massachusetts* v. *Mellon*, 262 U.S. 447: 1923). Despite recurrent criticism, this power, moreover, has been acquiesced in by the other departments of government and by the people. Even when the judiciary itself seemed disposed to jeopardize its authority and prestige by unabashed forays into politics, as during the years immediately preceding the Civil War, in the early 1930s, and since 1954, powerful friends both in Congress and in the private sector have come to its defense.

The most clear-cut illustration of the way in which Congress may strike at judicial power through control over jurisdiction is *Yakus* v. *U.S.* (321 U.S. 414: 1944). The case arose under the Emergency Price Control Act of January 30, 1942, an act setting up the Emergency Court of Appeals and conferring upon it "exclusive jurisdiction to determine the validity of any regulation or order of the Price Administrator." The act declared that "no Court, Federal, State or Territorial, shall have jurisdiction or power to restrain, enjoin, or set aside any provision of this Act." In the criminal prosecution brought by the United States in a federal district court, Yakus argued in defense that the Price Control Act, as interpreted and applied in certain orders of the Price Administrator, deprived him of his property without due process of law. A sharply divided Court rejected his plea, holding that the provisions of the Price Control Act were "broad enough in terms to deprive the district court of power to consider the validity of the Administrative regulation or orders as a defense to a criminal prosecution for its violation." The defendant's constitutional rights were not infringed, the Court said, since he might have brought a suit for injunction in the Emergency Court of Appeals prior to conviction. Thus, even in the defense of criminal actions, the constitutional issue could not be raised in the lower federal courts. Justices Roberts and Rutledge dissented.

Standing to Sue and Other Requirements.   In many cases where the federal courts, including the Supreme Court, would appear to have jurisdiction one or more other requirements may prevent a court from accepting and deciding the case. Some of these self-denying ordinances were set forth by Justice Brandeis, concurring, in *Ashwander* v. *TVA* (297 U.S. 288: 1936). Summarized briefly, these rules are:

1. The Court will not pass upon the constitutionality in a friendly, nonadversary, proceeding.
2. The Court will not anticipate a question of constitutional law in advance of the necessity for deciding it.
3. The Court will not formulate a rule of law broader than the facts of the case require.
4. If possible, the Court will dispose of a case on nonconstitutional grounds.
5. The Court will not pass upon the validity of a statute on complaint of one who fails to show injury to person or property.
6. The Court will not pass upon the constitutionality of a statute at the instance of one who has accepted its benefits.
7. Whenever possible, statutes will be construed so as to avoid a constitutional issue.

Judicial modesty pervades these self-denials, but justices differ markedly in applying rules governing access to the court. Judicial activists are inclined to gloss over the problems of jurisdiction as "technical," while those who favor judicial self-restraint can frequently avoid a decision on the merits by insisting that the petitioner has run afoul of one or more limiting rules.

A commonly invoked rule is that requiring standing to sue, that is, a direct personal interest on the part of the litigant allegedly infringed by the law or governmental action. In *Massachusetts* v. *Mellon* (262 U.S. 447: 1923) a state was not allowed to challenge the validity of the Federal Maternity Act on behalf of its citizens. And although state taxpayers are allowed to bring suit in state courts based on the unconstitutionality of state laws and official acts, *Frothingham* v. *Mellon* (262 U.S. 447: 1923) denied standing to a federal taxpayer who sought to challenge the Federal Maternity Act. The Court distinguished the status of federal and state taxpayers by concluding that the interest of the former was minute and indeterminable. In spite of this decision, the Court in 1968 conceded standing to a federal taxpayer who sought to challenge an alleged breach of the First Amendment's establishment-of-religion clause through federal expenditures under a 1965 act for textbooks and instructional costs in sectarian schools (*Flast* v. *Cohen,* 392 U.S. 83). The Court distinguished this situation from the typical taxpayer suit by viewing the establishment clause itself as a limitation on the taxing and spending power of Congress, hence a taxpayer can urge more than his general interest in the expenditure of federal funds.

The tendency in the modern era has been to lower standing barriers. Federal statutes allowing access were upheld in *Data Processing Service* v. *Camp* (397 U.S. 150: 1970). Slight economic, and even noneconomic interests, have been held to justify standing (*Sierra Club* v. *Morton,* 405 U.S. 727: 1972; *United States* v. *SCRAP,* 412 U.S. 669: 1973). The Burger Court, however, has shown a tendency to cut back on standing. In *United States* v. *Richardson* (418 U.S. 166: 1974), the Court refused to allow standing to a taxpayer who challenged provisions of the Central Intelligence Act of 1949 that seemed to run counter to Article 1, Section 9, Clause 7, requiring a published statement and account of all expenditures. In a 1975 case, the Court held, 6–3, that various minority and low-income petitioners lacked standing to challenge a zoning ordinance that allegedly excluded them and other low-income groups from living in the town involved (*Warth* v. *Seldin,* 422 U.S. 490).

Another requirement is that the case must present a "live" dispute. In *De Funis* v. *Odegaard* (416 U.S. 312: 1974) the Court held, 5–4, that a case brought by a white law student, challenging a University of Washington preferential admissions program for minorities was moot. *De Funis* aroused national interest, with 26 amicus curiae briefs, yet the Burger majority concluded that the fact that the student had been admitted to law school by court order and was about to graduate eliminated any injury to him. Justice Douglas, whose order allowed De Funis to enter and continue in school while the case proceeded up to the Supreme Court, was the only Justice to deal with the merits, condemning use of race as an admissions criterion. His opinion is reprinted in chapter 11.

A case must also have reached a certain stage of maturity before the Court will hear and determine it on the merits. *United Public Workers* v. *Mitchell* (330 U.S. 75: 1947) refused to examine the constitutionality of the Hatch Act prohibition against certain kinds of political activities by federal employees, since the employee bringing suit had not in fact violated the law, and thus had not yet suffered injury. A 1972 decision, *Laird* v. *Tatum* (408 U.S. 1), held, 5–4, that the petitioners' attack on the army civilian surveillance system was not, in Chief Justice Burger's view, ripe. For the Chief Justice, allegations of a "subjective chill [of First Amendment rights] are not an adequate substitute for a claim of objective harm or a threat of specific future harm."

Nor will the Court commonly rule on most of the questions a case conceivably presents. Much is usually left unsaid. In *Rostker* v. *Goldberg,* decided late in the 1980–81 term (reprinted in chapter 11) the statute providing for all-male draft registration survived attack on equal protection grounds. In dissent, Justice Marshall itemized the questions the Court was *not* answering.

It bears emphasis . . . that the only question presented by this case is whether the exclusion of women from registration under the Military Selective Service Act . . . contravenes the equal protection component of the Due Process Clause of the Fifth Amendment. Although the purpose of registration is to assist preparations for drafting civilians into the military, *we are not asked to rule on the constitutionality of a statute governing conscription. . . .* Consequently, we are not called upon to decide whether either men or women can be drafted at all, whether they must be drafted in equal numbers, in what order they should be drafted, or once inducted, how they are to be trained for their respective functions. In addition, this case does not involve a challenge to the statutes or policies that prohibit female members of the Armed Forces from serving in combat. . . .

Similarly, the Court will not render decision where nonjusticiable issues are involved. This merges into the "political questions" issue discussed in *Baker* v. *Carr.*

Law Applied by Federal Courts.   In matters of purely local importance, the federal courts are supposed to follow decisions of state courts, but as a practical matter they are bound by the rule chiefly in cases dealing with rights in real property. Under the now discarded doctrine of *Swift* v. *Tyson* (16 Pet. 1: 1842), federal courts were not required to follow state court decisions in matters of general jurisprudence and commercial law, but could determine such cases according to their own view of common-law principles. In the face of persistent criticism, the federal courts continued to make their own decisions in the field of insurance, in various branches of contract law, and in cases of tort.

In 1933, however, the Court manifested a desire to restrict the application of the doctrine and to follow decisions of state courts whenever possible. Five years later the Court in *Erie* v. *Tompkins* (304 U.S. 64: 1938) reversed the century-old precedent of *Swift* v. *Tyson.* "Experience in applying the doctrine of *Swift* v. *Tyson,*" Justice Brandeis said, "had revealed its defects, political and social; and the benefits expected to flow from the rule did not accrue. Persistence of state courts in their own opinions on questions of common law prevented uniformity; and the impossibility of discovering a satisfactory line of demarcation between the province of general law and that of local law developed a new well of uncertainties."

The Judicial Code now provides that "the laws of the several states . . . shall be regarded as rules of decision in trials at common law in the courts of the United States." Equity, admiralty, and criminal cases are excluded from the operation of this clause, and its scope was further limited by construing the word "laws" to mean only state statutes. However, since the judicial interpretation of a statute is an integral part of that statute, federal courts follow the decisions of the highest court of the state in construing a state statute.

SUPREME COURT PROCEDURE

Article III of the Constitution establishes "the judicial power of the United States" in "one Supreme Court." Since 1869 this Supreme Court has consisted of nine Justices; in 1891 their circuit duties were curtailed. The tenor of congressional action throughout the years (especially the Act of 1925) has been to contract the obligatory jurisdiction of the Supreme Court in order to enable it to concentrate on constitutional issues of wide public interest and importance.

The present method of Supreme Court review (Chapter 81, Title 28, United States Code) is essentially as listed below.

On appeal (a review by right, similar to the old writ of error):
  From the state courts and the District of Columbia Court of Appeals

1. Where a state court has invalidated a federal statute or treaty provision.
2. Where a state court has upheld a state law or state constitutional provision allegedly in conflict with the federal Constitution, laws, or treaties.

From the courts of appeals

1. Where a federal law or treaty is held unconstitutional.
2. Where a state law or constitutional provision is held invalid because of a conflict with a federal law, treaty, or constitutional provision.
3. Where questions certified from district courts concerning the constitutionality of provisions of the Federal Election Campaign Act of 1971, as amended, have been answered.

From the district courts (direct appeal to the Supreme Court)

1. Where a federal statute is held unconstitutional in a civil action to which the United States is a party.
2. Where a statute explicitly provides for the convening of a three-judge district court. (Three-judge district courts are authorized in only a few situations today, including cases involving the apportionment of congressional or state legislative districts and certain provisions of the Civil Rights Act of 1964 and the Voting Rights Act of 1965.)
3. Where in specified situations a final judgment has been entered in a civil antitrust case brought by the United States. (In all other cases, decisions by district courts are appealable only to the courts of appeals. From there they may go to the Supreme Court on certiorari or in one of the narrow categories of appeal.)

On certiorari (review granted or denied at the discretion of the Supreme Court):
From the state courts and the District of Columbia Court of Appeals

1. Where in all cases involving federal constitutional, statutory or treaty provisions, the decision is favorable to the claim under federal law.
2. Where a federal constitutional, statutory, or treaty provision has been construed.
3. Where "any title, right, privilege or immunity" is claimed under the Constitution, statutes, or treaties of the United States.

From the courts of appeals

1. Where a decision involves interpretation or application of the Constitution or federal laws or treaties.
2. Where state laws and constitutional provisions have been challenged as being contrary to federal law, and the court of appeals has held otherwise.

(The certiorari jurisdiction of the Supreme Court also extends to decisions of the Court of Claims and the Court of Custom and Patent Appeals.)

On certification: Where, at the initiation of a court of appeals, instructions on a point of law are desired.

In the 1980–81 term, there were 152 decisions announced with full opinions (including 8 lengthy per curiam, or unsigned, opinions), but 7 were decided on the basis of threshold questions without reaching the merits. A total of 122 other cases were summarily decided. In contrast, 3,967 cases were disposed of by denial of certiorari or dismissal of appeal. Some 786 cases (including 17 cases claiming the Court's original jurisdiction) were carried over into the 1981–82 term for disposition.

Appeals are commonly regarded as review by right, but are frequently dismissed because of the "failure to state a substantial federal question." Review on certiorari "is not a matter of right . . . and will be granted only when there are special or important reasons therefor." The bulk of applications are rejected because the petitions are defective in form, fail to present an issue of importance, or are not distinguishable from well-established precedents. For example, on June 15, 1981, the Court denied certiorari in No. 80–1722, *Sharrow* v. *Holtzman,* where the question was whether use of the word "he" in Article I, Section 3, of the Constitution establishes a gender qualification for United States senators. The Court of Appeals for the Second Circuit had ruled that it did not. On certiorari and appeal, at least four Justices must vote to accept jurisdiction if the case is to be reviewed on the merits. Deciding what to decide is therefore an important part of the judicial process. Statements by counsel, in losing causes in state and lower federal courts, that they will "take the case to the Supreme Court" should, therefore, be taken as threats, not promises. The Supreme Court is a very special court, with very particular legal concerns.

The actual work of the Supreme Court falls under four headings; reading various papers, oral argument, conference, opinions and decisions.

The Reading Stage.   Each petition for certiorari and application for appeal generates extensive reading material for the Justices and their law clerks. In briefs requesting review, counsel submit lengthy statements and cite substantial portions of the lower court record to demonstrate why the Court should (or should not) accept the case for decision. (A denial of certiorari or a dismissal of the appeal leaves in force the decision of the most immediate court below.) When the Justices accept a case for review, opposing counsel submit yet another round of briefs. Persons and organizations interested in, but not parties to, a case may add to the Justices' reading assignments still further by filing their own briefs as amici curiae, or "friends of the Court."

Oral Argument.   In addition to reading the printed briefs submitted by counsel, the Court listens to oral argument. During the Chief Justiceship of John Marshall (1801–1835) arguments were well-nigh interminable. Daniel Webster used to run on for days. In 1849, the Court reduced the time for oral argument to two hours: one for appellant or petitioner (the party seeking the review) and one for appellee or respondent (the defendant on review). More recently, opposing counsel must be content with dividing an hour between themselves. The Court allots additional time only in exceptional circumstances. The Court sits from October through June and sometimes into early July, with arguments being heard from October until the end of April. Monday, Tuesday, and Wednesday of two consecutive weeks are set aside for oral argument, with at least two weeks following being reserved for the preparation of opinions. The Justices hear arguments on those days from 10:00 A.M. until 3:00 P.M., with an hour recess at noon for lunch. "This is not an eight-hour day, to be sure," Justice John H. Clarke commented in 1932, "but I was occasionally obliged to listen to an argument which made those four hours stretch out as if to the crack of doom." Asked why he stood behind his chair "oftener and longer than any other Justice," Clarke replied: "When I became a judge I resolved that so long as a lawyer was permitted to address any court of which I should be a member I would keep awake and at least maintain the appearance of listening to him. . . . I preferred to stand and keep awake rather than show discourtesy to my brethren of the bar by sleeping, more or less fitfully, in my chair, as judges of some courts . . . have sometimes been known to do.''

Conference.   Friday is the principal conference day—the time set apart primarily for discussion and decision of cases argued during the week and other cases that may have passed from earlier argument. Recently, the Justices have added a Wednesday afternoon conference, to avoid a Saturday or Sunday conference. According to Justice Rehnquist,

> As soon as we come off the bench Wednesday afternoon around three o'clock, we go into private 'conference' in a room adjoining the chambers of the Chief Justice. At our Wednesday afternoon meeting we deliberate and vote on the four cases which we heard argued the preceding Monday. The Chief Justice begins the discussion of each case with a summary of the facts, his analysis of the law, and an announcement of his proposed vote (that is, whether to affirm, reverse, modify, etc.). The discussion then passes to the senior Associate Justice, presently Mr. Justice Brennan, who does likewise. It then goes on down the line to the junior Associate Justice. When the discussion of one case is concluded, the discussion of the next one is immediately taken up, until all the argued cases on the agenda for that particular Conference have been disposed of.
>
> On Thursday during a week of oral argument we have neither oral arguments nor Conference scheduled, but on the Friday of that week we begin a Conference at 9:30 in the morning, go until 12:30 in the afternoon, take 45 minutes for lunch, and return to continue our deliberations until the middle or late part of the afternoon. At this Conference we dispose of the eight cases which we heard argued on the preceding Tuesday and Wednesday. We likewise dispose of all of the petitions for certiorari and appeals which are before us that particular week. (''Sunshine in the Third Branch,'' 16 *Washburn Law Journal* 559, 559–660, n. 1: 1977).

If Monday or Tuesday of an argument week happen to be a holiday, there is no Wednesday conference. The Friday conference shifts to Thursday in May and June, giving the printer a longer lead time for opinions coming down the following Monday. The conference in Thanksgiving week takes place on Wednesday rather than Friday. Since conference meeting times are set by the Court and not by statute, the next Chief Justice may change this system. The current system, for example, varies in some respects from that which was in use during Chief Justice Warren's day. In cases of great importance, discussion may take place at more than one conference before the Justices are prepared to reach a decision. All cases are decided by majority vote of the Justices after such study and discussion as each case seems to require. For conference action on petitions for certiorari and jurisdictional statements for appeal, the Chief Justice uses a ''Discuss List.'' This is a timesaving device. Any Justice may add a case to the ''Discuss List,'' but unless a case makes the list—and about 70 percent do not—review is automatically denied, without discussion.

Opinions and Decisions.   On Saturday or early in the week after a two-week session of oral argument the Chief Justice circulates an assignment list to the Justices. If the Chief Justice is of the majority, he assigns the task of writing the opinion for the Court; if not, the senior Justice of the majority makes the assignment. In the latter case, the opinion assignment is often made right at the conference table. Preparation of the majority opinion necessarily represents much ''give and take.'' Greatest possible criticism is allowed. ''The opinion, when prepared,'' wrote Justice Harlan, ''is privately printed, and a copy placed in the hands of each member of the court for examination and criticism. It is examined by each Justice and returned to the author with such criticisms as are deemed necessary. If these objections are of a serious kind, affecting the general trend of the opinion, the writer calls the attention of the Justices to them, that they may be passed upon. The author adopts such suggestions of mere form as meet his views. If objections are made to which the writer does not agree, they are considered in conference, and are sustained or overruled, as the majority may determine. The opinion is reprinted so as to express the final conclusions of the court, and is then filed." Thus each majority opinion represents the consensus of the majority, not merely the opinion of the writer. A decision for which no majority opinion can be agreed upon is referred to as "the judgment of the Court."

If there are dissents, the senior member of the dissenting group may assign the opinion-writing duty; however, the prevalence of highly diverse viewpoints often makes this unnecessary, as each dissenter may choose to write a separate opinion of his own. Concurring opinions, increasingly prevalent in recent years, indicate the acceptance by a Justice of the majority decision but unwillingness to adopt all the reasoning contained in the opinion of the Court, or a desire to say something additionally.

Dissenting and concurring opinions are frequently worthy of close study, as indications of what the law may yet become. The dissenting opinion is often a warning against pressing any particular legal doctrine too far; and it is not unusual for the dissents of one generation to become the dominant opinions of the next. Sometimes a reversal has taken place within a few years.

After the opinion or opinions are written and circulated—a process that can drag on for weeks and even months—it is possible for a member of the Court to change his vote and decide to adhere to an opinion contrary to the one he originally supported. Up to the moment at which the writer of the opinion announces it in open Court, the Justices are free to change their positions. Ultimately, the alignment of the Justices becomes firm, and at a subsequent session the Court announces its decision. The Court is a fast track, and it takes some scrambling to keep up.

The primary purpose of this complex and time-consuming procedure is to furnish to litigants the solution of a "case" or "controversy." Decisions and opinions are also addressed to courts generally, and to the legal profession, as well as to all others who study the workings of the Supreme Court.

While the number of cases the Court decides with formal written opinion has not changed significantly during the past two or three decades, the number of cases from which the Justices choose this number has grown drastically. In 1930, the Justices found 1,039 cases on their docket. In 1951, about 1,200 cases were filed. By 1970 the number had tripled to 3,600. The 1979–80 docket contained 3,985 new filings, with 796 additional cases carried over from prior terms. This trend has led some to worry about the Court's work load and its ability to do its work competently. Chief Justice Burger has warned that it may become "impossible" for a Chief Justice "to perform his duties well and survive very long." Justice Blackmun has worried "about the cases that we 'barely' do not take, namely, those that almost assuredly would have been taken twenty years ago." Justice Douglas, by contrast, considered "the case for our 'overwork' . . . a myth." Acknowledging that "our time is largely spent in the fascinating task of reading petitions for certiorari and jurisdictional statements," he still maintained that "we are, if anything, underworked, not overworked."

To deal with the case load, a study group headed by Professor Paul A. Freund and selected by Chief Justice Burger recommended in 1972 the establishment of a National Court of Appeals to share the task of screening requests for High Court action each year. The new court would review the Supreme Court docket, referring only the most important cases to the Justices and disposing of the rest itself.

The proposal has stirred controversy within the Court and among lawyers and lower-court judges. Without formal endorsement, Chief Justice Burger presses for action to relieve the Court's burden, citing the Freund Commission's recommendations as worthy of consideration. The Chief Justice also encouraged the establishment of a federal commission, headed by Nebraska Senator Roman L. Hruska, which recommended an intermediate court to decide about 150 cases a year referred to it either by the Supreme Court or existing courts of appeals. However, all its rulings would be subject to Supreme Court review. Other proposals call for eliminating categories of cases that currently qualify for Supreme Court review. While no major changes have yet occurred, it is certain that debate on the Court's work load and various remedies will continue. Proposals to change the jurisdiction of the Supreme Court and the organization of the federal court system throughout American history have always been controversial, because such changes involve considerations of access and power, as well as efficiency.

SOURCE MATERIALS

Court Decisions.   The reported opinions of the Supreme Court form the basic material for the study of constitutional law. There are three editions of these reports.

1. *United States Reports* (the official edition, now published by the Government Printing Office, Washington, D.C.). Until 1875, the reports were cited according to the name of the reporter, with the reporter's name usually abbreviated. Beginning with Volume 91 in 1875, the reports have been cited only by volume number and the designation "U.S." (For example, a case cited as 444 U.S. 130 is located in volume 444 of the *U.S. Reports,* beginning on page 130.)

1789–1800	Dallas	(1–4 Dall., 1–4 U.S.)
1801–1815	Cranch	(1–9 Cr., 5–13 U.S.)
1816–1827	Wheaton	(1–12 Wheat., 14–25 U.S.)
1828–1842	Peters	(1–16 Pet., 26–41 U.S.)
1843–1860	Howard	(1–24 How., 42–65 U.S.)
1861–1862	Black	(1–2 Bl., 66–67 U.S.)
1863–1874	Wallace	(1–23 Wall., 68–90 U.S.)
1875–		(91– U.S.)

The number of volumes of the *United States Reports* has now passed the 450 mark.

2. *United States Supreme Court Reports, Lawyers' Edition* (published by the Lawyers' Cooperative Publishing Company, Rochester, New York, a commercial publisher). The advantage of this complete edition lies in the inclusion of material from the briefs of opposing counsel, and a substantial number of notes and annotations on various topics of constitutional law. Lawyers' Edition is cited as L.Ed. (e.g., 96 L.Ed. 954).

3. *Supreme Court Reporter* (published by West Publishing Company, St. Paul, Minnesota). This is similar in concept to the Lawyers' Edition, but is not a complete edition of all cases since 1789. It is cited as S.Ct. (e.g., 58 S.Ct. 166).

All of the foregoing publishers issue preliminary or advance sheets of the reports, those of the commercial publishers appearing much earlier than the government's. The earliest publication of the full opinions appears on the day following a decision in the *United States Law Week,* published by the Bureau of National Affairs, and in *Supreme*

Court Bulletin, published by Commerce Clearing House. Some very recent cases cited in this volume carry the *Law Week* citation (e.g., 49 LW 4685).

Lower federal court opinions are published by a private publisher: the decisions of the courts of appeals appear in *Federal Reporter* in 300 numbered volumes, subsequently numbered in a second series; they are cited as F. or F. 2d. Selected decisions of the district courts appear in *Federal Supplement,* cited as F. Supp.

The "record" of each decided case contains valuable material in the form of briefs of counsel, proceedings in lower courts, and exhibits. Unfortunately, these are not nearly so widely available as the Supreme Court decisions themselves. Some twenty-five law libraries across the nation are designated depositories and routinely receive copies of such documents from the clerk of the Supreme Court. Other libraries may subscribe to microfiche editions. University Publications of America in Washington, D.C., publishes *Landmark Briefs and Arguments of the Supreme Court of the United States: Constitutional Law.* Numbering over 112 volumes, and growing, this set contains the complete extant record, plus transcripts of oral arguments where available, of major constitutional decisions of the Supreme Court, beginning in 1793. It includes many of the cases selected for this book.

Legislative and Administrative Records.   The statutes may be found chronologically in *United States Statutes at Large,* of which a new volume appears annually, and are available in an analytical form in *United States Code Annotated* (West Publishing Co.) and in *United States Code Service* (Lawyers' Cooperative Publishing Co.).

Debates in Congress are available under the following titles and have been officially published since 1873:

Annals of Congress, 1789–1824
Register of Debates in Congress, 1824–1837
Congressional Globe, 1833–1873
Congressional Record, 1873–

Administrative rules and orders are published chronologically in the *Federal Register,* and are presented analytically in the *Code of Federal Regulations.* There is also a commercially published annotated edition of the Code. Administrative and congressional activity is also followed by *Congressional Quarterly Weekly Report* (published by Congressional Quarterly, Inc., of Washington, D.C.) and by *National Journal* (published by Government Research Corp., of Washington, D.C.).

State Court Decisions.   The decisions of the highest state courts are published separately by either the state or a commercial publisher. A sectional reporter system, which combines selected decisions of the courts of several states in one publication, is also available in most law libraries.

Law Review Material.   In addition to a substantial body of books and monographs, many of which are cited at the ends of essays throughout this book, there is a vast output of articles in legal periodicals on all phases of constitutional law. The student will find relevant law review articles more readily by referring to the *Index to Legal Periodicals* (published by H. W. Wilson Co. of New York City), which is organized on a subject-matter and author basis. The *Law Review Digest* (published by Bakken, Watt, Peterson, Inc., of Minneapolis) contains, as the name suggests, digests of selected articles published in American legal periodicals.

SELECTED READINGS

BRENNAN, W. J., JR., "Inside View of the High Court," *New York Times Magazine,* Oct. 6, 1963.

CASPER, GERHARD and RICHARD A. POSNER, *The Workload of the Supreme Court.* Chicago: American Bar Foundation, 1976.

CLARKE, JOHN H., "Reminiscences of Courts and the Law," 5 *Proceedings* of the Fifth Annual Meeting of the State Bar of California 20 (1932).

FISH, PETER G., *The Politics of Federal Judicial Administration.* Princeton: Princeton University Press, 1973.

FRANKFURTER, FELIX, and J. M. LANDIS, *The Business of the Supreme Court.* New York: Macmillan, 1928.

HARLAN, JOHN M., "What Part Does Oral Argument Play in the Conduct of an Appeal?" 41 *Cornell Law Quarterly* 6 (1955).

HOWARD, J. WOODFORD JR., *Courts of Appeals in the Federal Judicial System.* Princeton: Princeton University Press, 1981.

MASON, ALPHEUS THOMAS, "Eavesdropping on Justice: A Review Essay," 95 *Political Science Quarterly* 295 (1980).

PROVINE, DORIS MARIE, *Case Selection in the United States Supreme Court.* Chicago: University of Chicago Press, 1980.

STEPHENSON, D. GRIER, JR., Review of *The Brethren,* 46 *Brooklyn Law Review* 373 (1980).

STERN, ROBERT L., and EUGENE GRESSMAN, *Supreme Court Practice,* 5th ed. Washington: Bureau of National Affairs, 1978.

Structure and Internal Procedures: Recommendations for Change. Washington: Commission on Revision of the Federal Court Appellate System, 1975.

Report of the Study Group on the Caseload of the Supreme Court. Washington: Administrative Office of the U.S. Courts, 1972.

WOODWARD, BOB, and SCOTT ARMSTRONG, *The Brethren: Inside the Supreme Court.* New York: Simon and Schuster, 1979.

TWO

The Constitution,
the Supreme Court,
and Judicial Review

The Constitution of 1787 and its 26 amendments can be read in about half an hour. One could memorize the written document word for word, as many school children once did, and still know little or nothing of its meaning. The reason is that the formal body of rules known as constitutional law consists primarily of decisions and opinions of the United States Supreme Court—the gloss that the Justices have spread on the formal document. Charles Warren asks us not to forget that "however the Court may interpret the provisions of the Constitution, it is still the Constitution which is law and not decisions of the Court." But Charles Evans Hughes bluntly asserted that "The Constitution is what the Judges say it is." Myth wars with reality both within and without the Court.

GRANTING AND LIMITING POWER

In the United States the Constitution alone is supreme. All agencies of government stand in the relationship of creator to creatures. There is, Woodrow Wilson observed, "no sovereign government in America." But Wilson was not blind to the fact that government means action. "Power belongs to government, is lodged in organs of initiative; control belongs to the community, is lodged with the voters"—and the courts.

American constitutionalism deals with the problem James Madison posed in *The Federalist,* No. 51: "In framing a government which is to be administered by men over men, the great difficulty lies in this: you must first enable the government to control the governed; and in the next place oblige it to control itself." The Constitution both grants and limits power. Article I lists the powers of Congress; Article II invests executive power in the President; Article III confers judicial power of the United States on one Supreme Court and on such other courts as Congress may establish. Article I, Section 9, sets limits on national power; Article I, Section 10, restricts the states. Chief Justice Marshall called this section, the only one in the original Constitution limiting state power, "a bill of rights for the people of the states.'' The Constitution provides no definition of either powers or limitations.

In ways both obvious and subtle, the Constitution appears to be an instrument of rights, of limitations, rather than of powers. Certain things Congress is expressly forbidden to do. It may not pass an ex post facto law or a bill of attainder; it may not tax exports from any state; and it may not—except in great emergencies—suspend the writ of habeas corpus. The Bill of Rights (Amendments I through VIII) contains a longer list of things the national government is powerless to do. The state governments are likewise forbidden to do specific things. Article I, Section 10, declares that a state may not enact ex post facto laws, impair the obligation of contracts, coin money, emit bills of credit, or enter into any treaty or alliance with a foreign state. Certain restrictions imposed by the Bill of Rights on the national government have now been largely ''incorporated'' in the Fourteenth Amendment as limits on the states.

Government is circumscribed in less specific ways. The principles of separation of powers and of federalism, the ''due process'' clauses of the Constitution, and the doctrine of judicial review all manifest determination to oblige government to control itself. None of these limiting principles is spelled out; they are either implicit in the organization and structure of the Constitution, or, as with judicial review, deducible from ''the theory of our government.''

The Constitution separates and limits power, even as it confers it. Congress is endowed with ''legislative'' power; it may not, therefore (except as a result of a specific grant or by implication), exercise executive or judicial power. The same restrictions apply to the other branches of the national government: the terms *judicial power* and *executive power,* like *legislative power,* have a technical meaning. In the exercise of their respective functions, neither Congress, President, nor judiciary may, under the principle of separation of powers, encroach on fields allocated to the other branches of government. Instead of requiring that the departments be kept absolutely separate and distinct, however, the Constitution mingles their functions. Congress is granted legislative power, but the grant is not exclusive. Law making is shared by the President in his exercise of the veto. The appointing authority is vested in the President; but on certain appointments the Senate must give its advice and consent.

The second power-limiting principle, federalism, means a constitutional system in which two authorities, each having a complete governmental system, exist in the same territory and act on the same people. In its American manifestation, federalism is a complicated arrangement whereby the national government exercises enumerated, implied, and inherent powers, all others being ''reserved to the States respectively, or to the people.'' Each government is supreme within its own sphere; neither is supreme within the sphere of the other. Federalism, like separation of powers and checks and balances, is a means of obliging government to control itself.

Madison and the Founding Fathers generally called this intricate system ''free government.'' The power surrendered by the people is first divided between two distinct governments (the national government and the states) and then the portion allotted to each subdivided among distinct and separate departments. Hence a double security is provided for the rights of the people. Distinct governments will exercise control over each other and at the same time each will be checked by itself. ''Vibrations of power'' (the ''genius'' of free government, Hamilton called it) is inherent in this complexus of restraints. Just how such controls were to be enforced the Constitution does not specify.

Not only is each government, national and state, bound to restrain itself lest the operations of one encroach upon the sphere of the other, but each government must heed the injunction that "no person" may be deprived of life, liberty, or property "without due process of law." The Fifth Amendment limits the national government in this respect; the Fourteenth Amendment controls the states. Applying standards drawn from these vague words, the Supreme Court is the ultimate guardian of individual privilege and governmental prerogative alike. It is, Woodrow Wilson observed, "the balance-wheel of our entire system."

THE DOCTRINE OF JUDICIAL REVIEW

For correctives against abuse of power, Americans have not been content to rely on political checks. Public opinion and the ballot box, the essential safeguards in most free societies, are not enough. In America, government is kept within bounds, not only by the electoral process, but also through separation of powers, federalism, "due process of law," and (as an adjunct to all these) judicial review.

The Founding Fathers made the Constitution "the supreme law of the land," but they left unanswered the question of who was to sustain this supremacy. In the Philadelphia Convention debates of 1787, it was suggested that each House of Congress might, when in doubt, call upon the judges for an opinion as to the validity of national legislation. Madison declared that a "law violating a constitution established by the people themselves would be considered by the judges as null and void." It was repeatedly urged that Supreme Court Justices be joined with the executive in a council of revision and be empowered to veto congressional legislation. Certain delegates objected to this proposal, contending that the Justices would have this power anyway in cases properly before them. Any such provision would give the Court a double check. It would compromise "the impartiality of the Court by making them go on record before they were called in due course, to give . . . their exposition of the laws, which involved a power of deciding on their constitutionality." Other members of the Convention, though not denying that the Court could exercise such power, asserted that it would violate the principle of separation of powers and have the effect, as Elbridge Gerry remarked, of "making statesmen of judges." In the end the power of judicial review was not expressly authorized.

Professor Corwin suggests that for the Constitution's framers, judicial review rests "upon certain general principles [government under law, separation of powers, federalism, Bill of Rights] which, in their estimation, made specific provision for it unnecessary." It may be significant that the legitimacy of judicial review became a topic for scholarly investigation only after 1890, when judicial review threatened to become the judicial *supremacy* Robert Yates had warned against. Alexander Hamilton, noting that "some perplexity respecting the rights of Courts to pronounce legislative acts void . . . has arisen," replied in *Federalist,* No. 78. This unstaged debate is excerpted in this chapter.

James Wilson, Oliver Ellsworth, and John Marshall, all destined for appointment to the Supreme Court, subscribed to the doctrine of judicial review in their respective ratifying conventions. On January 7, 1788, Ellsworth of Connecticut declared:

> If the United States go beyond their powers, if they make a law which the constitution does not authorize, it is void; and the judicial power, the national judges, who, to secure their impartiality, are to be made independent, will declare it to be void. On the other hand, if the States

go beyond their limits, if they make a law which is an usurpation upon the general government, the law is void; and upright independent judges will declare it so.

James Wilson was equally emphatic in Pennsylvania. Marshall was on record in favor of judicial review nearly 15 years before, as Chief Justice of the United States, he asserted the doctrine in *Marbury* v. *Madison*. It was not, however, until 1803 that this American way of obliging government to control itself was firmly established. As propounded by Marshall, judicial review means the power of the Supreme Court to pass on the validity of legislation in cases and controversies actually before it. The standard is the Constitution, thought of as higher law and deemed to be binding on government at all levels.

The American Constitution, unlike the British, cannot be changed by an ordinary act of legislation; this is its distinctive feature, not that it is written. No constitution, including our own, is either altogether written or altogether unwritten. The British constitution, though supposedly made up of custom and tradition, is partly written. Magna Charta, Petition of Right, Bill of Rights, Act of Settlement, and Parliament Act of 1911 are written. In the Constitution, there is no mention of the president's cabinet and no reference to senatorial courtesy, to political parties, or to the national nominating conventions for choosing candidates for election. The electoral college is expressly provided for in the written Constitution; usage has, for all practical purposes, discarded it. Thus the Constitution is only the original trunk. Important new branches have been added, through formal amendment, custom and usage, and above all, judicial interpretation. The American Constitution "in operation," Woodrow Wilson writes, "is manifestly a very different thing from the Constitution of the books."

Amendments to the Constitution have been proposed by the hundreds, more than 1,800 in its first century; but formal amendment is a rare event—only 26 to date. The Constitution's most significant growth comes from its definition and extension by the Supreme Court. In applying the broad provisions of the Constitution to particular cases, it determines the source of powers sought to be exercised and, by construing the relevant clauses, decides how far those powers extend. It must also protect individual rights against arbitrary government action. Chief Justice Marshall frequently warned against parsimonious construction of national power. A constitution, Hamilton observed, cannot "limit a nation's needs." *Needs* manifest themselves in terms of power and limits on power. Just as the powers of government must be expanded to meet changed conditions, so limits on power must also be accommodated to changed circumstances and conditions.

The most distinctive feature of our Constitution is that it is *law*, paramount, supreme law, and subject to interpretation by the Supreme Court in cases properly before it. Judicial review is an implied, not a substantive power; it is implied from, and is incidental to, the Court's judicial power—the power to interpret law and decide cases. Chief Justice Marshall portrayed judicial review as a necessary adjunct to both a written Constitution and a government deriving its power from the people. Nor does judicial power, he maintained, give the Supreme Court any practical or real omnipotence. The Court is simply exercising judicial power conferred by the Constitution and sustained by the principle of separation of powers. "It is, emphatically, the province and duty of the Judicial department to say what the law is." The effect, in theory, is not to elevate Court over legislature, but rather to make "the power of the people superior to both."

Marshall's argument was not unanswerable, as Justice Gibson's trenchant criticism in *Eakin* v. *Raub* makes clear. In 1803, and for quite some time thereafter, *Marbury* v. *Madison* aroused comment and criticism, not because the "great Chief Justice" asserted the power of judicial review, but because he went out of his way to read a lecture to President Jefferson and Secretary of State Madison as to their official duties under the Constitution. Earlier, Democratic-Republicans had severely criticized the Alien-Sedition Law and incorporation of the national bank as unconstitutional. The effects of judicial review are both negative and positive: it can veto as well as authenticate.

Jefferson himself never denied the power of the Supreme Court to pass on the validity of acts of Congress in the course of deciding cases. But he did deny that such a decision was binding on the President in the performance of his purely executive function. Jefferson stated his position in 1804: "The judges, believing the [Alien-Sedition] law constitutional, had a right to pass a sentence of fine and imprisonment, because that power was placed in their hands by the Constitution. But the Executive, believing the law to be unconstitutional, was bound to remit the execution of it, because that power has been confided to him by the Constitution. That instrument meant that its coordinate branches should be checks on each other. But the opinion which gives to the judges the right to decide what laws are constitutional, and what not, not only for themselves in their own sphere of action, but for the legislative and Executive also in their spheres, would make the Judiciary a despotic branch." Jefferson accepted the finality of judicial *decisions* in cases where their effects were primarily on the judiciary, as in *Marbury;* he rejected their binding effect on coordinate branches of the government.

The "despotic" potentialities of the judicial veto, at least in Marshall's time, were less onerous than is sometimes imagined. It was not until 1857 and the ill-fated Dred Scott decision that the second act of Congress ran afoul of the Constitution. Rejecting Marshall's view of a constitution intended to endure, Chief Justice Taney affirmed that the Constitution "speaks not only with the same words, but with the same meaning and intent" as when it came from the hands of the Framers. Taney did not confine his opinion to the question of Negro citizenship, but proceeded to discuss the extent of congressional power over the territories. Congress had no power to prohibit slavery in the territories and therefore the Missouri Compromise of 1820 violated the constitution.

Dred Scott marked a major expansion in the scope of judicial review. Unlike the statute in *Marbury,* the invalidated act did not pertain to the Judicial Department, nor contravene a precise, unambiguous provision of the Constitution. The Court vetoed a major legislative policy, forestalling future congressional efforts to deal with the foremost political issue of the day. *Dred Scott,* not *Marbury,* foreshadowed future controversies concerning the scope of judicial review.

Chief Justice Marshall had been content to defer to "the wisdom and discretion of Congress," checked by the controls voters possess at elections, as "the sole restraints" to secure the people from abuse. For Marshall's doctrine of *national* supremacy, Taney substituted *judicial* supremacy.

More important than judicial review of acts of Congress is the control federal courts exercise over state acts and state court decisions. The number of congressional acts invalidated has been comparatively small, just over a hundred to date. Quite otherwise has been the effect of judicial review of state action. Between 1889 and 1937 hundreds of state acts were disallowed. In the same period, only 69 acts of Congress were overturned, 13 being vetoed between June 1, 1934, and June 1, 1936. The seeming inconsistency between the doctrine of judicial review of congressional legislation and the need for effective government did not become a serious public issue until the last quarter of the nineteenth century. Prior to 1900 the Court had invoked its authority against Congress so sparingly that Justice Holmes could predict that "the United States would not come to an end if we lost our power to declare an Act of Congress void." "I do think," Holmes added, "the Union would be imperilled if we could not make that declaration as to the laws of the several states." One in his position could observe "how often a local policy prevails with those who are not trained to national views."

During the formative period of our history, it was of first importance to establish an effective barrier against state action hostile to the Constitution and the Union it created. Thomas Jefferson voiced the hope "that some peaceable means should be contrived for the federal head to enforce compliance on the part of the States." The Philadelphia Convention delegates, keenly aware of the necessity of establishing external control over state action, suggested various limitations. One proposal gave Congress a negative on state laws; another provided for federal appointment of state governors and gave the general government a negative on state acts. All these were rejected. In its final form "this Constitution," and the laws "made in pursuance thereof, and all treaties made, or which shall be made, under the authority of the United States," are declared to be "the supreme law of the land; and the judges in every state are bound thereby, anything in the Constitution or laws of any State to the contrary notwithstanding."

In the Virginia Ratifying Convention, John Marshall had envisioned judicial review as an alternative to revolution. "What is the service or purpose of a judiciary but to execute the laws in a peaceful, orderly manner, without shedding blood, or creating a contest, or availing yourselves of force?" Madison reinforced Marshall: "A political system that does not provide for a peaceable and effectual decision of all controversies arising among the parties is not a Government, but a mere Treaty between independent nations, without any resort for terminating disputes but negotiations, and that failing, the sword." Failure to lodge this power in the federal judiciary, he added in 1832, "would be as much a mockery as a scabbard put into the hands of a soldier without a sword in it."

The first Congress, apparently believing that the purpose of the supremacy clause (Art. VI, Para. 2) was to make the judiciary the final resort for all cases arising in the states, enacted Section 25, Judiciary Act of 1789, authorizing the Supreme Court to pass upon the validity of state legislation and to review decisions of state tribunals wherein constitutional questions had been answered in favor of the state, or adversely to national power. Though Section 25 recognized the important role that state courts might play in interpreting and applying the Constitution, federal law, and treaties, it had the effect of strengthening national power by making explicit a function of the Supreme Court left to inference in the Constitution itself.

In a period of Democratic-Republican dominance, during which only the judiciary remained in Federalist hands, invalidation of state acts and acceptance of jurisdiction of appeals on writ of error to a "sovereign" state court aroused strong states' rights resentment. *Fletcher* v. *Peck* (6 Cr. 87: 1810), the first case in which the Supreme Court declared a state act violative of the provisions of the federal Constitution, must have exceeded all expectations. Representatives in Congress condemned the ruling as "sapping the foundations of all our Constitutions," and Marshall's associate, Mr. Justice Johnson, intimated in dissent that the Chief Justice had seized an opportunity to assert judicial review of state acts in a moot case. There was less antagonism toward the Court's decision in states other than Georgia, but no one failed to recognize that power in the Supreme Court to review state acts would vitally affect our constitutional development.

After almost two centuries of experience with judicial power, judicial review is firmly entrenched as a part of the American political system. Within consensus, however, lies conflict. To believe that the Court *can* exercise judicial review is not necessarily to acknowledge that the Court always *should*. To recognize the Court's place in principle is not to approve its intervention in particular cases or in particular arenas of public policy. What was true in the time of Yates, Hamilton, and Marshall remains true today. Constitutional law in the American context is concerned with the nature and scope of judicial power. That concern finds its way explicitly or implicitly into every case reprinted in this book. The concern is no idle, useless relic from eighteenth century minds and jurisprudence. It remains indisputably alive in the ninth decade of the twentieth century. Variation on the differences among Justices Roberts, Sutherland, and Stone as to the nature and scope of judicial power, expressed in the context of *U.S.* v. *Butler* and reprinted in this chapter, are conspicuous in judicial opinions. Two books, published in 1932 and 1977 respectively, are entitled "Government by Judiciary" indicating that the label is not entirely idle speculation.

JUDGING SELF-JUDGED

Justice Brewer maintained in the late 1800s that judges "make no laws, establish no policy, never enter into the domain of popular action. They do not govern." "All the court does, or can do," Justice Roberts declared in 1936, "is to announce its considered judgment. . . . The only power it has, if such it may be called, is the power of judgment. This court neither approves nor condemns any legislative policy." Through the years, Supreme Court Justices have continued to profess judicial impotence, but hardly ever without rousing incredulity.

"I have never known any judges," Justice John H. Clarke observed, "who discharged their judicial duties in an atmosphere of pure, unadulterated reason. Alas, we are all 'the common growth of Mother Earth,' even those of us who wear the long robe." In its dual role of symbol and instrument of authority, the Supreme Court has always been confronted with the difficult task of reconciling the profession of judicial aloofness with the reality of personal discretion and political power. With refreshing candor, Justice Jackson observed: "We are not final because we are infallible, but we are infallible only because we are final" (*Brown* v. *Allen,* 344 U.S. 443: 1953).

Supreme Court justices are appointed for life—or during "good behavior." They may be impeached, but impeachment proved in practice to be not even a "scarecrow," as Jefferson said. Nevertheless, the Court is subject to various direct and indirect controls. The dramatic repudiation of its own decisions, on the heels of President Roosevelt's Court-packing threat, contradicts Justice Stone's self-effacing dictum that "the only check upon our own exercise of power is our own sense of self-restraint." Decisions on constitutional issues may be changed, by constitutional amendment, as in the Income Tax Case of 1895. Decisions involving statutory interpretation can be altered by an act of Congress, as was done after the judgment of *U.S.* v. *Southeastern Underwriters* (322 U.S. 533: 1944) and *Jencks* v. *U.S.* (353 U.S. 657: 1957).

The Constitution expressly gives Congress control over the Court's appellate jurisdiction. To prevent the Court from passing on the constitutionality of the Reconstruction Acts, Congress denied the Court's jurisdiction in a case then pending. "What, then, is the effect of the Repealing Act?" Chief Justice Chase asked deferentially. "We cannot doubt as to this. Without jurisdiction the Court cannot proceed at all in any cause. Jurisdiction is power to declare the law; when it ceases to exist, the only function remaining to the Court is that of announcing the fact and dismissing the cause'' (*Ex parte McCardle*).

The Court's appellate jurisdiction can be cut off any time the Congress sees fit. Such action was threatened in 1957, when the Jenner-Butler Bill withdrew the Court's jurisdiction in certain civil rights cases. During the latter years of the Warren Court, various bills were introduced to strike at judicial review itself by placing limits on the Court's appellate jurisdiction.

The summer of 1981 witnessed a new rash of Court-curbing bills—23 in the House and four in the Senate. Relying on the congressional victory in *Ex parte McCardle*, most of these would restrict the Court by selectively withdrawing jurisdiction on volatile issues like abortion, school segregation, and prayer in the public schools (*Congressional Quarterly Weekly Report*, May 30, 1981, p. 967). Each bill finds support in the outcry which has followed decisions by the Supreme Court in these areas. ''If Congress can decide willy-nilly that the Supreme Court and the federal appellate courts have no appellate jurisdiction by a simple majority vote,'' argues Congressman Robert Kastenmeier in opposition, ''then we have arrogated to ourselves considerable power.''

Still another bill would attack the Court on abortion by seeking to overturn the 1973 decision of *Roe* v. *Wade*, which established abortion as a Fourteenth Amendment right. Rather than withdrawing jurisdiction, this legislation—pushed by Senator Helms and Representative Hyde—would simply declare, by act of Congress, that life begins at conception. Since the Fourteenth Amendment protects ''life,'' the states could then pass antiabortion statutes. Raised was the specter of district attorneys investigating the circumstances of miscarriages. Inspiration for this approach comes apparently from *Katzenbach* v. *Morgan* (384 U.S. 641: 1966) when the Court acknowledged congressional authority to define constitutional rights. Whatever the approach or outcome, Senator Leahy of Vermont expressed the apprehension of many: ''I hope in the ensuing months we do not conclude that what is permissible is always wise.''

These efforts, old and new, fly in the face of one of the oldest and most religiously observed tenets in American constitutional interpretation. It goes back to 1793 and *Chisholm* v. *Georgia*, reprinted in chapter 4. In that case an ill-received Supreme Court decision on the nature of the Union was reversed by constitutional amendment—the Eleventh. About a century later the Court achieved considerable notoriety by overturning —five votes to four—a law which established a national income tax (*Pollock* v. *Farmers' Loan and Trust Co.*, reprinted in chapter 7). Many responsible observers denounced the Court for being wrong. The question was what to do about it. President Taft, among others, insisted that a constitutional amendment was necessary to erase it. He explained: ''A mature consideration has satisfied me that an amendment is the only proper course. . . . This course is much to be preferred to the one proposed of re-enacting a law once judicially declared to be unconstitutional. For the Congress to assume that the Court will reverse itself, and to enact legislation on such an assumption, will not strengthen popular confidence in the stability of judicial construction of the Constitution. It is much wiser policy to accept the decision and remedy the effect by an amendment in due and regular course.''

Taft placed high value on maintaining the fiction of an unchanging Constitution, even in the face of judicial action that was in error. The notion that Congress could reverse an objectionable decision by an ordinary act of Congress might threaten the popular image that the judicial version of the Constitution *is* the Constitution. This was an image Taft thought important to maintain.

After a lapse of twenty years the income tax was legitimized by the Sixteenth Amendment and therefore could be levied "without apportionment among the several states, and without regard to any census or enumeration." The cumbersome and time-consuming amendment procedure mandated by the Constitution suggests, however, that those opposed to the abortion decision may have long years of struggle and waiting ahead. Herein lies the attractiveness of the statutory devices proposed in 1981.

Moreover, a president may, by discriminating appointments, if the opportunity presents itself, change the voting balance within the Court. This occurred in the *Legal Tender Cases* (12 Wall. 457: 1871), and after John F. Kennedy's replacement of Felix Frankfurter with Arthur Goldberg. President Roosevelt's Court-packing proposal failed of enactment, but it was not without effect. Justice Roberts told a congressional committee in 1954 that he had been "fully conscious of the tremendous strain and threat to the existing court," stemming from F.D.R.'s audacious assault. Ours is "a government of laws and not of men" only in a qualified sense. As noted, President Nixon had occasion to make four appointments and was thereby able to alter the tone of constitutional jurisprudence as it had prevailed in Chief Justice Warren's day.

ENTERING THE "POLITICAL THICKET"

If "judges can open it [the Constitution] at all," Chief Justice Marshall commented in *Marbury* v. *Madison*, "what part of it are they forbidden to read or obey?" A self-disabling answer, at odds with the Chief Justice's inference, was given in *Luther* v. *Borden* (7 How. 1: 1849). The Justices, speaking through Chief Justice Taney, decided that the question whether the government of Rhode Island or any other state is "republican" (as guaranteed by Article IV, Section 4) was "political" in nature, and must be determined either by Congress through its acceptance or rejection of state representatives or by presidential acts in response to requests for assistance in putting down domestic violence. Decisions of the political departments concerning the international relations of the United States are likewise considered binding on the Court. Another question termed "political," and therefore requiring solution, if at all, through political agencies, is determination of whether a state has ratified a proposed constitutional amendment (*Coleman* v. *Miller,* 307 U.S. 433: 1939). The Court has refused to decide whether use by a state of the initiative and referendum is a denial of "a republican form of government" (*Pacific States Tel. & Tel. Co.* v. *Oregon,* 223 U.S. 118: 1912).

One of the most important fields in which the Court once invoked this self-imposed limitation upon judicial power is legislative apportionment. In *Colegrove* v. *Green* (328 U.S. 549: 1946), Justice Frankfurter termed this issue one "of a peculiarly political nature and therefore not meet for judicial determination." Voters seeking relief from Illinois's malapportioned congressional districts must turn to the state legislature or Congress, not to the Court. "Courts ought not to enter this 'political thicket,'" Frankfurter warned. "It is hostile to a democratic system to involve the judiciary in the politics of the people. . . . The remedy for unfairness in districting is to secure state legislatures that will apportion properly, or to invoke the ample powers of Congress."

Three Justices (Black, Douglas, and Murphy) dissented, arguing that equal protection required the election of Congressmen from districts generally equal in population. Said Justice Black,

> What is involved here is the right to vote guaranteed by the Federal Constitution. It has always been the rule that where a federally protected right has been invaded the federal courts will provide the remedy to rectify the wrong done. Federal courts have not hesitated to exercise their equity power in cases involving deprivation of property and liberty. . . . There is no reason why they should do so where the case involves the right to choose representatives that make laws affecting liberty and property. . . .

A majority of Supreme Court Justices refused to do their duty, as interpreted by a minority of three, until *Gomillion* v. *Lightfoot* (364 U.S. 339: 1960). Involved was an act of the Alabama legislature changing the boundaries in the city of Tuskegee from a simple square into a 28-sided monster. The result was to remove from the city all but a handful of black voters, while leaving white voters unaffected. Justice Frankfurter, in spite of a contention made in his *Colegrove* opinion, that this was a "political question," ruled that the Fifteenth Amendment guarantee against racial discrimination justified judicial action. Left unanswered was the question of whether the Fourteenth Amendment's Equal Protection Clause might provide a basis for judicial remedy of nonracial discrimination, specifically that based on urban versus rural residence.

An affirmative answer was given on March 26, 1962, in the landmark case of *Baker* v. *Carr*. Finding no obstacle in the "political question" doctrine, Justice Brennan ruled that malapportionment of state legislatures may constitute a violation of the Equal Protection Clause, that federal courts are empowered to provide a remedy.

In making belated entrance into this "political thicket," the Justices neglected (or refused) to lay down guidelines along which reapportionment might proceed. That came the next year, in *Gray* v. *Sanders* (372 U.S. 368: 1963), in which the Court, applying the one-man-one-vote principle, invalidated the Georgia County unit system of primary election in state-wide offices. Said Justice Douglas: "Once the geographical unit for which a representative is to be chosen is designated, all who participate in the election are to have an equal vote—whatever their race, whatever their sex, whatever their occupation, whatever their income, and wherever their home may be in that geographical unit. This is required by the equal protection clause of the Fourteenth Amendment."

In 1964, the Court (*Wesberry* v. *Sanders,* 376 U.S. 1: 1964) extended the same principle to congressional districts, holding that the Constitution had the "plain objective of making equal representation for equal numbers of people the fundamental goal for the House of Representatives." "As nearly as practicable," the Court declared, "one man's vote in a congressional election is to be worth as much as another's." In overruling *Colegrove*, Justice Black, relying on the Records of the Constitutional Convention and *The Federalist,* virtually repeated his dissenting opinion of 1946.

The conclusion of the three-round battle, set in motion by *Baker* v. *Carr,* came in *Reynolds* v. *Sims*. By applying the now familiar principle of one man, one vote, the Justices challenged the constitutionality of at least 40 state legislatures.

When Chief Justice Warren left the Court, he was asked to identify his major contribution. The somewhat surprising answer was categorical: reapportionment, especially *Reynolds* v. *Sims*. Why? The right to vote freely and equitably for the candidates of one's choice is the essence of a democratic society. Untrammeled exercise of this right is essential to the preservation of all others—''the bedrock of our political system,'' he called it. To hold that a vote in one county or electoral district is worth 10 times as much as the vote in another runs counter to ''our fundamental ideas of democratic representation.''

In the reapportionment decisions, as in those on race relations and rules of criminal procedure, the Court made new law, fashioned a new Constitution. ''For when, in the name of constitutional interpretation,'' dissenting Justice Harlan complained in *Reynolds,* ''the Court adds something to the Constitution that was deliberately excluded from it, the Court in reality substitutes its view of what should be so for the amending process.''

But judicial amendments, unlike those accomplished by the formal process prescribed in Article V, can be altered with relative ease. The changes made by one Court can be revised, thanks to new personnel, by a later Court. Said Justice Douglas: ''All constitutional questions are always open.''

Justice Douglas's assertion found qualified endorsement after he left the Court. Some members of the Court are by no means convinced that the political question doctrine has no force. When Senator Goldwater and other senators and representatives sued President Carter for giving notice to terminate the Mutual Defense Treaty with Taiwan without first coming to Congress, six Justices voted to dismiss the case altogether, without addressing the constitutional issue of presidential power it raised (*Goldwater* v. *Carter,* 444 U.S. 996: 1979). Four of them expressly held that the President's action constituted a nonjusticiable political question. Only Justice Brennan, author of the Court's opinion in *Baker* v. *Carr,* addressed the merits. (The treaty-termination issue is discussed in the following chapter.)

JUDICIAL REVIEW—A DISTINCTIVELY AMERICAN CONTRIBUTION

In a provocative statement revealing his nationalist preferences, the late Edward S. Corwin delineated four periods of constitutional interpretation. The first, reaching to the end of Chief Justice Marshall's long regime (1801–1835) features ''the dominance of the Constitutional Document.'' To support his nationalist bias, Marshall frequently cited theories of the Constitution.

The second period, stretching from 1835 to about 1895, is marked by ''the *par excellence* of the constitutional theory.'' Using dual federalism, due process of law, the conception of liberty as ''freedom of contract,'' and other judicial penumbra, the Justices put ''the national law-making power into a straitjacket so far as the regulation of business was concerned.''

Corwin calls the third period, 1895–1937, ''judicial review pure and simple.'' By this time, the Court found itself heir to such ''a variety of instruments of constitutional exegesis that it was often able to achieve almost any result . . . it considered desirable, and that without flagrant departure from good form.''

During the fourth period, 1937–1969, Supreme Court Justices led a revolution. A new Constitution emerged. After 1937, the Court stopped vetoing social and economic legislation, apparently content to leave protection of property rights to the mercy of the political controls. Justification for acquiescence in vastly increased government power over the economy was found in the slogan ''back to the Constitution'' (the Constitution as it was before 1890). Having abandoned guardianship of property, the Court became increasingly preoccupied with human beings and their rights as people—freedom of speech and press, rights of the accused and of the poor, freedom from racial discrimination, and the right to political equality in legislative districting.

The new Constitution emerged gradually. Vigorous protest has marked every step, particularly in relation to those dramatic shifts made after the appointment in 1953 of Earl Warren as Chief Justice. The new Constitution protects civil liberties against bigots, defends the right to a fair trial of indigent and ignorant persons accused of crime, guarantees the right of a majority to prevail over entrenched minorities in an election.

The Court's work load reflected this change. Of the 160 decisions in which opinions were written in the 1935–36 term, only two were in the area of civil rights. In 1960–61, 54 of the 120 decisions in which opinions were prepared concerned civil liberties. Disproportionate judicial concern for civil liberties continues.

The Constitution was not intended to be, nor in practice has it proved to be, a straitjacket. Constitutional interpretation has been infinitely variable. Since judges do not live in a vacuum, their decisions are influenced by inheritance, education, and the pressures of economic and social forces. The Court may restrain, as during the years 1890–1936, as well as initiate, as in cases such as *Brown* v. *Board of Education* and *Baker* v. *Carr*. The innovations that marked the regime of Chief Justice Warren, though diminished, have not disappeared. One would be hard pressed to find ultimate and thoroughly satisfactory justification for some of them in constitutional terms. In *Reynolds* v. *Sims* the Court plainly reached out for a desired result. This reach was even more obvious in the abortion decision. Still, a majority of the Justices through the years have felt authorized to intervene where injustices exist for which there is no perceived and probable remedy by other institutions. Debate on the nature and scope of judicial power continues not only within the confines of the Court but in the give-and-take of the political system. American constitutional law has been shaped by the Court, of course. Sometimes forgotten is the role of the people and the substance of decisions they will accept.

The pervasiveness of judicial power is now one of the most conspicuous aspects of the Supreme Court. It is hard to think of a feature of American life left untouched by its decrees. Its docket reads like a policy agenda for the nation. This development is all the more extraordinary in light of the fact that it is the work of a Court, four of whose members were appointed by President Nixon, who pledged himself to curb judicial activism, taking as his model the apostle of judicial self-restraint, Justice Frankfurter. It is hardly too much to say that Robert Yates's prediction of 1788 that the Court would finally expand its power so as to be able to "mould" the Constitution into any shape it pleased has been fulfilled. It remains to be seen whether President Reagan, successor to a president who did not appoint a single Supreme Court Justice, will reverse this trend. As of now, Reagan's opportunity, in bold contrast to that of Carter, will be surpassed only by that of Franklin Roosevelt. As history abundantly demonstrates, this does not necessarily mean a change of judicial direction. Prediction of judicial conduct is risky.

By and large, the effect of judicial decisions has been to expand and enlarge the sphere of government, rather than to qualify and restrict it. "The restraining power of the judiciary does not manifest its chief worth," Judge Cardozo observed, "in the few cases in which the legislature has gone beyond the lines that mark the limits of discretion." Its primary value has been in "making vocal and audible the ideals that might otherwise be silenced. . . . " Had this not been so, a document framed in the context of agrarianism, and largely unamended except by constitutional interpretation, could not serve the expanding needs of government in a complex industrialized society.

"The greatest statesmen," Woodrow Wilson observed, "are always those who attempt their task with imagination, with a large vision of things to come. . . . And so, whether by force of circumstance or by deliberate design, we have married legislation with adjudication and look for statesmanship in our courts."

Thanks largely to statesmanship within the Supreme Court, the Constitution has been more than "a mere lawyer's document." It has been "a vehicle of the nation's life."

SELECTED READINGS

BERGER, RAOUL, *Congress and the Supreme Court*. Cambridge: Harvard University Press, 1969.

————, *Government by Judiciary; The Transformation of the Fourteenth Amendment*. Cambridge: Harvard University Press, 1977.

BOUDIN, L. B., *Government by Judiciary*. 2 vols. New York: Godwin, 1932.

BURTON, HAROLD H., "The Cornerstone of Constitutional Law: The Extraordinary Case of Marbury v. Madison," 36 *American Bar Association Journal* 805 (1950).

CARDOZO, BENJAMIN N., *Nature of the Judicial Process*. New Haven: Yale University Press, 1932.

CHOPER, JESSE H., *Judicial Review and the National Political Process: A Functional Reconsideration*. Chicago: University of Chicago Press, 1980.

CORWIN, EDWARD S., *The Constitution and What It Means Today*, 14th ed. Revised by Harold W. Chase and Craig R. Ducat. Princeton: Princeton University Press, 1978.

————, *The Doctrine of Judicial Review*. Princeton: Princeton University Press, 1914.

DIXON, ROBERT, JR., *Democratic Representation in Law and Politics*. New York: Oxford University Press, 1969.

DOUGLAS, WILLIAM O., "Stare Decisis," 4 *Record of the Bar Association of the City of New York* 152 (1949).

ELLIOTT, WARD E. Y., *The Rise of Guardian Democracy: The Supreme Court's Role in Voting Rights Disputes*. Cambridge: Harvard University Press, 1974.

ELY, JOHN HART, *Democracy and Distrust: A Theory of Judicial Review*. Cambridge: Harvard University Press, 1980.

FRIEDMAN, LEON, and FRED L. ISRAEL, *The Justices of the United States Supreme Court 1789–1969: Their Lives and Major Opinions*. 4 vols. New York: Chelsea House, 1969. A useful Appendix includes Length of Service, Data on Age, The Presidents, The Justices and Their Politics, Geographical Background, Family Data, Legal Education, Occupational Background and Post-Judicial Activities. A fifth volume, edited by Friedman, covers the years 1969–1978 and supplements the first four.

HENKIN, LOUIS, "Is There a 'Political Question' Doctrine?" 85 *Yale Law Journal* 597 (1971).

HOBSON, CHARLES F., "The Negative on State Laws: James Madison, the Constitution, and the Crisis of Republican Government," 36 *William and Mary Quarterly* (3rd series) 215 (1979).

JACKSON, ROBERT H., *The Struggle for Judicial Supremacy*. New York: Knopf, 1941.

_____, *The Supreme Court and the American System of Government*. Cambridge: Harvard University Press, 1955.

LEVY, LEONARD, ed., *American Constitutional Law: Historical Essays*. New York: Harper Torchbooks, 1966.

LOSS, RICHARD, ed., *Corwin on the Constitution: Volume One, The Foundations of American Constitutional and Political Thought, the Powers of Congress, and the President's Power of Removal*. Ithaca: Cornell University Press, 1981.

MASON, ALPHEUS THOMAS, "Myth and Reality in Supreme Court Decisions," 48 *Virginia Law Review* 1385 (1962).

_____, *The Supreme Court: Palladium of Freedom*. Ann Arbor: University of Michigan Press, 1962.

_____, *The Supreme Court from Taft to Burger*. Baton Rouge: Louisiana State Press, 1979.

_____, "Owen Josephus Roberts," *Dictionary of American Biography*, Supplement 5, 1951–1955, pp. 571–578.

_____, and D. GRIER STEPHENSON, JR., Comps., *American Constitutional Development*. Arlington Heights, Ill.: AHM Publishing Co., 1977.

MCCLOSKEY, R. G., "Foreword: The Reapportionment Case," 75 *Harvard Law Review* 54 (1962).

_____, *The American Supreme Court*. Chicago: University of Chicago Press, 1960.

MILLER, CHARLES A., *The Supreme Court and the Uses of History*. Cambridge: Harvard University Press, 1969.

MORGAN, DONALD G., "The Origin of Supreme Court Dissent," 10 *William and Mary Quarterly* (3rd series) 353 (1953).

MURPHY, WALTER F., *Elements of Judicial Strategy*. Chicago: University of Chicago Press, 1964.

_____, and C. HERMAN PRITCHETT, *Courts, Judges, and Politics,* 3rd ed. New York: Random House, 1979.

SEDDIG, ROBERT G., "John Marshall and the Origins of Supreme Court Leadership," 36 *University of Pittsburgh Law Review* 785 (1975).

STEPHENSON, D. GRIER, JR., *The Supreme Court and the American Republic: An Annotated Bibliography*. New York: Garland Publishing, Inc., 1981.

TRIBE, LAURENCE, *American Constitutional Law*. Mineola, N.Y.: Foundation Press, 1978.

WARREN, CHARLES, "Legislative and Judicial Attacks on the Supreme Court of the United States," 47 *American Law Review* 1 (1913).

_____, *The Supreme Court in United States History*. Boston: Little, Brown, 1928.

WECHSLER, HERBERT, "Toward Neutral Principles of Constitutional Law," 73 *Harvard Law Review* 1 (1959). For a perceptive critique of Wechsler, see Arthur Miller and Ronald Howell, "The Myth of Neutrality in Constitutional Adjudication," 27 *University of Chicago Law Review* 661 (1960).

WESTIN, ALAN F., ed., *An Autobiography of the Supreme Court*. New York: Macmillan, 1963.

SELECTED BIOGRAPHIES

BEVERIDGE, ALBERT J., *The Life of John Marshall*. 4 vols. Boston: Houghton Mifflin, 1916.

CORWIN, EDWARD S., *John Marshall and the Constitution*. New Haven: Yale University Press, 1919.

DANELSKI, DAVID J., and JOSEPH F. TULCHIN, eds., *The Autobiographical Notes of Charles Evans Hughes*. Cambridge: Harvard University Press, 1973.

DILLIARD, IRVING, ed., *One Man's Stand for Freedom: Justice Black and the Bill of Rights*. New York: Knopf, 1963.

DUNNE, GERALD T., *Justice Joseph Story and the Rise of the Supreme Court*. New York: Simon and Schuster, 1970.

———, *Hugo Black and the Judicial Revolution*. New York: Simon and Schuster, 1977.

FAIRMAN, CHARLES, *Mr. Justice Miller and the Supreme Court, 1862-1890*. Cambridge: Harvard University Press, 1939.

HENDEL, SAMUEL, *Charles Evans Hughes and the Supreme Court*. New York: Columbia University Press, 1951.

HIGHSAW, ROBERT B., *Edward Douglass White; Defender of the Conservative Faith*. Baton Rouge: Louisiana State University Press, 1981.

HIRSCH, H. N., *The Enigma of Felix Frankfurter*. New York: Basic Books, 1981.

HOWARD, J. WOODFORD, *Mr. Justice Murphy: A Political Biography*. Princeton: Princeton University Press, 1968.

KING, WILLARD L., *Melville Weston Fuller*. New York: Macmillan, 1950.

LASH, JOSEPH P., ed., *Diaries of Felix Frankfurter* (1882–1965). New York: Norton, 1975.

LERNER, MAX, *The Mind and Faith of Mr. Justice Holmes*. Garden City, N.Y.: Halcyon House Reprint, 1948.

MAGRATH, C. PETER, *Morrison D. Waite*. New York: Macmillan, 1963.

MASON, ALPHEUS THOMAS, *Brandeis: A Free Man's Life*. New York: Viking, 1946.

———, *Harlan Fiske Stone: Pillar of the Law*. New York: Viking, 1956.

———, *William Howard Taft: Chief Justice*. New York: Simon and Schuster, 1964.

PASCHAL, J. FRANCIS, *Mr. Justice Sutherland*. Princeton: Princeton University Press, 1951.

SHAPIRO, DAVID L., ed., *Evolution of a Judicial Philosophy: Selected Opinions and Papers of Justice John Marshall Harlan*. Cambridge: Harvard University Press, 1969.

SIMON, JAMES F., *Independent Journey: The Life of William O. Douglas*. New York: Harper and Row, 1980.

SWISHER, CARL B., *Roger B. Taney*. Washington: Brookings, 1935.

———, *Stephen J. Field: Craftsman of the Law*. Washington: Brookings, 1930.

Unstaged Debate of 1788:
Robert Yates v. *Alexander Hamilton*

*This power in the judicial will enable them [judges] to mould the
Government into almost any shape they please*

ROBERT YATES, *Letters of Brutus,* 1788*

BRUTUS, NO. XI   31 January 1788

. . . Much has been said and written upon the
subject of this new system on both sides, but I
have not met with any writer, who has discussed
the judicial powers with any degree of accuracy.
And yet it is obvious, that we can form but very
imperfect ideas of the manner in which this
government will work, or the effect it will have
in changing the internal police and mode of
distributing justice at present subsisting in the
respective states, without a thorough investigation of the powers of the judiciary and of the
manner in which they will operate. This government is a complete system, not only for making,
but for executing laws. And the courts of law,
which will be constituted by it, are not only to
decide upon the constitution and the laws made
in pursuance of it, but by officers subordinate to
them to execute all their decisions. The real effect of this system of government will therefore
be brought home to the feelings of the people
through the medium of the judicial power. It is,
moreover, of great importance, to examine with
care the nature and extent of the judicial power,
because those who are to be vested with it, are to
be placed in a situation altogether unprecedented in a free country. They are to be
rendered totally independent, both of the people and the legislature, both with respect to
their offices and salaries. No errors they may
commit can be corrected by any power above

them, if any such power there be, nor can they
be removed from office for making ever so many
erroneous adjudications.

The only causes for which they can be displaced, is, conviction of treason, bribery, and
high crimes and misdemeanors.

This part of the plan is so modelled, as to
authorize the courts, not only to carry into execution the powers expressly given, but where
these are wanting or ambiguously expressed,
to supply what is wanting by their own decisions. . . .

They [the courts] will give the sense of every
article of the constitution, that may from time
to time come before them. And in their decisions they will not confine themselves to any
fixed or established rules, but will determine,
according to what appears to them, the reason
and spirit of the constitution. The opinions of
the supreme court, whatever they may be, will
have the force of law, because there is no power
provided in the constitution, that can correct
their errors, or controul their adjudications.
From this court there is no appeal. And I conceive the legislature themselves, cannot set aside
a judgment of this court, because they are
authorized by the constitution to decide in the
last resort. The legislature must be controuled
by the constitution, and not the constitution by
them. They have therefore no more right to set
aside any judgment pronounced upon the construction of the constitution, than they have to
take from the president, the chief command of
the army and navy, and commit it to some other
person. The reason is plain; the judicial and executive derive their authority from the same
source, that the legislature do theirs; and there-

* Published in the *New York Journal and Weekly Regis-
ter,* Numbers 11, 12, and 15. Reprinted in E. S. Corwin,
Court over Constitution (Princeton, N.J.: Princeton
University Press, 1938), Appendix, pp. 231–62.

fore in all cases, where the constitution does not make the one responsible to, or controulable by the other, they are altogether independent of each other.

The judicial power will operate to effect, in the most certain, but yet silent and imperceptible manner, what is evidently the tendency of the constitution:—I mean, an entire subversion of the legislative, executive and judicial powers of the individual states. Every adjudication of the supreme court, on any question that may arise upon the nature and extent of the general government, will affect the limits of the state jurisdiction. In proportion as the former enlarge the exercise of their powers, will that of the latter be restricted.

That the judicial power of the United States, will lean strongly in favour of the general government, and will give such an explanation to the constitution, as will favour an extension of its jurisdiction, is very evident from a variety of considerations.

1st. The constitution itself strongly countenances such a mode of construction. Most of the articles in this system, which convey powers of any considerable importance, are conceived in general and indefinite terms, which are either equivocal, ambiguous, or which require long definitions to unfold the extent of their meaning . . . . The clause which vests the power to pass all laws which are proper and necessary, to carry the powers given into execution . . . leaves the legislature at liberty, to do every thing, which in their judgment is best. It is said, I know, that this clause confers no power on the legislature, which they would not have had without it—though I believe this is not the fact, yet, admitting it to be, it implies that the constitution is not to receive an explanation strictly, according to its letter; but more power is implied than is expressed. . . .

This constitution gives sufficient colour for adopting an equitable construction, if we consider the great end and design it professedly has in view—this appears from its preamble to be, 'to form a more perfect union, establish justice, insure domestic tranquility, provide for the common defense, promote the general welfare,

and secure the blessings of liberty to ourselves and posterity.' The design of this system is here expressed, and it is proper to give such a meaning to the various parts, as will best promote the accomplishment of the end: this idea suggests itself naturally upon reading the preamble, and will countenance the court in giving the several articles such a sense, as will the most effectually promote the ends the constitution had in view. . . .

2d. Not only will the constitution justify the courts in inclining to this mode of explaining it, but they will be interested in using this latitude of interpretation. Every body of men invested with office are tenacious of power; they feel interested, and hence it has become a kind of maxim, to hand down their offices, with all its rights and privileges, unimpaired to their successors; the same principle will influence them to extend their power, and increase their rights; this of itself will operate strongly upon the courts to give such a meaning to the constitution in all cases where it can possibly be done, as will enlarge the sphere of their own authority. Every extension of the power of the general legislature, as well as of the judicial powers, will increase the powers of the courts; and the dignity and importance of the judges, will be in proportion to the extent and magnitude of the powers they exercise. I add, it is highly probable that emolument of the judges will be increased, with the increase of the business they will have to transact and its importance. From these considerations the judges will be interested to extend the powers of the courts, and to construe the constitution as much as possible, in such a way as to favour it; and that they will do it, appears probable.

3d. Because they will have precedent to plead, to justify them in it. It is well known, that the courts in England, have by their own authority, extended their jurisdiction far beyond the limits set them in their original institution, and by the laws of the land. . . .

When the courts will have a president [precedent] before them of a court which extended its jurisdiction in opposition to an act of the legislature, is it not to be expected that they will extend theirs, especially when there is nothing in the constitution expressly against it? and they are authorized to construct its meaning, and are not under any controul?

This power in the judicial, will enable them to mould the government, into almost any shape they please. . . .

BRUTUS, NO. XV   20 March 1788

I do not object to the judges holding their commissions during good behaviour. I suppose it a proper provision provided they were made properly responsible. But I say, this system has followed the English government in this, while it has departed from almost every other principle of their jurisprudence, under the idea, of rendering the judges independent; which, in the British constitution, means no more than that they hold their places during good behaviour, and have fixed salaries, they have made the judges *independent,* in the fullest sense of the word. There is no power above them, to controul any of their decisions. There is no authority that can remove them, and they cannot be controuled by the laws of the legislature. In short, they are independent of the people, of the legislature, and of every power under heaven. Men placed in this situation will generally soon feel themselves independent of heaven itself. . . .

The supreme court then have a right, independent of the legislature, to give a construction of the constitution and every part of it, and there is no power provided in this system to correct their construction or do it away. If, therefore, the legislature pass any laws, inconsistent with the sense the judges put upon the constitution, they will declare it void; and therefore in this respect their power is superior to that of the legislature. . . .

I have, in the course of my observation on this constitution, affirmed and endeavored to shew, that it was calculated to abolish entirely the state governments, and to melt down the states into one entire government, for every purpose as well internal and local, as external and national. . . .

Perhaps nothing could have been better conceived to facilitate the abolition of the state government than the constitution of the judicial. They will be able to extend the limits of the general government gradually, and by insensible degrees, and to accommodate themselves to the temper of the people. . . .

Had the construction of the constitution been left with the legislature, they would have explained it at their peril; if they exceeded their powers, or sought to find, in the spirit of the constitution, more than was expressed in the letter, the people from whom they derived their power could remove them, and do themselves right; and indeed I can see no other remedy that the people can have against their rulers for encroachments of this nature. A constitution is a compact of a people with their rulers; if the rulers break the compact, the people have a right and ought to remove them and do themselves justice; but in order to enable them to do this with the greater facility, those whom the people chuse at stated periods, should have the power in the last resort to determine the sense of the compact; if they determine contrary to the understanding of the people, an appeal will lie to the people at the period when the rulers are to be elected, and they will have it in their power to remedy the evil; but when this power is lodged in the hands of men independent of the people, and of their representatives, and who are not, constitutionally, accountable for their opinions, no way is left to controul them but *with a high hand and an outstretched arm.*

The Judiciary is beyond comparison the weakest of the three departments of power

ALEXANDER HAMILTON, *The Federalist*, No. 78*

HAMILTON'S REPLY TO 'BRUTUS'

We proceed now to an examination of the judiciary department of the proposed government. . . .

Whoever attentively considers the different departments of power must perceive, that, in a government in which they are separated from each other, the judiciary, from the nature of its functions, will always be the least dangerous to the political rights of the Constitution; because it will be least in a capacity to annoy or injure them. . . . The judiciary . . . has no influence over either the sword or the purse; no direction either of the strength or of the wealth of the society; and can take no active resolution whatever. It may truly be said to have neither FORCE nor WILL, but merely judgment; and must ultimately depend upon the aid of the executive arm even for the efficacy of its judgments.

This simple view of the matter suggests several important consequences. It proves incontestably, that the judiciary is beyond comparison the weakest of the three departments of power; that it can never attack with success either of the other two; and that all possible care is requisite to enable it to defend itself against their attacks. It equally proves, that though individual oppression may now and then proceed from the courts of justice, the general liberty of the people can never be endangered from that quarter; I mean so long as the judiciary remains truly distinct from both the legislature and the Executive. . . .

Some perplexity respecting the right of courts to pronounce legislative acts void, because contrary to the Constitution, has arisen

* Henry Cabot Lodge, ed., *The Federalist* (New York: G. P. Putnam's Sons, 1904).

from an imagination that the doctrine would imply a superiority of the judiciary to the legislative power. It is urged that the authority which can declare the acts of another void, must necessarily be superior to the one whose acts may be declared void. As this doctrine is of great importance in all the American constitutions, a brief discussion of the ground on which it rests cannot be unacceptable.

There is no position which depends on clearer principles, than that every act of a delegated authority, contrary to the tenor of the commission under which it is exercised, is void. No legislative act, therefore, contrary to the Constitution, can be valid. To deny this, would be to affirm, that the deputy is greater than his principal; that the servant is above his master; that the representatives of the people are superior to the people themselves; that men acting by virtue of powers, may do not only what their powers do not authorize, but what they forbid.

If it be said that the legislative body are themselves the constitutional judges of their own powers, and that the construction they put upon them is conclusive upon the other departments, it may be answered, that this cannot be the natural presumption, where it is not to be collected from any particular provisions in the Constitution. It is not otherwise to be supposed, that the Constitution could intend to enable the representatives of the people to substitute their *will* to that of their constituents. It is far more rational to suppose, that the courts were designed to be an intermediate body between the people and the legislature, in order, among other things, to keep the latter within the limits assigned to their authority. The interpretation of the laws is the proper and peculiar province of the courts. A constitution is, in fact, and must be regarded by the judges, as a fundamental law. It therefore belongs to them to ascertain its meaning, as well as the meaning of any particular act proceeding from the legislative body. If there should happen to be an irreconcilable variance between the two, that which has the superior obligation and validity ought, of course, to be preferred; or, in other words, the Constitution ought to be preferred to the statute, the intention of the people to the intention of their agents.

Nor does this conclusion by any means suppose a superiority of the judicial to the legislative power. It only supposes that the power of the people is superior to both; and that where the will of the legislature, declared in its statutes, stands in opposition to that of the people, declared in the Constitution, the judges ought to be governed by the latter rather than the former. They ought to regulate their decisions by the fundamental laws, rather than by those which are not fundamental. . . .

If, then, the courts of justice are to be considered as the bulwarks of a limited Constitution against legislative encroachments, this consideration will afford a strong argument for the permanent tenure of judicial offices, since nothing will contribute so much as this to that independent spirit in the judges which must be essential to the faithful performance of so arduous a duty.

This independence of the judges is equally requisite to guard the Constitution and the rights of individuals from the effects of those ill humors, which the arts of designing men, or the influence of particular conjunctures, sometimes disseminate among the people themselves, and which, though they speedily give place to better information, and more deliberate reflection, have a tendency, in the meantime, to occasion dangerous innovations in the government, and serious oppressions of the minor party in the community. . . .

But it is not with a view to infractions of the Constitution only, that the independence of the judges may be an essential safeguard against the effects of occasional ill humors in the society. These sometimes extend no farther than to the injury of the private rights of particular classes of citizens, by unjust and partial laws. Here also the firmness of the judicial magistracy is of vast importance in mitigating the severity and confining the operation of such laws. . . . This is a circumstance calculated to have more influence upon the character of our governments, than but few may be aware of. The benefits of the integrity and moderation of the judiciary have already been felt in more States than one; and though they may have displeased those whose sinister expectations they may have disappointed, they must have commanded the esteem and applause of all the virtuous and disinterested. . . .

There is yet a further and a weightier reason for the permanency of the judicial offices, which is deducible from the nature of the qualifications they require. It has been frequently remarked, with great propriety, that a voluminous code of laws is one of the inconveniences necessarily connected with the advantages of a free government. To avoid an arbitrary discretion in the courts, it is indispensable that they should be bound down by strict rules and precedents, which serve to define and point out their duty in every particular case that comes before them; and it will readily be conceived from the variety of controversies which grow out of the folly and wickedness of mankind, that the records of those precedents must unavoidably swell to a very considerable bulk, and must demand long and laborious study to acquire a competent knowledge of them. Hence it is, that there can be but few men in the society who will have sufficient skill in the laws to qualify them for the stations of judges. And making the proper deductions for the ordinary depravity of human nature, the number must be still smaller of those who unite the requisite integrity with the requisite knowledge. These considerations apprise us, that the government can have no great option between fit character; and that a temporary duration in office, which would naturally discourage such characters from quitting a lucrative line of practice to accept a seat on the bench, would have a tendency to throw the administration of justice into hands less able, and less well qualified, to conduct it with utility and dignity. . . .

Marbury v. Madison
1 Cranch (5 U.S.) 137, 2 L.Ed. 60 (1803)

Shortly before the end of President Adams's term, he nominated Marbury and three others to be justices of the peace in the District of Columbia. Their nominations were confirmed and commissions signed by the President, but the Secretary of State, John Marshall, had not delivered them. Jefferson's new Secretary of State, James Madison, refused to deliver the commissions, claiming that delivery was necessary to complete the appointments. The four men asked the Supreme Court to issue a writ of mandamus ordering delivery in the exercise of its original jurisdiction. Mandamus was not sought from lower federal courts.

The opinion of the court was delivered by the CHIEF JUSTICE [MARSHALL]. . . .

The first object of inquiry is—Has the applicant a right to the commission he demands? . . . [The court finds that as Marbury's appointment was complete he has a right to the commission.]

2. This brings us to the second inquiry; which is: If he has a right, and that right has been violated, do the laws of this country afford him a remedy? . . . [The court finds that they do.]

3. It remains to be inquired whether he is entitled to the remedy for which he applies? This depends on 1st. The nature of the writ applied for; and 2d. The power of this court.

1st. . . . This, then, is a plain case for a *mandamus,* either to deliver the commission, or a copy of it from the record; and it only remains to be inquired, whether it can issue from this court.

The act to establish the judicial courts of the United States authorizes the supreme court "to issue writs of *mandamus,* in cases warranted by the principles and usages of law, to any courts appointed, or persons holding office, under the authority of the United States." . . . The constitution vests the whole judicial power of the United States in one supreme court, and such inferior courts as congress shall, from time to time, ordain and establish. This power is expressly extended to all cases arising under the laws of the United States; and consequently, in some form, may be exercised over the present case; because the right claimed is given by a law of the United States.

In the distribution of this power, it is declared, that "the supreme court shall have original jurisdiction, in all cases affecting ambassadors, other public ministers and consuls, and those in which a state shall be a party. In all other cases, the supreme court shall have appellate jurisdiction." . . . If it has been intended to leave it in the discretion of the legislature, to apportion the judicial power between the supreme and inferior courts, according to the will of that body, it would certainly have been useless to have proceeded further than to have defined the judicial power, and the tribunals in which it should be vested. The subsequent part of the section is mere surplusage—is entirely without meaning, if such is to be the construction. If congress remains at liberty to give this court appellate jurisdiction, where the constitution has declared their jurisdiction shall be original; and original jurisdiction where the constitution has declared it shall be appellate; the distribution of jurisdiction, made in the constitution, is form without substance. . . . To enable this court, then, to issue a *mandamus,* it must be shown to be an exercise of appellate jurisdiction, or to be necessary to enable them to exercise appellate jurisdiction. . . . It is the essential criterion of appellate jurisdiction, that it revises and corrects the proceedings in a cause already instituted, and does not create that cause. Although therefore, a *mandamus* may be directed to courts, yet to issue such a writ to an officer, for the delivery of a paper, is, in effect, the same as to sustain an original action for that paper, and therefore, seems not to belong to appellate, but to original jurisdiction. Neither is it necessary in such a case as this, to enable the court to exercise its appellate jurisdiction. The authority, therefore, given to the supreme court, by the act establishing the judicial courts of the United States, to issue writs of *mandamus* to public officers, appears not to be warranted by the constitution; and it becomes necessary to inquire whether a jurisdiction so conferred can be exercised.

The question, whether an act, repugnant to the constitution, can become the law of the land, is a question deeply interesting to the United States: but, happily, not of an intricacy proportioned to its interest. It seems only necessary to recognize certain principles, supposed to have been long and well established, to decide it. That the people have an original right to establish, for their future government, such principles as, in their opinion, shall most conduce to their own happiness, is the basis on which the whole American fabric has been erected. The exercise of this original right is a very great exertion; nor can it, nor ought it, to be frequently repeated. The principles, therefore, so established, are deemed fundamental: and as the authority from which they proceed is supreme, and can seldom act, they are designed to be permanent.

This original and supreme will organizes the government, and assigns to different departments their respective powers. It may either stop here, or establish certain limits not to be transcended by those departments. The government of the United States is of the latter description. The powers of the legislature are defined and limited; and that those limits may not be mistaken, or forgotten, the constitution is written. To what purpose are powers limited, and to what purpose is that limitation committed to writing, if these limits may, at any time, be passed by those intended to be restrained? The distinction between a government with limited and unlimited powers is abolished, if those limits do not confine the persons on whom they are imposed, and if acts prohibited and acts allowed, are of equal obligation. It is a proposition too plain to be contested, that the constitution controls any

legislative act repugnant to it; or, that the legislature may alter the constitution by an ordinary act.

Between these alternatives, there is no middle ground. The constitution is either a superior paramount law, unchangeable by ordinary means, or it is on a level with ordinary legislative acts, and, like other acts, is alterable when the legislature shall please to alter it. If the former part of the alternative be true, then a legislative act, contrary to the constitution, is not law; if the latter part be true, then written constitutions are absurd attempts, on the part of the people, to limit a power, in its own nature, illimitable.

Certainly, all those who have framed written constitutions contemplate them as forming the fundamental and paramount law of the nation, and consequently, the theory of every such government must be, that an act of the legislature, repugnant to the constitution, is void. This theory is essentially attached to a written constitution, and is, consequently, to be considered, by this court, as one of the fundamental principles of our society. It is not, therefore, to be lost sight of, in the further consideration of this subject.

If an act of the legislature, repugnant to the constitution, is void, does it, notwithstanding its invalidity, bind the courts, and oblige them to give it effect? Or, in other words, though it be not law, does it constitute a rule as operative as if it was a law? This would be to overthrow, in fact, what was established in theory; and would seem, at first view, an absurdity too gross to be insisted on. It shall, however, receive a more attentive consideration.

It is, emphatically, the province and duty of the judicial department, to say what the law is. Those who apply the rule to particular cases, must of necessity expound and interpret that rule. If two laws conflict with each other, the courts must decide on the operation of each. So, if a law be in opposition to the constitution; if both the law and the constitution apply to a particular case, so that the court must either decide that case, conformably to the law, disregarding the constitution; or comformably to the constitution, disregarding the law; the court must determine which of these conflicting rules governs the case: this is of the very essence of judicial duty. If then, the courts are to regard the constitution, and the constitution is superior to any ordinary act of the legislature, the constitution, and not such ordinary act, must govern the case to which they both apply.

Those, then, who controvert the principle, that the constitution is to be considered, in court, as a paramount law, are reduced to the necessity of maintaining that courts must close their eyes on the constitution, and see only the law. This doctrine would subvert the very foundation of all written constitutions. It would declare that an act which, according to the principles and theory of our government, is entirely void, is yet, in practice, completely obligatory. It would declare, that if the legislature shall do what is expressly forbidden, such act, notwithstanding the express prohibition, is in reality effectual. It would be giving to the legislature a practical and real omnipotence, with the same breath which professes to restrict their powers within narrow limits. It is prescribing limits, and declaring that those limits may be passed at pleasure. That it thus reduces to nothing, what we have deemed the greatest improvement on political institutions, a written constitution, would, of itself, be sufficient, in America, where written constitutions have been viewed with so much reverence, for rejecting the construction. But the peculiar expressions of the constitution of the United States furnish additional arguments in favor of its rejection. The judicial power of the United States is extended to all cases arising under the constitution. Could it be the intention of those who gave this power, to say, that in using it, the constitution should not be looked into? That a case arising under the constitution should be decided, without examining the instrument under which it arises? This is too extravagant to be maintained. In some cases, then, the constitution must be looked into by the judges. And if they can open it at all, what part of it are they forbidden to read or to obey?

There are many other parts of the constitu-

tion which serve to illustrate this subject. It is declared, that "no tax or duty shall be laid on articles exported from any state." Suppose, a duty on the export of cotton, of tobacco, or of flour; and a suit instituted to recover it. Ought judgment to be rendered in such a case? Ought the judges to close their eyes on the constitution, and only see the law?

The constitution declares "that no bill of attainder or *ex post facto* law shall be passed." If, however, such a bill should be passed, and a person should be prosecuted under it, must the court condemn to death those victims whom the constitution endeavors to preserve?

"No person," says the constitution, "shall be convicted of treason, unless on the testimony of two witnesses to the same overt act, or on confession in open court." Here, the language of the constitution is addressed especially to the courts. It prescribes, directly for them, a rule of evidence not to be departed from. If the legislature should change that rule, and declare one witness, or a confession out of court, sufficient for conviction, must the constitutional principle yield to the legislative act?

From these, and many other selections which might be made, it is apparent, that the framers of the constitution contemplated that instrument as a rule for the government of courts, as well as of the legislature. Why otherwise does it direct the judges to take an oath to support it? This oath certainly applies, in an especial manner, to their conduct in their official character. How immoral to impose it on them, if they were to be used as the instruments, and the knowing instruments, for violating what they swear to support!

The oath of office, too, imposed by the legislature, is completely demonstrative of the legislative opinion on this subject. It is in these words: "I do solemnly swear, that I will administer justice, without respect to persons, and do equal right to the poor and to the rich; and that I will faithfully and impartially discharge all the duties incumbent on me as———, according to the best of my abilities and understanding, agreeable to the constitution and laws of the United States." Why does a judge swear to discharge his duties agreeably to the constitution of the United States, if that constitution forms no rule for his government? If it is closed upon him, and cannot be inspected by him? If such be the real state of things, this is worse than solemn mockery. To prescribe, or to take this oath, becomes equally a crime.

It is also not entirely unworthy of observation, that in declaring what shall be the supreme law of the land, the constitution itself is first mentioned; and not the laws of the United States, generally, but those only which shall be made in pursuance of the constitution, have that rank.

Thus, the particular phraseology of the constitution of the United States confirms and strengthens the principle, supposed to be essential to all written constitutions, that a law repugnant to the constitution is void; and that courts, as well as other departments, are bound by that instrument.

The rule must be discharged.

Eakin v. Raub
12 Sergeant and Rawle (Pennsylvania Supreme Court) 330 (1825)

The dissenting opinion by Justice Gibson of the Pennsylvania Supreme Court in this unimportant 1825 case is generally recognized as the most effective answer to Marshall's famous argument supporting judicial review. Justice Gibson's opinion, Professor J. B. Thayer observed, "has fallen strangely out of sight. It is much the ablest discussion of the question [of the power of the judiciary to declare legislative acts unconstitutional] which I have ever seen, not excepting the judgment of Marshall in *Marbury* v. *Madison,* which as I venture to think has been overpraised." Justice Gibson's bold and impressive argument was a substantial factor in preventing his own appointment to the Supreme Court on the death of Justice Washington in 1830. In 1845 Gibson himself recanted, because the legislature of Pennsylvania had "sanctioned the pretensions of the courts to deal freely with the acts of the legislature, and from experience of the necessity of the case" (see *Norris* v. *Clymer,* 2 Pa. 281).

GIBSON, J....
I am aware, that a right [in the judiciary] to declare all unconstitutional acts void ... is generally held as a professional dogma, but, I apprehend, rather as a matter of faith than of reason. I admit that I once embraced the same doctrine, but without examination, and I shall therefore state the arguments that impelled me to abandon it, with great respect for those by whom it is still maintained. But I may premise, that it is not a little remarkable, that although the right in question has all along been claimed by the judiciary, no judge has ventured to discuss it, except Chief Justice Marshall, and if the argument of a jurist so distinguished for the strength of his ratiocinative powers be found inconclusive, it may fairly be set down to the weakness of the position which he attempts to defend....

I begin, then, by observing that in this country, the powers of the judiciary are divisible into those that are POLITICAL and those that are purely civil. Every power by which one organ of the government is enabled to control another, or to exert an influence over its acts, is a political power....

The constitution and the right of the legislature to pass the act, may be in collision. But is that a legitimate subject for judicial determination? If it be, the judiciary must be a peculiar organ, to revise the proceedings of the legislature, and to correct its mistakes; and in what part of the constitution are we to look for this proud pre-eminence? Viewing the matter in the opposite direction, what would be thought of an act of assembly in which it should be declared that the supreme court had, in a particular case, put a wrong construction on the constitution of the United States, and that the judgment should therefore be reversed? It would doubtless be thought a usurpation of judicial power. But it is by no means clear, that to declare a law void which has been enacted according to the forms prescribed in the constitution, is not a usurpation of legislative power. . . .

But it has been said to be emphatically the business of the judiciary, to ascertain and pronounce what the law is; and that this necessarily involves a consideration of the constitution. It does so: but how far? If the judiciary will inquire into anything besides the form of enactment, where shall it stop? . . .

. . . In theory, all the organs of the government are of equal capacity; or, if not equal, each must be supposed to have superior capacity only for those things which peculiarly belong to it; and as legislation peculiarly involves the consideration of those limitations which are put on the law-making power, and the interpretation of the laws when made, involves only the construction of the laws themselves, it follows that the construction of the constitution in this particular belongs to the legislature, which ought therefore to be taken to have superior capacity to judge of the constitutionality of its own acts. But suppose all to be of equal capacity in every respect, why should one exercise a controlling power over the rest? That the judiciary is of superior rank, has never been pretended, although it has been said to be co-ordinate. It is not easy, however, to comprehend how the power which gives law to all the rest, can be of no more than equal rank with one which receives it,

and is answerable to the former for the observance of its statutes. Legislation is essentially an act of sovereign power; but the execution of the laws by instruments that are governed by prescribed rules and exercise no power of volition, is essentially otherwise. . . . It may be said, the power of the legislature, also, is limited by prescribed rules. It is so. But it is nevertheless, the power of the people, and sovereign as far as it extends. It cannot be said, that the judiciary is co-ordinate merely because it is established by the constitution. If that were sufficient, sheriffs, registers of wills, and recorders of deeds, would be so too. Within the pale of their authority, the acts of these officers will have the power of the people for their support; but no one will pretend, they are of equal dignity with the acts of the legislature. Inequality of rank arises not from the manner in which the organ has been constituted, but from its essence and the nature of its functions; and the legislative organ is superior to every other, inasmuch as the power to will and to command, is essentially superior to the power to act and to obey. . . .

Everyone knows how seldom men think exactly alike on ordinary subjects; and a government constructed on the principle of assent by all its parts, would be inadequate to the most simple operations. The notion of a complication of counter checks has been carried to an extent in theory, of which the framers of the constitution never dreamt. When the entire sovereignty was separated into its elementary parts, and distributed to the appropriate branches, all things incident to the exercise of its powers were committed to each branch exclusively. The negative which each part of the legislature may exercise, in regard to the acts of the other, was thought sufficient to prevent material infractions of the restraints which were put on the power of the whole; for, had it been intended to interpose the judiciary as an additional barrier, the matter would surely not have been left in doubt. The judges would not have been left to stand on the insecure and ever shifting ground of public opinion as to constructive powers; they would have been placed on the impregnable ground of an express grant. They would not have been compelled to resort to debates in the convention, or the opinion that was generally entertained at the time. . . .

The power is said to be restricted to cases that are free from doubt or difficulty. But the abstract existence of a power cannot depend on the clearness or obscurity of the case in which it is to be exercised; for that is a consideration that cannot present itself, before the question of the existence of the power shall have been determined; and, if its existence be conceded, no considerations of policy arising from the obscurity of the particular case, ought to influence the exercise of it. . . .

To say, therefore, that the power is to be exercised but in perfectly clear cases, is to betray a doubt of the propriety of exercising it at all. Were the same caution used in judging of the existence of the power that is inculcated as to the exercise of it, the profession would perhaps arrive at a different conclusion. The grant of a power so extraordinary ought to appear so plain, that he who should run might read. . . .

What I have in view in this inquiry, is the supposed right of the judiciary to interfere, in cases where the constitution is to be carried into effect through the instrumentality of the legislature, and where that organ must necessarily first decide on the constitutionality of its own act. The oath to support the constitution is not peculiar to the judges, but is taken indiscriminately by every officer of the government, and is designed rather as a test of the political principles of the man, than to bind the officer in the discharge of his duty: otherwise it is difficult to determine what operation it is to have in the case of a recorder of deeds, for instance, who, in the execution of his office, has nothing to do with the constitution. But granting it to relate to the official conduct of the judge, as well as every other officer, and not to his political principles, still it must be understood in reference to supporting the constitution, *only as far as that may be involved in his official duty;* and, consequently, if his official duty does not comprehend an inquiry into the authority of the legislature, neither does his oath. . . .

But do not the judges do a positive act in violation of the constitution, when they give effect to an unconstitutional law? Not if the law has been passed according to the forms established in the constitution. The fallacy of the question is, in supposing that the judiciary adopts the acts of the legislature as its own; whereas the enactment of a law and the interpretation of it are not concurrent acts, and as the judiciary is not required to concur in the enactment, neither is it in the breach of the constitution which may be the consequence of the enactment. The fault is imputable to the legislature, and on it the responsibility exclusively rests. . . .

But it has been said, that this construction would deprive the citizen of the advantages which are peculiar to a written constitution, by at once declaring the power of the legislature in practice to be illimitable. . . . But there is no magic or inherent power in parchment and ink, to command respect and protect principles from violation. In the business of government a recurrence to first principles answers the end of an observation at sea with a view to correct the dead reckoning; and for this purpose, a written constitution is an instrument of inestimable value. It is of inestimable value, also, in rendering its first principles familiar to the mass of people; for, after all, there is no effectual guard against legislative usurpation but public opinion, the force of which, in this country is inconceivably great. . . . Once let public opinion be so corrupt as to sanction every misconstruction of the constitution and abuse of power which the temptation of the moment may dictate, and the party which may happen to be predominant, will laugh at the puny efforts of a dependent power to arrest it in its course.

For these reasons, I am of [the] opinion that it rests with the people, in whom full and absolute sovereign power resides, to correct abuses in legislation, by instructing their representatives to repeal the obnoxious act. What is wanting to plenary power in the govenment, is reserved by the people for their own immediate use; and to redress an infringement of their rights in this respect, would seem to be an accessory of the power thus reserved. It might, perhaps, have been better to vest the power in the judiciary; as it might be expected that its habits of deliberation, and the aid derived from the arguments of counsel, would more frequently lead to accurate conclusions. On the other hand, the judiciary is not infallible; and an error by it would admit of no remedy but a more distinct expression of the public will, through the extraordinary medium of a convention; whereas, an error by the legislature admits of a remedy by an exertion of the same will, in the ordinary exercise of the right of suffrage,—a mode better calculated to attain the end, without popular excitement. It may be said, the people would probably not notice an error of their representatives. But they would as probably do so, as notice an error of the judiciary; and, besides, it is a postulate in the theory of our government, and the very basis of the superstructure, that the people are wise, virtuous, and competent to manage their own affairs; and if they are not so, in fact, still every question of this sort must be determined according to the principles of the constitution, as it came from the hands of the framers, and the existence of a defect which was not foreseen, would not justify those who administer the government, in applying a corrective in practice, which can be provided only by convention. . . .

But in regard to an act of [a state] assembly, which is found to be in collision with the constitution, laws, or treaties of the *United States,* I take the duty of the judiciary to be exactly the reverse. By becoming parties to the federal constitution, the states have agreed to several limitations of their individual sovereignty, to enforce which, it was thought to be absolutely necessary to prevent them from giving effect to laws in violation of those limitations, through the instrumentality of their own judges. Accordingly, it is declared in the sixth article and second section of the federal constitution, that "This constitution, and the laws of the *United States* which shall be made in pursuance thereof, and all treaties made, or which shall be made under the authority of the *United States,* shall be the *supreme* law of the land; and the *judges* in every *state* shall be BOUND thereby: anything in the *laws* or *constitution* of any *state* to the contrary notwithstanding." . . .

Dred Scott v. *Sandford*
19 Howard (60 U.S.) 393, 15 L.Ed. 691 (1857)

In 1834, Dred Scott, a Negro slave belonging to Dr. Emerson, a surgeon in the United States Army, was taken by his master to Illinois, where slavery was forbidden. Later on, Scott was taken to Fort Snelling, in the territory of Louisiana, north of 36° 30', an area in which slavery was forbidden by the Missouri Compromise. Having been taken back to Missouri, the Negro brought suit in United States Circuit Court in Missouri to recover his freedom, basing his action on the claim that residence in a free territory conferred freedom. On a writ of error, from an adverse judgment, Dred Scott appealed to the Supreme Court.

MR. CHIEF JUSTICE TANEY delivered the opinion of the court.

. . . The question is simply this: Can a negro, whose ancestors were imported into this country, and sold as slaves, become a member of the political community formed and brought into existence by the Constitution of the United States, and as such become entitled to all the rights, and privileges, and immunities, guarantied (sic) by that instrument to the citizen? One of which rights is the privilege of suing in a court of the United States in the cases specified in the Constitution.

We think . . . [the people of the negro race] . . . are not included, and were not intended to be included, under the words ''citizens'' in the Constitution, and can therefore claim none of the rights and privileges which that instrument provides for and secures to citizens of the United States. On the contrary, they were at that time considered as a subordinate and inferior class of beings, who had been subjugated by the dominant race, and, whether emancipated or not, yet remained subject to their authority, and had no rights or privileges but such as those who held the power and the Government might choose to grant them.

It is not the province of the court to decide upon the justice or injustice, the policy or impolicy, of these laws. The decision of that question belonged to the political or law-making power; to those who formed the sovereignty and framed the Constitution. The duty of the court is, to interpret the instrument they have framed, with the best lights we can obtain on the subject, and to administer it as we find it, according to its true intent and meaning when it was adopted. . . .

The question then arises, whether the provisions of the Constitution, in relation to the personal rights and privileges to which the citizen of a State should be entitled, embraced the negro African race, at that time in this country, or who might afterwards be imported, who had then or should afterwards be made free in any State; and to put it in the power of a single State to make him a citizen of the United States, and endue him with the full rights of citizenship in every other State without their consent? Does the Constitution of the United States act upon him whenever he shall be made free under the laws of a State, and raised there to the rank of a citizen, and immediately clothe him with all the privileges of a citizen in every other State, and in its own courts?

The court thinks the affirmative of these propositions cannot be maintained. And if it cannot, the plaintiff in error could not be a citizen of the State of Missouri, within the meaning of the Constitution of the United States, and, consequently, was not entitled to sue in its courts. . . .

In the opinion of the court, the legislation and histories of the times, and the language used in the Declaration of Independence, show, that neither the class of persons who had been imported as slaves, nor their descendants, whether they had become free or not, were then acknowledged as a part of the people, nor intended to be included in the general words used in that memorable instrument. . . .

They had for more than a century before been regarded as beings of an inferior order, and altogether unfit to associate with the white race, either in social or political relations; and so far inferior, that they had no rights which the white man was bound to respect; and that the negro might justly and lawfully be reduced to slavery for his benefit. He was bought and sold, and treated as an ordinary article of merchandise and traffic, whenever a profit could be made by it. This opinion was at that time fixed and universal in the civilized portion of the white race. It was regarded as an axiom in morals as well as in politics, which no one thought of disputing, or supposed to be open to dispute; and men in every grade and position in society daily and habitually acted upon it in their private pursuits, as well as in matters of public concern, without doubting for a moment the correctness of this opinion. . . .

The only two provisions [of the Constitution] which point to them and include them [Art. I, Sec. 9, and Art. IV, Sec. 2], treat them as property, and make it the duty of the Government to protect it; no other power, in relation to this race, is to be found in the Constitution; and as it is a Government of special, delegated, powers, no authority beyond these two provisions can be constitutionally exercised. The Government of the United States had no right to interfere for any other purpose but that of protecting the rights of the owner, leaving it altogether with the several States to deal with this race, whether emancipated or not, as each State may think justice, humanity, and the interests and safety of society, require. The States evidently intended to reserve this power exclusively to themselves.

No one, we presume, supposes that any change in public opinion or feeling, in relation to this unfortunate race, in the civilized nations of Europe or in this country, should induce the court to give to the words of the Constitution a more liberal construction in their favor than they were intended to bear when the instrument was framed and adopted. Such an argument would be altogether inadmissible in any tribunal called on to interpret it. If any of its provisions are deemed unjust, there is a mode prescribed in the instrument itself by which it may be amended; but while it remains unaltered, it must be construed now as it was understood at the time of its adoption. It is not only the same in words, but the same in meaning, and delegates the same powers to the Government, and reserves and secures the same rights and privileges to the citizen; and as long as it continues to exist in its present form, it speaks not only in the same words, but with the same meaning and intent with which it spoke when it came from the hands of its framers, and was voted on and adopted by the people of the United States. Any other rule of construction would abrogate the judicial character of this court, and make it the mere reflex of the popular opinion of the day. . . .

What the construction was at that time, we think can hardly admit of doubt. We have the language of the Declaration of Independence and of the Articles of Confederation, in addition to the plain words of the Constitution itself; we have the legislation of the different States, before, about the time, and since, the Constitution was adopted; we have the legislation of Congress, from the time of its adoption to a recent period; and we have the constant and uniform action of the Executive Department, all concurring together, and leading to the same result. And if anything in relation to the construction of the Constitution can be regarded as settled, it is that which we now give to the word "citizen" and the word "people." . . .

The act of Congress, upon which the plaintiff relies, declares that slavery and involuntary servitude, except as a punishment for crime, shall be forever prohibited in all that part of the territory ceded by France, under the name of Louisiana, which lies north of thirty-six degrees thirty minutes north latitude, and not included within the limits of Missouri. And the . . . inquiry is whether Congress was authorized to pass this law under any of the powers granted to it by the Constitution; for if the authority is not given by that instrument, it is the duty of this court to declare it void and inoperative, and incapable of conferring freedom upon any one who is held as a slave under the laws of any one of the States.

The counsel for the plaintiff has laid much stress upon that article in the Constitution which confers on Congress the power "to dispose of and make all needful rules and regulations respecting the territory or other property belonging to the United States," but, in the judgment of the court, that provision has no bearing on the present controversy, and the power there given, whatever it may be, is confined, and was intended to be confined, to the territory which at that time belonged to, or was claimed by the United States, and was within their boundaries as settled by the treaty with Great Britain, and can have no influence upon a territory afterwards acquired from a foreign Government. It was a special provision for a known and particular territory, and to meet a present emergency, and nothing more.

. . . The powers of the Government and the rights and privileges of the citizen are regulated and plainly defined by the Constitution itself. And when the Territory becomes a part of the United States, the Federal Government enters into possession in the character impressed upon it by those who created it. It enters upon it with its powers over the citizen strictly defined, and limited by the Constitution, from which it derives its own existence, and by virtue of which alone it continues to exist and act as a Government and sovereignty. It has no power of any kind beyond it; and it cannot, when it enters a Territory of the United States, put off its character and assume discretionary or despotic powers which the Constitution has denied to it.

It cannot create for itself a new character separated from the citizens of the United States, and the duties it owes them under the provisions of the Constitution. The Territory being a part of the United States, the Government and the citizen both enter it under the authority of the Constitution, with their respective rights defined and marked out; and the Federal Government can exercise no power over his person or property, beyond what that instrument confers, nor lawfully deny any right which it has reserved. . . .

. . . An Act of Congress which deprives a citizen of the United States of his liberty or property, merely because he came himself or brought his property into a particular Territory of the United States, and who had committed no offense against the laws, could hardly be dignified with the name of due process of law.

The powers over person and property of which we speak are not only not granted to Congress, but are in express terms denied, and they are forbidden to exercise them. And this prohibition is not confined to the States, but the words are general, and extend to the whole territory over which the Constitution gives it power to legislate, including those portions of it remaining under Territorial Government, as well as that covered by States. It is a total absence of power everywhere within the dominion of the United States, and places the citizens of a Territory, so far as these rights are concerned, on the same footing with citizens of the States and guards them as firmly and plainly against any inroads which the General Government might attempt, under the plea of implied or incidental powers. And if Congress itself cannot do this—if it is beyond the powers conferred on the Federal Government—it will be admitted, we presume, that it could not authorize a Territorial Government to exercise them. It would confer no power on any local Government, established by its authority, to violate provisions of the Constitution. . . .

Upon these considerations, it is the opinion of the court that the act of Congress which prohibited a citizen from holding and owning property of this kind in the territory of the United States north of the line therein mentioned, is not warranted by the Constitution, and is therefore void; and that neither Dred Scott himself, nor any of his family, were made free by being carried into this territory; even if they had been carried there by the owner, with the intention of becoming a permanent resident. . . .

MR. JUSTICE CURTIS, joined by MR. JUSTICE MCLEAN, dissenting:

I dissent from the opinion pronounced by the Chief Justice, and from the judgment which the majority of the court think it proper to render in this case. . . .

To determine whether any free persons, descended from Africans held in slavery, were citizens of the United States under the Confederation, and consequently at the time of the adoption of the Constitution of the United States, it is only necessary to know whether any such persons were citizens of either of the States under the Confederation, at the time of the adoption of the Constitution.

Of this there can be no doubt. At the time of the ratification of the Articles of Confederation, all free native-born inhabitants of the States of New Hampshire, Massachusetts, New York, New Jersey, and North Carolina, though descended from African slaves, were not only citizens of those States, but such of them as had the other necessary qualifications possessed the franchise of electors, on equal terms with other citizens. . . .

I dissent, therefore, from that part of the opinion of the majority of the court, in which it is held that a person of African descent cannot be a citizen of the United States; and I regret I must go further, and dissent both from what I deem their assumption of authority to examine the constitutionality of the act of Congress commonly called the Missouri Compromise act, and the grounds and conclusions announced in their opinion.

Having first decided that they were bound to consider the sufficiency of the plea to the jurisdiction of the Circuit Court, and having decided that this plea showed that the Circuit Court had no jurisdiction, and consequently that this is a case to which the judicial power of the United States does not extend, they have gone on to examine the merits of the case as they appeared on the trial before the court and jury, on the issues joined on the pleas in bar, and so have reached the question of the power of Congress to pass the act of 1820. On so grave a subject as this, I feel obliged to say that, in my opinion, such an exertion of judicial power transcends the limits of the authority of the court, as described by its repeated decisions and, as I understand, acknowledged in this opinion of the majority of the court. . . .

Nor, in my judgment, will the position, that a prohibition to bring slaves into a Territory deprives any one of his property without due process of law, bear examination. . . .

Ex Parte McCardle
7 Wall. (74 U.S.) 506, 19 L.Ed. 264 (1869)

During Reconstruction after the Civil War, a newspaper editor in Mississippi named William McCardle was jailed by a military commander for trial before a military commission for publishing "incendiary and libelous" articles. McCardle was a civilian and sought release on *habeas corpus* in the Circuit Court for the Southern District of Mississippi. After hearing his case, the judge remanded McCardle to the custody of the military authorities. McCardle then took an appeal to the Supreme Court authorized by a statute passed by Congress in 1867. Following argument of his case in the Supreme Court and while the Justices had it under advisement, Congress overrode President Johnson's veto and repealed the statute in 1868 (15 Stat. 44). The majority in Congress apparently feared that the constitutionality of much of its Reconstruction program was at stake in the litigation. Chief Justice Chase noted in his opinion that decision in the case had been delayed by his participation in the President's impeachment trial in the Senate. The *McCardle* case should be read in the light of *Ex parte Yerger* (8 Wall. 85: 1869) and *United States* v. *Klein* (13 Wall. 128: 1872).

MR. CHIEF JUSTICE CHASE delivered the opinion of the Court. . . .

The first question necessarily is that of jurisdiction; for, if the act of March, 1868, takes away the jurisdiction defined by the act of February, 1867, it is useless, if not improper, to enter into any discussion of other questions.

It is quite true, as was argued by the counsel for the petitioner, that the appellate jurisdiction of this court is not derived from acts of Congress. It is, strictly speaking, conferred by the Constitution. But it is conferred "with such exceptions and under such regulations as Congress shall make."

It is unnecessary to consider whether, if Congress had made no exceptions and no regulations, this court might not have exercised general appellate jurisdiction under rules prescribed by itself. For among the earliest acts of the first Congress, at its first session, was the act of September 24th, 1789, to establish the judicial courts of the United States. That act provided for the organization of this court, and prescribed regulations for the exercise of its jurisdiction.

The source of that jurisdiction, and the limitations of it by the Constitution and by statute, have been on several occasions subjects of consideration here. . . .

The principle that the affirmation of appellate jurisdiction implies the negation of all such jurisdiction not affirmed having been thus established, it was an almost necessary consequence that acts of Congress, providing for the exercise of jurisdiction, should come to be spoken of as acts granting jurisdiction, and not as acts making exceptions to the constitutional grant of it.

The exception to appellate jurisdiction in the case before us, however, is not an inference from the affirmation of other appellate jurisdiction. It is made in terms. The provision of the act of 1867, affirming the appellate jurisdiction of this court in cases of *habeas corpus* is expressly repealed. It is hardly possible to imagine a plainer instance of positive exception.

We are not at liberty to inquire into the motives of the legislature. We can only examine into its power under the Constitution; and the power to make exceptions to the appellate jurisdiction of this court is given by express words.

What, then, is the effect of the repealing act upon the case before us? We cannot doubt as to this. Without jurisdiction the court cannot proceed at all in any cause. Jurisdiction is power to declare the law, and when it ceases to exist, the only function remaining to the court is that of announcing the fact and dismissing the cause. And this is not less clear upon authority than upon principle. . . .

It is quite clear, therefore, that this court cannot proceed to pronounce judgment in this case, for it has no longer jurisdiction of the appeal; and judicial duty is not less fitly performed by declining ungranted jurisdiction than in exercising firmly that which the Constitution and the laws confer.

Counsel seem to have supposed, if effect be given to the repealing act in question, that the whole appellate power of the court, in cases of *habeas corpus,* is denied. But this is an error. The act of 1868 does not except from that jurisdiction any cases but appeals from Circuit Courts under the act of 1867. It does not affect the jurisdiction which was previously exercised.

The appeal of the petitioner in this case must be dismissed for want of jurisdiction.

United States v. *Butler*
297 U.S. 1, 56 S.Ct. 312, 80 L.Ed. 477 (1936)

In 1933 Congress attempted to benefit farm producers through the Agricultural Adjustment Act. The basic scheme adopted was the payment of various amounts to farmers in return for the farmers' promise to reduce crop acreage. A processing tax designed to finance the program of benefit payments was levied on the first processor of the commodity involved, and was to be measured by the difference between current average farm prices and the price prevailing in an earlier base period (1909–1914). Butler, the receiver for a processor, refused to pay the tax. The District Court ordered it paid, but the Circuit Court of Appeals reversed the order. The government appealed.

The primary criteria for inclusion of cases in this book are, among other things, significance of the decision and quality of the reasoning in its support. Certain cases, however, may not meet these tests and yet be worthy of space for instructional purposes. A striking example is *United States* v. *Butler*. In an opinion by Justice Roberts, the Court considers three theories of the taxing power. Rejecting the theory bearing the name Madison, he embraces the Hamiltonian doctrine only to formulate one of his own, completely at odds with Hamilton's broad conception of national power. The essence of his argument is that if it is within the reserved powers of the states to do something on a local scale, the national government is not permitted to attempt a comparable end on a more general scale. In other words, the Tenth Amendment limits national power. (The essay in chapter 7 discusses both *Butler* and the taxing power.)

To support this line of reasoning, Justice Roberts invoked the so-called mechanical theory of judicial interpretation. The effect is to make a very delicate process comparable to the task of the dry-goods clerk measuring calico or the grocer weighing coffee. Speaking for a minority of three, Justice Stone attacked this simplistic approach in his famous observation: "The only check upon our . . . power is our own sense of self-restraint."

Stone's seemingly realistic approach provoked Justice Sutherland a year later to use his dissenting opinion in *West Coast Hotel* v. *Parrish* (300 U.S. 379: 1937) to revive judicial orthodoxy. Thus we have, brought into juxtaposition, three different theories of judicial review, all within the short span of fifteen months. (*West Coast Hotel* and its significance in constitutional theory are discussed in chapter 8.)

MR. JUSTICE ROBERTS delivered the opinion of the Court. . . .

It is inaccurate and misleading to speak of the exaction from processors prescribed by the challenged act as a tax, or to say that as a tax it is subject to no infirmity. A tax, in the general understanding of the term, and as used in the Constitution, signifies an exaction for the support of the government. The word has never been thought to connote the expropriation of money from one group for the benefit of another. We may concede that the latter sort of imposition is constitutional when imposed to effectuate regulation of a matter in which both groups are interested and in respect of which there is a power of legislative regulation. But manifestly no justification for it can be found unless as an integral part of such regulation. The exaction cannot be wrested out of its setting, denominated an excise for raising revenue and legalized by ignoring its purpose as a mere instrumentality for bringing about a desired end. To do this would be to shut our eyes to what all others than we can see and understand. *Child*

Labor Tax Case [*Bailey* v. *Drexel Furniture Co.*]. . . .

We conclude that the act is one regulating agricultural production; that the tax is a mere incident of such regulation; and that the respondents have standing to challenge the legality of the exaction.

It does not follow that as the act is not an exertion of the taxing power and the exaction not a true tax, the statute is void or the exaction uncollectible. For, to paraphrase what was said in the Head Money cases, 112 U.S. 580, if this is an expedient regulation by Congress, of a subject within one of its granted powers, "and the end to be attained is one falling within that power, the act is not void, because, within a loose and more extended sense than was used in the Constitution," the exaction is called a tax.

The Government asserts that even if the respondents may question the propriety of the appropriation embodied in the statute, their attack must fail because Article 1, § 8 of the Constitution, authorizes the contemplated expenditure of the funds raised by the tax. This contention presents the great and the controlling question in the case. We approach its decision with a sense of our grave responsibility to render judgment in accordance with the principles established for the governance of all three branches of the Government.

There should be no misunderstanding as to the function of this court in such a case. It is sometimes said that the court assumes a power to overrule or control the action of the people's representatives. This is a misconception. The Constitution is the supreme law of the land ordained and established by the people. All legislation must conform to the principles it lays down. When an act of Congress is appropriately challenged in the courts as not conforming to the constitutional mandate, the judicial branch of the Government has only one duty—to lay the article of the Constitution which is invoked beside the statute which is challenged and to decide whether the latter squares with the former. All the court does, or can do, is to announce its considered judgment upon the question. The only power it has, if such it may be called, is the power of judgment. This court neither approves nor condemns any legislative policy. Its delicate and difficult office is to ascertain and declare whether the legislation is in accordance with, or in contravention of, the provisions of the Constitution; and having done that, its duty ends. . . .

Article 1, § 8, of the Constitution vests sundry powers in the Congress. But two of its clauses have any bearing upon the validity of the statute under review.

The third clause endows the Congress with power "to regulate commerce . . . among the several States." Despite reference in its first section to a burden upon, and an obstruction of the normal currents of commerce, the act under review does not purport to regulate transactions in interstate or foreign commerce. Its stated purpose is the control of agricultural production, a purely local activity, in an effort to raise the prices paid the farmer. Indeed, the Government does not attempt to uphold the validity of the act on the basis of the commerce clause, which, for the purpose of the present case, may be put aside as irrelevant.

The clause thought to authorize the legislation—the first—confers upon the Congress power "to lay and collect Taxes, Duties, Imposts and Excises, to pay the Debts and provide for the common Defense and general Welfare of the United States. . . ." It is not contended that this provision grants power to regulate agricultural production upon the theory that such legislation would promote the general welfare. The government concedes that the phrase "to provide for the general welfare" qualifies the power "to lay and collect taxes." The view that the clause grants power to provide for the general welfare, independently of the taxing power, has never been authoritatively accepted. Mr. Justice Story points out that, if it were adopted, "it is obvious that under color of the generality of the words, to 'provide for the common defence and general welfare,' the government of the United States is, in reality, a government of general and unlimited powers, notwithstanding the subsequent enumeration of specific powers." The true construction undoubtedly is that the only thing granted is the power to tax for the purpose of providing funds for payment of the nation's debts and making provision for the general welfare.

Nevertheless, the Government asserts that warrant is found in this clause for the adoption of the Agricultural Adjustment Act. The argument is that Congress may appropriate and authorize the spending of moneys for the "general welfare"; that the phrase should be liberally construed to cover anything conducive to national welfare; that decision as to what will promote such welfare rests with Congress alone, and the courts may not review its determination; and, finally, that the appropriation under attack was in fact for the general welfare of the United States.

The Congress is expressly empowered to lay taxes to provide for the general welfare. Funds in the Treasury as a result of taxation may be expended only through appropriation. (Article 1, § 9, cl. 7.) They can never accomplish the objects for which they were collected, unless the power to appropriate is as broad as the power to tax. The necessary implication from the terms of the grant is that the public funds may be appropriated ''to provide for the general welfare of the United States.'' These words cannot be meaningless, else they would not have been used. The conclusion must be that they were intended to limit and define the granted power to raise and to expend money. How shall they be construed to effectuate the intent of the instrument?

Since the foundation of the nation, sharp differences of opinion have persisted as to the true interpretation of the phrase. Madison asserted it amounted to no more than a reference to the other powers enumerated in the subsequent clauses of the same section; that, as the United States is a government of limited and enumerated powers, the grant of power to tax and spend for the general national welfare must be confined to the enumerated legislative fields committed to the Congress. In this view the phrase is mere tautology, for taxation and appropriation are or may be necessary incidents of the exercise of any of the enumerated legislative powers. Hamilton, on the other hand, maintained the clause confers a power separate and distinct from those later enumerated, is not restricted in meaning by the grant of them, and Congress consequently has a substantive power to tax and to appropriate, limited only by the requirement that it shall be exercised to provide for the general welfare of the United States. Each contention has had the support of those whose views are entitled to weight. This court has noticed the question, but has never found it necessary to decide which is the true construction. Mr. Justice Story, in his Commentaries, espouses the Hamiltonian position. We shall not review the writings of public men and commentators or discuss the legislative practice. Study of all these leads us to conclude that the reading advocated by Mr. Justice Story is the correct one. While, therefore, the power to tax is not unlimited, its confines are set in the clause which confers it and not in those of Section 8 which bestow and define the legislative powers of the Congress. It results that the power of Congress to authorize expenditure of public moneys for public purposes is not limited by the direct grants of legislative power found in the Constitution.

But the adoption of the broader construction leaves the power to spend subject to limitations. . . .

Story says that if the tax be not proposed for the common defence or general welfare, but for other objects wholly extraneous, it would be wholly indefensible upon constitutional principles. And he makes it clear that the powers of taxation and appropriation extend only to matters of national, as distinguished from local welfare. . . .

We are not now required to ascertain the scope of the phrase ''general welfare of the United States'' or to determine whether an appropriation in aid of agriculture falls within it. Wholly apart from that question, another principle embedded in our Constitution prohibits the enforcement of the Agricultural Adjustment Act. The act invades the reserved rights of the states. It is a statutory plan to regulate and control agricultural production, a matter beyond the powers delegated to the federal government. The tax, the appropriation of the funds raised, and the direction for their disbursement, are but parts of the plan. They are but means to an unconstitutional end.

From the accepted doctrine that the United States is a government of delegated powers, it follows that those not expressly granted, or reasonably to be implied from such as are conferred, are reserved to the states or to the people. To forestall any suggestion to the contrary, the Tenth Amendment was adopted. The same proposition, otherwise stated, is that powers not granted are prohibited. None to regulate agricultural production is given, and therefore legislation by Congress for that purpose is forbidden. . . .

If the taxing power may not be used as the instrument to enforce a regulation of matters of state concern with respect to which the Congress has no authority to interfere, may it, as in the present case, be employed to raise the money necessary to purchase a compliance which the Congress is powerless to command? The Government asserts that whatever might be said against the validity of the plan, if compulsory, it is constitutionally sound because the end is accomplished by voluntary cooperation. There are two sufficient answers to the contention. The regulation is not in fact voluntary. The farmer, of course, may refuse to comply, but the price of such refusal is the loss of benefits. The amount offered is intended to be sufficient to exert pressure on him to agree to the proposed regulation. The power to confer or withhold unlimited benefits is the power to coerce or destroy. If the cotton grower elects not to accept the benefits, he will receive less for his crops; those who receive payments will be able to undersell him. The result may well be financial ruin. The coercive purpose and intent of the statute is not obscured by the fact that it has not been perfectly successful. It is pointed out that, because there still remained a minority whom the rental and benefit payments were insufficient to induce to surrender their independence of action, the Congress has gone further and, in the Bankhead Cotton Act, used the taxing power in a more directly minatory fashion to compel submission. This progression only serves more fully to expose the coercive purpose of the so-called tax imposed by the present act. It is clear that the Department of Agriculture has properly described the plan as one to keep a noncooperating minority in line. This is coercion by economic pressure. The asserted power of choice is illusory. . . .

Congress has no power to enforce its commands on the farmer to the ends sought by the Agricultural Adjustment Act. It must follow that it may not indirectly accomplish those ends by taxing and spending to purchase compliance. The Constitution and the entire plan of our government negative any such use of the power to tax and to spend as the act undertakes to authorize. It does not help to declare that local conditions throughout the nation have created a situation of national concern; for this is but to say that whenever there is a widespread similarity of local conditions, Congress may ignore constitutional limitations upon its own powers and usurp those reserved to the states. If, in lieu of compulsory regulation of subjects within the states' reserved jurisdiction, which is prohibited, the Congress could invoke the taxing and spending power as a means to accomplish the same end, clause 1 of § 8 of article 1 would become the instrument for total subversion of the governmental powers reserved to the individual states.

If the act before us is a proper exercise of the federal taxing power, evidently the regulation of all industry throughout the United States may be accomplished by similar exercises of the same power. . . .

Until recently no suggestion of the existence of any such power in the federal government has been advanced. The expressions of the framers of the Constitution, the decisions of this court interpreting that instrument and the writings of great commentators will be searched in vain for any suggestion that there exists in the clause under discussion or elsewhere in the Constitution, the authority whereby every provision and every fair implication from that instrument may be subverted, the independence of the individual states obliterated, and the United States converted into a central government exercising uncontrolled police power in every state of the Union, superseding all local control or regulation of the affairs or concerns of the states. . . .

Affirmed.

MR. JUSTICE STONE, dissenting. . . .

1. The power of courts to declare a statute unconstitutional is subject to two guiding principles of decision which ought never to be absent from judicial consciousness. One is that courts are concerned only with the power to enact statutes, not with their wisdom. The other is that while unconstitutional exercise of power by the executive and legislative branches of the government is subject to judicial restraint, the only check upon our own exercise of power is our own sense of self-restraint.* For the removal of unwise laws from the statute books appeal lies

---

* This familiar line, frequently quoted, rarely if ever queried, is too sweeping. It overlooks the control Congress and the president may exert. In less than a year after Stone uttered these words, President Roosevelt demonstrated how a president may influence judicial decisions merely by threatening to ''pack'' the Court with justices of his own political persuasion.

not to the courts but to the ballot and to the processes of democratic government.

2. The constitutional power of Congress to levy an excise tax upon the processing of agricultural products is not questioned. The present levy is held invalid, not for any want of power in Congress to lay such a tax to defray public expenditures, including those for the general welfare, but because the use to which its proceeds are put is disapproved.

3. As the present depressed state of agriculture is nationwide in its extent and effects, there is no basis for saying that the expenditure of public money in aid of farmers is not within the specifically granted power of Congress to levy taxes to "provide for the . . . general welfare." The opinion of the Court does not declare otherwise.

4. No question of a variable tax fixed from time to time by fiat of the Secretary of Agriculture, or of unauthorized delegation of legislative power, is now presented. The schedule of rates imposed by the Secretary in accordance with the original command of Congress has since been specifically adopted and confirmed by Act of Congress, which has declared that it shall be the lawful tax. . . .

It is with these preliminary and hardly controverted matters in mind that we should direct our attention to the pivot on which the decision of the Court is made to turn. It is that a levy unquestionably within the taxing power of Congress may be treated as invalid because it is a step in a plan to regulate agricultural production and is thus a forbidden infringement of state power. The levy is not any the less an exercise of taxing power because it is intended to defray an expenditure for the general welfare rather than for some other support of government. Nor is the levy and collection of the tax pointed to as affecting the regulation. While all federal taxes inevitably have some influence on the internal economy of the states, it is not contended that the levy of a processing tax upon manufacturers using agricultural products as raw material has any perceptible regulatory effect upon either their production or manufacture. . . .

Of the assertion that the payments to farmers are coercive, it is enough to say that no such contention is pressed by the taxpayer, and no such consequences were to be anticipated or appear to have resulted from the administration of the Act. The suggestion of coercion finds no support in the record or in any data showing the actual operation of the Act. Threat of loss, not hope of gain, is the essence of economic coercion. . . .

It is upon the contention that state power is infringed by purchased regulation of agricultural production that chief reliance is placed. It is insisted that, while the Constitution gives to Congress, in specific and unambiguous terms, the power to tax and spend, the power is subject to limitations which do not find their origin in any express provision of the Constitution and to which other expressly delegated powers are not subject. . . .

The spending power of Congress is in addition to the legislative power and not subordinate to it. This independent grant of the power of the purse, and its very nature, involving in its exercise the duty to insure expenditure within the granted power presuppose freedom of selection among diverse ends and aims, and the capacity to impose such conditions as will render the choice effective. It is a contradiction in terms to say that there is power to spend for the national welfare, while rejecting any power to impose conditions reasonably adapted to the attainment of the end which alone would justify the expenditure.

The limitation now sanctioned must lead to absurd consequences. The government may give seeds to farmers, but may not condition the gift upon their being planted in places where they are most needed or even planted at all. The government may give money to the unemployed, but may not ask that those who get it shall give labor in return, or even use it to support their families. It may give money to sufferers from earthquake, fire, tornado, pestilence or flood, but may not impose conditions—health precautions designed to prevent the spread of disease, or induce the movement of population to safer or more sanitary areas. All that, because it is purchased regulation infringing state powers, must be left for the states, who are unable or unwilling to supply the necessary relief. . . .

That the governmental power of the purse is a great one is not now for the first time announced. Every student of the history of government and economics is aware of its magnitude and of its existence in every civilized government. Both were well understood by the framers of the Constitution when they sanctioned the grant of the spending power to the federal government, and both were recognized by Hamilton and Story, whose views of the spending power as standing on a parity with the other powers specifically granted, have hitherto been generally accepted.

The suggestion that it must now be curtailed by judicial fiat because it may be abused by unwise use hardly rises to the dignity of the arguments. So may judicial power be abused. ''The power to tax is the power to destroy,'' but we do not, for that reason, doubt its existence, or hold that its efficacy is to be restricted by its incidental or collateral effects upon the states. . . . The power to tax and spend is not without constitutional restraints. One restriction is that the purpose must be truly national. Another is that it may not be used to coerce action left to state control. Another is the conscience and patriotism of Congress and the Executive. ''It must be remembered that legislators are the ultimate guardians of the liberties and welfare of the people in quite as great a degree as the courts.'' Justice Holmes, in *Missouri, Kansas & Texas Ry. Co.* v. *May*, 194 U.S. 267, 270.

A tortured construction of the Constitution is not to be justified by recourse to extreme examples of reckless congressional spending which might occur if courts could not prevent expenditures which, even if they could be thought to effect any national purpose, would be possible only by action of a legislature lost to all sense of public responsibility. Such suppositions are addressed to the mind accustomed to believe that it is the business of courts to sit in judgment on the wisdom of legislative action. Courts are not the only agency of government that must be assumed to have capacity to govern. Congress and the courts both unhappily may falter or be mistaken in the performance of their constitutional duty. But interpretation of our great charter of government which proceeds on any assumption that the responsibility for the preservation of our institutions is the exclusive concern of any one of the three branches of government, or that it alone can save them from destruction is far more likely, in the long run, ''to obliterate the constituent members'' of ''an indestructible union of indestructible states'' than the frank recognition that language, even of a constitution, may mean what it says: that the power to tax and spend includes the power to relieve a nationwide economic maladjustment by conditional gifts of money.

MR. JUSTICE BRANDEIS and MR. JUSTICE CARDOZO joined in this opinion.

MR. JUSTICE SUTHERLAND, dissenting in *West Coast Hotel* v. *Parrish*. . . .

Under our form of government, where the written Constitution, by its own terms is the supreme law, some agency of necessity, must have the power to say the final word as to the validity of a statute assailed as unconstitutional. The Constitution makes it clear that the power has been intrusted to this court when the question arises in a controversy within its jurisdiction; and so long as the power remains there, its exercise cannot be avoided without betrayal of the trust.

It has been pointed out many times, as in the Adkins case, that this judicial duty is one of gravity and delicacy; and that rational doubts must be resolved in favor of the constitutionality of the statute. But whose doubts, and by whom resolved? Undoubtedly it is the duty of a member of the court, in the process of reaching a right conclusion, to give due weight to the opposing views of his associates; but in the end, the question which he must answer is not whether such views seem sound to those who entertain them, but whether they convince him that the statute is constitutional or engender in his mind a rational doubt upon that issue. The oath which he takes as a judge is not a composite oath, but an individual one. And in passing upon the validity of a statute, he discharges a duty imposed upon *him,* which cannot be consummated justly by an automatic acceptance of the views of others which have neither convinced, nor created a reasonable doubt in his mind. If upon a question so important he thus surrender his deliberate judgment, he stands forsworn. He cannot subordinate his convictions to that extent and keep faith with his oath or retain his judicial and moral independence.

The suggestion that the only check upon the exercise of the judicial power, when properly invoked, to declare a constitutional right superior to an unconstitutional statute is the judge's own faculty of self-restraint, is both ill considered and mischievous. Self-restraint belongs in the domain of will and not of judgment. The check upon the judge is that imposed by his oath of office, by the Constitution and by his own conscientious and informed convictions; and since he has the duty to make up his own mind and adjudge accordingly, it is hard to see how there could be any other restraint. . . .

It is urged that the question involved should now receive fresh consideration, among other reasons, because of "the economic conditions which have supervened"; but the meaning of the Constitution does not change with the ebb and flow of economic events. We frequently are told in more general words that the Constitu-

tion must be construed in the light of the present. If by that it is meant that the Constitution is made up of living words that apply to every new condition which they include, the statement is quite true. But to say, if that be intended, that the words of the Constitution mean today what they did not mean when written—that is, that they do not apply to a situation now to which they would have applied then—is to rob that instrument of the essential element which continues it in force as the people have made it until they, and not their official agents, have made it otherwise. . . .

The judicial function is that of interpretation; it does not include the power of amendment under the guise of interpretation. To miss the point of difference between the two is to miss all that the phrase "supreme law of the land" stands for and to convert what was intended as inescapable and enduring mandates into mere moral reflections.

If the Constitution, intelligently and reasonably construed in the light of these principles, stands in the way of desirable legislation, the blame must rest upon that instrument, and not upon the court for enforcing it according to its terms. The remedy in that situation—and the only true remedy—is to amend the Constitution. . . .

Baker v. *Carr*
369 U.S. 186, 82 S.Ct. 691, 7 L.Ed. 2d 663 (1962)

Appellants brought suit in Federal District Court in Tennessee, under the Civil Rights Acts of 1875, to redress alleged violations of constitutional rights. They charged that a 1901 Tennessee statute arbitrarily and capriciously apportioned the seats in the General Assembly among the state's 95 counties. Failure subsequently to reapportion the seats, notwithstanding substantial growth and redistribution of the state's population, debased their votes and thus denied them equal protection of the laws guaranteed by the Fourteenth Amendment. The District Court dismissed the complaint, ruling that it lacked jurisdiction of the subject matter and that no claim was stated upon which relief could be granted.

JUSTICE BRENNAN delivered the opinion of the Court. . . .

The complaint alleges that the 1901 statute effects an apportionment that deprives the appellants of the equal protection of the laws in violation of the Fourteenth Amendment. Dismissal of the complaint upon the ground of lack of jurisdiction of the subject matter would, therefore, be justified only if that claim were "so attenuated and unsubstantial as to be absolutely devoid of merit," . . . Since the District Court obviously and correctly did not deem the asserted federal constitutional claim unsubstantial and frivolous, it should not have dismissed the complaint for want of jurisdiction of the subject matter. . . .

We hold that the appellants do have standing to maintain this suit. Our decisions plainly support this conclusion. Many of the cases have assumed rather than articulated the premise in deciding the merits of similar claims. And *Colegrove* v. *Green,* . . . squarely held that voters who allege facts showing disadvantage to themselves as individuals have standing to sue. [A footnote points out that the concurring opinion of Justice Rutledge and Justice Black's dissenting opinion held there was standing, and expressed doubt whether Justice Frankfurter's opinion . . . intimated lack of it.]

. . . The mere fact that the suit seeks protection of a political right does not mean it presents a political question. Such an objection "is little more than a play upon words." . . . Rather, it is argued that apportionment cases, whatever the actual wording of the complaint, can involve no federal constitutional right except one resting on the guaranty of a republican form of government, and that complaints based on that clause have been held to present political questions which are nonjusticiable.

We hold that the claim pleaded here neither rests upon nor implicates the Guaranty Clause and that its justiciability is therefore not foreclosed by our decisions of cases involving that clause. The District Court misinterpreted *Colegrove* v. *Green* and other decisions of this Court on which it relied. Appellants' claim that they are being denied equal protection is justi-

ciable, and if "discrimination is sufficiently shown, the right to relief under the equal protection clause is not diminished by the fact that the discrimination relates to political rights." . . . To show why we reject the argument based on the Guaranty Clause, we must examine the authorities under it. But because there appears to be some uncertainty as to why those cases did present political questions, and specifically as to whether this apportionment case is like those cases, we deem it necessary first to consider the contours of the "political question" doctrine . . . . [The opinion proceeds to a consideration of foreign relations, "durations of hostilities," validity of enactments of constitutional amendments and the status of Indian tribes.]

It is apparent that several formulations which vary slightly according to the settings in which the questions arise may describe a political question, although each has one or more elements which identifies it as essentially a function of the separation of powers. Prominent on the surface of any case held to involve a political question is found a textually demonstrable constitutional commitment of the issue to a coordinate political department; or a lack of judicially discoverable and manageable standards for resolving it; or the impossibility of deciding without an initial policy determination of a kind clearly for nonjudicial discretion; or the impossibility of a court's undertaking independent resolution without expressing lack of the respect due coordinate branches of government; or an unusual need for unquestioning adherence to a political decision already made; or the potentiality of embarrassment from multifarious pronouncements by various departments on one question.

Unless one of these formulations is inextricable from the case at bar, there should be no dismissal for nonjusticiability on the ground of a political question's presence. The doctrine of which we treat is one of "political questions," not one of "political cases." The courts cannot reject as "no lawsuit" a bona fide controversy as to whether some action denominated "political" exceeds constitutional authority. . . .

Several factors were thought by the Court in

Luther [*Luther* v. *Borden*] to make the question there "political": the commitment to the other branches of the decision as to which is the lawful state government; the unambiguous action by the President, in recognizing the charter government as the lawful authority; the need for finality in the executive's decision; and the lack of criteria by which a court could determine which form of government was republican.

But the only significance that Luther could have for our immediate purposes is in its holding that the Guaranty Clause is not a repository of judicially manageable standards which a court could utilize independently in order to identify a State's lawful government. The Court has since refused to resort to the Guaranty Clause—which alone had been invoked for the purpose—as the source of a constitutional standard for invalidating state action. . . .

We come, finally to the ultimate inquiry whether our precedents as to what constitutes a nonjusticiable "political question" bring the case before us under the umbrella of that doctrine. A natural beginning is to note whether any of the common characteristics which we have been able to identify and label descriptively are present. We find none: The question here is the consistency of state action with the Federal Constitution. We have no question decided, or to be decided, by a political branch of government coequal with this Court. Nor do we risk embarrassment of our government abroad, or grave disturbance at home if we take issue with Tennessee as to the constitutionality of her action here challenged. Nor need the appellants, in order to succeed in this action, ask the Court to enter upon policy determinations for which judicially manageable standards are lacking. Judicial standards under the Equal Protection Clause are well developed and familiar, and it has been open to courts since the enactment of the Fourteenth Amendment to determine, if on the particular facts they review, that a discrimination reflects no policy, but simply arbitrary and capricious action.

This case does, in one sense, involve the allocation of political power within a State, and

the appellants might conceivably have added a claim under the Guaranty Clause. Of course, as we have seen, any reliance on that clause would be futile. But because any reliance on the Guaranty Clause could not have succeeded, it does not follow that appellants may not be heard on the equal protection claim which in fact they tender. True, it must be clear that the Fourteenth Amendment claim is not so enmeshed with those political question elements which render Guaranty Clause claims nonjusticiable as actually to present a political question itself. But we have found that not to be the case here. . . .

We conclude then that the nonjusticiability of claims resting on the Guaranty Clause which arises from their embodiment of questions that were thought "political," can have no bearing upon the justiciability of the equal protection claim presented in this case. Finally, we emphasize that it is the involvement in Guaranty Clause claims of the elements thought to define "political questions," and no other feature, which could render them nonjusticiable. Specifically, we have said that such claims are not held nonjusticiable because they touch matters of state governmental organization. . . .

Article 1, Sections 2, 4, and 5 and Amendment 14, Section 2 relate only to congressional elections and obviously do not govern apportionment of state legislatures. However, our decisions in favor of justiciability even in light of those provisions plainly afford no support for the District Court's conclusion that the subject matter of this controversy presents a political question. Indeed, the refusal to award relief in Colegrove resulted only from the controlling view of a want of equity. . . .

We conclude that the complaint's allegations of a denial of equal protection present a justiciable constitutional cause of action upon which appellants are entitled to a trial and a decision. The right asserted is within the reach of judicial protection under the Fourteenth Amendment. . . .

MR. JUSTICE WHITTAKER did not participate.

MR. JUSTICE FRANKFURTER dissenting, joined by MR. JUSTICE HARLAN.

The Court today reverses a uniform course of decision established by a dozen cases, including one by which the very claim now sustained was unanimously rejected only five years ago. . . . Such a massive repudiation of the experience of our whole past in asserting destructively novel judicial power demands a detailed analysis of the role of this Court in our constitutional scheme. Disregard of inherent limits in the effective exercise of the Court's "judicial Power" not only presages the futility of judicial intervention in the essentially political conflict of forces by which the relation between population and representation has time out of mind been and now is determined. It may well impair the Court's position as the ultimate organ of "the supreme Law of the Land" in that vast range of legal problems, often strongly entangled in popular feeling, on which this Court must pronounce. The Court's authority—possessed neither of the purse nor the sword—ultimately rests on sustained public confidence in its moral sanction. Such feeling must be nourished by the Court's complete detachment, in fact and in appearance, from political entanglements and by abstention from injecting itself into the clash of political forces in political settlements. . . .

For this Court to direct the District Court to enforce a claim to which the Court has over the years consistently found itself required to deny legal enforcement and at the same time to find it necessary to withhold any guidance to the lower court how to enforce this turnabout, new legal claim, manifests an odd—indeed an esoteric—conception of judicial propriety. . . .

Even assuming the indispensable intellectual disinterestedness on the part of judges in such matters, they do not have accepted legal standards or criteria or even reliable analogies to draw upon for making judicial judgments. To charge courts with the task of accommodating the incommensurable factors of policy that underlie these mathematical puzzles is to attribute, however flatteringly, omnicompetence to judges. . . .

We are soothingly told at the bar of this Court that we need not worry about the kind of remedy a court could effectively fashion once the abstract constitutional right to have courts pass on a state-wide system of electoral districting is recognized as a matter of judicial rhetoric, because legislatures would heed the Court's admonition. This is not only an euphoric hope. It implies a sorry confession of judicial impotence in place of a frank acknowledgment that there is not under our Constitution a judicial remedy for every political mischief, for every undesirable exercise of legislative power. The Framers carefully and with deliberate forethought refused so to enthrone the judiciary. In this situation, as in others of like nature, appeal for relief does not belong here. Appeal must be to an informed, civically militant electorate. In a democratic society like ours, relief must come through an aroused popular conscience that sears the conscience of the people's representatives. In any event there is nothing judicially more unseemly nor more self-defeating than for this Court to make interrorem pronouncements, to indulge in merely empty rhetoric, sounding a word of promise to the ear, sure to be disappointing to the hope. . . .

What, then, is this question of legislative apportionment? Appellants invoke the right to vote and to have their votes counted. But they are permitted to vote and their votes are counted. They go to the polls, they cast their ballots, they send their representatives to the state councils. Their complaint is simply that the representatives are not sufficiently numerous or powerful—in short, that Tennessee has adopted a basis of representation with which they are dissatisfied. Talk of "debasement" or "dilution" is circular talk. One cannot speak of "debasement" or "dilution" of the value of a vote until there is first defined a standard of reference as to what a vote should be worth. What is actually asked of the Court in this case is to choose among competing bases of representation—ultimately, really, among competing theories of political philosophy—in order to establish an appropriate frame of government for the State of Tennessee and thereby for all the States of the Union. . . .

. . . What Tennessee illustrates is an old and still widespread method of representation—

representation by local geographical division, only in part respective of population—in preference to others, others, forsooth, more appealing. Appellants contest this choice and seek to make this Court the arbiter of the disagreement. They would make the Equal Protection Clause the charter of adjudication, asserting that the equality which it guarantees comports, if not the assurance of equal weight to every voter's vote, at least the basic conception that representation ought to be proportionate to population, a standard by reference to which the reasonableness of apportionment plans may be judged.

To find such a political conception legally enforceable in the broad and unspecific guarantee of equal protection is to rewrite the Constitution. . . .

Dissenting opinion of MR. JUSTICE HARLAN, joined by MR. JUSTICE FRANKFURTER. . . .

From a reading of the majority and concurring opinions one will not find it difficult to catch the premises that underlie this decision. The fact that the appellants have been unable to obtain political redress of their asserted grievances appears to be regarded as a matter which should lead the Court to stretch to find some basis for judicial intervention. While the Equal Protection Clause is invoked, the opinion for the Court notably eschews explaining how, consonant with past decisions, the undisputed facts in this case can be considered to show a violation of that constitutional provision. . . .

In conclusion, it is appropriate to say that one need not agree, as a citizen, with what Tennessee has done or failed to do, in order to deprecate, as a judge, what the majority is doing today. Those observers of the Court who see it primarily as the last refuge for the correction of all inequality or injustice, no matter what its nature or source, will no doubt applaud this decision and its break with the past. Those who consider that continuing national respect for the Court's authority depends in large measure upon its wise exercise of self-restraint and discipline in constitutional adjudication, will view the decision with deep concern.

I would affirm.

MR. JUSTICE DOUGLAS, concurring. . . .

MR. JUSTICE STEWART, concurring. . . .

MR. JUSTICE CLARK, concurring.

One emerging from the rash of opinions with their accompanying clashing of views may well find himself suffering a mental blindness. The Court holds that the appellants have alleged a cause of action. However, it refuses to award relief here—although the facts are undisputed—and fails to give the District Court any guidance whatever. One dissenting opinion, bursting with words that go through so much and conclude with so little, condemns the majority action as "a massive repudiation of the experience of our whole past." Another describes the complaints as merely asserting conclusory allegations that Tennessee's apportionment is "incorrect," "arbitrary," "obsolete," and "unconstitutional." I believe it can be shown that this case is distinguishable from earlier cases dealing with the distribution of political power by a State, that a patent violation of the Equal Protection Clause of the United States Constitution has been shown, and that an appropriate remedy may be formulated. . . .

Although I find the Tennessee apportionment statute offends the Equal Protection Clause, I would not consider intervention by this Court into so delicate a field if there were any other relief available to the people of Tennessee. But the majority of the people of Tennessee have no "practical opportunities for exerting their political weight at the polls" to correct the existing "invidious discrimination." Tennessee has no initiative and referendum. I have searched diligently for other "practical opportunities" present under the law. I find none other than through the federal courts. The majority of the voters have been caught up in a legislative straitjacket. Tennessee has an "informed, civically militant electorate" and "an aroused popular conscience," but it does not sear "the conscience of the people's representatives." . . . It is said that there is recourse in Congress and perhaps that may be, but from a practical standpoint this is without substance. To date Congress has never undertaken such a task in any State. We therefore must conclude that the people of Tennessee are stymied and without judicial intervention will be saddled with the present discrimination in the affairs of their state government. . . .

As John Rutledge (later Chief Justice) said 175 years ago in the course of the Constitutional Convention, a chief function of the Court is to secure the national rights. Its decision today supports the proposition for which our forebears fought and many died, namely that "to be fully conformable to the principle of right, the form of government must be representative." That is the keystone upon which our government was founded and lacking which no republic can survive. It is well for this Court to practice self-restraint and discipline in constitutional adjudication, but never in its history have those principles received sanction where the national rights of so many have been so clearly infringed for so long a time. National respect for the courts is more enhanced through the forthright enforcement of those rights rather than by rendering them nugatory through the interposition of subterfuges. In my view the ultimate decision today is in the greatest tradition of this Court.

Reynolds v. Sims
377 U.S. 533, 84 S.Ct. 1362, 12 L.Ed. 2d 506 (1964)

The climax of a series of cases involving challenges to state apportionment arrangements came on June 15, 1964, when the Court invalidated the legislative apportionments of Alabama, Colorado, Delaware, Maryland, New York, and Virginia. The majority opinion in Reynolds v. Sims sets forth the basic principles applied in each of the six cases. In addition to excerpts from the dissenting opinion of Justice Harlan in Reynolds, included here, is a substantial excerpt from the opinion by Justice Stewart, who dissented in the Colorado and New York cases chiefly because he thought the deviations from equality in their legislative apportionment had a rational basis. In the Colorado case (Lucas v. Forty-Fourth General Assembly of Colorado, 377 U.S. 713), the apportionment plan rejected by the Court had been approved by the Colorado voters by a margin of over 2 to 1 in the November 1962 general election. The Court was not persuaded by this expression of popular views, and observed that both the apportionment plan in effect at the time of the election and an alternative plan rejected by the voters had provided for at-large election of Senators in multimember counties. Hence, the voters may have selected the lesser of evils. More basically, the conclusion was that the courts must apply the equal protection clause to protect voting rights and that voter approval of an unconstitutional scheme "is without federal constitutional significance. . . ."

MR. CHIEF JUSTICE WARREN delivered the opinion of the Court. . . .

Plaintiffs below alleged that the last apportionment of the Alabama Legislature was based on the 1900 federal census, despite the requirement of the State Constitution that the legislature be reapportioned decennially. They asserted that, since the population growth in the State from 1900 to 1960 had been uneven, Jefferson and other counties were now victims of serious discrimination with respect to the allocation of legislative representation. As a result of the failure of the legislature to reapportion itself, plaintiffs asserted, they were denied "equal suffrage in free and equal elections . . . and the equal protection of the laws" in violation of the Alabama Constitution and the Fourteenth Amendment to the Federal Constitution. The complaint asserted that plaintiffs had no other adequate remedy, and that they had exhausted all forms of relief other than that available through the federal courts. . . .

Undeniably the Constitution of the United States protects the right of all qualified citizens to vote, in state as well as in federal elections. A consistent line of decisions by this Court in cases involving attempts to deny or restrict the right of suffrage has made this indelibly clear. . . . The right to vote can neither be denied outright, *Guinn* v. *United States*, 238 U.S. 347, . . . *Lane* v. *Wilson*, 307 U.S. 268, . . . nor can it be destroyed by alteration of ballots, see *United States* v. *Classic*, 313 U.S. 299, 315, . . . nor diluted by ballot-box stuffing, *Ex parte Siebold*, 100 U.S. 371. . . . The right to vote freely for the candidate of one's choice is of the essence of a democratic society, and any restrictions on that right strike at the heart of representative government. And the right of suffrage can be denied by a debasement or dilution of the weight of a citizen's vote just as effectively as by wholly prohibiting the free exercise of the franchise. . . .

. . . In these cases we are faced with the problem . . . of determining the basic standards and stating the applicable guidelines for implementing our decision in *Baker* v. *Carr*. . . .

A predominant consideration in determining whether a State's legislative apportionment scheme constitutes an invidious discrimination violative of rights asserted under the Equal Protection Clause is that the rights allegedly impaired are individual and personal in nature. . . . Undoubtedly, the right of suffrage is a fundamental matter in a free and democratic society. Especially since the right to exercise the franchise in a free and unimpaired manner is preservative of other basic civil and political rights, any alleged infringement of the right of

citizens to vote must be carefully and meticulously scrutinized. . . .

Legislators represent people, not trees or acres. Legislators are elected by voters, not farms or cities or economic interests. As long as ours is a representative form of government, and our legislatures are those instruments of government elected directly by and directly representative of the people, the right to elect legislators in a free and unimpaired fashion is a bedrock of our political system. It could hardly be gainsaid that a constitutional claim had been asserted by an allegation that certain otherwise qualified voters had been entirely prohibited from voting for members of their state legislature. And, if a State should provide that the votes of citizens in one part of the State should be given two times, or five times, or 10 times the weight of votes of citizens in another part of the State, it could hardly be contended that the right to vote of those residing in the disfavored areas had not been effectively diluted. It would appear extraordinary to suggest that a state could be constitutionally permitted to enact a law providing that certain of the state's voters could vote two, five, or 10 times for their legislative representatives, while voters living elsewhere could vote only once. And it is inconceivable that a state law to the effect that, in counting votes for legislators, the votes of citizens in one part of the State would be multiplied by two, five or 10, while the votes of persons in another area would be counted only at face value, could be constitutionally sustainable. Of course, the effect of state legislative districting schemes which give the same number of representatives to unequal numbers of constituents is identical.[1] Over-

---

[1] As stated by Mr. Justice Black in *Colegrove* v. *Green*, 328 U.S. 549, 569–571:

"No one would deny that the equal protection clause would . . . prohibit a law that would expressly give certain citizens a half-vote and others a full vote. . . . [T]he constitutionally guaranteed right to vote and the right to have one's vote counted clearly imply the policy that state election systems, no matter what their form, should be designed to give approximately equal weight to each vote cast. . . . [A] state legislature cannot deny eligible voters the right to

weighting and overvaluation of the votes of those living here has the certain effect of dilution and undervaluation of the votes of those living there. The resulting discrimination against those individual voters living in disfavored areas is easily demonstrable mathematically. Their right to vote is simply not the same right to vote as that of those living in a favored part of the State. Two, five, or 10 of them must vote before the effect of their voting is equivalent to that of their favored neighbor. Weighting the votes of citizens differently, by any method or means, merely because of where they happen to reside, hardly seems justifiable. One must be ever aware that the Constitution forbids "sophisticated as well as simple-minded modes of discrimination." *Lane* v. *Wilson,* 307 U.S. 268, 275. . . . As we stated in *Wesberry* v. *Sanders,* supra:

> We do not believe that the Framers of the Constitution intended to permit the same vote-diluting discrimination to be accomplished through the device of districts containing widely varied numbers of inhabitants. To say that a vote is worth more in one district than in another would . . . run counter to our fundamental ideas of democratic government. . . .[2]

State legislatures are, historically, the fountainhead of representative government in this country. A number of them have their roots in colonial times, and substantially antedate the creation of our Nation and our Federal Government. In fact, the first formal stirrings of American political independence are to be found, in large part, in the views and actions of several of the colonial legislative bodies. With the birth of our National Government, and the adoption and ratification of the Federal Constitution, state legislatures retained a most important place in our Nation's governmental structure. But representative government is in essence self-government through the medium of elected representatives of the people, and each and every citizen has an inalienable right to full and effective participation in the political processes of his State's legislative bodies. Most citizens can achieve this participation only as qualified voters through the election of legislators to represent them. Full and effective participation by all citizens in state government requires, therefore, that each citizen have an equally effective voice in the election of members of his state legislature. Modern and viable state government needs, and the Constitution demands, no less.

Logically, in a society that is ostensibly grounded on representative government, it would seem reasonable that a majority of the people of a State could elect a majority of that State's legislators. To conclude differently, and to sanction minority control of state legislative bodies, would appear to deny majority rights in a way that far surpasses any possible denial of minority rights that might otherwise be thought to result. Since legislatures are responsible for enacting laws by which all citizens are to be governed, they should be bodies which are collectively responsive to the popular will. And the concept of equal protection has been traditionally viewed as requiring the uniform treat-

---

vote for Congressmen and the right to have their vote counted. It can no more destroy the effectiveness of their vote in part and no more accomplish this in the name of 'apportionment' than under any other name." (Black, J., dissenting.)

[2] And, as stated by Mr. Justice Douglas in *MacDougall* v. *Green,* 355 U.S., at 288, 290:

"[A] regulation . . . [which] discriminates against the residents of the populous counties of the state in favor of rural sections . . . lacks the equality to which the exercise of political rights is entitled under the Fourteenth Amendment.

"Free and honest elections are the very foundation of our republican form of government. . . . Discrimination against any group or class of citizens in the exercise of these constitutionally protected rights of citizenship deprives the electoral process of integrity. . . .

"None would deny that a state law giving some citizens twice the vote of other citizens in either the primary or general election would lack that equality which the Fourteenth Amendment guarantees. . . . The theme of the Constitution is equality among citizens in the exercise of their

---

political rights. The notion that one group can be granted greater voting strength than another is hostile to our standards for popular representative government." (Douglas, J., dissenting.)

ment of persons standing in the same relation to the governmental action questioned or challenged. With respect to the allocation of legislative representation, all voters, as citizens of a State, stand in the same relation regardless of where they live. Any suggested criteria for the differentiation of citizens are insufficient to justify any discrimination, as to the weight of their votes, unless relevant to the permissible purposes of legislative apportionment. Since the achieving of fair and effective representation for all citizens is concededly the basic aim of legislative apportionment, we conclude that the Equal Protection Clause guarantees the opportunity for equal participation by all voters in the election of state legislators. Diluting the weight of votes because of place of residence impairs basic constitutional rights under the Fourteenth Amendment just as much as invidious discrimination based upon factors such as race, *Brown* v. *Board of Education,* 347 U.S. 483, . . . or economic status, *Griffin* v. *Illinois,* 351 U.S. 12, . . . *Douglas* v. *California,* 372 U.S. 353. . . . Our constitutional system amply provides for the protection of minorities by means other than giving them majority control of state legislatures. And the democratic ideals of equality and majority rule, which have served this Nation so well in the past, are hardly of any less significance for the present and the future.

We are told that the matter of apportioning representation in a state legislature is a complex and many-faceted one. We are advised that States can rationally consider factors other than population in apportioning legislative representation. We are admonished not to restrict the power of the States to impose differing views as to political philosophy on their citizens. We are cautioned about the dangers of entering into political thickets and mathematical quagmires. Our answer is this: a denial of constitutionally protected rights demands judicial protection; our oath and our office require no less of us. As stated in *Gomillion* v. *Lightfoot,* supra,

When a State exercises power wholly within the domain of state interest, it is insulated from

federal judicial review. But such insulation is not carried over when state power is used as an instrument for circumventing a federally protected right.

To the extent that a citizen's right to vote is debased, he is that much less a citizen. The fact that an individual lives here or there is not a legitimate reason for overweighting or diluting the efficacy of his vote. The complexions of societies and civilizations change, often with amazing rapidity. A nation once primarily rural in character becomes predominantly urban. Representation schemes once fair and equitable become archaic and outdated. But the basic principle of representative government remains, and must remain, unchanged—the weight of a citizen's vote cannot be made to depend on where he lives. Population is, of necessity, the starting point for consideration and the controlling criterion for judgment in legislative apportionment controversies. A citizen, a qualified voter, is no more nor no less so because he lives in the city or on the farm. This is the clear and strong command of our Constitution's Equal Protection Clause. This is an essential part of the concept of a government of laws and not men. This is at the heart of Lincoln's vision of "government of the people, by the people, [and] for the people." The Equal Protection Clause demands no less than substantially equal state legislative representation for all citizens, of all places as well as of all races.

We hold that, as a basic constitutional standard, the Equal Protection Clause requires that the seats in both houses of a bicameral state legislature must be apportioned on a population basis. Simply stated, an individual's right to vote for state legislators is unconstitutionally impaired when its weight is in a substantial fashion diluted when compared with votes of citizens living in other parts of the State. Since, under neither the existing apportionment provisions nor under either of the proposed plans was either of the houses of the Alabama Legislature apportioned on a population basis, the District Court correctly held that all three of these schemes were constitutionally invalid. . . .

Legislative apportionment in Alabama is signally illustrative and symptomatic of the seriousness of this problem in a number of the States. At the time this litigation was commenced, there had been no reapportionment of seats in the Alabama Legislature for over 60 years. Legislative inaction, coupled with the unavailability of any political or judicial remedy, had resulted, with the passage of years, in the perpetuated scheme becoming little more than an irrational anachronism. . . .

Much has been written since our decision in *Baker* v. *Carr* about the applicability of the so-called federal analogy to state legislative apportionment arrangements. After considering the matter, the court below concluded that no conceivable analogy could be drawn between the federal scheme and the apportionment of seats in the Alabama Legislature under the proposed constitutional amendment. We agree with the District Court, and find the federal analogy inapposite and irrelevant to state legislative districting schemes. Attempted reliance on the federal analogy appears often to be little more than an after-the-fact rationalization offered in defense of maladjusted state apportionment arrangements. The original constitutions of 36 of our States provided that representation in both houses of the state legislatures would be based completely, or predominantly, on population. And the Founding Fathers clearly had no intention of establishing a pattern or model for the apportionment of seats in state legislatures when the system of representation in the Federal Congress was adopted. Demonstrative of this is the fact that the Northwest Ordinance, adopted in the same year, 1787, as the Federal Constitution, provided for the apportionment of seats in territorial legislatures solely on the basis of population.

The system of representation in the two Houses of the Federal Congress is one ingrained in our Constitution, as part of the law of the land. It is one conceived out of compromise and concession indispensable to the establishment of our federal republic. Arising from unique historical circumstances, it is based on the consideration that in establishing our type of federalism a group of formerly independent States bound themselves together under one national government. Admittedly, the original 13 States surrendered some of their sovereignty in agreeing to join together ''to form a more perfect Union.'' But at the heart of our constitutional system remains the concept of separate and distinct governmental entities which have delegated some, but not all, of their formerly held powers to the single national government. . . .

Political subdivisions of States—counties, cities, or whatever—never were and never have been considered as sovereign entities. Rather, they have been traditionally regarded as subordinate governmental instrumentalities created by the State to assist in the carrying out of state governmental functions. . . .

Since we find the so-called federal analogy inapposite to a consideration of the constitutional validity of state legislative apportionment schemes, we necessarily hold that the Equal Protection Clause requires both houses of a state legislature to be apportioned on a population basis. The right of a citizen to equal representation and to have his vote weighted equally with those of all other citizens in the election of members of one house of a bicameral state legislature would amount to little if States could effectively submerge the equal-population principle in the apportionment of seats in the other house. If such a scheme were permissible, an individual citizen's ability to exercise an effective voice in the only instrument of state government directly representative of the people might be almost as effectively thwarted as if neither house were apportioned on a population basis. Deadlock between the two bodies might result in compromise and concession on some issues. But in all too many cases the more probable result would be frustration of the majority will through minority veto in the house not apportioned on a population basis, stemming directly from the failure to accord adequate overall legislative representation to all of the State's citizens on a nondiscriminatory basis. In summary, we can perceive no constitutional difference, with respect to the geographical distribution of state legislative representation, between the two houses of a bicameral state legislature.

We do not believe that the concept of bicameralism is rendered anachronistic and meaningless when the predominant basis of representation in the two state legislative bodies is required to be the same—population. A prime reason for bicameralism, modernly considered, is to insure mature and deliberate consideration of, and to prevent precipitate action on, proposed legislative measures. Simply because the controlling criterion for apportioning representation is required to be the same in both houses does not mean that there will be no differences in the composition and complexion of the two bodies. Different constituencies can be represented in the two houses. One body could be composed of single-member districts while the other could have at least some multimember districts. The length of terms of the legislators in the separate bodies could differ. The numerical size of the two bodies could be made to differ, even significantly, and the geographical size of districts from which legislators are elected could also be made to differ. And apportionment in one house could be arranged so as to balance off minor inequities in the representation of certain areas in the other house. In summary, these and other factors could be, and are presently in many States, utilized to engender differing complexions and collective attitudes in the two bodies of a state legislature, although both are apportioned substantially on a population basis.

By holding that as a federal constitutional requisite both houses of a state legislature must be apportioned on a population basis, we mean that the Equal Protection Clause requires that a State make an honest and good faith effort to construct districts, in both houses of its legislature, as nearly of equal population as is practicable. We realize that it is a practical impossibility to arrange legislative districts so that each one has an identical number of residents, or citizens, or voters. Mathematical exactness or precision is hardly a workable constitutional requirement.

MR. JUSTICE HARLAN, dissenting.

... With these cases the Court approaches the end of the third round set in motion by the complaint filed in *Baker* v. *Carr.* What is done today deepens my conviction that judicial entry into this realm is profoundly ill-advised and constitutionally impermissible. As I have said before, *Wesberry* v. *Sanders,* supra, 376 U.S. at 48, I believe that the vitality of our political system, on which in the last analysis all else depends, is weakened by reliance on the judiciary for political reform; in time a complacent body politic may result.

These decisions also cut deeply into the fabric of our federalism. What must follow from them may eventually appear to be the product of State Legislatures. Nevertheless, no thinking person can fail to recognize that the aftermath of these cases, however desirable it may be thought in itself, will have been achieved at the cost of a radical alteration in the relationship between the States and the Federal Government, more particularly the Federal Judiciary. Only one who has an overbearing impatience with the federal system and its political processes will believe that that cost was not too high or was inevitable.

Finally, these decisions give support to a current mistaken view of the Constitution and the constitutional function of this Court. This view, in a nutshell, is that every major social ill in this country can find its cure in some constitutional "principle," and that this Court should "take the lead" in promoting reform when other branches of government fail to act. The Constitution is not a panacea for every blot upon the public welfare, nor should this Court, ordained as a judicial body, be thought of as a general haven for reform movements. The Constitution is an instrument of government, fundamental to which is the premise that in a diffusion of governmental authority lies the greatest promise that this Nation will realize liberty for all its citizens. This Court, limited in function in accordance with that premise, does not serve its high purpose when it exceeds its authority, even to satisfy justified impatience with the slow workings of the political process. For when, in the name of constitutional interpretation, the

Court *adds* something to the Constitution that was deliberately excluded from it, the Court in reality substitutes its view of what should be so for the amending process. . . .

MR. JUSTICE STEWART, whom MR. JUSTICE CLARK joins, dissenting.

. . . Simply stated, the question [in these cases] is to what degree, if at all, the Equal Protection Clause of the Fourteenth Amendment limits each sovereign State's freedom to establish appropriate electoral constituencies from which representatives to the State's bicameral legislative assembly are to be chosen. The Court's answer is a blunt one, and, I think, woefully wrong. The Equal Protection Clause, said the Court, "requires that the seats in both houses of a bicameral state legislature must be apportioned on a population basis.". . .

With all respect, I think that this is not correct, simply as a matter of fact. It has been unanswerably demonstrated before now that this "was not the colonial system, it was not the system chosen for the national government by the Constitution, it was not the system exclusively or even predominantly practiced by the States at the time of adoption of the Fourteenth Amendment, it is not predominantly practiced by the States today." Secondly, says the Court, unless legislative districts are equal in population, voters in the more populous districts will suffer a "debasement" amounting to a constitutional injury. . . .

The Court's draconian pronouncement, which makes unconstitutional the legislatures of most of the 50 States, finds no support in the words of the Constitution, in any prior decision of this Court, or in the 175-year political history of our Federal Union. With all respect, I am convinced these decisions mark a long step backward into that unhappy era when a majority of the members of this Court were thought by many to have convinced themselves and each other that the demands of the Constitution were to be measured not by what it says, but by their own notions of wise political theory. The rule announced today is at odds with long-established principles of constitutional adjudication under the Equal Protection Clause, and it stifles

values of local individuality and initiative vital to the character of the Federal Union which it was the genius of our Constitution to create.

What the Court has done is to convert a particular political philosophy into a constitutional rule, binding upon each of the 50 States, from Maine to Hawaii, from Alaska to Texas, without regard and without respect for the many individualized and differentiated characteristics stemming from each State's distinct history, distinct geography, distinct distribution of population, and distinct political heritage. My own understanding of the various theories of representative government is that no one theory has ever commanded unanimous assent among political scientists, historians, or others who have considered the problem. But even if it were thought that the rule announced today by the Court is, as a matter of political theory, the most desirable general rule which can be devised as a basis for the make-up of the representative assembly of a typical State, I could not join in the fabrication of a constitutional mandate which imports and forever freezes one theory of political thought into our Constitution, and forever denies to every State any opportunity for enlightened and progressive innovation in the design of its democratic institutions, so as to accommodate within a system of representative government the interests and aspirations of diverse groups of people, without subjecting any group or class to absolute domination by a geographically concentrated or highly organized majority.

Representative government is a process of accommodating group interests through democratic institutional arrangements. Its function is to channel the numerous opinions, interests, and abilities of the people of a State into the making of the State's public policy. Appropriate legislative apportionment, therefore, should ideally be designed to insure effective **representation in the State's legislature, in cooperation with other organs of political power,** of the various groups and interests making up the electorate. In practice, of course, this ideal is approximated in the particular apportionment system of any State by a realistic accommodation of the diverse and often con-flicting political forces operating within the State. . . .

The Court today declines to give any recognition to these considerations and countless others, tangible and intangible, in holding unconstitutional the particular systems of legislative apportionment which these States have chosen. Instead, the Court says that the requirements of the Equal Protection Clause can be met in any State only by the uncritical, simplistic, and heavy-handed application of sixth-grade arithmetic.

But legislators do not represent faceless numbers. They represent people, or, more accurately, a majority of the voters in their districts—people with identifiable needs and interests which require legislative representation, and which can often be related to the geographical areas in which these people live. The very fact of geographic districting, the constitutional validity of which the Court does not question, carries with it an acceptance of the idea of legislative representation of regional needs and interests. Yet if geographical residence is irrelevant, as the Court suggests,

and the goal is solely that of equally "weighted" votes, I do not understand why the Court's constitutional rule does not require the abolition of districts and the holding of all elections at large. . . .

I think that the Equal Protection Clause demands but two basic attributes of any plan of state legislative apportionment. First, it demands that, in the light of the State's own characteristics and needs, the plan must be a rational one. Secondly, it demands that the plan must be such as not to permit the systematic frustration of the will of a majority of the electorate of the State. I think it is apparent that any plan of legislative apportionment which could be shown to reflect no policy, but simply arbitrary and capricious action or inaction, and that any plan which could be shown systematically to prevent ultimate effective majority rule, would be invalid under accepted Equal Protection Clause standards. But, beyond this, I think there is nothing in the Federal Constitution to prevent a State from choosing any electoral legislative structure it thinks best suited to the interests, temper, and customs of its people. . . .

THREE

Congress, the Court,
and the President

The principle of separation of powers, propounded by seventeenth- and eighteenth-century political philosophers Harrington, Locke, and Montesquieu, was a device for limiting governmental power by taking from the monarch his ancient law-making power and vesting it in a legislature. The American development of this doctrine went much further. In place of the traditional division into legislative and executive, the American colonies adopted a threefold division, elevating the judiciary to coequal position and putting all three under the rule of law established by a written constitution.

SEPARATION OF POWERS

The federal Constitution contains no specific declaration concerning separation of powers. The principle is implicit in the organization of the first three articles: (1) "All legislative powers herein granted shall be vested in a Congress of the United States"; (2) "The executive power shall be vested in a President of the United States"; (3) "The judicial power shall be vested in one Supreme Court and in such inferior courts as the Congress shall . . . ordain and establish." From this separation is derived the doctrine that certain functions, because of their essential nature, may properly be exercised by only a particular branch of the government; that such functions cannot be delegated to any other branch; and that one department may not interfere with another by usurping its powers or by supervising their exercise.

At the Convention of 1787, separation of powers was endorsed with virtual unanimity. "No political truth," Madison said, "is of greater intrinsic value." In *Federalist* essays 47, 48 and 51 (excerpted in this chapter), Madison explored the principle. Inherited from Montesquieu, it is inspired by the conviction that "every man vested with power is apt to abuse it; and carry his authority as far as it will go." "Is it not strange," Montesquieu asked, "that virtue itself has need of limits?"

No precise line is or could be drawn between the three branches of the national government, nor between the respective domains of national and state authority. In *Federalist,* No. 37, also excerpted in this chapter, Madison explains why and underscores the resulting difficulty for constitutional interpretation.

Separation of powers is a misnomer. The Constitution separates organs of government; it fuses functions and powers. Because of frequently voiced criticism of the blending of executive, legislature, and judiciary in the proposed Constitution, Madison felt compelled to restate the traditional theory. The sharing of powers through the scheme of checks and balances was, Madison explained, a valuable additional restraint on government, which complemented the principle of separation of powers. Not only did the blending of powers limit government itself; it also provided weapons by which each department could defend its position in the constitutional system. The President's veto, it was urged, protected him against legislative encroachments, and his power of appointment gave him influence against judicial assault. The Court had the power to pass on legislation, and was protected by life tenure. The Congress could impeach a President and members of the Court. The national lawmakers controlled the purse upon which both the other departments depended, the Senate passed on presidential appointments, and the Congress controlled the appellate jurisdiction of the Supreme Court.

The legislature may exercise the executive power of pardon in the form of a grant of amnesty or immunity from prosecution. It may punish contempts, and may provide in minute detail the rules of procedure to be followed by the courts. The power of Congress to control the issuance of injunctions by federal courts and to restrict their power to punish disobedience has also been sustained. Although the courts do not legislate in the strict sense of the word, their decisions may be regarded from a realistic point of view as a form of law making. The courts, within limits, may exercise the executive power of appointment; and Congress may confer on them the power to suspend sentence, even though such power is legislative in nature. The President's power over foreign relations is such that the functions of advising and consenting to treaties and of "declaring" war, apparently entrusted by the Constitution to the legislature, have come largely under his control. Executive officers and administrative bodies also exercise functions that belong to other departments. Thus the commissioner of patents exercises judicial power in determining whether a patent shall be issued or renewed; members of the Tax Court make judicial decisions in tax cases; and the independent regulatory commissions and the cabinet departments themselves exercise legislative and judicial powers. Moreover, under *Katzenbach* v. *Morgan* (384 U.S. 641: 1966), which found constitutional the ban on literacy tests for voting in the Voting Rights Act of 1965, the Justices effectively shared the power of constitutional interpretation with Congress. The significance seems to be that Congress is as entitled to determine legislatively what the Fourteenth Amendment means as the Court is entitled to do so judicially. *Morgan* may play a major role in congressional efforts to restrict or even to overturn the Supreme Court's decision on abortion (*Roe* v. *Wade,* 410 U.S. 113: 1973).

In practice, separation of powers is a flexible principle. Chief Justice Marshall used it to bolster his argument for judicial review in *Marbury*. Judge Gibson relied heavily on that same principle to attack judicial review. Separation of powers was President Nixon's primary reliance in his struggle to withhold the tapes, but the Burger Court ruled that though executive privilege is "fundamental to the operation of government and inextricably rooted in the separation of powers under the Constitution," it cannot "sustain an absolute, unqualified presidential privilege of immunity from judicial process under all circumstances." Nor has the doctrine of separation of powers been a barrier against legislation by Congress (the Presidential Recordings and Materials Preservation Act, 88 Stat. 1965) specifying control over, and access to, the White House papers and tape recordings from President Nixon's five and a half years in office (*Nixon* v. *Administrator of General Services*, 433 U.S. 425: 1977). The majority reached this conclusion in face of Justice Rehnquist's charge that the statute, even though limited only to the Nixon materials, "poses a real threat to the ability of future Presidents to receive candid advice and to give candid instructions. This result . . . will daily stand as a veritable sword of Damocles over every succeeding President and his advisors." Nixon lost again when an equally divided Supreme Court, in *Kissinger* v. *Halperin* (49 LW 4782: 1981), upheld a decision by the Second Circuit Court of Appeals that a president and his top advisers do not enjoy an absolute immunity against suits alleging a violation of constitutional rights.

So far as the Constitution is concerned, the doctrine of separation of powers applies only to the national government and need not be adhered to by the states. Nor does the doctrine apply to the governments established by Congress for the territories and for the District of Columbia. Still, the importance of the freedom of one department from interference by another has been recognized. Sharing exists within separation. In *United States* v. *Nixon* Chief Justice Burger argued that acknowledgement of an unqualified executive privilege would hinder the judiciary in its conduct of a criminal trial. At one time, freedom of the courts from external control was carried so far as to prevent the levy of a nondiscriminatory income tax on the salaries of federal judges (*Evans* v. *Gore*, 253 U.S. 245: 1920).

THE CONGRESS

Delegation of Authority.   The rule prohibiting the delegation of legislative authority, already mentioned in connection with the separation of powers, has been necessarily relaxed when executive officers or boards have been the grantees of the power. Statutes cannot be so detailed as to contain every regulation and form of procedure by which the legislative policies set forth therein are to be carried out. The courts have consequently recognized that administrative officers must be permitted some discretion in the enforcement of laws, and that the effective operation of government often requires the exercise of legislative authority by the executive. Hence Congress may permit executive officers to determine when a given statute shall become operative, and fill in the details of legislative enactments by appropriate regulations. An early case, *The Aurora* v. *United States* (7 Cr. 382: 1813), sustained the grant of power to the President to revive the Non-Intercourse Act when he shall have ascertained that certain conditions exist. *Hampton & Co.* v. *United States* (276 U.S. 394: 1928) sustained a flexible tariff act authorizing the President to raise or lower tariff rates by 50 percent to equalize the costs of production in the United States and competing foreign countries. For a unanimous court, Chief Justice Taft wrote,

The well-known maxim *"Delegata potestas non potest delegari"* (a delegate cannot delegate, that is, transfer his powers), applicable to the law of agency in the general and common law, is well understood and has had wider application in the construction of our federal and state constitutions than it has in private law. . . .

The field of Congress involves all and many varieties of legislative action and Congress has found it frequently necessary to use officers of the executive branch within defined limits, to secure the exact effect intended by acts of legislation, by vesting discretion in such officers to make public regulations interpreting a statute and directing the details of its execution, even to the extent of providing for penalizing a breach of such regulations. . . .

Congress may feel itself unable conveniently to determine exactly when its exercise of the legislative power should become effective, because dependent on future conditions, and it may leave the determination of such time to the decision of an executive. . . .

Prior to 1935 no statute had ever been held invalid because of unconstitutional delegation of power to the executive. In each instance the standard set up by the legislature was held to be sufficiently definite, although some rather vague criteria were thus sustained. In *Panama Refining Co.* v. *Ryan* (Hot Oil Case) (293 U.S. 388: 1935), however, the Supreme Court held unconstitutional a provision of the National Industrial Recovery Act authorizing the President to prohibit the interstate shipment of oil produced or withdrawn in violation of state regulations. The Court declared that an absolute and uncontrolled discretion had been vested in the executive since the statute stated no policy and provided no standard by which the validity of the President's action could be judged. Justice Cardozo, dissenting, found that the declaration of policy in the Act's preamble provided a sufficiently definite standard, but the majority could see no relationship between the broad generalities of that section and the power sought for the President. The majority thought Congress had "left the matter to the President without standard or rule, to be dealt with as he pleased," but Cardozo feared lest classical separation of powers become "a doctrinaire concept to be made use of with pedantic rigor." "Discretion is not unconfined and vagrant," he concluded. "It is canalized within banks that keep it from overflowing."

In *Schechter Poultry Corporation* v. *United States* (295 U.S. 495: 1935) decided shortly after the Hot Oil decision, however, Cardozo joined his brethren in condemning the attempted delegation to the president of code-approving authority. The discretion of the president under the National Industrial Recovery Act was, the Court said, "virtually unfettered," and Cardozo, in a concurring opinion, termed it "delegation run riot." The infirmities of these laws with respect to the attempted delegations were for the most part the result of hasty and inefficient legislative draftsmanship. By 1938 both Congress and the Court had learned a lesson. In the Fair Labor Standards Act, Congress, by adding a rather detailed, though uninstructive, list of factors to guide the administrators' judgment, provided satisfactory limits within which administrative discretion was to be exercised. In *Opp Cotton Mills* v. *Administrator* (312 U.S. 126: 1941), the Court unanimously upheld regulations against the charge, among other things, that the Administrator was authorized to fix wages without adequate congressional guides or control. Justice Stone, ruling that there had been "no failure of performance of the legislative function," observed:

> In an increasingly complex society Congress obviously could not perform its functions if it were obliged to find all the facts subsidiary to the basic conclusions which support the defined legislative policy in fixing, for example, a tariff rate, a railroad rate, or the rate of wages to be applied in particular industries by a minimum wage law. The Constitution, viewed as a continually operative charter of Government, is not to be interpreted as demanding the impossible or impracticable. The essentials of the legislative function are the determination of the legislative policy and its formulation as a rule of conduct. These essentials are preserved when Congress specifies the basic conclusions of fact upon ascertainment of which, from rele-

vant data by a designated administrative agency, it ordains that its statutory command is to be effective.

In international relations the power delegated need not be encumbered by restrictions. *United States* v. *Curtiss-Wright Export Corp.* sustained an embargo on arms to warring South American countries proclaimed by the President pursuant to a joint resolution of Congress authorizing such action upon a finding that it "may contribute to the reestablishment of peace between those countries." The Justices distinguished delegations of power over internal affairs and those over foreign relations. In wartime, delegations must of necessity be made on a tremendous scale, with fewer standards than are contained in peacetime delegations. All such delegations have been sustained, both in and following World Wars I and II.

Whether in war or in peace, the Court now seems more kindly disposed toward the efforts of legislative bodies to accomplish policy objectives through delegation. The exercise of executive discretion is, however, subject to judicial review on the following questions: whether the standard is a reasonably definite one; if an administrative regulation is involved, whether it comes within the scope of the delegated authority; if the decision of an administrative body is involved, whether that body was acting within its proper jurisdiction (i.e., whether the facts of the case can reasonably be said to place it within the operative range of the statute that is being applied).

Legislative Investigations.   A function of Congress, vying in importance with law making itself, is investigation. Woodrow Wilson rated the "informing function" higher than that of legislation. In 1936 Senator Hugo L. Black, who the next year became a Supreme Court Justice, referred to congressional investigations as "among the most useful and fruitful functions of the national legislature." Though derived immediately from the "necessary and proper" clause, the investigatory power is also grounded in the fact that Congress, like Parliament and the early state legislatures, is a deliberative body. Each house, separately or concurrently, may pass resolutions expressing its views on any subject it sees fit. To inform itself on matters likely to become subjects of legislation, Congress may establish committees. Such committees may subpoena witnesses and take testimony. If witnesses refuse to cooperate, they may be punished for contempt. But legislative imprisonment may not extend beyond the session of Congress in which the offense was committed. Congress's investigatory power falls short of authority to make inquiry into the purely personal affairs of private individuals. Investigation must be related to some legislative purpose (*Kilbourn* v. *Thompson,* 103 U.S. 168: 1881).

In 1927 *McGrain* v. *Daugherty* (273 U.S. 135: 1927) upheld the resolution authorizing investigation of corruption in the Department of Justice, though it failed to mention possible legislation. The Court reasoned that "the subject was one on which legislation could be had, . . . the only legitimate object the Senate could have in ordering the investigation was to aid it in legislating; and . . . the subject matter was such that the presumption should be indulged that this was the real object." Twenty-five years later, amid the cold war, a 1953 decision indicated that a committee may not extend by its own interpretation the scope of investigation set forth in the resolution creating it (*United States* v. *Rumely,* 345 U.S. 41: 1953).

This case concerned a House resolution, empowering a committee to investigate all lobbying activities intended to influence legislation. Five Justices held that the investigation was limited, by the terms of the resolution, to activities constituting direct contact with Congress and did not extend to other lobbying activities, including attempts to influence congressional thinking through publication of books and pamphlets. In a concurring opinion, Justice Douglas suggested that the First Amendment might bar such investigations.

Without basing its decision on the First Amendment, the Court in *Watkins* v. *United States* questioned the authority of either house to delve into the private lives of individuals—to "expose for the sake of exposure," or to deny freedom of speech or right of association. The 6-to-1 majority agreed that the power to conduct investigations "is inherent in the legislative process," but insisted that as a matter of due process of law all witnesses must be informed of the pertinency of the questions put to them. Reaction to the decision was hotly critical. Two years later, by construing the Watkins precedent narrowly, a divided court in *Barenblatt* v. *United States* reached a different result. Similarly in rulings on state legislative investigations, the pattern has been bold judicial advance and apparent withdrawal (*Sweezy* v. *New Hampshire*, 354 U.S. 234: 1957 and *Uphaus* v. *Wyman*, 360 U.S. 72: 1959).

As congressional investigations increase in number and scope, it appears that actual legislative purpose becomes less significant. Committees have been balked increasingly by the refusal of witnesses to answer questions under the Fifth Amendment privilege against self-incrimination. The Supreme Court holds that the privilege may properly be used by witnesses even though hearings are not, strictly speaking, criminal proceedings (*Quinn* v. *United States*, 349 U.S. 155: 1955; *Emspak* v. *United States*, 349 U.S. 190: 1955).

A different problem arises when congressional committees seek to procure the attendance of executive officials, or to obtain documents in the possession of the President. Subordinate officials may be required by Congress to attend committee meetings. Until 1974 (*U.S.* v. *Nixon*) refusal of the President to yield subpoenaed documents had been conclusive.

Membership and Privilege.   May 21, 1969, the day President Nixon announced Chief Justice Warren's successor, disagreement between Warren and Burger was dramatically illustrated. On March 1, 1967, the House of Representatives had voted to exclude Harlem Congressman Adam Clayton Powell on the ground that he had misused public funds and was contemptuous of the New York courts and committees of Congress. By a vote of 7 to 1 (*Powell* v. *McCormack*, 395 U.S. 486), the Supreme Court held that the House of Representatives lacked power to *exclude* from its membership a person duly elected, who meets the age, citizenship, and residence requirements specified in Article I, Section 2 of the Constitution. The distinction between the power of the House to *exclude* must not be equated with its power to *expel*. Holding that "it is the responsibility of this Court to act as ultimate interpreter of the Constitution," Chief Justice Warren in his last major opinion, reversed the opinion of Judge Warren E. Burger, the man nominated to succeed him. Invoking separation of powers, Judge Burger, in his capacity as judge on the Court of Appeals, District of Columbia, joined by two associates, had dismissed Representative Powell's suit for reinstatement, contending that courts should not rule on a political issue fraught with possible conflict between Congress and courts. Chief Justice Warren disagreed:

"Our system of government requires that Federal Courts on occasion interpret the Constitution in a manner at variance with the construction given the document by another branch. The alleged conflict that such an adjudication may cause cannot justify the courts' avoiding their constitutional responsibility." Buttressing his opinion with history, and sounding the note that ran through his reapportionment rulings, Chief Justice Warren concluded,

Our examination of the relevant historical material leads us to the conclusions that petitioners are correct that the Constitution leaves the House without authority to *exclude* any person, duly elected by his constituents, who meets the requirements for membership expressly prescribed in the Constitution.

Not only the Constitution, but, also the theory underlying it, reenforced the Chief Justice's view.

Hamilton emphasized: "[T]he true principle of a republic is, that the people should choose whom they please to govern them. Representation is imperfect in proportion as the current of popular favor is checked. This great source of free government, popular election, should be perfectly pure, and the most unbounded liberty be allowed. . . . " Had the intent of the Framers emerged from this material with less clarity, we would nevertheless have been compelled to resolve any ambiguity in favor of a narrow construction of the scope of Congress' power to exclude members-elect. A fundamental principle of our representative democracy is, in Hamilton's words, "that the people should choose whom they please to govern them. . . . " As Madison pointed out in the Convention, this principle is undermined as much by limiting whom the people can elect as by limiting the franchise itself. In apparent agreement with this basic philosophy, the Convention adopted his suggestion limiting the power to expel. To allow essentially that same power to be exercised under the guise of judging qualifications, would be to ignore Madison's warning.

As in so many of the Warren Court's rulings, judicial review, apparently at odds with popular government, was invoked to sustain government by the people.

The Court has also declined to allow Congress to be the sole judge of the scope of the privilege enshrined in the Speech or Debate Clause (Art. I, Sec. 6) of the Constitution. The protection against being "questioned in any other Place" is a major resource of legislative power and independence. The privilege extends "not only to a member but also to his aides insofar as the conduct of the latter would be a protected legislative act if performed by the member himself" (*Gravel* v. *United States,* 408 U.S. 606: 1972), but not to the Superintendent of Documents and other officials of the Government Printing Office who have been directed by Congress to publish certain materials (*Doe* v. *McMillan,* 412 U.S. 306: 1973). The clause does not forbid indictment for accepting a bribe (*United States* v. *Brewster,* 408 U.S. 501: 1972), but it can prevent a prosecutor from introducing evidence of past legislative acts, as a way of establishing motive, when a member is on trial (*United States* v. *Helstoski,* 442 U.S. 477: 1979). Critical to the scope of the privilege is the definition of a "protected legislative act." As Chief Justice Burger's opinion in *Hutchinson* v. *Proxmire* indicates, the definition is by no means all-inclusive.

THE PRESIDENT

Addressing himself to the executive in *Federalist,* No. 70, Hamilton wrote,

There is an idea, which is not without its advocates, that a vigorous executive is inconsistent with the genius of republican government. The enlightened well-wishers to this species of government must at least hope that the supposition is destitute of foundation. Energy in the

Executive is a leading character in the definition of good government. It is essential to the protection of the community against foreign attacks; it is not less essential to the steady administration of the laws; to the protection of property against those irregular and high-handed combinations which sometimes interrupt the ordinary course of justice; to the security of liberty against the enterprises and assaults of ambition, of faction, and of anarchy.

A feeble executive implies a feeble execution of the government. A feeble execution is but another phrase for a bad execution; and a government ill executed, whatever it may be in theory, must be, in practice, a bad government.

The ingredients which constitute energy in the Executive are, first, unity: secondly, duration; thirdly, an adequate provision for its support; fourthly, competent powers. . . .

The ingredients which constitute safety in the republican sense are, first, a due dependence on the people, secondly, a due responsibility.

Like most modern governments, the United States has manifested a tendency toward concentration of power in the hands of the executive. The President is the political head of the country in extraconstitutional affairs; he exercises the power to pardon, the veto power, and extensive war powers, and has an almost absolute control over foreign relations. Moreover, under certain limitations, Congress may give the executive its own power for use when swift and coordinated action is required. Finally, the conduct of government, increasingly in the multiple hands of administrative authority, has given rise to the expressions "government by commission" and "government by executive order"—both indicative of aggrandizement as the characteristic mark of presidential power.

The members of the Convention of 1787 who feared that the President inevitably would succumb to an all-powerful legislature have proved to be poor prophets. Although the Supreme Court has from the time of Marshall asserted and maintained a role of great significance, it is the presidential office that has expanded most in power and shown the greatest increase in both the number and variety of its activities. This swelling of executive power is not unique to America. The grand age of the legislature, when the dominance of the concept of limited government both required and permitted long debate preceding any change in governmental policy, and the paucity of governmental programs facilitated legislative surveillance of administration, is past. War, economic crises, and the complexity of problems confronting industrialized societies have thrust upon the executive power and responsibility not contemplated in an earlier age. "Taken, by and large," Professor Corwin wrote in 1941, "the history of the presidency has been a history of aggrandizement." The years since have underscored this conclusion.

Three strikingly divergent theories purport to describe the nature and scope of presidential power: the constitutional theory, the stewardship theory, and the prerogative theory. The constitutional theory holds that Article II contains an enumeration of executive powers, and that the President must be prepared to justify all his actions on the basis of either enumerated or implied power. The best statement of the constitutional theory appears in W. H. Taft's book, *Our Chief Magistrate and His Powers* (1916). In opposition to Taft, Theodore Roosevelt contended that the President is a "steward of the people," and is therefore under the duty to do "anything that the needs of the nation demanded unless such action was forbidden by the Constitution and the laws." Taft denounced Roosevelt's theory as calculated to make the President a "universal Providence." As Chief Justice, however, he indicated greater sympathy for it (*Myers* v. *U.S.,* 272 U.S. 52: 1926). Going beyond the first Roosevelt's "stewardship" theory, Franklin D. Roosevelt's concept of his duties conforms essentially to John Locke's description of "prerogative"—"the power to act according to discretion for the public good, without the prescription of the law and sometimes even against it." During his long incumbency, President Roosevelt often sacrificed constitutional and legal restrictions on the altar of "emergency" and a commanding public interest.

Many dicta in the *Curtiss-Wright* case seem to justify "inherent" power, at least in foreign affairs, where the president speaks and acts for the nation. In the domestic sphere, however, this is, as the Steel Seizure Case suggests, a highly dubious rationale for presidential action (*Youngstown* v. *Sawyer*). When this case was before the District Court, counsel for the United States, asked by the bench to specify the source of the President's power to seize the steel mills in peacetime, declared: ". . . We base the President's power on Sections 1, 2, and 3 of Article II of the Constitution, and whatever inherent, implied or residual powers may flow therefrom." "So you contend the Executive has unlimited power in time of an emergency?" the judge inquired. Government counsel replied that the President "has the power to take such action as is necessary to meet the emergency," and indicated that the only limitations on executive power in an emergency are the ballot box and impeachment. In argument before the Supreme Court, however, government counsel stressed the president's specific powers derived from the duty to execute the laws, and as commander-in-chief. Only Justices Black and Douglas held that seizure of private property must in every instance be based on statute. The other concurring Justices reserved the question whether, in the absence of any legislation providing for seizure, presidential action based on inherent power would be constitutional. The Steel Case also demonstrates that, although the President may not be the subject of judicial orders limiting his actions in executing laws or implementing policy (*Mississippi* v. *Johnson*, 4 Wall. 475: 1867), his subordinate officers may be the objects of injunctive and other forms of relief, when they act, or threaten to act, illegally.

In its unanimous decision of July 24, 1974 (*United States* v. *Nixon*), the Court held that the President himself must respond to a subpoena issued in connection with a pending trial of former government officials. While sanctioning "executive privilege," the Justices ruled that neither the doctrine of separation of powers nor the alleged confidentiality of executive communications barred the federal courts from access to presidential tapes needed as evidence in a criminal case. Participating in the case were justices appointed by five presidents, three by President Nixon. In constitutional theory and political consequences, *United States* v. *Nixon* is among the most remarkable decisions in the Court's history. Vindicated was the ideal "government of laws and not of men."

Appointment and Removal of Officers.   The Constitution provides that the president, "shall nominate and, by and with the advice and consent of the Senate, shall appoint ambassadors . . . judges of the Supreme Court, and all other officers of the United States, whose appointments are not herein otherwise provided for and which shall be established by law; but the Congress may by law vest the appointment of such inferior officers, as they think proper, in the President alone, in the courts of law, or in the heads of departments" (Art II, Sec. 2, Cl. 2). Persons appointed in a manner not specified by the Constitution are not "officers of the United States"; and while no definition of the term "inferior officers" has ever been made by the courts, it would seem to include all except those in whom the power of appointment might be vested.

The Constitution makes no provision for the removal of officers appointed under the clause above quoted. While the power of removal is generally regarded as a power derived from the power to appoint, it rests within the sole discretion of the President only when exercised with respect to a purely executive or ministerial office.

Following the decision of *Myers* v. *United States,* (272 U.S. 52: 1926), it was generally thought that the power of the President to remove officials appointed by him was plenary, free from any limitations imposed by Congress. Dicta in Chief Justice Taft's opinion in the Myers case seem to suggest this doctrine. Former President Taft said,

> The vesting of the executive power in the President was essentially a grant of the power to execute the laws. But the President alone and unaided could not execute the laws. He must execute them by the assistance of subordinates. . . .
>
> The power to prevent the removal of an officer who has served under the President is different from the authority to consent to or reject his appointment. When a nomination is made, it may be presumed that the Senate is, or may become, as well advised as to the fitness of the nominee as the President, but in the nature of things the defects in ability or intelligence or loyalty in the administration of the laws of one who has served as an officer under the President are facts as to which the President, or his trusted subordinates, must be better informed than the Senate, and the power to remove him may therefore be regarded as confined for very sound and practical reasons, to the governmental authority which has administrative control. The power of removal is incident to the power of appointment, not to the power of advising and consenting to appointment, and when the grant of the executive power is enforced by the express mandate to take care that the laws be faithfully executed, it emphasizes the necessity for including within the executive power as conferred the exclusive power of removal. . . .

Justices Brandeis, Holmes, and McReynolds dissented. All denied that the President either possessed or required an unlimited authority to remove inferior officers. Taft stressed efficiency; Brandeis's primary concern was abuse of power.

> The doctrine of the separation of powers was adopted by the Conventions of 1787, not to promote efficiency but to preclude the exercise of arbitrary power. The purpose was, not to avoid friction, but by means of the inevitable friction incident to the distribution of governmental powers among three departments, to save the people from autocracy. . . .

Nine years after the Myers decision, the Court whittled down the broad rule, holding that the removal of officials from certain independent agencies, such as the Federal Trade Commission, could be limited to causes defined by Congress (*Humphrey's Executor* v. *United States,* 295 U.S. 602: 1934). The Court distinguished positions in the traditional executive departments, for whose administration the President assumed primary responsibility, from those in agencies established by Congress to carry out legislative policy essentially free from any executive influence other than that resulting from appointment. This distinction was maintained in *Wiener* v. *U.S.* (357 U.S. 349: 1958). The case involved President Eisenhower's removal of a member of the War Claims Commission. There were specific statutory limits on the removal of Federal Trade Commissioners, but none in the War Claims Act. Stressing the quasi-judicial nature of the agency, Justice Frankfurter minimized this distinction: "Congress did not wish to have hang over the Commission the Damocles' sword of removal by the President for no reason other than he preferred to have on that Commission men of 'his own choosing'."

Pardoning Power.   The President is empowered to grant "reprieves" (a suspension of legally imposed penalties) and "pardons" (a remission of sentence) except in cases of impeachment. Under Article II, Section 4, a President allegedly guilty of treason, bribery, or other high crimes and misdemeanors is subject to impeachment. The penalty is removal from office and disqualification for future office holding. An impeached president may be prosecuted and, if found guilty, the usual penalties are applicable. Without confessing criminal wrongdoing, President Nixon escaped impeachment by resignation. President Ford's "full, free and absolute" pardon saved his predecessor from prosecution for criminal conduct and also removed any political disqualification.

The Supreme Court has ruled that acceptance of a pardon implies confession of guilt (*Burdick* v. *U.S.*, 236 U.S. 79, 94: 1915). At a news conference, President Ford endorsed this interpretation and applied it to Richard Nixon.

In *Ex parte Grossman* (267 U.S. 87: 1925) the pardoning power of the President seemed to collide head on with the power of the courts to punish for contempt. Nevertheless, the Supreme Court, taking a generous view of the pardoning power, held that the President's power in this field was as great as that of the English kings, who had frequently pardoned those guilty of contempt of court. Applying this theory, a district court upheld as constitutional Ford's pardon of Nixon (*Murphy* v. *Ford,* 390 F. Supp. 1372: W.D. Mich, 1975).

Protection against Domestic Violence.   The President has the duty under Article IV, Section 4, to furnish military assistance to repress domestic violence upon call of a state legislature or governor. From the Whiskey Rebellion to the present, presidents have been called upon for aid, either because of insurrection against the lawful state government, or because of disorders arising from economic or social disputes. The action of the President in sending, or even agreeing to commit, troops to the aid of one of the contending factions in a state dispute is a recognition that there is a lawful government in that state (*Luther* v. *Borden*). If the disorder results in the violation of federal laws, the President may then act in accordance with his duty to "take care that the laws be faithfully executed. . . . " In either case, in the actual direction of troops he acts in his capacity of commander-in-chief.

Execution of the Laws.   With or without approval of a state governor, the president may use military force or any other means deemed necessary to fulfill his obligation faithfully to execute the laws of the United States (*In re Debs,* 158 U.S. 546: 1895). Earlier the Court had exempted from state prosecution a special officer appointed by direction of the President to guard Justice Field, when the officer shot and killed a man who had threatened and accosted the Supreme Court Justice (*In re Neagle,* 135 U.S. 1: 1890). The justification given in the Neagle case was the President's duty to execute the laws, which the Court interpreted broadly to include the protection of officials carrying out their lawful duties. In other words, the President was not required to cite a specific statute authorizing each of his actions. His power to protect the "peace" of the United States and execute the laws seemingly has no effective judicial limits. Martial law may be authorized whenever a state governor or the President considers it necessary for the restoration of order. (See *Moyer* v. *Peabody,* 212 U.S. 78: 1909 and *Sterling* v. *Constantin,* 287 U.S. 378: 1932).

Impoundment.   Particularly in recent years, the President, at political odds with Congress, has refused to spend appropriated funds. In 1967, President Johnson impounded billions of highway funds appropriated for the states. The Nixon Administration withheld 202 million from the congressional food stamp program. An even greater sum was withheld in 1972. Nixon directed the Administrator of the Environmental Protection Agency to allot to the states several billion dollars less than authorized by the Federal Water Pollution Control Act. In *Train* v. *City of New York* (420 U.S. 35: 1975), the Court, in an opinion by Justice White, avoided the constitutional issue of impoundment, but concluded as a matter of statutory interpretation that Congress had not intended to allow the President such discretion. In 1974, the Congressional Budget and Impoundment Control Act (88 Stat. 297) became law, as the senators and representatives attempted to strengthen their influence over the "purse." Title X of the statute creates a procedure for legislative review of impoundments. Involved is a complex political struggle that does not lend itself to easy judicial resolution.

Military Powers.   The power of the federal government over the armed forces of the nation is divided between the President and Congress. The legislature has been given the important powers of raising armies and providing a navy (Art. I, Sec. 8, Cl. 14); the President, as commander-in-chief of the armed forces (Art. II, Sec. 2, Cl. 1), may issue regulations of his own and may take charge of all military operations in time of peace as well as in war.

War does not suspend the guaranties of the Constitution. Speaking for the majority in the *Milligan* case Justice Davis observed: "No doctrine involving more pernicious consequences was ever invented by the wit of man than that any of its [the Constitution's] provisions can be suspended during any of the great emergencies of the government. Such a doctrine leads directly to anarchy or despotism, but the theory of necessity on which it is based is false; for the government, within the Constitution, has all the powers granted to it, which are necessary to preserve its existence; as has been happily proved by the result of the great effort [secession of the states] to throw off its just authority." Yet in the very case in which this hypocritical pronouncement was made the Constitution was suspended!

Echoing one aspect of Justice Davis's observation, Holmes remarked in 1919 (*Frohwerk* v. *U.S.,* 249 U.S. 204): "We do not lose our right to condemn either measures or men because the country is at war." Yet under the "inherent" powers doctrine Attorney General John Mitchell argued in 1971 that "the President, acting through the Attorney General, may constitutionally authorize the use of electronic surveillance in cases where he had determined that, in order to preserve national security the use of such surveillance is reasonable." Countervailing values were asserted in the Court's far-reaching decision in *United States* v. *United States District Court.*

Two different approaches to the problem of waging war successfully can be found in American history. Under Lincoln, Congress was ignored or asked to ratify executive actions already accomplished or under way. In World Wars I and II, on the other hand, Congress passed a vast number of general statutes of wide scope delegating to the President, or to persons designated by him, vast discretionary powers. The widest of these delegations was upheld (e.g., *Bowles* v. *Willingham,* 321 U.S. 503: 1944). When statutory authority is thus added to the President's already expansive powers as commander-in-chief, all constitutional limitations virtually disappear, as seen in the Japanese relocation cases. Even without the support of statute, presidential power in wartime is subject to few limitations. The President can control the movement of the armed forces and prescribe rules, including judicial procedures, for the government of captured territory. He may direct the seizure of former enemy officers and officials after the conclusion of hostilities, and set up military commissions to try them in proceedings that are not limited by the Constitution.

Article I, Section 9 of the Constitution seemingly limits Congress's power of suspending the writ of habeas corpus to "cases of rebellion or invasion." Yet Lincoln, during the Civil War, suspended the privilege of the writ without congressional authorization, and ordered his officers to refuse service of a writ of habeas corpus issued by Chief Justice Taney. Subsequently, Congress authorized the President to suspend the writ in certain cases; the Supreme Court, however, refused to pass on the validity of the President's action (*Ex parte Vallandigham,* 1 Wall. 243: 1864). Lincoln provided another extreme example of executive power when he imposed martial law on portions of the northern states and substituted trial by military commission for the regular processes of law in dealing with traitors and others charged with violations of wartime statutes.

In *Ex parte Milligan,* decided in 1866 after the end of hostilities, the Court held that Lincoln had exceeded his authority, the regular courts of Indiana, where the military commission had convicted Milligan, being open and prepared to handle the charges against him. Five members of the Court went further and stated that martial rule could never exist where the courts were open. Four members thought that Congress could have sanctioned what the executive could not.

In World War II a similar result followed, where the Governor-General of Hawaii, pursuant to presidential authorization, invoked martial rule and gave to military commissions jurisdiction over all criminal offenses. In a 6-to-2 decision, the Court held such action invalid on the basis of the Milligan decision (*Duncan* v. *Kahanamoku,* 327 U.S. 304: 1946).

The unique problem was presented at the end of World War II, when the Court was asked by the Japanese General Yamashita and other Japanese war leaders to review their trials by military commissions for violation of the laws of war, claiming serious procedural errors in the trial, as well as innocence of the charge. The Court decided that the findings of a military commission are not reviewable, thus in effect permitting these tribunals to follow rules that differ substantially from those required in the regular trial courts. Murphy and Rutledge, dissenting, pointed out that the Court's decision meant that minimal standards of fairness need not be followed by military commissions, and that such commissions are thus effectively placed beyond the ''rule of law'' (*In re Yamashita,* 327 U.S. 1: 1946).

While enemies of the United States could not successfully invoke constitutional guaranties, and were, in effect, subjected to the sense of justice of military tribunals, American citizens have been more successful in escaping military control. In *United States ex rel. Toth* v. *Quarles* (350 U.S. 11: 1955), the Court held that an honorably discharged serviceman was not subject to court-martial jurisdiction for offenses allegedly committed before discharge, and that a provision of the Uniform Code of Military Justice providing the contrary was invalid. In 1956 a sharply divided Court held that civilians accompanying the armed forces abroad were triable by courts-martial as provided by the Code (*Reid* v. *Covert,* 351 U.S. 487; *Kinsella* v. *Krueger,* 351 U.S. 470). On rehearing, the Court made a dramatic about-face and held that Congress could not deprive a civilian citizen of the United States of his constitutional guaranties of trial by jury and other rights in capital cases, regardless of the difficulties in making a civil trial available (*Reid* v. *Covert* and *Kinsella* v. *Krueger,* 354 U.S. 1: 1967). Subsequently the rule was extended to noncapital cases (*Kinsella* v. *Singleton,* 361 U.S. 234: 1960).

Although civilians accompanying the armed forces were thus able to preserve their constitutional rights, a serviceman in Japan seeking trial by court-martial under the Uniform Code of Military Justice found that by executive agreement or treaty the United States could provide for trial in foreign courts of military personnel charged with certain offenses not of a purely military nature (*Wilson* v. *Girard,* 354 U.S. 524: 1957).

Foreign Affairs.   In foreign affairs, presidential power again is limited by Congress only with great difficulty and on rare occasions. Congressional control of the purse provides a check of growing importance at a time when foreign aid is an important consideration in diplomatic relations. The Court has upheld, as we have seen, delegation of power by Congress to the President that would have been invalidated if it had been made in domestic legislation. More important to presidential power, however, is the theory of sovereignty set forth in Justice Sutherland's *Curtiss-Wright* opinion, and the great reservoir of inherent power possessed by the President as representative of the United States in dealing with other nations. Treaties, it is true, must receive the consent of two-thirds of the Senate. Once it is passed, a treaty may then be the basis of implementing legislation that otherwise would not be within the power of Congress (*Missouri* v. *Holland*). On the other hand, Congress may by statute alter or negate the effect of a treaty on domestic law.

The tendency of modern presidents to use executive agreements in place of the treaty has freed them from dependency on the Senate. Such agreements have the same legal effect as treaties (*United States* v. *Belmont,* 301 U.S. 324: 1937; *United States* v. *Pink* 315 U.S. 203: 1942). In 1952 and again in 1953 resolutions were introduced in the Senate providing among other things, that "A treaty shall become effective as internal law in the United States only through legislation which would be valid in absence of the treaty." These efforts were resisted primarily because of the serious adverse impact such an amendment would inevitably exert on the President's control of foreign relations. With the increasing importance and complexity of foreign policy, the President has found it necessary to play a role unhindered by the ability of one-third-plus-one of the Senate to frustrate his actions.

A case in point was President Carter's notification in December 1978 to terminate this country's Mutual Defense Treaty with Taiwan on January 1, 1980, without congressional approval. Opponents of his efforts couched their objections in constitutional terms. The Senate had ratified the treaty, and even though its terms provided for termination on a year's notice by either signatory, they claimed the President could not do it alone. So they filed suit. After a defeat in the district court (481 F. Supp. 949: 1979), the court of appeals upheld Carter's unilateral authority (617 F. 2d 697: 1979). The Senate's authority to ratify does not imply a role in termination, the judges held. The Senate had approved a treaty that provided for terms of a year's notice. It was up to President to give that notice, as the nation's representative in foreign affairs.

In *Goldwater* v. *Carter* (444 U.S. 996: 1979), the Court, without hearing oral argument, refused to address the merits of the suit. Six Justices directed the lower court to dismiss the complaint. Two would have assigned the case for full review and decision. Only Justice Brennan reached the merits, siding with the President.

In this situation as in many others in American constitutional interpretation, the past informs the present and the present sheds light on the past. Bearing on the Taiwan treaty termination is *Myers* v. *United States,* reviewed earlier in this essay. President Wilson had fired Myers, an executive officer, without approval of Congress. Voting 6 to 3, the Supreme Court found the President's power of removal to be incident to his power of appointment, not to the Senate's power of advising and consenting to the appointment. If the removal power is incident to appointment, may not the termination of a treaty be considered incident to negotiation? The fact that the *Myers* case involved internal rather than external affairs strengthened the constitutional case for President Carter. The President, declared Justice Sutherland in *Curtiss-Wright,* "makes treaties with the advice and consent of the Senate; but he alone negotiates. Into the field of negotiation the Senate cannot intrude; the Congress itself is powerless to invade it."

Landmark decisions like *Curtiss-Wright* and *Youngstown* found renewed application in 1981 when the Court on the last day of its term upheld the legality of President Carter's extraordinary financial actions in the Iranian Hostage Affair (*Dames & Moore* v. *Regan,* 49 LW 4969: 1981). Agreeing with Justice Frankfurter's words in *Youngstown* that the Framers "did not make the judiciary the overseer of our government," Justice Rehnquist and an all but unanimous bench moved at great lengths to justify Carter's steps in this troubled matter. Strengthened was the constitutional status of executive agreements. Emphasized was the idea that congressional acquiescense or inaction constitutes congressional approval. Demonstrated was the considerable deference the Court is inclined to show to the executive branch in foreign relations.

The Framers made war making a joint enterprise. Congress is authorized to "declare war"; the President is designated "commander in chief." Technology has expanded the President's role and correspondingly curtailed the power of Congress. In recognition of vastly changed conditions after World War II, Congress itself endorsed executive aggrandizement. Only recently have the legislators attempted to regain their constitutional share of war making, or war avoiding.

In the face of rising public protest against the undeclared Vietnam War, New York Senator Javits sponsored congressional hearings leading to legislation designed to curb presidential power. The result is the controversial War Powers Resolution of 1973 (87 Stat. 555), a far cry from the 1964 Gulf of Tonkin Resolution (78 Stat. 384), which declared "that Congress approves and supports the determination of the President as commander-in-chief, to take all necessary measures to repel any armed attack against the forces of the United States and to prevent further aggression." Whether or not the Javits resolution can be effectively enforced remains to be seen.

The President is under a positive obligation "to take care that the laws be faithfully executed." His power must be adapted to changed and changing conditions. But, in fulfilling this responsibility, he must also take into account those principles and provisions of the Constitution which restrict as well as enlarge his powers. As commander-in-chief, he cannot pick and choose the provisions of the Constitution he executes. Congress's share in war making must be adapted to unforeseen developments. Otherwise, technological evolution alone makes emergence of a totalitarian system inevitable.

Of course the Framers could not have foreseen conditions as they exist today, but the underlying principles of their handiwork are clear. As to war making, they intended Congress to participate. Early in the Philadelphia Convention debates, Madison observed: "A rupture with other powers is among the greatest national calamities. It ought therefore to be effectually provided that no part of a nation shall have it in its power to bring them [wars] on the whole." Madison was referring to the possibility that individual states might unwittingly involve the country in war, but his conviction that the war-making power should be shared is clear.

The power of Congress in this sensitive area was not meant to cripple and impede; it was designed to produce a wiser course of action. Sound in 1787, it is no less so today.

SELECTED READINGS

BARBER, S. A., *The Constitution and the Delegation of Congressional Power.* Chicago: University of Chicago Press, 1975.

BARTH, ALAN, *Government by Investigation.* New York: Viking, 1955.

BERGER, RAOUL, *Executive Privilege: A Constitutional Myth.* Cambridge: Harvard University Press, 1974.

———, *Impeachment: The Constitutional Problem.* Cambridge: Harvard University Press, 1973.

CORWIN, EDWARD S., *The President, Office and Powers,* 4th ed. New York: New York University Press, 1957.

———, "The Steel Seizure Case: Judicial Bricks without Straw," 53 *Columbia Law Review* 53 (1953).

FELLMAN, DAVID, "The Separation of Powers and the Judiciary," 37 *Review of Politics* 357 (1975).

FISHER, LOUIS, *The Constitution Between Friends; Congress, the President, and the Law.* New York: St. Martin's Press, 1978.

FRIEDMAN, JAMES D., "Review: Delegation of Power and Institutional Competence," 43 *University of Chicago Law Review* 307 (1976).

GWYN, W. B., *The Meaning of Separation of Powers.* The Hague: Martinus Na'jhoff, 1965.

HENKIN, LOUIS, *Foreign Affairs and the Constitution.* New York: Foundation Press, 1972.

LOFGREN, CHARLES A., "*U.S.* v. *Curtiss-Wright Export Corporation:* An Historical Reassessment," 83 *Yale Law Review* 1 (1973).

MARCUS, MAEVA, *Truman and the Steel Seizure Case: The Limits of Presidential Power.* New York: Columbia University Press, 1977.

RANDALL, J. G., *Constitutional Problems under Lincoln,* rev. ed. Urbana: University of Illinois Press, 1951.

REVELEY, W. T. III, "Presidential War-Making: Constitutional Prerogative or Usurpation," 55 *Virginia Law Review* 1243 (1969).

ROSSITER, CLINTON, *The Supreme Court and the Commander-in-Chief.* Ithaca: Cornell University Press, 1951.

SCIGLIANO, ROBERT, *The Supreme Court and the Presidency.* New York: Free Press, 1972.

SPINDLER, JOHN F., "Executive Agreements and the Proposed Constitutional Amendments to the Treaty Power," 51 *Michigan Law Review* 1202 (1953).

SPONG, W. B., JR., "Can Balance be Restored in the Constitutional War Powers of the President and Congress?" 6 *University of Richmond Law Review* 11 (1971).

STEPHENSON, D. GRIER, JR., "'The Mild Magistracy of the Law': *U.S.* v. *Richard Nixon,*" 103 *Intellect* 288 (1975).

TAYLOR, TELFORD. *The Grand Inquest: The Story of Congressional Investigations.* New York: Simon and Schuster, 1955.

The novelty of the undertaking immediately strikes us. It has been shown in the course of these papers, that the existing Confederation is founded on principles which are fallacious; that we must consequently change this first foundation, and with it the superstructure resting upon it. . . .

Among the difficulties encountered by the convention, a very important one must have lain in combining the requisite stability and energy in government, with the inviolable attention due to liberty and to the republican form. Without substantially accomplishing this part of their undertaking, they would have very imperfectly fulfilled the object of their appointment, or the expectation of the public; yet that it could not be easily accomplished, will be denied by no one who is unwilling to betray his ignorance of the subject. Energy in government is essential to the security against external and internal danger, and to that prompt and salutary execution of the laws which enter into the very definition of good government. Stability in government is essential to national character and to the advantages annexed to it, as well as to that repose and confidence in the minds of the people, which are among the chief blessings of civil society. An irregular and mutable legislation is not more an evil in itself than it is odious to the people; and it may be pronounced with assurance that the people of this country, enlightened as they are with regard to the nature, and interested, as the great body of them are, in the effects of good government, will never be satisfied till some remedy be applied to the vicissitudes and uncertainties which characterize the State administrations. On comparing, however, these valuable ingredients with the vital principles of liberty, we must perceive at once the difficulty of mingling them together in their due proportions. The genius of republican liberty seems to demand on one side, not only that all power should be derived from the people, but that those intrusted with it should be kept in dependence on the people, by a short duration of their appointments; and that even during this short period the trust should be placed not in a few, but a number of hands. Stability, on the contrary, requires that the hands in which power is lodged should continue for a length of time the same. A frequent change of men will result from a frequent return of elections; and a frequent change of measures from a frequent change of men: whilst energy in government requires not only a certain duration of power, but the execution of it by a single hand.

How far the convention may have succeeded in this part of their work, will better appear on a more accurate view of it. From the cursory view here taken, it must clearly appear to have been an arduous part.

Not less arduous must have been the task of marking the proper line of partition between the authority of the general and that of the State governments. Every man will be sensible of this difficulty, in proportion as he has been accustomed to contemplate and discriminate objects extensive and complicated in their nature. The faculties of the mind itself have never yet been distinguished and defined, with satisfactory precision, by all the efforts of the most acute and metaphysical philosophers. Sense, perception, judgment, desire, volition, memory, imagination, are found to be separated by such delicate shades and minute gradations that their boundaries have eluded the most subtle investigations, and remain a pregnant source of ingenious disquisition and controversy. The boundaries between the great kingdom of nature, and, still more, between the various provinces, and lesser portions into which they are subdivided, afford another illustration of the same important truth. . . .

When we pass from the works of nature, in which all the delineations are perfectly accurate, and appear to be otherwise only from the imperfection of the eye which surveys them, to the institutions of man, in which the obscurity arises as well from the object itself as from the organ by which it is contemplated, we must perceive the necessity of moderating still further our expectations and hopes from the efforts of human sagacity. Experience has instructed us that no skill in the science of government has yet been able to discriminate and define, with sufficient certainty, its three great provinces—the legislative, executive, and judiciary; or even the privileges and powers of the different legislative branches. Questions daily occur in the course of practice, which prove the obscurity which reigns in these subjects, and which puzzle the greatest adepts in political science. . . .

Besides the obscurity arising from the complexity of objects, and the imperfection of the human faculties, the medium through which the conceptions of men are conveyed to each other adds a fresh embarrassment. The use of words is to express ideas. Perspicuity, therefore, requires not only that the ideas should be distinctly formed, but that they should be expressed by words distinctly and exclusively appropriate to them. But no language is so copious as to supply words and phrases for every complex idea, or so correct as not to include many equiv-

ocally denoting different ideas. Hence it must happen that however accurately objects may be discriminated in themselves, and however accurately the discrimination may be considered, the definition of them may be rendered inaccurate by the inaccuracy of the terms in which it is delivered. And this unavoidable inaccuracy must be greater or less, according to the complexity and novelty of the objects defined. When the Almighty himself condescends to address mankind in their own language, his meaning, luminous as it must be, is rendered dim and doubtful by the cloudy medium through which it is communicated.

Here, then, are three sources of vague and incorrect definitions: indistinctness of the object, imperfection of the organ of conception, inadequateness of the vehicle of ideas. Any one of these must produce a certain degree of obscurity. The convention, in delineating the boundary between the federal and State jurisdictions, must have experienced the full effect of them all. . . .

The Federalist, No. 47 (Madison)

One of the principal objections inculcated by the more respectable adversaries to the Constitution, is its supposed violation of the political maxim, that the legislative, executive, and judiciary departments ought to be separate and distinct. In the structure of the federal government, no regard, it is said, seems to have been paid to this essential precaution in favor of liberty. The several departments of power are distributed and blended in such a manner as at once to destroy all symmetry and beauty of form, and to expose some of the essential parts of the edifice to the danger of being crushed by the disproportionate weight of other parts.

No political truth is certainly of greater in-

trinsic value, or is stamped with the authority of more enlightened patrons of liberty, than that on which the objection is founded. The accumulation of all powers, legislative, executive, and judiciary, in the same hands, whether of one, a few, or many, and whether hereditary, self-appointed, or elective may justly be pronounced the very definition of tyranny. . . .

The oracle who is always consulted and cited on this subject is the celebrated Montesquieu. If he be not the author of this invaluable precept in the science of politics, he has the merit at least of displaying and recommending it most effectually to the attention of mankind. . . . In saying "There can be no liberty where the legislative and executive powers are united in the same person, or body of magistrates," or, "if the power of judging be not separated from the legislative and executive powers," he did not mean that these departments ought to have no PARTIAL AGENCY in, or no CONTROL over, the acts of each other. His meaning, as his own words import, and still more conclusively as illustrated by the example in his eye, can amount to no more than this, that where the WHOLE power of one department is exercised by the same hands which possess the WHOLE power of another department, the fundamental principles of a free constitution are subverted. . . .

The reasons on which Montesquieu grounds his maxim are a further demonstration of his meaning. "When the legislative and executive powers are united in the same person or body," says he, "there can be no liberty, because apprehensions may arise lest THE SAME monarch or senate should ENACT tyrannical laws to EXECUTE them in a tyrannical manner." Again: "Were the power of judging joined with the legislative, the life and liberty of the subject would be exposed to arbitrary control, for THE JUDGE would then be THE LEGISLATOR. Were it joined to the executive power, THE JUDGE might behave with all the violence of AN OPPRESSOR." Some of these reasons are more fully explained in other passages; but briefly stated as they are here, they sufficiently establish the meaning which we have put on this celebrated maxim of the celebrated author.

The Federalist, No. 48 (Madison)

It is agreed on all sides, that the powers properly belonging to one of the departments ought not to be directly and completely administered by either of the other departments. It is equally evident, that none of them ought to possess, directly or indirectly, an overruling influence over the others, in the administration of their respective powers. It will not be denied, that power is of an encroaching nature, and that it ought to be effectually restrained from passing the limits assigned to it. After discriminating, therefore, in theory, the several classes of power, as they may in their nature be legislative, executive, or judiciary, the next and most difficult task is to provide some practical security for each, against the invasion of the others. What this security ought to be, is the great problem to be solved.

Will it be sufficient to mark, with precision, the boundaries of these departments, in the constitution of the government, and to trust to these parchment barriers against the encroaching spirit of power? This is the security which appears to have been principally relied on by the compilers of most of the American constitutions. But experience assures us, that the efficacy of the provision has been greatly overrated; and that some more adequate defense is indispensably necessary for the more feeble, against the more powerful, members of the government. The legislative department is everywhere extending the sphere of its activity, and drawing all power into its impetuous vortex.

The legislative department derives a superiority in our governments from other circumstances. Its constitutional powers being at once more extensive, and less susceptible of precise limits, it can, with the greater facility, mask, under complicated and indirect measures, the encroachments which it makes on the coordinate departments. It is not unfrequently a question of real nicety in legislative bodies, whether the operation of a particular measure will, or will not, extend beyond the legislative sphere. On the other side, the executive power being restrained within a narrower compass, and being more simple in its nature, and the judiciary being described by landmarks still less uncertain, projects of usurpation by either of these departments would immediately betray and defeat themselves. Nor is this all: as the legislative department alone has access to the pockets of the people, and has in some constitutions full discretion, and in all a prevailing influence, over the pecuniary rewards of those who fill the other departments, a dependence is thus created in the latter, which gives still greater facility to encroachments of the former. . . .

The conclusion which I am warranted in drawing from these observations is, that a mere demarcation on parchment of the constitutional limits of the several departments, is not a sufficient guard against those encroachments which lead to a tyrannical concentration of all the powers of government in the same hands.

The Federalist, No. 51 (Madison)

To what expedient, then, shall we finally resort, for maintaining in practice the necessary partition of power among the several departments, as laid down in the Constitution? The only answer that can be given is, that as all these exterior provisions are found to be inadequate, the defect must be supplied, by so contriving the interior structure of the government as that its several constituent parts may, by their mutual relations, be the means of keeping each other in their proper places. . . .

In order to lay a due foundation for that separate and distinct exercise of the different powers of government, which to a certain extent is admitted on all hands to be essential to the preservation of liberty, it is evident that each department should have a will of its own; and consequently should be so constituted that the members of each should have as little agency as possible in the appointment of the members of the others. . . .

But the great security against a gradual concentration of the several powers in the same department, consists in giving to those who administer each department the necessary constitutional means and personal motives to resist encroachments of the others. The provision for defence must in this, as in all other cases, be made commensurate to the danger of attack. Ambition must be made to counteract ambition. The interest of the man must be connected with the constitutional rights of the place. It may be a reflection on human nature, that such devices should be necessary to control the abuses of government. But what is government itself, but the greatest of all reflections on human nature? If men were angels, no government would be necessary. If angels were to govern men, neither external nor internal controls on government would be necessary. In framing a government which is to be administered by men over men, the great difficulty lies in this: you must first enable the government to control the governed; and in the next place oblige it to control itself. A dependence on the people is, no doubt, the primary control on the government; but experience has taught mankind the necessity of auxiliary precautions.

This policy of supplying, by opposite and rival interests, the defect of better motives, might be traced through the whole system of human affairs, private as well as public. We see it particularly displayed in all the subordinate distributions of power, where the constant aim is to divide and arrange the several offices in such a manner as that each may be a check on the other—that the private interest of every individual may be a sentinel over the public rights. These inventions of prudence cannot be less requisite in the distribution of the supreme powers of the State. . . .

Watkins v. *United States*
354 U.S. 178, 77 S.Ct. 1173, I L.Ed. 2d 1273 (1957)

The broad investigating power of Congress had been upheld in *McGrain* v. *Daugherty*, 273 U.S. 135 (1927), where the purpose was to obtain information about alleged wrongdoing by the Attorney General and the Department of Justice. Increasingly in the period after World War II, Congress turned its attention to the activities within the United States of alleged members and officers of the Communist party. Frequently, witnesses invoked the Fifth Amendment, in refusing to answer committee questions. In *Watkins,* the witness based this refusal to answer on different grounds. The facts are given in the opinion below.

MR. CHIEF JUSTICE WARREN delivered the opinion of the Court. . . .

On April 29, 1954, petitioner appeared as a witness in compliance with a subpoena issued by a Subcommittee of the Committee on Un-American Activities of the House of Representatives. . . .

We start with several basic premises on which there is general agreement. The power of the Congress to conduct investigations is inherent in the legislative process. That power is broad. It encompasses inquiries concerning the administration of existing laws as well as proposed or possibly needed statutes. It includes surveys of defects in our social, economic or political system for the purpose of enabling the Congress to remedy them. It comprehends probes into departments of the Federal Government to expose corruption, inefficiency or waste. But broad as is this power of inquiry, it is not unlimited. There is no general authority to expose the private affairs of individuals without justification in terms of the functions of the Congress. This was freely conceded by the Solicitor General in his argument of this case. . . .

It is unquestionably the duty of all citizens to cooperate with the Congress in its efforts to obtain the facts needed for intelligent legislative action. It is their unremitting obligation to respond to subpoenas, to respect the dignity of the Congress and its committees and to testify fully with respect to matters within the province of proper investigation. This, of course, assumes that the constitutional rights of witnesses will be respected by the Congress as they are in a court of justice.

In the decade following World War II, there appeared a new kind of congressional inquiry unknown in prior periods of American history. Principally this was the result of the various investigations into the threat of subversion of the United States Government, but other subjects of congressional interest also contributed to the changed scene. This new phase of legislative inquiry involved a broad-scale intrusion into the lives and affairs of private citizens. It brought before the courts novel questions of the appropriate limits of congressional inquiry. Prior cases, like *Kilbourn, McGrain* and *Sinclair,* had defined the scope of investigative power in terms of the inherent limitations of the sources of that power. In the more recent cases, the emphasis shifted to problems of accommodating the interest of the Government with the rights and privileges of individuals. The central theme was the application of the Bill of Rights as a restraint upon the assertion of governmental power in this form.

It was during this period that the Fifth Amendment privilege against self-incrimination was frequently invoked and recognized as a legal limit upon the authority of a committee to require that a witness answer its questions. Some early doubts as to the applicability of the privilege before a legislative committee never matured. When the matter reached this Court, the Government did not challenge in any way that the Fifth Amendment protection was available to the witness, and such a challenge could not have prevailed. It confined its argument to the character of the answers sought and to the adequacy of the claim of privilege. . . .

A far more difficult task evolved from the claim by witnesses that the committees' interrogations were infringements upon the freedoms of the First Amendment. Clearly, an investigation is subject to the command that the Congress shall make no law abridging freedom of speech or press or assembly. While it is true that there is no statute to be reviewed, and that an investigation is not a law, nevertheless an investigation is part of lawmaking. It is justified solely as an adjunct to the legislative process. The First Amendment may be invoked against infringement of the protected freedoms by law or by lawmaking.

Abuses of the investigative process may imperceptibly lead to abridgement of protected freedoms. The mere summoning of a witness and compelling him to testify, against his will, about his beliefs, expressions or associations is a measure of governmental interference. And when those forced revelations concern matters that are unorthodox, unpopular, or even hateful to the general public, the reaction in the life of the witness may be disastrous. This effect is even more harsh when it is past beliefs, expressions or associations that are disclosed and judged by current standards rather than those

contemporary with the matters exposed. Nor does the witness alone suffer the consequences. Those who are identified by witnesses and thereby placed in the same glare of publicity are equally subject to public stigma, scorn and obloquy. Beyond that, there is the more subtle and immeasurable effect upon those who tend to adhere to the most orthodox and uncontroversial views and associations in order to avoid a similar fate at some future time. That this impact is partly the result of nongovernmental activity by private persons cannot relieve the investigators of their responsibility for initiating the reaction. . . .

We have no doubt that there is no congressional power to expose for the sake of exposure. The public is, of course, entitled to be informed concerning the workings of its government. That cannot be inflated into a general power to expose where the predominant result can only be an invasion of the private rights of individuals. But a solution to our problem is not to be found in testing the motives of committee members for this purpose. Such is not our function. Their motives alone would not vitiate an investigation which had been instituted by a House of Congress if that assembly's legislative purpose is being served.

. . . It is the responsibility of the Congress, in the first instance, to insure that compulsory process is used only in furtherance of a legislative purpose. That requires that the instructions to an investigating committee spell out that group's jurisdiction and purpose with sufficient particularity. Those instructions are embodied in the authorizing resolution. That document is the committee's charter. Broadly drafted and loosely worded, however, such resolutions can leave tremendous latitude to the discretion of the investigators. The more vague the committee's charter is, the greater becomes the possibility that the committee's specific actions are not in conformity with the will of the parent House of Congress.

The authorizing resolution of the Un-American Activities Committee was adopted in 1938 when a select committee, under the chairmanship of Representative Dies, was created. Several years later, the Committee was made a standing organ of the House with the same mandate. It defines the Committee's authority as follows:

[Rule XI]
The Committee on Un-American Activities, as a whole or by subcommittee, is authorized to make from time to time investigations of (i) the extent, character, and objects of un-American propaganda activities in the United States, (ii) the diffusion within the United States of subversive and un-American propaganda that is instigated from foreign countries or of a domestic origin and attacks the principle of the form of government as guaranteed by our Constitution, and (iii) all other questions in relation thereto that would aid Congress in any necessary remedial legislation.

It would be difficult to imagine a less explicit authorizing resolution. Who can define the meaning of "un-American"? What is that single, solitary "principle of the form of government as guaranteed by our Constitution"? There is no need to dwell upon the language, however. At one time, perhaps, the resolution might have been read narrowly to confine the Committee to the subject of propaganda. The events that have transpired in the fifteen years before the interrogation of petitioner make such a construction impossible at this date. . . .

No doubt every reasonable indulgence of legality must be accorded to the actions of a coordinate branch of our Government. But such deference cannot yield to an unnecessary and unreasonable dissipation of precious constitutional freedoms.

It is, of course, not the function of this Court to prescribe rigid rules for the Congress to follow in drafting resolutions establishing investigating committees. That is a matter peculiarly within the realm of the legislature, and its decisions will be accepted by the courts up to the point where their own duty to enforce the constitutionally protected rights of individuals is affected.

. . . Plainly these committees are restricted to the missions delegated to them, i.e., to acquire certain data to be used by the House or the Senate in coping with a problem that falls within its legislative sphere. No witness can be compelled to make disclosures on matters outside that area. This is a jurisdictional concept of pertinency drawn from the nature of a congressional committee's source of authority. It is not wholly different from nor unrelated to the element of pertinency embodied in the criminal statute under which petitioner was prosecuted. When the definition of jurisdictional pertinency is as uncertain and wavering as in the case of the Un-American Activities Committee, it becomes extremely difficult for the Committee to limit its inquiries to statutory pertinency.

In fulfillment of their obligation under this statute, the courts must accord to the defendants every right which is guaranteed to defendants in all other criminal cases. Among these is the right to have available, through a sufficiently precise statute, information revealing the standard of criminality before the commission of the alleged offense. Applied to persons prosecuted under § 192, this raises a special problem in that the statute defines the crime as refusal to answer "any question pertinent to the question under inquiry." Part of the standard of criminality, therefore, is the pertinency of the questions propounded to the witness.

The problem attains proportion when viewed from the standpoint of the witness who appears before a congressional committee. He must decide at the time the questions are propounded whether or not to answer. . . .

It is obvious that a person compelled to make this choice is entitled to have knowledge of the subject to which the interrogation is deemed pertinent. That knowledge must be available with the same degree of explicitness and clarity that the Due Process Clause requires in the expression of any element of a criminal offense. The "vice of vagueness" must be avoided here as in all other crimes. There are several sources that can outline the "question under inquiry" in such a way that the rules against vagueness are satisfied. The authorizing resolution, the remarks of the chairman or members of the committee, or even the nature of the proceedings themselves might sometimes make the topic clear. This case demonstrates, however, that these sources often leave the matter in grave doubt.

The statement of the Committee Chairman in this case, in response to petitioner's protest, was woefully inadequate to convey sufficient information as to the pertinency of the questions to the subject under inquiry. Petitioner was thus not accorded a fair opportunity to determine whether he was within his rights in refusing to answer, and his conviction is necessarily invalid under the Due Process Clause of the Fifth Amendment.

. . . The conclusions which we have reached in this case will not prevent the Congress, through its committees, from obtaining any information it needs for the proper fulfillment of its role in our scheme of government. The legislature is free to determine the kinds of data that should be collected. It is only those investigations that are conducted by use of compulsory process that give rise to a need to protect the rights of individuals against illegal encroachment. That protection can be readily achieved through procedures which prevent the separation of power from responsibility and which provide the constitutional requisites of fairness for witnesses. A measure of added care on the part of the House and the Senate in authorizing the use of compulsory process and by their committees in exercising that power would suffice. That is a small price to pay if it serves to uphold the principles of limited, constitutional government without constricting the power of the Congress to inform itself.

The judgment of the Court of Appeals is reversed, and the case is remanded to the District Court with instructions to dismiss the indictment.

It is so ordered.

MR. JUSTICE BURTON and MR. JUSTICE WHITTAKER took no part in the consideration or decision of this case.

MR. JUSTICE FRANKFURTER, concurring. . . .

MR. JUSTICE CLARK, dissenting.

As I see it the chief fault in the majority opinion is its mischievous curbing of the informing function of the Congress. While I am not versed in its procedures, my experience in the executive branch of the Government leads me to believe that the requirements laid down in the opinion for the operation of the committee system of inquiry are both unnecessary and unworkable. . . .

It may be that at times the House Committee on Un-American Activities has, as the Court says, "conceived of its task in the grand view of its name." And, perhaps, as the Court indicates, the rules of conduct placed upon the Committee by the House admit of individual abuse and unfairness. But that is none of our affair. So long as the object of a legislative inquiry is legitimate and the questions propounded are pertinent thereto, it is not for the courts to interfere with the committee system of inquiry. To hold otherwise would be an infringement on the power given the Congress to inform itself, and thus a trespass upon the fundamental American principle of separation of powers. The majority has substituted the judiciary as the grand inquisitor and supervisor of congressional investigations. It has never been so. . . .

The Court condemns the long-established and long-recognized committee system of inquiry of the House because it raises serious questions concerning the protection it affords to constitutional rights. . . . In effect the Court honors Watkins' claim of a "right to silence" which brings all inquiries, as we know, to a "dead end." I do not see how any First Amendment rights were endangered here. There is nothing in the First Amendment that provides the guarantees Watkins claims. . . .

Barenblatt v. United States
360 U.S. 109, 79 S.Ct. 1081, 3 L.Ed. 2d 1115 (1959)

Lloyd Barenblatt, a former college teacher, was called as a witness before a subcommittee of the House Un-American Activities Committee investigating Communist infiltration in education. Disclaiming any reliance on the Fifth Amendment,
he refused to answer questions regarding past affiliation with the Communist party,
contending that the subcommittee has no power to inquire into political beliefs and
associations. The Supreme Court vacated his conviction for contempt of Congress,
remanding the case for further consideration in light of the *Watkins* decision. His
conviction was again upheld by the Court of Appeals and the Supreme Court
granted certiorari.

MR. JUSTICE HARLAN delivered the opinion of
the Court.

Once more the Court is required to resolve
the conflicting constitutional claims of congressional power and of an individual's right to
resist its exercise. The congressional power in
question concerns the internal process of Congress in moving within its legislative domain; it
involves the utilization of its committees to
secure "testimony needed to enable it effi-
ciently to exercise a legislative function belonging to it under the Constitution." . . .

Broad as it is, the power is not, however,
without limitations. Since Congress may only
investigate into those areas in which it may
potentially legislate or appropriate, it cannot inquire into matters which are within the exclusive
province of one of the other branches of the
Government. . . . And the Congress, in common with all branches of the Government, must
exercise its powers subject to the limitations
placed by the Constitution on governmental action, more particularly in the context of this
case the relevant limitations of the Bill of
Rights. . . .

In the present case congressional efforts to
learn the extent of a nationwide, indeed world-
wide, problem have brought one of its investigating committees into the field of education.
Of course, broadly viewed, inquiries cannot be
made into the teaching that is pursued in any of
our educational institutions. When academic
teaching-freedom and its corollary learning-

freedom, so essential to the well-being of the
Nation, are claimed, this Court will always be
on the alert against intrusion by Congress into
this constitutionally protected domain. But this
does not mean that the Congress is precluded
from interrogating a witness merely because he
is a teacher. An educational institution is not a
constitutional sanctuary from inquiry into matters that may otherwise be within the constitutional legislative domain merely for the reason
that inquiry is made of someone within its
walls. . . .

At the outset it should be noted that Rule XI
authorized this Subcommittee to compel testimony within the framework of the investigative
authority conferred on the Un-American Activities Committee. Petitioner contends that
Watkins v. *United States* . . . nevertheless held
the grant of this power in all circumstances ineffective because of the vagueness of Rule XI in
delineating the Committee jurisdiction to
which its exercise was to be appurtenant. . . .

The Watkins case cannot properly be read as
standing for such a proposition. A principal
contention in *Watkins* was that the refusals to
answer were justified because the requirement
. . . that the questions asked be "pertinent to
the question under inquiry" had not been
satisfied. . . . This Court reversed the conviction
solely on that ground, holding that Watkins
had not been adequately apprised of the subject
matter of the Subcommittee's investigation or
the pertinency thereto of the questions he re-

fused to answer. . . . In so deciding the Court drew upon Rule XI only as one of the facets in the total *mise en scène* in its search for the "question under inquiry" in that particular investigation. . . . In short, while *Watkins* was critical of Rule XI, it did not involve the broad and inflexible holding petitioner now attributes to it. . . .

In *Watkins* the petitioner had made specific objection to the Subcommittee's questions on the ground of pertinency; the questions under inquiry had not been disclosed in any illuminating manner; and the questions asked the petitioner were not only amorphous on their face, but in some instances clearly foreign to the alleged subject matter of the investigation— "communism in labor. . . ."

Here "pertinency" was made to appear "with undisputable clarity." What we deal with here is whether petitioner was sufficiently apprised of "the topic under inquiry" thus authorized "and the connective reasoning whereby the precise questions asked related to it." . . . In light of this prepared memorandum of constitutional objectives there can be no doubt that this petitioner was well aware of the Subcommittee's authority and purpose to question him as it did. . . . In addition the other sources of this information which we recognized in *Watkins* . . . leave no room for a "pertinency" objection on this record. The subject matter of the inquiry had been identified at the commencement of the investigation as Communist infiltration into the field of education. . . . Further, petitioner had stood mute in the face of the Chairman's statement as to why he had been called as a witness by the Subcommittee. And lastly unlike Watkins, . . . petitioner refused to answer questions as to his own Communist Party affiliations, whose pertinency of course was clear beyond doubt. . . .

Our function, at this point, is purely one of constitutional adjudication in the particular case and upon the particular record before us, not to pass judgment upon the general wisdom or efficacy of the activities of this Committee in a vexing and complicated field. . . .

The protections of the First Amendment, unlike a proper claim of the privilege against self-incrimination under the Fifth Amendment, do not afford a witness the right to resist inquiry in all circumstances. Where First Amendment rights are asserted to bar governmental interrogation, resolution of the issue always involves a balancing by the courts of the competing private and public interests at stake in the particular circumstances shown. These principles were recognized in the Watkins case, where, in speaking of the First Amendment in relation to congressional inquiries, we said: . . . "It is manifest that despite the adverse effects which follow upon compelled disclosure of private matters, not all such inquiries are barred. . . . The critical element is the existence of, and the weight to be ascribed to, the interest of the Congress in demanding disclosures from an unwilling witness." . . .

We think that investigatory power in this domain is not to be denied Congress solely because the field of education is involved. . . . Indeed we do not understand petitioner here to suggest that Congress in no circumstances may inquire into Communist activity in the field of education. Rather, his position is in effect that this particular investigation was aimed not at the revolutionary aspects but at the theoretical classroom discussion of communism.

In our view this position rests on a too constricted view of the nature of the investigatory process, and is not supported by a fair assessment of the record before us. An investigation of advocacy or of preparation for overthrow certainly embraces the right to identify a witness as a member of the Communist Party . . . and to inquire into various manifestations of the Party's tenets. The strict requirements of a prosecution under the Smith Act . . . are not the measure of the permissible scope of a congressional investigation into "overthrow," for of necessity the investigatory process must proceed step by step. Nor can it fairly be concluded that this investigation was directed at controlling what is being taught at our universities rather than at overthrow. The statement of the Subcommittee Chairman at the opening of the investigation evinces no such intention, and so far as this record reveals nothing thereafter transpired which would justify our holding that the thrust of the investigation later changed. . . .

Nor can we accept the further contention that this investigation should not be deemed to have been in furtherance of a legislative purpose because the true objective of the Committee and of the Congress was purely "exposure." So long as Congress acts in pursuance of its constitutional power, the Judiciary lacks authority to intervene on the basis of the motives which spurred the exercise of that power. . . .

We conclude that the balance between the individual and the governmental interests here at stake must be struck in favor of the latter, and that therefore the provisions of the First Amendment have not been offended. . . .

MR. JUSTICE BLACK, with whom the CHIEF JUSTICE and MR. JUSTICE DOUGLAS concur, dissenting. . . .

I do not agree that laws directly abridging First Amendment freedoms can be justified by a congressional or judicial balancing process. . . .

To apply the Court's balancing test under such circumstances is to read the First Amendment to say "Congress shall pass no law abridging freedom of speech, press, assembly and petition, unless Congress and the Supreme Court reach the joint conclusion that on balance the interest of the Government in stifling these freedoms is greater than the interest of the people in having them exercised." This is closely akin to the notion that neither the First Amendment nor any other provision of the Bill of Rights should be enforced unless the Court believes it is reasonable to do so. Not only does this violate the genius of our written Constitution, but it runs expressly counter to the injunction to Court and Congress made by Madison when he introduced the Bill of Rights. "If they [the first ten amendments] are incorporated into the Constitution, independent tribunals of justice will consider themselves in a peculiar manner the guardians of those rights: they will be an impenetrable bulwark against every assumption of power in the Legislative or Executive; they will be naturally led to resist every encroachment upon rights expressly stipulated

for in the Constitution by the declaration of rights." Unless we return to this view of our judicial function, unless we once again accept the notion that the Bill of Rights means what it says and that this Court must enforce that meaning, I am of the opinion that our great charter of liberty will be more honored in the breach than in the observance.

But even assuming what I cannot assume, that some balancing is proper in this case, I feel that the Court after stating the test ignores it completely. At most it balances the right of the Government to preserve itself, against Barenblatt's right to refrain from revealing Communist affiliations. Such a balance, however, mistakes the factors to be weighed. In the first place, it completely leaves out the real interest in Barenblatt's silence, the interest of the people as a whole in being able to join organizations, advocate causes and make political "mistakes" without later being subjected to governmental penalties for having dared to think for themselves. It is this right, the right to err politically, which keeps us strong as a Nation. For no number of laws against communism can have as much effect as the personal conviction which comes from having heard its arguments and rejected them, or from having once accepted its tenets and later recognized their worthlessness. Instead, the obloquy which results from investigations such as this not only stifles "mistakes" but prevents all but the most courageous from hazarding any views which might at some later time become disfavored. This result, whose importance cannot be overestimated, is doubly crucial when it affects the universities, on which we must largely rely for the experimentation and development of new ideas essential to our country's welfare. It is these interests of society, rather than Barenblatt's own right to silence, which I think the Court should put on the balance against the demands of the Government, if any balancing process is to be tolerated. Instead they are not mentioned, while on the other side, the demands of the Government are vastly overstated and called "self-preservation." . . .

No matter how often or how quickly we

repeat the claim that the Communist Party is not a political party, we cannot outlaw it, as a group, without endangering the liberty of all of us. The reason is not hard to find, for mixed among those aims of communism which are illegal are perfectly normal political and social goals. And muddled with its revolutionary tenets is a drive to achieve power through the ballot, if it can be done. These things necessarily make it a political party whatever other, illegal, aims it may have. . . .

The fact is that once we allow any group which has some political aims or ideas to be driven from the ballot and from the battle for men's minds because some of its members are bad and some of its tenets are illegal, no group is safe. . . . History should teach us . . . that in times of high emotional excitement minority parties and groups which advocate extremely unpopular social or governmental innovations will always be typed as criminal gangs and attempts will always be made to drive them out. It was knowledge of this fact, and of its great dangers, that caused the Founders of our land to enact the First Amendment as a guarantee that neither Congress nor the people would do anything to hinder or destroy the capacity of individuals and groups to seek converts and votes for any cause, however radical or unpalatable their principles might seem under the accepted notions of the time. Whatever the States were left free to do, the First Amendment sought to leave Congress devoid of any kind or quality of power to direct any type of national laws against the freedom of individuals to think what they please, advocate whatever policy they choose, and join with others to bring about the social, religious, political and governmental changes which seem best to them. Today's holding, in my judgment, marks another major step in the progressively increasing retreat from the safeguards of the First Amendment. . . .

The Court today fails to see what is here for all to see—that exposure and punishment is the aim of this Committee and the reason for its existence. To deny this is to ignore the Committee's own claims and the reports it has issued ever since it was established. I cannot believe that the nature of our judicial office requires us to be so blind, and must conclude that the Un-American Activities Committee's "identification" and "exposure" of Communists and suspected Communists . . . amount to an encroachment on the judiciary which bodes ill for the liberties of the people of this land.

Ultimately all the questions in this case really boil down to one—whether we as a people will try fearfully and futilely to preserve democracy by adopting totalitarian methods, or whether in accordance with our traditions and our Constitution we will have the confidence and courage to be free.

MR. JUSTICE BRENNAN, dissenting. . . .

Hutchinson v. *Proxmire*
443 U.S. 111, 99 S.Ct. 2675, 61 L.Ed. 2d 411 (1979)

Senator William Proxmire established the "Golden Fleece of the Month Award" to point out what he felt were the most egregious examples of wasteful spending by federal agencies. The senator named Ronald R. Hutchinson, a researcher, as one of the recipients of this award. Funded by the National Science Foundation, the National Aeronautics and Space Administration, and the Office of Naval Research, Hutchinson had studied the behavior patterns of certain animals, including the clenching of jaws when the animals were exposed to various stimuli. In a speech in the Senate, Proxmire referred to the research as, among other things, "monkey business,'' and claimed that the studies had ''made a monkey out of the American taxpayer.'' The essence of the speech reappeared in a press release, a newsletter, and a television interview. Hutchinson then sued Proxmire and an aide for damages. The district court and the court of appeals both held that Proxmire's actions were covered by a combination of the Speech or Debate Clause and the First Amendment. Reference to the latter was important because the lower courts agreed that Hutchinson was a ''public figure'' within the meaning of *New York Times Co.* v. *Sullivan* (376 U.S. 254; 1964). That decision broadened the protection of free speech and press and correspondingly narrowed the situations in which one could constitutionally sue for libel. The Supreme Court granted certiorari.

MR. CHIEF JUSTICE BURGER delivered the opinion of the Court. . . .

In support of the Court of Appeals holding that newsletters and press releases are protected by the Speech or Debate Clause, respondents rely upon both historical precedent and present-day congressional practices. They contend that impetus for the Speech or Debate Clause privilege in our Constitution came from the history of parliamentary efforts to protect the right of members to criticize the spending of the Crown and from the prosecution of a Speaker of the House of Commons for publication of a report outside of Parliament. Respondents also contend that in the modern day very little speech or debate occurs on the floor of either House; from this they argue that press releases and newsletters are necessary for Members of Congress to communicate with other Members. . . . Respondents also argue that an essential part of the duties of a Member of Congress is to inform constituents, as well as other Members, of the issues being considered.

The Speech or Debate Clause has been directly passed on by this Court relatively few times in 190 years. . . . Literal reading of the Clause would, of course, confine its protection narrowly to a ''Speech or Debate in either House.'' But the Court has given the Clause a practical rather than a strictly literal reading which would limit the protection to utterances made within the four walls of either Chamber. Thus, we have held that committee hearings are protected, even if held outside the Chambers; committee reports are also protected. . . .

The gloss going beyond a strictly literal reading of the Clause has not, however, departed from the objective of protecting only legislative activities. In Thomas Jefferson's view:

> [The privilege] is restrained to things done in the House in a Parliamentary course . . . For [the Member] is not to have privilege contra morem parliamentarium, to exceed the bounds and limits of his place and duty. . . .

One of the draftsmen of the Constitution, James Wilson, expressed a similar thought in lectures delivered between 1790 and 1792 while he was a Justice of this Court. He rejected Blackstone's statement . . . that Parliament's privileges were preserved by keeping them indefinite:

> Very different is the case with regard to the legislature of the United States. . . . The great maxims, upon which our law of parliament is founded, are defined and ascertained in our constitutions. The arcana of privilege, and the arcana of prerogative, are equally unknown to our system of jurisprudence. . . .

In this respect, Wilson was underscoring the very purpose of our Constitution—inter alia, to provide *written* definitions of the powers, privileges, and immunities granted rather than rely on evolving constitutional concepts identified from diverse sources as in English law. . . .

Nearly a century ago, . . . this Court held that the Clause extended ''to things generally done in a session of the House by one of its members *in relation to the business before it."* (Emphasis added.) More recently we expressed a similar definition of the scope of the Clause:

> Legislative acts are not all-encompassing. The heart of the Clause is speech or debate in either House. Insofar as the Clause is construed to reach other matters, *they must be an integral part of the deliberative and communicative processes* by which Members participate *in committee and House proceedings* with respect to the consideration and passage or rejection of proposed legislation or with respect to other matters which the Constitution places within the jurisdiction of either House. As the Court of Appeals put it, the courts have extended the privilege to matters beyond pure speech or debate in either House, but "only when necessary to prevent indirect impairment of such deliberations." (Gravel v. United States, 408 U.S., at 625: emphasis added) . . .

Whatever imprecision there may be in the term "legislative activities," it is clear that nothing in history or in the explicit language of the Clause suggests any intention to create an absolute privilege from liability or suit for defamatory statements made outside the Chamber. . . . A speech by Proxmire in the Senate would be wholly immune and would be available to other Members of Congress and the public in the Congressional Record. But neither the newsletters nor the press release was "essential to the deliberations of the Senate" and neither was part of the deliberative process.

Respondents, however, argue that newsletters and press releases are essential to the functioning of the Senate; without them, they assert, a Senator cannot have a significant impact on the other Senators. We may assume that a Member's published statements exert some influence on other votes in the Congress and therefore have a relationship to the legislative and deliberative process. But in *Brewster,* 408 U.S., at 512, we rejected the respondents' expansive reading of the Clause.

> It is well known, of course, that Members of the Congress engage in many activities other than the purely legislative activities protected by the Speech or Debate Clause. These include . . . preparing so-called 'news letters' to constituents, news releases, and speeches delivered outside the Congress. . . .

We are unable to discern any "conscious choice" [by the Framers of the Constitution] to grant immunity for defamatory statements scattered far and wide by mail, press, and the electronic media.

Respondents also argue that newsletters and press releases are privileged as part of the "informing function" of Congress. Advocates of a broad reading of the "informing function" sometimes tend to confuse two uses of the term "informing." In one sense, Congress informs itself collectively by way of hearings of its committees. It was in that sense that Woodrow Wilson used "informing" in a statement related to congressional efforts to learn of the activities of the Executive Branch and administrative agencies; he did not include wide-ranging inquiries by individual Members on subjects of their choice. Moreover, Wilson's statement itself clearly implies a distinction between the *informing* function and the *legislative* function:

> Unless Congress have and use every means of acquainting itself with the acts and the disposition of the administrative agents of the government, the country must be helpless to learn how it is being served; and unless Congress both scrutinize these things and sift them by every form of discussion, the country must remain in embarrassing, crippling ignorance of the very affairs which it is most important that it should understand and direct. The informing function of Congress should be preferred even to its legislative function. . . . [T]he only really self-governing people is that people which discusses and interrogates its administration. . . .

It is in this narrower Wilsonian sense that this Court has employed "informing" in previous cases holding that congressional efforts to inform itself through committee hearings are part of the legislative function.

The other sense of the term, and the one relied upon by respondents, perceives it to be the duty of Members to tell the public about their activities. Valuable and desirable as it may be in broad terms, the transmittal of such information by individual Members in order to inform the public and other Members is not a part of the legislative function or the deliberations that make up the legislative process. As a result, transmittal of such information by press releases and newsletters is not protected by the Speech or Debate Clause.

Doe v. *McMillan* . . . is not to the contrary. It dealt only with reports from congressional committees, and held that Members of Congress could not be held liable for voting to publish a report. Voting and preparing committee reports are the individual and collective expressions of opinion within the legislative process. As such, they are protected by the Speech or Debate Clause. Newsletters and press releases, by contrast, are primarily means of informing those outside the legislative forum; they represent the views and will of a single Member. It does not disparage either their value or their importance to hold that they are not entitled to the protection of the Speech or Debate Clause. . . . [In the rest of his opinion, Chief Justice Burger maintained that Hutchinson was not a "public figure" within the terms of *New York Times Co.* v. *Sullivan.* The Court reversed the Court of Appeals and remanded the case for a trial on the merits.]

MR. JUSTICE STEWART, concurring and dissenting. . . .

MR. JUSTICE BRENNAN, dissenting. . . .

The Prize Cases
2 Black (67 U.S.) 635, 17 L.Ed. 459 (1863)

The Prize Cases represent the challenge to Lincoln's proclamation in 1861 of a blockade of Confederate ports prior to any action by Congress. The owners of various captured vessels appealed from adverse judgments in district courts.

MR. JUSTICE GRIER delivered the opinion of the Court. There are certain propositions of law which must necessarily affect the ultimate decision of these cases, and many others, which it will be proper to discuss and decide before we notice the special facts peculiar to each.

They are, 1st. Had the President a right to institute a blockade of ports in possession of persons in armed rebellion against the government, on the principles of international law, as known and acknowledged among civilized States?

2d. Was the property of persons domiciled or residing within those States a proper subject of capture on the sea as "enemies' property"? . . .

That a blockade *de facto* actually existed, and was formally declared and notified by the President on the 27th and 30th of April, 1861, is an admitted fact in these cases.

That the President, as the Executive Chief of the Government and Commander-in-Chief of the Army and Navy, was the proper person to make such notification, has not been and cannot be disputed.

The right of prize and capture has its origin in the *jus belli,* and is governed and adjudged under the law of nations. To legitimate the capture of a neutral vessel or property on the high seas, a war must exist *de facto,* and the neutral must have a knowledge or notice of the intention of one of the parties belligerent to use this mode of coercion against a port, city, or territory, in possession of the other.

Let us enquire whether, at the time this blockade was instituted, a state of war existed which would justify a resort to these means of subduing the hostile force.

War has been well defined to be, ''That state in which a nation prosecutes its right by force.''

The parties belligerent in a public war are independent nations. But it is not necessary to constitute war, that both parties should be acknowledged as independent nations or sovereign States. A war may exist where one of the belligerents claims sovereign rights as against the other.

Insurrection against a government may or may not culminate in an organized rebellion, but a civil war always begins by insurrection against the lawful authority of the Government. A civil war is never solemnly declared; it becomes such by its accidents—the number, power, and organization of the persons who originate and carry it on. . . .

As a civil war is never publicly proclaimed, *eo nomine* against insurgents, its actual existence is a fact in our domestic history which the Court is bound to notice and to know.

The true test of its existence, as found in the writing of the sages of the common law, may be thus summarily stated: ''When the regular course of justice is interrupted by revolt, rebellion, or insurrection, so that the Courts of Justice cannot be kept open, *civil war exists* and hostilities may be prosecuted on the same footing as if those opposing the Government were foreign enemies invading the land.''

By the Constitution, Congress alone has the power to declare a national or foreign war. It cannot declare war against a State, or any number of States, by virtue of any clause in the Constitution. The Constitution confers on the President the whole Executive power. He is bound to take care that the laws be faithfully executed. He is Commander-in-Chief of the Army and Navy of the United States, and of the militia of the several States when called into the actual service of the United States. He has no power to initiate or declare a war either against a foreign nation or a domestic State. But by the Acts of Congress of February 28th, 1795, and 3rd of March, 1807, he is authorized to call out the militia and use the military and naval forces of the United States in case of invasion by foreign nations, and to suppress insurrection against the government of a State or of the United States.

If a war be made by invasion of a foreign nation, the President is not only authorized but bound to resist force by force. He does not initiate the war, but is bound to accept the challenge without waiting for any special legislative authority. And whether the hostile party be a foreign invader, or States organized in rebellion, it is none the less a war, although the declaration of it be ''unilateral.'' . . .

As soon as the news of the attack on Fort Sumter, and the organization of a government by the seceding States, assuming to act as belligerents, could become known in Europe, to wit, on the 13th of May, 1861, the Queen of England issued her proclamation of neutrality, ''recognizing hostilities as existing between the government of the United States of America and *certain States* styling themselves the Confederate States of America.'' This was immediately followed by similar declarations or silent acquiescence by other nations.

After such an official recognition by the sovereign, a citizen of a foreign State is estopped to deny the existence of a war with all its consequences as regards neutrals. They cannot ask a Court to affect a technical ignorance of the existence of a war, which all the world acknowledges to be the greatest civil war known in the history of the human race, and thus cripple the arm of the government and paralyze its power by subtle definitions and ingenious sophisms. . . .

Whether the President in fulfilling his duties, as Commander-in-Chief, is suppressing an insurrection, has met with such armed hostile resistance, and a civil war of such alarming proportions as will compel him to accord to them the character of belligerents, is a question to be decided *by him,* and this court must be governed by the decisions and acts of the political department of the government to which this power was intrusted. ''He must determine what degree of force the crisis demands.'' The proclamation of blockade is itself official and conclusive evidence to the court that a state of war existed which demanded and authorized a recourse to such a measure, under the circumstances peculiar to the case. . . .

If it were necessary to the technical existence of a war, that it should have a legislative sanction, we find it in almost every act passed at the extraordinary session of the legislature of 1861, which was wholly employed in enacting laws to enable the government to prosecute the war with vigor and efficiency. And finally, in 1861, we find Congress ''*ex majore cautela*'' and in anticipation of such astute objections, passing an act ''approving, legalizing, making valid all the acts, proclamations, and orders of the President, etc., as if they had been *issued and done under the previous express authority and* directions of the Congress of the United States.'' . . .

On this first question therefore we are of the opinion that the President had a right, *jure belli,* to institute a blockade of ports in possession of the States in rebellion, which neutrals are bound to regard.

II. We come now to the consideration of the second question. What is included in the term ''enemies' property''?

Whether property be liable to capture as ''enemies' property'' does not in any manner depend on the personal allegiance of the owner. ''It is the illegal traffic that stamps it as ''enemies' property.'' It is of no consequence whether it belongs to an ally or a citizen. . . .

MR. JUSTICE NELSON, dissenting. . . .

This great and pervading change in the existing condition of a country, and in the relations of all her citizens or subjects, external and internal, from a state of peace, is the immediate effect and result of a state of war: and hence the same code which has annexed to the existence of a war all these disturbing consequences has declared that the right of making war belongs exclusively to the supreme or sovereign power of the State.

This power in all civilized nations is regulated by the fundamental laws or municipal constitution of the country.

By our Constitution this power is lodged in Congress. Congress shall have power ''to declare war, grant letters of marque and reprisal, and make rules concerning captures on land and water.'' . . .

In the case of a rebellion or resistance of a portion of the people of a country against the established government, there is no doubt, if in its progress and enlargement the government, thus sought to be overthrown sees fit, it may by the competent power recognize or declare the existence of a state of civil war, which will draw after it all the consequences and rights of war between the contending parties as in the case of a public war. . . . It is not to be denied, therefore, that if a civil war existed between that portion of the people in organized insurrection to overthrow this Government at the time this vessel and cargo were seized, and if she was guilty of a violation of the blockade, she would be lawful prize of war. But before this insurrection against the established Government can be dealt with on the footing of a civil war, within the meaning of the law of nations and the Constitution of the United States, and which will draw after it belligerent right, it must be recognized or declared by the war-making power of the Government. No power short of this can change the legal status of the Government or the relations of its citizens from that of peace to a state of war, or bring into existence all those duties and obligations of neutral third parties growing out of a state of war. The war power of the Government must be exercised before this changed condition of the Government and people and of neutral third parties can be admitted. There is no difference in this respect between a civil or a public war. . . .

An idea seemed to be entertained that all that was necessary to constitute a war was organized hostility in the district or country in a state of rebellion—that conflicts on land and on sea—the taking of towns and capture of fleets—in fine, the magnitude and dimensions of the resistance against the Government—constituted war with all the belligerent rights belonging to civil war. . . .

Now, in one sense, no doubt this is war, and may be a war of the most extensive and threatening dimensions and effects, but it is a statement simply of its existence in a material sense, and has no relevancy or weight when the question is what constitutes war in a legal sense, in the sense of the law of nations, and of the Constitution of the United States? For it must be a war in this sense to attach to it all the consequences that belong to belligerent rights. Instead, therefore, of inquiring after armies and navies, and victories lost and won, or organized rebellion against the general Government, the inquiry should be into the law of nations and into the municipal fundamental laws of the Government. For we find there that to constitute a civil war in the sense in which we are speaking, before it can exist, in contemplation of law, it must be recognized or declared by the sovereign power of the State, and which sovereign power by our Constitution is lodged in the Congress of the United States—civil war, therefore, under our system of government, can exist only by an act of Congress, which requires the assent of two of the great departments of the Government, the Executive and Legislative. . . .

So the war carried on by the President against insurrectionary districts in the Southern States, as in the case of the King of Great Britain in the American Revolution, was a personal war against those in rebellion, and with encouragement and support of loyal citizens with a view to their co-operation and aid in suppressing the insurgents, with this difference, as the war-making power belonged to the King, he might have recognized or declared the war at the beginning to be a civil war which would draw after it all the rights of a belligerent, but in the case of the President no such power existed: the war therefore from necessity was a personal war, until Congress assembled and acted upon this state of things. . . .

Upon the whole, after the most careful consideration of this case which the pressure of other duties has admitted, I am compelled to the conclusion that no civil war existed between this Government and the States in insurrection till recognized by the Act of Congress 13th of July, 1861; that the President does not possess the power under the Constitution to declare war or recognize its existence within the meaning of the law of nations, which carries with it belligerent rights, and thus change the country and all its citizens from a state of peace to a state of war; that this power belongs exclusively to the Congress of the United States, and consequently, that the President had no power to set on foot a blockade under the law of nations, and that the capture of the vessel and cargo in this case, and in all cases before us in which the capture occurred before the 13th of July 1861, for breach of blockade, or as enemies' property, are illegal and void and that the decrees of condemnation should be reversed and the vessel and cargo restored.

MR. CHIEF JUSTICE TANEY, MR. JUSTICE CATRON and MR. JUSTICE CLIFFORD, concurred in the dissenting opinion of MR. JUSTICE NELSON.

Ex Parte Milligan
4 Wall (71 U.S.) 2, 18 L.Ed. 281 (1866)

In 1864, Lambdin P. Milligan, self-educated teacher and lawyer, a Southern sympathizer living in Indiana, was seized and tried on charges of disloyalty by a military commission in the military district of Indiana. Not in the military forces, a citizen of Indiana, in which neither war nor insurrection existed and in which the civil courts were functioning, Milligan objected to the jurisdiction of the military commission and sought a writ of habeas corpus in the circuit court. An Act of 1863 had authorized suspension of the writ, but Milligan still insisted that the commission had no jurisdiction of his case. Sharply divided, the circuit court judges decided that this important case should be heard by the highest court in the land. The following questions were therefore certified by the Supreme Court: 1. Ought a writ of habeas corpus be issued? 2. Should the petitioner be discharged from custody? 3. Had the military commission jurisdiction to try and sentence Milligan? Read by Justice Davis, a personal friend of Lincoln, in a crowded courtroom of lawyers and congressmen, the majority opinion held that Milligan's trial by military commission was illegal. He was therefore ordered released. Davis ruled that Congress had no authority to establish military commissions, even if it decided to do so. Concurring justices, objecting to such a sweeping denial of congressional power, dissented on this point.

MR. JUSTICE DAVIS delivered the opinion of the court. . . .

During the late wicked Rebellion, the temper of the times did not allow that calmness and deliberation in discussion so necessary to a correct conclusion of a purely judicial question. *Then,* considerations of safety were mingled with the exercise of power, and feelings and interests prevailed which are happily terminated. *Now* that the public safety is assured, this question, as well as all others, can be discussed and decided without passion or the admixture of any element not required to form the legal judgment. We approach the investigation of this case, fully sensible of the magnitude of the inquiry and of the necessity of full and cautious deliberation.

The controlling question in the case is this: Upon the facts stated in Milligan's petition, and the exhibits filed, had the military commission mentioned in it jurisdiction, legally, to try and sentence him? Milligan, not a resident of one of the rebellious States, or a prisoner of war, but a citizen of Indiana for twenty years past, and never in the military or naval service, is while at his home, arrested by the military power of the United States, imprisoned, and, on certain criminal charges preferred against him, tried, convicted, and sentenced to be hanged by a military commission, organized under the direction of the military commander of the military district of Indiana. Had this tribunal the legal power and authority to try and punish this man? . . .

The Constitution of the United States is a law for rulers and people, equally in war and in peace, and covers with the shield of its protection all classes of men, at all times, and under all circumstances. No doctrine involving more pernicious consequences was ever invented by the wit of man than that any of its provisions can be suspended during any of the great exigencies of government. Such a doctrine leads directly to anarchy or despotism, but the theory of necessity on which it is based is false; for the government, within the Constitution, has all the powers granted to it which are necessary to preserve its existence; as has been happily proved by the result of the great effort to throw off its just authority.

Have any of the rights guaranteed by the Constitution been violated in the case of Milligan? and if so, what are they?

Every trial involves the exercise of judicial power; and from what source did the military commission that tried him derive their authority? Certainly no part of the judicial power of the country was conferred on them; because the Constitution expressly vests it "in one supreme court and such inferior courts as the Congress may from time to time ordain and establish," and it is not pretended that the commission was a court ordained and established by Congress. They cannot justify on the mandate of the President, because he is controlled by law, and has his appropriate sphere of duty, which is to execute, not to make, the laws; and there is "no unwritten criminal code to which resort can be had as a source of jurisdiction."

But it is said that the jurisdiction is complete under the "laws and usages of war."

It can serve no useful purpose to inquire what those laws and usages are, whence they originated, where found, and on whom they operate; they can never be applied to citizens in States which have upheld the authority of the government, and where the courts are open and their process unobstructed. This court has judicial knowledge that in Indiana the Federal authority was always unopposed, and its courts always open to hear criminal accusations and redress grievances; and no usage of war could sanction a military trial there for any offense whatever of a citizen in civil life, in nowise connected with the military service. Congress could grant no such power; and to the honor of our national legislature be it said, it has never been provoked by the state of the country even to attempt its exercise. One of the plainest constitutional provisions was, therefore, infringed when Milligan was tried by a court not ordained and established by Congress, and not composed of judges appointed during good behavior.

Why was he not delivered to the Circuit Court of Indiana to be proceeded against according to law? No reason of necessity could be urged against it; because Congress had declared penalties against the offenses charged, provided for their punishment, and directed that court to hear and determine them. And soon after this military tribunal was ended, the Circuit Court met, peacefully transacted its business, and adjourned. It needed no bayonets to protect it, and required no military aid to execute its judgments. It was held in a State, eminently distinguished for patriotism, by judges commissioned during the Rebellion, who were provided with juries, upright, intelligent, and selected by a marshal appointed by the President. The government had no right to conclude that Milligan, if guilty, would not receive in that court merited punishment. . . .

Another guarantee of freedom was broken when Milligan was denied a trial by jury. The great minds of the country have differed on the correct interpretation to be given to the various provisions of the Federal Constitution; and judicial decision has been often invoked to settle their true meaning; but until recently no one ever doubted that the right of trial by jury was fortified in the organic law against the power of attack. It is now assailed; but if ideas can be expressed in words, and language has any meaning, this right—one of the most valuable in a free country—is preserved to every one accused of crime who is not attached to the army, or navy, or militia in actual service. . . .

The discipline necessary to the efficiency of the army and navy required other and swifter modes of trial than are furnished by the common-law courts; and, in pursuance of the power conferred by the Constitution, Congress has declared the kinds of trial, and the manner in which they shall be conducted, for offenses committed while the party is in the military or naval service. Every one connected with these branches of the public service is amenable to the jurisdiction which Congress has created for their government, and, while thus serving, surrenders his right to be tried by the civil courts. All other persons, citizens of States where the courts are open, if charged with crime, are guaranteed the inestimable privilege of trial by jury. . . .

It is claimed that martial law covers with its broad mantle the proceedings of this military commission. The proposition is this: that in a time of war the commander of an armed force (if, in his opinion, the exigencies of the country demand it, and of which he is the judge) has the power, within the lines of his military district, to suspend all civil rights and their remedies, and subject citizens as well as soldiers to the rule of his will; and in the exercise of his lawful authority cannot be restrained, except by his superior officer or the President of the United States.

If this position is sound to the extent claimed, then when war exists, foreign or domestic, and the country is subdivided into military departments for mere convenience, the commander of one of them can, if he chooses, within his limits, on the plea of necessity, with the approval of the Executive, substitute military force for, and to the exclusion of, the laws, and punish all persons, as he thinks right and proper, without fixed or certain rules.

The statement of this proposition shows its importance; for, if true, republican government is a failure, and there is an end of liberty regulated by law. Martial law, established on such a basis, destroys every guarantee of the Constitution, and effectually renders the "military independent of, and superior to, the civil power,"—the attempt to do which by the King of Great Britain was deemed by our fathers such an offense, that they assigned it to the world as one of the causes which impelled them to declare their independence. Civil liberty and this kind of martial law cannot endure together; the antagonism is irreconcilable; and, in the conflict, one or the other must perish. . . .

The two remaining questions in this case must be answered in the affirmative. The suspension of the privilege of the writ of *habeas corpus* does not suspend the writ itself. The writ issues as a matter of course; and on the return made to it the court decides whether the party applying is denied the right of proceeding any further with it.

If the military trial of Milligan was contrary to law, then he was entitled, on the facts stated in his petition, to be discharged from custody by

the terms of the act of Congress of March 3, 1863. . . .

THE CHIEF JUSTICE [CHASE] delivered the following opinion. . . .

We agree in the proposition that no department of the government of the United States—neither President, nor Congress, nor the Courts—possesses any power not given by the Constitution. . . .

We think, . . . that the power of Congress, in the government of the land and naval forces and of the militia, is not at all affected by the fifth or any other amendment. It is not necessary to attempt any precise definition of the boundaries of this power. But may it not be said that government includes protection and defence as well as the regulation of the internal administration? And is it impossible to imagine cases in which citizens conspiring or attempting the destruction or great injury of the national forces may be subjected by Congress to military trial and punishment in the just exercise of this undoubted constitutional power? Congress is but the agent of the nation, and does not the security of individuals against the abuse of this, as of every other power, depend on the intelligence and virtue of the people, on their zeal for public and private liberty, upon official responsibility secured by law, and upon the frequency of elections, rather than upon doubtful constructions of legislative powers? . . .

In Indiana, for example, at the time of the arrest of Milligan and his co-conspirators, it is established by the papers in the record, that the state was a military district, was the theatre of military operations, had been actually invaded, and was constantly threatened with invasion. It appears, also, that a powerful secret association, composed of citizens and others, existed within the state, under military organization, conspiring against the draft, and plotting insurrection, the liberation of the prisoners of war at various depots, the seizure of the state and national arsenals, armed cooperation with the enemy, and war against the national government.

We cannot doubt that, in such a time of public danger, Congress had power, under the Constitution, to provide for the organization of a military commission, and for trial by that commission of persons engaged in this conspiracy. The fact that the Federal courts were open was regarded by Congress as a sufficient reason for not exercising the power; but that fact could not deprive Congress of the right to exercise it. Those courts might be open and undisturbed in the execution of their functions, and yet wholly incompetent to avert threatened danger, or to punish, with adequate promptitude and certainty, the guilty conspirators.

In Indiana, the judges and officers of the courts were loyal to the government. But it might have been otherwise. In times of rebellion and civil war it may often happen, indeed, that judges and marshals will be in active sympathy with the rebels, and courts their most efficient allies.

We have confined ourselves to the question of power. It was for Congress to determine the question of expediency. And Congress did determine it. That body did not see fit to authorize trials by military commission in Indiana, but by the strongest implication prohibited them. With that prohibition we are satisfied, and should have remained silent if the answers to the questions certified had been put on that ground, without denial of the existence of a power which we believe to be constitutional and important to the public safety—a denial which, as we have already suggested, seems to draw in question the power of Congress to pro-

tect from prosecution the members of military commissions who acted in obedience to their superior officers, and whose action, whether warranted by law or not, was approved by that upright and patriotic President under whose administration the Republic was rescued from threatened destruction. . . .

We think that the power of Congress, in such times and in such localities, to authorize trials for crimes against the security and safety of the national forces, may be derived from its constitutional authority to raise and support armies and to declare war, if not from its constitutional authority to provide for governing the national forces.

We have no apprehension that this power, under our American system of government, in which all official authority is derived from the people, and exercised under direct responsibility to the people, is more likely to be abused than the power to regulate commerce, or the power to borrow money. And we are unwilling to give our assent by silence to expressions of opinion which seem to us calculated, though not intended, to cripple the constitutional powers of the government, and to augment the public dangers in times of invasion and rebellion.

MR. JUSTICE WAYNE, MR. JUSTICE SWAYNE, and MR. JUSTICE MILLER concur with me in these views.

Missouri v. Holland
252 U.S. 416, 40 S.Ct. 382, 64 L.Ed. 641 (1920)

By a treaty of 1916 the United States and Great Britain undertook the regulation and protection of birds migrating between Canada and various parts of the United States. An act of 1918 gave effect to the treaty by establishing closed seasons and other rules. The state of Missouri brought a bill in equity to prevent a game warden of the United States from enforcing the act, and appealed from the District Court's dismissal of the bill.

MR. JUSTICE HOLMES delivered the opinion of the court. . . .

. . . The question raised is the general one whether the treaty and statute are void as an interference with the rights reserved to the States.

To answer this question it is not enough to refer to the Tenth Amendment, reserving the powers not delegated to the United States, because by Article II, § 2, the power to make treaties is delegated expressly, and by Article VI treaties made under the authority of the United States, along with the Constitution and laws of the United States made in pursuance thereof, are declared the supreme law of the land. If the treaty is valid there can be no dispute about the validity of the statute under Article I, § 8, as a necessary and proper means to execute the powers of the Government. The language of the Constitution as to the supremacy of treaties being general, the question before us is narrowed to an inquiry into the ground upon which the present supposed exception is placed.

It is said that a treaty cannot be valid if it infringes the Constitution, that there are limits, therefore, to the treaty-making power, and that one such limit is that what an act of Congress could not do unaided, in derogation of the powers reserved to the States a treaty cannot do. An earlier act of Congress that attempted by itself and not in pursuance of a treaty to regulate the killing of migratory birds within the States had been held bad in the District Court. *United States* v. *Shauver,* 214 Fed. Rep. 154. *United States* v. *McCullagh,* 221 Fed. Rep. 288. Those decisions were supported by arguments that migratory birds were owned by the States in their sovereign capacity for the benefit of their people and that under cases like *Geer* v. *Connecticut,* 161 U.S. 519, this control was one that Congress had no power to displace. The same argument is supposed to apply now with equal force.

Whether the two cases cited were decided rightly or not they cannot be accepted as a test of the treaty power. Acts of Congress are the supreme law of the land only when made in pursuance of the Constitution, while treaties are declared to be so when made under the authority of the United States. It is open to question whether the authority of the United States means more than the formal acts prescribed to make the convention. We do not mean to imply that there are no qualifications to the treaty-making power; but they must be ascertained in a different way. It is obvious that there may be matters of the sharpest exigency for the national well-being that an act of Congress could not deal with but that a treaty followed by such an act could, and it is not lightly to be assumed that, in matters requiring national action, "a power which must belong to and somewhere reside in every civilized government" is not to be found. *Andrews* v. *Andrews,* 188 U.S. 14, 33. What was said in that case with regard to the powers of the States applies with equal force to the powers of the nation in cases where the States individually are incompetent to act. We are not yet discussing the particular case before us but only are considering the validity of the test proposed. With regard to that we may add that when we are dealing with words that also are a constituent act, like the Constitution of the

United States, we must realize that they have called into life a being the development of which could not have been foreseen completely by the most gifted of its begetters. It was enough for them to realize or to hope that they had created an organism; it has taken a century and has cost their successors much sweat and blood to prove that they created a nation. The case before us must be considered in the light of our whole experience and not merely in that of what was said a hundred years ago. The treaty in question does not contravene any prohibitory words to be found in the Constitution. The only question is whether it is forbidden by some invisible radiation from the general terms of the Tenth Amendment. We must consider what this country has become in deciding what that Amendment has reserved.

The State as we have intimated founds its claim of exclusive authority upon an assertion of title to migratory birds, an assertion that is embodied in statute. No doubt it is true that as between a State and its inhabitants the State may regulate the killing and sale of such birds, but it does not follow that its authority is exclusive of paramount powers. To put the claim of the State upon title is to lean upon a slender reed. Wild birds are not in the possession of anyone; and possession is the beginning of ownership. The whole foundation of the State's rights is the presence within their jurisdiction of birds that yesterday had not arrived, tomorrow may be in another State and in a week a thousand miles away. If we are to be accurate we cannot put the case of the State upon higher ground than that the treaty deals with creatures that for the moment are within the State borders, that it must be carried out by officers of the United States within the same territory, and that but for the treaty the State would be free to regulate this subject itself. . . .

Here a national interest of very nearly the first magnitude is involved. It can be protected only by national action in concert with that of another power. The subject matter is only transitorily within the State and has no permanent habitat therein. But for the treaty and the statute there soon might be no birds for any powers to deal with. We see nothing in the Constitution that compels the Government to sit by while a food supply is cut off and the protectors of our forests and our crops are destroyed. It is not sufficient to rely upon the States. The reliance is vain, and were it otherwise, the question is whether the United States is forbidden to act. We are of opinion that the treaty and statute must be upheld.

Decree affirmed.

MR. JUSTICE VAN DEVANTER and MR. JUSTICE PITNEY dissent.

United States v. Curtiss-Wright
299 U.S. 304, 57 S.Ct. 216, 81 L.Ed. 255 (1936)

This landmark case involving the powers of the President in foreign affairs grew out of the efforts of Congress to limit a war between Bolivia and Paraguay, by granting to the President the power to prohibit the sale of arms and munitions to the warring nations. The defendant corporation, charged with conspiring to sell fifteen machine guns to Bolivia, demurred to the indictment on the ground that the delegation of power to the President was invalid. The district court sustained the demurrer, and the United States appealed.

MR. JUSTICE SUTHERLAND delivered the opinion of the Court. . . .

First. It is contended that by the Joint Resolution the going into effect and continued operation of the resolution was conditioned (a) upon the President's judgment as to its beneficial effect upon the re-establishment of peace between the countries engaged in armed conflict in the Chaco; (b) upon the making of a proclamation, which was left to his unfettered discretion, thus constituting an attempted substitution of the President's will for that of Congress; (c) upon the making of a proclamation putting an end to the operation of the resolution, which again was left to the President's unfettered discretion; and (d) further, that the extent of its operation in particular cases was subject to limitation and exception by the President, controlled by no standard. In each of these particulars, appellees urge that Congress abdicated its essential functions and delegated them to the Executive.

Whether, if the Joint Resolution had related solely to internal affairs, it would be open to the challenge that it constituted an unlawful delegation of legislative power to the Executive, we find it unnecessary to determine. The whole aim of the resolution is to affect a situation entirely external to the United States, and falling within the category of foreign affairs. The determination which we are called to make, therefore, is whether the Joint Resolution, as applied to that situation, is vulnerable to attack under the rule that forbids a delegation of the lawmaking power. In other words, assuming (but not deciding) that the challenged delegation, if it were confined to internal affairs, would be invalid, may it nevertheless be sustained on the ground that its exclusive aim is to afford a remedy for a hurtful condition within foreign territory?

It will contribute to the elucidation of the question if we first consider the differences between the powers of the federal government in respect of foreign or external affairs and those in respect of domestic or internal affairs. That there are differences between them, and that these differences are fundamental, may not be doubted.

The two classes of powers are different, both in respect of their origin and their nature. The broad statement that the federal government can exercise no powers except those specifically enumerated in the Constitution, and such implied powers as are necessary and proper to carry into effect the enumerated powers, is categorically true only in respect of our internal affairs. In that field, the primary purpose of the Constitution was to carve from the general mass of legislative powers *then possessed by the states* such portions as it was thought desirable to vest in the federal government leaving those not included in the enumeration still in the states. . . . That this doctrine applies only to powers which the states had is self-evident. And since the states severally never possessed international powers, such powers could not have been carved from the mass of state powers but obviously were transmitted to the United States from some other source. During the Colonial period, those powers were possessed exclusively by and were entirely under the control of the Crown. By the Declaration of Independence, "the Representatives of the United States of America" declared the United (not the several) Colonies to be free and independent states, and as such to have "full Power to levy War, conclude Peace, contract Alliances, establish Commerce and to do all other Acts and Things which Independent States may of right do."

As a result of the separation from Great Britain by the colonies, acting as a unit, the powers of external sovereignty passed from the Crown not to the colonies severally, but to the colonies in their collective and corporate capacity as the United States of America. Even before the Declaration, the colonies were a unit in foreign affairs, acting through a common agency—namely, the Continental Congress, composed of delegates from the thirteen colonies. That agency exercised the powers of war and peace, raised an army, created a navy, and finally adopted the Declaration of Independence. Rulers come and go; governments end and forms of government change; but sovereignty survives. A political society cannot endure without a supreme will somewhere. Sovereignty is never held in suspense. When, therefore, the external sovereignty of Great Britain in respect of the colonies ceased, it immediately passed to the Union. . . . That fact was given practical application almost at once. The treaty of peace, made on September 3, 1783, was concluded between his Britannic Majesty and the "United States of America." . . .

The Union existed before the Constitution, which was ordained and established among other things to form "a more perfect Union." Prior to that event, it is clear that the Union declared by the Articles of Confederation to be "perpetual," was the sole possessor of external sovereignty, and in the Union it remained without change save in so far as the Constitution in express terms qualified its exercise. The Framers' Convention was called and exerted its powers upon the irrefutable postulate that though the states were several their people in respect of foreign affairs were one. . . .

It results that the investment of the federal government with the powers of external sovereignty did not depend upon the affirmative grants of the Constitution. The powers to declare and wage war, to conclude peace, to make treaties, to maintain diplomatic relations with other sovereignties, if they had never been mentioned in the Constitution, would have vested in the federal government as necessary concomitants of nationality. Neither the Constitution nor the laws passed in pursuance of it have any force in foreign territory unless in respect of our own citizens; and operations of the nation in such territory must be governed by treaties, international understandings and compacts, and the principles of international law. As a member of the family of nations, the right and power of the United States in that field are equal to the right and power of the other members of the international family. Otherwise, the United States is not completely sovereign. . . .

Not only, as we have shown, is the federal power over external affairs in origin and essential character different from that over internal affairs, but participation in the exercise of the power is significantly limited. In this vast external realm, with its important, complicated, delicate and manifold problems, the President alone has the power to speak or listen as a representative of the nation. He *makes* treaties with the advice and consent of the Senate; but he alone negotiates. Into the field of negotiation the Senate cannot intrude; and Congress itself is powerless to invade it. . . .

It is important to bear in mind that we are here dealing not alone with an authority vested in the President by an exertion of legislative power, but with such an authority plus the very delicate, plenary and exclusive power of the President as the sole organ of the federal government in the field of international relations—a power which does not require as a basis for its exercise an act of Congress, but which, of course, like every other governmental power, must be exercised in subordination to the applicable provisions of the Constitution. It is quite apparent that if, in the maintenance of our international relations, embarrassment—perhaps serious embarrassment—is to be avoided and success for our aims achieved, congressional legislation which is to be made effective through negotiation and inquiry within the international field must often accord to the President a degree of discretion and freedom from statutory restriction which would not be admissible were domestic affairs alone involved. Moreover, he, not Congress, has the better opportunity of knowing the conditions which prevail in foreign countries, and especially is this true in time of war. He has his confidential sources of information. He has his agents in the form of diplomatic, consular and other officials. Secrecy in respect of information gathered by them may be highly necessary, and the premature disclosure of it productive of harmful results. Indeed, so clearly is this true that the first President refused to accede to a request to lay before the House of Representatives the instructions, correspondence and documents relating to the negotiation of the Jay Treaty—a refusal the wisdom of which was recognized by the House itself and has never been doubted.

The marked difference between foreign affairs and domestic affairs in this respect is recognized by both houses of Congress in the very form of their requisitions for information from the executive departments. In the case of every department except the Department of State, the resolution *directs* the official to furnish the information. In the case of the State Department, dealing with foreign affairs, the President is *requested* to furnish the information "if not incompatible with the public interest." A statement that to furnish the information is not compatible with the public interest rarely, if ever, is questioned.

When the President is to be authorized by legislation to act in respect to a matter intended to affect a situation in foreign territory, the legislator, properly bears in mind the important consideration that the form of the President's action—or, indeed, whether he shall act at all—may well depend, among other things, upon the nature of the confidential information which he has or may thereafter receive, or upon

the effect which his action may have upon our foreign relations. This consideration, in connection with what we have already said on the subject, discloses the unwisdom of requiring Congress in this field of governmental power to lay down narrowly defined standards by which the President is to be governed. As this court said in *Mackenzie* v. *Hare,* 239 U.S. 299, 311, "As a government, the United States is invested with all the attributes of sovereignty. As it has the character of nationality it has the powers of nationality, especially those which concern its relations and intercourse with other countries. *We should hesitate long before limiting or embarrassing such powers.*" (Italics supplied.) . . .

The result of holding that the joint resolution here under attack is void and unenforceable as constituting an unlawful delegation of legislative power would be to stamp this multitude of comparable acts and resolutions as likewise invalid. And while this court may not, and should not, hesitate to declare acts of Congress, however many times repeated, to be unconstitutional if beyond all rational doubt it finds them to be so, an impressive array of legislation such as we have just set forth, enacted by nearly every Congress from the beginning of our national existence to the present day, must be given unusual weight in the process of reaching a correct determination of the problem. A legislative practice such as we have here, evidenced not by only occasional instances, but marked by the movement of a steady stream for a century and a half of time, goes a long way in the direction of proving the presence of unassailable ground for the constitutionality of the practice, to be found in the origin and history of the power involved, or in its nature, or in both combined. . . .

Both upon principle and in accordance with precedent, we conclude there is sufficient warrant for the broad discretion vested in the President to determine whether the enforcement of the statute will have a beneficial effect upon the reestablishment of peace in the affected countries; whether he shall make proclamation to bring the resolution into operation; whether and when the resolution shall cease to operate and to make proclamation accordingly; and to prescribe limitations and exceptions to which the enforcement of the resolution shall be subject. . . .

Reversed.

MR. JUSTICE MCREYNOLDS does not agree.

He is of opinion that the court below reached the right conclusion and its judgment ought to be affirmed.

MR. JUSTICE STONE took no part in the consideration or decision of this case.

Korematsu v. *United States*
323 U.S. 214, 65 S.Ct. 193, 89 L.Ed. 194 (1944)

Shortly after America entered World War II, the President issued an executive order authorizing creation of military areas from which persons suspected of sabotage and espionage might be excluded. In pursuance of this order, military commanders were authorized to prescribe regulations controlling the right of persons to enter, leave, or remain in the areas. For violation of these regulations, Congress provided penalties.

Acting under these executive and congressional authorizations, the Western Defense Command divided the Pacific Coast into two military areas, imposing restrictions on persons living in them, including a curfew that applied only to aliens and persons of Japanese ancestry. The curfew was upheld (*Hirabayashi* v. *United States,* 320 U.S. 81: 1943) as a legitimate wartime measure.

Later on, the commanding general removed all Japanese to War Relocation Centers. Korematsu, an American citizen who refused to leave his home, was convicted in a federal district court for violation of the restriction order. When a circuit court of appeals affirmed his conviction, Korematsu, on writ of certiorari, brought the case to the Supreme Court.

MR. JUSTICE BLACK delivered the opinion of the Court.

. . . In the light of the principles we announced in the Hirabayashi Case, we are unable to conclude that it was beyond the war power of Congress and the Executive to exclude those of Japanese ancestry from the West Coast war area at the time they did. True, exclusion from the area in which one's home is located is a far greater deprivation than constant confinement to the home from 8 p.m. to 6 a.m. Nothing short of apprehension by the proper military authorities of the gravest imminent danger to the public safety can constitutionally justify either. But exclusion from a threatened area, no less than curfew, has a definite and close relationship to the prevention of espionage and sabotage. The military authorities, charged with the primary responsibility of defending our shores, concluded that curfew provided inadequate protection and ordered exclusion. They did so, as pointed out in our Hirabayashi opinion, in accordance with congressional authority to the military to say who should, and who should not, remain in the threatened areas.

In this case the petitioner challenges the assumptions upon which we rested our conclusions in the Hirabayashi Case. He also urges that by May 1942, when Order No. 34 was promulgated, all danger of Japanese invasion of the

West Coast had disappeared. After careful consideration of these contentions we are compelled to reject them.

Here, as in the Hirabayashi Case . . . "we cannot reject as unfounded the judgment of the military authorities and of Congress that there were disloyal members of that population, whose number and strength could not be precisely and quickly ascertained. We cannot say that the war-making branches of the Government did not have ground for believing that in a critical hour such persons could not readily be isolated and separately dealt with, and constituted a menace to the national defense and safety, which demanded that prompt and adequate measures be taken to guard against it."

Like curfew, exclusion of those of Japanese origin was deemed necessary because of the presence of an unascertaind number of disloyal members of the group, most of whom we have no doubt were loyal to this country. It was because we could not reject the finding of the military authorities that it was impossible to bring about an immediate segregation of the disloyal from the loyal that we sustained the validity of the curfew order as applying to the whole group. In the instant case, temporary exclusion of the entire group was rested by the military on the same ground. The judgment that exclusion of the whole group was for the same reason a military imperative answers the contention that the exclusion was in the nature of group punishment based on antagonism to those of Japanese origin. That there were members of the group who retained loyalties to Japan has been confirmed by investigations made subsequent to the exclusion. Approximately five thousand American citizens of Japanese ancestry refused to swear unqualified allegiance to the United States and to renounce allegiance to the Japanese Emperor, and several thousand evacuees requested repatriation to Japan.

We uphold the exclusion order as of the time it was made and when the petitioner violated it. . . . In doing so, we are not unmindful of the hardships imposed by it upon a large group of American citizens. . . . But hardships are part of war, and war is an aggregation of hardships. All citizens alike, both in and out of uniform, feel the impact of war in greater or lesser measure. Citizenship has its responsibilities as well as its privileges, and in time of war the burden is always heavier. Compulsory exclusion of large groups of citizens from their homes, except under circumstances of direst emergency and peril, is inconsistent with our basic governmental institutions. But when under conditions of modern warfare our shores are threatened by hostile forces, the power to protect must be commensurate with the threatened danger. . . .

We are . . . being asked to pass at this time upon the whole subsequent detention program in both assembly and relocation centers, although the only issues framed at the trial related to petitioner's remaining in the prohibited area in violation of the exclusion order. Had petitioner here left the prohibited area and gone to an assembly center we cannot say either as a matter of fact or law, that his presence in that center would have resulted in his detention in a relocation center. Some who did report to the assembly center were not sent to relocation centers, but were released upon condition that they remain outside the prohibited zone until the military orders were modified or lifted. This illustrates that they pose different problems and may be governed by different principles. The lawfulness of one does not necessarily determine the lawfulness of the others. This is made clear when we analyze the requirements of the separate provisions of the separate orders. These separate requirements were that those of Japanese ancestry (1) depart from the area; (2) report to and temporarily remain in an assembly center; (3) go under military control to a relocation center there to remain for an indeterminate period until released conditionally or unconditionally by the military authorities. Each of these requirements, it will be noted, imposed distinct duties in connection with the separate steps in a complete evacuation program. Had Congress directly incorporated into one Act the language of these separate orders, and provided sanctions for their violations, disobedience of any one would have constituted a separate of-fense. . . . There is no reason why violations of these orders, insofar as they were promulgated pursuant to congressional enactment, should not be treated as separate offenses. . . .

It is said that we are dealing here with the case of imprisonment of a citizen in a concentration camp solely because of his ancestry, without evidence or inquiry concerning his loyalty and good disposition towards the United States. Our task would be simple, our duty clear, were this a case involving the imprisonment of a loyal citizen in a concentration camp because of racial prejudice. Regardless of the true nature of the assembly and relocation centers—and we deem it unjustifiable to call them concentration camps with all the ugly connotations that term implies—we are dealing specifically with nothing but an exclusion order. To cast this case into outlines of racial prejudice, without reference to the real military dangers which were presented, merely confuses the issue. Kore-matsu was not excluded from the Military Area because of hostility to him or his race. He *was* ex-cluded because we are at war with the Japanese Empire, because the properly constituted military authorities feared an invasion of our West Coast and felt constrained to take proper security measures, because they decided that the military urgency of the situation demanded that all citizens of Japanese ancestry be segregated from the West Coast temporarily, and finally, because Congress, reposing its confidence in this time of war in our military leaders—as in-evitably it must—determined that they should have the power to do just this. . . . We can-not—by availing ourselves of the calm perspec-tive of hindsight—now say that at that time these actions were unjustified.

Affirmed.

MR. JUSTICE FRANKFURTER concurred in a separate opinion.

MR. JUSTICE JACKSON, dissenting:

The limitation under which courts always will labor in examining the necessity for a military order are illustrated by this case. How does the Court know that these orders have a reasonable basis in necessity? No evidence

whatever on that subject has been taken by this or any other court. There is sharp controversy as to the credibility of the DeWitt report. So the Court, having no real evidence before it, has no choice but to accept General DeWitt's own unsworn, self-serving statement, untested by any cross-examination, that what he did was reasonable. And thus it will always be when courts try to look into the reasonableness of a military order.

In the very nature of things military decisions are not susceptible of intelligent judicial ap-praisal. They do not pretend to rest on evidence, but are made on information that often would not be admissible and on assumptions that could not be proved. Information in support of an order could not be disclosed to courts without danger that it would reach the enemy. Neither can courts act on communications made in con-fidence. Hence courts can never have any real alternative to accepting the mere declaration of the authority that issued the order that it was reasonably necessary from a military viewpoint.

Much is said of the danger to liberty from the Army program for deporting and detaining these citizens of Japanese extraction. But a judicial construction of the due process clause that will sustain this order is a far more subtle blow to liberty than the promulgation of the order itself. A military order, however un-constitutional, is not apt to last longer than the military emergency. Even during that period a succeeding commander may revoke it all. But once a judicial opinion rationalizes such an order to show that it conforms to the Constitu-tion, or rather rationalizes the Constitution to show that the Constitution sanctions such an order, the Court for all time has validated the principle of racial discrimination in criminal procedure and of transplanting American citizens. The principle then lies about like a loaded weapon ready for the hand of any authority that can bring forward a plausible claim of an urgent need. Every repetition im-beds that principle more deeply in our law and thinking and expands it to new purposes. All who observe the work of the courts are familiar with what Judge Cardozo described as ''the tendency of a principle to expand itself to the limit of its logic." A military commander may overstep the bounds of constitutionality, and it is an incident. But if we review and approve, that passing incident becomes the doctrine of the Constitution. There it has a generative power of its own, and all that it creates will be in its own image. Nothing better illustrates this danger than does the Court's opinion in this case.

It argues that we are bound to uphold the conviction of Korematsu because we upheld one in *Hirabayashi* v. *United States,* 320 U.S. 81, . . . when we sustained these orders in so far as they applied a curfew requirement to a citizen of Japanese ancestry. I think we would learn something from that experience.

In that case we were urged to consider only the curfew feature, that being all that technically was involved, because it was the only count necessary to sustain Hirabayashi's conviction and sentence. We yielded, and the Chief Justice guarded the opinion as carefully as language will do. He said: "Our investigation here does not go beyond the inquiry whether, in the light of all the relevant circumstances preceding and attending their promulgation, the challenged orders and statute *afforded a reasonable basis for the action taken in imposing the curfew.*" . . . "We decide only the issue as we have defined it—we decide only that the *curfew order* as applied, and at the time it was applied, was within the boundaries of the war power." . . . And again: "It is unnecessary to consider whether or to what extent *such findings would support orders differing from the curfew order.*" . . . [Italics supplied.] However, in spite of our limiting words we did validate a discrimination on the basis of ancestry for mild and temporary deprivation of liberty. Now the principle of racial discrimination is pushed from support of mild measures to very harsh ones, and from temporary deprivations to indeterminate ones. And the precedent which it is said requires us to do so is *Hirabayashi.* The Court is now saying that in *Hirabayashi* we did decide the very things we there said we were not

deciding. Because we said that these citizens could be made to stay in their homes during the hours of dark, it is said we must require them to leave home entirely; and if that, we are told they may also be taken into custody for deportation; and if that, it is argued they may also be held for some undetermined time in detention camps. How far the principle of this case would be extended before plausible reasons would play out, I do not know.

I should hold that a civil court cannot be made to enforce an order which violates constitutional limitations even if it is a reasonable exercise of military authority. The courts can exercise only the judicial power, can apply only law, and must abide by the Constitution, or they cease to be civil courts and become instruments of military policy.

Of course the existence of a military power resting on force, so vagrant, so centralized, so necessarily heedless of the individual, is an inherent threat to liberty. But I would not lead people to rely on this Court for a review that seems to me wholly delusive. The military reasonableness of these orders can only be determined by military superiors. If the people ever let command of the war power fall into irresponsible and unscrupulous hands, the courts wield no power equal to its restraint. The chief restraint upon those who command the physical forces of the country, in the future as in the past, must be their responsibility to the political judgments of their contemporaries and to the moral judgments of history.

My duties as a justice as I see them do not require me to make a military judgment as to whether General DeWitt's evacuation and detention program was a reasonable military necessity. I do not suggest that the courts should have attempted to interfere with the Army in carrying out its task. But I do not think they may be asked to execute a military expedient that has no place in law under the Constitution. I would reverse the judgment and discharge the prisoner.

[JUSTICES MURPHY and ROBERTS dissented and wrote separate opinions.]

Youngstown Co. v. Sawyer
343 U.S. 579, 72 S.Ct. 863, 96 L.Ed. 1153 (1952)

A labor dispute in the steel industry, which began in 1951, resulted ultimately in 1952 in a presidential order authorizing the Secretary of Commerce to seize and operate the steel mills. The presidential order was not based on any statutory authority, but rather was premised on the national emergency created by the threatened strike in an industry vital to defense production. Additional details are contained in the opinion. The steel companies then obtained an injunction from a federal district court restraining Secretary of Commerce Sawyer. The Supreme Court granted certiorari to review a court of appeals decision staying the injunction. The Supreme Court acted with unusual speed: it granted certiorari on May 3, heard the argument on May 12, and handed down the decision on June 2, 1952. It should be noted also that each of the six members of the majority delivered an opinion and that Mr. Justice Clark concurred only in the result.

MR. JUSTICE BLACK delivered the opinion of the Court.

We are asked to decide whether the President was acting within his constitutional power when he issued an order directing the Secretary of Commerce to take possession of and operate most of the Nation's steel mills. The mill owners argue that the President's order amounts to law making, a legislative function which the Constitution has expressly confided to the Congress and not to the President. The Government's position is that the order was made on findings of the President that his action was necessary to avert a national catastrophe which would inevitably result from a stoppage of steel production, and that in meeting this grave emergency the President was acting within the aggregate of his constitutional powers as the Nation's Chief Executive and the Commander in Chief of the Armed Forces of the United States. . . .

The President's power, if any, to issue the order must stem either from an act of Congress or from the Constitution itself. There is no statute that expressly authorizes the President to take possession of property as he did here. Nor is there any act of Congress to which our attention has been directed from which such a power can fairly be implied. Indeed, we do not understand the Government to rely on statutory authorization for this seizure. . . .

Moreover, the use of the seizure technique to solve labor disputes in order to prevent work stoppages was not only unauthorized by any congressional enactment; prior to this controversy, Congress had refused to adopt that method of settling labor disputes. When the Taft-Hartley Act was under consideration in 1947, Congress rejected an amendment which would have authorized such governmental seizures in case of emergency. . . .

It is clear that if the President had authority to issue the order he did, it must be found in some provision of the Constitution. And it is not claimed that express constitutional language grants this power to the President. The contention is that presidential power should be implied from the aggregate of his powers under the Constitution. Particular reliance is placed on provisions in Article II which say that "the executive Power shall be vested in a President . . ."; that "he shall take Care that the Laws be faithfully executed"; and that he "shall be Commander in Chief of the Army and Navy of the United States."

The order cannot properly be sustained as an exercise of the President's military power as Commander in Chief of the Armed Forces. The Government attempts to do so by citing a number of cases upholding broad powers in military commanders engaged in day-to-day

125

fighting in a theater of war. Such cases need not concern us here. Even though "theater of war" be an expanding concept, we cannot with faithfulness to our constitutional system hold that the Commander in Chief of the Armed Forces has the ultimate power as such to take possession of private property in order to keep labor disputes from stopping production. This is a job for the Nation's lawmakers, not for its military authorities.

Nor can the seizure order be sustained because of the several constitutional provisions that grant executive power to the President. In the framework of our Constitution, the President's power to see that the laws are faithfully executed refutes the idea that he is to be a lawmaker. The Constitution limits his functions in the law-making process to the recommending of laws he thinks wise and the vetoing of laws he thinks bad. And the Constitution is neither silent nor equivocal about who shall make laws which the President is to execute. The first section of the first article says that "All legislative Powers herein granted shall be vested in a Congress of the United States. . . . " After granting many powers to the Congress, Article I goes on to provide that Congress may "make all Laws which shall be necessary and proper for carrying into Execution the foregoing Powers and all other Powers vested by this Constitution in the Government of the United States, or in any Department or Officer thereof." . . .

It is said that other Presidents without congressional authority have taken possession of private business enterprises in order to settle labor disputes. But even if this be true, Congress has not thereby lost its exclusive constitutional authority to make laws necessary and proper to carry out the powers vested by the Constitution "in the Government of the United States, or any Department or Officer thereof."

The Founders of this Nation entrusted the lawmaking power to the Congress alone in both good and bad times. It would do no good to recall the historical events, the fears of power and the hopes for freedom that lay behind their choice. Such a review would but confirm our holding that this seizure order cannot stand.

The judgment of the District Court is

Affirmed.

MR. JUSTICE FRANKFURTER, concurring. . . .

MR. JUSTICE BURTON, concurring in both the opinion and judgment of the Court. . . .

MR. JUSTICE CLARK, concurring in the judgment of the Court. . . .

MR. JUSTICE JACKSON, concurring in the judgment and opinion of the Court. . . .

A judge, like an executive adviser, may be surprised at the poverty of really useful and unambiguous authority applicable to concrete problems of executive power as they actually present themselves. Just what our forefathers did envision, or would have envisioned had they foreseen modern conditions, must be divined from materials almost as enigmatic as the dreams Joseph was called upon to interpret for Pharaoh. A century and a half of partisan debate and scholarly speculation yields no net result but only supplies more or less apt quotations from respected sources on each side of any question. They largely cancel each other. And court decisions are indecisive because of the judicial practice of dealing with the largest questions in the most narrow way.

The actual art of governing under our Constitution does not and cannot conform to judicial definitions of the power of any of its branches based on isolated clauses or even single Articles torn from context. While the Constitution diffuses power the better to secure liberty, it also contemplates that practice will integrate the dispersed powers into a workable government. It enjoins upon its branches separateness but interdependence, autonomy but reciprocity. Presidential powers are not fixed but fluctuate, depending upon their disjunction or conjunction with those of Congress. We may well begin by a somewhat oversimplified grouping of practical situations in which a President may doubt, or others may challenge, his powers. . . .

1. When the President acts pursuant to an express or implied authorization of Congress his authority is at its maximum, for it includes all that he possesses in his own right plus all that Congress can delegate. In these circumstances, and in these only, may he be said (for what it

may be worth) to personify the federal sovereignty. If his act is held unconstitutional under these circumstances, it usually means that the Federal Government as an undivided whole lacks power. A seizure executed by the President pursuant to an Act of Congress would be supported by the strongest of presumptions and the widest latitude of judicial interpretation, and the burden of persuasion would rest heavily upon any who might attack it.

2. When the President acts in absence of either a congressional grant or denial of authority, he can only rely upon his own independent powers, but there is a zone of twilight in which he and Congress may have concurrent authority, or in which its distribution is uncertain. Therefore, congressional inertia, indifference or quiescence may sometimes, at least as a practical matter, enable, if not invite, measures on independent presidential responsibility. In this area, any actual test of power is likely to depend on the imperatives of events and contemporary imponderables rather than on abstract theories of law.

3. When the President takes measures incompatible with the expressed or implied will of Congress, his power is at its lowest ebb, for then he can rely only upon his own constitutional powers minus any constitutional powers of Congress over the matter. Courts can sustain exclusive presidential control in such a case only by disabling the Congress from acting upon the subject. Presidential claim to a power at once so conclusive and preclusive must be scrutinized with caution, for what is at stake is the equilibrium established by our constitutional system.

Into which of these classifications does this executive seizure of the steel industry fit? It is eliminated from the first by admission, for it is conceded that no congressional authorization exists for this seizure. That takes away also the support of the many precedents and declarations which were made in relation, and must be confined, to this category.

Can it then be defended under flexible tests available to the second category? It seems clearly eliminated from that class because Congress has not left seizure of private property an open field but has covered it by three statutory policies inconsistent with this seizure. In cases where the purpose is to supply needs of the Government itself, two courses are provided: one, seizure of a plant which fails to comply with obligatory orders placed by the Government, another, condemnation of facilities, including temporary use under the power of eminent domain. The third is applicable where it is the general economy of the country that is to be protected rather than exclusive governmental interests. None of these were invoked. In choosing a different and inconsistent way of his own, the President cannot claim that it is necessitated or invited by failure of Congress to legislate upon the occasions, grounds and methods for seizure of industrial properties. . . .

The Solicitor General seeks the power of seizure in three clauses of the Executive Article, the first reading, ''The executive Power shall be vested in a President of the United States of America.'' Lest I be thought to exaggerate, I quote the interpretation which his brief puts upon it: ''In our view, this clause constitutes a grant of all the executive powers of which the Government is capable.'' If that be true, it is difficult to see why the forefathers bothered to add several specific items, including some trifling ones.

The example of such unlimited executive power that must have most impressed the forefathers was the prerogative exercised by George III, and the description of its evils in the Declaration of Independence leads me to doubt that they were creating their new Executive in his image. Continental European examples were no more appealing. And if we seek instruction from our own times, we can match it only from the executive powers in those governments we disparagingly describe as totalitarian. I cannot accept the view that this clause is a grant in bulk of all conceivable executive power but regard it as an allocation to the presidential office of the generic powers thereafter stated.

The clause on which the Government next relies is that ''The President shall be Commander in Chief of the Army and Navy of the

United States. . . . '' These cryptic words have given rise to some of the most persistent controversies in our constitutional history. Of course, they imply something more than an empty title. But just what authority goes with the name has plagued presidential advisers who would not waive or narrow it by nonassertion yet cannot say where it begins or ends. It undoubtedly puts the Nation's armed forces under presidential command. Hence, this loose appellation is sometimes advanced as support for any presidential action, internal or external, involving use of force, the idea being that it vests power to do anything, anywhere, that can be done with an army or navy.

That seems to be the logic of an argument tendered at our bar—that the President having, on his own responsibility, sent American troops abroad derives from that act ''affirmative power'' to seize the means of producing a supply of steel for them. To quote, ''Perhaps the most forceful illustration of the scope of presidential power in this connection is the fact that American troops in Korea, whose safety and effectiveness are so directly involved here, were sent to the field by an exercise of the President's constitutional powers.'' Thus, it is said he has invested himself with ''war powers.''

I cannot foresee all that it might entail if the Court should indorse this argument. Nothing in our Constitution is plainer than that declaration of a war is entrusted only to Congress. Of course, a state of war may in fact exist without a formal declaration. But no doctrine that the Court could promulgate would seem to me more sinister and alarming than that a President whose conduct of foreign affairs is so largely uncontrolled, and often even is unknown, can vastly enlarge his mastery over the internal affairs of the country by his own commitment of the Nation's armed forces to some foreign venture. I do not, however, find it necessary or appropriate to consider the legal status of the Korean enterprise to discountenance argument based on it. . . .

There are indications that the Constitution did not contemplate that the title Commander-in-Chief *of the Army and Navy* will constitute him also Commander-in-Chief of the country, its industries and its inhabitants. He has no monopoly of ''war powers,'' whatever they are. While Congress cannot deprive the President of the command of the army and navy, only Congress can provide him an army or navy to command. It is also empowered to make rules for the ''Government and Regulation of land and naval Forces,'' by which it may to some unknown extent impinge upon even command functions.

That military powers of the Commander-in-Chief were not to supersede representative government of internal affairs seems obvious from the Constitution and from elementary American History. Time out of mind, and even now in many parts of the world, a military commander can seize private housing to shelter his troops. Not so, however, in the United States, for the Third Amendment says, ''No Soldier shall, in time of peace be quartered in any house, without the consent of the Owner, nor in time of war, but in a manner to be prescribed by law.'' Thus, even in war time his seizure of needed military housing must be authorized by Congress. It also was expressly left to Congress to ''provide for calling forth the Militia to execute the Laws of the Union, suppress Insurrections and repel Invasions. . . .'' Such a limitation on the command power, written at a time when the militia rather than a standing army was contemplated as the military weapon of the Republic, underscores the Constitution's policy that Congress, not the Executive, should control utilization of the war power as an instrument of domestic policy. Congress, fulfilling that function, has authorized the President to use the army to enforce certain civil rights. On the other hand, Congress has forbidden him to use the army for the purpose of executing general laws except when *expressly* authorized by the Constitution or by Act of Congress.

While broad claims under this rubric often have been made, advice to the President in specific matters usually has carried overtones that powers, even under this head, are measured by the command functions usual to the topmost officer of the army and navy. Even then, heed has been taken of any efforts of Congress to negative his authority.

We should not use this occasion to circumscribe, much less to contract, the lawful role of the President as Commander-in-Chief. I should indulge the widest latitude of interpretation to sustain his exclusive function to command the instruments of national force, at least when turned against the outside world for the security of our society. But, when it is turned inward, not because of rebellion but because of a lawful economic struggle between industry and labor, it should have no such indulgence. His command power is not such an absolute as might be implied from that office in a militaristic system but is subject to limitations consistent with a constitutional Republic whose law and policy-making branch is a representative Congress. The purpose of lodging dual titles in one man was to insure that the civilian would control the military, not to enable the military to subordinate the presidential office. No penance would ever expiate the sin against free government of holding that a President can escape control of executive powers by law through assuming his military role. What the power of command may include I do not try to envision, but I think it is not a military prerogative, without support of law, to seize persons or property because they are important or even essential for the military and naval establishment.

The third clause in which the Solicitor General finds seizure powers is that ''he shall take Care that the Laws be faithfully executed. . . .'' That authority must be matched against words of the Fifth Amendment that ''No person shall be . . . deprived of life, liberty or property, without due process of law. . . .''

One gives a governmental authority that reaches so far as there is law, the other gives a private right that authority shall go no farther. These signify about all there is of the principle that ours is a government of laws, not of men, and that we submit ourselves to rulers only if under rules.

The Solicitor General lastly grounds support of the seizure upon nebulous, inherent powers never expressly granted but said to have accrued to the office from the customs and claims of preceding administrations. The plea is for a resulting power to deal with a crisis or an emergency according to the necessities of the case, the unarticulated assumption being that necessity knows no law. . . .

Contemporary foreign experience may be inconclusive as to the wisdom of lodging emergency powers somewhere in a modern government. But it suggests that emergency powers are consistent with free government only when their control is lodged elsewhere than in the Executive who exercises them. That is the safeguard that would be nullified by our adoption of the ''inherent powers'' formula. . . .

In the practical working of our Government we already have evolved a technique within the framework of the Constitution by which normal executive powers may be considerably expanded to meet an emergency. Congress may and has granted extraordinary authorities which lie dormant in normal times but may be called into play by the Executive in war or upon proclamation of a national emergency. In 1939, upon congressional request, the Attorney General listed ninety-nine such separate statutory grants by Congress of emergency or wartime executive powers. They were invoked from time to time as need appeared. Under this procedure we retain Government by law—special, temporary law, perhaps, but law nonetheless. The public may know the extent and limitations of the powers that can be asserted, and persons affected may be informed from the statute of their rights and duties.

In view of the ease, expedition and safety with which Congress can grant and has granted large emergency powers, certainly ample to embrace this crisis, I am quite unimpressed with the argument that we should affirm possession of them without statute. Such power either has no beginning or it has no end. If it exists, it need submit to no legal restraint. I am not alarmed that it would plunge us straightway into dictatorship, but it is at least a step in that wrong direction. . . .

Executive power has the advantage of concentration in a single head in whose choice the whole Nation has a part, making him the focus of public hopes and expectations. In drama, magnitude and finality his decisions so far overshadow any others that almost alone he fills the public eye and ear. No other personality in public life can begin to compete with him in access to the public mind through modern methods of communications. By his prestige as head of state and his influence upon public opinion he exerts a leverage upon those who are supposed to check and balance his power which often cancels their effectiveness. . . .

But I have no illusion that any decision by this Court can keep power in the hands of Congress if it is not wise and timely in meeting its problems. A crisis that challenges the President equally, or perhaps primarily, challenges Congress. If not good law, there was worldly wisdom in the maxim attributed to Napoleon that ''The tools belong to the man who can use them.'' We may say that power to legislate for emergencies belongs in the hands of Congress, but only Congress itself can prevent power from slipping through its fingers.

The essence of our free Government is ''leave to live by no man's leave, underneath the law''—to be governed by those impersonal forces which we call law. Our Government is fashioned to fulfill this concept so far as humanly possible. The Executive, except for recommendation and veto, has no legislative power. The executive action we have here originates in the individual will of the President and represents an exercise of authority without law. No one, perhaps not even the President, knows the limits of the power he may seek to exert in this instance and the parties affected cannot learn the limit of their rights. We do not know today what powers over labor or property would be claimed to flow from Government possession if we should legalize it, what rights to compensation would be claimed or recognized, or on what contingency it would end. With all its defects, delays and inconveniences, men

have discovered no technique for long preserving free government except that the Executive be under the law, and that the law be made by parliamentary deliberations.

Such institutions may be destined to pass away. But it is the duty of the Court to be last, not first, to give them up.

MR. JUSTICE DOUGLAS, concurring. . . .

MR. CHIEF JUSTICE VINSON, with whom MR. JUSTICE REED and MR. JUSTICE MINTON join, dissenting. . . .

Those who suggest that this is a case involving extraordinary powers should be mindful that these are extraordinary times. A world not yet recovered from the devastation of World War II has been forced to face the threat of another and more terrifying global conflict. . . .

The steel mills were seized for a public use. The power of eminent domain, invoked in this case, is an essential attribute of sovereignty and has long been recognized as a power of the Federal Government. . . .

Admitting that the Government could seize the mills, plaintiffs claim that the implied power of eminent domain can be exercised only under an Act of Congress; under no circumstances, they say, can that power be exercised by the President unless he can point to an express provision in enabling legislation. This was the view adopted by the District Judge when he granted the preliminary injunction. Without an answer, without hearing evidence, he determined the issue on the basis of his ''fixed conclusion . . . that defendant's acts are illegal'' because the President's only course in the face of an emergency is to present the matter to Congress and await the final passage of legislation which will enable the Government to cope with threatened disaster.

Under this view, the President is left powerless at the very moment when the need for action may be most pressing and when no one, other than he, is immediately capable of action. Under this view, he is left powerless because a power not expressly given to Congress is nevertheless found to rest exclusively with Congress. . . .

In passing upon the grave constitutional

question presented in this case, we must never forget, as Chief Justice Marshall admonished, that the Constitution is "intended to endure for ages to come, and, consequently, to be adapted to the various *crises* of human affairs," and that "[i]ts means are adequate to its ends." Cases do arise presenting questions which could not have been foreseen by the Framers. In such cases, the Constitution has been treated as a living document adaptable to new situations. But we are not called upon today to expand the Constitution to meet a new situation. For, in this case, we need only look to history and time-honored principles of constitutional law—principles that have been applied consistently by all branches of the Government throughout our history. It is those who assert the invalidity of the Executive Order who seek to amend the Constitution in this case. . . .

A review of executive action demonstrates that our Presidents have on many occasions exhibited the leadership contemplated by the Framers when they made the President Commander in Chief, and imposed upon him the trust to "take care that the Laws be faithfully executed." With or without explicit statutory authorization, Presidents have at such times dealt with national emergencies by acting promptly and resolutely to enforce legislative programs, at least to save those programs until Congress could act. Congress and the courts have responded to such executive initiative with consistent approval. . . .

The absence of a specific statute authorizing seizure of the steel mills as a mode of executing the laws—both the military procurement program and the anti-inflation program—has not until today been thought to prevent the president from executing the laws.

United States v. United States District Court *
407 U.S. 297, 92 S.Ct. 2125, 32 L.Ed. 2d 752 (1972)

During pretrial proceedings in a prosecution in the United States District Court for the Eastern District of Michigan for conspiracy to destroy government property, the court ordered the government to make full disclosure to one of the defendants of his conversations overheard by electronic surveillance instituted without a search warrant. The United States Court of Appeals for the Sixth Circuit denied the government's petition for a writ of mandamus to compel the district judge to vacate the disclosure order.

On certiorari, the United States Supreme Court affirmed. In an opinion by Justice Powell expressing the views of six members of the court, it was held that the customary Fourth Amendment requirement of judicial approval before initiation of a search or surveillance applies in domestic security cases.

JUSTICE DOUGLAS, while joining in the court's opinion, filed a separate concurring opinion. JUSTICE WHITE concurred on the ground that the surveillance was statutorily prohibited. CHIEF JUSTICE BURGER concurred in the result. JUSTICE REHNQUIST did not participate.

MR. JUSTICE POWELL delivered the opinion of the Court.

The issue before us is an important one for

* This case should also be read in connection with Chapter 9.

[margin notes, handwritten]: Presi. authority to use elect. surveillance in internal sec. matters w/o prior judicial approval / warrant; his right to protection, v. citizen's rt to security against unreasonable Govt intrusion

the people of our country and their Government. It involves the delicate question of the President's power, acting through the Attorney General, to authorize electronic surveillance in internal security matters without prior judicial approval. Successive Presidents for more than one-quarter of a century have authorized such surveillance in varying degrees, without guidance from the Congress or a definitive decision of this Court. This case brings the issue here for the first time. Its resolution is a matter of national concern, requiring sensitivity both to the Government's right to protect itself from unlawful subversion and attack and to the citizen's right to be secure in his privacy against unreasonable Government intrusion. . . .

Title III of the Omnibus Crime Control and Safe Streets Act . . . authorizes the use of electronic surveillance for classes of crimes carefully specified. . . . The Act represents a comprehensive attempt by Congress to promote more effective control of crime while protecting the privacy of individual thought and expression. . . .

Together with the elaborate surveillance requirements in Title III, there is the following proviso, 18 USC § 2511 (3):

> Nothing contained in this chapter or in section 605 of the Communications Act of 1934 (48 Stat 1143; 47 USC 605) shall limit the constitutional power of the President to take such measures as he deems necessary to protect the Nation against actual or potential attack or other hostile acts of a foreign power, to obtain foreign intelligence information deemed essential to the security of the United States, or to protect national security information against foreign intelligence activities. *Nor shall anything contained in this chapter be deemed to limit the constitutional power of the President to take such measures as he deems necessary to protect the United States against the overthrow of the Government by force or other unlawful means, or against any other clear and present danger to the structure or existence of the Government.* The contents of any wire or oral communication intercepted by authority of the President in the exercise of the foregoing powers may be received in evidence in any

trial hearing or other proceeding only where such interception was reasonable, and shall not be otherwise used or disclosed except as is necessary to implement that power. (Emphasis supplied.)

The Government relies on § 2511 (3). It argues that "in excepting national security surveillances from the Act's warrant requirement Congress recognized the President's authority to conduct such surveillances without prior judicial approval." . . . The section thus is viewed as a recognition or affirmance of a constitutional authority in the President to conduct warrantless domestic security surveillance such as that involved in this case.

We think the language of § 2511 (3), as well as the legislative history of the statute, refutes this interpretation. The relevant language is that:

> Nothing contained in this chapter. . . . shall limit the constitutional power of the President to take such measures as he deems necessary to protect . . .

against the dangers specified. At most, this is an implicit recognition that the President does have certain powers in the specified areas. Few would doubt this, as the section refers—among other things—to protection "against actual or potential attack or other hostile acts of a foreign power." But so far as the use of the President's electronic surveillance power is concerned, the language is essentially neutral.

Section 2511 (3) certainly confers no power, as the language is wholly inappropriate for such a purpose. It merely provides that the Act shall not be interpreted to limit or disturb such power as the President may have under the Constitution. In short, Congress simply left presidential powers where it found them. . . .

. . . [N]othing in § 2511 (3) was intended to *expand* or to *contract* or to *define* whatever presidential surveillance powers existed in matters affecting the national security. If we could accept the Government's characterization of § 2511 (3) as a congressionally prescribed exception to the general requirement of a warrant, it

§2511 is merely a congressional disclaimer

would be necessary to consider the question of whether the surveillance in this case came within the exception and, if so, whether the statutory exception was itself constitutionally valid. But viewing § 2511 (3) as a congressional disclaimer and expression of neutrality, we hold that the statute is not the measure of the executive authority asserted in this case. Rather, we must look to the constitutional powers of the President.

It is important at the outset to emphasize the limited nature of the question before the Court. This case raises no constitutional challenge to electronic surveillance as specifically authorized by Title III of the Omnibus Crime Control and Safe Streets Act of 1968. Nor is there any question or doubt as to the necessity of obtaining a warrant in the surveillance of crimes unrelated to the national security interest. . . . Further, the instant case requires no judgment on the scope of the President's surveillance power with respect to the activities of foreign powers, within or without this country. The Attorney General's affidavit in this case states that the surveillances were "deemed necessary to protect the nation from attempts of *domestic organizations* to attack and subvert the existing structure of Government" (emphasis supplied). There is no evidence of any involvement, directly or indirectly, of a foreign power.

Our present inquiry, though important, is therefore a narrow one. . . .

"Whether safeguards other than prior authorization by a magistrate would satisfy the Fourth Amendment in a situation involving the national security. . . ." The determination of this question requires the essential Fourth Amendment inquiry into the "reasonableness" of the search and seizure in question, and the way in which that "reasonableness" derives content and meaning through reference to the warrant clause. . . .

We begin the inquiry by noting that the President of the United States has the fundamental duty, under Art. II, § 1, of the Constitution, to "preserve, protect, and defend the Constitution of the United States." Implicit in that duty is the power to protect our Govern-

ment against those who would subvert or overthrow it by unlawful means. In the discharge of this duty, the President—through the Attorney General—may find it necessary to employ electronic surveillance to obtain intelligence information on the plans of those who plot unlawful acts against the Government. . . .

Though the Government and respondents debate their seriousness and magnitude, threats and acts of sabotage against the Government exist in sufficient number to justify investigative powers with respect to them. The covertness and complexity of potential unlawful conduct against the Government and the necessary dependency of many conspirators upon the telephone make electronic surveillance an effective investigatory instrument in certain circumstances. The marked acceleration in technological developments and sophistication in their use have resulted in new techniques for the planning, commission and concealment of criminal activities. It would be contrary to the public interest for Government to deny to itself the prudent and lawful employment of those very techniques which are employed against the Government and its law-abiding citizens. . . .

But a recognition of these elementary truths does not make the employment by Government of electronic surveillance a welcome development—even when employed with restraint and under judicial supervision. There is, understandably, a deep-seated uneasiness and apprehension that this capability will be used to intrude upon cherished privacy of law-abiding citizens.

We look to the Bill of Rights to safeguard this privacy. Though physical entry of the home is the chief evil against which the working of the Fourth Amendment is directed, its broader spirit now shields private speech from unreasonable surveillance. . . .

History abundantly documents the tendency of Government—however benevolent and benign its motives—to view with suspicion those who most fervently dispute its policies. Fourth Amendment protections become the more necessary when the targets of official surveillance may be those suspected of unorthodoxy in

court should be able to use electronic surveillance against domestic threats their political beliefs. The danger to political dissent is acute where the Government attempts to act under so vague a concept as the power to protect "domestic security." Given the difficulty of defining the domestic security interest, the danger of abuse in acting to protect that interest becomes apparent. . . . The price of lawful public dissent must not be a dread of subjection to an unchecked surveillance power. Nor must the fear of unauthorized official eavesdropping deter vigorous citizen dissent and discussion of Government action in private conversation. For private dissent, no less than open public discourse, is essential to our free society.

As the Fourth Amendment is not absolute in its terms, our task is to examine and balance the basic values at stake in this case: the duty of Government to protect the domestic security, and the potential danger posed by unreasonable surveillance to individual privacy and free expression. If the legitimate need of Government to safeguard domestic security requires the use of electronic surveillance, the question is whether the needs of citizens for privacy and free expression may not be better protected by requiring a warrant before such surveillance is undertaken. We must also ask whether a warrant requirement would unduly frustrate the efforts of Government to protect itself from acts of subversion and overthrow directed against it. . . .

. . . Fourth Amendment freedoms cannot properly be guaranteed if domestic security surveillances may be conducted solely within the discretion of the executive branch. The Fourth Amendment does not contemplate the executive officers of Government as neutral and disinterested magistrates. Their duty and responsibility is to enforce the laws, to investigate and to prosecute. . . . But those charged with this investigative, and prosecutorial duty should not be the sole judges of when to utilize constitutionally sensitive means in pursuing their tasks. The historical judgment, which the Fourth Amendment accepts, is that unreviewed executive discretion may yield too readily to pressures to obtain incriminating evidence and overlook potential invasions of privacy and protected speech. . . .

The Fourth Amendment contemplates a prior judicial judgment, not the risk that executive discretion may be reasonably exercised. This judicial role accords with our basic constitutional doctrine that individual freedoms will best be preserved through a separation of powers and division of functions among the different branches and levels of Government. . . . The independent check upon executive discretion is not satisfied, as the Government argues, by "extremely limited" post-surveillance judicial review. Indeed, post-surveillance review would never reach the surveillances which failed to result in prosecutions. Prior review by a neutral and detached magistrate is the time-tested means of effectuating Fourth Amendment rights. . . .

The Government argues that the special circumstances applicable to domestic security surveillances necessitate a further exception to the warrant requirement. It is urged that the requirement of prior judicial review would obstruct the President in the discharge of his constitutional duty to protect domestic security. We are told further that these surveillances are directed primarily to the collecting and maintaining of intelligence with respect to subversive forces and are not an attempt to gather evidence for specific criminal prosecutions. It is said that this type of surveillance should not be subject to traditional warrant requirements which were established to govern investigation of criminal activity, not on-going intelligence gathering. . . .

The Government further insists that courts "as a practical matter would have neither the knowledge nor the techniques necessary to determine whether there was probable cause to believe that surveillance was necessary to protect national security." These security problems, the Government contends, involve "a large number of complex and subtle factors" beyond the competence of courts to evaluate. . . .

As a final reason for exemption from a warrant requirement, the Government believes that disclosure to a magistrate of all or even a significant portion of the information involved in domestic security surveillances "would create serious potential dangers to the national security and to the lives of informants and agents. . . . Secrecy is the essential ingredient in intelligence gathering; requiring prior judicial authorization would create a greater 'danger of leaks . . . , because in addition to the judge, you have the clerk, the stenographer and some other official like a law assistant or bailiff who may be apprised of the nature' of the surveillance.'' . . .

These contentions in behalf of a complete exemption from the warrant requirement, when urged on behalf of the President and the national security in its domestic implications, merit the most careful consideration. We certainly do not reject them lightly, especially at a time of worldwide ferment and when civil disorders in this country are more prevalent than in the less turbulent periods of our history. There is, no doubt, pragmatic force to the Government's position.

But we do not think a case has been made for the requested departure from Fourth Amendment standards. The circumstances described do not justify complete exemption of domestic security surveillance from prior judicial scrutiny. Official surveillance, whether its purpose be criminal investigation or on-going intelligence gathering, risks infringement of constitutionally protected privacy of speech. Security surveillances are especially sensitive because of the inherent vagueness of the domestic security concept, the necessarily broad and continuing nature of intelligence gathering, and the temptation to utilize such surveillances to oversee political dissent. We recognize, as we have before, the constitutional basis of the President's domestic security role, but we think it must be exercised in a manner compatible with the Fourth Amendment. In this case we hold that this requires an appropriate prior warrant procedure.

We cannot accept the Government's argument that internal security matters are too subtle and complex for judicial evaluation. Courts regularly deal with the most difficult issues of our society. There is no reason to believe that federal judges will be insensitive to or uncomprehending of the issues involved in domestic security cases. Certainly courts can recognize that domestic security surveillance involves different considerations from the surveillance of ordinary crime. If the threat is too subtle or complex for our senior law enforcement officers to convey its significance to a court, one may question whether there is probable cause for surveillance.

Nor do we believe prior judicial approval will fracture the secrecy essential to official intelligence gathering. The investigation of criminal activity has long involved imparting sensitive information to judicial officers who have respected the confidentialities involved. Judges may be counted upon to be especially conscious of security requirements in national security cases. . . .

Thus, we conclude that the Government's concerns do not justify departure in this case from the customary Fourth Amendment requirement of judicial approval prior to initiation of a search or surveillance. Although some added burden will be imposed upon the Attorney General, this inconvenience is justified in a free society to protect constitutional values. Nor do we think the Government's domestic surveillance powers will be impaired to any significant degree. A prior warrant establishes presumptive validity of the surveillance and will minimize the burden of justification in post-surveillance judicial review. By no means of least importance, will be the reassurance of the public generally that indiscriminate wiretapping and bugging of law-abiding citizens cannot occur. . . .

danger in: 1) Vagueness of "security"
2) nature of intelligence gathering
3) temptation to use it to oversee political dissent

United States v. Nixon
418 U.S. 683, 94 S.Ct. 3090, 41 L.Ed. 2d 1039 (1974)

Following the indictment of seven high-ranking White House officials—including former presidential assistants H. R. Haldeman and John Ehrlichman and former Attorney General John Mitchell—for conspiracy to defraud the U.S. government and obstruction of justice, the Special Prosecutor obtained a subpoena *duces tecum* directing President Richard M. Nixon to deliver to the trial judge certain tape recordings and memoranda of conversations held in the White House. Nixon produced some of the subpoenaed material, but withheld other portions, invoking the so-called doctrine of executive privilege, which, he claimed, placed confidential presidential documents beyond judicial control. The trial judge denied the President's claim, and he appealed to the court of appeals. The Special Prosecutor asked the Supreme Court to review the case before the court of appeals had passed judgment, and the Justices agreed.

MR. CHIEF JUSTICE BURGER delivered the opinion of the Court. . . .

We turn to the claim that the subpoena should be quashed because it demands "confidential conversations between a President and his close advisors that it would be inconsistent with the public interest to produce." . . . The first contention is a broad claim that the separation of powers doctrine precludes judicial review of a President's claim of privilege. The second contention is that if he does not prevail on the claim of absolute privilege, the court should hold as a matter of constitutional law that the privilege prevails over the subpoena duces tecum.

In the performance of assigned constitutional duties each branch of the Government must initially interpret the Constitution, and the interpretation of its powers by any branch is due great respect from the others. The President's counsel . . . reads the Constitution as providing an absolute privilege of confidentiality for all presidential communications. Many decisions of this Court, however, have unequivocally reaffirmed the holding of *Marbury* v. *Madison* . . . (1803), that "it is emphatically the province and duty of the judicial department to say what the law is." . . .

No holding of the Court has defined the scope of judicial power specifically relating to the enforcement of a subpoena for confidential presidential communications for use in a criminal prosecution, but other exercises of powers by the Executive Branch and the Legislative Branch have been found invalid as in conflict with the Constitution. . . . Since this Court has consistently exercised the power to construe and delineate claims arising under express powers, it must follow that the Court has authority to interpret claims with respect to powers alleged to derive from enumerated powers.

In support of his claim of absolute privilege, the President's counsel urges two grounds, one of which is common to all governments and one of which is peculiar to our system of separation of powers. The first ground is the valid need for protection of communications between high government officials and those who advise and assist them in the performance of their manifold duties; the importance of this confidentiality is too plain to require further discussion. . . . Whatever the nature of the privilege of confidentiality of presidential communications in the exercise of Art. II powers, the privilege can be said to derive from the supremacy of each branch within its own assigned area of constitutional duties. Certain powers and privileges flow from the nature of enumerated powers; the protection of the confidentiality of presidential communications has similar constitutional underpinnings.

The second ground asserted by the President's counsel in support of the claim of absolute privilege rests on the doctrine of separation of powers. Here it is argued that the independence of the Executive Branch within its own sphere . . . insulates a president from a judicial subpoena in an ongoing criminal prosecution, and thereby protects confidential presidential communications.

However, neither the doctrine of separation of powers, nor the need for confidentiality of high level communications, without more, can sustain an absolute, unqualified presidential privilege of immunity from judicial process under all circumstances. The President's need for complete candor and objectivity from advisers calls for great deference from the courts. However, when the privilege depends solely on the broad, undifferentiated claim of public interest in the confidentiality of such conversations, a confrontation with other values arises. Absent a claim of need to protect military, diplomatic or sensitive national security secrets, we find it difficult to accept the argument that even the very important interest in confidentiality of presidential communications is significantly diminished by production of such material for *in camera* inspection with all the protection that a district court will be obliged to provide.

The impediment that an absolute, unqualified privilege would place in the way of the primary constitutional duty of the Judicial Branch to do justice in criminal prosecutions would plainly conflict with the function of the courts under Art. III. In designing the structure of our Government and dividing and allocating the sovereign power among three coequal branches, the Framers of the Constitution sought to provide a comprehensive system, but the separate powers were not intended to operate with absolute independence.

> While the Constitution diffuses power the better to secure liberty, it also contemplates that practice will integrate the dispersed powers into a workable government. It enjoins upon its branches separateness but interdependence, autonomy but reciprocity." *Youngstown Sheet & Tube Co.* v. *Sawyer* . . . (1952) (Jackson, J., concurring). . . .

Since we conclude that the legitimate needs of the judicial process may outweigh presidential privilege, it is necessary to resolve those competing interests in a manner that preserves the essential functions of each branch. The right and indeed the duty to resolve that question does not free the judiciary from according high respect to the representations made on behalf of the President. *United States* v. *Burr* . . . (1807).

The expectation of a President to the confidentiality of his conversations and correspondence, like the claim of confidentiality of judicial deliberations, for example, has all the values to which we accord deference for the privacy of all citizens and added to those values the necessity for protection of the public interest in candid, objective, and even blunt or harsh opinions in presidential decision making. . . . These are the considerations justifying a presumptive privilege for presidential communications. The privilege is fundamental to the operation of government and inextricably rooted in the separation of powers under the Constitution. In *Nixon* v. *Sirica* . . . (1973), the Court of Appeals held that such presidential communications are "presumptively privileged," . . . and this position is accepted by both parties in the present litigation. We agree with Mr. Chief Justice Marshall's observation, therefore, that "in no case of this kind would a court be required to proceed against the President as against an ordinary individual." *United States* v. *Burr*. . . .

But this presumptive privilege must be considered in light of our historic commitment to the rule of law. This is nowhere more profoundly manifest than in our view that "the twofold aim of criminal justice is that guilt shall not escape or innocence suffer." *Berger* v. *United States* . . . (1935). We have elected to employ an adversary system of criminal justice in which the parties contest issues before a court of law. The need to develop all relevant facts in the adversary system is both fundamental and comprehensive. The ends of criminal justice would be defeated if judgments were to be founded on a partial or speculative presentation of the facts. The very integrity of the judicial system and public confidence in the system depend on full disclosure of all the facts, within the framework of the rules of evidence. To ensure that justice is done, it is imperative to the function of courts that compulsory process be available for the production of evidence needed either by the prosecution or by the defense. . . .

In this case the President challenges a subpoena served on him as a third party requiring the production of materials for use in a criminal prosecution on the claim that he has a privilege against disclosure of confidential communications. He does not place his claim of privilege on the ground they are military or diplomatic secrets. As to these areas of Art. II duties, the courts have traditionally shown the utmost deference to presidential responsibilities. . . . No case of the Court . . . has extended this high degree of deference to a President's generalized interest in confidentiality. Nowhere in the Constitution . . . is there any explicit reference to a privilege of confidentiality, yet to the extent this interest relates to the effective discharge of a President's powers, it is constitutionally based.

The right to the production of all evidence at a criminal trial similarly has constitutional dimensions. The Sixth Amendment explicitly confers upon every defendant in a criminal trial the right "to be confronted with the witnesses against him" and "to have compulsory process for obtaining witnesses in his favor." Moreover, the Fifth Amendment also guarantees that no person shall be deprived of liberty without due process of law. It is the manifest duty of the courts to vindicate those guarantees and to accomplish that it is essential that all relevant and admissible evidence be produced.

In this case we must weigh the importance of the general privilege of confidentiality of presidential communications in performance of his responsibilities against the inroads of such a privilege on the fair administration of criminal justice. The interest in preserving confidentiality is weighty indeed and entitled to great respect. However, we cannot conclude that advisers will be moved to temper the candor of their remarks by the infrequent occasions of disclosure because of the possibility that such conversations will be called for in the context of a criminal prosecution.

On the other hand, the allowance of the privilege to withhold evidence that is demonstrably relevant in a criminal trial would cut deeply into the guarantee of due process of law and gravely impair the basic function of the courts. A President's acknowledged need for confidentiality in the communications of his office is general in nature, whereas the constitutional need for production of relevant evidence in a criminal proceeding is specific and central to the fair adjudication of a particular criminal case in the administration of justice. Without access to specific facts a criminal prosecution may be totally frustrated. . . .

We conclude that when the ground for asserting privilege as to subpoenaed materials sought for use in a criminal trial is based only on the generalized interest in confidentiality, it cannot prevail over the fundamental demands of due process of law in the fair administration of criminal justice. The generalized assertion of privilege must yield to the demonstrated, specific need for evidence in a pending criminal trial. . . .*

Affirmed.

MR. JUSTICE REHNQUIST took no part in the consideration or decision of these cases.

* In his book, *Witness to Power,* John D. Erlichman alleges that Chief Justice Burger "openly discussed the pros and cons of issues before the Court" with President Nixon. Maybe so, but Nixon's influence was apparently ineffective in this most crucial case. (*The New York Times,* Dec. 11, 1981, p. 1.)

FOUR

Federalism

Although judicial review has been considered America's unique contribution to political science, it may be that federalism will continue to be of greater influence on other nations, and of unending concern at home. With growing interest in world organization after World War II, attention again centered on American experience. Unfortunately for those who look upon federalism as the key to world order under law, our history—unless one takes the long view—is not reassuring.

The United States is governed by federalism—that is, a dual system in which governmental powers are distributed between central (national) and local (state) authorities. The reasons for the adoption of such a government are both historical and rational. During the revolutionary period the states regarded themselves as independent sovereignties. Under the Articles of Confederation, little of their power over internal affairs was surrendered to the Continental Congress. In the face of proved inability of the Confederation to cope with the problems confronting it, local patriotism had to yield.

When the Constitutional Convention met, compromise between the advocates of a strong central government and supporters of states' rights was necessary. Federalism fitted into Madison's basic requirement, reflecting his purpose, as stated in the *Federalist,* No. 51, to so contrive "the interior structure of the government as that its several constituent parts may, by their mutual relations, be the means of keeping each other in their proper places."

Hamilton, in the *Federalist,* No. 23, listed four chief purposes to be served by union: common defense, public peace, regulation of commerce, and foreign relations. General agreement that these objectives required unified government drew together representatives of small and large states alike. To Madison and other nationalists, it seemed certain that the people would remain firmly attached to their state governments. In the *Federalist,* No. 46, he affirmed that the ability of state governments to resist encroachments by the central government was immeasurably greater than the national government's capacity to withstand adverse state action.

One point on which the nationalists remained firm was their determination that no precise line should be drawn delineating national power vis-à-vis the states. The powers of the national government were enumerated but not defined. Alert to possible inroads on the states, Hugh Williamson of North Carolina objected that the effect might be to "restrain the States from regulating their internal affairs." Elbridge Gerry objected that indefinite power in the central authority might "enslave the States." Hamilton, Madison, and James Wilson would not budge, contending that a line dividing state and national power would unduly weaken national authority.

"When we come near the line," Wilson explained, "it cannot be found. . . . A discretion must be left on one side or the other. . . . Will it not be most safely lodged on the side of the National Government? . . . What danger is there that the whole will un-necessarily sacrifice a part? But reverse the case, and leave the whole at the mercy of each part, and will not the general interest be continually sacrificed to local interests?" Hamilton denied any intention to create a consolidated system. "By an abolition of the states, he meant that no boundary could be drawn between the National and State legislatures; that the former must therefore have indefinite authority. If it [National authority] were limited at all, the rivalry of the States would gradually subvert it."

The states were retained, as Madison said, insofar as they could be "subordinately useful." "It was impossible," he told the first Congress, "to confine a government to the exercise of express powers; there must necessarily be admitted powers by implication, unless the Constitution descended to recount every minutia." The Tenth Amendment does not limit national power.

What Madison said on the floor of Congress about the Tenth Amendment bears out Chief Justice Marshall's observation in *McCulloch* v. *Maryland*. It was designed, Marshall said, "for the purpose of quieting excessive jealousy which had been excited." In the House of Representatives debates, Madison explained that the amendment was intended "to extinguish from the bosom of every member of the community any apprehensions that there are those among his countrymen who wish to deprive them of the liberty for which they valiantly fought and honorably bled. And if there are amendments desired, of such a nature as will not injure the Constitution, and they can be ingrafted so as to give satisfaction to the doubting part of our fellow citizens, the friends of the Federal Government will evince that spirit of deference and concession for which they have hitherto been distinguished." Madison stated his position more tersely on August 15, 1789: "While I approve of these amendments [the Ninth and Tenth] I should oppose the consideration at this time of such as are likely to change the principles of the government." And when, three days later, Mr. Tucker proposed to add the word "expressly" to the proposed Tenth Amendment, making it read, "the powers not *expressly* delegated by this Constitution," Madison objected. "It was impossible," he explained, "to confine a Government to the exercise of express powers; there must necessarily be admitted powers by implication." Tucker's motion was defeated. Mr. Gerry's effort of August 21, to get the word "expressly" inserted, suffered the same fate, the vote being 32 to 17.

In *Federalist,* No. 39, Madison anticipated the judiciary's role under a federal system.

[T]he proposed government cannot be deemed a NATIONAL one; since its jurisdiction extends to certain enumerated objects only, and leaves to the several States a residuary and inviolable sovereignty over all other objects. It is true that in controversies relating to the boundary between the two jurisdictions, the tribunal which is ultimately to decide, is to be established under the general government. But this does not change the principle of the case. The decision is to be impartially made, according to the rules of the Constitution; and all the usual and most effectual precautions are taken to secure this impartiality. Some such tribunal is clearly essential to prevent an appeal to the sword and a dissolution of the compact; and that it ought to be established under the general rather than under the local governments, or, to speak more properly, that it could be safely established under the first alone, is a position not likely to be combated.

The distribution of powers agreed upon in the Convention, and the reassurance given the states by the Ninth and Tenth Amendments, did not preclude conflict. The struggle continued in politics, in the courts, and when prolonged debate and bitter controversy failed to yield a conclusive verdict, the contestants carried this baffling issue of political and constitutional theory to the battlefield for settlement by the arbitrament of the sword. Even this holocaust was not conclusive.

The problem of determining the extent of national and state power and of resolving the conflicts between the two centers of authority was ultimately left to the Supreme Court.

NATURE OF NATIONAL AUTHORITY

Delegated and Reserved Powers.   Theoretically, the powers of the national government are limited to those delegated to it by the Constitution, expressly or by implication; the powers "not delegated . . . nor prohibited by it to the states" are "reserved to the states respectively or to the people" (Tenth Amendment).

Express and Implied Powers.   As a sort of second dimension, the national government may use any and all means to give effect to any power specifically granted. This doctrine of implied powers finds its verbal basis in the power granted to Congress to make all laws necessary and proper for carrying into execution those powers expressly delegated to it (Art. I., Sec. 8, Cl. 18). No new or additional powers are granted by the "necessary and proper" clause; it merely enables the federal government to maintain its supremacy in the limited sphere of its activity. Article VI, Paragraph 2, the keystone of the federal system, supplies a third dimension of national power. It indicates that if the legitimate powers of state and nation conflict, that of the national government shall prevail. As Professor Corwin put it: "When national and state power, correctly defined in all other respects, come into conflict in consequence of attempting to govern simultaneously the same subject-matter, the former has always the right of way."

Thus national power is of three dimensions: (1) the enumeration in which the grant of power is couched; (2) the discretionary choice of means that Congress has for carrying its enumerated powers into execution; (3) the fact of supremacy (Art. VI, Para. 2). Under this three-dimensional theory of national authority, no subject matter whatever is withdrawn from control or regulation by the United States simply because it also lies within the usual domain of state power. Since, as pointed out above, the Tenth Amendment merely asserts a truism—powers not delegated are reserved—the coexistence of state governments does not limit national power.

Resulting Powers.   These are derived by implication from the mass of delegated powers or from a group of them. Such powers include the taking of property by eminent domain for a purpose not specified in the Constitution, the power to carry into effect treaties entered into by the United States, the power to maintain the supremacy of the national government within its sphere of authority, and the power to control relations with the Indians.

Exclusive and Concurrent Powers.   The powers of the national government may also be classified as exclusive or concurrent. Powers delegated to Congress by the Constitution are exclusive under the following conditions:

1. Where the right to exercise the power is made exclusive by express provision of the Constitution. Article I, Sec. 8, Cl. 17, for example, gives Congress exclusive power over the District of Columbia and over property purchased from a state with the consent of the legislature.

2. Where one section of the Constitution grants an express power to Congress and another section prohibits the states from exercising a similar power. For example, Congress is given the power to coin money (Art. I, Sec. 8, Cl. 5), and the states are expressly prohibited from exercising such power (Art. I, Sec. 10, Cl. 1).

3. Where the power granted to Congress, though not in terms exclusive, is such that the exercise of a similar power by the states would be utterly incompatible therewith. In *Cooley* v. *Board of Wardens* the Court admitted the existence of a concurrent power to control interstate commerce, but limited state power to matters of local concern. Where the subject matter is national in scope and requires uniform legislative treatment, such as the federal government alone can provide, the power of Congress is exclusive. "Exclusive" is here used in a special sense, since the disability of the states arises not from the Constitution but from the nature of the subject matter to which the power is applied. Such power has been termed "latent concurrent power," since Congress may consent to its exercise by the state.

CONCEPTS OF FEDERALISM

As was inevitable, the formal distribution of powers between the national government and the states proved to be a subject of diverse interpretations. Those who strove to safeguard state sovereignty feared broad construction of national powers; those who viewed the continuance of state power as the enemy of vested rights and of national strength, tended for tactical reasons to conceal their satisfaction with the increased scope of national authority.

The Federalism of John Marshall.   As John Adams left the presidency, he installed John Marshall, a strong party man and an ardent nationalist, as Chief Justice. Marshall read into our constitutional law a concept of federalism that magnified national at the expense of state power. Important precedents existed to aid his pro-nationalist labors. Besides the House of Representatives debates out of which the Tenth Amendment emerged, there was the leading case of *Chisholm* v. *Georgia,* in which state sovereignty pretensions were denied by a vote of 4 to 1.

Taking up the cudgels in behalf of state sovereignty, Justice Iredell summarized his dissenting views as follows: "The Constitution, so far as it respects the judicial authority, can only be carried into effect by acts of legislature . . . prescribing their methods of proceeding. . . . Congress has provided no new law in regard to this case, but referred us to the old [common law]. . . . No principles of the old law . . . authorize the present suit. . . ."

Justice Iredell's states' rights bias, like the nationalistic leanings of Justice Wilson's majority opinion, is rooted in a theory of the Constitution and of the Union: "A State does not [Iredell reasoned] owe its origin to the government of the United States. . . . It derives its authority from the same . . . source [as the government of the Union]: the voluntary and deliberate choice of the people. . . . A state, though subject in certain specified particulars to the authority of the government of the United States, is in every other respect totally independent. The people of the State created, the people of the State can only change, its Constitution.''

The Court's decision holding the ''sovereign'' state of Georgia amenable to the jurisdiction of the national judiciary and suable by a citizen of another state in the federal courts provoked prompt and largely unfavorable reaction. One newspaper saw it as a veiled attempt to reduce the states to mere corporations; another saw it as part of a grand design to bring about eventual monarchy. The *Independent Chronicle* of July 25, 1793, divined the practical grounds of attack—fear of the ''numerous prosecutions that will immediately issue from the various claims of refugees, Tories, etc., that will introduce a series of litigations as will throw every State in the Union into the greatest confusion.'' Therefore the apparent soundness of the Court's reading of the Constitution prompted immediate steps toward constitutional amendment. On January 8, 1798, three years before Marshall was appointed Chief Justice, the Eleventh Amendment became a part of the Constitution. Nearly a decade before Chief Justice Marshall's assertion of judicial review in *Marbury* v. *Madison* the Court's version of the Constitution was equated with the document itself.

Marshall's tenure (1801–1835), covering a period in which his political enemies dominated the political branches of the government, made his fervent nationalism stand out even more dramatically than if he had represented merely the judicial element in a broad nationalist movement. It was not until 1819, however, that the Chief Justice found himself face to face with the dreaded issue of ''clashing sovereignties'' (*McCulloch* v. *Maryland*). The Constitution, Marshall argued, was ''ordained and established in the name of the people''; it was not a compact among states, as counsel for Maryland contended. Nor did it result from the action of the people of the states or of their governments. The Constitution, he declared, altered the former position of the states as sovereign entities. Unlike the Congress under the Articles of Confederation, the national government operated directly on individuals. Within the sphere of its enumerated powers Congress was supreme. Furthermore, the ''necessary and proper clause'' gave Congress a discretionary choice of means for implementing the granted powers, and the Tenth Amendment served in no way to limit this freedom of selection. In reply to the argument that the taxing power was reserved to the states by the Tenth Amendment, and hence could operate even against a legitimate national instrumentality, Marshall demonstrated that the supremacy clause did not permit such a conclusion. At the same time, he went out of his way to deny state power to tax national instrumentalities. Thus, Marshall established not only the proposition that national powers must be liberally construed, but the equally decisive principle that the Tenth Amendment does not create in the states an independent limitation on such authority.

In *Cohens* v. *Virginia,* two years later, the Chief Justice refuted the argument that the highest state court had a power coequal with that of the Supreme Court in interpreting and applying the Constitution. ''The American States,'' he said, ''as well as the American People, have believed a close and firm Union to be essential to their liberty, and to their happiness.'' As a consequence the people had surrendered portions of state sovereignty to the national government. Finally, the supremacy clause and the principle of judicial review required that final decisions on constitutional issues ''arising'' in the state courts be made only by the Supreme Court.

Albert J. Beveridge described Marshall's opinion as "one of the strongest and most enduring strands of that mighty cable woven to hold the American people together as a united and imperishable nation." Jefferson condemned it as indicating judicial determination "to undermine the foundations of our confederated fabric." Denouncing the Justices as a "subtle corps of sappers and miners constantly working underground," Jefferson charged that they had transformed the federal system into "a general and supreme one alone." Marshall's ruling did have consolidating effects. However, one may doubt the correctness of Jefferson's charge that this result had been achieved by spurious judicial interpretation rather than by the Constitution.

In *Gibbons* v. *Ogden* Marshall again seized the opportunity to expound the nature of the Union. "It has been contended," he observed, "that if a law, passed by a state in the exercise of its acknowledged sovereignty, comes in conflict with a law passed by Congress in pursuance of the Constitution they affect the subject, and each other, like equal opposing powers." This was not true, Marshall maintained. "The framers of the Constitution foresaw this state of things, and provided for it, by declaring the supremacy not only of itself, but of laws made in pursuance of it." Marshall warned of the danger that the powers granted by the Constitution might by petty or scholastic construction prove inadequate to the exigencies of future years. "Powerful and ingenious minds," he wrote in *Gibbons* v. *Ogden,* "taking as postulates, that the powers expressly granted to the government of the Union, are to be contracted, by construction, into the narrowest possible compass, and that the original powers of the states are retained if any possible construction will retain them, may, by a course of well-digested but refined and metaphysical reasoning, founded on these premises, explain away the Constitution of our country, and leave it, a magnificent structure, indeed, to look at, but totally unfit for use."

Marshall's doctrine of national supremacy builds on the proposition that the central government and states confront each other in the relationship of superior and subordinate—if the exercise of Congress's enumerated powers be legitimate, the fact that their exercise encroaches on the states' traditional authority is of no significance. Finally, the Court's duty as arbiter of the federal system is not to preserve state sovereignty but to protect national power against state encroachments. As to federalism, the Court functions not as an umpire, but as an agency of national authority. For Marshall, as for Madison in 1788, the principal danger of the federal system lay in erosive state action. Effective political limitations existed against national efforts to impinge on state power, but only the Supreme Court could peacefully restrain state action from infringing upon the authority of the national government.

Marshall's doctrine of federalism did not go unchallenged. Madison, who became an increasingly severe critic of national power, as interpreted by Chief Justice Marshall, wrote that "the very existence of the local sovereignties was a control on the pleas for a constructive amplification of national power" (*Writings,* Vol. 8, pp. 447–453). The eminent states' rights theorist, John Taylor, thought that Marshall's doctrine destroyed the distribution of powers set forth in the Constitution. In a review of Kent's *Commentaries* in 1828, Hugh Swinton Legaré, later Attorney General and Secretary of State under President Tyler, commented: "The government has been fundamentally altered by the progress of opinion—that instead of being any longer one of enumerated powers and a circumscribed sphere, as it was beyond all doubt intended to be, it knows absolutely no bounds but the will of a majority of Congress . . . and threatens in the course of a few years, to control in the most offensive and despotic manner, all the pursuits, the interests, the opinions and the conduct of men." "That argument," Legaré concluded, "cannot be sound which necessarily converts a government of enumerated into one of indefinite powers, and a confederacy of republics into a gigantic and consolidated empire.'' As if to answer these fears, Marshall's successor, Roger Brooke Taney of Maryland, strove valiantly during his long tenure (1836–1864) to redefine federalism in terms more favorable to state power.

Taney and Dual Federalism.   The concept of federalism common to Marshall's critics insisted that the Constitution was a compact of sovereign states, not an ordinance of the people. This idea had been embodied in the Virginia-Kentucky Resolutions of 1798; it was the premise of John Taylor's view that the national government and the states face each other as equals across a precise constitutional line defining their respective jurisdictions. This concept of national-state equality had been the basis of Virginia's anarchical arguments in *Cohens* v. *Virginia*. It was argued that state courts had a power equal with that of the United States Supreme Court to interpret and apply the Constitution; and that in all cases "arising" in their courts, state judges had authority to interpret, with finality, the Constitution and the United States laws and treaties made under its authority. In pointed retort, the Chief Justice said:

> No government ought to be so defective in its organization, as not to contain within itself, the means of securing the execution of its own laws against other dangers than those which occur every day.
>
> Courts of justice are the means most usually employed; and it is reasonable to expect that a government should repose on its own courts, rather than on others. There is certainly nothing in the circumstances under which our constitution was formed; nothing in the history of the times, which would justify the opinion that the confidence reposed in the states was so implicit as to leave in them and their tribunals the power of resisting or defeating, in the form of law, the legitimate measures of the Union.

Accepting the basic creed of nation-state equality, the Taney Court stripped it of its anarchic implications. Within the powers reserved by the Tenth Amendment the states were sovereign, but final authority to determine the scope of state powers rested with the national judiciary, an arbitrator standing aloof from the sovereign pretensions of both nation and states. "This judicial power [Taney wrote in *Ableman* v. *Booth* (21 How. 506: 1859)] was justly regarded as indispensable, not merely to maintain the supremacy of the laws of the United States, but also to guard the states from any encroachment upon their reserved rights by the general government. . . . So long . . . as this Constitution shall endure, this tribunal must exist with it, deciding in the peaceful forum of judicial proceeding the angry and irritating controversies between sovereignties, which in other countries have been determined by the arbitrament of force." Marshall and Taney were agreed on one essential point: The Supreme Court provided a forum for keeping "revolution" within peaceful bounds.

For John Marshall's concept of national supremacy, the Taney Court substituted a theory of federal equilibrium. This doctrine, later called "dual sovereignty," is well expressed by Justice Daniel in upholding state action affecting commerce in the *License Cases* (5 How. 504: 1847): "Every power delegated to the federal government must be expounded in coincidence with a perfect right in the states to all that they have not delegated; in coincidence, too, with the possession of every power and right necessary for their existence and preservation." In contrast to Marshall's theory of a basic law "intended to endure for all ages," Taney thought of the Constitution as speaking "not only in the same words, but with the same meaning and intent with which it spoke when it came from the hands of the framers . . .'' (*Dred Scott* v. *Sandford*). Taney considered his position consistent with basic principles. Yet it was his arbitrary determination in the *Dred Scott* case to apply a theory of federalism no longer relevant to rapidly changing American society that served to discredit the Supreme Court as an arbiter of the federal system.

Taney's passionate concern for states' rights and the preservation of state control of slavery should not, however, obscure the fact that in the context of his times, state police power was the only available weapon with which government could face the pressing problems of the day. In a period in which the national government was not yet prepared to deal realistically with economic and social problems, the theory of national supremacy had the effect of posing the unexercised commerce power of Congress, or the contract clause (Art. I, Sec. 10), as barriers to any governmental action. Taney's dual federalism in the period 1837–1855 enabled the states to deal experimentally with problems that the national government would not face until another half-century had elapsed.

Marshall headed the Court for 34 years, Taney for 28, leaving two official conceptions of federalism succeeding Justices were free to apply as their inclinations or needs of the time dictated.

National Supremacy and Dual Federalism, 1864–1937.   Chief Justice Chase's observation (*Texas* v. *White*) that the Constitution ''in all its provisions, looks to an indestructible Union, composed of indestructible states'' was not mere rhetoric. In a series of cases arising under the Civil War amendments and various laws designed to fasten national standards on state political and social systems, the Supreme Court displayed stubborn resistance to extreme theories of national supremacy (e.g., *Slaughterhouse Cases; Civil Rights Cases*). As a corollary, the Court tended to regard state police power legislation with a generous eye (*Munn* v. *Illinois*). When state power ran into preferred judicial values, however, the Court did not hesitate to impose a constitutional check, especially after 1890 (e.g., *Lochner* v. *New York*.) With national legislation, the Marshall and Taney theories of federalism were called into service alternately, depending on judicial agreement with the policy objectives Congress sought. Cases such as *Swift* v. *United States* (196 U.S. 375: 1905) and *Hoke* v. *United States* (227 U.S. 308: 1913), which dealt with meat packing and prostitution respectively, looked to Marshall. In contrast, decisions such as *Bailey* v. *Drexel Furniture Co.* (involving child labor) looked to Taney. This wavering fealty to national supremacy lay bare a truth in debates on constitutional theory: one concept of federalism or another was chosen because of the policies it would in turn encourage or discourage. Flirtation with Taney's ''dual federalism'' reached a peak during the 1930s, resulting in the court-packing fight discussed in chapter 6. As a consequence, the Court embraced Marshall's doctrine of national supremacy after 1937, even going so far in *United States* v. *Darby Lumber Co.* to declare the Tenth Amendment to be no more than ''a truism.''

Independence of State and National Governments.   In addition to the express limitations and prohibitions on national and state power contained in the Constitution, the Justices have developed a considerable number of limitations stemming from federalism itself. Practical considerations involved in the maintenance of a federal form of government in which two sovereignties must operate side by side led to the adoption of the doctrine that neither government may interfere with the governmental functions of the other, nor with the agencies and officials through which those functions are executed.

The doctrine of governmental immunity had its inception in *McCulloch* v. *Maryland*. On the premise that ''the power to tax involves the power to destroy,'' Chief Justice Marshall declared: ''There is a plain repugnance, in conferring on one government a power to control the constitutional measures of another, which other, with respect to those very measures, is declared to be supreme over that which exerts the control. . . . If the states may tax one instrument employed by the [national] government in the execution of its powers, they may tax any and every instrument [and] they may tax all the means employed by the government, to an excess which would defeat all the ends of government. . . . The states have no power, by taxation or otherwise, to retard, impede, burden, or in any manner control the operations of the constitutional laws enacted by Congress to carry into execution the powers vested in the general government.''

Marshall's immunity doctrine was based upon the theory of the supremacy of the national government in its sphere of activity. Regarded in this light, it is quite consistent with his attitude toward the role of the central government in a federal system. Accordingly, he denied emphatically the proposition that ''every argument which would sustain the right of the general government to tax banks chartered by the states will equally sustain the right of the state to tax banks chartered by the general government.'' ''The difference,'' he explained, ''is that which always exists, and always must exist, between the action of the whole on the part, and the part on the whole—between the laws of a government declared to be supreme, and those of a government, which, when in opposition to those laws, is not supreme.''

In *Collector* v. *Day* (11 Wall. 113: 1871), however, the Court repudiated Marshall's obiter dictum. Ruling that the salaries of state court judges were immune from a national income tax, the Justices established the doctrine of reciprocal immunity, based on the theory of the equality of national and state authority under the federal system. In time, the doctrine of reciprocal immunity was carried to such lengths as to deny both governments fruitful sources of taxation. *Graves* v. *New York* (306 U.S. 466: 1939) overruled *Day* so far as it recognized ''an implied constitutional immunity from income taxation of salaries of officers or employees of the national or state government or their instrumentalities.'' The immunity doctrine as to the states had been qualified even earlier in *South Carolina* v. *United States* (199 U.S. 437: 1905), which upheld a federal tax on South Carolina's liquor-dispensing business. In *New York* v. *United States* (326 U.S. 572: 1946) the Court refused to distinguish South Carolina's traffic in liquor from New York's traffic in mineral water.

The Treaty-Making Power and the States.   The treaty-making power belongs exclusively to the national government, since the Constitution expressly delegates the power to the President and the Senate (Art. II, Sec. 2, Cl. 2) and prohibits its exercise by the states (Art. I, Sec. 10). Treaties entered into by the national government are ''the supreme law of the land,'' standing on a parity, insofar as their operative effect is concerned, with acts of Congress (Art. VI, Sec. 2)

By virtue of the treaty-making power, the national government may exercise greater power over the states than can Congress under its specific grants of power. The ordinary legislative power of Congress, for example, does not permit regulation of migratory birds (*Missouri* v. *Holland*), nor of the rights of aliens to own or inherit property, nor of a business that is purely intrastate in character. Yet in each of these cases, treaties in conflict with state laws have been held valid and supreme despite their obvious encroachment on the reserved powers of the states. But this does not mean that the constitutional distribution of powers between the states and the national government has been destroyed by an unlimited treaty power. The power is impliedly limited by the fact that it can be exercised only in relation to matters that are common subjects of international agreements. That is to say, the power may be used only in connection with foreign relations; it may not be used in violation of an express constitutional prohibition.

Cooperative Federalism.   Although conflicts between the two governments are sometimes avoided by maintaining the independence of each, there are times when cooperation is both desirable and necessary. The Constitution does not prevent such comity. The interaction of the two governments is most apparent where concurrent legislative power is exercised. Congress may choose to leave the states free to act, either by failing to legislate itself or by specifically consenting to state legislation in the field. On the other hand, state laws may be adopted outright, or Congress may provide that the operation of its law shall depend upon or be qualified by existing state laws.

In the zeal to examine the niceties of legal conflict, the constructive purposes federalism may serve have sometimes been overlooked. Of greatest significance is the use of grants-in-aid by the national government to the states in initiating and administering welfare programs. The national government may appropriate funds in aid of such state activities as education, road building, and unemployment relief. It may grant such funds to the respective states upon condition that a like amount or a specified proportion thereof be raised by them for similar purposes, or upon condition that the funds be spent in ways specified by federal law.

Cooperative federalism has received judicial endorsement (*Carmichael* v. *Southern Coal and Coke Co., 301* U.S. 495: 1937). Beneath the shift in judicial decision has been a significant change of political theory. Originally, the existence of national powers and a national government was used to inhibit the exercise of state power, and vice versa, by those who found all government regulation distasteful. Today, the Court has approved cooperative solutions that seem more adequate to the necessities of modern times. The Supreme Court has helped to vindicate Justice Cardozo's conviction that the Constitution was "framed on the theory that the people of the several states must sink or swim together, and that in the long run, prosperity and salvation are in union and not in division." Cooperative federalism, surrendering neither to the full claims of states' rights partisans nor to the extreme followers of John Marshall and Alexander Hamilton, gives full scope, as the decision in *Pennsylvania* v. *Nelson* shows, to the power entrusted to the national government. But one notes certain exceptions. In the Avocado Pear case (*Florida Avocado Growers* v. *Paul,* 373 U.S. 132: 1963) a majority of five, invoking the spirit of cooperative federalism, upheld state regulations, in spite of conflict with standards set by federal authority. A minority, moved by considerations of preemptive federalism underscored in *Pennsylvania* v. *Nelson* argued that the conflicting state law being pre-empted by federal regulation, "exclusive in its application," should give way.

The ascendancy gained by the Bill of Rights in the Warren Court agitated the issue of federalism and states' rights. "We are accustomed," Justice Harlan observed in 1964, "to speak of the Bill of Rights and the Fourteenth Amendment as the principal guarantees of personal liberty. Yet it would surely be shallow not to recognize that the structure of our political system accounts no less for the free society we have." The Founding Fathers "staked their faith that liberty would prosper in the new nation not primarily upon declarations of individual rights but upon the kind of government the Union was to have." "No view of the Bill of Rights or interpretation of any of its provisions," the Justice warns, "which fails to take due account of [federalism and separation of powers] can be considered constitutionally sound."

Reactivated was a variant of "dual federalism." It is "the very essence of our federalism," Justice Harlan declared, "that the states should have the widest latitude in the administration of their own systems of criminal justice." Moreover, Harlan's vehement strictures revived the eighteenth-century debate between Federalists and Antifederalists as to whether a bill of rights was necessary as a supplement to the protection against abuse of power afforded by federalism and separation of powers. In 1789, Alexander Hamilton and James Wilson said "no"; Jefferson and Madison said "yes."

It was largely to "take account" of federalism that the Court, 5 to 4, upheld a Georgia constitutional provision empowering the legislature to elect a governor, when no candidate obtained a majority at the general election. Against the challenge that the action of a malapportioned legislature, the majority of whose members were pledged to support the Democratic candidate, would violate the one-man-one-vote principle, the Court found no impediment in the United States Constitution to Georgia's continued use of a method of election antedating the Revolutionary War (*Fortson* v. *Morris,* 385 U.S. 231: 1966). In spite of this pro-state position, the Court was willing to intervene when the Georgia legislature refused to seat a successful black candidate who had supported statements by a national organization, and personally expressed views hostile to American policy in Vietnam. The different result in *Bond* v. *Floyd* (385 U.S. 116: 1966) is explainable in terms of the First Amendment freedom asserted by the rejected legislator, and the massive adverse impact on freedom of speech that would result if a legislative majority were free to impose its own conception of acceptable views on those seeking legislative seats. The decision in *Bond* was unanimous.

In 1962 "states' rights" was asserted with a defiance that recalls Appomattox. The picture widely broadcast, on June 12, 1963, of Alabama Governor George C. Wallace standing at the entrance of the State University determined to prevent the admission of blacks acting under federal court orders dramatically highlighted the issue. The controversy was, however, more broadly based.

Seared by Supreme Court decisions touching areas long considered sacrosanct, the states, speaking through the powerful Council of State Governments, proposed three far-reaching amendments. (For the text of these proposals, see *State Government* [Winter 1963], xxxvi, 10–15.) One proposal would undo the 1962 Supreme Court decision in *Baker* v. *Carr* in which the Court, striking at the rotten borough scandal, asserted its responsibility for more equitable apportionment of seats in the state legislatures. Another would permit state legislatures to amend the federal Constitution without consideration or discussion in any national forum. The third would set up a super-Supreme Court—"Court of the Union"—consisting of the chief justices of the 50 states, empowered to overrule Supreme Court decisions in cases involving federal-state relations. Proponents of these amendments moved so stealthily that 12 states approved one or more of them before the most informed citizen knew what was going on. Noting widespread apathy, Chief Justice Warren, addressing the American Law Institute on May 22, 1963, admonished members of the bar for not having initiated a "great national debate." "If proposals of this magnitude had been made in the early days of the Republic," the Chief Justice lamented, "the great debate would be resounding in every legislative hall and in every place where lawyers, scholars, and statesmen gather." The threat was to turn back the clock. These proposals, if adopted, would have returned us to the monstrous *imperium in imperio* so convincingly discredited under the Articles of Confederation.

Nearly a decade later, President Nixon, proclaiming a "New Revolution," conjured up a vision "more splendid than any in our history," "a revolution as profound, as far-reaching, as exciting" as that of 1776. Involved were: (1) sorting out and clarifying governmental responsibilities among the various levels of government; (2) improving the performance of those tasks which clearly belong to the central government; (3) strengthening the capacity of state and local governments in areas where decision making and administration are their primary responsibility. Fitting into this ambitious program were the four-billion-dollar Family Assistance Act, revenue-sharing—five billion dollars a year in five years—and the administration's comprehensive Manpower Act. While projecting a larger financial role for the national government, these measures were designed to enhance leadership capacity in state and local governments.

In much the same vein, although more successfully, President Reagan attempted to "revitalize" federalism by shifting both power and spending back to the states and localities. Early in his administration, he appointed a federalism task force consisting of an "inner wheel" (the Coordinating Task Force on Federalism) and an "outer wheel" (the President's Advisory Committee on Federalism) to make recommendations on "restructuring" the federal system. Many observers could recall no prior advisory group on federalism with such proximity to the highest councils of the administration (*National Journal*, May 2, 1981, p. 785).

The states' rights debate continues. Whether in terms of the differing visions of Chief Justices John Marshall and Roger Taney or of Presidents Franklin Roosevelt and Ronald Reagan, federalism remains a prominent feature of American politics and government. Its prominence springs from the fact that federalism concerns the allocation of power. This allocation is important because it helps to determine which of the many contending political groups will have the dominant voice and, therefore, which of many possible policy objectives government will pursue. Deciding *who* will act often decides *what* will be done.

Initially, it was said that the powers of the national government were "enumerated," those of the states "reserved." Beginning with Taney, this order of things began to change; the Tenth Amendment was turned upside down. Thanks to judicial review, Congress no longer enjoyed a discretionary choice of means for carrying its enumerated powers into execution. The Justices ruled, for example, that there were certain subject matters "expressly" reserved to the states, and, therefore, beyond national control. Besides slavery, these included manufacturing (*United States* v. *E. C. Knight*), employer-employee relations (*Hammer* v. *Dagenhart*), and agriculture (*United States* v. *Butler*). In these areas, the states enjoyed enumerated powers, not by the Constitution but by judicial mandate. The Supremacy Clause, apparently, recognized no distinction between laws of the states which would have to yield and those which would not have to yield to a conflicting exercise of national power by Congress. The effect was to eliminate the second dimension of national power in these areas. This judicial revolution reached a high point in 1937.

In 1941, the Court made a complete about-face, labeling the Tenth Amendment "a truism." Justice Stone merely expressed in a single word Madison's conception of the Tenth Amendment as superfluous when, yielding to heavy pressure from advocates of states' rights, he proposed it in the First Congress.

> I find, from looking into the amendments proposed by the State conventions, that several are particularly anxious that it should be declared in the constitution, that the powers not therein delegated should be reserved to the several States. Perhaps words which may define this more precisely than the whole of the instrument now does, may be considered as superfluous. I admit they may be deemed unnecessary; but there can be no harm in making such a declaration, if gentlemen will allow that the fact is as stated. I am sure I understand it so, and do therefore propose it. (Quoted in A. T. Mason, *The States Rights Debate*, 2nd ed., p. 188.)

Echoing Madison, the pronouncement by a unanimous Court in *United States* v. *Darby* seemed to mark the effective end not only of an important provision of the Constitution, but also of a theory, "dual federalism," for which it had supplied major support since the Taney era. Reviewing this development, the eminent scholar Edward S. Corwin, who had himself coined the expression, entitled an article "The Passing of Dual Federalism" (36 *Virginia Law Review* 1: 1950). His prognosis now seems as mistaken as the title was premature. Within a decade after *Darby,* certain Supreme Court Justices, notably William O. Douglas, invoked the Tenth Amendment in dissent as if it were still an effective check on national power. Ignoring the death knell of the Tenth Amendment Justice Stone had sounded in the *Darby Lumber* case of 1940, Douglas wrote:

> The notion that the sovereign position of the States must find its protection in the will of a transient majority of Congress is foreign to and a negation of our constitutional system. There will often be vital regional interests represented by no majority in Congress. The Constitution was designed to keep the balance between the States and the Nation outside the field of legislative controversy.
>
> The immunity of the States from federal taxation is no less clear because it is implied. . . . The Constitution is a compact between sovereigns. The power of one sovereign to tax another is an innovation so startling as to require explicit authority if it is to be allowed. If the power of the federal government to tax the States is conceded, the reserved power of the States guaranteed by the Tenth Amendment does not give them the independence which they have always been assumed to have. They are relegated to a more servile status. They become subject to interference and control both in the functions which they exercise and the methods which they employ. They must pay the federal government for the privilege of exercising the powers of sovereignty guaranteed them by the Constitution, whether, as here, they are disposing of their natural resources, or tomorrow they issue securities or perform any other acts within the scope of their police power. (Douglas dissenting in *New York* v. *United States,* 326 U.S. 572: 1946).

It was not until our own time, however, that a Justice once again employed the Tenth Amendment as an effective check on national power (*The National League of Cities* v. *Usery*). The conclusion is that, although the Tenth Amendment may be a "truism," it nevertheless remains a continuing force, a compelling reminder of America's search for *union* without *unity*.

Almost eight decades ago, Woodrow Wilson wrote:

> The question of the relation of the States to the federal government is the cardinal question of our constitutional system. At every turn of our national development we have been brought face to face with it, and no definition either of statesmen or of judges has ever quieted or decided it. It cannot, indeed, be settled by the opinion of any one generation, because it is a question of growth, and every successive stage of our political and economic development gives it a new aspect, makes it a new question. The general lines of definition which were to run between the powers granted to Congress and the powers reserved to the States the makers of the Constitution were able to draw with their characteristic foresight and lucidity; but the subject-matter of that definition is constantly changing, for it is the life of the nation itself. Our activities change alike their scope and their character with every generation. The old measures of the Constitution are every day to be filled with new grain as the varying crop of cir-

cumstances comes to maturity. (*Constitutional Government in the United States*, 1908, p. 173.)

Wilson grasped both the subtleties and the realities of America's major contribution to the governing process.

SELECTED READINGS

ANONYMOUS, "Judge Spencer Roane of Virginia: Champion of States' Rights—Foe of John Marshall," 66 *Harvard Law Review* 1242 (1953).

BERNS, WALTER, "The Meaning of the 10th Amendment," in *A Nation of States,* ed. R. A. Goldwin. Chicago: Rand McNally, 1963.

BORDEN, MORTON, *The Anti-Federalist Papers.* East Lansing, Mich.: Michigan State University Press, 1965.

CLARK, JANE P., *The Rise of a New Federalism.* New York: Columbia University Press, 1938.

CORWIN, EDWARD S., *Constitutional Revolution, Ltd.* Westport, Conn.: Greenwood Press, 1977 (reissue of 1941 edition).

———, "The Passing of Dual Federalism," 36 *Virginia Law Review* 1 (1950).

ELAZAR, D. J., *American Federalism: A View from the States,* 2nd ed. New York: Crowell, 1972.

GOLDWIN, ROBERT, ed., *A Nation of States: Essays on the American Federal System.* Chicago: Rand McNally. 1974. See especially Martin Diamond, "What the Framers Meant by Federalism."

HOWARD, A. E. DICK, "The Supreme Court and Federalism," in *The Courts: The Pendulum of Federalism. Final Report; Annual Chief Justice Earl Warren Conference on Advocacy in the United States.* Washington: The Roscoe Pound–American Trial Lawyers Foundation, 1979.

KENYON, CECELIA M., ed., *The Antifederalists.* New York: Bobbs Merrill, 1964.

LOFGREN, CHARLES A., "The Origins of the Tenth Amendment; History, Sovereignty and the Problem of Constitutional Intention," in Ronald K. L. Collins, ed., *Constitutional Government in America.* Durham, N.C.: Carolina Academic Press, 1980, p. 331.

MARSHALL, BURKE, *Federalism and Civil Rights.* New York: Columbia University Press, 1964.

MASON, ALPHEUS THOMAS, *The States Rights Debate: Antifederalism and the Constitution.* New York: Oxford University Press, 1972.

MATHIS, DOYLE, "*Chisholm* v. *Georgia:* Background and Settlement," 54 *Journal of American History* 19 (1967).

MICHELMAN, FRANK I., "States' Rights of 'Sovereignty' in *National League of Cities* v. *Usery,*" 86 *Yale Law Journal* 1165 (1977).

RANNEY, JOHN C., "The Basis of American Federalism," 3 *William and Mary Quarterly* (3rd series) 1 (1946).

SCHMIDHAUSER, JOHN R., *The Supreme Court as Final Arbiter in Federal-State Relations, 1789–1957.* Chapel Hill: The University of North Carolina Press, 1958.

STORING, HERBERT J., ed., *The Complete Anti-Federalist.* 7 vols. Chicago: University of Chicago Press, 1981.

Chisholm v. Georgia
2 Dall. (2 U.S.) 419, 1 L.Ed. 440 (1793)

On October 31, 1777, the Executive Council of Georgia authorized State Commissioners Thomas Stone and Edward Davies to purchase much needed supplies from Robert Farquhar, a Charleston, South Carolina, merchant. For his merchandise, Stone and Davies agreed to pay Farquhar $169,613.33 in Continental Currency or in indigo at Carolina prices, if currency was not available. Farquhar never received payment. His claims were still unsatisfied when he was hit by the boom of a pilot boat headed for Savannah. A short time after his death, Alexander Chisholm, a Charleston merchant, was qualified as Farquhar's executor, and began to press for payment of Farquhar's claim. When Georgia refused to pay it, the executor brought suit against the state in the United States Circuit Court for the District of Georgia, the case being listed as *Farquhar's Executor* v. *Georgia.* Alleging its sovereign and independent status under the federal Constitution, Georgia answered that it could not be made a party to any suit by a South Carolina citizen, and Judges James Iredell and Nathaniel Pendleton, sitting as Circuit Court judges, upheld, for different reasons, Georgia's objections. In a communication to the Georgia legislature, the state's attorney general declared that it could not have been the intention of "those persons delegated from the different States of the Union to form the Federal compact, to subject the government of each or either of the States to be impleaded in the District, Circuit, or Supreme Federal Court."

In 1792, Chisholm, nevertheless, filed suit in the Supreme Court. When Georgia failed to appear, the Court pointedly asked that "Any person having authority to speak for the State of Georgia is required to come forth and appear accordingly." When Georgia persisted in her refusal, the case again was postponed until February 4, 1793. No one appeared, and again the Justices issued another invitation. Still nothing happened, and the decision came down February 19, 1793. All five Justices delivered opinions; only Justice Iredell, holding to the view announced in the circuit court opinion, dissented. In the face of assurances made by Hamilton, Madison, and Marshall during the ratification debates that a state could not, without its consent, be made party defendant in the federal courts by a citizen of another state, the Court took jurisdiction and decided against the state.

The negative reaction was strong and prompt. A House resolution calling for amendment to the Constitution was filed the day of the decision, followed the next day by a supportive Senate resolution. The Eleventh Amendment was proposed and ratified in less than two years, being proclaimed as part of the Constitution on January 8, 1798.

Several points mark the case. It was not an original suit in the Supreme Court, as usually supposed, but a continuation of the case decided in the circuit court, under the title *Farquhar* v. *Georgia.* The Justices revealed their own feelings as to the momentous nature of the issue by their pressure on Georgia to appear in defense. In a sense, the suit was lost by default. Finally, the Congress's prompt resort to the formal amending process as a corrective for a decision, flying in the face of reassurances made while ratification of the Constitution was pending, is a testimonial to the stature of the judiciary. Significant is the fact that Congress, in proposing the Eleventh Amendment, and the states, in ratifying it, had within a markedly short time equated the Court's interpretation of the Constitution with the document itself.

WILSON, JUSTICE:—This is a case of uncommon magnitude. One of the parties to it is a state; certainly respectable, claiming to be sovereign. The question to be determined is whether this state, so respectable, and whose claim soars so high, is amenable to the jurisdiction of the supreme court of the United States? This question, important in itself, will depend on others, more important still; and, may, perhaps, be ultimately resolved into one, no less radical than this—"do the people of the United States form a nation?" . . .

To the Constitution of the United States the term sovereign is totally unknown. There is but one place where it could have been used with propriety. But, even in that place it would not, perhaps, have comported with the delicacy of those who ordained and established that constitution. They might have announced themselves "sovereign" people of the United States: But serenely conscious of the fact, they avoided the ostentatious declaration. . . .

In one sense, the term sovereign has for its correlative, subject. In this sense, the term can receive no application; for it has no object in the Constitution of the United States. Under that constitution there are citizens, but no subjects. "Citizens of the United States." "Citizens of another state." "Citizens of different states." "A state or citizen thereof." The term, subject, occurs indeed, once in the instrument; but to make the contrast strongly, the epithet "foreign" is prefixed. In this sense, I presume the state of Georgia has no claim upon her own citizens: In this sense, I am certain, she can have no claim upon the citizens of another state. . . .

As a judge of this court, I know, and can decide upon the knowledge, that the citizens of Georgia, when they acted upon the large scale of the union, as part of the "People of the United States," did not surrender the supreme or sovereign power to that state; but, as to the purposes of the union, retained it to themselves. As to the purposes of the union, therefore, Georgia is not a sovereign state. . . .

Under this view, the question is naturally subdivided into two others. 1. Could the Constitution of the United States vest a jurisdiction over the State of Georgia? 2. Has that constitution vested such jurisdiction in this court? I have already remarked, that in the practice, and even in the science of politics, there has been frequently a strong current against the natural order of things; and an inconsiderate or an interested disposition to sacrifice the end to the means. This remark deserves a more particular illustration. Even in almost every nation, which has been denominated free, the state has assumed a supercilious preeminence above the people who have formed it: Hence the haughty notions of state independence, state sovereignty, and state supremacy. In despotic governments, the Government has usurped, in a similar manner, both upon the state and the people: Hence all arbitrary doctrines and pretensions concerning the supreme, absolute, and incontrollable power of government. In each, man is degraded from the prime rank, which he ought to hold in human affairs; In the latter, the state as well as the man is degraded. Of both degradations, striking instances occur in history, in politics, and in common life. . . .

In the United States, and in the several states which compose the union, we go not so far; but still we go one step farther than we ought to go in this unnatural and inverted order of things. The states, rather than the people, for whose sakes the states exist, are frequently the objects which attract and arrest our principal attention. This, I believe, has produced much of the confusion and perplexity, which have appeared in several proceedings and several publications on state politics, and on the politics, too, of the United States. Sentiments and expressions of this inaccurate kind prevail in our common, even in our convivial, language. Is a toast asked? "The United States" instead of the "People of the United States," is the toast given. This is not politically correct. The toast is meant to present to view the first great object in the union: It presents only the second; It presents only the artificial person, instead of the natural persons, who spoke it into existence. A state I cheerfully admit, is the noblest work of man: But man himself, free and honest, is, I speak as to this world, the noblest work of God. . . .

With the strictest propriety, therefore, classical and political, our national scene opens with the most magnificent object which the nation could present. "The people of the United States" are the first personages introduced. Who were those people? They were the citizens of thirteen states, each of which had a separate constitution and government, and all of which were connected together by articles of confederation. To the purposes of public strength and felicity that confederacy was totally inadequate. A requisition on the several states terminated its legislative authority; executive or judicial authority it had none. In order, therefore, to form a more perfect union, to establish justice, to insure domestic tranquility, to provide for common defense, and to secure the blessings of liberty, those people, among whom were the people of Georgia, ordained and established the present constitution. By that constitution, legislative power is vested, executive power is vested, judicial power is vested.

The question now opens fairly to our view, could the people of those states, among whom were those of Georgia, bind those states, and Georgia, among the others, by the legislative, executive, and judicial power so vested? If the principles on which I have founded myself are just and true, this question must, unavoidably, receive an affirmative answer. If those States were the work of those people, those people, and that I may apply the case closely, the people of Georgia, in particular, could alter, as they pleased, their former work; to any given degree, they could diminish as well as enlarge it. Any or all of the former State powers they could extinguish or transfer. The inference which necessarily results is, that the constitution ordained and established by those people; and still closely to apply the case, in particular, by the people of Georgia, could vest jurisdiction or judicial

power over those states, and over the state of Georgia in particular.

The next question under this head is—Has the constitution done so? Did those people mean to exercise this, their undoubted power? These questions may be resolved, either by fair and conclusive deductions, or by direct and explicit declarations. In order, ultimately, to discover, whether the people of the United States intended to bind those states by the judicial power vested by the national constitution, a previous inquiry will naturally be: Did those people intend to bind those states by the legislative power vested by that constitution? The articles of confederation, it is well known, did not operate upon individual citizens, but operated only upon states. This defect was remedied by the national constitution, which, as all allow, has an operation on individual citizens. But if an opinion, which some seem to entertain, be just; the defect remedied, on one side, was balanced by a defect introduced on the other: for they seem to think, that the present constitution operates only on individual citizens, and not on states. This opinion, however, appears to be altogether unfounded. When certain laws of the states are declared to be "subject to the revision and control of the congress"; it cannot, surely be contended, that the legislative power of the national government was meant to have no operation on the several states. The fact, uncontrovertibly established in one instance, proves the principle in all other instances, to which the facts will be found to apply. We may then infer, that the people of the United States intended to bind the several states, by the legislative power of the national government. . . .

Whoever considers, in a combined and comprehensive view, the general texture of the constitution, will be satisfied that the people of the United States intended to form themselves into a nation for national purposes. They instituted, for such purposes, a national government complete in all its parts, with powers legislative, executive and judiciary; and in all those powers extending over the whole nation. Is it congruous that, with regard to such purposes, any man or body of men, any person, natural or artificial, should be permitted to claim successfully an entire exemption from the jurisdiction of the national government? Would not such claims, crowned with success, be repugnant to our very existence as a nation? When so many trains of deduction, coming from different quarters, converge and unite at last in the same point, we may safely conclude, as the legitimate result of this constitution, that the State of Georgia is amenable to the jurisdiction of this court.

But, in my opinion, this doctrine rests not upon the legitimate result of fair and conclusive deduction from the constitution; it is confirmed, beyond all doubt, by the direct and explicit declaration of the constitution itself. "The judicial power of the United States shall extend to controversies between two States." Two States are supposed to have a controversy between them; this controversy is supposed to be brought before those vested with the judicial power of the United States; can the most consummate degree of professional ingenuity devise a mode by which this "controversy between two States" can be brought before a court of law, and yet neither of those States be a defendant? "The judicial power of the United States shall extend to controversies between a State and citizens of another State." Could the strictest legal language; could even that language which is peculiarly appropriated to an art, deemed by a great master to be one of the most honorable, laudable, and profitable things in our law; could this strict and appropriate language describe with more precise accuracy the cause now pending before the tribunal? Causes, and not parties to causes, are weighed by justice in her equal scales; on the former, solely, her attention is fixed; to the latter she is, as she is painted, blind. . . .

JAY, CHIEF JUSTICE:—The question we are now to decide has been accurately stated, viz.: Is a state suable by individual citizens of another state? . . .

The revolution, or rather the Declaration of Independence, found the people already united for general purposes, and at the same time, providing for their more domestic concerns, by state conventions, and other temporary arrangements. From the crown of Great Britain, the sovereignty of their country passed to the people of it; and it was then not an uncommon opinion, that the unappropriated lands, which belonged to that crown, passed, not to the people of the colony or states within whose limits they were situated, but to the whole people; on whatever principles this opinion rested, it did not give way to the other, and thirteen sovereignties were considered as emerged from the principles of the revolution, combined with local convenience and considerations; the people nevertheless continued to consider themselves, in a national point of view, as one people; and they continued without interruption to manage their national concerns accordingly; afterwards, in the hurry of the war, and in the warmth of mutual confidence, they made a confederation of the States, the basis of a general Government. Experience disappointed the expectations they had formed from it; and then the people, in their collective and national capacity, established the present Constitution. It is remarkable that in establishing it, the people exercised their own rights, and their own proper sovereignty, and conscious of the plenitude of it, they declared with becoming dignity, "We the people of the United States," "do ordain and establish this Constitution." Here we see the people acting as sovereigns of the whole country; and in the language of sovereignty, establishing a Constitution by which it was their will, that the State Governments should be bound, and to which the State Constitutions should be made to conform. Every State Constitution is a compact made by and between the citizens of a state to govern themselves in a certain manner; and the Constitution of the United States is likewise a compact made by the people of the United States to govern themselves as to general objects, in a certain manner. By this great compact however, many prerogatives were transferred to the national Government, such as those of making war and peace, contracting alliances, coining money, &c. . . .

It may be asked, What is the precise sense and latitude in which the words "to establish justice," as here used, are to be understood? The answer to this question will result from the provisions made in the constitution on this head. They are specified in the 2d section of the 3d article, where it is ordained, that the judicial power of the United States shall extend to . . . controversies between two or more states; because domestic tranquillity requires, that the contentions of states should be peaceably terminated by the common judicatory; and because, in a free country, justice ought not to depend on the will of either of the litigants. . . .

It is politic, wise and good, that not only the controversies in which a state is plaintiff, but also those in which a state is defendant, should be settled; both cases, therefore, are within the reason of the remedy; and ought to be so adjudged, unless the obvious, plain and literal sense of the words forbid it. If we attend to the words, we find them to be express, positive, free from ambiguity, and without room for such implied expressions: "The judicial power of the United States shall extend to controversies between a state and citizens of another state." If the constitution really meant to extend these powers only to those controversies in which a state might be plaintiff, to the exclusion of those in which citizens had demands against a state, it is inconceivable, that it should have attempted to convey that meaning in words, not only so incompetent, but also repugnant to it; if it meant to exclude a certain class of these controversies, why were they not expressly excepted; on the contrary, not even an intimation of such intention appears in any part of the Constitution. It cannot be pretended, that where citizens urge and insist upon demands against a state, which the state refuses to admit and comply with, that there is no controversy between them. If it is a controversy between them, then it clearly falls not only within the spirit, but the very words of the Constitution. What is it to the cause of justice, and how can it affect the definition of the word controversy, whether the demands which cause the dispute, are made by a state against citizens of another state, or by the latter against the former? When power is thus extended to a controversy, it necessarily, as to all judicial purposes, is also extended to those between whom it subsists. . . .

I perceive, and therefore candor urges me to mention, a circumstance, which seems to favor the opposite side of the question. It is this: the same section of the Constitution which extends the judicial power to controversies "between a state and the citizens of another state," does also extend that power to controversies to which the United States are a party. Now, it may be said, if the word party comprehends both plaintiff and defendant, it follows, that the United States may be sued by any citizen, between whom and them there may be a controversy. This appears to me to be fair reasoning; but the same principles of candor which urge me to mention this objection, also urge me to suggest an important difference between the two cases. It is this, in all cases of actions against states or individual citizens, the national courts are supported in all their legal and constitutional proceedings and judgments, by the arm of the executive power of the United States; but in cases of actions against the United States, there is no power which the courts can call to their aid. From this distinction, important conclusions are deducible, and they place the case of a state, and the case of the United States, in very different points of view. . . .

IREDELL, JUSTICE, dissented. . . .

McCulloch v. Maryland
4 Wheat. (17 U.S.) 316, 4 L.Ed. 579 (1819)

This famous case resulted from the attempt of the Maryland legislature in 1818 to tax banks and bank branches not chartered by the state legislature. McCulloch, cashier of the Baltimore branch of the Bank of the United States, against which the law was directed, failed to pay the $15,000 annual fee, or comply with the alternative requirement by affixing tax stamps to the bank notes issued. McCulloch brought a writ of error against the Court of Appeals of the State of Maryland, which had upheld a lower court judgment against him.

MARSHALL, CHIEF JUSTICE, delivered the opinion of the court.

In the case now to be determined, the defendant, a sovereign state, denies the obligation of a law enacted by the legislature of the Union; and the plaintiff, on his part, contests the validity of an act which has been passed by the legislature of that state. The constitution of our country, in its most interesting and vital parts, is to be considered; the conflicting powers of the government of the Union and of its members, as marked in that constitution, are to be discussed; and an opinion given, which may essentially influence the great operations of the government. No tribunal can approach such a question without a deep sense of its importance, and of the awful responsibility involved in its decision. But it must be decided peacefully, or remain a source of hostile legislation, perhaps of hostility of a still more serious nature; and if it is to be so decided, by this tribunal alone can the decision be made. On the supreme court of the United States has the constitution of our country devolved this important duty.

The first question made in the case is, has congress power to incorporate a bank? It has been truly said, that this can scarcely be considered as an open question, entirely unprejudiced by the former proceedings of the nation respecting it. The principle now contested was introduced at a very early period of our history, has been recognized by many successive legislatures, and has been acted upon by the judicial department, in cases of peculiar delicacy, as a law of undoubted obligation. . . .

In discussing this question, the counsel for the state of Maryland have deemed it of some importance, in the construction of the constitution, to consider that instrument not as emanating from the people, but as the act of sovereign and independent states. The powers of the general government, it has been said, are delegated by the states, who alone are truly sovereign; and must be exercised in subordination to the states, who alone possess supreme dominion. It would be difficult to sustain this proposition. The convention which framed the constitution was, indeed, elected by the state legislatures. But the instrument, when it came from their hands, was a mere proposal, without obligation, or pretensions to it. It was reported to the then existing congress of the United States, with a request that it might "be submitted to a convention of delegates, chosen in each state by the people thereof, under the recommendation of its legislature, for their assent and ratification." This mode of proceeding was adopted; and by the convention, by congress, and by the state legislatures, the instrument was submitted to the *people*. They acted upon it, in the only manner in which they can act safely, effectively, and wisely, on such a subject by assembling in convention. It is true, they assembled in their several states; and where else should they have assembled? No political dreamer was ever wild enough to think of breaking down the lines which separate the states, and of compounding the American people into one common mass. Of consequence, when they act, they act in their states. But the measures they adopt do not, on that account, cease to be the measures of the people themselves, or become the measures of the state governments.

From these conventions the constitution derives its whole authority. The government proceeds directly from the people; is "ordained and established" in the name of the people; and is declared to be ordained, "in order to form a more perfect union, establish justice, insure domestic tranquillity, and secure the blessings of liberty, to themselves and to their posterity." The assent of the States, in their sovereign capacity, is implied in calling a convention, and thus submitting that instrument to the people. But the people were at perfect liberty to accept or reject it; and their act was final. It required not the affirmance, and could not be negatived, by the state governments. The constitution, when thus adopted, was of complete obligation, and bound the state sovereignties. . . .

To the formation of a league, such as was the confederation, the State sovereignties were certainly competent. But when "in order to form a more perfect union," it was deemed necessary to change this alliance into an effective government, possessing great and sovereign powers, and acting directly on the people, the necessity of referring it to the people, and of deriving its powers directly from them, was felt and acknowledged by all.

The government of the Union, then (whatever may be the influence of this fact on the case), is emphatically and truly a government of the people. In form and in substance it emanates from them, its powers are granted by them, and are to be exercised directly on them, and for their benefit.

This government is acknowledged by all to be one of enumerated powers. The principle, that it can exercise only the powers granted to it, would seem too apparent, to have required to be enforced by all those arguments, which its enlightened friends, while it was pending before the people, found it necessary to urge; that principle is now universally admitted. But the question respecting the extent of the powers actually granted, is perpetually arising, and will probably continue to arise, as long as our system shall exist. In discussing these questions, the conflicting powers of the general and state governments must be brought into view, and the supremacy of their respective laws, when they are in opposition, must be settled.

If any one proposition could command the universal assent of mankind, we might expect that it would be this—that the government of the Union, though limited in its powers, is supreme within its sphere of action. This would seem to result, necessarily, from its nature. It is the government of all; its powers are delegated by all; it represents all, and acts for all. Though any one state may be willing to control its operations, no state is willing to allow others to control them. The nation, on those subjects on which it can act, must necessarily bind its component parts. But this question is not left to mere reason: the people have, in express terms, decided it, by saying, "this constitution, and the laws of the United States, which shall be made in pursuance thereof," "shall be the supreme law of the land," and by requiring that the members of the state legislatures, and the officers of the executive and judicial departments of the states, shall take the oath of fidelity to it. The government of the United States, then, though limited in its powers, is supreme; and its laws, when made in pursuance of the constitution, form the supreme law of the land, "anything in the constitution or laws of any state, to the contrary notwithstanding."

Among the enumerated powers, we do not find that of establishing a bank or creating a corporation. But there is no phrase in the instrument which, like the articles of confederation, excludes incidental or implied powers; and which requires that everything granted shall be expressly and minutely described. Even the 10th amendment, which was framed for the purpose of quieting the excessive jealousies which had been excited, omits the word "expressly," and declares only that the powers "not delegated to the United States, nor prohibited to the states, are reserved to the states or to the people;" thus leaving the question, whether the particular power which may become the subject of contest, has been delegated to the one government, or prohibited to the other, to depend on a fair construction of the whole instrument. The men who drew and adopted this amendment had experienced the embarrassments resulting from the insertion of this word in the articles of confederation, and probably omitted it, to avoid those embarrassments. A constitution, to contain an accurate detail of all the subdivisions of which its great powers will admit, and of all the means by which they may be carried into execution, would partake of the prolixity of a legal code, and could scarcely be embraced by the human mind. It would, probably, never be understood by the public. Its nature, therefore, requires, that only its great outlines should be marked, its important objects designated, and the minor ingredients which compose those objects, be deduced from the nature of the objects themselves. That this idea was entertained by the framers of the American constitution, is not only to be inferred from the nature of the instrument, but from the language. Why else were some of the limitations, found in the 9th section of the 1st article, introduced? It is also, in some degree, warranted, by their having omitted to use any restrictive term which might prevent its receiving a fair and just interpretation. In considering this question, then, we must never forget, that it is *a constitution* we are expounding.

Although, among the enumerated powers of government, we do not find the word "bank," or "incorporation," we find the great powers, to lay and collect taxes; to borrow money; to regulate commerce; to declare and conduct war; and to raise and support armies and navies. The sword and the purse, all the external relations, and no inconsiderable portion of the industry of the nation, are intrusted to its government. It can never be pretended, that these vast powers draw after them others of inferior importance, merely because they are inferior. Such an idea can never be advanced. But it may with great reason be contended, that a government, intrusted with such ample powers, on the due execution of which the happiness and prosperity of the nation so vitally depends, must also be intrusted with ample means for their execution.

The power being given, it is the interest of the nation to facilitate its execution. It can never be their interest, and cannot be presumed to have been their intention, to clog and embarrass its execution, by withholding the most appropriate means. Throughout this vast republic, from the St. Croix to the Gulf of Mexico, from the Atlantic to the Pacific, revenue is to be collected and expended, armies are to be marched and supported. The exigencies of the nation may require, that the treasure raised in the north should be transported to the south, that raised in the east, conveyed to the west, or that this order should be reversed. Is that construction of the constitution to be preferred, which would render these operations difficult, hazardous, and expensive? Can we adopt that construction (unless the words imperiously require it), which would impute to the framers of that instrument, when granting these powers for the public good, the intention of impeding their exercise by withholding a choice of means? If, indeed, such be the mandate of the constitution, we have only to obey; but that instrument does not profess to enumerate the means by which the powers it confers may be executed; nor does it prohibit the creation of a corporation, if the existence of such a being be essential to the beneficial exercise of those powers. It is, then, the subject of fair inquiry, how far such means may be employed.

It is not denied, that the powers given to the government imply the ordinary means of execution. That, for example, of raising revenue, and applying it to national purposes, is admitted to imply the power of conveying money from place to place, as the exigencies of the nation may require, and of employing the usual means of conveyance. But it is denied, that the government has its choice of means; or, that it may employ the most convenient means, if, to employ them, it be necessary to erect a corporation. On what foundation does this argument rest? On this alone: the power of creating a corporation, is one appertaining to sovereignty, and is not expressly conferred on congress. This is true. But all legislative powers appertain to sovereignty. The original power of giving the law on any subject whatever, is a sovereign power; and if the government of the Union is restrained from creating a corporation, as a means for performing its functions, on the single reason that the creation of a corporation is an act of sovereignty; if the sufficiency of this reason be acknowledged, there would be some difficulty in sustaining the authority of congress to pass other laws for the accomplishment of the same objects. The government which has a right to do an act, and has imposed on it, the duty of performing that act, must, according to the dictates of reason, be allowed to select the means; and those who contend that it may not select any appropriate means, that one particular mode of effecting the object is expected, take upon themselves the burden of establishing that exception. . . .

. . . The power of creating a corporation, though appertaining to sovereignty, is not, like the power of making war, or levying taxes, or of regulating commerce, a great substantive and independent power, which cannot be implied as incidental to other powers, or used as a means of executing them. It is never the end for which other powers are exercised, but a means by which other objects are accomplished. No contributions are made to charity, for the sake of an incorporation, but a corporation is created to administer the charity; no seminary of learning is instituted, in order to be incorporated, but the corporate character is conferred to subserve the purposes of education. No city was ever built, with the sole object of being incorporated, but is incorporated as affording the best means of being well governed. The power of creating a corporation is never used for its own sake, but for the purpose of effecting something else. No sufficient reason is, therefore, perceived, why it may not pass as incidental to those powers which are expressly given, if it be a direct mode of executing them.

But the constitution of the United States has not left the right of congress to employ the necessary means, for the execution of the powers conferred on the government, to general reasoning. To its enumeration of powers is added, that of making "all laws which shall be necessary and

proper, for carrying into execution the foregoing powers, and all other powers vested by this constitution, in the government of the United States, or in any department thereof." The counsel for the state of Maryland has urged various arguments, to prove that this clause, though, in terms, a grant of power, is not so in effect; but is really restrictive of the general right, which might otherwise be implied, of selecting means for executing the enumerated powers. In support of this proposition, they have found it necessary to contend, that this clause was inserted for the purpose of conferring on congress the power of making laws. That, without it, doubts might be entertained whether congress could exercise its powers in the form of legislation.

But could this be the object for which it was inserted? . . . Could it be necessary to say, that a legislature should exercise legislative powers, in the shape of legislation? After allowing each house to prescribe its own course of proceeding, after describing the manner in which a bill should become a law, would it have entered into the mind of a single member of the convention, that an express power to make laws was necessary to enable the legislature to make them? That a legislature, endowed with legislative powers, can legislate, is a proposition too self-evident to have been questioned.

But the argument on which most reliance is placed, is drawn from the peculiar language of this clause. Congress is not empowered by it to make all laws, which may have relation to the powers conferred on the government, but only such as may be "necessary and proper" for carrying them into execution. The word "necessary" is considered as controlling the whole sentence, and as limiting the right to pass laws for the execution of the granted powers, to such as are indispensable, and without which the power would be nugatory. That it excludes the choice of means, and leaves to congress, in each case, that only which is most direct and simple.

Is it true, that this is the sense in which the word "necessary" is always used? Does it always import an absolute physical necessity, so strong, that one thing, to which another may be termed necessary, cannot exist without that other? We think it does not. If reference be had to its use, in the common affairs of the world, or in approved authors, we find that it frequently imports no more than that one thing is convenient, or useful, or essential to another. To employ the means necessary to an end, is generally understood as employing any means calculated to produce the end, and not as being confined to those single means, without which the end would be entirely unattainable. . . . It is, we think, impossible to compare the sentence which prohibits a State from laying "imposts, or duties on imports or exports, except what may be *absolutely* necessary for executing its inspection laws," with that which authorizes congress "to make all laws which shall be necessary and proper for carrying into execution" the powers of the general government, without feeling a conviction, that the convention understood itself to change materially the meaning of the word "necessary" by prefixing the word "absolutely." This word, then, like others, is used in various senses; and, in its construction, the subject, the context, the intention of the person using them, are all to be taken into view.

Let this be done in the case under consideration. The subject is the execution of those great powers on which the welfare of a nation essentially depends. It must have been the intention of those who gave these powers, to insure, as far as human prudence could insure, their beneficial execution. This could not be done, by confining the choice of means to such narrow limits as not to leave it in the power of congress to adopt any which might be appropriate, and which were conducive to the end. This provision is made in a constitution, intended to endure for ages to come, and consequently to be adapted to the various *crises* of human affairs. To have prescribed the means by which government should, in all future times, execute its powers, would have been to change, entirely, the character of the instrument, and give it the properties of a legal code. It would have been an unwise attempt to provide, by immutable rules, for exigencies which, if foreseen at all, must have been seen dimly, and which can be best

provided for as they occur. To have declared, that the best means shall not be used, but those alone, without which the power given would be nugatory, would have been to deprive the legislature of the capacity to avail itself of experience, to exercise its reason, and to accommodate its legislation to circumstances. If we apply this principle of construction to any of the powers of the government, we shall find it so pernicious in its operation that we shall be compelled to discard it. . . .

In ascertaining the sense in which the word "necessary" is used in this clause of the constitution, we may derive some aid from that with which it is associated. Congress shall have power "to make all laws which shall be necessary and proper to carry into execution" the powers of the government. If the word "necessary" was used in that strict and rigorous sense for which the counsel for the state of Maryland contend, it would be an extraordinary departure from the usual course of the human mind, as exhibited in composition, to add a word, the only possible effect of which is, to qualify that strict and rigorous meaning; to present to the mind the idea of some choice of means of legislation, not straitened and compressed within the narrow limits for which gentlemen contend.

But the argument which most conclusively demonstrates the error of the construction contended for by the counsel for the state of Maryland, is founded on the intention of the convention, as manifested in the whole clause. To waste time and argument in proving that, without it, congress might carry its powers into execution, would be not much less idle than to hold a lighted taper to the sun. As little can it be required to prove, that in the absence of this clause, congress would have some choice of means. That it might employ those which, in its judgment, would most advantageously effect the object to be accomplished. That any means adapted to the end, any means which tended directly to the execution of the constitutional powers of the government, were in themselves constitutional. This clause, as construed by the state of Maryland, would abridge, and almost annihilate, this useful and necessary right of the legislature to select its means. That this could not be intended is, we should think, had it not been already controverted, too apparent for controversy.

We think so for the following reasons: 1st. The clause is placed among the powers of congress, not among the limitations on those powers. 2d. Its terms purport to enlarge, not to diminish the powers vested in the government. It purports to be an additional power, not a restriction on those already granted. No reason has been, or can be assigned, for thus concealing an intention to narrow the discretion of the national legislature, under words which purport to enlarge it. The framers of the constitution wished its adoption, and well knew that it would be endangered by its strength, not by its weakness. Had they been capable of using language which would convey to the eye one idea, and, after deep reflection, impress on the mind, another, they would rather have disguised the grant of power, than its limitation. If then, their intention had been, by this clause, to restrain the free use of means which might otherwise have been implied, that intention would have been inserted in another place, and would have been expressed in terms resembling these. "In carrying into execution the foregoing powers and all others," &c., "no laws shall be passed but such as are necessary and proper." Had the intention been to make this clause restrictive, it would unquestionably have been so in form as well as in effect. . . .

We admit, as all must admit, that the powers of the government are limited, and that its limits are not to be transcended. But we think the sound construction of the constitution must allow to the national legislature that discretion, with respect to the means by which the powers it confers are to be carried into execution, which will enable that body to perform the high duties assigned to it, in the manner most beneficial to the people. Let the end be legitimate, let it be within the scope of the constitution, and all means which are appropriate, which are plainly adapted to that end, which are not prohibited, but consistent with the letter and spirit of the constitution, are constitutional. . . .

It being the opinion of the court, that the act incorporating the bank is constitutional; and that the power of establishing a branch in the state of Maryland might be properly exercised by the bank itself, we proceed to inquire—

Whether the state of Maryland may, without violating the constitution, tax that branch? That the power of taxation is one of vital importance; that it is retained by the states; that it is not abridged by the grant of a similar power to the government of the Union; that it is to be concurrently exercised by the two governments are truths which have never been denied. But such is the paramount character of the constitution, that its capacity to withdraw any subject from the action of even this power, is admitted. . . .

On this ground, the counsel for the bank place its claim to be exempted from the power of a state to tax its operations. There is no express provision for the case, but the claim has been sustained on a principle which so entirely pervades the constitution, is so intermixed with the materials which compose it, so interwoven with its web, so blended with its texture, as to be incapable of being separated from it, without rending it into shreds. This great principle is, that the constitution and the laws made in pursuance thereof are supreme; that they control the constitution and laws of the respective states, and cannot be controlled by them. From this, which may be almost termed an axiom, other propositions are deduced as corollaries, on the truth or error of which, and on their application to this case, the cause has been supposed to depend. These are, 1st: That a power to create implies a power to preserve: 2d. That a power to destroy, if wielded by a different hand, is hostile to, and incompatible with, these powers to create and preserve: 3d. That where this repugnancy exists, that authority which is supreme must control, not yield to that over which it is supreme. . . .

The power of Congress to create, and of course, to continue, the bank, was the subject of the preceding part of this opinion; and is no longer to be considered as questionable. That the power of taxing it by the states may be exercised so as to destroy it, is too obvious to be denied. But taxation is said to be an absolute power, which acknowledges no other limits than those expressly prescribed in the constitution, and like sovereign power of every other description, is trusted to the discretion of those who use it. But the very terms of this argument admit, that the sovereignty of the state, in the article of taxation itself, is subordinate to, and may be controlled by, the constitution of the United States. How far it has been controlled by that instrument must be a question of construction. In making this construction, no principle not declared, can be admissible, which would defeat the legitimate operations of a supreme government. It is of the very essence of supremacy, to remove all obstacles to its action within its own sphere, and so to modify every power vested in subordinate governments, as to exempt its own operations from their own influence. . . .

The sovereignty of a state extends to everything which exists by its own authority, or is introduced by its permission; but does it extend to those means which are employed by Congress to carry into execution—powers conferred on that body by the people of the United States? We think it demonstrable that it does not. Those powers are not given by the people of a single state. They are given by the people of the United States, to a government whose laws, made in pursuance of the constitution, are declared to be supreme. Consequently, the people of a single state cannot confer a sovereignty which will extend over them.

If we measure the power of taxation residing in a state, by the extent of sovereignty which the people of a single state possess, and can confer on its government, we have an intelligible standard, applicable to every case to which the power may be applied. We have a principle which leaves the power of taxing the people and property of a state unimpaired; which leaves to a state the command of all its resources, and which places beyond its reach, all those powers which are conferred by the people of the United States on the government of the Union, and all those means which are given for the purpose of carrying those powers into execution. We have a principle which is safe for the states, and safe for the Union. We are relieved, as we ought to be, from clashing sovereignty; from interfering powers; from a repugnancy between a right in one government to pull down, what there is an acknowledged right in another to build up; from the incompatibility of a right in one government to destroy, what there is a right in another to preserve. We are not driven to the perplexing inquiry, so unfit for the judicial department, what degree of taxation is a legitimate use, and what degree may amount to the abuse of the power. The attempt to use it on the means employed by the government of the Union, in pursuance of the constitution, is itself an abuse, because it is the usurpation of a power, which the people of a single state cannot give. We find, then, on just theory, a total failure of this original right to tax the means employed by the government of the Union, for the execution of its powers. The right never existed, and the question whether it has been surrendered, cannot arise.

But, waiving this theory for the present, let us resume the inquiry, whether this power can be exercised by the respective states, consistently with a fair construction of the constitution? That the power to tax involves the power to destroy; that the power to destroy may defeat and render useless the power to create; that there is a plain repugnancy in conferring on one government a power to control the constitutional measures of another, which other, with respect to those very measures, is declared to be supreme over that which exerts the control, are propositions not to be denied. But all inconsistencies are to be reconciled by the magic of the word *confidence*. Taxation, it is said, does not necessarily and unavoidably destroy. To carry it to the excess of destruction, would be an abuse, to presume which, would banish that confidence which is essential to all government. But is this a case of confidence? Would the people of any one state trust those of another with a power to control the most significant operations of their state government? We know they would not. Why, then, should we suppose, that the people of any one state should be willing to trust those of another with a power to control the operations of a government to which they have confided their most important and most valuable interests? In the legislature of the Union alone, all are represented. The legislature of the Union alone, therefore, can be trusted by the people with the power of controlling measures which concern all, in the confidence that it will not be abused. This, then is not a case of confidence, and we must consider it as it really is.

If we apply the principle for which the state of Maryland contends, to the constitution generally, we shall find it capable of changing totally the character of that instrument. We shall find it capable of arresting all the measures of the government, and of prostrating it at the foot of the states. The American people have declared their constitution and the laws made in pursuance thereof, to be supreme; but this principle would transfer the supremacy, in fact, to the states. If the states may tax one instrument, employed by the government in the execution of its powers, they may tax any and every other instrument. They may tax the mail; they may tax the mint; they may tax patent rights; they may tax the papers of the custom-house; they may tax judicial process; they may tax all the means employed by the government, to an excess which would defeat all the ends of government. This was not intended by the American people. They did not design to make their government dependent on the states. . . .

. . . If the controlling power of the states be established; if their supremacy as to taxation be acknowledged; what is to restrain their exercising this control in any shape they may please to give it? Their sovereignty is not confined to taxation; that is not the only mode in which it might be displayed. The question is, in truth, a question of supremacy, and if the right of the states to tax the means employed by the general government be conceded, the declaration that the constitution, and the laws made in pursuance thereof, shall be the supreme law of the land, is empty and unmeaning declamation. . . .

It has also been insisted, that, as the power of taxation in the general and state governments is

acknowledged to be concurrent, every argument which would sustain the right of the general government to tax banks chartered by the states, will equally sustain the rights of the states to tax banks chartered by the general government. But the two cases are not on the same reason. The people of all the states have created the general government, and have conferred upon it the general power of taxation. The people of all the states, and the states themselves, are represented in congress, and, by their representatives, exercise this power. When they tax the chartered institutions of the states, they tax their constituents; and these taxes must be uniform. But when a state taxes the operations of the government of the United States, it acts upon institutions created, not by their own constitutents, but by people over whom they claim no control. It acts upon the measures of a government created by others as well as themselves, for the benefit of others in common with themselves. The difference is that which always exists, and always must exist, between the action of the whole on a part, and the action of a part on the whole—between the laws of a government declared to be supreme, and those of a government which, when in opposition to those laws, is not supreme.

The court has bestowed on this subject its most deliberate consideration. The result is a conviction that the states have no power, by taxation or otherwise, to retard, impede, burden, or in any manner control, the operations of the constitutional laws enacted by congress to carry into execution the powers vested in the general government. This is, we think, the unavoidable consequence of that supremacy which the constitution has declared. We are unanimously of opinion, that the law passed by the legislature of Maryland, imposing a tax on the Bank of the United States, is unconstitutional and void.

This opinion does not deprive the states of any resources which they orginally possessed. It does not extend to a tax paid by the real property of the bank, in common with the other real property within the state, nor to a tax imposed on the interest which the citizens of Maryland may hold in this institution, in common with other property of the same description throughout the state. But this is a tax on the operations of the bank, and is, consequently, a tax on the operation of an instrument employed by the government of the Union to carry its powers into execution. Such a tax must be unconstitutional.

Cohens v. *Virginia*
6 Wheaton (19 U.S.) 264, 5 L.Ed. 257 (1821)

In 1802 Congress passed a law authorizing the District of Columbia to conduct a lottery. The Cohens were arrested in Virginia and convicted of selling lottery tickets in violation of a state statute. On the merits of the case, the Court upheld the conviction, declaring that the federal law afforded no immunity to prosecution beyond the limits of the District of Columbia. The portion of the opinion excerpted below pertains solely to the question of jurisdiction.

MR. CHIEF JUSTICE MARSHALL delivered the opinion of the court.

This is a writ of error to a judgment rendered in the Court of Hustings for the borough of Norfolk, on an information for selling lottery tickets, contrary to an act of the legislature in Virginia. In the state court, the defendant claimed the protection of an act of congress. A case was agreed between the parties, which states the act of assembly on which the prosecution was founded, and the act of congress on which the defendant relied, and concludes in these words: "If upon this case the court shall be of opinion that the acts of congress before mentioned were valid, and, on the true construction of those acts, the lottery tickets sold by the defendants as aforesaid, might lawfully be sold within the state of Virginia, notwithstanding the act or statute of the general assembly of Virginia prohibiting such sale, then judgment to be entered for the defendants: And if the court should be of opinion that the statute or act of the general assembly of the state of Virginia, prohibiting such sale, is valid, notwithstanding the said acts of congress, then judgment to be entered that the defendants are guilty, and that the commonwealth recover against them one hundred dollars and cost.''

Judgment was rendered against the defendants; and the court in which it was rendered being the highest court of the state in which the cause was cognizable, the record has been brought into this court by a writ of error.

The defendant in error moves to dismiss this writ, for want of jurisdiction.

In support of this motion, three points have been made, and argued with the ability which the importance of the question merits. These points are—

1st. That a state is a defendant.

2nd. That no writ of error lies from this court to a state court.

[Point 3 has been omitted].

The questions presented to the court by the two first points made at the bar are of great magnitude, and may truly be said vitally to affect the Union. They exclude the inquiry whether the constitution and laws of the United States have been violated by the judgment which the plaintiffs in error seek to review; and maintain that, admitting such violation, it is not in the power of the government to apply a corrective. They maintain that the nation does not possess a department capable of restraining, peaceably, and by authority of law, any attempts which may be made, by a part, against the legitimate powers of the whole; and that the government is reduced to the alternative of submitting to such attempts, or of resisting them by force. They maintain that the constitution of the United States has provided no tribunal for the final construction of itself, or of the laws or treaties of the nation; but that this power may be exercised in the last resort by the courts of every state of the Union. That the constitution, laws and treaties may receive as many constructions as there are states; and that this is not a mischief, or, if a mischief is irremediable. . . .

1st. The first question to be considered is, whether the jurisdiction of this court is excluded by the character of the parties, one of them being a state, and the other a citizen of that state?

The 2d section of the third article of the constitution defines the extent of the judicial power of the United States. Jurisdiction is given to the courts of the Union in two classes of cases. In the first, their jurisdiction depends on the character of the cause, whoever may be the parties. This class comprehends "all cases in law and equity arising under this constitution, the laws of the United States, and treaties made, or which shall be made, under their authority." This clause extends the jurisdiction of the court to all the cases described, without making in its terms any exception whatever, and without any regard to the condition of the party. If there be any exception, it is to be implied against the express words of the article.

In the second class, the jurisdiction depends entirely on the character of the parties. In this are comprehended "controversies between two or more States, between a State and citizens of another State," "and between a State and foreign states, citizens, or subjects." If these be the parties, it is entirely unimportant what may be the subject of controversy. Be it what it may, these parties have a constitutional right to come into the courts of the Union. . . .

If . . . a case arising under the constitution, or a law, must be one in which a party comes into court to demand something conferred on him by the constitution or a law, we think the construction too narrow. A case in law or equity consists of the right of the one party, as well as of the other, and may truly be said to arise under the constitution or a law of the United States, whenever its correct decision depends on the construction of either. . . .

The jurisdiction of the court, then, being extended by the letter of the constitution to all cases arising under it, or under the laws of the United States, it follows that those who would withdraw any case of this description from that jurisdiction, must sustain the exemption they claim, on the spirit and true meaning of the constitution, which spirit and true meaning must be so apparent as to overrule the words which its framers have employed. The counsel for the defendant in error have undertaken to do this; and have laid down the general proposition, that a sovereign independent state is not suable, except by its own consent.

This general proposition will not be controverted. But its consent is not requisite in each particular case. It may be given in a general law. And if a state has surrendered any portion of its sovereignty, the question whether a liability to suit be a part of this portion, depends on the instrument by which the surrender is made. If upon a just construction of that instrument, it shall appear that the state has submitted to be sued, then it has parted with this sovereign right of judging in every case on the justice of its own pretensions, and has intrusted that power to a tribunal in whose impartiality it confides.

The American states, as well as the American people, have believed a close and firm Union to be essential to their liberty and to their happiness. They have been taught by experience, that this Union cannot exist without a government for the whole; and they have been taught by the same experience that this government would be a mere shadow, that must disappoint all their hopes, unless invested with large portions of that sovereignty which belongs to independent states. Under the influence of this opinion, and thus instructed by experience, the American people, in the conventions of their respective states, adopted the present constitution.

If it could be doubted whether, from its nature, it were not supreme in all cases where it is empowered to act, that doubt would be removed by the declaration that "this constitution, and the laws of the United States which shall be made in pursuance thereof and all treaties made, or which shall be made, under the authority of the United States, shall be the supreme law of the land; and the judges in every state shall be bound thereby, anything in the constitution or laws of any state to the contrary notwithstanding."

This is the authoritative language of the American people; and, if gentlemen please, of the American states. It marks with lines too strong to be mistaken, the characteristic distinction between the government of the Union and those of the states. The general government, though limited as to its objects, is supreme with respect to those objects. This principle is a part of the constitution; and if there be any who deny its necessity, none can deny its authority.

To this supreme government ample powers are confided; and if it were possible to doubt the great purposes for which they were so confided, the people of the United States have declared that they are given "in order to form a more perfect union, establish justice, insure domestic tranquillity, provide for the common defense, promote the general welfare, and secure the blessings of liberty to themselves and their posterity."

With the ample powers confided to this supreme government, for these interesting purposes, are connected many express and important limitations on the sovereignty of the states, which are made for the same purposes. The powers of the Union on the great subjects of war, peace, and commerce, and on many others, are in themselves limitations of the sovereignty of the states; but in addition to these, the sovereignty of the states is surrendered in many instances where the surrender can only operate to the benefit of the people, and where, perhaps, no other power is conferred on congress than a conservative power to maintain the principles established in the constitution. The maintenance of these principles in their purity is certainly among the great duties of the government. One of the instruments by which this duty may be peaceably performed is the judicial department. It is authorized to decide all cases, of every description, arising under the constitution or laws of the United States. From this general grant of jurisdiction, no exception is made of those cases in which a state may be a party. When we consider the situation of the government of the Union and of a state, in relation to each other; the nature of our constitution; the subordination of the state governments to that constitution; the great purpose for which jurisdiction over all cases arising under the constitution and laws of the United States, is confided to the judicial department; are we at liberty to insert in this general grant, an exception of those cases in which a state may be a party? Will the spirit of the constitution justify this attempt to control its words? We think it will not. We think a case arising under the constitution or laws of the United States, is cognizable in the courts of the Union, whoever may be the parties of that case. . . .

One of the express objects, then, for which the judicial department was established, is the decision of controversies between states, and between a state and individuals. The mere circumstance, that a state is a party, gives jurisdiction to the court. How, then, can it be contended, that the very same instrument, in the very same section, should be so construed, as that this same circumstance should withdraw a case from the jurisdiction of the court, where the constitution or laws of the United States are supposed to have been violated? . . .

The mischievous consequences of the construction contended for on the part of Virginia, are also entitled to great consideration. It would prostrate, it has been said, the government and its laws at the feet of every state in the Union. And would not this be its effect? What power of the government could be executed by its own means, in any state disposed to resist its execution by a course of legislation? The laws must be executed by individuals acting within the several states. If these individuals may be exposed to penalties, and if the courts of the Union cannot correct the judgments by which these penalties may be enforced, the course of the government may be, at any time, arrested by the will of one of its members. Each member will possess a *veto* on the will of the whole. . . .

These collisions may take place in times of no extraordinary commotion. But a constitution is framed for ages to come, and is designed to approach immortality as nearly as human institutions can approach it. Its course cannot always be tranquil. It is exposed to storms and tempests, and its framers must be unwise statesmen indeed, if they have not provided it, as far as its nature will permit, with the means of self-preservation from the perils it may be destined to encounter. No government ought to be so defective in its organization, as not to contain within itself the means of securing the execution of its own laws against other dangers than those which occur every day. Courts of justice are the means most usually employed; and it is reasonable to expect that a government should repose on its own courts, rather than on others. There is certainly nothing in the circumstances under which our constitution was formed; nothing in the history of the times, which would justify the opinion that the confidence reposed in the states was so implicit as to leave in them and their tribunals the power of resisting or defeating, in the form of law, the legitimate measures of the Union. . . .

. . . If jurisdiction depended entirely on the character of the parties, and was not given where the parties have not an original right to come into court, that part of the 2d section of the 3d article, which extends the judicial power to all cases arising under the constitution and laws of the United States, would be surplusage. It is to give jurisdiction where the character of the parties would not give it, that this very important part of the clause was inserted. It may be true, that the partiality of the state tribunals, in ordinary controversies between a state and its citizens, was not apprehended, and therefore the judicial power of the Union was not extended to such cases; but this was not the sole nor the greatest object for which this department was created. A more important, a much more interesting object, was the preservation of the constitution and laws of the United States,

so far as they can be preserved by judicial authority; and therefore the jurisdiction of the courts of the Union was expressly extended to all cases arising under that constitution and those laws. If the constitution or laws may be violated by proceedings instituted by a state against its own citizens, and if that violation may be such as essentially to affect the constitution and the laws, such as to arrest the progress of governments in its constitutional course, why should these cases be excepted from the provision which expressly extends the judicial power of the Union to *all* cases arising under the constitution and laws? . . .

It is most true, that this court will not take jurisdiction if it should not: but it is equally true, that it must take jurisdiction, if it should. The judiciary cannot, as the legislature may, avoid a measure, because it approaches the confines of the constitution. We cannot pass it by, because it is doubtful. With whatever doubts, with whatever difficulties, a case may be attended, we must decide it, if it be brought before us. We have no more right to decline the exercise of jurisdiction which is given, than to usurp that which is not given. The one or the other would be treason to the constitution. Questions may occur, which we would gladly avoid; but we cannot avoid them. All we can do is, to exercise our best judgment, and conscientiously to perform our duty. In doing this, on the present occasion, we find this tribunal invested with appellate jurisdiction in all cases arising under the constitution and laws of the United States. We find no exception to this grant, and we cannot insert one. . . .

This leads to a consideration of the 11th amendment. It is in these words: ''The judicial power of the United States shall not be construed to extend to any suit in law or equity commenced or prosecuted against one of the United States, by citizens of another state, or by citizens or subjects of any foreign state.'' It is a part of our history, that, at the adoption of the constitution, all the states were greatly indebted; and the apprehension that these debts might be prosecuted in the federal courts, formed a very serious objection to that instrument. Suits were instituted; and the court maintained its jurisdiction. The alarm was general; and, to quiet the apprehensions that were so extensively entertained, this amendment was proposed in Congress, and adopted by the state legislatures.* That its motive was not to maintain the sovereignty of a state from the degradation supposed to attend a compulsory appearance before the tribunal of the nation, may be inferred from the terms of the amendment. It does not comprehend controversies between two or more states, or between a state and a foreign state. The jurisdiction of the court still extends to these cases: and in these a state may still be sued. We must ascribe the amendment, then, to some other cause than the dignity of a state. There is no difficulty in finding this cause. Those who were inhibited from commencing a suit against a state, or from prosecuting one which might be commenced before the adoption of the amendment, were persons who might probably be its creditors. There was not much reason to fear that foreign or sister states would be creditors to any considerable amount, and there was reason to retain the jurisdiction of the court in those cases, because it might be essential to the preservation of peace. The amendment, therefore, extended to suits commenced or prosecuted by individuals, but not to those brought by states. . . .

A general interest might well be felt in leaving to a state the full power of consulting its convenience in the adjustment of its debts, or of other claims upon it; but no interest could be felt in so changing the relations between the whole and its parts, as to strip the government of the means of protecting, by the instrumentality of its courts, the constitution and laws from active violation. . . .

Under the Judiciary Act, the effect of a writ of error is simply to bring the record into court, and submit the judgment of the inferior tribunal to reexamination. It does not in any manner act upon the parties; it acts only on the record. It removes the record into the supervising tribunal. Where, then, a state obtains a judgment against an individual, and the court rendering such judgment overrules a defense set up under the constitution or laws of the United States, the transfer of this record into the supreme court for the sole purpose of inquiring whether the judgment violates the constitution of the United States, can, with no propriety, we think, be denominated a suit commenced or prosecuted against the state whose judgment is so far reexamined. Nothing is demanded from the state. No claim against it of any description is asserted or prosecuted. The party is not to be restored to the possession of anything. Essentially, it is an appeal on a single point; and the defendant who appeals from a judgment rendered against him, is never said to commence or prosecute a suit against the plaintiff who has obtained the judgment. . . .

It is, then, the opinion of the court, that the defendant who removes a judgment rendered against him by a state court into this court, for the purpose of reexamining the question, whether that judgment be in violation of the constitution or laws of the United States, does not commence or prosecute a suit against the state. . . .

2d. The second objection to the jurisdiction of the court is, that its appellate power cannot be exercised, in any case, over the judgment of a state court.

This objection is sustained chiefly by arguments drawn from the supposed total separation of the judiciary of a state from that of the Union, and their entire independence of each other. The argument considers the federal judiciary as completely foreign to that of a state; and as being no more connected with it, in any respect whatever, than the court of a foreign state. If this hypothesis be just, the argument founded on it is equally so; but if the hypothesis be not supported by the constitution, the argument fails with it.

This hypothesis is not founded on any words in the constitution, which might seem to countenance it, but on the unreasonableness of giving a contrary construction to words which seem to require it; and on the incompatibility of

---

* The 11th Amendment was proposed and ratified shortly after the Court's decision in *Chisholm* v. *Ga.*

the application of the appellate jurisdiction to the judgments of state courts, with that constitutional relation which subsists between the government of the Union and the governments of those states which compose it.

Let this unreasonableness, this total incompatibility, be examined.

That the United States form, for many, and for most important purposes, a single nation, has not yet been denied. In war, we are one people. In making peace, we are one people. In all commercial regulations, we are one and the same people. In many other respects, the American people are one; and the government which is alone capable of controlling and managing their interests in all these respects, is the government of the Union. It is their government, and in that character, they have no other. America has chosen to be, in many respects, and to many purposes, a nation; and for all these purposes, her government is complete; to all these objects it is competent. The people have declared, that in the exercise of all powers given for these objects, it is supreme. It can, then, in effecting these objects, legitimately control all individuals or governments within the American territory. The constitution and laws of a state, so far as they are repugnant to the constitution and laws of the United States, are absolutely void. These states are constituent parts of the United States; they are members of one great empire—for some purposes sovereign, for some purposes subordinate.

In a government so constituted, is it unreasonable, that the judicial power should be competent to give efficacy to the constitutional laws of the legislature? That department can decide on the validity of the constitution or law of a state, if it be repugnant to the constitution or to a law of the United States. Is it unreasonable, that it should also be empowered to decide on the judgment of a state tribunal enforcing such unconstitutional law? . . .

The propriety of entrusting the construction of the constitution, and laws made in pursuance thereof, to the judiciary of the Union has not, we believe, as yet, been drawn into question. It seems to be a corollary from this political axiom, that the federal courts should either possess exclusive jurisdiction in such cases, or a power to revise the judgment rendered in them, by the state tribunals. If the federal and state courts have concurrent jurisdiction in all cases arising under the constitution, laws, and treaties of the United States; and if a case of this description brought in a state court cannot be removed before judgment, nor revised after judgment, then the construction of the constitution, laws, and treaties of the United States is not confided particularly to their judicial department, but is confided equally to that department and to the state courts, however they may be constituted. ''Thirteen independent courts,'' says a very celebrated statesman (and we have now more than twenty such courts), ''of final jurisdiction over the same causes, arising upon the same laws, is a hydra in government, from which nothing but contradiction and confusion can proceed.''

Dismissing the unpleasant suggestion, that any motives which may not be fairly avowed, or which ought not to exist, can ever influence a state or its courts, the necessity of uniformity, as well as correctness in expounding the constitution and laws of the United States, would itself suggest the propriety of vesting in some single tribunal the power of deciding, in the last resort, all cases in which they are involved.

We are not restrained, then, by the political relations between the general and state governments, from construing the words of the constitution, defining the judicial power, in their true sense. We are not bound to construe them more restrictively than they naturally import.

They give to the supreme court appellate jurisdiction in all cases arising under the constitution, laws, and treaties of the United States. The words are broad enough to comprehend all cases of this description, in whatever court they may be decided. . . .

This opinion has been already drawn out to great length to admit of entering into a particular consideration of the various forms in which the counsel who made this point has, with much ingenuity, presented his argument to the court. The argument, in all its forms, is essentially the same. It is founded, not on the words of the constitution, but on its spirit—a spirit extracted, not from the words of the instrument, but from his view of the nature of our Union, and of the great fundamental principles on which the fabric stands. To this argument, in all its forms, the same answer must be given. Let the nature and objects of our Union be considered; let the great fundamental principles, on which the fabric stands, be examined; and we think, the result must be, that there is nothing so extravagantly absurd, in giving to the court of the nation the power of revising the decisions of local tribunals, on questions which affect the nation, as to require the words which import this power should be restricted by a forced construction. . . .

Judgment affirmed.

[On the merits of the case, the Court held that the federal statute authorizing a lottery in the District of Columbia had no effect outside the limits of the District, and therefore upheld the conviction under the Virginia statute.]

Texas v. White
7 Wall. (74 U.S.) 700, 19 L.Ed. 227 (1869)

In 1851 Congress had provided that $10 million in United States bonds should be transferred to the state of Texas, payable to the state or bearer, and redeemable in 1864. In receiving the bonds, the Texas legislature by statute stipulated that endorsement by the governor of the state was necessary to make any of the bonds valid in the hands of individual holders. This act was repealed in 1862 by the insurgent Texas legislature, which authorized use of the bonds to obtain war supplies. In 1866 the reconstruction government sought to reclaim bonds in the hands of White and others. The defense interposed was that the Supreme Court lacked jurisdiction to entertain this original action because the plaintiff was not a state of the Union. The Supreme Court heard the case on an original bill.

THE CHIEF JUSTICE [CHASE] delivered the opinion of the court. . . .

The first inquiries to which our attention was directed by counsel, arose upon the allegations of the answer of Chiles (1) that no sufficient authority is shown for the prosecution of the suit in the name and on the behalf of the State of Texas; and (2) that the State, having severed her relations with a majority of the States of the Union, and having by her ordinance of secession attempted to throw off her allegiance to the Constitution and government of the United States, has so far changed her status as to be disabled from prosecuting suits in the National courts. . . .

It [the word *state*] describes sometimes a people or community of individuals united more or less closely in political relations, inhabiting temporarily or permanently the same country; often it denotes only the country or territorial region, inhabited by such a community; not unfrequently it is applied to the government under which the people live; at other times it represents the combined idea of people, territory, and government. . . .

In the Constitution the term state most frequently expresses the combined idea just noticed, of people, territory, and government. A state, in the ordinary sense of the Constitution, is a political community of free citizens, occupying a territory of defined boundaries, and organized under a government sanctioned and limited by a written constitution, and established by the consent of the governed. It is the union of such states, under a common constitution, which forms the distinct and greater political unit, which that Constitution designates as the United States, and makes of the people and states which compose it one people and one country. . . .

Texas took part, with the other Confederate States, in the war of the rebellion, which these events made inevitable. During the whole of that war there was no governor, or judge, or any other State official in Texas, who recognized the National authority. Nor was any officer of the United States permitted to exercise any authority whatever under the National government within the limits of the State, except under the immediate protection of the National military forces.

Did Texas, in consequence of these acts, cease to be a State? Or, if not, did the State cease to be a member of the Union?

It is needless to discuss, at length, the question whether the right of a State to withdraw from the Union for any cause, regarded by herself as sufficient, is consistent with the Constitution of the United States.

The Union of the States never was a purely artificial and arbitrary relation. It began among the Colonies, and grew out of common origin, mutual sympathies, kindred principles, similar interests, and geographical relations. It was confirmed and strengthened by the necessities of war, and received definite form, and character, and sanction from the Articles of Confederation. By these the Union was solemnly declared to "be perpetual." And when these Articles were found to be inadequate to the exigencies of the country, the Constitution was ordained "to form a more perfect Union." It is difficult to convey the idea of indissoluble unity more clearly than by these words. What can be indissoluble if a perpetual Union, made more perfect, is not?

But the perpetuity and indissolubility of the Union, by no means implies the loss of distinct

and individual existence, or of the right of self-government by the States. Under the Articles of Confederation, each State retained its sovereignty, freedom, and independence, and every power, jurisdiction, and right not expressly delegated to the United States. Under the Constitution, though the powers of the States were much restricted, still, all powers not delegated to the United States, nor prohibited to the States, are reserved to the States respectively, or to the people. And we have already had occasion to remark at this term, that "the people of each State compose a State, having its own government, and endowed with all the functions essential to separate and independent existence," and that "without the States in union, there could be no such political body as the United States." *County of Lane* v. *Oregon,* 7 Wallace, 76. Not only therefore can there be no loss of separate and independent autonomy to the States, through their union under the Constitution, but it may be not unreasonably said the preservation of the States, and the maintenance of their governments, are as much within the design and care of the Constitution as the preservation of the Union and the maintenance of the National government. The Constitution, in all its provisions, looks to an indestructible Union, composed of indestructible States.

When, therefore, Texas became one of the United States, she entered into an indissoluble relation. All the obligations of perpetual union and all the guarantees of republican government in the Union, attached at once to the State. The act which consummated her admission into the Union was something more than a compact; it was the incorporation of a new member into the political body. And it was final. The union between Texas and the other States was as complete, as perpetual, and as indissoluble as the union between the original States. There was no place for reconsideration, or revocation, except through revolution, or through consent of the States.

Considered therefore as transactions under the Constitution, the ordinance of secession, adopted by the convention and ratified by a majority of the citizens of Texas, and all the acts of her legislature intended to give effect to that ordinance, were absolutely null. They were utterly without operation in law. The obligations of the State, as a member of the Union, and of every citizen of the State, as a citizen of the United States, remained perfect and unimpaired. It certainly follows that the State did not cease to be a State, nor her citizens to be citizens of the Union. If this were otherwise, the State must have become foreign, and her citizens foreigners. The war must have ceased to be a war for the suppression of rebellion, and must have become a war for conquest and subjugation.

Our conclusion therefore is, that Texas continued to be a State, and a State of the Union, notwithstanding the transactions to which we have referred. And this conclusion, in our judgment, is not in conflict with any act or declaration of any department of the National government, but entirely in accordance with the whole series of such acts and declarations, since the first outbreak of rebellion.

But in order to the exercise, by a State, of the right to sue in this court, there needs to be a State government, competent to represent the State in its relations with the National government, so far at least as the institution and prosecution of a suit is concerned.

And it is by no means a logical conclusion, from the premises which we have endeavored to establish, that the governmental relations of Texas to the Union remained unaltered. Obligations often remain unimpaired, while relations are greatly changed. The obligations of allegiance to the State, and of obedience to her laws, subject to the Constitution of the United States, are binding upon all citizens, whether faithful or unfaithful to them; but the relations which subsist while these obligations are performed, are essentially different from those which arise when they are disregarded and set at naught. And the same must necessarily be true of the obligations and relations of States and citizens of the Union. No one has been bold enough to contend that, while Texas was controlled by a government hostile to the United States, and in affiliation with a hostile con-

federation, waging war upon the United States, senators chosen by her legislature, or representatives elected by her citizens, were entitled to seats in Congress; or that any suit, instituted in her name, could be entertained in this court. All admit that, during this condition of civil war, the rights of the State as a member, and her people as citizens of the Union, were suspended. The government and the citizens of the State, refusing to recognize their constitutional obligations, assumed the character of enemies, and incurred the consequences of rebellion.

These new relations imposed new duties upon the United States. The first was that of suppressing the rebellion. The next was that of reestablishing the broken relations of the State with the Union. The first of these duties having been performed, the next necessarily engaged the attention of the National government. . . .

There being then no government in Texas in constitutional relations with the Union, it became the duty of the United States to provide for the restoration of such a government. But the restoration of the government which existed before the rebellion, without a new election of officers, was obviously impossible; and before any such election could be properly held, it was necessary that the old constitution should receive such amendments as would conform its provisions to the new conditions created by emancipation, and afford adequate security to the people of the State.

In the exercise of the power conferred by the guaranty clause, as in the exercise of every other constitutional power, a discretion in the choice of means is necessarily allowed. It is essential only that the means must be necessary and proper for carrying into execution the power conferred, through the restoration of the State to its constitutional relations, under a republican form of government, and that no acts be done, and no authority exerted, which is either prohibited or unsanctioned by the Constitution. . . .

Nothing in the case before us requires the court to pronounce judgment upon the constitutionality of any particular provision of these acts.

But it is important to observe that these acts themselves show that the governments, which had been established and had been in actual operation under executive direction, were recognized by Congress as provisional, as existing, and as capable of continuance. . . .

[The right of Texas to bring suit was affirmed, and a decree issued enjoining White and others from setting up any claim to the bonds.]

MR. JUSTICE GRIER, dissenting. . . .

The original jurisdiction of this court can be invoked only by one of the United States. The Territories have no such right conferred on them by the Constitution, nor have the Indian tribes who are under the protection of the military authorities of the government.

Is Texas one of these United States? Or was she such at the time the bill was filed, or since?

This is to be decided as *a political fact,* not as *a legal fiction.* This court is bound to know and notice the public history of the nation.

If I regard the truth of history for the last eight years, I cannot discover the State of Texas as one of these United States. . . .

[JUSTICES SWAYNE and MILLER agreed with JUSTICE GRIER in denying the capacity of Texas to bring suit.].

Pennsylvania v. *Nelson*
350 U.S. 497, 76 S.Ct. 477, 100 L.Ed. 640 (1956)

In 1940, Congress passed the Smith Act, prohibiting the "knowing advocacy" of the overthrow of the government of the United States by force and violence. Many states have enacted laws punishing sedition against the state or the United States. Nelson, an acknowledged member of the Communist party, was convicted of a violation of the Pennsylvania Sedition Act. The Supreme Court of Pennsylvania, with only one dissent, reversed the conviction on the ground that the evidence against Nelson failed to reveal any act hostile to the state and that prosecutions for sedition against the United States were controlled by the Smith Act. Pennsylvania's petition for certiorari was granted.

MR. CHIEF JUSTICE WARREN delivered the opinion of the Court. . . .

The precise holding of the [Pennsylvania] court, and all that is before us for review, is that the Smith Act of 1940, as amended in 1948, which prohibits the knowing advocacy of the overthrow of the Government of the United States by force and violence, supersedes the enforceability of the Pennsylvania Sedition Act which proscribes the same conduct. . . .

It should be said at the outset that the decision in this case does not affect the right of States to enforce their sedition laws at times when the Federal Government has not occupied the field and is not protecting the entire country from seditious conduct. The distinction between the two situations was clearly recognized by the court below. Nor does it limit the jurisdiction of the States where the Constitution and Congress have specifically given them concurrent jurisdiction, as was done under the Eighteenth Amendment and the Volstead Act. . . . Neither does it limit the right of the State to protect itself at any time against sabotage or attempted violence of all kinds. Nor does it prevent the State from prosecuting where the same act constitutes both a federal offense and a state offense under the police power. . . .

Where, as in the instant case, Congress has not stated specifically whether a federal statute has occupied a field in which the States are otherwise free to legislate, different criteria have furnished touchstones for decision. Thus,

This Court, in considering the validity of state laws in the light of . . . federal laws touching the same subject, has made use of the following expressions: conflicting; contrary to; occupying the field; repugnance; difference; irreconcilability; inconsistency; violation; curtailment; and interference. But none of these expressions provides an infallible constitutional test or an exclusive constitutional yardstick. In the final analysis, there can be no one crystal clear, distinctly marked formula. (*Hines* v. *Davidowitz*, 312 U.S. 52.)

[In a footnote, Chief Justice Warren dismisses a point treated as crucial near the end of Justice Reed's dissenting opinion, namely, that Congress specifically showed its intention not to supersede state criminal statutes by any provision of Title 18 USC, where the Smith Act appears. The Chief Justice points out that Section 3231 provides for the original jurisdiction of the district courts, followed immediately by the provision cited by Justice Reed. "Nothing in this Title shall be held to take away or impair the jurisdiction of the courts of the several States under the laws thereof." The Chief Justice concludes that "the office of the second sentence is merely to limit the effect of the jurisdictional grant of the first sentence. There was no intention to resolve particular supersession questions by the Section."]

. . . In this case, we think that each of several tests of supersession is met.

First. "The scheme of federal regulation is so pervasive as to make reasonable the inference that Congress left no room for the States to supplement it. . . ."

. . . Looking to all of [the federal acts] in the aggregate, the conclusion is inescapable that Congress has intended to occupy the field of sedition. Taken as a whole, they evince a congressional plan which makes it reasonable to determine that no room has been left for the

States to supplement it. Therefore, a state sedition statute is superseded regardless of whether it purports to supplement the federal law. . . .

Second, the federal statutes "touch a field in which the federal interest is so dominant that the federal system [must] be assumed to preclude enforcement of state laws on the same subject." . . .

Third, enforcement of state sedition acts presents a serious danger of conflict with the administration of the federal program. Since 1939, in order to avoid a hampering of uniform enforcement of its program by sporadic local prosecutions, the Federal Government has urged local authorities not to intervene in such matters, but to turn over to the federal authorities immediately and unevaluated all information concerning subversive activities.

Since we find that Congress has occupied the field to the exclusion of parallel state legislation, that the dominant interest of the Federal Government precludes state intervention, and that administration of state Acts would conflict with the operation of the federal plan, we are convinced that the decision of the Supreme Court of Pennsylvania is unassailable.

We are not unmindful of the risk of compounding punishments which would be created by finding concurrent state power. In our view of the case, we do not reach the question whether double or multiple punishment for the same overt acts directed against the United States has constitutional sanction. Without compelling indication to the contrary, we will not assume that Congress intended to permit the possibility of double punishment. . . .

The judgment of the Supreme Court of Pennsylvania is

Affirmed.

MR. JUSTICE REED, with whom MR. JUSTICE BURTON, and MR. JUSTICE MINTON, join, dissenting . . . .

Congress has not, in any of its statutes relating to sedition, specifically barred the exercise of state power to punish the same acts under state law. And, we read the majority opinion to assume for this case that, absent federal legislation, there is no constitutional bar to punishment of sedition against the United States by both a State and the Nation. The majority limits to the federal courts the power to try charges of sedition against the Federal Government.

. . . It is quite apparent that since 1940 Congress has been keenly aware of the magnitude of existing state legislation proscribing sedition. It may be validly assumed that in these circumstances this Court should not void state legislation without a clear mandate from Congress.

We cannot agree that the federal criminal sanctions against sedition directed at the United States are of such a pervasive character as to indicate an intention to void state action.

Secondly, the Court states that the federal sedition statutes touch a field "in which the federal interest is so dominant" they must preclude state laws on the same subject. This concept is suggested in a comment on *Hines* v. *Davidowitz*. The Court in *Davidowitz* ruled that federal statutes compelling alien registration preclude enforcement of state statutes requiring alien registration. We read *Davidowitz* to teach nothing more than that when the Congress provided a single nation-wide integrated system of regulation so complete as that for aliens' registration (with fingerprinting, a scheduling of activities, and continuous information as to their residence), the Act bore so directly on our foreign relations as to make it evident that Congress intended only one uniform national alien registration system. . . .

Thirdly, the Court finds ground for abrogating Pennsylvania's anti-sedition statute because, in the Court's view, the State's administration of the Act may hamper the enforcement of the federal law. Quotations are inserted from statements of President Roosevelt and Mr. Hoover, the Director of the Federal Bureau of Investigation, to support the Court's position. But a reading of the quotations leads us to conclude their purpose was to gain prompt knowledge of evidence of subversive activities so that the federal agency could be fully advised. We find no suggestion from any official source that state officials should be less alert to ferret out or punish subversion. The Court's attitude as to interference seems to us quite contrary to that of the Legislative and Executive Departments. Congress was advised of the existing state sedition legislation when the Smith Act was enacted and has been kept current with its spread. No declaration of exclusiveness followed . . . .

Finally, and this one point seems in and of itself decisive, there is an independent reason for reversing the Pennsylvania Supreme Court. The Smith Act appears in Title 18 of the United States Code, which Title codifies the federal criminal laws. Section 3231 of that Title provides:

"Nothing in this title shall be held to take away or impair the jurisdiction of the courts of the several states under the laws thereof."

That declaration springs from the federal character of our Nation. It recognizes the fact that maintenance of order and fairness rests primarily with the States. The section was first enacted in 1825 and has appeared successively in the federal criminal laws since that time. 18 USCA § 3231 (Historical and Revision Notes). This Court has interpreted the section to mean that States may provide concurrent legislation in the absence of explicit congressional intent to the contrary. . . . The majority's position in this case cannot be reconciled with that clear authorization of Congress. . . .

The National League of Cities v. Usery
426 U.S. 833, 96 S.Ct. 2465, 49 L.Ed. 2d 245 (1976)

Individual cities and states, and organizations thereof, sued in the United States District Court for the District of Columbia to test the validity of 1974 amendments of the Fair Labor Standards Act extending the statutory minimum wage and maximum hour provisions to employees of states and their political subdivisions. A three-judge court dismissed the complaint for failure to state a claim on which relief could be granted.

On direct appeal, the United States Supreme Court reversed. An opinion by Rehnquist expressed the views of five members of the Court. Justice Blackmun joined in the Court's opinion with the understanding that it does not outlaw federal power in areas such as environmental protection. Justice Brennan, joined by White and Marshall, dissented. Justice Stevens wrote a dissenting opinion.

MR. JUSTICE REHNQUIST delivered the opinion of the Court.

Nearly 40 years ago Congress enacted the Fair Labor Standards Act, and required employers covered by the Act to pay their employees a minimum hourly wage and to pay them at one and one-half times their regular rate of pay for hours worked in excess of 40 during a work week.... This Court unanimously upheld the Act as valid exercise of congressional authority under the commerce power in *United States* v. *Darby*, 312 U.S. 100.

The original Fair Labor Standards Act passed in 1938 specifically excluded the States and their political subdivisions from its coverage....

In a series of amendments beginning in 1961 Congress began to extend the provisions of the Fair Labor Standards Act to some types of public employees. The 1961 amendment to the Act extended its coverage to persons who were employed in "enterprises" engaged in commerce or in the production of goods for commerce. And in 1966, with the amendment of the definition of employers under the Act, the exemption heretofore extended to the States and their political subdivisions was removed with respect to employees of state hospitals, institutions, and schools. We nevertheless sustained the validity of the combined effect of these two amendments in *Maryland* v. *Wirtz*, 392 U.S. 183....

... By its 1974 amendments, ... Congress has now entirely removed the exemption previously afforded States and their political subdivisions....

The Act thus imposes upon almost all public employment the minimum wage and maximum hour requirements previously restricted to employees engaged in interstate commerce. These requirements are essentially identical to those imposed upon private employers, although the Act does attempt to make some provision for public employment relationships which are without counterpart in the private sector, such as those presented by fire protection and law enforcement personnel....

Appellants in no way challenge these decisions establishing the breadth of authority granted Congress under the commerce power. Their contention, on the contrary, is that when Congress seeks to regulate directly the activities of States as public employers, it transgresses an affirmative limitation on the exercise of its power akin to other commerce power affirmative limitations contained in the Constitution....

This Court has never doubted that there are limits upon the power of Congress to override state sovereignty, even when exercising its otherwise plenary powers to tax or to regulate commerce which are conferred by Art. I of the Constitution. In *Wirtz,* for example, the Court took care to assure the appellants that it had "ample power to prevent . . . 'the utter destruction of the State as a sovereign political entity,'" which they feared.

In *Fry* (421 U.S. 541: 1975) the Court recognized that an express declaration of this limitation is found in the Tenth Amendment.

> While the Tenth Amendment has been characterized as a "truism," stating merely that "all is retained which has not been surrendered," *United States* v. *Darby,* 312 U.S. . . . the Amendment expressly declares the constitutional policy that Congress may not exercise power in a fashion that impairs the States' integrity or their ability to function effectively in a federal system. . . .

Appellee Secretary argues that the cases in which this Court has upheld sweeping exercises of authority by Congress, even though those exercises preempted state regulation of the private sector, have already curtailed the sovereignty of the States quite as much as the 1974 amendments to the Fair Labor Standards Act. We do not agree. It is one thing to recognize the authority of Congress to enact laws regulating individual businesses necessarily subject to the dual sovereignty of the government of the Nation and of the State in which they reside. It is quite another to uphold a similar exercise of congressional authority directed not to private citizens, but to the States as States. We have repeatedly recognized that there are attributes of sovereignty attaching to every state government which may not be impaired by Congress, not because Congress may lack an affirmative grant of legislative authority to reach the matter, but because the Constitution prohibits it from exercising the authority in that manner. . . .

One undoubted attribute of state sovereignty is the States' power to determine the wages which shall be paid to those whom they employ in order to carry out their governmental functions, what hours those persons will work, and what compensation will be provided where these employees may be called upon to work overtime. The question we must resolve in this case, then, is whether these determinations are "functions essential to separate and independent existence," . . . so that Congress may not abrogate the States' otherwise plenary authority to make them. . . .

Quite apart from the substantial costs imposed upon the States and their political subdivisions, the Act displaces state policies regarding the manner in which they will structure delivery of those governmental services which their citizens require. The Act, speaking directly to the States qua States, requires that they shall pay all but an extremely limited minority of their employees the minimum wage rates currently chosen by Congress. It may well be that as a matter of economic policy it would be desirable that States, just as private employers, comply with these minimum wage requirements. But it cannot be gainsaid that the federal requirement directly supplants the considered policy choices of the States' elected officials and administrators as to how they wish to structure pay scales in state employment. The State might wish to employ persons with little or no training, or those who wish to work on a casual basis, or those who for some reason do not possess minimum employment requirements, and pay them less than the federally prescribed minimum wage. It may wish to offer part time or summer employment to teenagers at a figure less than the minimum wage, and if unable to do so may decline to offer such employment at all. But the Act would forbid such choices by the States. The only "discretion" left to them under the Act is either to attempt to increase their revenue to meet the additional financial burden imposed upon them by paying congressionally prescribed wages to their existing complement of employees, or to reduce that complement to a number which can be paid the federal minimum wage without increasing revenue.

This dilemma presented by the minimum wage restrictions may seem not immediately different from that faced by private employers, who have long been covered by the Act and who must find ways to increase their gross income if they are to pay higher wages while maintaining current earnings. The difference, however, is that a State is not merely a factor in the "shifting economic arrangements" of the private sector of the economy . . . but is itself a coordinate element in the system established by the framers for governing our federal union. . . .

We do not doubt that this may be a salutary result, and that it has a sufficiently rational relationship to commerce to validate the application of the overtime provisions to private employers. But, like the minimum wage provisions, the vice of the Act as sought to be applied here is that it directly penalizes the States for choosing to hire governmental employees on terms different from those which Congress has sought to impose.

This congressionally imposed displacement of state decisions may substantially restructure traditional ways in which the local governments have arranged their affairs. Although at this point many of the actual effects under the proposed Amendments remain a matter of some dispute among the parties, enough can be satisfactorily anticipated for an outline discussion of their general import. The requirement imposing premium rates upon any employment in excess of what Congress has decided is appropriate for a governmental employee's workweek, for example, appears likely to have the effect of coercing the States to structure work periods in some employment areas, such as police and fire protection, in a manner substantially different from practices which have long been commonly accepted among local governments of this Nation. . . .

Our examination of the effect of the 1974 amendments, as sought to be extended to the States, and their political subdivisions, satisfies us that both the minimum wage and the maximum hour provisions will impermissibly interfere with the integral governmental functions of these bodies. . . . If Congress may withdraw from the States the authority to make those fundamental employment decisions upon which their systems for performance of these functions must rest, we think there would be little left of the States' "separate and independent existence." . . . Congress has attempted to exer-

cise its Commerce Clause authority to prescribe minimum wages and maximum hours to be paid by the States in their capacities as sovereign governments. In so doing, Congress has sought to wield its power in a fashion that would impair the States' "ability to function effectively within a federal system." . . .

MR. JUSTICE BRENNAN, with whom MR. JUSTICE WHITE and MR. JUSTICE MARSHALL join, dissenting.

The Court concedes, as of course it must, that Congress enacted the 1974 amendments pursuant to its exclusive power under Art. I, § 8, cl. 3, of the Constitution "To regulate Commerce . . . among the several States." It must therefore be surprising that my Brethren should choose this Bicentennial year of our independence to repudiate principles governing judicial interpretation of our Constitution settled since the time of Chief Justice John Marshall, discarding his postulate that the Constitution contemplates that restraints upon exercise by Congress of its plenary commerce power lie in the political process and not in the judicial process. For 152 years ago Chief Justice Marshall enunciated that principle to which, until today, his successors on this Court have been faithful.

[T]he power over commerce . . . is vested in Congress as absolutely as it would be in a single government, having in its constitution the same restrictions on the exercise of the power as are found in the constitution of the United States. *The wisdom and the discretion of Congress, their identity with the people, and the influence which their constituents possess at elections, are . . . the sole restraints on which they have relied, to secure them from its abuse. They are the restraints on which the people must often rely solely, in all representative governments. . . .*

There is no restraint based on state sovereignty requiring or permitting judicial enforcement anywhere expressed in the Constitution; our decisions over the last century and a half have explicitly rejected the existence of any such restraint on the commerce power.

We said in *United States* v. *California,* 297

U.S. 175, . . . that "[t]he sovereign power of the states is necessarily diminished to the extent of the grants of power to the federal government in the Constitution. . . . [T]he power of the state is subordinate to the constitutional exercise of the granted federal power." . . .

My Brethren thus have today manufactured an abstraction without substance, founded neither in the words of the Constitution nor on precedent. An abstraction having such profoundly pernicious consequences is not made less so by characterizing the 1974 amendments as legislation directed against the "States qua States." . . .

Clearly, therefore, my Brethren are also repudiating the long line of our precedents holding that a judicial finding that Congress has not unreasonably regulated a subject matter of "commerce" brings to an end the judicial role. "Let the end be legitimate, let it be within the scope of the constitution, and all means which are appropriate, which are plainly adapted to that end, which are not prohibited, but consist with the letter and spirit of the constitution, are constitutional." *McCulloch* v. *Maryland*, . . .

The reliance of my Brethren upon the Tenth Amendment as "an express declaration of [a state sovereignty] limitation," . . . not only suggests that they overrule governing decisions of this Court that address this question but must astound scholars of the Constitution. . . .

My Brethren do not successfully obscure today's patent usurpation of the role reserved for the political process by their purported discovery in the Constitution of a restraint derived from sovereignty of the States on Congress' exercise of the commerce power. . . .

Today's repudiation of this unbroken line of precedents that firmly reject my Brethren's ill-conceived abstraction can only be regarded as a transparent cover for invalidating a congressional judgment with which they disagree. The only analysis even remotely resembling that adopted today is found in a line of opinions dealing with the Commerce Clause and the Tenth Amendment that ultimately provoked a constitutional crisis for the Court in the 1930's. . . . We tend to forget that the Court invalidated legislation during the Great Depression, not solely under the Due Process Clause, but also and primarily under the Commerce Clause and the Tenth Amendment. It may have been the eventual abandonment of that overly restrictive construction of the commerce power that spelled defeat for the Court-packing plan, and preserved the integrity of this institution. . . . My Brethren today are transparently trying to cut back on that recognition of the scope of the commerce power. My Brethren's approach to this case is not far different from the dissenting opinions in the cases that averted the crisis. . . .

My Brethren do more than turn aside long-standing constitutional jurisprudence that emphatically rejects today's conclusion. More alarming is the startling restructuring of our federal system, and the role they create therein for the federal judiciary. This Court is simply not at liberty to erect a mirror of its own conception of a desirable governmental structure. If the 1974 amendments have any "vice," . . . my Brother Stevens is surely right that it represents "merely . . . a policy issue which has been firmly resolved by the branches of government having power to decide such questions." . . . It bears repeating "that effective restraints on . . . exercise [of the Commerce power] must proceed from political rather than from judicial processes." . . .

It is unacceptable that the judicial process should be thought superior to the political process in this area. Under the Constitution the judiciary has no role to play beyond finding that Congress has not made an unreasonable legislative judgment respecting what is "commerce." My Brother Blackmun suggests that controlling judicial supervision of the relationship between the States and our National Government by use of a balancing approach diminishes the ominous implications of today's decision. Such an approach, however, is a thinly veiled rationalization for judicial supervision of a policy judgment that our system of government reserves to Congress.

Judicial restraint in this area merely recognizes that the political branches of our

Government are structured to protect the interests of the States, as well as the Nation as a whole, and that the States are fully able to protect their own interests in the premises. Congress is constituted of representatives in both Senate and House elected from the States. . . .

Decisions upon the extent of federal intervention under the Commerce Clause into the affairs of the States are in that sense decisions of the States themselves. Judicial redistribution of powers granted the National Government by the terms of the Constitution violates the fundamental tenet of our federalism that the extent of federal intervention into the State's affairs in the exercise of delegated powers shall be determined by the States' exercise of political power through their representatives in Congress. . . .

There is no reason whatever to suppose that in enacting the 1974 amendments Congress, even if it might extensively obliterate state sovereignty by fully exercising its plenary power respecting commerce, had any purpose to do so. Surely the presumption must be to the contrary. Any realistic assessment of our federal political system, dominated as it is by representatives of the people *elected from the States,* yields the conclusion that it is highly unlikely that those representatives will ever be motivated to disregard totally the concerns of these States. . . .

MR. JUSTICE STEVENS, dissenting. . . .

FIVE

Commerce Power
and State Power

Removal of the obstructions on commercial relations imposed by the "sovereign" states was a moving cause of the Philadelphia Convention. For protection against these burdens and restrictions, Madison, as a member of the Continental Congress, had advocated general authority over commerce. Later on he was conspicuous among those who set in motion the sequence of events leading to the successful meeting at Philadelphia. There seems to be no doubt that the commerce clause was inserted in the Constitution primarily to prevent the states from interfering with the freedom of commercial intercourse. Yet all the plans offered by the Convention apparently envisioned a positive power in the national government to regulate commerce, and subsequent developments converted this clause into a most important source of national authority. Was this the intention of the men who framed the Constitution? The record of the Convention of 1787 affords no conclusive answer.

On September 15, 1787, Madison, commenting on the question whether, under Article I, Section 10, a tonnage tax could be levied by the states for purposes of clearing and dredging harbors, said: "It depends on the extent of the commerce power. These terms—to regulate commerce—are vague but seem to exclude this power of the states. He [Madison] was more and more convinced that the regulation of commerce was in its nature indivisible and ought to be wholly under one authority." Immediately following this statement, Sherman of Connecticut observed "The Power of the United States to regulate trade, being Supreme, can control interferences of the State regulations where such interferences happen; so that there is no danger to be apprehended from a concurrent jurisdiction."

"Had the issue been clearly posed and unequivocally settled," Albert S. Abel has commented, "it must perhaps have eliminated decades of judicial groping and guessing; on the other hand it might have broken up the convention."

Certain inferences about the nature and scope of the commerce power may be drawn from changes the Convention made in the wording of the commerce clause itself. In the Pinckney Plan the word ''exclusive'' was used before ''power.'' Draft VII of the Committee of Detail used ''exclusive,'' but in Draft IX it was deleted and reported out in its present form. No evidence has been presented concerning the significance of this deletion. ''Exclusive'' is used as a description of congressional power only in Clause 17 (laws for the District of Columbia). Even the power of Congress to declare war is not stated to be ''exclusive,'' but Article I, Section 10 explicitly limits state action.

One becomes aware of a noticeable lack of specific restraints, such as those spelled out in Article I, Section 10. The only restriction of a commercial nature forbids duty on imports (or exports), except for the amount necessary to meet inspection cost. This seems to suggest freedom of the states to pass other laws regulating commerce.

Because of the partisan motives of the speakers, contemporary opinion on the meaning of the clause is no sure guide. Those opposed to the new Constitution stressed its centralizing tendencies in lurid colors; supporters, on the other hand, minimized the significance of the commerce power. James McHenry of the Maryland delegation said: ''We almost shuddered at the fate of commerce of Maryland should we be unable to make any change in this extraordinary power.'' In the Virginia ratifying convention, Edmund Randolph agreed that the broad power over commerce was a sine qua non of the union, and yet he favored a two-thirds vote by Congress for national commerce acts. Richard Henry Lee, also of Virginia, reported a widespread fear that the clause would be used to discriminate against Southern states by the establishment of Northern monopolies.

The writers of that skillful campaign document *The Federalist* employed their usual tactics. They made clear the dangers of not giving a broad power over commerce to the general government, but blurred the precise limits of national power. In No. 7 Hamilton states: ''The competitions of commerce would be another fruitful source of contention. . . . Each state or separate confederacy would pursue a system of commercial policy peculiar to itself. . . . The infraction of these [state] regulations on one side, the efforts to prevent and repel them on the other, would naturally lead to outrages, and these to reprisals and war.'' In No. 42 Madison glosses over the nature of the commerce power by discussing it chiefly as a supplement to the power over foreign commerce, and by stressing the unfairness of permitting coastal states to levy a toll on states in the interior. In No. 45 Madison again hints that the commerce power will be exercised chiefly on foreign commerce.

Many years later, in 1829, after the ''Father of the Constitution'' had become a proponent of states' rights, he wrote J. C. Cabell that the power to regulate commerce was designed to prevent abuses by the states rather than for positive purposes of the national government: ''I always foresaw,'' Madison wrote, ''that difficulties might be started in relation to this power which could not be fully explained without recurring to views of it, which, however just, might give birth to specious though unsound objections. Being in the same terms with the power over foreign commerce, the same extent, if taken literally, would belong to it. Yet it is very certain that it grew out of the abuse of the power of the importing state in taxing the non-importing, and was intended as a negative and preventive provision against injustice among the States themselves, rather than as a power to be used for the positive purposes of the General Government, in which alone, however, the remedial power could be lodged.'' For those opposed to the use of the commerce power as a basis for positive national regulation, Madison's words have done yeoman service.

THE MARSHALL DOCTRINE

The intriguing question, What does the commerce clause mean? was first presented to the Court in 1824. *Gibbons* v. *Ogden* involved the unpopular New York "steamboat monopoly." Chancellor Kent, in upholding the monopoly, maintained that Congress did not have any direct jurisdiction over internal commerce or waters. Webster, arguing for Gibbons on appeal to the Supreme Court, asserted that Congress alone could regulate "high branches" of commerce. Counsel for the monopoly claimed that a concurrent power existed whenever such a power was not clearly denied by the Constitution. Webster's prophetic construction of commerce as comprehending "almost all the business and intercourse of life" was countered by the definition of commerce as "the transportation and sale of commodities." Both sides agreed that if an actual collision of state and national power occurred the latter must prevail, but the spokesman for the monopoly held that state power gave way only to the extent needed to give effect to the federal law. Accordingly navigation on state waters remained under state control.

Marshall could have solved the case simply by finding that both state and nation had acted within their powers, but since the state law conflicted with the federal licensing act it must give way. He chose instead to examine the nature of the commerce power before finding the existence of a conflict. Commerce was more than traffic; "it is intercourse," and comprehended navigation. He reiterated the point that commerce "among" the states cannot stop at state lines but "may be introduced into the interior." The power to regulate was "complete in itself, may be exercised to its utmost extent, and acknowledges *no limitations,* other than are prescribed in the Constitution." Though the states retained authority to enact inspection, pilotage, and health laws, even here Congress could enter the field if it chose.

In a separate opinion, Justice Johnson went beyond Marshall. Even in the absence of the licensing act, the state monopoly must give way. Johnson's forthright remarks on the effect of the coasting license stand in bold contrast to those of Marshall. The national commerce power, Johnson contended, embraces all the power enjoyed by the states before the Constitution. It is a grant of the whole power carrying the whole subject exclusively into the hands of the national government.

With the exception of monopolists and southern slave-owner spokesmen who feared the consequence of a broad definition of national power over commerce, public opinion welcomed the rebuke given holders of special privilege. Following the decision, the number of steamboats plying in and out of New York harbor increased in one year from six to 43.

Three years later, in *Brown* v. *Maryland* (12 Wheat. 419: 1827) the Court held that national power over foreign commerce excluded state regulation in the form of licensing and taxing importers. Marshall pointed out that state actions of this nature violated both the prohibition of state taxes on imports (Art. I, Sec. 10) and the limitations on state power implicit in the commerce clause. In his effort to draw a line between commerce that could be regulated by the states and commerce that could not, he formulated the "original package" doctrine, adding the dictum, "we suppose the principles laid down in this case to apply equally to importations from a sister state." Two generations later, in *Brown* v. *Houston* the Court, refusing to follow Marshall, established another rule for drawing the line between national control over commerce "among the states" and the state taxing power. Whenever an article shipped from another state reaches its final destination or is interrupted for business purposes, it loses its national immunity from state taxation—"in the absence of Congressional action."

Though Marshall described the subject matter of commerce and national power to regulate it in the most sweeping terms, he did not overlook the tremendous power reserved to the states. As to the "inspection laws," he said in *Gibbons* v. *Ogden:* "They form a portion of that immense mass of legislation which embraces everything within the territory of the State not surrendered to the general government; all which can be most advantageously exercised by the States themselves. Inspection laws, quarantine laws, health laws of every description, as well as laws for regulating the internal commerce of the State, and those which respect turnpike-roads, ferries, etc. are component parts of this mass." Commerce wholly within a state, which did not affect more than one state, was not within national authority, unless and until Congress acted positively.

"It has been observed," Marshall commented in *Brown* v. *Maryland* "that the powers remaining with the States may be so exercised as to come in conflict with those vested in Congress. When this happens, that which is not supreme must yield to that which is supreme. . . . The taxing power of the States . . . cannot interfere with any regulation of commerce." Marshall reiterated the point established in the Gibbons case, that wherever a conflict exists between national and state authority, the state must yield. But did the Constitution, in conferring upon Congress the power to regulate commerce, deny to the states all concurrent authority?

Marshall's view on this question comes out most clearly in *Willson* v. *Black Bird Creek Marsh Co.* (2 Pet. 245: 1829). The Delaware legislature had authorized the Black Bird Creek Marsh Company to build a dam across the creek for the purpose of redeeming marshland. Willson, who owned a sloop licensed under national authority, broke through the dam and continued to navigate the creek. The company sued for trespass. Upholding the Delaware Act, Marshall ruled:

> The act of assembly by which the plaintiffs were authorized to construct their dam, shows plainly that this is *one of those many creeks,* passing through a deep, level marsh, adjoining the Delaware, up which the tide flows for some distance. The value of the property on its banks must be enhanced by excluding the water from the marsh, and the *health of the inhabitants probably improved.* Measures calculated to produce these objects, provided they do not come into collision with the powers of the general government, are undoubtedly within those which are reserved to the states. . . .
>
> The counsel for the plaintiffs in error insist that it comes in conflict with the power of the United States "to regulate commerce . . . among the several states." If Congress had passed any act which bore upon the case; any act in execution of the power to regulate commerce, the object of which was to control state legislation over *those small navigable creeks* into which the tide flows, and *which abound throughout the lower country of the middle and southern states,* we should feel not much difficulty in saying that a state law coming in confict with such act would be void. But Congress has passed no such act. . . .
>
> We do not think, that the act empowering the Black Bird Creek Marsh company to place a dam across the creek, can, *under all the circumstances of the case,* be considered as repugnant to the power to regulate commerce in its dormant state, or as being in conflict with any law passed on the subject. [Italics are the authors'.]

Marshall is at pains to show the bearing of the dam on land values and the health of the community. As a health measure, enacted under the police power, the act was valid until it collided with national authority. One notes also that he passes over the fact that the sloop in question was licensed under an act of Congress—the vital consideration in the Gibbons case.

THE DOCTRINE OF THE TANEY COURT

During Taney's tenure as Chief Justice (1836–1864) the Court squarely faced the question Marshall had pointedly sidestepped in *Gibbons* v. *Ogden:* May the states regulate commerce in the absence of federal regulation? The importance of the answer cannot be overstressed. Congress was not likely to react positively during this period. Thus the invalidation of state laws regulating commerce meant that commerce was likely to be free from all regulation.

In *New York* v. *Miln* (11 Pet. 102: 1837), the Taney Court, in a confused set of opinions, upheld as a police-power regulation a state act requiring the ship's master on incoming vessels to furnish information concerning his passengers. Justice Thompson, originally assigned the task of writing the opinion, treated the state act as a police measure and permissible—in the absence of national action. Because four members of the Court balked at Thompson's analysis, Justice Barbour wrote an opinion holding the state law valid purely as a police measure. In his opinion, however, Barbour added some expressions about the commerce power with which other members did not agree, but since it was delivered on the last day of the term, they could do nothing to show their displeasure. Barbour's gratuitous remarks on commerce, with which Taney later indicated agreement, stated in effect that persons were not "subjects of commerce," a pronouncement highly pleasing to the slave states.

In 1847, the even more confused opinions in the License Cases (5 How. 504) revealed how difficult it was for the Court to settle on any one view of commerce power. Taney favored state regulation of the liquor trade. In one case, upholding a state act, he adopted the "original package" doctrine. In another he said that a state could regulate articles in original packages in the absence of national regulation, thus countering Marshall's dictum in *Brown* v. *Maryland,* a case in which Taney had been counsel for the state. Some members of the Court reasoned in terms of "police power"; others argued that only intrastate commerce was involved.

In the Passenger Cases (7 How. 283: 1849), taxes on passengers on incoming vessels were challenged. These cases were argued on three different occasions over a four-year period. Webster, who as counsel opposed the state acts, was convinced of the accuracy of his position, but feared the absence of a "strong and leading mind" on the Court. Van Buren, for the states, stressed the popular support for the state acts and state sovereignty. Webster won a 5-to-4 decision. Each of the five Justices stated his views in such a way, however, that the reporter could enter as a headnote only that the act was invalid. Three of the four dissenters wrote separate opinions. Taney held that since states could expel undesirable immigrants, they could reject them in the first place, and cited *New York* v. *Miln* to the effect that persons were not "subjects of commerce." The majority split—two Justices ruling congressional power over foreign commerce to be exclusive, three holding that this was unnecessary for the decision since the state act conflicted with existing national legislation. The one happy note in this confusion was that the judges did not follow sectional or party lines. Nevertheless, disappointment and frustration greeted the decision.

The law was in this muddle when President Fillmore, in 1851, appointed Benjamin R. Curtis to the Court. Curtis, a brilliant Massachusetts lawyer, was destined to be the mediator between the two tenuous coalitions, and the effective medium through whom a compromise was reached. In the famous case of *Cooley* v. *Board of Port Wardens* a state pilotage fee was declared valid against the charge that it conflicted with the national commerce power. Complicating the situation was a congressional act of 1789 stating that pilots should be regulated in conformity ''with such laws as the states may hereafter enact . . . until further legislative provision shall be made by Congress.'' Curtis, combining elements of the ''exclusive'' and ''concurrent'' doctrines, fashioned a new formula. His middle ground was this: Subjects national in scope admit only of uniform regulation; these require congressional legislation, and in the absense of such legislation the states cannot act. As to subjects of a local character, not requiring uniform legislation, the states may legislate (according to Curtis) until Congress, by acting on the same subject, displaces the state law. Where national and state laws are in conflict, the federal rule prevails. Though Taney did not agree with Curtis's analysis, he silently joined in the opinion.

The opinions delivered under the leadership of Marshall and Taney contained ammunition for those advocating or opposing commercial regulation by either state or nation. For future courts, however, substantial difficulties existed, despite the ''balanced'' formula fashioned in the *Cooley* case. What was a subject matter requiring a national (or uniform) regulation? When was a state law affecting commerce in conflict with national legislation? The awkward question of the extent of state power to tax one or more aspects of interstate commerce was left to the future. The answers the Court might give had more than logical or semantic importance because, with the national government incapable or unwilling to regulate, a theory of broad national power, combined with a narrow definition of what required local regulation, meant that commerce would be free of all regulation.

COMMERCE POWER AND STATE ACTION: 1865–1890

Under the Cooley doctrine, in the absence of congressional legislation, the Court's first duty was to determine the nature of the subject matter regulated. If it required national regulation, then state action was foreclosed. If the subject matter permitted state or local regulation, two questions remained: Did the state law discriminate against interstate commerce, and in favor of local commerce? Did the state act, although nondiscriminatory, place an unreasonable burden on interstate commerce? Socioeconomic fact and theory, flavored by judicial bias, entered inevitably into the attempt to answer these questions. Until 1937, as we shall see, theories of federalism and theories of laissez-faire marched hand in hand.

A variety of aims motivate state governments in passing laws affecting interstate commerce. Invocation of the ''police power,'' to protect the public health, safety, morals, and general welfare, frequently has the effect of prescribing a rule affecting one or more aspects of commerce. Legislation requiring trains to have certain lights, to sound horns, and to proceed at limited speeds has this effect, as does legislation forbidding the sale of harmful food or drink.

Another state purpose is to create, protect, and foster intrastate commerce, and to construct and improve roads, canals, and streams. In the consideration of all such measures, the line between intra- and interstate activities is hard to draw. A third objective is to tax commercial activities within the state in order to raise revenue and, in many instances, to compensate the state for services rendered those using its commercial facilities. A tax on gasoline, for example, provides revenue for road repairs.

In the post-Civil War period, especially, state legislatures were under pressure to solve the problems arising from a burgeoning industrialism. It seemed not unlikely, at least prior to 1880, that regulation, if it were to come at all, had to be state regulation. Such legislation had first to run the gauntlet of challenge on the ground of invalidity under state constitutions. Then it was possible for its opponents to invoke the Constitution of the United States, especially the commerce clause, and later the due process clause of the Fourteenth Amendment, as weapons against the state action. Since due process in the federal courts before 1890 had only procedural significance, the commerce clause was the chief weapon to frustrate state efforts to regulate the growing world of business and commerce.

In the 1869 case of *Paul* v. *Virginia* (8 Wall. 168) the Court upheld a state act requiring all insurance companies to obtain a license before issuing policies within the state. State power was sustained against the contention that insurance is essentially an interstate business, and in the absence of national legislation could not be regulated by the states. Justice Field, speaking for a unanimous court, met this argument by declaring that insurance transactions are local in character because, technically considered, the delivery of the contract took place in Virginia. That the Justices did not take a narrow view of national power when Congress chose to act was shown by the decision holding a federal licensing act applicable to a steamboat engaged in carrying goods and passengers on a navigable river between two points wholly within a state (*The Daniel Ball,* 10 Wall. 557: 1871). The river was a "highway of commerce," Justice Field said, and the federal licensing act was an appropriate means of insuring the safety of navigation. Even though the steamer did not itself travel in interstate commerce, it was an "instrument" by which such commerce was carried on, since some of the persons and goods continued across state lines. A Missouri statute that licensed and taxed peddlers of goods not grown or produced in Missouri was invalidated in 1876 (*Welton* v. *Missouri,* 91 U.S. 275). Here the Court emphasized discrimination against interstate commerce.

After 1870, state legislation regulating the railroads focused judicial attention on the limits of state power in the absence of congressional action. In *Munn* v. *Illinois* and the other "Granger" cases (94 U.S. 77, 155, 179, 180, 187: 1877) the Court upheld an Illinois regulation of elevator and railroad rates. Although "instruments" of interstate commerce were the subject of the legislation and "may become connected with interstate commerce," they were not necessarily so; until Congress acted, the states could control the rates, even though this regulation had an indirect effect on interstate commerce. Shortly after this decision the Court held that (in the absence of congressional legislation) the states were free to tax goods held within a state even if the goods were subjects of interstate commerce (*Brown* v. *Houston*). By 1886, however, the Court shifted ground. The facts in the historic Wabash case (*Wabash, St. Louis & Pacific Ry. Co.* v. *Illinois,* 118 U.S. 557: 1886) showed that the railroad charged 15 cents per pound from Peoria, Illinois, and 25 cents per pound from Gilman, Illinois, on shipments of similar chattels to New York City. The state court had allowed the application of the state law forbidding price discrimination by measuring the discrimination on the intrastate portion of the journey, but the Supreme Court held that since these were single trips such measurement was invalid. "This is commerce of national character," Justice Miller said, "and national regulation is required."

Bradley, Waite, and Gray objected, stating that in the absence of congressional action the states should be allowed to act so long as the effect on interstate commerce was indirect. It is noteworthy that between 1877 and 1886 the Court set aside 14 state commercial regulations; in only two instances was national legislation involved.

While state railroad rate regulation became virtually meaningless with the passage of the Interstate Commerce Act in 1887, state police-power legislation affecting transportation continued unabated. In 1888 (*Smith* v. *Alabama*, 124 U.S. 465) a state law requiring a license for locomotive drivers was accepted as a police regulation, despite its effect on interstate commerce. In 1890 a state law requiring railroads carrying passengers in the state to provide equal but separate facilities for Negroes was upheld (*Louisville Railway* v. *Mississippi*, 133 U.S.587).

STATE LEGISLATION AND THE COMMERCE POWER:
1890–1981

After 1890, two dominant themes pervade the application of the commerce clause: (1) use of the commerce power by Congress to accomplish broad social and economic purposes; (2) continuation and further development of the commerce clause as a restriction on state action affecting interstate commerce.

At the outset, cases on the second subject reveal no clear pattern. In *Leisy* v. *Hardin* (135 U.S. 100: 1890) the Taney Court's ruling in the License Cases was rejected on the ground that beer was a genuine article of commerce, the sale of which could be prohibited only by congressional action. Yet four years later in *Plumley* v. *Massachusetts* the Court held that a Massachusetts law prohibiting the sale of colored oleo only "incidentally affected" trade between states and was, therefore, a legitimate police measure to prevent the defrauding of purchasers. Increasingly, the Court, after ascertaining that the subject matter was not one requiring national regulation, examined the state law to see whether it discriminated against or burdened interstate commerce. Whether the statute challenged was labeled a police regulation, a tax law, or an attempt to control intrastate commerce is largely irrelevant, although the language of the decisions is frequently confused on this point.

The Court has been rather generous in upholding state acts regulating motor transportation, such as the licensing of vehicles using state roads (*Buck* v. *Kuykendall*, 267 U.S. 307: 1925). In the important 1938 case of *South Carolina* v. *Barnwell* (303 U.S. 177) a statute prohibiting trucks with loads over 20,000 pounds and widths exceeding 90 inches from using state roads was upheld. Justice Stone thought that in the absence of congressional legislation it was a reasonable measure to protect roads built and maintained by the state, especially since no discrimination or attempt to burden interstate commerce had been shown. Similarly state taxes ostensibly designed to force interstate traffic to bear its share of the cost of maintaining and policing highways were upheld (in 11 of 16 cases, 1915–1950) on the theory that they neither discriminated against interstate vehicles nor imposed unreasonable burdens on interstate commerce. However, where the tax is viewed as one on the privilege of doing business within the state (*Spector Motor Service* v. *O'Connor*, 340 U.S. 602: 1951), or where the tax formula bears no resemblance to highway use (*McCarroll* v. *Dixie Greyhound Lines*, 309 U.S. 176: 1940), state legislation has been invalidated.

Problems of a different nature have been presented by state police regulations, such as that challenged successfully in *Di Santo* v. *Pennsylvania* (273 U.S. 34: 1927), where the state tried to license sellers of steamship tickets. The Di Santo decision itself was overturned in *California* v. *Thompson* (313 U.S. 109: 1941), which involved a law requiring licenses for those selling interstate bus tickets. "In the absence of pertinent congressional legislation there is constitutional power in the states to regulate interstate commerce by motor vehicles whenever it affects the safety of the public or the safety and convenient use of the highways, provided only that the regulation does not in any other respect unnecessarily obstruct interstate commerce."

Most often today in such situations the Justices are inclined toward a balancing-of-interests approach. This is the method reflected in Justice Stone's majority opinion in *Southern Pacific* v. *Arizona* (the train limit case). In recent truck-length cases, the Court has ruled that state bans on 65-foot double trailers, especially where neighboring states permit them on the highways, violate the commerce clause (*Raymond Motor Transportation, Inc.* v. *Rice*, 434 U.S. 429: 1978; *Kassel* v. *Consolidated Freightways Corp.*, 49 LW 4328: 1981). As Justice Powell maintained in *Kassel*, "[T]he incantation of a purpose to promote the public health or safety does not insulate a state law from Commerce Clause attack. Regulations designed for that salutary purpose nevertheless may further the purpose so marginally, and interfere with commerce so substantially, as to be invalid. . . ." The judicial task in these cases is at heart both empirical and political—a weighing of one benefit against another.

That should not be, Brennan responded. For himself and for Justice Marshall, Brennan agreed that the Iowa regulation in question in *Kassel* offended the commerce clause, but "with all respect, my Brothers ask and answer the wrong question."

> For me, analysis of Commerce Clause challenges to state regulations must take into account three principles: (1) The courts are not empowered to second-guess the empirical judgments of lawmakers concerning the utility of legislation. (2) The burdens imposed on commerce must be balanced against the local benefits actually sought to be achieved by the State's lawmakers, and not against those suggested after the fact by counsel. (3) Protectionist legislation is unconstitutional under the Commerce Clause, even if the burdens and benefits are related to safety rather than economics.

Parker v. *Brown* is one of the most extreme instances of permissible state regulation. It should be read in conjunction with *Hood* v. *Dumond*. Both cases involved attempts by states to regulate local agricultural markets, yet the Court gave opposite responses under the commerce clause. The ambivalence which these decisions created is evidence that the line dividing permissible regulation from impermissible is by no means distinct.

Yet, articulation of worthy purposes may run counter to the need for national standardization. The Court, moreover, remains especially sensitive to efforts by states and localities to foster "protectionism," or "Balkanization," as Justice Brennan's concurrence in *Kassel* indicates. The same concern is reflected in the majority and dissenting opinions in *Reeves, Inc.* v. *Stake*, where the Justices examined the sales policies of a state-owned cement plant.

State and local regulations to protect the environment or to improve the quality of life may meet similar challenges under the commerce clause. In light of President Reagan's drive for a "revitalized federalism," such cases may become more frequent. In *City of Burbank* v. *Lockheed Air Terminal* (411 U.S. 624: 1973), the Court struck down an ordinance banning takeoffs and landings by certain jet aircraft at an airport during late-night hours. While finding no express pre-emption by national statutes, Justice Douglas for the Court found an implied one. ''If we were to uphold the Burbank ordinance and a significant number of municipalities followed suit, it is obvious that fractionalized control of the timing of takeoffs and landings would severely limit the flexibility of the FAA in controlling air traffic flow. The difficulties of scheduling flights to avoid congestion and the concomitant decrease in safety would be compounded.''

More recently, Justice Stewart spoke for a seven-member majority in overturning a New Jersey statute which prohibited the importation of most ''solid or liquid waste which originated or was collected outside the territorial limits of the State'' (*City of Philadelphia* v. *New Jersey*, 437 U.S. 617: 1978). The obvious intent of the law was to prevent the state from becoming a dumping ground for its more populous neighbors of New York and Pennsylvania. ''The New Jersey law blocks the importation of waste in an . . . effort to saddle those outside the State with the entire burden of slowing the flow of refuse into New Jersey's remaining landfill sites. That legislative effort is clearly impermissible under the Commerce Clause. . . .'' Referring to decisions which had upheld state quarantine laws against similar attacks, Chief Justice Burger joined Justice Rehnquist in asking in dissent ''why a State may ban the importation of items whose movement risks contagion, but cannot ban the importation of items which, although they may be transported into the State without undue danger, will then simply pile up in an ever increasing danger to the public's health and safety. The Commerce Clause was not drawn with a view to having the validity of state laws turn on such pointless distinctions.''

In recent years, few commerce cases have stimulated greater controversy than *United States* v. *South-Eastern Underwriters* (322 U.S. 533: 1944). Here the Court, speaking through Justice Black, ruled that insurance is commerce, and thus supposedly overturned a 75-year-old precedent (*Paul* v. *Virginia*). In Black's view, the commerce clause does not of itself appropriate anything exclusively to the national government—except possibly the duty to see to it that state laws do not discriminate against interstate commerce. Black's opinion in the South-Eastern Underwriters case is the first since Marshall's day to give the commerce clause an all-embracing yet state-power-saving construction. The confusion throughout seems to have arisen from the Court's persistent tendency to consider state regulation ''affecting'' interstate commerce as though it involved power in the states to regulate such commerce. In Marshall's view, as in Black's, such regulating power as the states possess derives from their police power. Furthermore, state legislation enacted thereunder will prevail unless and until supplanted by national legislation. In a word, the states possess, as Marshall said, that ''immense mass'' of power designated ''police''; Congress has the power to regulate commerce. When the two conflict, that which is ''supreme'' must prevail over that which is not supreme. The question turns, therefore, on whether there is a conflict, or whether state action ''burdens'' interstate commerce.

In a different sphere, the Court has also employed the commerce clause as a weapon against racial discrimination. Drawing on Justice Stone's ''balancing-of-interests'' test from the Arizona Train Limit case of 1945, Justice Reed for the majority wrote that a state ''Jim Crow'' law could not be enforced against bus passengers in interstate commerce (*Morgan* v. *Virginia*, 328 U.S. 373: 1946). Following the reasoning of the Morgan case, the Court in 1960 ordered desegregation of bus station terminals and restaurants, holding that segregation was in violation of the Interstate Commerce Act and unduly burdened interstate commerce (*Boynton* v. *Virginia*, 364 U.S. 454: 1960). As to the expanding use of the commerce clause to enforce desegregation, the Court has declared, ''We have settled beyond question that no state may require racial segregation of interstate or intrastate transportation facilities. . . . The question is no longer open; it is foreclosed as a litigable issue'' (*Bailey* v. *Patterson,* 369 U.S. 31: 1962).

Constitutional considerations have also intruded on the "national pastime." In 1922 professional baseball, despite the "reserve clause" by which one team gains exclusive rights to a player's services, was held immune from the Sherman Act on the ground that organized baseball is not interstate commerce (*Federal Baseball Club of Baltimore* v. *National League,* 259 U.S. 200). Many thought that the interstate and commercial character of professional baseball had become more apparent with time, and that the *South-Eastern Underwriters* decision portended a shift of judicial opinion. But in *Toolson* v. *New York Yankees* (346 U.S. 356: 1953), the Court adhered to the legal fiction that baseball is not interstate commerce, a position it refused to take in cases involving other professional sports. Football (*Radovich* v. *National Football League,* 352 U.S. 445: 1957) and boxing (*United States* v. *International Boxing Club,* 348 U.S. 236: 1955) were held to be activities in interstate commerce and hence subject to the antitrust laws. *Flood* v. *Kuhn* (407 U.S. 258: 1972) found five Justices willing to place professional baseball within interstate commerce but nonetheless unwilling to include the sport within the scope of federal antitrust laws. "The Court," Justice Blackmun argued, "has concluded that Congress as yet has had no intention to subject baseball's reserve system to the reach of the antitrust statutes. This, obviously, has been deemed to be something other than mere congressional silence and passivity.. . . If there is any inconsistency or illogic in all this, it is an inconsistency and illogic of long standing that is to be remedied by the Congress and not by this Court.''

From this survey certain conclusions can be drawn. First, the rule in the Cooley case has not been used to frustrate state legislation simply because one might argue that a national rule would be more efficient or desirable. Second, judicial generosity toward state action has in fact permitted the erection of certain trade barriers (motor carrier limitations, taxes, inspection laws, safety laws). Third, Congress for many reasons has not chosen to regulate all subjects that lie within the reach of its commerce power. Fourth, the permissible limits of the state taxing power are not clearly defined, although, in general, nondiscriminatory and apportioned taxes have a good chance of being upheld.

The commonly held view that the growth of the national commerce power has completely displaced state power is far from true. To be sure, the Supreme Court has undertaken the role of guardian of the national market against obviously discriminatory and parochial efforts to re-erect the type of trade barriers that marked the preconstitutional era. But the Court has increasingly recognized the danger of leaving large areas of commercial activity free from all regulation, which would be the inescapable result if Congress cannot or will not act and the states are forbidden to act.

SELECTED READINGS

BENSON, PAUL R., JR., *The Supreme Court and the Commerce Clause, 1937–1970.* Cambridge, Mass.: Dunellen, 1970.

CORWIN, EDWARD S., *The Commerce Power Versus States Rights.* Princeton: Princeton University Press, 1936.

———, "The Schechter Case—Landmark or What?," 13 *New York University Law Quarterly Review* 151 (1936).

DOWLING, NOEL T., Interstate Commerce and the State Power," 27 *Virginia Law Review* 1 (1940).

———, "Interstate Commerce and State Power," revised version, 47 *Columbia Law Review* 547 (1947).

FRANKFURTER, FELIX, *The Commerce Clause under Marshall, Taney and Waite.* Chapel Hill: University of North Carolina Press, 1937.

POWELL, THOMAS REED, "Commerce, Pensions, and Codes," 49 *Harvard Law Review* 1, 193 (Nov., Dec. 1935).

STERN, ROBERT L., "That Commerce Which Concerns More States Than One," 47 *Harvard Law Review* 1375 (1934).

A steamboat monopoly granted by the state of New York gave rise to the first important case involving the commerce clause. Gibbons, whose vessels were licensed under a 1793 federal act, attempted to navigate in New York State waters, disregarding an exclusive right held in Ogden, the assignee of the original right. The injunction that issued against Gibbons was sustained by the highest state court. Gibbons appealed.

MARSHALL, CH. J., delivered the opinion of the court. . . .

As preliminary to the very able discussions of the constitution, which we have heard from the bar, and as having some influence on its construction, reference has been made to the political situation of these states, anterior to its formation. It has been said, that they were sovereign, were completely independent, and were connected with each other only by a league. This is true. But when these allied sovereigns converted their league into a government, when they converted their congress of ambassadors, deputed to deliberate on their common concerns, and to recommend measures of general utility, into a legislature, empowered to enact laws on the most interesting subjects, the whole character in which the states appear, underwent a change, the extent of which must be determined by a fair consideration of the instrument by which that change was effected.

This instrument contains an enumeration of powers expressly granted by the people to their government. It has been said, that these powers ought to be construed strictly. But why ought they to be so construed? Is there one sentence in the constitution which gives countenance to this rule? In the last of the enumerated powers, that which grants, expressly, the means for carrying all others into execution, congress is authorized "to make all laws which shall be necessary and proper" for the purpose. But this limitation on the means which may be used, is not extended to the powers which are conferred; nor is there one sentence in the constitution, which has been pointed out by the gentlemen of the bar, or which we have been able to discern, that prescribes this rule. We do not, therefore, think ourselves justified in adopting it. What do gentlemen mean, by a strict construction? If they contend only against that enlarged construction, which would extend words beyond their natural and obvious import, we might question the application of the term, but should not controvert the principle. If they contend for that narrow construction which, in support of some theory not to be found in the constitution, would deny to the government those powers which the words of the grant, as usually understood, import, and which are consistent with the general views and objects of the instrument—for that narrow construction, which would cripple the government, and render it unequal to the objects for which it is declared to be instituted, and to which the powers given, as fairly understood, render it competent—then we cannot perceive the propriety of this strict construction, nor adopt it as the rule by which the constitution is to be expounded. As men whose intentions require no concealment, generally employ the words which most directly and aptly express the ideas they intend to convey, the enlightened patriots who framed our constitution, and the people who adopted it, must be understood to have employed words in their natural sense, and to have intended what they have said. If, from the imperfection of human language, there should be serious doubts respecting the extent of any given power, it is a well settled rule, that the objects for which it was given, especially, when those objects are expressed in the instrument itself, should have great influence in the construction. . . . We know of no rule for construing the extent of such powers, other than is given by the language of the instrument which confers them, taken in connection with the purposes for which they were conferred.

The words are: "Congress shall have power to regulate commerce with foreign nations, and among the several states, and with the Indian tribes." The subject to be regulated is commerce; and our constitution being, as was aptly said at the bar, one of enumeration, and not of definition, to ascertain the extent of the power, it becomes necessary to settle the meaning of the word. The counsel for the appellee would limit it to traffic, to buying and selling, or the interchange of commodities, and do not admit that it comprehends navigation. This would restrict a general term, applicable to many objects, to one of its significations. Commerce, undoubtedly, is traffic, but it is something more—it is intercourse. It describes the commercial intercourse between nations, and parts of nations, in all its branches, and is regulated by prescribing rules for carrying on that intercourse. The mind can scarcely conceive a system for regulating commerce between nations which shall exclude all laws concerning navigation, which shall be silent on the admission of the vessels of the one nation into the ports of the other, and confined to prescribing rules for the conduct of individuals, in the actual employment of buying and selling or of barter. If commerce does not include navigation, the government of the Union has no direct power over that subject, and can make no law prescribing what shall constitute American vessels, or requiring that they shall be navigated by American seamen. Yet this power has been exercised from the commencement of the government, has been exercised with the consent of all, and has been understood by all to be a commercial regulation. All America understands, and has uniformly understood, the word "commerce," to comprehend navigation. It was so understood, and must have been so understood, when the constitution was framed. The power over commerce, including navigation, was one of the primary objects for which

the people of America adopted their government, and must have been contemplated in forming it. The convention must have used the word in that sense, because all have understood it in that sense; and the attempt to restrict it comes too late. If the opinion that "commerce," as the word is used in the constitution, comprehends navigation also, requires any additional confirmation, that additional confirmation is, we think, furnished by the words of the instrument itself. It is a rule of construction, acknowledged by all, that the exceptions from a power mark its extent: for it would be absurd, as well as useless, to except from a granted power, that which was not granted—that which the words of the grant could not comprehend. If, then, there are in the constitution plain exceptions from the power over navigation, plain inhibitions to the exercise of that power in a particular way, it is a proof that those who made these exceptions, and prescribed these inhibitions, understood the power to which they applied as being granted. The 9th section of the last article declares, that "no preference shall be given, by any regulation of commerce or revenue, to the ports of one state over those of another." This clause cannot be understood as applicable to those laws only which are passed for the purposes of revenue, because it is expressly applied to commercial regulations; and the most obvious preference which can be given to one port over another, in regulating commerce, relates to navigation. But the subsequent part of the sentence is still more explicit. It is, "nor shall vessels bound to or from one state, be obliged to enter, clear or pay duties in another." These words have a direct reference to navigation. . . .

The word used in the constitution, then, comprehends, and has been always understood to comprehend, navigation within its meaning; and a power to regulate navigation, is as expressly granted, as if that term had been added to the word "commerce." To what commerce does this power extend? The constitution informs us, to commerce "with foreign nations, and among the several states, and with the Indian tribes." It has, we believe, been universally admitted, that these words comprehend every species of commercial intercourse between the United States and foreign nations. No sort of trade can be carried on between this country and any other, to which this power does not extend. It has been truly said, that commerce, as the word is used in the constitution, is a unit, every part of which is indicated by the term.

If this be the admitted meaning of the word, in its application to foreign nations, it must carry the same meaning throughout the sentence, and remain a unit, unless there be some plain intelligible cause which alters it. The subject to which the power is next applied, is to commerce, ''among the several states.'' The word ''among'' means intermingled with. A thing which is among others, is intermingled with them. Commerce among the states, cannot stop at the external boundary line of each state, but may be introduced into the interior. It is not intended to say, that these words comprehend that commerce, which is completely internal, which is carried on between man and man in a state, or between different parts of the same state, and which does not extend to or affect other states. Such a power would be inconvenient, and is certainly unnecessary. Comprehensive as the word ''among'' is, it may very properly be restricted to that commerce which concerns more states than one. The phrase is not one which would probably have been selected to indicate the completely interior traffic of a state, because it is not an apt phrase for that purpose; and the enumeration of the particular classes of commerce to which the power was to be extended, would not have been made, had the intention been to extend the power to every description. The enumeration presupposes something not enumerated; and that something, if we regard the language or the subject of the sentence, must be the exclusively internal commerce of a state. The genius and character of the whole government seem to be, that its action is to be applied to all the external concerns of the nation, and to those internal concerns which affect the states generally; but not to those which are completely within a particular state, which do not affect other states, and with

which it is not necessary to interfere, for the purpose of executing some of the general powers of the government. The completely internal commerce of a state, then, may be considered as reserved for the state itself.

But, in regulating commerce with foreign nations, the power of congress does not stop at the jurisdictional lines of the several states. It would be a very useless power, if it could not pass those lines. The commerce of the United States with foreign nations is that of the whole United States; every district has a right to participate in it. The deep streams which penetrate our country in every direction pass through the interior of almost every state in the Union, and furnish the means of exercising this right. If congress has the power to regulate it, that power must be exercised whenever the subject exists. If it exists within the states, if a foreign voyage may commence or terminate at a port within a state, then the power of congress may be exercised within a state.

This principle is, if possible, still more clear, when applied to commerce ''among the several states.'' They either join each other, in which case they are separated by a mathematical line, or they are remote from each other, in which case other states lie between them. What is commerce ''among'' them; and how is it to be conducted? Can a trading expedition between two adjoining states, commence and terminate outside of each? And if the trading intercourse be between two states remote from each other, must it not commence in one, terminate in the other, and probably pass through a third? Commerce among the states must of necessity, be commerce with the states. In the regulation of trade with the Indian tribes, the action of the law, especially, when the constitution was made, was chiefly within a state. The power of congress, then, whatever it may be, must be exercised within the territorial jurisdiction of the several states. The sense of the nation on this subject, is unequivocally manifested by the provisions made in the laws for transporting goods, by land, between Baltimore and Providence, between New York and Philadelphia, and between Philadelphia and Baltimore.

We are now arrived at the inquiry—what is this power? It is the power to regulate; that is, to prescribe the rule by which commerce is to be governed. This power, like all others vested in congress, is complete in itself, may be exercised to its utmost extent, and acknowledges no limitations, other than are prescribed in the constitution. These are expressed in plain terms, and do not affect the questions which arise in this case, or which have been discussed at the bar. If, as has always been understood, the sovereignty of congress, though limited to specified objects, is plenary as to those objects, the power over commerce with foreign nations, and among the several states, is vested in congress as absolutely as it would be in a single government, having in its constitution the same restrictions on the exercise of the power as are found in the constitution of the United States. The wisdom and the discretion of congress, their identity with the people, and the influence which their constituents possess at elections, are, in this, as in many other instances, as that, for example, of declaring war, the sole restraints on which they have relied, to secure them from its abuse. They are the restraints on which the people must often rely solely, in all representative governments. . . .

But it has been urged, with great earnestness, that although the power of congress to regulate commerce with foreign nations, and among the several states, be co-extensive with the subject itself, and have no other limits than are prescribed in the constitution, yet the states may severally exercise the same power within their respective jurisdictions. In support of this argument, it is said that they possessed it as an inseparable attribute of sovereignty before the formation of the constitution, and still retain it, except so far as they have surrendered it by that instrument; that this principle results from the nature of the government, and is secured by the tenth amendment; that an affirmative grant of power is not exclusive, unless in its own nature it be such that the continued exercise of it by the former possessor is inconsistent with the grant, and that this is not of that description. The appellant conceding these postulates, except the

last, contends that full power to regulate a particular subject implies the whole power, and leaves no residuum; that a grant of the whole is incompatible with the existence of a right in another to any part of it. Both parties have appealed to the constitution, to legislative acts, and judicial decisions; and have drawn arguments from all these sources to support and illustrate the propositions they respectively maintain.

The grant of the power to lay and collect taxes is, like the power to regulate commerce, made in general terms, and has never been understood to interfere with the exercise of the same power by the states; and hence has been drawn an argument which has been applied to the question under consideration. But the two grants are not, it is conceived, similar in their terms or their nature. Although many of the powers formerly exercised by the states are transferred to the government of the Union, yet the state governments remain, and constitute a most important part of our system. The power of taxation is indispensable to their existence, and is a power which, in its own nature, is capable of residing in, and being exercised by, different authorities at the same time. We are accustomed to see it placed, for different purposes, in different hands. Taxation is the simple operation of taking small portions from a perpetually accumulating mass, susceptible of almost infinite division; and a power in one to take what is necessary for certain purposes, is not in its nature incompatible with a power in another to take what is necessary for other purposes. Congress is authorized to lay and collect taxes, etc., to pay the debts, and provide for the common defense and general welfare of the United States. This does not interefere with the power of the states to tax for the support of their own governments; nor is the exercise of that power by the states an exercise of any portion of the power that is granted to the United States. In imposing taxes for state purposes, they are not doing what congress is empowered to do. Congress is not empowered to tax for those purposes which are within the exclusive province of the States. When, then, each government exercises the power of taxation, neither is exercising the power of the other. But when a state proceeds to regulate commerce with foreign nations, or among the several states, it is exercising the very power that is granted to congress, and is doing the very thing which congress is authorized to do. There is no analogy then, between the power of taxation and the power of regulating commerce. . . .

But the inspection laws are said to be regulations of commerce, and are certainly recognized in the constitution as being passed in the exercise of a power remaining with the states.

That inspection laws may have a remote and considerable influence on commerce, will not be denied; but that a power to regulate commerce is the source from which the right to pass them is derived, cannot be admitted. The object of inspection laws, is to improve the quality of articles produced by the labor of a country; to fit them for exportation; or it may be, for domestic use. They act upon the subject, before it becomes an article of foreign commerce, or of commerce among the states, and prepare it for that purpose. They form a portion of that immense mass of legislation, which embraces everything within the territory of a state, not surrendered to a general government; all of which can be most advantageously exercised by the states themselves. Inspection laws, quarantine laws, health laws of every description, as well as laws for regulating the internal commerce of a state, and those which respect turnpike roads, ferries, etc., are component parts of this mass.

No direct general power over these objects is granted to congress, and, consequently, they remain subject to state legislation. If the legislative power of the Union can reach them, it must be, where the power is expressly given for a special purpose, or is clearly incidental to some power which is expressly given. It is obvious, that the government of the Union, in the exercise of its express powers, that, for example, of regulating commerce with foreign nations and among the states, may use means that may also be employed by a state, in the exercise of its acknowledged powers; that, for example, of

regulating commerce within the state. If congress licenses vessels to sail from one port to another, in the same state, the act is supposed to be, necessarily, incidental to the power expressly granted to congress, and implies no claim of a direct power to regulate the purely internal commerce of a state, or to act directly on its system of police. So, if a state, in passing laws on subjects acknowledged to be within its control, and with a view to those subjects, shall adopt a measure of the same character with one which congress may adopt, it does not derive its authority from the particular power which has been granted, but from some other which remains with the state. All experience shows that the same measures, or measures scarcely distinguishable from each other, may flow from distinct powers; but this does not prove that the powers themselves are identical. Although the means used in their execution may sometimes approach each other so nearly as to be confounded, there are other situations in which they are sufficiently distinct to establish their individuality.

In our complex system, presenting the rare and difficult scheme of one general government whose action extends over the whole, but which possesses only certain enumerated powers; and of numerous state governments, which retain and exercise all powers not delegated to the Union, contests respecting power must arise. Were it even otherwise, the measures taken by the respective governments to execute their acknowledged powers would often be of the same description, and might sometimes interfere. This, however, does not prove that the one is exercising, or has a right to exercise, the powers of the other.

It has been said that the act of August 7, 1789, acknowledges a concurrent power in the states to regulate the conduct of pilots, and hence is inferred an admission of their concurrent right with congress to regulate commerce with foreign nations, and amongst the states. But this inference is not, we think, justified by the fact. Although congress cannot enable a state to legislate, congress may adopt the provisions of a state on any subject. When the government of the Union was brought into existence, it found a system for the regulation of its pilots in full force in every state. The act which has been mentioned, adopts this system, and gives it the same validity as if its provisions had been specially made by congress. But the act, it may be said, is prospective also, and the adoption of laws to be made in future, presupposes the right in the maker to legislate on the subject. The act unquestionably manifests an intention to leave this subject entirely to the states, until congress should think proper to interpose; but the very enactment of such a law indicates an opinion that it was necessary; that the existing system would not be applicable to the new state of things, unless expressly applied to it by congress. . . . The acknowledged power of a state to regulate its police, its domestic trade and to govern its own citizens, may enable it to legislate on this subject to a considerable extent; and the adoption of its system by congress, and the application of it to the whole subject of commerce, does not seem to the court to imply a right in the states so to apply it of their own authority. . . .

Since, however, in exercising the power of regulating their own purely internal affairs, whether of trading or police, the states may sometimes enact laws, the validity of which depends on their [not] interfering with, and being contrary to, an act of congress passed in pursuance of the constitution, the court will enter upon the inquiry whether the laws of New York, as expounded by the highest tribunal of that state, have, in their application to this case, come into collision with an act of congress, and deprived a citizen of a right to which that act entitles him. Should this collision exist, it will be immaterial whether those laws were passed in virtue of a concurrent power "to regulate commerce with foreign nations and among the several States," or, in virtue of a power to regulate their domestic trade and police. In one case and the other, the acts of New York must yield to the law of congress, and the decision sustaining the privilege they confer, against a right given by a law of the Union, must be erroneous. This opinion has been frequently expressed in this court,

and is founded, as well on the nature of the government, as on the words of the constitution. In argument, however, it has been contended, that if a law passed by a state, in the exercise of its acknowledged sovereignty comes into conflict with a law passed by congress in pursuance of the constitution, they affect the subject, and each other, like equal opposing powers. But the framers of our constitution foresaw this state of things, and provided for it, by declaring the supremacy not only of itself, but of the laws made in pursuance of it.

The nullity of any act, inconsistent with the constitution, is produced by the declaration, that the constitution is the supreme law. . . . In every such case, the act of congress, or the treaty, is supreme; and the law of the state, though enacted in the exercise of powers not controverted, must yield to it. . . .

Johnson, Justice. . . .

The history of the times will . . . sustain the opinion, that the grant of power over commerce, if intended to be commensurate with the evils existing, and the purpose of remedying those evils, could be only commensurate with the power of the states over the subject. . . .

The "power to regulate commerce," here meant to be granted, was that power to regulate commerce which previously existed in the states. But what was that power? The states were unquestionably, supreme; and each possessed that power over commerce, which is acknowledged to reside in every sovereign state. The definition and limits of that power are to be sought among the features of international law; and, as it was not only admitted, but insisted on by both parties, in argument, that, "unaffected by a state of war, by treaties, or by municipal regulations, all commerce among independent states was legitimate," there is no necessity to appeal to the oracles of the *jus commune* for the correctness of that doctrine. The law of nations, regarding man as a social animal, pronounces all commerce legitimate, in a state of peace, until prohibited by positive law. The power of a sovereign state over commerce, therefore, amounts to nothing more than a power to limit and restrain it at pleasure. And since the power to prescribe the limits to its freedom, necessarily implies the power to determine what shall remain unrestrained it follows, that the power must be exclusive; it can reside but in one potentate; and hence, the grant of this power carries with it the whole subject, leaving nothing for the state to act upon. . . .

. . . Power to regulate foreign commerce, is given in the same words, and in the same breath, as it were, with that over the commerce of the states and with the Indian tribes. But the power to regulate foreign commerce is necessarily exclusive. The states are unknown to foreign nations; their sovereignty exists only with relation to each other and the general government. Whatever regulations foreign commerce should be subjected to in the ports of the Union, the general government would be held responsible for them; and all other regulations, but those which congress had imposed, would be regarded by foreign nations as trespasses and violations of national faith and comity.

But the language which grants the power as to one description of commerce, grants it as to all; and, in fact, if ever the exercise of a right, or acquiescence in a construction, could be inferred from contemporaneous and continued assent, it is that of the exclusive effect of this grant.

A right over the subject has never been pretended to, in any instance, except as incidental to exercise of some other unquestionable power. . . .

When speaking of the power of congress over navigation, I do not regard it as a power incidental to that of regulating commerce; I consider it as the thing itself; inseparable from it as vital motion is from vital existence.

Commerce, in its simplest signification, means an exchange of goods: but in the advancement of society, labor, transportation, intelligence, care, and various mediums of exchange, become commodities, and enter into commerce; the subject, the vehicle, the agent, and their various operations, become the objects of commercial regulation. Shipbuilding, the carrying trade, and propagation of seamen, are such vital agents of commercial prosperity, that the nation which could not legislate over these subjects, would not possess power to regulate commerce. . . .

It is impossible, with the views which I entertain of the principle on which the commercial privileges of the people of the United States among themselves, rests [sic], to concur in the view which this court takes of the effect of the coasting license in this cause. I do not regard it as the foundation of the right set up in behalf of the appellant. If there was any one object riding over every other in the adoption of the constitution, it was to keep the commercial intercourse among the states free from all invidious and partial restraints. And I cannot overcome the conviction, that if the licensing act was repealed tomorrow, the rights of the appellant to a reversal of the decision complained of, would be as strong as it is under this license. . . .

. . . This court doth further direct, order and decree, that the bill of the said Aaron Ogden be dismissed, and the same is hereby dismissed accordingly.

Cooley v. Board of Wardens
12 How. (53 U.S.) 299, 13 L.Ed. 996 (1851)

A state pilotage law of 1803 required that vessels leaving Philadelphia should pay a one-half fee if a pilot were not hired. An act of the United States of 1789 declared that state pilotage acts should continue in effect. Cooley, the consignee of two vessels outward bound from Philadelphia, refused to pay the state fee. From judgments against him in the state courts, he brought writs of error.

MR. JUSTICE CURTIS delivered the opinion of the court. . . .

It remains to consider the objection that it [the state act] is repugnant to the third clause of the eighth section of the first article. "The Congress shall have power to regulate commerce with foreign nations and among the several states, and with the Indian tribes."

That the power to regulate commerce includes the regulation of navigation, we consider settled. And when we look to the nature of the service performed by pilots, to the relations which that service and its compensations bear to navigation between the several states, and between the ports of the United States and foreign countries, we are brought to the conclusion, that the regulation of the qualifications of pilots, of the modes and times of offering and rendering their services, of the responsibilities which shall rest upon them, of the powers they shall possess, of the compensation they may demand, and of the penalties by which their rights and duties may be enforced, do constitute regulations of navigation, and consequently of commerce, within the just meaning of this clause of the Constitution.

The power to regulate navigation is the power to prescribe rules in conformity with which navigation must be carried on. It extends to the persons who conduct it, as well as to the instruments used. Accordingly, the first Congress assembled under the Constitution passed laws requiring the masters of ships and vessels of the United States to be citizens of the United States, and established many rules for the government and regulation of officers and seamen. . . . These have been from time to time added to and changed, and we are not aware that their validity has been questioned. . . .

The act of 1789 . . . already referred to, contains a clear legislative exposition of the Constitution by the first Congress, to the effect that the power to regulate pilots was conferred on Congress by the Constitution; as does also the act of March the 2d, 1837, the terms of which have just been given. The weight to be allowed to this contemporaneous construction, and the practice of Congress under it, has, in another connection, been adverted to. And a majority of the court are of opinion that a regulation of pilots is a regulation of commerce, within the grant to Congress of the commercial power, contained in the third clause of the eighth section of the first article of the Constitution.

It becomes necessary, therefore, to consider whether this law of Pennsylvania, being a regulation of commerce, is valid.

The act of Congress of the 7th of August, 1789, sec. 4, is as follows:

That all pilots in the bays, inlets, rivers, harbors, and ports of the United States shall continue to be regulated in conformity with the existing laws of the states, respectively wherein such pilots may be, or with such laws as the states may respectively hereafter enact for the purpose, until further legislative provision shall be made by Congress.

If the law of Pennsylvania, now in question, had been in existence at the date of this act of Congress, we might hold it to have been adopted by Congress, and thus made a law of the United States, and so valid. Because this act does, in effect, give the force of an act of Congress, to the then existing state laws on this subject, so long as they should continue unrepealed by the state which enacted them.

But the law on which these actions are founded was not enacted till 1803. What effect then can be attributed to so much of the act of 1789, as declares, that pilots shall continue to be regulated in conformity "with such laws as the states may respectively hereafter enact for the purpose, until further legislative provision shall be made by Congress"?

If the states were divested of the power to legislate on this subject by the grant of the commercial power to Congress, it is plain this act could not confer upon them power thus to legislate. If the Constitution excluded the states from making any law regulating commerce, certainly Congress cannot regrant, or in any manner reconvey to the states that power. And yet this act of 1789 gives its sanction only to laws enacted by the States. This necessarily implies a constitutional power to legislate; for only a rule created by the sovereign power of a state acting in its legislative capacity, can be deemed a law enacted by a state; and if the state has so limited its sovereign power that it no longer extends to a particular subject, manifestly it cannot, in any proper sense, be said to enact law thereon. Entertaining these views, we are brought directly and unavoidably to the consideration of the question, whether the grant of the commercial power to congress, did per se deprive the states of all power to regulate pilots. This question has never been decided by this court, nor, in our judgment, has any case depending upon all the considerations which must govern this one, come before this court. The grant of commercial power to Congress does not contain any terms which expressly exclude the states from exercising an authority over its subject matter. If they are excluded, it must be because the nature of the power, thus granted to Congress, requires that a similar authority should not exist in the states. If it were conceded on the one side, that the nature of this power, like that to legislate for the District of Columbia, is absolutely and totally repugnant to the existence of similar power in the states, probably no one would deny that the grant of the power to Congress, as effectually and perfectly excludes the states from all future legislation on the subject, as if express words had been used to exclude them. And on the other hand, if it were admitted that the existence of this power in Congress, like the power of taxation, is compatible with the existence of a similar power in the states, then it would be in conformity with the contemporary exposition of the Constitution (Federalist, No. 32), and with the judicial construction, given from time to time by this court, after the most deliberate consideration, to hold that the mere grant of such a power to Congress, did not imply a prohibition on the states to exercise the same power; that it is not the mere existence of such a power, but its exercise by Congress, which may be incompatible with the exercise of the same power by the states, and that the states may legislate in the absence of congressional regulations. . . .

The diversities of opinion, therefore, which have existed on this subject, have arisen from the different views taken of the nature of this power. But when the nature of a power like this is spoken of, when it is said that the nature of the power requires that it should be exercised exclusively by Congress, it must be intended to refer to the subjects of that power, and to say they are of such a nature as to require exclusive legislation by Congress. Now the power to regulate commerce embraces a vast field, containing not only many, but exceedingly various subjects, quite unlike in their nature; some imperatively demanding a single uniform rule, operating equally on the commerce of the United States in every port; and some, like the subject now in question, as imperatively demanding that diversity which alone can meet the local necessities of navigation.

Either absolutely to affirm, or deny that the nature of this power requires exclusive legislation by Congress, is to lose sight of the nature of the subjects of this power, and to assert concerning all of them, what is really applicable but to a part. Whatever subjects of this power are in their nature national, or admit only of one uniform system, or plan of regulation, may justly be said to be of such a nature as to require exclusive legislation by Congress. That this cannot be affirmed of laws for the regulation of pilots and pilotage is plain. The act of 1789 contains a clear and authoritative declaration by the first Congress that the nature of this subject is such that until Congress should find it necessary to exert its power, it should be left to the legislation of the states; that it is local and not national; that it is likely to be the best provided for, not by one system, or plan or regulation but by as many as the legislative discretion of the several states should deem applicable to the local peculiarities of the ports within their limits.

Viewed in this light, so much of this act of 1789 as declares that pilots shall continue to be regulated "by such laws as the states may respectively hereafter enact for that purpose," instead of being held to be inoperative, as an attempt to confer on the states a power to legislate, of which the Constitution had deprived them, is allowed an appropriate and important signification. It manifests the understanding of Congress, at the outset of the government, that the nature of this subject is not such as to require its exclusive legislation. The practice of the states, and of the national government, has been in conformity with this declaration, from the origin of the national government to this time; and the nature of the subject when examined is such as to leave no doubt of the superior fitness and propriety, not to say the absolute necessity, of different systems of regulation, drawn from local knowledge and experience, and conformed to local wants. How, then, can we say that, by the mere grant of power to regulate commerce, the states are deprived of all the power to legislate on this subject, because from the nature of the power the legislation of Congress must be exclusive? This would be to affirm that the nature of the power is, in this case, something different from the nature of the subject to which, in such case, the power extends, and that the nature of the power necessarily demands, in all cases, exclusive legislation by Congress, while the nature of one of the subjects of that power, not only does not require such exclusive legislation but may be best provided for by many different systems enacted by the states, in conformity

with the circumstances of the ports within their limits. In construing an instrument designed for the formation of a government, and in determining the extent of one of its important grants of power to legislate, we can make no such distinction between the nature of the power and the nature of the subject on which that power was intended practically to operate, nor consider the grant more extensive by affirming of the power, what is not true of its subject now in question.

It is the opinion of a majority of the court that the mere grant to Congress of the power to regulate commerce did not deprive the states of power to regulate pilots, and that although Congress has legislated on this subject, its legislation manifests an intention, with a single exception, not to regulate this subject, but to leave its regulation to the several states. To these precise questions, which are all we are called on to decide, this opinion must be understood to be confined. It does not extend to the question what other subjects, under the commercial power, are within the exclusive control of Congress, or may be regulated by the states in the absence of all congressional legislation; nor to the general question, how far any regulation of a subject by Congress, may be deemed to operate as an exclusion of all legislation by the states upon the same subject. We decide the precise questions before us, upon what we deem sound principles, applicable to this particular subject in the state in which the legislation of Congress has left it. We go no further. . . .

We are of opinion that this state law was enacted by virtue of a power, residing in the state to legislate; that it is not in conflict with any law of Congress; that it does not interfere with any system which Congress has established by making regulations, or by intentionally leaving individuals to their own unrestricted action: that this law is therefore valid, and the judgment of the Supreme Court of Pennsylvania in each case must be affirmed.

MR. JUSTICE MCLEAN and MR. JUSTICE WAYNE dissented; and MR. JUSTICE DANIEL although he concurred in the judgment of the court, yet dissented from its reasoning. . . .

Brown v. Houston
114 U.S. 622, 5 S.Ct. 1091, 29 L.Ed. 257 (1885)

Coal, shipped by a mining company in Pennsylvania to an agent in New Orleans, was subjected to a Louisiana annual tax on movable property while it remained on flat boats awaiting sale to whatever customers appeared. The company resisted payment on various grounds, but chiefly on the ground that the tax was an improper regulation of interstate commerce. From an adverse decision in the Supreme Court of Louisiana, Brown brought his case to the Supreme Court on a writ of error.

MR. JUSTICE BRADLEY delivered the opinion of the court. . . .

The power to regulate commerce among the several States is granted to Congress in terms as absolute as is the power to regulate commerce with foreign nations. If not in all respects an exclusive power; if, in the absence of Congressional action, the States may continue to regulate matters of local interest only incidentally affecting foreign and inter-state commerce, such as pilots, wharves, harbors, roads, bridges, tolls, freights, etc., still, according to the rule laid down in *Cooley* v. *Board of Wardens of Philadelphia* . . . the power of Congress is exclusive wherever the matter is national in its character or admits of one uniform system or plan of regulation; and is certainly so far exclusive that no State has power to make any law or regulation which will affect the free and unrestrained intercourse and trade between the States, as Congress has left it, or which will impose any discriminating burden or tax upon the citizens or products of other States, coming or brought within its jurisdiction. All laws and regulations are restrictive of natural freedom to some extent, and where no regulation is imposed by the government which has the exclusive power to regulate, it is an indication of its will that the matter shall be left free. So long as Congress does not pass any law to regulate commerce among the several States, it thereby indicates its will that that commerce shall be free and untrammelled; and any regulation of the subject by the State is repugnant to such freedom. . . . It may be laid down as the settled doctrine of this court, at this day, that a State can no

more regulate or impede commerce among the several States than it can regulate or impede commerce with foreign nations.

This being the recognized law, the question then arises whether the assessment of the tax in question amounted to any interference with, or restriction upon the free introduction of the plaintiffs' coal from the State of Pennsylvania into the State of Louisiana, and the free disposal of the same in commerce in the latter State; in other words, whether the tax amounted to a regulation of, or restriction upon, commerce among the States; or only to an exercise of local administration under the general taxing power, which, though it may incidentally affect the subjects of commerce, is entirely within the power of the State until Congress shall see fit to interfere and make express regulations on the subject.

As to the character and mode of the assessment, little need be added to what has already been said. It was not a tax imposed upon the coal as a foreign product, or as the product of another State than Louisiana, nor a tax imposed by reason of the coal being imported or brought into Louisiana, nor a tax imposed whilst it was in a state of transit through that State to some other place of destination. It was imposed after the coal had arrived at its destination and was put up for sale. The coal had come to its place of rest, for final disposal or use, and was a commodity in the market of New Orleans. It might continue in that condition for a year or two years, or only for a day. It had become a part of the general mass of property in the state, and as such it was taxed for the current year (1880), as all other property in the City of New Orleans was taxed. Under the law, it could not be taxed again until the following year. It was subjected to no discrimination in favor of goods which were the product of Louisiana, or goods which were the property of citizens of Louisiana. It was treated in exactly the same manner as such goods were treated.

It cannot be seriously contended, at least in the absence of any Congressional legislation to the contrary, that all goods which are the product of other States are to be free from taxation in the State to which they may be carried for use or sale.

. . . The taxing of goods from other States, as such, or by reason of their so coming, would be a discriminating tax against them as imports, and would be a regulation of inter-State commerce, inconsistent with that perfect freedom of trade which Congress has seen fit should remain undisturbed. But if, after their arrival within the State,—that being to which they may be carried for use or trade,—if, after this, they are subjected to a general tax laid alike on all property within the city, we fail to see how such a taxing can be deemed a regulation of commerce which would have the objectionable effect referred to. . . .

When Congress shall see fit to make a regulation on the subject of property transferred from one State to another, which may have the effect to give it a temporary exemption from taxation in the State to which it is transported, it will be time enough to consider any conflict that may arise between such regulation and the general taxing laws of the State. In the present case we see no such conflict, either in the law itself or in the proceedings which have been had under it and sustained by the State tribunals, nor any conflict with the general rule that a State cannot pass a law which shall interfere with the unrestricted freedom of commerce between the States. . . .

Affirmed.

Plumley v. Massachusetts
155 U.S. 461, 15 S.Ct. 154, 39 L.Ed. 223 (1894)

A Massachusetts statute of 1891 prohibited the manufacture or sale of oleomargarine colored like butter. Plumley, an agent of a Chicago firm that manufactured colored oleomargarine, was convicted of making a sale in violation of the act, and brought a writ of error to review the affirming judgment of the Supreme Judicial Court of Massachusetts.

MR. JUSTICE HARLAN delivered the opinion of the court. . . .

The petitioner claimed that the statute of Massachusetts was repugnant to the clause of the Constitution providing that the Congress shall have power to regulate commerce among the several States; to the clause declaring that the citizens of each State shall be entitled to all the privileges and immunities of citizens in the several States; to the clause providing that no State shall make or enforce any law which shall abridge the privileges or immunities of citizens of the United States, nor deprive any person of life, liberty, or property without due process of law, nor deny to any person within its jurisdiction the equal protection of the laws; to the clause declaring that private property shall not be taken for public purposes; and to the act of Congress of August 2, 1886, entitled ''An act defining butter, also imposing a tax upon and regulating the manufacture, sale, importation, and exportation of oleomargarine." . . .

The learned counsel for the appellant states that Congress in the act of August 2, 1886, has legislated fully on the subject of oleomargarine. This may be true so far as the purposes of that act are concerned. But there is no ground to suppose that Congress intended in that enactment to interfere with the exercise by the States of any authority they could rightfully exercise over the sale within their respective limits of the article defined as oleomargarine. . . . Congress had no purpose to restrict the power of the States over the subject of the manufacture and sale of oleomargarine within their respective limits. The taxes prescribed by that act were imposed for national purposes, and their imposition did not give authority to those who paid them to engage in the manufacture or sale of oleomargarine in any State which lawfully forbade such manufacture or sale, or to disregard any regulations which a State might lawfully prescribe in reference to that article. . . .

Nor was the act of Congress relating to oleomargarine intended as a regulation of commerce among the States. Its provisions do not have special application to the transfer of oleomargarine from one State of the Union to another. They relieve the manufacturer or seller, if he conforms to the regulations prescribed by Congress or by the Commissioner of Internal Revenue under the authority conferred upon him in that regard, from penalty or punishment so far as the general government is concerned, but they do not interfere with the exercise by the States of any authority they possess of preventing deception or fraud in the sales of property within their respective limits.

The vital question in this case is, therefore, unaffected by the act of Congress or by any regulations that have been established in execution of its provisions. That question is, whether, as contended by the petitioner, the statute under examination in its application to sales of oleomargarine brought into Massachusetts from other States is in conflict with the clause of the Constitution of the United States investing Congress with power to regulate commerce among the several States. . . .

It will be observed that the statute of Massachusetts which is alleged to be repugnant to the commerce clause of the Constitution does not prohibit the manufacture or sale of all oleomargarine, but only such as is colored in imitation of yellow butter produced from pure unadulterated milk or cream of such milk. If free from coloration or ingredient that "causes it to look like butter," the right to sell it "in a separate and distinct form, and in such manner as will advise the consumer of its real character," is neither restricted nor prohibited. It appears, in this case, that oleomargarine, in its natural condition, is of "a light yellowish color," and that the article sold by the accused was artificially colored "in imitation of yellow butter." Now, the real object of coloring oleomargarine so as to make it look like genuine butter is that it may appear to be what it is not, and thus induce unwary purchasers who do not closely scrutinize the label upon the package in which it is contained, to buy it as and for butter produced from unadulterated milk or cream from such milk. The suggestion that oleomargarine is artificially colored so as to render it more palatable and attractive can only mean that customers are deluded, by such coloration, into believing that they are getting genuine butter. If any one thinks that oleomargarine, not artificially colored so as to cause it to look like butter, is as palatable or as wholesome for purposes of food as pure butter, he is, as already observed, at liberty under the state of Massachusetts to manufacture it in that State or to sell it there in such a manner as to inform the customer of its real character. He is only forbidden to practice, in such matter, a fraud upon the general public. The statute seeks to suppress false pretenses and to promote fair dealing in the sale of an article of food. It compels the sale of oleomargarine for what it really is, by preventing its sale for what it is not. Can it be that the Constitution of the United States secures to any one the privilege of manufacturing an article of food in such a manner as to induce the mass of people to believe that they are buying something which, in fact, is wholly different from that which is offered for sale? Does the freedom of commerce among the States demand a recognition of the right to practice a deception upon the public in the sale of any articles, even those that may have become the subject of trade in different parts of the country? . . .

If there be any subject over which it would seem the States ought to have plenary control, and the power to legislate in respect to which it ought not to be supposed was intended to be surrendered to the general government, it is the protection of the people against fraud and deception in the sale of food products. Such legislation may, indeed, indirectly or incidentally affect trade in such products transported from one State to another State. But that circumstance does not show that laws of the character alluded to are inconsistent with the power of Congress to regulate commerce among the States. . . .

But the case most relied on by the petitioner to support the proposition that oleomargarine, being a recognized article of commerce, may be introduced into a State and there sold in original packages, without any restriction being imposed by the State upon such sale, is *Leisy* v. *Hardin*. . . .

It is sufficient to say of *Leisy* v. *Hardin* that it did not in form or in substance present the particular question now under consideration. The article which the majority of the court in that case held could be sold in Iowa in original packages, the statute of the State to the contrary notwithstanding, was beer manufactured in Illinois and shipped to the former State to be there sold in such packages. So far as the record disclosed, and so far as the contentions of the parties were concerned, the article there in question was what it appeared to be, namely, genuine beer, and not a liquid or drink colored artificially so as to cause it to look like beer. . . .

We are of opinion that it is within the power of a State to exclude from its markets any compound manufactured in another State, which has been artificially colored or adulterated so as to cause it to look like an article of food in general use, and the sale of which may, by reason of such coloration or adulteration, cheat the general public into purchasing that which they may not intend to buy. The Constitution of the United States does not secure to any one the

privilege of defrauding the public. The deception against which the statute of Massachusetts is aimed is an offense against society; and the States are as competent to protect their people against such offenses or wrongs as they are to protect them against crimes or wrongs of more serious character. And this protection may be given without violating any right secured by the national Constitution, and without infringing the authority of the general government. A State enactment forbidding the sale of deceitful imitations of articles of food in general use among the people does not abridge any privilege secured to citizens of the United States, nor, in any just sense, interfere with the freedom of commerce among the several States. It is legislation which "can be most advantageously exercised by the States themselves." *Gibbons* v. *Ogden*. . . .

We are not unmindful of the fact—indeed, this court has often had occasion to observe—that the acknowledged power of the States to protect the morals, the health, and safety of their people by appropriate legislation, sometimes touches, in its exercise, the line separating the respective domains of national and state authority. But in view of the complex system of government which exists in this country, "presenting," as this court, speaking by Chief Justice Marshall, has said, "the rare and difficult scheme of one general government, whose action extends over the whole, but which possesses only certain enumerated powers, and of numerous state governments which retain and exercise all powers not delegated to the Union," the judiciary of the United States should not strike down a legislative enactment of a State—especially if it has direct connection with the social order, the health, and the morals of its people—unless such legislation plainly and palpably violates some right granted or secured by the national Constitution or encroaches upon the authority delegated to the United States for the attainment of objects of national concern.

We cannot adjudge in reference to the statute of Massachusetts, and as the court below correctly held that the plaintiff in error was not restrained of his liberty in violation of the Constitution of the United States, the judgment must be affirmed.

MR. JUSTICE JACKSON, now absent, was present at the argument and participated in the decision of this case. He concurs in this opinion.

Judgment affirmed.

MR. CHIEF JUSTICE FULLER . . . dissenting.

The power vested in Congress to regulate commerce among the several States is the power to prescribe the rule by which that commerce is to be governed, and, as that commerce is national in its character and must be governed by a uniform system, so long as Congress does not pass any law to regulate it, or allowing the States to do so, it thereby indicates its will that such commerce shall be free and untrammelled. Manifestly, whenever State legislation comes in conflict with that will, it must give way.

In whatever language such legislation may be framed, its purpose must be determined by its natural and reasonable effect, and the presumption that it was enacted in good faith cannot control the determination of the question whether it is or is not repugnant to the Constitution of the United States.

Upon this record oleomargarine is conceded to be a wholesome, palatable, and nutritious article of food, in no way deleterious to the public health or welfare. It is of the natural color of but-

ter, and looks like butter, and is often colored, as butter is, by harmless ingredients, a deeper yellow, to render it more attractive to consumers. The assumption that it is thus colored to make it appear to be a different article, generically, than it is, has no legal basis in this case to rest on. It cannot be denied that oleomargarine is a recognized article of commerce, and moreover, it is regulated as such, for revenue purposes, by the act of Congress of August 2, 1886. . . .

I deny that a State may exclude from commerce legitimate subjects of commercial dealings because of the possibility that their appearance may deceive purchasers in regard to their qualities. . . .

The right to import, export, or sell oleomargarine in the original package under the regulations prescribed by Congress cannot be inhibited by such legislation as that before us. Fluctuation in decision in respect of so vital a power as that to regulate commerce among the several States, is to be deprecated, and the opinion and judgment in this case seem to me clearly inconsistent with settled principles. I dissent from the opinion and judgment, and am authorized to say that MR. JUSTICE FIELD and MR. JUSTICE BREWER concur with me in so doing.

Parker v. *Brown*
317 U.S. 341, 63 S.Ct. 307, 87 L.Ed. 315 (1943)

The California Agricultural Prorate Act of 1933 created a program by which competition among growers was restricted in order to maintain prices in the distribution of their products. The complainant Brown, a raisin producer, obtained a decree in a district court enjoining the enforcement of the program on the ground that he was suffering irreparable injury under the program because of his inability to fulfill his contracts except at heavy financial loss. The Supreme Court, on appeal, held that the state act was neither contrary to the Sherman Anti-Trust Act nor in conflict with the Agricultural Adjustment Act of 1938. It then considered the issue of constitutionality under the commerce clause. Parker, the California representative, appealed.

MR. CHIEF JUSTICE STONE delivered the opinion of the Court. . . .

Validity of the Program under the Commerce Clause. . . .

The question is thus presented whether in the absence of congressional legislation prohibiting or regulating the transactions affected by the state program, the restrictions which it imposes upon the sale within the state of a commodity by its producer to a processor who contemplates doing, and in fact does work upon the commodity before packing and shipping it in interstate commerce, violate the Commerce Clause. . . .

The governments of the states are sovereign within their territory save only as they are subject to the prohibitions of the Constitution or as their action in some measure conflicts with powers delegated to the National Government, or with Congressional legislation enacted in the exercise of those powers. This Court has repeatedly held that the grant of power to Congress by the Commerce Clause did not wholly withdraw from the states the authority to regulate the commerce with respect to matters of local concern, on which Congress has not spoken. *A fortiori* there are many subjects and transactions of local concern not themselves interstate commerce or a part of its operations which are within the regulatory and taxing power of the states, so long as state action serves local ends and does not discriminate against the commerce, even though the exercise of those powers may materially affect it. Whether we resort to the mechanical test sometimes applied by this Court in determining when interstate commerce begins with respect to a commodity grown or manufactured within a state and then sold and shipped out of it—or whether we consider only the power of the state in the absence of Congressional action to regulate matters of local concern, even though the regulation affects or in some measure restricts the commerce—we think the present regulation is within state power. . . .

In applying the mechanical test to determine when interstate commerce begins and ends . . . this Court has frequently held that for purposes of local taxation or regulation "manufacture" is not interstate commerce even though the manufacturing process is of slight extent. . . . And such regulations of manufacture have been sustained where, aimed at matters of local concern, they had the effect of preventing commerce in the regulated article. . . . A state is also free to license and tax intrastate buying where the purchaser expects in the usual course of business to resell in interstate commerce. . . . And no case has gone so far as to hold that a state could not license or otherwise regulate the sale of articles within the state because the buyer, after processing and packing them, will, in the normal course of business, sell and ship them in interstate commerce.

All of these cases proceed on the ground that the taxation or regulation involved, however drastically it may affect interstate commerce, is nevertheless not prohibited by the Commerce Clause where the regulation is imposed before any operation of interstate commerce occurs. Applying that test, the regulation here controls the disposition, including the sale and purchase of raisins before they are processed and packed preparatory to interstate sale and shipment. The regulation is thus applied to transactions wholly intrastate before the raisins are ready for shipment in interstate commerce. . . .

This distinction between local regulation of those who are not engaged in commerce, although the commodity which they produce and sell to local buyers is ultimately destined for interstate commerce, and the regulation of those who engage in the commerce of selling the produce interstate, has in general served, and serves here, as a ready means of distinguishing those local activities which, under the Commerce Clause, are the appropriate subject of state regulation despite their effect on interstate commerce. But courts are not confined to so mechanical a test. When Congress has not exerted its power under the Commerce Clause, and state regulation of matters of local concern is so related to interstate commerce that it also operates as a regulation of that commerce, the reconciliation of the power thus granted with that reserved to the state is to be attained by the accommodation of the competing demands of the state and national interests involved. . . .

Such regulations by the state are to be sustained, not because they are ''indirect'' rather than ''direct'' . . . not because they control interstate activities in such a manner as only to affect the commerce rather than to command its operations. But they are to be upheld because upon a consideration of all the relevant facts and circumstances it appears that the matter is one which may appropriately be regulated in the interest of the safety, health and well-being of local communities, and which, because of its local character and the practical difficulties involved, may never be adequately dealt with by Congress. Because of its local character also there may be wide scope for local regulation without substantially impairing the national interest in the regulation of commerce by a single authority and without materially obstructing the free flow of commerce, which were the principal objects sought to be secured by the Commerce Clause. . . . There may also be, as in the present case, local regulations whose effect upon the national commerce is such as not to conflict but to coincide with a policy which Congress has established with respect to it. . . .

In comparing the relative weights of the conflicting local and national interests involved, it is significant that Congress, by its agricultural legislation, has recognized the distressed condition of much of the agricultural production of the United States, and has authorized marketing procedures, substantially like the California prorate program, for stabilizing the marketing of agricultural products. Acting under this legislation the Secretary of Agriculture has established a large number of market stabilization programs for agricultural commodities moving in interstate commerce in various parts of the country, including seven affecting California crops. All involved attempt in one way or another to prevent overproduction of agricultural products and excessive competition in marketing them, with price stabilization as the ultimate objective. Most if not all had a like effect in restricting shipments and raising or maintaining prices of agricultural commodities in interstate commerce.

It thus appears that whatever effect the operation of the California program may have on interstate commerce, it is one which it has been the policy of Congress to aid and encourage through federal agencies in conformity to the Agricultural Marketing Agreement Act, and § 302 of the Agricultural Adjustment Act. Nor is the effect on the commerce greater than or substantially different in kind from that contemplated by the stabilization programs authorized by federal statutes. As we have seen, the Agricultural Marketing Agreement Act is applicable to raisins only on the direction of the Secretary of Agriculture who, instead of establishing a federal program has, as the statute authorizes, cooperated in promoting the state program and aided it by substantial federal loans. Hence we cannot say that the effect of the state program on interstate commerce is one which conflicts with Congressional policy or is such as to preclude the state from this exercise of its reserved power to regulate domestic agricultural production.

We conclude that the California prorate program for the 1940 raisin crop is a regulation of state industry of local concern which, in all the circumstances of this case which we have detailed, does not impair national control over the commerce in a manner or to a degree forbidden by the Constitution.

Reversed.

Southern Pacific v. Arizona
325 U.S. 761, 65 S.Ct. 1515, 89 L.Ed. 1915 (1945)

The Arizona Train Limit Law of 1912 made it unlawful to operate within the state a railroad train of more than 14 passenger or 70 freight cars. In 1940, when the state sought to collect penalties for violations of the act, the appellant company objected, claiming that the act was unconstitutional. The Supreme Court of Arizona upheld the constitutionality of the law, and the company appealed. The portion of the opinion of Chief Justice Stone holding that there was no conflict between the state act and federal legislation has been omitted.

MR. CHIEF JUSTICE STONE delivered the opinion of the Court. . . .

. . . We are . . . brought to appellant's contention, that the state statute contravenes the commerce clause of the Federal Constitution.

Although the commerce clause conferred on the national government power to regulate commerce, its possession of the power does not exclude all state power of regulation. Ever since *Willson* v. *Black Bird Creek Marsh Co.*, 2 Pet. 245, and *Cooley* v. *Board of Wardens* . . . it has been recognized that, in the absence of conflicting legislation by Congress, there is a residuum of power in the state to make laws governing matters of local concern which nevertheless in some measure affect interstate commerce or even, to some extent, regulate it. . . . Thus the states may regulate matters which, because of their number and diversity, may never be adequately dealt with by Congress. . . . When the regulation of matters of local concern is local in character and effect, and its impact on the national commerce does not seriously interfere with its operation, and the consequent incentive to deal with them nationally is light, such regulation has been generally held to be within state authority. . . .

But ever since *Gibbons* v. *Ogden* . . . the states have not been deemed to have authority to impede substantially the free flow of commerce from state to state, or to regulate those phases of the national commerce which, because of the need of national uniformity, demand that their regulation, if any, be prescribed by a single authority. . . .

In the application of these principles some enactments may be found to be plainly within and others plainly without state power. But between these extremes lies the infinite variety of cases, in which regulation of local matters may also operate as a regulation of commerce, in which reconciliation of the conflicting claims of state and national power is to be attained only by some appraisal and accommodation of the competing demands of the state and national interests involved. . . .

For a hundred years it has been accepted constitutional doctrine that the commerce clause, without the aid of Congressional legislation, thus affords some protection from state legislation inimical to the national commerce, and that in such cases, where Congress has not acted, this Court, and not the state legislature, is under the commerce clause the final arbiter of the competing demands of state and national interests. . . .

Congress has undoubted power to redefine the distribution of power over interstate commerce. It may either permit the states to regulate the commerce in a manner which would otherwise not be permissible . . . or exclude state regulation even of matters of peculiarly local concern which nevertheless affect interstate commerce. . . .

But in general Congress has left it to the courts to formulate the rules thus interpreting the commerce clause in its application, doubtless because it has appreciated the destructive consequences to the commerce of the nation if their protection were withdrawn and has been aware that in their application state laws will not be invalidated without the support of relevant factual material which will ''afford a sure basis'' for an informed judgment.

. . . Meanwhile, Congress has accommodated its legislation, as have the states, to these rules as an established feature of our constitutional system. There has thus been left to the state wide scope for the regulation of matters of local state concern, even though it in some measure affects the commerce, provided it does not materially restrict the free flow of commerce across state lines, or interfere with it in matters with respect to which uniformity of regulation is of predominant national concern.

Hence the matters for ultimate determination here are the nature and extent of the burden which the state regulation of interstate trains, adopted as a safety measure, imposes on interstate commerce, and whether the relative weights of the state and national interests involved are such as to make inapplicable the rule, generally observed, that the free flow of interstate commerce and its freedom from local restraints in matters requiring uniformity of regulation are interests safeguarded by the commerce clause from state interference. . . .

The findings show that the operation of long trains, that is trains of more than fourteen passenger and more than seventy freight cars, is standard practice over the main lines of the railroads of the United States, and that, if the length of trains is to be regulated at all, national uniformity in the regulation adopted, such as only Congress can prescribe, is practically indispensable to the operation of an efficient and economical national railway system. . . .

The unchallenged findings leave no doubt that the Arizona Train Limit Law imposes a serious burden on the interstate commerce conducted by appellant. It materially impedes the movement of appellant's interstate trains through that state and interposes a substantial obstruction to the national policy proclaimed by Congress, to promote adequate, economical and efficient railway transportation service. . . . Enforcement of the law in Arizona, while train

lengths remain unregulated or are regulated by varying standards in other states, must inevitably result in an impairment of uniformity of efficient railroad operation because the railroads are subjected to regulation which is not uniform in its application. Compliance with a state statute limiting train lengths requires interstate trains of a length lawful in other states to be broken up and reconstituted as they enter each state according as it may impose varying limitations upon train lengths. The alternative is for the carrier to conform to the lowest train limit restriction of any of the states through which its trains pass, whose laws thus control the carriers' operations both within and without the regulating state. . . .

If one state may regulate train lengths, so may all the others, and they need not prescribe the same maximum limitation. The practical effect of such regulation is to control train operations beyond the boundaries of the state exacting it because of the necessity of breaking up and reassembling long trains at the nearest terminal points before entering and after leaving the regulating state. The serious impediment to the free flow of commerce by the local regulation of train lengths and the practical necessity that such regulation, if any, must be prescribed by a single body having a nationwide authority are apparent.

The trial court found that the Arizona law had no reasonable relation to safety, and made train operation more dangerous. Examination of the evidence and the detailed findings makes it clear that this conclusion was rested on facts found which indicate that such increased danger of accident and personal injury as may result from the greater length of trains is more than offset by the increase in the number of accidents resulting from the larger number of trains when train lengths are reduced. In considering the effect of the statute as a safety measure, therefore, the factor of controlling significance for present purposes is not whether there is basis for the conclusion of the Arizona Supreme Court that the increase in length of trains beyond the statutory maximum has an adverse effect upon safety of operation. The decisive question is whether in the circumstances the total effect of the law as a safety measure in reducing accidents and casualties is so slight or problematical as not to outweigh the national interest in keeping interstate commerce free from interferences which seriously impede it and subject it to local regulation which does not have a uniform effect on the interstate train journey which it interrupts. . . .

We think, as the trial court found, that the Arizona Train Limit Law, viewed as a safety measure, affords at most slight and dubious advantage, if any, over unregulated train lengths, because it results in an increase in the number of trains and train operations and the consequent increase in train accidents of a character generally more severe than those due to slack action. Its undoubted effect on the commerce is the regulation, without securing uniformity, of the length of trains operated in interstate commerce, which lack is itself a primary cause of preventing the free flow of commerce by delaying it and by substantially increasing its cost and impairing its efficiency. In these respects the case differs from those where a state, by regulatory measures affecting the commerce, has removed or reduced safety hazards without substantial interference with the interstate movement of trains. . . .

The principle that, without controlling Congressional action, a state may not regulate interstate commerce so as substantially to affect its flow or deprive it of needed uniformity in its regulation is not to be avoided by "simply invoking the convenient apologetics of the police power." . . .

Appellees especially rely on the full train crew cases, *Chicago, R. I. & P. R. Co.* v. *Arkansas*, 219 U.S. 453 . . . and also on *South Carolina State Highway Dept.* v. *Barnwell Bros.*, 303 U.S. 177, as supporting the state's authority to regulate the length of interstate trains. While the full train crew laws undoubtedly placed an added financial burden on the railroads in order to serve a local interest, they did not obstruct interstate transportation or seriously impede it. *South Carolina State Highway Dept.* v.

Barnwell Bros., was concerned with the power of the state to regulate the weight and width of motor cars passing interstate over its highways, a legislative field over which the state has a far more extensive control than over interstate railroads. In that case . . . we were at pains to point out that there are few subjects of state regulation affecting interstate commerce which are so peculiarly of local concern as is the use of the state's highways. Unlike the railroads local highways are built, owned and maintained by the state or its municipal subdivisions. The state is responsible for their safe and economical administration. Regulations affecting the safety of their use must be applied alike to intrastate and interstate traffic. The fact that they affect alike shippers in interstate and intrastate commerce in great numbers, within as well as without the state, is a safeguard against regulatory abuses. Their regulation is akin to quarantine measures, game laws, and like local regulations of rivers, harbors, piers, and docks, with respect to which the state has exceptional scope for the exercise of its regulatory power, and which, Congress not acting, have been sustained even though they materially interfere with interstate commerce.

The contrast between the present regulation and the full train crew laws in point of their effects on the commerce, and the like contrast with the highway safety regulations, in point of the nature of the subject of regulation and the state's interest in it, illustrate and emphasize the considerations which enter into a determination of the relative weights of state and national interests where state regulation affecting commerce is attempted. Here examination of all the relevant factors makes it plain that the state interest is outweighed by the interest of the Nation in an adequate, economical and efficient railway transportation service, which must prevail.

Reversed.

MR. JUSTICE RUTLEDGE concurs in the result.

MR. JUSTICE BLACK, dissenting.

The determination of whether it is in the interest of society for the length of trains to be governmentally regulated is a matter of public policy. Someone must fix that policy—either the Congress, or the state, or the courts. A century and a half of constitutional history and government admonishes this Court to leave that choice to the elected legislative representatives of the people themselves, where it properly belongs both on democratic principles and the requirements of efficient government.

I think that legislatures, to the exclusion of courts, have the constitutional power to enact laws limiting train lengths, for the purpose of reducing injuries brought about by "slack movements." Their power is not less because a requirement of short trains might increase grade crossing accidents. This latter fact raises an entirely different element of danger which is itself subject to legislative regulation. For legislatures may, if necessary, require railroads to take appropriate steps to reduce the likelihood of injuries at grade crossings. . . . And the fact that grade-crossing improvements may be expensive is no sufficient reason to say that an unconstitutional "burden" is put upon a railroad even though it be an interstate road. . . .

There have been many sharp divisions of this Court concerning its authority, in the absence of congressional enactment, to invalidate state laws as violating the Commerce Clause. . . . That discussion need not be renewed here, be-

cause even the broadest exponents of judicial power in this field have not heretofore expressed doubt as to a state's power, absent a paramount congressional declaration, to regulate interstate trains in the interest of safety. . . .

This record in its entirety leaves me with no doubt whatever that many employees have been seriously injured and killed in the past, and that many more are likely to be so in the future, because of "slack movement" in trains. Everyday knowledge as well as direct evidence presented at the various hearings, substantiates the report of the Senate Committee that danger from slack movement is greater in long trains than in short trains. It may be that offsetting dangers are possible in the operation of short trains. The balancing of these probabilities, however, is not in my judgment a matter for judicial determination, but one which calls for legislative consideration. Representatives elected by the people to make their laws, rather than judges appointed to interpret those laws, can best determine the policies which govern the people. That at least is the basic principle on which our democratic society rests. I would affirm the judgment of the Supreme Court of Arizona.

MR. JUSTICE DOUGLAS also dissented.

Hood v. Dumond
336 U.S. 525, 69 S.Ct. 657, 93 L.Ed. 865 (1949)

The Hood Company, a Massachusetts corporation, distributed in Boston milk collected at the company's three milk-receiving stations in the lower state of New York. When Hood sought a license for an additional receiving station in New York, the State Commissioner of Agriculture and Markets refused on the ground that an expansion of Hood's facilities would reduce the supply of milk for local markets and would result in destructive competition in a market area already well served. The company petitioned for certiorari from an adverse judgment in the New York Court of Appeals.

MR. JUSTICE JACKSON delivered the opinion of the Court. . . .

The desire of the Forefathers to federalize regulation of foreign and interstate commerce stands in sharp contrast to their jealous preservation of the State's power over its internal affairs. No other federal power was so universally assumed to be necessary, no other State power was so readily relinquished. There was no desire to authorize federal interference with social conditions or legal institutions of the States. Even the Bill of Rights amendments were framed only as a limitation upon the powers of Congress. The States were quite content with their several and diverse controls over most matters, but, as Madison has indicated, "want of a general power over Commerce led to an exercise of this power separately, by the States, which not only proved abortive, but engendered rival, conflicting and angry regulations." 3 Farrand, *Records of the Federal Convention*, 547. . . .

The Commerce Clause is one of the most prolific sources of national power and an equally prolific source of conflict with legislation of the State. While the Constitution vests in Congress the power to regulate commerce among the States, it does not say what the States may or may not do in the absence of congressional action, nor how to draw the line between what is and what is not commerce among the States. Perhaps even more than by interpretation of its written word, this Court has advanced the solidarity and prosperity of this Nation by the meaning it has given to these great silences of the Constitution. . . .

The material success that has come to inhabitants of the states which make up this federal free trade unit has been the most impressive in the history of commerce, but the established interdependence of the States only emphasizes the necessity of protecting interstate movement of goods against local burdens and repressions. We need only consider the consequences if each of the few states that produce copper, lead, high-grade iron ore, timber, cotton, oil or gas should decree that industries located in that state shall have priority. What fantastic rivalries and dislocations and reprisals would ensue if such practices were begun! Or suppose that the field of discrimination and retaliation be industry. May Michigan provide that automobiles cannot be taken out of that State until local dealers' demands are fully met? Would she not have every argument in the favor of such a statute that can be offered in support of New York's limiting sales of milk for out-of-state shipment to protect the economic interests of her competing dealers and local consumers? Could Ohio then pounce upon the rubber tire industry, on which she has a substantial grip, to retaliate for Michigan's auto monopoly?

Our system, fostered by the Commerce Clause, is that every farmer and every craftsman shall be encouraged to produce by the certainty that he will have free access to every market in the Nation, that no home embargoes will withhold his exports, and no foreign state will by customs duties or regulations exclude them. Likewise, every consumer may look to the free competition from every producing area in the Nation to protect him from exploitation by any. Such was the vision of the Founders; such has been the doctrine of this Court, which has given it reality. . . .

The State, however, contends that such restraint or obstruction as its order imposes on interstate commerce does not violate the Commerce Clause because the State regulation coincides with, supplements and is part of the federal regulatory scheme. This contention that Congress has taken possession of "the field" but shared it with the state, it is to be noted, reverses the contention usually made in comparable cases, which is that Congress has not fully occupied the field and hence the State may fill the void.

Congress, as a part of its Agricultural Marketing Agreement Act, authorizes the Secretary of Agriculture to issue orders regulating the handling of several agricultural products, including milk, when they are within the reach of its commerce power. . . .

The Congressional regulation contemplates and permits a wide latitude in which the State may exercise its police power over the local facilities for handling milk. We assume, though it is not necessary to decide, that the Federal Act does not preclude a state from placing restrictions and obstructions in the way of interstate commerce for the ends and purposes always held permissible under the Commerce Clause. But here the challenge is the sole and specific ground that it will subject others to competition and take supplies needed locally, an end, as we have shown, always held to be precluded by the Commerce Clause. We have no doubt that Congress in the national interest could prohibit or curtail shipments of milk in interstate commerce, unless and until local demands are met. Nor do we know of any reason why Congress may not, if it deems it in the national interest, authorize the state to place similar restraints on movement of articles of commerce. And the provisions looking to state cooperation may be sufficient to warrant the state in imposing regulations approved by the federal authorities, even if they otherwise might run counter to the decisions that coincidence is as fatal as conflict when Congress acts. . . .

Moreover, we can hardly assume that the challenged provisions of this order advance the federal scheme of regulation because Congress forbids inclusion of such a policy in a federal milk order. Section 8c (5) (G) of the Act provides:

> No marketing agreement or order applicable to milk and its products in any marketing area shall prohibit or in any manner limit, in the case of the products of milk, the marketing in the area of any milk or product thereof produced in any production area in the United States.

While there may be difference of opinion as to whether this authorizes the Federal Order to limit, so long as it does not prohibit, interstate shipment of milk . . . a question upon which we express no opinion—it is clear that the policy of the provision is inconsistent with the State's contention that it may, in its own interest, impose such a limitation as a coincident or supplement to federal regulation. . . .

. . . The judgment is reversed and the cause remanded for proceedings not inconsistent with this opinion.

It is so ordered.

MR. JUSTICE BLACK, dissenting.

In this case the Court sets up a new constitutional formula for invalidation of state laws regulating local phases of interstate commerce. I believe the New York law is invulnerable to constitutional attack under constitutional rules which the majority of this Court have long accepted. The new formula subjects state regulations of local business activities to greater constitutional hazards than they have ever had to meet before. The consequences of the new formula, as I understand it, will not merely leave a large area of local business activities free from state regulation. . . .

That part of the regulatory plan challenged here bars issuance of licenses for additional milk-handling plants if new plants would "tend to destructive competition in a market already adequately served" or would be contrary to "the public interest." In determining whether a milk market is "adequately served," the state follows a plan similar to the federal law in that both divide the country into "marketing areas." . . .

. . . The commissioner found that more plants would bring about the kind of destructive competition against which the law was aimed. That finding is not challenged. Nor is it charged that the order was prompted by desire to prevent New York milk from going to Boston. . . .

The language of this state Act is not discriminatory, the legislative history shows it was not so intended, and the commissioner has not administered it with a hostile eye. The Act must stand or fall on this basis notwithstanding the overtones of the Court's opinion. If petitioner and other interstate milk dealers are to be placed above and beyond this law, it must be done solely on this Court's new constitutional formula which bars a state from protecting itself against local destructive competitive practices so far as they are indulged in by dealers who ship their milk into other states. . . .

It seems to me that the Court now steps in

where Congress wanted it to stay out. The Court puts itself in the position of guardian of interstate trade in the milk industry. Congress, with full constitutional power to do so, selected the Secretary of Agriculture to do this job. Maybe this Court would be a better guardian, but it may be doubted that authority for the Court to undertake the task can be found in the Constitution—even in its "great silences." At any rate, I had supposed that this Court would not find conflict where Congress explicitly has commanded cooperation.

. . . The gravity of striking down state regulations is immeasurably increased when it results as here in leaving a no-man's land immune from any effective regulation whatever. It is dangerous to assume that the aggressive cupidity of some need never be checked by government in the interest of all.

The judicially directed march of due process philosophy as an emancipator of business from regulation appeared arrested a few years ago. That appearance was illusory. That philosophy continues its march. The due process clause and commerce clause have been used like Siamese twins in a never-ending stream of challenges to government regulation. . . . The reach of one twin may appear to be longer than that of the other, but either can easily be turned to remedy this apparent handicap.

Both the commerce and due process clauses serve high purposes when confined within their proper scope. But a stretching of either outside its sphere can paralyze the legislative process, rendering the people's legislative representatives impotent to perform their duty of providing appropriate rules to govern this dynamic civilization. Both clauses easily lend themselves to inordinate expansions of this Court's power at the expense of legislative power. For under the prevailing due process rule, appeals can be made to the "fundamental principles of liberty and justice" which our "fathers" wished to preserve. In commerce clause cases reference can appropriately be made to the far-seeing wisdom of the "fathers" in guarding against commercial and even shooting wars among the states. Such arguments have strong emotional appeals and when skillfully utilized they sometimes obscure the vision. . . .

. . . Any doubt I may have concerning the wisdom of New York's law is far less, however, than is my skepticism concerning the ability of the Federal Government to reach out and effectively regulate all the local business activities in the forty-eight states.

I would leave New York's law alone.

MR. JUSTICE MURPHY joins in this opinion.

[MR. JUSTICE FRANKFURTER wrote a dissenting opinion in which MR. JUSTICE RUTLEDGE joined.]

Reeves, Inc. v. Stake
447 U.S. 429, 100 S.Ct. 2271, 65 L.Ed. 2d 244 (1980)

For many years the state of South Dakota has operated a cement plant. Between 1970 and 1977, some 40 percent of the plant's production was shipped to buyers outside the state. Reeves, Inc., is a ready-mix concrete distributor in Wyoming, which from 1958 until 1978 obtained 95 percent of its cement from the state-owned plant. In 1978, various difficulties at the cement plant forced a cut in production. The State Cement Commission chose to supply all South Dakota customers first and to honor other contract commitments. Being out of state and lacking a long-term contract, Reeves was unable to purchase any more cement and was obliged to reduce its own concrete production by 76 percent when no other adequate suppliers could be found. Reeves then sued the commission in U.S. district court, which "reasoned that South Dakota's 'hoarding' was inimical to the national free market envisioned by the Commerce Clause." The Court of Appeals for the Eighth Circuit reversed, and the Supreme Court granted certiorari. After a detailed review of the commission's policy and Reeves's plight, Justice Blackmun's majority opinion turned to a review of *Hughes* v. *Alexandria Scrap Corp.*, 426 U.S. 794 (1976). In this earlier case Justice Powell wrote the opinion of the Court, while Justices Brennan, White, and Marshall dissented.

MR. JUSTICE BLACKMUN delivered the opinion of the court. . . .

Alexandria Scrap concerned a Maryland program designed to remove abandoned automobiles from the State's roadways and junkyards. To encourage recycling, a "bounty" was offered for every Maryland-titled junk car converted into scrap. Processors located both in and outside Maryland were eligible to collect these subsidies. The legislation, as initially enacted in 1969, required a processor seeking a bounty to present documentation evidencing ownership of the wrecked car. This requirement however, did not apply to "hulks," inoperable automobiles over eight years old. In 1974, the statute was amended to extend documentation requirements to hulks, which comprised a large majority of the junk cars being processed. Departing from prior practice, the new law imposed more exacting documentation requirements on out-of-state than in-state processors. By making it less remunerative for suppliers to transfer vehicles outside Maryland, the reform triggered a "precipitate decline in the number of bounty-eligible hulks supplied to appellee's [Virginia] plant from Maryland sources." . . . Indeed, "[t]he practical effect was substantially the same as if Maryland had withdrawn altogether the availability of bounties on hulks delivered by unlicensed suppliers to licensed non-Maryland processors."

Invoking the Commerce Clause, a three-judge District Court struck down the legislation. . . . It observed that the amendment imposed "substantial burdens upon the free flow of interstate commerce," . . . and reasoned that the discriminatory program was not the least

disruptive means of achieving the State's articulated objective. . . .

This Court reversed. It recognized the persuasiveness of the lower court's analysis if the inherent restrictions of the Commerce Clause were deemed applicable. In the Court's view, however, *Alexandria Scrap* did not involve "the kind of action with which the Commerce Clause is concerned." . . .

Having characterized Maryland as a market participant, rather than as a market regulator, the Court found no reason to "believe the Commerce Clause was intended to require independent justification for [the State's] action." . . . The Court couched its holding in unmistakably broad terms. "Nothing in the purposes animating the Commerce Clause prohibits a State, in the absence of congressional action, from participating in the market and exercising the right to favor its own citizens over others." . . .

The basic distinction drawn in *Alexandria Scrap* between States as market participants and States as market regulators makes good sense and sound law. As that case explains, the Commerce Clause responds principally to state taxes and regulatory measures impeding free private trade in the national marketplace. . . . There is no indication of a constitutional plan to limit the ability of the States themselves to operate freely in the free market. . . .

Restraint in this area is also counseled by considerations of state sovereignty, the role of each State " 'as guardian and trustee for its people,' " . . . and "the long recognized right of trader or manufacturer, engaged in an entirely private business, freely to exercise his own independent discretion as to parties with whom he will deal." . . . Moreover, state proprietary activities may be, and often are, burdened with the same restrictions imposed on private market participants. Evenhandedness suggests that, when acting as proprietors, States should similarly share existing freedoms from federal constraints, including the inherent limits of the Commerce Clause. . . . Finally, as this case illustrates, the competing considerations in cases involving state proprietary action often will be subtle, complex, politically charged, and difficult to assess under traditional Commerce Clause analysis. Given these factors, *Alexandria Scrap* wisely recognizes that, as a rule, the adjustment of interests in this context is a task better suited for Congress than this Court.

South Dakota, as a seller of cement, unquestionably fits the "market participant" label more comfortably than a State acting to subsidize local scrap processors. Thus, the general rule of *Alexandria Scrap* plainly applies here. . . .

In finding a Commerce Clause violation, the District Court emphasized "that the Commission . . . made an election to become part of the interstate commerce system." . . . The gist of this reasoning, repeated by petitioner here, is that one good turn deserves another. Having long exploited the interstate market, South Dakota should not be permitted to withdraw from it when a shortage arises. This argument is not persuasive. It is somewhat self-serving to say that South Dakota has "exploited" the interstate market. An equally fair characterization is that neighboring States have long benefited from South Dakota's foresight and industry. . . .

Our rejection of petitioner's market-exploitation theory fundamentally refocuses analysis. It means that to reverse we would have to void a South Dakota "residents only" policy even if it had been enforced from the plant's very first days. Such a holding, however, would interfere significantly with a State's ability to structure relations exclusively with its own citizens. It would also threaten the future fashioning of effective and creative programs for solving local problems and distributing government largesse. . . . A healthy regard for federalism and good government renders us reluctant to risk these results.

To stay experimentation in things social and economic is a grave responsibility. Denial of the right to experiment may be fraught with serious consequences to the Nation. It is one of the happy incidents of the federal system that a single courageous State may, if its citizens choose, serve as a laboratory; and try novel social and economic experiments without risk to the rest of the country. *New State Ice Co.* v. *Liebmann*, 285 U.S. 262, 311 (1932) (Brandeis, J., dissenting).

Undaunted by these considerations, petitioner advances four more arguments for reversal:

First, petitioner protests that South Dakota's preference for its residents responds solely to the "non-governmental objective" of protectionism. . . . Therefore, petitioner argues the policy is *per se* invalid. . . .

We find the label "protectionism" of little help in this context. The State's refusal to sell to buyers other than South Dakotans is "protectionist" only in the sense that it limits benefits generated by a state program to those who fund the state treasury and whom the State was created to serve. Petitioner's argument apparently also would characterize as "protectionist" rules restricting to state residents the enjoyment of state educational institutions, energy generated by a state-run plant, police and fire protection, and agricultural improvement and business development programs. Such policies, while perhaps "protectionist" in a loose sense, reflect the essential and patently unobjectionable purpose of state government—to serve the citizens of the State.

Second, petitioner echoes the District Court's warning.

If a state in this union, were allowed to hoard its commodities or resources for the use of their own residents only, a drastic situation might evolve. For example, Pennsylvania or Wyoming might keep their coal, the northwest its timber, and the mining states their minerals. The result being that embargo may be retaliated by embargo and commerce would be halted at state lines. . . .

This argument, although rooted in the core purpose of the Commerce Clause, does not fit the present facts. Cement is not a natural resource, like coal, timber, wild game, or minerals. . . . It is the end-product of a complex process whereby a costly physical plant and human labor act on raw materials. South Dakota has not sought to limit access to the State's limestone or other materials used to make cement. Nor has it restricted the ability of private firms or sister States to set up plants within its borders. . . .

Third, it is suggested that the South Dakota program is infirm because it places South Dakota suppliers of ready-mix concrete at a competitive advantage in the out-of-state market; Wyoming suppliers, such as petitioner, have little chance against South Dakota suppliers who can purchase cement from the State's plant and freely sell beyond South Dakota's borders.

The force of this argument is seriously diminished, if not eliminated, by several considerations. The argument necessarily implies that the South Dakota scheme would be unobjectionable if sales in other States were totally barred. It therefore proves too much, for it would tolerate even a greater measure of protectionism and stifling of interstate commerce than the challenged system allows. . . . Finally, the competitive plight of out-of-state ready-mix suppliers cannot be laid solely at the feet of South Dakota. It is attributable as well to their own States' not providing or attracting alternative sources of supply and to the suppliers' own failure to guard against shortages by executing long-term supply contracts with the South Dakota plant.

In its last argument, petitioner urges that, had South Dakota not acted, free market forces would have generated an appropriate level of supply at free market prices for all buyers in the region. Having replaced free market forces,

South Dakota should be forced to replicate how the free market would have operated under prevailing conditions.

This argument appears to us to be simplistic and speculative. The very reason South Dakota built its plant was because the free market had failed adequately to supply the region with cement. . . .

We conclude, then, that the arguments for invalidating South Dakota's resident-preference program are weak at best. Whatever residual force inheres in them is more than offset by countervailing considerations of policy and fairness. Reversal would discourage similar state projects, even though this project demonstrably has served the needs of state residents and has helped the entire region for more than a half century. Reversal also would rob South Dakota of the intended benefit of its foresight, risk, and industry. Under these circumstances, there is no reason to depart from the general rule of *Alexandria Scrap*.

The judgment of the United States Court of Appeals is affirmed.

It is so ordered.

MR. JUSTICE POWELL, with whom MR. JUSTICE BRENNAN, MR. JUSTICE WHITE, and MR. JUSTICE STEVENS join, dissenting. . . .

The need to ensure unrestricted trade among the States created a major impetus for the drafting of the Constitution. "The power over commerce . . . was one of the primary objects for which the people of America adopted their government. . . ." *Gibbons* v. *Ogden*. . . . Indeed, the Constitutional Convention was called after an earlier convention on trade and commercial problems proved inconclusive. . . . In the subsequent debate over ratification, Alexander Hamilton emphasized the importance of unrestricted interstate commerce:

An unrestrained intercourse between the States themselves will advance the trade of each, by an interchange of their respective productions. . . . Commercial enterprise will have much greater scope, from the diversity in the productions of different States. When the staple of one fails . . . it can call to its aid the staple of another. *The Federalist*, No. 11. . . .

The Commerce Clause has proved an effective weapon against protectionism. The Court has used it to strike down limitations on access to local goods, be they animal, . . . vegetable, . . . or mineral. . . .

This case presents a novel constitutional question. The Commerce Clause would bar legislation imposing on private parties the type of restraint on commerce adopted by South Dakota. . . . Conversely, a private business constitutionally could adopt a marketing policy that excluded customers who come from another State. This case falls between those polar situations. The State, through its Commission, engages in a commercial enterprise and restricts its own interstate distribution. The question is whether the Commission's policy should be treated like state regulation of private parties or like the marketing policy of a private business.

The application of the Commerce Clause to this case should turn on the nature of the governmental activity involved. If a public enterprise undertakes an "integral operatio[n] in areas of traditional governmental functions," . . . the Commerce Clause is not directly relevant. If, however, the State enters the private market and operates a commercial enterprise for the advantage of its private citizens, it may not evade the constitutional policy against economic balkanization.

This distinction derives from the power of governments to supply their own needs, . . . and from the purpose of the Commerce Clause itself, which is designed to protect "the natural functioning of the interstate market," *Hughes* v. *Alexandria Scrap*. . . . In procuring goods and services for the operation of government, a State may act without regard to the private marketplace and remove itself from the reach of the Commerce Clause. . . . But when a State itself becomes a participant in the private market for other purposes, the Constitution forbids actions that would impede the flow of interstate com-

merce. These categories recognize no more than the "constitutional line between the State as Government and the State as trader." *New York* v. *United States*. . . .

The threshold issue is whether South Dakota has undertaken integral government operations in an area of traditional governmental functions, or whether it has participated in the marketplace as a private firm. If the latter characterization applies, we also must determine whether the State Commission's marketing policy burdens the flow of interstate trade. This analysis highlights the differences between the state action here and that before the Court in *Hughes* v. *Alexandria Scrap Corp*. . . .

As the Court today notes, *Alexandria Scrap* determined that Maryland's bounty program constituted direct state participation in the market for automobile hulks. . . . But the critical question—the second step in the opinion's analysis—was whether the bounty program constituted an impermissible burden on interstate commerce. Recognizing that the case did not fit neatly into conventional Commerce Clause theory. . . . we found no burden on commerce. . . .

Unlike the market subsidies at issue in *Alexandria Scrap,* the marketing policy of the South Dakota Cement Commission has cut off interstate trade. . . . The effect on interstate trade is the same as if the state legislature had imposed the policy on private cement producers. The Commerce Clause prohibits this severe restraint on commerce.

I share the Court's desire to preserve state sovereignty. But the Commerce Clause long has been recognized as a limitation on that sovereignty, consciously designed to maintain a national market and defeat economic provincialism. The Court today approves protectionist state policies. In the absence of contrary congressional action, those policies now can be implemented as long as the State itself directly participates in the market.

By enforcing the Commerce Clause in this case, the Court would work no unfairness on the people of South Dakota. They still could reserve cement for public projects and share in whatever return the plant generated. They could not, however, use the power of the State to furnish themselves with cement forbidden to the people of neighboring States.

The creation of a free national economy was a major goal of the States when they resolved to unite under the Federal Constitution. The decision today cannot be reconciled with that purpose.

SIX

Congressional Power
under the Commerce Clause

Until 1890 the Supreme Court was concerned with the commerce clause primarily as it limited state action affecting interstate commerce. By and large, the Court was generous in its view of state power. In 1876, for example, the Justices held that the states—in the absence of legislation by Congress—could regulate railroad and other rates for interstate as well as for intrastate shipments. This led to such great confusion that ten years later the Court, in the history-making Wabash case (*Wabash Railway Co.* v. *Illinois,* 118 U.S. 557: 1886), was obliged to repudiate its former view.

THE NEED FOR NATIONAL ACTION

The Illinois act under consideration in the Wabash case had been applied as a corrective of long- and short-haul rate discriminations on shipments originating in Illinois and terminating in New York City. "As restricted to a transportation which begins and ends within the limits of the state," the Court said, "it may be very just and equitable. . . . But when it is attempted to apply to transportation through an entire series of states a principle of this kind, and each one of the states shall attempt to establish its own rates of transportation . . . the deleterious influence upon the freedom of commerce among the states . . . cannot be overestimated." The Court concluded by suggesting that since the subject was of "national character" any regulation "should be done by the Congress of the United States under the commerce clause of the Constitution." Enacted the next year was the Interstate Commerce Act—the first major effort by Congress under the commerce power to achieve regulatory purpose.

Three years later the Sherman Anti-Trust Act showed that Congress was determined to use its commerce power to accomplish purposes far beyond anything hitherto attempted. The business community strenuously resisted this bold national effort to control American industrial and commercial life, finding useful constitutional weapons in both the due process and commerce clauses. In the survey that follows, the conventional measures regulating commerce (e.g., acts and administrative orders prescribing rules for railroads, motor carriers, aircraft, and the telephone and other industries) have of necessity been ignored. We shall consider only major cases involving acts of a controversial nature by which the national government attempted to accomplish various far-reaching economic or social objectives.

Difficult questions arose at the very outset concerning the applicability of the Sherman Anti-Trust Act (1890) to industrial and commercial enterprise. The rationale of the Act was that certain combinations and conspiracies that had the effect of restraining or monopolizing interstate commerce should be prohibited. In *United States* v. *E. C. Knight,* known as the Sugar Trust case, a monopoly in the production of refined sugar was held exempt from the Sherman Act. To Chief Justice Fuller, commerce meant primarily transportation—the physical movement of goods following manufacture. The effect of contracts and combinations to control manufacture, ''however inevitable and whatever its extent,'' would be ''indirect,'' the Chief Justice held, and therefore beyond congressional reach. Yet he recognized that goods are manufactured *only* because they can be sold, that manufacture and commerce are part of a seamless web. Much disturbed by the implications of an integrated national economy for federal power, the Chief Justice said: ''Slight reflection will show that if the national power extends to all contracts and combinations in manufacture, agriculture, mining, and other productive industries, whose ultimate result may affect external commerce, comparatively little of business operations and affairs would be left for state control.''

In 1904, however (*Northern Securities Co.* v. *United States,* 193 U.S. 197), a scheme by which a holding company had been established to hold the stock of competing railroads was held contrary to the Sherman Act. In another broad interpretation of the commerce power (*Swift* v. *United States,* 196 U.S. 375: 1905), a combination of meat packers was held unlawful under the Act, on the ground that their activities, though geographically ''local,'' were important incidents in a current of interstate commerce. ''Although the combination alleged,'' Justice Holmes observed, ''embraces restraint and monopoly of trade within a single state, its effect upon commerce among the states is not accidental, secondary, remote or merely probable. . . . Here the subject matter is sales and the very point of the combination is to restrain and monopolize commerce among the states in respect to such sales.'' Although not expressly overruled, the Sugar Trust case was seriously undermined.

Of *Swift* v. *United States,* Chief Justice Taft said in 1923 (*Board of Trade of Chicago* v. *Olsen,* 262 U.S. 1: 1923): ''That case was a milestone in the interpretation of the commerce clause of the Constitution. It recognized the great changes and development in the business of this vast country and drew again the dividing line between interstate and intrastate commerce where the Constitution intended it to be. It refused to permit local incidents of great interstate movement, which, taken alone, were intrastate, to characterize the movement as such. The Swift case merely fitted the commerce clause to the real and practical essence of modern business growth.''

JUDICIAL CHOICES IN CONSTITUTIONAL INTERPRETATION

But only three years after the Swift case, the Court refused to find sufficient connection between membership in a labor organization and the free flow of commerce (*Adair* v. *United States,* 208 U.S. 161: 1908). The federal act in dispute had made it unlawful for railroad employers to discharge employees because of their union membership, a frequent source of strikes in this period. Apart from his view that the government should not interfere with an alleged "equality" of bargaining between employer and employees, Justice Harlan expressed ideas on the scope of the commerce clause frequently repeated in later cases. The rules prescribed by Congress under the commerce power must, he said, have a "real" or "substantial" relation to the commerce regulated. In other words, Harlan narrowed Marshall's broad definition of commerce by determining in each case, according to standards created by the Supreme Court, whether the congressional conception of commerce squared with its own. Justice McKenna, dissenting, thought that removing a cause of frequent strikes was more important to the health of commerce than most safety regulations, and Holmes, also dissenting, chided the majority for confusing questions of economic policy with those of constitutional power.

A series of cases between 1903 and World War I clearly established the principle that the commerce power could be used as a device for accomplishing purely social goals. In the first case (*Champion* v. *Ames,*) a federal act prohibiting the interstate shipment of lottery tickets was upheld. While the opinion contained frequent references to the evil quality of these tickets, the dissent pointed out that the evil began only with their illegal use at the point of destination. On similar grounds, the Pure Food and Drug Act withstood attack in 1911 (*Hipolite Egg Co.* v. *United States,* 220 U.S. 45). In *Hoke* v. *United States* (227 U.S. 308: 1913), the Court approved the Mann Act, making it a felony to transport a woman from one state to another for immoral purposes. In the *Shreveport* case, the Court upheld an Interstate Commerce Commission order fixing intrastate railroad rates because of their effect on interstate commerce, suggesting a return to Marshall's view that national commerce power extends to all commerce that "affects more than one state."

After 1918 the pattern is confused. In the frequently cited decision in *Hammer* v. *Dagenhart* the Court, following the Sugar Trust case, again drew a distinction between commerce and manufacturing. Congress had prohibited the transportation in interstate commerce of products produced by child labor (age 16 in mines, age 14 in factories, or more than 48 hours a week for the age group 14–16 years). Justice Day, for the Court, characterized the precedents involving lotteries, food, and white slavery as attempts to regulate where transportation was used to accomplish harmful results; production and its incidents, on the other hand, were (in Day's opinion) local matters. Holmes, dissenting, countered: "The states . . . may regulate their internal affairs and their domestic commerce as they like. But when they seek to send their products across the state line they are no longer within their rights." To Holmes there was no greater justification for examining the motives of Congress in this case than in those involving lottery tickets, food, or women. Holmes made clear his view that the different result followed from the Justices' ideas on social policy.

Two subsequent cases seemed to indicate once again that the Court might be prepared to accept a broad construction of the commerce power. In *Stafford* v. *Wallace* Chief Justice Taft delivered an opinion upholding the Packers and Stockyards Act of 1921, an attempt to regulate trade practices in the Chicago meat-packing industry. Taft stated that although in a geographic sense the packers were conducting a local business, in an economic sense their activities were but an incident in a continuing interstate market. Justice Holmes' "clear and comprehensive exposition" in the *Swift* case, Taft said, "leaves to us in this case little but the obvious application of the principles there declared." The application of the commerce clause in the *Swift* case, Taft continued, was "the result of the natural development of interstate commerce under modern conditions. It was the inevitable recognition of the great central fact that such streams of commerce from one part of the country to another, which are ever flowing, are, in their very essence, the commerce among the states and with foreign nations which historically it was one of the chief purposes of the Constitution to bring under national protection and control.''

Following the same line of reasoning, the Court in 1925 upheld the National Motor Theft Act, making it a crime to transport or conceal a stolen automobile (*Brooks* v. *United States,* 267 U.S. 432). These cases cast grave doubt on the value of *Hammer* v. *Dagenhart* as a precedent and seemed to portend a return to the broad doctrines of Chief Justice Marshall. In 1935, when the Court was faced with the necessity of passing on the New Deal legislation enacted under the commerce clause, it had before it two viable lines of precedents: (1) The doctrines established by John Marshall, which had inspired the Court's decisions in *Swift* v. *United States* and *Stafford* v. *Wallace;* and (2) the restrictive interpretations of the Sugar Trust case and *Hammer* v. *Dagenhart.*

THE NEW DEAL IN COURT

The first New Deal reform measure reached the Supreme Bench on December 10, 1934, under circumstances that did not augur well for the validity of executive orders issued under NIRA. The Panama Refining Company had challenged the Act's prohibition against shipment of ''hot oil'' (that exceeding state allowances) across state lines. Early in the argument government counsel disclosed that criminal penalties attaching to the violation of the relevant code provisions had been inadvertently omitted from the executive order. Judicial curiosity was immediately aroused, and concern deepened when opposing counsel bitterly complained that his client had been arrested, indicted, and held several days in jail for violating this nonexistent ''law.'' With these points against it the government was at a disadvantage in pressing its argument that Congress could constitutionally empower the President in his discretion to ban ''hot oil'' from interstate commerce. Hughes and seven other Justices held Section 9(c) of the NIRA invalid as an unconstitutional delegation of legislative power to the chief executive (*Panama Refining Co.* v. *Ryan,* 293 U.S. 388: 1935). Congress, they said, established no ''primary standard,'' thus leaving ''the matter to the President without standard or rule, to be dealt with as he pleased.'' For the first time the maxim *delegata potestas non potest delegari,* a principle not found in the Constitution, formed the basis of a judicial decision overturning an act of Congress.

Before the dust thrown up by the ''hot oil'' decision had fairly settled, the Court made headlines again in its 5-to-4 decision scuttling the recently enacted railroad retirement scheme, which required the carriers to subscribe to a pension plan for old employees (*Railroad Retirement Board* v. *Alton R. R. Co.,* 295 U.S. 330: 1935). For the majority, Mr. Justice Roberts ridiculed the statute. Brushing the legislation aside as based on ''the contentment and satisfaction theory'' of social progress, he inquired: ''Is it not apparent that they [pensions] are really and essentially related solely to the social welfare of the worker, and therefore remote from any regulation of commerce as such?'' Congress might, he agreed, require outright dismissal of all aged workers, but it could not give them pensions. If superannuation is a danger, Roberts argued in effect, the commerce clause authorizes compulsory retirement—without a pension! Congressional effort to compel railroads to pension off older workers must fail for want of any relation between the pensioning system and the efficiency or safety of the national rail network.

The discouraging aspect of Justice Roberts's opinion is implicit in Hughes's dissent:

". . . the majority finally raise a barrier against all legislative action of this nature by declaring that the subject matter itself lies beyond the reach of the congressional authority to regulate interstate commerce. In that view, no matter how suitably limited . . . or how appropriate the measure of retirement allowances, or how sound actuarially the plan, or how well adjusted the burden, still under this decision Congress could not be at liberty to enact such a measure. . . . I think that the conclusion thus reached is a departure from sound principles and places an unwarranted limitation upon the commerce clause of the Constitution."

Taken together, the Panama Refining and the Railroad Retirement cases forecast the New Deal's doom. The blow fell on May 27, 1935, "Black Monday," when NIRA (symbolized by the Blue Eagle) was guillotined out of the recovery program (*Schechter Poultry Co.* v. *United States,* 295 U.S. 495: 1935).

The Schechter brothers, wholesale poultry dealers in Brooklyn, were charged with violating NIRA's Live Poultry Code by ignoring minimum wage and maximum hour requirements, and by giving special treatment to preferred customers. The Court, speaking through Chief Justice Hughes, found the act wanting as an unconstitutional delegation of legislative power. Government counsel conceded that congressional authority to regulate the Schechter business had to be based on the commerce clause, but the Court held the defendants' business was neither interstate commerce in itself, nor closely enough connected with it to "affect" such commerce.

"In determining how far the Federal Government may go in controlling intrastate transactions, upon the ground that they 'affect' interstate commerce," the Chief Justice declared, "there is a necessary and well-established distinction between direct and indirect effects. The precise line can be drawn only as individual cases arise, but the distinction is clear in principle. . . ." For supporting authority, Hughes went back to 1890 and the Sugar Trust decision. Curiously enough, he did not cite that case, but he did mention *Brown* v. *Houston,* and in so doing suffered a strange oversight. In that case the Court had ruled that barges of coal shipped down the river to New Orleans, even though the coal remained in its "original package," were subject to local taxation—"in the absence of congressional action." In a brief opinion, Justice Bradley mentioned the qualification five times. The Chief Justice ignored it, though the very question in the case before him concerned the validity of "congressional action."

Stone and Cardozo, in a separate opinion written by the latter, agreed with the Court's disposition of the case. "This," they said, "is delegation running riot." Nor could they find support in the commerce clause "for the regulation of wages and hours of labor in the intrastate transactions that make up the defendants' business." Without characterizing all production as "local," Stone and Cardozo rejected "a view of causation that would obliterate the distinction between what is national and what is local in the activities of commerce." Somewhat more cautious than their brethren, however, they subtly indicated a desire to treat such problems as they arose without anticipating and deciding in sweeping language all the constitutional issues of the decade.

On May 18, 1935, the Justices ruled, 6 to 3, that Congress had failed in its effort to salvage NRA remedies for the notoriously distressed bituminous coal industry (*Carter* v. *Carter Coal Co.*). The situation was so urgent and the benefits of the legislation so evident that President Roosevelt had taken the unusual step of asking the congressional subcommittee, while the Guffey Coal Act was pending, not to "permit doubts as to constitutionality, however reasonable," to block the suggested legislation. Five Justices, apparently undisturbed by the consequences of inaction, were moved by considerations (to them) of even greater concern: ". . . it is of vital moment," Justice Sutherland said for the majority, "that, in order to preserve the fixed balance intended by the Constitution, the powers of the general government be not so extended as to embrace any not within the express terms of the several grants or the implications necessary to be drawn therefrom."

Sutherland's opinion is clear-cut and unequivocal on one point that Chief Justice Hughes had left obscure—the nature of the distinction between direct and indirect effects. "The local character of mining, of manufacturing, and of crop growing is a fact, and remains a fact, whatever may be done with the products," Sutherland said. Going back to Chief Justice Fuller's opinion in the Sugar Trust case and paraphrasing his words, Sutherland declared: "Such effect as they [working conditions] may have upon commerce, however extensive it may be, is secondary and indirect. An increase in the greatness of the effect adds to its importance. It does not alter its character." In the teeth of the congressional declaration that the Act's price-fixing and labor provisions were separable, Sutherland held that they were united inextricably, and therefore must stand or fall together. They must fall, he ruled, because the labor provisions here, like those involved in the Schechter case, bore no "direct" relation to interstate commerce.

Chief Justice Hughes wrote a separate opinion. He maintained that Justice Sutherland was in error in denying the separability of price-fixing and hours of labor regulation, but he apparently agreed with Sutherland's contention that mining is not commerce. The distinction between direct and indirect being one of kind rather than degree, national regulation must await the cumbersome process of constitutional amendment. "If the people desire to give Congress the power to regulate industries within the State, and the relations of employers and employees in those industries," Hughes wrote, "they are at liberty to declare their will in the appropriate manner, but it is not for the Court to amend the Constitution by judicial decision."

To maintain his concept of the federal system Hughes, in effect, returned to the formula Chief Justice Fuller had invoked in 1895: "The distinction between direct and indirect effects of intrastate transactions upon interstate commerce must be recognized as a fundamental one, essential to the maintenance of our constitutional system. Otherwise, as we have said, there would be virtually no limit to the federal power and for all practical purposes we should have a completely centralized government." The Chief Justice was merely enforcing the views he had expressed as a private citizen in 1928.

> The *dual system of government* implies the maintenance of the constitutional restrictions of the powers of Congress as well as those of the States. The existence of the function of the Supreme Court is a constant monition to Congress. A judicial, as distinguished from a mere political, solution of the questions arising from time to time has its advantages in a more philosophical and uniform exposition of constitutional principles than would otherwise be probable. Moreover, the expansion of the country has vastly increased the volume of legislative measures and there is severe pressure toward an undue centralization. In Congress, theories of State autonomy, strongly held so far as profession goes, may easily yield to the demands of interests seeking Federal support. Many of our citizens in their zeal for particular measures have little regard for any of the limitations of Federal authority. We have entered upon an era of regulation with a great variety of legislative proposals, constantly multiplying governmental contacts with the activities of industry and trade. These proposals raise more frequently than in the past questions of National, as opposed to State, power. If our *dual system* with its recognition of local authority in local concerns is worth maintaining, *judicial review is*

likely to be of increasing value (*The Supreme Court of the United States*, pp. 95–96). [Italics added.]

Yet even as the Court exalted the "constitutional system" (construed as dual federalism) to outlaw major New Deal enactments, it handed down two decisions— *Whitfield* v. *Ohio* (297 U.S. 431: 1936) and *Kentucky Whip and Collar Co.* v. *Illinois Central Railroad Co.* (299 U.S. 334: 1937)—that seemed to revitalize national authority at the expense of the states. The first involved the constitutionality of a congressional act which, following the pattern of the Wilson Act of 1890, deprived convict-made goods of their interstate character and submitted them to state regulation upon arrival, "in the same manner as though such goods . . . had been manufactured, produced or mined in such state." The Whip and Collar Company case involved the validity of another congressional enactment, modeled after the Webb-Kenyon Act of 1913, prohibiting transportation in interstate or foreign commerce of convict-made goods "into any state where the goods are intended to be received, possessed, sold, or used in violation of its laws." Upholding this Act, Chief Justice Hughes declared that "in certain circumstances an absolute prohibition of interstate transportation is constitutional regulation. . . . The contention is inadmissible that the Act of Congress is invalid merely because the horse collars and harness which petitioner manufactures and sells are useful and harmless articles. . . . The pertinent point is that where the subject of commerce is one as to which the power of the state may constitutionally be exerted by restriction or prohibition in order to prevent harmful consequences, the Congress may, if it sees fit, put forth its power to regulate interstate commerce so as to prevent that commerce from being used to impede the carrying out of the state policy."

After these decisions what, one may ask, is left of the doctrines of *Sugar Trust* and *Hammer* v. *Dagenhart?* A negative answer would seem reasonable. Nor is this all. Only 12 months before the Schechter decision, the broad scope of the national commerce power was again recognized in *Baldwin* v. *Seelig* (294 U.S. 511: 1935). Here the Court invalidated a New York law prohibiting the sale in New York of milk purchased outside the state at prices lower than those fixed by local law for similar purchases within the state. Upholding "our national solidarity" and deploring "nice distinctions . . . made at times between direct and indirect burdens," the Court declared the New York act void, whether applied to milk out of the original package or enforced against milk while so packaged. The Court's decision stood on the proposition that the national commerce power operated to destroy the states' power to establish "an economic barrier against competition with the products of another state or the labor of its residents."

It is hard to make out any differences between the Schechter and Seelig businesses. The contradictory rulings in the two cases are all the more puzzling when one takes into account the fact that in *Baldwin* v. *Seelig* the national commerce power was "dormant," whereas in Schechter it had been exercised, only to encounter "nice distinctions . . . between direct and indirect burdens" and the sanctity of a preconceived theory of "our constitutional system."

So far as the commerce power was concerned, the Court by 1936 seemed to have adopted the view that certain subjects were local in nature and beyond the power of Congress even though they required national or uniform regulations if they were to be regulated at all. On the other hand, effective state-by-state regulation was clearly impossible; even if it were attempted it might, if any state regulation were found to have any substantial effect on interstate commerce, run afoul (as in *Baldwin* v. *Seelig*) of the "silence of Congress" doctrine. The Court thus had narrowed the commerce doctrines of Marshall by withdrawing from congressional power certain subject matters, such as production, agriculture, and the employer-employee relationship. In effect, the Court had created a category other than those enumerated in the Cooley case, viz., those objects which could not in practice be regulated by either government—a "twilight zone," a "no man's land."

CONSTITUTION OF POWERS OR OF RIGHTS?

By the spring of 1936 it looked as if the Court had put the New Deal firmly on the rack of unconstitutionality. Loud acclaim resounded in the ranks of the Old Guard. Addressing the 1936 Republican National Convention, Herbert Hoover expressed heartfelt thanks "to Almighty God for the Constitution and the Supreme Court." Chief Justice Hughes joined in this triumphant chorus. "I am happy to report," he remarked in his American Law Institute address, "that the Supreme Court is still functioning." Members and guests of the Institute vigorously applauded the announcement, obliging the speaker "to pause for more than two minutes."

All this rejoicing was in response to the stark fact that nine Supreme Court Justices, sometimes only five, had rendered government impotent. The entire legislative program overwhelmingly approved by the American people in 1932, 1934, and 1936 was, as Assistant Attorney General Jackson said, in danger of being lost in "a maze of constitutional metaphors."

This crucial impasse between Congress and the Court had not occurred overnight, nor had it come about without persistent protest within the Court itself. Justice Brandeis had railed against the Court's exercise of "the powers of a super-legislature," and Justice Holmes had deplored the lack of any limit to the Court's willingness to invalidate legislation that struck a "majority of this Court as for any reason undesirable." Justice Stone had accused his colleagues of torturing the Constitution, and warned that "Courts are not the only agency of government that must be assumed to have the capacity to govern." The Constitution as a straitjacket or "vehicle of the Nation's life"—that was the basic issue. "With a competent, detached and courageous judiciary," Justice Stone said, "most of the problems of adequate administration would disappear." In case after case, Stone had alerted his colleagues to the perils of "self-inflicted" wounds. Time and time again writers and speakers alluded to or quoted from his dissents to prove from the mouth of this "most highly respected Justice" how the majority had perverted the judicial function.

By January 1936, with popular pressure rising, the constitutional crisis reached the explosive stage. "The way out will be found shortly," the *St. Louis Star-Times* predicted, "because it must be found." "The time has come," the *New York Post* proclaimed in March 1936, "for a showdown with Judicial autocracy."

A legislative groundswell mounted perilously after the Agricultural Adjustment Act case (*United States* v. *Butler*). "This detached group," Oregon's Representative Walter M. Pierce said of the Court majority, "did not hold the Triple A Act was in contravention of the rights of man or the laws of God, but it did say that by its passage the Congress had interfered with the rights of the states. What an arbitrary, unjust, and reactionary opinion it seems to those of us who hold that the minority opinion is more logical, more legally sound, more just, and helpfully constructive in a changing social order!''

Legislators mentioned several nostrums for the constitutional impasse. One innovator, reproached for suggesting a remedy that meant ''putting the Court on the spot,'' heatedly replied: ''Exactly . . . the Court ought to be put on the spot when it subscribes to such labored and far-fetched opinions as that of the Chief Justice in the poultry case.''

Nor were the militant lawmakers without press support. A small but remarkably vocal group of newspapers took up the cry: ''Curb this Court before it destroys the nation.'' The people should bring the Justices down from ''the pedestal of fetish and deal with them as men and not supermen,'' clamored the *Philadelphia Record*. In the same vein the obscure Danville, Pennsylvania, *Morning News* editorialized: ''Everybody knows there will be nothing the Court can do about it when elected officials finally say to it: 'Your ruling is stupid and doesn't make sense, according to our opinion and according to the bristling protests of four of your number. Therefore we shall ignore you.''' ''By their own admission,'' the *Philadelphia Record* observed, drawing on Stone's outraged dissents, ''they read their personal bias, their individual economic predilections into our fundamental law. Instead of utilizing their unequaled independence to serve the Constitution, they twist the Constitution to serve their notions. And today the document dedicated to the general welfare is employed to destroy the general welfare. . . . The Supreme Court's usurpation of power is the issue of the hour.''

Various correctives were open. The President and Congress might limit the jurisdiction of the Supreme Court, increase the number of judges to override the present arrogant majority, or sponsor constitutional amendments limiting the Court's power. Though many Congressmen urged that something be done, they were uncertain what to do, not quite sure whether the trouble was the fault of the Constitution or of judges, ''callously insensible to the needs and demands of our people.'' The President and his party were uncertain, too, at least on the most feasible remedy politically. The Democratic Party Platform in 1936 said: ''If these problems [social and economic] cannot be effectively solved by legislation within the Constitution, we shall seek such clarifying amendments as [we] . . . shall find necessary, in order adequately to regulate commerce, protect public health and safety and safeguard economic liberty. Thus we propose to maintain the letter and spirit of the Constitution.'' Throughout the campaign Democratic orators muted the discord, giving no hint that President Roosevelt would, if reelected, wage all-out war on the judiciary.

THE COURT PACKING THREAT

Even in the face of his overwhelming electoral triumph, the President could not be sure that the Court would give ground. Did not the traditional theory insist that the Justices are, and must be, immune to election returns? In no mood to take chances, the President, on February 5, 1937, sent to Congress his message proposing a drastic shake-up in the judiciary. In a word, the President's solution was to give a Supreme Court Justice past 70 six months in which to retire. A Justice who failed to retire within the appointed time could continue in office, but the Chief Executive would appoint an additional Justice—presumably younger and better able to carry the heavy load. Since there were six Justices in this category, Roosevelt would make six appointments at once.

In presenting his proposal the President gave no hint of wishing to stem the tide of anti-New Deal decisions. He tendered the hemlock cup to the elderly jurists on the elevated ground that they slowed the efficient dispatch of judicial business. "Can it be said," the President observed, "that full justice is achieved when a court is forced by the sheer necessity of keeping up with its business to decline, without even an explanation, to hear 87 percent of the cases presented to it by private litigants?"

Roosevelt had awaited the propitious moment. Early February of 1937 seemed well-nigh perfect. The election had, as one newspaper said, yielded "a roar in which cheers for the Supreme Court were drowned out." Congressional opinion appeared overtly hostile. One news commentator reported in January 1936 that "The boys on Capitol Hill have their knives out, and how they do ache to use them."

Yet from the very start "Courtpacking" ran into terrific public opposition. Overnight, Supreme Court Justices were again pictured as demigods far above the sweaty crowd, weighing public policy in the delicate scales of the law. "Constitutionality" was talked about as if it were a tangible fact, undeviating and precise, not merely the current judicial theory of what ought and what ought not to be done. The same Congressmen who, prior to the President's message, had demanded the scalps of reactionary Justices, were "shocked beyond measure" and turned upon Roosevelt in an attitude of anguished surprise. Closing ranks with Bar Associations, the newspapers lined up almost solidly against courtpacking. The idea implicit in Roosevelt's scheme, that the Court may change its interpretation in such a way as to sustain legislative power to meet national needs, was called as "false in theory, as it would be ruinous in practice." The press and the bar had hit a responsive chord. Said Walter Lippmann: "No issue so great or so deep has been raised in America since secession." Throughout the ensuing months debate waxed furiously. Clergymen, educators, businessmen, and lawyers trekked to Washington and testified for or against the plan.

Everyone who could read knew that the Justices were not the vestal virgins of the Constitution. Yet, through the years, and despite increasing evidence that judicial interpretation and not Fundamental Law shackled the power to govern, the American people had come to regard the Court as the symbol of their freedom. Tarnished though the symbol was, it made, like the English monarchy, for national stability and poise in crisis; moreover, like its English counterpart, the Supreme Court commanded the loyalty of the citizenry, providing perhaps an impregnable barrier against dictatorship and personal government. "The President wants to control the Supreme Court" was hammered home incessantly. If the plan were accepted, the anti-New Deal press averred, nothing would stand between Roosevelt and the absolute dictatorship of the United States.

Roosevelt, quick to sense that his initial approach had been a major blunder, moved closer to the real issue on March 4, when he likened the judiciary to an unruly horse on the government gang plough, unwilling to pull with its teammates, the executive and Congress. As he saw it now, the crucial question was not whether the Court had kept up with its calendar, but whether it had kept up with the country. The President's false assertion that the judges lagged in their work blurred the issue, diverting public attention so completely that his later effort to face the difficulty squarely never quite succeeded.

In a nationwide Fireside Chat on March 9, the President threw off the cloak of sophistry and frankly explained: "The Court has been acting not as a judicial body, but as a policy-making body. . . . That is not only my accusation, it is the accusation of most distinguished Justices of the present Supreme Court. . . . In holding the AAA unconstitutional, Justice Stone said of the majority opinion that it was 'a tortured construction of the

Constitution' and two other Justices agreed with him. In the case holding the New York Minimum Wage Law unconstitutional [*Morehead* v. *New York ex rel. Tipaldo,* 298 U.S. 587: 1936], Justice Stone said that the majority were actually reading into the Constitution their own 'personal economic predilections' . . . and two other Justices agreed with him.''

A vigorous campaign against the President's bill was being waged in the Senate under the leadership of Senator Burton K. Wheeler. Tom Corcoran, then a White House adviser, tried vainly to dissuade the Montana Senator from making a fight; the President himself told Wheeler of the futility of opposing a measure certain to pass in any event. ''A liberal cause,'' Wheeler explained bluntly, ''was never won by stacking a deck of cards, by stuffing a ballot box or packing a Court.''

Meanwhile, those able to make the most realistic estimate of the condition of the Court's docket—the Justices themselves—maintained a discreet silence. Finally, Senator Wheeler nervously sought an interview with Justice Brandeis.

Much to his surprise he found Brandeis most cooperative. ''Why don't you call on the Chief Justice?'' Brandeis suggested. ''But I don't know the Chief Justice,'' the Montana Senator demurred. ''Well,'' said Brandeis, somewhat impatiently, ''the Chief Justice knows you and knows what you are doing.''

This was late Friday afternoon. The next day Senator Wheeler went to see Chief Justice Hughes. The Senator wanted to know from the Justices themselves whether the President's oft-repeated allegations about the swollen Court docket, lack of efficiency, and so on had any basis in fact. As Brandeis had indicated, the Chief Justice was not only enlisted but enthusiastic. Though Wheeler had not reached him until Saturday, March 20, he was able somehow to prepare a long and closely reasoned document for the Senator's use the following Monday, March 22. ''The baby is born,'' he said with a broad smile, as he put the letter into Wheeler's hand late Sunday afternoon.

Hughes's letter not only scotched the President's charge that the ''old men'' were not abreast of their docket, but also revealed its composer as a canny dialectician. Though carefully refraining from open opposition to the plan, the letter suggests that the President's idea of an enlarged Court and the hearing of cases in divisions might run counter to the constitutional provision for ''one Supreme Court.'' It was extraordinary enough, some of his colleagues thought, for a Justice to go out of his way to meet constitutional issues unnecessary for deciding a case; Hughes went further and handed down advisory opinion on a burning political issue, and did so, moreover, in flat opposition to the stand he had taken in his book of 1928, *The Supreme Court of the United States.*

Hughes also managed to convey the erroneous impression that the entire Court endorsed his statement. Ignoring the customary disavowal of authority to speak for members of a body not consulted, he was ''confident that it [the statement] is in accord with the views of the justices,'' though he admitted ''on account of the shortness of time, I have not been able to consult with members of the Court generally.'' We know that Cardozo and Stone, at least, objected strongly to Hughes's ''extra-official-expression on a constitutional question.'' ''I did not see the Chief Justice's letter, or know of it until I read it in the papers,'' Stone exploded; ''I certainly would not have joined in that part of it which undertakes to suggest, what is and what is not constitutional.''

The Chief Justice's letter, combined with the Court's dramatic about-face, put a fatal crimp in the President's project. The Court's victory was not, however, unmixed. Roosevelt's plan was defeated but, without the appointment of a single new Justice, he won from the embattled Court decisions favorable to the New Deal. As Robert Jackson put it, ''In politics the black-robed reactionary Justices had won over the master liberal politician of our day. In law the President defeated the recalcitrant Justices in their own Court.''* As the fight raged about them, the Justices began destruction of their most recent handiwork.

A SWITCH IN TIME

At the end of the 1935–36 term, the really big issue facing Court and country was posed by the Wagner Labor Relations Act. Would the Justices turn their backs on the Schechter and Guffey Coal rulings and permit the national government to substitute law for naked force in labor relations? Several cases were argued on February 10 and 11, 1937. In the heat of the court fight, industrial peace—or war—seemed to hang in the balance. Then, on April 12, 1937, Chief Justice Hughes put forward a broad and encompassing definition of interstate commerce and conceded to Congress the power to protect the lifelines of the national economy from private industrial warfare (*National Labor Relations Board* v. *Jones & Laughlin Steel Corp.*).

Arguments that had proved effective in the Schechter and Guffey Coal cases now availed nothing. ''Those cases,'' the Chief Justice commented summarily, ''are not controlling here.'' They were not controlling because he now chose to consider that ''fundamental'' distinction between ''direct and indirect effects'' as one of degree rather than kind. They were not binding now because he minimized the point much stressed in the Schechter case, namely, that the ''fundamental'' nature of the distinction between direct and indirect effects of intrastate transactions upon interstate commerce arises from the fact that it is ''essential'' to the maintenance of ''our constitutional system.'' Since interstate commerce was now seen as a ''practical conception,'' interference with that commerce ''must be appraised by a judgment that does not ignore actual experience.''

Treating the earlier approach somewhat disdainfully, the Chief Justice declared that, in light of the industry's ''farflung activities,'' it was ''idle to say'' that interference by strikes or other labor disturbances ''would be indirect or remote. It is obvious that it would be immediate and might be catastrophic.'' ''We are asked to shut our eyes to the

---

* In an effort to prevent a repetition of the 1937 Court ''fight,'' and to remove the Court permanently from the political arena, Senator Butler of Maryland in 1953 introduced a joint resolution proposing a constitutional amendment fixing the composition and jurisdiction of the Supreme Court. The Senator's purpose was ''to forestall future efforts by a President or a Congress seeking to nullify or impair the power of the judicial branch of the Government.'' His proposed amendment would fix the number of Justices at nine; make retirement of Supreme Court Justices and all federal judges compulsory at the age of 75; render the Justices ineligible to become President or Vice-President; and, in constitutional cases, prevent Congress from restricting the authority of the Supreme Court to consider constitutional issues within its appellate jurisdiction. On May 11, 1954, after a desultory debate in which only a handful of Senators participated, the Senate approved the proposed amendment by a vote of 58 to 19, deleting only the provision concerning the ineligibility of Justices to become President or Vice-President. The measure had less success in the House of Representatives and never emerged from committee.

Is the Butler amendment a wise measure? In the past, as during the administrations of Jefferson, Jackson, Lincoln, and the two Roosevelts, when judges, ignoring their professed ''self-restraint,'' interposed the judicial arm to impede democratic solution of vital issues of the day, the power of Congress to determine the size of the Court and control its appellate jurisdiction has been resorted to effectively. The Butler amendment seems to rest on two assumptions: (a) that the Court has not been in politics, except as drawn in by the political organs of government; (b) that the proposed amendment, by increasing their independence, would keep the Justices above the swirling waters of politics. There is little or nothing in United States history to justify this expectation.

plainest facts of our national life,'' the Chief Justice continued, ''and to deal with the question of direct and indirect effects in an intellectual vacuum.''

''When industries organize themselves on a national scale, making their relation to interstate commerce the dominant factor in their activities, how can it be maintained that their industrial labor relations constitute a forbidden field into which Congress may not enter when it is necessary to protect interstate commerce from the paralyzing consequences of industrial war?'' The Chief Justice's sweeping doctrine did not apply solely to large-scale industries, such as steel. He proceeded immediately to apply the same doctrine to two small concerns, a trailer company and a men's clothing manufacturer. By a vote of 5 to 4 a major New Deal enactment was sustained.

The Chief Justice's colleagues naturally supposed that the man who took a position apparently so completely at odds with his earlier pronouncements must have seen a new light. ''Every consideration brought forward to uphold the act before us was applicable to support the acts held unconstitutional in cases decided within two years,'' Justice McReynolds countered in dissent. The four dissenters bemoaned this flagrant departure from Schechter and Carter. No ''direct'' and ''material'' interference was threatened here, they argued, and nothing could be more remote and indirect than the relation between the regulation of hours and wages of labor and the flow of interstate commerce.

Chief Justice Hughes's insistence that these reversals and new interpretations, while the Court was under fire, were unrelated to the President's bold determination to reorganize the judiciary provoked cynical reaction among both professional and lay commentators. ''We are told,'' a skeptical paragrapher noted, ''that the Supreme Court's about-face was not due to outside clamor. It seems that the new building has a sound-proof room, to which the Justices may retire to change their minds.''

Two things should be noted: First, there is nothing in the majority opinion that does not find its counterpart in *Gibbons* v. *Ogden*. Second, this was not a ''packed'' Court. The same Justices had defeated the NRA and the Guffey Coal Act.

THE NATIONAL VIEW OF COMMERCE

In *United States* v. *Darby* Justice Stone, in upholding the Fair Labor Standards Act, which fixed minimum wages and maximum hours for producers of goods shipped in interstate commerce, added this significant comment: ''The motive and purpose of a regulation of interstate commerce are matters for the legislative judgment upon the exercise of which the Constitution places no restriction and over which the Courts are given no control.'' *Hammer* v. *Dagenhart,* he said, was overruled. Finally, in *Wickard* v. *Filburn* the Court went full circle by upholding the validity of the wheat-marketing provisions of the Agricultural Adjustment Act as applied to wheat grown for home consumption.

Filburn ran a small wheat farm in Ohio. Each year he planted some acres of wheat for his poultry. After accepting an Agricultural Marketing Agreement Allotment of 11 acres, he planted 23 and raised 269 bushels of wheat in excess of his assigned quota. The penalty provisions of the act were invoked by the Secretary of Agriculture and suit was brought to collect penalties. In defense, Filburn argued that national regulation could not be applied to him since he had grown the wheat for his own chickens, not for a national market. In rejecting this argument Justice Jackson, speaking for the Court, threw out all the old distinctions of ''direct,'' ''indirect,'' ''production,'' ''commerce,'' and emphasized the economic effect upon interstate commerce as the true test of whether local activities could be regulated by Congress under the commerce power. Even if we assume, Jackson reassured, the wheat is never marketed, ''it supplies a need of the man who grew it which would otherwise be reflected by purchases in the open market. Home grown wheat in this sense competes with wheat in commerce.''

Decisions upholding the 1964 Civil Rights Act (78 Stat. 241) cast further light on the modern Court's conception of congressional power over commerce. In *Heart of Atlanta Motel* v. *United States* and in *Katzenbach* v. *McClung* the Justices upheld the application of provisions of the Act barring racial discrimination not only to an establishment serving interstate travelers (*Atlanta Motel*), but to a local restaurant using food that had ''moved'' in commerce between the states (*McClung*). Although the Court makes no reference to the compatibility of its earlier decision in Schechter Poultry with the McClung decision, it may be asked whether, in spite of Justice Black's disclaimer, there is now any commercial activity beyond the reach of congressional power.

The extensive reach of the 1964 Act is manifest in *Daniel* v. *Paul* (395 U.S. 298: 1969), where a recreational facility near Little Rock, Arkansas, was found to be a ''public accommodation'' affecting commerce. The entire 232-acre establishment with its golf, swimming, dancing, and other activities was held to be within the act's provisions because three of the four items sold at the snack bar had originated outside of the state, thus making it a public accommodation.

Various anticrime statutes provide other examples of how congressional control of the channels and instrumentalities of interstate commerce can be used to regulate or prohibit activities formerly considered essentially local. As the earlier lottery, oleomargarine, and Mann Act decisions indicate, congressional control based on the commerce clause seems virtually unlimited. In 1961 Congress passed antiracketeering acts, forbidding traveling in interstate commerce with intent to do a number of enumerated crime-related acts, such as sending or carrying book-making articles in interstate commerce or receiving a firearm shipped in interstate commerce if the recipient has been convicted of a crime. Two provisions of the 1968 Civil Rights Act (82 Stat. 73) adopt the same format. One prohibits traveling in interstate commerce, or using its instrumentalities, with intent to cause a riot, the law which provided the basis for the Chicago Seven Trial following the turbulent 1968 Democratic Party Convention. Another is directed against those who, by teaching or acts, contribute to a civil disorder that may ''obstruct, delay, or adversely affect commerce.'' Clearly, there are almost endless opportunities to extend federal power against antisocial behavior, using the techniques of the 1961 and 1968 acts.

So far as the commerce power is concerned, the so-called constitutional revolution thus appears not so much a revolution as a counterrevolution. In the period from 1890 to 1936, when the Court began to develop a series of implied limitations on the exercise of the commerce power, it was not doing so in response to any rule of law announced by the Marshall or Taney Courts. Marshall, while not denying the power of the states to regulate certain local matters, defined the commerce power broadly. Taney's Court, although more generous to local regulation, in the absence of federal legislation, made it clear that Congress's power was broad and to the extent exercised would be upheld, and that the Court would undertake to determine the validity of state acts by measuring the need for uniform regulation in each case. The Court, in other words, would play the difficult role of ascertaining the limits of state power over commerce until Congress should act.

In the period 1890–1936 the Court inverted the role of the Taney Court. At one time it would use the commerce power to frustrate state acts where they interfered with national commerce; but at other times it would imply limits on the national power to regulate certain aspects of commerce by evolving rules denying to mining, agriculture, and manufacturing any relationship with interstate commerce.

If one is inclined to protest that the founders never dreamed of AAA, FLSA, and NLRA, the answer is that of course they did not. This argument, it might be pointed out, could be used to reject the great bulk of modern state and national regulatory acts. But, as Marshall said in *McCulloch* v. *Maryland:* "This provision [necessary and proper clause] is made in a constitution, intended to endure for ages to come, and, consequently, to be adapted to the various crises of human affairs. To have prescribed the means by which government should, in all future time, execute its powers, would have been to change, entirely, the character of the instrument, and give it the properties of a legal code. It would have been an unwise attempt to provide, by immutable rules, for exigencies which, if foreseen at all, must have been seen dimly, and which can be best provided for as they occur." In the light of this philosophy the growth of national power through the commerce clause can be described as the necessary response by government to economic and social change. Those adversely affected by regulation clamored "back to the Constitution." Back to which constitution—that of 1787, as interpreted by John Marshall, or that of 1890–1936?

Until 1976, events dictated the answer. Then, in an extraordinary about-face, the Justices voted, 5 to 4, that the 1974 amendment of the Fair Labor Standards Act extending the minimum wage and maximum hour provisions to employees of states and their subdivisions exceeded congressional power under the commerce clause. For the majority, the constitutional barrier was the Tenth Amendment. Revived was the Court-created doctrine of dual federalism. Noting that the decision flew in the face of the commerce power as enunciated by Chief Justice Marshall 152 years ago and reaffirmed since 1937, dissenting Justice Brennan, joined by Justices Marshall and White, commented: "The reliance of my brethren upon the Tenth Amendment, as 'an express declaration of a state sovereignty limitation,' not only suggests that they overrule governing decisions of this Court, but must astound scholars of the Constitution." The Court's 1976 decision also flew in the face of what Madison said in the Congress which framed the Tenth Amendment: "If the power was not given, Congress could not exercise it, if given, they might exercise it, although it should interfere with the laws, or even the Constitution of the states."

Although this extraordinary case involved exercise of the commerce power, the decision turned on the Court-created doctrine of dual federalism. It is therefore included in the chapter on federalism.

SELECTED READINGS

ANNOTATION, "Federal Police Power," 81 *Lawyers' Edition, United States Supreme Court Reports* 938 (1937).

CORWIN, EDWARD S., *Constitutional Revolution, Ltd.* Westport, Conn.: Greenwood Press, 1977 (reissue of 1941 edition).

———, *The Commerce Power Versus States Rights.* Princeton: Princeton University Press, 1936.

CUSHMAN, ROBERT E., "National Police Power under the Commerce Clause," in *3 Selected Essays on Constitutional Law*, pp. 62–79. Chicago: Foundation Press, 1938.

HAMILTON, WALTON H., and DOUGLASS ADAIR, *The Power to Govern.* New York: W. W. Norton Co., Inc., 1937.

MASON, ALPHEUS T., "Charles Evans Hughes: An Appeal to the Bar of History," 6 *Vanderbilt Law Review* 1 (1952).

———, "Harlan Fiske Stone and FDR's Court Plan," 61 *Yale Law Journal* 791 (1952).

———, *The Supreme Court: Instrument of Power or of Revealed Truth, 1930-1937.* Boston: Boston University Press, 1953.

SCHLESINGER, JR. ARTHUR, *The Politics of Upheaval.* Boston: Houghton Mifflin, 1960.

STEAMER, ROBERT J., *Supreme Court in Crisis.* Amherst: University of Massachusetts Press, 1971.

United States v. *E. C. Knight*
156 U.S. 1, 15 S.Ct. 249, 39 L.Ed. 325 (1895)

The American Sugar Refining Company, which controlled a majority of the sugar-refining companies of the United States, attempted to attain an almost complete monopoly by purchasing control of the E. C. Knight Company and three other companies, which together produced about one-third of the national output. Alleging that the defendant companies (American Sugar, E. C. Knight, and three others) had entered into contracts that constituted combinations in restraint of trade, and that these companies had conspired to restrain trade, both contrary to the Sherman Anti-Trust Act of 1890, the government sought to obtain a court order canceling the various agreements. The lower federal courts refused to grant this relief on the ground that the combination or conspiracy involved in this case pertained to manufacturing, and not to interstate commerce. The United States appealed.

MR. CHIEF JUSTICE FULLER . . . delivered the opinion of the court.

By the purchase of the stock of the four Philadelphia refineries, with shares of its own stock, the American Sugar Refining Company acquired nearly complete control of the manufacture of refined sugar within the United States. The bill charged that the contracts under which these purchases were made constituted combinations in restraint of trade, and that in entering into them the defendants combined and conspired to restrain the trade and commerce in refined sugar among the several States and with foreign nations, contrary to the act of Congress of July 2, 1890. . . .

The fundamental question is, whether conceding that the existence of a monopoly in manufacture is established by the evidence, that monopoly can be directly suppressed under the act of Congress in the mode attempted by this bill.

It cannot be denied that the power of a state to protect the lives, health, and property of its citizens, and to preserve good order and the public morals, "the power to govern men and things within the limits of its dominion," is a power originally and always belonging to the States, not surrendered by them to the general government, nor directly restrained by the Constitution of the United States, and essentially exclusive. The relief of the citizens of each State from the burden of monopoly and the evils resulting from the restraint of trade among such citizens was left with the States to deal with, and this court has recognized their possession of that power even to the extent of holding that an employment or business carried on by private individuals, when it becomes a matter of such public interest and importance as to create a common charge or burden upon the citizen; in other words, when it becomes a practical monopoly, to which the citizen is compelled to resort and by means of which a tribute can be exacted from the community, is subject to regulation by state legislative power. On the other hand, the power of Congress to regulate commerce among the several States is also exclusive. The Constitution does not provide that interstate commerce shall be free, but, by the grant of this exclusive power to regulate it, it was left free except as Congress might impose restraints. Therefore it has been determined that the failure of Congress to exercise this exclusive power in any case is an expression of its will that the subject shall be free from restrictions or impositions upon it by the several States, and if a law passed by a State in the exercise of its acknowledged powers comes into conflict with that will, the Congress and the State cannot occupy the position of equal opposing sovereignties, because the Constitution declares its supremacy and that of the laws passed in pursuance thereof; and that which is not supreme must yield to that which is supreme. "Commerce, undoubtedly, is traffic," said Chief Justice Marshall, "but it is something more; it is intercourse. It describes the commercial intercourse between nations and parts of nations in all its branches, and is regulated by prescribing rules for carrying on that intercourse." That which belongs to commerce is within the jurisdiction of the United States, but that which does not belong to commerce is within the jurisdiction of the police power of the State. . . .

The argument is that the power to control the manufacture of refined sugar is a monopoly over a necessary of life, to the enjoyment of which by a large part of the population of the United States interstate commerce is indispensable, and that, therefore, the general government in the exercise of the power to regulate commerce may repress such monopoly directly and set aside the instruments which have created it. But this argument cannot be confined to necessaries of life merely, and must include all articles of general consumption. Doubtless the power to control the manufacture of a given thing involves in a certain sense the control of its disposition, but this is a secondary and not the primary sense; and although the exercise of that power may result in bringing the operation of commerce into play, it does not control it, and affects it only incidentally and indirectly. Commerce succeeds to manufacture, and is not a part of it. The power to regulate commerce is the power to prescribe the rule by which commerce shall be governed, and is a power independent of the power to suppress monopoly. But it may operate in repression of monopoly whenever that comes within the rules by which commerce is governed or whenever the transaction is itself a monopoly of commerce. . . .

It is vital that the independence of the commercial power and of the police power, and the delimitation between them, however sometimes perplexing, should always be recognized and observed, for while the one furnishes the strongest bond of union, the other is essential to the preservation of the autonomy of the States as required by our dual form of government; and

acknowledged evils, however grave and urgent they may appear to be, had better be borne, than the risk be run, in the effort to suppress them, of more serious consequences by resort to expedients of even doubtful constitutionality. . . .

Contracts, combinations, or conspiracies to control domestic enterprise in manufacture, agriculture, mining, production in all its forms, or to raise or lower prices or wages, might unquestionably tend to restrain external as well as domestic trade, but the restraint would be an indirect result, however inevitable and whatever its extent, and such result would not necessarily determine the object of the contract, combination, or conspiracy.

Again, all the authorities agree that in order to vitiate a contract or combination it is not essential that its result should be a complete monopoly; it is sufficient if it really tends to that end and to deprive the public of the advantages which flow from free competition. Slight reflection will show that if the national power extends to all contracts and combinations in manufacture, agriculture, mining, and other productive industries, whose ultimate result may affect external commerce, comparatively little of business operations and affairs would be left for state control.

It was in the light of well-settled principles that the act of July 2, 1890, was framed. Congress did not attempt thereby to assert the power to deal with monopoly directly as such; or to limit and restrict the rights of corporations created by the States or the Citizens of the States in the acquisition, control, or disposition of property; or to regulate or prescribe the price or prices at which such property or the products thereof should be sold; or to make criminal the acts of persons in the acquisition and control of property which the States of their residence or creation sanctioned or permitted. Aside from the provisions applicable where Congress might exercise municipal power, what the law struck at was combinations, contracts, and conspiracies to monopolize trade and commerce among the several States or with foreign nations; but the contracts and acts of the defendants related exclusively to the acquisition of the Philadelphia refineries and the business of sugar refining in Pennsylvania, and bore no direct relation to commerce between the States or with foreign nations. . . . There was nothing in the proofs to indicate any intention to put a restraint upon trade or commerce, and the fact, as we have seen, that trade or commerce might be indirectly affected was not enough to entitle complainants to a decree. . . .

Decree affirmed.

MR. JUSTICE HARLAN, dissenting. . . .

. . . In its consideration of the important constitutional question presented, this court assumes on the record before us that the result of the transactions disclosed by the pleadings and proof was the creation of a monopoly in the manufacture of a necessary of life. If this combination, so far as its operations necessarily or directly affect interstate commerce, cannot be restrained or suppressed under some power granted to Congress, it will be cause for regret that the patriotic statesmen who framed the Constitution did not foresee the necessity of investing the national government with power to deal with gigantic monopolies holding in their grasp, and injuriously controlling in their own interest, the entire trade *among the States* in food products that are essential to the comfort of every household in the land. . . .

The power of Congress covers and protects the absolute freedom of such intercourse and trade among the States as may or must succeed manufacture and precede transportation from the place of purchase. This would seem to be conceded; for, the court in the present case expressly declares that *"contracts to buy,* sell, or exchange goods *to be transported among the several States,* the transportation and its instrumentalities, and articles bought, sold, or exchanged for the purpose of such transit among the States, or put in the way of transit, *may be regulated,* but this is *because they form part of interstate trade or commerce."* Here is a direct admission—one which the settled doctrines of this court justify—that contracts to buy and the purchasing of goods *to be transported from one State to another,* and transportation, with its in-

strumentalities, are all *parts* of interstate trade or commerce. Each part of such trade is then under the protection of Congress. And yet, by the opinion and judgment in this case, if I do not misapprehend them, Congress is without power to protect the commercial intercourse that such purchasing necessarily involves against the restraints and burdens arising from the existence of *combinations* that meet purchasers, from whatever State they come, with the threat —for it is nothing more nor less than a threat— that they *shall not* purchase what they desire to purchase, *except at the prices fixed by such combinations.*

To the general government has been committed the control of commercial intercourse among the States, to the end that it may be free at all times from any restraints except such as Congress may impose or permit for the benefit of the whole country. The common government of all the people is the only one that can adequately deal with a matter which directly and injuriously affects the entire commerce of the country, which concerns equally all the people of the Union, and which, it must be confessed, cannot be adequately controlled by any one State. Its authority should not be so weakened by construction that it cannot reach and eradicate evils that, beyond all question, tend to defeat an object which that government is entitled, by the Constitution, to accomplish. "Powerful and ingenious minds," this court has said, "taking, as postulates, that the powers expressly granted to the government of the Union, are to be contracted by construction into the narrowest possible compass, and that the original powers of the States are retained if any possible construction will retain them, may, by a course of well digested, but refined and metaphysical reasoning, founded on these premises, explain away the Constitution of our country, and leave it, a magnificent structure, indeed, to look at, but totally unfit for use. They may so entangle and perplex the understanding as to obscure principles which were before thought quite plain, and induce doubts where, if the mind were to pursue its own course, none would be perceived." *Gibbons* v. *Ogden.* . . .

Champion v. Ames
(The Lottery Case)
188 U.S. 321, 23 S.Ct. 321, 47 L.Ed. 492 (1903)

An Act of Congress of 1895 made it an offense to send or conspire to send lottery tickets in interstate commerce. The defendants, who were convicted under the statute, appealed from a circuit court order dismissing a writ of habeas corpus.

MR. JUSTICE HARLAN . . . delivered the opinion of the court.

The appellant insists that the carrying of lottery tickets from one State to another State by an express company engaged in carrying freight and packages, from State to State, although such tickets may be contained in a box or package, does not constitute, and cannot by any act of Congress be legally made to constitute, *commerce* among the states within the meaning of the clause of the Constitution of the United States providing that Congress shall have power "to regulate commerce with foreign nations, and among the several states, and with the Indian tribes"; consequently, that Congress cannot make it an offense to cause such tickets to be carried from one State to another.

The government insists that express companies, when engaged, for hire, in the business of transportation from one State to another, are instrumentalities of commerce among the States; that the carrying of lottery tickets from one State to another is commerce which Congress may regulate; and that as a means of executing the power to regulate interstate commerce Congress may make it an offense against the United States to cause lottery tickets to be carried from one State to another.

The questions presented by these opposing contentions are of great moment, and are entitled to receive, as they have received, the most careful consideration.

What is the import of the word "commerce" as used in the Constitution? It is not defined by that instrument. Undoubtedly, the carrying from one State to another by independent carriers of things or commodities that are ordinary subjects of traffic, and which have in themselves a recognized value in money, constitutes interstate commerce. But does not commerce among the several States include something more? Does not the carrying from one State to another, by independent carriers, of lottery tickets that entitle the holder to the payment of a certain amount of money therein specified, also constitute commerce among the States? . . .

The leading case under the commerce clause of the Constitution is *Gibbons* v. *Ogden*. . . . Referring to that clause, Chief Justice Marshall said: "The subject to be regulated is commerce; and our Constitution being, as was aptly said at the bar, one of enumeration, and not of definition, to ascertain the extent of the power, it becomes necessary to settle the meaning of the word. . . . Commerce, undoubtedly is traffic, but it is something more; it is intercourse. It describes the commercial intercourse between nations, and parts of nations, in all its branches, and is regulated by prescribing rules for carrying on that intercourse. . . ."

Again: "We are now arrived at the inquiry—what is this power? It is the power to regulate; that is, to prescribe the rule by which commerce is to be governed. This power, like all others vested in congress, is *complete in itself,* may be exercised *to its utmost extent,* and acknowledges *no limitations, other than are prescribed in the Constitution.*" . . .

. . . The cases cited . . . show that commerce among the States embraces navigation, intercourse, communication, traffic, the transit of persons, and the transmission of messages by telegraph. They also show that the power to regulate commerce among the several States is vested in Congress as absolutely as it would be in a single government, having in its constitution the same restrictions on the exercise of the power as are found in the Constitution of the United States; that such power is plenary, complete in itself, and may be exerted by Congress to its utmost extent, subject *only* to such limitations as the Constitution imposes upon the exercise of the powers granted by it; and that in determining the character of the regulations to be adopted Congress has a large discretion which is not to be controlled by the courts, simply because, in their opinion, such regulations may not be the best or most effective that could be employed.

We come then to inquire whether there is any solid foundation upon which to rest the contention that Congress may not regulate the carrying of lottery tickets from one State to another, at least by corporations or companies whose business it is, for hire, to carry tangible property from one State to another.

It was said in argument that lottery tickets are not of any real or substantial value in themselves, and therefore are not subjects of commerce. If that were conceded to be the only legal test as to what are to be deemed subjects of the commerce that may be regulated by Congress, we cannot accept as accurate the broad statement that such tickets are of no value. Upon their face they showed that the lottery company offered a large capital prize, to be paid to the holder of the ticket winning the prize at the drawing advertised to be held at Asuncion, Paraguay. . . .

We are of opinion that lottery tickets are subjects of traffic, and therefore are subjects of commerce, and the regulation of the carriage of such tickets from State to State, at least by independent carriers, is a regulation of commerce among the several States.

But it is said that the statute in question does not regulate the carrying of lottery tickets from State to State, but by punishing those who cause them to be so carried Congress in effect prohibits such carrying; that in respect of the carrying from one State to another of articles or things that are, in fact, or according to usage in business, the subjects of commerce, the authority given Congress was not to *prohibit,* but only to *regulate.* . . .

If a State, when considering legislation for the suppression of lotteries within its own limits, may properly take into view the evils that inhere in the raising of money, in that mode, why may not Congress, invested with the power to regulate commerce among the several States, provide that such commerce shall not be polluted by the carrying of lottery tickets from one State to another? In this connection it must not be forgotten that the power of Congress to regulate commerce among the States is plenary, is complete in itself, and is subject to no limitations except such as may be found in the Constitution. What provision in that instrument can be regarded as limiting the exercise of the power granted? . . .

If it be said that the act of 1895 is inconsistent with the Tenth Amendment, reserving to the States respectively, or to the people, the powers not delegated to the United States, the answer is that the power to regulate commerce among the States has been expressly delegated to Congress.

Besides, Congress, by that act, does not assume to interfere with traffic or commerce in lottery tickets carried on exclusively within the limits of any State, but has in view only commerce of that kind among the several States. It has not assumed to interfere with the completely internal affairs of any State, and has only legislated in respect of a matter which concerns the people of the United States. As a State may, for the purpose of guarding the morals of its own people, forbid all sales of lottery tickets within its limits, so Congress, for the purpose of guarding the people of the United States against the ''widespread pestilence of lotteries'' and to protect the commerce which concerns all the States, may prohibit the carrying of lottery tickets from one State to another. In legislating upon the subject of the traffic in lottery tickets, as carried on through interstate commerce, Congress only supplemented the action of those States— perhaps all of them—which, for the protection of the public morals, prohibit the drawing of lotteries, as well as the sale or circulation of lottery tickets, within their respective limits. It said, in effect, that it would not permit the declared policy of the States, which sought to protect their people against the mischiefs of the lottery business, to be overthrown or disregarded by the agency of interstate commerce. We should hesitate long before adjudging that an evil of such appalling character, carried on through interstate commerce, cannot be met and crushed by the only power competent to that end....

It is said, however, that if, in order to suppress lotteries carried on through interstate commerce, Congress may exclude lottery tickets from such commerce, that principle leads necessarily to the conclusion that Congress may arbitrarily exclude from commerce among the States any article, commodity, or thing, of whatever kind or nature, or however useful or valuable, which it may choose, no matter with what motive, to declare shall not be carried from one State to another. It will be time enough to consider the constitutionality of such legislation when we must do so. The present case does not require the court to declare the full extent of the power that Congress may exercise in the regulation of commerce among the States. We may, however, repeat, in this connection, what the court has heretofore said, that the power of Congress to regulate commerce among the States, although plenary, cannot be deemed arbitrary, since it is subject to such limitations or restrictions as are prescribed by the Constitution....

The whole subject is too important, and the questions suggested by its consideration are too difficult of solution, to justify any attempt to lay down a rule for determining in advance the validity of every statute that may be enacted under the commerce clause. We decide nothing more in the present case than that lottery tickets are subjects of traffic among those who choose to sell or buy them; that the carriage of such tickets by independent carriers from one State to another is therefore interstate commerce; that under its power to regulate commerce among the several States Congress—subject to the limitations imposed by the Constitution upon the exercise of the powers granted—has plenary authority over such commerce, and may prohibit the carriage of such tickets from State to State; and that legislation to that end, and of that character, is not inconsistent with any limitation or restriction imposed upon the exercise of the powers granted to Congress....

Affirmed.

MR. CHIEF JUSTICE FULLER ... dissenting: ...

The power of the State to impose restraints and burdens on persons and property in conservation and promotion of the public health, good order, and prosperity is a power originally and always belonging to the States, not surrendered by them to the general government, nor directly restrained by the Constitution of the United States, and essentially exclusive, and the suppression of lotteries as a harmful business falls within this power, commonly called, of police. *Douglas* v. *Kentucky,* 168 U.S. 488.

It is urged, however, that because Congress is empowered to regulate commerce between the several States, it, therefore, may suppress lotteries by prohibiting the carriage of lottery matter. Congress may, indeed, make all laws necessary and proper for carrying the powers granted to it into execution, and doubtless an act prohibiting the carriage of lottery matter would be necessary and proper to the execution of a power to suppress lotteries; but that power belongs to the States and not to Congress. To hold that Congress has general police power would be to hold that it may accomplish objects not intrusted to the General Government, and to defeat the operation of the Tenth Amendment, declaring that: "The powers not delegated to the United States by the Constitution, nor prohibited by it to the States, are reserved to the States respectively, or to the people."...

... To say that the mere carrying of an article which is not an article of commerce in and of itself nevertheless becomes such the moment it is to be transported from one State to another, is to transform a non-commercial article into one simply because it is transported. I cannot conceive that any such result can properly follow.

It would be to say that everything is an article of commerce the moment it is taken to be transported from place to place, and of interstate commerce if from State to State.

An invitation to dine, or to take a drive, or a note of introduction, all become articles of commerce under the ruling in this case, by being deposited with an express company for transportation. This in effect breaks down all the differences between that which is, and that which is not, an article of commerce, and the necessary consequence is to take from the States all jurisdiction over the subject so far as interstate communication is concerned. It is a long step in the direction of wiping out all traces of state lines, and the creation of a centralized Government.

Does the grant to Congress of the power to regulate interstate commerce impart the absolute power to prohibit it? . . .

The power to prohibit the transportation of diseased animals and infected goods over railroads or on steamboats is an entirely different thing, for they would be in themselves injurious to the transaction of interstate commerce, and, moreover, are essentially commercial in their nature. And the exclusion of diseased persons rests on different ground, for nobody would pretend that persons could be kept off the trains because they were going from one state to another to engage in the lottery business. However enticing that business may be, we do not understand how these pieces of paper themselves can communicate bad principles by contact. . . .

I regard this decision as inconsistent with the views of the framers of the Constitution, and of Marshall, its great expounder. Our form of government may remain notwithstanding legislation or decision, but, as long ago observed, it is with governments, as with religions, the form may survive the substance of the faith.

In my opinion the act in question in the particular under consideration is invalid, and the judgments below ought to be reversed, and my brothers Brewer, Shiras and Peckham concur in this dissent.

The Shreveport Case
(*Houston, E. & W. Texas Ry. Co.* v. *United States*)
234 U.S. 342, 34 S.Ct. 833, 58 L.Ed. 1341 (1914)

This case represents an appeal from a judgment of the United States Commerce Court dismissing the petitions in suits to set aside an order of the Interstate Commerce Commission regulating railway rates. The complaint stated that a railroad operating between Shreveport, La., and Dallas, Tex., charged more for haulage between Shreveport and points west in Texas than it did between points at a greater distance within Texas. For example, the rate on furniture from Shreveport, La., to Longview, Tex., 65.7 miles, was 35 cents, while the rate from Longview to Dallas, Tex., 124 miles, was 24.8 cents. The Interstate Commerce Commission had approved the interstate rates out of Shreveport, but in order to remove the disparity between inter- and intrastate rates, ordered the railroads to charge no higher rate from Shreveport to Dallas or intermediate points than it charged from Dallas eastwards for an equal distance. The railroads claimed the Interstate Commerce Commission had no jurisdiction over intrastate rates.

MR. JUSTICE HUGHES delivered the opinion of the court. . . .

The point of the objection to the order is that, as the discrimination found by the Commission to be unjust arises out of the relation of intrastate rates, maintained under state authority, to interstate rates that have been upheld as reasonable, its correction is beyond the Commission's power. Manifestly the order might be complied with, and the discrimination avoided either by reducing the interstate rates from Shreveport to the level of the competing intrastate rates, or by raising these intrastate rates to the level of the interstate rates, or by such reduction in the one case and increase in the other as would result in equality. But it is urged that, so far as the interstate rates were sustained by the Commission as reasonable, the Commission was without authority to compel their reduction in order to equalize them with the lower intrastate rates. The holding of the commerce court was that the order relieved the appellants from further obligation to observe the intrastate rates, and that they were at liberty to comply with the Commission's requirements by increasing these rates sufficiently to remove the forbidden discrimination. The invalidity of the order in this aspect is challenged upon two grounds:

1. That Congress is impotent to control the intrastate charges of an interstate carrier even to the extent necessary to prevent injurious discrimination against interstate traffic; and

2. That, if it be assumed that Congress has this power, still it has not been exercised, and hence the action of this commission exceeded the limits of the authority which has been conferred upon it. . . .

Congress is empowered to regulate—that is, to provide the law for the government of interstate commerce; to enact "all appropriate legislation" for its "protection and advancement" (*The Daniel Ball*, 10 Wall. 557, 564); to adopt measures "to promote its growth and insure its safety" (*Mobile County* v. *Kimball*, 102 U.S. 691, 696); "to foster, protect, control, and restrain" (*Second Employers' Liability Cases*

[*Mondou* v. *New York, N. H. & H. R. Co.*], 223 U.S. 1, 47, 53, 54). Its authority, extending to these interstate carriers as instruments of interstate commerce, necessarily embraces the right to control their operations in all matters having such a close and substantial relation to interstate traffic that the control is essential or appropriate to the security of that traffic, to the efficiency of the interstate service, and to the maintenance of conditions under which interstate commerce may be conducted upon fair terms and without molestation or hindrance. As it is competent for Congress to legislate to these ends, unquestionably it may seek their attainment by requiring that the agencies of interstate commerce shall not be used in such manner as to cripple, retard, or destroy it. The fact that carriers are instruments of intrastate commerce, as well as of interstate commerce, does not derogate from the complete and paramount authority of Congress over the latter or preclude the Federal power from being exerted to prevent the intrastate operations of such carriers from being made a means of injury to that which has been confided to Federal care. Wherever the interstate and intrastate transactions of carriers are so related that the government of the one involves the control of the other, it is Congress, and not the State, that is entitled to prescribe the final and dominant rule, for otherwise Congress would be denied the exercise of its constitutional authority, and the State, and not the Nation, would be supreme within the national field.

. . . This is not to say that Congress possesses the authority to regulate the internal commerce of a State, as such, but that it does possess the power to foster and protect interstate commerce, and to take all measures necessary or appropriate to that end, although intrastate transactions of interstate carriers may thereby be controlled.

This principle is applicable here. We find no reason to doubt that Congress is entitled to keep the highways of interstate communication open to interstate traffic upon fair and equal terms. That an unjust discrimination in the rates of a common carrier, by which one person or locality is unduly favored as against another under substantially similar conditions of traffic, constitutes an evil is undeniable; and where this evil consists in the action of an interstate carrier in unreasonably discriminating against interstate traffic over its line, the authority of Congress to prevent it is equally clear. It is immaterial, so far as the protecting power of Congress is concerned, that the discrimination arises from intrastate rates as compared with interstate rates. The use of the instrument of interstate commerce in a discriminatory manner so as to inflict injury upon that commerce, or some part thereof, furnishes abundant ground for Federal intervention. Nor can the attempted exercise of state authority alter the matter, where Congress has acted, for a State may not authorize a carrier to do that which Congress is entitled to forbid and has forbidden.

It is also clear that, in removing the injurious discriminations against interstate traffic arising from the relation of intrastate to interstate rates, Congress is not bound to reduce the latter below

what it may deem to be a proper standard fair to the carrier and to the public. Otherwise, it could prevent the injury to interstate commerce only by the sacrifice of its judgment as to interstate rates. Congress is entitled to maintain its own standard as to these rates and to forbid any discriminatory action by interstate carriers which will obstruct the freedom of movement of interstate traffic over their lines in accordance with the terms it establishes.

Having this power, Congress could provide for its execution through the aid of a subordinate body; and we conclude that the order of the Commission now in question cannot be held invalid upon the ground that it exceeded the authority which Congress could lawfully confer. . . .

The decree of the Commerce Court is affirmed in each case.

Affirmed.

MR. JUSTICE LURTON and MR. JUSTICE PITNEY dissent.

Hammer v. Dagenhart
247 U.S. 251, 38 S.Ct. 529, 62 L.Ed. 1101 (1918)

An Act of Congress of 1916 forbade the shipment in interstate commerce of products of child labor. A father of two children who worked in a North Carolina cotton mill sought and obtained an injunction against enforcement of the Act, on the ground that it was unconstitutional. The Government appealed.

MR. JUSTICE DAY delivered the opinion of the Court. . . .

The controlling question for decision is: Is it within the authority of Congress in regulating commerce among the States to prohibit the transportation in interstate commerce of manufactured goods, the product of a factory in which, within thirty days prior to their removal therefrom, children under the age of fourteen have been employed or permitted to work, or children between the ages of fourteen and six-

teen years have been employed or permitted to work more than eight hours in any day, or more than six days in any week, or after the hour of 7 o'clock P.M. or before the hour of 6 o'clock A.M.?

The power essential to the passage of this act, the Government contends, is found in the commerce clause of the Constitution which authorizes Congress to regulate commerce with foreign nations and among the States.

In *Gibbons* v. *Ogden* . . . Chief Justice Marshall, speaking for this court, and defining the extent and nature of the commerce power, said, "It is the power to regulate, that is, to prescribe the rule by which commerce is to be governed." In other words, the power is one to control the means by which commerce is carried on, which is directly the contrary of the assumed right to forbid commerce from moving and thus destroy it as to particular commodities. But it is insisted that adjudged cases in this court establish the doctrine that the power to regulate given to Congress incidentally includes the authority to prohibit the movement of ordinary commodities and therefore that the subject is not open for discussion. The cases demonstrate the contrary. They rest upon the character of the particular subjects dealt with and the fact that the scope of governmental authority, state or national, possessed over them is such that the authority to prohibit is as to them but the exertion of the power to regulate.

The first of these cases is *Champion* v. *Ames,* . . . the so-called Lottery Case, in which it was held that Congress might pass a law having the effect to keep the channels of commerce free from use in the transportation of tickets used in the promotion of lottery schemes. In *Hipolite Egg Co.* v. *United States,* 220 U.S. 45, this court sustained the power of Congress to pass the Pure Food and Drug Act, which prohibited the introduction into the States by means of interstate commerce of impure foods and drugs. . . .

In *Caminetti* v. *United States,* 242 U.S. 470, we held that Congress might prohibit the transportation of women in interstate commerce for the purpose of debauchery and kindred purposes. In *Clark Distilling Co.* v. *Western Maryland Railway Co.,* 242 U.S. 311 . . . concluding the discussion which sustained the authority of the government to prohibit the transportation of liquor in interstate commerce, the court said: "The exceptional nature of the subject here regulated is the basis upon which the exceptional power exerted must rest and affords no ground for any fear that such power may be constitutionally extended to things which it may not, consistently with the guaranties of the Constitution, embrace."

In each of these instances the use of interstate transportation was necessary to the accomplishment of harmful results. In other words, although the power over interstate transportation was to regulate, that could only be accomplished by prohibiting the use of the facilities of interstate commerce to effect the evil intended.

This element is wanting in the present case. The thing intended to be accomplished by this statute is the denial of the facilities of interstate commerce to those manufacturers in the States who employ children within the prohibited ages. The act in its effect does not regulate transportation among the States, but aims to standardize the ages at which children may be employed in mining and manufacturing within the States. The goods shipped are of themselves harmless. The act permits them to be freely shipped after thirty days from the time of their removal from the factory. When offered for shipment, and before transportation begins, the labor of their production is over, and the mere fact that they were intended for interstate commerce transportation does not make their production subject to federal control under the commerce power.

Commerce "consists of intercourse and traffic . . . and includes the transportation of persons and property, as well as the purchase, sale and exchange of commodities." The making of goods and the mining of coal are not commerce, nor does the fact that these things are to be afterwards shipped or used in interstate commerce, make their production a part thereof. . . .

The grant of power to Congress over the subject of interstate commerce was to enable it to regulate such commerce, and not to give it authority to control the States in the exercise of the police power over local trade and manufacture.

The grant of authority over a purely federal matter was not intended to destroy the local power always existing and carefully reserved to the States in the Tenth Amendment to the Constitution. . . .

That there should be limitations upon the right to employ children in mines and factories in the interest of their own and the public welfare, all will admit. That such employment is generally deemed to require regulation is shown by the fact that the brief of counsel states that every State in the Union has a law upon the subject, limiting the right to thus employ children. In North Carolina, the State wherein is located the factory in which the employment was had in the present case, no child under twelve years of age is permitted to work.

It may be desirable that such laws be uniform, but our Federal Government is one of enumerated powers; "this principle," declared Chief Justice Marshall in *McCulloch* v. *Maryland* . . . "is universally admitted." . . .

In interpreting the Constitution it must never be forgotten that the nation is made up of States to which are entrusted the powers of local government. And to them and to the people the powers not expressly [sic] delegated to the national government are reserved. . . . To sustain this statute would not be in our judgment a recognition of the lawful exertion of congressional authority over interstate commerce, but would sanction an invasion by the federal power of the control of a matter purely local in its character, and over which no authority has been delegated to Congress in conferring the power to regulate commerce among the States.

We have neither authority nor disposition to question the motives of Congress in enacting this legislation. The purposes intended must be attained consistently with constitutional limitations and not by an invasion of the powers of the States. This court has no more important function than that which devolves upon it the obligation to preserve inviolate the constitutional limitations upon the exercise of authority, federal and state, to the end that each may continue to discharge, harmoniously with the other, the duties entrusted to it by the Constitution.

In our view the necessary effect of this act is, by means of a prohibition against the movement in interstate commerce of ordinary commercial commodities, to regulate the hours of labor of children in factories and mines within the States, a purely state authority. Thus the act in a twofold sense is repugnant to the Constitu-

tion. It not only transcends the authority delegated to Congress over commerce but also exerts a power as to a purely local matter to which the federal authority does not extend. The far-reaching result of upholding the act cannot be more plainly indicated than by pointing out that if Congress can thus regulate matters entrusted to local authority by prohibition of the movement of commodities in interstate commerce, all freedom of commerce will be at an end, and the power of the states over local matters may be eliminated, and thus our system of government be practically destroyed.

For these reasons we hold that this law exceeds the constitutional authority of Congress. It follows that the decree of the District Court must be

Affirmed.

MR. JUSTICE HOLMES, dissenting. . . .

The first step in my argument is to make plain what no one is likely to dispute—that the statute in question is within the power expressly given to Congress if considered only as to its immediate effects and that if invalid it is so only upon some collateral ground. The statute confines itself to prohibiting the carriage of certain goods in interstate or foreign commerce. Congress is given power to regulate such commerce in unqualified terms. It would not be argued today that the power to regulate does not include the power to prohibit. Regulation means the prohibition of something, and when interstate commerce is the matter to be regulated I cannot doubt that the regulation may prohibit any part of such commerce that Congress sees fit to forbid. At all events it is established by the Lottery Case and others that have followed it that a law is not beyond the regulative power of Congress merely because it prohibits certain transportation out and out. . . . So I repeat that this statute in its immediate operation is clearly within the Congress's constitutional power.

The question then is narrowed to whether the exercise of its otherwise constitutional power by Congress can be pronounced unconstitutional because of its possible reaction upon the conduct of the States in a matter upon which I have admitted that they are free from direct control. I should have thought that that matter had been disposed of so fully as to leave no room for doubt. I should have thought that the most conspicuous decisions of this Court had made it clear that the power to regulate commerce and other constitutional powers could not be cut down or qualified by the fact that it might interfere with the carrying out of the domestic policy of any State. . . .

The notion that prohibition is any less prohibition when applied to things now thought evil I do not understand. But if there is any matter upon which civilized countries have agreed —far more unanimously than they have with regard to intoxicants and some other matters over which this country is now emotionally aroused—it is the evil of premature and excessive child labor. I should have thought that if we were to introduce our own moral conceptions where in my opinion they do not belong, this was preeminently a case for upholding the exercise of all its powers by the United States.

But I had thought that the propriety of the exercise of a power admitted to exist in some cases was for the consideration of Congress alone and that this Court always had disavowed the right to intrude its judgment upon questions of policy or morals. It is not for this Court to pronounce when prohibition is necessary to regulation if it ever may be necessary—to say that it is permissible as against strong drink but not as against the product of ruined lives.

The act does not meddle with anything belonging to the States. They may regulate their internal affairs and their domestic commerce as they like. But when they seek to send their products across the state line they are no longer within their rights. If there were no Constitution and no Congress their power to cross the line would depend upon their neighbors. Under the Constitution such commerce belongs not to the States but to Congress to regulate. It may carry out its views of public policy whatever indirect effect they may have upon the activities of the States. Instead of being encountered by a prohibitive tariff at her boundaries, the State encounters the public policy of the United States which it is for Congress to express. The public policy of the United States is shaped with a view to the benefit of the nation as a whole. If, as has been the case within the memory of men still living, a State should take a different view of the propriety of sustaining a lottery from that which generally prevails, I cannot believe that the fact would require a different decision from that reached in *Champion* v. *Ames*. Yet in that case it would be said with quite as much force as in this that Congress was attempting to intermeddle with the State's domestic affairs. The national welfare as understood by Congress may require a different attitude within its sphere from that of some self-seeking State. It seems to me entirely constitutional for Congress to enforce its understanding by all the means at its command.

MR. JUSTICE MCKENNA, MR. JUSTICE BRANDEIS and MR. JUSTICE CLARKE concur in this opinion.

Stafford v. Wallace
258 U.S. 495, 42 S.Ct. 397, 66 L.Ed. 735 (1922)

The Packers and Stockyards Act of 1921 attempted to regulate certain practices of meat packers that allegedly restricted and burdened interstate commerce in meat products. Stafford sought an interlocutory injunction against the enforcement of the act and appealed from a denial of his application.

MR. CHIEF JUSTICE TAFT . . . delivered the opinion of the court. . . .

The Packers and Stockyards Act of 1921 seeks to regulate the business of the packers done in interstate commerce and forbids them to engage in unfair, discriminatory or deceptive practices in such commerce, or to subject any person to unreasonable prejudice therein, or to do any of a number of acts to control prices or establish a monopoly in the business. . . .

The object to be secured by the act is the free and unburdened flow of live stock from the ranges and farms of the West and the Southwest through the great stockyards and slaughtering centers on the borders of that region, and thence in the form of meat products to the consuming cities of the country in the Middle West and East, or, still as live stock, to the feeding places and fattening farms in the Middle West or East for further preparation for the market.

The chief evil feared is the monopoly of the packers, enabling them unduly and arbitrarily to lower prices to the shipper who sells, and unduly and arbitrarily to increase the price to the consumer who buys. Congress thought that the power to maintain this monopoly was aided by control of the stockyards. Another evil which it sought to provide against by the act, was exorbitant charges, duplication of commissions, deceptive practices in respect of prices, in the passage of the live stock through the stockyards, all made possible by collusion between the stockyards management and the commission men, on the one hand, and the packers and dealers on the other.

The stockyards are not a place of rest or final destination. Thousands of head of live stock arrive daily by carload and trainload lots, and must be promptly sold and disposed of and moved out to give place to the constantly flowing traffic that presses behind. The stockyards are but a throat through which the current flows, and the transactions which occur therein are only incident to this current from the West to the East, and from one State to another. Such transactions cannot be separated from the movement to which they contribute and necessarily take on its character. The commission men are essential in making the sales without which the flow of the current would be obstructed, and this, whether they are made to packers or dealers. The dealers are essential to the sales to the stock farmers and feeders. The sales are not in this aspect merely local transactions. They create a local change of title, it is true, but they do not stop the flow; they merely change the private interests in the subject of the current, not interfering with, but, on the contrary, being indispensable to its continuity. The origin of the live stock is in the West, its ultimate destination known to, and intended by, all engaged in the business is in the Middle West and East either as meat products or for feeding and fattening. This is the definite and well-understood course of business. The stockyards and the sales are necessary factors in the middle of this current of commerce.

The act, therefore, treats the various stockyards of the country as great national public utilities to promote the flow of commerce from the ranges and farms of the West to the consumers in the East. It assumes that they conduct a business affected by a public use of a national character and subject to national regulation. That it is a business within the power of regulation by legislative action needs no discussion.

That has been settled since the case of *Munn* v. *Illinois*. . . . Nor is there any doubt that in the receipt of live stock by rail and in their delivery by rail the stockyards are an interstate commerce agency. . . . The only question here is whether the business done in the stockyards between the receipt of the live stock in the yards and the shipment of them therefrom is a part of interstate commerce, or is so associated with it as to bring it within the power of national regulation. A similar question has been before this court and had great consideration in *Swift & Co.* v. *United States,* 196 U.S. 375. The judgment in that case gives a clear and comprehensive exposition which leaves to us in this case little but the obvious application of the principles there declared. . . .

The application of the commerce clause of the Constitution in the Swift Case was the result of the natural development of interstate commerce under modern conditions. It was the inevitable recognition of the great central fact that such streams of commerce from one part of the country to another which are ever flowing are in their very essence the commerce among the States and with foreign nations which historically it was one of the chief purposes of the Constitution to bring under national protection and control. This court declined to defeat this purpose in respect of such a stream and take it out of complete national regulation by a nice and technical inquiry into the non-interstate character of some of its necessary incidents and facilities when considered alone and without reference to their association with the movement of which they were an essential but subordinate part. . . .

Of course, what we are considering here is not a bill in equity or an indictment charging conspiracy to obstruct interstate commerce, but a law. The language of the law shows that what Congress had in mind primarily was to prevent such conspiracies by supervision of the agencies which would be likely to be employed in it. If Congress could provide for punishment or restraint of such conspiracies after their formation through the Anti-Trust Law as in the Swift Case, certainly it may provide regulation to prevent their formation. The reasonable fear by Congress that such acts, usually lawful and affecting only intrastate commerce when considered alone, will probably and more or less constantly be used in conspiracies against interstate commerce or constitute a direct and undue burden on it, expressed in this remedial legislation, serves the same purpose as the intent charged in the Swift indictment to bring acts of a similar character into the current of interstate commerce for federal restraint. Whatever amounts to more or less constant practice, and threatens to obstruct or unduly to burden the freedom of interstate commerce is within the regulatory power of Congress under the commerce clause, and it is primarily for Congress to consider and decide the fact of danger and meet it. This court will certainly not substitute its judgment for that of Congress in such a matter unless the relation of the subject to interstate commerce and its effect upon it are clearly nonexistent. . . .

The orders of the District Court refusing the interlocutory injunctions are

Affirmed.

Mr. Justice McReynolds dissents.

Mr. Justice Day did not sit in these cases and took no part in their decision.

Carter v. Carter Coal Co.
298 U.S. 238, 56 S.Ct. 855, 80 L.Ed. 1160 (1936)

In the Bituminous Coal Conservation Act of 1935 Congress attempted to stabilize the production and marketing of coal. The Act provided for a National Bituminous Coal Commission with general supervisory powers over the industry through a Bituminous Coal Code. In each of 23 districts, boards were to be given the power to fix minimum coal prices. National hours of labor agreements and district minimum wage agreements were to be effective when the producers of two-thirds of the annual tonnage and representatives of more than one-half of the employed workers agreed to terms. A labor board in the Department of Labor was given the duty of protecting the collective bargaining process and adjudicating labor disputes.

Producers were to be induced to accept these codes by a tax provision that allowed 90 percent of a tax of 15 percent on sales at the mines to be refunded to those producers who accepted the code provisions. In the Act, Congress also stated that the provisions of the Act were separable, and the possible invalidity of one should not affect the constitutionality of other sections. A number of cases involving suits to bar payment of the tax and acceptance of the Code were consolidated on certiorari from circuit courts of appeals and from district courts. The majority of the Supreme Court held the delegation of code-drafting power to a part of the producers and workers to be invalid. The following excerpts from the opinion deal principally with the issue of whether federal regulation of mining activities was permissible under the commerce clause.

MR. JUSTICE SUTHERLAND delivered the opinion of the Court. . . .

The general rule with regard to the respective powers of the national and the state governments under the Constitution is not in doubt. The States were before the Constitution; and, consequently, their legislative powers antedated the Constitution. Those who framed and those who adopted that instrument meant to carve from the general mass of legislative powers, then possessed by the States, only such portions as it was thought wise to confer upon the federal government; and in order that there should be no uncertainty in respect of what was taken and what was left, the national powers of legislation were not aggregated but enumerated —with the result that what was not embraced by the enumeration remained vested in the States without change or impairment. . . . While the States are not sovereign in the true sense of that term, but only *quasi*-sovereign, yet in respect of all powers reserved to them they are supreme—

"as independent of the general government as that government within its sphere is independent of the States." *The Collector* v. *Day*, 11 Wall. 113, 124. And since every addition to the national legislative power to some extent detracts from or invades the power of the States, it is of vital moment that, in order to preserve the fixed balance intended by the Constitution, the powers of the general government be not so extended as to embrace any not within the express terms of the several grants or implications necessarily to be drawn therefrom. It is no longer open to question that the general government, unlike the States . . . possesses no *inherent* power in respect of the internal affairs of the States; and emphatically not with regard to legislation. The question in respect of the inherent power of that government as to the external affairs of the nation and in the field of international law is a wholly different matter which it is not necessary now to consider. . . .

The determination of the Framers Convention and the ratifying conventions to preserve complete and unimpaired state self-government in all matters not committed to the general government is one of the plainest facts which emerges from the history of their deliberations. And adherence to that determination is incumbent equally upon the federal government and the States. State powers can neither be appropriated on the one hand nor abdicated on the other. . . . Every journey to a forbidden end begins with the first step; and the danger of such a step by the federal government in the direction of taking over the powers of the states is that the end of the journey may find the states so despoiled of their powers, or—what may amount to the same thing—so relieved of the responsibilities which possession of the powers necessarily enjoins, as to reduce them to little more than geographical subdivisions of the national domain. It is safe to say that if, when the Constitution was under consideration, it had been thought that any such danger lurked behind its plain words, it would never have been ratified. . . .

. . . Since the validity of the act depends upon whether it is a regulation of interstate commerce, the nature and extent of the power conferred upon Congress by the commerce clause becomes the determinative question in this branch of the case. . . . We first inquire, then—What is commerce? The term, as this court many times has said, is one of extensive import. No all-embracing definition has ever been formulated. The question is to be approached both affirmatively and negatively—that is to say, from the points of view as to what it includes and what it excludes. . . .

As used in the Constitution, the word "commerce" is the equivalent of the phrase "intercourse for the purposes of trade," and includes transportation, purchase, sale, and exchange of commodities between the citizens of the different States. And the power to regulate commerce embraces the instruments by which commerce is carried on. . . . In *Veazie* v. *Moor,* 14 How. 568, 573–574, this court, after saying that the phrase could never be applied to transac-

tions wholly internal, significantly added: "Nor can it be properly concluded, that, because the products of domestic enterprise in agriculture or manufactures, or in the arts, may ultimately become the subjects of foreign commerce, that the control of the means or the encouragements by which enterprise is fostered and protected, is legitimately within the import of the phrase *foreign commerce,* or fairly implied in any investiture of the power to regulate such commerce. A pretension as far-reaching as this, would extend to contracts between citizen and citizen of the same State, would control the pursuits of the planter, the grazier, the manufacturer, the mechanic, the immense operations of the collieries and mines and furnaces of the country; for there is not one of these avocations, the results of which may not become the subjects of foreign commerce, and be borne either by turnpikes, canals, or railroads, from point to point within the several States, towards an ultimate destination, like the one above mentioned." . . .

Chief Justice Fuller, speaking for this court in *United States* v. *E. C. Knight,* . . . said:

"Doubtless the power to control the manufacture of a given thing involves in a certain sense the control of its disposition, but this is secondary and not the primary sense; and although the exercise of that power may result in bringing the operation of commerce into play, it does not control it, and affects it only incidentally and indirectly. Commerce succeeds to manufacture, and is not a part of it. . . ."

That commodities produced or manufactured within a State are intended to be sold or transported outside the State does not render their production or manufacture subject to federal regulation under the commerce clause. . . .

We have seen that the word "commerce" is the equivalent of the phrase "intercourse for the purposes of trade." Plainly, the incidents leading up to and culminating in the mining of coal do not constitute such intercourse. The employment of men, the fixing of their wages, hours of labor, and working conditions, the bargaining in respect of these things—whether carried on separately or collectively—each and all constitute intercourse for the purposes of production, not of trade. The latter is a thing apart from the relation of employer and employee, which in all producing occupations is purely local in character. Extraction of coal from the mine is the aim and the completed result of local activities. Commerce in the coal mined is not brought into being by force of these activities, but by negotiations, agreements and circumstances entirely apart from production. Mining brings the subject matter of commerce into existence. Commerce disposes of it.

A consideration of the foregoing, and of many cases which might be added to those already cited, renders inescapable the conclusion that the effect of the labor provisions of the act, including those in respect of minimum wages, wage agreements, collective bargaining, and the Labor Board and its powers, primarily falls upon production and not upon commerce; and confirms the further resulting conclusion that production is a purely local activity. It follows that none of these essential antecedents of production constitutes a transaction in or forms any part of interstate commerce. *Schechter Corp.* v. *United States*. . . . Everything which moves in interstate commerce has had a local origin. Without local production somewhere, interstate commerce, as now carried on, would practically disappear. Nevertheless, the local character of mining, of manufacturing, and of crop growing is a fact, and remains a fact, whatever may be done with the products. . . .

But § 1 (the preamble) of the act now under review declares that all production and distribution of bituminous coal "bear upon and directly affect its interstate commerce"; and that regulation thereof is imperative for the protection of such commerce. The contention of the government is that the labor provisions of the act may be sustained in that way.

That the production of every commodity intended for interstate sale and transportation has some effect upon interstate commerce may be,

if it has not already been, freely granted: and we are brought to the final and decisive inquiry, whether here that effect is direct, as the "preamble" recites, or indirect. The distinction is not formal, but substantial in the highest degree as we pointed out in the Schechter case, . . . "If the commerce clause were construed," we there said, "to reach all enterprises and transactions which could be said to have an indirect effect upon interstate commerce, the federal authority would embrace practically all the activities of the people and the authority of the State over its domestic concerns would exist only by sufferance of the federal government. Indeed, on such a theory, even the development of the State's commercial facilities would be subject to federal control." It was also pointed out, . . . "that the distinction between direct and indirect effects of intrastate transactions upon interstate commerce must be recognized as a fundamental one, essential to the maintenance of our constitutional system."

Whether the effect of a given activity or condition is direct or indirect is not always easy to determine. The word "direct" implies that the activity or condition invoked or blamed shall operate proximately—not mediately, remotely, or collaterally—to produce the effect. It connotes the absence of an efficient intervening agency or condition. And the extent of the effect bears no logical relation to its character. The distinction between a direct and an indirect effect turns, not upon the magnitude of either the cause or the effect, but entirely upon the manner in which the effect has been brought about. If the production by one man of a single ton of coal intended for interstate sale and shipment, and actually so sold and shipped, affects interstate commerce indirectly, the effect does not become direct by multiplying the tonnage, or increasing the number of men employed, or adding to the expense or complexities of the business, or by all combined. It is quite true that rules of law are sometimes qualified by considerations of degree, as the government argues. But the matter of degree has no bearing upon the question here, since that question is not—What is the *extent* of the local activity or condition, or the *extent* of the effect produced upon interstate commerce? but—What is the *relation* between the activity or condition and the effect?

Much stress is put upon the evils which come from the struggle between employers and employees over the matter of wages, working conditions, the right of collective bargaining, etc., and the resulting strikes, curtailment, and irregularity of production and effect on prices; and it is insisted that interstate commerce is greatly affected thereby. But, in addition to what has just been said, the conclusive answer is that the evils are all local evils over which the federal government has no legislative control. The relation of employer and employee is a local relation. At common law, it is one of the domestic relations. The wages are paid for the doing of local work. Working conditions are obviously local conditions. The employees are not engaged in or about commerce, but exclusively in producing a commodity. And the controversies and evils, which it is the object of the act to regulate and minimize, are local controversies and evils affecting local work undertaken to accomplish that local result. Such effect as they may have upon commerce, however extensive it may be, is secondary and indirect. An increase in the greatness of the effect adds to its importance. It does not alter its character. . . .

. . . Finally, we are brought to the price-fixing provisions of the code. The necessity of considering the question of their constitutionality will depend upon whether they are separable from the labor provisions so that they can stand independently. . . .

Since both were adopted, we must conclude that both were thought essential. The regulations of labor on the one hand and prices on the other furnish mutual aid and support; and their associated force—not one or the other but both combined—was deemed by Congress to be necessary to achieve the end sought. The statutory mandate for a code upheld by two legs at once suggests the improbability that Congress would have assented to a code supported by only one. . . .

. . . The conclusion is unavoidable that the price-fixing provisions of the code are so related to and dependent upon the labor provisions as considerations or compensations, as to make it clearly probable that the latter being held bad, the former would not have been passed. The fall of the latter, therefore, carries down with it the former. . . .

The price-fixing provisions of the code are thus disposed of without coming to the question of their constitutionality; but neither this disposition of the matter, nor anything we have said, is to be taken as indicating that the court is of opinion that these provisions, if separately enacted, could be sustained. . . .

It is so ordered.

Separate opinion of MR. CHIEF JUSTICE HUGHES.

I agree that the stockholders were entitled to bring their suit; that, in view of the question whether any part of the Act could be sustained, the suits were not premature; that the so-called tax is not a real tax, but a penalty; that the constitutional power of the Federal Government to impose this penalty must rest upon the commerce clause, as the Government concedes; that production—in this case mining—which precedes commerce, is not itself commerce; and that the power to regulate commerce among the several States is not a power to regulate industry within the State.

The power to regulate interstate commerce embraces the power to protect that commerce from injury, whatever may be the source of the dangers which threaten it, and to adopt any appropriate means to that end. . . . Congress thus has adequate authority to maintain the orderly conduct of interstate commerce and to provide for the peaceful settlement of disputes which threaten it. . . . But Congress may not use this protective authority as a pretext for the exertion of power to regulate activities and relations within the States which affect interstate commerce only indirectly. Otherwise, in view of the multitude of indirect effects, Congress in its discretion could assume control of virtually all the activities of the people to the subversion of the fundamental principle of the Constitution.

If the people desire to give Congress the power to regulate industries within the State, and the relations of employers and employees in those industries, they are at liberty to declare their will in the appropriate manner, but it is not for the Court to amend the Constitution by judicial decision. . . .

But that is not the whole case. The Act also provides for the regulation of the prices of bituminous coal sold in interstate commerce and prohibits unfair methods of competition in interstate commerce. Undoubtedly transactions in carrying on interstate commerce are subject to the federal power to regulate that commerce, and the control of charges and the protection of fair competition in that commerce are familiar illustrations of the exercise of the power, as the Interstate Commerce Act, the Packers and Stockyards Act, and the Anti-Trust Acts abundantly show. . . .

Whether the policy of fixing prices of commodities sold in interstate commerce is a sound policy is not for our consideration. The question of that policy, and of its particular applications, is for Congress. The exercise of the power of regulation is subject to the constitutional restriction of the due process clause, and if in fixing rates, prices or conditions of competition, that requirement is transgressed, the judicial power may be invoked to the end that the constitutional limitation may be maintained . . . .

Upon what ground, then, can it be said that this plan for the regulation of transactions in interstate commerce in coal is beyond the constitutional power of Congress? The Court reaches that conclusion in the view that the invalidity of the labor provisions requires us to condemn the Act in its entirety. I am unable to concur in that opinion. I think that the express provisions of the Act preclude such a finding of inseparability . . . .

MR. JUSTICE CARDOZO (dissenting).

. . . I am satisfied that the Act is within the power of the central government in so far as it provides for minimum and maximum prices upon sales of bituminous coal in the transactions of interstate commerce and in those of intrastate commerce where interstate commerce is directly or intimately affected. Whether it is valid also in other provisions that have been considered and condemned in the opinion of the court, I do not find it necessary to determine at this time. Silence must not be taken as importing acquiescence. Much would have to be written if the subject, even as thus restricted, were to be explored through all its implications, historical and economic as well as strictly legal. The fact that the prevailing opinion leaves the price provisions open for consideration in the future makes it appropriate to forego a fullness of elaboration that might otherwise be necessary. As a system of price fixing the Act is challenged upon three grounds: (1) because the governance of prices is not within the commerce clause; [(2) and (3) omitted].

(1) With reference to the first objection, the obvious and sufficient answer is, so far as the Act is directed to interstate transactions, that sales made in such conditions constitute interstate commerce, and do not merely "affect" it . . . . To regulate the price for such transactions is to regulate commerce itself, and not alone its antecedent conditions or its ultimate consequences. The very act of sale is limited and governed. Prices in interstate transactions may not be regulated by the States. *Baldwin* v. *Seelig,* 294 U.S. 511. They must therefore be subject to the power of the nation unless they are to be withdrawn altogether from governmental supervision . . . . If such a vacuum were permitted, many a public evil incidental to interstate transactions would be left without a remedy. This does not mean, of course, that prices may be fixed for arbitrary reasons or in an arbitrary way. The commerce power of the nation is subject to the requirement of due process like the police power of the states . . . . Heed must be given to similar considerations of social benefit or detriment in marking the division between reason and oppression. The evidence is overwhelming that Congress did not ignore those considerations in the adoption of this Act. What is to be said in that regard may conveniently be postponed to the part of the opinion dealing with the Fifth Amendment.

Regulation of prices being an exercise of the

commerce power in respect of interstate transactions, the question remains whether it comes within that power as applied to intrastate sales where interstate prices are directly or intimately affected. Mining and agriculture and manufacture are not interstate commerce considered by themselves, yet their relation to that commerce may be such that for the protection of the one there is need to regulate the other . . . . Sometimes it is said that the relation must be ''direct'' to bring that power into play. In many circumstances such a description will be sufficiently precise to meet the needs of the occasion. But a great principle of constitutional law is not susceptible of comprehensive statement in an adjective. The underlying thought is merely this, that ''the law is not indifferent to considerations of degree.'' . . . It cannot be indifferent to them without an expansion of the commerce clause that would absorb or imperil the reserved powers of the States. At times, as in the case cited, the waves of causation will have radiated so far that their undulatory motion, if discernible at all, will be too faint or obscure, too broken by crosscurrents, to be heeded by the law. In such circumstances the holding is not directed at prices or wages considered in the abstract, but at prices or wages in particular conditions. The relation may be tenuous or the opposite according to the facts. Always the setting of the facts is to be viewed if one would know the closeness of the tie. Perhaps, if one group of adjectives is to be chosen in preference to another, ''intimate'' and ''remote'' will be found to be as good as any. At all events, ''direct'' and ''indirect,'' even if accepted as sufficient, must not be read too narrowly. Cf. Stone, J., in *DiSanto* v. *Pennsylvania*, 273 U.S. 34, 44. A survey of the cases shows that the words have been interpreted with suppleness of adaptation and flexibility of meaning. The power is as broad as the need that evokes it . . . .

I am authorized to state that MR. JUSTICE BRANDEIS and MR. JUSTICE STONE join in this opinion.

National Labor Relations Board v. Jones & Laughlin Steel Corporation
301 U.S. 1, 57 S.Ct. 615, 81 L.Ed. 893 (1937)

The National Labor Relations Act of 1935 was designed to protect the right of workers to organize and to encourage collective bargaining procedures. In this case the National Labor Relations Board had ordered the defendant corporation to cease and desist from certain ''unfair labor practices,'' and, when the corporation failed to comply, had petitioned the circuit court of appeals (as provided in the Act) to enforce the Board's order. The Supreme Court granted certiorari from the court's refusal to issue the order.

MR. CHIEF JUSTICE HUGHES delivered the opinion of the Court. . . .

The Scope of the Act. The Act is challenged in its entirety as an attempt to regulate all industry, thus invading the reserved powers of the States over their local concerns. It is asserted that the references in the Act to interstate and foreign commerce are colorable at best; that the Act is not a true regulation of such commerce or of matters which directly affect it but on the contrary has the fundamental object of placing under the compulsory supervision of the federal government all industrial labor relations within the nation. The argument seeks support in the broad words of the preamble (section one) and in the sweep of the provisions of the Act, and it is further insisted that its legislative history shows an essential universal purpose in the light of which its scope cannot be limited by either construction or by the application of the separability clause.

If this conception of terms, intent and consequent inseparability were sound, the Act would necessarily fall by reason of the limitation upon the federal power which inheres in the constitutional grant, as well as because of the explicit reservation of the Tenth Amendment. *Schechter Corp.* v. *United States.* . . . The authority of the federal government may not be pushed to such an extreme as to destroy the distinction, which the commerce clause itself establishes, between commerce "among the several States" and the internal concerns of a State. That distinction between what is national and what is local in the activities of commerce is vital to the maintenance of our federal system.

But we are not at liberty to deny effect to specific provisions, which Congress has constitutional power to enact, by superimposing upon them inferences from general legislative declarations of an ambiguous character, even if found in the same statute. The cardinal principle of statutory construction is to save and not to destroy. We have repeatedly held that as between two possible interpretations of a statute, by one of which it would be unconstitutional and by the other valid, our plain duty is to adopt that which will save the act. . . .

We think it clear that the National Labor Relations Act may be construed so as to operate within the sphere of constitutional authority. The jurisdiction conferred upon the Board, and invoked in this instance, is found in § 10 (a), which provides:

"Sec. 10(a). The Board is empowered, as hereinafter provided, to prevent any person from engaging in any unfair labor practice (listed in § 8) affecting commerce."

The critical words of this provision, prescribing the limits of the Board's authority in dealing with the labor practices, are "affecting commerce." . . .

There can be no question that the commerce thus contemplated by the Act (aside from that within a Territory or the District of Columbia) is interstate and foreign commerce in the constitutional sense. The Act also defines the term "affecting commerce" (§ 2(6)):

"The term 'affecting commerce' means in commerce, or burdening or obstructing commerce or the free flow of commerce, or having led or tending to lead to a labor dispute burdening or obstructing commerce or the free flow of commerce."

This definition is one of exclusion as well as inclusion. The grant of authority to the Board does not purport to extend to the relationship between all industrial employees and employers. Its terms do not impose collective bargaining upon all industry regardless of effects upon interstate or foreign commerce. It purports to reach only what may be deemed to burden or obstruct that commerce and, thus qualified, it must be construed as contemplating the exercise of control within constitutional bounds. It is a familiar principle that acts which directly burden or obstruct interstate or foreign commerce, or its free flow, are within the reach of the congressional power. Acts having that effect are not rendered immune because they grow out of labor disputes. . . . Whether or not particular action does affect commerce in such a close and intimate fashion as to be subject to federal control, and hence to lie within the authority conferred upon the Board, is left by the statute to be determined as individual cases arise. . . .

The Application of the Act to Employees Engaged in Production.—The Principle Involved. Respondent says that whatever may be said of employees engaged in interstate commerce, the industrial relations and activities in the manufacturing department of respondent's enterprise are not subject to federal regulation. The argument rests upon the proposition that manufacturing in itself is not commerce. . . .

. . . Reference is made to our decision sustaining the Packers and Stockyards Act. *Stafford* v. *Wallace*. . . . The Court found that the stockyards were but a "throat" through which the current of commerce flowed and the transactions which there occurred could not be separated from that movement. Here the sales at the stockyards were not regarded as merely local transactions, for while they created "a local change of title" they did not "stop the flow," but merely changed the private interests in the subject of the current. Distinguishing the cases which upheld the power of the State to impose a non-discriminatory tax upon property which the owner intended to transport to another State, but which was not in actual transit and was held within the State subject to the disposition of the owner, the Court remarked: "The question, it should be observed, is not with respect to the extent of the power of Congress to regulate interstate commerce, but whether a particular exercise of state power in view of its nature and operation must be deemed to be in conflict with this paramount authority." . . .

Respondent contends that the instant case presents material distinction. Respondent says that the Aliquippa plant is extensive in size and represents a large investment in buildings, machinery and equipment. The raw materials which are brought to the plant are delayed for long periods and, after being subjected to manufacturing processes "are changed substantially as to character, utility and value." . . .

We do not find it necessary to determine whether these features of defendant's business dispose of the asserted analogy to the "stream of commerce" cases. The instances in which that metaphor has been used are but particular, and not exclusive, illustrations of the protective power which the Government invokes in support of the present Act. The congressional authority to protect interstate commerce from burdens and obstructions is not limited to transactions which can be deemed to be an essential part of a "flow" of interstate or foreign commerce. Burdens and obstructions may be due to injurious action springing from other sources. The fundamental principle is that the power to regulate commerce is the power to enact "all appropriate legislation" for "its protection and advancement". . . . That power is plenary and may be exerted to protect interstate commerce "no matter what the source of the dangers which threaten it." *Second Employers' Liability Cases*, . . . *Schechter Corporation* v. *United States*. Although activities may be intrastate in character when separately considered, if they have such a close and substantial relation to interstate commerce that their control is essential or appropriate to protect that commerce from burdens and obstructions, Congress cannot be denied the power to exercise that control. . . . Undoubtedly the scope of this power must be considered in the light of our dual system of government and may not be extended so as to embrace effects upon interstate commerce so indirect and remote that to embrace them, in view of our complex society, would effectually obliterate the distinction between what is national and what is local and create a completely centralized government. . . . The question is necessarily one of degree. As the Court said in *Chicago Board of Trade* v. *Olsen*, 262 U.S. 37, repeating what had been said in *Stafford* v. *Wallace*; . . . "Whatever amounts to more or less constant practice, and threatens to obstruct or unduly to burden the freedom of interstate commerce is within the regulatory power of Congress under the commerce clause and it is primarily for Congress to consider and decide the fact of the danger and meet it."

That intrastate activities, by reason of close and intimate relation to interstate commerce, may fall within federal control is demonstrated in the case of carriers who are engaged in both interstate and intrastate transportation. There federal control has been found essential to secure the freedom of interstate traffic from interference or unjust discrimination and to promote the efficiency of the interstate service. . . .

The close and intimate effect which brings the subject within the reach of federal power may be due to activities in relation to productive industry although the industry when separately viewed is local. This has been abundantly illustrated in the application of the federal Anti-

Trust Act. In the Standard Oil and American Tobacco cases, 221 U.S. 1, 106, that statute was applied to combinations of employers engaged in productive industry. Counsel for the offending corporations strongly urged that the Sherman Act had no application because the acts complained of were not acts of interstate or foreign commerce, nor direct and immediate in their effect on interstate or foreign commerce, but primarily affected manufacturing and not commerce. . . .

It is thus apparent that the fact that the employees here concerned were engaged in production is not determinative. The question remains as to the effect upon interstate commerce of the labor practice involved. In the Schechter case, we found that the effect there was so remote as to be beyond the federal power. To find "immediacy or directness" there was to find it "almost everywhere," a result inconsistent with the maintenance of our federal system. In the Carter case, the Court was of the opinion that the provisions of the statute relating to production were invalid upon several grounds—that there was improper delegation of legislative power, and that the requirements not only went beyond any sustainable measure of protection of interstate commerce but were also inconsistent with due process. These cases are not controlling here.

Effects of the Unfair Labor Practice in Respondent's Enterprise. Giving full weight to respondent's contention with respect to a break in the complete continuity of the "stream of commerce" by reason of respondent's manufacturing operations, the fact remains that the stoppage of those operations by industrial strife would have a most serious effect upon interstate commerce. In view of respondent's far-flung activities, it is idle to say that the effect would be indirect or remote. It is obvious that it would be immediate and might be catastrophic. We are asked to shut our eyes to the plainest facts of our national life and to deal with the question of direct and indirect effects in an intellectual vacuum. Because there may be but indirect and remote effects upon interstate commerce in connection with a host of local enter-

prises throughout the country, it does not follow that other industrial activities do not have such a close and intimate relation to interstate commerce as to make the presence of industrial strife a matter of the most urgent national concern. When industries organize themselves on a national scale, making their relation to interstate commerce the dominant factor in their activities, how can it be maintained that their industrial labor relations constitute a forbidden field into which Congress may not enter when it is necessary to protect interstate commerce from the paralyzing consequences of industrial war? We have often said that interstate commerce itself is a practical conception. It is equally true that interferences with that commerce must be appraised by a judgment that does not ignore actual experience. . . .

Our conclusion is that the order of the Board was within its competency and that the Act is valid as here applied. The judgment of the Circuit Court of Appeals is reversed and the case is remanded for further proceedings in conformity with this opinion.

Reversed.

MR. JUSTICE MCREYNOLDS delivered the following dissenting opinion. . . .

MR. JUSTICE VAN DEVANTER, MR. JUSTICE SUTHERLAND, MR. JUSTICE BUTLER and I are unable to agree with the decisions just announced. . . .

The Court as we think departs from well-established principles followed in *A. L. A. Schechter Poultry Corp.* v. *United States* . . . and *Carter* v. *Carter Coal Co.* . . . Every consideration brought forward to uphold the Act before us was applicable to support the Acts held unconstitutional in causes decided within two years. And the lower courts rightly deemed them controlling.

By its terms the Labor Act extends to employers—large and small—unless excluded by definition, and declares that if one of these interferes with, restrains, or coerces any employee regarding his labor affiliations, etc., this shall be regarded as unfair labor practice. . . .

The three respondents happen to be manufacturing concerns—one large, two relatively small. The Act is now applied to each upon grounds common to all. Obviously what is determined as to these concerns may gravely affect a multitude of employers who engage in a great variety of private enterprises—mercantile, manufacturing, publishing, stockraising, mining, etc. It puts into the hands of a Board control over purely local industry beyond anything heretofore deemed permissible.

The argument in support of the Board affirms: "Thus the validity of any specific application of the preventive measures of this Act depends upon whether industrial strife resulting from the practices in the particular enterprise under consideration would be of the character which Federal power could control if it occurred. If strife in that enterprise could be controlled, certainly it could be prevented."

Manifestly that view of Congressional power would extend it into almost every field of human industry. . . .

Any effect on interstate commerce by the discharge of employees shown here, would be indirect and remote in the highest degree, as consideration of the facts will show. In No. 419 (*National Labor Relations Board* v. *Jones & Laughlin Steel Corp.*) ten men out of ten thousand were discharged; in the other cases only a few. The immediate effect in the factory may be to create discontent among all those employed and a strike may follow, which, in turn, may result in reducing production, which ultimately may reduce the volume of goods moving in interstate commerce. By this chain of indirect and progressively remote events we finally reach the evil with which it is said the legislation under consideration undertakes to deal. A more remote and indirect interference with interstate commerce or a more definite invasion of the powers reserved to the States is difficult, if not impossible, to imagine.

The Constitution still recognizes the existence of States with indestructible powers; the Tenth Amendment was supposed to put them beyond controversy.

United States v. Darby
312 U.S. 100, 61 S.Ct. 451, 85 L.Ed. 609 (1941)

The Fair Labor Standards Act of 1938 provided for the fixing of minimum wages and maximum hours for employees in industries whose products were shipped in interstate commerce. The Act declared that the production of goods for commerce under substandard conditions causes the channels of commerce to be used to "spread and perpetuate such labor conditions among the workers of the several States; burdens commerce and the free flow of goods in commerce; constitutes an unfair method of competition in commerce; leads to labor disputes burdening and obstructing commerce; and interferes with the orderly and fair marketing of goods in commerce." From a district court judgment quashing an indictment against an alleged violator of the Act, the government appealed.

MR. JUSTICE STONE delivered the opinion of the court.

The two principal questions raised by the record in this case are, *first,* whether Congress has constitutional power to prohibit the shipment in interstate commerce of lumber manufactured by employees whose wages are less than a prescribed minimum or whose weekly hours of labor at that wage are greater than a prescribed maximum, and, *second,* whether it has power to prohibit the employment of workmen in the production of goods "for interstate commerce" at other than prescribed wages and hours.

The demurrer, so far as now relevant to the appeal, challenged the validity of the Fair Labor Standards Act under the Commerce Clause and the Fifth and Tenth Amendments. The district court quashed the indictment in its entirety upon the broad grounds that the Act, which it interpreted as a regulation of manufacture within the states, is unconstitutional. It declared that manufacture is not interstate commerce and that the regulation by the Fair Labor Standards Act of wages and hours of employment of those engaged in the manufacture of goods which it is intended at the time of production "may or will be" after production "sold in interstate commerce in part or in whole" is not within the congressional power to regulate interstate commerce.

The effect of the court's decision and judgment are thus to deny the power of Congress to prohibit shipment in interstate commerce of lumber produced for interstate commerce under the proscribed substandard labor conditions of wages and hours, its power to penalize the employer for his failure to conform to the wage and hour provisions in the case of employees engaged in the production of lumber which he intends thereafter to ship in interstate commerce in part or in whole according to the normal course of his business and its power to compel him to keep records of hours of employment as required by the statute and the regulations of the administrator. . . .

While manufacture is not of itself interstate commerce the shipment of manufactured goods interstate is such commerce and the prohibition of such shipment by Congress is indubitably a regulation of the commerce. The power to regulate commerce is the power "to prescribe the rule by which commerce is governed." *Gibbons* v. *Ogden.* . . . It extends not only to those regulations which aid, foster and protect the commerce, but embraces those which prohibit it. . . . It is conceded that the power of Congress

to prohibit transportation in interstate commerce includes noxious articles, *Lottery Case;* . . . stolen articles, *Brooks* v. *United States,* 267 U.S. 432; kidnapped persons, *Gooch* v. *United States;* 297 U.S. 124, and articles such as intoxicating liquor or convict made goods, traffic in which is forbidden or restricted by the laws of the state of destination. *Kentucky Whip & Collar Co.* v. *Illinois Central R. R. Co.,* 299 U.S. 334.

But it is said that the present prohibition falls within the scope of none of these categories; that while the prohibition is nominally a regulation of the commerce its motive or purpose is regulation of wages and hours of persons engaged in manufacture, the control of which has been reserved to the states and upon which Georgia and some of the states of destination have placed no restriction; that the effect of the present statute is not to exclude the prescribed articles from interstate commerce in aid of state regulation as in *Kentucky Whip & Collar Co.* v. *Illinois Central R. R. Co.,* . . . but instead, under the guise of a regulation of interstate commerce, it undertakes to regulate wages and hours within the state contrary to the policy of the state which has elected to leave them unregulated. . . .

The motive and purpose of the present regulation is plainly to make effective the Congressional conception of public policy that interstate commerce should not be made the instrument of competition in the distribution of goods produced under substandard labor conditions, which competition is injurious to the commerce and to the states from and to which the commerce flows. The motive and purpose of a regulation of interstate commerce are matters for the legislative judgment upon the exercise of which the Constitution places no restriction and over which the courts are given no control. . . . Whatever their motive and purpose, regulations of commerce which do not infringe some constitutional prohibition are within the plenary power conferred on Congress by the Commerce Clause. Subject only to that limitation, . . . we conclude that the prohibition of the shipment interstate of goods produced under the forbidden substandard labor conditions is within the constitutional authority of Congress.

In the more than a century which has elapsed since the decision of *Gibbons* v. *Ogden,* these principles of constitutional interpretation have been so long and repeatedly recognized by this Court as applicable to the Commerce Clause, that there would be little occasion for repeating them now were it not for the decision of this Court twenty-two years ago in *Hammer* v. *Dagenhart.* . . . In that case it was held by a bare majority of the Court over the powerful and now classic dissent of Mr. Justice Holmes setting forth the fundamental issues involved, that Congress was without power to exclude the products of child labor from interstate commerce. The reasoning and conclusion of the Court's opinion there cannot be reconciled with the conclusion which we have reached, that the power of Congress under the Commerce Clause is plenary to exclude any article from interstate commerce subject only to specific prohibitions of the Constitution.

Hammer v. *Dagenhart* has not been followed. The distinction on which the decision was rested that Congressional power to prohibit interstate commerce is limited to articles which in themselves have some harmful or deleterious property—a distinction which was novel when made and unsupported by any provision of the Constitution—has long since been abandoned. . . .

The conclusion is inescapable that *Hammer* v. *Dagenhart* was a departure from the principles which have prevailed in the interpretation of the commerce clause both before and since the decision and that such vitality, as a precedent, as it then had has long since been exhausted. It should be and now is overruled.

Validity of the wage and hour requirements. Section 15(a) (2) and §§ 6 and 7 require employers to conform to the wage and hour provisions with respect to all employees engaged in the production of goods for interstate commerce. As appellees' employees are not alleged to be "engaged in interstate commerce" the validity of the prohibition turns on the question whether the employment, under other than the prescribed labor standards, of employees engaged in the production of goods for interstate commerce is so related to the commerce and so affects it as to be within the reach of the power of Congress to regulate it. . . .

Congress, having by the present Act adopted the policy of excluding from interstate commerce all goods produced for the commerce which do not conform to the specified labor standards, it may choose the means reasonably adapted to the attainment of the permitted end, even though they involve control of intrastate activities. Such legislation has often been sustained with respect to powers, other than the commerce power granted to the national government, when the means chosen, although not themselves within the granted power, were nevertheless deemed appropriate aids to the accomplishment of some purpose within an admitted power of the national government. . . .

The Sherman Act and the National Labor Relations Act are familiar examples of the exertion of the commerce power to prohibit or control activities wholly intrastate because of their effect on interstate commerce. . . .

So far as *Carter* v. *Carter Coal Co.* . . . is inconsistent with this conclusion, its doctrine is limited in principle by the decisions under the Sherman Act and the National Labor Relations Act, which we have cited and which we follow. . . .

Our conclusion is unaffected by the Tenth Amendment which provides: "The powers not delegated to the United States by the Constitution nor prohibited by it to the states are reserved to the states respectively or to the people." The amendment states but a truism that all is retained which has not been surrendered. There is nothing in the history of its adoption to suggest that it was more than declaratory of the relationship between the national and state governments as it had been established by the Constitution before the amendment or that its purpose was other than to allay fears that the new national government might seek to exercise powers not granted, and that the states might not be able to exercise fully their reserved powers. See e.g., II Elliot's Debates, 123, 131; III *id.* 450, 464, 600; IV *id.* 140, 149; I Annals of Congress, 432, 761, 767–768; Story, *Commentaries on the Constitution,* §§ 1907–1908. . . .

The Act is sufficiently definite to meet constitutional demands. One who employs persons, without conforming to the prescribed wage and hour conditions, to work on goods which he ships or expects to ship across state lines, is warned that he may be subject to the criminal penalties of the Act. No more is required. . . .

We have considered, but find it unnecessary to discuss other contentions.

Reversed.

Wickard v. *Filburn*
317 U.S. 111, 63 S.Ct. 82, 87 L.Ed. 122 (1942)

The Agricultural Adjustment Act of 1938 was passed by Congress in an effort to stabilize agricultural production. The basic scheme as applied to wheat involved an annual proclamation by the Secretary of Agriculture of a national acreage allotment, which was then apportioned to states, and eventually passed on in the form of quotas to the individual farmer. If more than one-third of the farmers subject to the Act disapproved by referendum the proposed national quota, the effect of the Act was to be suspended. Penalties were imposed for production in excess of an agreed-upon quota. Filburn, a wheat farmer, produced wheat in excess of his quota for use on his own farm, and resisted payment of the penalty by seeking an injunction against Secretary of Agriculture Wickard and other officials. A three-judge district court issued the injunction on the ground that the Secretary of Agriculture had made an improper and misleading speech in supporting the adoption of the quota by referendum, and further, that a retroactive increase in the penalty for excess production and marketing violated the Fifth Amendment. On appeal the Supreme Court rejected both of these lower-court holdings. The opinion excerpts that follow deal with the main constitutional issue of whether the regulation involved here was within the commerce power.

MR. JUSTICE JACKSON delivered the opinion of the Court. . . .

It is urged that under the Commerce Clause of the Constitution, Art. I, § 8, Cl. 3, Congress does not possess the power it has in this instance sought to exercise. The question would merit little consideration since our decision in *United States* v. *Darby* . . . sustaining the federal power to regulate production of goods for commerce except for the fact that this Act extends federal regulation to production not intended in any part for commerce but wholly for consumption on the farm. The Act includes a definition of "market" and its derivatives so that as related to wheat in addition to its conventional meaning it also means to dispose of "by feeding (in any form) to poultry or livestock which, or the products of which, are sold, bartered, or exchanged, or to be so disposed of." Hence, marketing quotas not only embrace all that may be sold without penalty but also what may be consumed on the premises. Wheat produced on excess acreage is designated as "available for marketing" as so defined and the penalty is imposed thereon. Penalties do not depend upon whether any part of the wheat either within or without the quota is sold or intended to be sold. The sum of this is that the Federal Government fixes a quota including all that the farmer may harvest for sale or for his own farm needs, and declares that wheat produced on excess acreage may neither be disposed of nor used except upon payment of the penalty or except it is stored as required by the Act or delivered to the Secretary of Agriculture.

Appellee says that this is a regulation of production and consumption of wheat. Such activities are, he urges, beyond the reach of Congressional power under the Commerce Clause, since they are local in character, and their effects upon interstate commerce are at most "indirect." In answer the Government argues that the statute regulates neither production nor consumption, but only marketing; and, in the alternative, that if the Act does go beyond the regulation of marketing it is sustainable as a "necessary and proper" implementation of the power of Congress over interstate commerce.

The Government's concern lest the Act be held to be a regulation of production or consumption rather than of marketing is attributable to a few dicta and decisions of this Court which might be understood to lay it down that activities such as "production," "manufacturing," and "mining" are strictly "local" and, except in special circumstances which are not present here, cannot be regulated under the commerce power because their effects upon interstate commerce are, as matter of law, only "indirect." Even today, when this power has been held to have great latitude, there is no decision of this Court that such activities may be regulated where no part of the product is intended for interstate commerce or intermingled with the subjects thereof. We believe that a review of the course of decision under the Commerce Clause will make plain, however, that questions of the power of Congress are not to be decided by reference to any formula which would give controlling force to nomenclature

such as "production" and "indirect" and foreclose consideration of the actual effects of the activity in question upon interstate commerce. . . .

The Court's recognition of the relevance of the economic effects in the application of the Commerce Clause . . . has made the mechanical application of legal formulas no longer feasible. Once an economic measure of the reach of the power granted to Congress in the Commerce Clause is accepted, questions of federal power cannot be decided simply by finding the activity in question to be "production" nor can consideration of its economic effects be foreclosed by calling them "indirect." The present Chief Justice has said in summary of the present state of the law: "The commerce power is not confined in its exercise to the regulation of commerce among the states. It extends to those activities intrastate which so affect interstate commerce, or the exertion of the power of Congress over it, as to make regulation of them appropriate means to the attainment of a legitimate end, the effective execution of the granted power to regulate interstate commerce. . . . The power of Congress over interstate commerce is plenary and complete in itself, may be exercised to its utmost extent, and acknowledges no limitations other than are prescribed in the Constitution. . . . It follows that no form of state activity can constitutionally thwart the regulatory power granted by the commerce clause to Congress. Hence the reach of that power extends to those intrastate activities which in a substantial way interfere with or obstruct the exercise of the granted power." . . .

Whether the subject of the regulation in question was "production," "consumption," or "marketing" is, therefore, not material for purposes of deciding the question of federal power before us. That an activity is of local character may help in a doubtful case to determine whether Congress intended to reach it. The same consideration might help in determining whether in the absence of Congressional action it would be permissible for the state to exert its power on the subject matter, even though in so doing it to some degree affected interstate commerce. But even if appellant's activity be local and though it may not be regarded as commerce, it may still, whatever its nature, be reached by Congress if it exerts a substantial economic effect on interstate commerce and this irrespective of whether such effect is what might at some earlier time have been defined as "direct" or "indirect." . . .

The effect of consumption of home-grown wheat on interstate commerce is due to the fact that it constitutes the most variable factor in the disappearance of the wheat crop. Consumption on the farm where grown appears to vary in an amount greater than 10 per cent of average production. The total amount of wheat consumed as food varies but relatively little, and use as seed is relatively constant. . . .

It is well established by decisions of this Court that the power to regulate commerce includes the power to regulate the prices at which commodities in that commerce are dealt in and practices affecting such prices. One of the primary purposes of the Act in question was to increase the market price of wheat and to that end to limit the volume thereof that could affect the market. It can hardly be denied that a factor of such volume and variability as home-consumed wheat would have a substantial influence on price and market conditions. This may arise because being in marketable condition such home-grown wheat overhangs the market and if induced by rising prices tends to flow into the market and check price increases. But if we assume that it is never marketed, it supplies a need of the man who grew it which would otherwise be reflected by purchases in the open market. Home-grown wheat in this sense competes with wheat in commerce. The stimulation of commerce is a use of a regulatory function quite as definitely as prohibitions or restrictions thereon. This record leaves us in no doubt that Congress may properly have considered that wheat consumed on the farm where grown if wholly outside the scheme of regulation would have a substantial effect in defeating and obstructing its purpose to stimulate trade therein at increased prices.

It is said, however, that this Act, forcing some farmers into the market to buy what they could provide for themselves, is an unfair promotion of the markets and prices of specializing wheat growers. It is of the essence of regulation that it lays a restraining hand on the self-interest of the regulated and that advantages from the regulation commonly fall to others. The conflicts of economic interest between the regulated and those who advantage by it are wisely left under our system to resolution by the Congress under its more flexible and responsible legislative process. Such conflicts rarely lend themselves to judicial determination. And with the wisdom, workability, or fairness, of the plan of regulation we have nothing to do. . . .

Reversed.

Heart of Atlanta Motel v. United States
379 U.S. 241, 85 S.Ct. 348, 13 L.Ed. 2d 258 (1964)
Katzenbach v. McClung
379 U.S. 294, 85 S.Ct. 377, 13 L.Ed. 2d 290 (1964)

In the Civil Rights Act of 1964 Congress sought, among other purposes, to eliminate racial discrimination in hotels, motels, restaurants and similar places, basing its action on both the equal protection of the laws clause and Section 5 of the Fourteenth Amendment and the commerce clause. In the Atlanta Motel case, the Act was applied to an establishment, 75 percent of whose guests were from out-of-state. McClung's Barbecue, in Birmingham, Alabama, was a local restaurant, to which the Act was applied under a provision covering any restaurant that "serves or offers to serve interstate travelers or a substantial portion of the food which it serves . . . has moved in commerce." Approximately half of the food served at the Barbecue, though purchased within Alabama, had "moved" in commerce. Although two Justices, Douglas and Goldberg, would have upheld the Act under the Fourteenth Amendment provisions as well as the commerce clause, the commerce clause was chosen by the majority as justifying the Act, and the portions of the opinions reproduced below deal principally with the commerce power. The Motel appealed from a three-man district court injunction against its refusal to accept black lodgers, while the Attorney General appealed in McClung from a three-judge district court holding that the Act could not be applied to the restaurant. A brief excerpt from Justice Clark's opinion for the Court in *Atlanta Motel* is followed by a somewhat longer extract from his opinion in the *McClung* case. Justice Black's concurring opinion, a portion of which follows, is interesting because of the comments concerning the limits, if any, on congressional power to regulate commercial activities within a state. Justice Douglas states his preference for relying on the equal protection clause.

MR. JUSTICE CLARK delivered the opinion of the Court. . . . (*Heart of Atlanta*)

It is admitted that the operation of the motel brings it within the provisions of § 201(a) of the Act and that appellant refused to provide lodging for transient Negroes because of their race or color and that it intends to continue that policy unless restrained. . . .

. . . The determinative test of the exercise of power by the Congress under the Commerce Clause is simply whether the activity sought to be regulated is "commerce which concerns more than one state" and has a real and substantial relation to the national interest. . . .

It is said that the operation of the motel here is of a purely local character. But, assuming this to be true, 'if it is interstate commerce that feels the pinch, it does not matter how local the operation that applies the squeeze." . . .

. . . The power of Congress to promote interstate commerce also includes the power to regulate the local incidents thereof, including local activities in both the States of origin and destination, which might have a substantial and harmful effect upon that commerce. One need only examine the evidence which we have discussed above to see that Congress may—as it has—prohibit racial discrimination by motels serving travelers, however "local" their operations may appear. . . .

Affirmed.

MR. JUSTICE CLARK delivered the opinion of the Court. . . . (*Katzenbach* v. *McClung*)

. . . The activities that are beyond the reach of

Congress are "those which are completely within a particular State, which do not affect other States, and with which it is not necessary to interfere, for the purpose of executing some of the general powers of the government." ... *Gibbons* v. *Ogden*. This rule is as good today as it was when Chief Justice Marshall laid it down almost a century and a half ago.

This Court has held time and again that this power extends to activities of retail establishments, including restaurants, which directly or indirectly burden or obstruct interstate commerce. We have detailed the cases in *Heart of Atlanta Motel*, . . . , and will not repeat them here.

Nor are the cases holding that interstate commerce ends when goods come to rest in the state of destination apposite here. That line of cases has been applied with reference to state taxation or regulation but not in the field of federal regulation. . . .

Here, as there, Congress has determined for itself that refusals of service to Negroes have imposed burdens both upon the interstate flow of food and upon the movement of products generally. Of course, the mere fact that Congress has said when particular activity shall be deemed to affect commerce does not preclude further examination by this Court. But where we find that the legislators, in light of the facts and testimony before them, have a rational basis for finding a chosen regulatory scheme necessary to the protection of commerce, our investigation is at an end. The only remaining question—one answered in the affirmative by the court below—is whether the particular restaurant either serves or offers to serve interstate travelers or serves food a substantial portion of which has moved in interstate commerce. . . .

Confronted as we are with the facts laid before Congress, we must conclude that it had a rational basis for finding that racial discrimination in restaurants had a direct and adverse effect on the free flow of interstate commerce. . . .

The absence of direct evidence connecting discriminatory restaurant service with the flow of interstate food, a factor on which the appellees place much reliance, is not, given the

evidence as to the effect of such practices on other aspects of commerce, a crucial matter.

The power of Congress in this field is broad and sweeping; where it keeps within its sphere and violates no express constitutional limitation it has been the rule of this Court, going back almost to the founding days of the Republic, not to interfere. The Civil Rights Act of 1964, as here applied, we find to be plainly appropriate in the resolution of what the Congress found to be a national commercial problem of the first magnitude. We find it in no violation of any express limitations of the Constitution and we therefore declare it valid.

MR. JUSTICE BLACK, concurring. . . .

It requires no novel or strained interpretation of the Commerce Clause to sustain Title II as applied in either of these cases. At least since *Gibbons* v. *Ogden* . . . it has been uniformly accepted that the power of Congress to regulate commerce among the States is plenary, "complete in itself, may be exercised to its utmost extent, and acknowledges no limitations, other than are prescribed in the constitution." . . . Nor is "Commerce" as used in the Commerce Clause to be limited to a narrow, technical concept. It includes not only, as Congress has enumerated in the Act, "travel, trade, traffic, commerce, transportation, or communication," but also all other unitary transactions and activities that take place in more States than one. That some parts or segments of such unitary transactions may take place only in one State cannot, of course, take from Congress its plenary power to regulate them in the national interest. The facilities and instrumentalities used to carry on this commerce, such as railroads, truck lines, ships, rivers, and even highways are also subject to congressional regulation, so far as is necessary to keep interstate traffic upon fair and equal terms. . . .

Furthermore, it has long been held that the Necessary and Proper Clause, Art. 1, § 8, cl. 18, adds to the commerce power of Congress the power to regulate local instrumentalities operating within a single state if their activities burden the flow of commerce among the States. Thus in the Shreveport Case . . . this Court recognizes that Congress could not fully carry out its responsibility to protect interstate commerce were its constitutional power to regulate that commerce to be strictly limited to prescribing the rules for controlling the things actually moving in such commerce or the contracts, transactions, and other activities, immediately concerning them. Regulation of purely intrastate railroad rates is primarily a local problem for state rather than national control. But the Shreveport Case sustained the power of Congress under the Commerce Clause and the Necessary and Proper Clause to control purely intrastate rates, even though reasonable, where the effect of such rates was found to impose a discrimination injurious to interstate commerce. This holding that Congress had power under these clauses, not merely to enact laws governing interstate activities and transactions, but also to regulate even purely local activities and transactions where necessary to foster and protect interstate commerce, was amply supported by Mr. Justice (later Mr. Chief Justice) Hughes' reliance upon many prior holdings of this Court extending back to *Gibbons* v. *Ogden*, . . . And since the Shreveport Case this Court has steadfastly followed, and indeed has emphasized time and time again, that Congress has ample power to protect interstate commerce from activities adversely and injuriously affecting it, which but for this adverse effect on interstate commerce would be beyond the power of Congress to regulate. . . .

. . . I recognize that every remote possible, speculative effect on commerce should not be accepted as an adequate constitutional ground to uproot and throw into the discard all our traditional distinctions between what is purely local, and therefore controlled by state laws, and what affects the national interest and is therefore subject to control by federal laws. I recognize too that some isolated and remote lunch room which sells only to local people and buys almost all its supplies in the locality may possibly be beyond the reach of the power of Congress to regulate commerce, just as such an establishment is not covered by the present Act. But in deciding the constitutional power of Congress in cases like the two before us we do not consider the effect on interstate commerce of only one isolated, individual, local event, without regard to the fact that this single local event when added to many others of a similar nature may impose a burden on interstate commerce by reducing its volume or distorting its flow. . . .

Long ago this Court, again speaking through Mr. Chief Justice Marshall, said:

> Let the end be legitimate, let it be within the scope of the constitution, and all means which are appropriate, which are plainly adapted to that end, which are not prohibited, but consistent with the letter and spirit of the constitution, are constitutional. (*McCulloch* v. *Maryland*. . . .)

By this standard Congress acted within its power here. In view of the Commerce Clause it is not possible to deny that the aim of protecting interstate commerce from undue burdens is a legitimate end. In view of the Thirteenth, Fourteenth and Fifteenth Amendments, it is not possible to deny that the aim of protecting Negroes from discrimination is also a legitimate end. The means adopted to achieve these ends are also appropriate, plainly adopted to achieve them and not prohibited by the Constitution but consistent with both its letter and spirit. . . .

MR. JUSTICE DOUGLAS, concurring.

Though I join the Court's opinion, I am somewhat reluctant here, as I was in *Edwards* v. *California*, 314 U.S. 160, . . . to rest solely on the Commerce Clause. My reluctance is not due to any conviction that Congress lacks power to regulate commerce in the interests of human rights. It is rather my belief that the right of people to be free of state action that discriminates against them because of race, like the "right to persons to move freely from State to State" . . . "occupies a more protected position in our constitutional system than does the movement of cattle, fruit, steel and coal across state lines." . . .

Hence I would prefer to rest on the assertion of legislative power contained in § 5 of the Fourteenth Amendment which states: "The Congress shall have power to enforce, by appropriate legislation, the provisions of this article''—a power which the Court concedes was exercised at least in part in this Act.

A decision based on the Fourteenth Amendment would have a more settling effect, making unnecessary litigation over whether a particular restaurant or inn is within the commerce definition of the Act or whether a particular customer is an interstate traveler. Under my construction, the Act would apply to all customers in all the enumerated places of public accommodation. And that construction would put an end to all obstructionist strategies and finally close one door on a bitter chapter in American history.

SEVEN

National Taxing
and Spending Power

Government, like individual citizens, must have regular income to pay bills and maintain credit. In addition, government must have coercive power to collect taxes. No government can carry on if it has to depend, as did the Congress under the Articles of Confederation, on requisitions and voluntary contributions. Indeed, the principal weakness of the central government under the Articles was want of power to levy taxes. National expenditures were defrayed out of a common treasury, supplied by the states in proportion to the occupied land in each state, and upon requisition of Congress. The states reserved the right to levy taxes for this purpose and were, in fact, delinquent in making payments.

Therefore, it is not surprising that, although members of the Federal Convention were sharply divided on many issues, they were almost unanimous in their insistence that Congress should have broad power to tax and spend. Heading the list of enumerated powers in Article I, Section 8, stands the provision that Congress shall have power ''to lay and collect taxes, duties, imposts and excises, to pay the debts and provide for the common defense and general welfare of the United States.''

It would be difficult to fashion more sweeping language. In the exercise of its taxing and spending power, the national government acts directly on individual citizens and their property, acts as directly as though there were no states. Nor are there any limits (apart from those imposed on Congress at the ballot box) on the amount Congress may attempt to collect through taxation. The only limitations on taxing power are those which the Constitution specifically provides in Article I, Section 9, and those which the Supreme Court has established through its various decisions. Article I, Section 9, specifically prohibits the national government from granting a preference to one state's ports over another's, and forbids a tax on exports (a concession made in 1787 to southern exporters). These provisions have occasioned no difficulties.

LIMITATIONS THROUGH INTERPRETATION

In addition to express limitations, the Supreme Court has developed two others through interpretation. The first is the doctrine of reciprocal immunity of the state and national governments and their instrumentalities from taxation by the other. Originally, Marshall argued that this immunity was enjoyed only by the national government (*McCulloch* v. *Maryland*), but, with the ascendancy of the concept of dual federalism, the Court extended the immunity to state governments and their instrumentalities. *Collector* v. *Day,* in which the Court recognized an implied immunity of state and municipal officers from income taxation, was finally overruled in *Graves* v. *New York.* The immunity of the states, however, was qualified in 1905. In *South Carolina* v. *United States* (199 U.S. 437: 1905), involving a federal tax on the state of South Carolina's liquor-dispensing business, the state claimed immunity under the doctrine of *Collector* v. *Day,* but without success. In denying immunity, the Court made this distinction: whenever the state embarks on a business enterprise, in contrast to what the Court called the exercise of governmental functions, the state loses its Court-created immunity. This is still good law, though what is and what is not a governmental function is not easily decided today, with state governments entering more and more fields previously under private management (e.g., water and power utilities and transit systems). In the New York Mineral Waters case, as we have seen, the Court split three ways. The Justices were so sharply divided that no ''opinion of the Court'' was possible.

A second judge-made limitation, first considered in the Child Labor Tax case of 1922 (*Bailey* v. *Drexel Furniture Co.*) was not fully developed until 1936 in the famous AAA case (*United States* v. *Butler*). Justice Roberts, speaking for the Court, declared that the reserved powers of the states (Tenth Amendment) prevented Congress from using the taxing and spending power as an indirect method of regulating certain activities that traditionally belonged to the states, of which agricultural production was one example. His opinion is curious: Although he declares that the taxing and spending power may be used for any purpose that concerns the general welfare, thus adopting the broad view of Hamilton and Story, he then proceeds to hold that this power does not authorize supporting legislation to achieve any purpose not specifically included within one of the enumerated powers, thus embracing the narrow construction of James Madison. In effect, the opinion uses ''dual federalism,'' utilizing the Tenth Amendment, as a restriction on national taxing power.

This view was hardly announced, however, before it was retracted. One year later, in *Steward Machine Company* v. *Davis* (301 U.S. 548) and *Helvering* v. *Davis* (301 U.S. 619), Justice Cardozo set forth a strongly nationalistic theory of the taxing power which, in effect, held that Congress has full power to tax and spend for the general welfare. Represented in these decisions was a significant shift in political theory as well as constitutional interpretation.

The Social Security Act of 1935 levied a tax on employers of eight or more persons, measured by a prescribed percentage of the wages paid. A credit of 90 percent of the tax was allowed for amounts paid into an approved state employment fund. Steward Machine company paid the tax under protest and sued to recover.

Assailants of the Act argued that its dominant end and aim was to force the states to enact unemployment laws at the behest of the federal government. The Act's supporters insisted that the goal was not constraint, but a larger freedom, the states and nation joining in a cooperative endeavor to avert a common evil and achieve a common end.

"Who then is coerced through the operation of this statute?" Justice Cardozo asked. "Not the taxpayer. He pays in fulfillment of the mandate of the local legislature. Not the state. Even now she does not offer a suggestion that in passing the unemployment law she was affected by duress. . . . For all that appears she is satisfied with her choice, and would be sorely disappointed if it were now annulled."

Against this remarkable example of cooperative federalism to achieve a common goal—promotion of the general welfare—diehard Justices McReynolds, Sutherland, Van Devanter, and Butler dissented.

DIRECT AND INDIRECT TAXES

The constitution also declares that taxes are of two kinds, and sets forth briefly the rules by which Congress may use each. Article I, Section 9 declares that direct taxes shall be levied according to the rule of apportionment among the several states on the basis of census enumeration or population. Indirect taxes shall be levied according to the rule of uniformity, which means geographical uniformity, as *Knowlton* v. *Moore,* (178 U.S. 41: 1900) made clear. That is to say, a tax must be laid at the same rate and on the same basis in all parts of the United States. The meaning of indirect taxes, which include all excises and duties, has rarely troubled the Court, but the definition of direct taxes has provided substantial difficulties.

Madison's notes throw no light on the mystery of what is a direct tax. The single entry on this question runs: "Mr. Davies of North Carolina rose to ask the meaning of the direct taxes. Mr. King said he did not know." Like so many other terms in the Constitution, the meaning of direct taxes had to be spelled out by judicial construction. The Court first spoke on the subject in 1796 in the leading case of *Hylton* v. *United States* where a federal tax on carriages was held to be an indirect tax, and therefore not subject to apportionment. The Court's holding was based first on the nature of the carriage tax, which it considered a levy on the privilege of using carriages; and second, on the impossibility of fairly apportioning a tax of this kind, since the ratio of carriages to population was obviously not the same in each state. The Justices agreed that the only direct taxes were capitation and land taxes, and these categories remained frozen for a century.

In accordance with its belief that the Court would adhere to this definition, Congress levied an income tax during the Civil War. It was challenged unsuccessfully in *Springer* v. *United States* (102 U.S. 586: 1881), and stood until the 1890s, when Congress enacted another income tax law, levied, as the Civil War tax had been, as if it were indirect. This time, in *Pollock* v. *Farmers' Loan and Trust Co.,* the Court changed its mind, boldly correcting the definition of direct taxes given in *Hylton,* thus righting, by a margin of one vote, "a century of error." In his brief attacking the validity of the income tax (on the theory that it was direct and had to be apportioned), Joseph H. Choate, one of the leaders of the American bar, referred to the tax in violent terms—he called it "communism," "socialism," and "populism." Adopting Choate's sulphurous language, Justice Field, in a concurring opinion, warned that "The present assault upon capital is but the beginning . . . the stepping stone to others . . . till our political contests will become a war of the poor against the rich." He insisted that this kind of class struggle had to be stopped.

The dissenting judges decried in equally fervent language what they deemed a disastrous blow at congressional power, and an unwarranted expansion of judicial review.

The immediate effect of this decision was to add income taxes to the category of direct taxes, and, since it was not feasible to apportion income taxes, Congress was deprived of this fruitful source of revenue for nearly 20 years. To correct this judge-made amendment of the Constitution, Congress and the states resorted finally to the cumbersome formal amending process, which in 1913 resulted in the Sixteenth Amendment: "The Congress shall have power to lay and collect taxes on incomes, from whatever source derived, without apportionment among the several states, and without regard to any census of enumeration."

This seemingly comprehensive language, however, was not allowed to mean all that it seemed to say. By judicial construction, the Amendment was held to mean only that income taxes need not be apportioned, and was not interpreted as authorizing taxes on all incomes. The salaries of federal judges, the Court ruled in 1920 in *Evans* v. *Gore* (253 U.S. 245) were still exempt from the income tax—the Justices thus preferred their own judge-made exemption to the clear language of a constitutional amendment! However, without any revision of the Sixteenth Amendment, *Evans* v. *Gore* was overruled in 1939. In *O'Malley* v. *Woodrough* (307 U.S. 277), where the judges changed their minds again, Justice Frankfurter observed: "To suggest that it [a non-discriminatory income tax] makes inroads upon the independence of judges . . . by making them bear their aliquot share of the cost of maintaining the government is to trivialize the great historic experience on which the framers based the safeguards of Article 3, Section 1."

REGULATION THROUGH TAXATION

The most obvious and normal purpose of taxation is the raising of revenue, but this is not taxation's only legitimate purpose. Whether a tax is primarily for revenue or regulation is frequently a difficult question, a matter of degree, for, strictly speaking, no tax is or can be solely a revenue measure. The taxes open to challenge by the taxpayer are also those laid in such circumstances or of such a nature that their primary purpose is clearly regulation rather than revenue.

One aspect of this question has been definitely settled: Congress may use its taxing power primarily for purposes of regulation, or even destruction, when the tax serves to aid Congress in exercising one of its other delegated powers, such as regulating interstate commerce, controlling the currency, or maintaining a postal service. An illustrative case is *Veazie Bank* v. *Fenno* (8 Wall. 533: 1869), involving an act of Congress placing a 10 percent tax on state bank note issues in order to protect the notes of the new national banks from the state banks' competition. The tax was, of course, destructive, as it was intended to be; yet the Court upheld it on the ground that Congress could have achieved the same end by absolute prohibition of state bank notes under the currency power.

A more controversial question remains. May Congress use a tax primarily as a regulatory device, that is, to enforce some social or economic policy, when no enumerated power of Congress can be invoked in justification? For a long period the Court's answers to this question wavered between a clear "yes" and an equally clear "no."

The leading affirmative case is *McCray* v. *United States,* which concerned the validity of a destructive tax on oleomargarine colored to resemble butter. That the primary pur-

pose of the tax was regulation and not revenue was clear from the much higher tax on colored oleomargarine (10 cents per pound) as compared with uncolored oleomargarine (¼
cent per pound). Yet, the Court held that, since Congress had virtually unlimited discretion in the selection of the objects of taxation, it was no part of the judicial function to explore congressional motives. Under this judicial hands-off policy, Congress proceeded to
regulate by taxation the manufacture of phosphorus matches and narcotics, and the retail
sale of certain firearms. It should be observed that the doctrine of the McCray case, acceptable as it was to those who felt that Congress should use all regulatory weapons available to
it, came close to making the question of the validity of destructive and regulatory taxation a
political question.

In due course, the Court evolved a more effective technique for imposing limitations
upon the destructive use of the federal taxing power for purposes of social control and
regulation. The change came in 1922 in the second child labor case (*Bailey* v. *Drexel Furniture Co.*), which involved the constitutionality of a 10 percent federal tax on the net income of any employer of child labor, regardless of the number of children employed. In
addition the Act set up an elaborate code for regulating each employer's conduct, a matter
over which Congress admittedly had no direct control. Speaking through Chief Justice
Taft, an all but unanimous Court condemned the Act primarily because it was a ''penalty''
and not a tax, and secondarily because by regulating production the Act invaded the reserved powers of the states. Justice Clarke dissented without opinion. Soon thereafter he
resigned and, in response to Woodrow Wilson's request for an explanation, poured out his
disillusionment with the Court, including Justice Brandeis. (The letter is reproduced in
Mason, *William Howard Taft: Chief Justice,* 1965, pp. 165–67.)

In 1935–36, when the New Deal program based on the taxing power, as under the
commerce clause, was tested, two lines of precedents were available. If the Court chose to
sustain a measure under the taxing power, it could employ the generous principle of the
McCray case. If, on the other hand, the Court chose to set aside the legislation, it could
look upon the tax—as Chief Justice Taft did in the Bailey case—as a ''penalty,'' a form of
''regulation,'' an invasion of domain reserved to the states.

One of the planks in the platform on which FDR was elected—a commitment equal
in emphasis to the Democratic candidate's campaign promise to balance the budget—was
his solemn vow to restore agricultural prosperity. Under the famous Agricultural Adjustment Act (AAA), a processing tax was levied on basic commodities such as wheat, corn,
and cotton. From the funds thus accumulated, money was paid out to farmers as ''inducement'' to reduce their acreage. Here, at long last, was a self-financing scheme to subsidize
farmers as the protective tariff had long subsidized industry.

High expectations arose from the first years of its administration, until one
December day in 1935 the entire scheme became shrouded in constitutional doubt. Attacking the Act's constitutionality was Philadelphia's most eminent lawyer, George Whar-
ton Pepper. Perfectly cast for the role, Pepper observed: ''I have tried very hard to argue
this case calmly and dispassionately, because it seems to me that this is the best way in
which an advocate can discharge his duty to this Court. But I do not want Your Honors to
think my feelings are not involved and that my emotions are not deeply stirred. Indeed,
may it please Your Honors, I believe I am standing here today to plead the cause of the
America I have loved; and I pray Almighty God that not in my time may 'the land of the
regimented' be accepted as a worthy substitute for 'the land of the free.''' For Pepper,
economic dogma, no less than congressional taxing power, was at stake.

The former Senator's prayer was soon answered. Within a month, on January 6,
1936, the Court announced its decision in *United States* v. *Butler.* Justice Roberts,

Pepper's former student at the University of Pennsylvania Law School, spoke for the majority, which included Chief Justice Hughes. The vote was 6 to 3, Brandeis, Cardozo, and Stone dissenting. This case is reprinted in chapter 2.

The keystone of AAA, the processing tax, could not be upheld as a tax. "The word has never been thought to connote the expropriation of money from one group for the benefit of another," the Court ruled. If valid, the exaction could be supported only as an exercise of the disputed power to tax and spend for the general welfare. The Court was thus face to face with an unresolved issue dating from Washington's first administration.

Was the power to tax and spend for the general welfare a substantive, independent power, as Hamilton maintained? Or was it no power at all, but rather an appendage of Congress's other enumerated powers, as Madison contended? Through many administrations, regardless of party, appropriations of money had been made to accomplish purposes not identified with those which Congress is authorized to promote under its other powers. Hamilton had upheld this view in his famous *Report on Manufactures,* and Justice Roberts emphatically embraced it in *United States* v. *Butler.* No sooner had he adopted the Hamiltonian theory, however, than the Justice proceeded to enforce, for all practical purposes, the narrow Madisonian theory he had just repudiated. Congress, the Justice agreed, might appropriate money for an objective designated as the general welfare, but it could attach no terms or conditions to the use of funds so appropriated unless such terms or conditions were themselves authorized by another specific congressional grant. Federal money might be spent for the broad purposes outlined by Hamilton, but Congress could control the expenditure only if the objectives were within the narrow scope Madison gave the general welfare clause.

Probing deeply into congressional motives, Justice Roberts discovered that this was not a tax at all, but payment of benefits to farmers to induce (or coerce) them into curtailing production. Congress, he said, has no power to regulate production. The tax was thus in effect an ingenious disguise of such regulation, an invalid invasion of the reserved domain of the states. "From the accepted doctrine that the United States is a government of delegated powers," Roberts reasoned, "it follows that those not expressly granted, or reasonably to be implied from such as are conferred, are reserved to the states or to the people. To forestall any suggestion to the contrary, the Tenth Amendment was adopted. The same proposition, otherwise stated, is that powers not granted are prohibited. None to regulate agricultural production is given, and therefore legislation by Congress for that purpose is forbidden."

Justice Roberts thus placed the taxing and spending provisions in a special category, doing for Congress's power to tax and spend what Justice Day had done in 1918 for Congress's power to regulate interstate commerce. In both instances the judiciary wrote "expressly" into the Tenth Amendment. "It is an established principle," Justice Roberts concluded, "that the attainment of a prohibited end may not be accomplished under the pretext of the exertion of powers which are granted."

The intramural judicial war, developing since 1930, now reached its climax. Six Justices, including Hughes and Roberts, were solidly united against the power to govern. Accordingly, Justice Stone in his dissent does more than attack the majority's view of the taxing and spending power. He blasts judicial usurpation as such. Justice Roberts had raised the specter of "legislative power, without restriction or limitation," "vested in a parliament . . . subject to no restrictions except the discretion of its members." But, Stone countered, consider the status of our own power. While the Executive and Congress are restrained by "the ballot box and the processes of democratic government [and] subject to judicial restraint, the only check upon our own exercise of power is our own sense of self-restraint." Precisely because it is unfettered, Stone argued, judicial responsibility should be discharged with finer conscience and humility than that of any other agency of government.

Of course, "governmental power of the purse" was, as Stone conceded, fraught with frightening possibilities of abuse. But the majority's inference that such power, unless judicially limited, might be put to undesirable and constitutionally prohibited ends, Stone said, "hardly rises to the dignity of argument." "So may judicial power be abused," he commented curtly.

Thus in *United States* v. *Butler* the Court chose to follow Taft's narrow construction of the taxing power, only to revert back, in upholding the Social Security Act, to the more generous rule of the McCray case. An event not unrelated to this remarkable judicial about-face was President Roosevelt's proposal to "pack" the Court. The magnitude of this change was acknowledged in *Sonzinsky* v. *United States* (300 U.S. 506: 1937), which upheld the prohibitive tax on certain classes of firearms: "We are not free to speculate as to the motives which moved Congress to impose it, or as to the extent to which it may operate to restrict the activities taxed. . . . Since it operates as a tax, it is within the national taxing power."

Justice Roberts's opinion in *United States* v. *Butler* is among the most remarkable in the Court's history. Taking into account three theories of the national taxing power, he added one of his own. While carrying to the limit judicial review (for Judge Gibson a "proud pre-eminence") Roberts reduced the Court's function to the status of a grocer weighing coffee or the dry goods clerk measuring calico. It was merely a matter of laying "the article of the Constitution which is invoked beside the statute which is challenged and to decide whether the latter squares with the former."

Three years after the Butler case, the Court, with Justice Roberts again writing the majority opinion, sustained a second attempt to regulate agricultural production (*Mulford* v. *Smith* [307 U.S. 38: 1939]). This time Congress had relied on its commerce power to reach the desired end and, with the fall of the Tenth Amendment as a bar to national action, the effort was successful.

An interesting subsequent congressional regulation through taxation is the Act of 1951 requiring gamblers to procure a license and pay a substantial tax. This act was declared invalid by a federal district judge, but it was upheld by the Supreme Court (*United States* v. *Kahriger* [345 U.S. 22: 1953]). As Chief Justice Taft anticipated in the Bailey case, the taxing power has been used by the national government as a weapon to take over, one by one, subjects traditionally within the orbit of state police power.

The theme in *United States* v. *Kahriger* that there is "no constitutional right to gamble" is no longer persuasive. In *Marchetti* v. *United States* (390 U.S. 39: 1968) the Court held, 7 to 1, that the Fifth Amendment privilege against self-incrimination provides a complete defense against prosecution for violation of the Federal Wagering Tax statutes. Vindicated were the dissenting opinions of Justices Black, Douglas, and Frankfurter in *Kahriger*.

Marchetti was convicted of conspiring to evade payment under a 1951 federal law requiring gamblers to register with the government each year, buy and display a $50 gambling stamp, and pay a 10 percent excise tax on their gross wagers. Reversing *Kahriger*, Justice Harlan for the majority ruled that the statutory obligation to register and pay the tax created hazards of self-incrimination. In effect, the federal law converted a local offense—gambling—into a federal crime by taxing it and imposing a one-year prison term for failure to pay. But if gamblers obeyed the law, they confessed violation of state gambling laws, being damned if they did, and damned if they didn't.

Pondering the effect of the decision, while admitting its soundness, Henry E. Petersen, chief of the Justice Department's organized crime section, declared: "I feel like I have lost my right arm." In one year an "unconstitutional" federal law had produced 491 convictions. Softening the blow, Justice Harlan declared that taxpayers not confronted by substantial hazards of self-incrimination would not be shielded from the penalties prescribed by wagering tax legislation. But the same day *Marchetti* came down, the Court (*Haynes* v. *U.S., 390* U.S. 85) invalidated, 8 to 1, a section of the National Firearms Act, making it a crime to buy a sawed-off shotgun or automatic weapon without notifying the government. A provision punishing possession of an unregistered gun was also declared unconstitutional, since registration would violate the privilege against self-incrimination.

Chief Justice Warren, the sole dissenter, would have affirmed Marchetti's conviction on the basis of *Kahriger*. The Chief Justice was concerned lest the Court open to attack other federal registration statutes touching allegedly illegal activities. Among the legislation in jeopardy was the Federal Marijuana Tax Act, prohibiting sale of the drug without an official order form. In an opinion expressing the views of six members (*Minor* v. *U.S.*, 396 U.S. 87: 1969) Justice White held that conviction under the Act was not invalid under the seller's Fifth Amendment privilege against self-incrimination. Justice Douglas, joined by Black, dissented: "The Government is punishing an individual for failing to do something that the Government has made it impossible for him to do—that is, obtain an order form, from the prospective purchaser prior to making a sale of heroin. . . . Thus it is the order form—not the mere sale—that constitutes the heart of the offense for which this petitioner is convicted. I do not see how the Government can make a crime out of not receiving an order form and at the same time allow no order forms for this category of sales."

Now, with a largely reconstituted Court, there are many areas in which constitutional issues will receive further definition, hopefully clarification. Surely, none is more confused than use of the national taxing power to achieve the objective to which the Nixon administration was rhetorically committed—"law and order." It seems ironical that Chief Justice Warren, who had supposedly "unbalanced" the peace-making forces in favor of criminality, should have been the sole dissenter in *Marchetti*.

SELECTED READINGS

ANNOTATION, "Power of Congress to exercise its taxing power to restrict or suppress the thing taxed, or to accomplish some ulterior purpose," 81 *U.S. Supreme Court Reports, Lawyer's Edition* 776.

CORWIN, EDWARD S., *Court over Constitution*. Princeton: Princeton University Press, 1938.

——, "The Spending Power of Congress," 36 *Harvard Law Review* 548 (1923).

CUSHMAN, ROBERT E., "Social and Economic Control Through Federal Taxation," 18 *Minnesota Law Review* 757 (1934).

LAWSON, J. F., *The General Welfare Clause*. Washington: published by the author, 1926.

MASON, A. T., "Owen Josephus Roberts," *Dictionary of American Biography, Supplement Five*. New York: Charles Scribner's Sons, 1977.

Hylton v. *United States*
3 Dall. (3 U.S.) 171, 1 L.Ed. 556 (1796)

Hylton claimed that a congressional act of 1794 levying a tax of $16 on each carriage was a direct tax and must be laid in proportion to the census. On the theory of an ownership of 125 carriages, Hylton obtained a review, on error, of an adverse judgment in the circuit court.

CHASE, JUSTICE.—By the case stated, only one question is submitted to the opinion of this court—whether the law of Congress of the 5th of June 1794, entitled, ''An act to lay duties upon carriages for the conveyance of persons,'' is unconstitutional and void?

The principles laid down, to prove the above law void, are these: that a tax on carriages is a direct tax, and, therefore, by the constitution, must be laid according to the census, directed by the constitution to be taken, to ascertain the number of representatives from each state. And that the tax in question on carriages is not laid by that rule of apportionment, but by the rule of uniformity, prescribed by the constitution in the case of duties, imposts and excises; and a tax on carriages is not within either of those descriptions . . . .

It appears to me, that a tax on carriages cannot be laid by the rule of apportionment, without very great inequality and injustice. For example: suppose, two states, equal in census, to pay $80,000 each, by a tax on carriages, of eight dollars on every carriage; and in one state, there are 100 carriages, and in the other 1000. The owners of carriages in one state, would pay ten times the tax of owners in the other. A. in one state, would pay for his carriage eight dollars, but B. in the other state would pay for his carriage, eighty dollars . . . .

I think, an annual tax on carriages for the conveyance of persons, may be considered as within the power granted to congress to lay duties. The term *duty,* is the most comprehensive, next to the general term *tax;* and practically, in Great Britain (whence we take our general ideas of taxes, duties, imposts, excises, customs, &c.), embraces taxes on stamps, tolls for passage, &c., and is not confined to taxes on importation only. It seems to me, that a tax on expense is an indirect tax; and I think, an annual tax on a carriage for conveyance of persons, is of that kind; because a carriage is a consumable commodity; and such annual tax on it, is on the expense of the owner.

I am inclined to think but of this I do not give a judicial opinion, that the direct taxes contemplated by the constitution, are only two, to wit, a capitation or poll tax, simply, without regard to property, profession or any other circumstance; and a tax on land. I doubt, whether a tax, by a general assessment of personal property, within the United States, is included within the term direct tax . . . .

PATERSON, JUSTICE.— . . .

. . . Whether direct taxes, in the sense of the constitution, comprehend any other tax than a capitation tax, and tax on land, is a questionable point. If congress, for instance, should tax, in the aggregate or mass, things that generally pervade all the states in the Union, then, perhaps, the rule of apportionment would be the most proper, especially, if an assessment was to intervene. This appears by the practice of some of the states, to have been considered as a direct tax. Whether it be so, under the constitution of the United States, is a matter of some difficulty; but as it is not before the court, it would be improper to give any decisive opinion upon it. I never entertained a doubt that the principal, I will not say, the only, objects, that the framers of the constitution contemplated, as falling within the rule of apportionment, were a capitation tax and a tax on land. Local considerations, and the particular circumstances, and relative situation of the states, naturally lead to this view of the subject. The provision was made in favor of the southern states; they possessed a large number of slaves; they had extensive tracts of territory, thinly settled, and not very productive. A majority of the states had but few slaves, and several of them a limited territory, well settled, and in a high state of cultivation. The southern states, if no provision had been introduced in the constitution, would have been wholly at the mercy of the other states. Congress in such case, might tax slaves, at discretion or arbitrarily, and land in every part of the Union, after the same rate or measure: so much a head in the first instance, and so much an acre, in the second. To guard them against imposition, in these particulars, was the reason of introducing the clause in the constitution, which directs that representatives and direct taxes shall be apportioned among the states, according to their respective numbers. . . .

IREDELL, JUSTICE.— . . .

As all direct taxes must be apportioned, it is evident, that the constitution contemplated none as direct, but such as could be apportioned. If this cannot be apportioned, it is, therefore, not a direct tax in the sense of the constitution.

That this tax cannot be apportioned, is evident. Suppose, ten dollars contemplated as a tax on each chariot, or post chaise, in the United States, and the number of both in all the United States be computed at 105, the number of representatives in congress.

This would produce in the whole . . . $1,050.00
The share of Virginia being 19/105 parts, would be $190.00
The share of Connecticut being 7/105 parts, would be 70.00
Then suppose Virginia had 50 carriages, Connecticut 2,
The share of Virginia being $190, this must, of course, be collected from the owners of carriages, and there would, therefore, be collected from each carriage 3.80
The share of Connecticut being $70, each carriage would pay 35.00

If any state had no carriages, there could be no apportionment at all. This mode is too manifestly absurd to be supported, and has not even been attempted in debate. . . .

BY THE COURT.—Let the judgment of the circuit court be affirmed.

[JUSTICES WILSON AND CUSHING did not deliver opinions.]

Pollock v. *Farmers' Loan and Trust Company*
158 U.S. 601, 15 S.Ct. 673, 39 L.Ed. 1108 (1895) (Rehearing)

An Act of Congress of 1894 imposed a tax on income derived from various classes of property as well as that resulting from personal services. In the first decision (April 8, 1895) involving the Act, the Court, with one Justice absent, declared the Act invalid insofar as it was applied to the income from real estate or the interest on municipal bonds. The Court had split on other questions presented. In May 1895, the Court granted a rehearing in order that these questions might receive authoritative answers.

MR. CHIEF JUSTICE FULLER delivered the opinion of the court. . . .

. . . The Constitution divided Federal taxation into two great classes, the class of direct taxes and the class of duties, imposts, and excises, and prescribed two rules which qualified the grant of power as to each class.

The power to lay direct taxes, apportioned

among the several States in proportion to their representation in the popular branch of Congress, a representation based on population as ascertained by the census, was plenary and absolute, but to lay direct taxes without apportionment was forbidden. The power to lay duties, imposts, and excises was subject to the qualification that the imposition must be uniform throughout the United States.

Our previous decision was confined to the consideration of the validity of the tax on the income from real estate, and on the income from municipal bonds. The question thus limited was whether such taxation was direct or not, in the meaning of the Constitution; and the court went no farther, as to the tax on the incomes from real estate, than to hold that it fell within the same class as the source whence the income was derived, that is, that a tax upon the realty and a tax upon the receipts therefrom were alike direct; while as to the income from municipal bonds, that could not be taxed because of want of power to tax the source, and no reference was made to the nature of the tax being direct or indirect.

We are now permitted to broaden the field of inquiry, and determine to which of the two great classes a tax upon a person's entire income, whether derived from rents, or products, or otherwise, of real estate, or from bonds, stocks or other forms of personal property, belongs; and we are unable to conclude that the enforced subtraction from the yield of all the owner's real or personal property, in the manner prescribed, is so different from a tax upon the property itself, that it is not a direct, but an indirect tax, in the meaning of the Constitution. . . .

We know of no reason for holding otherwise than that the words "direct taxes" on the one hand, and "duties, imposts, and excises" on the other, were used in the Constitution in their natural and obvious sense, nor, in arriving at what those terms embrace, do we perceive any ground for enlarging them beyond, or narrowing them within, their natural and obvious import at the time the Constitution was framed and ratified. . . .

In the light of the struggle in the convention as to whether or not the new Nation should be empowered to levy taxes directly on the individual until after the States had failed to respond to requisitions—a struggle which did not terminate until the amendment to that effect, proposed by Massachusetts and concurred in by South Carolina, New Hampshire, New York, and Rhode Island, had been rejected—it would seem beyond reasonable question that direct taxation, taking the place as it did of requisitions, was purposely restrained to apportionment according to representation, in order that the former system as to ratio might be retained, while the mode of collection was changed. . . .

The reasons for the clauses of the Constitution in respect of direct taxation are not far to seek. The States, respectively, possessed plenary powers of taxation. They could tax the property of their citizens in such manner and to such extent as they saw fit; they had unrestricted powers to impose duties or imposts on imports from abroad, and excises on manufactures, consumable commodities, or otherwise. They gave up the great sources of revenue derived from commerce; they retained the concurrent power of levying excises, and duties if covering anything other than excises; but in respect of them the range of taxation was narrowed by the power granted over interstate commerce, and by the danger of being put at disadvantage in dealing with excises on manufactures. They retained the power of direct taxation, and to that they looked as their chief resource; but even in respect of that, they granted the concurrent power, and if the tax were placed by both governments on the same subject, the claim of the United States had preference. Therefore, they did not grant the power of direct taxation without regard to their own condition and resources as States; but they granted the power of apportioned direct taxation, a power just as efficacious to serve the needs of the general government, but securing to the States the opportunity to pay the amount apportioned, and to recoup from their own citizens in the most feasible way, and in harmony with their systems of local self-government. If, in the changes of wealth and population in particular States, apportionment produced inequality, it was an inequality stipulated for, just as the equal representation . . . in the Senate, was stipulated for. The Constitution ordains affirmatively that each State shall have two members of that body, and negatively that no State shall by amendment be deprived of its equal suffrage in the Senate without its consent. The Constitution ordains affirmatively that representatives and direct taxes shall be apportioned among the several States according to numbers, and negatively that no direct tax shall be laid unless in proportion to the enumeration. . . .

It is said that a tax on the whole income of property is not a direct tax in the meaning of the Constitution, but a duty, and, as a duty, leviable without apportionment, whether direct or indirect. We do not think so. Direct taxation was not restricted in one breath, and the restriction blown to the winds in another. . . .

. . . Thus we find Mr. Hamilton, while writing to induce the adoption of the Constitution, *first,* dividing the power of taxation into *external* and *internal,* putting into the former the power of imposing duties on imported articles and into the latter all remaining powers; and, *second,* dividing the latter into *direct* and *indirect,* putting into the latter, duties and excises on articles of consumption.

It seems to us to inevitably follow that in Mr. Hamilton's judgment at that time all internal taxes, except duties and excises on articles of consumption, fell into the category of direct taxes. . . .

. . . He gives, however, it appears to us, a definition which covers the question before us. A tax upon one's whole income is a tax upon the annual receipts from his whole property, and as such falls within the same class as a tax upon that property, and is a direct tax, in the meaning of the Constitution. And Mr. Hamilton in his report on the public credit, in referring to contracts with citizens of a foreign country, said: "This principle, which seems critically correct, would exempt as well the income as the capital

of the property. It protects the use, as effectually as the thing. What, in fact, is property, but a fiction, without the beneficial use of it? In many cases, indeed, the *income* or *annuity* is the property itself." 3 Hamilton's Works, 34. . . .

The Constitution prohibits any direct tax, unless in proportion to numbers as ascertained by the census; and, in the light of the circumstances to which we have referred, is it not an evasion of that prohibition to hold that a general unapportioned tax, imposed upon all property owners as a body for or in respect of their property, is not direct, in the meaning of the Constitution, because confined to the income therefrom?

Whatever the speculative views of political economists or revenue reformers may be, can it be properly held that the Constitution, taken in its plain and obvious sense, and with due regard to the circumstances attending the formation of the government, authorizes a general unapportioned tax on the products of the farm and the rents of real estate, although imposed merely because of ownership and with no possible means of escape from payment, as belonging to a totally different class from that which includes the property from which the income proceeds?

There can be only one answer, unless the constitutional restriction is to be treated as utterly illusory and futile, and the object of its framers defeated. We find it impossible to hold that a fundamental requisition, deemed so important as to be enforced by two provisions, one affirmative and one negative, can be refined away by forced distinctions between that which gives value to property and the property itself.

Nor can we perceive any ground why the same reasoning does not apply to capital in personality held for the purpose of income or ordinarily yielding income, and to the income therefrom. All the real estate of the country, and all its invested personal property, are open to the direct operation of the taxing power if an apportionment be made according to the Constitution. The Constitution does not say that no direct tax shall be laid by apportionment on any other property than land; on the contrary, it forbids all unapportioned direct taxes; and we know of no warrant for excepting personal property from the exercise of the power, or any reason why an apportioned direct tax cannot be laid and assessed. . . .

We have considered the act only in respect of the tax on income derived from real estate, and from invested personal property, and have not commented on so much of it as bears on gains or profits from business, privileges, or employments, in view of the instances in which taxation on business, privileges, or employments has assumed the guise of an excise tax and been sustained as such.

Being of opinion that so much of the sections of this law as lays a tax on income from real and personal property is invalid, we are brought to the question of the effect of that conclusion upon these sections as a whole.

It is elementary that the same statute may be in part constitutional and in part unconstitutional, and if the parts are wholly independent of each other, that which is constitutional may stand while that which is unconstitutional will be rejected. And in the case before us there is no question as to validity of this act, except sections twenty-seven to thirty-seven inclusive, which relate to the subject which has been under discussion; and as to them we think that the rule laid down by Chief Justice Shaw [of the Massachusetts Supreme Court] in *Warren* v. *Charlestown*, 2 Gray, 84, is applicable, that if the different parts ''are so mutually connected with and dependent on each other, as conditions, considerations or compensations for each other, as to warrant the belief that the legislature intended them as a whole, and that, if all could not be carried into effect, the legislature would not pass the residue independently, and some parts are unconstitutional, all the provisions which are thus dependent, conditional or connected, must fall with them.'' . . .

Our conclusions may, therefore, be summed up as follows:

First. We adhere to the opinion already announced, that, taxes on real estate being indisputably direct taxes, taxes on the rents or incomes of real estate are equally direct taxes.

Second. We are of opinion that taxes on personal property, or on the income of personal property, are likewise direct taxes.

Third. The tax imposed by sections twenty-seven to thirty-seven, inclusive, of the act of 1894, so far as it falls on the income of real estate and of personal property, being a direct tax within the meaning of the Constitution, and, therefore, unconstitutional and void because not apportioned according to representation, all those sections, constituting one entire scheme of taxation, are necessarily invalid.

The decrees hereinbefore entered in this court will be vacated; the decrees below will be reversed, and the case remanded, with instructions to grant the relief prayed.

MR. JUSTICE HARLAN dissenting. . . .

In my judgment a tax on *income* derived from real property ought not to be, and until now has never been, regarded by any court as a direct tax on such property within the meaning of the Constitution. As the great mass of lands in most of the States do not bring any rents, and as incomes from rents vary in different States, such a tax cannot possibly be apportioned among the States on the basis merely of numbers with any approach to equality of right among taxpayers, any more than a tax on carriages or other personal property could be so apportioned. And, in view of former adjudications, beginning with the Hylton case and ending with the Springer case, a decision now that a tax on income from real property can be laid and collected only by apportioning the same among the States, on the basis of numbers, may, not improperly, be regarded as a judicial revolution, that may sow the seeds of hate and distrust among the people of different sections of our common country. . . .

In determining whether a tax on income from rents is a direct tax, within the meaning of the Constitution, the inquiry is not whether it may in some way indirectly affect the land or the land owner, but whether it is a *direct* tax *on the thing taxed, the land.* The circumstance that such a tax may possibly have the effect to diminish the value of the use of the land is neither decisive of the question nor important.

While a tax *on the land* itself, whether at a fixed rate applicable to all lands without regard to their value, or by the acre or according to their market value, might be deemed a direct tax within the meaning of the Constitution as interpreted in the Hylton case, a duty on rents is a duty on something distinct and entirely separate from, although issuing out of, the land. . . .

In my judgment—to say nothing of the disregard of the former adjudications of this court, and of the settled practice of the government—this decision may well excite the gravest apprehensions. It strikes at the very foundations of national authority, in that it denies to the general government a power which is, or may become, vital to the very existence and preservation of the Union in a national emergency, such as that of war with a great commercial nation, during which the collection of all duties upon imports will cease or be materially diminished. It tends to reestablish that condition of helplessness in which Congress found itself during the period of the Articles of Confederation, when it was without authority by laws operating directly upon individuals, to lay and collect, through its own agents, taxes sufficient to pay the debts and defray the expenses of government, but was dependent, in all such matters, upon the good will of the States, and their promptness in meeting requisitions made upon them by Congress.

Why do I say that the decision just rendered impairs or menaces the national authority? The reason is so apparent that it need only be stated. In its practical operation this decision withdraws from national taxation not only all incomes derived from real estate, but tangible personal property, *invested* personal property, bonds, stocks, investments of all kinds, and the income that may be derived from such property. This results from the fact that by the decision of the court, all such personal property and all incomes from real estate and personal property are placed beyond national taxation otherwise than by *apportionment* among the States *on the basis* simply *of population*. No such apportionment can possibly be made without doing gross injustice to the many for the benefit of the favored few in particular States. Any attempt upon the part of Congress to apportion among the States, upon the basis simply of their population, taxation of personal property or of incomes, would tend to arouse such indignation among the freemen of America that it would never be repeated. When therefore, this court adjudges, as it does now adjudge, that Congress cannot impose a duty or tax upon personal property, or upon income arising either from rents of real estate or from personal property, including invested personal property, bonds, stocks, and investments of all kinds, except by apportioning the sum to be so raised among the States according to population, it *practically* decides that, *without an amendment of the Constitution*—two-thirds of both Houses of Congress and three-fourths of the States concurring—such property and incomes can never be made to contribute to the support of the national government. . . .

I dissent from the opinion and judgment of the court.

[The separate dissenting opinions of JUSTICES BROWN, JACKSON, and WHITE have been omitted.]

McCray v. United States
195 U.S. 27, 24 S.Ct. 769, 49 L.Ed. 78 (1904)

The Oleomargarine Act, passed by Congress in 1886 and amended in 1902, levied a tax of 1/4 cent per pound on uncolored oleomargarine and 10 cents per pound on oleomargarine colored yellow. McCray, a licensed dealer, failed to pay the higher tax in making sales of the colored product and was fined. McCray sought review by writ of error to the district court.

MR. JUSTICE WHITE . . . delivered the opinion of the court. . . .

Did Congress in passing the acts which are assailed, exert a power not conferred by the Constitution?

That the acts in question on their face impose excise taxes which Congress had the power to levy is so completely established as to require only statement. *Patton* v. *Brady,* 184 U.S. 608, 619; *Knowlton* v. *Moore,* 178 U.S. 41; *Nicol* v. *Ames,* 173 U.S. 509; *In re Kollock,* 165 U.S. 526.

The last case referred to (*In re Kollock*) involved the act of 1886, and the court, speaking through Mr. Chief Justice Fuller, said:

The act before us is on its face an act for levying taxes, and although it may operate in so doing to prevent deception in the sale of oleomargarine as and for butter, its primary object must be assumed to be the raising of revenue. . . .

It is, however, argued if a lawful power may be exerted for an unlawful purpose, and thus by abusing the power it may be made to accomplish a result not intended by the Constitution, all limitations of power must disappear, and the grave function lodged in the judiciary, to confine all the departments within the authority conferred by the Constitution, will be of no avail. This, when reduced to its last analysis, comes to this, that, because a particular department of the government may exert its lawful powers with the object or motive of reaching an end not justified, therefore it becomes the duty of the judiciary to restrain the exercise of a lawful power wherever it seems to the judicial mind that such lawful power has been abused. But this reduces itself to the contention that, under our constitutional system, the abuse by one department of the government of its lawful powers is to be corrected by the abuse of its powers by another department. . . .

It is, of course, true, as suggested, that if there be no authority in the judiciary to restrain a lawful exercise of power by another department of the government, where a wrong motive or purpose has impelled to the exertion of the power, that abuses of a power conferred may be temporarily effectual. The remedy for this, however, lies, not in the abuse by the judicial authority of its functions, but in the people, upon whom, after all, under our institutions, reliance must be placed for the correction of abuses committed in the exercise of a lawful power. . . .

It being thus demonstrated that the motive or purpose of Congress in adopting the acts in question may not be inquired into, we are brought to consider the contentions relied upon to show that the acts assailed were beyond the power of Congress, putting entirely out of view all considerations based upon purpose or motive.

Undoubtedly, in determining whether a particular act is within a granted power, its scope and effect are to be considered. Applying this rule to the acts assailed, it is self-evident that on their face they levy excise tax. That being their necessary scope and operation, it follows that the acts are within the grant of power. The argument to the contrary rests on the proposition that, although the tax be within the power, as enforcing it will destroy or restrict the manufacture of artificially colored oleomargarine, therefore the power to levy the tax did not obtain. This, however, is but to say that the question of power depends, not upon the authority conferred by the Constitution, but upon what may be the consequence arising from the exercise of the lawful authority.

Since, as pointed out in all the decisions referred to, the taxing power conferred by the Constitution knows no limits except those expressly stated in that instrument, it must follow, if a tax be within the lawful power, the exertion of that power may not be judicially restrained because of the results to arise from its exercise. . . .

Whilst undoubtedly both the Fifth and Tenth Amendments qualify, in so far as they are applicable, all the provisions of the Constitution, nothing in those amendments operates to take away the grant of power to tax conferred by the Constitution upon Congress. The contention on this subject rests upon the theory that the purpose and motive of Congress in exercising its undoubted powers may be inquired into by the courts, and the proposition is therefore disposed of by what has been said on that subject.

The right of Congress to tax within its delegated powers being unrestrained, except as limited by the Constitution, it was within the authority conferred on Congress to select the objects upon which an excise should be laid. It therefore follows that, in exerting its power, no want of due process of law could possibly result, because that body chose to impose an excise on artificially colored oleomargarine and not upon natural butter artificially colored. The judicial power may not usurp the functions of the legislative in order to control that branch of the government in the performance of its lawful duties. This was aptly pointed out in the extract heretofore made from the opinion in *Treat* v. *White,* 181 U.S. 264. . . .

Let us concede that if a case was presented where the abuse of the taxing power was so extreme as to be beyond the principles which we have previously stated, and where it was plain to the judicial mind that the power had been called into play not for revenue but solely for the purpose of destroying rights which could not be rightfully destroyed consistently with the principles of freedom and justice upon which the Constitution rests, that it would be the duty of the courts to say that such an arbitrary act was not merely an abuse of a delegated power, but was the exercise of an authority not conferred. This concession, however, like the one previously made, must be without influence upon the decision of this case for the reasons previously stated; that is, that the manufacture of artificially colored oleomargarine may be prohibited by a free government without a violation of fundmental rights.

Affirmed.

THE CHIEF JUSTICE [FULLER], MR. JUSTICE BROWN and MR. JUSTICE PECKHAM dissent.

Bailey v. Drexel Furniture Company
(Child Labor Tax Case)
259 U.S. 20, 42 S.Ct. 449, 66 L.Ed. 817 (1922)

In the Revenue Act of 1919 Congress imposed a tax on mine and quarry employers of children under 16, and mill and factory owners who employed children under 14, or who permitted children between 14 and 16 to work more than an eight-hour day and a six-day week. The tax was levied on net profits. The Drexel Furniture Company, which had employed a boy under 14, paid the tax under protest and then sued to recover the amount paid. The district court sustained the company and the collector obtained a writ of error.

MR. CHIEF JUSTICE TAFT delivered the opinion of the court.

This case presents the question of the constitutional validity of the Child Labor Tax Law. . . .

The law is attacked on the ground that it is a regulation of the employment of child labor in the States—an exclusively state function under the Federal Constitution and within the reservations of the Tenth Amendment. It is defended on the ground that it is a mere excise tax levied by the Congress of the United States under its broad power of taxation conferred by § 8, Article I, of the Federal Constitution. We must construe the law and interpret the intent and meaning of Congress from the language of the act. The words are to be given their ordinary meaning unless the context shows that they are differently used. Does this law impose a tax with only that incidental restraint and regulation which a tax must inevitably involve? Or does it regulate by the use of the so-called tax as a penalty? If a tax, it is clearly an excise. If it were an excise on a commodity or other thing of value we might not be permitted under previous decisions of this court to infer solely from its heavy burden that the act intends a prohibition instead of a tax. But this act is more. It provides a heavy exaction for a departure from a detailed and specified course of conduct in business. That course of business is that employers shall employ in mines and quarries, children of an age greater than sixteen years; in mills and factories, children of an age greater than fourteen years, and shall prevent children of less than sixteen years in mills and factories from working more than eight hours a day or six days in the week. If an employer departs from his prescribed course of business, he is to pay the Government one-tenth of his entire net income in the business for a full year. The amount is not to be proportioned in any degree to the extent or frequency of the departures, but is to be paid by the employer in full measure whether he employs five hundred children for a year, or employs only one for a day. Moreover, if he does not know the child is within the named age limit, he is not to pay; that is to say, it is only where he knowingly departs from the prescribed course that payment is to be exacted. Scienter is associated with penalties not with taxes. The employer's factory is to be subject to inspection at any time not only by the taxing officers of the Treasury, the Department normally charged with the collection of taxes, but also by the Secretary of Labor and his subordinates whose normal function is the advancement and protection of the welfare of the workers. In the light of these features of the act, a court must be blind not to see that the so-called tax is imposed to stop the employment of children within the age limits prescribed. Its prohibitory and regulatory effect and purpose are palpable. All others can see and understand this. How can we properly shut our minds to it?

It is the high duty and function of this court in cases regularly brought to its bar to decline to recognize or enforce seeming laws of Congress, dealing with subjects not entrusted to Congress but left or commited by the supreme law of the land to the control of the States. We can not avoid the duty even though it require us to refuse to give effect to legislation designed to promote the highest good. The good sought in unconstitutional legislation is an insidious feature because it leads citizens and legislators of good purpose to promote it without thought of the serious breach it will make in the ark of our covenant or the harm which will come from breaking down recognized standards. In the maintenance of local self-government, on the one hand, and the national power, on the other, our country has been able to endure and prosper for near a century and a half.

Out of a proper respect for the acts of a coordinate branch of the Government, this court has gone far to sustain taxing acts as such, even though there has been ground for suspecting from the weight of the tax it was intended to destroy its subject. But, in the act before us, the presumption of validity cannot prevail, because the proof of the contrary is found on the very face of its provisions. Grant the validity of this law, and all that Congress would need to do, hereafter, in seeking to take over to its control any one of the great number of subjects of public interest, jurisdiction of which the States have never parted with, and which are reserved to them by the Tenth Amendment, would be to enact a detailed measure of complete regulation of the subject and enforce it by so-called tax upon departures from it. To give such magic to the word "tax" would be to break down all constitutional limitation of the powers of Congress and completely wipe out the sovereignty of the States.

The difference between a tax and a penalty is sometimes difficult to define and yet the consequences of the distinction in the required method of their collection often are important. Where the sovereign enacting the law has power to impose both tax and penalty the difference between revenue production and mere regulation may be immaterial, but not so when one sovereign can impose a tax only, and the power of regulation rests in another. Taxes are occasionally imposed in the discretion of the legislature on proper subjects with the primary motive of obtaining revenue from them and with the incidental motive of discouraging them by making their continuance onerous. They do not lose their character as taxes because of the incidental motive. But there comes a time in the extension of the penalizing features of the so-called tax when it loses its character as such and becomes a mere penalty with the characteristics of regulation and punishment. Such is the case in the law before us. Although Congress does not invalidate the contract of employment or expressly declare that the employment within the mentioned ages is illegal, it does exhibit its intention practically to achieve the latter result by adopting the criteria of wrongdoing and imposing its principal consequence on those who transgress its standard.

The case before us can not be distinguished from that of *Hammer* v. *Dagenhart*. . . . Congress there enacted a law to prohibit transportation in interstate commerce of goods made at a factory in which there was employment of children with the same ages and for the same number of hours a day and days in a week as are penalized by the act in this case. . . .

In the case at the bar, Congress in the name of a tax which on the face of the act is a penalty seeks to do the same thing, and the effort must be equally futile. . . .

But it is pressed upon us that this court has gone so far in sustaining taxing measures the effect or tendency of which was to accomplish purposes not directly within congressional power that we are bound by authority to maintain this law.

The first of these is *Veazie Bank* v. *Fenno*, 8 Wall. 533. . . .

The next case is that of *McCray* v. *United States*. . . . In neither of these cases did the law objected to show on its face as does the law before us the detailed specifications of a regulation of a state concern and business with a heavy exaction to promote the efficacy of such regulation. . . .

. . . *United States* v. *Doremus*, 249 U.S. 86 . . . involved the validity of the Narcotic

Drug Act, 38 Stat. 785, which imposed a special tax on the manufacture, importation and sale or gift of opium or coca leaves or their compounds or derivatives. . . .

The court said that the act could not be declared invalid just because another motive than taxation, not shown on the face of the act, might have contributed to its passage. This case does not militate against the conclusion we have reached in respect of the law now before us. The court, there, made manifest its view that the provisions of the so-called taxing act must be naturally and reasonably adapted to the collection of the tax and not solely to the achievement of some other purpose plainly within state power. . . .

For the reasons given, we must hold the Child Labor Tax Law invalid and the judgment of the District Court is

Affirmed.

MR. JUSTICE CLARKE dissents.

United States v. Butler
297 U.S. 1, 56 S.Ct. 312, 80 L.Ed. 477 (1936)

This case is reprinted in chapter 2, beginning on page 58.

EIGHT

Contract Clause, Vested Rights, and the Development of Due Process

Heretofore we have been concerned with national power—the power of Congress to regulate commerce and to tax and spend, and the relation of congressional authority to state power in the same areas. Out of the Court's interpretation of national power emerged one of the first great antinomies of constitutional law—national supremacy versus dual federalism. By 1937 the Court had largely resolved that conflict in favor of national power.

This chapter features another major antinomy—the doctrines of vested rights versus state police power. Throughout much of our history, the state police power (the power to promote the health, safety, morals, and general welfare) has been limited by the commerce clause. We are now to explore the limitations of state power that flow from the doctrine of vested rights.

The struggle between vested rights and police power is a variant of the earlier conflict between theories of natural rights, on the one hand, and the principle of legislative supremacy on the other. On this side of the Atlantic, these two doctrines represent the reaction upon each other of the prerevolutionary contest between the natural rights of the colonists and parliamentary supremacy. The same phenomenon was manifest after 1776 in the efforts of state legislative majorities to regulate the property and contract rights of individual citizens.

THE DOCTRINE OF VESTED RIGHTS

Of the two doctrines, that of vested rights is of earlier origin, being rooted in the notion that property is the basic social institution. Antedating civil society itself, property fixes the limits within which even supreme legislative authority may properly operate. Indeed, the main function of government, its *raison d'être,* is to protect property. ''The right of acquiring and possessing property and having it protected,'' Justice Paterson wrote in an early circuit court opinion, ''is one of the natural inherent and unalienable rights of man. Men have a sense of property: property is necessary to their subsistence, and correspondent to their natural wants and desires; its security was one of the objects that induced them to unite in society. No man would become a member of a community in which he could not enjoy the fruits of his honest labor and industry. The preservation of property, then, is a primary object of the social compact'' (*Van Horne's Lessee* v. *Dorrance*, 2 Dall. 304, 310: 1795).

James Madison elaborated this doctrine in his 1792 *Essay on Property*.

> This term means ''that dominion which one man claims and exercises over the external things of the world, in exclusion of every other individual.'' But in its larger and juster meaning, it embraces everything to which a man may attach a value and have a right; and which leaves to every one else the like advantage. In the former sense, a man's land, or merchandise, or money is called his property. In the latter sense, a man has property in his opinions and a free communication of them. He has a property of peculiar value in his religious opinions, and in the profession and practice dictated by them. He has property dear to him in the safety and liberty of his person. He has equal property in the free use of his faculties and free choice of the objects on which to employ them. In a word, as a man is said to have a right to his property, he may be equally said to have a property in his rights. . . . If there be a government then which prides itself on maintaining the inviolability of property, which provides that none shall be taken directly even for public use without indemnification to the owner, and yet directly violates the property which individuals have in their opinions, their religion, their person and their faculties, nay more which directly violates their property in their actual possessions, in the labor that acquires their daily subsistence, and in the hallowed remnant of time which ought to relieve their fatigues and soothe their cares, the inference will have been anticipated that such a government is not a pattern for the United States. If the United States mean to obtain or deserve the full praise due to wise and just governments they will equally respect the rights of property and the property in rights. *

Madison defined property broadly, as did John Locke—''lives, liberties and estates, which I call by the general name—property.''

Among the major causes of the Federal Convention of 1787 was the ''injustice'' of state laws concerning property, bringing into question ''the fundamental principle of republican government, that the majority who rule in such governments are the safest guardians both of public good and private rights.'' The point is illustrated in the colloquy that occurred in the early days of the Philadelphia Convention between Roger Sherman and James Madison. Sherman had enumerated the objects of the Convention as defense

---

* In 1972 (*Lynch* v. *Household Finance Corp.*, 405 U.S. 538), Justice Stewart, speaking for the Court, echoed Madison:

> The dichotomy between personal liberties and property rights is a false one. Property does not have rights. People have rights. The right to enjoy property without unlawful deprivation, no less than the right to speak or right to travel, is in truth a ''personal right,'' whether the ''property'' in question be a welfare check, a home, or a savings account. In fact, a fundamental interdependence exists between the personal right to liberty and the personal right in property. Neither could have meaning without the other. That rights in property are basic civil rights has long been recognized.

The dichotomy Justice Stewart adumbrated is increasingly evident in the Burger Court.

against foreign danger and internal disputes, and the need for a central authority to make treaties with foreign nations and to regulate foreign commerce. Madison agreed that these objects were important, but insisted on combining with them "the necessity of providing more effectually for *the security of private rights* and the steady dispensation of justice within the states." "Interferences with these," Madison added, "were evils which had, more perhaps than anything else, produced this convention." What Madison had in mind was state legislation on behalf of the financially embarrassed but politically dominant small-farmer class, led by such rabble-rousers as Daniel Shays in Massachusetts—men seeking special legislation to alter under the standing law the rights of designated parties; intervention by state legislatures in private controversies pending in, or already decided by, the ordinary courts; and legislation setting aside judgments, granting new hearings, voiding valid wills, or validating void wills. Those who wished to see the menace of special legislation and state legislative supremacy abated, those who felt the need for outside protection of the rights of property and of contract, naturally supported the movement afoot for a Constitutional Convention.

But how were the Framers to secure such protection? Various measures were proposed, but every motion looking to the imposition of property qualification for suffrage or office-holding failed. The suggestion that the Senate be organized as a barrier for property was also defeated. The difficult and delicate matter of suffrage was ultimately left to the states. As the Constitution came from the hands of the Framers, it contained only one brief clause that might afford vested rights protection against state legislative majorities— Art. 1, Sec. 10: "No State shall . . . pass any . . . ex post facto law or laws impairing the obligation of contracts. . . ." When it came up for interpretation in *Calder* v. *Bull,* even this clause was given a very narrow interpretation. Confining the application of ex post facto to retroactive penal legislation, the Court held that it was not "inserted to secure the citizen in his private rights of either property or contracts." This decision, creating a wide breach in the constitutional protection afforded civil rights, aroused widespread criticism. Even Justice Chase, who delivered the opinion, seemed apologetic, suggesting that legislation adversely affecting vested rights might be set aside as violation of natural law. "There are certain vital principles," Chase observed, "in our free republican governments which will determine and overrule an apparent and flagrant abuse of legislative power. An act of the legislature (for I cannot call it a law) contrary to the great principles of social compact cannot be considered a rightful exercise of the legislative authority."

But Chase's associate, Justice Iredell, questioned the validity of natural law limitations on legislative power. He characterized such talk as the plaything of "some speculative jurists," and said that if the Constitution itself imposed no checks on legislative power, "whatever the legislature chose to enact would be lawfully enacted, and the judicial power could never interpose to pronounce it void." "The ideas of natural justice are regulated by no fixed standard," Iredell commented. "The ablest and purest of men have differed upon the subject, and all that the Court could properly say in such an event would be that the legislature . . . had passed an act which, in the opinion of the judges, was inconsistent with abstract principles of justice."

Which of these views on the scope of judicial power has prevailed? In appearance Iredell's, but (as we shall see) at the end of the century Chase's views were for all practical purposes triumphant. By 1890 the Court achieved, under the due process clause of the Fourteenth Amendment, the very power to supervise and control legislative action in relation to abstract principles of justice against which Iredell had so strongly protested.

EXPANSION OF THE CONTRACT CLAUSE

Calder v. *Bull* was a binding precedent in 1810, when the leading case of *Fletcher* v. *Peck* (6 Cr. 87) came before Chief Justice Marshall. "Marshall," Professor Corwin has written, found in *Fletcher* v. *Peck* "a task of restoration awaiting him in that great field of Constitutional Law which defines state power in relation to private rights." Hamilton had laid solid foundations for an effective national government; no such preliminary work had been done in the task now confronting the Chief Justice. Indeed, *Calder* v. *Bull* presented a well-nigh insuperable barrier.

Fletcher v. *Peck* illustrates the speculative spirit rife in America at the close of the 1700s. Land companies found Georgia an especially inviting field. Between 1789 and 1795 speculators badgered the Georgia legislators without success. Finally, however, on January 7, 1795, the Governor of Georgia signed a bill granting the greater part of what is now Alabama and Mississippi to four groups of purchasers, known as the Yazoo Land Companies, at 1 ½ cents per acre. The "purchasers" included men of national reputation and local politicians (all but one member of the Georgia legislature who voted for the act held shares in one or more of the companies). Indignation ran high and in 1796 a new legislature repealed the land-grab act. By the time of repeal some of the lands had passed into the hands of purchasers, mostly Boston capitalists, who in turn sold extensively to investors in New England and the Middle Atlantic States.

Contending that the repeal act of 1796 could not constitutionally divest them of their titles, these innocent purchasers decided to test their rights in the federal courts. The case, an "arranged" suit, first came before the Supreme Court in the 1809 term; it was re-argued the next year, and a decision was rendered on March 16, 1810. Sustaining the contention of the Yazoo claimants, Chief Justice Marshall held that the 1796 repeal act was an unconstitutional impairment of the obligation of a contract. At the outset Marshall suggested that the rescinding act of the Georgia legislature was void as a violation of vested rights, and hence contrary to the underlying principles of society and government. But, apparently realizing that a decision based on such flimsy ground would be less secure than one grounded in the Constitution, he turned to the contract clause. In doing this, he was confronted with two difficulties; first, the sort of contract the Framers had in mind must have been executory—a contract in which the obligation of performance is still to be discharged. Marshall got around this by saying that every grant is attended by an implied contract on the part of the grantor not to reassert his right to the thing granted. Therefore, the clause covered executed contracts in which performance has been fulfilled as well as executory contracts.

The greater difficulty was that the contract before the Court was *public,* not private. In private contracts it is easy enough to distinguish the contract as an agreement between the parties from the obligation which comes from the law and holds the parties to their agreement. Who, in this case, was to hold Georgia to its engagement? Certainly not Georgia, which had passed the rescinding act, or the Georgia state court. Marshall escaped the dilemma by ruling that Georgia's obligation was moral, and that this moral injunction had been elevated to legal status by Article 1, Section 10—"a Bill of Rights for the people of each State," Marshall called it.

But the Chief Justice was uncertain at the very end. The last paragraph of his opinion states that Georgia was restrained from passing the rescinding act "either by general principles that are common to our free institutions, or by particular provisions of the Constitution."

Fletcher v. *Peck* went a long way toward bridging the gap opened by *Calder* v. *Bull* in the constitutional protection of private rights. But, since Marshall's ruling was somewhat ambiguous, there remained the question of whether the obligation-of-contract clause safeguarded corporate charters as well as public grants against legislative interference. In 1819, by his opinion in the Dartmouth College case, Marshall filled in the breach Justice Chase had created in the constitutional protection of vested rights.

The college's original charter was granted by the King of England. Parliament could have destroyed it at any time before 1776, and before 1788 the state of New Hampshire could have wiped it out. After that year, Marshall held that it must continue in perpetuity. His opinion adds up to these propositions: The college was not public, but a "private eleemosynary institution"; its charter was the outgrowth of a contract between the original donors and the Crown; the trustees represented the interest of the donors; the Constitution protects this representative interest.

Marshall agonized at only one point. The requirement of the obligation-of-contract clause was admittedly designed to protect those having a vested beneficial interest. No one then living, not even the trustees, had any such interest in Dartmouth College. But Marshall held that the case came within the spirit, if not the words, of the Constitution.

The nub of Marshall's decision is the proposition that any ambiguity in a charter must be construed in favor of the adventurers and against the state. With perpetuity thus implied, the college charter was placed beyond the reach of the legislature. By that same token, the charters of profit-seeking corporations were likewise beyond the control of legislative majorities. In short, the doctrine of vested rights, heretofore having no safeguard except the principles of natural law, now enjoyed the solid protection of a specific provision of the Constitution—the impairment-of-contract clause.

In a separate opinion in the Dartmouth College case, Marshall's scholarly colleague Joseph Story suggested the means by which states might in the future avoid the restrictive effect of Marshall's holding. Speaking of the state's power over corporations, Story observed that there was "no other control, than what is expressly or implicitly reserved by the charter itself."

As early as 1805 Virginia had used a reservation clause (reserving to the state the power to alter, amend, or repeal a charter) in special incorporation acts. In 1827, following the Dartmouth decision, New York enacted a general law making all charters "hereafter granted . . . subject to alteration, suspension and repeal, in the discretion of the legislature." All states now have such a provision in their constitutions, in general acts, or in both.

Could any society, particularly an industrialized society claiming to rest on the foundation of popular sovereignty, hold rigidly to the doctrine of vested rights? Even John Marshall seemed unwilling to go quite so far. In *Fletcher* v. *Peck,* the doctrine of the public interest gave way to the doctrine of vested rights. But 11 years later, in the Dartmouth College case, Marshall suggested an opposing idea, the idea later designated as "police power." "The framers of the Constitution," he observed, "did not intend to restrain the states in the regulation of the civil institutions adopted for internal government." In *Gibbons* v. *Ogden,* the police-power concept became quite explicit: "The acknowledged power of the state to regulate its police, its domestic trade and to govern its own citizens may enable it to legislate on this subject [commerce] to a considerable extent." Referring to "inspection laws," Marshall conceded that they "form a portion of that immense mass of legislation, which embraces everything within the territory of a state, not surrendered to the general government." The term "police power" itself appears in *Brown* v. *Maryland*

(12 Wheat. 419: 1827). Marshall speaks of the police power as residual, comprising what is left over of the state's power beyond those other great prerogatives, eminent domain and taxation.

By 1830, the doctrine of vested rights, as limiting legislative power, was nevertheless accepted in a majority of the states and by leading lawyers and judges—especially by the eminent jurist Chancellor Kent of New York. Kent conceded that the state had the power to "prescribe the mode and manner of using it [property] so far as may be necessary to prevent the abuse of the right to the injury or annoyance of others or to the public." But he denied state power to destroy property values in the hands of owners without paying for them. Implicit in Kent's doctrine was his theory of social progress. "A state of equality as to property is impossible to be maintained, for it is against the laws of our nature; and if it could be reduced to practice, it would place the human race in a restless enjoyment and stupid inactivity which would degrade the mind and destroy the happiness of social life."

The fierceness of the battle between public power and vested rights at the state level was highlighted in *Wilkinson* v. *Leland* (2 Pet. 627: 1829). Daniel Webster, attorney for the defendant in error, insisted that: "If at this period, there is not a general restraint on legislatures in favor of private rights, there is an end to private property. Though there may be no prohibition in the constitution, the legislature is restrained from acts subverting the great principles of republican liberty and of the social compact." To this contention Webster's opponent, William Wirt, responded: "Who is the sovereign? Is it not the legislature of the state and are not its acts effectual unless they come in contact with the great principles of the social compact?" Justice Story, speaking for the Court, upheld the retrospective legislation in question, yet he too supported vested rights: "That government can scarcely be deemed to be free where the rights of property are left solely dependent upon the will of a legislative body without any restraint. The fundamental maxims of a free government seem to require that the rights of personal liberty and private property should be sacred."

What these pronouncements mean is that property rights fix the contours within which the legislature may exercise its powers. The Court felt obliged to enforce these limitations even in the absence of specific provisions of the Constitution. These were America's "preferred freedoms"—values so generally recognized and accepted that no such phrase was needed to describe them.

DEVELOPMENT OF THE POLICE POWER

Meanwhile political forces of great significance for the development of constitutional law were taking shape. The year 1828 saw the election as President of the democratically inclined Andrew Jackson; in the same decade Massachusetts, New York, and Virginia met in convention to remove certain constitutional safeguards for economic privilege and to liberalize the suffrage. Out of all this emerged the doctrine of popular sovereignty, the notion that the will of the people is to be discovered at the ballot box, not merely in a document framed in 1787. The juristic expression of popular sovereignty is the doctrine of the police power, which was given classic expression and interpretation in 1837 by Jackson's appointee and Marshall's successor, Roger Brooke Taney.

The two cases of Dartmouth College and Charles River Bridge illustrate two alternate approaches to progress. Chief Justice Marshall's thoughts turned toward security of property and contract rights against government encroachment. Without losing sight of these values, Chief Justice Taney argued that the community also has rights and it is the object and end of government to promote the prosperity and happiness of all. Paul Freund sums up the contrasting theories: "Where Marshall heard only a single voice emanating from the contract clause, his successors have attuned themselves to stereophonic sound, to counter pressures from public and general welfare interests."

In the License Cases of 1847, Taney gave the state police power succinct definition: "The power to *govern men and things* within the limits of its own dominion." A concept of incalculable potentialities, "police power" came to mean not only legislative authority to remove government-created privilege, as in the Charles River Bridge case, but also provided sanction for state legislation having broad social purpose. Coming in 1837 at the peak of Jackson's power and prestige, Taney's doctrine of the police power did in fact stimulate considerable legislative activity.

Many years later, in one of the first cases foreshadowing the ultimately favorable constitutional fate of the New Deal (*Home Building and Loan Association* v. *Blaisdell*), the Justices, voting 5 to 4, refused to hold that the contract clause had been breached by a state statute changing the terms of mortgage contracts. The legislation seemed to fly in the face of Article 1, Section 10. Distinguishing between the *obligation* of the contract and the *remedy,* Chief Justice Hughes tried to demonstrate that the moratorium placed on mortgage foreclosures did not impair the obligation; the statute merely modified the remedy, explaining that "while emergency does not create power, emergency may furnish the occasion for the exercise of power." Justices Cardozo and Stone read the Chief Justice's first draft with misgivings so serious that each considered writing a concurring opinion. The former actually prepared a draft (reprinted in this chapter), and Stone submitted a long memorandum.

The Chief Justice's opinion, as finally announced, included long passages from Cardozo's unpublished concurring opinion and from Stone's memorandum. But he kept intact the legalistic logomachy about "emergency," thus exposing himself to dissenting Justice Sutherland's broadside.

After the Charles River Bridge decision, the contract clause never regained its earlier stature as a barrier against legislative encroachment on property rights. In *Stone* v. *Mississippi* (101 U.S. 814: 1880) the Court refused to limit state police power by applying the protection of the contract clause to a lottery company charter. The reason for the police-power rule, said Chief Justice Waite in delivering the opinion of the Court, lies in the fact that "the power of governing is a trust, committed by the people to the government, no part of which can be granted away. . . . [The agencies of government established by the people] can govern according to their discretion, if within the scope of their general authority, while in power; but they cannot give away or sell the discretion of those that are to come after them, in respect to matters the government of which, from the very nature of things, must 'vary with varying circumstances.' . . . The contracts which the Constitution protects are those that relate to property rights, not governmental." The Court's task was eased by the character of the property right involved, but in terming police power "governmental," in speaking of an "implied understanding" that a grant might be altered, the Court obscured the real clash of interests between property rights and legislative power.

In *El Paso* v. *Simmons* (379 U.S. 497: 1965), the Court's flexible interpretation of the obligation-of-contract clause won well-nigh unanimous support. Eight Justices, only Black dissenting, held that not every modification of a contractual promise, even one embodied in a state statute, impairs the obligation of contract. Denying that the Minnesota Moratorium decision furnished foundations for the majority's decision, Justice Black accused his colleagues of "balancing away the plain guarantee of Article 1, Section 10. . . ," of justifying a state in taking "a man's private property for public use without compensation in violation of the plain guarantee of the Fifth Amendment, made applicable to the States by the Fourteenth. . . ." That some life remains in the contract clause is evident from Justice Blackmun's opinion in *United States Trust Co.* v. *New Jersey,* decided in 1977 and reprinted in this chapter.

THE ORIGINS OF DUE PROCESS

Meanwhile a new judicial formula had been found for defeating government action under the police power. The 1830s had seen the establishment of the public school system; the 1840s witnessed the first steps toward regulation of the liquor traffic and primitive factory legislation. The character and volume of social legislation created the need for a new constitutional weapon. Special credit for the invention of that weapon must go to the New York Court of Appeals—and to the leading case of *Wynehamer* v. *New York* (13 New York 378: 1856).

The defendant, Wynehamer, was indicted and convicted by a common-law jury in the Court of Sessions of Erie County for selling liquor in small quantities contrary to the act, passed April 9, 1855, "for the prevention of intemperance, pauperism and crime." It was admitted that the defendant owned the liquors in question before and at the time the law took effect. But Wynehamer's counsel insisted that he was entitled to an acquittal on the ground, among others, that the statute was unconstitutional and void. The Court invalidated the act, but the complexity of the issue and the diversity of judicial opinion concerning it are indicated by the fact that the Judges split three ways.

Judge Comstock, who spoke for the Court, noted that, though "the legislative power" is vested in the legislature, it is subject to special constitutional limitations, "which are of very great interest and importance" in that they prohibit the deprivation of life, liberty, and property without due process of law.

The Justice had thus introduced a constitutional injunction of tremendous possibilities—"due process." What does it mean? To the lay mind this phrase suggests procedural limitations—that is, if it limits legislative power at all, it does so in terms not of what can be done, but of *how* something must be done. Comstock and the concurring Justices made clear that they had something more sweeping in mind. Since the legislature has only limited powers, it cannot encroach, Comstock contended, on the rights of any species of property, even where the action would be of "absolute benefit" to the people of the state. To allow the legislature such a power, even in the public interest, would "subvert the fundamental idea of property." "In a government like ours," Comstock observed, "theories of public good or public necessity may be so plausible, or even so truthful, as to command popular majorities. But whether truthful or plausible merely, and by whatever numbers they are assented to, there are some absolute private rights beyond their reach, and among these the constitution places the right of property."

Two concurring opinions rejected Comstock's notion of "higher law," i.e., of extraconstitutional limitations, and held that the only limits on legislative power are those stated in the Constitution. The legislature, they said, could regulate property, even to the extent of rendering it virtually worthless; but they, too, held that the present act involved destruction rather than regulation, and was therefore void. The form of the declaration—''No person shall be deprived of life, liberty or property without due process of law''—Justice A. S. Johnson commented, ''necessarily imports that the legislature cannot make the mere existence of the rights secured the occasion of depriving a person of any of them, *even by the forms which belong to 'due process of law'*. For if it does not necessarily import this, then the legislative power is absolute.''

In his dissenting opinion, Justice T. A. Johnson emphasized the idea that legislative power is supreme except where specifically limited by the Constitution. Judicial review based upon judges' views of what is reasonable would constitute usurpation, a ''veto or dispensing power'' that does not ''pertain to the judicial functions.'' More than this, said Johnson, the courts should approach even doubtful legislation with the greatest of restraint, remembering that their primary function is vigilantly and fearlessly to uphold legislative enactments. ''The people have a far more certain and reliable security and protection against mere impolitic, overstringent or uncalled-for legislation than courts can ever afford, in their reserved power of changing . . . the representatives of their legislative sovereignty; and to that final and ultimate tribunal should all such errors and mistakes in legislation be referred for correction.'' As to the rights of property, they had long been subject to popular control; and if they could ever have been enjoyed as a natural right, that right had long since ceased to exist. Without such governmental control of the misuses of property, those putative rights would be superior to liberty itself.

Due process of law also received a different emphasis in Johnson's hands: it must be considered as protecting physical property itself rather than any rights thereof. To proscribe governmental controls that decrease the value of property would, after all, ''place the right of traffic above every other right, and render it independent of the power of government.'' ''A government,'' the dissenting Justice concluded, ''which does not have power to make all needful rules with respect to internal trade and commerce, to impose such restrictions upon it as may be deemed necessary for the good of all, and even to prohibit and suppress entirely any particular traffic which is found to be injurious and demoralizing in its tendencies and consequences, is no government.''

Reflected in the various Wynehamer opinions are differences that recall the unstaged debate between Chief Justice Marshall and Judge Gibson concerning the nature and scope of judicial review, and also the conflict between Justices Chase and Iredell regarding natural law—''certain vital principles in our free republican governments''—as a viable check on legislative power vis-à-vis property rights.

Impressive support for the Wynehamer decision is found in an anonymous *American Law Magazine* article of July 1843. Written under the title ''The Security of Private Property,'' this paper argued that property needs ''every parchment barrier which has been or can be thrown around it.'' ''In a republic, where the legislature . . . is annually elected, and where . . . legislation partakes . . . of the passions and impulses of the moment, it is important to inquire into the extent of the power possessed by the majority to encroach upon the fruits of honest industry, or interfere with the proprietor in his free and undisturbed possession and enjoyment.''

''What,'' the writer asks, ''are the general powers of government in a civilized society? Is there no *lex legum,* independent of express Constitutional restrictions?'' The answer is cautious, but decisive. ''It may be a wide and dangerous door to open to judicial discretion, to say that they shall apply to the question of validity or invalidity of legislative acts, the general principles of just government as laid down by the most eminent jurists and text writers. Yet suppose the legislature to pass a law arbitrarily depriving a citizen of life or liberty, without fault or crime, must we look to the Constitution for an express disaffirmance of such power? There exists a disaffirmance of it, clear, positive, and unequivocal in the words Magna Carta transferred into the Bill of Rights. . . . The same provision which secures our lives and liberties against an arbitrary exercise of power . . . extends to our property.''

The constitutional protection this writer found so fully supported in authoritative texts was enforceable, he said, ''through an independent judiciary.'' The article concludes with the happy thought that ''the reader . . . will lay it aside with the reflection that the liberty of the republican states of America will owe their perpetuity to their courts, executing the supreme will of the people against acts of tyranny and oppression, whether proceeding from the executive or the legislator.''

In 1856, the year *Wynehamer* came down, the Supreme Court of the United States had occasion to define due process in the Fifth Amendment. In *Murray* v. *Hoboken* (18 How. 272), only a process in conflict with a provision of the Constitution, or in conflict with ''settled usages and modes of proceeding existing in the common and statute law of England, before the emigration of our ancestors and which are . . . not . . . unsuited to their civil and political conditions'' lacked due process. ''That all men of that day,'' the late Judge Charles M. Hough commented, ''had no conception of due process other than a summary description of a fairly tried action at law, is not asserted; but I do submit that reports before the Civil War yield small evidence that there was any professional conviction that it was more than that.''

Contemporaneously with the Wynehamer decision, ''several other state courts were deciding similar issues in precisely the opposite way, and invoking the police power in justification.'' Thus, by mid-nineteenth century two great forces were meeting head on: the doctrine of vested rights and the doctrine of the police power. Professor Corwin suggests that on the eve of the Civil War, courts and country were faced with a reincarnation of the old conundrum: What happens when an irresistible force—the doctrine of the police power—meets an immovable object—the doctrine of vested rights? What, moreover, was to be the role of the courts in this situation?

Confronted with cases such as that of Charles River Bridge, Corwin suggests that the courts might have done one of two things: surrender the view that rights of property and of contract set absolute barriers against the exercise of public power; or cast about for a new constitutional formula to protect vested rights against regulatory legislative power. Would the phrase ''due process'' serve this purpose? Could a term suggesting procedural limitations only be fashioned into a limitation on substantive law making? The great significance of the Wynehamer case is that it evoked in 1856 due process of law as a constitutional measure not only of *how,* but of *what* legislative power should be exercised.

JUDICIAL RESTRAINT AND THE FOURTEENTH AMENDMENT

Two major events made 1868 a landmark in the development of ''due process'': the publication of Thomas M. Cooley's classic work *Constitutional Limitations* and the adoption of the Fourteenth Amendment. Cooley's treatise contains chapters of special interest: Chapter 11, ''Protection of Property by the Law of the Land''; and Chapter 16, ''The Police Power and the States.'' ''Thus was the national Supreme Court,'' Corwin observed,

"... supplied with a double set of answers, each duly authenticated by supporting precedents ... touching the vital problem of the relation of legislative power to the property right." The Fourteenth Amendment added a weapon of untold potentialities to the judicial arsenal; henceforth the battles to protect property rights against state regulation were destined to revolve around "due process." Accordionlike in its contour, it was broad enough to embrace the concept of natural law.

Despite the unlimited potentiality latent in the Fourteenth Amendment for the enhancement of the Court's supervisory power, the Justices seemed reluctant to exploit this new source of authority. In the Slaughterhouse Cases, Justice Miller and four colleagues refused to construe the privileges-and-immunities clause as breaking down the distinction between state and national citizenship. The purpose of the framers of the Fourteenth Amendment was not to confer on the national government the duty of protecting both kinds of citizenship. National citizenship included the right of coming to the seat of the government, the right to enjoy government offices, and the right to government protection on the high seas, whereas state citizenship included, among other rights, the fundamental right to acquire and possess property. Since the rights allegedly infringed in the Slaughterhouse Cases were derived from state citizenship, the butchers of New Orleans could not, in Miller's opinion, look beyond the state for protection.

Justice Miller was equally cool to the application of the equal protection and due process clauses. As for equal protection, he doubted its relevance except in cases involving the rights of Negroes. Due process had not yet been the subject of much construction, but under no interpretation he had yet seen could the challenged statute be held lacking in due process. Why did Miller take such a narrow view of judicial power? Essentially, it grew out of his conception of the Union—"the structure and spirit of our institutions." The Fourteenth Amendment did not change "the whole theory of the relations of the State and Federal governments to each other and of both these governments to the people." "Such a ruling," Miller said, "would constitute this Court a perpetual censor upon all legislation of the states on the civil rights of their own citizens, with authority to nullify such as it did not approve."

Involved was a theory of federalism. Justice Miller noted that the Framers had "divided on the line which should separate the powers of the national government from those of the state governments." The prevailing sense of danger from federal power had motivated the drive for adoption of the first 11 amendments. The Civil War alerted the nation to the fact that "the true danger to the perpetuity of the Union" was "the capacity of the state organizations ... for determined resistance to the General Government." The Civil War amendments, especially the Fourteenth, reflect this fear. Now, the Court felt duty-bound to curb any effort to change the federal balance, even by the amending process.

Four Justices, including Chief Justice Chase and headed by Justice Field, dissented vehemently and at great length. Field said that the issues were "of the gravest importance, not merely to the parties ... but to the whole country. It is nothing less than the question whether the recent amendments ... protect the *citizens of the United States against the deprivation of their common rights by state legislation*" (editors' italics). Field thought that the amendment was intended "to place the common rights of American citizens under the protection of the national government." Nor was the Louisiana act invalid solely as violating the Fourteenth Amendment. "Grants of exclusive privilege," Field contended, "... are opposed to the whole theory of free government, and it requires no aid from any bill of rights to render them void. That only is a free government, in the

American sense of the term, under which the inalienable right of every citizen to pursue his happiness is unrestrained, except by just, equal and impartial laws." The Court's narrow construction of the amendment made it, in Field's opinion, a "vain and idle enactment."

Despite Field's protest, judicial hands-off was maintained four years later in *Munn* v. *Illinois* where a statute fixing rates for grain elevators was challenged. Harking back to principles of common law, Chief Justice Waite reasoned that when a man devotes his property to a use in which the public has an interest, the property ceases to be private; it becomes "affected with a public interest," and hence subject to a greater degree of regulation. The legislature, not the Court, was to determine how much regulation was permissible, whether it was arbitrary and whether the business was so affected. Against this refusal to censor state legislation, dissenting Justice Field objected strongly. "This decision," he said, "was subversive of the rights of private property." The principles of "free government" fixed absolute limits on legislative power, and these limits could not be altered even by organic law. "There is no magic in the language," Field commented, "though used by a constitutional convention, which can change a private business into a public one. . . ."

For almost a century the existence of the "due process" clause in the Fifth Amendment had not created any serious limitation on the substance of national legislation. But the clause was no sooner inserted in the Fourteenth Amendment than it became a rallying point for those who resisted the effort of government to regulate and control the expanding industrial economy. This strange turn of events puzzled Supreme Court Justices no less than commentators. Speaking for the Court in *Davidson* v. *New Orleans* (96 U.S. 97, 103–4: 1878), Justice Miller noted that,

> While it [due process] has been a part of the Constitution, as a restraint upon the power of the States, only a very few years, the docket of this court is crowded with cases in which we are asked to hold that State courts and State legislatures have deprived their own citizens of life, liberty, and property without due process of law. There is here abundant evidence that there exists some strange misconception of the scope of this provision as found in the Fourteenth Amendment. In fact, it would seem from the character of many of the cases before us, and the arguments made in them, that the clause under consideration is looked upon as a means of bringing to the test of the decision of this court the abstract opinions of every unsuccessful litigant in a State court of the justice of the decision against him, and of the merits of the legislation on which such a decision may be founded.

But what was "remarkable" about the notion that the property right is basic? What is "strange" about the view that vested rights set limits on what the government may do, even though those boundaries are not specifically drawn in the Constitution itself? The notion that due process fixes substance as well as procedural limitations on the law-making authority was not lacking in respectable support. In 1953, Howard Jay Graham observed: "Americans may be proud and thankful to discover, certainly in these times, that broadened and discretionary due process, far from being an excrescence or tool of ambition, is in reality so deeply enrooted in our national consciousness that its judicial achievement was quite as much a result as a cause of widespread popular usage."

Though the Court persisted in its refusal to use the due process clause as a means of censoring state legislation, another decade was to see the views of Field and the other dissenters prevail. Thus the breach left by the Munn and Davidson cases and others in the wall of protection around vested rights was destined to be closed, just as the same breach had been bridged by Chief Justice Marshall when he expanded the scope of the contract clause to overcome the decision in *Calder* v. *Bull*. Various forces and factors were joined in this movement.

FACTORS LEADING TO JUDICIAL CENSORSHIP

In 1878, one year after the Munn and Davidson decisions, the American Bar Association was organized. By 1881 it was embarked on a deliberate and persistent campaign of education designed to reverse the Court's broad conception of legislative power. The chief burden of the association's campaign was to convince the nation that judges "discover" law rather than "make" it. In the annual addresses of the president and the titles of various papers, it is evident that the association stood with John Stuart Mill for individualism, agreed with Darwin's view of the inevitability of the human struggle, and accepted Herbert Spencer's evolutionary theories of politics. Extracts from addresses reveal such thoughts as: "The great curse of the world is too much government"; "Forces which make for growth should be left absolutely free to all"; "Ownership and responsibility are now individual"; "If trusts are a defensive weapon of property interests against the communistic trend, they are desirable"; "Monopoly is often a necessity and an advantage."

In the *Princeton Review* for March 1878, Judge Cooley suggested two safeguards against the rising threat of popular power. One was the Constitution—"if properly construed." "If principles are not fixed and permanent," he wrote, "they are not constitutional." The second was "higher law," "natural law." Cooley treated the "laws" of supply and demand as if they were part of the Constitution itself. Free government could not support any fixing of prices for service, even if monopoly existed. "Does . . . the *mere* fact," he inquired, "that one owns the whole supply of anything, confer upon the state the authority to interfere and limit the price he may set upon his wares or his services?" Anyone inclined to give an affirmative response should be expected to show how the power may be harmonized with the general "principles of free government." Private monopolists could thus effect regulations of individual rights in ways not open to public and politically responsible government.

It is difficult to square Cooley's ideas on the requirements of free government with the facts. The volume *Laws and Liberties of Massachusetts,* published in 1648, shows that price-fixing and wage-fixing were quite common in colonial days. Prior to 1787 at least eight of the 13 states passed laws fixing the prices of almost everything from butter and beans to shoes and steel. "This," Justice Robert H. Jackson observed, "was the atmosphere in which the fathers of the Constitution were brought up; this is the way they acted when left to their own devices. Is it likely, then, that when they adopted the Fifth Amendment they meant to select for outlawry that form of legislation which fixed wages or prices? And if they had no such intention, did the states which ratified the due process clause of the Fourteenth Amendment understand that they were renouncing the power?"

Whatever the correct answer, a shift in the Court's view, embodied in *Munn* v. *Illinois,* came swiftly. In 1882, Roscoe Conkling made his famous argument in *San Mateo Co.* v. *Southern Pacific R.R.* (116 U.S. 138: 1883). Conkling, who had been a member of the Joint Congressional Committee that drafted the Fourteenth Amendment in 1866, revealed for the first time a manuscript Journal of the Joint Committee. From this authoritative source he selected extensive quotations to show that he and his colleagues in drafting the equal protection and the due process clauses purposely used the word "person" as including corporations. "At the time the Fourteenth Amendment was ratified,"

Conkling told the Justices, ''individuals and joint stock companies were appealing for congressional and administrative protection against invidious and discriminating State and local taxes. . . . Those who devised the Fourteenth Amendment . . . planted in the Constitution a monumental truth to stand foursquare to whatever wind might blow.'' . . .

Conkling's testimony was impressive. In addition to his role in drafting the amendment for submission to both houses of Congress, he had twice refused appointment—once the Chief Justiceship—to the Supreme Court itself. For whatever reason, within a few years after Conkling's revelations, the Court began veering away from the narrow Negro-race protection theory expounded by Miller in the Slaughterhouse cases, away from the narrow conception of judicial review under due process propounded by Waite in *Munn* v. *Illinois,* and accepted Conkling's theory that corporations were persons under the due process clause (*Santa Clara Co.* v. *Southern Pacific R.R.;* 118 U.S. 394: 1886). Yet scholarly research has revealed that Conkling sold the Court a constitutional bill of goods. In 1938, Howard Jay Graham showed that Conkling's ''conspiracy'' theory of the Fourteenth Amendment was a fraud, or at least a trick unworthy of a great lawyer. At certain points in his peroration in the San Mateo case, Conkling indicated that surmise, not factual knowledge, was the basis of his theory. (''Those who devised the Fourteenth Amendment may have builded better than they knew. . . . To some of them the sunset of life may have given mystical lore.'') Graham's conclusion is that Conkling ''suppressed'' pertinent facts and misrepresented others; he ''deliberately misquoted the Journal [of the Joint Committee] and even arranged his excerpts so as to give his listeners a false impression of the record and his own relation thereto.''

Nevertheless, Conkling's argument received strong support. The impending shift for which the dissenters in the Munn and Slaughterhouse cases had argued was evidenced in majority opinions. *Hurtado* v. *California* illustrated judicial protection, via due process, for the rights of individuals and minorities, while *Mugler* v. *Kansas* foreshadowed judicial safeguards for property rights.

Speaking for the Court in the Hurtado case, Justice Matthews sustained an act of California substituting a prosecutor's information for grand jury indictment against the charge that it violated due process. But he warned: ''The limitations imposed by our constitutional law upon the action of the government, both state and national, are essential to the preservation of public and private rights. . . . The enforcement of these limitations by judicial process is the device of self-governing communities to protect the rights of individuals and minorities . . . against the power of numbers.''

Similarly, Justice Harlan, speaking for the Court in *Mugler* v. *Kansas,* commented: ''It does not at all follow that every statute enacted ostensibly for the promotion of these ends [morals and welfare] is to be accepted as a legitimate exertion of the police powers of the state.'' Legitimacy was to be determined by the Court. ''The courts are not bound by mere forms, nor are they to be misled by mere pretenses. They are at liberty—indeed, are under a solemn duty—to look at the substance of things.''

THE FOURTEENTH AMENDMENT JUDICIALLY AMENDED

Three factors had been at work to effect this judicial revolution—the bar association's propaganda campaign, Conkling's so-called conspiracy theory of the Fourteenth Amendment, and powerful dissenting opinions. In 1887 and 1890 a fourth element was added—change in judicial personnel. Between 1877 and 1890 seven Justices who had participated in the Slaughterhouse and Munn cases resigned or died. Field lived on, and in 1888 he was joined by his nephew David J. Brewer and Chief Justice Melville W. Fuller. It is ironic that, at the very time this judicial turnover was completed, Charles C. Marshall supplied impressive historical and analytical justification for the Court's resistance to the use of the Fourteenth Amendment as a barrier against social legislation. A lawyer of conservative sympathies, Marshall said that the police power—the power to govern men and things—hitherto exercised by various ruling classes, belonged to the legislature. Property, previously regarded as an absolute right, was (in Marshall's opinion) legitimately subject to control by the legislature.

"It is clear," Marshall wrote, "that if, according to law, all property affected by a public use or interest, is in its very nature subject to legislative control, then for the legislature to control its use is in no sense to deprive a citizen of such property contrary to the law of the land. What the citizen owns is not absolute property but a *qualified and contingent interest in property.* Control by the legislature is its necessary incident, and such control, when exercised through a statute, is in its very self 'due process of law.' It is equally clear, for the same reasons, that such legislative control is not the appropriation of private property to public use. When the legislature exercises such control it does not appropriate property, for up to the extent of such control there is no property."

Two great questions, Marshall commented, had vexed the American people: personal liberty and property. The Dred Scott decision opened the first, the Munn decision the second. Each decision left "a wide section of human rights unprotected by the constitutional guaranties." These opinions were products of divided courts, and both stimulated great controversy. "In a commercial emergency," Marshall continues, "the oracles of law have been approached. Dumb for almost a century on the questions involved because no inquirer had sought the shrine, they now give forth a response which startles lawyers and laymen and startles them the more they read and examine. For the first time it is appreciated that there has lain dormant for a century a vigorous principle of the Common Law, an element of Anglo-Saxon government, which in the hands of an aristocracy has often been an instrument of wrong and oppression and which may in the hands of 'the people' effect a despoliation of property owners surpassing the encroachments of the crown at the worst periods of English history."

The implications of the Munn decision were terrifying. "Our boasted security in property rights falls away for the lack of a constitutional guaranty against this sovereign power thus discovered in our legislatures. It is apparent that against the whim of a temporary majority, inflamed with class prejudice, envy or revenge, the property of no man is safe. And the danger is even greater in an age teeming with shifting theories of social reform and economic science, which seem to have but one common principle—the subjection of private property to governmental control for the good—or alleged good—of the public."

Marshall did not question the soundness of the Court's decision in the Munn case. On the contrary, he argued that the doctrine of legislative supremacy is well established, both historically and constitutionally. But he was concerned about the "wide section of human rights" left unprotected by that decision. Nor did the "higher law principles," featured in the dissenting opinions of Justice Field, provide any safeguard. The Munn decision had, Marshall concluded, revealed "a defect where all was supposed to be perfection." That defect is "properly remedied only by constitutional amendment." "The possibility of retracing steps," Marshall wrote emphatically, "of reversing or distinguishing, or otherwise nullifying [the Munn doctrine] through the courts is put quite beyond possibility.''

Six months before Marshall's article saw the light of day, what he said must be done by resort to the formal amending process had already been accomplished by the Court's decision in *Chicago, Milwaukee and St. Paul R. R. Co.* v. *Minnesota.* By a vote of 6 to 3 the Justices decided, against vehemently protesting dissenters, that the question of the reasonableness of rates could not be left by the legislature to a state commission, but must be subject to judicial review. This decision completed a judicial revolution. The Court had now become what Justice Miller had feared—a ''perpetual censor'' of state legislation under the due process clause of the Fourteenth Amendment. ''From that decision,'' Judge Charles M. Hough has written, ''I date the flood.''

This outcome might have been anticipated. As early as 1875, Justice Miller had remarked: ''It is vain to contend with Judges who have been at the bar the advocates for forty years of railroad companies, and all forms of associated capital, when they are called upon to decide cases where such interests are in contest. All their training, all their feelings are from the start in favor of those who need no such influence.''

''I am losing interest in these matters,'' Miller concluded wearily. ''I will do my duty, but will fight no more.''

The liberal battle within the judiciary had been lost. In the Supreme Court, powerful vested interests found ''a bulwark of defense against the subtle and skillful manipulation of democratic processes to achieve unsanctioned theories.'' Just as political democracy was coming into its own, the Supreme Court, equating the laissez-faire dogma with the Constitution, safeguarded industrial might against the force of ''mere numbers, whether organized in trade unions or in legislative assemblies.'' In 1893, as if to demonstrate that he had learned the American Bar Association's lesson, Justice Henry Billings Brown, of the United States Supreme Court, interrupted his judicial labors to discuss ''The Distribution of Property.''

> While enthusiasts may picture to us an ideal state of society where neither riches nor poverty shall exist, wherein all shall be comfortably housed and clad, and what are called the useless luxuries of life are unknown, such a utopia is utterly inconsistent with human character as at present constituted; and it is at least doubtful whether upon the whole it would conduce as much to the general happiness and contentment of the community which excites the emulation and stimulates the energies, even if it also awakens the envy, of the less prosperous. Rich men are essential even to the well-being of the poor. . . . One has but to consider for a moment the immediate consequence of the abolition of large private fortunes to appreciate the danger which lurks in any radical disturbance of the present social system.

Momentarily doffing judicial robes in 1893, Justice David J. Brewer addressed the New York Bar Association on ''The Nation's Safeguard.'' Linking Herbert Spencer, the British sociologist, with Plato, taking account of the state of affairs, and of popular and professional protest against the expansion of judicial power, Brewer advocated judicial activism—''Strengthening the judiciary.''

Brewer believed with Judge John F. Dillon that the Supreme Court was ''the only breakwater against the haste and the passions of the people—against the tumultuous ocean of democracy.'' But certain eminent lawyers, including Conrad Reno and Richard C. McMurtrie, warned against judicial intervention. ''Who shall determine questions of public necessity under our form of government,'' Reno inquired, ''the legislature or the courts?'' Taking a restrictive view of judicial power, Reno argued that ''[p]rogress along economic lines must cease if the Courts have the power to seize upon vague clauses in the constitution to perpetuate the economic views of the past, and to fasten them upon the present as matters of constitutional law, of which the courts are the final judge.''

In a similar vein, McMurtrie, eminent Philadelphia lawyer, argued that: ''The mistake is in forgetting that legislature within the limits of its power is the final arbitrator of what is right or proper, and its power extends to determining what are the proper limits of the natural rights of pursuing happiness, exercising liberty and even retaining life, or it ceases to be sovereign, and thus *legislative* power is transferred to the Court.''

The most reasoned response to Justice Brewer's advocacy of judicial activism came from Harvard law professor James Bradley Thayer. In an unstaged debate, excerpted in this chapter, Thayer proclaimed the standard for judicial self-restraint. Speaking in Chicago, a storm center of social conflict, Thayer, unlike Brewer, rose above it. The late Justice Frankfurter rated Thayer's article of 1893 ''the most important single essay in constitutional law . . . , the great guide for judges, and the great guide for understanding by non-judges.''

MEASURING THE IMMEASURABLE

Until 1937, Thayer's sober counsel was to no avail. Armed with the power to decide matters of ''right'' and ''wrong,'' the Court played a role it had earlier spurned. President Arthur Twining Hadley of Yale, presuming to correct the record, wrote in 1908,

> When it is said, as it commonly is, that the fundamental division of powers in the modern State is into legislative, executive and judicial, the student of American institutions may fairly note an exception. The fundamental division of powers in the Constitution of the United States is between voters on the one hand and property owners on the other. The forces of democracy on one side, divided between the executive and the legislature, are set over against the forces of property on the other side, with the judiciary as arbiter between them; the Constitution itself not only forbidding the legislature and executive to trench upon the rights of property, but compelling the judiciary to define and uphold those rights in a manner provided by the Constitution itself. . . . The voter was omnipotent—within a limited area. He could make what laws he pleased, as long as those laws did not trench upon property rights. He could elect what officers he pleased, as long as those officers did not try to do certain duties confided by the Constitution to the property holders. Democracy was complete as far as it went, but constitutionally it was bound to stop short of social democracy.

Hadley summarized the extant situation; what he neglected to state was that the Court's ''proud pre-eminence'' was a recent development, dating from the 1890s.

In 1897, five years before he became a Supreme Court Justice, O. W. Holmes explained the forces and fears which converted judicial review into judicial supremacy.

> When socialism first began to be talked about, the comfortable classes of the community were a good deal frightened. I suspect that this fear has influenced judicial action. . . . I think something similar has led people who no longer hope to control the legislatures to look to the Courts as expounders of the Constitution, and that in some courts, new principles have

been discovered outside the bodies of those instruments, which may be generalized into acceptance of economic doctrines which prevailed about fifty years ago, and a wholesale prohibition of what a tribunal of lawyers does not think about right. [*Collected Legal Papers,* New York: Harcourt, Brace, 1920, p. 184.]

Broadening the context in which the "judicial revolution" (Justice Harlan's expression, dissenting in *Pollock*) occurred, James Bradley Thayer wrote,

The legislatures are growing accustomed to distrust of [democracy] and more and more readily inclined to justify it, and to shed the considerations of constitutional restraints,—certainly as concerning the exact extent of these restrictions,—turning that subject over to the courts; and what is worse, they insensibly fall into the habit of assuming that whatever they could constitutionally do they may do,—as if honor and fair dealing and common honesty were not relevant to their inquiries. The people, all this while, become careless as to whom they send to the legislature; too often they cheerfully vote for men whom they would not trust with an important private affair, and when these unfit persons are found to pass foolish and bad laws, and the courts step in and disregard them, the people are glad that these few wiser gentlemen on the bench are so ready to protect them against their more immediate representatives. . . . It should be remembered that the exercise of it [the power of judicial review], even when unavoidable, is always attended with a serious evil, namely, that the correction of legislative mistake comes from the outside, and that the people thus lose the political experience, and the moral education and stimulus that comes from fighting the question out in the ordinary way and correcting their own errors. The tendency of a common and easy resort to this great function, now lamentably too common, is to dwarf the political capacity of the people, and to deaden its sense of moral responsibility. It is no light thing to do that. [*John Marshall,* Boston: Houghton Mifflin, 1901, pp. 103–107.]

Virtually a superlegislature, the Court proceeded to discharge the delicate responsibility of mediating between public power and private rights. Due process was a poor measuring instrument because it varied according to the user. But its very uncertainty as a test of what the legislatures might do was useful for judges who wanted to be able to say "no," and yet plead inability to say what might be done in the future, or precisely what was wrong with that which had been done in the past. It would seem, then, that Justice Iredell's scorn of natural law as a limitation on state legislative power might be applied equally well to due process. Since this concept provided no "fixed standard," all the Court could properly say in raising it as a constitutional bar was that the legislature had passed an act which, in the opinion of the judges, was inconsistent with abstract principles of justice.

Once the Court abandoned its previous attitude of judicial self-restraint, how could the Justices avoid reading their own predilections into the Constitution? The problem was squarely presented in the famous New York Bake Shop case (*Lochner* v. *New York*). Justice Peckham's measure of "due process" in delivering the Court's opinion contrasts sharply with that of Holmes in dissent. Peckham invoked that most unscientific test, "common understanding"; "to common understanding," said Peckham, "the trade of a baker has never been regarded as an unhealthy one." A few excerpts from his opinion suggest ingrained predilections: "It might be safely affirmed that almost all occupations more or less affect the health. But are we all, on that account, at the mercy of legislative majorities?" "This interference on the part of legislatures of the several states with the ordinary trades and occupations of the people seems to be on the increase." Peckham hastened to add that he did "not believe in the soundness of the views" in support of such legislation.

Justice Peckham's predilections were so outspoken as to arouse curiosity. Responding to an inquiry from Professor Frankfurter, Justice Holmes wrote on May 28, 1922: "You ask me about Peckham. I used to say his major premise was 'God damn it,' meaning thereby that emotional predilection somewhat governed him on social themes."

Holmes denounced any such use of due process; the Constitution had not enacted Herbert Spencer's social statics or any other social or economic theory. Against Peckham's test of "common understanding," Holmes argued for the "natural outcome of a dominant opinion." Although the legislature was limited by prohibitory words in the Constitution, and by whether "a rational and fair man necessarily would admit that the statute proposed would infringe fundamental principles as they have been understood by the traditions of our people and our law," the presumed reasonableness of legislative majorities should be the rule; unreasonableness the exception. But was it not somewhat presumptuous for Holmes to suggest that the five Justices in the majority were less "rational and fair" than himself and the three who agreed with him?

Justice Harlan, also dissenting, came to grips more effectively than Holmes with the central issue in the case: What is the proper scope of judicial power in this area, and how should this power be exercised? Granting, as Peckham did, that "liberty of contract" is subject to such regulations as the state may reasonably prescribe for the common good and well-being of society, what are the conditions under which the judiciary may declare regulations in excess of legislative authority void? "If," Harlan answered, "the end the legislature seeks to accomplish be one to which its power extends, and if the means employed to that end, although not the wisest or best, are yet not plainly and palpably unauthorized by law, then the Court cannot interfere."

The dissenter was not content to let the matter rest there. Peckham indicated that if a real and substantial relation between the health of bakers and the hours they worked could be shown, the New York act might be sustained. Acting on this suggestion, meeting the majority on its own grounds, Justice Harlan proceeded to demonstrate by recourse to nonlegal sources (ignored by both Peckham and Holmes) that "'the labor of the bakers is among the hardest and most laborious imaginable.'" Not only had hours of labor long been "a subject of consideration among civilized people," but "we also judicially know that the number of hours that should constitute a day's labor in particular occupations . . . has been the subject of enactments by Congress and by nearly all the states." Therefore, the New York statute could "not be held to be in conflict with the Fourteenth Amendment, without enlarging the scope of the amendment far beyond its original purpose, and without bringing under the supervision of this court matters which have been supposed to belong exclusively to the legislative departments of the several states when exerting their conceded power to guard the health and safety of their citizens by such regulations as they in their wisdom deem best."

"Let the state alone in the management of its purely domestic affairs," Harlan implored, "so long as it does not appear beyond all question that it has violated the Federal Constitution."

THE BRANDEIS BRIEF

From the Lochner decision Justice Harlan anticipated "consequences of a far-reaching and mischievous character." Reformers shared these forebodings; they realized that, if social legislation were to be saved from judicial obscurantism, a different approach would have to be made. In 1907 the National Consumers League, learning that the Oregon ten-hour law for women was soon to be contested in the Supreme Court, began a search for outstanding counsel to present the case in support of the Oregon law. Joseph H. Choate, one of the most distinguished and successful lawyers of his time, the man who had blocked the "march of Communism" in the Income Tax Case of 1895, refused a retainer, saying that he saw no reason why "a big husky Irish woman should not work more than ten hours in a laundry if she and her employers so desired." The day after Choate's refusal, Louis D. Brandeis of Boston accepted the retainer and began work on his now famous factual brief.

At the turn of the century judges generally disliked hours-of-labor regulation, even for women. In 1895 the Illinois Supreme Court invalidated an eight-hour law for women, and in 1907 the New York Court of Appeals set aside a similar law, saying: "When it is sought under the guise of a labor law, arbitrarily as here to prevent an adult female citizen from working any time of day that suits her, . . . it is time to call a halt." The Lochner decision followed this trend. "In our judgment," Peckham had said, "it is not possible *in fact* to discover the connection between the number of hours a baker must work in a bakery and the healthful quality of the bread made by the workman." Brandeis, accepting this challenge, took a bold and unprecedented step: he furnished the Court with the requisite social and economic statistics to *demonstrate* this factual relationship between working hours and public health and safety. Heretofore no lawyer had had confidence in his ability to make the judges see a "reasonable" relation grounded in facts whether they wanted to see it or not. Brandeis had confidence in both himself and the judges.

Instead of the usual array of legal precedents, Brandeis produced facts and statistics on women's health needs in order to show that the legislation was within the legal principles already enumerated by the Court. Playing down the revolutionary aspects of his brief (*Muller* v. *Oregon,* 208 U.S. 412: 1908), Brandeis made use of established legal rules. In a daring move, he agreed with Peckham's opinion in the Lochner case that "no law limiting the liberty of contract ought to go beyond necessity." He diverged from Peckham in urging that neither logic nor "common understanding" was a sufficient test. Following the line suggested by Justice Harlan, he asserted that "no logic is properly applicable to these laws, except the logic of facts."

Brandeis's brief was revolutionary; it brought to a court disposed to make economic and social judgments—a power, one may well argue, never intended—a method for performing its task more intelligently and more fairly. His Muller brief contains two pages of conventional legal arguments and over one hundred pages of factual data drawn from the reports and studies of governmental bureaus, legislative committees, commissions on hygiene, and factory inspections—all proving that long hours are, *as a matter of fact,* dangerous to women's health, safety, and morals, and that short hours result in general social and economic benefits.

The ten-hour law was upheld; Justice Brewer took the unusual step of commenting on Brandeis's novel technique: "It may not be amiss in the present case, before examining the constitutional question, to notice the course of legislation, as well as expressions of opinion from other than judicial sources. In the brief filed by Mr. Louis D. Brandeis . . . is a very copious collection of all these matters." The remainder of Justice Brewer's comment clearly indicates that he did not consider Brandeis's "facts" conclusive. The Court's opinion in the Muller case, like that of Peckham in *Lochner,* was based essentially on "common knowledge."

> That woman's physical structure and the performance of maternal functions place her at a
> disadvantage in the struggle for subsistence is obvious. . . . Some legislation to protect her

seems necessary to secure a real equality of right. . . . It is impossible to close one's eyes to the fact that she still looks to her brother and depends upon him. A wide-spread and long-continued belief concerning [a fact] is worthy of consideration. We take judicial cognizance of all matters of general knowledge.

A more tolerant judicial attitude soon became apparent. In 1917 the Court upheld (*Bunting* v. *Oregon,* 243 U.S. 426) a ten-hour-day law with an overtime provision for men. "There is a contention made," the Court observed, "that the law, even regarded as regulating hours of service, is not either necessary or useful for the preservation of the health of employees in mills, factories and manufacturing establishments. The record contains no facts to support the contention and against it is the judgment of the legislature and the Supreme Court [of Oregon]." The burden of proof had been shifted from the state to those contesting the legislation.

. . . We need not cast about for reasons for the legislative judgment. We are not required to be sure of the precise reason for its exercise or be convinced of the wisdom of its exercise. . . . It is enough for our decision if the legislation under review was passed in the exercise of an admitted power of government; and that it is not as complete as it might be, not as rigid in its prohibitions as might be, gives, perhaps, evasion too much play, is lighter in its penalties than it might be, is no impeachment of its legality. This may be a blemish, giving opportunity for criticism and difference in characterization, but the constitutional validity of legislation cannot be determined by the degree of exactness of its provisions or remedies. New policies are usually tentative in their beginnings, advance in firmness as they advance in acceptance. They do not at a particular moment of time spring full-perfect in extent or means from the legislative brain. Time may be necessary to fashion them to precedent customs and conditions. . . .

Such "liberalism" was short-lived. Brandeis himself was appointed to the bench in 1916, but his appointment did little more than balance Wilson's earlier elevation of his attorney general, James R. McReynolds, to Associate Justice. Within a few years Warren G. Harding succeeded Wilson and named William Howard Taft Chief Justice and George Sutherland Associate Justice.

STUBBORN THEORY CONQUERS PLIABLE FACTS

Skepticism continued to mark the conservative Justices' attitudes toward facts. In 1921 Justice Holmes cited the "publicly notorious and almost worldwide fact" of housing shortages following World War I to help justify a rent control act for the District of Columbia (*Block* v. *Hirsh,* 256 U.S. 135: 1921). But Justice Sutherland, confronted in 1923 with a mass of sociological data in support of the validity of a District of Columbia act regulating women's wages, brushed all such extralegal matter aside as "interesting, but only mildly persuasive" (*Adkins* v. *Children's Hospital*). "Freedom of contract is the general rule," Sutherland commented in setting aside the wage law, "restraint the exception." The wage and price features of contract seemed to enjoy special constitutional sanctity in the eyes of the conservative majority. But the Constitution itself says nothing of freedom of contract, nor of the general rule or exceptions to it. And one looks in vain to the Constitution itself for Sutherland's principle of opposition to wage-fixing and price-fixing. "Contract is not specifically mentioned in the text that we have to construe," Holmes said in dissent, "and contract is no more exempt from law than other acts.'' Even Chief Justice Taft disapproved of Sutherland's disinterment of the discredited Lochner precedent. Commenting informally on the minimum wage decision, Holmes said: ''It was intended inter alia to dethrone liberty of contract from its ascendancy in the liberty of business.''

In 1923 also the Court narrowed the scope of the concept ''business affected with a public interest.'' Chief Justice Taft, speaking for a unanimous court in *Wolff Packing Co. v. Court of Industrial Relations* (262 U.S. 522: 1923), said that the legislature's declaration of the fact was not conclusive. His contempt for whatever facts Kansas might produce to justify price regulation of butchering and other activities was expressed in the sweeping statement: ''It is manifest . . . that mere declaration by a legislature that a business is affected with a public interest is not conclusive whether its attempted regulation on that ground is justified. The circumstances of its alleged change from the status of a private business and its freedom from regulation into one in which the public have come to have an interest are always a subject of judicial inquiry. . . . It has never been supposed, since the adoption of the Constitution, that the business of the butcher, or the baker, the tailor, the wood chopper, the mining operator or the miner was clothed with such a public interest that the price of his product or his wages could be fixed by state regulation.'' Yet the Justices three years earlier (*Green* v. *Frazier,* 253 U.S. 233) had upheld a series of North Dakota acts setting up a comprehensive scheme of public ownership of utilities and industries against the charge that taxation for these purposes was not a ''public purpose'' and therefore violated due process. Speaking through Justice Day, the Court took the position that the due process clause did not empower the Supreme Court to interfere with a declaration of the ''people, the legislature, and the highest court of the state'' that the purposes were of a ''public nature.''

In later cases, notably *Jay Burns & Co.* v. *Bryan* (264 U.S. 504: 1924), facts proved to be a double-edged sword. In this case, which involved a statute fixing the weight of loaves of bread to prevent fraud, each side confronted the Court with equally competent experts. Before the case was disposed of, the Justices themselves had achieved considerable competence in the science (or art) of bread making. But the Court was as divided as the experts.

Justice Brandeis, dissenting, set in clearer focus the proper role of social and economic statistics in the judicial process.

> Put at its highest, our function is to determine, in the light of all facts which may enrich our knowledge and enlarge our understanding, whether the measure, enacted in the exercise of the police power and of a character inherently unobjectionable, transcends the bounds of reason. That is, whether the provision as applied is so clearly arbitrary or capricious that legislators acting reasonably could not have believed it to be necessary or appropriate for the public welfare.
>
> To decide, as a fact, that the prohibition of excess weights ''is not necessary for the protection of the purchasers against imposition and fraud by short weights''; that it ''is not calculated to effectuate that purpose''; and that it ''subjects bakery and sellers of bread'' to heavy burdens, is, in my opinion, an exercise of the power of a super-legislature—not the performance of the constitutional function of judicial review.

Brandeis considered the Court's function equally circumscribed when confronted with a legislative policy he disapproved. In 1925 the Oklahoma legislature provided that no one could engage in the manufacture of ice for sale without obtaining a license. If on investigation the State Commission found that the community was adequately served, it might turn down the bid of a would-be competitor, and in this way, perhaps, advance monopoly. On its face, this legislation encouraged precisely the trend Brandeis had tried to prevent. "The control here asserted," the Court ruled in a 6-to-2 opinion setting aside the act, "does not protect against monopoly, but tends to foster it." Yet Brandeis, in dissent, voted to uphold the regulation. "Our function," he wrote, "is only to determine the reasonableness of the legislature's belief in the existence of evils and in the effectiveness of the remedy provided." Amid economic emergency "more serious than war," Brandeis observed,

> There must be power in the States and the Nation to remould, through experimentation, our economic practices and institutions to meet changing social and economic needs. . . . This Court has the power to prevent an experiment. We may strike down the statute which embodies it on the ground that, in our opinion, the measure is arbitrary, capricious, or unreasonable. . . . But in the exercise of this high power, we must be ever on guard, lest we erect our prejudices into legal principles. If we would guide by the light of reason, we must let our minds be bold. (*New State Ice Co.* v. *Liebmann*, 285 U.S. 262: 1932.)

Brandeis's factual brief in 1908 had been in response to a particular need. At the turn of the century, the evils of long hours, low wages, and improper working conditions were well known. His brief had challenged Justice Peckham's disregard of the presumptive principle in the Lochner case. For effective remedial action, social facts had to be marshaled on a specific front and given moral voltage. In the decision-making process, however, social science data are only one among the factors requiring consideration. "Government," Brandeis observed, "is not an exact science." The social sciences are "largely uncharted seas."

Social and economic data rarely exhibit the convincing proof usually afforded by scientific demonstrations in a laboratory. One can never be sure that all the facts are assembled; and even a full set of facts rarely points to only one conclusion. Brandeis himself realized this when asked by a friend, "How can you be so sure that a particular course of action is the right one?" Brandeis replied, "When you are 51 percent sure, then go ahead." If government had to await the certainty achieved by the physical scientist, political action would be paralyzed.

Facts do not speak for themselves; they must be interpreted. Judges may select their own facts as preference dictates, and when facts, however voluminous, are confronted with a "stubborn theory," the latter usually wins. "Facts," as Professor Morris R. Cohen has said, "are more pliable than stubborn theories. Facts can be ignored, explained away, or denied. But theories are mental habits which cannot be changed at will."

On the altar of stubborn theory, and in the face of its own settled principle of "presumption of constitutionality," the Court had fashioned the paralyzing rule that "freedom is the rule, regulation is the exception." By narrow margins the Justices singled out the price and wage feature of a contract as its "heart," and therefore entitled to special constitutional immunity. That category of business which, by changed circumstances, became "affected with a public interest" was by 1923 for all practical purposes closed. Various state statutes—a New York act designed to protect the public against theater ticket scalpers (*Tyson* v. *Banton*, 273 U.S. 418: 1927), a New Jersey statute to protect employees from the rascality of private employment agencies (*Ribnik* v. *McBride*, 277 U.S. 350: 1928)—fell under the ban of one or the other of these judge-made principles. Justice

Holmes, supported by Justices Brandeis and Stone, reacted strongly to all such judicial obtuseness.

> We fear to grant power and are unwilling to recognize it when it exists. . . . The police power often is used in a wide sense to cover and . . . apologize for the general power of the Legislature to make a part of the community uncomfortable by a change.
>
> I do not believe in such apologies. I think the proper course is to recognize that a State Legislature can do whatever it sees fit to do unless it is restrained by some express prohibition in the Constitution of the United States or of the State, and that Courts should be careful not to extend such prohibitions beyond their obvious meaning by reading into them conceptions of public policy that the particular Court may happen to entertain. . . . (*Tyson* v. *Banton*, 273 U.S. 418: 1927.)

Dissenting Justices Holmes, Stone, and Brandeis made it quite clear that the only way to make the Court a constructive partner in the governing process was to return to the judicial self-restraint doctrine Chief Justice Morrison R. Waite proclaimed in the Munn opinion of 1877.

THE DECLINE OF SUBSTANTIVE DUE PROCESS

Two cases decided in 1934 indicated a return to that position. In the Blaisdell case (*Home Building and Loan Assn.* v. *Blaisdell*) a Minnesota emergency statute postponing the foreclosure of farm loans was upheld. In *Nebbia* v. *New York* the Court sustained a New York statute fixing minimum and maximum milk prices. Justice Roberts, rejecting the old ''business affected with a public interest'' concept as a limitation on state action, observed: ''There is no closed class or category of business affected with a public interest.'' Concerning the high barrier Justice Sutherland had erected about wages and prices, Roberts observed: ''The due process clause makes no mention of sales or of prices any more than it speaks of business or contract. . . . The thought seems nevertheless to have persisted that there is something peculiarly sacrosanct about the price one may charge for what he makes or sells.''

Though the majority upheld price regulation on principle, Justice McReynolds in dissent implied that the legislation somehow gained support because of the exigency of the times. Sounding the usual stoic note, he said,

> The exigency is of the kind which inevitably arises when one set of men continue to produce more than all others can buy. The distressing result to the producer followed his ill-advised but voluntary effort. . . . If here we have an emergency sufficient to empower the legislature to fix sales prices, then whenever there is too much or too little of an essential thing—whether of milk or grain or pork or coal or shoes or clothes—constitutional provisions may be declared inoperative. . . . If now liberty or property may be struck down because of difficult circumstance, we must expect that hereafter every right must yield to the voice of an impatient majority when stirred by distressful exigency. . . . Certain fundamentals have been set beyond experimentation; the Constitution has released them from control by the state.

"With the wisdom of the policy adopted," Justice Roberts had said, "the Courts are both incompetent and unauthorized to deal." "But plainly," Justice McReynolds retorted, "I think this Court must have regard to the wisdom of the enactment."

Both the Blaisdell and Nebbia cases had been decided by votes of 5 to 4, but in 1936 (*Morehead* v. *New York ex rel. Tipaldo,* 298 U.S. 587) the Justices virtually returned, in the face of these more recent rulings, to the discredited Adkins precedent of 1923. Nevertheless, it was soon evident that the Nebbia decision had marked the beginning of the end of "due process" as a substantive limitation on legislation affecting economic rights. The death blow came in 1937 in *West Coast Hotel Co.* v. *Parrish* (300 U.S. 379), where the Adkins case was expressly overruled. Upholding the minimum wage for women, Chief Justice Hughes asked: "What is freedom? The Constitution does not speak of liberty of contract. It speaks of liberty and prohibits the deprivation of liberty without due process of law. In prohibiting that deprivation, the Constitution does not recognize an absolute and uncontrollable liberty. Liberty in each of its phases has its history and connotation. But the liberty safeguarded is liberty in a social organization which requires the protection of law against the evils which menace the health, safety, morals and welfare of the people." Liberty could be infringed by forces other than government, and infringement by those forces may require the affirmative action of government for its protection. Justice Sutherland's dissent appears in chapter 2 on page 64.

This change in constitutional interpretation had to await a shift in political theory. After 1932 the orientation of political theory became increasingly collectivistic. Thereafter it was recognized that no individual, no group, can profit or suffer without affecting the interests of all. In *Home Building and Loan Association* v. *Blaisdell,* Chief Justice Hughes referred to "the growing appreciation of public needs and of the necessity of finding ground for a rational compromise between individual rights and public welfare." The question was "no longer merely that of one party to a contract as against another, but of the use of reasonable means to safeguard the economic structure upon which the good of all depends."

A more generous attitude toward government regulation of the economy was soon manifest in other fields. "The Constitution does not bind rate-making bodies to the service of any single formula or combination of formulas," the Court concluded in 1942 (*Federal Power Commission* v. *Natural Gas Pipeline Co.,* 315 U.S. 575). "If the total effect of the rate order cannot be said to be unjust and unreasonable, judicial inquiry . . . is at an end." In 1944 the Court abandoned the confused but stringent standards set forth in *Smyth* v. *Ames* (169 U.S. 466: 1898), and agreed to accept administratively determined rates (*Federal Power Commission* v. *Hope Gas Co.,* 320 U.S. 591). Where former due process decisions had balked state and national regulation of social and economic matters, the reconstituted Court of 1941 made it clear that a different judicial philosophy was to prevail.

Justice Stone had expressed the new approach. Speaking for the Court in *United States* v. *Carolene Products Co.* (304 U.S. 144: 1938), he upheld an act of Congress prohibiting the shipment of "filled milk" against due process, as well as against other objections. "The existence of facts supporting the legislative judgment is to be presumed," he said, "for regulatory legislation affecting ordinary commercial transactions is not to be pronounced unconstitutional unless in the light of the facts made known or generally assumed it is of such a character as to preclude the assumption that it rests upon some rational basis within the knowledge and experience of the legislators."

Due process no longer served as a shield against commercial regulations. As to economic affairs, "the laissez-faire principle of non-interference . . . withered." Social advancement could now be sought, as Justice Jackson remarked in 1943, "through closer integration of society and through expanded and strengthened government controls." It is equally immaterial, the Court had ruled in 1939, "that State action may run counter to the economic wisdom either of Adam Smith or of John Maynard Keynes" (*Osborn* v. *Ozlin*, 310 U.S. 53: 1940). "The day is gone," Justice Douglas announced, "when this Court uses the Due Process Clause of the Fourteenth Amendment to strike down State laws . . . because they may be unwise, improvident or out of harmony with a particular school of thought" (*Williamson* v. *Lee Optical of Oklahoma,* 348 U.S. 483: 1955). The Justices have been equally generous in acknowledging state power over land use, as such cases as *Penn Central Transportation Co.* v. *New York City* (438 U.S. 104: 1978) and *Agins* v. *City of Tiburon* (447 U.S. 255: 1980) amply show.

If it would be extreme to say that the Court has completely abandoned its supervisory role in such matters, decisions since 1937 point strongly toward the position advocated by Holmes, Brandeis, and Stone. As Justice Black emphasized in 1963 (*Ferguson* v. *Skrupa*), "The doctrine that prevailed in Lochner, . . . and like cases—that due process authorizes courts to hold laws unconstitutional when they believe the legislature has acted unwisely—has long since been discarded. We have returned to the original constitutional proposition that courts do not substitute their social and economic beliefs for the judgment of legislative bodies, who are elected to pass laws."

SEARCH FOR A ROLE

At the very moment the Court relaxed its supervisory control over social and economic policy, Justice Stone outlined "an affirmative thrust" for due process. In contrast with his expression of judicial tolerance of economic regulation, he suggested that political freedoms enjoy a special status in the Bill of Rights. In reviewing state or national action affecting speech, press, or religion, for instance, should the Court employ assumptions and presumptions that differ from those relied upon in other cases where the question of constitutionality was raised? In other words, does the Court envision a hierarchy of Constitution-protected values, with the First Amendment freedoms at the apex and property rights placed further down?

In the otherwise obscure case of *United States* v. *Carolene Products Co.,* Justice Stone tentatively explored the subject. In the body of his opinion, he wrote,

> Regulatory legislation affecting ordinary commercial transactions is not to be pronounced unconstitutional unless in the light of the facts made known or generally assumed it is of such a character as to preclude the assumption that it rests upon some rational basis within the knowledge and experience of the legislators.

He would not go so far as to say that no economic legislation would ever violate constitutional restraints, but he did suggest strictly confining the Court's role. Attached to this proposition was footnote four:

> There may be narrower scope for operation of the presumption of constitutionality when legislation appears on its face to be within a specific prohibition of the Constitution, such as

those of the first ten amendments, which are deemed equally specific when held to be embraced within the Fourteenth. . . .

It is unnecessary to consider now whether legislation which restricts those political processes which can ordinarily be expected to bring about repeal of undesirable legislation, is to be subjected to more exacting judicial scrutiny under the general prohibitions of the Fourteenth Amendment than are most other types of legislation. . . .

Nor need we enquire whether similar considerations enter into the review of statutes directed at particular religious . . . or national . . . or racial minorities . . . whether prejudice against discrete and insular minorities may be a special condition, which tends seriously to curtail the operation of those political processes ordinarily to be relied upon to protect minorities, and which may call for a correspondingly more searching judicial inquiry. . . .

This footnote of three paragraphs contains a corresponding number of ideas. The first suggests that when legislation, on its face, contravenes the specific constitutional negatives set out in the Bill of Rights, the usual presumption of constitutionality may be curtailed or even waived. The second paragraph indicates that the judiciary has a special responsibility as defender of those liberties prerequisite to the effective functioning of political processes. The Court thus becomes the ultimate guardian against abuses that would poison the primary check on government—the ballot box. It must protect those liberties on which the effectiveness of political action depends. The third paragraph suggests a special role for the Court as protector of minorities and of unpopular groups peculiarly helpless at the polls in the face of discriminatory or repressive assault.

Until 1937, judicial activism in defense of property and contract rights was, as we have seen, the Court's posture. Within a year, without a single change in judicial personnel, "self-restraint" became the order of the day. Only President Roosevelt's Court-packing threat had intervened.

Any inference, however, that the Justices abdicated is in error. The Court had merely relinquished a self-acquired guardianship. Under the self-restraint banner, the Justices would leave protection of property to what Madison called the "primary control," "dependence on the people"—the ballot box. Judicial activism old-style was dead; judicial activism new-style was just around the corner.

Shortly after the judicial backtrack in 1937, Princeton's Professor Edward S. Corwin suggested what lay ahead. The Court, having abandoned its role as defender of property, would thereafter "be free, as it had not been in many years, to support the humane values of free thought, free utterance, and fair play." Corwin predicted that surrender of the Court's protective role for economic privilege would allow the justices "to give voice to the conscience of the country." The Court would have plenty to do if it intervened "on behalf of the helpless and oppressed against local injustice and prejudice rather than intervening in the assertion of out-of-date economic theories as it has done too often since 1890."

The same year that Professor Corwin made these prognostications, Justice Stone, leader of the drive for judicial self-restraint before 1937, pondered, as we have seen, the Court's future course. If the judicial baby was not to be thrown out with the bath water, the Court must find other interests to guard.

Professor Frankfurter, writing Justice Stone on April 27, 1938, praised the Justice's "admirable opinion," adding: "I was especially excited by your note 4." It is "extremely suggestive and opens up new territory."

Stone was quick to disavow pioneering. The doctrine of political restraints went back to Chief Justice Marshall; groundwork for the Carolene Products footnote had been laid by

Brandeis, Holmes, and Hughes, the real pathbreakers being Cardozo and Holmes. Judicial supervision would continue to be an important part of the political system, but new concerns would replace the old.

SELECTED READINGS

ACKERMAN, BRUCE, *Private Property and the Constitution*. New Haven: Yale University Press, 1977.

ANONYMOUS, ''The Security of Private Property,'' 1 *American Law Magazine* 318 (1843).

BIXBY, DAVID M., ''The Roosevelt Court, Democratic Ideology, and Minority Rights: Another look at *United States* v. *Classic*,'' 90 *Yale Law Journal* 741 (1981).

BREWER, DAVID J., ''The Nation's Safeguard,'' 16 *Report of the New York State Bar Association* 37 (1893).

COOLEY, THOMAS M., *Constitutional Limitations*, 1st ed. Boston: Little, Brown, 1868.

——, ''Limits to State Control of Private Business,'' *Princeton Review*, March 1878, p. 233.

CORWIN, EDWARD S., ''The Basic Doctrine of American Constitutional Law,'' 12 *Michigan Law Review* 247 (1914). Reprinted in Mason and Garvey, eds., *American Constitutional History: Essays by Edward S. Corwin*. Gloucester, Mass.: Peter Smith, 1970.

——, ''The Doctrine of Due Process of Law before the Civil War,'' 24 *Harvard Law Review* 366 (1911).

DILLON, JOHN F., ''Address of the President,'' *Report of the Fifteenth Annual Meeting of the American Bar Association* (1892), pp. 167–211.

FAIRMAN, CHARLES, *Mr. Justice Miller and the Supreme Court, 1862–1890*. Cambridge: Harvard University Press, 1939.

FLACK, HORACE, *The Adoption of the Fourteenth Amendment*. Baltimore: Johns Hopkins Press, 1908.

GABIN, SANFORD B., ''Judicial Review, James Bradley Thayer and the 'Reasonable Doubt' Test,'' 3 *Hastings Constitutional Law Quarterly* 96 (1976).

GRAHAM, HOWARD JAY, *Everyman's Constitution*. Madison: State Historical Society of Wisconsin, 1968. A collection of outstanding articles dealing with the origins and proper interpretation of the Fourteenth Amendment.

——, ''Procedure to Substance—Extra-Judicial Role of Due Process,'' 40 *California Law Review* 483 (1952–53).

HADLEY, A. T., ''The Constitutional Position of Property in America,'' 64 *The Independent* 834 (1908).

HAMILTON, WALTON, ''The Path of Due Process of Law,'' in Conyers Read, ed., *The Constitution Reconsidered*. New York: Columbia University Press, 1938.

HOUGH, CHARLES, ''Due Process of Law Today,'' 32 *Harvard Law Review* 218 (1919).

MCCLOSKEY, ROBERT G., "Economic Due Process and the Supreme Court: An Exhumation and Reburial," 1962 *Supreme Court Review* 34.

MCLAUGHLIN, ANDREW C., "The Court, the Corporation, and Conkling," 46 *American Historical Review* 45 (1940).

MCMURTRIE, RICHARD C., "The Jurisdiction to Declare Void Acts of Legislation—When Is It Legitimate and When Mere Usurpation of Sovereignty?" 32 *American Law Register* 1093 (1893).

MAGRATH, C. PETER, *Yazoo—Law and Politics in the New Republic: The Case of Fletcher* v. *Peck*. Providence, Rhode Island: Brown University Press, 1966.

MARSHALL, CHARLES C., "A New Constitutional Amendment," 24 *American Law Review* 908 (1890)

MASON, ALPHEUS T., "The Conservative World of Mr. Justice Sutherland," 32 *American Political Science Review* 443 (1938).

——, *Brandeis, Lawyer and Judge in the Modern State*, Chapter VI, "The Brandeis Brief." Princeton: Princeton University Press, 1933.

——, "The Case of the Overworked Laundress," in John Garraty, ed., *Quarrels That Have Shaped the Constitution*. New York: Harper and Row, 1964.

——, "Judicial Activism: Old and New," *55 Virginia Law Review* 385 (1969).

MORIN, RICHARD W., "Will to Resist: The Dartmouth College Case," *Dartmouth College Alumni Magazine*, April 1969.

PAUL, ARNOLD M., *Conservative Crisis and Rule of Law: Attitudes of Bar and Bench, 1887–1895*. Ithaca: Cornell University Press, 1960.

SIEGAN, BERNARD H., *Economic Liberties and the Constitution*. Chicago: University of Chicago Press, 1981.

STEPHENSON, D. GRIER, JR., "The Supreme Court and Constitutional Change: *Lochner* v. *New York* Revisited," 21 *Villanova Law Review* 217 (1976).

THAYER, JAMES BRADLEY, "The Origin and Scope of the American Doctrine of Constitutional Law," 7 *Harvard Law Review* 129 (1893).

TRIBE, LAURENCE, "Toward a Model of Roles in the Due Process of Life and Law," 87 *Harvard Law Review* 1 (1973).

TWISS, BENJAMIN R., *Lawyers and the Constitution*. Princeton: Princeton University Press, 1942.

WRIGHT, BENJAMIN F., *The Contract Clause of the Constitution*. Cambridge: Harvard University Press, 1938.

Calder v. Bull
3 Dall. (3 U.S.) 386, 1 L.Ed. 648 (1798)

The legislature of Connecticut passed a law granting a new hearing to Bull and his wife, after their right to appeal a probate court decree had expired. At the second hearing, Bull was successful, and Calder, the other claimant, after appealing unsuccessfully to the highest Connecticut court, brought his case to the Supreme Court on a writ of error. The opinions of the Justices are important, not only for their definition of ex post facto laws, but for the views expressed about natural law and judicial review.

CHASE, JUSTICE— . . .

The counsel for the plaintiffs in error contend, that the . . . law of the legislature of Connecticut, granting a new hearing, in the above case, is an *ex post facto* law, prohibited by the constitution of the United States; that any law of the federal government, or of any of the state governments, contrary to the constitution of the United States, is void; and that this court possesses the power to declare such law void.

It appears to me a self-evident proposition, that the several state legislatures retain all the powers of legislation, delegated to them by the state constitutions; which are not expressly taken away by the constitution of the United States. The establishing courts of justice, the appointment of judges, and the making regulations for the administration of justice within each state, according to its laws, on all subjects not intrusted to the federal government, appears to me to be the peculiar and exclusive province and duty of the state legislatures. All the powers delegated by the people of the United States to the federal government are defined, and no *constructive* powers can be exercised by it, and all the powers that remain in the state governments are indefinite. . . . The sole inquiry is, whether this resolution or law of Connecticut . . . is an *ex post facto* law, within the prohibition of the federal constitution.

Whether the legislature of any of the states can revise and correct by law, a decision of any of its courts of justice, although not prohibited by the constitution of the state, is a question of very great importance, and not necessary now to be determined; because the resolution or law in question does not go so far. I cannot subscribe to the omnipotence of a state legislature, or that it is absolute and without control; although its authority should not be expressly restrained by the constitution, or fundamental law of the state. The people of the United States erected their constitutions or forms of government, to establish justice, to promote the general welfare, to secure the blessings of liberty, and to protect their persons and property from violence. The purposes for which men enter into society will determine the nature and terms of the social compact; and as they are the foundation of the legislative power, they will decide what are the proper objects of it. The nature and ends of legislative power will limit the exercise of it. This fundamental principle flows from the very nature of our free republican governments, that no man should be compelled to do what the laws do not require, nor to refrain from acts which the laws permit. There are acts which the federal or state legislature cannot do, without exceeding their authority. There are certain vital principles in our free republican governments which will determine and overrule an apparent and flagrant abuse of legislative power; as to authorize manifest injustice by positive law; or to take away that security for personal liberty, or private property, for the protection whereof the government was established. An act of the legislature (for I cannot call it a law), contrary to the great first principles of the social compact, cannot be considered a rightful exercise of legislative authority. The obligation of a law in governments established on express compact, and on republican principles, must be determined by the nature of the power on which it is founded.

A few instances will suffice to explain what I mean. A law that punished a citizen for an innocent action, or, in other words, for an act which, when done, was in violation of no existing law; a law that destroys, or impairs, the lawful private contracts of citizens; a law that makes a man a judge in his own cause; or a law that takes property from A, and gives it to B. It is against all reason and justice for a people to intrust a legislature with such powers; and, therefore, it cannot be presumed that they have done it. The genius, the nature, and the spirit of our state governments amount to a prohibition of such acts of legislation; and the general principles of law and reason forbid them. The legislature may enjoin, permit, forbid and punish; they may declare new crimes, and establish rules of conduct for all its citizens in future cases; they may command what is right, and prohibit what is wrong; but they cannot change innocence into guilt, or punish innocence as a crime; or violate the right of an antecedent lawful private contract; or the right of private property. To maintain that our federal or state legislature possesses such powers, if they had not been expressly restrained, would, in my opinion, be a political heresy altogether inadmissible in our free republican governments. . . .

The Constitution of the United States, Art. 1, § 9, prohibits the legislature of the United States from passing an *ex post facto* law; and in section 10 lays several restrictions on the authority of the legislatures of the several states; and among them, "that no state shall pass any *ex post facto* law." . . .

I will state what laws I consider *ex post facto* laws, within the words and the intent of the prohibition. 1st. Every law that makes an action done before the passing of the law, and which was innocent when done, criminal; and punishes such action. 2d. Every law that aggravates a crime, or makes it greater than it was, when committed. 3d. Every law that changes the punishment, and inflicts a greater punishment,

than the law annexed to the crime, when committed. 4th. Every law that alters the legal rules of evidence, and receives less, or different testimony, than the law required at the time of the commission of the offense, in order to convict the offender. All these, and similar laws, are manifestly unjust and oppressive. In my opinion, the true distinction is between *ex post facto* laws, and retrospective laws. Every *ex post facto* law must necessarily be retrospective; but every retrospective law is not an *ex post facto* law; the former only are prohibited. Every law that takes away or impairs rights vested, agreeably to existing laws, is retrospective, and is generally unjust, and may be oppressive; and it is a good general rule, that a law should have no retrospect; but there are cases in which laws may justly, and for the benefit of the community, and also of individuals, relate to a time antecedent to their commencement; as statutes of oblivion or of pardon. They are certainly retrospective, and literally both concerning and after the facts committed. But I do not consider any law *ex post facto,* within the prohibition, that mollifies the rigor of the criminal law; but only those that create or aggravate the crime; or increase the punishment, or change the rules of evidence, for the purpose of conviction. Every law that is to have an operation before the making thereof, as to commence at an antecedent time; or to save time from the statute of limitations; or to excuse acts which were unlawful, and before committed, and the like, is retrospective. But such laws may be proper or necessary, as the case may be. There is a great and apparent difference between making an unlawful act lawful; and the making an innocent action criminal, and punishing it as a crime. The expressions "*ex post facto* laws" are technical, they had been in use long before the revolution, and had acquired an appropriate meaning by legislators, lawyers and authors. The celebrated and judicious Sir William Blackstone, in his Commentaries, considers an *ex post facto* law precisely in the same light I have done. His opinion is confirmed by his successor, Mr. Wooddeson; and by the author of *The Federalist,* who I esteem superior to both, for his extensive and accurate knowledge of the true principles of government. . . . If the term *ex post facto* law is to be construed to include and to prohibit the enacting any law after the fact, it will greatly restrict the power of the federal and state legislatures; and the consequences of such a construction may not be foreseen. . . .

It is not to be presumed that the federal or state legislatures will pass laws to deprive citizens of rights vested in them by existing laws; unless for the benefit of the whole community; and on making full satisfaction. The restraint against making any *ex post facto* laws was not considered, by the framers of the constitution, as extending to prohibit the depriving a citizen even of a vested right to property; or the provision, ''that private property should not be taken for public use, without just compensation,'' was unnecessary.

It seems to me that the right of property, in its origin, could only arise from compact express or implied, and I think it the better opinion, that the right, as well as the mode or manner of acquiring property, and of alienating or transferring, inheriting or transmitting it, is conferred by society, is regulated by civil institution, and is always subject to the rules prescribed by positive law. When I say that a right is vested in a citizen, I mean, that he has the power to do certain actions, or to possess certain things, according to the law of the land. . . .

I am of opinion that the decree of the supreme court of errors of Connecticut be affirmed, with costs.

IREDELL, JUSTICE.— . . .

If . . . a government, composed of legislative, executive and judicial departments, were established, by a constitution which imposed no limits on the legislative power, the consequence would inevitably be, that whatever the legislative power chose to enact, would be lawfully enacted, and the judicial power could never interpose to pronounce it void. It is true, that some speculative jurists have held, that a legislative act against natural justice must, in itself, be void; but I cannot think that, under such a government any court of justice would

possess a power to declare it so. Sir William Blackstone, having put the strong case of an act of parliament, which authorizes a man to try his own cause, explicitly adds, that even in that case, ''there is no court that has power to defeat the intent of the legislature, when couched in such evident and express words, as leave no doubt whether it was the intent of the legislature or no.'' 1 Bl. Com. 91.

In order, therefore, to guard against so great an evil, it has been the policy of all the American states, which have, individually, framed their state constitutions, since the revolution, and of the people of the United States, when they framed the federal constitution, to define with precision the objects of legislative power, and to restrain its exercise within marked and settled boundaries. If any act of congress, or of the legislature of a state, violates those constitutional provisions, it is unquestionably void; though, I admit, that as the authority to declare it void is of a delicate and awful nature, the court will never resort to that authority, but in a clear and urgent case. If, on the other hand, the legislature of the Union, or the legislature of any member of the Union, shall pass a law, within the general scope of their constitutional power, the court cannot pronounce it to be void, merely because it is, in their judgment, contrary to the principles of natural justice. The ideas of natural justice are regulated by no fixed standard: the ablest and the purest men have differed upon the subject; and all that the court could properly say, in such an event, would be, that the legislature (possessed of an equal right of opinion) had passed an act which, in the opinion of the judges, was inconsistent with the abstract principles of natural justice. There are then but two lights, in which the subject can be viewed: 1st. If the legislature pursue the authority delegated to them, their acts are valid. 2d. If they transgress the boundaries of that authority, their acts are invalid. In the former case, they exercise the discretion vested in them by the people, to whom alone they are responsible for the faithful discharge of their trust: but in the latter case, they violate a fundamental law, which must be our guide, whenever we are called upon as judges, to determine the validity of a legislative act.

Still, however, in the present instance, the act or resolution of the legislature of Connecticut, cannot be regarded as an *ex post facto* law; for the true construction of the prohibition extends to criminal, not to civil issues. . . .

The policy, the reason and humanity of the prohibition, do not . . . extend to civil cases, to cases that merely affect the private property of citizens. Some of the most necessary and important acts of legislation are, on the contrary, founded upon the principle, that private rights must yield to public exigencies. Highways are run through private grounds; fortifications, lighthouses, and other public edifices, are necessarily sometimes built upon the soil owned by individuals. In such, and similar cases, if the owners should refuse voluntarily to accommodate the public, they must be constrained, so far as the public necessities require; and justice is done, by allowing them a reasonable equivalent. Without the possession of this power, the operations of government would often be obstructed, and society itself would be endangered. It is not sufficient to urge, that the power may be abused, for such is the nature of all power—such is the tendency of every human institution: and, it might as fairly be said, that the power of taxation, which is only circumscribed by the discretion of the body in which it is vested, ought not to be granted, because the legislature, disregarding its true objects, might, for visionary and useless projects, impose a tax to the amount of nineteen shillings in the pound. We must be content to limit power, where we can, and where we cannot, consistently with its use, we must be content to repose a salutary confidence. It is our consolation, that there never existed a government, in ancient or modern times, more free from danger in this respect, than the governments of America. . . .

Judgment affirmed.

Dartmouth College v. Woodward
4 Wheat. (17 U.S.) 518, 4 L.Ed. 629 (1819)

The famous Dartmouth College case involved rival claimants to the records, the seal, and other objects signifying control of the college. The trustees of the college, basing their claim on a charter granted in 1769 by King George III, sought to regain control from a group whose authority had been created by three legislative acts of 1816 that amended the original charter by increasing the number of trustees and vesting the future power of appointment of trustees in the governor and his council. The New Hampshire superior court of judicature upheld Woodward and the new control group.

The opinion of the court was delivered by MARSHALL, CH. J.— . . .

It can require no argument to prove, that the circumstances of this case constitute a contract. An application is made to the crown for a charter to incorporate a religious and literary institution. In the application, it is stated, that large contributions have been made for the object, which will be conferred on the corporation, as soon as it shall be created. The charter is granted, and on its faith the property is conveyed. Surely, in this transaction every ingredient of a complete and legitimate contract is to be found. The points for consideration are, 1. Is this contract protected by the constitution of the United States? 2. Is it impaired by the acts under which the defendant holds? . . .

The parties in this case differ less on general principles, less on the true construction of the constitution in the abstract, than on the application of those principles to this case, and on the true construction of the charter of 1769. This is the point on which the cause essentially depends. If the act of incorporation be a grant of political power, if it creates a civil institution, to be employed in the administration of the government, or if the funds of the college be public property, or if the state of New Hampshire, as a government, be alone interested in its transactions, the subject is one in which the legislature of the state may act according to its judgment, unrestrained by any limitation of its power imposed by the constitution of the United States.

But if this be a private eleemosynary institution, endowed with a capacity to take property, for objects unconnected with government, whose funds are bestowed by individuals, on the faith of the charter; if the donors have stipulated for the future disposition and management of those funds, in the manner prescribed by themselves; there may be more difficulty in the case, although neither the persons who have made these stipulations, nor those for whose benefit they were made, should be parties to the cause. Those who are no longer interested in the property, may yet retain such an interest in the preservation of their own arrangements, as to have a right to insist, that those arrangements shall be held sacred. Or, if they have themselves disappeared, it becomes a subject of serious and anxious inquiry, whether those whom they have legally empowered to represent them forever, may not assert all the rights which they possessed while in being: whether, if they be without personal representatives, who may feel injured by a violation of the compact, the trustees be not so completely their representatives, in the eye of the law, as to stand in their

place, not only as respects the government of the college, but also as respects the maintenance of the college charter. It becomes then the duty of the court, most seriously to examine this charter, and to ascertain its true character. . . .

A corporation is an artificial being, invisible, intangible, and existing only in contemplation of law. Being the mere creature of law, it possesses only those properties which the charter of its creation confers upon it, either expressly or as incidental to its very existence. These are such as are supposed best calculated to effect the object for which it was created. Among the most important are immortality, and, if the expression may be allowed, individuality; properties by which a perpetual succession of many persons are considered as the same, and may act as a single individual. . . . It is no more a state instrument than a natural person exercising the same powers would be. If, then, a natural person, employed by individuals in the education of youth, or for the government of a seminary in which youth is educated, would not become a public officer, or be considered as a member of the civil government, how is it that this artificial being, created by law for the purpose of being employed by the same individuals for the same purposes, should become a part of the civil government of the country? Is it because its existence, its capacities, its powers, are given by law? Because the government has given it the power to take and to hold property in a particular form and for particular purposes, has the government a consequent right substantially to change that form, or to vary the purposes to which the property is to be applied? This principle has never been asserted or recognized, and is supported by no authority. Can it derive aid from reason?

The objects for which a corporation is created are universally such as the government wishes to promote. . . . The benefit to the public is considered as an ample compensation for the faculty it confers, and the corporation is created. If the advantages to the public constitute a full compensation for the faculty it gives, there can be no reason for exacting a further compensation, by claiming a right to exercise over this artificial being a power which changes its nature, and touches the fund for the security and application of which it was created. There can be no reason for implying in a charter, given for a valuable consideration, a power which is not only not expressed, but is in direct contradiction to its express stipulations.

From the fact, then, that a charter of incorporation has been granted, nothing can be inferred which changes the character of the institution, or transfers to the government any new power over it. The character of civil institutions does not grow out of their incorporation, but out of the manner in which they are formed, and the objects for which they are created. The right to change them is not founded on their being incorporated, but on their being the instruments of government, created for its purpose. The same institutions, created for the same objects, though not incorporated, would be public institutions, and, of course, be controllable by the legislature. The incorporating act neither gives nor prevents this control. Neither, in reason, can the incorporating act change the character of a private eleemosynary institution. . . .

From this review of the charter, it appears that Dartmouth College is an eleemosynary institution, incorporated for the purpose of perpetuating the application of the bounty of the donors to the specified objects of the bounty; that its trustees or governors were originally named by the founder, and invested with the power of perpetuating themselves; that they are not public officers, nor is it a civil institution, participating in the administration of government; but a charity school, or a seminary of education, incorporated for the preservation of its property, and the perpetual application of that property to the objects of its creation.

Yet a question remains to be considered of more real difficulty, on which more doubt has been entertained than on all that have been discussed. The founders of the college, at least those whose contributions were in money, have parted with the property bestowed upon it, and their representatives have no interest in that property. The donors of land are equally with-

out interest so long as the corporation shall exist. Could they be found, they are unaffected by any alteration in its constitution, and probably regardless of its form or even of its existence. The students are fluctuating, and no individual among our youth has a vested interest in the institution which can be asserted in a court of justice. Neither the founders of the college, nor the youth for whose benefit it was founded, complain of the alteration made in its charter, or think themselves injured by it. The trustees alone complain, and the trustees have no beneficial interest to be protected. Can this be such a contract as the constitution intended to withdraw from the power of state legislation? Contracts, the parties to which have a vested beneficial interest, and those only, it has been said, are the objects about which the constitution is solicitous, and to which its protection is extended.

The court has bestowed on this argument the most deliberate consideration, and the result will be stated. Dr. Wheelock, acting for himself and for those who, at his solicitation, had made contributions to his school, applied for this charter, as the instrument which should enable him and them to perpetuate their beneficent intention. It was granted. An artificial, immortal being was created by the crown, capable of receiving and distributing forever, according to the will of the donors, the donations which should be made to it. On this being, the contributions which had been collected were immediately bestowed. These gifts were made, not indeed to make a profit for the donors or their posterity, but for something, in their opinion, of inestimable value; for something which they deemed a full equivalent for the money with which it was purchased. The consideration for which they stipulated, is the perpetual application of the fund to its objects, in the mode prescribed by themselves. Their descendants may take no interest in the preservation of this consideration. But in this respect their descendants are not their representatives. They are represented by the corporation. The corporation is the assignee of their rights, stands in their place, and distributes their bounty, as they would themselves have distributed it had they been immortal. So with respect to the students who are to derive learning from this source. The corporation is a trustee for them also. Their potential rights, which, taken distributively, are imperceptible, amount collectively to a most important interest. These are, in the aggregate, to be exercised, asserted, and protected by the corporation. They were as completely out of the donors, at the instant of their being vested in the corporation, and as incapable of being asserted by the students, as at present. . . .

This is plainly a contract to which the donors, the trustees, and the crown (to whose rights and obligations New Hampshire succeeds) were the original parties. It is a contract made on a valuable consideration. It is a contract for the security and disposition of property. It is a contract on the faith of which real and personal estate has been conveyed to the corporation. It is then a contract within the letter of the constitution, and within its spirit also, unless the fact that the property is invested by the donors in trustees, for the promotion of religion and education, for the benefit of persons who are perpetually changing, though the objects remain the same, shall create a particular exception, taking this case out of the prohibition contained in the constitution. . . .

It is more than possible that the preservation of rights of this description was not particularly in the view of the framers of the constitution, when the clause under consideration was introduced into that instrument. It is probable that interferences of more frequent recurrence, to which the temptation was stronger, and of which the mischief was more extensive, constituted the great motive for imposing this restriction on the state legislatures. But although a particular and a rare case may not, in itself, be of sufficient magnitude to induce a rule, yet it must be governed by the rule, when established, unless some plain and strong reason for excluding it can be given. It is not enough to say, that this particular case was not in the mind of the Convention when the article was framed, nor of the American people when it was adopted. It is necessary to go further, and to say

that, had this particular case been suggested, the language would have been so varied as to exclude it, or it would have been made a special exception. The case being within the words of the rule, must be within its operation likewise, unless there be something in the literal construction so obviously absurd or mischievous, or repugnant to the general spirit of the instrument, as to justify those who expound the constitution in making it an exception.

On what safe and intelligible ground can this exception stand? There is no expression in the constitution, no sentiment delivered by its contemporaneous expounders, which would justify us in making it. In the absence of all authority of this kind, is there, in the nature and reason of the case itself, that which would sustain a construction of the constitution not warranted by its words? Are contracts of this description of a character to excite so little interest that we must exclude them from the provisions of the constitution, as being unworthy of the attention of those who framed the instrument? Or does public policy so imperiously demand their remaining exposed to legislative alteration as to compel us, or rather permit us to say, that these words, which were introduced to give stability to contracts, and which in their plain import comprehend this contract, must yet be so construed as to exclude it? . . .

If the insignificance of the object does not require that we should exclude contracts respecting it from the protection of the constitution, neither, as we conceive, is the policy of leaving them subject to legislative alteration so apparent, as to require a forced construction of that instrument, in order to effect it. These eleemosynary institutions do not fill the place, which would otherwise be occupied by government, but that which would otherwise remain vacant. They are complete acquisitions to literature. They are donations to education; donations, which any government must be disposed rather to encourage than to discountenance. It requires no very critical examination of the human mind, to enable us to determine, that one great inducement to these gifts is the conviction felt by the giver, that the disposition he makes of them is immutable. It is probable, that no man was, and that no man ever will be, the founder of a college, believing at the time, that an act of incorporation constitutes no security for the institution; believing, that it is immediately to be deemed a public institution, whose funds are to be governed and applied, not by the will of the donor, but by the will of the legislature. All such gifts are made in the pleasing, perhaps delusive hope, that the charity will flow forever in the channel which the givers have marked out for it. If every man finds in his own bosom strong evidence of the universality of this sentiment, there can be but little reason to imagine, that the framers of our constitution were strangers to it, and that, feeling the necessity and policy of giving permanence and security to contracts, of withdrawing them from the influence of legislative bodies, whose fluctuating policy, and repeated interferences, produced the most perplexing and injurious embarrassments, they still deemed it necessary to leave these contracts subject to those interferences. The motives for such an exception must be very powerful, to justify the construction which makes it. . . .

2. We next proceed to the inquiry, whether its obligation has been impaired by those acts of the legislature of New Hampshire, to which the special verdict refers? . . .

It has been already stated, that the act "to amend the charter, and enlarge and improve the corporation of Dartmouth College," increases the number of trustees of twenty-one, gives the appointment of the additional members to the executive of the state, and creates a board of overseers, to consist of twenty-five persons, of whom twenty-one are also appointed by the executive of New Hampshire, who have power to inspect and control the most important acts of the trustees.

On the effect of this law [of 1816], two opinions cannot be entertained. Between acting directly, and acting through the agency of trustees and overseers, no essential difference is perceived. The whole power of governing the college is transferred from trustees appointed according to the will of the founder, expressed in the charter, to the executive of New Hampshire. The management and application of the funds of this eleemosynary institution, which are placed by the donors in the hands of trustees named in the charter, and empowered to perpetuate themselves, are placed by this act under the control of the government of the state. The will of the state is substituted for the will of the donors, in every essential operation of the college. This is not an immaterial change. The founders of the college contracted not merely for the perpetual application of the funds which they gave to the object for which those funds were given; they contracted, also, to secure that application by the constitution of the corporation. They contracted for a system which should, as far as human foresight can provide, retain forever the government of the literary institution they had formed, in the hands of persons approved by themselves. This system is totally changed. The charter of 1769 exists no longer. It is reorganized; and reorganized in such a manner as to convert a literary institution, moulded according to the will of its founders, and placed under the control of private literary men, into a machine entirely subservient to the will of government. This may be for the advantage of this college in particular, and may be for the advantage of literature in general; but it is not according to the will of the donors, and is subversive of that contract on the faith of which their property was given. . . .

It results from this opinion, that the acts of the legislature of New Hampshire, which are stated in the special verdict found in this cause, are repugnant to the constitution of the United States; and that the judgment on this special verdict ought to have been for the plaintiffs. The judgment of the State Court must, therefore, be reversed.

[JUSTICES WASHINGTON and STORY delivered separate opinions with the same holding. JUSTICE DUVALL dissented.]

Charles River Bridge v. Warren Bridge
11 Pet. (36 U.S.) 420, 9 L.Ed. 773 (1837)

In 1785 the Massachusetts legislature granted to the Charles River Bridge Company the right to construct a bridge between Charlestown and Boston, with the power to collect tolls for 40 years (later extended to 70 years). This franchise replaced an exclusive ferry right formerly possessed by Harvard College, but which the college yielded in return for annual payments during the life of the bridge charter. In 1828, the legislature chartered the Warren Bridge Company, with the power to collect tolls on a bridge which it constructed sufficiently close to the Charles River Bridge to deprive its owners of their anticipated tolls. When a state court rejected the plaintiff company's bill for an injunction and other relief, review was sought on a writ of error. A very short excerpt from the 65-page dissenting opinion of Justice Story is given below, following Taney's opinion for the Court.

MR. CHIEF JUSTICE TANEY delivered the opinion of the court. . . .

Upon what ground can the plaintiffs in error contend that the ferry rights of the college have been transferred to the proprietors of the bridge? If they have been thus transferred, it must be by some mode of transfer known to the law; and the evidence relied on to prove it, can be pointed out in the record. How was it transferred? It is not suggested that there ever was, in point of fact, a deed of conveyance executed by the college to the bridge company. Is there any evidence in the record from which such a conveyance may, upon legal principle, be presumed? The testimony before the court, so far from laying the foundation for such a presumption, repels it in the most positive terms. The petition to the legislature, in 1785, on which the charter was granted, does not suggest an assignment, nor any agreement or consent on the part of the college; and the petitioners do not appear to have regarded the wishes of that institution, as by any means necessary to ensure their success. They place their application entirely on considerations of public interest and public convenience, and the superior advantages of a communication across Charles River by a bridge, instead of a ferry. . . .

This brings us to the act of the legislature of Massachusetts, of 1785, by which the plaintiffs were incorporated by the name of "The Proprietors of the Charles River Bridge"; and it is here, and in the law of 1792, prolonging their charter, that we must look for the extent and nature of the franchise conferred upon the plaintiffs.

Much has been said in the argument of the principles of construction by which this law is to be expounded, and what undertakings, on the part of the state, may be implied. The court thinks there can be no serious difficulty on that head. It is the grant of certain franchises by the public to a private corporation, and in a matter where the public interest is concerned. The rule of construction in such cases is well settled, both in England and by the decisions of our own tribunals. In 2 Barn. & Adol., 793, in the case of the *Proprietors of the Stourbridge Canal* v. *Wheeley and others,* the court says, "The canal having been made under an act of parliament, the rights of the plaintiffs are derived entirely from that act. This, like many other cases, is a bargain between a company of adventurers and the public, the terms of which are expressed in the statute; and the rule of construction, in all such cases, is now fully established to be this; that any ambiguity in the terms of the contract must operate against the adventurers, and in favor of the public, and the plaintiffs can claim nothing that is not clearly given them by the act.'' And the doctrine thus laid down is abundantly sustained by the authorities referred to in this decision.

. . . The argument in favour of the proprietors of the Charles River bridge, is . . . that the power claimed by the state, if it exists, may be so used as to destroy the value of the franchise they have granted to the corporation. . . . The existence of the power does not, and cannot depend upon the circumstance of its having been exercised or not. . . .

. . . The object and end of all government is to promote the happiness and prosperity of the community by which it is established, and it can never be assumed, that the government intended to diminish its powers of accomplishing the end for which it was created. And in a country like ours, free, active, and enterprising, continually advancing in numbers and wealth, new channels of communication are daily found necessary, both for travel and trade; and are essential to the comfort, convenience, and prosperity of the people. A state ought never to be presumed to surrender this power, because, like the taxing power, the whole community has an interest in preserving it undiminished. And when a corporation alleges, that a state has surrendered, for seventy years, its power of improvement and public accommodation, in a great and important line of travel, along which a vast number of its citizens must daily pass, the community has a right to insist, in the language of this court above quoted, ''that its abandonment ought not to be presumed in a case in which the deliberate purpose of the state to abandon it does not appear.'' The continued existence of a government would be of no great value, if by implications and presumptions it was disarmed of the powers necessary to accomplish the ends of its creation; and the functions it was designed to perform, transferred to the hands of privileged corporations. The rule of construction announced by the court was not confined to the taxing power; nor is it so limited in the opinion delivered. On the contrary, it was distinctly placed on the ground that the interests of the community were concerned in

preserving, undiminished, the power then in question; and whenever any power of the state is said to be surrendered and diminished, whether it be the taxing power or any other affecting the public interest, the same principle applies, and the rule of construction must be the same. No one will question that the interests of the great body of the people of the state would, in this instance, be affected by the surrender of this great line of travel to a single corporation, with the right to exact toll, and exclude competition for seventy years. While the rights of private property are sacredly guarded, we must not forget that the community also has rights, and that the happiness and well-being of every citizen depends on their faithful preservation.

Adopting the rule of construction above stated as the settled one, we proceed to apply it to the charter of 1785, to the proprietors of the Charles River bridge. This act of incorporation is in the usual form, and the privileges such as are commonly given to corporations of that kind. It confers on them the ordinary faculties of a corporation, for the purpose of building the bridge; and establishes certain rates of toll, which the company is authorized to take: this is the whole grant. There is no exclusive privilege given to them over the water of Charles River, above or below their bridge; no right to erect another bridge themselves, nor to prevent other persons from erecting one, no engagement from the state, that another shall not be erected; and no undertaking not to sanction competition, nor to make improvements that may diminish the amount of its income. Upon all these subjects, the charter is silent; and nothing is said in it about a line of travel, so much insisted on in the argument, in which they are to have exclusive privileges. . . .

. . . In short, all the franchises and rights of property, enumerated in the charter, and there mentioned to have been granted to it, remain unimpaired. But its income is destroyed by the Warren bridge; which, being free, draws off the passengers and property which would have gone over it, and renders their franchise of no value. This is the gist of the complaint. For it is not pretended, that the erection of the Warren bridge would have done them any injury, or in any degree affected their right of property, if it had not diminished the amount of their tolls. In order, then, to entitle themselves to relief, it is necessary to show, that the legislature contracted not to do the act of which they complain; and that they impaired, or in other words, violated, that contract by the erection of the Warren bridge.

The inquiry, then, is, does the charter contain such a contract on the part of the state? Is there any such stipulation to be found in that instrument? It must be admitted on all hands, that there is none; no words that even relate to another bridge, or to the diminution of their tolls, or to the line of travel. If a contract on that subject can be gathered from the charter, it must be by implication; and cannot be found in the words used. Can such an agreement be implied? The rule of construction before stated is an answer to the question; in charters of this description, no rights are taken from the public, or given to the corporation, beyond those which the words of the charter, by their natural and proper construction, purport to convey. There are no words which import such a contract as the plaintiffs in error contend for, and none can be implied. . . .

Indeed, the practice and usage of almost every state in the Union, old enough to have commenced the work of internal improvement, is opposed to the doctrine contended for on the part of the plaintiffs in error. Turnpike roads have been made in succession, on the same line of travel; the later ones interfering materially with the profits of the first. These corporations have, in some instances, been utterly ruined by the introduction of newer and better modes of transportation and traveling. In some cases, railroads have rendered the turnpike roads on the same line of travel so entirely useless, that the franchise of the turnpike corporation is not worth preserving. Yet in none of these cases have the corporations supposed that their privileges were invaded, or any contract violated on the part of the state. Amid the multitude of cases which have occurred, and have been daily occurring for the last forty or fifty years, this is the first instance in which such an implied contract has been contended for, and this court called upon to infer it, from an ordinary act of incorporation, containing nothing more than the usual stipulations and provisions to be found in every such law. The absence of any such controversy, when there must have been so many occasions to give rise to it, proves that neither states, nor individuals, nor corporations, ever imagined that such a contract could be implied from such charters. It shows, that the men who voted for these laws never imagined that they were forming such a contract; and if we maintain that they have made it, we must create it by a legal fiction, in opposition to the truth of the fact, and the obvious intention of the party. We cannot deal thus with the rights reserved to the states; and by legal intendments and mere technical reasoning, take away from them any portion of that power over their own internal police and improvement, which is so necessary to their well-being and prosperity.

And what would be the fruits of this doctrine of implied contracts, on the part of the states, and of property in a line of travel by a corporation, if it should now be sanctioned by this court? To what results would it lead us? If it is to be found in the charter to this bridge, the same process of reasoning must discover it, in the various acts which have been passed, within the last forty years, for turnpike companies. And what is to be the extent of the privileges of exclusion on the different sides of the road? The counsel who have so ably argued this case, have not attempted to define it by any certain boundaries. How far must the new improvement be distant from the old one? How near may you approach, without invading its rights in the privileged line? If this court should establish the principles now contended for, what is to become of the numerous railroads established on the same line of travel with turnpike companies; and which have rendered the franchise of the turnpike corporations of no value? Let it once be understood, that such charters carry with them these implied contracts, and give this unknown and undefined property in a line of travelling;

and you will soon find the old turnpike corporations awakening from their sleep and calling upon this court to put down the improvements which have taken their place. The millions of property which have been invested in railroads and canals, upon lines of travel which had been before occupied by turnpike corporations, will be put in jeopardy. We shall be thrown back to the improvements of the last century, and obliged to stand still, until the claims of the old turnpike corporations shall be satisfied; and they shall consent to permit these states to avail themselves of the lights of modern science, and to partake of the benefit of those improvements which are now adding to the wealth and prosperity, and the convenience and comfort, of every other part of the civilized world. Nor is this all. This court will find itself compelled to fix, by some arbitrary rule, the width of this new kind of property in a line of travel; for if such a right of property exists, we have no lights to guide us in marking out its extent, unless, indeed, we resort to the old feudal grants, and to the exclusive rights of ferries, by prescription, between towns; and are prepared to decide that when a turnpike road from one town to another, had been made, no railroad or canal, between these two points, could afterwards be established. This court is not prepared to sanction principles which must lead to such results. . . .

The judgment of the supreme judicial court of the commonwealth of Massachusetts, dismissing the plaintiffs' bill, must therefore, be affirmed with costs.

[MR. JUSTICE MCLEAN delivered an opinion in which he urged that the bill be dismissed for want of jurisdiction, although he thought that the plaintiffs' claim had merit.]

MR. JUSTICE STORY, dissenting. . . .

The present . . . is not the case of a royal grant, but of a legislative grant, by a public statute. The rules of the common law in relation to royal grants have, therefore, in reality, nothing to do with the case. We are to give this act of incorporation a rational and fair construction, according to the general rules which govern in all cases of the exposition of public statutes. We are to ascertain the legislative intent; and that once ascertained, it is our duty to give it a full and liberal operation. . . .

I admit, that where the terms of a grant are to impose burdens upon the public, or to create a restraint injurious to the public interests, there is sound reason for interpreting the terms, if ambiguous, in favour of the public. But at the same time, I insist, that there is not the slightest reason for saying, even in such a case, that the grant is not to be construed favourably to the grantee, so as to secure him in the enjoyment of what is actually granted. . . .

. . . Our legislatures neither have, nor affect to have any royal prerogatives. There is no provision in the constitution authorizing their grants to be construed differently from the grants of private persons, in regard to the like subject matter. The policy of the common law, which gave the crown so many exclusive privileges, and extraordinary claims, different from those of the subject, was founded in a good measure, if not altogether, upon the divine right of kings, or at least upon a sense of their exalted dignity and preeminence over all subjects, and upon the notion, that they are entitled to peculiar favour, for the protection of their kingly privileges. They were always construed according to common sense and common reason, upon their language and their intent. What reason is there, that our legislative acts should not receive a similar interpretation? Is it not at least as important in our free governments, that a citizen should have as much security for his rights and estate derived from the grants of the legislature, as he would have in England? What solid ground is there to say, that the words of a grant in the mouth of a citizen, shall mean one thing, and in the mouth of the legislature shall mean another thing? That in regard to the grant of a citizen, every word shall in case of any question of interpretation or implication be construed against him, and in regard to the grant of the government, every word shall be construed in its favour? That language shall be construed, not according to its natural import and implications from its own proper sense, and the objects of the instrument; but shall change its meaning, as it is spoken by the whole people, or by one of them?

There may be very solid grounds to say, that neither grants nor charters ought to be extended beyond the fair reach of their words; and that no implications ought to be made, which are not clearly deducible from the language, and the nature and objects of the grant. . . .

But it has been argued, and the argument has been pressed in every form which ingenuity could suggest, that if grants of this nature are to be construed liberally, as conferring any exclusive rights on the grantees, it will interpose an effectual barrier against all general improvements of the country. . . . For my own part, I can conceive of no surer plan to arrest all public improvements, founded on private capital and enterprise, than to make the outlay of that capital uncertain, and questionable both as to security, and as to productiveness. No man will hazard his capital in any enterprise, in which, if there be a loss, it must be borne exclusively by himself; and if there be success, he has not the slightest security of enjoying the rewards of that success for a single moment. . . .

Upon the whole, my judgment is that the act of the legislature of Massachusetts granting the charter of Warren Bridge, is an act impairing the obligation of the prior contract and grant to the proprietors of Charles River bridge; and, by the Constitution of the United States, it is, therefore, utterly void. I am for reversing the decree of the state court (dismissing the bill), and for remanding the cause to the state court for further proceedings. . . .

MR. JUSTICE THOMPSON concurred in this opinion. . . .

Home Building & Loan Association v. *Blaisdell*
290 U.S. 398, 54 S.Ct. 231, 78 L.Ed. 413 (1934)

The Minnesota Mortgage Moratorium Law, passed in 1933, was designed to prevent the foreclosure of mortgages during the emergency produced by economic depression. The Act authorized judicial action by which the redemption period of mortgages could be extended under conditions set by the court. The Act was to remain in effect "only during the continuance of the emergency and in no event beyond May 1, 1935." Blaisdell had mortgaged a house and lot to the appellant company; when the company foreclosed, Blaisdell sought an extension of the period of redemption on the ground that he would not be able to redeem by the date fixed by the law in effect when the mortgage had been foreclosed. The court extended the redemption period on condition that certain monthly payments be made. The Supreme Court of Minnesota affirmed the judgment. The Loan Company appealed.

MR. CHIEF JUSTICE HUGHES delivered the opinion of the Court. . . .

The state court upheld the statute as an emergency measure. Although conceding that the obligations of the mortgage contract were impaired, the court decided that what it thus described as an impairment was, notwithstanding the contract clause of the Federal Constitution, within the police power of the state as that power was called into exercise by the public economic emergency which the legislature had found to exist. Attention is thus directed to the preamble and first section of the statute which described the existing emergency in terms that were deemed to justify the temporary relief which the statute affords. The state court, declaring that it could not say that this legislative finding was without basis, supplemented that finding by its own statement of conditions of which it took judicial notice. The court said:

"In addition to the weight to be given the determination of the Legislature that an economic emergency exists which demands relief, the court must take notice of other considerations. The members of the Legislature come from every community of the state and from all the walks of life. They are familiar with conditions generally in every calling, occupation, profession, and business in the state. Not only they, but the courts must be guided by what is common knowledge. It is common knowledge that in the last few years land values have shrunk enormously. Loans made a few years ago upon the basis of the then going values cannot possibly be replaced on the basis of present values. We all know that when this law was enacted the large financial companies which had made it their business to invest in mortgages, had ceased to do so. No bank would directly or indirectly loan on real estate mortgages. Life insurance companies, large investors on such mortgages, had even declared a moratorium as to the loan provisions of the policy contracts. The President had closed banks temporarily. The Congress, in addition to many extraordinary measures looking to the relief of the economic emergency, had passed an act to supply funds whereby mortgagors may be able within a reasonable time to refinance their mortgages or redeem from sales where the redemption has not expired. With this knowledge the court cannot well hold that the Legislature had no basis in fact for the conclusion that an economic emergency existed which called for the exercise of the police power to grant relief." . . .

The statute does not impair the integrity of the mortgage indebtedness. The obligation for interest remains. The statute does not affect the validity of the sale or the right of a mortgagee-purchaser to title in fee, or his right to obtain a deficiency judgment, if the mortgagor fails to redeem within the prescribed period. Aside from the extension of time, the other conditions of redemption are unaltered. While the mortgagor remains in possession, he must pay the rental value as that value has been determined, upon notice and hearing, by the court. The rental value so paid is devoted to the carrying of the property by the application of the required payments to taxes, insurance, and interest on the mortgage indebtedness. While the mortgagee-purchaser is debarred from actual possession, he has, so far as rental value is concerned, the equivalent of possession during the extended period.

In determining whether the provision for this temporary and conditional relief exceeds the power of the state by reason of the clause in the Federal Constitution prohibiting impairment of the obligations of contracts, we must consider the relation of emergency to constitutional power, the historical setting of the contract clause, the development of the jurisprudence of this Court in the construction of that clause, and the principles of construction which we may consider to be established.

Emergency does not create power. Emergency does not increase granted power or remove or diminish the restrictions imposed upon power granted or reserved. The Constitution was adopted in a period of grave emergency. Its grants of power to the Federal Government and its limitations of the power of the states were determined in the light of emergency, and they are not altered by emergency. What power was thus granted and what limitations were thus imposed are questions which have always been, and always will be, the subject of close examination under our constitutional system.

While emergency does not create power, emergency may furnish the occasion for the exercise of power. "Although an emergency may not call into life a power which has never lived, nevertheless emergency may afford a reason for the exertion of a living power already enjoyed." *Wilson* v. *New,* 243 U.S. 332, 348. The constitutional question presented in the light of an emergency is whether the power possessed embraces the particular exercise of it in response to particular conditions. Thus, the war power of the federal government is not created by the emergency of war, but it is a power given to meet that emergency. It is a power to wage war successfully, and thus it permits the harnessing of the entire energies of the people in a supreme cooperative effort to preserve the nation. But even the war power does not remove constitutional limitations safeguarding essential liberties. When the provisions of the Constitution, in grant or restriction, are specific, so particularized as not to admit of construction, no question is presented. Thus, emergency would not permit a state to have more than two Senators in the Congress, or permit the election of a President by a general popular vote without regard to the number of electors to which the states are respectively entitled, or permit the states to "coin money" or to "make anything but gold and silver coin a tender in payment of debts." But, where constitutional grants and limitations of power are set forth in general clauses, which afford a broad outline, the process of construction is essential to fill in the details. That is true of the contract clause. . . .

In the construction of the contract clause, the debates in the Constitutional Convention are of little aid. But the reasons which led to the adoption of that clause, and of the other prohibitions of Section 10 of Article I, are not left in doubt, and have frequently been described with eloquent emphasis. The widespread distress following the revolutionary period, and the plight of debtors had called forth in the state an ignoble array of legislative schemes for the defeat of creditors and the invasion of contractual obligations. Legislative interferences had been so numerous and extreme that the confidence essential to prosperous trade had been undermined and the utter destruction of credit was threatened. "The sober people of America" were convinced that some "thorough reform" was needed which would "inspire a general prudence and industry, and give a regular course to the business of society." *The Federalist,* No. 44. . . .

The inescapable problems of construction have been: What is a contract? What are the obligations of contracts? What constitutes impairment of these obligations? What residuum of power is there still in the states, in relation to the operation of contracts, to protect the vital interests of the community? Questions of this character, "of no small nicety and intricacy, have vexed the legislative halls, as well as the judicial tribunals, with an uncounted variety and frequency of litigation and speculation." Story on the Constitution, § 1375. . . .

It is manifest . . . that there has been a growing appreciation of public needs and of the necessity of finding ground for a rational compromise between individual rights and public welfare. . . . Pressure of a constantly increasing density of population, the interrelation of the activities of our people and the complexity of our economic interests, have inevitably led to an increased use of the organization of society in order to protect the very bases of individual opportunity. Where, in earlier days, it was thought that only the concerns of individuals or of classes were involved, and that those of the state itself were touched only remotely, it has later been found that the fundamental interests of the state are directly affected; and that the question is no longer merely that of one party to a contract as against another, but of the use of reasonable means to safeguard the economic structure upon which the good of all depends.

It is no answer to say that this public need was not apprehended a century ago, or to insist that what the provision of the Constitution meant to the vision of that day it must mean to the vision of our time. If by the statement that what the Constitution meant at the time of its adoption it means today, it is intended to say that the great clauses of the Constitution must be confined to the interpretation which the framers, with the conditions and outlook of their time, would have placed upon them, the statement carries its own refutation. It was to guard against such a narrow conception that Chief Justice Marshall uttered the memorable warning: "We must never forget, that it is *a constitution* we are expounding" (*McCulloch* v. *Maryland* . . .); "a constitution intended to endure for ages to come, and, consequently, to be adapted to the various *crises* of human affairs.'' ... ''When we are dealing with the words of the Constitution,'' said this Court in *Missouri* v. *Holland* ... ''we must realize that they have called into life a being the development of which could not have been foreseen completely by the most gifted of its begetters. . . . The case before us must be considered in the light of our whole experience and not merely in that of what was said a hundred years ago.''

Nor is it helpful to attempt to draw a fine distinction between the intended meaning of the words of the Constitution and their intended application. When we consider the contract clause and the decisions which have expounded it in harmony with the essential reserved power of the states to protect the security of their peoples, we find no warrant for the conclusion that the clause has been warped by these decisions from its proper significance or that the founders of our government would have interpreted the clause differently had they had occasion to assume that responsibility in the conditions of the later day. The vast body of law which has been developed was unknown to the fathers, but it is believed to have preserved the essential content and the spirit of the Constitution. With a growing recognition of public needs and the relation of individual right to public security, the Court has sought to prevent the perversion of the clause through its use as an instrument to throttle the capacity of the states to protect their fundamental interests. . . .

We are of the opinion that the Minnesota statute as here applied does not violate the contract clause of the Federal Constitution. Whether the legislation is wise or unwise as a matter of policy is a question with which we are not concerned. . . .

The judgment of the Supreme Court of Minnesota is affirmed.

Judgment affirmed.

MR. JUSTICE SUTHERLAND, dissenting.

Few questions of greater moment than that just decided have been submitted for judicial inquiry during this generation. He simply closes his eyes to the necessary implications of the decision who fails to see in it the potentiality of future gradual but ever-advancing encroachments upon the sanctity of private and public contracts. The effect of the Minnesota legislation, though serious enough in itself, is of trivial significance compared with the far more serious and dangerous inroads upon the limitations of the Constitution which are almost certain to ensue as a consequence naturally following any step beyond the boundaries fixed by that instrument. And those of us who are thus apprehensive of the effect of this decision would, in a matter so important, be neglectful of our duty should we fail to spread upon the permanent records of the court the reasons which move us to the opposite view.

A provision of the Constitution, it is hardly necessary to say, does not admit of two distinctly opposite interpretations. It does not mean one thing at one time and an entirely different thing at another time. If the contract impairment clause, when framed and adopted, meant that the terms of a contract for the payment of money could not be altered *in invitum* by a state statute enacted for the relief of hardly pressed debtors to the end and with the effect of postponing payment or enforcement during and because of an economic or financial emergency, it is but to state the obvious to say that it means the same now. This view, at once so rational in its application to the written word, and so necessary to the stability of constitutional principles, though from time to time challenged, has never, unless recently, been put within the realm of doubt by the decisions of this court. . . .

The provisions of the Federal Constitution, undoubtedly, are pliable in the sense that in appropriate cases they have the capacity of bringing within their grasp every new condition which falls within their meaning. But, their *meaning* is changeless; it is only their *application* which is extensible. . . . Constitutional grants of power and restrictions upon the exercise of power are not flexible as the doctrines of the common law are flexible. These doctrines, upon the principles of the common law itself, modify or abrogate themselves whenever they are or whenever they become plainly unsuited to different or changed conditions. . . .

The whole aim of construction, as applied to

a provision of the Constitution, is to discover the meaning, to ascertain and give effect to the intent, of its framers and the people who adopted it. . . . And if the meaning be at all doubtful, the doubt should be resolved, wherever reasonably possible to do so, in a way to forward the evident purpose with which the provision was adopted. . . .

A candid consideration of the history and circumstances which led up to and accompanied the framing and adoption of this clause will demonstrate conclusively that it was framed and adopted with the specific and studied purpose of preventing legislation designed to relieve debtors *especially* in time of financial distress. Indeed, it is not probable that any other purpose was definitely in the minds of those who composed the framers' convention or the ratifying state conventions which followed, although the restriction has been given a wider application upon principles clearly stated by Chief Justice Marshall in the Dartmouth College Case. . . .

The present exigency is nothing new. From the beginning of our existence as a nation, periods of depression, of industrial failure, of financial distress, of unpaid and unpayable indebtedness, have alternated with years of plenty. The vital lesson that expenditure beyond income begets poverty, that public or private extravagance, financed by promises to pay, either must end in complete or partial repudiation or the promises be fulfilled by self-denial and painful effort, though constantly taught by bitter experience, seems never to be learned; and the attempt by legislative devices to shift the misfortune of the debtor to the shoulders of the creditor without coming into conflict with the contract impairment clause has been persistent and oft-repeated.

The defense of the Minnesota law is made upon grounds which were discountenanced by the makers of the Constitution and have many times been rejected by this court. That defense should not now succeed, because it constitutes an effort to overthrow the constitutional provision by an appeal to facts and circumstances identical with those which brought it into existence. With due regard for the process of logical thinking, it legitimately cannot be urged that conditions which produced the rule may now be invoked to destroy it.

. . . The opinion concedes that emergency does not create power, or increase granted power, or remove or diminish restrictions upon power granted or reserved. It then proceeds to say, however, that while emergency does not create power, it may furnish the occasion for the exercise of power. I can only interpret what is said on that subject as meaning that while an emergency does not diminish a restriction upon power it furnishes an occasion for diminishing it; and this, as it seems to me, is merely to say the same thing by the use of another set of words, with the effect of affirming that which has just been denied. . . .

The Minnesota statute either impairs the obligation of contracts or it does not. If it does not, the occasion to which it relates becomes immaterial, since then the passage of the statute is the exercise of a normal, unrestricted, state power and requires no special occasion to render it effective. If it does, the emergency no more furnishes a proper occasion for its exercise than if the emergency were nonexistent. And so, while, in form, the suggested distinction seems to put us forward in a straight line, in reality it simply carries us back in a circle, like bewildered travelers lost in a wood, to the point where we parted company with the view of the state court. . . .

I quite agree with the opinion of the court that whether the legislation under review is wise or unwise is a matter with which we have nothing to do. Whether it is likely to work well or work ill presents a question entirely irrelevant to the issue. The only legitimate inquiry we can make is whether it is constitutional. If it is not, its virtues, if it have any, cannot save it; if it is, its faults cannot be invoked to accomplish its destruction. If the provisions of the Constitution be not upheld when they pinch as well as when they comfort, they may as well be abandoned. Being unable to reach any other conclusion than that the Minnesota statute infringes the constitutional restriction under review, I have no choice but to say so.

I am authorized to say that MR. JUSTICE VAN

DEVANTER, MR. JUSTICE MCREYNOLDS and MR. JUSTICE BUTLER concur in this opinion.

HARLAN FISKE STONE PAPERS. LIBRARY OF CONGRESS.

MR. JUSTICE CARDOZO concurring in an *unpublished* opinion.

"We must never forget that it is *a constitution* we are expounding." Marshall, C. J., in *McCulloch* v. *Maryland*. . . . "A constitution [is] intended to endure for ages to come, and consequently, to be adapted to the various *crises* of human affairs." *Ibid*. . . .

"The case before us must be considered in the light of our whole experience and not merely in that of what was said a hundred years ago." *Holmes, J. in Missouri* v. *Holland*. . . .

A hundred years ago when this court decided *Bronson* v. *Kinzie* . . . property might be taken without due process of law through the legislation of the states, and the courts of the nation were powerless to give redress, unless indeed they could find that a contract had been broken. *Dartmouth College* v. *Woodward* . . . ; *Fletcher* v. *Peck*. . . . The judges of those courts had not yet begun to speak of the police power * except in an off hand way or in expounding the effect of the commerce clause upon local regulations. The License Cases. . . . Due process in the states was whatever the states ordained. In such circumstances there was jeopardy, or the threat of it, in encroachment, however slight, upon the obligation to adhere to the letter of a contract. Once reject that test, and no other was available, or so it might well have seemed. The states could not be kept within the limits of reason and fair dealing for such restraints were then unknown as curbs upon their power. It was either all or nothing.

The Fourteenth Amendment came, and with it a profound change in the relation between the federal government and the governments of the states. No longer were the states invested with arbitrary power. Their statutes affecting property or liberty were brought within supervision of independent courts and subjected to the rule of reason. The dilemma of "all or nothing" no longer stared us in the face.

Upon the basis of that amendment, a vast body of law unknown to the fathers has been built in treatise and decision. The economic and social changes wrought by the industrial revolution and by the growth of population have made it necessary for government at this day to [do] a thousand things that were beyond the experience or the thought of a century ago. With the growing recognition of this need, courts have awakened to the truth that the contract clause is perverted from its proper meaning when it throttles the capacity of the states to exert their governmental power in response to crying needs. . . . The early cases dealt with the problem as one affecting the conflicting rights and interests of individuals and classes. This was the attitude of the courts up to the Fourteenth Amendment; and the tendency to some extent persisted even later. . . . The rights and interests of the state itself were involved, as it seemed, only indirectly and remotely, if they were thought to be involved at all. We know better in these days, with the passing of the frontier and of the unpeopled spaces of the west. With these and other changes, the welfare of the social organism in any of its parts is bound up more inseparably than ever with the welfare of the whole. A gospel of *laissez-faire*—of individual initiative—of thrift and industry and sacrifice— may be inadequate in that great society we live in to point the way to salvation, at least for economic life. The state when it acts today by statutes like the one before us is not furthering the selfish good of individuals or classes as ends of ultimate validity. It is furthering its own good by maintaining the economic structure on which the good of all depends. Such at least is its endeavor, however much it miss the mark. The attainment of that end, so august and impersonal, will not be barred and thwarted by the obstruction of a contract set up along the way.

Looking back over the century, one perceives a process of evolution too strong to be set back. The decisions brought together by the Chief

---

* The use of this term is traced to its origins with copious citations in Mott, Due Process of Law, pp. 300, 302 (1926).

Justice [Hughes] show with impressive force how the court in its interpretation of the contract clause has been feeling its way toward a rational compromise between private rights and public welfare. From the beginning it was seen that something must be subtracted from the words of the Constitution in all their literal and stark significance. This was forcefully pointed out by Johnson, J., in *Ogden* v. *Saunders,* 12 Wheat. 213, 286. At first refuge was found in the distinction between right and remedy with all its bewildering refinements. Gradually the distinction was perceived to be inadequate. The search was for a broader base, for a division that would separate the lawful and the forbidden by lines more closely in correspondence with the necessities of government. The Fourteenth Amendment was seen to point the way. Contracts were still to be preserved. There was to be no arbitrary destruction of their binding force, nor any arbitrary impairment. There was to be no impairment, even though not arbitrary, except with the limits of fairness, of moderation,

and of pressing and emergent need. But a promise exchanged between individuals was not to paralyze the state in its endeavor in times of direful crisis to keep its life-blood flowing.

To hold this may be inconsistent with things that men said in 1787 when expounding to compatriots the newly written constitution. They did not see the changes in the relation between states and nation or in the play of social forces that lay hidden in the womb of time. It may be inconsistent with things that they believed or took for granted. Their beliefs to be significant must be adjusted to the world they knew. It is not in my judgment inconsistent with what they would say today, nor with what today they would believe, if they were called upon to interpret "in the light of our whole experience" the constitution that they framed for the needs of an expanding future.

With this supplemental statement I concur in all that has been written in the opinion of the court.

United States Trust Co. of New York v. *New Jersey*
431 U.S. 1, 97 S.Ct. 1505, 52 L.Ed. 2d 92 (1977)

The Port Authority of New York and New Jersey was established by the two states to coordinate and improve commerce in the port of New York. In 1962 an agreement between the two states, growing out of a construction project and the acquisition of a railroad, limited the ability of the Port Authority to subsidize rail passenger transportation from revenues and reserves pledged as security for bonds floated by the Authority. In 1974, in the wake of a national energy crisis, the states repealed the 1962 covenant. The bank brought suit in the New Jersey Superior Court alleging an unconstitutional impairment of the states' contract with the bondholders. The state court dismissed the complaint after trial, and the New Jersey Supreme Court affirmed. When the case reached the United States Supreme Court on appeal, two Justices did not take part in the decision. Justice Blackmun's opinion speaks for himself and three others—a majority of the bench participating in this case.

MR. JUSTICE BLACKMUN delivered the opinion of the Court. . . . [The first part of Justice Blackmun's opinion contains a lengthy statement of the facts and background of the case.]

At the time the Constitution was adopted, and for nearly a century thereafter, the Contract Clause was one of the few express limitations on state power. The many decisions of this Court involving the Contract Clause are evidence of its important place in our constitutional jurisprudence. Over the last century, however, the Fourteenth Amendment has assumed a far larger place in constitutional adjudication concerning the States. We feel that the present role of the Contract Clause is largely illuminated by two of this Court's decisions. In each, legislation was sustained despite a claim that it had impaired the obligations of contracts.

Home Building & Loan Assn. v. *Blaisdell* . . . is regarded as the leading case in the modern era of Contract Clause interpretation. At issue was the Minnesota Mortgage Moratorium Law, enacted in 1933, during the depth of the Depression and when that State was under severe economic stress, and appeared to have no effective alternative. . . .

This Court's most recent Contract Clause decision is *El Paso* v. *Simmons.* . . . That case concerned a 1941 Texas statute that limited to a 5-year period the reinstatement rights of an interest-defaulting purchaser of land from the State. . . . The Court recognized that "the power of a State to modify or affect the obligation of contract is not without limit," but held that "the objects of the Texas statute make abundantly clear that it impairs no protected right under the Contract Clause." . . .

Both of these cases eschewed a rigid application of the Contract Clause to invalidate state legislation. Yet neither indicated that the Contract Clause was without meaning in modern constitutional jurisprudence, or that its limitation on state power was illusory. Whether or not the protection of contract rights comports with current views of wise public policy, the Contract Clause remains a part of our written Constitution. . . .

Although the Contract Clause appears literally to proscribe "any" impairment, this Court observed in *Blaisdell* that "the prohibition is not an absolute one and is not to be read with literal exactness like a mathematical formula." . . . Thus, a finding that there has been a technical impairment is merely a preliminary step in resolving the more difficult question whether that impairment is permitted under the Constitution. . . .

Mass transportation, energy conservation, and environmental protection are goals that are important and of legitimate public concern. Appellees contend that these goals are so important that any harm to bondholders from repeal of the 1962 covenant is greatly outweighed by the public benefit. We do not accept this invitation to engage in a utilitarian comparison of public benefit and private loss. Contrary to Mr. Justice Black's fear . . . expressed in sole dissent in *El Paso* v. *Simmons* . . . the Court has not "balanced away" the limitation on state action imposed by the Contract Clause. Thus a State cannot refuse to meet its legitimate financial obligations simply because it would prefer to spend the money to promote the public good rather than the private welfare of its creditors. We can only sustain the repeal of the 1962 covenant if that impairment was both reasonable and necessary to serve the admittedly important purposes claimed by the State.*

The more specific justification offered for the repeal of the 1962 covenant was the States' plan for encouraging users of private automobiles to shift to public transportation. The States intended to discourage private automobile use by raising bridge and tunnel tolls and to use the extra revenue from those tolls to subsidize improved commuter railroad service. Appellees contend that repeal of the 1962 covenant was necessary to implement this plan because the new mass transit facilities could not possibly be

---

* The dissent suggests . . . that such careful scrutiny is unwarranted in this case because the harm to bondholders is relatively small. For the same reason, however, contractual obligations of this magnitude need not impose barriers to changes in public policy. The States remain free to exercise their powers of eminent domain to abrogate such contractual rights, upon payment of just compensation. . . .

self-supporting and the covenant's "permitted deficits" level had already been exceeded. We reject this justification because the repeal was neither necessary to achievement of the plan nor reasonable in light of the circumstances.

The determination of necessity can be considered on two levels. First, it cannot be said that total repeal of the covenant was essential; a less drastic modification would have permitted the contemplated plan without entirely removing the covenant's limitations on the use of Port Authority revenues and reserves to subsidize commuter railroads. Second, without modifying the covenant at all, the States could have adopted alternative means of achieving their twin goals of discouraging automobile use and improving mass transit. Appellees contend, however, that choosing among these alternatives is a matter for legislative discretion. But a State is not completely free to consider impairing the obligations of its own contracts on a par with other policy alternatives. Similarly, a State is not free to impose a drastic impairment when an evident and more moderate course would serve its purposes equally well. In *El Paso* v. *Simmons* . . . the imposition of a five-year statute of limitations on what was previously a perpetual right of redemption was regarded by this Court as "quite clearly necessary" to achieve the State's vital interest in the orderly administration of its school lands program. . . . In the instant case the State has failed to demonstrate that repeal of the 1962 covenant was similarly necessary.

We also cannot conclude that repeal of the covenant was reasonable in light of the surrounding circumstances. In this regard a comparison with *El Paso* v. *Simmons* . . . again is instructive. There a 19th century statute had effects that were unforeseen and unintended by the legislature when originally adopted. As a result speculators were placed in a position to obtain windfall benefits. The Court held that adoption of a statute of limitation was a reasonable means to "restrict a party to those gains reasonably to be expected from the contract" when it was adopted. . . .

By contrast, in the instant case the need for

mass transportation in the New York metropolitan area was not a new development, and the likelihood that publicly owned commuter railroads would produce substantial deficits was well known. As early as 1922, over a half century ago, there were pressures to involve the Port Authority in mass transit. It was with full knowledge of these concerns that the 1962 covenant was adopted. Indeed, the covenant was specifically intended to protect the pledged revenues and reserves against the possibility that such concerns would lead the Port Authority into greater involvement in deficit mass transit.

During the 12-year period between adoption of the covenant and its repeal, public perception of the importance of mass transit undoubtedly grew because of increased general concern with environmental protection and energy conservation. But these concerns were not unknown in 1962, and the subsequent changes were of degree and not of kind. We cannot say that these changes caused the covenant to have a substantially different impact in 1974 than when it was adopted in 1962. And we cannot conclude that the repeal was reasonable in the light of changed circumstances.

We therefore hold that the Contract Clause of the United States Constitution prohibits the retroactive repeal of the 1962 covenant. The judgment of the Supreme Court of New Jersey is reversed.

It is so ordered.

MR. JUSTICE STEWART took no part in the decision of this case.

MR. JUSTICE POWELL took no part in the consideration or decision of this case.

MR. CHIEF JUSTICE BURGER, concurring. . . .

MR. JUSTICE BRENNAN, with whom MR. JUSTICE WHITE and MR. JUSTICE MARSHALL join, dissenting.

Decisions of this Court for at least a century have construed the Contract Clause largely to be powerless in binding a State to contracts limiting the authority of successor legislatures to enact laws in furtherance of the health, safety, and similar collective interests of the polity. In short, those decisions established the principle that lawful exercises of a State's police powers stand paramount to private rights held under contract. Today's decision, in invalidating the New Jersey Legislature's 1974 repeal of its predecessor's 1962 covenant, rejects this previous understanding and remolds the Contract Clause into a potent instrument for overseeing important policy determinations of the state legislature. At the same time, by creating a constitutional safe haven for property rights embodied in a contract, the decision substantially distorts modern constitutional jurisprudence governing regulation of private economic interests. I might understand, though I could not accept, this revival of the Contract Clause were it in accordance with some coherent and constructive view of public policy. But elevation of the Clause to the status of regulator of the municipal bond market at the heavy price of frustration of sound legislative policy-making is as demonstrably unwise as it is unnecessary. The justification for today's decision, therefore, remains a mystery to me. . . .

Nowhere are we told why a state policy, no matter how responsive to the general welfare of its citizens, can be reasonable only if it confronts issues that previously were absolutely unforeseen. Indeed, this arbitrary perspective seems peculiarly inappropriate in a case like this where at least three new and independent congressional enactments between the years 1962 and 1974 summoned major urban centers like New York and New Jersey to action in the environmental, energy, and transportation fields. In short, on this record, I can neither understand nor accept the Court's characterization of New Jersey's action as unreasonable.

If the Court's treatment of New Jersey's legitimate policy interests is inadequate, its consideration of the countervailing injury ostensibly suffered by the appellant is barely discernible at all. For the Court apparently holds that a mere "technical impairment" of contract suffices to subject New Jersey's repealer to serious judicial scrutiny and invalidation under the Contract Clause. . . . The Court's modest statement of the economic injury that today attracts its judicial intervention is, however, understandable. For fairly read, the record before us

makes plain that the repeal of the 1962 covenant has occasioned only the most minimal damage on the part of the Authority's bondholders.

Obviously, the heart of the obligation to the bondholders—and the interests ostensibly safeguarded by the 1962 covenant—is the periodic payment of interest and the repayment of principal when due. The Court does not, and indeed cannot, contend that either New Jersey or the Authority has called into question the validity of these underlying obligations. No creditor complains that public authorities have defaulted on a coupon payment or failed to redeem a bond that has matured. In fact, the Court does not even offer any reason whatever for fearing that, as a result of the covenant's repeal, the securities in appellant's portfolio are jeopardized. . . .

The Court today dusts off the Contract Clause and thereby undermines the bipartisan policies of two States that manifestly seek to further the legitimate needs of their citizens. The Court's analysis, I submit, fundamentally misconceives the nature of the Contract Clause guarantee.

One of the fundamental premises of our popular democracy is that each generation of representatives can and will remain responsive to the needs and desires of those whom they represent. Crucial to this end is the assurance that new legislators will not automatically be bound by the policies and undertakings of earlier days. In accordance with this philosophy, the Framers of our Constitution conceived of the Contract Clause primarily as protection for economic transactions entered into by purely private parties, rather than obligations involving the State itself. . . . The Framers fully recognized that nothing would so jeopardize the legitimacy of a system of government that relies upon the ebbs and flows of politics to "clean out the rascals" than the possibility that those same rascals might perpetuate their policies simply by locking them into binding contracts.

Following an early opinion of the Court, however, that took the first step of applying the Contract Clause to public undertakings,

Fletcher v. *Peck* . . . , later decisions attempted to define the reach of the Clause consistently with the demands of our governing processes. The central principle developed by these decisions, beginning at least a century ago, has been that Contract Clause challenges such as that raised by appellant are to be resolved by according unusual deference to the lawmaking authority of state and local governments. Especially when the State acts in furtherance of the variety of broad social interests that came clustered together under the rubric of ''police powers,'' . . . in particular, matters of health, safety, and the preservation of natural resources—the decisions of this Court pursued a course of steady return to the intention of the Constitution's Framers by closely circumscribing the scope of the Contract Clause.

This theme of judicial self-restraint and its underlying premise that a State always retains the sovereign authority to legislate in behalf of its people was commonly expressed by the doctrine that the Contract Clause will not even recognize efforts of a State to enter into contracts limiting the authority of succeeding legislators to enact laws in behalf of the health,

safety, and similar collective interests of the polity—in short, that that State's police power is inalienable by contract. . . .

I would not want to be read as suggesting that the States should blithely proceed down the path of repudiating their obligations, financial or otherwise. Their credibility in the credit market obviously is highly dependent on exercising their vast lawmaking powers with self-restraint and discipline, and I, for one, have little doubt that few, if any, jurisdictions would choose to use their authority ''so foolish[ly] as to kill a goose that lays golden eggs for them.'' . . . But in the final analysis, there is no reason to doubt that appellant's financial welfare is being adequately policed by the political processes and the bond marketplace itself. The role to be played by the Constitution is at most a limited one. . . . For this Court should have learned long ago that the Constitution—be it through the Contract or Due Process Clause—can actively intrude into such economic and policy matters only if my Brethren are prepared to bear enormous institutional and social costs. Because I consider the potential dangers of such judicial interference to be intolerable, I dissent.

Slaughterhouse Cases
16 Wall. (83 U.S.) 36, 21 L.Ed. 394 (1873)

In 1869 the Louisiana legislature granted a monopoly to a slaughterhouse company with a schedule of fees for the sheltering and slaughtering of animals within the city limits of New Orleans. Various butchers then sought an injunction against the monopoly in the state courts and, when unsuccessful, obtained a writ of error from the Supreme Court.

MR. JUSTICE MILLER . . . delivered the opinion of the Court. . . .

The statute is denounced not only as creating a monopoly and conferring odious and exclusive privileges upon a small number of persons at the expense of the great body of the community of

New Orleans, but it is asserted that it deprives a large and meritorious class of citizens—the whole of the butchers of the city—of the right to exercise their trade, the business to which they have been trained and on which they depend for the support of themselves and their families;

and that the unrestricted exercise of the business of butchering is necessary to the daily subsistence of the population of the city. . . .

It is not, and cannot be successfully controverted, that it is both the right and the duty of the legislative body—the supreme power of the State or municipality—to prescribe and determine the localities where the business of slaughtering for a great city may be conducted. To do this effectively it is indispensable that all persons who slaughter animals for food shall do it in those places *and nowhere else.*

The statute under consideration defines these localities and forbids slaughtering in any other. It does not, as has been asserted, prevent the butcher from doing his own slaughtering. On the contrary, the Slaughter House Company is required, under a heavy penalty, to permit any person who wishes to do so, to slaughter in their houses; and they are bound to make ample provision for the convenience of all slaughtering for the entire city. The butcher then is still permitted to slaughter, to prepare, and to sell his own meats; but he is required to slaughter at a specified place and to pay reasonable compensation for the use of the accommodations furnished him at that place.

The wisdom of the monopoly granted by the legislature may be open to question, but it is difficult to see a justification for the assertion that the butchers are deprived of the right to labor in their occupation, or the people of their daily service in preparing food, or how this statute, with the duties and guards imposed upon the company, can be said to destroy the business of the butcher, or seriously interfere with its pursuit.

The power here exercised by the legislature of Louisiana is, in its essential nature, one which has been, up to the present period in the constitutional history of this country, always conceded to belong to the States, however it may *now* be questioned in some of its details. . . .

Unless, therefore, it can be maintained that the exclusive privilege granted by this charter to the corporation is beyond the power of the legislature of Louisiana, there can be no just exception to the validity of the statute. And in this respect we are not able to see that these

privileges are especially odious or objectionable. The duty imposed as a consideration for the privilege is well defined, and its enforcement well guarded. The prices or charges to be made by the company are limited by the statute, and we are not advised that they are on the whole exorbitant or unjust.

The proposition is, therefore, reduced to these terms: Can any exclusive privileges be granted to any of its citizens, or to a corporation, by the legislature of a State? . . .

The plaintiffs in error accepting this isssue, allege that the statute is a violation of the Constitution of the United States in these several particulars:

That it creates an involuntary servitude forbidden by the thirteenth article of amendment;
That it abridges the privileges and immunities of citizens of the United States;
That it denies to the plaintiffs the equal protection of the laws; and,
That it deprives them of their property without due process of law; contrary to the provisions of the first section of the fourteenth article of amendment.

This court is thus called upon for the first time to give construction to these articles.

. . . On the most casual examination of the language of these amendments [the 13th, 14th, and 15th], no one can fail to be impressed with the one pervading purpose found in them all, lying at the foundation of each, and without which none of them would have even been suggested; we mean the freedom of the slave race, the security and firm establishment of that freedom, and the protection of the newly-made freeman and citizen from the oppressions of those who had formerly exercised unlimited dominion over him. It is true that only the fifteenth amendment, in terms, mentions the negro by speaking of his color and his slavery. But it is just as true that each of the other articles was addressed to the grievances of that race, and designed to remedy them as the fifteenth.

We do not say that no one else but the negro can share in this protection. Both the language and spirit of these articles are to have their fair and just weight in any question of construction. Undoubtedly while negro slavery alone was in the mind of the Congress which proposed the thirteenth article, it forbids any other kind of slavery, now or hereafter. If Mexican peonage or the Chinese cooly labor system shall develop slavery of the Mexican or Chinese race within our territory, this amendment may safely be trusted to make it void. And so if other rights are assailed by the States which properly and necessarily fall within the protection of these articles, that protection will apply, though the party interested may not be of African descent. But what we do say, and what we wish to be understood is, that in any fair and just construction of any section or phrase of these amendments, it is necessary to look to the purpose which we have said was the pervading spirit of them all, the evil which they were designed to remedy, and the process of continued addition to the Constitution, until that purpose was supposed to be accomplished, as far as constitutional law can accomplish it. . . .

The next observation is more important in view of the arguments of counsel in the present case. It is, that the distinction between citizenship of the United States and citizenship of a State is clearly recognized and established. Not only may a man be a citizen of the United States without being a citizen of a State, but an important element is necessary to convert the former into the latter. He must reside within the State to make him a citizen of it, but it is only necessary that he should be born or naturalized in the United States to be a citizen of the Union.

It is quite clear, then, that there is a citizenship of the United States, and a citizenship of a State, which are distinct from each other, and which depend upon different characteristics or circumstances in the individual.

We think this distinction and its explicit recognition in this amendment of great weight in this argument, because the next paragraph of this same section, which is the one mainly relied on by the plaintiffs in error, speaks only of privileges and immunities of citizens of the United States, and does not speak of those of citizens of the several States. The argument, however, in favor of the plaintiffs rests wholly on the assumption that the citizenship is the same, and the privileges and immunities guaranteed by the clause are the same.

The language is, "No State shall make or enforce any law which shall abridge the privileges or immunities of citizens of *the United States*." It is a little remarkable, if this clause was intended as a protection to the citizen of a State against the legislative power of his own State, that the word citizen of the State should be left out when it is so carefully used, and used in contradistinction to citizens of the United States, in the very sentence which precedes it. It is too clear for argument that the change in phraseology was adopted understandingly and with a purpose.

Of the privileges and immunities of the citizen of the United States, and of the privileges and immunities of the citizen of the State, and what they respectively are, we will presently consider; but we wish to state here that it is only the former which are placed by this clause under the protection of the Federal Constitution, and that the latter, whatever they may be, are not intended to have any additional protection by this paragraph of the amendment.

If, then, there is a difference between the privileges and immunities belonging to a citizen of the United States as such, and those belonging to the citizen of the States as such the latter must rest for their security and protection where they have heretofore rested; for they are not embraced by this paragraph of the amendment. . . .

Fortunately we are not without judicial construction of this clause of the Constitution. The first and the leading case on the subject is that of *Corfield* v. *Coryell,* 6 Fed. Cas. 3230, decided by Mr. Justice Washington in the Circuit Court for the District of Pennsylvania in 1823.

"The inquiry," he says, "is, what are the privileges and immunities of citizens of the several States? We feel no hesitation in confining these expressions to those privileges and immunities which are fundamental; which belong of right to the citizens of all free governments, and which have at all times been enjoyed by citizens of the several States which compose this Union, from the time of their becoming free, independent, and sovereign. What these fundamental principles are, it would be more tedious than difficult to enumerate. They may all, however, be comprehended under the following general heads: protection by the government, with the right to acquire and possess property of every kind, and to pursue and obtain happiness and safety, subject, nevertheless, to such restraints as the government may prescribe for the general good of the whole." . . .

It would be the vainest show of learning to attempt to prove by citations of authority, that up to the adoption of the recent amendments, no claim or pretense was set up that those rights depended on the Federal government for their existence or protection, beyond the very few express limitations which the Federal Constitution imposed upon the States—such, for instance, as the prohibition against ex post facto laws, bills of attainder, and laws impairing the obligation of contracts. But with the exception of these and a few other restrictions, the entire domain of the privileges and immunities of the citizens of the States, as above defined, lay within the constitutional and legislative power of the States, and without that of the Federal government. Was it the purpose of the Fourteenth Amendment, by the simple declaration that no State should make or enforce any law which shall abridge the privileges and immunities of *citizens of the United States,* to transfer the security and protection of all the civil rights which we have mentioned, from the States to the Federal government? And where it is declared that Congress shall have the power to enforce that article, was it intended to bring within the power of Congress the entire domain of civil rights heretofore belonging exclusively to the States?

All this and more must follow, if the proposition of the plaintiffs in error be sound. For not only are these rights subject to the control of Congress whenever in its discretion any of them are supposed to be abridged by State legislation, but that body may also pass laws in advance,

limiting and restricting the exercise of legislative power by the States, in their most ordinary and usual functions, as in its judgment it may think proper on all such subjects. And still further, such a construction followed by the reversal of the judgments of the Supreme Court of Louisiana in these cases, would constitute this court a perpetual censor upon all legislation of the States, on the civil rights of their own citizens, with authority to nullify such as it did not approve as consistent with those rights, as they existed at the time of the adoption of this amendment. The argument we admit is not always the most conclusive which is drawn from the consequences urged against the adoption of a particular construction of an instrument. But when, as in the case before us, these consequences are so serious, so far-reaching and pervading, so great a departure from the structure and spirit of our institutions; when the effect is to fetter and degrade the State governments by subjecting them to the control of Congress, in the exercise of powers heretofore universally conceded to them of the most ordinary and fundamental character; when in fact it radically changes the whole theory of the relations of the State and Federal governments to each other and of both these governments to the people; the argument has a force that is irresistible, in the absence of language which expresses such a purpose too clearly to admit of doubt.

We are convinced that no such results were intended by the Congress which proposed these amendments, nor by the legislatures of the States which ratified them.

Having shown that the privileges and immunities relied on in the argument are those which belong to citizens of the States as such, and that they are left to the State governments for security and protection, and not by this article placed under the special care of the Federal government, we may hold ourselves excused from defining the privileges and immunities of citizens of the United States which no State can abridge, until some case involving those privileges may make it necessary to do so.

But lest it be said that no such privileges and immunities are to be found if those we have been considering are excluded, we venture to suggest some which owe their existence to the Federal government, its National character, its Constitution, or its laws.

One of these is well described in the case of *Crandall* v. *Nevada,* 6 Wall. 35. It is said to be the right of the citizens of this great country, protected by implied guarantees of its Constitution, "to come to the seat of government to assert any claim he may have upon that government, to transact any business he may have with it, to seek its protection, to share its offices, to engage in administering its functions. He has the right of free access to its seaports, through which all operations of foreign commerce are conducted, to the subtreasuries, land offices, and courts of justice in the several States." And quoting from the language of Chief Justice Taney in another case, it is said "that for all the great purposes for which the Federal government was established, we are one people, with one common country, we are all citizens of the United States"; and it is, as such citizens, that their rights are supported in this court in *Crandall* v. *Nevada. . . .*

The argument has not been much pressed in these cases that the defendant's charter deprives the plaintiffs of their property without due process of law, or that it denies to them the equal protection of the law. The first of these paragraphs has been in the Constitution since the adoption of the fifth amendment, as a restraint upon the Federal power. It is also to be found in some form of expression in the constitutions of nearly all the states, as a restraint upon the power of the States. This law, then, has practically been the same as it now is during the existence of the government except so far as the present amendment may place the restraining power over the States in this matter in the hands of the Federal government.

We are not without judicial interpretation, therefore, both State and National, of the meaning of this clause. And it is sufficient to say that under no construction of that provision that we have ever seen, or any that we deem admissible, can the restraint imposed by the State of Louisiana upon the exercise of their trade by the butchers of New Orleans be held to be a deprivation of property within the meaning of that provision.

"Nor shall any State deny to any person within its jurisdiction the equal protection of the laws."

In the light of the history of these amendments, and the pervading purpose of them, which we have already discussed, it is not difficult to give a meaning to this clause. The existence of laws in the States where the newly emancipated negroes resided, which discriminated with gross injustice and hardship against them as a class, was the evil to be remedied by this clause, and by it such laws are forbidden.

If, however, the States did not conform their laws to its requirements, then by the fifth section of the article of amendment Congress was authorized to enforce it by suitable legislation. We doubt very much whether any action of a State not directed by way of discrimination against the negroes as a class, or on account of their race, will ever be held to come within the purview of this provision. It is so clearly a provision for that race and that emergency, that a strong case would be necessary for its application to any other. But as it is a State that is to be dealt with, and not alone the validity of its laws, we may safely leave that matter until Congress shall have exercised its power, or some case of State oppression, by denial of equal justice in its courts, shall have claimed a decision at our hands. We find no such case in the one before us, and do not deem it necessary to go over the argument again, as it may have relation to this particular clause of the amendment. . . .

The judgments of the Supreme Court of Louisiana in these cases are

Affirmed.

MR. JUSTICE FIELD, dissenting: . . .

The question presented is . . . one of the gravest importance, not merely to the parties here, but to the whole country. It is nothing less than the question whether the recent amendments to the Federal Constitution protect the citizens of the United States against the deprivation of their common rights by State legislation. In my judgment the fourteenth amendment does afford such protection, and was so intended by the Congress which framed and the States which adopted it.

The amendment does not attempt to confer any new privileges or immunities upon citizens, or to enumerate or define those already existing. It assumes that there are such privileges and immunities which belong of right to citizens as such, and ordains that they shall not be abridged by State legislation. If this inhibition has no reference to privileges and immunities of this character, but only refers, as held by the majority of the court in their opinion, to such privileges and immunities as were before its adoption specially designated in the Constitution or necessarily implied as belonging to citizens of the United States, it was a vain and idle enactment, which accomplished nothing, and most unnecessarily excited Congress and the people on its passage. With privileges and immunities thus designated or implied no State could ever have interfered by its laws and no new constitutional provision was required to inhibit such interference. The supremacy of the Constitution and the laws of the United States always controlled any State legislation of that character. But if the amendment refers to the natural and inalienable rights which belong to all citizens, the inhibition has a profound significance and consequence.

What, then, are the privileges and immunities which are secured against abridgment by State legislation? . . .

The terms, "privileges and immunities" are not new in the Amendment; they were in the Constitution before the Amendment was adopted. They are found in the 2d section of the 4th article, which declares that "the citizens of each State shall be entitled to all privileges and immunities of citizens in the several States," and they have been the subject of frequent consideration in judicial decisions. In *Corfield* v. *Coryell*, . . . Mr. Justice Washington said he had "no hesitation in confining these expressions to those privileges and immunities which were, in their nature, fundamental; which belong of right to citizens of all free governments, and which have at all times been enjoyed by the citizens of the several States which compose the Union, from the time of their becoming free, independent, and sovereign"; and in considering what those fundamental privileges were, he said that perhaps it would be more tedious than difficult to enumerate them, but that they might be "all comprehended under the following general heads: protection by the government; the enjoyment of life and liberty, with the right to acquire and possess property of every kind, and to pursue and obtain happiness and safety, subject, nevertheless, to such restraints as the government may justly prescribe for the general good of the whole." This appears to me to be a sound construction of the clause in question. The privileges and immunities designated are those *which of right belong to the citizens of all free governments*. Clearly among these must be placed the right to pursue a lawful employment in a lawful manner, without other restraint than such as equally affects all persons. In the discussions in Congress upon the passage of the Civil Rights Act repeated reference was made to this language of Mr. Justice Washington. It was cited by Senator Trumbull with the observation that it enumerated the very rights belonging to a citizen of the United States set forth in the first section of the act, and with the statement that all persons born in the United States, being declared by the act citizens of the United States, would thenceforth be entitled to the rights of citizens, and that these were the great fundamental rights set forth in the act; and that they were set forth "as appertaining to every freeman." . . .

This equality of right, with exemption from all disparaging and partial enactments, in the lawful pursuits of life, throughout the whole country, is the distinguishing privilege of citizens of the United States. To them, everywhere, all pursuits, all professions, all avocations are open without other restrictions than such as are imposed equally upon all others of the same age, sex, and condition. The State may prescribe such regulations for every pursuit and calling of life as will promote the public health, secure the good order and advance the general prosperity of society, but when once prescribed, the pursuit or calling must be free to be followed by every citizen who is within the conditions designated, and will conform to the regulations. This is the fundamental idea upon which our institutions rest, and unless adhered to in the legislation of the country our government will be a republic only in name. The fourteenth amendment, in my judgment, makes it essential to the validity of the legislation of every State that this equality of right should be respected. How widely this equality has been departed from, how entirely rejected and trampled upon by the act of Louisiana, I have already shown. And it is to me a matter of profound regret that its validity is recognized by a majority of this court, for by it the right of free labor, one of the most sacred and imprescriptible rights of man, is violated. . . .

I am authorized by the CHIEF JUSTICE [CHASE], MR. JUSTICE SWAYNE, and MR. JUSTICE BRADLEY, to state that they concur with me in this dissenting opinion.

MR. JUSTICE BRADLEY, also dissenting: . . .

The right of a State to regulate the conduct of its citizens is undoubtedly a very broad and extensive one, and not to be lightly restricted. But there are certain fundamental rights which this right of regulation cannot infringe. It may prescribe the manner of their exercise, but it cannot subvert the rights themselves. . . .

The granting of monopolies, or exclusive privileges to individuals or corporations, is an invasion of the right of another to choose a lawful calling, and an infringement of personal liberty. It was so felt by the English nation as far back as the reigns of Elizabeth and James. A fierce struggle for the suppression of such monopolies, and for abolishing the prerogative of creating them, was made and was successful . . . . And ever since that struggle no English-speaking people have ever endured such an odious badge of tyranny. . . .

Lastly: Can the Federal courts administer relief to citizens of the United States whose privileges and immunities have been abridged by a State? Of this I entertain no doubt. Prior to the Fourteenth Amendment this could not be done, except in a few instances, for the want of the requisite authority. . . .

Admitting, therefore, that formerly the States were not prohibited from infringing any fundamental privileges and immunities of citizens of the United States, except in a few specified cases, that cannot be said now, since the adoption of the Fourteenth Amendment. In my judgment, it was the intention of the people of this country in adopting that amendment to provide National security against violation by the States of the fundamental rights of the citizen. . . .

In my opinion the judgment of the Supreme Court of Louisiana ought to be reversed.

[MR. JUSTICE SWAYNE also delivered a dissenting opinion.]

Munn v. *Illinois*
94 U.S. 113, 24 L.Ed. 77 (1877)

Article XIII of the Constitution of Illinois, adopted in 1870, declared grain elevators to be "public warehouses" and gave to the general assembly the power of passing laws relating to the storage of grain. An act of 1871 fixed the rates which warehouse owners might charge, required licenses, and made other regulations governing the conduct of warehousemen. Munn, who was convicted of operating a warehouse without a license and other unlawful practices, sought review on a writ of error from an adverse judgment in the Illinois Supreme Court.

MR. CHIEF JUSTICE WAITE delivered the opinion of the court.

The question to be determined in this case is whether the general assembly of Illinois can, under the limitations upon the legislative powers of the States imposed by the Constitution of the United States, fix by law the maximum of charges for the storage of grain in warehouses at Chicago and other places in the State having not less than one hundred thousand inhabitants, "in which grain is stored in bulk, and in which the grain of different owners is mixed together, or in which grain is stored in such a manner that the identity of different lots or parcels cannot be accurately preserved."

It is claimed that such a law is repugnant:

1. To that part of Sect. 8, Art. I, of the Constitution of the United States which confers upon Congress the power "to regulate commerce with foreign nations and among the several States";

2. To that part of Sect. 9 of the same article, which provides that "no preference shall be given by any regulation of commerce or revenue to the ports of one State over those of another"; and

3. To that part of amendment 14 which ordains that no State shall "deprive any person of life, liberty, or property, without due process of law, nor deny to any person within its jurisdiction the equal protection of the laws."

We will consider the last of these objections first. . . .

The Constitution contains no definition of the word "deprive," as used in the Fourteenth Amendment. To determine its signification, therefore, it is necessary to ascertain the effect which usage has given it, when employed in the same or a like connection.

While this provision of the amendment is new in the Constitution of the United States, as a limitation upon the powers of the States, it is old as a principle of civilized government. It is found in Magna Charta, and, in substance if not in form, in nearly or quite all the constitutions that have been from time to time adopted by the several States of the Union. By the Fifth Amendment, it was introduced into the Constitution of the United States as a limitation upon the powers of the national government, and by the Fourteenth, as a guaranty against any encroachments upon an acknowledged right of citizenship by the legislatures of the States. . . .

When one becomes a member of society, he necessarily parts with some rights or privileges which, as an individual not affected by his relations to others, he might retain. "A body politic," as aptly defined in the preamble of the Constitution of Massachusetts, "is a social compact by which the whole people covenants with each citizen, and each citizen with the whole people, that all shall be governed by certain laws for the common good." This does not confer power upon the whole people to control rights which are purely and exclusively private, . . . but it does authorize the establishment of laws requiring each citizen to so conduct himself, and so use his own property, as not unnecessarily to injure another. This is the very essence of government, and has found expression in the maxim, *sic utere tuo ut alienum non laedas*. [So use your own as not to injure others.] From this source come the police powers, which, as was said by Mr. Chief Justice Taney in the License Cases, 5 How. 583, ''are nothing more or less than the powers of government inherent in every sovereignty . . . that is to say . . . the power to govern men and things.'' Under these powers the government regulates the conduct of its citizens one towards another, and the manner in which each shall use his own property, when such regulation becomes necessary for the public good. In their exercise it has been customary in England from time immemorial, and in this country from its first colonization, to regulate ferries, common carriers, hackmen, bakers, millers, wharfingers, innkeepers, &c., and in so doing to fix a maximum of charge to be made for services rendered, accommodations furnished, and articles sold. To this day, statutes are to be found in many of the States upon some or all these subjects; and we think it has never yet been successfully contended that such legislation came within any of the constitutional prohibitions against interference with private property. With the Fifth Amendment in force, Congress in 1820 conferred power upon the city of Washington ''to regulate . . . the rates of wharfage at private wharves, . . . the sweeping of chimneys, and to fix the rates of fees therefor, . . . and the weight and quality of bread,'' . . . and, in 1848, ''to make all necessary regulations respecting hackney carriages and the rates of fare of the same, and the rates of hauling by cartmen, wagoners, carmen, and draymen, and the rates of commission of auctioneers.'' . . .

From this it is apparent that, down to the time of the adoption of the Fourteenth Amendment, it was not supposed that statutes regulating the use, or even the price of the use, of private property necessarily deprived an owner of his property without due process of law. Under some circumstances they may, but not under all. The amendment does not change the law in this particular: it simply prevents the States from doing that which will operate as such a deprivation.

This brings us to inquire as to the principles upon which this power of regulation rests, in order that we may determine what is within and what is without its operative effect. Looking, then, to the common law, from whence came the right which the Constitution protects, we find that when private property is ''affected with a public interest, it ceases to be *juris privati* only.'' This was said by Lord Chief Justice Hale more than two hundred years ago, in his treatise *De Portibus Maris,* . . . , and has been accepted without objection as an essential element in the law of property ever since. Property does become clothed with a public interest when used in a manner to make it of public consequence, and affect the community at large. When, therefore, one devotes his property to a use in which the public has an interest, he, in effect, grants to the public an interest in that use, and must submit to be controlled by the public for the common good, to the extent of the interest he has thus created. He may withdraw his grant by discontinuing the use; but, so long as he maintains the use, he must submit to the control. . . .

. . . Enough has already been said to show that, when private property is devoted to a public use, it is subject to public regulation. It remains only to ascertain whether the warehouses of these plaintiffs in error, and the business which is carried on there, come within the operation of this principle. . . .

. . . It is difficult to see why, if the common carrier, or the miller, or the ferryman, or the innkeeper, or the wharfinger, or the baker, or the cartman, or the hackney-coachman, pursues a public employment and exercises ''a sort of public office,'' these plaintiffs in error do not. They stand, to use again the language of their counsel, in the very ''gateway of commerce,'' and take toll from all who pass. Their business most certainly ''tends to a common charge, and has become a thing of public interest and use.'' Every bushel of grain for its passage ''pays a toll, which is a common charge,'' and, therefore, according to Lord Hale, every such warehouseman ''ought to be under public regulation, viz., that he . . . take but reasonable toll.'' Certainly, if any business can be clothed ''with a public interest and cease to be *juris privati* only," this has been. It may not be made so by the operation of the Constitution of Illinois or this statute, but it is by the facts.

We also are not permitted to overlook the fact that, for some reason, the people of Illinois, when they revised their Constitution in 1870, saw fit to make it the duty of the general assembly to pass laws "for the protection of producers, shippers, and receivers of grain and produce." . . .

. . . For our purposes we must assume that, if a state of facts could exist that would justify such legislation, it actually did exist when the statute now under consideration was passed. For us the question is one of power, not of expediency. If no state of circumstances could exist to justify such a statute, then we may declare this one void, because in excess of the legislative power of the State. But if it could, we must presume it did. Of the propriety of legislative interference within the scope of legislative power, the legislature is the exclusive judge.

Neither is it a matter of any moment that no precedent can be found for a statute precisely like this. It is conceded that the business is one of recent origin, that its growth has been rapid, and that it is already of great importance. And it must also be conceded that it is a business in which the whole public has a direct and positive interest. It presents, therefore, a case for the application of a long-known and well-established principle in social science, and this statute simply extends the law so as to meet this new development of commercial progress. There is no attempt to compel these owners to grant the public an interest in their property, but to declare their obligations, if they use it in this particular manner. . . .

It is insisted, however, that the owner of property is entitled to a reasonable compensation for its use, even though it be clothed with a public interest, and that what is reasonable is a judicial and not a legislative question.

As has already been shown, the practice had been otherwise. In countries where the common law prevails, it has been customary from time immemorial for the legislature to declare what

shall be a reasonable compensation under such circumstances, or, perhaps more properly speaking, to fix a maximum beyond which any charge made would be unreasonable. Undoubtedly, in mere private contracts, relating to matters in which the public has no interest, what is reasonable must be ascertained judicially. But this is because the legislature has no control over such a contract. So, too, in matters which do affect the public interest, and as to which legislative control may be exercised, if there are no statutory regulations upon the subject, the courts must determine what is reasonable. The controlling fact is the power to regulate at all. If that exists, the right to establish the maximum of charge, as one of the means of regulation, is implied. In fact, the common-law rule, which requires the charge to be reasonable, is itself a regulation as to price. Without it the owner could make his rates at will, and compel the public to yield to his terms, or forego the use.

But a mere common-law regulation of trade or business may be changed by statute. A person has no property, no vested interest, in any rule of the common law. That is only one of the forms of municipal law, and is no more sacred than any other. Rights of property which have been created by the common law cannot be taken away without due process; but the law itself, as a rule of conduct, may be changed at the will, or even at the whim, of the legislature, unless prevented by constitutional limitations. Indeed, the great office of statutes is to remedy defects in the common law as they are developed, and to adapt it to the changes of time and circumstance. To limit the rate of charge for services rendered in a public employment, or for the use of property in which the public has an interest, is only changing a regulation which existed before. It establishes no new principle in the law, but only gives a new effect to an old one.

We know that this is a power which may be abused; but that is no argument against its existence. For protection against abuses by legislatures the people must resort to the polls, not to the courts.

We come now to consider the effect upon this

statute of the power of Congress to regulate commerce.

It was very properly said in the case of the State Tax on Railway Gross Receipts, 15 Wall. 293, that "it is not everything that affects commerce that amounts to a regulation of it, within the meaning of the Constitution." The warehouses of these plaintiffs in error are situated and their business carried on exclusively within the limits of the State of Illinois. They are used as instruments by those engaged in State as well as those engaged in interstate commerce, but they are no more necessarily a part of commerce itself than the dray or the cart by which, but for them, grain would be transferred from one railroad station to another. Incidentally they may become connected with interstate commerce, but not necessarily so. Their regulation is a thing of domestic concern, and, certainly, until Congress acts in reference to their interstate relations, the State may exercise all the powers of government over them, even though in so doing it may indirectly operate upon commerce outside its immediate jurisdiction. We do not say that a case may not arise in which it will be found that a State, under the form of regulating its own affairs, has encroached upon the exclusive domain of Congress, in respect to interstate commerce, but we do say that, upon the facts as they are presented to us in this record, that has not been done....

Judgment affirmed.

MR. JUSTICE FIELD. I am compelled to dissent from the decision of the court in this case, and from the reasons upon which that decision is founded. The principle upon which the opinion of the majority proceeds is, in my judgment, subversive of the rights of private property, heretofore believed to be protected by constitutional guaranties against legislative interference, and is in conflict with the authorities cited in its support....

The declaration of the Constitution of 1870, that private buildings used for private purposes shall be deemed public institutions, does not make them so. The receipt and storage of grain in a building erected by private means for that purpose does not constitute the building a public warehouse. There is no magic in the language, though used by a constitutional convention, which can change a private business into a public one, or alter the character of the building in which the business is transacted. A tailor's or a shoemaker's shop would still retain its private character, even though the assembled wisdom of the State should declare, by organic act or legislative ordinance, that such a place was a public workshop, and that the workmen were public tailors or public shoemakers. One might as well attempt to change the nature of colors, by giving them a new designation. The defendants were no more public warehousemen, as justly observed by counsel, than the merchant who sells his merchandise to the public is a public merchant, or blacksmith who shoes horses for the public is a public blacksmith and it was a strange notion that by calling them so they would be brought under legislative control....

... The doctrine declared is that property "becomes clothed with a public interest when used in a manner to make it of public consequence, and affect the community at large"; and from such clothing the right of the legislature is deduced to control the use of the property, and to determine the compensation which the owner may receive for it. When Sir Matthew Hale, and the sages of the law in his day, spoke of property as affected by a public interest, and ceasing from that cause to be *juris privati* solely, that is ceasing to be held merely in private right, they referred to property dedicated by the owner to public uses, or to property the use of which was granted by the government, or in connection with which special privileges were conferred. Unless the property was thus dedicated or some right bestowed by the government was held with the property, either by specific grant or by prescription of so long a time as to imply a grant originally, the property was not affected by any public interest so as to be taken out of the category of property held in private right. But it is not in any such sense that the terms "clothing property with a public interest" are used in this case. From the nature of the business under consideration—the storage of grain—which, in any sense in which the words can be used, is a private business, in which the public are interested only as they are interested in the storage of other products of the soil, or in articles of manufacture, it is clear that the court intended to declare that, whenever one devotes his property to a business which is useful to the public—"affects the community at large,"—the legislature can regulate the compensation which the owner may receive for its use, and for his own services in connection with it. . . .

If this be sound law, if there be no protection, either in the principles upon which our republican government is founded, or in the prohibitions of the Constitution against such invasion of private rights, all property and all business in the State are held at the mercy of a majority of its legislature. The public has no greater interest in the use of buildings for the storage of grain than it has in the use of buildings for the residences of families, nor, indeed, any thing like so great an interest; and, according to the doctrine announced, the legislature may fix the rent of all tenements used for residences, without reference to the cost of their erection. If the owner does not like the rates prescribed, he may cease renting his houses. He has granted to the public, says the court, an interest in the use of the buildings, and "he may withdraw his grant by discontinuing the use; but, so long as he maintains the use, he must submit to the control." The public is interested in the manufacture of cotton, woolen, and silken fabrics, in the construction of machinery, in the printing and publication of books and periodicals, and in the making of utensils of every variety, useful and ornamental; indeed, there is hardly an enterprise or business engaging the attention and labor of any considerable portion of the community, in which the public has not an interest in the sense in which that term is used by the court in its opinion; and the doctrine which allows the legislature to interfere with and regulate the charges which the owners of property thus employed shall make for its use, that is, the rates at which all these different kinds of business shall be carried on, has never

before been asserted, so far as I am aware, by any judicial tribunal in the United States. . . .

No State "shall deprive any person of life, liberty, or property without due process of law," says the Fourteenth Amendment to the Constitution. . . .

By the term "liberty," as used in the provision, something more is meant than mere freedom from physical restraint or the bounds of a prison. It means freedom to go where one may choose, and to act in such manner, not inconsistent with the equal rights of others, as his judgment may dictate for the promotion of his happiness; that is, to pursue such callings and avocations as may be most suitable to develop his capacities, and give to them their highest enjoyment.

The same liberal construction which is required for the protection of life and liberty, in all particulars in which life and liberty are of any value, should be applied to the protection of private property. If the legislature of a State, under pretense of providing for the public good, or for any other reason, can determine, against the consent of the owner, the uses to which private property shall be devoted, or the prices which the owner shall receive for its uses, it can deprive him of the property as completely as by a special act for its confiscation or destruction. If, for instance, the owner is prohibited from using his building for the purposes for which it was designed, it is of little consequence that he is permitted to retain the title and possession; or, if he is compelled to take as compensation for its use less than the expenses to which he is subjected by its ownership, he is, for all practical purposes, deprived of the property, as effectually as if the legislature had ordered his forcible dispossession. If it be admitted that the legislature has any control over the compensation, the extent of that compensation becomes a mere matter of legislative discretion. . . .

There is nothing in the character of the business of the defendants as warehousemen which called for the interference complained of in this case. Their buildings are not nuisances; their occupation of receiving and storing grain infringes upon no rights of others, disturbs no neighborhood, infects not the air, and in no respect prevents others from using and enjoying their property as to them may seem best. The legislation in question is nothing less than a bold assertion of absolute power by the state to control at its discretion the property and business of the citizen, and fix the compensation he shall receive. . . .

I deny the power of any legislature under our government to fix the price which one shall receive for his property of any kind. If the power can be exercised as to one article, it may as to all articles, and the prices of every thing, from a calico gown to a city mansion, may be the subject of legislative direction. . . .

I am of opinion that the judgment of the Supreme Court of Illinois should be reversed.

[MR. JUSTICE STRONG concurred in the opinion of MR. JUSTICE FIELD.]

Mugler v. Kansas
123 U.S. 623, 8 S.Ct. 273, 31 L.Ed. 205 (1887)

An article of the constitution of Kansas, adopted in 1880, prohibited the manufacture and sale of intoxicating liquors except for certain restricted purposes, and a statute of 1881 provided sanctions. Mugler, who had erected a brewery in 1877, was convicted of selling and manufacturing beer after the effective date of the statute. He sought on writ of error to review the affirmance of his conviction.

MR. JUSTICE HARLAN delivered the opinion of the court. . . .

The general question in each case is, whether the foregoing statutes of Kansas are in conflict with that clause of the Fourteenth Amendment, which provides that "no State shall make or enforce any law which shall abridge the privileges or immunities of citizens of the United States; nor shall any State deprive any person of life, liberty, or property, without due process of law."

That legislation by a State prohibiting the manufacture within her limits of intoxicating liquors, to be there sold or bartered for general use as a beverage, does not necessarily infringe any right, privilege, or immunity secured by the Constitution of the United States, is made clear by the decisions of this court, rendered before and since the adoption of the Fourteenth Amendment. . . .

. . . These cases rest upon the acknowledged right of the States of the Union to control their purely internal affairs, and, in so doing, to protect the health, morals, and safety of their people by regulations that do not interfere with the execution of the powers of the general government, or violate rights secured by the Constitution of the United States. The power to establish such regulations, as was said in *Gibbons* v. *Ogden* . . . reaches everything within the territory of a State not surrendered to the national government.

It is, however, contended that, although the State may prohibit the manufacture of intoxicating liquors for sale or barter within her limits, for general use as a beverage, "no convention or legislature has the right, under our form of government, to prohibit any citizen from manufacturing for his own use, or for export, or storage, any article of food or drink not endangering or affecting the rights of others." The argument made in support of the first branch of this proposition, briefly stated, is, that in the implied compact between the State and the citizen certain rights are reserved by the latter, which are guaranteed by the constitutional provision protecting persons against being deprived of life, liberty, or property, without due process of law, and with which the State cannot interfere; that among those rights is that of manufacturing for one's use either food or drink; and that while according to the doctrines of the Commune, the State may control the tastes, appetites, habits, dress, food, and drink of the people, our system of government, based upon the individuality and intelligence of the citizen, does not claim to control him, except as to his conduct to others, leaving him the sole judge as to all that only affects himself. . . .

But by whom, or by what authority, is it to be determined whether the manufacture of particular articles of drink, either for general use or for the personal use of the maker, will injuriously affect the public? Power to determine such questions, so as to bind all, must exist somewhere; else society will be at the mercy of the few, who, regarding only their own appetites or passions, may be willing to imperil the peace and security of the many, provided only they are permitted to do as they please. Under our system that power is lodged with the legislative branch of the government. It belongs to that department to exert what are known as the police powers of the State, and to determine, primarily what measures are appropriate or needful for the protection of the public morals, the public health, or the public safety.

It does not at all follow that every statute enacted ostensibly for the promotion of these ends is to be accepted as a legitimate exertion of the police powers of the State. There are, of necessity, limits beyond which legislation cannot rightfully go. . . . The courts are not bound by mere forms, nor are they to be misled by mere pretenses. They are at liberty—indeed, are under a solemn duty—to look at the substance of things, whenever they enter upon the inquiry whether the legislature has transcended the limits of its authority. If, therefore, a statute purporting to have been enacted to protect the public health, the public morals, or the public

safety, has no real or substantial relation to those objects, or is a palpable invasion of rights secured by the fundamental law, it is the duty of the courts to so adjudge, and thereby give effect to the Constitution.

Keeping in view these principles, as governing the relations of the judicial and legislative departments of government with each other, it is difficult to perceive any ground for the judiciary to declare that the prohibition by Kansas of the manufacture or sale, within her limits, of intoxicating liquors for general use there as a beverage, is not fairly adapted to the end of protecting the community against the evils which confessedly result from the excessive use of ardent spirits. . . . Indeed, it is a fundamental principle in our institutions, indispensable to the preservation of public liberty, that one of the separate departments of government shall not usurp powers committed by the Constitution to another department. And so, if, in the judgment of the legislature, the manufacture of intoxicating liquors for the maker's own use, as a beverage, would tend to cripple, if it did not defeat, the effort to guard the community against the evils attending the excessive use of such liquors, it is not for the courts, upon their views as to what is best and safest for the community, to disregard the legislative determination of that question. So far from such a regulation having no relation to the general end sought to be accomplished, the entire scheme of prohibition, as embodied in the Constitution and laws of Kansas, might fail, if the right of each citizen to manufacture intoxicating liquors for his own use as a beverage were recognized. Such a right does not inhere in citizenship. Nor can it be said that government interferes with or impairs any one's constitutional rights of liberty or of property, when it determines that the manufacture and sale of intoxicating drinks, for general or individual use, as a beverage, are, or may become, hurtful to society, and constitute, therefore, a business in which no one may lawfully engage. Those rights are best secured, in our government, by the observance, upon the part of all, of such regulations as are established by competent authority to promote the common good. No one may rightfully do that which the law-making power, upon reasonable grounds, declares to be prejudicial to the general welfare. . . .

. . . A prohibition simply upon the use of property for purposes that are declared, by valid legislation, to be injurious to the health, morals, or safety of the community, cannot, in any just sense, be deemed a taking or an appropriation of property for the public benefit. Such legislation does not disturb the owner in the control or use of his property for lawful purposes, nor restrict his right to dispose of it, but is only a declaration by the State that its use by any one, for certain forbidden purposes, is prejudicial to the public interests. . . .

A portion of the argument in behalf of the defendants is to the effect that the statutes of Kansas forbid the manufacture of intoxicating liquors to be exported, or to be carried to other States, and, upon that ground, are repugnant to the clause of the Constitution of the United States giving Congress power to regulate commerce with foreign nations and among the several States. We need only say, upon this point, that there is no intimation in the record that the beer which the respective defendants manufactured was intended to be carried out of the State or to foreign countries. And, without expressing an opinion as to whether such facts would have constituted a good defence, we observe that it will be time enough to decide a case of that character when it shall come before us.

Affirmed.

[MR. JUSTICE FIELD delivered a separate opinion, dissenting in part.]

Chicago, Milwaukee and St. Paul Railway Co. v. Minnesota
134 U.S. 418, 10 S.Ct. 462, 702, 33 L.Ed. 970 (1890)

A Minnesota act of 1887 established a railroad and warehouse commission with the power to set "equal and reasonable rates of charges for the transportation of property." In this case the commission had ordered a decrease in the rate charged for milk transportation from 4 and 3 cents between specified places to 2½ cents. In upholding the commission's order the Supreme Court of Minnesota refused to permit a judicial hearing on the question of reasonableness. The railroad brought writ of error.

MR. JUSTICE BLATCHFORD . . . delivered the opinion of the court. . . .

The construction put upon the statute by the Supreme Court of Minnesota must be accepted by this court, for the purposes of the present case, as conclusive and not to be reexamined here as to its propriety or accuracy. The Supreme Court authoritatively declares that it is the expressed intention of the legislature of Minnesota, by the statute, that the rates recommended and published by the commission, if it proceeds in the manner pointed out by the act, are not simply advisory, nor merely *prima facie* equal and reasonable, but final and conclusive as to what are equal and reasonable, charges; that the law neither contemplates nor allows any issue to be made or inquiry to be had as to their equality or reasonableness in fact; that, under the statute, the rates published by the commission are the only ones that are lawful, and, therefore, in contemplation of law the only ones that are equal and reasonable; and that, in a proceeding for a mandamus under the statute, there is no fact to traverse except the violation of law in not complying with the recommendations of the commission. In other words, although the railroad company is forbidden to establish rates that are not equal and reasonable, there is no power in the courts to stay the hands of the commission, if it chooses to establish rates that are unequal and unreasonable.

This being the construction of the statute by which we are bound in considering the present case, we are of opinion that, so construed, it conflicts with the Constitution of the United States in the particulars complained of by the railroad company. It deprives the company of its right to a judicial investigation by due process of law, under the forms and with the machinery provided by the wisdom of successive ages for the investigation judicially of the truth of a matter in controversy, and substitutes therefore, as an absolute finality, the action of a railroad commission which, in view of the powers conceded to it by the state court, cannot be regarded as clothed with judicial functions or possessing the machinery of a court of justice.

Under Section 8 of the statute, which the Supreme Court of Minnesota says is the only one which relates to the matter of the fixing by the commission of general schedules of rates, and which section, it says, fully and exclusively provides for that subject, and is complete in itself, all that the commission is required to do is, on the filing with it by a railroad company of copies of its schedules of charges, to "find" that any part thereof is in any respect unequal or unreasonable, and then it is authorized and directed to compel the company to change the same and adopt such charge as the commission "shall declare to be equal and reasonable," and, to that end, it is required to inform the company in writing in what respect its charges are unequal and unreasonable. No hearing is provided for, no summons or notice to the company before the commission has found what it is to find and declared what it is to declare, no opportunity provided for the company to introduce witnesses before the commission, in fact, nothing which has the semblance of due

process of law; and although, in the present case, it appears that, prior to the decision of the commission, the company appeared before it by its agent, and the commission investigated the rates charged by the company for transporting milk, yet it does not appear what the character of the investigation was or how the result was arrived at.

By the second section of the statute in question, it is provided that all charges made by a common carrier for the transportation of passengers or property shall be equal and reasonable. Under this provision, the carrier has a right to make equal and reasonable charges for such transportation. In the present case, the return alleged that the rate of charge fixed by the commission was not equal or reasonable, and the Supreme Court held that the statute deprived the company of the right to show that judicially. The question of the reasonableness of a rate of charge for transportation by a railroad company, involving as it does the element of reasonableness both as regards the company and as regards the public, is eminently a question for judicial investigation, requiring due process of law for its determination. If the company is deprived of the power of charging reasonable rates for the use of its property, and such deprivation takes place in the absence of an investigation by judicial machinery, it is deprived of the lawful use of its property, and thus, in substance and effect, of the property itself, without due process of law and in violation of the Constitution of the United States; and in so far as it is thus deprived, while other persons are permitted to receive reasonable profits upon their invested capital, the company is deprived of the equal protection of the laws. . . .

. . . *Reversed, and remanded with an instruction for further proceedings not inconsistent with the opinion of this court.*

MR. JUSTICE MILLER [concurred].

MR. JUSTICE BRADLEY (with whom concurred MR. JUSTICE GRAY and MR. JUSTICE LAMAR) dissenting.

I cannot agree to the decision of the court in this case. It practically overrules *Munn* v. *Illinois*, . . . , and the several railroad cases that were decided at the same time. The governing principle of those cases was that the regulation and settlement of the fares of railroads and other public accommodations is a legislative prerogative and not a judicial one. . . .

But it is said that all charges should be reasonable, and that none but reasonable charges can be exacted; and it is urged that what is a reasonable charge is a judicial question. On the contrary, it is preeminently a legislative one, involving considerations of a policy as well as of remuneration; and is usually determined by the legislature, by fixing a maximum of charges in the charter of the company, or afterwards, if its hands are not tied by contract. . . .

Thus, the legislature either fixes the charges at rates which it deems reasonable; or merely declares that they shall be reasonable; and it is only in the latter case, where what is reasonable is left open, that the courts have jurisdiction of the subject. I repeat: When the legislature declares that the charges shall be reasonable, or, which is the same thing, allows the common-law rule to that effect to prevail, and leaves the matter there; then resort may be had to the courts to inquire judicially whether the charges are reasonable. Then, and not till then, is it a judicial question. But the legislature has the right, and it is its prerogative, if it chooses to exercise it, to declare what is reasonable. . . .

It is always a delicate thing for the courts to make an issue with the legislative department of the government, and they should never do so if it is possible to avoid it. By the decision now made we declare, in effect, that the judiciary, and not the legislature, is the final arbiter in the regulation of fares and freights of railroads and the charges of other public accommodations. It is an assumption of authority on the part of the judiciary which, it seems to me, with all due deference to the judgment of my brethren, it has no right to make. . . .

I think it is perfectly clear, and well settled by the decisions of this court, that the legislature might have fixed the rates in question. If it had done so, it would have done it through the aid of committees appointed to investigate the subject, to acquire information, to cite parties, to get all the facts before them, and finally to decide and report. No one could have said that this was not due process of law. And if the legislature itself could do this, acting by its committees, and proceeding according to the usual forms adopted by such bodies, I can see no good reason why it might not delegate the duty to a board of commissioners, charged, as the board in this case was, to regulate and fix the charges so as to be equal and reasonable. . . .

It may be that our legislatures are invested with too much power, open, as they are, to influences so dangerous to the interests of individuals, corporations and society. But such is the Constitution of our republican form of government; and we are bound to abide by it until it can be corrected in a legitimate way. If our legislatures become too arbitrary in the exercise of their powers, the people always have a remedy in their hands; they may at any time restrain them by constitutional limitations. But so long as they remain invested with the powers that ordinarily belong to the legislative branch of government, they are entitled to exercise those powers, amongst which, in my judgment, is that of the regulation of railroads and other public means of intercommunication, and the burdens and charges which those who own them are authorized to impose upon the public. . . .

Unstaged Debate of 1893:
Justice Brewer v. *Professor Thayer*

JUSTICE DAVID J. BREWER, *The Movement of Coercion,*
an address before the New York State Bar Association,
17 January 1893

The salvation of the nation—a strengthened judiciary

Three things differentiate the civilized man from the savage—that which he knows, that which he is, and that which he has. That which he knows: The Knowledge of the savage is limited to the day, and bounded by the visible horizon. The civilized man looks backward through all history, and beholds the present limits of the universe. The accumulations of the centuries are his. The logic of Aristotle and Bacon determines the processes of his mind. The philosophy of Plato and Herbert Spencer is his wisdom. . . .

It is the unvarying law, that the wealth of a community will be in the hands of a few; and the greater the general wealth, the greater the individual accumulations. The large majority of men are unwilling to endure that long self-denial and saving which makes accumulation possible; they have not the business tact and sagacity which bring about large combinations and great financial results; and hence it always has been, and until human nature is remodeled always will be true, that the wealth of a nation is in the hands of a few, while the many subsist upon the proceeds of their daily toil. But security is the chief end of government; and other things being equal, that government is best which protects to the fullest extent each individual, rich or poor, high or low, in the possession of his property and the pursuit of his business. It was the boast of our ancestors in the old country, that they were able to wrest from the power of the king so much security for life, liberty and property. . . .

Here there is no monarch threatening trespass upon the individual. The danger is from the multitudes—the majority, with whom is the power. . . .

This movement expresses itself in two ways: First, in the improper use of labor organizations to destroy the freedom of the laborer, and control the uses of capital. . . . When a thousand laborers gather around a railroad track, and say to those who seek employment that they had better not, and when that advice is supplemented every little while by a terrible assault on one who disregards it, every one knows that something more than advice is intended. It is coercion, force; it is the effort of the many, by the mere weight of numbers, to compel the one to do their bidding. It is a proceeding outside of the law, in defiance of the law, and in spirit and effect—an attempt to strip from one that has that which of right belongs to him—the full and undisturbed use and enjoyment of his own. . . . It is the attempt to give to the many a control over the few—a step toward despotism. Let the movement succeed; let it once be known that the individual is not free to contract for his personal services. . . and the next step will be a direct effort on the part of the many to seize the property of the few.

The other form of this movement assumes the guise of a regulation of the charges for the use of property subjected, or supposed to be, to a public use. This acts in two directions: One by extending the list of those things, charges for whose use the government may prescribe; until now we hear it affirmed that whenever property is devoted to a use in which the public has an interest, charges for that use may be fixed by law. And if there be any property in the use of which the public or some portion of it has no interest, I hardly know what it is or where to find it. And second, in so reducing charges for the use of property, which in fact is subjected to a public use, that no compensation or income is received by those who have so invested their property. By the one it subjects all property and its uses to the will of the majority; by the other it robs property of its value. Statutes and decisions both disclose that this movement, with just these results, has a present and alarming existence. . . .

. . . It may be said that that majority will not be so foolish, selfish and cruel as to strip that property of its earning capacity. I say that so long as constitutional guaranties lift on American soil their buttresses and bulwarks against wrong, and so long as the American judiciary breathes the free air of courage, it cannot. . . .

As might be expected, they who wish to push this movement to the extreme, who would brook no restraint on aught that seems to make for their gain, are unanimous in crying out against judicial interference, and are constantly seeking to minimize the power of the courts. . . . The argument is that judges are not adapted by their education and training to settle such matters as these; that they lack acquaintance with affairs and are tied to precedents; that the procedure in the courts is too slow and that no action could be had therein until long after the need of action has passed. It would be folly to assert that this argument is barren of force. . . . But the great body of judges are as well versed in the affairs of life as any, and they who unravel all the mysteries of accounting between partners, settle the business of the largest corporations and extract all the truth from the mass of scholastic verbiage that falls from the lips of expert witnesses in patent cases, will have no difficulty in determining what is right and wrong between employer and employees, and whether proposed rates of freight and fare are reasonable as between the public and the owners; while as for speed, is there anything quicker than a writ of injunction? . . .

The mischief-makers in this movement ever strive to get away from courts and judges, and to place the power of decision in the hands of those who will the more readily and freely yield to the pressure of numbers, that so-called demand of the majority. . . .

And so it is, that because of the growth of this movement, of its development in many directions, and the activity of those who are in it, and especially because of the further fact that, carrying votes in its hand, it ever appeals to the trimming politician and time-serving demagogue, and thus enters into so much of legislation, arises the urgent need of giving to the judiciary the utmost vigor and efficiency. Now, if ever in the history of this country, must there be somewhere and somehow a controlling force which speaks for justice, and for justice only. . . .

What, then, ought to be done? My reply is, strengthen the judiciary. . . .

It may be said that this is practically substituting government by the judges for government by the people, and thus turning back the currents of history. The world has seen government by chiefs, by kings and emperors, by priests and by nobles. All have failed, and now government by the people is on trial. Shall we abandon that and try government by judges? But this involves a total misunderstanding of the relations of judges to government. There is nothing in this power of the judiciary detracting in the least from the idea of government of and by the people. The courts hold neither purse nor sword; they cannot corrupt nor arbitrarily control. They make no laws, they establish no policy, they never enter into the domain of popular action. They do not govern. Their functions in relation to the State are limited to seeing that popular action does not trespass upon right and justice as it exists in written constitutions and natural law. So it is that the utmost power of the courts and judges works no interference with true liberty, no trespass on the fullest and highest development of government of and by the people; it only means security to personal rights—the inalienable rights, life, liberty and the pursuit of happiness. . . .

Who does not hear the old demagogic

cry—*vox populi vox dei* (paraphrased today, the majority are always right)—constantly invoked to justify disregard of those guaranties which have hitherto been deemed sufficient to give protection to private property? . . .

I am firmly persuaded that the salvation of the Nation, the permanence of government of and by the people, rests upon the independence and vigor of the judiciary. To stay the waves of popular feeling, to restrain the greedy hand of the many from filching from the few that which they have honestly acquired, and to protect in every man's possession and enjoyment, be he rich or poor, that which he hath, demands a tribunal as strong as is consistent with the freedom of human action, and as free from all influences and suggestions other than is compassed in the thought of justice, as can be created out of the infirmities of human nature. To that end the courts exist, and for that let all the judges be put beyond the reach of political office, and all fear of losing position or compen-sation during good behavior. It may be that this is not popular doctrine to-day. . . . The black flag of anarchism, flaunting destruction to property, and therefore relapse of society to bar-barism; the red flag of socialism, inviting a redistribution of property, which, in order to secure the vaunted equality, must be repeated again and again at constantly decreasing inter-vals, and that colorless piece of baby-cloth, which suggests that the State take all property and direct all the work and life of individuals, as if they were little children, may seem to fill the air with their flutter. But as against these schemes, or any other plot or vagary of fiend, fool or fanatic, the eager and earnest protest and cry of the Anglo-Saxon is for individual freedom and absolute protection of all his rights of per-son and property. . . . And to help and strengthen that good time, we shall yet see in every State an independent judiciary, made as independent of all outside influences as is possi-ble . . . supreme in fact as in name. . . .

JAMES BRADLEY THAYER, *The Origin and Scope of the American Doctrine of Constitutional Law,* an address before the Congress on Jurisprudence and Law Reform, 9 August 1893. *Harvard Law Review,* vol. VII, 25 October 1893, pp. 129–56 *passim*

Fixing the outside border of reasonable legislative action leaves the Court a great and stately jurisdiction.

How did our American doctrine, which allows to the judiciary the power to declare legislative Acts unconstitutional, and to treat them as null, come about, and what is the true scope of it? . . .

It is plain that where a power so momentous as this primary authority to interpret is given, the actual determinations of the body to whom it is intrusted are entitled to a corresponding respect; and this not on mere grounds of courtesy or conventional respect, but on very solid and significant grounds of policy and law. The judiciary may well reflect that if they had been regarded by the people as the chief protec-tion against legislative violation of the constitu-tion, they would not have been allowed merely this incidental and postponed control. They would have been let in, as it was sometimes endeavored in the conventions to let them in, to a revision of the laws before they began to operate. As the opportunity of the judges to check and correct unconstitutional Acts is so limited, it may help us to understand why the extent of their control, when they do have the opportunity, should also be narrow.

It was, then, all along true, and it was foreseen, that much which is harmful and unconstitutional may take effect without any capacity in the courts to prevent it, since their whole power is a judicial one. Their interference was but one of many safeguards, and its scope was narrow.

The rigor of this limitation upon judicial action is sometimes freely recognized, yet in a perverted way which really operates to extend the judicial function beyond its just bounds. The court's duty, we are told, is the mere and simple office of construing two writings and comparing one with another, as two contracts or two statutes are construed and compared when they are said to conflict; of declaring the true meaning of each, and, if they are opposed to each other, of carrying into effect the constitution as being of superior obligation—an ordinary and humble judicial duty, as the courts sometimes describe it. This way of putting it easily results in the wrong kind of disregard of legislative considerations; not merely in refusing to let them directly operate as grounds of judgment, but in refusing to consider them at all. Instead of taking them into account and allowing for them as furnishing possible grounds of legislative action, there takes place a pedantic and academic treatment of the texts of the constitution and the laws. And so we miss that combination of a lawyer's rigor with a statesman's breadth of view which should be found in dealing with this class of questions in constitutional law. . . .

The courts have perceived with more or less distinctness that this exercise of the judicial function does in truth go far beyond the simple business which judges sometimes describe. If their duty were in truth merely and nakedly to ascertain the meaning of the text of the constitu-

tion and of the impeached Act of the legislature, and to determine, as an academic question, whether in the court's judgment the two were in conflict, it would, to be sure, be an elevated and important office, one dealing with great matters, involving large public considerations, but yet a function far simpler than it really is. Having ascertained all this, yet there remains a question—the really momentous question—whether, after all, the court can disregard the Act. It cannot do this as a mere matter of course —merely because it is concluded that upon a just and true construction the law is unconstitutional. That is precisely the significance of the rule of administration that the courts lay down. It can only disregard the Act when those who have the right to make laws have not merely made a mistake, but have made a very clear one —so clear that it is not open to rational question. That is the standard of duty to which the courts bring legislative Acts; that is the test which they apply—not merely their own judgment as to constitutionality, but their conclusion as to what judgment is permissible to another department which the constitution has charged with the duty of making it. This rule recognizes that, having regard to the great, complex, ever-unfolding exigencies of government, much which will seem unconstitutional to one man, or body of men, may reasonably not seem so to another; that the constitution often admits of different interpretations; that there is often a range of choice and judgment; that in such cases the constitution does not impose upon the legislature any one specific opinion, but leaves open this range of choice; and that whatever choice is rational is constitutional. . . . [A legislator] may vote against a measure as being, in his judgment, unconstitutional; and, being subsequently placed on the bench, when this measure, having been passed by the legislature in spite of his opposition, comes before him judicially, may there find it his duty, although he has in no degree changed his opinion, to declare it constitutional . . . .

The legislature in determining what shall be done, what it is reasonable to do, does not divide its duty with the judges, nor must it conform to their conception of what is prudent or reasonable legislation. The judicial function is merely that of fixing the outside border of reasonable legislative action, the boundary beyond which the taxing power, the power of eminent domain, police power, and legislative power in general, cannot go without violating the prohibitions of the constitution or crossing the line of its grants. . . .

. . . [T]*he ultimate question is not what is the true meaning of the constitution, but whether legislation is sustainable or not.* . . .

. . . What really took place in adopting our theory of constitutional law was this: we introduced for the first time into the conduct of government through its great departments a judicial sanction, as among these departments, not full and complete, but partial. The judges were allowed, indirectly and in a degree, the power to revise the action of other departments and to pronounce it null. In simple truth, while this is a mere judicial function, it involves, owing to the subject matter with which it deals, taking a part, a secondary part, in the political conduct of government. If that be so, then the judges must apply methods and principles that befit their task. In such a work there can be no permanent or fitting *modus vivendi* between the different departments unless each is sure of the full cooperation of the others, so long as its own action conforms to any reasonable and fairly permissible view of its constitutional power. The ultimate arbiter of what is rational and permissible is indeed always the courts, so far as litigated cases bring the question before them. This leaves to our courts a great and stately jurisdiction. It will only imperil the whole of it if it is sought to give them more. They must not step into the shoes of the lawmaker. . . .

I am not stating a new doctrine, but attempting to restate more exactly and truly an admitted one. If what I have said be sound, it is greatly to be desired that it should be more emphasized by our courts, in its full significance. It has been often remarked that private rights are more respected by the legislatures of some countries which have no written constitution, than by ours. No doubt our doctrine of constitutional law had had a tendency to drive out questions of justice and right, and to fill the mind of legislators with thoughts of mere legality, of what the constitution allows. And, moreover, even in the matter of legality, they have felt little responsibility; if we are wrong, they say, the courts will correct it. If what I have been saying is true, the safe and permanent road towards reform is that of impressing upon our people a far stronger sense than they have of the great range of possible harm and evil that our system leaves open, and must leave open, to the legislatures, and of the clear limits of judicial power; so that responsibility may be brought sharply home where it belongs. The checking and cutting down of legislative power, by numerous detailed prohibitions in the constitution, cannot be accomplished without making the government petty and incompetent. This process has already been carried much too far in some of our States. Under no system can the power of courts go far to save a people from ruin; our chief protection lies elsewhere. . . .

Court Actively ~~Take~~ removes an attempt of invasion by State

Lochner v. New York
198 U.S. 45, 25 S.Ct. 539, 49 L.Ed. 937 (1905)

Lochner, a bakery owner, was convicted of violating a New York law that limited the hours of employment in bakeries and confectionery establishments to 10 hours a day and 60 hours a week. The New York appellate courts sustained the conviction, and Lochner sought review by writ of error.

MR. JUSTICE PECKHAM . . . delivered the opinion of the court. . . .

. . . The mandate of the statute that "no employé shall be required or permitted to work," is the substantial equivalent of an enactment that "no employé shall contract or agree to work" more than ten hours per day, and as there is no provision for special emergencies the statute is mandatory in all cases. It is not an act merely fixing the number of hours which shall constitute a legal day's work, but an absolute prohibition upon the employer permitting, under any circumstances, more than ten hours' work to be done in his establishment. The employé may desire to earn the extra money, which would arise from his working more than the prescribed time, but this statute forbids the employer from permitting the employé to earn it.

The statute necessarily interferes with the right of contract between the employer and employés, concerning the number of hours in which the latter may labor in the bakery of the employer. The general right to make a contract in relation to his business is part of the liberty of the individual protected by the Fourteenth Amendment of the federal Constitution. *Allgeyer* v. *Louisiana,* 165 U.S. 578. Under that provision no state can deprive any person of life, liberty, or property without due process of law. The right to purchase or to sell labor is part of the liberty protected by this amendment, unless there are circumstances which exclude the right. There are, however, certain powers, existing in the sovereignty of each state in the Union, somewhat vaguely termed police powers, the exact description and limitation of which have not

been attempted by the courts. Those powers, broadly stated, and without, at present, any attempt at a more specific limitation, relate to the safety, health, morals and general welfare of the public. Both property and liberty are held on such reasonable conditions as may be imposed by the governing power of the state in the exercise of those powers, and with such conditions the Fourteenth Amendment was not designed to interfere. . . .

The state, therefore, has power to prevent the individual from making certain kinds of contracts, and in regard to them the federal Constitution offers no protection. If the contract be one which the state, in the legitimate exercise of its police power, has the right to prohibit, it is not prevented from prohibiting it by the Fourteenth Amendment. Contracts in violation of a statute, either of the federal or state government, or a contract to let one's property for immoral purposes, or to do any other unlawful act, could obtain no protection from the federal Constitution, as coming under the liberty of person or of free contract. Therefore, when the state, by its legislature, in the assumed exercise of its police powers, has passed an act which seriously limits the right to labor or the right of contract in regard to their means of livelihood between persons who are sui juris (both employer and employé), it becomes of great importance to determine which shall prevail—the right of the individual to labor for such time as he may choose, or the right of the state to prevent the individual from laboring, or from entering into any contract to labor, beyond a certain time prescribed by the state.

This court has recognized the existence and

366

upheld the exercise of the police powers of the states in many cases which might fairly be considered as border ones, and it has, in the course of its determination of questions regarding the asserted invalidity of such statutes, on the ground of their violation of the rights secured by the federal Constitution, been guided by rules of a very liberal nature, the application of which has resulted, in numerous instances, in upholding the validity of state statutes thus assailed. Among the later cases where the state law has been upheld by this court is that of *Holden* v. *Hardy*, 169 U.S. 366. A provision in the act of the legislature of Utah was there under consideration, the act limiting the employment of workmen in all underground mines or workings, to eight hours per day, ''except in cases of emergency, where life or property is in imminent danger.'' It also limited the hours of labor in smelting and other institutions for the reduction or refining of ores or metals to eight hours per day, except in like cases of emergency. The act was held to be a valid exercise of police powers of the state. A review of many of the cases on the subject, decided by this and other courts, is given in the opinion. It was held that the kind of employment, mining, smelting, etc., and the character of the employés in such kinds of labor, were such as to make it reasonable and proper for the state to interfere to prevent the employés from being constrained by the rules laid down by the proprietors in regard to labor. . . .

It must, of course, be conceded that there is a limit to the valid exercise of the police power by the state. There is no dispute concerning this general proposition. Otherwise the Fourteenth Amendment would have no efficacy and the legislatures of the states would have unbounded power, and it would be enough to say that any piece of legislation was enacted to conserve the morals, the health, or the safety of the people; such legislation would be valid, no matter how absolutely without foundation the claim might be. The claim of the police power would be a mere pretext—become another and delusive name for the supreme sovereignty of the state to be exercised free from constitutional restraint. This is not contended for. In every case that comes before this court, therefore, where legislation of this character is concerned, and where the protection of the federal Constitution is sought, the question necessarily arises: Is this a fair, reasonable, and appropriate exercise of the police power of the state, or is it an unreasonable, unnecessary, and arbitrary interference with the right of the individual to his personal liberty, or to enter into those contracts in relation to labor which may seem to him appropriate or necessary for the support of himself and his family? Of course the liberty of contract relating to labor includes both parties to it. The one has as much right to purchase as the other to sell labor.

This is not a question of substituting the judgment of the court for that of the legislature. If the act be within the power of the state it is valid, although the judgment of the court might be totally opposed to the enactment of such a law. But the question would still remain: Is it within the police power of the state? and that question must be answered by the court.

The question whether this act is valid as a labor law, pure and simple, may be dismissed in a few words. There is no reasonable ground for interfering with the liberty of person or the right of free contract, by determining the hours of labor, in the occupation of a baker. There is no contention that bakers as a class are not equal in intelligence and capacity to men in other trades or manual occupations, or that they are not able to assert their rights and care for themselves without the protecting arm of the state, interfering with their independence of judgment and of action. They are in no sense wards of the state. Viewed in the light of a purely labor law, with no reference whatever to the question of health, we think that a law like the one before us involves neither the safety, the morals, nor the welfare, of the public, and that the interest of the public is not in the slightest degree affected by such an act. The law must be upheld, if at all, as a law pertaining to the health of the individual engaged in the occupation of a baker.

It does not affect any other portion of the public than those who are engaged in that occupation. Clean and wholesome bread does not depend upon whether the baker works but ten hours per day or only sixty hours a week. The limitation of the hours of labor does not come within the police power on that ground.

It is a question of which of two powers or rights shall prevail—the power of the state to legislate or the right of the individual to liberty of person and freedom of contract. The mere assertion that the subject relates, though but in a remote degree, to the public health, does not necessarily render the enactment valid. The act must have a more direct relation, as a means to an end, and the end itself must be appropriate and legitimate, before an act can be held to be valid which interferes with the general right of an individual to be free in his person and in his power to contract in relation to his own labor. . . .

We think that there can be no fair doubt that the trade of a baker, in and of itself, is not an unhealthy one to that degree which would authorize the legislature to interfere with the right to labor, and with the right of free contract on the part of the individual, either as employer or employé. In looking through statistics regarding all trades and occupations, it may be true that the trade of a baker does not appear to be as healthy as some other trades, and is also vastly more healthy than still others. To the common understanding the trade of a baker has never been regarded as an unhealthy one. Very likely physicians would not recommend the exercise of that or of any other trade as a remedy for ill health. Some occupations are more healthy than others, but we think there are none which might not come under the power of the legislature to supervise and control the hours of working therein, if the mere fact that the occupation is not absolutely and perfectly healthy is to confer that right upon the legislative department of the government. It might be safely affirmed that almost all occupations more or less affect the health. There must be more than the mere fact of the possible existence of some small amount of unhealthiness to warrant legislative interference with liberty. It is unfortunately true that labor, even in any department, may possibly carry with it the seeds of unhealthiness. But are we all, on that account, at the mercy of legislative majorities? . . .

We do not believe in the soundness of the views which uphold this law. On the contrary we think that such a law as this, although passed in the assumed exercise of the police power, and as relating to the public health, or the health of the employés named, is not within that power, and is invalid. The act is not, within any fair meaning of the term, a health law, but is an illegal interference with the rights of individuals, both employers and employés, to make contracts regarding labor upon such terms as they may think best, or which they may agree upon with the other parties to such contracts.

Statutes of the nature of that under review, limiting the hours in which grown and intelligent men may labor to earn their living, are mere meddlesome interferences with the rights of the individual, and they are not saved from condemnation by the claim that they are passed in the exercise of the police power. . . .

It was further urged . . . that restricting the hours of labor in the case of bakers was valid because it tended to cleanliness on the part of the workers, as a man was more apt to be cleanly when not overworked, and if cleanly then his "output" was also more likely to be so. . . . We do not admit the reasoning to be sufficient to justify the claimed right of such interference. The state in that case would assume the position of a supervisor, or *pater familias,* over every act of the individual, and its right of governmental interference with his hours of labor, his hours of exercise, the character thereof, and the extent to which it shall be carried would be recognized and upheld. In our judgment it is not possible in fact to discover the connection between the number of hours a baker may work in the bakery and the healthy quality of the bread made by the workman. The connection, if any exists, is too shadowy and thin to build any argument for the interference of the legislature. If the man works ten hours a day it is all right, but if ten and a half or eleven his health is in danger and his bread may be unhealthful, and, therefore, he shall not be permitted to do it. This, we think, is unreasonable and entirely arbitrary. . . .

This interference on the part of the legislatures of the several states with the ordinary trades and occupations of the people seems to be on the increase. . . .

It is impossible for us to shut our eyes to the fact that many of the laws of this character, while passed under what is claimed to be the police power for the purpose of protecting the public health or welfare, are, in reality, passed from other motives. We are justified in saying so when, from the character of the law and the subject upon which it legislates, it is apparent that the public health or welfare bears but the most remote relation to the law. The purpose of a statute must be determined from the natural and legal effect of the language employed; and whether it is or is not repugnant to the Constitution of the United States must be determined from the natural effect of such statutes when put into operation, and not from their proclaimed purpose.

Reversed.

MR. JUSTICE HARLAN, with whom MR. JUSTICE WHITE and MR. JUSTICE DAY concurred [dissented].

MR. JUSTICE HOLMES, dissenting.

I regret sincerely that I am unable to agree with the judgment in this case, and that I think it is my duty to express my dissent.

This case is decided upon an economic theory which a large part of the country does not entertain. If it were a question whether I agreed with that theory, I should desire to study it further and long before making up my mind. But I do not conceive that to be my duty, because I strongly believe that my agreement or disagreement has nothing to do with the right of a majority to embody their opinions in law. It is settled by various decisions of this court that state Constitutions and state laws may regulate life in many ways which we as legislators might think as injudicious, or if you like as tyrannical as this, and which, equally with this, interfere with the liberty to contract. Sunday laws and usury laws are ancient examples. A more modern one is the prohibition of lotteries. The liberty of the citizen to do as he likes so long as he does not interfere with the liberty of others to do the same, which has been a shibboleth for some well-known writers, is interefered with by school laws, by the post office, by every state or municipal institution which takes his money for purposes thought desirable, whether he likes it or not. The Fourteenth Amendment does not enact Mr. Herbert Spencer's Social Statics. The other day we sustained the Massachusetts vaccination law. *Jacobson* v. *Massachusetts,* 197 U.S. 11. . . . United States and state statutes and decisions cutting down the liberty to contract by way of combination are familiar to this court. *Northern Securities Co.* v. *United States,* 193 U.S. 197. . . . Two years ago we upheld the prohibition of sales of stock on margins, or for future delivery, in the Constitution of California. *Otis* v. *Parker,* 187 U.S. 606. . . . The decision sustaining an eight-hour law for miners is still recent. *Holden* v. *Hardy,* 169 U.S. 366. . . . Some of these laws embody convictions or prejudices which judges are likely to share. Some may not. But a constitution is not intended to embody a particular economic theory, whether of paternalism and the organic relation of the citizen to the state or of *laissez faire.* It is made for people of fundamentally differing views, and the accident of our finding certain opinions natural and familiar, or novel, and even shocking, ought not to conclude our judgment upon the question whether statutes embodying them conflict with the Constitution of the United States.

General propositions do not decide concrete cases. The decision will depend on a judgment or intuition more subtle than any articulate major premise. But I think that the proposition just stated, if it is accepted, will carry us far toward the end. Every opinion tends to become a law. I think that the word "liberty," in the Fourteenth Amendment, is perverted when it is held to prevent the natural outcome of a dominant opinion, unless it can be said that a rational and fair man necessarily would admit that the statute proposed would infringe fundamental principles as they have been understood by the traditions of our people and our law. It does not need research to show that no such sweeping condemnation can be passed upon the statute before us. A reasonable man might think it a proper measure on the score of health. Men whom I certainly could not pronounce unrea-sonable would uphold it as a first instalment of a general regulation of the hours of work. Whether in the latter aspect it would be open to the charge of inequality I think it unnecessary to discuss.

Adkins v. Children's Hospital
261 U.S. 525, 43 S.Ct. 394, 67 L.Ed. 785 (1923)

In 1918 Congress sought to protect the standard of living of women and minor workers in the District of Columbia by authorizing a board to set minimum wages for such workers. A hospital and a woman hotel worker sought and obtained injunctions against the enforcement of the Act by Adkins and other board members. Adkins appealed.

MR. JUSTICE SUTHERLAND delivered the opinion of the court. . . .

The judicial duty of passing upon the constitutionality of an act of Congress is one of great gravity and delicacy. The statute here in question has successfully borne the scrutiny of the legislative branch of the government, which, by enacting it, has affirmed its validity; and that determination must be given great weight. This court, by an unbroken line of decisions from Chief Justice Marshall to the present day, has steadily adhered to the rule that every possible presumption is in favor of the validity of an act of Congress until overcome beyond rational doubt. But if by clear and indubitable demonstration a statute be opposed to the Constitution we have no choice but to say so. The Constitution, by its own terms, is the supreme law of the land, emanating from the people, the repository of ultimate sovereignty under our form of government. A congressional statute, on the other hand, is the act of an agency of this sovereign authority, and if it conflict with the Constitution must fall; for that which is not supreme must yield to that which is. . . .

The statute now under consideration is attacked upon the ground that it authorizes an unconstitutional interference with the freedom of contract included within the guaranties of the due process clause of the Fifth Amendment. That the right to contract about one's affairs is a part of the liberty of the individual protected by this clause is settled by the decisions of this Court and is no longer open to question. . . . Within this liberty are contracts of employment of labor. In making such contracts, generally speaking, the parties have an equal right to obtain from each other the best terms they can as the result of private bargaining. . . .

There is, of course, no such thing as absolute freedom of contract. It is subject to a great variety of restraints. But freedom of contract is, nevertheless, the general rule and restraint the exception; and the exercise of legislative authority to abridge it can be justified only by the existence of exceptional circumstances. Whether these circumstances exist in the present case constitutes the question to be answered. . . .

In the Muller case, 208 U.S. 412, the validity

of an Oregon statute, forbidding the employment of any female in certain industries more than ten hours during any one day was upheld. The decision proceeded upon the theory that the difference between the sexes may justify a different rule respecting hours of labor in the case of women than in the case of men. It is pointed out that these consist in differences of physical structure, especially in respect of the maternal functions, and also in the fact that historically woman has always been dependent upon man, who has established his control by superior physical strength.... But the ancient inequality of the sexes, otherwise than physical, as suggested in the Muller case has continued "with diminishing intensity." In view of the great—not to say revolutionary—changes which have taken place since that utterance, in the contractual, political, and civil status of women, culminating in the Nineteenth Amendment, it is not unreasonable to say that these differences have now come almost, if not quite, to the vanishing point. In this aspect of the matter, while the physical differences must be recognized in appropriate cases, and legislation fixing hours or conditions of work may properly take them into account, we cannot accept the doctrine that women of mature age, *sui juris,* require or may be subjected to restrictions upon their liberty of contract which could not lawfully be imposed in the case of men under similar circumstances. To do so would be to ignore all the implications to be drawn from the present-day trend of legislation, as well as that of common thought and usage, by which woman is accorded emancipation from the old doctrine that she must be given special protection or be subjected to special restraint in her contractual and civil relationships. In passing, it may be noted that the instant statute applies in the case of a woman employer contracting with a woman employee as it does when the former is a man.

The essential characteristics of the statute now under consideration, which differentiate it from the laws fixing hours of labor, will be made to appear as we proceed. It is sufficient now to point out that the latter ... deal with incidents of the employment having no necessary effect upon the heart of the contract; that is, the amount of wages to be paid and received. A law forbidding work to continue beyond a given number of hours leaves the parties free to contract about wages and thereby equalize whatever additional burdens may be imposed upon the employer as a result of the restrictions as to hours, by an adjustment in respect of the amount of wages. Enough has been said to show that the authority to fix hours of labor cannot be exercised except in respect of those occupations where work of long continued duration is detrimental to health. This court has been careful in every case where the question has been raised, to place its decision upon this limited authority of the legislature to regulate hours of labor and to disclaim any purpose to uphold the legislation as fixing wages, thus recognizing an essential difference between the two. It seems plain that these decisions afford no real support for any form of law establishing minimum wages.

If now, in the light furnished by the foregoing exceptions to the general rule forbidding legislative interference with freedom of contract, we examine and analyze the statute in question, we shall see that it differs from them in every material respect.... It is simply and exclusively a price-fixing law, confined to adult women (for we are not now considering the provisions relating to minors), who are legally as capable of contracting for themselves as men. It forbids two parties having lawful capacity—under penalties as to the employer—to freely contract with one another in respect of the price for which one shall render service to the other in a purely private employment where both are willing, perhaps anxious, to agree, even though the consequence may be to oblige one to surrender a desirable engagement and the other to dispense with the services of a desirable employee....

The standard furnished by the statute for the guidance of the board is so vague as to be impossible of practical application with any reasonable degree of accuracy. What is sufficient to supply the necessary cost of living for a woman worker and maintain her in good health and protect her morals is obviously not a precise or unvarying sum—not even approximately so. The amount will depend upon a variety of circumstances: the individual temperament, habits of thrift, care, ability to buy necessaries intelligently, and whether the woman lives alone or with her family. To those who practice economy, a given sum will afford comfort, while to those of contrary habit the same sum will be wholly inadequate. The cooperative economies of the family group are not taken into account though they constitute an important consideration in estimating the cost of living, for it is obvious that the individual expense will be less in the case of a member of a family than in the case of one living alone. The relation between earnings and morals is not capable of standardization. It cannot be shown that well paid women safeguard their morals more carefully than those who are poorly paid. Morality rests upon other considerations than wages; and there is, certainly, no such prevalent connection between the two as to justify a broad attempt to adjust the latter with reference to the former. . . .

The law takes account of the necessities of only one party to the contract. It ignores the necessities of the employer by compelling him to pay not less than a certain sum, not only whether the employee is capable of earning it, but irrespective of the ability of his business to sustain the burden, generously leaving him, of course, the privilege of abandoning his business as an alternative for going on at a loss. Within the limits of the minimum sum, he is precluded, under penalty of fine and imprisonment, from adjusting compensation to the differing merits of his employees. It compels him to pay at least the sum fixed in any event, because the employee needs it, but requires no service of equivalent value from the employee. . . . To the extent that the sum fixed exceeds the fair value of the services rendered, it amounts to a compulsory exaction from the employer for the support of a partially indigent person, for whose condition there rests upon him no peculiar responsibility, and therefore, in effect, arbitrarily shifts to his shoulders a burden which, if it belongs to anybody, belongs to society as a whole.

The feature of this statute which, perhaps more than any other, puts upon it the stamp of invalidity is that it exacts from the employer an arbitrary payment for a purpose and upon a basis having no causal connection with his business, or the contract or the work the employee engages to do. . . . The ethical right of every worker, man or woman, to a living wage may be conceded. One of the declared and important purposes of trade organizations is to secure it. And with that principle and with every legitimate effort to realize it in fact, no one can quarrel; but the fallacy of the proposed method of attaining it is that it assumes that every employer is bound at all events to furnish it. The moral requirement implicit in every contract of employment, viz., that the amount to be paid and the service to be rendered shall bear to each other some relation of just equivalence, is completely ignored. . . . Certainly the employer by paying a fair equivalent for the service rendered, though not sufficient to support the employee, has neither caused nor contributed to her poverty. On the contrary, to the extent of what he pays he has relieved it. In principle, there can be no difference between the case of selling labor and the case of selling goods. If one goes to the butcher, the baker or grocer to buy food, he is morally entitled to obtain the worth of his money but he is not entitled to more. If what he gets is worth what he pays he is not justified in demanding more simply because he needs more; and the shopkeeper, having dealt fairly and honestly in that transaction, is not concerned in any peculiar sense with the question of his customer's necessities. . . . A statute which prescribes payment without regard to any of these things and solely with relation to circumstances apart from the contract of employment, the business affected by it and the work done under it, is so clearly the product of a naked, arbitrary exercise of power that it cannot be allowed to stand under the Constitution of the United States. . . .

We are asked, upon the one hand, to consider the fact that several states have adopted similar statutes, and we are invited, upon the other hand, to give weight to the fact that three times as many states, presumably as well informed and as anxious to promote the health and morals of their people, have refrained from enacting such legislation. We have also been furnished with a large number of printed opinions approving the policy of the minimum wage, and our own reading has disclosed a large number of the contrary. These are all proper enough for the consideration of the law-making bodies, since their tendency is to establish the desirability or undesirability of the legislation; but they reflect no legitimate light upon the question of its validity, and that is what we are called upon to decide. The elucidation of that question cannot be aided by counting heads.

It is said that great benefits have resulted from the operation of such statutes, not alone in the District of Columbia but in the several states where they have been in force. A mass of reports, opinions of special öbservers and students of the subject, and the like, has been brought before us in support of this statement, all of which we have found interesting, but only mildly persuasive. That the earnings of women now are greater than they were formerly, and that conditions affecting women have become better in other respects, may be conceded; but convincing indications of the logical relation of these desirable changes to the law in question are significantly lacking. They may be, and quite probably are, due to other causes. . . .

Finally, it may be said that if, in the interest of the public welfare, the police power may be invoked to justify the fixing of a minimum wage, it may, when the public welfare is thought to require it, be invoked to justify a maximum wage. The power to fix high wages connotes, by like course of reasoning, the power to fix low wages. If in the face of the guaranties of the Fifth Amendment, this form of legislation shall be legally justified, the field for the operation of the police power will have been widened to a great and dangerous degree. If, for example, in the opinion of future lawmakers, wages in the building trades shall become so high as to preclude people of ordinary means from building and owning homes, an authority which sustains the minimum wage will be invoked to support a maximum wage for building laborers and artisans, and the same argument which has been here urged to strip the employer of his constitutional liberty of contract in one direction will be utilized to strip the employee of his constitutional liberty of contract in the opposite direction. A wrong decision does not end with itself: it is a precedent, and, with the swing of sentiment, its bad influence may run from one extremity of the arc to the other.

It has been said that legislation of the kind now under review is required in the interest of social justice, for whose ends freedom of contract may lawfully be subjected to restraint. The liberty of the individual to do as he pleases, even in innocent matters, is not absolute. It must frequently yield to the common good, and the line beyond which the power of interference may not be pressed is neither definite nor unalterable but may be made to move, within limits not well defined, with changing need and circumstances. Any attempt to fix a rigid boundary would be unwise as well as futile. But, nevertheless, there are limits to the power, and when these have been passed, it becomes the plain duty of the courts in the proper exercise of their authority to so declare. To sustain the individual freedom of action contemplated by the Constitution, is not to strike down the common good but to exalt it; for surely the good of society as a whole cannot be better served than by the preservation against arbitrary restraint of the liberties of its constituent members.

It follows from what has been said that the act in question passes the limit prescribed by the Constitution, and, accordingly, the decrees of the court below are

Affirmed.

MR. JUSTICE BRANDEIS took no part in the consideration or decision of these cases.

MR. CHIEF JUSTICE TAFT, dissenting.

I regret much to differ from the Court in these cases.

The boundary of the police power beyond which its exercise becomes an invasion of the guaranty of liberty under the Fifth and Fourteenth Amendments of the Constitution is not easy to mark. Our Court has been laboriously engaged in pricking out a line in successive cases. We must be careful, it seems to me, to follow that line as well as we can and not to depart from it by suggesting a distinction that is formal rather than real.

Legislatures in limiting freedom of contract between employee and employer by a minimum wage proceed on the assumption that employees, in the class receiving least pay, are not upon a full level of equality of choice with their employer and in their necessitous circumstances are prone to accept pretty much anything that is offered. They are peculiarly subject to the overreaching of the harsh and greedy employer. The evils of the sweating system and of the long hours and low wages which are characteristic of it are well known. Now, I agree that it is a disputable question in the field of political economy how far a statutory requirement of maximum hours or minimum wages may be a useful remedy for these evils, and whether it may not make the case of the oppressed employee worse than it was before. But it is not the function of this Court to hold congressional acts invalid simply because they are passed to carry out economic views which the Court believes to be unwise or unsound. . . .

The right of the legislature under the Fifth and Fourteenth Amendments to limit the hours of employment on the score of the health of the employee, it seems to me, has been firmly established. As to that, one would think, the line had been pricked out so that it has become a well formulated rule. . . . It is impossible for me to reconcile the Bunting case and the Lochner case and I have always supposed that the Lochner case was thus overruled *sub silentio*. Yet the opinion of the Court herein in support of its conclusion quotes from the opinion in the Lochner case as one which has been sometimes distinguished but never overruled. Certainly there was no attempt to distinguish it in the Bunting case.

However, the opinion herein does not overrule the Bunting case in express terms, and therefore I assume that the conclusion in this case rests on the distinction between a minimum of wages and a maximum of hours in the limiting of liberty to contract. I regret to be at variance with the Court as to the substance of this distinction. In absolute freedom of contract the one term is as important as the other for both enter equally into the consideration given and received, a restriction as to one is not any greater in essence than the other, and is of the same kind. One is the multiplier and the other the multiplicand.

If it be said that long hours of labor have a more direct effect upon the health of the employee than the low wage, there is very respectable authority from close observers, disclosed in the record and in the literature on the subject quoted at length in the briefs, that they are equally harmful in this regard. Congress took this view and we can not say it was not warranted in so doing. . . .

I am authorized to say that MR. JUSTICE SANFORD concurs in this opinion.

MR. JUSTICE HOLMES, dissenting.

The question in this case is the broad one, whether Congress can establish minimum rates of wages for women in the District of Columbia with due provision for special circumstances, or whether we must say that Congress has no power to meddle with the matter at all. To me, notwithstanding the deference due to the prevailing judgment of the Court, the power of Congress seems absolutely free from doubt. The end, to remove conditions leading to ill health, immorality and the deterioration of the race, no one would deny to be within the scope of constitutional legislation. The means are means that have the approval of Congress, of many States, and of those governments from which we have learned our greatest lessons. When so many intelligent persons who have studied the matter more than any of us can, have thought that the means are effective and are worth the price, it seems to me impossible to deny that the belief reasonably may be held by reasonable men. If the law encountered no other objection than that the means bore no relation to the end or that they cost too much I do not suppose that anyone would venture to say that it was bad. I agree, of course, that a law answering the foregoing requirements might be invalidated by specific provisions of the constitution. For instance it might take private property without just compensation. But in the present instance the only objection that can be urged is found within the vague contours of the Fifth Amendment, prohibiting the depriving any person of liberty or property without due process of law. To that I turn.

The earlier decisions upon the same words in the Fourteenth Amendment began within our memory and went no farther than an unpretentious assertion of the liberty to follow the ordinary callings. Later that innocuous generality was expanded into the dogma, Liberty of Contract. Contract is not specially mentioned in the text that we have to construe. It is merely an example of doing what you want to do, embodied in the word liberty. But pretty much all law consists in forbidding men to do some things that they want to do, and contract is no more exempt from law than other acts. Without enumerating all the restrictive laws that have been upheld I will mention a few that seem to me to have interfered with liberty of contract quite as seriously and directly as the one before us. Usury laws prohibit contracts by which a man receives more than so much interest for the money that he lends. Statutes of frauds restrict many contracts to certain forms. Some Sunday laws prohibit practically all contracts during one-seventh of our whole life. Insurance rates may be regulated. *German Alliance Insurance Co.* v. *Lewis*, 233 U.S. 389. . . . Finally women's hours of labor may be fixed . . . and the principle was extended to men with the allowance of a limited overtime to be paid for "at the rate of time and one-half of the regular wage," in *Bunting* v. *Oregon*. . . .

I confess that I do not understand the principle on which the power to fix a minimum for the wages of women can be denied by those who admit the power to fix a maximum for their hours of work. I fully assent to the proposition that here as elsewhere the distinctions of the law are distinctions of degree, but I perceive no difference in the kind or degree of interference with liberty, the only matter with which we have any concern, between the one case and the other. The bargain is equally affected whichever half you regulate. *Muller* v. *Oregon,* I take it, is as good law today as it was in 1908. It will need more than the Nineteenth Amendment to convince me that there are no differences between men and women, or that legislation cannot take those differences into account. I should not hesitate to take them into account if I thought it necessary to sustain this act. . . . But after *Bunting* v. *Oregon* . . . I had supposed that it was not necessary, and that *Lochner* v. *New York* . . . would be allowed a deserved repose. . . . I am of opinion that the statute is valid and that the decree should be reversed.

Nebbia v. *New York*
291 U.S. 502, 54 S.Ct. 505, 78 L.Ed. 940 (1934)

To combat some of the effects of economic depression on the milk industry, the legislature of New York in 1933 adopted a Milk Control Law under which minimum prices could be set. The board constituted by the law set a minimum price for the retail sale of milk, which Nebbia, a grocery store proprietor, violated. The New York Court of Appeals affirmed his conviction and Nebbia appealed. Many commentators saw the Court's decision in this case, especially the proposition that "the power to promote the general welfare is inherent in government," as indicating judicial approval of the New Deal.

MR. JUSTICE ROBERTS delivered the opinion of the Court. . . .

Under our form of government the use of property and the making of contracts are normally matters of private and not of public concern. The general rule is that both shall be free of governmental interference. But neither property rights nor contract rights are absolute; for government cannot exist if the citizen may at will use his property to the detriment of his fellows, or exercise his freedom of contract to work them harm. Equally fundamental with the private right is that of the public to regulate it in the common interest. . . .

Thus has this court from the early days affirmed that the power to promote the general welfare is inherent in government. Touching the matters committed to it by the Constitution, the United States possesses the power, as do the states in their sovereign capacity touching all subjects jurisdiction of which is not surrendered to the federal government, as shown by the quotations above given. These correlative rights, that of the citizen to exercise exclusive dominion over property and freely to contract about his affairs, and that of the state to regulate the use of property and the conduct of business, are always in collision. No exercise of the private right can be imagined which will not in some respect, however slight, affect the public; no exercise of the legislative prerogative to regulate the conduct of the citizen which will not to some extent abridge his liberty or affect his property. But subject only to constitutional restraint the private right must yield to the public need.

The Fifth Amendment, in the field of federal activity, and the Fourteenth, as respects state action, do not prohibit governmental regulation for the public welfare. They merely condition the exertion of the admitted power, by securing that the end shall be accomplished by methods consistent with due process. And the guaranty of due process, as has often been held, demands only that the law shall not be unreasonable, arbitrary, or capricious, and that the means selected shall have a real and substantial relation to the object sought to be attained. It results that a regulation valid for one sort of business, or in given circumstances, may be invalid for another sort, or for the same business under other circumstances, because the reasonableness of each regulation depends upon the relevant facts. . . .

The Constitution does not guarantee the unrestricted privilege to engage in a business or to conduct it as one pleases. Certain kinds of business may be prohibited; and the right to conduct a business, or to pursue a calling, may be conditioned. Regulation of a business to prevent waste of the state's resources may be justified. And statutes prescribing the terms upon which those conducting certain businesses may contract, or imposing terms if they do enter into agreements, are within the state's competency. . . .

But we are told that because the law essays to control prices it denies due process. Notwithstanding the admitted power to correct existing economic ills by appropriate regulation of business, even though an indirect result may be a restriction of the freedom of contract or a modification of charges for services or the price of commodities, the appellant urges that direct fixation of prices is a type of regulation absolutely forbidden. His position is that the Fourteenth Amendment requires us to hold the challenged statute void for this reason alone. The argument runs that the public control of rates or prices is per se unreasonable and unconstitutional, save as applied to businesses affected with a public interest; that a business so affected is one in which property is devoted to an enterprise of a sort which the public itself might appropriately undertake, or one whose owner relies on a public grant or franchise for the right to conduct the business, or in which he is bound to serve all who apply; in short, such as is commonly called a public utility; or a business in its nature a monopoly. The milk industry, it is said, possesses none of these characteristics, and, therefore, not being affected with a public interest, its charges may not be controlled by the state. Upon the soundness of this contention the appellant's case against the statute depends.

We may as well say at once that the dairy industry is not, in the accepted sense of the phrase, a public utility. We think the appellant is also right in asserting that there is in this case no suggestion of any monopoly or monopolistic practice. It goes without saying that those engaged in the business are in no way dependent upon public grants or franchises for the privilege of conducting their activities. But if, as must be conceded, the industry is subject to regulation in the public interest, what constitutional principle bars the state from correcting existing maladjustments by legislation touching prices? We think there is no such principle. The due process clause makes no mention of sales or prices any more than it speaks of business or contracts or buildings or other incidents of property. The thought seems nevertheless to have persisted that there is something peculiarly sacrosanct about the price one may charge for what he makes or sells, and that, however able to regulate other elements of manufacture or trade, with incidental effect upon price, the state is incapable of directly controlling the price itself. This view was negatived many years ago. *Munn* v. *Illinois*. . . .

It is clear that there is no closed class or category of businesses affected with a public interest, and the function of courts in the application of the Fifth and Fourteenth Amendments is to determine in each case whether circumstances vindicate the challenged regulation as a reasonable execution of governmental authority or condemn it as arbitrary or discriminatory. . . . The phrase "affected with a public interest" can, in the nature of things, mean no more than that an industry, for adequate reason, is subject to control for the public good. In several of the decisions of this court wherein the expressions "affected with a public interest," and "clothed with a public use," have been brought forward as the criteria of the validity of price control, it has been admitted that they are not susceptible of definition and form an unsatisfactory test of the constitutionality of legislation directed at business practices or prices. These decisions must rest, finally, upon the basis that the requirements of due process were not met because the laws were found arbitrary in their operation and effect. But there can be no doubt that upon

proper occasion and by appropriate measures the state may regulate a business in any of its aspects, including the prices to be charged for the products or commodities it sells.

So far as the requirement of due process is concerned, and in the absence of other constitutional restriction, a state is free to adopt whatever economic policy may reasonably be deemed to promote public welfare, and to enforce that policy by legislation adapted to its purpose. The courts are without authority either to declare such policy, or, when it is declared by the legislative arm, to override it. If the laws passed are seen to have a reasonable relation to a proper legislative purpose and are neither arbitrary nor discriminatory, the requirements of due process are satisfied, and judicial determination to that effect renders a court *functus officio*. "Whether the free operation of the normal laws of competition is a wise and wholesome rule for trade and commerce is an economic question which this court need not consider or determine." . . . And it is equally clear that if the legislative policy be to curb unrestrained and harmful competition by measures which are not arbitrary or discriminatory it does not lie with the courts to determine that the rule is unwise. With the wisdom of the policy adopted, with the adequacy or practicability of the law enacted to forward it, the courts are both incompetent and unauthorized to deal. . . .

Price control, like any other form of regulation, is unconstitutional only if arbitrary, discriminatory, or demonstrably irrelevant to the policy the legislature is free to adopt, and hence an unnecessary and unwarranted interference with individual liberty.

Tested by these considerations we find no basis in the due process clause of the Fourteenth Amendment for condemning the provision of the Agriculture and Markets Law here drawn into question.

The judgment is

Affirmed.

Separate opinion of MR. JUSTICE MC-REYNOLDS. . . .

If . . . liberty or property may be struck down because of difficult circumstances, we must expect that hereafter every right must yield to the voice of an impatient majority when stirred by distressful exigency. . . . Certain fundamentals have been set beyond experimentation; the Constitution has released them from control by the state. . . .

The exigency is of a kind which inevitably arises when one set of men continue to produce more than all others can buy. The distressing result of the producer followed his ill-advised but voluntary effort. . . .

Of the assailed statute the Court of Appeals says . . . "With the wisdom of the legislation we have naught to do. . . ."

But plainly, I think, this Court must have regard to the wisdom of the enactment.

The Legislature cannot lawfully destroy guaranteed rights of one man with the prime purpose of enriching another, even if for the moment, this may seem advantageous to the public. And the adoption of any "concept of jurisprudence" which permits facile disregard of the Constitution as long interpreted and

respected will inevitably lead to its destruction. Then, all rights will be subject to the caprice of the hour; government by stable laws will pass.

The somewhat misty suggestion below that condemnation of the challenged legislation would amount to holding "that the due process clause has left milk producers unprotected from oppression," I assume, was not intended as a material contribution to the discussion upon the merits of the cause. Grave concern for embarrassed farmers is everywhere; but this should neither obscure the rights of others nor obstruct judicial appraisement of measures proposed for relief. The ultimate welfare of the producer, like that of every other class, requires dominance of the Constitution. And zealously to uphold this in all its parts is the highest duty intrusted to the courts.

The judgment of the court below should be reversed.

MR. JUSTICE VAN DEVANTER, MR. JUSTICE SUTHERLAND, and MR. JUSTICE BUTLER authorize me to say that they concur in this opinion.

Ferguson v. Skrupa
372 U.S. 726, 83 S.Ct. 1028, 10 L.Ed. 2d 93 (1963)

The relevant facts are included in the opinion.

MR. JUSTICE BLACK delivered the opinion of the Court.

In this case, properly here on appeal . . . , we are asked to review the judgment of a three-judge District Court enjoining, as being in violation of the Due Process Clause of the Fourteenth Amendment, a Kansas statute making it a misdemeanor for any person to engage "in the business of debt adjusting" except as an incident to "the lawful practice of law in this state." The statute defines "debt adjusting" as "the making of a contract, express, or implied with a particular debtor whereby the debtor agrees to

pay a certain amount of money periodically to the person engaged in the debt adjusting business who shall for a consideration distribute the same among certain specified creditors in accordance with a plan agreed upon."

The complaint, filed by appellee Skrupa doing business as "Credit Advisor," alleged that Skrupa was engaged in the business of "debt adjusting" as defined by the statute, that his business was a "useful and desirable" one, that his business activities were not "inherently immoral or dangerous" or in any way contrary to the public welfare, and that therefore the business could not be "absolutely prohibited" by Kansas. The three-judge court heard evidence by Skrupa tending to show the usefulness and desirability of his business and evidence by the state officials tending to show that "debt adjusting" lends itself to grave abuses against distressed debtors, particularly in the lower income brackets, and that these abuses are of such gravity that a number of States have strictly regulated "debt adjusting" or prohibited it altogether. The court found that Skrupa's business did fall within the Act's proscription and concluded, one judge dissenting, that the Act was prohibitory, not regulatory, but that even if construed in part as regulatory it was an unreasonable regulation of a "lawful business," which the court held amounted to a violation of the Due Process Clause of the Fourteenth Amendment. The court accordingly enjoined enforcement of the statute. . . .

Under the system of government created by our Constitution, it is up to legislatures, not courts, to decide on the wisdom and utility of legislation. There was a time when the Due Process Clause was used by this Court to strike down laws which were thought unreasonable, that is, unwise or incompatible with some particular economic or social philosophy. In this manner the Due Process Clause was used, for example, to nullify laws prescribing maximum hours for work in bakeries, *Lochner* v. *New York*, . . . outlawing "yellow dog" contracts, *Coppage* v. *Kansas*, . . . , setting minimum wages for women, *Adkins* v. *Children's Hospital* . . . , and fixing the weight of loaves of bread, *Jay Burns Baking Co.* v. *Bryan*. . . . This intrusion by the judiciary into the realm of legislative value judgments was strongly objected to at the time, particularly by Mr. Justice Holmes and Mr. Justice Brandeis.

The doctrine that prevailed in Lochner, Coppage, Adkins, Burns, and like cases—that due process authorizes courts to hold laws unconstitutional when they believe the legislature has acted unwisely—has long since been discarded. We have returned to the original constitutional proposition that courts do not substitute their social and economic beliefs for the judgment of legislative bodies, who are elected to pass laws. As this Court stated in a unanimous opinion in 1941, "We are not concerned . . . with the wisdom, need, or appropriateness of the legislation." Legislative bodies have broad scope to experiment with economic problems, and this Court does not sit to "subject the State to an intolerable supervision hostile to the basic principles of our Government and wholly beyond the protection which the general clause of the Fourteenth Amendment was intended to secure." It is now settled that States "have power to legislate against what are found to be injurious practices in their internal commercial and business affairs, so long as their laws do not run afoul of some specific federal constitutional prohibition or of some valid federal law."

In the face of our abandonment of the use of the "vague contours" of the Due Process Clause to nullify laws which a majority of the Court believed to be economically unwise, reliance on *Adams* v. *Tanner* is as mistaken as would be adherence to *Adkins* v. *Children's Hospital*, overruled by *West Coast Hotel Co.* v. *Parrish*. . . . Not only has the philosophy of Adams been abandoned, but also this Court almost 15 years ago expressly pointed to another opinion of this Court as having "clearly undermined" Adams. We conclude that the Kansas Legislature was free to decide for itself that legislation was needed to deal with the business of debt adjusting. Unquestionably, there are arguments showing that the business of debt adjusting has social utility, but such arguments are properly addressed to the legislature, not to us. We refuse to sit as a "superlegislature to weigh the wisdom of legislation," and we emphatically refuse to go back to the time when courts used the Due Process Clause "to strike down state laws, regulatory of business and industrial conditions, because they may be unwise, improvident, or out of harmony with a particular school of thought." Nor are we able or willing to draw lines by calling a law "prohibitory" or "regulatory." Whether the legislature takes for its textbook Adam Smith, Herbert Spencer, Lord Keynes, or some other is no concern of ours. The Kansas debt adjusting statute may be wise or unwise. But relief, if any be needed, lies not with us but with the body constituted to pass laws for the State of Kansas.

Nor is the statute's exception of lawyers a denial of equal protection of the laws to non-lawyers. Statutes create many classifications which do not deny equal protection; it is only "invidious discrimination" which offends the Constitution. If the State of Kansas wants to limit debt adjusting to lawyers, the Equal Protection Clause does not forbid. We also find no merit in the contention that the Fourteenth Amendment is violated by the failure of the Kansas statute's title to be as specific as appellee thinks it ought to be under the Kansas Constitution.

Reversed.

MR. JUSTICE HARLAN concurs in the judgment on the ground that this state measure bears a rational relation to a constitutionally permissible objective. . . .

NINE

Criminal Procedure and the Nationalization of the Bill of Rights

State constitutions adopted in 1776 and in subsequent years usually contained either a separate bill of rights or other provisions that achieved the same objective. As a member of the First Congress elected under the new Constitution, Madison drew up seventeen amendments. After a two-year delay, ten were ratified. The first eight constitute the Bill of Rights.

Proposed but not ratified was Madison's Number 14: "No state shall infringe the right of trial by jury in criminal cases, nor the right of conscience, nor the freedom of speech or press." Believing that there was more danger of abuse of power by state governments than by the government of the United States, Madison conceived Number 14 to be "the most valuable amendment in the whole list. If there were any reason to restrain the Government of the United States from infringing these essential rights, it was equally necessary that they should be secured against the State governments." (Annals of Congress, 440: Giles & Seaton eds. 1789)

Madison's concern was prophetic. It anticipated the adoption of the Fourteenth Amendment 79 years later. It foreshadowed the drive to apply the specific provisions of the Bill of Rights to state action under the Fourteenth Amendment's due process clause. Incorporation was significant. Without application of the Bill of Rights to the states, the full impact of Justice Stone's *Carolene Products* footnote, discussed in the previous chapter, could not be felt.

THE ARGUMENT FOR INCORPORATION

It was not until 1833 that the Supreme Court answered the question of whether the first eight amendments limited state as well as national action. To Marshall this was a question "of great importance, but not of much difficulty" (*Barron* v. *Baltimore*, 7 Pet. 243). The

City of Baltimore, under acts of the Maryland legislature, had diverted the flow of several streams. As a result of the changes, silt was deposited around Barron's wharf, making it unfit for shipping and, in Barron's opinion, depriving him of property without just compensation. Denying the Supreme Court's jurisdiction to declare the state acts repugnant to the Constitution, Marshall observed: "We are of the opinion, that the provision in the Fifth Amendment to the Constitution, declaring that private property shall not be taken for public use without just compensation is intended solely as a limitation of the power of the United States, and is not applicable to the legislation of the states." In support of this conclusion, the Chief Justice pointed out that the limitations set forth in the Constitution in general terms, as well as the powers conferred, applied to the "government created by the instrument." In addition, he cited proceedings in the state ratifying conventions culminating in the demand for a bill of rights to furnish "security against the apprehended encroachments of the general government."

A contrary ruling would have had immense consequences for the jurisdiction of the Court. As it was, most legal disputes between a state government and one of its citizens remained outside the federal judicial system, unless the commerce or contract clauses were at issue. This is important to remember, because until recent decades government action and government policy largely meant the action and policy of state and local governments.

Shortly after the end of the Civil War, the question of the applicability of the Bill of Rights to the states reappeared. This time there was a difference. The Fourteenth Amendment had become part of the Constitution in 1868. Did it have the effect of incorporating the Bill of Rights, either through the privileges and immunities clause or by virtue of the due process clause? Suitors pressed upon the Court arguments showing that one or more guaranties were included in the phrase "due process of law," now protected by the new amendment against state action. In the Slaughterhouse Cases, reprinted in chapter 8, Justice Miller and his slim majority displayed little patience with efforts by the butchers from New Orleans to use the Fourteenth Amendment as a barrier against state economic regulation. Dictum suggested, however, that the newly ratified addition to the Constitution was not barren of meaning. "The right to peaceably assemble and petition for redress of grievances, the privilege of the writ of habeas corpus, are rights of the citizen guaranteed by the Federal Constitution." The Supreme Court eventually displayed willingness to incorporate the First Amendment rights in the Fourteenth Amendment, and later on extended its protection to other provisions of the Bill of Rights. Until 1961, however, incorporation moved at a glacial pace.

In the 1884 case of *Hurtado* v. *California* the Court refused to hold that the due process clause of the Fourteenth Amendment prevented the substitution by a state of a prosecutor's affidavit (information) for grand jury indictment in criminal cases. Later, the Court cast doubt on its adherence to the Hurtado doctrine by holding that the due process clause limited taking property without just compensation (*Chicago, Milwaukee & St. Paul Railway Co.* v. *Minnesota*). With this exception in favor of property rights, the Court was unwilling to depart from its basic position that due process—being enumerated in the Fifth Amendment as a separate right, distinct from the various other procedural rights of the Bill of Rights—could not be treated as a shorthand expression of all procedural rights required of the states by the Fourteenth Amendment.

Thus, states were allowed to weaken the protection against self-incrimination (*Twining* v. *New Jersey,* 211 U.S. 78:1908), and to alter the common-law trial by jury (*Maxwell* v. *Dow,* 176 U.S. 581: 1900). By 1937, long after the Court had agreed that the "liberty" protected by the Fourteenth Amendment included some of the First Amendment freedoms, the Supreme Court, speaking through Justice Cardozo in *Palko* v. *Connecticut*, reaffirmed its long-held view that the entire Bill of Rights was not incorporated in the Fourteenth Amendment and attempted to justify its selective process.

> There emerges the perception of a rationalizing principle which gives to discrete instances a proper order and coherence. The right to trial by jury and the immunity from prosecution except as the result of an indictment may have value and importance. Even so, they are not of the very essence of a scheme of ordered liberty. To abolish them is not to violate a ''principle of justice so rooted in the traditions and conscience of our people as to be ranked as fundamental. . . .''

> We reach a different plane of social and moral values when we pass to the privileges and immunities that have been taken over from the earlier articles of the Federal Bill of Rights and brought within the Fourteenth Amendment by a process of absorption. These in their origin were effective against the federal government. If the Fourteenth Amendment has absorbed them, the process of absorption has had its source in the belief that neither liberty nor justice would exist if they were sacrificed.

This ''natural law'' method of selecting and discarding rights has not gone unchallenged. From 1884 to the present time, various Justices have argued that the entire Bill of Rights should be incorporated in the Fourteenth Amendment. Consider Justice Black's dissenting opinion in *Adamson* v. *California*.

> My study of the historical events that culminated in the Fourteenth Amendment, and the expressions of those who sponsored and favored, as well as those who opposed its submission and passage, persuades me that one of the chief objects that the provisions of the Amendment's first section, separately, and as a whole were intended to accomplish, was to make the Bill of Rights applicable to the states. . . . The ''natural law'' formula should be abandoned as an incongruous excrescence on our Constitution. I believe that formula to be itself a violation of our Constitution, in that it subtly conveys to courts, at the expense of legislatures, ultimate power over public policies in fields where no specific provision of the Constitution limits legislative power. . . . I fear to see the consequences of the Court's practice of substituting its own concept of decency and fundamental justice for the language of the Bill of Rights as its point of departure in interpreting and enforcing that Bill of Rights.

Justice Frankfurter's reading of history led him to exactly the opposite conclusion. In the 70 years following the adoption of the Fourteenth Amendment, he reports, its scope was passed upon by 53 judges. Only one of these—an ''eccentric exception'' at that (Justice Harlan)—ever indicated that the Fourteenth Amendment was a ''shorthand summary'' of the first eight amendments.

Yet the reader may want to ponder whether the *Palko* doctrine which Frankfurter adopted or the total incorporation doctrine which Black espoused was thoroughly satisfactory in coping with the outrageous facts of the ''stomach pump case'' (*Rochin* v. *California*), reprinted in this chapter. Each Justice was convinced the police had violated the Constitution, but Frankfurter and Black arrived at that conclusion by altogether different routes.

Justice Black's strictures on the Court's use of the ''natural law'' formula as an instrument of judicial decision recall Justice Iredell's misgivings in *Calder* v. *Bull*. Similarly,

Justice Field's inclination in the Granger decision and other cases to invoke ''the structure and spirit of our institutions'' as a bar to legislative action regulating rights of property provoked critical comment from both within and without the Court. After extensive research Professor Charles Fairman concludes that ''the record of history is against him [Black].'' Fairman describes the evidence against the Justice as ''a high mountain'' and the evidence supporting him as ''a few pebbles and stones.''

Today, almost all of the provisions of the Bill of Rights which possess contemporary significance have been brought to bear against the states. The consequences for federalism and judicial power have been enormous, especially when coupled with an increased sensitivity to police and courtroom procedure during the second half of the Warren Court (1961–1969). Incorporation was so nearly complete that Justice Black observed with some relish in *Duncan* v. *Louisiana* that the process of selectivity had finally accomplished piecemeal what he would have done at once in *Adamson*. Of greater significance today are the protections enshrined in due process beyond those strictly enumerated in the Bill of Rights. It is here that Justice Black's total incorporation approach (this much, and no more) stops, and a variation on Justice Cardozo's fairness doctrine from *Palko* begins. If the Fourteenth Amendment's due process clause is not bound to the meaning of the Bill of Rights, then it remains a source of inspiration for those who wish to enlarge the list of constitutionally protected liberties.

THE DOUBLE STANDARD—STATE AND FEDERAL CRIMINAL JUSTICE

For a long time, not only did the Court refuse to incorporate the entire Bill of Rights, or even its more important procedural guarantees, but also it refrained for several decades from any realistic review of state convictions to determine whether ''due'' or ''fair'' process had been followed. Until the 1920s the Court reviewed state criminal trials only to the extent necessary to determine that the state court had exercised jurisdiction properly and provided a corrective process for possible trial errors (*Frank* v. *Mangum*, 237 U.S. 309:1915). In other words, a state trial that seemingly complied with the state's formal rules as interpreted by the state's highest court satisfied the Supreme Court's Fourteenth Amendment standard of due process of law. This superficial and essentially meaningless federal review began to change with *Moore* v. *Dempsey* (261 U.S. 86: 1923). In this case, the Court, speaking through Justice Holmes, held that the federal district court was duty-bound to conduct a hearing on the facts, where state prisoners alleged that their trial and conviction lacked due process as the result of mob pressure and inflammatory newspaper accounts.

Typically, even the *Dempsey* rule meant that citizens were still subject to a double standard of justice under the United States Constitution. For a defendant standing trial, the federal constitutional rights one enjoyed depended on whether the trial was in state or federal court. Supreme Court review was far more demanding of the latter than the former.

During this period, the Supreme Court tended to impose on federal officials and federal trial courts rules which on the whole were more protective of individual rights than those applied by state courts under their own legal systems. The Supreme Court even went beyond the Bill of Rights and federal statutes by invoking its supervisory powers as the highest court in the federal judicial system to justify prescribing rules of procedure and penalties for improper conduct which were not required by any constitutional provision.

For example, one of the thorniest problems in criminal procedure has resulted from the Supreme Court's decision in 1914 to impose an exclusionary rule as a means of enforcing the Fourth Amendment's protection against unreasonable searches and seizures. In English common law, material and relevant evidence has always been held admissible at a trial even though officials may have obtained it through an improper search and seizure. In an early case, *Boyd* v. *United States* (116 U.S. 616: 1886), the Court refused to allow the government to compel an individual to produce papers that might help convict him of a violation of customs law, combining the protections against self-incrimination and unreasonable seizures. *Weeks* v. *United States* (232 U.S. 383: 1914) laid down the broad rule that evidence produced by illegal searches was inadmissible at federal trials. The Sixth Amendment guaranty of the right to the assistance of counsel was construed as a mandate that every defendant in federal criminal trials be offered counsel (*Johnson* v. *Zerbst*, 304 U.S. 458: 1938). Later *McNabb* v. *United States* (318 U.S. 332: 1943) and *Mallory* v. *United States* (354 U.S. 449: 1957) regarded the federal rule requiring prompt arraignment of the defendant as mandatory, so that even a voluntary confession made between arrest and delayed arraignment before the federal commissioner was inadmissible at the trial, a view that elicited strong protests from some federal law enforcement officials.

The Court also aided law enforcement. With the development of technical means of surveillance, the Court was faced with difficult questions as to what kind of official invasions violate the Fourth Amendment. In 1928 (*Olmstead* v. *United States*), a sharply divided Court held that wiretapping did not violate the Fourth Amendment guaranty against unreasonable searches and seizures because there was no seizure of papers, tangible material effects, or actual physical invasion of the house.

Justice Brandeis's spirited dissenting opinion in *Olmstead* gave Chief Justice Marshall's famous dictum— "We must never forget it is a Constitution we are expounding"— a new twist. Just as grants of power, as Marshall had reasoned, must be adapted to changed conditions, so Brandeis insisted that the Court take into account altered conditions in interpreting limitations on power. Here, too, Brandeis argued, "Time works changes. . . . Discovery and invention have made it possible for the government by means far more effective than stretching upon the rack to obtain disclosures in court of what is whispered in the closet." Forty years later, in *Katz* v. *United States*, Brandeis's dissent became the law of the land. The unanimous decision in *United States* v. *U. S. District Court* follows in the Brandeis tradition.

But the history of federal criminal procedure in the intervening years is not so easily brushed aside. *Olmstead* was widely criticized. When later cases involving evidence obtained by wiretapping came before the Court, generous interpretation was given a provision of the Federal Communications Act of 1934. Under that legislation interception and divulgence of messages were prohibited; thus federal officials were prohibited from bringing evidence obtained through wiretapping (*Nardone* v. *United States*, 302 U.S. 379:1937; *Nardone* v. *United States*, 308 U.S. 338: 1939).

Later on, the Court veered back toward a more restrictive view. The protection of the Federal Communications Act was held inapplicable to a person not a party to a phone conversation (*Goldstein* v. *United States*, 316 U.S. 114:1942), so that wiretapping retained its value as an informatory device. Even more striking was the Court's refusal to outlaw the use by federal agents of a detectaphone placed on the adjacent wall of a suspect's office. A majority of five refused to overrule *Olmstead,* citing the lack of any trespass in placing the detectaphone (*Goldman* v. *United States,* 316 U.S. 129: 1942), a point that Chief Justice Taft had stressed in *Olmstead.* In a later case, the Supreme Court condemned police use of a spike microphone, driven into a row house wall so that it made contact with a heating conduit, thus enabling the officers to hear all conversations in a suspect's house (*Silverman* v. *United States,* 365 U.S. 505: 1961). Justice Stewart, speaking for all the Justices but Justice Douglas (who wanted *Olmstead* overruled), emphasized the mechanical nature of the trespass.

Once the Supreme Court and lower federal courts abandoned their hands-off policy and began a more realistic, if restrained, examination of state criminal proceedings, they found many discrepancies between state practices and due process standards. The 1931 Report of the Wickersham Commission, *Lawlessness in Law Enforcement,* documented the use by the police of physical and psychological coercion in inducing confessions, detention incommunicado of suspects, unfairness in prosecutor bargaining and other departures from fair procedures in the period before trial. In the following year, a landmark decision revealed how the widely assumed right of indigent defendants to have the assistance of counsel could be frustrated even in the most serious state cases. *Powell* v. *Alabama* held that in capital cases, indigent, young, inexperienced, and illiterate defendants had to receive the assistance of counsel appointed by the state, and the appointment had to be one that made possible a reasonably efficient defense. In the course of reaching its decision, which on its face dealt principally with the issue of adequate defense during trial, a subject that fell rather naturally within the ambit of appellate review, the Supreme Court revealed again, as in the earlier Frank and Moore cases, some of the realities of pretrial procedure in the states, especially in those cases where authorities were under pressure to obtain convictions.

The problem confronting counsel who sought review of state convictions was to convince the Supreme Court that their clients had been denied a "fair trial" as the result of the denial of one or more procedural steps, use of improper enforcement tactics, or denial of counsel. The nature of the fair trial rule is clearly revealed in the right to counsel cases. The 1938 decision in *Johnson* v. *Zerbst* (304 U.S. 458) made clear the rule that all criminal defendants in federal courts had to be offered appointed counsel, if through poverty they were unable to retain a lawyer. But when the Court was asked in 1942 to extend that holding to noncapital state cases, the Court refused (*Betts* v. *Brady,* 316 U.S. 455). The Fourteenth Amendment did not incorporate any Sixth Amendment right as such, said Justice Roberts for the Court. It was only "in certain circumstances, or in connection with other elements" that denial of a specific provision of the Bill of Rights was also a denial of due process. In the Court's eyes, Betts, a mature man, in a relatively simple case, had been given a fair trial even though he had been compelled to defend himself. Obviously, the adoption of the fair trial rule was explainable both in terms of the Palko rationale, and its appeal to Justice Frankfurter and other justices who were concerned lest the traditional balance between state and national power should be substantially altered. Under the fair trial rule, state convictions were reversible in the occasional "bad" cases, while the states retained effective control of their own criminal proceedings.

Thus the Court, applying the fair trial rule, upheld many state actions contrary to federal standards. In *Adamson* v. *California* it continued to uphold a state prosecutor's comment on the failure of a defendant to take the witness stand. A conviction based on evidence obtained by illegal entry of a home and use of a hidden microphone was sustained (*Irvine* v. *California,* 347 U.S. 128: 1954). In federal trials, the Fourth Amendment's provision against unreasonable searches and seizures forbade the use of illegally obtained evidence. But *Wolf* v. *Colorado* (338 U.S. 25: 1949) held that the "exclusionary" rule was not applicable in state courts. By a 5 to 4 vote the Court held that counsel retained by a defendant had no right to see him until the police had finished a reasonable period of interrogation. (*Crooker* v. *California,* 357 U.S. 433: 1958).

Increasing review of state convictions was, however, having an effect on judicial perceptions. As the Court paid ever closer attention to the detailed facts in each case, it inevitably found many cases where pretrial actions or failure to appoint counsel resulted in what in retrospect appeared to be a serious element of unfairness in the proceedings. Increasingly, the Court gave weight (excessive, according to the critics) to the misbehavior of law enforcement officers, with the result that a number of demonstrably guilty defendants gained new trials. In *Rochin* v. *California* the Court found police use of a stomach pump on a suspect who had swallowed narcotics capsules to be offensive "to a sense of justice." In numerous cases involving allegedly coerced confessions the Court invalidated the conviction, even though the facts in the confession were verifiable and the probability of the accused's guilt extremely high (e.g. *Ashcraft* v. *Tennessee,* 322 U.S. 143: 1944; *Watts* v. *Indiana,* 338 U.S. 49: 1949; *Culombe* v. *Connecticut,* 367 U.S. 568: 1961).

During the entire period from 1940 to 1960, two or more Justices believed in total incorporation of the Bill of Rights (Black, Douglas, Murphy, Rutledge), and Justices Warren and Brennan subscribed to selective incorporation. Thus it required only an additional vote or two, recruited from the "fair trial" adherents, to command a majority. Depending on the factual situation, one or more of the "fair trial" advocates, Chief Justice Vinson, Justices Clark, Minton, Burton, Harlan, Reed, or Frankfurter, the most articulate exponent of its virtues, might join the incorporators to form a majority. In spite of professed concern of the fair trial adherents for the value of federalism, the Supreme Court's reversal of a substantial number of state convictions aroused the ire of state judges. In 1958, the Conference of State Chief Justices passed an unprecedented resolution severely criticizing the United States Supreme Court, one of the specific grievances being the high court's growing tendency to reverse state criminal convictions as the result of an independent examination of the facts. The decisions in subsequent years suggest that the Supreme Court was not persuaded by the state justices' broadside.

Only in one sense has the trend of decisions after 1958 met the complaint of state judicial spokesmen. By incorporating into the Fourteenth Amendment several of the more crucial procedural guaranties of the Bill of Rights, and by insisting that the states meet federal standards for these rights as developed by the Court over the years, the Court has moved a long way toward providing more explicit standards for official behavior in contrast to the loose measures of the retrospectively applied "fair trial" rule.

THE MERGING OF STATE AND FEDERAL CRIMINAL JUSTICE

As the crime rate rose dramatically in the 1960s, the Supreme Court devoted more and more time to criminal cases, both state and national. And many Congressmen, aggrieved by the Court's desegregation decisions, reapportionment requirements, or decisions allegedly protecting communists and radicals, found new allies for an assault on the Warren Court.

Fred Graham of the *New York Times* called this revolution in criminal justice "the self-inflicted wound," equating unpopular prodefendant holdings with *Dred Scott,* the Legal Tender Cases of the 1870s, and the 1895 invalidation of the federal income tax. The analogy may not be altogether apt. Earlier wounds, unlike the criminal justice cases, struck directly at the power to govern and involved the Court in partisan political controversy.

For obvious reasons, criminal defendants and prisoners are among the least effective interest groups. Small wonder the Warren Court's stance in these cases received limited popular support. Moreover, by the end of the 1960s, more crucial issues had come to the fore—rights of political offenders, conscientious objectors, and "end the war" campaigns.

Persons convicted of serious crimes have little to lose by attempting to convince an appellate court that the trial court or law enforcement officials committed an error of constitutional significance. Trial judges faced with questions involving the admissibility of evidence obtained in unique ways may rule incorrectly. Zealous federal law enforcement officials may exceed constitutional limits in their efforts to obtain convictions, although they are much less prone to err than their state counterparts.

Many national and state officials and a large part of the public look upon certain of these constitutional guaranties as socially undesirable. Newspaper editors are prone to deplore "technicalities" of the law, by which improperly seized evidence is held inadmissible or an improperly admitted confession produced by coercive police methods is the cause of reversal by an appellate court. The frequent use by witnesses before grand juries and legislative investigation committees of the self-incrimination clause of the Fifth Amendment has resulted from time to time in public clamor that the scope of the right be narrowed. Since the numerous instances in which these guaranties have been invoked by persons later proved innocent have received virtually no publicity, there is fostered in the public mind the picture of large numbers of guilty persons escaping punishment through constitutionally created loopholes in the law.

Another line of reasoning, taking an historical approach, concludes that the democratic character of American institutions obviates the need for devices that admittedly fulfilled a valuable function as a check on the absolutist tendencies of English monarchs. This argument is easily answered: There are thousands of cases on record in which American officials, either from zeal to enforce the law or solve a crime, or from a basic dislike of members of certain minority groups, have committed acts that no civilized nation can permit. The dangers to personal liberties that would follow abandonment of these constitutional guaranties are incalculable. "The greatest dangers to liberty lurk in insidious encroachment by men of zeal, well-meaning, but without understanding" (Justice Brandeis, dissenting in *Olmstead* v. *U.S.*).

The conflict of interests presented in these pages is frequently stated in misleading terms. Involved is not, as sometimes appears, freedom versus security. Rather, it is a struggle between two cherished and not necessarily antithetical values, a clash of rights, not of wrongs. The judicial task is one of determining how much protection can be accorded each individual without unduly hampering the effort of government to maintain order and peace, without which there can be no freedom. Small wonder the framers of our national and state constitutions gave special attention to procedural rights. Far from demonstrating fondness for technicalities, this emphasis on procedural guaranties highlights the conviction that "The history of American freedom is in no small measure the history of procedure" (Justice Frankfurter in *Malinski* v. *New York,* 324 U.S. 401, 419: 1945).

Once the Supreme Court decided that the Constitution protected the rights of state defendants, and that federal courts were available to those seeking vindication of their rights, the pattern was set for a continuing feud between state and federal judges and officials. The states were upset by the application of the fair trial rule, allowing federal judges to examine the totality of the facts and circumstances of each case. More disturbing were the bombshells in the 1960s by which virtually all of the procedural guaranties of the Bill of Rights were incorporated into the Fourteenth Amendment. The conservative line which had been drawn in *Palko* v. *Connecticut,* and maintained in *Adamson* v. *California* was thus breached in a series of decisions beginning with *Mapp* v. *Ohio.* Justice White recapitulated the entire incorporation process in *Duncan* v. *Louisiana,* where the Court held that the federal right to trial by jury in all but petty cases was applicable to the states. This process of nationalizing the Bill of Rights and imposing the various interpretations that evolved from federal cases has been especially galling to the states.

At the same time, a review of Court decisions over the past three decades makes it clear that not all decisions of the Warren Court had the effect of hampering law enforcement, any more than decisions of the Burger Court have all leaned toward crime control. Critics have a way of selecting their ammunition, and critics of the Warren and Burger courts, though usually quite different in their politics, have been no exception in this respect. Since the Court has no public relations staff to place its decisions in the most favorable light, it is no wonder that opinion polls revealed popular dislike for the Court's handling of criminal justice problems in the 1960s and suspicion among fans of the Warren Court that its successor was throwing the Bill of Rights to the wind in the 1970s and 1980s.

What follows is a brief survey of some of the topics in criminal procedure, with a review of the major cases. The field is too vast to include them all. Cases on criminal procedure are as myriad as the variety of citizen-police-courtroom encounters themselves.

The Exclusionary Rule.   Since 1914 federal courts had excluded from trial evidence obtained illegally. In the 1949 decision in *Wolf* v. *Colorado* (338 U.S. 25), the Court had held the Fourth Amendment guaranty against unreasonable search and seizure applicable to the states, but refrained from imposing the federal exclusionary rule, asserting with more confidence than accuracy, that other remedies were available to state victims of illegal searches and seizures. By 1961 the Supreme Court had learned what others had long known—civil tort remedies against offending police officers or criminal prosecution failed to provide redress. *Mapp* v. *Ohio* marked the beginning of heightened concern with the realities of criminal justice at the state level, and abandonment of the fair trial approach. The impact of *Mapp* was mitigated by *Linkletter* v. *Walker* (381 U.S. 618:1965), ruling that *Mapp* should apply only to cases pending on direct review at the time of the 1961 decision.

Mapp remains the linchpin for much of the due process revolution set loose by the Warren Court. Most citizen encounters with law enforcement authorities are with state and local police. Court decisions specifying proper procedure for stops, searches, and arrests thus have real impact on the criminal justice system when coupled with the exclusionary rule. Yet, because of the social costs of the rule—one does not benefit from its operation unless incriminating evidence is found—it remains a center of controversy. *Stone* v. *Powell,* reprinted in this chapter, reveals much discomfort and some dissatisfaction with the rule among the majority of the Court's present membership.

Furthermore, *Rakas* v. *Illinois* (439 U.S. 128: 1978) applied a contracted principle of standing to reduce the number of situations in which a defendant can invoke the exclusionary rule. After receiving a robbery report, police stopped and searched a car in which Rakas and others were riding, and found a sawed-off rifle and rifle shells which were later introduced as evidence against them. Neither Rakas nor any of the other petitioners in the case owned the car or the rifle and shells. The Illinois courts held that they lacked standing to raise a Fourth Amendment objection to the allegedly unlawful search and seizure, and five Justices of the Supreme Court affirmed. As spokesman, Justice Rehnquist refused to accept the proposition that anyone against whom a search is directed has standing to contest its validity. Rather, " 'Fourth Amendment rights are personal rights which . . . may not be vicariously asserted.' . . . A person who is aggrieved by an illegal search and seizure only through the introduction of damaging evidence secured by a search of a third person's premises or property has not had any of his Fourth Amendment rights infringed." Petitioners would need a property interest either in the automobile or in the materials seized. Failing this, they would have to have "a constitutionally protected expectation of privacy" in the place searched.

In a dissent joined by Justices Brennan, Marshall, and Stevens, Justice White protested vigorously.

> . . . The ruling today undercuts the force of the exclusionary rule in the one area in which its use is most certainly justified—the deterrence of bad-faith violations of the Fourth Amendment. . . . This decision invites police to engage in patently unreasonable searches every time an automobile contains more than one occupant. Should something be found, only the owner of the vehicle, or of the item, will have standing to seek suppression, and the evidence will presumably be usable against the other occupants.

The Right to Counsel.   The fair trial rule with respect to counsel in state noncapital cases was overturned by *Gideon* v. *Wainwright* (372 U.S. 335: 1963), which now imposed the federal rule on state procedures. Justice Black sought to give the impression that the *Betts* v. *Brady* rule (316 U.S. 455), requiring appointment of counsel only where the totality of circumstances made it necessary for a fair trial, was a prior break with the precedents. To one who reexamines *Powell* v. *Alabama* and subsequent decisions, Black's reasoning was contrived. Yet, Black was correct in stating:" . . . The right of one charged with crime to counsel may not be deemed fundamental and essential to fair trials in some countries, but it is in ours." *Douglas* v. *California* (372 U.S. 353: 1963) upheld the right of indigents to have the assistance of counsel for appeal. In doing so it relied on the equal protection argument which had led the Court to require free transcripts for indigent defendants who wanted to appeal (*Griffin* v. *Illinois,* 351 U.S. 12: 1956). Where the appeal is discretionary, rather than of right, the rule for appointed counsel does not apply (*Ross* v. *Moffitt,* 417 U.S. 600: 1974). Similarly, counsel is not constitutionally required in *habeas corpus* cases, when a defendant attacks his conviction collaterally instead of on direct appeal.

In other significant rulings, a defendant was held entitled to counsel at the arraignment (*Hamilton* v. *Alabama,* 368 U.S. 52: 1961), and at a deferred sentencing-probation revocation proceeding after trial (*Mempa* v. *Rhay,* 389 U.S. 128: 1967). After sentencing however, counsel is provided indigents at such hearings only on a "case-by-case" basis (*Gagnon* v. *Scarpelli,* 411 U.S. 778: 1973). For counsel at trial, the Burger Court has broadened the *Gideon* rule to include petty offenses, where confinement for any period is part of the sentence. The trial judge's decision to appoint counsel thus affects the sentence imposed later if the defendant is found guilty (*Scott* v. *Illinois,* 440 U.S. 367: 1979, clarifying *Argersinger* v. *Hamlin,* 407 U.S. 25: 1972). Nevertheless, a defendant has a constitutional right to refuse counsel if the choice is made voluntarily and intelligently (*Faretta* v. *California,* 422 U.S. 806: 1975).

Self-Incrimination and Identification of the Accused.   The earlier decisions of *Twining* v. *New Jersey* (211 U.S. 78: 1908) and *Adamson* v. *California,* which had refused to extend to state proceedings the federal Fifth Amendment privilege against self-incrimination, were overruled in *Malloy* v. *Hogan* (378 U.S. 1: 1964), where a witness refused to testify, and in *Griffin* v. *California* (380 U.S. 609: 1965), where a state judge commented adversely on a defendant's refusal to take the stand and testify in his own behalf. Once again, the Court tried to soften the blow by making the Griffin decision applicable only to cases pending on direct appeal at the time of the overruling decision (*Tehan* v. *Shott,* 382 U.S. 406: 1966).

The extent of the guard against self-incrimination has presented the Court with questions. Again, the tension is between the needs of law enforcement and the freedom properly to be accorded the individual. Fifth Amendment protection may be claimed by a witness to justify refusal to testify before a grand jury, jury, or legislative committee, or to prevent being compelled to produce papers or other evidence (*Counselman* v. *Hitchcock,* 142 U.S. 547: 1892). Although an investigating committee hearing is not a criminal proceeding, the Court recognized in 1955 that the consequences to the witness of compelled testimony might be the same as in judicial proceedings (*Quinn* v. *United States,* 349 U.S. 155; *Emspak* v. *United States,* 349 U.S. 190). In an effort to make available testimony of reluctant witnesses concerning Communist party activities and organized crime, Congress then resorted to a technique used in earlier periods to facilitate enforcement of specific statutes. A witness could be granted immunity from prosecution with respect to the matters about which he testified. The Immunity Act of 1954 and the administrative procedures set forth in the Act were upheld in *Ullman* v. *United States* (350 U.S. 422: 1956). The Organized Crime Control Act of 1970 (84 Stat. 927) allows a federal court, grand jury, administrative agency, or congressional committee to offer "use" as opposed to "transactional" immunity in exchange for compelled testimony. The former is less extensive than the latter, and five of seven participating Justices found this arrangement harmonious with the Fifth Amendment (*Kastigar* v. *United States,* 406 U.S. 441: 1972).

Other examples demonstrate that constitutional rights are not self-defining. The Court has generally interpreted the protection against self-incrimination to include testimonial, but not nontestimonial, evidence. So, in *Schmerber* v. *California* (384 U.S. 757: 1966), a five-man majority upheld a conviction for drunken driving based on a blood sample taken without the defendant's permission. In a case with strong overtones of the testimonial, a badly divided Court refused to void a California statute which required the driver of an automobile involved in an accident to stop and leave his name and address with the owner of the property he had damaged (*California* v. *Byers,* 402 U.S. 424: 1971).

The most devastating decision from the law enforcement viewpoint was *Miranda* v. *Arizona* whose pronouncements were foreshadowed by a 1964 right-to-counsel case, *Escobedo* v. *Illinois* (378 U.S. 478). In overruling *Crooker* v. *California* (357 U.S. 433: 1958) and *Cicenia* v. *LaGay* (357 U.S. 504: 1958), the Court in *Escobedo* condemned the police practice of preventing a suspect from consulting with his lawyer until his interrogation was ended. This and numerous other cases over the previous three decades had made the Court aware of a variety of law enforcement practices that seemed unfair to the accused, many of whom were young, ignorant, and members of minority groups. The Court, which had been inching toward what Herbert Packer termed the "due process model" of criminal justice, in contrast to the older "crime control model," now proceeded in *Miranda* v. *Arizona* to require federal and state officials to give suspects specified warnings or equivalent advice before beginning to interrogate them about alleged crimes. The Warren

Court held that the privilege against self-incrimination can be secured in no other way. The Justices were joining the Sixth Amendment's provisions for right to counsel with the Fifth Amendment's guard against self-incrimination. The belief was that events transpiring in the station house greatly influence the outcome of events in the courthouse.

As *Rhode Island* v. *Innis,* reprinted in this chapter, shows, statements made by a suspect after requesting a lawyer may still be used under certain circumstances. In cases today, the debate turns on whether the suspect has in fact waived his *Miranda* rights, or on whether a *Miranda*-type "interrogation" has in fact occurred. Recognizing the explosive quality of its decision (general "jail delivery" if *Miranda* were applied to past convictions), the Court gave the decision only limited retroactive application: to those defendants whose trials began after June 13, 1966, the day *Miranda* came down. It was retroactive because for many the interrogations had occurred much earlier (*Johnson* v. *New Jersey,* 384 U.S. 719:1966).

In a related development, the Court held that defendant had a right to have retained or appointed counsel present at police lineups, federal or state, because of the danger of faulty identification (*U.S.* v. *Wade,* 388 U.S. 218: 1967 and *Gilbert* v. *California,* 388 U.S. 263: 1967). However, as in *Miranda,* a suspect might choose to waive his right to have counsel present at a lineup, a practice which has been very common; and *Wade,* too, was given only prospective application (*Stovall* v. *Denno,* 388 US. 293: 1967). In addition, the Court offered legislatures and enforcement officials an invitation to provide truly fair lineup procedures that would eliminate the need for counsel's presence, but this suggestion was viewed by critics as less than helpful, since the Court avoided specific recommendations. Moreover, the *Wade* requirement has been held not to apply to informal identification which occurs prior to the initiation of formal criminal prosecution against a suspect (*Kirby* v. *Illinois,* 406 U.S. 682: 1972).

On the basis of experience under *Miranda* and *Wade,* revealed in empirical studies and statements and writings of participants in the process of law enforcement and trial, suspects waiving their rights to silence and counsel continue to make confessions and appear at lineups as in the past. In only a small number of cases do the Miranda warnings seem to make a difference, where, as the result of the suspect's insistence on having counsel before answering questions, the state comes away empty-handed.

A clear indication that the Burger Court has less affection for *Miranda* than did its predecessor is evidenced by the 5-to-4 decision in *Harris* v. *New York* (401 U.S. 22: 1971). Statements made by Harris, inadmissible in direct testimony because of failure of the police to inform him of his Miranda rights, were used to attack the credibility of assertions he made on the witness stand. The Chief Justice conceded that questioning Harris about his statement to police "undoubtedly provided valuable aid to the jury in assessing credibility, and the benefits of this process should not be lost, in our view, because of the speculative possibility that impermissible police conduct will be encouraged thereby." Attempting, apparently, to minimize what for the four dissenters marked a significant and regrettable regression, the Chief Justice observed,

> Some comments in the Miranda opinion can indeed be read as indicating a bar to use of an uncounseled statement for any purpose, but discussion of that issue was not at all necessary to the court's holding and cannot be regarded as controlling. . . . The shield provided by Miranda cannot be perverted into a license to use perjury by way of defense, free from risk of confrontation with prior inconsistent utterances.

For Justice Brennan, joined by Douglas and Marshall, *Harris* v. *New York* ''goes far toward undoing much of the progress made in conforming police methods to the Constitution. . . . The Court today tells the police that they may freely interrogate an accused incommunicado and without counsel and know that although any statement they obtain in violation of *Miranda* can't be used in the State's direct testimony, it may be introduced if the defendant has the temerity to testify in his own defense. . . . It is monstrous that Courts should aid or abet the law-breaking police officers.'' The *Harris* exception to Miranda was continued in *Oregon* v. *Hass* (420 U.S. 714: 1975).

Arrests, Searches and Seizures—Old and New Style.   Few areas of the law are as confusing as the law growing out of the Fourth Amendment guaranties against unreasonable searches and seizures and establishing requirements for the issuance of warrants. *Mapp* v. *Ohio* extended the exclusionary rule to the states, but in itself did nothing to clarify the relevant law. In subsequent decisions, the Supreme Court resolved some issues in ways favoring law enforcement, though others added grounds to the critics' attack on the Court for ''coddling criminals.''

One of the recurrent problems is: When does probable cause exist to justify the issuance of an arrest or search warrant, or to justify an arrest without a warrant? The Court has almost always shown a preference in this century for searches and seizures authorized by warrants, as opposed to warrantless intrusions. Situations can be anticipated, however, where the requirement for a warrant would be so impractical as seriously to hamper law enforcement. So, over the years the Justices have created exceptions to the warrant requirement, and as one might suppose, the scope and application of the various exceptions have been the source of much litigation.

An important exception to the proviso for a search warrant was the curiously evolved doctrine that those places under the control of the arrestee could be searched in order to avoid the danger of concealed weapons or to prevent destruction of crime-related items. In *United States* v. *Rabinowitz* (339 U.S. 56: 1950) an entire office was thoroughly searched incident to a lawful arrest, and the admission at trial of forged stamps discovered during the search was approved. The 1969 decision in *Chimel* v. *California* represents the Court's effort to narrow the area subject to a warrantless search incident to an arrest. Justice Stewart's opinion for the majority shows both the wavering development of the law and judicial determination to induce greater use of search warrants by the police.

The *Chimel* majority split in *United States* v. *Robinson*, however. Robinson was arrested by a policeman in the District of Columbia for driving with a revoked license. A warrantless search of his person incident to the arrest turned up heroin. For the dissenters in *Robinson*, unrefined application of *Chimel* now seemed to grant police too much discretion.

The automobile itself has long been an exception to the general rule that warrants are needed in advance of searches. *Carroll* v. *United States* (267 U.S. 132: 1925) allowed the warrantless search of a car where there was probable cause to believe it was carrying contraband or was being used to violate the law. But the ''automobile exception'' may be in trouble, as the opinions in *Arkansas* v. *Sanders* suggest. There, a majority refused to approve a warrantless search of luggage taken from the trunk of a car.

An important pro-police decision justifying search procedures when part of a ''hot pursuit'' of a suspect, and, more importantly allowing seizure of ''mere evidence'' of crime, was *Warden* v. *Hayden* (387 U.S. 294: 1967). Prior to this ruling, searches could be directed only toward contraband, fruits, or instrumentalities of crime, a limitation which the Court now found lacking in rationality, and not derived from any principle of the Fourth Amendment. In the Warden case, police, while searching a house during "hot pursuit," discovered clothing worn by the defendant. Obviously, abandonment of the "mere evidence" rule assists the police both in use of warrants and in searches incident to a lawful arrest, as well as in exigent situations like that of *Warden*.

In an outgrowth of this case, with First Amendment implications as well, the Court upheld a third-party search by warrant of a newspaper office and files. Law enforcement officers were looking for unpublished photographs which they thought would help them identify assailants of a policeman injured during a demonstration. No one at the newspaper office, however, was suspected of the crime (*Zurcher* v. *Stanford Daily,* 436 U.S. 547: 1978). An outcry by news organizations led Congress to pass a bill overturning *Zurcher,* by barring federal, state, and local police from using warrants to search news offices, subject to very narrow exceptions (*Congressional Quarterly Weekly Report,* Oct. 4, 1980; p. 2897). Note that Congress limited *Zurcher* only for the benefit of the news media, not for citizens generally or other professions. In a related matter, police with an arrest warrant must now, the Court has decided, have a search warrant as well before entering the residence of a third party not named in the former. Allowed are the usual exceptions of consent and "exigent circumstances" (*Steagald* v. *United States,* 49 LW 4418: 1981).

A factor complicating judicial oversight of police practices and behavior is the use of anonymous informers in establishing probable cause. Many of the affidavits signed by police officers recite certain details they learned secondhand from such people, anonymous even to the magistrate issuing the warrant. Key to preventing anonymity from becoming a shield for fictitiousness is the requirement that the officer demonstrate the informant's reliability to the magistrate. The Justices have differed over the degree to which the government must demonstrate the informant's reliability when obtaining a warrant. *Spinelli* v. *United States* (393 U.S. 410: 1969) demanded more than *United States* v. *Harris* (403 U.S. 573: 1971). The constitutional objection to the use of informers on the ground that one cannot confront his accusers was overcome by the Court in *McCray* v. *Illinois* (386 U.S. 300: 1967). So, as *Chimel* called for a greater use of search warrants, *McCray* made it easier to get them.

Electronic eavesdropping and wiretapping gave the Court difficulty from the beginning. In the absence of an official physical trespass to the property subject to the wiretap or bugging, the Court had refused to find a Fourth Amendment violation. Critics, inspired by Brandeis's dissent in *Olmstead,* showed how eavesdropping could take place without violating the Fourth Amendment, as Chief Justice Taft had construed it. Both libertarians and law enforcement officials welcomed *Katz* v. *United States,* which expressly overruled *Olmstead.*

Following *Katz,* the 1968 Omnibus Crime Control and Safe Streets Act (82 Stat. 212) authorized electronic surveillance in a wide variety of cases, but the statute by no means answered all the constitutional questions. In a highly significant interpretation of the Act in 1972, all eight Justices participating rejected the federal government's claim that electronic surveillance, endorsed by the Attorney General but without judicial approval, was lawful under the President's power to protect national security at home (*United States* v. *U.S. District Court,* reprinted in chapter 3). Congressional action to legitimize electronic surveillance in national security matters came in the Foreign Intelligence Surveillance Act of 1978 (92 Stat. 1783). Special courts created by the Act hear requests by the government for warrants to conduct electronic surveillance of "U.S. persons" believed to be working on behalf of a foreign power. More relaxed controls are allowed when the target of the surveillance is a "foreign power" or "agent of a foreign power."

The impact of such legislation on individual privacy can be heavy. As Justice Powell noted in his opinion in *U.S. District Court,* "Though the total number of intercepts authorized by state and federal judges pursuant to . . . the 1968 . . . Act was 597 in 1970, each surveillance may involve hundreds of different conversations. The average intercept in 1970 involved 44 people and 655 conversations, of which 295 or 45 percent were incriminating." Moreover, the use of "pen registers" to determine the numbers dialed from a telephone has not been considered subject to the particular warrant requirements of the 1968 Act (*United States* v. *New York Telephone Co.,* 434 U.S. 159: 1977).

Informers and electronic surveillance combine where an agent or informer is "wired for sound" while talking with a suspect. *On Lee* v. *United States* (343 U.S. 747: 1952) and *Lopez* v. *United States* (373 U.S. 427: 1963) upheld the lawfulness of such police techniques. Even after *Katz,* with its emphasis on "expectation of privacy," the practice survived a constitutional challenge over pronounced dissents in *United States* v. *White* (401 U.S. 745: 1971). In effect, a majority seems to have concluded that one takes his chances when he talks with anyone, in these situations at any rate. But the government's prerogative is severely limited once formal judicial proceedings against a suspect have been launched (*Massiah* v. *United States,* 377 U.S. 201: 1964).

For many years police had engaged in the practice of stopping persons behaving suspiciously and, to protect themselves, patting down or searching those who might be armed. Most civil libertarians criticized this process, since the police normally lacked probable cause for an arrest and the law simply had no provision for a detention process less restrictive than arrest. The critics also claimed that stopping, questioning, and frisking for weapons was a police tactic too often directed toward racial and other minority groups. In *Terry* v. *Ohio,* reprinted here, this practice was upheld by the Warren Court against the charge that it violated the Fourth Amendment. In so doing, the Justices authenticated an important police tactic in the prevention and solution of crimes.

Building on *Terry,* Justice Rehnquist carried police frisking even further (*Adams* v. *Williams,* 407 U.S. 143: 1972). The presence of an informer's tip admittedly insufficiently reliable to constitute probable cause was nonetheless allowed to help establish the "reasonable suspicion"—a standard less demanding on police than probable cause—which *Terry* approved. In dissent, Justice Marshall reminded the majority that Douglas, the sole dissenter in *Terry,* had warned of "powerful hydraulic pressures throughout our history that bear heavily on the Court to water down constitutional guarantees." "Today's decision," Marshall concluded, "demonstrates how prescient Douglas was."

Justice Brennan's dissent in *Adams* drew on Judge Friendly's opinion in the case when it was heard by the Second Circuit. "There is too much danger," Friendly contended, "that, instead of the stop being the object and the protective frisk an incident thereto, the reverse will be true. . . . *Terry* will have opened the sluicegates for serious and unintended erosion of the protection of the Fourth Amendment." Still, the *Adams* dissenters, less Douglas, joined the rest of the Court in stamping as constitutionally permissible a brief stop of vehicles near American borders to ask occupants questions about their citizenship (*United States* v. *Brignoni-Ponce,* 422 U.S. 873: 1975).

Police may make felony arrests in public places without warrants where probable cause exists (*United States* v. *Watson,* 423 U.S. 411: 1976), but arrest warrants are required when police make routine felony arrests in a private residence (*Payton* v. *New York,* 445

U.S. 573: 1980). Again, the usual exceptions of consent and exigent circumstances apply. Detention, short of formal arrest and based on less than probable cause, is permitted in a *Terry*-type stop, but anything longer becomes questionable. The variety of possible situations has made it difficult for the Justices to write precise guidelines, but two examples may be instructive. In *Dunaway* v. *New York* (422 U.S. 200: 1979), the Court excluded the fruits of an interrogation which occurred at the police station even though Dunaway had received his *Miranda* warnings. He was not formally under arrest, but his detention was lengthy and the police admitted that he was not free to go and that they lacked probable cause for arrest. Yet in *Michigan* v. *Summers* (49 LW 4776: 1981) the majority approved the detention of the occupants of a dwelling while police conducted a proper search with warrant. Reviewing recent cases, Justice Stevens recognized

> that some seizures admittedly covered by the Fourth Amendment constitute such limited intrusions on the personal security of those detained and are justified by such substantial law enforcement interests that they may be made on less than probable cause, so long as police have an articulable basis for suspecting criminal activity. In these cases, as in *Dunaway,* the Court was applying the ultimate standard of reasonableness embodied in the Fourth Amendment. They are consistent with the general rule that every arrest, and every seizure having the essential attributes of a formal arrest, is unreasonable unless it is supported by probable cause. But they demonstrate that the exception for limited intrusions that may be justified by special law enforcement interests is not confined to the momentary, on-the-street detention accompanied by a frisk for weapons involved in *Terry* and *Adams*.

In the last dissent he announced from the Supreme Court bench, Justice Stewart joined by Justices Brennan and Marshall thought the majority had gone too far in accommodating law enforcement needs.

> If the police, acting without probable cause, can seize a person to make him available for arrest in case probable cause is later developed to arrest him, the requirement of probable cause for arrest has been turned upside down. And if the police may seize a person without probable cause in order to "facilitate" the execution of a warrant that did not authorize his arrest, the fundamental principle that the scope of a search and seizure can be justified only by the scope of the underlying warrant has suffered serious damage. There is no authority in this Court for the principle that the police can engage in searches and seizures without probable cause simply because to do so enhances their ability to conduct investigations which may eventually lead to probable cause.

Even with the obvious public interest in traffic safety, the Fourth Amendment standard of reasonableness blocks the "random" stop by a police officer on the highway to check for a valid license and registration (*Delaware* v. *Prouse*, 440 U.S. 648: 1979). The significance of this decision is seen in the facts of the case. As the policeman approached the automobile he had stopped, he smelled marijuana smoke and then seized marijuana he saw lying in "plain view" on the floor of the car. Since a policeman must be lawfully present for a search and arrest to be valid, a contrary ruling in *Prouse* would have greatly expanded police powers. Observing that the majority explicitly refused to ban checking all traffic at roadblock-type stops, Justice Rehnquist countered in dissent that "a highway patrolman needs neither probable cause nor articulable suspicion to stop *all* motorists on a particular thoroughfare, but he cannot without articulable suspicion stop *less* than all motorists.''

Other Incorporation Issues.   *Duncan* v. *Louisiana* made jury trial mandatory in all serious state, as well as federal, cases, although a six-man jury is permissible (*Williams* v. *Florida*, 399 U.S. 78: 1970). The speedy trial guaranty was similarly applied to the states in *Klopfer* v. *North Carolina* (386 U.S. 213: 1967). The Sixth Amendment right to confront witnesses was incorporated in *Pointer* v. *Texas* (380 U.S. 400: 1965). One aspect of the confrontation clause, the right of the accused to be present in the courtroom, can be forfeited by unruly behavior of the type that occurred frequently in the late 1960s. In *Illinois* v. *Allen* (397 U.S. 337: 1970) the Court held that if a defendant, after being warned that he will be removed if disruptive behavior continues, persists in such behavior, he can be removed from the courtroom while the trial continues.

The Sixth Amendment right to have compulsory process in obtaining witnesses was incorporated by *Washington* v. *Texas* (388 U.S. 14: 1967). The double jeopardy protection was applied to the states by *Benton* v. *Maryland* (395 U.S. 784: 1969), which involved retrial of a man for both larceny and burglary after he had been acquitted of larceny and convicted of burglary in the first trial.

Capital and Other Punishment.   Reading the opinions from *Gregg* v. *Georgia* reprinted in this chapter may leave the impression that a majority of the Supreme Court does not find the death penalty a violation *per se* of the Eighth and Fourteenth amendments. That impression is correct. In the wake of *Gregg*, hundreds of convicted felons have been placed on "death row." Still, there have been very few executions in the United States during the years since the Court first began looking carefully at capital punishment well over a decade ago. While a majority gives constitutional approval to capital punishment, in principle, their decisions have raised substantial obstacles to carrying it out. *Furman* v. *Georgia* (408 U.S. 238: 1972) mandates standards to limit the discretion of judges and juries, yet complete removal of discretion by making capital punishment mandatory also violates the Eighth Amendment's ban on cruel and unusual punishment (*Woodson* v. *North Carolina*, 428 U.S. 280: 1976). A state must allow for the introduction of any mitigating circumstances (*Roberts* v. *Louisiana*, 431 U.S. 635: 1977), and may not impose the death penalty for rape (*Coker* v. *Georgia*, 433 U.S. 584: 1977). The Court will scrutinize application of a state's own *Furman* standards (*Godfrey* v. *Georgia*, 446 U.S. 420: 1980), and will overturn a death sentence in cases where a jury was not given an opportunity to find the accused guilty of a "lesser included offense." That is, the jury must be able to choose between more than guilt of a capital offense and no guilt at all (*Beck* v. *Alabama*, 447 U.S. 625: 1980). Moreover, the Fifth and Sixth amendments impose particular requirements on the prosecution when evidence from a state-initiated psychiatric interview is introduced at the penalty phase of a capital trial (*Estelle* v. *Smith*, 49 LW 4490: 1981).

The cumulative effect of these and other decisions on capital punishment has been to make the death penalty an unusually costly objective for prosecutors to pursue, in terms of time, energy, and staff. Since lives are at stake, this is as it should be. Yet a practical argument against attempts to impose the ultimate penalty in most instances where it might apply comes from the fact that relative to all criminal cases, capital cases amount to only a tiny fraction of the whole. Given the effort which the state must now mount, the enormous quantity of public resources required in capital cases might otherwise be employed elsewhere in the criminal justice system. Present rules permit defense counsel to wage a procedural war of attrition on the death penalty.

As severely as the Court has examined state practices in capital cases, a majority of the Justices has thus far been unwilling to apply the same scrutiny to noncapital sentences that might violate the Eighth Amendment because they are excessive. The fear seems to be that the floodgates of litigation will be opened if they do. Determination not to accept the burden was displayed graphically in *Rummel* v. *Estelle* (445 U.S. 263: 1980). Five Justices led by Rehnquist refused to consider the application of the Texas recidivist statute an instance of cruel and unusual punishment when, on conviction for his third felony for defrauding others, Rummel was sentenced to life imprisonment. The total amount in question from Rummel's three run-ins with the law was about $230. Justice Stevens admitted in dissent "that the difference between the petitioner's grossly disproportionate sentence and other prisoners' constitutionally valid sentences is not separated by the clear distinction that separates capital from noncapital punishment." Still, he protested that "'the fact that a line has to be drawn somewhere does not justify its being drawn anywhere.' . . . The Court has, in my view, chosen the easiest line rather than the best."

> We are construing a living Constitution. The sentence imposed upon the petitioner would be viewed as grossly unjust by virtually every layman and lawyer. In my view, objective criteria clearly establish that a mandatory life sentence for defrauding persons of about $230 crosses any rationally drawn line separating punishment that lawfully may be imposed from that which is proscribed by the Eighth Amendment.

The decision in *Rummel* was anticipated by *Ingraham* v. *Wright* (430 U.S. 651: 1977), where Justice Powell for a majority of five refused to consider corporal punishment in public schools, no matter how severe, an issue under the Eighth Amendment. Neither did the due process clause require notice and a prior hearing before paddling could commence. Noting that "corporal punishment in the public schools implicates a constitutionally protected interest, . . . the traditional common-law remedies are fully adequate to afford due process." In dissent Justice White rejoined that the record in the case revealed "beatings so severe that if they had been inflicted on a hardened criminal for the commission of a serious crime, they might not pass constitutional muster."

Unfair Trial Publicity.   Two important cases in the 1960s clarified limitations on the reporting of criminal trials, a process that inevitably presents a clash of constitutional values—free press versus fair trial. Television was the culprit in the pretrial and trial of Billie Sol Estes (*Estes* v. *Texas,* 381 U.S. 532: 1965). The Court split 5 to 4. In a plurality opinion, Justice Clark confessed that "one cannot put his finger on [the] specific mischief and prove with particularity wherein he [Estes] was prejudiced." Then both he and Chief Justice Warren, in a concurring opinion set forth a number of hypotheses concerning the bad effects of television on perceptive jurors and the various other trial participants. In 1981, however, all eight participating Justices in *Chandler* v. *Florida* (49 LW 4141) concluded that televised coverage of a trial does not, by itelf, necessarily amount to a violation of the Constitution. Left open was the opportunity for the defendant to demonstrate adverse impact on the fairness of proceedings in individual cases, but the burden of proof dramatically moved away from those who advocate a greater presence of cameras in the courtroom.

Excessive "trial by newspaper" was the grounds for reversing the second-degree murder conviction of Dr. Samuel H. Sheppard (*Sheppard* v. *Maxwell,* 384 U.S. 333: 1966), but the Court devoted considerable attention to failure of the trial judge to take positive steps to control the courtroom behavior of media representatives, to insulate witnesses, and to prevent counsel, police, and witnesses from passing tidbits of information to the press.

To ensure freedom of the press, the Burger Court spoke out emphatically in striking down unanimously the Nebraska gag order of October 1975 issued by a district court judge in a sensational murder trial (*Nebraska Press Association* v. *Stuart*). Writing for the Court, Chief Justice Burger called prior restraint "the most serious and least tolerable infringement of First Amendment rights." Joined by Marshall and Stewart, Justice Brennan declared that prior restraints on the press are "constitutionally impermissible" even as a means of trying to assure a fair trial.

Gannett Co. v. DePasquale (443 U.S. 368: 1979) presented an issue which *Nebraska Press* did not. In *Gannett,* a judge closed a pretrial suppression hearing for the purpose of keeping possibly prejudicial material out of public view. In upholding this technique as a device to help assure a fair trial, Justice Stewart for the majority seemed to extend the same judicial prerogative to the trial itself. Justice Blackmun, writing for himself and Justices White, Brennan, and Marshall, argued persuasively that the Sixth Amendment's guaranty of a public trial was a right belonging not only to the defendant but to the public generally and that judicial proceedings could be closed only in extraordinary situations. A year later, the Court shifted position in *Richmond Newspapers, Inc.* v. *Virginia* (448 U.S. 555: 1980). Here a judge had closed a trial to the public. In a decision with far-reaching implications, a unanimous bench mandated an open trial on a First Amendment right of access, rather than on Sixth Amendment grounds. What remains unclear is the degree to which *Richmond Newspapers* applies to pretrial proceedings of the sort at issue in *Gannett.*

Juvenile Justice.   At the time of their establishment, separate courts for handling offenses by juveniles, using procedures markedly less formal and accusatorial than the regular courts, were heralded as a significant humanitarian breakthrough. Increasingly over time, however, critics began to point to conspicuous shortcomings, frequently resulting in arbitrary and unfair treatment of juveniles.

In 1966 the Supreme Court revealed its concern in *Kent* v. *United States* (383 U.S. 541), when in deciding a District of Columbia case on a statutory basis, the Court stressed fairness and due process. *In re Gault* (387 U.S. 1: 1967), a significant breakthrough, involved an Arizona juvenile proceeding. A 15-year-old boy had been charged with making indecent remarks in a phone call to a neighbor. No notice of his arrest had been given to the boy's parents, nor were they informed of the charge filed with the court. The complainant was not present at his hearing, of which no memorandum or record was made. At a second hearing, conflicting testimony was given, and a probation officer's "referral report" was filed with the court, with no copy available to the parents or the accused. At the conclusion, Gerald Gault was committed as a juvenile delinquent until he reached the age of 21. Under Arizona law, no appeal was possible. Applying due process standards, the Supreme Court found a lack of notice, a denial of the right to counsel (appointed or retained), failure to allow confrontation and cross-examination of witnesses, as well as a denial of the privilege against self-incrimination.

A further step was taken in 1970, when the burden of proving a juvenile's guilt beyond a reasonable doubt was placed upon the state when it charged an offense that would have constituted a crime if committed by an adult (*In re Winship,* 397 U.S. 358). Chief Justice Burger, in dissent, viewed the Court's action as "evading the differences between juvenile courts and traditional courts," a step which "turns the clock back to the pre-juvenile court era."

In 1971 (*McKeiver* v. *Pennsylvania,* 403 U.S. 528: 1971) Chief Justice Burger's cautionary attitude became the law of the land. Announcing the judgment of the Court in a 6-to-3 ruling, Justice Blackmun called a halt to the judicial march started in 1967 by Justice Fortas. Refusing to add trial by jury to the list of procedural safeguards extended to juveniles, Justice Blackmun argued that "a jury trial might remake the juvenile proceedings into a fully adversary process" and thereby "put an effective end to what has been the idealistic prospect of an intimate, informal protective proceeding." In a vigorously elaborate dissent, Justice Douglas pointed out that a youth about to be deprived of his liberty for five or six years has a powerful claim for full due process. Douglas believed that juveniles, no less than adults, are entitled to "the guarantees of the Bill of Rights, made applicable to the States by the Fourteenth Amendment," including jury trial.

Federal Control of State Criminal Proceedings.   There have always been two methods by which criminal defendants could seek a federal remedy for alleged unconstitutional state action—through regular review by appeal or certiorari and, with certain exceptions, through a writ of *habeas corpus.* An early case (*Ex parte Young,* 209 U.S. 123: 1908) established the general authority of federal courts to issue an injunction against actions taken, or threatened, by state officers in violation of the Constitution. In the years following *Young* the Supreme Court and lower federal courts pursued a hands-off policy, refusing to enjoin criminal prosecutions. A 1965 case, *Dombrowski* v. *Pfister* (380 U.S. 479) portended a loosening of this attitude. The unusual facts, involving continued harassment by Louisiana officers, and the vagueness of the offenses charged against petitioner and other NAACP officials caused the Court to conclude that a lack of good faith was shown in charging the petitioner and that the adverse effect on petitioner's First Amendment rights was clear. The Burger Court, in *Younger* v. *Harris* (401 U.S. 37: 1971), displayed greater deference to the states. In the absence of unusual facts, federal courts are to avoid actions that intrude on a state's authority to try all offenses against state law.

In *Stone* v. *Powell* the Burger Court denied federal *habeas corpus* rights to a state prisoner who had been previously afforded litigation of his claim in the state court. Does the judge-made rule excluding evidence obtained by an unconstitutional search and seizure introduced at the trial, presumably designed to deter crime, "outweigh the rule's heavy cost to a rational enforcement of criminal law?" In opinions charged with overtones of dual federalism, the Court's answer was "no." If prisoners had received a full and fair hearing in state courts, they could not bring federal *habeas corpus* proceedings to test the constitutionality of searches leading to their conviction.

One other important development is worthy of mention. During the Warren Court, a majority often found itself pushing state criminal justice systems to provide a longer list of rights for the accused. A pro-prosecution ruling by a state supreme court stood a good chance of being reversed on appeal. As the past decade has witnessed less enthusiasm among a majority of the Burger Court for the rights of criminal defendants, many state courts have maintained or enlarged these rights as a matter of state constitutional law. Although Justice Brennan, for one, has opposed, sometimes stridently, this trend in recent Supreme Court decisions to withhold application of the federal Bill of Rights, he applauds this newer tendency in state courts. Reflected in this development is a tribute, as he sees it, to James Madison and the federal system he helped to establish.

Doffing judicial robes in January 1977, the Justice presented his views in the philosophical tone of a scholar in the pages of the *Harvard Law Review.* His remarkable article was prompted by the "occasion" or "excuse" of having reached the biblical summit of three score years and ten. "The essential point I am making," Brennan wrote, " . . . is not that the United States Supreme Court is necessarily wrong in its interpretation of the federal Constitution, or that ultimate constitutional truths invariably come prepackaged in the dissents, including my own, from decisions of the Court. It is simply that the decisions of the Court are not, and should not be, dispositive of questions regarding rights guaranteed by counterpart provisions of state law.'' As a result, he maintained,

> . . . [s]tate courts cannot rest when they have afforded their citizens the full protections of the federal Constitution. State constitutions, too, are a font of individual liberties, their protections often extending beyond those required by the Supreme Court's interpretation of federal law. The legal revolution which has brought federal law to the fore must not be allowed to inhibit the independent protective force of state law—for without it, the full realization of our liberties cannot be guaranteed.
>
> (William J. Brennan, Jr., ''State Constitutions and the Protection of Individual Rights,'' 90 *Harvard Law Review* 489, 491, 502: 1977.)

Criminal justice has become a paramount concern of constitutional law and now comprises a single body of national jurisprudence with respect to the rights of defendants. Decisions since 1969 represent a withdrawal from certain ''advanced'' positions taken or implied by the Warren Court. Yet, while some of the Warren Court's opinions in criminal procedure cases have been subjected to restrictions, none has been expressly overruled. This is all the more significant in light of the fact that the Warren Court's so-called advances in this area had been bitterly criticized by a minority of four and were thus the most fragile of its judicial creations.

In terms of impact on day-to-day law enforcement, however, it is doubtful whether dramatic judicial pronouncements have had serious negative effects. Confessions, waiver of rights, guilty pleas, and the ''harmless error'' rule combine to keep the conviction rate relatively high. Solution of the crime problem lies elsewhere than through the adoption of rules more favorable to law enforcement. Despite grave misgivings expressed in recent Burger Court decisions, the Warren Court's insistence on fairer, more humane rules for police behavior has contributed to greater police efficiency—a development which, more logically, might have been achieved through administrative controls.

SELECTED READINGS

ALLEN, FRANCIS A., ''Federalism and the Fourth Amendment: A Requiem for Wolf,'' *1961 Supreme Court Review* 1.

AVINS, ALFRED, ed., *The Reconstruction Amendment Debate: The Legislative History in Congress on the 13th, 14th, 15th Amendments*. Richmond: Virginia Commission on Constitutional Government, 1967.

BARNETT, EDWARD L., JR., ''Personal Rights, Property Rights and the Fourth Amendment,'' *1960 Supreme Court Review* 46.

BEANEY, WILLIAM M., *The Right to Counsel in American Courts*. Ann Arbor: University of Michigan Press, 1955.

BEYTAGH, F. X., "Ten Years of Non-Retroactivity: a Critique and a Proposal," *61 Virginia Law Review* 1557 (1975).

BLACK, CHARLES L., *Capital Punishment: The Inevitability of Caprice and Mistake*. New York: W. W. Norton & Co., 1974.

BRANT, IRVING, *The Bill of Rights*. Indianapolis: Bobbs-Merrill, 1965.

CORTNER, RICHARD C., *The Supreme Court and the Second Bill of Rights: The Fourteenth Amendment and the Nationalization of Civil Liberties*. Madison: University of Wisconsin Press, 1981.

FAIRMAN, CHARLES, "Does the Fourteenth Amendment Incorporate the Bill of Rights: The Original Understanding," 2 *Stanford Law Review* 5 (1949).

FELLMAN, DAVID, *The Defendant's Rights Today*. Madison: University of Wisconsin Press, 1976.

GRAHAM, FRED P. *The Self-Inflicted Wound*. New York: Macmillan, 1970.

GRISWOLD, ERWIN N., *Search and Seizure: A Dilemma of the Supreme Court*. Lincoln: University of Nebraska Press, 1975.

KAMISAR, YALE, WAYNE R. LA FAVE, AND JEROLD H. ISRAEL, *Basic Criminal Procedure*, 5th ed. St. Paul, Minn.: West Publishing Co., 1980.

KAPLAN, JOHN, "The Limits of the Exclusionary Rule," 26 *Stanford Law Review* 1027 (1974).

LANDYNSKI, JACOB W., *Searches and Seizures and the Supreme Court*. Baltimore: Johns Hopkins University Press, 1966.

MELTSNER, MICHAEL, *Cruel and Unusual Punishment*. New York: Random House, 1973.

OAKS, DALLIN, "Studying the Exclusionary Rule in Searches and Seizures," 37 *University of Chicago Law Review* 665 (1970).

ROSSUM, R. A., "New Rights and Old Wrongs: The Supreme Court and the Problem of Retroactivity," 23 *Emory Law Journal* 381 (1974).

STEPHENSON, D. GRIER, JR., "Fair Trial–Free Press: Rights in Continuing Tension," 46 *Brooklyn Law Review* 39 (1979).

I. Nationalization
of The Bill of Rights

Hurtado v. *California*
110 U.S. 516, 4 S.Ct. 111, 28 L.Ed. 232 (1884)

The Constitution of California, adopted in 1879, provided that criminal offenses could be prosecuted by information instead of the older form of grand jury indictment. Hurtado brought a writ of error to review the affirmance of his conviction for murder.

MR. JUSTICE MATTHEWS delivered the opinion of the court. . . .

It is claimed on behalf of the prisoner that the conviction and sentence are void, on the ground that they are repugnant to that clause of the Fourteenth Article of Amendment of the Constitution of the United States which is in these words:

"Nor shall any State deprive any person of life, liberty, or property without due process of law."

The proposition of law we are asked to affirm is that an indictment or presentment by a grand jury, as known to the common law of England, is essential to that "due process of law," when applied to prosecutions for felonies, which is secured and guaranteed by this provision of the Constitution of the United States, and which accordingly it is forbidden to the States respectively to dispense with in the administration of criminal law. . . .

The Constitution of the United States was ordained, it is true, by descendants of Englishmen, who inherited the traditions of English law and history; but it was made for an undefined and expanding future, and for a people gathered and to be gathered from many nations and of many tongues. And while we take just pride in the principles and institutions of the common law, we are not to forget that in lands where other systems of jurisprudence prevail, the ideas and processes of civil justice are also not unknown. Due process of law, in spite of the absolutism of continental governments, is not alien to that code which survived the Roman Empire as the foundation of modern civilization in Europe, and which has given us that fundamental maxim of distributive justice—*suum cuique tribuere*. There is nothing in Magna Charta, rightly construed as a broad charter of public right and law, which ought to exclude the best ideas of all systems and of every age; and as it was the characteristic principle of the common law to draw its inspiration from every fountain of justice, we are not to assume that the sources of its supply have been exhausted. On the contrary, we should expect that the new and various experiences of our own situation and system will mould and shape it into new and not less useful forms.

In this country written constitutions were deemed essential to protect the rights and liberties of the people against the encroachments of power delegated to their governments, and the provisions of Magna Charta were incorporated into Bills of Rights. They were limitations upon all the powers of government, legislative as well as executive and judicial.

It necessarily happened, therefore, that as these broad and general maxims of liberty and justice held in our system a different place and performed a different function from their position and office in English constitutional history and law, they would receive and justify a corresponding and more comprehensive interpretation. Applied in England only as guards against executive usurpation and tyranny, here they have become bulwarks also against arbitrary legislation; but, in that application, as it would be incongruous to measure and restrict them by ancient customary English law, they must be held to guarantee, not particular forms of procedure, but the very substance of individual rights to life, liberty, and property. . . .

We are to construe [the due process] . . . phrase in the Fourteenth Amendment by the *usus loquendi* of the Constitution itself. The same words are contained in the Fifth Amendment. That article makes specific and express provision for perpetuating the institution of the grand jury, so far as relates to prosecutions for the more aggravated crimes under the laws of the United States. . . .

According to a recognized canon of interpretation, especially applicable to formal and solemn instruments of constitutional law, we are forbidden to assume, without clear reason to the contrary, that any part of this most important amendment is superfluous. The natural and obvious inference is, that in the sense of the Constitution, "due process of law" was not meant or intended to include, *ex vi termini*, the institution and procedure of a grand jury in any case. The conclusion is equally irresistible, that when the same phrase was employed in the Fourteenth Amendment to restrain the action of the States, it was used in the same sense and with no greater extent; and that if in the adoption of that amendment it had been part of its purpose to perpetuate the institution of the grand jury in all the States, it would have embodied, as did the Fifth Amendment, express declarations to that effect. Due process of law in the latter refers to that law of the land which derives its authority from the legislative powers conferred upon Congress by the Constitution of the United States, exercised within the limits therein prescribed, and interpreted according to the principles of the common law. In the Fourteenth Amendment, by parity of reason, it refers to that law of the land in each State which derives its authority from the inherent and reserved powers of the State, exerted within the limits of those fundamental principles of liberty and justice which lie at the base of all our civil and political institutions, and the greatest

security for which resides in the right of the people to make their own laws, and alter them at their pleasure. . . .

But it is not to be supposed that these legislative powers are absolute and despotic, and that the amendment prescribing due process of law is too vague and indefinite to operate as a practical restraint. It is not every act, legislative in form, that is law. Law is something more than mere will exerted as an act of power. It must be not a special rule for a particular person or a particular case, but, in the language of Mr. Webster, in his familiar definition, "the general law, a law which hears before it condemns, which proceeds upon inquiry, and renders judgment only after trial," so "that every citizen shall hold his life, liberty, property and immunities under the protection of the general rules which govern society," and thus excluding, as not due process of law, acts of attainder, bills of pains and penalties, acts of confiscation, acts reversing judgments, and acts directly transferring one man's estate to another, legislative judgments and decrees, and other similar special, partial and arbitrary exertions of power under the forms of legislation. Arbitrary power, enforcing its edicts to the injury of the persons and property of its subjects, is not law, whether manifested as the decree of a personal monarch or of an impersonal multitude. And the limitations imposed by our constitutional law upon the action of the governments, both State and national, are essential to the preservation of public and private rights, notwithstanding the representative character of our political institutions. The enforcement of these limitations by judicial process is the device of self-governing communities to protect the rights of individuals and minorities, as well against the power of numbers as against the violence of public agents transcending the limits of lawful authority, even when acting in the name and wielding the force of the government. . . .

It follows that any legal proceeding enforced by public authority, whether sanctioned by age and custom, or newly devised in the discretion of the legislative power, in furtherance of the general public good, which regards and preserves these principles of liberty and justice, must be held to be due process of law. . . .

Tried by these principles, we are unable to say that the substitution for a presentment or indictment by a grand jury of the proceeding by information, after examination and commitment by a magistrate, certifying to the probable guilt of the defendant, with the right on his part to the aid of counsel, and to the cross examination of the witnesses produced for the prosecution, is not due process of law. It is, as we have seen, an ancient proceeding at common law, which might include every case of an offense of less grade than a felony, except misprision of treason; and in every circumstance of its administration, as authorized by the statute of California, it carefully considers and guards the substantial interests of the prisoner. It is merely a preliminary proceeding, and can result in no final judgment, except as a consequence of a regular judicial trial, conducted precisely as in cases of indictments. . . .

For these reasons, finding no error therein, the judgment of the Supreme Court of California is

Affirmed.

MR. JUSTICE HARLAN, dissenting. . . .

"Due process of law," within the meaning of the national Constitution, does not import one thing with reference to the powers of the States, and another with reference to the powers of the general government. If particular proceedings conducted under the authority of the general government, and involving life, are prohibited, because not constituting that due process of law required by the Fifth Amendment of the Constitution of the United States, similar proceedings, conducted under the authority of a State, must be deemed illegal as not being due process of law within the meaning of the Fourteenth Amendment. What, then, is the meaning of the words, "due process of law" in the latter amendment?

In seeking that meaning we are, fortunately, not left without authoritative directions as to the source, and the only source, from which the necessary information is to be obtained. In *Mur-*

ray v. *Hoboken,* 18 How. 272, 276–7, it was said,

The Constitution contains no description of those processes which it was intended to allow or forbid. It does not even declare what principles are to be applied to ascertain whether it be due process. It is manifest that it was not left to the legislative power to enact any process which might be devised. The article is a restraint on the legislative as well as on the executive and judicial powers of the government, and cannot be so construed as to leave Congress free to make any process "due process of law" by its mere will. To what principles are we to resort to ascertain whether this process enacted by Congress is due process? To this the answer must be two-fold. We must examine the Constitution itself to see whether this process be in conflict with any of its provisions. If not found to be so, we must look *to those settled usages and modes of proceeding existing in the common and statute law of England before the emigration of our ancestors, and which are shown not to have been unsuited to their civil and political condition by having been acted on by them after the settlement of this country. . . .*

[Harlan next cites various authorities.]

I omit further citations of authorities, which are numerous, to prove that, according to the settled usages and modes of proceeding existing under the common and statute law of England at the settlement of this country, information in capital cases was not consistent with the "law of the land," or with "due process of law." Such was the understanding of the patriotic men who established free institutions upon this continent. Almost the identical words of Magna Charta were incorporated into most of the State Constitutions before the adoption of our national Constitution. When they declared, in substance, that no person should be deprived of life, liberty, or property, except by the judgment of his peers or the law of the land, they intended to assert his right to the same guaranties that were given in the mother country by the great charter and the laws passed in furtherance of its fundamental principles. . . .

But it is said that the framers of the Constitution did not suppose that due process of law necessarily required for a capital offence the institution and procedure of a grand jury, else they would not in the same amendment prohibiting the deprivation of life, liberty, or property, without due process of law, have made specific and express provision for a grand jury where the crime is capital or otherwise infamous; therefore, it is argued, the requirement by the Fourteenth Amendment of due process of law in all proceedings involving life, liberty, and property, without specific reference to grand juries in any case whatever, was not intended as a restriction upon the power which it is claimed the States previously had, so far as the express restrictions of the national Constitution are concerned, to dispense altogether with grand juries.

This line of argument, it seems to me, would lead to results which are inconsistent with the vital principles of republican government. If the presence in the Fifth Amendment of a specific provision for grand juries in capital cases, alongside the provision for due process of law in proceedings involving life, liberty, or property, is held to prove that "due process of law" did not, in the judgment of the framers of the Constitution, necessarily require a grand jury in capital cases, inexorable logic would require it to be, likewise, held that the right not to be put twice in jeopardy of life and limb for the same offense, nor compelled in a criminal case to testify against one's self—rights and immunities also specifically recognized in the Fifth Amendment—were not protected by that due process of law required by the settled usages and proceedings existing under the common and statute law of England at the settlement of this country. More than that, other amendments of the Constitution proposed at the same time, expressly recognize the right of persons to just compensation for private property taken for public use; their right, when accused of crime, to be informed of the nature and cause of the accusation against them, and to a speedy and public trial, by an impartial jury of the State and district wherein the crime was committed: to be confronted by the witnesses against them; and to have compulsory process for obtaining witnesses in their favor. Will it be claimed that these rights were not secured by the "law of the land" or by "due process of law," as declared and established at the foundation of our government? Are they to be excluded from the enumeration of the fundamental principles of liberty and justice, and, therefore, not embraced by "due process of law?" If the argument of my brethren be sound, those rights—although universally recognized at the establishment of our institutions as secured by that due process of law which for centuries had been the foundation of Anglo-Saxon liberty—were not deemed by our fathers as essential in the due process of law prescribed by our Constitution; because—such seems to be the argument—had they been regarded as involved in due process of law they would not have been specifically and expressly provided for, but left to the protection given by the general clause forbidding the deprivation of life, liberty, or property without due process of law. Further, the reasoning of the opinion indubitably leads to the conclusion that but for the specific provisions made in the Constitution for the security of the personal rights enumerated, the general inhibition against deprivation of life, liberty and property without due process of law would not have prevented Congress from enacting a statute in derogation of each of them. . . .

To these considerations may be added others of very great significance. When the Fourteenth Amendment was adopted, all the States of the Union, some in terms, all substantially, declared, in their constitutions, that no person shall be deprived of life, liberty, or property, otherwise than "by the judgment of his peers, or the law of the land," or "without due process of law." When that Amendment was adopted, the constitution of each State, with few exceptions, contained, and still contains, a Bill of Rights, enumerating the rights of life, liberty and property which cannot be impaired or destroyed by the legislative department. In some of them, as in those of Pennsylvania, Kentucky, Ohio, Alabama, Illinois, Arkansas,

Florida, Mississippi, Missouri and North Carolina, the rights so enumerated were declared to be embraced by "the general, great and essential principles of liberty and free government"; in others, as in those of Connecticut, in 1818, and Kansas, in 1857, to be embraced by "the great and essential principles of free government." Now, it is a fact of momentous interest in this discussion, that, when the Fourteenth Amendment was submitted and adopted, the Bill of Rights and the constitutions of twenty-seven States expressly forbade criminal prosecutions, by information, for capital cases; while, in the remaining ten states, they were impliedly forbidden by a general clause declaring that no person should be deprived of life otherwise than by "the judgment of his peers or the law of the land," or "without due process of law." It may be safely affirmed that, when that Amendment was adopted, a criminal prosecution, by information, for a crime involving life, was not permitted in any one of the States composing the Union. So that the court, in this case, while conceding that the requirement of due process of law protects the fundamental principles of liberty and justice, adjudges, in effect, that an immunity or right, recognized at the common law to be essential to personal security, jealously guarded by our national Constitution against violation by any tribunal or body exercising authority under the general government, and expressly or impliedly recognized, *when the Fourteenth Amendment was adopted,* in the Bill of Rights or Constitution of every State in the Union, is, yet, not a fundamental principle in governments established, as those of the States of the Union are, to secure to the citizen liberty and justice, and, therefore, is not involved in that due process of law required in proceedings conducted under the sanction of a State. My sense of duty constrains me to dissent from this interpretation of the supreme law of the land.

MR. JUSTICE FIELD did not take part in the decision of this case.

grand jury now recognized as important by common law, the basis of constitution, by state before 14th amend.

Palko v. Connecticut
302 U.S. 319, 58 S.Ct. 149, 82 L.Ed. 288 (1937)

By statute Connecticut permitted the state to appeal from rulings and decisions in its criminal courts on points of law. Palko, convicted of murder in the second degree and given a life sentence, was retried after a successful state appeal. His second trial, held in spite of his objection that he was being placed in jeopardy twice, resulted in a conviction for first-degree murder and a death sentence. Palko appealed.

MR. JUSTICE CARDOZO delivered the opinion of the Court. . . .

The argument for appellant is that whatever is forbidden by the Fifth Amendment is forbidden by the Fourteenth Amendment also. The Fifth Amendment, which is not directed to the states, but solely to the federal government, creates immunity from double jeopardy. No person shall be "subject for the same offense to be twice put in jeopardy of life or limb." The Fourteenth Amendment ordains, "nor shall any State deprive any person of life, liberty, or property without due process of law." To retry a defendant, though under one indictment and only one, subjects him, it is said, to double jeopardy in violation of the Fifth Amendment,

Does double jeopardy clause apply to states?.

[handwritten margin note: Is the law fundamental to truth & conscience of people? Would justice be fair w/o them]

if the prosecution is one on behalf of the United States. From this the consequence is said to follow that there is a denial of life or liberty without due process of law, if the prosecution is one on behalf of the people of a state. . . .

[The] thesis is even broader. Whatever would be a violation of the original bill of rights (Amendments I to VIII) if done by the federal government is now equally unlawful by force of the Fourteenth Amendment if done by a state. There is no such general rule.

The Fifth Amendment provides, among other things, that no person shall be held to answer for a capital or otherwise infamous crime unless on presentment or indictment of a grand jury. This court has held that, in prosecutions by a state, presentment or indictment by a grand jury may give way to informations at the instance of a public officer. . . . The Fifth Amendment provides also that no person shall be compelled in any criminal case to be a witness against himself. This court has said that, in prosecutions by a state, the exemption will fail if the state elects to end it. . . . The Sixth Amendment calls for a jury trial in criminal cases and the Seventh for a jury trial in civil cases of common law where the value in controversy shall exceed twenty dollars. This court has ruled that consistently with those amendments trial by jury may be modified by a state or abolished altogether. . . .

On the other hand, the due process clause of the Fourteenth Amendment may make it unlawful for a state to abridge by its statutes the freedom of speech which the First Amendment safeguards against encroachment by the Congress . . . or the like freedom of the press . . . or the right of peaceable assembly, without which speech would be unduly trammeled. . . .

The line of division may seem to be wavering and broken if there is a hasty catalogue of the cases on the one side and the other. Reflection and analysis will induce a different view. There emerges the perception of a rationalizing principle which gives to discrete instances a proper order and coherence. The right to trial by jury and the immunity from prosecution except as the result of an indictment may have value and importance. Even so, they are not of the very essence of a scheme of ordered liberty. To abolish them is not to violate a "principle of justice so rooted in the traditions and conscience of our people as to be ranked as fundamental." . . . Few would be so narrow or provincial as to maintain that a fair and enlightened system of justice would be impossible without them. What is true of jury trials and indictments is true also, as the cases show, of the immunity from compulsory self-incrimination. . . . This too might be lost, and justice still be done. Indeed, today as in the past there are students of our penal system who look upon the immunity as a mischief rather than a benefit, and who would limit its scope, or destroy it altogether. No doubt there would remain the need to give protection against torture, physical or mental. . . . Justice, however, would not perish if the accused were subject to a duty to respond to orderly inquiry. The exclusion of these immunities and privileges from the privileges and immunities protected against the action of the states has not been arbitrary or casual. It has been dictated by a study and appreciation of the meaning, the essential implications, of liberty itself.

We reach a different plane of social and moral values when we pass to the privileges and immunities that have been taken over from the earlier articles of the Federal Bill of Rights and brought within the Fourteenth Amendment by a process of absorption. These in their origin were effective against the federal government alone. If the Fourteenth Amendment has absorbed them, the process of absorption has had its source in the belief that neither liberty nor justice would exist if they were sacrificed. . . . This is true, for illustration, of freedom of thought and speech. Of that freedom one may say that it is the matrix, the indispensable condition, of nearly every other form of freedom. With rare aberrations a pervasive recognition of that truth can be traced in our history, political and legal. So it has come about that the domain of liberty, withdrawn by the Fourteenth Amendment from encroachment by the states, has been enlarged by latter-day judgments to include liberty of the mind as well as liberty of action. . . .

Our survey of the cases serves, we think, to justify the statement that the dividing line between them, if not unfaltering throughout its course, has been true for the most part to a unifying principle. On which side of the line the case made out by the appellant has appropriate location must be the next inquiry and the final one. Is that kind of double jeopardy to which

the statute has subjected him a hardship so acute and shocking that our polity will not endure it? Does it violate those "fundamental principles of liberty and justice which lie at the base of all our civil and political institutions?" . . . The answer surely must be "no."

The judgment is

Affirmed.

MR. JUSTICE BUTLER dissents.

Adamson v. California
332 U.S. 46, 67 S.Ct. 1672, 91 L.Ed. 1903 (1947)

Adamson appealed from a judgment of the Supreme Court of California affirming his conviction of murder. The basis of his appeal was the alleged invalidity of a California code provision that permitted the prosecution and the court to comment on the failure of a defendant to take the witness stand to explain or deny evidence against him. In his trial Adamson, who had a record of three previous felony convictions, chose not to take the stand, thus causing adverse comments by the district attorney and court. However, if he had chosen to testify the district attorney could then have revealed his record of previous convictions in order to impeach his testimony. It should be noted that the majority of state jurisdictions and the federal courts did not permit comment on a defendant's failure to testify.

MR. JUSTICE REED delivered the opinion of the Court. . . .

In the first place, appellant urges that the provision of the Fifth Amendment that no person "shall be compelled in any criminal case to be a witness against himself" is a fundamental national privilege or immunity protected against state abridgment by the Fourteenth Amendment or a privilege or immunity secured, through the Fourteenth Amendment, against deprivation by state action because it is a personal right, enumerated in the federal Bill of Rights.

Secondly, appellant relies upon the due process of law clause of the Fourteenth Amendment to invalidate the provisions of the California law, . . . and as applied (a) because comment on

failure to testify is permitted, (b) because appellant was forced to forego testimony in person because of danger of disclosure of his past convictions through cross-examination, and (c) because the presumption of innocence was infringed by the shifting of the burden of proof to appellant in permitting comment on his failure to testify.

We shall assume, but without any intention thereby of ruling upon the issue, that permission by law to the court, counsel and jury to comment upon and consider the failure of defendant "to explain or to deny by his testimony any evidence of facts in the case against him" would infringe defendant's privilege against self-incrimination under the Fifth Amendment if this were a trial in a court of the United States under similar law. Such an assumption does not determine appellant's rights under the Fourteenth Amendment. It is settled law that the clause of the Fifth Amendment, protecting a person against being compelled to be a witness against himself, is not made effective by the Fourteenth Amendment as a protection against state action on the ground that freedom from testimonial compulsion is a right of national citizenship, or because it is a personal privilege or immunity secured by the Federal Constitution as one of the rights of man that are listed in the Bill of Rights.

The reasoning that leads to those conclusions starts with the unquestioned premise that the Bill of Rights, when adopted, was for the protection of the individual against the federal government and its provisions were inapplicable to similar actions done by the states. . . . With the adoption of the Fourteenth Amendment, it was suggested that the dual citizenship recognized by its first sentence secured for citizens federal protection for their elemental privileges and immunities of state citizenship. The Slaughterhouse cases decided, contrary to the suggestion, that these rights, as privileges and immunities of state citizenship, remained under the sole protection of the state governments. This Court, without the expression of a contrary view upon that phase of the issues before the Court, has approved this determination. The power to free defendants in state trials from self-incrimination was specifically determined to be beyond the scope of the privileges and immunities clause of the Fourteenth Amendment in *Twining* v. *New Jersey*, 211 U.S. 78, 91–98. ''The privilege against self-incrimination may be withdrawn and the accused put upon the stand as a witness for the state.'' The Twining case likewise disposed of the contention that freedom from testimonial compulsion, being specifically granted by the Bill of Rights, is a federal privilege or immunity that is protected by the Fourteenth Amendment against state invasion. This Court held that the inclusion in the Bill of Rights of this protection against the power of the national government did not make

the privilege a federal privilege or immunity secured to citizens by the Constitution against state action. *Twining* v. *New Jersey*, . . . ; *Palko* v. *Connecticut*. . . . After declaring that state and national citizenship co-exist in the same person, the Fourteenth Amendment forbids a state from abridging the privileges and immunities of citizens of the United States. As a matter of words, this leaves a state free to abridge, within the limits of the due process clause, the privileges and immunities flowing from state citizenship. This reading of the Federal Constitution has heretofore found favor with the majority of this Court as a natural and logical interpretation. It accords with the constitutional doctrine of federalism by leaving to the states the responsibility of dealing with the privileges and immunities of their citizens except those inherent in national citizenship. It is the construction placed upon the amendment by justices whose own experience had given them contemporaneous knowledge of the purposes that led to the adoption of the Fourteenth Amendment. This construction has become embedded in our federal system as a functioning element in preserving the balance between national and state power. We reaffirm the conclusion of the Twining and Palko cases that protection against self-incrimination is not a privilege or immunity of national citizenship.

Appellant secondly contends that if the privilege against self-incrimination is not a right protected by the privileges and immunities clause of the Fourteenth Amendment against state action, this privilege, to its full scope under the Fifth Amendment, inheres in the right to a fair trial. A right to a fair trial is a right admittedly protected by the due process clause of the Fourteenth Amendment. Therefore, appellant argues, the due process clause of the Fourteenth Amendment protects his privilege against self-incrimination. The due process clause of the Fourteenth Amendment, however, does not draw all the rights of the federal Bill of Rights under its protection. That contention was made and rejected in *Palko* v. *Connecticut*. . . . It was rejected with citation of the cases excluding several of the rights, protected by the Bill of

Rights, against infringement by the National Government. Nothing has been called to our attention that either the framers of the Fourteenth Amendment or the states that adopted it intended its due process clause to draw within its scope the earlier amendments to the Constitution. Palko held that such provisions of the Bill of Rights as were "implicit in the concept of ordered liberty," p. 325, became secure from state interference by the clause. But it held nothing more.

Specifically, the due process clause does not protect, by virtue of its mere existence, the accused's freedom from giving testimony by compulsion in state trials that is secured to him against federal interference by the Fifth Amendment. . . . For a state to require testimony from an accused is not necessarily a breach of a state's obligation to give a fair trial. . . .

California, however, is one of a few states that permit limited comment upon a defendant's failure to testify. That permission is narrow. The California law is set out in note 3 and authorizes comment by court and counsel upon the "failure of the defendant to explain or to deny by his testimony any evidence or facts in the case against him." This does not involve any presumption, rebuttable or irrebuttable, either of guilt or of the truth of any fact, that is offered in evidence. It allows inferences to be drawn from proven facts. Because of this clause, the court can direct the jury's attention to whatever evidence there may be that a defendant could deny and the prosecution can argue as to inferences that may be drawn from the accused's failure to testify. . . . It seems quite natural that when a defendant has opportunity to deny or explain facts and determines not to do so, the prosecution should bring out the strength of the evidence by commenting upon defendant's failure to explain or deny it. The prosecution evidence may be of facts that may be beyond the knowledge of the accused. If so, his failure to testify would have little if any weight. But the facts may be such as are necessarily in the knowledge of the accused. In that case a failure to explain would point to an inability to explain. . . .

It is true that if comment were forbidden, an accused in this situation could remain silent and avoid evidence of former crimes and comment upon his failure to testify. We are of the view, however, that a state may control such a situation in accordance with its own ideas of the most efficient administration of criminal justice. The purpose of due process is not to protect an accused against a proper conviction but against an unfair conviction. When evidence is before a jury that threatens conviction, it does not seem unfair to require him to choose between leaving the adverse evidence unexplained and subjecting himself to impeachment through disclosure of former crimes. Indeed, this is a dilemma with which any defendant may be faced. If facts, adverse to the defendant, are proven by the prosecution, there may be no way to explain them favorably to the accused except by a witness who may be vulnerable to impeachment on cross-examination. The defendant must then decide whether or not to use such a witness. The fact that the witness may also be the defendant makes the choice more difficult but a denial of due process does not emerge from the circumstances. . . .

We find no other error that gives ground for our intervention in California's administration of criminal justice.

Affirmed.

MR. JUSTICE FRANKFURTER, concurring.

Less than ten years ago, Mr. Justice Cardozo announced as settled constitutional law that while the Fifth Amendment, "which is not directed to the states, but solely to the federal government," provides that no person shall be compelled in any criminal case to be a witness against himself, the process of law assured by the Fourteenth Amendment does not require such immunity from self-incrimination: "in prosecutions by a state, the exemption will fail if the state elects to end it." *Palko* v. *Connecticut.* . . . Mr. Justice Cardozo spoke for the Court, consisting of Mr. Chief Justice Hughes, and McReynolds, Brandeis, Sutherland, Stone, Roberts, Black, JJ. (Mr. Justice Butler dissented.) The matter no longer called for discussion; a reference to *Twining* v. *New*

Jersey, 211 U.S. 78, decided thirty years before the Palko case, sufficed.

Decisions of this Court do not have equal intrinsic authority. The Twining case shows the judicial process at its best—comprehensive briefs and powerful arguments on both sides, followed by long deliberation, resulting in an opinion by Mr. Justice Moody which at once gained and has ever since retained recognition as one of the outstanding opinions in the history of the Court. After enjoying unquestioned prestige for forty years, the Twining case should not now be diluted, even unwittingly, either in its judicial philosophy or in its particulars. As the surest way of keeping the Twining case intact, I would affirm this case on its authority. . . .

MR. JUSTICE BLACK, dissenting. . . .

This decision reasserts a constitutional theory spelled out in *Twining* v. *New Jersey*, . . . that this Court is endowed by the Constitution with boundless power under ''natural law'' periodically to expand and contract constitutional standards to conform to the Court's conception of what at a particular time constitutes ''civilized decency'' and ''fundamental liberty and justice.'' Invoking this Twining rule, the Court concludes that although comment upon testimony in a federal court would violate the Fifth Amendment, identical comment in a state court does not violate today's fashion in civilized decency and fundamentals and is therefore not prohibited by the Federal Constitution as amended.

The Twining case was the first, as it is the only decision of this Court which has squarely held that states were free, notwithstanding the Fifth and Fourteenth Amendments, to extort evidence from one accused of crime. I agree that if Twining be reaffirmed, the result reached might appropriately follow. But I would not reaffirm the Twining decision. I think that decision and the ''natural law'' theory of the Constitution upon which it relies degrade the constitutional safeguards of the Bill of Rights and simultaneously appropriate for this Court a broad power which we are not authorized by the Constitution to exercise. . . .

My study of the historical events that culminated in the Fourteenth Amendment, and the expressions of those who sponsored and favored, as well as those who opposed its submission and passage, persuades me that one of the chief objects that the provisions of the Amendment's first section, separately, and as a whole, were intended to accomplish was to make the Bill of Rights applicable to the states. With full knowledge of the import of the Barron decision, the framers and backers of the Fourteenth Amendment proclaimed its purpose to be to overturn the constitutional rule that case had announced. This historical purpose has never received full consideration or exposition in any opinion of this Court interpreting the Amendment. . . .

In the Twining case itself, the Court was cited to a then recent book, Guthrie, *Fourteenth Amendment to the Constitution* (1898). A few pages of that work recited some of the legislative background of the Amendment, emphasizing the speech of Senator Howard. But Guthrie did not emphasize the speeches of Congressman Bingham, nor the part he played in the framing and adoption of the first section of the Fourteenth Amendment. Yet Congressman Bingham may, without extravagance, be called the Madison of the first section of the Fourteenth Amendment. In the Twining opinion, the Court explicitly declined to give weight to the historical demonstration that the first section of the Amendment was intended to apply to the states the several protections of the Bill of Rights. It held that that question was ''no longer open'' because of previous decisions of this Court which, however, had not appraised the historical evidence on that subject. The Court admitted that its action had resulted in giving ''much less effect to the Fourteenth Amendment than some of the public men active in framing it'' had intended it to have. . . . With particular reference to the guarantee against compelled testimony, the Court stated that ''Much might be said in favor of the view that the privilege was guaranteed against state impairment as a privilege and immunity of National citizenship, but, as has been shown, the decisions of this court have foreclosed that view." Thus the Court declined, and again today declines, to appraise the relevant historical evidence of the intended scope of the first section of the Amendment. Instead it relied upon previous cases, none of which had analyzed the evidence showing that one purpose of those who framed, advocated, and adopted the Amendment had been to make the Bill of Rights applicable to the States. None of the cases relied upon by the Court today made such an analysis.

For this reason, I am attaching to this dissent an appendix which contains a resumé, by no means complete, of the Amendment's history. In my judgment that history conclusively demonstrates that the language of the first section of the Fourteenth Amendment taken as a whole, was thought by those responsible for its submission to the people, and by those who opposed its submission, sufficiently explicit to guarantee that thereafter no state could deprive its citizens of the privileges and protections of the Bill of Rights. Whether this Court ever will, or whether it now should, in the light of past decisions, give full effect to what the Amendment was intended to accomplish is not necessarily essential to a decision here. However that may be, our prior decisions, including Twining, do not prevent our carrying out that purpose, at least to the extent of making applicable to the states, not a mere part, as the Court has, but the full protection of the Fifth Amendment's provision against compelling evidence from an accused to convict him of crime. And I further contend that the "natural law" formula which the Court uses to reach its conclusion in this case should be abandoned as an incongruous excrescence on our Constitution. I believe that formula to be itself a violation of our Constitution, in that it subtly conveys to courts, at the expense of legislatures, ultimate power over public policies in fields where no specific provision of the Constitution limits legislative power. And my belief seems to be in accord with the views expressed by this Court, at least for the first two decades after the Fourteenth Amendment was adopted. . . .

I cannot consider the Bill of Rights to be an outworn 18th-century "straight jacket" as the Twining opinion did. Its provisions may be thought outdated abstractions by some. And it is true that they were designed to meet ancient evils. But they are the same kind of human evils that have emerged from century to century wherever excessive power is sought by the few at the expense of the many. In my judgment the people of no nation can lose their liberty so long as a Bill of Rights like ours survives and its basic purposes are conscientiously interpreted, enforced and respected so as to afford continuous protection against old, as well as new, devices and practices which might thwart those purposes. I fear to see the consequences of the Court's practice of substituting its own concepts of decency and fundamental justice for the language of the Bill of Rights as its point of departure in interpreting and enforcing that Bill of Rights. If the choice must be between the selective process of the Palko decision applying some of the Bill of Rights to the States, or the Twining rule applying none of them, I would choose the Palko selective process. But rather than accept either of these choices, I would follow what I believe was the original purpose of the Fourteenth Amendment—to extend to all the people of the nation the complete protection of the Bill of Rights. To hold that this Court can determine what, if any, provisions of the Bill of Rights will be enforced, and if so to what degree, is to frustrate the great design of a written Constitution.

Conceding the possibility that this Court is now wise enough to improve on the Bill of Rights by substituting natural law concepts for the Bill of Rights, I think the possibility is entirely too speculative to agree to take that course. I would therefore hold in this case that the full protection of the Fifth Amendment's proscription against compelled testimony must be afforded by California. This I would do because of reliance upon the original purpose of the Fourteenth Amendment.

It is an illusory apprehension that literal application of some or all of the provisions of the Bill of Rights to the States would unwisely increase the sum total of the powers of this Court to invalidate state legislation. The Federal

Does lack of Incorporation
give too much power to courts;
Black says Yes, Frankfurter
says incorporation gives too much power
to courts

Government has not been harmfully burdened by the requirement that enforcement of federal laws affecting civil liberty conform literally to the Bill of Rights. Who would advocate its repeal? It must be conceded, of course, that the natural-law-due-process formula, which the Court today reaffirms, has been interpreted to limit substantially this Court's power to prevent state violations of the individual civil liberties guaranteed by the Bill of Rights. But this formula also has been used in the past, and can be used in the future, to license this Court, in considering regulatory legislation, to roam at large in the broad expanses of policy and morals and to trespass, all too freely, on the legislative domain of the States as well as the Federal Government. . . .

To pass upon the constitutionality of statutes by looking to particular standards enumerated in the Bill of Rights and other parts of the Constitution is one thing; to invalidate statutes because of application of "natural law" deemed to be above and undefined by the Constitution is another. "In the one instance, courts proceeding within clearly marked constitutional boundaries seek to execute policies written into the Constitution; in the other they roam at will in the limitless area of their own beliefs as to reasonableness and actually select policies, a responsibility which the Constitution entrusts to the legislative representatives of the people.''

MR. JUSTICE DOUGLAS joins in this opinion.

MR. JUSTICE MURPHY, with whom MR. JUSTICE RUTLEDGE concurs, dissenting.

While in substantial agreement with the views of MR. JUSTICE BLACK, I have one reservation and one addition.

I agree that the specific guarantees of the Bill of Rights should be carried over intact into the first section of the Fourteenth Amendment. But I am not prepared to say that the latter is entirely and necessarily limited by the Bill of Rights. Occasions may arise where a proceeding falls so far short of conforming to fundamental standards of procedure as to warrant constitutional condemnation in terms of a lack of due process despite the absence of a specific provision in the Bill of Rights. . . .

Rochin v. California
342 U.S. 165, 72 S.Ct. 205, 96 L.Ed. 183
(1952)

In 1949 three deputy sheriffs of Los Angeles County unlawfully forced their way into Rochin's room. They found him sitting partly dressed on the bed where his wife was lying. A deputy spotted two capsules on a nearby nightstand. When asked whose they were, Rochin put them in his mouth. As described by the majority opinion, "A struggle ensued, in the course of which the three officers 'jumped upon him' and attempted to extract the capsules. The force they applied proved unavailing against Rochin's resistance. He was handcuffed and taken to a hospital. At the direction of one of the officers a doctor forced an emetic solution through a tube into Rochin's stomach against his will. This 'stomach pumping' produced vomiting. In the vomited matter were found two capsules which proved to contain morphine." On this evidence he was convicted and sentenced to sixty days imprisonment. The district court of appeal affirmed the judgment and the California Supreme Court denied review. The Supreme Court granted certiorari "because a serious question *exercise Powerful duties w/ care. It is a narrow field that the SC has jurisdiction over*

Criminal Procedure and the Nationalization of the Bill of Rights   415

is raised as to the limitations which the Due Process Clause of the Fourteenth Amendment imposes on the conduct of criminal proceedings by the state." *Talk again of notion of justice*

MR. JUSTICE FRANKFURTER delivered the opinion of the Court. . . .

In our federal system the administration of criminal justice is predominantly committed to the care of the States. The power to define crimes belongs to Congress only as an appropriate means of carrying into execution its limited grant of legislative powers. . . . Broadly speaking, crimes in the United States are what the laws of the individual States make them, subject to the limitations of Art. 1 § 10[1], in the original Constitution, prohibiting bills of attainder and ex post facto laws, and of the Thirteenth and Fourteenth Amendments.

These limitations, in the main, concern not restrictions upon the powers of the States to define crime, except in the restricted area where federal authority has preempted the field, but restrictions upon the manner in which the States may enforce their penal codes. Accordingly, in reviewing a State criminal conviction under a claim of right guaranteed by the Due Process Clause of the Fourteenth Amendment, from which is derived the most far-reaching and most frequent federal basis of challenging State criminal justice, "we must be deeply mindful of the responsibilities of the States for the enforcement of criminal laws, and exercise with due humility our merely negative function in subjecting convictions from state courts to the very narrow scrutiny which the Due Process Clause of the Fourteenth Amendment authorizes." Due process of law, "itself a historical product," . . . is not to be turned into a destructive dogma against the States in the administration of their systems of criminal justice.

However, this Court too has its responsibility. Regard for the requirements of the Due Process Clause "inescapably imposes upon this Court an exercise of judgment upon the whole course of the proceedings [resulting in a conviction] in order to ascertain whether they offend those canons of decency and fairness which express the notions of justice of English-speaking peoples even toward those charged with the most heinous offenses." . . . These standards of justice are not authoritatively formulated anywhere as though they were specifics. Due process of law is a summarized constitutional guarantee of respect for those personal immunities which, as Mr. Justice Cardozo twice wrote for the Court, are "so rooted in the traditions and conscience of our people as to be ranked as fundamental," *Snyder* v. *Massachusetts*, . . . or are "implicit in the concept of ordered liberty." *Palko* v. *Connecticut*. . . . *contra Black*

The vague contours of the Due Process Clause do not leave judges at large. We may not draw on our merely personal and private notions and disregard the limits that bind judges in their judicial function. Even though the concept of due process of law is not final and fixed, these limits are derived from considerations that are fused in the whole nature of our judicial process. . . .

Due process of law thus conceived is not to be derided as resort to a revival of "natural law." To believe that this judicial exercise of judgment could be avoided by freezing "due process of law" at some fixed stage of time or thought is to suggest that the most important aspect of constitutional adjudication is a function for inanimate machines and not for judges, for whom the independence safeguarded by Article 3 of the Constitution was designed and who are presumably guided by established standards of judicial behavior. Even cybernetics has not yet made that haughty claim. To practice the requisite detachment and to achieve sufficient objectivity no doubt demands of judges the habit of self-discipline and self-criticism, incertitude that one's own views are incontestable and alert tolerance toward views not shared. But these are precisely the presuppositions of our judicial process. They are precisely the qualities society has a right to expect from those entrusted with ultimate judicial power. *law interpretation should be able to change w/ times*

need humility. Can't pin down an exact meaning of due process

Restraints on our jurisdiction are self-imposed only in the sense that there is from our decisions no immediate appeal short of impeachment or constitutional amendment. But that does not make due process of law a matter of judicial caprice. The faculties of the Due Process Clause may be indefinite and vague, but the mode of their ascertainment is not self-willed. In each case "due process of law" requires an evaluation based on a disinterested inquiry pursued in the spirit of science, on a balanced order of facts exactly and fairly stated, on the detached consideration of conflicting claims . . . on a judgment not ad hoc and episodic but duly mindful of reconciling the needs both of continuity and of change in a progressive society.

Applying these general considerations to the circumstances of the present case, we are compelled to conclude that the proceedings by which this conviction was obtained do more than offend some fastidious squeamishness or private sentimentalism about combatting crime too energetically. This is conduct that shocks the conscience. Illegally breaking into the privacy of the petitioner, the struggle to open his mouth and remove what was there, the forcible extraction of his stomach's contents—this course of proceeding by agents of government to obtain evidence is bound to offend even hardened sensibilities. They are methods too close to the rack and the screw to permit of constitutional differentiation. . . .

On the facts of this case the conviction of the petitioner has been obtained by methods that offend the Due Process Clause. The judgment below must be

Reversed.

MR. JUSTICE MINTON took no part in the consideration or decision of this case.

MR. JUSTICE BLACK, concurring.

Adamson v. *California* . . . sets out reasons for my belief that state as well as federal courts and law enforcement officers must obey the Fifth Amendment's command that "No person . . . shall be compelled in any criminal case to be a witness against himself." I think a person is compelled to be a witness against himself not only when he is compelled to testify, but also when as here, incriminating evidence is forcibly

taken from him by a contrivance of modern science. . . .

In the view of a majority of the Court, however, the Fifth Amendment imposes no restraint of any kind on the states. They nevertheless hold that California's use of this evidence violated the Due Process Clause of the Fourteenth Amendment. Since they hold as I do in this case, I regret my inability to accept their interpretation without protest. But I believe that faithful adherence to the specific guarantees in the Bill of Rights insures a more permanent protection of individual liberty than that which can be afforded by the nebulous standards stated by the majority.

What the majority hold is that the Due Process Clause empowers this Court to nullify any state law if its application "shocks the conscience," offends "a sense of justice" or runs counter to the "decencies of civilized conduct." The majority emphasize that these statements do not refer to their own consciences or to their senses of justice and decency. For we are told that "we may not draw on our merely personal and private notions"; our judgment must be grounded on "considerations deeply rooted in reason, and in the compelling traditions of the legal profession." We are further admonished to measure the validity of state practices, not by our reason, or by the traditions of the legal profession, but by "the community's sense of fair play and decency"; by the "traditions and conscience of our people"; or by "those canons of decency and fairness which express the notions of justice of English-speaking peoples." These canons are made necessary, it is said, because of "interests of society pushing in opposite directions."

If the Due Process Clause does vest this Court with such unlimited power to invalidate laws, I am still in doubt as to why we should consider only the notions of English-speaking peoples to determine what are immutable and fundamental principles of justice. Moreover, one may well ask what avenues of investigation are open to discover "canons" of conduct so universally favored that this Court should write them into the Constitution? All we are told is that the discovery must be made by an "evaluation based on a disinterested inquiry pursued in the spirit of science on a balanced order of facts." . . .

Some constitutional provisions are stated in absolute and unqualified language such, for illustration, as the First Amendment stating that no law shall be passed prohibiting the free exercise of religion or abridging the freedom of speech or press. Other constitutional provisions do require courts to choose between competing policies, such as the Fourth Amendment which, by its terms, necessitates a judicial decision as to what is an "unreasonable" search or seizure. There is, however, no express constitutional language granting judicial power to invalidate *every* state law of *every* kind deemed "unreasonable" or contrary to the Court's notion of civilized decencies; yet the constitutional philosophy used by the majority has, in the past, been used to deny a state the right to fix the price of gasoline, . . . and even the right to prevent bakers from palming off smaller for larger loaves of bread. . . . These cases, and others, show the extent to which the evanescent standards of the majority's philosophy have been used to nullify state legislative programs passed to suppress evil economic practices. What paralyzing role this same philosophy will play in the future economic affairs of this country is impossible to predict. Of even graver concern, however, is the use of the philosophy to nullify the Bill of Rights. I long ago concluded that the accordion-like qualities of this philosophy must inevitably imperil all the individual liberty safeguards specifically enumerated in the Bill of Rights. Reflection and recent decisions of this Court sanctioning abridgment of the freedom of speech and press have strengthened this conclusion.

MR. JUSTICE DOUGLAS, concurring. . . .

Duncan v. *Louisiana*
391 U.S. 145, 88 S.Ct. 1444, 20 L.Ed. 2d 491 (1968)

Duncan was convicted of simple battery, a misdemeanor punishable under Louisiana law by two years' imprisonment and a $300 fine. His request for trial by jury was denied because the state constitution restricted trial by jury to capital offenses and those punishable by hard labor. The Louisiana Supreme Court denied his claim that his right to jury trial under the Sixth and Fourteenth Amendments had been violated. Duncan appealed.

[*Note:* Bracketed comments, appearing in the footnotes of this case, have been added by the editors.]

MR. JUSTICE WHITE delivered the opinion of the Court. . . .

The Fourteenth Amendment denies the States the power to "deprive any person of life, liberty, or property, without due process of law." In resolving conflicting claims concerning the meaning of this spacious language, the Court has looked increasingly to the Bill of Rights for guidance; many of the rights guaranteed by the first eight Amendments to the Constitution have been held to be protected against state action by the Due Process Clause of

[handwritten annotation: Test is now American scheme of Justice, not natural law]

the Fourteenth Amendment. That clause now protects the right to compensation for property taken by the State;[1] the rights of speech, press, and religion covered by the First Amendment;[2] the Fourth Amendment rights to be free from unreasonable searches and seizures and to have excluded from criminal trials any evidence illegally seized;[3] the right guaranteed by the Fifth Amendment to be free of compelled self-incrimination;[4] and the Sixth Amendment rights to counsel,[5] to a speedy[6] and public[7] trial, to confrontation of opposing witnesses,[8] and a compulsory process for obtaining witnesses.[9]

The test for determining whether a right extended by the Fifth and Sixth Amendments with respect to federal criminal proceedings is also protected against state action by the Fourteenth Amendment has been phrased in a variety of ways in the opinions of this Court. The question has been asked whether a right is among those "'fundamental principles of liberty and justice which lie at the base of all our civil and political institutions,'" *Powell* v. *Alabama*, 287 U.S. 45, 67 (1932);[10] whether it is "basic in our system of jurisprudence," *In re Oliver*, 333 U.S. 257, 273 (1948); and whether it is "a fundamental right, essential to a fair trial," *Gideon* v. *Wainwright*, 372 U.S. 335, 343–344 (1963); *Malloy* v. *Hogan*, 378 U.S. 1, 6

(1964); *Pointer* v. *Texas*, 380 U.S. 400, 403 (1965). The claim before us is that the right to trial by jury guaranteed by the Sixth Amendment meets these tests. The position of Louisiana, on the other hand, is that the Constitution imposes upon the States no duty to give a jury trial in any criminal case, regardless of the seriousness of the crime or the size of the punishment which may be imposed. Because we believe that trial by jury in criminal cases is fundamental to the American scheme of justice, we hold that the Fourteenth Amendment guarantees a right of jury trial in all criminal cases which—were they to be tried in a federal court—would come within the Sixth Amendment's guarantee.[11]

---

[1] *Chicago, B. & Q. R. Co.* v. *Chicago*, 166 U.S. 226 (1897).

[2] See, e.g., *Fiske* v. *Kansas*, 274 U.S. 380 (1927) [anticipated in *Gitlow* v. *New York*, 268 U.S. 652 (1925).]

[3] See *Mapp* v. *Ohio*, 367 U.S. 643 (1961) [overruling *Wolf* v. *Colorado*, 338 U.S. 35 (1949)].

[4] *Malloy* v. *Hogan*, 378 U.S. 1 (1964) [reversing *Twining* v. *New Jersey*, 211 U.S. 78 (1908)].

[5] *Gideon* v. *Wainwright*, 372 U.S. 335 (1963) [anticipated in *Powell* v. *Alabama*, 287 U.S. 45 (1932); spelled out in *Miranda*; qualified in *Harris* v. *New York* (401 U.S. 222: 1971)].

[6] *Klopfer* v. *North Carolina*, 386 U.S. 213 (1967).

[7] *In re Oliver*, 333 U.S. 257 (1948).

[8] *Pointer* v. *Texas*, 380 U.S. 400 (1965) [qualified in *Dutton* v. *Evans*, 400 U.S. 74 (1970)].

[9] *Washington* v. *Texas*, 388 U.S. 14 (1967).

[10] Quoting from *Hebert* v. *Louisiana*, 272 U.S. 312, 316 (1926).

[11] In one sense recent cases applying provisions of the first eight Amendments to the States represent a new approach to the "incorporation" debate. Earlier the Court can be seen as having asked, when inquiring into whether some particular procedural safeguard was required of a state, if a civilized system could be imagined that would not accord the particular protection. For example, *Palko* v. *Connecticut*, 302 U.S. 319, 325 (1937) [*Palko* was itself overruled in *Benton* v. *Maryland* (395 U.S. 781: 1969), evoking from Justice Harlan: "Today *Palko* becomes another casualty in the so far unchecked march toward 'incorporating' much, if not all, of the Federal Bill of Rights into the Due Process Clause . . . eroding many of the basics of our federal system."] stated: "The right to trial by jury and the immunity from prosecution except as the result of an indictment may have value and importance. Even so, they are not the very essence of a scheme of ordered liberty. . . . Few would be so narrow or provincial as to maintain that a fair and enlightened system of justice would be impossible without them." The recent cases, on the other hand, have proceeded upon the valid assumption that state criminal processes are not imaginary and theoretical schemes but actual systems bearing virtually every characteristic of the common-law system that has been developing contemporaneously in England and in this country. The question thus is whether given this kind of system a particular procedure is fundamental—whether, that is, a procedure is necessary to an Anglo-American regime of ordered liberty. It is this sort of inquiry that can justify the conclusions that state courts must exclude evidence seized in violation of the Fourth Amendment. *Mapp* v. *Ohio*, 367 U.S. 643 (1961); that state prosecutors may not comment on a defendant's failure to testify, *Griffin* v. *California*, 380 U.S. 609 (1965); and that criminal punishment may not be imposed for the status of narcotics addiction, *Robinson* v. *California*, 370 U.S. 660 (1962). [In the Robinson case, this was ruled "cruel and unusual" punishment in violation of the Eighth Amendment (incor-

Since we consider the appeal before us to be such a case, we hold that the Constitution was violated when appellant's demand for jury trial was refused.

MR. JUSTICE BLACK, with whom MR. JUSTICE DOUGLAS joins, concurring.

The Court today holds that the right to trial by jury guaranteed defendants in criminal cases in federal courts by Art. III of the United States Constitution and by the Sixth Amendment is also guaranteed by the Fourteenth Amendment to defendants tried in state courts. With this holding I agree for reasons given by the Court. I also agree because of reasons given in my dissent in *Adamson* v. *California*, 332 U.S. 46, . . . And I am very happy to support this selective process through which our Court has since the

porated into the due process clause of the Fourteenth). But in 1968 (*Powell* v. *Texas,* 392 U.S. 514) a divided Court (5–4) decided that the conviction, under a Texas statute, of a chronic alcoholic for the crime of public drunkenness is not cruel and unusual punishment proscribed by the Eighth Amendment]. Of immediate relevance for this case are the Court's holdings that the States must comply with certain provisions of the Sixth Amendment, specifically that the States may not refuse a speedy trial, confrontation of witnesses, and the assistance, at state expense if necessary, of counsel. . . . Of each of these determinations that a constitutional provision originally written to bind the Federal Government should bind the States as well it might be said that the limitation in question is not necessarily fundamental to fairness in every criminal system that might be imagined but is fundamental in the context of the criminal processes maintained by the American States.

When the inquiry is approached in this way the question whether the States can impose criminal punishment without granting a jury trial appears quite different from the way it appeared in the older cases opining that States might abolish jury trial. See, e.g., *Maxwell* v. *Dow,* 176 U.S. 581 (1900) [Here virtually overruled]. A criminal process which was fair and equitable but used no juries is easy to imagine. It would make use of alternative guarantees and protections which would serve the purposes that the jury serves in the English and American systems. Yet no American State has undertaken to construct such a system. Instead, every American State, including Louisiana, uses the jury extensively, and imposes very serious punishments only after a trial at which the defendant has a right to a jury's verdict. In every state, including Louisiana, the structure and style of the criminal process—the supporting framework and the subsidiary procedures—are of the sort that naturally complement jury trial, and have developed in connection with and in reliance upon jury trial.

Adamson case held most of the specific Bill of Rights' protections applicable to the States to the same extent they are applicable to the Federal Government. . . .

What I wrote there in 1947 was the product of years of study and research. My appraisal of the legislative history followed 10 years of legislative experience as a Senator of the United States, not a bad way, I suspect, to learn the value of what is said in legislative debates, committee discussions, committee reports, and various other steps taken in the course of passage of bills, resolutions, and proposed constitutional amendments. My Brother Harlan's objections to my Adamson dissent history, like that of most of the objectors, relies most heavily on a criticism written by Professor Charles Fairman and published in the *Stanford Law Review*. 2 Stan. L. Rev. 5 (1949). I have read and studied this article extensively, including the historical references, but am compelled to add that in my view it has completely failed to refute the inferences and arguments that I suggested in my Adamson dissent. Professor Fairman's "history" relies very heavily on what was *not* said in the state legislatures that passed on the Fourteenth Amendment. Instead of relying on this kind of negative pregnant, my legislative experience has convinced me that it is far wiser to rely on what *was* said, and most importantly, said by the men who actually sponsored the Amendment in the Congress. I know from my years in the United States Senate that it is to men like Congressman Bingham, who steered the Amendment through the House, and Senator Howard, who introduced it in the Senate, that members of Congress look when they seek the real meaning of what is being offered. And they vote for or against a bill based on what the sponsors of that bill and those who oppose it tell them it means. . . .

While I do not wish at this time to discuss at length my disagreement with Brother Harlan's forthright and frank restatement of the now discredited Twining doctrine, I do want to point out what appears to me to be the basic difference between us. His view, as was indeed the view of Twining, is that "due process is an evolving concept'' and therefore that it entails a ''gradual process of judicial inclusion and exclusion'' to ascertain those ''immutable principles of free government which no member of the Union may disregard.'' Thus the Due Process Clause is treated as prescribing no specific and clearly ascertainable constitutional command that judges must obey in interpreting the Constitution, but rather as leaving judges free to decide at any particular time whether a particular rule or judicial formulation embodies an ''immutable principle of free government'' or ''is implicit in the concept of ordered liberty,'' or whether certain conduct ''shocks the judge's conscience'' or runs counter to some other similar, undefined and undefinable standard. Thus due process, according to my Brother Harlan, is to be a word with no permanent meaning, but one which is found to shift from time to time in accordance with judges' predilections and understandings of what is best for the country. If due process means this, the Fourteenth Amendment, in my opinion, might as well have been written that ''no person shall be deprived of life, liberty or property except by laws that the judges of the United States Supreme Court shall find to be consistent with the immutable principles of free government.'' It is impossible for me to believe that such unconfined power is given to judges in our Constitution that is a written one in order to limit governmental power. . . .

Finally I want to add that I am not bothered by the argument that applying the Bill of Rights to the States, ''according to the same standards that protect those rights against federal encroachment,'' interferes with our concept of federalism in that it may prevent States from trying novel social and economic experiments. I have never believed that under the guise of federalism the States should be able to experiment with the protections afforded our citizens through the Bill of Rights. As Justice Goldberg said so wisely in his concurring opinion in *Pointer* v. *Texas,* 380 U.S. 400, ''. . . to deny to the States the power to impair a fundamental constitutional right is not to increase federal power, but, rather, to limit the power of both

federal and state governments in favor of safeguarding the fundamental rights and liberties of the individual. In my view this promotes rather than undermines the basic policy of avoiding excess concentration of power in government, federal or state, which underlies our concepts of federalism.'' 380 U.S., at 414. . . . It seems to me totally inconsistent to advocate on the one hand, the power of this Court to strike down any state law or practice which it finds ''unreasonable'' or ''unfair,'' and on the other hand urge that the States be given maximum power to develop their own laws and procedures. . . . No one is more concerned than I that the States be allowed to use the full scope of their powers as their citizens see fit. And that is why I have continually fought against the expansion of this Court's authority over the States through the use of a broad, general interpretation of due process that permits judges to strike down state laws they do not like.

In closing I want to emphasize that I believe as strongly as ever that the Fourteenth Amendment was intended to make the Bill of Rights applicable to the States. I have been willing to support the selective incorporation doctrine, however, as an alternative, although perhaps less historically supportable than complete incorporation. The selective incorporation process, if used properly, does limit the Supreme Court in the Fourteenth Amendment field to specific Bill of Rights' protections only and keeps judges from roaming at will in their own notions of what policies outside the Bill of Rights are desirable and what are not. And, most importantly for me, the selective incorporation process has the virtue of having already worked to make most of the Bill of Rights' protections applicable to the States.

MR. JUSTICE HARLAN, whom MR. JUSTICE STEWART joins, dissenting. . . .

The Court's approach to this case is an uneasy and illogical compromise among the views of various Justices on how the Due Process Clause should be interpreted. The Court does not say that those who framed the Fourteenth Amendment intended to make the Sixth Amendment applicable to the States. And the Court concedes that it finds nothing unfair about the procedure by which the present appellant was tried. Nevertheless, the Court reverses his conviction: it holds, for some reason not apparent to me, that the Due Process Clause incorporates the particular clause of the Sixth Amendment that requires trial by jury in federal criminal cases—including, as I read its opinion, the sometimes trivial accompanying baggage of judicial interpretation in federal contexts. I have raised my voice many times before against the Court's continuing undiscriminating insistence upon fastening on the States federal notions of criminal justice, and I must do so again in this instance. With all respect, the Court's approach and its reading of history are altogether topsy-turvy.

I believe I am correct in saying that every member of the Court for at least the last 135 years has agreed that our Founders did not consider the requirements of the Bill of Rights so fundamental that they should operate directly against the States. They were wont to believe rather that the security of liberty in America rested primarily upon the dispersion of governmental power across a federal system. The Bill of Rights was considered unnecessary by some but insisted upon by others in order to curb the possibility of abuse of power by the strong central government they were creating.

The Civil War Amendments dramatically altered the relation of the Federal Government to the States. The first section of the Fourteenth Amendment imposes highly significant restrictions on state action. But the restrictions are couched in very broad and general terms: citizenship; privileges and immunities; due process of law; equal protection of the laws....

A few members of the Court have taken the position that the intention of those who drafted the first section of the Fourteenth Amendment was simply, and exclusively, to make the provisions of the first eight amendments applicable to state action. This view has never been accepted by this Court. In my view, ... the first section of the Fourteenth Amendment was meant neither to incorporate, nor to be limited to, the specific guarantees of the first eight amendments. The overwhelming historical evidence marshalled by Professor Fairman demonstrates, to me conclusively, that the Congressmen and state legislators who wrote, debated, and ratified the Fourteenth Amendment did not think they were "incorporating" the Bill of Rights and the very breadth and generality of the Amendment's provisions suggest that its authors did not suppose that the Nation would always be limited to mid-19th century conceptions of "liberty" and "due process of law" but that the increasing experience and evolving conscience of the American people would add new "intermediate premises." In short, neither history, nor sense, supports using the Fourteenth Amendment to put the States in a constitutional strait-jacket with respect to their own development in the administration of criminal or civil law.

Although I therefore fundamentally disagree with the total incorporation view of the Fourteenth Amendment, it seems to me that such a position does at least have the virtue, lacking in the Court's selective incorporation approach, of internal consistency: we look to the Bill of Rights, word for word, clause for clause, precedent for precedent because, it is said, the men who wrote the Amendment wanted it that way. For those who do not accept this "history," a different source of "intermediate premises" must be found. The Bill of Rights is not necessarily irrelevant to the search for guidance in interpreting the Fourteenth Amendment, but the reason for and the nature of its relevance must be articulated.

Apart from the approach taken by the absolute incorporationists, I can see only one method of analysis that has any internal logic. That is to start with the words "liberty" and "due process of law" and attempt to define them in a way that accords with American traditions and our system of government. This approach, involving a much more discriminating process of adjudication than does "incorporation," is, albeit difficult, the one that was followed throughout the nineteenth and most of the present century. It entails a "gradual process of judicial inclusion and exclusion,'' seeking, with due recognition of constitutional tolerance for state experimentation and disparity, to ascertain those ''immutable principles of free government which no member of the Union may disregard.'' Due process was not restricted to rules fixed in the past, for that ''would be to deny every quality of the law but its age, and to render it incapable of progress or improvement.'' Nor did it impose nationwide uniformity in details, for ''[t]he Fourteenth Amendment does not profess to secure to all persons in the United States the benefit of the same laws and the same remedies. Great diversities in these respects may exist in two States separated only by an imaginary line. On one side of the line there may be a right of trial by jury, and on the other side there may be no such right. Each State prescribes its own modes of judicial proceeding.''

Through this gradual process, this Court sought to define ''liberty'' by isolating freedoms that Americans of the past and of the present considered more important than any suggested countervailing public objective. The Court also, by interpretation of the phrase ''due process of law,'' enforced the Constitution's guarantee that no State may imprison an individual except by fair and impartial procedures.

The relationship of the Bill of Rights to this ''gradual process'' seems to me to be twofold. In the first place it has long been clear that the Due Process Clause imposes some restrictions on state action that parallel Bill of Rights restrictions on federal action. Second, and more important than this accidental overlap, is the fact that the Bill of Rights is evidence, at various points, of the content Americans find in the term ''liberty'' and of American standards of fundamental fairness. . . .

Today's Court still remains unwilling to accept the total incorporationists' view of the history of the Fourteenth Amendment. This, if accepted, would afford a cogent reason for applying the Sixth Amendment to the States. The Court is also, apparently, unwilling to face the task of determining whether denial of trial by jury in the situation before us, or in other situations, is fundamentally unfair. Consequently, the Court has compromised on the ease of the incorporationist position, without its internal logic. It has simply assumed that the question before us is whether the Jury Trial Clause of the Sixth Amendment should be incorporated into the Fourteenth, jot-for-jot and case-for-case, or ignored. Then the Court merely declares that the clause in question is ''in'' rather than ''out.''

The Court has justified neither its starting place nor its conclusion. If the problem is to discover and articulate the rules of fundamental fairness in criminal proceedings, there is no reason to assume that the whole body of rules developed in this Court constituting Sixth Amendment jury trial must be regarded as a unit. The requirement of trial by jury in federal criminal cases has given rise to numerous subsidiary questions respecting the exact scope and content of the right. It surely cannot be that every answer the Court has given, or will give, to such a question is attributable to the Founders; or even that every rule announced carries equal conviction of this Court; still less can it be that every such subprinciple is equally fundamental to ordered liberty. . . .

Even if I could agree that the question before us is whether Sixth Amendment jury trial is totally ''in'' or totally ''out,'' I can find in the Court's opinion no real reasons for concluding that it should be ''in.'' The basis for differentiating among clauses in the Bill of Rights cannot be that only some clauses are in the Bill of Rights, or that only some are old and much praised, or that only some have played an important role in the development of federal law. These things are true of all. The Court says that some clauses are more ''fundamental'' than others, but it turns out to be using this word in a sense that would have astonished Mr. Justice Cardozo and which, in addition, is of no help. The word does not mean ''analytically critical to procedural fairness'' for no real analysis of the role of the jury in making procedures fair is even attempted. Instead, the word turns out to mean ''old,'' ''much praised,'' and ''found in the

Bill of Rights.'' The definition of ''fundamental'' thus turns out to be circular. . . .

The argument that jury trial is not a requisite of due process is quite simple. The central proposition of *Palko*, . . . a proposition to which I would adhere, is that ''due process of law'' requires only that criminal trials be fundamentally fair. As stated above, apart from the theory that it was historically intended as a mere shorthand for the Bill of Rights, I do not see what else ''due process of law'' can intelligibly be thought to mean. If due process of law requires only fundamental fairness, then the inquiry in each case must be whether a state trial process was a fair one. The Court has held, properly I think, that in an adversary process it is a requisite of fairness, for which there is no adequate substitute, that a criminal defendant be afforded a right to counsel and to cross-examine opposing witnesses. But it simply has not been demonstrated, nor, I think, can it be demonstrated, that trial by jury is the only fair means of resolving issues of fact. . . .

In sum, there is a wide range of views on the desirability of trial by jury, and on the ways to make it most effective when it is used; there is also considerable variation from State to State in local conditions such as the size of the criminal caseload, the ease or difficulty of summoning jurors, and other trial conditions bearing on fairness. We have before us, therefore, an almost perfect example of a situation in which the celebrated dictum of Mr. Justice Brandeis should be invoked. It is, he said, ''one of the happy incidents of the federal system that a single courageous State may, if its citizens choose, serve as a laboratory. . . .'' *New State Ice Co.* v. *Liebmann,* 285 U.S. 262, 311. . . .

II. The Exclusionary Rule

Mapp v. *Ohio*
367 U.S. 643, 81 S.Ct. 1684, 6 L.Ed. 2d 1081 (1961)

Cleveland police officers, acting on information that a bombing-case suspect and betting equipment might be found in Mrs. Mapp's house, forced their way in after being refused admission and, without a search warrant, subjected the house and its contents to thorough search. In a basement trunk materials were found which provided the basis for her conviction of possessing obscene materials. The Ohio Supreme Court upheld the conviction on the grounds that state law did not require the exclusion of illegally obtained evidence and that *Wolf* v. *Colorado* did not prevent Ohio from adopting such a rule.

MR. JUSTICE CLARK delivered the opinion of the Court. . . .

In 1949, . . . this Court, in *Wolf* v. *Colorado,* 338 U.S. 25, . . . discussed the effect of the Fourth Amendment upon the States through the operation of the Due Process Clause of the Fourteenth Amendment. It said,

[W]e have no hesitation in saying that were a State affirmatively to sanction such police incursion into privacy it would run counter to the guaranty of the Fourteenth Amendment.

. . . The Court's reasons for not considering essential to the right to privacy, as a curb im-

*4th amend. does apply
but does exc. rule apply? in Wolf. Court
said other means were
ok to enforce 4th*

posed upon the States by the Due Process Clause, that which decades before had been posited as part and parcel of the Fourth Amendment's limitation upon federal encroachment of individual privacy, were bottomed on factual considerations.

While they are not basically relevant to a decision that the exclusionary rule is an essential ingredient of the Fourth Amendment as the right it embodies is vouchsafed against the States by the Due Process Clause, we will consider the current validity of the factual grounds upon which *Wolf* was based.

The Court in *Wolf* first stated that "[t]he contrariety of views of the States" on the adoption of the exclusionary rule of *Weeks* was "particularly impressive" and, in this connection, that it could not "brush aside the experience of States which deem the incidence of such conduct by the police too slight to call for a deterrent remedy . . . by overriding the [States'] relevant rules of evidence." . . . While in 1949, prior to the Wolf case, almost two-thirds of the States were opposed to the use of the exclusionary rule, now, despite the Wolf case, more than half of those since passing upon it, by their own legislative or judicial decision, have wholly or partly adopted or adhered to the Weeks rule. . . . Significantly, among those now following the rule is California which, according to its highest court, was "compelled to reach that conclusion because other remedies have completely failed to secure compliance with the constitutional provisions. . . ." . . . In connection with this California case, we note that the second basis elaborated in *Wolf* in support of its failure to enforce the exclusionary doctrine against the States was that "other means of protection" have been afforded "the right to privacy." 338 U.S. at 30. The experience of California that such other remedies have been worthless and futile is buttressed by the experience of other States. The obvious futility of relegating the Fourth Amendment to the protection of other remedies has, moreover, been recognized by this Court since *Wolf*. . . .

Likewise, time has set its face against what

Wolf called the "weighty testimony" of *People v. Defore*, 242 N.Y. 13, 150 N.E. 585 (1926). There Justice (then Judge) Cardozo, rejecting adoption of the Weeks exclusionary rule in New York, had said that "[t]he Federal rule as it stands is either too strict or too lax." However, the force of that reasoning has been largely vitiated by later decisions of this Court. . . .

It, therefore, plainly appears that the factual considerations supporting the failure of the Wolf Court to include the Weeks exclusionary rule when it recognized the enforceability of the right to privacy against the States in 1949, while not basically relevant to the constitutional consideration, could not, in any analysis, now be deemed controlling. . . .

. . . Today we once again examine *Wolf*'s constitutional documentation of the right to privacy free from unreasonable state intrusion, and, after its dozen years on our books, are led by it to close the only courtroom door remaining open to evidence secured by official lawlessness in flagrant abuse of that basic right, reserved to all persons as a specific guarantee against that very same unlawful conduct. We hold that all evidence obtained by searches and seizures in violation of the Constitution is, by that same authority, inadmissible in a state court.

Since the Fourth Amendment's right of privacy has been declared enforceable against the States through the Due Process Clause of the Fourteenth, it is enforceable against them by the same sanction of exclusion as is used against the Federal Government. Were it otherwise, then just as without the *Weeks* rule the assurance against unreasonable federal searches and seizures would be "a form of words," valueless and undeserving of mention in a perpetual charter of inestimable human liberties, so too, without that rule the freedom from state invasions of privacy would be so ephemeral and so neatly severed from its conceptual nexus with the freedom from all brutish means of coercing evidence as not to merit this Court's high regard as a freedom "implicit in the concept of ordered liberty." At the time that the Court held in *Wolf* that the Amendment was ap-

*Facts have
proved that exc.
rule is necessary*

[Handwritten margin notes: "recognized right of privacy demands that illegaly obtained evidence should be excluded" and "w/o exe rule; law & constitut protection means nothing"]

plicable to the States through the Due Process Clause, the cases of this Court, as we have seen, had steadfastly held that as to federal officers the Fourth Amendment included the exclusion of the evidence seized in violation of its provisions. Even *Wolf* "stoutly adhered" to that proposition. The right to privacy, when conceded operatively enforceable against the States, was not susceptible of destruction by avulsion of the sanction upon which its protection and enjoyment had always been deemed dependent under the Boyd, Weeks and Silverthorne cases. Therefore, in extending the substantive protections of due process to all constitutionally unreasonable searches—state or federal—it was logically and constitutionally necessary that the exclusion doctrine—an essential part of the right to privacy—be also insisted upon as an essential ingredient of the right newly recognized by the Wolf case. In short, the admission of the new constitutional right by *Wolf* could not consistently tolerate denial of its most important constitutional privilege, namely, the exclusion of the evidence which an accused had been forced to give by reason of the unlawful seizure. To hold otherwise is to grant the right but in reality to withhold its privilege and enjoyment. . . .

Indeed, we are aware of no restraint, similar to that rejected today, conditioning the enforcement of any other basic constitutional right. The right to privacy, no less important than any other right carefully and particularly reserved to the people, would stand in marked contrast to all other rights declared as "basic to a free society." *Wolf* v. *Colorado* . . . (338 U.S. at 27). This Court has not hesitated to enforce as strictly against the State as it does against the Federal Government the rights of free speech and of a free press, the rights to notice and to a fair, public trial, including, as it does, the right not to be convicted by use of a coerced confession, however logically relevant it be, and without regard to its reliability. . . . And nothing could be more certain than that when a coerced confession is involved, "the relevant rules of evidence" are overridden without regard to

"the incidence of such conduct by the police," slight or frequent. Why should not the same rule apply to what is tantamount to coerced testimony by way of unconstitutional seizure of goods, papers, effects, documents, etc.? . . .

The ignoble shortcut to conviction left open to the State tends to destroy the entire system of constitutional restraints on which the liberties of the people rest. Having once recognized that the right to privacy embodied in the Fourth Amendment is enforceable against the States and that the right to be secure against rude invasions of privacy by state officers is, therefore, constitutional in origin, we can no longer permit that right to remain an empty promise. Because it is enforceable in the same manner and to like effect as other basic rights secured by the Due Process Clause, we can no longer permit it to be revocable at the whim of any police officer who, in the name of law enforcement itself, chooses to suspend its enjoyment. Our decision, founded on reason and truth, gives to the individual no more than that which the Constitution guarantees him, to the police officer no less than that to which honest law enforcement is entitled, and, to the courts, that judicial integrity so necessary in the true administration of justice. . . .

Reversed and remanded.

MR. JUSTICE BLACK, concurring. . . .

I am still not persuaded that the Fourth Amendment, standing alone, would be enough to bar the introduction into evidence against an accused of papers and effects seized from him in violation of its commands. For the Fourth Amendment does not itself contain any provisions expressly precluding the use of such evidence, and I am extremely doubtful that such a provision could properly be inferred from nothing more than the basic command against unreasonable searches and seizures. Reflection on the problem, however, in the light of cases coming before the Court since Wolf, has led me to conclude that when the Fourth Amendment's ban against unreasonable searches and seizures is considered together with the Fifth Amendment's ban against compelled self-incrimination, a constitutional basis emerges which not only justifies but actually requires the exclusionary rule. . . .

[MR. JUSTICE DOUGLAS wrote a separate concurring opinion.]

MR. JUSTICE HARLAN, whom MR. JUSTICE FRANKFURTER and MR. JUSTICE WHITTAKER join, dissenting.

In overruling the Wolf case the Court, in my opinion, has forgotten the sense of judicial restraint which, with the due regard for stare decisis, is one element that should enter into deciding whether a past decision of this Court should be overruled. Apart from that I also believe that the *Wolf* rule represents sounder Constitutional doctrine than the new rule which now replaces it. . . .

At the heart of the majority's opinion in this case is the following syllogism: (1) the rule excluding in federal criminal trials evidence which is the product of an illegal search and seizure is a "part and parcel" of the Fourth Amendment; (2) Wolf held that the "privacy" assured against federal action by the Fourth Amendment is also protected against state action by the Fourteenth Amendment; and (3) it is therefore "logically and constitutionally necessary" that the Weeks exclusionary rule should also be enforced against the States.

This reasoning ultimately rests on the unsound premise that because *Wolf* carried into the States, as part of "the concept of ordered liberty" embodied in the Fourteenth Amendment . . . , it must follow that whatever configurations of the Fourth Amendment have been developed in the particularizing federal precedents are likewise to be deemed a part of "ordered liberty," and as such are enforceable against the States. For me, this does not follow at all.

It cannot be too much emphasized that what was recognized in *Wolf* was not that the Fourth Amendment *as such* is enforceable against the States as a facet of due process, a view of the Fourteenth Amendment which, as *Wolf* itself pointed out . . . , has long since been discredited, but the principle of privacy "which is at the core of the Fourth Amendment."

. . . It would not be proper to expect or impose any precise equivalence, either as regards the scope of the right or the means of its implementation, between the requirements of the Fourth and Fourteenth Amendments. For the Fourth, unlike what was said in *Wolf* of the Fourteenth, does not state a general principle only; it is a particular command, having its setting in a preexisting legal context on which both interpreting decisions and enabling statutes must at least build. . . .

The preservation of a proper balance between state and federal responsibility in the administration of criminal justice demands patience on the part of those who might like to see things move faster among the States in this respect. Problems of criminal law enforcement vary widely from State to State. One State, in considering the totality of its legal picture, may conclude that the need for embracing the *Weeks* rule is pressing because other remedies are unavailable or inadequate to secure compliance with the substantive constitutional principle involved. Another, though equally solicitous of constitutional rights, may choose to pursue one purpose at a time, allowing all evidence relevant to guilt to be brought into a criminal trial, and dealing with constitutional infractions by other means. Still another may consider the exclusionary rule too rough and ready a remedy, in that it reaches only unconstitutional intrusions which eventuate in criminal prosecution of the victims. Further, a State after experimenting with the Weeks rule for a time may, because of unsatisfactory experience with it, decide to revert to a nonexclusionary rule. And so on. From the standpoint of constitutional permissibility in pointing a State in one direction or another, I do not see at all why "time has set its face against" the considerations which led Mr. Justice Cardozo, then chief judge of the New York Court of Appeals, to reject for New York in *People* v. *Defore,* . . . the Weeks exclusionary rule. For us the question remains, as it has always been, one of state power, not one of passing judgment on the wisdom of one state course or another. In my view this Court should continue to forbear from fettering the States with an adamant rule which may embarrass them in coping with their own peculiar problems in criminal law enforcement....

Stone v. Powell
428 U.S. 465, 96 S. Ct. 3037, 49 L.Ed. 2d 1067 (1976)

Two state prisoners, both convicted of homicide, sought federal habeas corpus relief in separate state court proceedings in California and Nebraska on the ground that in the state trials evidence obtained by an unconstitutional search and seizure was introduced. The petition for habeas corpus was denied by a United States district court in one case and granted by another district court in the second case. The Court of Appeals for the Ninth Circuit reversed in the first instance, and the Court of Appeals for the Eighth Circuit affirmed in the second.

On a writ of certiorari, the Supreme Court reversed. An opinion by Justice Powell expressed the views of six Justices. Chief Justice Burger concurred; Justices Brennan, Marshall, and White dissented.

MR. JUSTICE POWELL delivered the opinion of the Court.

The question presented is whether a federal court should consider, in ruling on a petition for habeas corpus relief filed by a state prisoner, a claim that evidence obtained by an unconstitutional search or seizure was introduced at his trial, when he has previously been afforded an opportunity for full and fair litigation of his claim in the state courts. The issue is of considerable importance to the administration of criminal justice.

The Mapp majority justified the application of the rule [requiring the exclusion of unconstitutionally seized evidence in state criminal trials] on several grounds, but relied principally upon the belief that exclusion would deter future unlawful police conduct....

The primary justification for the exclusionary rule then is the deterrence of police conduct that violates Fourth Amendment rights. Post-Mapp decisions have established that the rule is not a personal constitutional right. It is not calculated to redress the injury to the privacy of the victim of the search or seizure, for any "[r]eparation

comes too late." ... Instead, "the rule is a judicially created remedy designed to safeguard Fourth Amendment rights generally through its deterrent effect." ...

... But despite the broad deterrent purpose of the exclusionary rule, it has never been interpreted to proscribe the introduction of illegally seized evidence in all proceedings or against all persons. As in the case of any remedial device, "the application of the rule has been restricted to those areas where its remedial objectives are thought most efficaciously served." ...

Our refusal to extend the exclusionary rule to grand jury proceedings was based on a balancing of the potential injury to the historic role and function of the grand jury by such extension against the potential contribution to the effectuation of the Fourth Amendment through deterrence of police misconduct.

Any incremental deterrent effect which might be achieved by extending the rule to grand jury proceedings is uncertain at best. Whatever deterrence of police misconduct may result from the exclusion of illegally seized evidence from criminal trials, it is unrealistic to assume that the application of the rule to grand jury proceedings would significantly further that goal. Such an extension would deter only police investigation consciously directed toward the discovery of evidence solely for use in a grand jury investigation. . . .

We therefore decline to embrace a view that would achieve a speculative and undoubtedly minimal advance in the deterrence of police misconduct at the expense of substantially impeding the role of the grand jury. [*U.S.* v. *Calandra*, 414 U.S. 338: 1974.]

We turn now to the specific question presented by these cases. Respondents allege violations of Fourth Amendment rights guaranteed them through the Fourteenth Amendment. The question is whether state prisoners—who have been afforded the opportunity for full and fair consideration of their reliance upon the exclusionary rule with respect to seized evidence by the state courts at trial and on direct review—may invoke their claim again on federal habeas corpus review. The answer is to be found by weighing the utility of the exclusionary rule against the costs of extending it to collateral review of Fourth Amendment claims.

The costs of applying the exclusionary rule even at trial and on direct review are well known. The focus of the trial, and the attention of the participants therein, is diverted from the ultimate question of guilt or innocence that should be the central concern in a criminal proceeding. Moreover, the physical evidence sought to be excluded is typically reliable and often the most probative information bearing on the guilt or innocence of the defendant. As Mr. Justice Black emphasized in his dissent in *Kaufman,*

A claim of illegal search and seizure under the Fourth Amendment is crucially different from many other constitutional rights; ordinarily the evidence seized can in no way have been rendered untrustworthy by the means of its seizure and indeed often this evidence alone establishes beyond virtually any shadow of a doubt that the defendant is guilty. (394 U.S., at 237) . . .

Application of the rule thus deflects the truthfinding process and often frees the guilty. The disparity in particular cases between the error committed by the police officer and the windfall afforded a guilty defendant by application of the rule is contrary to the idea of proportionality that is essential to the concept of justice. Thus, although the rule is thought to deter unlawful police activity in part through the nurturing of respect for Fourth Amendment values, if applied indiscriminately it may well have the opposite effect of generating disrespect for the law and administration of justice. These long-recognized costs of the rule persist when a criminal conviction is sought to be overturned on collateral review on the ground that a search-and-seizure claim was erroneously rejected by two or more tiers of state courts.

Evidence obtained by police officers in violation of the Fourth Amendment is excluded at trial in the hope that the frequency of future violations will decrease. Despite the absence of supportive empirical evidence, we have assumed that the immediate effect of exclusion will be to discourage law enforcement officials from violating the Fourth Amendment by removing the incentive to disregard it. More importantly, over the long term, this demonstration that our society attaches serious consequences to violation of constitutional rights is thought to encourage those who formulate law enforcement policies, and the officers who implement them, to incorporate Fourth Amendment ideals into their value system.

We adhere to the view that these considerations support the implementation of the exclusionary rule at trial and its enforcement on direct appeal of state court convictions. But the additional contribution, if any, of the consideration of search-and-seizure claims of state prisoners on collateral review is small in relation to the costs. . . . The view that the deterrence of Fourth Amendment violations would be furthered rests on the dubious assumption that law enforcement authorities would fear that federal habeas corpus review might reveal flaws in a search or seizure that went undetected at trial and on appeal. Even if one rationally could assume that some additional incremental deterrent effect would be present in isolated cases, the resulting advance of the legitimate goal of furthering Fourth Amendment rights would be outweighed by the acknowledged costs to other values vital to a rational system of criminal justice.

In sum, we conclude that where the State has provided an opportunity for full and fair litigation of a Fourth Amendment claim, a state prisoner may not be granted federal habeas corpus relief on the ground that evidence obtained in an unconstitutional search or seizure was introduced at his trial. In this context the contribution of the exclusionary rule, if any, to the effectuation of the Fourth Amendment is minimal and the substantial societal costs of application of the rule persist with special force.

MR. CHIEF JUSTICE BURGER, concurring. . . .

Despite its avowed deterrent objective, proof is lacking that the exclusionary rule, a purely judge-created device based on "hard cases," serves the purpose of deterrence. Notwithstanding Herculean efforts, no empirical study has been able to demonstrate that the rule does in fact have any deterrent effect. In the face of dwindling support for the rule some would go so far as to extend it to civil cases. *United States* v. *Janis*, . . .

To vindicate the continued existence of this judge-made rule, it is incumbent upon those who seek its retention—and surely its *extension*—to demonstrate that it serves its declared deterrent purpose and to show that the results outweigh the rule's heavy costs to rational enforcement of the criminal law. . . . The burden rightly rests upon those who ask society to ignore trustworthy evidence of guilt, at the expense of setting obviously guilty criminals free to ply their trade.

In my view, it is an abdication of judicial responsibility to exact such exorbitant costs from society purely on the basis of speculative and unsubstantiated assumptions. . . .

It can no longer be assumed that other branches of government will act while judges cling to this Draconian, discredited device in its present absolutist form. Legislatures are un-

likely to create statutory alternatives, or impose direct sanctions on errant police officers or on the public treasury by way of tort actions, so long as persons who commit serious crimes continue to reap the enormous and undeserved benefits of the exclusionary rule. And of course, by definition the direct beneficiaries of this rule can be none but persons guilty of crimes. With this extraordinary "remedy" for Fourth Amendment violations, however slight, inadvertent or technical, legislatures might assume that nothing more should be done, even though a grave defect of the exclusionary rule is that it offers no relief whatever to victims of overzealous police work who never appear in court. . . . And even if legislatures were inclined to experiment with alternative remedies, they have no assurance that the judicially created rule will be abolished or even modified in response to such legislative innovations. The unhappy result, as I see it, is that alternatives will inevitably be stymied by rigid adherence on our part to the exclusionary rule. I venture to predict that overruling this judicially contrived doctrine—or limiting its scope to egregious, bad-faith conduct—would inspire a surge of activity toward providing some kind of statutory remedy for persons injured by police mistakes or misconduct.

The Court's opinion today eloquently reflects something of the dismal social costs occasioned by the rule. . . .

From its genesis in the desire to protect private papers, the exclusionary rule has now been carried to the point of potentially excluding from evidence the traditional corpus delicti in a murder or kidnapping case. . . .

Expansion of the reach of the exclusionary rule has brought Cardozo's grim prophecy in *People* v. *Defore*, 242 N.Y. 12, 150 N.E. 585, 588 (1926), nearer to fulfillment.

A room is searched against the law, and the body of a murdered man is found. If the place of discovery may not be proved, the other circumstances may be insufficient to connect the defendant with the crime. The privacy of the home has been infringed, and the murderer goes free. . . . We may not subject society to these dangers until the Legislature has spoken with a clearer voice. . . .

MR. JUSTICE BRENNAN, with whom MR. JUSTICE MARSHALL concurs, dissenting. . . .

The Court today holds ''that where the State has provided an opportunity for full and fair litigation of a Fourth Amendment claim, a state prisoner may not be granted federal habeas corpus relief on the ground that evidence obtained in an unconstitutional search or seizure was introduced at his trial.'' . . . To be sure, my Brethren are hostile to the continued vitality of the exclusionary rule as part and parcel of the Fourth Amendment's prohibition of unreasonable searches and seizures, as today's decision in *United States* v. *Janis,* . . . confirms. But these cases, despite the veil of Fourth Amendment terminology employed by the Court, plainly do not involve any question of the right of a defendant to have evidence excluded from use against him in his criminal trial when that evidence was seized in contravention of rights ostensibly secured by the Fourth and Fourteenth Amendments. Rather, they involve the question of the availability of a *federal forum* for vindicating those federally guaranteed rights. Today's holding portends substantial evisceration of federal habeas corpus jurisdiction, and I dissent.

MR. JUSTICE WHITE, dissenting.

For many of the reasons stated by Mr. Justice Brennan, I cannot agree that the writ of habeas corpus should be any less available to those convicted of state crimes where they allege Fourth Amendment violations than where other constitutional issues are presented to the federal court. . . .

Under the present habeas corpus statute, neither Rice's nor Powell's applications for habeas corpus should be dismissed on the grounds now stated by the Court. I would affirm the judgments of the Courts of Appeals as being acceptable applications of the exclusionary rule applicable in state criminal trials by virtue of *Mapp* v. *Ohio,* 367 U.S. 643. . . .

I feel constrained to say, however, that I would join four or more other Justices in substantially limiting the reach of the exclusionary rule as presently administered under the Fourth Amendment in federal and state criminal trials.

Whether I would have joined the Court's opinion in *Mapp* v. *Ohio* . . . had I then been a member of the Court, I do not know. But as time went on after coming to this bench, I became convinced that both *Weeks* v. *United States,* 232 U.S. 383, . . . (1914), and *Mapp* v. *Ohio* had overshot their mark insofar as they aimed to deter lawless action by law enforcement personnel and that in many of its applications the exclusionary rule was not advancing that aim in the slightest and that in this respect it was a senseless obstacle to arriving at the truth in many criminal trials.

The rule has been much criticized and suggestions have been made that it should be wholly abolished, but I would overrule neither *Weeks* v. *United States* nor *Mapp* v. *Ohio.* I am nevertheless of the view that the rule should be substantially modified so as to prevent its application in those many circumstances where the evidence at issue was seized by an officer acting in the good-faith belief that his conduct comported with existing law and having reasonable grounds for this belief. These are recurring situations; and recurringly evidence is excluded without any realistic expectation that its exclusion will contribute in the slightest to the purposes of the rule, even though the trial will be seriously affected or the indictment dismissed. . . .

III. Electronic Surveillance and Unreasonable Searches and Seizures

Olmstead v. United States
277 U.S. 438, 48 S.Ct. 564, 72 L.Ed. 944 (1928)

Olmstead and others were charged and convicted of conspiring to violate the national Prohibition Act. Evidence proving the conspiracy had been obtained by four federal agents who tapped the telephone lines of several of the defendants, without, however, committing any trespass on their property. A statute of the state of Washington made it a misdemeanor to "intercept, read or in any way interrupt or delay the sending of a message over any telegraph or telephone line...." Olmstead and the others brought certiorari from adverse judgments in the Circuit Court of Appeals.

MR. CHIEF JUSTICE TAFT delivered the opinion of the court.

These cases are here by certiorari from the Circuit Court of Appeals for the Ninth Circuit. ... They were granted with the distinct limitation that the hearing should be confined to the single question whether the use of evidence of private telephone conversations between the defendants and others, intercepted by means of wire tapping, amounted to a violation of the Fourth and Fifth Amendments. ...

The Fourth Amendment provides: "The right of the people to be secure in their persons, houses, papers, and effects against unreasonable searches and seizures shall not be violated, and no warrants shall issue but upon probable cause, supported by oath or affirmation and particularly describing the place to be searched and the persons or things to be seized." And the Fifth: "No person ... shall be compelled, in any criminal case, to be a witness against himself." ...

There is no room in the present case for applying the Fifth Amendment unless the Fourth Amendment was first violated. There was no evidence of compulsion to induce the defendants to talk over their many telephones. They were continually and voluntarily transacting business without knowledge of the interception. Our consideration must be confined to the Fourth Amendment. ...

The well-known historical purpose of the Fourth Amendment, directed against general warrants and writs of assistance, was to prevent the use of governmental force to search a man's house, his person, his papers and his effects, and to prevent their seizure against his will. ...

A representative of the Intelligence Department of the army, having by stealth obtained admission to the defendant's office, seized and carried away certain private papers valuable for evidential purposes. This was held an unreasonable search and seizure within the Fourth Amendment. A stealthy entrance in such circumstances became the equivalent to an entry by force. There was actual entrance into the private quarters of defendant and the taking away of something tangible. Here we have testimony only of voluntary conversations secretly overheard.

The amendment itself shows that the search is to be of material things—the person, the house, his papers, or his effects. The description of the warrant necessary to make the proceeding lawful is that it must specify the place to be searched and the person or *things* to be seized. ... The language of the amendment cannot be extended and expanded to include telephone wires, reaching to the whole world from the defendant's house or office. The intervening wires are not part of his house or office, any more than are the highways along which they are stretched. ...

Congress may, of course, protect the secrecy

[handwritten margin note: listeners were never inside the house. everything done was done outside the realm of the home. it does not fall under 4th amend protection]

of telephone messages by making them, when intercepted, inadmissible in evidence in federal criminal trials, by direct legislation, and thus depart from the common law of evidence. But the courts may not adopt such a policy by attributing an enlarged and unusual meaning to the Fourth Amendment. The reasonable view is that one who installs in his house a telephone instrument with connecting wires intends to project his voice to those quite outside, and that the wires beyond his house, and messages while passing over them, are not within the protection of the Fourth Amendment. Here those who intercepted the projected voices were not in the house of either party to the conversation.

Neither the cases we have cited nor any of the many federal decisions brought to our attention hold the Fourth Amendment to have been violated as against a defendant, unless there has been an official search and seizure of his person or such a seizure of his papers or his tangible material effects or an actual physical invasion of his house ''or curtilage'' for the purpose of making a seizure.

We think, therefore, that the wire tapping here disclosed did not amount to a search or seizure within the meaning of the Fourth Amendment.

What has been said disposes of the only question that comes within terms of our order granting certiorari in these cases. But some of our number, departing from that order, have concluded that there is merit in the twofold objection, overruled in both courts below, that evidence obtained through intercepting of telephone messages by government agents was inadmissible, because the mode of obtaining it was unethical and a misdemeanor under the law of Washington. To avoid any misapprehension of our views of the objection we shall deal with it in both of its phases. . . .

Nor can we, without the sanction of congressional enactment, subscribe to the suggestion that the courts have a discretion to exclude evidence, the admission of which is not unconstitutional, because unethically secured. This would be at variance with the common-law doctrine generally supported by authority.

There is no case that sustains, nor any recognized textbook that gives color to, such a view. Our general experience shows that much evidence has always been receivable, although not obtained by conformity to the highest ethics. The history of criminal trials shows numerous cases of prosecutions of oathbound conspiracies for murder, robbery, and other crimes, where officers of the law have disguised themselves and joined the organizations, taken the oaths, and given themselves every appearance of active members engaged in the promotion of crime for the purpose of securing evidence. Evidence secured by such means has always been received.

A standard which would forbid the reception of evidence, if obtained by other than nice ethical conduct by government officials, would make society suffer and give criminals greater immunity than has been known heretofore. In the absence of controlling legislation by Congress, those who realize the difficulties in bringing offenders to justice may well deem it wise that the exclusion of evidence should be confined to cases where rights under the Constitution would be violated by admitting it. . . .

Affirmed.

MR. JUSTICE HOLMES: [dissenting]

My Brother Brandeis has given this case so exhaustive an examination that I desire to add but a few words. . . . It is desirable that criminals should be detected, and to that end that all available evidence should be used. It also is desirable that the Government should not itself foster and pay for other crimes, when they are the means by which the evidence is to be obtained. If it pays its officers for having got evidence by crime I do not see why it may not as well pay them for getting it in the same way, and I can attach no importance to protestations of disapproval if it knowingly accepts and pays and announces that in future it will pay for the fruits. We have to choose, and for my part I think it a less evil that some criminals should escape than that the Government should play an ignoble part. . . .

MR. JUSTICE BRANDEIS, dissenting. . . .

''We must never forget,'' said Mr. Chief

Justice Marshall in *McCulloch* v. *Maryland,* "that it is a constitution we are expounding." Since then, this Court has repeatedly sustained the exercise of power by Congress, under various clauses of that instrument, over objects of which the Fathers could not have dreamed. . . . We have likewise held that general limitations on the powers of Government, like those embodied in the due process clauses of the Fifth and Fourteenth Amendments, do not forbid the United States or the States from meeting modern conditions by regulations which "a century ago, or even half a century ago, probably would have been rejected as arbitrary and oppressive". . . . Clauses guaranteeing to the individual protection against specific abuses of power, must have a similar capacity of adaptation to a changing world. . . .

When the Fourth and Fifth Amendments were adopted, "the form that evil had theretofore taken," had been necessarily simple. Force and violence were then the only means known to man by which a Government could directly effect self-incrimination. It could compel the individual to testify—a compulsion effected, if need be, by torture. It could secure possession of his papers and other articles incident to his private life—a seizure effected, if need be, by breaking and entry. Protection against such invasion of "the sanctities of a man's home and the privacies of life" was provided in the Fourth and Fifth Amendments, by specific language. *Boyd* v. *United States,* 116 U.S. 616,630. But "time works changes, brings into existence new conditions and purposes." Subtler and more far-reaching means of invading privacy have become available to the government. Discovery and invention have made it possible for the government, by means far more effective than stretching upon the rack, to obtain disclosure in court of what is whispered in the closet.

Moreover, "in the application of a constitution, our contemplation cannot be only of what has been, but of what may be." The progress of science in furnishing the government with means of espionage is not likely to stop with wire-tapping. Ways may some day be developed by which the government, without removing papers from secret drawers, can reproduce them in court, and by which it will be enabled to expose to a jury the most intimate occurrences of the home. Advances in the psychic and related sciences may bring means of exploring unexpressed beliefs, thoughts and emotions.

. . . Can it be that the Constitution affords no protection against such invasions of individual security?

A sufficient answer is found in *Boyd* v. *United States,* . . . a case that will be remembered as long as civil liberty lives in the United States. This court there reviewed the history that lay behind the Fourth and Fifth Amendments. We said with reference to Lord Camden's judgment in *Entick* v. *Carrington,* 19 Howell's State Trials, 1030: "The principles laid down in this opinion affect the very essence of constitutional liberty and security. They reach farther than the concrete form of the case there before the court, with its adventitious circumstances; they apply to all invasions on the part of the Government and its employés of the sanctities of a man's home and the privacies of life. It is not the breaking of his doors, and the rummaging of his drawers, that constitutes the essence of the offence: but it is the invasion of his indefeasible right of personal security, personal liberty and private property, where that right has never been forfeited by his conviction of some public offence—it is the invasion of this sacred right which underlies and constitutes the essence of Lord Camden's judgment. Breaking into a house and opening boxes and drawers are circumstances of aggravation; but any forcible and compulsory extortion of a man's own testimony or of his private papers to be used as evidence of a crime or to forfeit his goods, is within the condemnation of that judgment. In this regard the Fourth and Fifth Amendments run almost into each other." . . .

Decisions of this Court applying the principle of the Boyd case have settled these things. Unjustified search and seizure violates the Fourth Amendment, whatever the character of the paper; whether the paper when taken by the federal officers was in the home, in an office or elsewhere; whether the taking was effected by force, by fraud, or in the orderly process of a court's procedure. From these decisions, it follows necessarily that the Amendment was violated by the officer's reading the paper without a physical seizure, without his even touching it; and that use, in any criminal proceeding, of the contents of the paper so examined—as where they are testified to by a federal officer who thus saw the document or where, through knowledge so obtained, a copy has been procured elsewhere—any such use constitutes a violation of the Fifth Amendment.

The protection guaranteed by the Amendments is much broader in scope. The makers of our Constitution undertook to secure conditions favorable to the pursuit of happiness. They recognized the significance of man's spiritual nature, of his feelings and of his intellect. They knew that only a part of the pain, pleasure and satisfactions of life are to be found in material things. They sought to protect Americans in their beliefs, their thoughts, their emotions and their sensations. They conferred, as against the Government, the right to be let alone—the most comprehensive of rights and the right most valued by civilized men. To protect that right, every unjustifiable intrusion by the Government upon the privacy of the individual, whatever the means employed, must be deemed a violation of the Fourth Amendment. And the use, as evidence in a criminal proceeding, of facts ascertained by such intrusion must be deemed a violation of the Fifth.

Applying to the Fourth and Fifth Amendments the established rule of construction, the defendant's objections to the evidence obtained by a wire-tapping must, in my opinion, be sustained. It is, of course, immaterial where the physical connection with the telephone wires leading into the defendants' premises was made. And it is also immaterial that the intrusion was in aid of law enforcement. Experience should teach us to be most on our guard to protect liberty when the government's purposes are beneficent. Men born to freedom are naturally alert to repel invasion of their liberty by evilminded rulers. The greatest dangers to liberty lurk in insidious encroachment by men of zeal, well-meaning, but without understanding. . . .

[JUSTICE BRANDEIS, in the remainder of his opinion, declared that the violation of the state statute by federal officers was an additional ground for holding the evidence to be inadmissible.]

[MR. JUSTICE BUTLER wrote a separate dissenting opinion. MR. JUSTICE STONE, dissenting, concurred in the opinions of HOLMES and BRANDEIS, and with that of BUTLER in part.]

DISSENT: court must repel any encroachment on liberty. Whether or not phone wires are placed inside or outside house is immaterial.

Katz v. *United States*
389 U.S. 347, 88 S.Ct. 507, 19 L.Ed. 2d 576 (1967)

The petitioner, Katz, was convicted of transmitting wagering information by telephone from Los Angeles to Miami and Boston in violation of a federal statute. At the trial, the Government was permitted to introduce evidence gathered from attaching an electronic listening device to the outside of a public telephone booth from which he placed his calls. The Supreme Court granted certiorari to determine if the recordings had been obtained in violation of the Fourth Amendment's "search and seizure" provisions.

MR. JUSTICE STEWART delivered the opinion of the Court. . . .

Because of the misleading way the issues have been formulated, the parties have attached great significance to the characterization of the telephone booth from which the petitioner placed his calls. The petitioner has strenuously argued that the booth was a "constitutionally protected area." The Government has maintained with equal vigor that it was not. But this effort to decide whether or not a given "area," viewed in the abstract, is "constitutionally protected" deflects attention from the problem presented by this case. For the Fourth Amendment protects people, not places. What a person knowingly exposes to the public, even in his own home or office, is not a subject of Fourth Amendment protection. . . . But what he seeks to preserve as private, even in an area accessible to the public, may be constitutionally protected. . . .

The Government stresses the fact that the telephone booth from which the petitioner made his calls was constructed partly of glass, so that he was as visible after he entered it as he would have been if he had remained outside. But what he sought to exclude when he entered the booth was not the intruding eye—it was the uninvited ear. He did not shed his right to do so simply because he made his calls from a place where he might be seen. No less than an individual in a business office, in a friend's apartment, or in a taxicab, a person in a telephone booth may rely upon the protection of the Fourth Amendment. One who occupies it, shuts the door behind him, and pays the toll that permits him to place a call, is surely entitled to assume that the words he utters into the mouthpiece will not be broadcast to the world. To read the Constitution more narrowly is to ignore the vital role that the public telephone has come to play in private communication.

The Government contends, however, that the activities of its agents in this case should not be tested by Fourth Amendment requirements, for the surveillance technique they employed involved no physical penetration of the telephone booth from which the petitioner placed his calls. It is true that the absence of such penetration was at one time thought to foreclose further Fourth Amendment inquiry, *Olmstead* v. *United States.* . . . That Amendment was thought to limit only searches and seizures of tangible property. But "[t]he premise that property interests control the right of the Government to search and seize has been discredited." Thus, although a closely divided Court supposed in *Olmstead* that surveillance without any trespass and without the seizure of any material object fell outside the ambit of the Constitution, we have since departed from the narrow view on which that decision rested. Indeed, we have expressly held that the Fourth Amendment governs not only the seizure of tangible items, but extends as well to the recording of oral statements, overheard without any "technical trespass under . . . local property law." *Silverman* v. *United States,* 365 U.S. 505. . . . Once this much is acknowledged, and once it is recognized that the Fourth Amend-

b eadoth of amendment cannot be determined by place since it is the person that matters

ment protects people—and not simply "areas"—against unreasonable searches and seizures, it becomes clear that the reach of that Amendment cannot turn upon the presence or absence of a physical intrusion into any given enclosure.

. . . We conclude that the underpinnings of *Olmstead* and *Goldman* [316 U.S. 129] have been so eroded by our subsequent decisions that the "trespass" doctrine there enunciated can no longer be regarded as controlling. The Government's activities in electronically listening to and recording the petitioner's words violated the privacy upon which he justifiably relied while using the telephone booth and thus constituted a "search and seizure" within the meaning of the Fourth Amendment. The fact that the electronic device employed to achieve that end did not happen to penetrate the wall of the booth can have no constitutional significance.

The question remaining for decision, then, is whether the search and seizure conducted in this case complied with constitutional standards. In that regard, the Government's position is that its agents acted in an entirely defensible manner: They did not begin their electronic surveillance until investigation of the petitioner's activities had established a strong probability that he was using the telephone in question to transmit gambling information to persons in other States, in violation of federal law. Moreover, the surveillance was limited, both in scope and in duration, to the specific purpose of establishing the contents of the petitioner's unlawful telephonic communications. The agents confined their surveillance to the brief periods during which he used the telephone booth, and they took great care to overhear only the conversations of the petitioner himself.

Accepting this account of the Government's actions as accurate, it is clear that this surveillance was so narrowly circumscribed that a duly authorized magistrate, properly notified of the need for such investigation, specifically informed of the basis on which it was to proceed, and clearly apprised of the precise intrusion it would entail, could constitutionally have authorized, with appropriate safeguards, the

very limited search and seizure that the Government asserts in fact took place. . . .

The Government urges that, because its agents relied upon the decisions in *Olmstead* and *Goldman*, and because they did no more here than they might properly have done with prior judicial sanction, we should retroactively validate their conduct. That we cannot do. It is apparent that the agents in this case acted with restraint. Yet the inescapable fact is that this restraint was imposed by the agents themselves, not by a judicial officer. They were not required, before commencing the search, to present their estimate of probable cause for detached scrutiny by a neutral magistrate. They were not compelled, during the conduct of the search itself, to observe precise limits established in advance by a specific court order. Nor were they directed, after the search had been completed, to notify the authorizing magistrate in detail of all that had been seized. In the absence of such safeguards, this Court has never sustained a search upon the sole ground that officers reasonably expected to find evidence of a particular crime and voluntarily confined their activities to the least intrusive means consistent with that end. Searches conducted without warrants have been held unlawful "notwithstanding facts unquestionably showing probable cause," . . . for the Constitution requires "that the deliberate, impartial judgment of a judicial officer . . . be interposed between the citizen and the police. . . ." . . . "Over and again this Court has emphasized that the mandate of the [Fourth] Amendment requires adherence to judicial processes," . . . and that searches conducted outside the judicial process, without prior approval by judge or magistrate, are per se unreasonable under the Fourth Amendment—subject only to a few specifically established and well-delineated exceptions.

It is difficult to imagine how any of those exceptions could ever apply to the sort of search and seizure involved in this case. Even electronic surveillance substantially contemporaneous with an individual's arrest could hardly be deemed an "incident" of that arrest. Nor could the use of electronic surveillance without prior authorization be justified on grounds of "hot pursuit.'' And, of course, the very nature of electronic surveillance precludes its use pursuant to the suspect's consent.

The Government . . . argues that surveillance of a telephone booth should be exempted from the usual requirement of advance authorization by a magistrate upon a showing of probable cause. We cannot agree. Omission of such authorization "bypasses the safeguards provided by an objective predetermination of probable cause, and substitutes instead the far less reliable procedure of an after-the-event justification for the . . . search, too likely to be subtly influenced by the familiar shortcomings of hindsight judgment." . . .

And bypassing a neutral predetermination of the *scope* of a search leaves individuals secure from Fourth Amendment violations "only in the discretion of the police." . . .

These considerations do not vanish when the search in question is transferred from the setting of a home, an office, or a hotel room, to that of a telephone booth. Wherever a man may be, he is entitled to know that he will remain free from unreasonable searches and seizures. The government agents here ignored "the procedure of antecedent justification . . . that is central to the Fourth Amendment," a procedure that we hold to be a constitutional precondition of the kind of electronic surveillance involved in this case. Because the surveillance here failed to meet that condition, and because it led to the petitioner's conviction, the judgment must be reversed.

It is so ordered.

MR. JUSTICE MARSHALL took no part in the consideration or decision of this case.

MR. JUSTICE DOUGLAS, with whom MR. JUSTICE BRENNAN joins, concurring.

While I join the opinion of the Court, I feel compelled to reply to the separate concurring opinion of my Brother White, which I view as a wholly unwarranted green light for the Executive Branch to resort to electronic eavesdropping without a warrant in cases which the Executive Branch itself labels "national security" matters.

Neither the President nor the Attorney General is a magistrate. In matters where they believe national security may be involved they are not detached, disinterested, and neutral as a court or magistrate must be. Under the separation of powers created by the Constitution, the Executive Branch is not supposed to be neutral and disinterested. Rather it should vigorously investigate and prevent breaches of national security and prosecute those who violate the pertinent federal laws. The President and Attorney General are properly interested parties, cast in the role of adversary, in national security cases. They may even be the intended victims of subversive action. Since spies and saboteurs are as entitled to the protection of the Fourth Amendment as suspected gamblers like petitioner, I cannot agree that where spies and saboteurs are involved adequate protection of Fourth Amendment rights is assured when the President and Attorney General assume both the position of adversary-and-prosecutor and disinterested, neutral magistrate.

There is, so far as I understand constitutional history, no distinction under the Fourth Amendment between types of crimes. Article III, § 3, gives "treason" a very narrow definition and puts restrictions on its proof. But the Fourth Amendment draws no lines between various substantive offenses. The arrests in cases of "hot pursuit," the arrests on visible or other evidence of probable cause cut across the board and are not peculiar to any kind of crime.

I would respect the present lines of distinction and not improvise because a particular crime seems particularly heinous. When the Framers took that step, as they did with treason, the worst crime of all, they made their purpose manifest.

MR. JUSTICE HARLAN, concurring. . . .

MR. JUSTICE WHITE, concurring.

In joining the Court's opinion, I note the Court's acknowledgment that there are circumstances in which it is reasonable to search without a warrant. In this connection, . . . the Court points out that today's decision does not reach national security cases. Wiretapping to protect the security of the Nation has been authorized by successive Presidents. The present Administration would apparently save national security cases from restrictions against wiretapping. . . . We should not require the warrant procedure and the magistrate's judgment if the President of the United States or his chief legal officer, the Attorney General, had considered the requirements of national security and authorized electronic surveillance as reasonable.

MR. JUSTICE BLACK, dissenting.

If I could agree with the Court that eavesdropping carried on by electronic means (equivalent to wiretapping) constitutes a "search" or "seizure," I would be happy to join the Court's opinion. For on that premise my brother Stewart sets out methods in accord with the Fourth Amendment to guide States in the enactment and enforcement of laws passed to regulate wiretapping by government. In this respect today's opinion differs sharply from *Berger* v. *New York*, 388 U.S. 41, . . . decided last term, which held void on its face a New York statute authorizing wiretapping on warrants issued by magistrates on showings of probable cause. The Berger case also set up what appeared to be insuperable obstacles to the valid passage of such wiretapping laws by States. The Court's opinion in this case, however, removes the doubts about state power in this field and abates to a large extent the confusion and near paralyzing effect of the Berger holding. Notwithstanding these good efforts of the Court, I am still unable to agree with its interpretation of the Fourth Amendment.

My basic objection is twofold: (1) I do not believe that the words of the Amendment will bear the meaning given them by today's decision, and (2) I do not believe that it is the proper role of this Court to rewrite the Amendment in order "to bring it into harmony with the times" and thus reach a result that many people believe to be desirable.

While I realize that an argument based on the meaning of words lacks the scope, and no doubt the appeal, of broad policy discussions and philosophical discourses on such nebulous subjects as privacy, for me the language of the Amendment is the crucial place to look in construing a written document such as our Constitution. The Fourth Amendment says that

"The right of the people to be secure in their persons, houses, papers, and effects, against unreasonable searches and seizures, shall not be violated, and no Warrants shall issue, but upon probable cause, supported by Oath or affirmation, and particularly describing the place to be searched, and the persons or things to be seized."

The first clause protects "persons, houses, papers, and effects, against unreasonable searches and seizures. . . ." These words connote the idea of tangible things with size, form, and weight, things capable of being searched, seized, or both. The second clause of the Amendment still further establishes its Framers' purpose to limit its protection to tangible things by providing that no warrants shall issue but those "particularly describing the place to be searched and the person or things to be seized." A conversation overheard by eavesdropping whether by plain snooping or wiretapping, is not tangible and, under the normally accepted meanings of the words, can neither be searched nor seized. In addition the language of the second clause indicates that the Amendment refers to something not only tangible so it can be seized but to something already in existence so it can be described. Yet the Court's interpretation would have the Amendment apply to overhearing future conversations which by their very nature are nonexistent until they take place. How can one "describe" a future conversation, and if not, how can a magistrate issue a warrant to eavesdrop one in the future? It is argued that information showing what is expected to be said is sufficient to limit the boundaries of what later can be admitted into evidence; but does such general information really meet the specific language of the Amendment which says "particularly describing"? Rather than using language in a completely artificial way, I must conclude that the Fourth Amendment simply does not apply to eavesdropping.

Tapping telephone wires, of course, was an unknown possibility at the time the Fourth Amendment was adopted. . . . "In those days the eavesdropper listened by naked ear under the eaves of houses or their windows, or beyond their walls seeking out private discourse." ... There can be no doubt that the Framers were aware of this practice, and if they had desired to outlaw or restrict the use of evidence obtained by eavesdropping, I believe that they would have used the appropriate language to do so in the Fourth Amendment. They certainly would not have left such a task to the ingenuity of language-stretching judges. No one, it seems to me, can read the debates on the Bill of Rights without reaching the conclusion that its Framers and critics well knew the meaning of the words they used, what they would be understood to mean by others, their scope and their limitations. Under these circumstances it strikes me as a charge against their scholarship, their commonsense and their candor to give the Fourth Amendment's language the eavesdropping meaning the Court imputes to it today.

I do not deny that common sense requires and that this Court often has said that the Bill of Rights' safeguards should be given a liberal construction. This principle, however, does not justify construing the search and seizure amendment as applying to eavesdropping or the "seizure" of conversations. The Fourth Amendment was aimed directly at the abhorred practice of breaking in, ransacking and searching homes and other buildings and seizing people's personal belongings without warrants issued by magistrates. The Amendment deserves, and this Court has given it, a liberal construction in order to protect against warrantless searches of buildings and seizures of tangible personal effects. But until today this Court has refused to say that eavesdropping comes within the ambit of Fourth Amendment restrictions. ...

In interpreting the Bill of Rights, I willingly go as far as a liberal construction of the language takes me, but I simply cannot in good conscience give a meaning to words which they have never before been thought to have and which they certainly do not have in common ordinary usage. I will not distort the words of the Amendment in order to "keep the Constitution up to date" or "to bring it into harmony with the times." It was never meant for this Court to have such power, which in effect would make us a continuously functioning constitutional convention.

With this decision the Court has completed, I hope, its rewriting of the Fourth Amendment, which started only recently when the Court began referring incessantly to the Fourth Amendment not so much as a law against *unreasonable* searches and seizures as one to protect an individual's privacy. By clever word juggling the Court finds it plausible to argue that language aimed specifically at searches and seizures of things that can be searched and seized may, to protect privacy, be applied to eavesdropped evidence of conversations that can neither be searched nor seized. Few things happen to an individual that do not affect his privacy in one way or another. Thus, by arbitrarily substituting the Court's language, designed to protect privacy, for the Constitution's language, designed to protect against unreasonable searches and seizures, the Court has made the Fourth Amendment its vehicle for holding all laws violative of the Constitution which offend the Court's broadest concept of privacy. ...

The Fourth Amendment protects privacy only to the extent that it prohibits unreasonable searches and seizures of "persons, houses, papers and effects." No general right is created by the Amendment so as to give this Court the unlimited power to hold unconstitutional everything which affects privacy. Certainly the Framers, well acquainted as they were with the excesses of governmental power, did not intend to grant this Court such omnipotent lawmaking authority as that. The history of governments proves that it is dangerous to freedom to repose such powers in courts.

For these reasons I respectfully dissent.

United States v. United States District Court
407 U.S. 297, 92 S.Ct. 2125, 32 L.Ed. 2d 752 (1972)

(This case is reprinted in chapter 3, beginning on page 131.)

Terry v. Ohio
392 U.S. 1, 88 S.Ct. 1868, 20 L.Ed. 2d 889 (1968)

This case examined the constitutionality of the "stop-and-frisk" by police, and presented the Warren Court with a Fourth Amendment dilemma. Was the situation Officer McFadden observed sufficient to establish probable cause for arrest? If so, what would such a ruling do to the limits imposed on police behavior by the Constitution? If the Court found McFadden's actions constitutionally unacceptable, could the Justices reasonably expect police officers in the future not to do precisely what McFadden had done? The reader should pay particular attention to Chief Justice Warren's recitation of, and emphasis on, the facts. Remember that the decision came down after several years of increasingly violent street crime. In the courts below, the convictions of Terry and his sidekick Chilton for carrying concealed weapons had been upheld.

MR. CHIEF JUSTICE WARREN delivered the opinion of the Court. . . .

Petitioner Terry was convicted of carrying a concealed weapon and sentenced to the statutorily prescribed term of one to three years in the penitentiary. Following the denial of a pretrial motion to suppress, the prosecution introduced in evidence two revolvers and a number of bullets seized from Terry and a codefendant, Richard Chilton, by Cleveland Police Detective Martin McFadden. At the hearing on the motion to suppress this evidence, Officer McFadden testified that while he was patrolling in plain clothes in downtown Cleveland at approximately 2:30 in the afternoon of October 31, 1963, his attention was attracted by two men, Chilton and Terry, standing on the corner of Huron Road and Euclid Avenue. He had never seen the two men before, and he was unable to say precisely what first drew his eye to them. However, he testified that he had been a policeman for 39 years and a detective for 35 and that he had been assigned to patrol this vicinity of downtown Cleveland for shoplifters and pickpockets for 30 years. . . .

His interest aroused, Officer McFadden took up a post of observation in the entrance to a store 300 to 400 feet away from the two men. . . . He saw one of the men leave the other one and walk southwest on Huron Road, past some stores. The man paused for a moment and looked in a store window, then walked on a short distance, turned around and walked back toward the corner, pausing once again to look in the same store window. He rejoined his companion at the corner, and the two conferred briefly. Then the second man went through the same series of motions, strolling down Huron Road, looking in the same window, walking on a short distance, turning back, peering in the store window again, and returning to confer with the first man at the corner. The two men repeated this ritual alternately between five and six times apiece—in all, roughly a dozen trips. At one point, while the two were standing together on the corner, a third man approached them and engaged them briefly in conversation. This man then left the two others and walked west on Euclid Avenue. Chilton and Terry resumed their measured pacing, peering, and conferring. After this had gone on for 10 to 12 minutes, the two men walked off together, heading west on Euclid Avenue, following the path taken earlier by the third man.

By this time Officer McFadden had become thoroughly suspicious. He testified that after observing their elaborately casual and oft-repeated reconnaissance of the store window on Huron Road, he suspected the two men of "casing a job, a stick-up," and that he considered it his duty as a police officer to investigate further. He added that he feared "they may have a gun." Thus, Officer McFadden followed Chilton and Terry and saw them stop in front of Zucker's store to talk to the same man who had conferred with them earlier on the street corner. Deciding that the situation was ripe for direct action, Officer McFadden approached the three men, identified himself as a police officer and asked for their names. At this point his knowledge was confined to what he had observed. He was not acquainted with any of the three men by name or by sight, and he had received no information concerning them from any other source. When the men "mumbled something" in response to his inquiries, Officer McFadden grabbed petitioner Terry, spun him around so that they were facing the other two, with Terry between McFadden and the others, and patted down the outside of his clothing. In the left breast pocket of Terry's overcoat Officer McFadden felt a pistol. He reached inside the overcoat pocket, but was unable to remove the gun. At this point, keeping Terry between himself and the others, the officer ordered all three men to enter Zucker's store. As they went in, he removed Terry's overcoat completely, removed a .38-caliber revolver from the pocket and ordered all three men to face the wall with their hands raised. Officer McFadden pro-

ceeded to pat down the outer clothing of Chilton and the third man, Katz. He discovered another revolver in the outer pocket of Chilton's overcoat, but no weapons were found on Katz. . . .

Our first task is to establish at what point in this encounter the Fourth Amendment becomes relevant. That is, we must decide whether and when Officer McFadden "seized" Terry and whether and when he conducted a "search." . . . It is quite plain that the Fourth Amendment governs "seizures" of the person which do not eventuate in a trip to the station house and prosecution for crime—"arrests" in traditional terminology. It must be recognized that whenever a police officer accosts an individual and restrains his freedom to walk away, he has "seized" that person. And it is nothing less than sheer torture of the English language to suggest that a careful exploration of the outer surfaces of a person's clothing all over his or her body in an attempt to find weapons is not a "search." Moreover, it is simply fantastic to urge that such a procedure performed in public by a policeman while the citizen stands helpless, perhaps facing a wall with his hands raised, is a "petty indignity." It is a serious intrusion upon the sanctity of the person, which may inflict great indignity and arouse strong resentment, and it is not to be undertaken lightly.

The danger in the logic which proceeds upon distinctions between a "stop" and an "arrest," or "seizure" of the person, and between a "frisk" and a "search" is twofold. It seeks to isolate from constitutional scrutiny the initial stages of the contact between the policeman and the citizen. And by suggesting a rigid all-or-nothing model of justification and regulation under the Amendment, it obscures the utility of limitations upon the scope, as well as the initiation, of police action as a means of constitutional regulation. . . .

The distinctions of classical "stop-and-frisk" theory thus serve to divert attention from the central inquiry under the Fourth Amendment—the reasonableness in all the circumstances of the particular governmental invasion of a citizen's personal security. "Search" is it a 4th amend. "search & seizure" violation? yes and "seizure" are not talismans. We therefore reject the notions that the Fourth Amendment does not come into play at all as a limitation upon police conduct if the officers stop short of something called a "technical arrest" or a "full-blown search." . . .

[W]e cannot blind ourselves to the need for law enforcement officers to protect themselves and other prospective victims of violence in situations where they may lack probable cause for an arrest. When an officer is justified in believing that the individual whose suspicious behavior he is investigating at close range is armed and presently dangerous to the officer or to others, it would appear to be clearly unreasonable to deny the officer the power to take necessary measures to determine whether the person is in fact carrying a weapon and to neutralize the threat of physical harm.

We must still consider, however, the nature and quality of the intrusion on individual rights which must be accepted if police officers are to be conceded the right to search for weapons in situations where probable cause to arrest for crime is lacking. Even a limited search of the outer clothing for weapons constitutes a severe, though brief, intrusion upon cherished personal security, and it must surely be an annoying, frightening, and perhaps humiliating experience. . . .

We conclude that the revolver seized from Terry was properly admitted in evidence against him. At the time he seized petitioner and searched him for weapons, Officer McFadden had reasonable grounds to believe that petitioner was armed and dangerous, and it was necessary for the protection of himself and others to take swift measures to discover the true facts and neutralize the threat of harm if it materialized. The policeman carefully restricted his search to what was appropriate to the discovery of the particular items which he sought. Each case of this sort will, of course, have to be decided on its own facts. We merely hold today that where a police officer observes unusual conduct which leads him reasonably to conclude in light of his experience that criminal activity may be afoot and that the persons with

whom he is dealing may be armed and presently dangerous, where in the course of investigating this behavior he identifies himself as a policeman and makes reasonable inquiries, and where nothing in the initial stages of the encounter serves to dispel his reasonable fear for his own or others' safety, he is entitled for the protection of himself and others in the area to conduct a carefully limited search of the outer clothing of such persons in an attempt to discover weapons which might be used to assault him.

Such a search is a reasonable search under the Fourth Amendment, and any weapons seized may properly be introduced in evidence against the person from whom they were taken.

Affirmed.

MR. JUSTICE BLACK concurs in the judgment. . . .

MR. JUSTICE HARLAN, concurring. . . .

MR. JUSTICE WHITE, concurring. . . .

MR. JUSTICE DOUGLAS, dissenting.

I agree that petitioner was "seized" within the meaning of the Fourth Amendment. I also agree that frisking petitioner and his companions for guns was a "search." But it is a mystery how that "search" and that "seizure" can be constitutional by Fourth Amendment standards, unless there was "probable cause" to believe that (1) a crime had been committed or (2) a crime was in the process of being committed or (3) a crime was about to be committed. . . .

The infringement on personal liberty of any "seizure" of a person can only be "reasonable" under the Fourth Amendment if we require the police to possess "probable cause" before they seize him. Only that line draws a meaningful distinction between an officer's mere inkling and the presence of facts within the officer's personal knowledge which would convince a reasonable man that the person seized has committed, is committing, or is about to commit a particular crime. "In dealing with probable cause, . . . as the very name implies, we deal with probabilities. These are not technical; they are the factual and practical considerations of everyday life on which reasonable and prudent

*giving police more
power than magistrate*

men, not legal technicians, act." *Brinegar* v.
United States. . . .

To give the police greater power than a
magistrate is to take a long step down the
totalitarian path. Perhaps such a step is
desirable to cope with modern forms of
lawlessness. But if it is taken, it should be the
deliberate choice of the people through a constitutional amendment. Until the Fourth
Amendment, which is closely allied with the
Fifth, is rewritten, the person and the effects of
the individual are beyond the reach of all
government agencies until there are reasonable
grounds to believe that a criminal venture has
been launched or is about to be launched.

There have been powerful hydraulic
pressures throughout our history that bear
heavily on the Court to water down constitutional guarantees and give the police the upper
hand. That hydraulic pressure has probably
never been greater than it is today.

Yet if the individual is no longer to be
sovereign, if the police can pick him up whenever they do not like the cut of his jib, if they can
"seize" and "search" him in their discretion,
we enter a new regime. The decision to enter it
should be made only after a full debate by the
people of this country.

Chimel v. *California*
395 U.S. 752, 89 S.Ct. 2034, 23 L.Ed. 2d 685 (1969)

After arresting the defendant in his home for burglary of a coin shop, police officers
conducted a search of his entire three-bedroom house, including the attic, the
garage, a small workshop, and various drawers. Certain items found through
the search were admitted into evidence against him and he was convicted. Both the
California Court of Appeal and the California Supreme Court affirmed the conviction, holding that although the officers had no search warrant, the search of the
defendant's home had been justified on the ground that it had been incident to a
valid arrest. The defendant appealed and the Supreme Court granted certiorari.

MR. JUSTICE STEWART delivered the opinion of
the Court.

This case raises basic questions concerning
the permissible scope under the Fourth Amendment of a search incident to a lawful arrest. . . .
. . . We proceed on the hypothesis that the
California courts were correct in holding that
the arrest of the petitioner was valid under
the Constitution. This brings us directly to the
question whether the warrantless search of the
petitioner's entire house can be constitutionally
justified as incident to that arrest. The decisions
of this Court bearing upon that question have

been far from consistent, as even the most cursory review makes evident. . . .

When an arrest is made, it is reasonable for
the arresting officer to search the person arrested
in order to remove any weapons that the latter
might seek to use in order to resist or effect his
escape. Otherwise, the officer's safety might
well be endangered, and the arrest itself
frustrated. In addition, it is entirely reasonable
for the arresting officer to search for and seize
any evidence on the arrestee's person in order to
prevent its concealment or destruction. And the
area into which an arrestee might reach in order

*Is a warrantless search
of house incident to arrest
constitutional?*

to grab a weapon or evidentiary items must, of course, be governed by a like rule. A gun on a table or in a drawer in front of one who is arrested can be as dangerous to the arresting officer as one concealed in the clothing of the person arrested. There is ample justification, therefore, for a search of the arrestee's person and the area "within his immediate control"—construing that phrase to mean the area from within which he might gain possession of a weapon or destructible evidence.

There is no comparable justification, however, for routinely searching through all the desk drawers or other closed or concealed areas in that room itself. Such searches, in the absence of well recognized exceptions, may be made only under the authority of a search warrant. The "adherence to judicial processes" mandated by the Fourth Amendment requires no less. . . .

It is argued in the present case that it is "reasonable" to search a man's house when he is arrested in it. But that argument is founded on little more than a subjective view regarding the acceptability of certain sorts of police conduct, and not on considerations relevant to Fourth Amendment interests. Under such an unconfined analysis, Fourth Amendment protection in this area would approach the evaporation point. It is not easy to explain why, for instance, it is less subjectively "reasonable" to search a man's house when he is arrested on his front lawn—or just down the street—than it is when he happens to be in the house at the time of arrest. . . .

Application of sound Fourth Amendment principles to the facts of this case produces a clear result. The search here went far beyond the petitioner's person and the area from within which he might have obtained either a weapon or something that could have been used as evidence against him. There was no constitutional justification, in the absence of a search warrant, for extending the search beyond that area. The scope of the search was, therefore, "unreasonable" under the Fourth and Fourteenth Amendments, and the petitioner's conviction cannot stand.

Reversed.

MR. JUSTICE HARLAN concurring. . . .

MR. JUSTICE WHITE, with whom JUSTICE BLACK joins, dissenting.

Few areas of the law have been as subject to shifting constitutional standards over the last 50 years as that of the search "incident to an arrest." There has been a remarkable instability in this whole area, which has seen at least four major shifts in emphasis. Today's opinion makes an untimely fifth. In my view, the Court should not now abandon the old rule. . . .

The rule which has prevailed, but for very brief or doubtful periods of aberration, is that a search incident to an arrest may extend to those areas under the control of the defendant and where items subject to constitutional seizure may be found. The justification for this rule must, under the language of the Fourth Amendment, lie in the reasonableness of the rule. *Terry* v. *Ohio*, 392 U.S. 1, . . .

. . . The Court must decide whether a given search is reasonable. The Amendment does not proscribe "warrantless searches" but instead it proscribes "unreasonable searches" and this Court has never held nor does the majority today assert that warrantless searches are necessarily unreasonable. . . .

The case provides a good illustration of my point that it is unreasonable to require police to leave the scene of an arrest in order to obtain a search warrant when they already have probable cause to search and there is a clear danger that the items for which they may reasonably search will be removed before they return with a warrant. Petitioner was arrested in his home after an arrest whose validity will be explored below, but which I will now assume was valid. There was doubtless probable cause not only to arrest petitioner, but also to search his house. He had obliquely admitted, both to a neighbor and to the owner of the burglarized store, that he had committed the burglary. In light of this, and the fact that the neighbor had seen other admittedly stolen property in petitioner's house, there was surely probable cause on which a warrant could have [been] issued to search the house for the stolen coins. Moreover, had the police simply arrested petitioner, taken him off to the station house, and later returned with a warrant, it seems very likely that petitioner's wife, who in view of petitioner's generally garrulous nature must have known of the robbery, would have removed the coins. For the police to search the house while the evidence they had probable cause to search out and seize was still there cannot be considered unreasonable.

This line of analysis, supported by the precedents of this Court, hinges on two assumptions. One is that the arrest of petitioner without a valid warrant was constitutional as the majority assumes; the other is that the police were not required to obtain a search warrant in advance, even though they knew that the effect of the arrest might well be to alert petitioner's wife that the coins had better be removed soon. Thus it is necessary to examine the constitutionality of the arrest since if it was illegal, the exigent circumstances which it created may not, as the consequences of a lawless act, be used to justify the contemporaneous warrantless search. But for the arrest, the warrantless search may not be justified. And if circumstances can justify the warrantless arrest, it would be strange to say that the Fourth Amendment bars the warrantless search, regardless of the circumstances, since the invasion and disruption of a man's life and privacy which stem from his arrest are ordinarily far greater than the relatively minor intrusions attending a search of his premises.

Congress has expressly authorized a wide range of officials to make arrests without any warrant in criminal cases. United States Marshals have long had this power, which is also vested in the agents of the Federal Bureau of Investigation, and in the Secret Service and the narcotics law enforcement agency. That warrantless arrest power may apply even when there is time to get a warrant without fear that the suspect may escape is made perfectly clear by the legislative history of the statute granting arrest power to the FBI. . . .

In the light of the uniformity of judgment of the Congress, past judicial decisions, and common practice rejecting the proposition that arrest warrants are essential wherever it is practicable to get them, the conclusion is inevitable that such arrests and accompanying searches are reasonable, at least until experience teaches the

contrary. It must very often be the case that by the time probable cause to arrest a man is accumulated, the man is aware of police interest in him or for other good reasons is on the verge of flight. Moreover, it will likely be very difficult to determine the probability of his flight. Given this situation, it may be best in all cases simply to allow the arrest if there is probable cause, especially since that issue can be determined very shortly after the arrest. . . .

If circumstances so often require the warrantless arrest that the law generally permits it, the typical situation will find the arresting officers lawfully on the premises without arrest or search warrant. Like the majority, I would permit the police to search the person of a suspect and the area under his immediate control either to assure the safety of the officers or to prevent the destruction of evidence. And like the majority, I see nothing in the arrest alone furnishing probable cause for a search of any broader scope. However, where as here the existence of probable cause is independently established and would justify a warrant for a broader search for evidence, I would follow past cases and permit such a search to be carried out without a warrant, since the fact of arrest supplies an exigent circumstance justifying police action before the evidence can be removed, and also alerts the suspect to the fact of the search so that he can immediately seek judicial determination of probable cause in an adversary proceeding, and appropriate redress.

This view, consistent with past cases, would not authorize the general search against which the Fourth Amendment was meant to guard, nor would it broaden or render uncertain in any way whatsoever the scope of searches permitted under the Fourth Amendment. The issue in this case is not the breadth of the search since there was clearly probable cause for the search which was carried out. No broader search than if the officers had a warrant would be permitted. The only issue is whether a search warrant was required as a precondition to that search. It is agreed that such a warrant would be required absent exigent circumstances. I would hold that the fact of arrest supplies such an exigent circumstance, since the police had lawfully gained entry to the premises to effect the arrest and since delaying the search to secure a warrant would have involved the risk of not recovering the fruits of the crime. . . .

An arrested man, by definition conscious of the police interest in him, and provided almost immediately with a lawyer and a judge, is in an excellent position to dispute the reasonableness of his arrest and contemporaneous search in a full adversary proceeding. I would uphold the constitutionality of this search contemporaneous with an arrest since there was probable cause both for the search and for the arrest, exigent circumstance involving the removal or destruction of evidence, and a satisfactory opportunity to dispute the issues of probable cause shortly thereafter. In this case, the search was reasonable.

United States v. Robinson
414 U.S. 218, 94 S.Ct. 467, 38 L.Ed. 2d 427 (1973)

On an April evening in 1968, Officer Jenks of the District of Columbia police force observed Willie Robinson driving a 1965 Cadillac. Because of prior investigation, Jenks had good reason to believe that Robinson's driver's license had been revoked. In the District of Columbia, driving after revocation of a license carried a mandatory jail sentence or fine, or both. Jenks signaled Robinson to stop and informed him that he was under arrest for "operating after revocation and obtaining a permit by misrepresentation." After Robinson got out of the car, Jenks searched him before taking him into custody. During the patdown, Jenks felt an object in the left breast pocket of the heavy coat Robinson was wearing, but could not tell what it was. He removed it from the pocket, and it turned out to be a crumpled cigarette package. Jenks then opened the pack and found 14 gelatin capsules containing white powder, which on analysis proved to be heroin. This heroin formed the basis for Robinson's conviction in the district court. The Court of Appeals for the District of Columbia Circuit reversed, and the Supreme Court granted certiorari.

MR. JUSTICE REHNQUIST delivered the opinion of the Court. . . .

It is well settled that a search incident to a lawful arrest is a traditional exception to the warrant requirement of the Fourth Amendment. This general exception has historically been formulated into two distinct propositions. The first is that a search may be made of the *person* of the arrestee by virtue of the lawful arrest. The second is that a search may be made of the area within the control of the arrestee.

Examination of this Court's decisions shows that these two propositions have been treated quite differently. The validity of the search of a person incident to a lawful arrest has been regarded as settled from its first enunciation, and has remained virtually unchallenged until the present case. The validity of the second proposition, while likewise conceded in principle, has been subject to differing interpretations as to the extent of the area which may be searched.

Because the rule requiring exclusion of evidence obtained in violation of the Fourth Amendment was first enunciated in *Weeks* v. *United States*, . . . it is understandable that virtually all of this Court's search-and-seizure law has been developed since that time. In *Weeks* the Court made clear its recognition of the validity of a search incident to a lawful arrest. . . .

Throughout the series of cases in which the Court has addressed the second proposition relating to a search incident to a lawful arrest—the permissible area beyond the person of the arrestee which such a search may cover—no doubt has been expressed as to the unqualified authority of the arresting authority to search the person of the arrestee. E.g., *Carroll* v. *United States* . . . , *Chimel* v. *California*. . . . In *Chimel*, where the Court overruled *Rabinowitz* and *Harris* as to the area of permissible search incident to a lawful arrest, full recognition was again given to the authority to search the person of the arrestee. . . .

Three years after the decision in *Chimel*, . . . we upheld the validity of a search in which heroin had been taken from the person of the defendant after his arrest on a weapons charge, in *Adams* v. *Williams*. . . .

The justification or reason for the authority to search incident to a lawful arrest rests quite as much on the need to disarm the suspect in order to take him into custody as it does on the need to preserve evidence on his person for later use at trial. . . . The standards traditionally governing a search incident to lawful arrest are not, therefore, commuted to the stricter Terry standards by the absence of probable fruits or further evidence of the particular crime for which the arrest is made.

Nor are we inclined, on the basis of what seems to us to be a rather speculative judgment, to qualify the breadth of the general authority to search incident to a lawful custodial arrest on an assumption that persons arrested for the offense of driving while their licenses have been revoked are less likely to possess dangerous weapons than are those arrested for other crimes. It is scarcely open to doubt that the danger to an officer is far greater in the case of the extended exposure which follows the taking of a suspect into custody and transporting him to the police station than in the case of the relatively fleeting contact resulting from the typical Terry-type stop. This is an adequate basis for treating all custodial arrests alike for purposes of search justification.

But quite apart from these distinctions, our more fundamental disagreement with the Court of Appeals arises from its suggestion that there must be litigated in each case the issue of whether or not there was present one of the reasons supporting the authority for a search of the person incident to a lawful arrest. We do not think the long line of authorities of this Court dating back to *Weeks*, or what we can glean from the history of practice in this country and in England, requires such a case-by-case adjudication. A police officer's determination as to how and where to search the person of a suspect whom he has arrested is necessarily a quick ad hoc judgment which the Fourth Amendment does not require to be broken down in each instance into an analysis of each step in the search. The authority to search the person incident to a lawful custodial arrest, while based upon the need to disarm and to discover evidence, does not depend on what a court may later decide was the probability in a particular arrest situation that weapons or evidence would in fact be found upon the person of the suspect. A custodial arrest of a suspect based on probable cause is a reasonable intrusion under the Fourth Amendment; that intrusion being lawful, a search incident to the arrest requires no additional justification. It is the fact of the lawful arrest which establishes the authority to search, and we hold that in the case of a lawful custodial arrest a full search of the person is not only an exception to the warrant requirement of the Fourth Amendment, but is also a "reasonable" search under that Amendment.

The search of respondent's person conducted by Officer Jenks in this case and the seizure from him of the heroin, were permissible under established Fourth Amendment law. While thorough, the search partook of none of the extreme or patently abusive characteristics which were held to violate the Due Process Clause of the Fourteenth Amendment in *Rochin* v. *California*. . . . Since it is the fact of custodial arrest which gives rise to the authority to search, it

[Handwritten annotations: "How can they use it to convict him", "NO.", "2nd search exceeded protective search?"]

is of no moment that Jenks did not indicate any subjective fear of the respondent or that he did not himself suspect that respondent was armed. Having in the course of a lawful search come upon the crumpled package of cigarettes, he was entitled to inspect it; and when his inspection revealed the heroin capsules, he was entitled to seize them as "fruits, instrumentalities, or contraband" probative of criminal conduct. . . . The judgment of the Court of Appeals holding otherwise is

Reversed.

MR. JUSTICE POWELL, concurring. . . .

MR. JUSTICE MARSHALL, with whom MR. JUSTICE DOUGLAS and MR. JUSTICE BRENNAN join, dissenting.

Certain fundamental principles have characterized this Court's Fourth Amendment jurisprudence over the years. Perhaps the most basic of these was expressed by Mr. Justice Butler, speaking for a unanimous Court in *Go-Bart Co.* v. *United States,* 282 U.S. 344 (1931): "There is no formula for the determination of reasonableness. Each case is to be decided on its own facts and circumstances." . . .

In the present case, however, the majority turns its back on these principles, holding that "the fact of the lawful arrest" always establishes the authority to conduct a full search of the arrestee's person, regardless of whether in a particular case "there was present one of the reasons supporting the authority for a search of the person incident to a lawful arrest." . . .

The majority opinion fails to recognize that the search conducted by Officer Jenks did not merely involve a search of respondent's person. It also included a separate search of effects found on his person. And even were we to assume, arguendo, that it was reasonable for Jenks to remove the object he felt in respondent's pocket, clearly there was no justification consistent with the Fourth Amendment which would authorize his opening the package and looking inside.

To begin with, after Jenks had the cigarette package in his hands, there is no indication that he had reason to believe or did in fact believe that the package contained a weapon. More im-

portantly, even if the crumpled-up cigarette package had in fact contained some sort of small weapon, it would have been impossible for respondent to have used it once the package was in the officer's hands. Opening the package, therefore, did not further the protective purpose of the search. Even the dissenting opinion in the Court of Appeals conceded that "since the package was now in the officer's possession, any risk of the prisoner's use of a weapon in this package had been eliminated." . . .

It is suggested, however, that since the custodial arrest itself represents a significant intrusion into the privacy of the person, any additional intrusion by way of opening or examining effects found on the person is not worthy of constitutional protection. But such an approach was expressly rejected by the Court in *Chimel.* . . . *Chimel* established the principle that the lawful right of the police to interfere with the security of the person did not, standing alone, automatically confer the right to interfere with the security and privacy of his house. Hence, the mere fact of an arrest should be no justification, in and of itself, for invading the privacy of the individual's personal effects.

The Government argues that it is difficult to see what constitutionally protected "expectation of privacy" a prisoner has in the interior of a cigarette pack. One wonders if the result in this case would have been the same were respondent a businessman who was lawfully taken into custody for driving without a license and whose wallet was taken from him by the police. Would it be reasonable for the police officer, because of the possibility that a razor blade was hidden somewhere in the wallet, to open it, remove all the contents, and examine each item carefully? Or suppose a lawyer lawfully arrested for a traffic offense is found to have a sealed envelope on his person. Would it be permissible for the arresting officer to tear open the envelope in order to make sure that it did not contain a clandestine weapon—perhaps a pin or a razor blade? . . . Would it not be more consonant with the purpose of the Fourth Amendment and the legitimate needs of the police to require the officer, if he has any question whatsoever about what the wallet or letter contains, to hold onto it until the arrestee is brought to the precinct station? . . .

The search conducted by Officer Jenks in this case went far beyond what was reasonably necessary to protect him from harm or to ensure that respondent would not effect an escape from custody. In my view, it therefore fell outside the scope of a properly drawn "search incident to arrest" exception to the Fourth Amendment's warrant requirement. I would affirm the judgment of the Court of Appeals holding that the fruits of the search should have been suppressed at respondent's trial.

Arkansas v. Sanders
442 U.S. 753, 99 S.Ct. 2586, 61 L.Ed. 2d 235 (1979)

An informant told police in Little Rock, Arkansas, that a suspect would arrive on a flight to the local airport carrying a green suitcase containing marijuana. Placing the air terminal under surveillance, police observed the suspect, Sanders, arrive and retrieve a green suitcase from the baggage service area. Sanders handed the suitcase to a companion named Rambo, who placed the suitcase in the trunk of a taxi. When the taxi drove away carrying Sanders, Rambo, and the green suitcase, the police gave chase and stopped the car. The taxi driver opened the trunk at the request of police and without asking either Sanders or Rambo for permission, they opened the unlocked suitcase and found 9.3 pounds of marijuana packed in ten plastic bags. On appeal, the Arkansas Supreme Court reversed their convictions, relying on *United States* v. *Chadwick* (433 U.S. 1: 1977) which overturned a conviction based on the contents of a footlocker lawfully seized, but unlawfully opened, from the open trunk of a parked automobile outside a train station. When the state asked the United States Supreme Court to review the decision by the Arkansas high court, the reliability of the informant was not an issue.

MR. JUSTICE POWELL delivered the opinion of the Court.

Although the general principles applicable to claims of Fourth Amendment violations are well settled, litigation over requests for suppression of highly relevant evidence continues to occupy much of the attention of courts at all levels of the state and federal judiciary. Courts and law enforcement officials often find it difficult to discern the proper application of these principles to individual cases, because the circumstances giving rise to suppression requests can vary almost infinitely. Moreover, an apparently small difference in the factual situation frequently is viewed as a controlling difference in determining Fourth Amendment rights. The present case presents an example. Only two Terms ago, we held that a locked footlocker could not lawfully be searched without a warrant, even though it had been loaded into the trunk of an automobile parked at a curb. *United States* v. *Chadwick*. . . . In earlier cases, on the other hand, the Court sustained the constitutionality of warrantless searches of automobiles and their contents under what has become known as the "automobile exception" to the warrant requirement. See, *e.g.*, *Chambers* v. *Maroney*, 399 U.S. 42 (1970); *Carroll* v. *United States*, 267 U.S. 132 (1925). We thus are presented with the task of determining whether the warrantless search of respondent's suitcase falls on the *Chadwick* or the *Chambers/Carroll* side of the Fourth Amendment line. Although in a sense this is a line-drawing process, it must be guided by established principles.

We commence with a summary of these principles. The Fourth Amendment protects the privacy and security of persons in two important ways. First, it guarantees "[t]he right of the people to be secure in their persons, houses, papers, and effects, against unreasonable searches and seizures." In addition, this Court has interpreted the Amendment to include the requirement that normally searches of private property be performed pursuant to a search warrant issued in compliance with the Warrant Clause. . . . In the ordinary case, therefore, a search of private property must be both reasonable and pursuant to a properly issued search warrant. The mere reasonableness of a search, assessed in the light of the surrounding circumstances, is not a substitute for the judicial warrant required under the Fourth Amendment. . . . The prominent place the warrant requirement is given in our decisions reflects the "basic constitutional doctrine that individual freedoms will best be preserved through a separation of powers and division of functions among the different branches and levels of Government." . . . By requiring that conclusions concerning probable cause and the scope of a search "be drawn by a neutral and detached magistrate instead of being judged by the officer engaged in the often competitive enterprise of ferreting out crime," . . . we minimize the risk of unreasonable assertions of executive authority. . . .

Nonetheless, there are some exceptions to the warrant requirement. These have been established where it was concluded that the public interest required some flexibility in the application of the general rule that a valid warrant is a prerequisite for a search. . . .

One of the circumstances in which the Constitution does not require a search warrant is when the police stop an automobile on the street or highway because they have probable cause to believe it contains contraband or evidence of a crime. . . . There are essentially

two reasons for the distinction between automobiles and other private property. First, as the Court repeatedly has recognized, the inherent mobility of automobiles often makes it impracticable to obtain a warrant. . . . In addition, the configuration, use, and regulation of automobiles often may dilute the reasonable expectation of privacy that exists with respect to differently situated property. See *Rakas v. Illinois*. . . .

In the present case, the State argues that the warrantless search of respondent's suitcase was proper under *Carroll* and its progeny. The police acted properly—indeed commendably—in apprehending respondent and his luggage. . . .

The only question, therefore, is whether the police, rather than immediately searching the suitcase without a warrant, should have taken it, along with respondent, to the police station and there obtained a warrant for the search. A lawful search of luggage generally may be performed only pursuant to a warrant. In *Chadwick*, we declined an invitation to extend the *Carroll* exception to all searches of luggage, noting that neither of the two policies supporting warrantless searches of automobiles applies to luggage. Here, as in *Chadwick*, the officers had seized the luggage and had it exclusively within their control at the time of the search. Consequently, "there was not the slightest danger that [the luggage] or its contents could have been removed before a valid search warrant could be obtained." . . . And, as we observed in that case, luggage is a common repository for one's personal effects, and therefore is inevitably associated with the expectation of privacy. . . .

In sum, we hold that the warrant requirement of the Fourth Amendment applies to personal luggage taken from an automobile to the same degree it applies to such luggage in other locations. Thus, insofar as the police are entitled to search such luggage without a warrant, their actions must be justified under some exception to the warrant requirement other than that applicable to automobiles stopped on the highway. Where—as in the present case—the police,

police should bring luggage for Judicial approval before searching it

without endangering themselves or risking loss of the evidence, lawfully have detained one suspected of criminal activity and secured his suitcase, they should delay the search thereof until after judicial approval has been obtained. In this way, constitutional rights of suspects to prior judicial review of searches will be fully protected.

The judgment of the Arkansas Supreme Court is

Affirmed.

Mr. Chief Justice Burger, with whom Mr. Justice Stevens joins, concurring in the judgment. . . .

Mr. Justice Blackmun, with whom Mr. Justice Rehnquist joins, dissenting. . . .

The impractical nature of the Court's line-drawing is brought into focus if one places himself in the position of the policeman confronting an automobile that properly has been stopped. In approaching the vehicle and its occupants, the officer must divide the world of personal property into three groups. If there is probable cause to arrest the occupants, then under *Chimel* v. *California*, . . . he may search objects within the occupants' immediate control, with or without probable cause. If there is probable cause to search the automobile itself, then under *Carroll* and *Chambers* the entire interior area of the automobile may be searched, with or without a warrant. But under *Chadwick* and the present case, if any suitcase-like object is found in the car outside the immediate control area of the occupants, it cannot be searched, in the absence of exigent circumstances, without a warrant.

The inherent opaqueness of these "principles," in terms of the policies underlying the Fourth and Fourteenth Amendments, and the confusion to be created for all concerned, are readily illustrated. Suppose a portable luggage-container-rack is affixed to the top of the vehicle. Is the arresting officer constitutionally able to open this on the spot, on the theory that it is

like the car's trunk, or must he remove it and take it to the station for a warrant, on the theory that it is like the 200-pound footlocker in *Chadwick?* Or suppose there is probable cause to arrest persons seated in the front seat of the automobile, and a suitcase rests on the back seat. Is that suitcase within the area of immediate control, such that the *Chadwick-Sanders* rules do not apply? Or suppose the arresting officer opens the car's trunk and finds that it contains an array of containers—an orange crate, a lunch bucket, an attache case, a duffelbag, a cardboard box, a backpack, a tote-bag, and a paper bag. Which of these may be searched immediately, and which are so "personal" that they must be impounded for future search only pursuant to a warrant? The problems of distinguishing between "luggage" and "some integral part of the automobile," . . . between luggage that is within the "immediate control" of the arrestee and luggage that is not; and between "personal luggage" and other "containers and packages" such as those most curiously described, . . . will be legion. The lines that will be drawn will not make much sense in terms of the policies of the Fourth and Fourteenth Amendments. And the heightened possibilities for error will mean that many convictions will be overturned, highly relevant evidence again will be excluded, and guilty persons will be set free in return for little apparent gain in precise and clearly understood constitutional analysis.

In my view, it would be better to adopt a clear-cut rule to the effect that a warrant should not be required to seize and search any personal property found in an automobile that may in turn be seized and searched without a warrant pursuant to *Carroll* and *Chambers.* . . . Such an approach would simplify the constitutional law of criminal procedure without seriously derogating from the values protected by the Fourth Amendment's prohibition of unreasonable searches and seizures.

Blackmun— no warrant should be necessary at all for automobiles.

IV. Right to Counsel

Powell v. Alabama
287 U.S. 45, 53 S.Ct. 55, 77 L.Ed. 158 (1932)

The 1931 conviction in Alabama courts of seven black men charged with the rape of two white women resulted in a series of legal tests in the Supreme Court of the United States, of which the instant case was the first. The Chief Justice of the Alabama Supreme Court had dissented from that court's affirmance of the conviction, chiefly because of the hostile atmosphere which surrounded the trial and the speed and casualness with which the trial judge had dealt with the question of counsel for the defendants. The defendants obtained certiorari.

MR. JUSTICE SUTHERLAND delivered the opinion of the court. . . .

In this court the judgments are assailed upon the grounds that the defendants, and each of them, were denied due process of law and the equal protection of the laws, in contravention of the Fourteenth Amendment, specifically as follows: (1) They were not given a fair, impartial, and deliberate trial; (2) they were denied the right of counsel, with the accustomed incidents of consultation and opportunity of preparation for trial; and (3) they were tried before juries from which qualified members of their own race were systematically excluded. These questions were properly raised and saved in the courts below.

The only one of the assignments which we shall consider is the second, in respect of the denial of counsel; and it becomes unnecessary to discuss the facts of the case or the circumstances surrounding the prosecution except in so far as they reflect light upon that question. . . .

First. The record shows that immediately upon the return of the indictment defendants were arraigned and pleaded not guilty. Apparently they were not asked whether they had, or were able to employ, counsel, or wished to have counsel appointed; or whether they had friends or relatives who might assist in that regard if communicated with. That it would not have been an idle ceremony to have given the defendants reasonable opportunity to communicate with their families and endeavor to obtain counsel is demonstrated by the fact that very soon after conviction, able counsel appeared in their behalf. This was pointed out by Chief Justice Anderson in the course of his dissenting opinion. "They were nonresidents," he said, "and had little time or opportunity to get in touch with their families and friends who were scattered throughout two other states, and time has demonstrated that they could or would have been represented by able counsel had a better opportunity been given by a reasonable delay in the trial of the cases judging from the number and activity of counsel that appeared immediately or shortly after their conviction."

It is hardly necessary to say that the right to counsel being conceded, a defendant should be afforded a fair opportunity to secure counsel of his own choice. Not only was that not done here, but such designation of counsel as was attempted was either so indefinite or so close upon the trial as to amount to a denial of effective and substantial aid in that regard. This will be amply demonstrated by a brief review of the record.

April 6, six days after indictment, the trials began. When the first case was called, the court inquired whether the parties were ready for trial. The state's attorney replied that he was ready to proceed. No one answered for the defendants or appeared to represent or defend them. Mr. Roddy, a Tennessee lawyer not a member of the local bar, addressed the court, saying that he had not been employed, but that people who were interested had spoken to him about the case. He was asked by the court whether he intended to appear for the defendants, and answered that he would like to appear along with counsel that the court might appoint. . . .

And in this casual fashion the matter of counsel in a capital case was disposed of.

It thus will be seen that until the very morning of the trial no lawyer had been named or definitely designated to represent the defendants. . . .

. . . [D]uring perhaps the most critical period of the proceedings against these defendants, that is to say, from the time of their arraignment until the beginning of their trial, when consultation, thorough-going investigation and preparation were vitally important, the defendants did not have the aid of counsel in any real sense, although they were as much entitled to such aid during that period as at the trial itself.

Second. The Constitution of Alabama provides that in all criminal prosecutions the accused shall enjoy the right to have the assistance of counsel; and a state statute requires the court in a capital case, where the defendant is unable to employ counsel, to appoint counsel for him. The state Supreme Court held that these provisions had not been infringed, and with that holding we are powerless to interfere. The question, however, which it is our duty, and within our power, to decide, is whether the denial of the assistance of counsel contravenes the due process clause of the Fourteenth Amendment to the Federal Constitution. . . .

An affirmation of the right to the aid of counsel in petty offenses, and its denial in the case of crimes of the gravest character, where such aid is most needed, is so outrageous and so obviously a perversion of all sense of proportion that the rule was constantly, vigorously and sometimes passionately assailed by English statesmen and lawyers. . . .

The rule was rejected by the colonies. . . .

It . . . appears that in at least twelve of the thirteen colonies the rule of the English common law, in the respect now under consideration, had been definitely rejected and the right to counsel fully recognized in all criminal prosecutions, save that in one or two instances the right was limited to capital offenses or to the more serious crimes; and this court seems to have been of the opinion that this was true in all the colonies. . . .

The Sixth Amendment, in terms, provides that in all criminal prosecutions the accused shall enjoy the right "to have the Assistance of Counsel for his defence." In the face of the reasoning of the Hurtado case, if it stood alone, it would be difficult to justify the conclusion that the right to counsel, being thus specifically granted by the Sixth Amendment, was also within the intendment of the due process of law clause. But the Hurtado case does not stand alone. In the later case of *Chicago, Burlington & Q. R. Co.* v. *Chicago,* 166 U.S. 226, 241, this court held that a judgment of a state court, even though authorized by statute, by which private property was taken for public use without just compensation, was in violation of the due process of law required by the Fourteenth Amendment, notwithstanding that the Fifth Amendment explicitly declares that private property shall not be taken for public use without just compensation. . . .

Likewise, this court has considered that freedom of speech and of the press are rights protected by the due process clause of the Fourteenth Amendment, although in the First Amendment, Congress is prohibited in specific terms from abridging the right. . . .

These later cases establish that notwithstanding the sweeping character of the language in the Hurtado case, the rule laid down is not without exceptions. The rule is an aid to construction, and in some instances may be conclusive; but it must yield to more compelling considerations whenever such considerations exist. The fact that the right involved is of such a character that it cannot be denied without violating those "fundamental principles of liberty and justice which lie at the base of all our civil and political institutions" (*Hebert* v. *Louisiana,* 272 U.S. 312, 316), is obviously one of those compelling considerations which must prevail in determining whether it is embraced within the due process clause of the Fourteenth Amendment, although it be specifically dealt with in another part of the Federal Constitution. Evidently this court, in the later cases enumerated, regarded the rights there under consideration as of this fundamental character. That some such distinction must be observed is foreshadowed in *Twining* v. *New Jersey,* 211 U.S. 78, 99, where Mr. Justice Moody, speaking for the court, said that: "... it is possible that some of the personal rights safeguarded by the first eight Amendments against national action may also be safeguarded against state action, because a denial of them would be a denial of due process of law, *Chicago, Burlington & Quincy Railroad* v. *Chicago,* 166 U.S. 226. If this is so, it is not because those rights are enumerated in the first eight Amendments, but because they are of such a nature that they are included in the conception of due process of law." While the question has never been categorically determined by this court, a consideration of the nature of the right and a review of the expressions of this and other courts makes it clear that the right to the aid of counsel is of this fundamental character. . . .

What, then, does a hearing include? Historically and in practice, in our own country at least, it has always included the right to the aid of counsel when desired and provided by the party asserting the right. The right to be heard would be, in many cases, of little avail if it did not comprehend the right to be heard by counsel. Even the intelligent and educated layman has small and sometimes no skill in the science of law. If charged with crime, he is incapable, generally, of determining for himself whether the indictment is good or bad. He is unfamiliar with the rules of evidence. Left without the aid of counsel he may be put on trial without a proper charge, and convicted upon incompetent evidence, or evidence irrelevant to the issue or otherwise inadmissible. He lacks both the skill and knowledge adequately to prepare his defense, even though he have a perfect one. He requires the guiding hand of counsel at every

step in the proceedings against him. Without it, though he be not guilty, he faces the danger of conviction because he does not know how to establish his innocence. If that be true of men of intelligence, how much more true is it of the ignorant and illiterate, or those of feeble intellect. If in any case, civil or criminal, a state or federal court were arbitrarily to refuse to hear a party by counsel, employed by and appearing for him, it reasonably may not be doubted that such a refusal would be a denial of a hearing, and, therefore, of due process in the constitutional sense. . . .

In the light of the facts outlined in the forepart of this opinion—the ignorance and illiteracy of the defendants, their youth, the circumstances of public hostility, the imprisonment and the close surveillance of the defendants by the military forces, the fact that their friends and families were all in other states and communication with them necessarily difficult, and above all that they stood in deadly peril of their lives—we think the failure of the trial court to give them reasonable time and opportunity to secure counsel was a clear denial of due process.

But passing that, and assuming their inability, even if opportunity had been given, to employ counsel, as the trial court evidently did assume, we are of opinion that, under the circumstances just stated, the necessity of counsel was so vital and imperative that the failure of the trial court to make an effective appointment of counsel was likewise a denial of due process within the meaning of the Fourteenth Amendment. Whether this would be so in other criminal prosecutions, or under other circumstances, we need not determine. All that it is necessary now to decide, as we do decide, is that in a capital case, where the defendant is unable to employ counsel, and is incapable adequately of making his own defense because of ignorance, feeblemindedness, illiteracy, or the like, it is the duty of the court, whether requested or not, to assign counsel for him as a necessary requisite of due process of law; and that duty is not discharged by an assignment at such a time or under such circumstances as to preclude the giving of effective aid in the preparation and trial of the case. To hold otherwise would be to ignore the fundamental postulate, already adverted to, "that there are certain immutable principles of justice which inhere in the very idea of free government which no member of the Union may disregard." *Holden* v. *Hardy*, 169 U.S. 366. In a case such as this, whatever may be the rule in other cases, the right to have counsel appointed, when nec-

essary, is a logical corollary from the constitutional right to be heard by counsel. . . .

The judgments must be reversed and the causes remanded for further proceedings not inconsistent with this opinion.

Judgments reversed.

[MR. JUSTICE BUTLER, with MR. JUSTICE MCREYNOLDS concurring, wrote a dissenting opinion.]

Gideon v. *Wainwright*
372 U.S. 335, 83 S.Ct. 792, 9 L.Ed. 2d 799 (1963)

Clarence Gideon was charged in a Florida state court with breaking and entering a poolroom with the intent to commit a crime. This was a felony under Florida law. He appeared in court without a lawyer, and when he requested that the trial court appoint one for him because he could not afford retained counsel, the judge refused. Florida law at the time provided appointed counsel for indigents only in capital cases. Following conviction, Gideon filed a petition for *habeas corpus* in the Florida Supreme Court, which denied relief without opinion. The United States Supreme Court granted certiorari.

MR. JUSTICE BLACK delivered the opinion of the Court. . . .

Since 1942, when *Betts* v. *Brady* . . . was decided by a divided Court, the problem of a defendant's federal constitutional right to counsel in a state court has been a continuing source of controversy and litigation in both state and federal courts. To give this problem another review here, we granted certiorari. . . . Since Gideon was proceeding in forma pauperis, we appointed counsel to represent him and requested both sides to discuss in their briefs and oral arguments the following: "Should this Court's holding in *Betts* v. *Brady*, . . . be reconsidered?"

The facts upon which Betts claimed that he had been unconstitutionally denied the right to have counsel appointed to assist him are strik-

ingly like the facts upon which Gideon here bases his federal constitutional claim. Betts was indicted for robbery in a Maryland state court. On arraignment, he told the trial judge of his lack of funds to hire a lawyer and asked the court to appoint one for him. Betts was advised that it was not the practice in that county to appoint counsel for indigent defendants except in murder and rape cases. He then pleaded not guilty, had witnesses summoned, crossexamined the State's witnesses, examined his own, and chose not to testify himself. He was found guilty by the judge, sitting without a jury, and sentenced to eight years in prison.

Like Gideon, Betts sought release by habeas corpus, alleging that he had been denied the right to assistance of counsel in violation of the Fourteenth Amendment. Betts was denied any

[handwritten top margin: fair trial cannot be assured unless w/o counsel]

relief, and on review this Court affirmed. It was held that a refusal to appoint counsel for an indigent defendant charged with a felony did not necessarily violate the Due Process Clause of the Fourteenth Amendment, which for reasons given the Court deemed to be the only applicable federal constitutional provision. The Court said,

> Asserted denial [of due process] is to be tested by an appraisal of the totality of facts in a given case. That which may, in one setting, constitute a denial of fundamental fairness, shocking to the universal sense of justice, may, in other circumstances, and in the light of other considerations, fall short of such denial. . . .

Treating due process as "a concept less rigid and more fluid than those envisaged in other specific and particular provisions of the Bill of Rights," the Court held that refusal to appoint counsel under the particular facts and circumstances in the Betts Case was not so "offensive to the common and fundamental ideas of fairness" as to amount to a denial of due process. . . .

We accept *Betts* v. *Brady's* assumption, based as it was on our prior cases, that a provision of the Bill of Rights which is "fundamental and essential to a fair trial" is made obligatory upon the States by the Fourteenth Amendment. We think the Court in *Betts* was wrong, however, in concluding that the Sixth Amendment's guarantee of counsel is not one of these fundamental rights. Ten years before *Betts* v. *Brady,* this Court, after full consideration of all the historical data examined in *Betts,* had unequivocally declared that "the right to the aid of counsel is of this fundamental character." *Powell* v. *Alabama.* . . . While the Court at the close of its *Powell* opinion did by its language, as this Court frequently does, limit its holding to the particular facts and circumstances of that case, its conclusions about the fundamental nature of the right to counsel are unmistakable. . . .

The fact is that in deciding as it did—that

[handwritten left margin: Betts v. Brady was wrong in saying that rt to counsel was not fundamental]

"appointment of counsel is not a fundamental right, essential to a fair trial"—the Court in *Betts* v. *Brady* made an abrupt break with its own well-considered precedents. In returning to these old precedents, sounder we believe than the new, we but restore constitutional principles established to achieve a fair system of justice. Not only these precedents but also reason and reflection require us to recognize that in our adversary system of criminal justice, any person haled into court, who is too poor to hire a lawyer, cannot be assured a fair trial unless counsel is provided for him. This seems to us to be an obvious truth. Governments, both state and federal, quite properly spend vast sums of money to establish machinery to try defendants accused of crime. Lawyers to prosecute are everywhere deemed essential to protect the public's interest in an orderly society. Similarly, there are few defendants charged with crime, few indeed, who fail to hire the best lawyers they can get to prepare and present their defenses. That government hires lawyers to prosecute and defendants who have the money hire lawyers to defend are the strongest indications of the widespread belief that lawyers in criminal courts are necessities, not luxuries. The right of one charged with crime to counsel may not be deemed fundamental and essential to fair trials in some countries, but it is in ours. From the very beginning, our state and national constitutions and laws have laid great emphasis on procedural and substantive safeguards designed to assure fair trials before impartial tribunals in which every defendant stands equal before the law. This noble ideal cannot be realized if the poor man charged with crime has to face his accusers without a lawyer to assist him.

The Court in *Betts* v. *Brady* departed from the sound wisdom upon which the Court's holding in *Powell* v. *Alabama* rested. Florida, supported by two other States, has asked that *Betts* v. *Brady* be left intact. Twenty-two States, as friends of the Court, argue that *Betts* was "an anachronism when handed down" and that it should now be overruled. We agree.

The judgment is reversed and the cause is

remanded to the Supreme Court of Florida for further action not inconsistent with this opinion.

Reversed.

MR. JUSTICE DOUGLAS, concurring. . . .

MR. JUSTICE CLARK, concurring in the result. . . .

MR. JUSTICE HARLAN, concurring.

I agree that *Betts* v. *Brady* should be overruled, but consider it entitled to a more respectful burial than has been accorded, at least on the part of those of us who were not on the Court when that case was decided.

I cannot subscribe to the view that *Betts* v. *Brady* represented "an abrupt break with its own well-considered precedents." . . . In 1932, in *Powell* v. *Alabama*, . . . a capital case, this Court declared that under the particular facts there presented—"the ignorance and illiteracy of the defendants, their youth, the circumstances of public hostility . . . and above all that they stood in deadly peril of their lives". . . —the state court had a duty to assign counsel for the trial as a necessary requisite of due process of law. It is evident that these limiting facts were not added to the opinion as an afterthought; they were repeatedly emphasized, . . . and were clearly regarded as important to the result.

Thus when this Court, a decade later, decided *Betts* v. *Brady,* it did no more than to admit of the possible existence of special circumstances in noncapital as well as capital trials, while at the same time insisting that such circumstances be shown in order to establish a denial of due process. The right to appointed counsel had been recognized as being considerably broader in federal prosecutions, see *Johnson* v. *Zerbst,* . . . but to have imposed these requirements on the States would indeed have been "an abrupt break" with the almost immediate past. The declaration that the right to appointed counsel in state prosecutions, as established in *Powell* v. *Alabama,* was not limited to capital cases was in truth not a departure from, but an extension of, existing precedent.

The principles declared in *Powell* and in *Betts,* however, have had a troubled journey throughout the years that have followed first the one case and then the other. . . .

In noncapital cases, the "special circumstances" rule has continued to exist in form while its substance has been substantially and steadily eroded. In the first decade after *Betts,* there were cases in which the Court found special circumstances to be lacking, but usually by a sharply divided vote. However, no such decision has been cited to us, and I have found none, after *Quicksall* v. *Michigan,* . . . decided in 1950. At the same time, there have been not a few cases in which special circumstances were found in little or nothing more than the "complexity" of the legal questions presented, although those questions were often of only routine difficulty. The Court has come to recognize, in other words, that the mere existence of a serious criminal charge constituted in itself special circumstances requiring the services of counsel at trial. In truth the *Betts* v. *Brady* rule is no longer a reality.

This evolution, however, appears not to have been fully recognized by many state courts, in this instance charged with the front-line responsibility for the enforcement of constitutional rights. To continue a rule which is honored by this Court only with lip service is not a healthy thing and in the long run will do disservice to the federal system. . . .

In agreeing with the Court that the right to counsel in a case such as this should now be expressly recognized as a fundamental right embraced in the Fourteenth Amendment, I wish to make a further observation. When we hold a right or immunity, valid against the Federal Government, to be "implicit in the concept of ordered liberty" and thus valid against the States, I do not read our past decisions to suggest that by so holding, we automatically carry over an entire body of federal law and apply it in full sweep to the States. Any such concept would disregard the frequently wide disparity between the legitimate interests of the States and of the Federal Government, the divergent problems that they face, and the significantly different consequences of their actions. . . . In what is done today I do not understand the Court to depart from the principles laid down in *Palko* v. *Connecticut*, . . . or to embrace the concept that the Fourteenth Amendment "incorporates" the Sixth Amendment as such.

On these premises I join in the judgment of the Court.

He doesn't believe in incorporation.

Miranda v. Arizona
384 U.S. 436, 86 S.Ct. 1602, 16 L.Ed. 2d 694 (1966)

In reviewing four state criminal convictions in 1966 (in three the convictions had been upheld; in one, reversed) the Supreme Court, as on earlier occasions, was presented in each case with the question of whether a defendant's confession made in police custody was admissible under constitutional requirements. In each of these cases defendant had not been advised of his right to remain silent and to consult counsel. Although the interrogations took place for varying periods in the cases, in none was there an allegation of violence or threat of violence. In the 1964 case of *Escobedo* v. *Illinois* (378 U.S. 478) the Court had reversed where the defendant was interrogated without being advised of his right to remain silent and to consult with counsel, but in addition his request to consult counsel was denied.

MR. CHIEF JUSTICE WARREN delivered the opinion of the Court.

. . . We start here, as we did in Escobedo, with the premise that our holding is not an innovation in our jurisprudence, but is an application of principles long recognized and applied in other settings. We have undertaken a thorough reexamination of the Escobedo decision and the principles it announced, and we reaffirm it. That case was but an explication of basic rights that are enshrined in our Constitution—that "No person . . . shall be compelled in any criminal case to be a witness against himself," and that "the accused shall . . . have the Assistance of Counsel"—rights which were put in jeopardy in that case through official overbearing. These precious rights were fixed in our Constitution only after centuries of persecution and struggle. And in the words of Chief Justice Marshall, they were secured "for ages to come and . . . designed to approach immortal-

ity as nearly as human institutions can approach it." . . .

Our holding . . . briefly stated . . . is this: the prosecution may not use statements, whether exculpatory or inculpatory, stemming from custodial interrogation of the defendant unless it demonstrates the use of procedural safeguards effective to secure the privilege against self-incrimination. By custodial interrogation, we mean questioning initiated by law enforcement officers after a person has been taken into custody or otherwise deprived of his freedom of action in any significant way. As for the procedural safeguards to be employed, unless other fully effective means are devised to inform accused persons of their right of silence and to assure a continuous opportunity to exercise it, the following measures are required. Prior to any questioning, the person must be warned that he has a right to remain silent, that any statement he does make may be used as

witness against self,
assistance of counsel

rt. to remain silent . . . etc

evidence against him, and that he has a right to the presence of an attorney, either retained or appointed. The defendant may waive effectuation of these rights, provided the waiver is made voluntarily, knowingly and intelligently. If, however, he indicates in any manner and at any stage of the process that he wishes to consult with an attorney before speaking there can be no questioning. Likewise, if the individual is alone and indicates in any manner that he does not wish to be interrogated, the police may not question him. The mere fact that he may have answered some questions or volunteered some statements on his own does not deprive him of the right to refrain from answering any further inquiries until he has consulted with an attorney and thereafter consents to be questioned.

The constitutional issue we decide in each of these cases is the admissibility of statements obtained from a defendant questioned while in custody and deprived of his freedom of action. In each, the defendant was questioned by police officers, detectives, or a prosecuting attorney in a room in which he was cut off from the outside world. In none of these cases was the defendant given a full and effective warning of his rights at the outset of the interrogation process. In all the cases, the questioning elicited oral admissions, and in three of them, signed statements as well which were admitted at their trials. They all thus share salient features—incommunicado interrogation of individuals in a police-dominated atmosphere, resulting in self-incriminating statements without full warnings of constitutional rights.

An understanding of the nature and setting of this in-custody interrogation is essential to our decisions today. The difficulty in depicting what transpires at such interrogations stems from the fact that in this country they have largely taken place incommunicado. From extensive factual studies undertaken in the early 1930s, including the famous Wickersham Report to Congress by a Presidential Commission, it is clear that police violence and the "third degree" flourished at that time. In a series of cases decided by this Court long after

these studies, the police resorted to physical brutality—beatings, hanging, whipping—and to sustained and protracted questioning incommunicado in order to extort confessions. The 1961 Commission on Civil Rights found much evidence to indicate that "some policemen still resort to physical force to obtain confessions." . . . The use of physical brutality and violence is not, unfortunately, relegated to the past or to any part of the country.

Again we stress that the modern practice of in-custody interrogation is psychologically rather than physically oriented. As we have stated before, "Since *Chambers* v. *Florida,* . . . this Court has recognized that coercion can be mental as well as physical, and that the blood of the accused is not the only hallmark of an unconstitutional inquisition." *Blackburn* v. *Alabama,* 361 U.S. 199, . . . Interrogation still takes place in privacy. Privacy results in secrecy and this in turn results in a gap in our knowledge as to what in fact goes on in the interrogation rooms. A valuable source of information about present police practices, however, may be found in various police manuals and texts which document procedures employed with success in the past, and which recommend various other effective tactics. [The opinion surveys manuals and texts.]

From these representative samples of interrogation techniques, the setting prescribed by the manuals and observed in practice becomes clear. In essence, it is this: To be alone with the subject is essential to prevent distraction and to deprive him of any outside support. The aura of confidence in his guilt undermines his will to resist. He merely confirms the preconceived story the police seek to have him describe. Patience and persistence, at times relentless questioning, are employed. To obtain a confession, the interrogator must "patiently maneuver himself or his quarry into a position from which the desired object may be obtained." When normal procedures fail to produce the needed result, the police may resort to deceptive stratagems such as giving false legal advice. It is important to keep the subject off balance, for example, by trading on his insecurity about himself or his surroundings. The police then persuade, trick, or cajole him out of exercising his constitutional rights.

Even without employing brutality, the "third degree" or the specific stratagems described above, the very fact of custodial interrogation exacts a heavy toll on individual liberty and trades on the weakness of individuals.

In these cases, we might not find the defendants' statements to have been involuntary in traditional terms. Our concern for adequate safeguards to protect precious Fifth Amendment rights is, of course, not lessened in the slightest. To be sure, the records do not evince overt physical coercion or patented psychological ploys. The fact remains that in none of these cases did the officers undertake to afford appropriate safeguards at the outset of the interrogation to insure that the statements were truly the product of free choice.

It is obvious that such an interrogation environment is created for no purpose other than to subjugate the individual to the will of his examiner. This atmosphere carries its own badge of intimidation. To be sure, this is not physical intimidation, but it is equally destructive of human dignity. The current practice of incommunicado interrogation is at odds with one of our Nation's most cherished principles—that the individual may not be compelled to incriminate himself. Unless adequate protective devices are employed to dispel the compulsion inherent in custodial surroundings, no statement obtained from the defendant can truly be the product of his free choice. . . .

Today . . . there can be no doubt that the Fifth Amendment privilege is available outside of criminal court proceedings and serves to protect persons in all settings in which their freedom of action is curtailed from being compelled to incriminate themselves. We have concluded that without proper safeguards the process of in-custody interrogation of persons suspected or accused of crime contains inherently compelling pressures which work to undermine the individual's will to resist and to compel him to speak where he would not otherwise do so freely. In order to combat these pressures and to permit a full opportunity to exercise the privilege against self-incrimination, the accused must be adequately and effectively apprised of his rights and the exercise of those rights must be fully honored. . . .

The circumstances surrounding in-custody interrogation can operate very quickly to overbear the will of one merely made aware of his privilege by his interrogators. Therefore, the right to have counsel present at the interrogation is indispensable to the protection of the Fifth Amendment privilege under the system we delineate today. Our aim is to assure that the individual's right to choose between silence and speech remains unfettered throughout the interrogation process. . . .

Our decision is not intended to hamper the traditional function of police officers in investigating crime. See *Escobedo* v. *Illinois*, . . . When an individual is in custody on probable cause, the police may, of course, seek out evidence in the field to be used at trial against him. Such investigation may include inquiry of persons not under restraint. General on-the-scene questioning as to facts surrounding a crime or other general questioning of citizens in the fact-finding process is not affected by our holding. It is an act of responsible citizenship for individuals to give whatever information they may have to aid in law enforcement. In such situations the compelling atmosphere inherent in the process of in-custody interrogation is not necessarily present.

In dealing with statements obtained through interrogation, we do not purport to find all confessions inadmissible. Confessions remain a proper element in law enforcement. Any statement given freely and voluntarily without any compelling influences is, of course, admissible in evidence. The fundamental import of the privilege while an individual is in custody is not whether he is allowed to talk to the police without the benefit of warnings and counsel, but whether he can be interrogated. There is no requirement that police stop a person who enters a police station and states that he wishes to confess to a crime, or a person who calls the police to offer a confession or any other statement he desires to make. Volunteered statements of any kind are not barred by the Fifth Amendment and their admissibility is not affected by our holding today. . . .

In announcing these principles, we are not unmindful of the burdens which law enforcement officials must bear, often under trying circumstances. We also fully recognize the obligation of all citizens to aid in enforcing the criminal laws. This court, while protecting individual rights, has always given ample latitude to law enforcement agencies in the legitimate exercise of their duties. The limits we have placed on the interrogation process should not constitute an undue interference with a proper system of law enforcement. As we have noted, our decision does not in any way preclude police from carrying out their traditional investigatory functions. . . .

MR. JUSTICE HARLAN, whom MR. JUSTICE STEWART and MR. JUSTICE WHITE join, dissenting.

I believe the decision of the Court represents poor constitutional law and entails harmful consequences for the country at large. How serious these consequences may prove to be only time can tell. . . . The new rules are not designed to guard against police brutality or other unmistakably banned forms of coercion. Those who use third-degree tactics and deny them in court are equally able and destined to lie as skillfully about warnings and waivers. Rather, the thrust of the new rules is to negate all pressures, to reinforce the nervous or ignorant suspect, and ultimately to discourage any confession at all. The aim in short is toward ''voluntariness'' in a utopian sense, or to view it from a different angle, voluntariness with a vengeance.

To incorporate this notion into the Constitution requires a strained reading of history and precedent and a disregard of the very pragmatic concerns that alone may on occasion justify such strains. I believe that reasoned examination will show that the Due Process Clause provides an adequate tool for coping with confessions and that, even if the Fifth Amendment privilege against self-incrimination be invoked, its

precedents taken as a whole do not sustain the present rules. Viewed as a choice based on pure policy, these new rules prove to be a highly debatable if not one-sided appraisal of the competing interests, imposed over widespread objection, at the very time when judicial restraint is most called for by the circumstances.

. . . The Court's opinion in my view reveals no adequate basis for extending the Fifth Amendment's privilege against self-incrimination to the police station. Far more important, it fails to show that the Court's new rules are well supported, let alone compelled, by Fifth Amendment precedents. Instead, the new rules actually derive from quotation and analogy drawn from precedents under the Sixth Amendment, which should properly have no bearing on police interrogation. . . .

The more important premise is that pressure on the suspect must be eliminated though it be only the subtle influence of the atmosphere and surroundings. The Fifth Amendment, however, has never been thought to forbid *all* pressure to incriminate oneself in the situations covered by it. . . . However, the Court's unspoken assumption that *any* pressure violates the privilege is not supported by the precedents and it has failed to show why the Fifth Amendment prohibits that relatively mild pressure the Due Process Clause permits. . . .

Examined as an expression of public policy, the Court's new regime proves so dubious that there can be no due compensation for its weakness in constitutional law. Foregoing discussion has shown, I think, how mistaken is the Court in implying that the Constitution has struck the balance in favor of the approach the Court takes. Rather, precedent reveals that the Fourteenth Amendment in practice has been construed to strike a different balance, that the Fifth Amendment gives the Court little solid support in this context, and that the Sixth Amendment should have no bearing at all. Legal history has been stretched before to satisfy deep needs of society. In this instance, however, the Court has not and cannot make the powerful showing that its new rules are plainly desirable in the context of our society, something which is surely demanded before those rules are engrafted onto the Constitution and imposed on every State and county in the land.

Without at all subscribing to the generally black picture of police conduct painted by the Court, I think it must be frankly recognized at the outset that police questioning allowable under due process precedents may inherently entail some pressure on the suspect and may seek advantage in his ignorance or weaknesses. The atmosphere and questioning techniques, proper and fair though they be, can in themselves exert a tug on the suspect to confess and in this light "[t]o speak of any confessions of crime made after arrest as being 'voluntary' or 'uncoerced' is somewhat inaccurate, although traditional. A confession is wholly and incontestably voluntary only if a guilty person gives himself up to the law and becomes his own accuser." *Ashcraft* v. *Tennessee,* 332 U.S. 143, . . . (Jackson, J., dissenting). Until today, the role of the constitution has been only to sift out *undue* pressure, not to assure spontaneous confessions.

The Court's new rules aim to offset these minor pressures and disadvantages intrinsic to any kind of police interrogation. The rules do not serve due process interests in preventing blatant coercion since, as I noted earlier, they do nothing to contain the policeman who is prepared to lie from the start. The rules work for reliability in confessions almost only in the Pickwickian sense that they can prevent some from being given at all.

It is no secret that concern has been expressed lest long-range and lasting reforms be frustrated by this Court's too-rapid departure from existing constitutional standards. Despite the Court's disclaimer, the practical effect of the decision made today must inevitably be to handicap seriously sound efforts at reform, not least by removing options necessary to a just compromise of competing interests. Of course, legislative reform is rarely speedy or unanimous, though this Court has been more patient in the past. But the legislative reforms when they come would have the vast advantage of empirical data and comprehensive study, they would allow experimentation and use of solutions not open to the courts, and they would restore initiative in criminal law reform to those forums where it truly belongs.

[The dissenting opinions of MR. JUSTICE CLARK and MR. JUSTICE WHITE are omitted.]

Rhode Island v. Innis
446 U.S. 291, 100 S.Ct. 1682, 64 L.Ed. 2d 297 (1980)

In January, 1975, a taxicab driver in Providence, Rhode Island, was killed by a shotgun blast aimed at the back of his head. Five days later, another Providence cab driver reported to police that he had just been robbed by a man wielding a sawed-off shotgun. This second driver identified a photograph of Innis as his assailant. In a matter of hours a patrolman spotted Innis, who was unarmed, arrested him, and advised him of his *Miranda* rights. A police sergeant arrived at the scene shortly, and he too read Innis the *Miranda* warnings. A police captain and other officers next appeared, and the captain also advised Innis of his rights under *Miranda*. Innis replied that he understood the rights and wanted to speak to a lawyer. Innis was placed in a police cruiser with three officers for the ride to the police station. The captain had instructed them not to question or intimidate Innis in any way. Driving to the station house, one policeman said to another, "I frequent this area while on patrol'' and (because there is a school for handicapped children nearby) ''there's a lot of handicapped children running around in this area, and God forbid one of them might find a weapon with shells and they might hurt themselves.'' (The police had yet to find the murder weapon.) Another officer responded that ''it would be too bad if the little—I believe he said girl—would pick up the gun, maybe kill herself.'' Innis interrupted the conversation at this point, telling the officers they should turn the car around so that he could show them the location of the gun. Advised of this development by radio, the captain met the car at the scene of the arrest and again advised Innis of his *Miranda* rights. Innis said that he understood his rights but wanted to get the gun out of the way because of the kids in the area of the school. Innis then led police to a spot by the side of the road where he pointed out the shotgun. At trial, the defendant moved to suppress the shotgun and the statements he had made to police about it. The trial court admitted the evidence, and a jury found him guilty. On appeal, the state supreme court set the conviction aside because police had interrogated him without the presence of counsel. The state court relied on *Brewer* v. *Williams* (430 U.S. 436: 1977), where the Supreme Court ruled out similar evidence but in a situation where the suspect had already been arraigned and counsel appointed. The Supreme Court granted Rhode Island's petition for certiorari to address the meaning of ''interrogation'' under *Miranda*.

MR. JUSTICE STEWART delivered the opinion of the Court. . . .

It is clear . . . that the special procedural safeguards outlined in *Miranda* are required not where a suspect is simply taken into custody, but rather where a suspect in custody is subjected to interrogation. ''Interrogation,'' as conceptualized in the *Miranda* opinion, must reflect a measure of compulsion above and beyond that inherent in custody itself.

We conclude that the *Miranda* safeguards come into play whenever a person in custody is subjected to either express questioning or its functional equivalent. That is to say, the term ''interrogation'' under *Miranda* refers not only to express questioning, but also to any words or actions on the part of the police (other than those normally attendant to arrest and custody) that the police should know are reasonably likely to elicit an incriminating response from the suspect. The latter portion of this definition focuses primarily upon the perceptions of the suspect, rather than the intent of the police. This focus reflects the fact that the *Miranda* safeguards were designed to vest a suspect in custody with an added measure of protection against coercive police practices, without regard to objective proof of the underlying intent of the police. A practice that the police should know is reasonably likely to evoke an incriminating response from a suspect thus amounts to interrogation. But, since the police surely cannot be held accountable for the unforeseeable results of their words or actions, the definition of interrogation can extend only to words or actions on the part of police officers that they *should have known* were reasonably likely to elicit an incriminating response.

Turning to the facts of the present case, we conclude that the respondent was not ''interrogated'' within the meaning of *Miranda*. It is undisputed that the first prong of the definition of ''interrogation'' was not satisfied, for the conversation between Patrolmen Gleckman and McKenna included no express questioning of the respondent. Rather, that conversation was, at least in form, nothing more than a dialogue between the two officers to which no response from the respondent was invited.

Moreover, it cannot be fairly concluded that the respondent was subjected to the ''functional equivalent'' of questioning. It cannot be said, in short, that Patrolmen Gleckman and McKenna should have known that their conversation was reasonably likely to elicit an incriminating response from the respondent. There is nothing in the record to suggest that the officers were aware that the respondent was peculiarly susceptible to an appeal to his conscience concerning the safety of handicapped children. Nor is there anything in the record to suggest that the police knew that the respondent was unusually disoriented or upset at the time of his arrest.

The case thus boils down to whether, in the context of a brief conversation, the officers should have known that the respondent would suddenly be moved to make a self-incriminating response. Given the fact that the entire conversation appears to have consisted of no more than a few off-hand remarks, we cannot say that the officers should have known that it was reasonably likely that Innis would so respond. This is not a case where the police carried on a lengthy harangue in the presence of the suspect. Nor does the record support the respondent's contention that, under the circumstances, the officers' comments were particularly "evocative." It is our view, therefore, that the respondent was not subjected by the police to words or actions that the police should have known were reasonably likely to elicit an incriminating response from him.

The Rhode Island Supreme Court erred, in short, in equating "subtle compulsion" with interrogation. That the officers' comments struck a responsive chord is readily apparent. Thus, it may be said, as the Rhode Island Supreme Court did say, that the respondent was subjected to "subtle compulsion." But that is not the end of the inquiry. It must also be established that a suspect's incriminating response was the product of words or actions on the part of the police that they should have known were reasonably likely to elicit an incriminating response. This was not established in the present case.

For the reasons stated, the judgment of the Supreme Court of Rhode Island is vacated, and the case is remanded to that court for further proceedings not inconsistent with this opinion. *It is so ordered.*

MR. JUSTICE WHITE, concurring. . . .

MR. CHIEF JUSTICE BURGER, concurring in the judgment. . . .

The meaning of *Miranda* has become reasonably clear and law enforcement practices have adjusted to its strictures; I would neither overrule *Miranda,* disparage it, nor extend it at this late date. I fear, however, that the . . . Court's opinion will not clarify the tension between this holding and *Brewer* v. *Williams,* . . . and our other cases. It may introduce new elements of uncertainty; under the Court's test, a police officer in the brief time available, apparently must evaluate the suggestibility and susceptibility of an accused. . . . Few, if any, police officers are competent to make the kind of evaluation seemingly contemplated; even a psychiatrist asked to express an expert opinion on these aspects of a suspect in custody would very likely employ extensive questioning and observation to make the judgment now charged to police officers.

Trial judges have enough difficulty discerning the boundaries and nuances flowing from post-*Miranda* opinions, and we do not clarify that situation today.

MR. JUSTICE MARSHALL, with whom MR. JUSTICE BRENNAN joins, dissenting.

I am substantially in agreement with the Court's definition of "interrogation" within the meaning of *Miranda* v. *Arizona.* . . . In my view, the *Miranda* safeguards apply whenever police conduct is intended or likely to produce a response from a suspect in custody. As I read the Court's opinion, its definition of "interrogation" for *Miranda* purposes is equivalent, for practical purposes, to my formulation, since it contemplates that "where a police practice is designed to elicit an incriminating response from the accused, it is unlikely that the practice will not also be one which the police should have known was reasonably likely to have that effect." . . . Thus, the Court requires an objective inquiry into the likely effect of police conduct on a typical individual, taking into account any special susceptibility of the suspect to certain kinds of pressure of which the police know or have reason to know.

I am utterly at a loss, however, to understand how this objective standard as applied to the facts before us can rationally lead to the conclusion that there was no interrogation. Innis was arrested at 4:30 a.m., handcuffed, searched, advised of his rights, and placed in the back seat of a patrol car. Within a short time he had been twice more advised of his rights and driven away in a four door sedan with three police officers. Two officers sat in the front seat and one sat beside Innis in the back seat. Since the car traveled no more than a mile before Innis agreed to point out the location of the murder weapon, Officer Gleckman must have begun almost immediately to talk about the search for the shotgun.

The Court attempts to characterize Gleckman's statements as "no more than a few off-hand remarks" which could not reasonably have been expected to elicit a response. . . . If the statements had been addressed to petitioner, it would be impossible to draw such a conclusion. The simple message of the "talking back and forth" between Gleckman and McKenna was that they had to find the shotgun to avert a child's death.

One can scarcely imagine a stronger appeal to the conscience of a suspect—*any* suspect—than the assertion that if the weapon is not found an innocent person will be hurt or killed. And not just any innocent person, but an innocent child—a little girl—a helpless, handicapped little girl on her way to school. The notion that such

an appeal could not be expected to have any effect unless the suspect were known to have some special interest in handicapped children verges on the ludicrous. As a matter of fact, the appeal to a suspect to confess for the sake of others, to "display some evidence of decency and honor," is a classic interrogation technique. . . .

Gleckman's remarks would obviously have constituted interrogation if they had been explicitly directed to petitioner, and the result should not be different because they were nominally addressed to McKenna. This is not a case where police officers speaking among themselves are accidentally overheard by a suspect.

MR. JUSTICE STEVENS, dissenting. . . .

. . . [T]he Court's test creates an incentive for police to ignore a suspect's invocation of his rights in order to make continued attempts to extract information from him. If a suspect does not appear to be susceptible to a particular type of psychological pressure, the police are apparently free to exert that pressure on him despite his request for counsel, so long as they are careful not to punctuate their statements with question marks. And if, contrary to all reasonable expectations, the suspect makes an incriminating statement, that statement can be used against him at trial. The Court thus turns *Miranda*'s unequivocal rule against any interrogation at all into a trap in which unwary suspects may be caught by police deception. . . .

V. Capital Punishment

Gregg v. Georgia
428 U.S. 153, 96 S.Ct. 2909, 49 L.Ed. 2d 859 (1976)

Furman v. *Georgia* (408 U.S. 238: 1972) held that, under Georgia's statutes, capital punishment constituted "cruel and unusual punishment," because juries had untrammeled discretion to impose or withhold the penalty. Georgia's amended statutory scheme, expressly drawn to meet the Court's objections, was sustained by the state court. On certiorari, the Supreme Court affirmed. Although unable to join in an opinion, seven members of the Court agreed that imposition of the death penalty for murder does not violate the Eighth and Fourteenth Amendments.

Justices Powell, Stewart, and Stevens announced the judgment of the Court in an opinion delivered by Justice Stewart. Chief Justice Burger and Justice Rehnquist, joining the opinion of Justice White, held that Georgia's system of capital punishment was consistent with the ruling in the Furman case. Justice Blackmun concurred in the judgment, referring to his dissenting opinion in the Furman case. Justices Brennan and Marshall dissented.

MR. JUSTICE STEWART:

. . . We address initially the basic contention that the punishment of death for the crime of murder is, under all circumstances, "cruel and unusual" in violation of the Eighth and Fourteenth Amendments of the Constitution. . . .

The Court on a number of occasions has both assumed and asserted the constitutionality of capital punishment. In several cases that assumption provided a necessary foundation for the decision, as the Court was asked to decide whether a particular method of carrying out a capital sentence would be allowed to stand under the Eighth Amendment. But until *Furman* v. *Georgia,* 408 U.S. 238 (1972), the Court never confronted squarely the fundamental claim that the punishment of death always, regardless of the enormity of the offense or the procedure followed in imposing the sentence, is cruel and unusual punishment in violation of the Constitution. . . .

Although this issue was presented and addressed in *Furman,* it was not resolved by the Court. Four Justices would have held that capital punishment is not unconstitutional per se; two Justices would have reached the opposite conclusion; and three Justices, while agreeing that the statutes then before the Court were invalid as applied, left open the question whether such punishment may ever be imposed. We now hold that the punishment of death does not invariably violate the Constitution. . . .

It is from the foregoing precedents that the Eighth Amendment has not been regarded as a static concept. As Chief Justice Warren said, in an oft-quoted phrase, "[the] amendment must draw its meaning from the evolving standards of decency that mark the progress of a maturing society." . . . Thus, an assessment of contemporary values concerning the infliction of a challenged sanction is relevant to the application of the Eighth Amendment. As we develop below more fully, this assessment does not call for a subjective judgment. It requires, rather, that we look to objective indicia that reflect the public attitude toward a given sanction. . . .

But our cases also make clear that public perceptions of standards of decency with respect to criminal sanctions are not conclusive. A penalty also must accord with "the dignity of man," which is the "basic concept underlying the Eighth Amendment." . . . This means, at least, that the punishment not be "excessive." When a form of punishment in the abstract (in this case, whether capital punishment may ever be imposed as a sanction for murder) rather than in the particular (the propriety of death as a penalty to be applied to a specific defendant for a specific crime) is under consideration, the inquiry into "excessiveness" has two aspects. First, the punishment must not involve the unnecessary and wanton infliction of pain. Second, the punishment must not be grossly out of proportion to the severity of the crime....

Of course, the requirements of the Eighth Amendment must be applied with an awareness of the limited role to be played by the courts. This does not mean that judges have no role to play, for the Eighth Amendment is a restraint upon the exercise of legislative power....

But, while we have an obligation to insure that constitutional bounds are not overreached, we may not act as judges as we might as legislators....

Therefore, in assessing a punishment by a democratically elected legislature against the constitutional measure, we presume its validity. We may not require the legislature to select the least severe penalty possible so long as the penalty selected is not cruelly inhumane or disproportionate to the crime involved. And a heavy burden rests on those who would attack the judgment of the representatives of the people.

This is true in part because the constitutional test is intertwined with an assessment of contemporary standards and the legislative judgment weighs heavily in ascertaining such standards....

The petitioners in the capital cases before the Court today renew the "standards of decency" argument, but developments during the four years since *Furman* have undercut substantially the assumptions upon which their argument rested. Despite the continuing debate, dating back to the 19th century, over the morality and utility of capital punishment, it is now evident that a large proportion of American society continues to regard it as an appropriate and necessary sanction.

The most marked indication of society's endorsement of the death penalty for murder is the legislative response to *Furman*. The legislatures of at least 35 states have enacted new statutes that provide for the death penalty for at least some crimes that result in the death of another person. And the Congress of the United States, in 1974, enacted a statute providing the death penalty for aircraft piracy that results in death....

As we have seen, however, the Eighth Amendment demands more than that a challenged punishment be acceptable to contemporary society. The Court also must ask whether it comports with the basic concept of human dignity at the core of the amendment. Although we cannot "invalidate a category of penalties because we deem less severe penalties adequate to serve the ends of penology," the sanction imposed cannot be so totally without penological justification that it results in the gratuitous infliction of suffering....

The death penalty is said to serve two principal social purposes: retribution and deterrence of capital crimes by prospective offenders.

In part, capital punishment is an expression of society's moral outrage at particularly offensive conduct. This function may be unappealing to many, but it is essential in an ordered society that asks its citizens to rely on legal processes rather than self-help to vindicate their wrongs....

Statistical attempts to evaluate the worth of the death penalty as a deterrent to crimes by potential offenders have occasioned a great deal of debate. The results simply have been inconclusive....

The deference we owe to the decisions of the state legislatures under our Federal system ... is enhanced where the specification of punishments is concerned, for "these are peculiarly questions of legislative policy." A decision that a given punishment is impermissible under the Eighth Amendment cannot be reversed short of a constitutional amendment. The ability of the people to express their preference through the normal democratic processes, as well as through ballot referenda, is shut off. Revisions cannot be made in the light of further experience. . . . We now consider specifically whether the sentence of death for the crime of murder is a per se violation of the Eighth and Fourteenth Amendments to the Constitution. . . . We note first that history and precedent strongly support a negative answer to this question.

The imposition of the death penalty for the crime of murder has a long history of acceptance both in the United States and in England. The common-law rule imposed a mandatory death sentence on all convicted murderers. . . . And the penalty continued to be used into the 20th century by most American states, although the breadth of the common-law rule was diminished, initially by narrowing the class of murders to be punished by death and subsequently by widespread adoption of laws expressly granting judges the discretion to recommend mercy. . . .

It is apparent from the text of the Constitution itself that the existence of capital punishment was accepted by the framers. At the time the Eighth Amendment was ratified, capital punishment was a common sanction in every state. Indeed, the first Congress of the United States enacted legislation providing death as the penalty for specified crimes. . . .

For nearly two centuries, this Court, repeatedly and often expressly, has recognized that capital punishment is not invalid per se. . . .

Four years ago, the petitioners in *Furman* and its companion cases predicated their argument primarily upon the asserted proposition that standards of decency had evolved to the point where capital punishment no longer could be tolerated. The petitioners in those cases said, in effect, that the evolutionary process had come to an end, and that standards of decency required that the Eighth Amendment be construed finally as prohibiting capital punishment for any crime regardless of its depravity and impact on society. . . .

Although some of the studies suggest that the death penalty may not function as a significantly greater deterrent than lesser penalties, there is no convincing empirical evidence either supporting or refuting this view.

We may nevertheless assume safely that there are murderers, such as those who act in passion, for whom the threat of death has little or no deterrent effect. But for many others, the death penalty undoubtedly is a significant deterrent. There are carefully contemplated murders, such as murder for hire, where the possible penalty of death may well enter into the cold calculus that precedes the decision to act. And there are some categories of murder, such as murder by a life prisoner, where other sanctions may not be adequate. . . .

In sum, we cannot say that the judgment of the Georgia Legislature that capital punishment may be necessary in some cases is clearly wrong. Considerations of federalism, as well as respect for the ability of a legislature to evaluate, in terms of its particular state the moral consensus concerning the death penalty and its social utility as a sanction, require us to conclude, in the absence of more convincing evidence, that the infliction of death as a punishment for murder is not without justification and thus is not unconstitutionally severe.

Finally, we must consider whether the punishment of death is disproportionate in relation to the crime for which it is imposed. There is no question that death as a punishment is unique in its severity and irrevocability. . . . When a defendant's life is at stake, the Court has been particularly sensitive to insure that every safeguard is observed. . . .

But we are concerned here only with the imposition of capital punishment for the crime of murder, and when a life has been taken deliberately by the offender, we cannot say that the punishment is invariably disproportionate to the crime. It is an extreme sanction, suitable to the most extreme of crimes.

We hold that the death penalty is not a form of punishment that may never be imposed, regardless of the circumstances of the offense, regardless of the character of the offender, and regardless of the procedure followed in reaching the decision to impose it.

We now consider whether Georgia may impose the death penalty on the petitioner in this case. . . .

The basic concern of *Furman* centered on those defendants who were being condemned to death capriciously and arbitrarily. Under the procedures before the Court in that case, sentencing authorities were not directed to give attention to the nature or circumstances of the crime committed or to the character or record of the defendant. Left unguided, juries imposed the death sentence in a way that could only be called freakish. The new Georgia sentencing procedures, by contrast, focus the jury's attention on the particularized nature of the crime and the particularized characteristics of the individual defendant. While the jury is permitted to consider any aggravating or mitigating circumstances, it must find and identify at least one statutory aggravating factor before it may impose a penalty of death. In this way the jury's discretion is channeled. No longer can a jury wantonly and freakishly impose the death sentence; it is always circumscribed by the legislative guidelines. In addition, the review function of the Supreme Court of Georgia affords additional assurance that the concerns that prompted our decision in *Furman* are not present to any significant degree in the Georgia procedure applied here.

For the reasons expressed in this opinion, we hold that the statutory system under which Gregg was sentenced to death does not violate the Constitution. Accordingly, the judgment of the Georgia Supreme Court is affirmed.

It is so ordered.

MR. JUSTICE BRENNAN, dissenting:

. . . This Court inescapably has the duty, as the ultimate arbiter of the meaning of our Constitution, to say whether, when individuals condemned to death stand before our bar, "moral concepts" require us to hold that the law has progressed to the point where we should declare that the punishment of death, like punishments on the rack, the screw and the wheel, is no longer morally tolerable in our civilized society. My opinion in *Furman* v. *Georgia* concluded that our civilization and the law had progressed to this point and therefore the punishment of death, for whatever crime and under all circumstances, is "cruel and unusual" in violation of the Eighth and Fourteenth Amendments of the Constitution. I shall not again canvass the reasons that led to that conclusion. I emphasize only that foremost among the "moral concepts" recognized in our cases and inherent in the clause is the primary moral principle that the state, even as it punishes, must treat its citizens in a manner consistent with their intrinsic worth as human beings—a punishment must not be so severe as to be degrading to human dignity. A judicial determination whether the punishment of death comports with human dignity is therefore not only permitted but compelled by the clause. . . .

Death is not only an unusually severe punishment, unusual in its pain, in its finality, and in its enormity, but it serves no penal purpose more effectively than a less severe punishment; therefore the principle inherent in the clause that prohibits pointless infliction of excessive punishment when less severe punishment can adequately achieve the same purposes invalidates the punishment. . . .

MR. JUSTICE MARSHALL, dissenting:

. . . My sole purposes here are to consider the suggestion that my conclusion in *Furman* has been undercut by developments since then, and briefly to evaluate the basis for my brethren's holding that the extinction of life is a permissible form of punishment under the cruel and unusual punishments clause.

In *Furman* I concluded that the death penalty is constitutionally invalid for two reasons. First, the death penalty is excessive. . . . And second, the American people, fully informed as to the purposes of the death penalty and its liabilities, would in my view reject it as morally unacceptable. . . .

Since the decision in *Furman,* the legislatures of 35 states have enacted new statutes authorizing the imposition of the death sentence for certain crimes, and Congress has enacted a law providing the death penalty for air piracy resulting in death. I would be less than candid if I did not acknowledge that these developments have a significant bearing on a realistic assessment of the moral acceptability of the death penalty to the American people. But if the constitutionality of the death penalty turns, as I have urged, on the opinion of an *informed* citizenry, then even the enactment of new death statutes cannot be viewed as conclusive. In *Furman,* I observed that the American people are largely unaware of the information critical to a judgment on the morality of the death penalty, and concluded that if they were better informed they would consider it shocking, unjust, and unacceptable. . . .

Even assuming, however, that the post-Furman enactment of statutes authorizing the death penalty renders the prediction of the views of an informed citizenry an uncertain basis for a constitutional decision, the enactment of those statutes has no bearing whatsoever on the conclusion that the death penalty is unconstitutional because it is excessive. An excessive penalty is invalid under the cruel and unusual punishments clause ''even though popular sentiment may favor'' it. The inquiry here, then, is simply whether the death penalty is necessary to accomplish the legitimate legislative purposes in punishment, or whether a less severe penalty such as life imprisonment would do as well. . . .

The two purposes that sustain the death penalty as nonexcessive in the court's view are general deterrence and retribution. . . .

The other principal purpose said to be served by the death penalty is retribution. The notion that retribution can serve as a moral justification for the sanction of death finds credence in the opinion of my brothers Stewart, Powell, and Stevens, and that of my brother White in *Roberts* v. *Louisiana.* It is this notion that I find to be the most disturbing aspect of today's unfortunate decision. . . .

The foregoing contentions that society's expression of moral outrage through the imposition of the death penalty preempts the citizenry from taking the law into its own hands and reinforces moral values—are not retributive in the purest sense. They are essentially utilitarian in that they portray the death penalty as valuable because of its beneficial results. These justifications for the death penalty are inadequate because the penalty is, quite clearly I think, not necessary to the accomplishment of those results.

There remains for consideration, however, what might be termed the purely retributive justification for the death penalty—that the death penalty is appropriate, not because of its beneficial effect on society, but because the taking of the murderer's life is itself morally good. Some of the language of the plurality's opinion appears positively to embrace this notion of retribution for its own sake as a justification for capital punishment. . . .

The mere fact that the community demands the murderer's life in return for the evil he has done cannot sustain the death penalty, for as the plurality reminds us, ''the Eighth Amendment demands more than that the challenged punishment be acceptable to contemporary society.'' . . . To be sustained under the Eighth Amendment, the death penalty must [''comport] with the basic concept of human dignity at the core of the amendment''; the objective in imposing it must be [''consistent] with our respect for the dignity of other men.'' Under these standards, the taking of life ''because the wrongdoer deserves it'' surely must fall, for such a punishment has as its very basis the total denial of the wrongdoer's dignity and worth.

The death penalty, unnecessary to promote the goal of deterrence or to further any legitimate notion of retribution, is an excessive penalty forbidden by the Eighth and Fourteenth Amendments. I respectfully dissent from the Court's judgment upholding the sentences of death imposed upon the petitioners in these cases.

TEN

First Amendment Freedoms and Privacy

The makers of our Constitution . . . conferred,
as against the government, the right to be
let alone—the most comprehensive of rights
and the right most valued by civilized men.

JUSTICE BRANDEIS, dissenting in
Olmstead v. *United States*

THE BILL OF RIGHTS

As the Constitution came from the hands of the Framers, the powers of the national government were enumerated but not defined. Without specification or definition, other powers were reserved to the states or to the people. The Constitution was drafted, submitted to state conventions, and ratified without a bill of rights. While the states pondered ratification, Jefferson urged specific restraints on national authority. Arguing that "a bill of rights is what the people are entitled to against every government on earth," he insisted that natural rights "should not be refused or rest on inference."

Alexander Hamilton and James Wilson demurred. Both contended that a bill of rights was unnecessary. Why make exceptions to power not granted? "In a government of enumerated powers," Wilson declared, "such a measure would not only be unnecessary, but preposterous and dangerous." For Hamilton, bills of rights "would sound much better in a treatise on ethics than in a constitution of government."

Thanks to Jefferson, these arguments did not prevail. Insisting on curbs over and beyond structural checks, he advocated "binding up the several branches of the government by certain laws, which when they transgress their acts become nullities." This would "render unnecessary an appeal to the people, or in other words a rebellion on every infraction of their rights." When a reluctant James Madison yielded to Jefferson's plea for a bill of rights and deduced supporting reasons, Jefferson singled out the argument of "great weight" for him—the legal check it puts in the hands of the judiciary. In presenting bill-of-rights amendments to the first Congress, Madison made Jefferson's argument his own. Thanks to the Bill of Rights, "independent tribunals of justice" would be "an impenetrable bulwark against every assumption of power in the legislative or executive." The Jefferson-Madison correspondence (1787–88) is excerpted before the cases in this chapter.

Fundamental rights gain no greater moral sanctity by being written into the Constitution, but individuals could thereafter look to courts for their protection. Rights formerly natural became civil.

THE NATIONALIZATION OF THE FIRST AMENDMENT

One of the most spectacular developments in American constitutional law has been the Supreme Court's expansion of the due process clause in the Fourteenth Amendment to include the Bill-of-Rights guarantees. Excepting the powerful dissenting opinion in the Slaughterhouse cases and in *Hurtado,* there was, at the outset, little hint of this evolution. The majority narrowed the scope of the privileges and immunities clause and, in passing, ridiculed the argument that due process meant more than "due procedure." *Davidson* v. *New Orleans* (96 U.S. 97: 1878), for example, held that a state is only required to grant an "appropriate hearing." Justice Bradley's concurrence proved prophetic. Due process, he said, was a standard by which the Court should examine the "reasonableness" of state legislation.

The Justices were not yet willing to become censors of state legislation. In *Hurtado* v. *California* they denied that anything in the due process clause prevented a state from substituting information (affidavit by the prosecutor) for grand jury indictment. Speaking for the Court, Justice Matthews argued that, since the Fifth Amendment contained a due process clause as one of many safeguards in the Bill of Rights, the same provision in the Fourteenth Amendment could not logically be held to include its other specific guaranties. Due process, he said, was the "law of the land in each state, exerted within the limits of those fundamental principles of liberty and justice which lie at the base of our civil and political institutions." Accordingly, these rights were best protected by the ballot box and the state legislatures. Justice Matthews' vague and sweeping "natural law" language provided a crude basis of review for later judges less hesitant to reverse the legislative judgment.

Justice Moody (*Twining* v. *New Jersey,* 211 U.S. 78: 1908) indicated a new trend: "It is possible that some of the personal rights safeguarded by the first eight amendments against national action may also be safeguarded against state action because a denial of them would be a denial of due process of law." Though Moody struggled to define such rights by references to "fundamental principles," "arbitrary action," "inalienable rights of mankind," and "immutable principles of justice," the precise meaning of "due process" eluded him. Justice Harlan dissented, as he had throughout this period, insisting that the Fourteenth Amendment incorporates the entire Bill of Rights.

From 1892 on, the Supreme Court displayed remarkable willingness to employ due process as a protective device against state action affecting property rights. "Liberty" became a highly meaningful concept as applied to the rights of an employer and employee to enter into contracts free from state interference (*Lochner* v. *New York*). At the same time, the Justices refused to expand the meaning of the due process clause where personal freedoms were at stake. Noting an apparent inconsistency, Professor Frankfurter tried to explain it.

That a majority of the Supreme Court which frequently disallowed restraint on economic powers should so consistently have sanctioned restraints of the mind is perhaps only a surface paradox. There is an underlying unity between fear of ample experimentation in economics and fear of the expression of ideas. (*Mr. Justice Holmes and the Supreme Court*, 1938, p. 62)

Frankfurter was both perceptive and prophetic. At that very moment, the Court was beginning to reassess constitutional priorities.

The Court's seemingly illogical position did not endure. The change began when Justice McKenna (*Gilbert* v. *Minnesota,* 254 U.S. 325: 1920) assumed for the sake of argument that freedom of speech guaranteed in the First Amendment was applicable to state action. Brandeis was more forthright, "I cannot believe," he declared, after citing a number of cases in which due process had been used to protect property rights, "that the liberty guaranteed by the Fourteenth Amendment includes only liberty to acquire and enjoy property." Three years later, *Meyer* v. *Nebraska* proclaimed a broader meaning of the "liberty" that could not be denied without due process.

A judicial about-face began in *Gitlow* v. *New York.* Gitlow had been convicted under the New York Criminal Anarchy Act of 1902 of circulating pamphlets urging workers to revolutionary mass action and "dictatorship of the proletariat." In Gitlow's defense his counsel argued that the New York statute deprived him of "liberty" without due process of law. Though the Court ruled that the 1902 Act, as applied to Gitlow, did not unduly restrict freedom of speech or press, it accepted the view that the freedoms guaranteed in the First Amendment are safeguarded by the due process clause of the Fourteenth Amendment: "For present purposes, we may and do assume that freedom of speech, and of the press—which are protected by the First Amendment from abridgement by Congress—are among the fundamental personal rights and 'liberties' protected by the due process clause of the Fourteenth Amendment from impairment by the states." Rejecting Holmes's "clear and present danger" test, the majority ruled that even though speeches and publications themselves create no immediate danger, the state may, under its police power, validly forbid them as having a "bad tendency"—that is, a tendency to bring about results dangerous to public security. Two years later, in *Fiske* v. *Kansas* (274 U.S. 380), the Court invalidated a similar state criminal syndicalism act as applied because it violated the Fourteenth Amendment's due process clause.

Incorporation of other First Amendment rights followed. In 1931 the Supreme Court voted 5 to 4 that freedom of the press is within the protection of the "liberty" guaranteed in the Fourteenth Amendment (*Near* v. *Minnesota,* 283 U.S. 697); in 1937 the right of peaceable assembly was included (*DeJonge* v. *Oregon,* 299 U.S. 353); and in 1940 the freedom-of-religion provision was used to invalidate a Connecticut statute requiring a permit of all solicitors for religious or charitable causes (*Cantwell* v. *Connecticut,* 310 U.S. 296).

Finally, in 1947, the Court, while upholding 5 to 4 a New Jersey act providing bus service to all children attending public and parochial schools, served notice that the First Amendment provision denying to Congress the power to pass laws respecting establishment of religion was within the scope of the Fourteenth Amendment, and was intended to create a "wall of separation" between church and state (*Everson* v. *Board of Education,* 330 U.S. 1: 1947). As a result of these and other cases of similar import, all the rights of the First Amendment have been absorbed into the due process clause of the Fourteenth, and now receive protection in federal courts against adverse action by the states or the national government.

THE TESTS OF FREEDOM

First Amendment freedoms confront the Court with a difficult task, one that is not present in all cases of judicial review. Where enumerated powers of Congress or the President are subject to interpretation, the Court's function is at an end when the action taken is found to be within the limits of constitutionally granted power. In reaching such a conclusion the Court is immeasurably aided by the well-established presumption of constitutionality that accompanies most legislative and executive actions.

In cases involving freedom of speech, of press, or of religion, the Court must interpret and apply a grant of power—frequently the "reserved" police power of the state—while at the same time it must interpret and apply a constitutional limitation on governmental power. Governments must have police power to maintain themselves against attacks from within, just as they must have military power to resist attacks from without. Police power, meaning in this context the authority necessary to maintain a peaceful and orderly society, is an obvious requisite of government. On the other hand, the Court is aware that the American political tradition has been opposed to unlimited governmental power, and that the Bill of Rights represents one of the "auxiliary precautions" against its emergence. Moreover, the guaranties of the First Amendment are fundamental—free speech, free press, and the right of assembly make possible a continuing debate on issues large and small, without which the electoral process becomes an empty ritual. The free exercise of religion and the separation of church and state represent the American solution to one of the basic issues in the Western political tradition—the proper relation of state and church, of individuals to their God and their government. The religion clauses are central to the protection of religious beliefs and to the maintenance of civil peace in a religiously diverse culture.

The easy path to constitutional decision by way of presumption of constitutionality of legislative or administrative action is not readily available in this field. When confronted with clashes between individual freedom and state power, the Court has formulated tests. Whatever measures are employed, the Court's answers depend ultimately on the Justice's view of correct social policy and their conception of the role of the judiciary in achieving balance between freedom and order. By 1925 the Court possessed two tests for First Amendment cases—"clear and present danger" (that seemed to express a preference for free speech) and "bad tendency" (a test more favorable to legislative action). Each emerged from post-World War I cases involving wartime national security legislation.

INTERNAL SECURITY AND FIRST AMENDMENT FREEDOMS

During the long period between 1787 and World War I, the First Amendment served as little more than a historical reminder of the lively concern for personal freedom expressed during the nation's formative years. Since the judicial revolution of 1937, however, the First Amendment has been one of the focal points of constitutional jurisprudence.

At the inception of our national government, the Federalists had, it is true, thought it necessary to curb the speech of their political opponents. Under the Alien and Sedition Acts scandalous criticism of the President or Congress with intent to bring them into disrepute was proscribed in sweeping terms. These laws, generally judged unconstitutional, were never tested because Jefferson and the Republicans feared that the federalist

Supreme Court would declare the laws valid, thus establishing an unfortunate precedent. It is noteworthy that the federalist proponents of these laws, many of whom had played leading roles in the dramatic formulation of the Constitution, used an argument that has become a familiar defense of speech limitations. Threats to national security, they argued, made restrictions inevitable; preservation of the Constitution is more important than protection of any one right it guaranties. Obviously, this logic may be used to justify destruction of all constitutional rights.

Barring Lincoln's unofficial suppression of Northern critics of governmental policies during the Civil War, there was no national government action raising free speech issues until World War I. In 1917 and 1918 Congress passed two laws that resulted in extensive litigation, focusing public attention on basic issues of freedom of speech in wartime. The so-called Espionage Act of 1917 prohibited and punished interferences with recruitment or acts adversely affecting military morale, and made the intent of the actor or speaker an essential element of the offense. This latter requirement was difficult to apply.

In *Schenck* v. *United States* Justice Holmes, in upholding the act as applied to antidraft leaflets, suggested the now famous ''clear and present danger'' test: ''The question in every case is whether the words used are used in such circumstances and are of such a nature as to create a clear and present danger that they will bring about the substantive evils that Congress has a right to prevent.'' Holmes's test invited more questions than it answered. Enmeshed with highly complex issues of proximity, degree, and content, it nevertheless displayed a preference for a wide latitude of speech.

In later cases rejecting Holmes's formula, the Court adopted a measure less generous to the speaker. A Socialist antiwar pamphlet was held within the 1917 law as having ''a tendency to cause insubordination, disloyalty, and refusal of duty.'' Holmes and Brandeis opposed the new rule because it eliminated both the speaker's intent and the likelihood of danger as relevant elements.

A Sedition Law of 1918 went far beyond the 1917 act, making punishable speech that in World War II would have been deemed mere political comment. It singled out for punishment any ''disloyal, profane, scurrilous, or abusive language about the form of government, the Constitution, soldiers and sailors, flag or uniform of the armed forces,'' and in addition made unlawful any ''word or act [favoring] the cause of the German Empire . . . or [opposing] the cause of the United States.'' This law was upheld, and its application sustained, in *Abrams* v. *United States* (250 U.S. 616: 1919), where pamphlets opposing the Allied (and American) intervention in Russia after the revolution were held to be within its terms. Holmes, dissenting, thought that the majority had inferred an intent not shown by evidence and that, in any event, no threat of ''clear and present danger'' to the war effort had been shown. The effect of this postwar litigation was to enlarge the importance of the free speech guaranty; however, it should be noted that the cases involved the proper application of federal statutes to specific forms of speech or writing rather than serious questions concerning the constitutionality of the statutes themselves. When this flurry of litigation subsided, cases involving federal action vis-à-vis First Amendment rights virtually disappeared until World War II.

In the period between World Wars I and II, the states were more active in seeking curbs against radical action, principally through efforts to enforce criminal syndicalism of the kind involved in *Gitlow* v. *New York*. The Supreme Court's reaction to such measures was mixed. In *Whitney* v. *California* the majority upheld a conviction under a state criminal syndicalism law, primarily because a criminal conspiracy was not within the bounds of free speech, a position echoed in Justice Jackson's concurring opinion in the

Dennis case. Brandeis, concurring, reasserted the merits of the clear-and-present-danger test. In 1931 (*Stromberg* v. *California,* 283 U.S. 359) the Court, invalidating for vagueness a state statute prohibiting the display of a red flag as a symbol of opposition to organized government, placed its decision squarely under the freedom-of-speech rubric.

By 1937 the Court was prepared to apply the clear-and-present-danger test to the legality of speeches and material disseminated by a Communist Party organizer, contrary to Georgia's criminal syndicalist law (*Herndon* v. *Lowry,* 301 U.S. 242). "...[T]he legislature of Georgia has not" the Court ruled, "made membership in the Communist Party unlawful by reason of its supposed dangerous tendency even in the remote future." Justice Roberts, speaking for the Court, found the act defective as applied because the judge and jury had not determined that the defendant's utterances constituted "a clear and present danger of forcible obstruction of a particular state function."

By World War II, "clear and present danger" was the accepted test of potential harm. Applied to both state and federal laws, it became the measure of the criminality of unpopular beliefs and potentially dangerous action.

It was not until the Court was confronted with a case testing the Smith Act of 1940, Section 1 of which made it a felony to advocate the violent overthrow of the government of the United States, or to conspire to organize a group advocating such violence, that the clear-and-present-danger test "bowed out." In upholding the Act as applied to 11 leaders of the American Communist Party (*Dennis* v. *United States*), the Supreme Court applied the test Judge Learned Hand suggested in his Second Circuit Court of Appeals opinion: "In each case Courts must ask whether the gravity of the 'evil,' discounted by its improbability, justifies such invasion of free speech as is necessary to avoid the danger." To Chief Justice Vinson, spokesman for the Court, the clear-and-present-danger test, while applicable to the isolated speech of individuals or small groups, was inappropriate for testing words associated with a large-scale conspiratorial movement: "The situation with which Justices Holmes and Brandeis were concerned in *Gitlow* was a comparatively isolated event, bearing little relation in their minds to any substantial threat to the safety of the community."

Apparently Vinson approved the trial judge's holding that as a matter of law, defendant's alleged activities presented "a sufficient danger of a substantive evil" to justify the application of the statute under the First Amendment. The Chief Justice's attempt to square Judge Hand's formula with the clear-and-present-danger test is highly reminiscent of the decisions obtained earlier by application of the "bad tendency" test.

In *Yates* v. *United States* the Court was again called upon to examine the scope of the Smith Act. Its decision, taking a strict view of the proof necessary to convict, made it impossible for the government to retry the *Yates* defendants and others whose trials were pending. In the light of this decision, many thought that the membership provisions of the Smith Act would be held invalid once the Court was confronted with the issues. But in *Scales* v. *United States* (367 U.S. 203: 1961) the Court saved the constitutionality of the challenged clause by insisting that only active and knowledgeable membership was within the act's coverage.

In another action directed against the Communist party, the United States ultimately gained Supreme Court approval of the 1950 Subversive Activities Control Act, which, as applied to the Communist party, required them to register with a government board as a "Communist-action" organization. Various handicaps, such as special stamping of a registered organization's mail, were imposed upon those held to be "Communist-action" groups. By a 5-to-4 majority, the Court in *Communist Party of the United States* v. *Subversive Activities Control Bd.* (367 U.S. 1: 1961) held the act to be regulatory, not punitive. After the Party refused to register, the SAC Board ordered individual members to register, as provided in the Act. Their refusal to register was upheld by the Court on the ground that their admission of Party membership would make them liable to prosecution under other statutes, and hence violated their privilege against self-incrimination (*Albertson* v. *Subversive Activities Control Board,* 382 U.S. 70: 1965).

In what was described at the time as a serious blow to those fighting Communist infiltration in education, the Court voided the automatic dismissal under a city ordinance of a City College of New York professor who invoked the Fifth Amendment at a congressional committee inquiry (*Slochower* v. *Board of Education,* 350 U.S. 551: 1956). The blow was softened two years later when the Court in 5-to-4 decisions upheld the dismissals of a public school teacher and a subway employee who refused to answer the questions of their superiors concerning possible subversive affiliation (*Beilan* v. *Board of Education,* 357 U.S. 399, 409: 1958; *Lerner* v. *Casey,* 357 U.S. 468, 409: 1958).

In a 1967 case, *Keyishian* v. *Board of Regents* (385 U.S. 589), the Court, finding overbreadth and vagueness in the statute, threw out a New York loyalty oath requiring a denial of Communist affiliation as a prerequisite to teaching at a state university. The Court relied on the fact that the statute could cover mere membership in a Communist organization, something less than the constitutionally required standard of membership *plus* a "specific intent to further the unlawful aims of an organization."

Arousing bitter criticism within bar association ranks were rulings invalidating state decisions that precluded admission to the practicing bar where applicants allegedly had not demonstrated good moral character, because of doubts as to their loyalty (*Konigsberg* v. *State Bar,* 353 U.S. 252: 1957; *Schware* v. *Board of Bar Examiners,* 353 U.S. 232: 1957). These decisions, rejecting the judgment of state courts on a matter traditionally within virtually complete state control, came hard on the heels of the Court's well-publicized holding in *Pennsylvania* v. *Nelson* that the states should abandon their efforts to protect the United States against seditious activities. Protesting angrily, the 1958 Conference of the State Chief Justices adopted a resolution criticizing Supreme Court decisions affecting the states. Shortly thereafter, the Court took a less offensive tack. In the second *Konigsberg* case (*Konigsberg* v. *State Bar,* 366 U.S. 36: 1961) and another involving rejection of a bar applicant (*In re Anastaplo,* 366 U.S. 82: 1961), the Court upheld rejections based on the refusal of the applicant to cooperate by answering questions about Communist party membership and other questions relevant to his moral character and other qualifications for practicing law.

In *Aptheker* v. *Secretary of State* (378 U.S. 500: 1964), the Court relied on the right to travel abroad in holding unconstitutional, on its face, an SACB order that permitted the revocation of passports held by Communist party members. The Court refused to interpret the statute to apply only to "active" members and voided the entire order as being overly broad and impinging on constitutionally protected freedoms. Similarly in *United States* v. *Robel* (389 U.S. 258: 1967), the Court invalidated a statute which made it a crime for any member of a Communist-action organization "to engage in any employment in a defense facility." The Government sought to defend the Subversive Activities Control Act under the war power, describing it as an "expression of the growing concern shown by the executive and legislative branches of government over the risks of internal subversion in plants on which the national defense depend(s)." As to this, Chief Justice Warren, for a 6–2 majority, observed:

> This concept of "national defense" cannot be deemed an end in itself, justifying any exercise of legislative power designed to promote such a goal. Implicit in the term "national defense"

is the notion of defending those values and ideals which set this Nation apart. . . . It would indeed be ironic if, in the name of national defense, we would sanction subversion of one of those liberties—the freedom of association—which makes the defense of the Nation worthwhile.

Yet the Court has upheld against First Amendment attack the implied statutory authority of the Secretary of State to revoke the passport of an American citizen whose actions abroad "are causing or are likely to cause serious danger to the national security or the foreign policy of the United States" (*Haig* v. *Agee,* 49 LW 4869: 1981). In this case a former employee of the Central Intelligence Agency had announced a campaign "to expose CIA officers and agents and to take the measures necessary to drive them out of the countries where they are operating." He then engaged in activities the State Department regarded as resulting in identification of alleged undercover CIA agents and other American intelligence sources in foreign countries. Over the objections of Justices Brennan and Marshall, the majority cited *Near* v. *Minnesota* (283 U.S. 697: 1931), concluding that "Agee's First Amendment claim has no foundation. . . . Agee's disclosures, among other things, have the declared purpose of obstructing intelligence operations and the recruiting of intelligence personnel. They are clearly not protected by the Constitution. The mere fact that Agee is also engaged in criticism of the Government does not render his conduct beyond the reach of the law."

A unique case, questioning the extent to which Congress may exercise its power to regulate and protect interstate commerce if such regulation affects the right of free speech, was resolved in favor of the government in *American Communications Association* v. *Douds* (339 U.S. 382: 1950). In this case the Taft-Hartley Act of 1947 requirement that labor leaders sign a non-Communist oath in order to qualify their union for participation under the act was held not to violate the First Amendment right of nonsigners. The dissenters tried in vain to invoke the clear-and-present-danger test. But in *United States* v. *Brown* (381 U.S. 437: 1965) the *Douds* decision was in effect overruled, since the Court held invalid a provision in the Labor-Management Reporting and Disclosure Act (1959), a successor provision to that in the 1947 act, making it a crime for a Communist party member to serve as a union officer or employee.

Many argued that the Court had moved too far ahead of dominant opinion in the late 1950s and early 1960s. Anti-Court legislation in Congress passed the House and failed by only one vote in the Senate. Sharp criticism came from those obsessed with the pressing need to ferret out persons allegedly guilty of subversive activities or associations, past or present. The American Bar Association, numerous state bar associations, a wide assortment of state associations, and the Conference of Chief Justices spoke out in vehement protest. Newspaper commentators, some of whom exhibited little knowledge of the actual decisions, and legal scholars who found technical as well as policy deficiencies in the opinions, were also aroused.

Voluble critics were more in evidence than the Court's defenders. Chief Justice Stone's *Carolene* footnote, discussed in chapter 8, suggests that constitutional rights are not rights against government so much as rights against the dominant majority represented by government. The Bill of Rights expresses the judgment of the founders that the majority is neither always right nor likely to be tolerant. Whether we adhere to that judgment will be determined by the reaction of the American people, who in the long run must choose between judicial protection of constitutional rights or unlimited majority rule.

THE RIGHT OF ASSOCIATION

Apart from special problems arising from the activities of the Communist party (USA) and its allies, the right of association and permissible state regulation of association present difficult questions in the United States, a nation of joiners, where associations of all kinds have traditionally flourished. Business corporations, and more recently, labor unions and allegedly subversive organizations have been subject to a variety of regulations. But, on the whole, private associations have flourished free of government interference. A New York law of 1923, requiring every society of more than 20 members bound by oaths to file a copy of its constitution, rules, and oath, as well as a list of officers and members, was upheld (*New York ex rel. Bryant* v. *Zimmerman,* 278 U.S. 63: 1928). The Court distinguished the Ku Klux Klan, the target of the law, from other groups with different objectives. The argument that liberty of the individual member was improperly affected was summarily brushed aside. In marked contrast is the decision in *NAACP* v. *Alabama.* Distinguishing an attack on the NAACP from New York's earlier effort to curb the Klan, the Court concluded that Alabama had failed to show justification for demanding information certain to deter exercise of the right of association. In another case, the Court upheld the refusal of NAACP officers to submit membership lists in accordance with ordinances of two Arkansas cities that required this and other information of all organizations functioning within the city (*Bates* v. *Little Rock,* 361 U.S. 516: 1960).

While the two preceding cases found the Court unanimous in striking down state efforts to compel disclosure of NAACP membership, the Court split 5 to 4 in the next case involving right of association (*Shelton* v. *Tucker,* 364 U.S. 479: 1960). An Arkansas statute compelled teachers in a state-supported school or college to file annually an affidavit listing every organization to which they had belonged or regularly contributed within the preceding five years. The dissenting opinions of Justices Frankfurter and Harlan emphasized the state's obvious interest in the qualifications of the teachers it hired, which in their view distinguished this from the two NAACP membership cases. The majority recognized this state interest but thought it could be achieved by a less sweeping demand for relevant information than was here evident.

The Court was unanimous again in invalidating two Louisiana acts as applied to the NAACP (*Louisiana ex rel. Gremillion* v. *NAACP,* 366 U.S. 293: 1961). One required every nontrading association within the state to file an affidavit that none of the officers or directors of its national organization were members of the Communist party or other subversive organizations. This obviously required knowledge that local officers could not be expected to possess. The other statute, enacted in 1924 supposedly to curb the Ku Klux Klan but never enforced against any organization until this action, required submission of a list of members and officers. This was set aside on the grounds raised in the earlier case.

A more difficult clash between a state's interests in obtaining information and the associational right to privacy occurred in *Gibson* v. *Florida Legislative Investigating Committee* (372 U.S. 539: 1963). In an earlier proceeding the Florida Supreme Court held that the committee could not demand the membership list of the NAACP but could compel a custodian of the organization's records to bring the list to a hearing held to determine whether certain named members of the NAACP were Communists. The case, coming to the Supreme Court, resulted from the refusal of the custodian to produce the list. The majority thought that the committee had not shown sufficient evidence of relationship between Communist activities and the branch of the NAACP under investigation. The dissenting Justices argued that testimony of state witnesses and an earlier "anti-Communist" Resolution of the NAACP were sufficient to show efforts by Communists to infiltrate the NAACP and hence justify the legislative demand for information.

Investigations by committees of Congress have raised issues of free speech and association. The difference is that the Court is inclined to show greater deference to a coordinate branch than to an agency of a state government. Contrast the opposing results and reasoning found in *Watkins* v. *United States* and *Barenblatt* v. *United States,* reprinted in chapter 3. Both date from the 1950s, when much congressional committee time was spent ferreting out suspected Communists.

SPEECH AND ASSEMBLY: THE RIGHT TO PROTEST

When the Supreme Court was confronted by state and federal laws directed against Communist party members, it dealt with a phenomenon of national and international significance. In applying variants of the clear-and-present-danger test, the Justices were asked to make assessments of the seriousness of the threat, the appropriateness of the governmental response, and the danger lest speech and association be unduly restricted. Viewed superficially, the Court should have an easier time in dealing with various municipal ordinances and administrative actions affecting freedom of speech and assembly. In practice the task has proved far from simple. The difficulties in appraising local situations and the many factors that necessarily affect local decision making are apparent in the many opinions upholding or invalidating local actions. The basic method has been one of balancing interests, while viewing with suspicion prior restraints on speech and assembly. Overly broad or vague ordinances and those which give unfettered discretion to administrators have been subject to "exacting scrutiny." While recognizing that speech and assembly can be the cause of riots and disorder, the Justices have sought to protect unpopular and contentious speech, since these are the forms of expression that most need protection. In practice, however, a risk of imminent danger to members of a crowd or to the speaker himself may present a dilemma to the police, in which their decision is bound to be viewed as wrong by those adversely affected.

A classic example is *Terminiello* v. *Chicago,* reprinted in this chapter, where the Court divided 5 to 4, reversing the conviction of a speaker for a "breach of peace." Although the majority utilized the clear-and-present-danger test and based its decision on the overly broad charge of the trial judge, the facts of the case (as Justice Jackson's dissenting opinon makes clear) raise fundamental issues concerning the maintenance of public order where speech threatens to disturb it.

In another close decision, *Feiner* v. *New York* (340 U.S. 315: 1951), the Court denied the free speech claim of a sidewalk orator who had used derogatory language about public officials (including the President) and the American Legion to a small crowd clustered around him. Unrest and threatening movements prompted a policeman to order the speaker to stop, and to arrest him when he refused. The Supreme Court, with three vehement dissenters, upheld the speaker's conviction. Citing with approval a statement in the Cantwell case, Chief Justice Vinson declared: "When clear and present danger of riot, disorder, interference with traffic upon the public streets, or other immediate threat to public safety, peace, or order, appears, the power of the state to prevent or punish is obvious" (*Cantwell* v. *Connecticut,* 310 U.S. 296: 1940). In this and similar cases, the confusion of facts that usually surrounds the allegedly illegal speech makes effective review by an appellate court extremely difficult, if not impossible. The trial court, by accepting the official version of the incidents involved, severely handicaps a speaker who wants to appeal his conviction.

Only where the Supreme Court is willing to review the facts in a civil liberties case may an appellant from a state conviction succeed in reversing that conviction. "Many times in the past," dissenting Justice Black commented in the Feiner case, "this Court has said that despite findings below, we will examine the evidence for ourselves to ascertain whether federally protected rights have been denied. . . . Even a partial abandonment of this rule marks a dark day for civil liberties in our nation." "But," Justice Black continued, "still more has been lost today. . . . In my judgment, today's holding means that as a practical matter, minority speakers can be silenced in any city. Hereafter, despite the First and Fourteenth Amendments, the policeman's club can take heavy toll of a current administration's public critics. Criticism of public officials will be too dangerous for all but the most courageous." Justice Black expressed the view that it was the duty of the police to protect the speaker rather than to arrest him. During his last years on the Court, however, Justice Black seemed to have lost his libertarian fervor, moving critics to level against him the charge of inconsistency, and stirring the Justice himself to an explanation, if not defense, of his position (*A Constitutional Faith,* 1968).

An exception to the application of the clear-and-present-danger test is that of "fighting words." In *Chaplinsky* v. *New Hampshire* (315 U.S. 568: 1942), the Court unanimously upheld the conviction of a speaker (a Jehovah's Witness) who, in a dispute with a policeman, used abusive language. The Court recognized Chaplinsky's words as "likely to provoke the average person to retaliation." In the opinion of Justice Murphy, certain utterances, of which fighting words are a part, "are no essential part of any exposition of ideas and are of such slight social value as a step to truth that any benefit that may be derived from them is clearly outweighed by the social interest in order and morality." Justice Murphy's reference to the lewd, obscene, and libelous as being in the same class as the "fighting words" exception has been the subject of much litigation, but the narrow exception, excluding fighting words from protection of the First Amendment, has retained its full force.

Even here, context is important. *Cohen* v. *California* (403 U.S. 15: 1971) found the Court reversing the conviction of a young man who, as a method of protest, emblazoned the words "F*** the draft" on his jacket. He was arrested in a courthouse corridor and charged with "disturbing the peace." The tables were turned, with Justice Harlan upholding the First Amendment claim and Justice Black (along with Justice White and Chief Justice Burger) joining Justice Blackmun's dissent. "No individual actually or likely to be present could reasonably have regarded the words . . . as a direct personal insult," wrote patrician Justice Harlan. "Nor do we have here an instance of the exercise of the State's police power to prevent a speaker from intentionally provoking a given group to hostile reaction. . . . [W]hile the particular four-letter word being litigated here is perhaps more distasteful than most others of its genre, it is nevertheless often true that one man's vulgarity is another's lyric. Indeed, . . . because government officials cannot make principled distinctions in this area . . . the Constitution leaves matters of taste and style so largely to the individual."

Regulation with a potential for restricting speech is not limited to statutes punishing breaches of the peace. A different type of statute—one requiring that licenses be obtained before a parade or assembly can be held—poses the danger of prior restraint on the expression of ideas. For this reason, such statutes require an unusually heavy justification under the First Amendment. In *Cox* v. *New Hampshire* (312 U.S. 569: 1941), the Court upheld a state statute requiring that a license be obtained from local authorities before a parade could be held on a public street. The state supreme court saved the statute from successful constitutional attack by construing the licensing authority of the local board narrowly, limited to considerations of time, place, and manner of parades and processions so as to safeguard public convenience. The Court reasoned that this type of regulation was entirely proper and necessary in order that the municipality might provide adequate policing for parades and processions and ensure safe and efficient use of public facilities. Thus construed, the statute left no discretion with the local board issuing permits to discriminate on any basis.

Admitting that a municipality can regulate parades and demonstrations as to time, place, and manner, what is the status of a defendant who marches in the face of an injunction issued pursuant to an arguably unconstitutional licensing procedure? *Walker* v. *City of Birmingham* (338 U.S. 307: 1967) held that demonstrators who had violated an *ex parte* injunction could not defend against contempt charges by asserting the unconstitutionality of the city ordinance under which they were charged. Yet two years later the Court held unconstitutional the ordinance under which Walker had been charged (*Shuttlesworth* v. *City of Birmingham*, 394 U.S. 147: 1969). Although the state court in *Shuttlesworth* tried to limit the authority of the licensing board to that approved by the Court in *Cox,* the Court held that the narrowing of the statute had come too late, since the petitioner had been informed that "under no circumstances would he be permitted to demonstrate in Birmingham." This was sufficient to distinguish this case from *Cox,* where there had been no prior administration of the statute before the narrowing construction.

Shuttlesworth illustrates a recent trend in free speech cases. The Court has fashioned new devices to protect expression: overbreadth of statutory restrictions; the possibility of alternative measures less burdensome to the exercise of constitutional rights; strict application of statutory requirements with respect to intent of the actors.

Edwards v. *South Carolina* (372 U.S. 229: 1963) reversed breach of peace convictions of black students who had gathered near the South Carolina State House to protest racial discrimination. The arrests followed the gathering of a hostile crowd and the demonstrators' rejection of a police order to disperse. Distinguishing this case from *Feiner,* the majority relied heavily on the fact that petitioners had been convicted under a breach of peace statute rather than under a narrowly drawn ordinance designed to regulate traffic or establish reasonable hours of access to the State House. In this case the state had made criminal (through the use of a broad breach of the peace statute) the expression of unpopular views. Justice Clark in dissent argued that the situation here was analogous to that in *Feiner* and that the breach of peace convictions should therefore stand. A similar result was reached in *Gregory* v. *Chicago* (394 U.S. 111: 1969), where breach of peace convictions of petitioners were reversed because the judge's instructions to the jury permitted it to convict on the basis of petitioners' having engaged in protected activity.

Another category of cases considers whether certain kinds of utterances are protected by the First Amendment, wholly apart from whether the language tends to incite others to violent acts. In *Watts* v. *United States* (394 U.S. 705: 1969), the Court reversed a conviction under a statute declaring it a felony to "knowingly and willfully" make a threat on the life of the President. Petitioner said, at a public rally, that if he had to carry a rifle, the first man he would like to get was L.B.J. The Court reasoned that speech such as this must be interpreted with the First Amendment clearly in mind, and that here the statement was "kind of political hyperbole." Hence, the prosecution had not established that a willful and knowing threat had been made on the life of the President.

Even though the clear-and-present-danger concept has become less important in free speech cases in recent years, it is still a relevant standard in some contexts. In *Brandenburg* v. *Ohio* (395 U.S. 444: 1969), a leader of the Ku Klux Klan was convicted under an Ohio criminal syndicalism statute of "advocating . . . the duty, necessity, or propriety of crime, sabotage, violence or unlawful methods of terrorism as a means of accomplishing industrial or political reform," and of "voluntarily assembling with a society, group or assemblage of persons formed to teach or advocate the doctrines of criminal syndicalism." The facts revealed that petitioner had informed newspapers of a scheduled Klan meeting, and later on broadcast portions of the rally over a local station and a national network. Petitioner had decried government repression of the Caucasian race and spoke of the possibility of revenge. Some participants carried weapons. The Court held the Ohio statute unconstitutional because it punished mere advocacy and impinged on protected speech, stating that "a state could not proscribe advocacy of the use of force or of law violation except when it was directed to inciting or producing imminent lawless action and is likely to incite or produce such action."

Increasingly, those protesting governmental policy resort to symbolic speech to make clear their position and influence others. The Supreme Court's reaction to these claims has varied. In *United States* v. *O'Brien* (391 U.S. 367: 1968), the Court sustained petitioner's conviction for destroying his draft card in violation of federal law. Petitioner claimed that prohibiting the burning of draft cards violated his rights of free speech and served no legitimate legislative function. The law as applied to O'Brien was sustained, the Court rejecting any inference that an "apparently limitless variety of conduct can be labeled 'speech' whenever a person engaging in the conduct intends to thereby express an idea." In this case the speech aspects of O'Brien's action ranked low in the Court's analysis of what it considered interference with a legitimate governmental purpose.

The Court reached a different conclusion in *Tinker* v. *Des Moines School District* (393 U.S. 503: 1971), upholding the right of school children to wear black armbands as a protest against the Vietnam War. In the same area is *Street* v. *New York* (394 U.S. 576: 1969), in which petitioner appealed conviction under a New York statute making it a misdemeanor publicly to defile the flag. Street, disturbed by recent political events, publicly burned a United States flag, expressing his contempt for an America that could not protect James Meredith from an assassination attempt. The Court did not broach the petitioner's argument that desecration of the flag in the abstract would constitute free speech, because it found that the statute as applied to petitioner permitted him to be punished merely for speaking contemptuously of the flag. The separate dissents of Justices Warren, Black, White, and Fortas expressed the view that Street had been punished for his conduct in burning the flag, and not for expressing his opinions.

Another cluster of free speech problems arises from efforts to regulate the media of speech and to draw the line between permissible and prohibited forums for the expression of ideas. *Adderley* v. *Florida* (385 U.S. 39: 1966) upheld trespass convictions of 32 persons who assembled on the grounds outside a county jail to protest the previous arrests of demonstrating students and to protest various forms of racial segregation. Justice Black, for the majority, reasoned that the state had a special interest in keeping demonstrators off the portion of the jail grounds reserved for jail use, and that the state's "malicious trespass" statute could be applied to this type of demonstration on public property. Justice Douglas, writing for four dissenters, viewed the majority position as improperly turning a legitimate protest into a trespass case. In stark opposition to Black, Douglas considered the jail a particularly appropriate place to demonstrate: "Those who do not control television and radio, those who cannot afford to advertise in newspapers or circulate elaborate pamphlets may have only a more limited type of access to public officials. Their methods should not be condemned as tactics of obstruction and harassment as long as the assembly and petition are peaceful, as these were." In *Brown* v. *Louisiana*, however, the Court reversed breach of peace convictions of five black males who protested the segregation of a county library by refusing to leave when asked.

As the Brown case indicates, freedom of speech is not restricted to purely verbal expression, but includes some forms of action accompanying speech. In "speech plus" cases the problem is to determine what actions associated with speech come within the ambit of constitutional protection. This issue arises in "picketing" to advertise the facts of a labor dispute, discouraging public contact with the "struck" enterprise.

After 1937, when the Court abandoned censorship of legislation regulating business, the Justices became more alert to acts limiting freedom of labor. In states where antilabor sentiment was strong, one of labor's principal weapons had been destroyed by forbidding picketing in labor disputes. In 1940 peaceful picketing was brought under the protection of freedom of speech (*Thornhill* v. *Alabama*, 310 U.S. 88). Setting aside an Alabama statute, Justice Murphy declared that abridgement of liberty in labor disputes was permissible "only where the clear danger of substantive evils arises under circumstances affording no opportunity to test the merits of ideas by competition for acceptance in the market of public opinion." This decision followed that of *Hague* v. *Committee for Industrial Organizations* (307 U.S. 496: 1939), where the Court upheld against repressive local action the right of a labor organization to hold public meetings for organizational and other purposes.

Later cases have modified some of the sweeping doctrines enunciated in the Thornhill case and permitted limitation of picketing where violence accompanied it (*Milkwagon Drivers Union* v. *Meadowmoor Dairies, Inc.*, 312 U.S. 287: 1941), or where it was used to achieve an unlawful objective (*Giboney* v. *Empire Storage & Ice Co.*, 336 U.S. 490: 1949; *International Brotherhood of Teamsters* v. *Hanke*, 339 U.S. 470: 1950; *International Brotherhood of Teamsters* v. *Vogt*, 354 U.S. 284: 1957).

In *Amalgamated Food Employees* v. *Logan Valley Plaza* (391 U.S. 308: 1968) the Court sustained, 6 to 3, the right of petitioners to picket at a privately owned shopping center. The majority reached back to *Marsh* v. *Alabama* (326 U.S. 501: 1946) for an analogy. In *Marsh*, the Court enforced the guaranties of the First Amendment on the streets of a "company town." "The similarities between the business block in Marsh and the shopping center in the present case are striking," Justice Marshall wrote. They were so striking that "the State may not delegate the power, through the use of its trespass laws, wholly to exclude those members of the public wishing to exercise their First Amendment rights on the premises in a manner and for a purpose generally consonant with the use to which the property is actually put." Marshall's reference to *Marsh* was galling to dissenting Justice Black, who had authored the majority opinion in the earlier case.

In *Logan Valley*, the picketing was labor related, directed against a store in the shopping center. Would the Court extend *Logan Valley* to include other kinds of picketing or leafleting aimed not at a store but at a larger political or social issue not necessarily connected with any particular business at a shopping center? Four years later, a majority answered in the negative (*Lloyd Corp.* v. *Tanner*, 407 U.S. 551: 1972), and *Logan Valley* was expressly overruled in *Hudgens* v. *NLRB* (424 U.S. 507: 1976). After a lapse of only eight years, Justice Black's dissenting opinion of 1968 became the law of the land.

It seems now, however, that free speech does not necessarily stop where the shopping mall begins. In *PruneYard Shopping Center* v. *Robins* (447 U.S. 74: 1980) a unanimous bench allowed a state-created constitutional right of free speech at shopping centers to prevail against a challenge that it amounted to an unconstitutional state interference with the owner's property rights under the Fourteenth Amendment. What the Supreme Court is unwilling to read into the First Amendment is perfectly acceptable when read into state constitutions by state courts. *Logan Valley* has, practically speaking, been revived, if on a hobbled, state-option basis.

Residential picketing is another troublesome area of First Amendment policy, which provokes a clash not usually with property rights but with privacy. Even when such expression is confined to the public streets and sidewalks, "preserving the sanctity of the home, the one retreat to which men and women can repair to escape from the tribulations of their daily pursuits, is surely an important value," Justice Brennan acknowledged in *Carey* v. *Brown* (447 U.S. 455: 1980). This case involved a Chicago ordinance which banned most forms of residential picketing, but exempted a few, including labor picketing, when the residence was being used as a place of business. Six Justices applied the equal protection clause and held that government could not discriminate in the ordinance on the basis of the content of expression. Strongly suggested was the constitutional infirmity of an absolute ban on all residential picketing at any time. The inference was that regulations governing time, place, and manner would be thoroughly permissible if applied on a non-discriminatory basis as to content.

COMMERCIAL SPEECH

First Amendment protections are by no means limited to political speech. Even though guarding the democratic process may have been uppermost in the minds of Madison and others who campaigned for the Amendment, the Supreme Court has enlarged the shield to cover "commercial speech" as well. In *Virginia State Board of Pharmacy* v. *Virginia Consumer Council* (425 U.S. 748: 1976), the Justices set aside legislation barring price advertising of prescription drugs. From the drugstore it was only a short distance to the law office the following year, and a state bar's ban against advertising the fees lawyers charged clients for routine services (*Bates* v. *State Bar of Arizona,* 433 U.S. 350: 1977). Even when a municipality prohibits the posting of "For Sale" or "Sold" signs to stem "white flight" from integrated neighborhoods, the First Amendment intervenes, said Justice Marshall for all eight participating Justices (*Linmark Associates, Inc.* v. *Township of Willingboro,* 431 U.S. 85: 1977).

In 1980, Justice Powell offered an overview of the Court's position on commercial speech (*Central Hudson Gas & Electric Corp.* v. *Public Service Commission of New York,* 447 U.S. 557: 1980).

> In commercial speech cases . . . a four-part analysis has developed. At the outset, we must determine whether the expression is protected by the First Amendment. For commercial speech to come within that provision, it at least must concern lawful activity and not be misleading. Next, we ask whether the asserted governmental interest is substantial. If both inquiries yield positive answers, we must determine whether the regulation directly advances the governmental interest asserted, and whether it is not more extensive than is necessary to serve that interest.

In this case the commission banned advertising by an electric utility which promoted the use of electricity. A majority found that the New York regulation failed on the fourth part of the standard.

cigarette ads?

The Commission . . . has not demonstrated that its interest in conservation cannot be protected adequately by more limited regulation of appellant's commercial expression. To further its policy of conservation, the Commission could attempt to restrict the format and content of Central Hudson's advertising. It might, for example, require that the advertisements include information about the relative efficiency and expense of the offered service, both under current conditions and for the foreseeable future. . . . In the absence of a showing that more limited speech regulation would be ineffective, we cannot approve the complete suppression of Central Hudson's advertising.

Justice Stevens, joined by Brennan, was more direct.

The justification for the regulation is nothing more than the expressed fear that the audience may find the utility's message persuasive. Without the aid of any coercion, deception, or misinformation, truthful communication may persuade some citizens to consume more electricity than they otherwise would. I assume that such a consequence would be undesirable and that government may therefore prohibit and punish the unnecessary or excessive use of electricity. But if the perceived harm associated with greater electrical usage is not sufficiently serious to justify direct regulation, surely it does not constitute the kind of clear and present danger that can justify the suppression of speech.

Dissenting, Justice Rehnquist claimed that ''the Court unleashed a Pandora's box when it 'elevated' commercial speech to the level of traditional political speech. . . .''

The line between ''commercial speech,'' and the kind of speech that those who drafted the First Amendment had in mind, may not be a technically or intellectually easy one to draw, but it surely produced far fewer problems than has the development of judicial doctrine in this area since *Virginia Board*. For in the world of political advocacy and *its* marketplace of ideas, there is no such thing as a ''fraudulent'' idea: there may be useless proposals, totally unworkable schemes, as well as very sound proposals that will receive the imprimatur of the ''marketplace of ideas'' through our majoritarian system of election and representative government. The free flow of information is important in this context not because it will lead to the discovery of any objective ''truth,'' but because it is essential to our system of self-government. . . .
     What time, legal decisions, and common sense have so widely severed, I declined to join in *Virginia Board,* and regret now to see the Court reaping the seeds that it there sowed. For in a democracy, the economic is subordinate to the political, a lesson that our ancestors learned long ago, and that our descendants will undoubtedly have to relearn many years hence.

THE ELECTORAL PROCESS

Restrictions on the source, amount, and use of funds in the political process also impact on the First Amendment. In *Buckley* v. *Valeo* (424 U.S. 1: 1976) the Court reviewed at length the constitutionality of the Federal Election Campaign Act, designed to reduce the influence of "big money" in national elections. In an extensive per curiam opinion and in a variety of concurring and dissenting opinions which consumed almost 300 pages in the *United States Reports,* the Court disallowed the provisions of the statute that put a limit of $50,000 on the use by a presidential candidate of his own or his immediate family's money. This was seen as an unconstitutional infringement on the First Amendment. Endorsed, however, were ceilings on contributions of $1,000 and $5,000 from individuals and groups, respectively, to candidates seeking federal office. This restriction was regarded as a less "direct and substantial" restraint on expression. Combined, these holdings gave a distinct advantage to families with considerable wealth and to candidates with high name recognition. Because of limitations imposed on both gifts and spending, the news media now had a more prominent role in campaigns, as candidates in many instances became dependent on news coverage as a kind of "free advertising."

State restrictions have received scrutiny too. In *First National Bank of Boston* v. *Bellotti* (435 U.S. 765: 1978), the First Amendment prevailed five votes to four over a Massachusetts statute which prohibited spending corporate funds "for the purpose of . . . influencing or affecting the vote on any question submitted to the voters, other than one materially affecting any of the property, business or assets of the corporation." The majority reasoned that such spending could be prohibited only if the state could demonstrate that "corporate advocacy threatened imminently to undermine democratic processes. . . ." In dissent, Justice White argued that corporate speech was "not fungible with communications emanating from individuals and is subject to restrictions which individual expression is not."

The First Amendment has brought the Court closer to the day-to-day world of American politics in other ways. In *Elrod* v. *Burns* (427 U.S. 347: 1976) six Justices invalidated "a practice as old as the Republic, a practice which has contributed significantly to the democratization of American politics," said Justice Powell in dissent. The practice at issue was the patronage system—discharging employees not on civil service because of their party affiliation. Burns and others were employees of the sheriff's department in Cook County, Illinois. They were also Republican. Elrod was the newly-elected sheriff, and a Democrat. For himself and three colleagues, Justice Brennan in a plurality opinion resisted the argument that judicial intervention would badly weaken the party system. Besides, "any contribution of patronage dismissals to the democratic process does not suffice to override their severe encroachment on First Amendment freedoms." Covered by this decision were "nonpolicy making, nonconfidential government employees."

Branti v. *Finkel* (445 U.S. 507: 1980) clarified somewhat the reach of *Elrod.* At issue were the dismissals on partisan grounds of two assistant public defenders in Rockland County, New York. For the majority, Justice Stevens explained: "[T]he question is whether the hiring authority can demonstrate that party affiliation is an appropriate requirement for the effective performance of the public office involved."

> Having thus framed the issue, it is manifest that the continued employment of an assistant public defender cannot properly be conditioned upon his allegiance to the political party in control of the county government. The primary, if not the only, responsibility of an assistant public defender is to represent individual citizens in controversy with the State.

Left in doubt by *Branti* was patronage *hiring.* More to the point, appointment of United States attorneys by the President often takes party affiliation into account. Under *Branti,* may they be discharged for partisan reasons? May they be hired for partisan reasons?

Other party practices have fared better. *Cousins* v. *Wigoda* (419 U.S. 477: 1975) placed the Justices in the midst of a credentials dispute from the 1972 Democratic National Convention. Wigoda was a member of the elected, but not seated, delegation from Cook County, Illinois. Cousins was a member of the defeated, but seated, delegation. Concluding that members of political parties enjoy a First Amendment right of association, the Court ruled for Cousins, according primacy to the national convention of a party in determining the qualifications and eligibility of its delegates. Similarly, the National Democratic Party's choice of closed presidential primaries prevailed when challenged by the open presidential primary preferred by Wisconsin (*Democratic Party* v. *LaFollette,* 49 LW 4178: 1981). The question was not whether Wisconsin could have an open primary. "Rather, the question is whether, once Wisconsin has opened its presidential preference primary to voters who do not publicly declare their party affiliation, it may then bind the National Party to honor the binding results, even though those results were reached in a manner contrary to National Party rules." *Wigoda* provided the answer. Careful students will want to examine the relationship between the Wisconsin primary case and the Jaybird party case (*Terry* v. *Adams,* 345 U.S. 461: 1953), mentioned in the following chapter. In the older case, the Court recognized no First Amendment associational rights, at least where racial discrimination was involved.

FREEDOM OF THE PRESS

In the landmark 5-to-4 decision of 1931 (*Near* v. *Minnesota*) Chief Justice Hughes, spokesman for the majority, held unconstitutional a Minnesota statute under which public authorities might call a newspaper to account for publishing scandalous and defamatory matter, and "unless the owner or publisher is able and disposed to bring competent evidence to satisfy the judge that the charges are true and are published with good motives, and justifiable ends, his newspaper or periodical is suppressed and further publication is made punishable as a contempt." "This," the Chief Justice declared, "is censorship." By the narrow margin of one vote, the Supreme Court advanced the cause of freedom.

In 1964 (*New York Times* v. *Sullivan*), the justices practically abolished the right of public officials to collect damages for libel. Under the *New York Times* decision, the press, and perhaps anyone else, has the right to publish libelous statements about public officials. "Actual malice" must be shown by a plaintiff under the *Sullivan* rule. In June 1967, the Court extended the *New York Times* rule to prominent people outside the government (*Curtis Publishing Co.* v. *Butts; Associated Press* v. *Walker,* 388 U.S. 130: 1967). The Court's rationale has been summed up this way: "What is added to the field of libel is taken from the arena of debate, and democracy calls for robust, wide-open debate about public issues. Libel, then, that deals with public affairs is not evil; it serves a socially useful function." In a related development, the Court limited the scope of a New York law protecting the "right to privacy" by holding that substantial inaccuracies in what purported to be an account of actual events did not invade "privacy" unless the publisher's misstatements were willful or reckless (*Time* v. *Hill,* 385 U.S. 374: 1967).

Yet, *Time, Inc.* v. *Firestone* (424 U.S. 448: 1976) maintained the publisher's liability in a libel action even though the action arose when the magazine reported judicial proceedings. Moreover, in a case involving the CBS television program "60 Minutes," the Court upheld a libel plaintiff's right to raise questions probing the minds of journalists in an effort to establish the "malice" the *Sullivan* rule requires (*Herbert* v. *Lando,* 441 U.S. 153: 1979).

In June 1971 (*New York Times Co.* v. *United States*), the United States sought to enjoin the *Times* from publishing the contents of a classified study entitled, "History of U.S. Decision-Making Process on Vietnam Policy." A brief per curiam opinion simply stated that the government had not met the necessary burden of "showing justification for the enforcement of such a restraint." The issue's complexity is exemplified in the nine opinions, six concurring and three dissenting, the Justices felt obliged to write.

Prior restraints on publication may be the hobgoblin of American constitutional interpretation, as some of the opinions in the Pentagon Papers case suggest, but this presumption received its severest test when the federal government sought to prevent publication of an issue of *The Progressive* magazine. Officials were distressed by an article it was to contain: "The H-Bomb Secret; How We Got It, Why We're Telling It." The fear was not that the article would enable anyone to build a hydrogen bomb in the basement, but that it contained information which would be a significant help to countries attempting to develop a nuclear capability. Unlike the government's position in the Pentagon Papers case, there seemed this time to be statutory authority for a court to issue an injunction. In *United States* v. *Progressive, Inc.* (467 F. Supp. 990: 1979), Judge Warren of the United States District Court for the Western District of Wisconsin did just that. Before argument on appeal in the court of appeals, however, the Madison (Wisconsin) *Press Connection* published an eighteen-page letter recounting much of the same information which was to have appeared in *The Progressive*. The issue of prior restraint therefore became moot, and the Justice Department withdrew its suit. While this case never received full judicial consideration higher than the district court level, it does illustrate the practical difficulties in trying to prevent publication of material people want to publish.

The national government and state governments are also involved in the less dramatic function of helping to protect the morals and welfare of their citizens. A state case, *Alberts* v. *California* (354 U.S. 476: 1957) accepted state action directed against "hard core" pornography. Its companion federal case, *Roth* v. *United States,* exploring the kind of printed matter that may be excluded from the mails and from interstate shipment, raised the problem of freedom and order most acutely. Justice Harlan stressed a point that goes to the heart of federal-state relations, underscoring the vastly greater consequences of national over state censorship, a difference that in his view justifies the Court in scrutinizing federal action more strictly. In *Roth* Justice Brennan wrote for the majority that "obscenity is utterly without redeeming social importance." Therefore, it "is not within the area of constitutionally protected speech or press." The key of course was to define the obscene, and the constitutional standard became "whether to the average person, applying contemporary community standards, the dominant theme of the material taken as a whole appeals to prurient interest." Almost a decade later, *Memoirs of a Woman of Pleasure* v. *Massachusetts* (383 U.S. 413: 1966) made it more difficult for government to maintain a successful obscenity prosecution. While formally endorsed only by a plurality, the elements of proof now included a demonstration that the material in question be "patently offensive" and "utterly without redeeming social value." Definitional problems abounded and as a result so did the number of obscenity cases on the Court's docket. Some of the Justices found themselves with no choice but to look at the material in question. The Court staff obligingly set up a special viewing room, complete with projector.

In 1969, *Stanley* v. *Georgia* (394 U.S. 557) gave the strong hint that all obscenity laws were living on borrowed time. The Court held that mere private possession of obscene materials was protected by the First Amendment. Said Justice Marshall for the majority: "If the First Amendment means anything, it means that a State has no business telling a man, sitting alone in his own house, what books he may read or what films he may watch." As to the state's contention that exposure to obscenity may lead to deviant sexual behavior or crimes of sexual violence, Marshall wrote: "Given the present state of knowledge, the State may no more prohibit mere possession of obscenity on the ground that it may lead to antisocial conduct than it may prohibit possession of chemistry books on the ground that they may lead to the manufacture of homemade spirits."

But the majority pulled back from the logical implications of *Stanley* in *Miller* v. *California,* and announced new definitional standards. Most significantly, the prosecution now had to show that the material in question lacked only "serious value," not that it was "utterly without" value. Justice Brennan, who wrote the majority opinion in *Roth,* admitted in dissent that "the approach initiated 15 years ago in *Roth* . . . and culminating in the Court's decision today, cannot bring stability to this area of the law without jeopardizing fundamental First Amendment values. . . ." He proposed instead a "significant departure." Justice Douglas reasserted his familiar position, as he and Black had done in *Memoirs* and *Roth,* that obscenity is speech and as such is protected by the First Amendment.

Questions on press freedom surfacing in litigation today tend to be of two types. The first and older involves some form of state restriction on what can be published, and the Justices have usually been sympathetic to press interests. *Miami Herald Publishing Co.* v. *Tornillo* (418 U.S. 241: 1974) voided a Florida statute which granted a "right of reply" to political candidates criticized in a newspaper. In a case which pitted privacy versus press freedom, the Court chose the latter, striking down a Georgia law which banned publishing the name of rape victims (*Cox Broadcasting Corp.* v. *Cohn,* 420 U.S. 469: 1975). A West Virginia statute which made it a misdemeanor to print the name of a youth charged with a juvenile offense without permission of juvenile court fared no better (*Smith* v. *Daily Mail Publishing Co.,* 443 U.S. 97: 1979). Nor can direct restraints on publication be regarded as constitutionally acceptable even when they are designed to avoid adverse publicity in an effort to obtain a fair trial for the accused (*Nebraska Press Association* v. *Stuart,* reprinted in this chapter).

The second and newer type of press litigation involves privilege and access. Here the government actions in question are not aimed at preventing or punishing publication of certain information. Rather, a policy impedes or obstructs the press in carrying out the tasks journalists assign to themselves. For example, in *Branzburg* v. *Hayes* the issue was a constitutional privilege for newspersons refusing to reveal the identity of confidential sources before a grand jury. The slim majority of five relied on the maxim that the law is entitled to "every man's evidence," a point which became of greater interest two years later in the Nixon tapes case. In the wake of *Branzburg,* some states enacted "shield" laws to do statutorily what the Court had declined to do constitutionally. Such laws even predated *Branzburg* in other states. A state "shield" law is still subordinate to the Sixth Amendment's guaranty of a fair trial and so may not always grant as full a privilege as journalists desire. This is a weakness reporter Myron Farber discovered (*Matter of Farber and the New York Times Co.,* 78 N.J. 259, 394 A. 2d 330: 1978) when the New Jersey Supreme Court refused to acknowledge a complete privilege under that state's "shield" law. Significantly perhaps, the Supreme Court of the United States denied certiorari.

Press interests lost again in *Houchins* v. *KQED* (438 U.S. 1: 1978), where a four to three majority ruled against a claim that newspersons had a First Amendment right of access to a county jail to interview prisoners and generally to investigate conditions in the aftermath of an inmate's suicide. The minority would have accorded access, temporarily at least, to both the press and the public. "The preservation of a full and free flow of information to the general public has long been recognized as a core objective of the First Amendment. . .," Justice Stevens argued. "It is for this reason that the First Amendment protects not only the dissemination but also the receipt of information and ideas." This minority point of view apparently won the approval of all eight participating Justices in *Richmond Newspapers, Inc.* v. *Virginia* (448 U.S. 555: 1980). The Court set aside on First Amendment grounds a trial judge's order to close a trial for the purpose of limiting publicity which might prove prejudicial to the rights of the accused. Said Justice Stevens, "This is a watershed case." It remains to be seen whether *Richmond Newspapers* will later be applied only to trials or whether the Court will extend its application to other arenas as well.

FREEDOM OF RELIGION

The free exercise provision of the First Amendment was incorporated into the Fourteenth Amendment in 1940 when the Court invalidated a Connecticut statute requiring a permit for all solicitors for religious or charitable causes (*Cantwell* v. *Connecticut,* 310 U.S. 296). In the same year, the Court, departing from the clear-and-present-danger test, sustained a state act requiring all schoolchildren, including Jehovah's Witnesses, to salute the flag (*Minersville School District* v. *Gobitis*).

   Joined in Justice Frankfurter's seemingly reactionary decision were Justices Black, Douglas, and Murphy. Only Justice Stone dissented. In an effort to win Stone's support, Frankfurter wrote (in a letter reprinted in this chapter) his colleague at length, arguing that the case be decided "in the particular setting of our time and circumstances." "It is relevant," he pleaded, "to make the adjustment we have to make within the framework of present circumstances and those that are clearly ahead of us."

   The year was 1940, a few months after Hitler unleashed his diabolical blitzkrieg in Europe. With the endorsement of eight Justices, judicial activism paraded under the banner of judicial self-restraint. But not for long. Two years later (*Jones* v. *Opelika,* 316 U.S. 584: 1942) Black, Douglas, and Murphy, in a remarkable about-face, recanted and explained.

> Since we joined in the opinion in the Gobitis case, we think this is an appropriate occasion to state that we now believe that it was also wrongly decided. Certainly our democratic form of government functioning under the historic Bill of Rights has a high responsibility to accommodate itself to the religious views of minorities however unpopular and unorthodox those views may be. The First Amendment does not put the right freely to exercise religion in a subordinate position. We fear, however, that the opinion in these and the Gobitis case do exactly that.

Encouraged by the *Opelika* dissent, and the appointment of two new Justices, Jackson and Rutledge, Walter Barnette and several other Jehovah's Witnesses brought suit to enjoin enforcement of the flag salute against their children. Voting 6 to 3 (*West Virginia*

Board of Ed. v. *Barnette*), the Court reversed itself, holding that First Amendment freedoms may be restricted "only to prevent grave and immediate dangers."

There are few instances in the Court's history in which the change of views and of judicial personnel were so quickly reflected in judicial decisions.

In 1947 the prohibition against any law respecting establishment of religion was also incorporated. The case, *Everson* v. *Board of Education* (330 U.S. 1), while allowing a state to pay the costs of bus transportation of children attending church-affiliated schools, set forth the principle that the religious clauses of the Constitution erected a "wall of separation" between church and state. Dissenting, Justice Rutledge issued a prophetic warning.

> Two great drives are constantly in motion to abridge, in the name of education, the complete division of religion and civil authority which our forefathers made. One is to introduce religious education and observances into the public schools. The other, to obtain public funds for the aid and support of various private religious schools. . . .
>
> In my opinion both avenues were closed by the Constitution. Neither should be opened by this Court. The matter is not one of quantity, to be measured by the amount of money expended. Now as in Madison's day it is one of principle, to keep separate the separate spheres as the First Amendment drew them; to prevent the first experiment upon our liberties; and to keep the question from becoming entangled in corrosive precedents. We should not be less strict to keep strong and untarnished the one side of the shield of religious freedom than we have been of the other.

The significance of the "wall" metaphor became more apparent in 1948, when the Court struck down a Champaign, Illinois, released-time program for religion in *McCollum* v. *Board of Education*. But only four years later, in *Zorach* v. *Clauson* (343 U.S. 306: 1952) the Court upheld a New York released-time program, basing its different conclusion on factual distinctions between the two programs. The practical effect of the second decision was to save religious released-time programs.

The satisfaction of proponents of religion in the schools, however, was short-lived. Prayers and Bible reading in schools next came under fire. *Engel* v. *Vitale* (370 U.S. 421: 1962) invalidated the use in New York public schools of a short prayer, approved by the Board of Regents, to be recited during opening exercises of each school day. Criticism of the decision and of the Justices by churchmen, congressmen, and the press was intense. Some religious leaders and certain newspapers defended the Court, but these comments hardly balanced the volume and heat generated by the decision's opponents. In 1963 the Court went further, deciding that Bible reading and recitation of the Lord's Prayer in class were also invalid. Only Justice Stewart dissented in *Abington Twp.* v. *Schempp* as he had in *Engel* v. *Vitale*.

In 1968 a state law requiring local public school authorities to lend textbooks free of charge to all students, including those attending private schools, was upheld (*Board of Education* v. *Allen*, 392 U.S. 236). Relying on the holding in *Everson*, Justice White restated the two-pronged test the Court had used in *Schempp*: "[T]o withstand the strictures of the Establishment Clause there must be a secular legislative purpose and a primary effect that neither advances nor inhibits religion."

Two years later, the Court upheld state tax exemptions for real property owned by religious organizations and used for religious purposes in *Walz* v. *Tax Commission* (397 U.S. 664: 1970). But the real significance of the case was the criteria established. The establishment clause was intended to afford protection against "sponsorship, financial support, and active involvement of the sovereign in religious activity." Further, the Court held that a state statute must not foster "an excessive government entanglement with religion." Recent decisions highlight difficulties in applying these cumulative criteria. In *Lemon* v. *Kurtzman* (403 U.S. 602: 1971), state aid to elementary and secondary nonpublic schools in Rhode Island and Pennsylvania was held violative of the religion clauses of the First Amendment. The aid was a 15 percent salary supplement to nonpublic school teachers, providing that teachers receiving such aid did not teach any religious subjects at the nonpublic school. The Court held that the cumulative impact of the entire relationship, arising under the state statute, was excessive entanglement between government and religion. In another decision, handed down the same day as *Lemon,* the Court held valid a congressional act which allowed funds for the construction of buildings on college and university campuses, even though private institutions were involved (*Tilton* v. *Richardson,* 403 U.S. 672: 1971). Distinguishing *Lemon,* the Court held that there was less danger here than in church-related primary and secondary schools dealing with impressionable children that religion would permeate the area of secular education, since religious indoctrination was not a substantial purpose or activity of these church-related colleges.

Litigation of various kinds of state aid to church-supported schools has become a fixture on the Court's docket. Because too strenuous an application of the ban on establishment might well amount to an infringement on free exercise, a majority of the Justices have allowed some forms of aid, but not most, to pass constitutional muster. Combining the holdings in *Meek* v. *Pittenger* (421 U.S. 349: 1975), *Wolman* v. *Walter* (433 U.S. 229: 1977) and *Committee for Public Education and Religious Liberty* v. *Regan* (444 U.S. 646: 1980) with earlier decisions, the Court will accept, for example, on-premises diagnostic and off-premises therapeutic services for parochial school students performed by state employees, supplemental grants to schools to pay for testing and scoring, textbook loans to pupils, and bus transportation to and from school (but not for field trips). Not acceptable to a majority in these cases are state tuition tax credits to parents of parochial school students, state funds for school building maintenance, supplements for teachers' salaries, and loans of instructional materials to the schools. At the same time, *Roemer* v. *Board of Public Works of Maryland,* reprinted in this chapter, indicates that the Court has been more generous with church-related colleges and universities. In any event, constitutional law in this area remains largely confused and unprincipled. The intensity of the drive to aid church schools with public funds is matched only by the energy expended in opposition to the practice.

State efforts to promote separation of church and state have been met by constitutional attack as well. *Widmar* v. *Vincent* (50 LW 4062: 1981) brought into play claims of free exercise, free speech, and non-establishment. Here, a policy of the University of Missouri at Kansas City denying use of University buildings and grounds "for purposes of religious worship or religious teaching" was struck down. Only Justice White dissented. Holding that a public university cannot "exclude groups because of the content of their speech," Justice Powell for the majority remained "unpersuaded that the primary effect of the public forum, open to all forms of discourse, would be to advance religion."

> We are not oblivious to the range of an open forum's likely effects. It is possible—perhaps even foreseeable—that religious groups will benefit from access to University facilities. But this Court has explained that a religious organization's enjoyment of merely "incidental" benefits does not violate the prohibition against the "primary advancement" of religion.

Freedom of religion is also invoked by the conscientious objector to military service. The Universal Military Service Act exempted from combatant military service those persons who are conscientiously opposed to participation in war in any form by reason of their "religious training and beliefs." The quoted phrase is defined as a "belief in a relation to a Supreme Being involving duties superior to those arising from a human relation, but [not including] essentially political, sociological, or philosophical views or a merely personal moral code." In *United States* v. *Seeger* (380 U.S. 163: 1965), this section was attacked on the grounds that it did not exempt nonreligious conscientious objectors and that it discriminated among different forms of religious expression. Holding that the petitioners were entitled to exemption, Justice Clark observed: "the test of belief 'in a relation to a Supreme Being' is whether a given belief that is sincere and meaningful occupies a place in the life of its possessor parallel to that filled by the orthodox belief in God of one who clearly qualifies for the exemption. Where such beliefs have parallel positions in the lives of their respective holders we cannot say that one is 'in a relation to a Supreme Being' and the other is not."

More recently, the Court held that conscientious objection to the Vietnam War, rather than to all war, was insufficient to warrant an exemption from the draft or a discharge from military service (*Gillette* v. *United States,* 401 U.S. 437: 1971). In *Clay* v. *United States* (403 U.S. 698: 1971), where the objection was upheld, the Court stated: "In order to qualify for classification as a conscientious objector, a registrant must satisfy three basic tests. He must show that he is conscientiously opposed to war in any form. He must show that this opposition is based upon religious training and belief, as the term has been construed in our decisions. And he must show that this objection is sincere. In applying these tests, the Selective Service System must be concerned with the registrant as an individual, not with its own interpretation of the dogma of the religious sect, if any, to which he may belong."

Religion has been highlighted in other decisions. Sunday closing laws have existed for decades, but in many instances have been loosely enforced or totally ignored. The emergence of large Sunday sellers in some localities aroused the opposition of store owners who observed conventional hours. In *McGowan* v. *Maryland* and companion cases (366 U.S. 420: 1961), they convinced the Court that the original religious motive behind Sunday closing laws had been dissipated, and that such laws represented nothing more than a general desire of the community to have one day of quiet and rest. Strong dissenting opinions indicated that all were not convinced, and other decisions reveal judicial alertness toward legislative requirements that penalize an individual for his religious beliefs or his secularist attitude. In *Torcaso* v. *Watkins* (367 U.S. 488: 1961) the Court unanimously held that Maryland could not constitutionally require an officeholder—in this case a notary public—to take an oath expressing a belief in God as a condition for taking office. And by a vote of 7 to 2, South Carolina was found to have inhibited the free exercise of religion by denying unemployment compensation to a Seventh Day Adventist because of her refusal to work on Saturday, which for those of her faith was observed as a Sabbath (*Sherbert* v. *Verner*). *Sherbert* called into question the logic of the Court's ruling in *Braunfeld* v. *Brown* (366 U.S. 599: 1961). As an Orthodox Jew, Abraham Braunfeld felt obliged to close his store from Friday evening until Saturday evening. The Sunday closing law in Pennsylvania required that he be closed on Sunday as well. He argued that the state law placed an unconstitutional burden on the exercise of his religious beliefs, but a majority held otherwise, regarding as important the distinction between making a religious practice unlawful and making it more expensive.

Braunfeld seemed to fade further in 1972 when the Court set aside the application to Amish youth of a Wisconsin law compelling children to attend public or private school until 16 years of age. The Justices found that the statute severely threatened the survival of an established religious faith (*Wisconsin* v. *Yoder*, reprinted in this chapter).

SPECIAL GOVERNMENTAL INTERESTS AND FIRST AMENDMENT RIGHTS

The Bill of Rights and other guaranties of the Constitution generally assume American citizenship (except where ''persons'' are mentioned) and the Fourteenth Amendment set at rest doubts concerning that status by virtue of birth within the United States. Naturalization provides a method of acquiring citizenship by those who are not native-born.

One of the difficult questions in modern times is whether citizenship status may be lost involuntarily, and how. By a 5-to-4 vote, *Trop* v. *Dulles* (356 U.S. 86: 1958) held a section of the Nationality Act of 1940 unconstitutional in providing loss of citizenship upon conviction and dishonorable discharge for wartime desertion, while at the same time upholding, 5 to 4, deprivation of citizenship of a native-born citizen who voted in Mexican elections while residing there (*Perez* v. *Brownell*, 356 U.S. 44: 1958). Justice Brennan, the swing-man, saw a rational connection between regulation of foreign policy and preventing citizens from voting in foreign elections. Deprivation of citizenship was not a reasonable means of exercising the war power.

Perez was overruled in *Afroyim* v. *Rusk* (387 U.S. 253: 1967) where a naturalized citizen who voted in an Israeli election was held not to have lost his citizenship. The majority of five, speaking through Justice Black, rejected the idea that citizenship could be lost except by a clearly voluntary decision of the citizen.

In 1971 the Court again grappled with this question, upholding a provision of the Immigration and Nationality Act that required a person born abroad, one of whose parents was American, to be physically present in the United States five continuous years between the ages of 14 and 28, or suffer loss of citizenship. In *Rogers* v. *Bellei* (401 U.S. 81: 1971), a majority of five found that Bellei was not a citizen as defined in the Fourteenth Amendment, and hence, Congress could give him provisional citizenship status subject to conditions which, in this case, he failed to meet. Four dissenters asserted that a person born abroad of an American parent is ''naturalized in the United States within the meaning of the Fourteenth Amendment.'' Mr. Justice Black, joined by Douglas and Marshall, was caustically critical: ''The Court today holds that Congress can indeed rob a citizen of his citizenship just so long as five members of this Court can satisfy themselves that the congressional action was not 'unreasonable, arbitrary,' . . . 'misplaced or arbitrary' . . . or 'irrational or arbitrary or unfair.' . . . Not one of these 'tests' appears in the Constitution. . . .''

Finally, some of the themes touched on in earlier chapters are relevant to the enjoyment of First Amendment rights. The war powers were invoked successfully in two World War II cases. One involved imposition of a Pacific Coast curfew on American citizens of Japanese ancestry (*Hirabayashi* v. *United States*, 320 U.S. 81: 1943). A second case (*Korematsu* v. *United States*) concerned an order excluding Japanese-Americans from defined coastal regions. This was also upheld over the powerful protest of Justice Murphy that the order went over "the very brink of constitutional power and falls into the abyss of racism." In a third case, *Ex parte Endo* (323 U.S. 283: 1944), the continued detention in relocation centers, or grants of leave on conditions, of Japanese-Americans found loyal was held in violation of the statutes involved. While commentators have almost universally condemned the deprivations of liberty resulting from these World War II programs, the Court's decisions remain on the books as a reminder of one additional casualty of war. It is worth noting that the Internal Security Act (1950), Title II, designated an Emergency Detention Act, provided that upon a proclamation of emergency by a President in the event of invasion, declaration of war, or insurrection in aid of a foreign enemy, the attorney general may "apprehend and by order detain . . . each person as to whom there is a reasonable ground to believe that such person probably will engage in, or probably will conspire with others to engage in, acts of espionage or of sabotage." There was no provision for judicial proceedings before detention and only a limited review after detention, one in which the government could choose to withhold evidence. This Act was repealed in 1971, with Congress declaring "No citizen shall be imprisoned or otherwise detained by the United States except pursuant to an Act of Congress" (85 Stat. 347).

PRIVACY

In 1965, Connecticut's anticontraceptive statute, though violative of no express provisions of the Constitution, foundered on the penumbral right of privacy. "Specific guarantees of the Bill of Rights," Justice Douglas reasoned for a majority of seven (mentioning Amendments 1, 3, 4, 5, 6, 8, 9, and 14), "have penumbras, formed by emanations from those guarantees that give them life and substance" (*Griswold* v. *Connecticut*).

"We do not sit," the justice observed, "as a super-legislature to determine the wisdom, need, and propriety of laws that touch economic problems, business affairs or social conditions. This law, however, operated directly on an intimate relation of husband and wife and their physician's role in one aspect of that relation."

The reasonable inference is that, in Justice Douglas's mind, the Court *does sit* as a super-legislature in safeguarding the penumbral right of privacy. The distinction thus sharply drawn between the Court's responsibility toward economic and personal rights, if legitimate, could be important, even crucial.

Dissenting justices, Black and Stewart, exploded. Black accused the majority of amending the Constitution under the guise of interpreting it, thus converting the Court into "a day-to-day Constitutional Convention." "I like my privacy as well as the next one," the eighty-year-old justice commented feelingly, "but I am, nevertheless, compelled to admit that government has a right to invade it unless prohibited by some specific constitutional provision." Sounding the note of "strict construction," Justice Black declared war on all penumbral embellishments.

Webster defines *penumbra* as a "marginal region or borderland of partial obscurity or some blighting influence as of doubt or chagrin." Small wonder Justice Black was outraged. Yet penumbra was not unprecedented. It is, in fact, among the most conspicuous weapons in the arsenal of constitutional interpretation.

In 1895, Chief Justice Fuller fashioned the "direct and indirect effects" penumbra to undermine the national commerce power, permitting a 95 percent monopoly in the manufacture of sugar to do what the Court denied to Congress—the power to regulate commerce. The penumbral doctrine of "dual federalism" cut two ways, denying both the national government and the states power to regulate the economy. To dilute the state police power, the Court invoked a penumbral right not mentioned in the Constitution—"liberty of contract." Scores of state statutes, including hours-of-labor and minimum-wage laws for women, fell under this nebulous label. The phony "separate but equal" formula kept public schools racially segregated for half a century. A newcomer in the ever-lengthening list of penumbra is "executive privilege." For none does Webster's foggy definition seem more apt.

Since *Griswold* the Supreme Court has enlarged on the constitutional right of privacy. Many cases in criminal procedure and free-press law concern individual privacy of course, so that subject is hardly new to the Justices. What is new after *Griswold* is the development of the right as it affects decisions one makes about his or her body. *Eisenstadt* v. *Baird* relied on both *Griswold* and the equal protection clause to void a Massachusetts statute which confined distribution of contraceptive devices to married persons (405 U.S. 438: 1972). As Justice Brennan concluded, "If the right of privacy means anything, it is the right of the *individual*, married or single, to be free from unwarranted governmental intrusion into matters so fundamentally affecting a person as the decision whether to bear or beget a child."

The landmark decision of *Roe* v. *Wade*, reprinted in this chapter, came the following year, stoking the flames of a national political blaze that shows no sign of diminishing. Justice Blackmun's majority opinion for seven colleagues acknowledged a constitutional right to abortion, calling forth Justice Rehnquist's retort in dissent that the result "partakes more of judicial legislation than it does of a determination of the intent of the drafters of the Fourteenth Amendment."

Reflecting the views of those who oppose the right created in *Roe* v. *Wade*, Congress and some state legislatures have attempted in various ways to limit the availability of abortion and to discourage its use. *Planned Parenthood of Central Missouri* v. *Danforth* (428 U.S. 52: 1976) knocked down the part of a state law requiring a married woman to obtain consent of her spouse in most instances before undergoing an abortion and voided a similar requirement for parental consent if an unmarried woman was under 18 years of age. A Utah statute, requiring physicians to "notify, if possible" the parents of minor women seeking abortions, received six affirmative votes (*H. L.* v. *Matheson*, 49 LW 4255: 1981). In *Maher* v. *Roe* (432 U.S. 464: 1977) the Court found no constitutional violation where states choose to pay for therapeutic abortions but not for elective ones, a conclusion extended to Congress in *Harris* v. *McRae* (448 U.S. 297: 1980), which upheld the spending of Medicaid funds for childbirth but not for most abortions (the "Hyde Amendment").

The birth control and abortion decisions came together in *Carey* v. *Population Services International* (431 U.S. 678: 1977). Here the Supreme Court invalidated a New York statute which, among other things, made it criminal to sell or distribute contraceptives to minors under sixteen years of age. According to Justice Brennan in a plurality opinion,

> Since the State may not impose a blanket prohibition, or even a blanket requirement of parental consent, on the choice of a minor to terminate her pregnancy, the constitutionality of a blanket prohibition of the distribution of contraceptives to minors is *a fortiori* foreclosed. The State's interests in protection of the mental and physical health of the pregnant minor, and in protection of potential life are clearly more implicated by the abortion decision than by the decision to use a nonhazardous contraceptive.

It may be that this line of privacy decisions calls into question the constitutionality of laws on statutory rape. Still, the Court has upheld such a statute on Equal Protection grounds (the sexual act was criminal for the male but not for the female), and has not considered the privacy aspects involved (*Michael M.* v. *Superior Court of Sonoma County,* 49 LW 4273: 1981). Possibly in doubt as well is the constitutionality of laws outlawing consensual homosexual acts in private, or so thought one member of a three-judge federal district court in Virginia (*Doe* v. *Commonwealth's Attorney,* 403 F. Supp. 1199: E.D. Va., 1975). On appeal, however, the Supreme Court affirmed without opinion the judgment of the district court, upholding the validity of the Virginia sodomy statute in question.

ARE THERE PREFERRED FREEDOMS?

During the past several decades the Court generally has maintained hostility to restrictions on free speech. Government policies or actions aimed at the content of speech—that is, at ideas or messages—enter the judicial process under heavy presumption of unconstitutionality. Only if the speech falls into one of several narrow exceptions is the Court inclined to be receptive to the government's position. Where a policy or action is not aimed at content of speech, but where the flow and distribution of speech are nonetheless inhibited, the Court weighs the effects of the former on the latter. Important in this calculus is the degree of constriction on speech and the importance of the interest the state is pursuing. Interpretation of the First Amendment does involve the balancing of recognized constitutional values. Its construction is not (as Justice Black sometimes used to insist over vigorous protest from Justice Harlan) the mechanical task of placing the Amendment alongside the challenged statute to decide whether they square.

If the balancing usually means that speech and other First Amendment rights prevail over competing interests, does this mean that the First Amendment is in a favored position? Are there preferred freedoms? Justice Stone's footnote four in *Carolene Products,* discussed near the end of the essay in chapter 8, suggests precisely that.

First Amendment freedoms lie at the heart of democratic values and the democratic process. So much of the Constitution deals not with substance, but with procedure. The Constitution speaks not nearly so often to *what* decisions are to be made as to *how* decisions are to be made. Freedom of expression and conscience are, therefore, integral components of democratic politics. Indeed, it is difficult to imagine politics being democratic where individuals with points of view in the minority cannot campaign to become the majority. Representative government and development of the human potential require a degree of tolerance for differing ideas, manners, and styles, and it is to forms of expression that the First Amendment largely addresses itself. Uncertainty arises, however, in deciding how much tolerance to extend to expression, especially when other important values seem threatened. Especially perplexing is the dilemma posed by persons who would use the freedoms of the democratic process as a means toward imposing antidemocratic and authoritarian policy on the nation.

In his *West Virginia Board of Ed.* v. *Barnette* opinion, Justice Jackson argued that more than a rational basis must support restrictions on freedom of speech, press, assembly, and worship. "The very purpose of a Bill of Rights was to withdraw certain subjects from the vicissitudes of political controversy, to place them beyond the reach of majorities." In 1945, Justice Rutledge stated the doctrine most clearly in *Thomas* v. *Collins* (323 U.S. 516): "The case confronts us again with the duty our system places on this Court to say where the individual's freedom ends and the state's power begins. Choice on that border, now as always delicate, is perhaps more so where the usual presumption supporting legislation [that it is constitutional] is balanced by the preferred place given in our scheme to the great, the indispensable democratic freedoms secured by the First Amendment.''

Justice Frankfurter, apparently recanting his initial approval, criticized judicial effort to create a preferred status for First Amendment freedoms and opposed Justice Reed's use of the ''preferred position'' concept (*Kovacs* v. *Cooper,* 336 U.S. 77: 1949). Deploring footnote 4 as ''the way of announcing a new constitutional doctrine,'' he wrote: ''This is a phrase that has uncritically crept into some recent opinions of this Court. I deem it a mischievous phrase, if it carries the thought, which it may safely imply, that any law touching communication is infected with presumptive invalidity.''

Frankfurter, joined by the majority, preferred to examine all legislative and official action against the standard of ''reasonableness,'' with the presumption of validity applying in freedom cases as in all others. Justices Black and Douglas, voting together in many instances, waged a rearguard action in support of the preferred freedoms doctrine. In 1945, Chief Justice Stone, whose Carolene Products footnote had laid certain foundations for preferred freedoms, expressed misgivings.

> My more conservative brethren in the old days enacted their own economic prejudice into law. What they did placed in jeopardy a great and useful institution of government. The pendulum has now swung to the other extreme, and history is repeating itself. The Court is now in as much danger of becoming a legislative Constitution-making body, enacting into law its own predilections, as it was then. (To Irving Brant, August 25, 1945. Quoted in Mason, *The Supreme Court from Taft to Burger,* 1979, p. 168.)

As has happened on earlier occasions in the long history of the Court, changes of personnel after 1953, and illusory lessening of international tensions, produced a judicial climate more favorable to freedom. At least four of the Justices—Chief Justice Warren, and Justices Black, Douglas, and Brennan—tended to give First Amendment freedoms a preferred position in the scale of constitutional values. With one additional vote, they were able to swing the Court toward a libertarian result. With the retirement of Justice Frankfurter—the intellectual leader of ''judicial restraint''—and appointment of Justice Goldberg in 1962, the tipping of the balance toward the libertarian group was realized. The appointment in 1965 of Abe Fortas as Justice Goldberg's successor, when the latter resigned to become ambassador to the United Nations, further tipped the liberal balance. President Johnson's selection of Thurgood Marshall in 1967 (the first black to sit on the Supreme Court), as successor to retiring Justice Tom Clark, gave the Court an even brighter liberal tinge.

While the 1970s initially seemed to signal a new era, decisions since Warren Burger's appointment as Chief Justice and into the 1980s indicate that the Court as a whole remains sensitive to governmental actions impinging on the First Amendment. Even in the context of a ruling against a claim of free speech, Justice Powell went out of his way to recognize ''a special solicitude'' which the courts have shown for ''the guarantees of the First Amendment'' (*Lloyd Corp.* v. *Tanner,* 407 U.S. 551: 1972).

SELECTED READINGS

ANASTAPOLO, GEORGE, *The Constitutionalist: Notes on the First Amendment.* Dallas: Southern Methodist University Press, 1971.

BEANEY, WILLIAM M., "The Constitutional Right to Privacy in the Supreme Court," 1962 *Supreme Court Review* 212.

BERNS, WALTER, *The First Amendment and the Future of American Democracy.* New York: Basic Books, 1976.

——, "Freedom of the Press and the Alien and Sedition Laws: a Reappraisal," 1970 *Supreme Court Review* 109.

BRANT, IRVING, *The Bill of Rights.* Indianapolis: Bobbs-Merrill, 1965.

CAHN, EDMOND, ed., *The Great Rights.* New York: Macmillan, 1963.

CANAVAN, FRANCIS, "Freedom of Speech and Press: For What Purpose?" 16 *American Journal of Jurisprudence* 95 (1971).

CHAFEE, ZECHARIAH, JR., *Free Speech in the United States.* Cambridge: Harvard University Press, 1942.

CORWIN, EDWARD S., "Bowing Out 'Clear and Present Danger,' " 27 *Notre Dame Lawyer* 325 (1952).

EMERSON, THOMAS I., "Colonial Intentions and Current Realities of the First Amendment," 125 *University of Pennsylvania Law Review* 737 (1977).

——, *The System of Freedom of Expression.* New York: Random House, 1970.

——, DAVID HABER, and NORMAN DORSEN, *Political and Civil Rights in the United States,* 3rd ed., 2 vols. Boston: Little, Brown, 1967.

FORTE, DAVID, ed., *The Supreme Court in American Politics: Judicial Activism vs. Judicial Self-Restraint.* Lexington, Mass.: Heath, 1972.

FRANK, JOHN P., "Review and Basic Liberties," in Edmond Cahn, ed., *Supreme Court and Supreme Law.* Bloomington, Ind.: Indiana University Press, 1954.

GELLHORN, WALTER, ed., *The States and Subversion.* Ithaca: Cornell University Press, 1952.

GUNTHER, GERALD, "Learned Hand and the Origins of Modern First Amendment Doctrine: Some Fragments of History," 27 *Stanford Law Review* 719 (1975).

HAND, LEARNED, *The Bill of Rights.* Cambridge: Harvard University Press, 1958.

HORN, ROBERT A., *Groups and the Constitution.* Stanford: Stanford University Press, 1956.

IRISH, MARIAN D., ed., *Continuing Crisis in American Politics.* Englewood Cliffs, N.J.: Prentice-Hall, 1962. See especially the chapter by A. T. Mason, "Constitutional Limitations in a World of Continuing Crisis," pp. 109–132.

KONVITZ, MILTON, *Expanding Liberties.* New York: Viking, 1966.

LEVENTHAL, HAROLD, "Courts and Political Thickets," 77 *Columbia Law Review* 345 (1977). Reviews court decisions on the electoral process.

LEVY, LEONARD W., *Legacy of Suppression: Freedom of Speech and Press in Early American History.* Cambridge: Harvard University Press, 1960.

LUSKY, LOUIS, *By What Right? A Commentary on the Supreme Court's Power to Revise the Constitution.* Charlottesville, Va.: The Michie Co., 1976.

MASON, ALPHEUS THOMAS, "The Burger Court in Historical Perspective," 89 *Political Science Quarterly* 27 (1974).

———, "Understanding the Warren Court: Judicial Self-Restraint and Judicial Duty," 81 *Political Science Quarterly* 523 (1966).

MEIKLEJOHN, ALEXANDER, "The First Amendment Is an Absolute," 1961 *Supreme Court Review* 245.

MENDELSON, WALLACE, "Clear and Present Danger—From Schenck to Dennis," 52 *Columbia Law Review* 313 (1952).

MURPHY, WALTER F., "Civil Liberties and the Japanese American Cases," 11 *Western Political Quarterly* 3 (1958).

O'BRIEN, DAVID M., *The Public's Right to Know: The Supreme Court and the First Amendment*. New York: Praeger, 1981.

PIPEL, HARRIET E., *Obscenity and the Constitution*. New York: R. R. Bowker, 1973.

PRITCHETT, C. HERMAN, *Civil Liberties and the Vinson Court*. Chicago: University of Chicago Press, 1954.

ROYSTER, VERMONT, *The American Press and the Revolutionary Tradition*. Washington, D.C.: American Enterprise Institute for Public Policy Research, 1974.

RUTLAND, ROBERT A., *The Birth of the Bill of Rights, 1776–1791*. Chapel Hill: University of North Carolina Press, 1955.

SHAPIRO, MARTIN, *The Pentagon Papers and the Courts: A Study in Foreign Policy Making and Freedom of the Press*. San Francisco: Chandler Publishing Co., 1972.

SORAUF, FRANK J., *The Wall of Separation; The Constitutional Politics of Church and State*. Princeton: Princeton University Press, 1976.

Symposium: Federal Election Laws, 29 *Emory Law Journal* 313 (1980).

Symposium: New Directions in Judicial Policy Making, 23 *Emory Law Journal* 643 (1974). Articles and comment by Gordon E. Baker, J. Woodford Howard, Jr., John R. Schmidhauser, and A. B. Winter.

"Toward a Constitutional Theory of Individuality: The Privacy Opinions of Justice Douglas," 87 *Yale Law Journal* 1579 (1978).

VALENTE, W. D. "Eccentric Constitutional Jurisprudence," 21 *Catholic Lawyer* 235 (1975).

WESTIN, ALAN F., *Privacy and Freedom*. New York: Atheneum, 1967.

YARBROUGH, T. E. "The Burger Court and Freedom of Expression," 33 *Washington and Lee Law Review* 37 (1976).

I. Drive for a Bill of Rights

Jefferson-Madison Correspondence, 1787–88

A bill of rights is what the people are entitled to against every government on earth

THOMAS JEFFERSON to James Madison, 20 December 1787

... I like much the general idea of framing a government which should go on of itself peaceably, without needing continual recurrence to the state legislatures. I like the organization of the government into Legislative, Judiciary and Executive.

... There are other good things of less moment. I will now add what I do not like. First the omission of a bill of rights providing clearly and without the aid of sophisms for freedom of religion, freedom of the press, protection against standing armies, restriction against monopolies, the eternal and unremitting force of the habeas corpus laws, and trials by jury in all matters of fact triable by the laws of the land and not by the law of Nations. To say, as Mr. Wilson does, that a bill of rights was not necessary because all is reserved in the case of the general government which is not given, while in the particular ones all is given which is not reserved might do for the Audience to whom it was addressed, but is surely gratis dictum, opposed by strong inferences from the body of the instrument, as well as from the omission of the clause of our present confederation which had declared that in express terms. It was a hard conclusion to say because there has been no uniformity among the states as to the cases triable by jury, because some have been so incautious as to abandon this mode of trial, therefore the more prudent states shall be reduced to the same level of calamity. It would have been much more just and wise to have concluded the other way that as most of the states had judiciously preserved this palladium, those who had wandered should be brought back to it, and to have established general right instead of general wrong. Let me add that a bill of rights is what the people are entitled to against every government on earth, general or particular, and what no just government should refuse, or rest on inference. . . .

I own I am not a friend to a very energetic government. It is always oppressive. The late rebellion in Massachusetts has given more alarm than I think it should have done. Calculate that one rebellion in 13 states in the course of 11 years, is but one for each state in a century and a half. No country should be so long without one. Nor will any degree of power in the hands of government prevent insurrections. . . . After all, it is my principle that the will of the Majority should always prevail. If they approve the proposed Constitution in all its parts, I shall concur in it cheerfully, in hopes that they will amend it whenever they shall find it works wrong. . . .

I have never found the omission of a bill of rights a material defect

JAMES MADISON to Thomas Jefferson, 17 October 1788

. . . My own opinion has always been in favor of a bill of rights, provided it be so framed as not to imply powers not meant to be included in the enumeration. At the same time I have never thought the omission a material defect, nor been anxious to supply it even by *subsequent* amendment, for any other reason than that it is anxiously desired by others. I have favored it because I supposed it might be of use, and if properly executed could not be of disservice. I have not viewed it in an important light—1. because I conceive that in a certain degree, though not in the extent argued by Mr. Wilson, the rights in question are reserved by the manner in which the federal powers are granted. 2. because there is great reason to fear that a positive declaration of some of the most essential rights could not be obtained in the requisite latitude. I am sure that the rights of conscience in particular, if submitted to public definition would be narrowed much more than they are likely ever to be by an assumed power. . . .

. . . Experience proves the inefficacy of a bill of rights on those occasions when its controul is most needed. Repeated violations of these parchment barriers have been committed by overbearing majorities in every State. In Virginia I have seen the bill of rights violated in every instance where it has been opposed to a popular current. Notwithstanding the explicit provision contained in that instrument for the rights of Conscience, it is well known that a religious establishment would have taken place in that State, if the Legislative majority had found as they expected, a majority of the people in favor of the measure; and I am persuaded that if a majority of the people were not of one sect, the measure would still take place and on narrower ground than was then proposed, notwithstanding the additional obstacle which the law has since created. Wherever the real power in a Government lies, there is the danger of oppression. In our Government, the real power lies in

the majority of the Community, and the invasion of private rights is *chiefly* to be apprehended, not from acts of government contrary to the sense of its constituents, but from acts in which the Government is the mere instrument of the major number of the Constituents. This is a truth of great importance, but not yet sufficiently attended to; and is probably more strongly impressed on my mind by facts, and reflections suggested by them, than on yours which has contemplated abuses of power issuing from a very different quarter. Wherever there is an interest and power to do wrong, wrong will generally be done, and not less readily by a powerful & interested party than by a powerful and interested prince. . . .

. . . What use then it may be asked can a bill of rights serve in popular Governments? I answer the two following which, though less essential than in other Governments, sufficiently recommend the precaution: 1. The political truths declared in that solemn manner acquire by degrees the character of fundamental maxims of free Governments, and as they become incorporated with the national sentiment, counteract the impulses of interest and passion. 2. Altho, it be generally true as above stated that the danger of oppression lies in the interested majorities of the people rather than in usurped acts of the Government, yet there may be occasions on which the evil may spring from the latter source; and on such, a bill of rights will be a good ground for an appeal to the sense of the community. Perhaps too there may be a certain degree of danger, that a succession of artful and ambitious rulers may by gradual & well timed advances, finally erect an independent Government on the subversion of liberty. Should this danger exist at all, it is prudent to guard against it, especially when the precaution can do no injury. At the same time I must own that I see no tendency in our Governments to danger on that side. It has been remarked that there is a tendency in all Governments to an augmentation of power at the expence of liberty. But the remark as usually understood does not appear to me well founded. Power when it has attained a certain degree of energy and independence goes on generally to further degrees. But when below that degree, the direct tendency is to further degrees of relaxation, until the abuses of liberty beget a sudden transition to an undue degree of power. With this explanation the remark may be true; and in the latter sense only is it, in my opinion applicable to the Governments in America. It is a melancholy reflection that liberty should be equally exposed to danger whether the Government have too much or too little power, and that the line which divides these extremes should be so inaccurately defined by experience. . . .

You omit an argument which has great weight with me

THOMAS JEFFERSON to James Madison, 15 March 1789

. . . Your thoughts on the subject of the Declaration of rights in the letter of Oct. 17, I have weighed with great satisfaction. Some of them had not occurred to me before, but were acknoleged [sic] just in the moment they were presented to my mind. In the arguments in favor of a declaration of rights, you omit one which has great weight with me, the legal check which it puts into the hands of the judiciary. This is a body, which if rendered independent, and kept strictly to their own department merits great confidence for their learning and integrity. In fact, what degree of confidence would be too much for a body composed of such men as Wythe, Blair, and Pendleton? On characters like these the 'civium ardor prava jubentium' would make no impression. I am happy to find that on the whole you are a friend to this amendment. The Declaration of rights is like all other human blessings alloyed with some inconveniences, and not accomplishing fully its object. But the good in this instance vastly overweighs the evil. . . .

. . . Experience proves the inefficacy of a bill of rights. True. But tho it is not absolutely efficacious under all circumstances, it is of great potency always, and rarely inefficacious. A brace the more will often keep up the building which would have fallen with that brace the less. There is a remarkable difference between the characters of the inconveniences which attend a Declaration of rights, and those which attend the want of it. The inconveniences of the Declaration are that it may cramp government in its useful exertions. But the evil of this is shortlived, moderate and reparable. The inconveniences of the want of a Declaration are permanent, afflicting and irreparable: they are in constant progression from bad to worse. The executive in our governments is not the sole, it is scarcely the principal object of my jealousy. The tyranny of the legislatures is the most formidable dread at present, and will be for long years. That of the executive will come in its turn, but it will be at a remote period. . . .

I am much pleased with the prospect that a declaration of rights will be added: and hope it will be done in that way which will not endanger the whole frame of the government, or any essential part of it. . . .

We act the part of wise and liberal men to make these alterations

JAMES MADISON, Speech Placing the Proposed Bill of Rights Amendments
before the House of Representatives, 8 June 1789

Mr. Madison rose, and reminded the House that this was the day that he had heretofore named for bringing forward amendments to the constitution, as contemplated in the fifth article of the constitution. . . .

The first of these amendments relates to what may be called a bill of rights. I will own that I never considered this provision so essential to the federal constitution, as to make it improper to ratify it, until such an amendment was added; at the same time, I always conceived, that in a certain form, and to a certain extent, such a provision was neither improper nor altogether useless. . . .

It has been said, that it is unnecessary to load the constitution with this provision, because it was not found effectual in the constitution of the particular States. It is true, there are a few particular States in which some of the most valuable articles have not, at one time or other, been violated; but it does not follow but they may have, to a certain degree, a salutary effect against the abuse of power. If they are incorporated into the constitution, independent tribunals of justice will consider themselves in a peculiar manner the guardians of those rights; they will be an impenetrable bulwark against every assumption of power in the legislative or executive; they will be naturally led to resist every encroachment upon rights expressly stipulated for in the constitution by the declaration of rights. Besides this security, there is a great probability that such a declaration in the federal system would be enforced; because the State Legislatures will jealously and closely watch the operations of this Government, and be able to resist with more effect every assumption of power, than any other power on earth can do; and the greatest opponents to a Federal Government admit the State Legislatures to be sure guardians of the people's liberty. I conclude, from this view of the subject, that it will be proper in itself, and highly politic, for the tranquility of the public mind, and the stability of the Government, that we should offer something, in the form I have proposed, to be incorporated in the system of Government, as a declaration of the rights of the people.

I wish also, in revising the constitution, we may throw into that section, which interdicts the abuse of certain powers in the State Legislatures, some other provisions of equal, if not greater importance than those already made. The words, 'No State shall pass any bill of attainder, *ex post facto* law,' &c. were wise and proper restrictions in the constitution. I think there is more danger of those powers being abused by the State Governments than by the Government of the United States. The same may be said of other powers which they possess, if not controlled by the general principle, that laws are unconstitutional which infringe the rights of the community. I should therefore wish to extend this interdiction, and add that no State shall violate the equal right of conscience, freedom of the press, or trial by jury in criminal cases; because it is proper that every Government should be disarmed of powers which trench upon those particular rights. I know, in some of the State constitutions, the power of the Government is controlled by such a declaration; but others are not. I cannot see any reason against obtaining even a double security on those points; and nothing can give a more sincere proof of the attachment of those who opposed this constitution to these great and important rights, than to see them join in obtaining the security I have now proposed: because it must be admitted, on all hands, that the State Governments are as liable to attack these invaluable privileges as the General Government is, and therefore ought to be as cautiously guarded against. . . . [An amendment providing for safeguards against the states was proposed, but it failed of adoption.]

II. Political Association and Advocacy

Schenck v. *United States*
249 U.S. 47, 39 S.Ct. 247, 63 L.Ed. 470 (1919)

Schenck and others were charged with conspiracy to obstruct the draft and other violations of the Espionage Act of 1917. Their specific offense was printing and distributing leaflets that opposed the war effort generally and conscription specifically. After conviction in the district court, Schenck brought a writ of error.

MR. JUSTICE HOLMES delivered the opinion of the court.

This is an indictment in three counts. . . . The defendants were found guilty on all the counts. They set up the First Amendment to the Constitution forbidding Congress to make any law abridging the freedom of speech, or of the press, and bringing the case here on that ground have argued some other points also of which we must dispose. . . .

The document in question upon its first printed side recited the first section of the Thirteenth Amendment, said that the idea embodied in it was violated by the Conscription Act, and that a conscript is little better than a convict. In impassioned language it intimated that conscription was despotism in its worst form and a monstrous wrong against humanity in the interest of Wall Street's chosen few. It said "Do not submit to intimidation," but in form at least confined itself to peaceful measures such as a petition for the repeal of the act. The other and later printed side of the sheet was headed "Assert Your Rights." It stated reasons for alleging that any one violated the Constitution when he refused to recognize "your right to assert your opposition to the draft," and went on "If you do not assert and support your rights, you are helping to deny or disparage rights which it is the solemn duty of all citizens and residents of the United States to retain." It described the arguments on the other side as coming from cunning politicians and a mercenary capitalist press, and even silent consent to the conscription law as helping to support an infamous conspiracy. It denied the power to send our citizens away to foreign shores to shoot up the people of other lands, and added that words could not express the condemnation such cold-blooded ruthlessness deserves, &c., winding up "You must do your share to maintain, support and uphold the rights of the people of this country." Of course the document would not have been sent unless it had been intended to have some effect, and we do not see what effect it could be expected to have upon persons subject to the draft except to influence them to obstruct the carrying out of it. The defendants do not deny that the jury might find against them on this point.

But it is said, suppose that that was the tendency of this circular, it is protected by the First Amendment to the Constitution. Two of the strongest expressions are said to be quoted respectively from well-known public men. It well may be that the prohibition of laws abridging the freedom of speech is not confined to previous restraints, although to prevent them may have been the main purpose, as intimated in *Patterson* v. *Colorado,* 205 U.S. 454, 462. We admit that in many places and in ordinary times the defendants in saying all that was said in the circular would have been within their constitutional rights. But the character of every act depends upon the circumstances in which it is done. . . . The most stringent protection of free speech would not protect a man in falsely shouting fire in a theatre and causing a panic. It does not even protect a man from an injunction against uttering words that may have all the effect of force. . . . The question in every case is whether the words are used in such circumstances and are of such a nature as to create a clear and present danger that they will bring about the substantive evils that Congress has a right to prevent. It is a question of proximity and degree. When a nation is at war many things that might be said in time of peace are such a hindrance to its effort that their utterance will not be endured so long as men fight and that no Court could regard them as protected by any constitutional right. It seems to be admitted that if an actual obstruction of the recruiting service were proved, liability for words that produced that effect might be enforced. The statute of 1917 in § 4 punishes conspiracies to obstruct as well as actual obstruction. If the act (speaking, or circulating a paper), its tendency and the intent with which it is done are the same, we perceive no ground for saying that success alone warrants making the act a crime.

Judgments affirmed.

Gitlow v. New York
268 U.S. 652, 45 S.Ct. 625, 69 L.Ed. 1138 (1925)

Gitlow, a member of the left-wing section of the Socialist party, was convicted of the New York State statutory crime of criminal anarchy. He brought writ of error to review judgments affirming his conviction.

MR. JUSTICE SANFORD delivered the opinion of the Court. . . .

The contention here is that the statute, by its terms and as applied in this case, is repugnant to the due process clause of the Fourteenth Amendment. . . .

The indictment was in two counts. The first charged that the defendant had advocated, advised and taught the duty, necessity and propriety of overthrowing and overturning organized government by force, violence and unlawful means, by certain writings therein set forth entitled ''The Left Wing Manifesto''; the second that he had printed, published and knowingly circulated and distributed a certain paper called ''The Revolutionary Age,'' containing the writings set forth in the first count, advocating, advising and teaching the doctrine that organized government should be overthrown by force, violence and unlawful means. . . .

The precise question presented, and the only question which we can consider under this writ of error, then is, whether the statute, as construed and applied in this case by the state courts, deprived the defendant of his liberty of expression in violation of the due process clause of the Fourteenth Amendment.

The statute does not penalize the utterance or publication of abstract ''doctrine'' or academic discussion having no quality of incitement to any concrete action. It is not aimed against mere historical or philosophical essays. It does not restrain the advocacy of changes in the form of government by constitutional and lawful means. What it prohibits is language advocating, advising or teaching the overthrow of organized government by unlawful means. . . .

The Manifesto, plainly, is neither the statement of abstract doctrine nor, as suggested by counsel, mere prediction that industrial disturbances and revolutionary mass strikes will result spontaneously in an inevitable process of evolution in the economic system. It advocates and urges in fervent language mass action which shall progressively foment industrial disturbances and through political mass strikes and revolutionary mass action overthrow and destroy organized parliamentary government. It concludes with a call to action in these words: "The proletariat revolution and the Communist reconstruction of society—*the struggle for these*—is now indispensable. . . . The Communist International calls the proletariat of the world to the final struggle!" This is not the expression of philosophical abstractions, the mere prediction of future events; it is the language of direct incitement. . . .

. . . That the jury were warranted in finding that the Manifesto advocated not merely the abstract doctrine of overthrowing organized government by force, violence and unlawful means, but action to that end is clear.

For present purposes we may and do assume that freedom of speech and of the press—which are protected by the First Amendment from abridgment by Congress—are among the fundamental personal rights and "liberties" protected by the due process clause of the Fourteenth Amendment from impairment by the states. . . .

It is a fundamental principle, long established, that the freedom of speech and of the press which is secured by the Constitution, does not confer an absolute right to speak or publish, without responsibility, whatever one may choose, or an unrestricted and unbridled license that gives immunity for every possible use of language and prevents the punishment of those who abuse this freedom. . . .

That a State in the exercise of its police power may punish those who abuse this freedom by utterances inimical to the public welfare, tending to corrupt public morals, incite to crime, or disturb the public peace, is not open to question. . . .

By enacting the present statute the State has determined, through its legislative body, that utterances advocating the overthrow of organized government by force, violence and unlawful means, are so inimical to the general welfare and involve such danger of substantive evil that they may be penalized in the exercise of its

police power. That determination must be given great weight. Every presumption is to be indulged in favor of the validity of the statute. . . . That utterances inciting to the overthrow of organized government by unlawful means, present a sufficient danger of substantive evil to bring their punishment within the range of legislative discretion, is clear. Such utterances, by their very nature, involve danger to the public peace and to the security of the State. They threaten breaches of the peace and ultimate revolution. And the immediate danger is none the less real and substantial, because the effect of a given utterance cannot be accurately foreseen. The State cannot reasonably be required to measure the danger from every such utterance in the nice balance of a jeweler's scale. A single revolutionary spark may kindle a fire that, smouldering for a time, may burst into a sweeping and destructive conflagration. It cannot be said that the State is acting arbitrarily or unreasonably when in the exercise of its judgment as to the measures necessary to protect the public peace and safety, it seeks to extinguish the spark without waiting until it has enkindled the flame or blazed into the conflagration. It cannot reasonably be required to defer the adoption of measures for its own peace and safety until the revolutionary utterances lead to actual disturbances of the public peace or imminent and immediate danger of its own destruction; but it may, in the exercise of its judgment, suppress the threatened danger in its incipiency. . . .

We cannot hold that the present statute is an arbitrary or unreasonable exercise of the police power of the State unwarrantably infringing the freedom of speech or press; and we must and do sustain its constitutionality. . . .

Affirmed.

MR. JUSTICE HOLMES, dissenting.

MR. JUSTICE BRANDEIS and I are of opinion that this judgment should be reversed. The general principle of free speech, it seems to me, must be taken to be included in the Fourteenth Amendment, in view of the scope that has been given to the word "liberty" as there used, although perhaps it may be accepted with a somewhat larger latitude of interpretation than is allowed to Congress by the sweeping language that governs or ought to govern the laws of the United States. If I am right, then I think that the criterion sanctioned by the full court in *Schenck* v. *United States* . . . applies. It is manifest that there was no present danger of an attempt to overthrow the government by force on the part of the admittedly small minority who shared the defendant's views. It is said that this manifesto was more than a theory, that it was an incitement. Every idea is an incitement. It offers itself for belief and if believed it is acted on unless some other belief outweighs it or some failure of energy stifles the movement at its birth. The only difference between the expression of an opinion and an incitement in the narrower sense is the speaker's enthusiasm for the result. Eloquence may set fire to reason. But whatever may be thought of the redundant discourse before us it had no chance of starting a present conflagration. If in the long run the beliefs expressed in proletarian dictatorship are destined to be accepted by the dominant forces of the community, the only meaning of free speech is that they should be given their chance and have their way.

If the publication of this document had been laid out as an attempt to induce an uprising against government at once and not at some indefinite time in the future it would have presented a different question. The object would have been one with which the law might deal, subject to the doubt whether there was any danger that the publication could produce any result, or in other words, whether it was not futile and too remote from possible consequences. But the indictment alleges the publication and nothing more.

[*The Court Reporter neglected to record the fact that Justice Stone did not participate in the consideration or the decision of the case*].

Whitney v. *California*
274 U.S. 357, 47 S.Ct. 641, 71 L.Ed. 1095 (1927)

The appellant, Anita Whitney, was charged and convicted of violating California's Criminal Syndicalism Act (1919) by organizing, assisting in organizing, and being a member of a group advocating unlawful force as a political weapon, contrary to the statute (the provisions of which are contained in the opinion). Specifically, Miss Whitney was charged with participating in a convention of the Communist Labor party of California, which was affiliated with the Communist International of Moscow. Evidence showed that she had personally proposed a resolution advocating a strictly political role for the Party, which the convention had rejected in favor of a national program advocating various revolutionary measures including national strikes. Appellant remained until the end of the convention, and did not withdraw from the Party. From a judgment of a California district court of appeal affirming her conviction, Miss Whitney brought the case to the Supreme Court on a writ of error.

MR. JUSTICE SANFORD delivered the opinion of the Court. . . .

The first count of the information, on which the conviction was had, charged that on or about November 28, 1919, in Alameda County, the defendant in violation of the Criminal Syndicalism Act, "did then and there unlawfully, willfully, wrongfully, deliberately and feloniously organize and assist in organizing, and was, is, and knowingly became a member of an organization, society, group and assemblage of persons organized and assembled to advocate, teach, aid and abet criminal syndicalism." . . .

1. While it is not denied that the evidence warranted the jury in finding that the defendant became a member of and assisted in organizing the Communist Labor Party of California, and that this was organized to advocate, teach, aid or abet criminal syndicalism as defined by the Act, it is urged that the Act, as here construed and applied, deprived the defendant of her liberty without due process of law in that it has made her action in attending the Oakland convention unlawful by reason of "a subsequent event brought about against her will, by the agency of others," with no showing of a specific intent on her part to join in the forbidden purpose of the association, and merely because, by reason of a lack of "prophetic" understanding, she failed to foresee the quality that others would give to the convention. The argument is, in effect, that the character of the state organization could not be forecast when she attended the convention; that she had no purpose of helping to create an instrument of terrorism and violence; that she "took part in formulating and presenting to the convention a resolution which, if adopted, would have committed the new organization to a legitimate policy of political reform by the use of the ballot"; that it was not until after the majority of the convention turned out to be "contrary minded, and other less temperate policies prevailed" that the convention could have taken on the character of criminal syndicalism; and that as this was done over her protest, her mere presence in the convention, however violent the opinions expressed therein, could not thereby become a crime.

2. It is clear that the Syndicalism Act is not repugnant to the due process clause by reason of vagueness and uncertainty of definitions. . . .

The Act, plainly, meets the essential requirement of due process that a penal statute be "sufficiently explicit to inform those who are subject to it what conduct on their part will render them liable to its penalties," and be couched in terms that are not "so vague that men of common intelligence must necessarily guess at its meaning and differ as to its application." . . .

3. Neither is the Syndicalism Act repugnant to the equal protection clause, on the ground that, as its penalties are confined to those who advocate a resort to violent and unlawful methods as a means of changing industrial and political conditions, it arbitrarily discriminates between such persons and those who may advocate a resort to these methods as a means of maintaining such conditions.

It is settled by repeated decisions of this Court that the equal protection clause does not take from a State the power to classify in the adoption of police laws, but admits of the exercise of a wide scope of discretion, and avoids what is done only when it is without any reasonable basis and therefore is purely arbitrary; and that one who assails the classification must carry the burden of showing that it does not rest upon any reasonable basis, but is essentially arbitrary. . . .

4. Nor is the Syndicalism Act as applied in this case repugnant to the due process clause as a restraint of the rights of free speech, assembly, and association.

That the freedom of speech which is secured by the Constitution does not confer an absolute right to speak, without responsibility, whatever one may choose, or an unrestricted and unbridled license giving immunity for every possible use of language and preventing the punishment of those who abuse this freedom; and that a State in the exercise of its police power may punish those who abuse this freedom by utterances inimical to the public welfare, tending to incite to crime, disturb the public peace, or endanger the foundations of organized government and threaten its overthrow by unlawful means, is not open to question. . . .

By enacting the provisions of the Syndicalism Act the State has declared, through its legislative body, that to knowingly be or become a member of or assist in organizing an association to advocate, teach or aid and abet the commission of crimes or unlawful acts of force, violence or terrorism as a means of accomplishing industrial or political changes, involves such danger to the public peace and the security of the State, that these acts should be penalized in the exercise of its police power.

That determination must be given great weight. Every presumption is to be indulged in favor of the validity of the statute, *Mugler* v. *Kansas* . . . and it may not be declared unconstitutional unless it is an arbitrary or unreasonable attempt to exercise the authority vested in the State in the public interest. . . .

Affirmed.

MR. JUSTICE BRANDEIS, concurring. . . .

Despite arguments to the contrary which had seemed to me persuasive, it is settled that the due process clause of the Fourteenth Amendment applies to matters of substantive law as well as to matters of procedure. Thus all fundamental rights comprised within the term liberty are protected by the federal Constitution from invasion by the states. The right of free speech, the right to teach and the right of assembly are, of course, fundamental rights. . . . These may not be denied or abridged. But, although the rights of free speech and assembly are fundamental, they are not in their nature absolute. Their exercise is subject to restriction, if the particular restriction proposed is required in order to protect the state from destruction or from serious injury, political, economic or moral. That the necessity which is essential to a valid restriction does not exist unless speech would produce, or is intended to produce, a clear and imminent danger of some substantive evil which the state constitutionally may seek to prevent has been settled. . . .

It is said to be the function of the Legislature to determine whether at a particular time and under the particular circumstances the formation of, or assembly with, a society organized to advocate criminal syndicalism constitutes a clear and present danger of substantive evil; and that enacting the law here in question the Legislature of California determined that question in the affirmative. . . . The legislature must obviously decide, in the first instance, whether a danger exists which calls for a particular protective measure. But where a statute is valid only in case certain conditions exist, the enactment of the statute cannot alone establish the facts which are essential to its validity. Prohibitory legislation has repeatedly been held invalid, because unnecessary, where the denial of liberty involved

was that of engaging in a particular business. The powers of the courts to strike down an offending law are no less when the interests involved are not property rights, but the fundamental personal rights of free speech and assembly.

This court has not yet fixed the standard by which to determine when a danger shall be deemed clear; how remote the danger may be and yet be deemed present; and what degree of evil shall be deemed sufficiently substantial to justify resort to abridgment of free speech and assembly as the means of protection. To reach sound conclusions on these matters, we must bear in mind why a state is, ordinarily, denied the power to prohibit dissemination of social, economic and political doctrine which a vast majority of its citizens believes to be false and fraught with evil consequence.

Those who won our independence believed that the final end of the state was to make men free to develop their faculties, and that in its government the deliberative forces should prevail over the arbitrary. They valued liberty both as an end and as a means. They believed liberty to be the secret of happiness and courage to be the secret of liberty. They believed that freedom to think as you will and to speak as you think are means indispensable to the discovery and spread of political truth; that without free speech and assembly discussion would be futile; that with them, discussion affords ordinarily adequate protection against the dissemination of noxious doctrine; that the greatest menace to freedom is an inert people; that public discussion is a political duty; and that this should be a fundamental principle of the American government. They recognized the risks to which all human institutions are subject. But they knew that order cannot be secured merely through fear of punishment for its infraction; that it is hazardous to discourage thought, hope and imagination; that fear breeds repression; that repression breeds hate; that hate menaces stable government; that the path of safety lies in the opportunity to discuss freely supposed grievances and proposed remedies; and that the fitting remedy for evil counsels is good ones. Believing in the power of reason as applied through public discussion, they eschewed silence coerced by law—the argument of force in its worst form. Recognizing the occasional tyrannies of governing majorities, they amended the Constitution so that free speech and assembly should be guaranteed.

Fear of serious injury cannot alone justify suppression of free speech and assembly. Men feared witches and burnt women. It is the function of speech to free men from the bondage of irrational fears. To justify suppression of free speech there must be reasonable ground to fear that serious evil will result if free speech is practiced. There must be reasonable ground to believe that the danger apprehended is imminent. There must be reasonable ground to believe that the evil to be prevented is a serious one. . . . The wide difference between advocacy and incitement, between preparation and attempt, between assembling and conspiracy, must be borne in mind. In order to support a finding of clear and present danger it must be shown either that immediate serious violence was to be expected or was advocated, or that the past conduct furnished reason to believe that such advocacy was then contemplated.

Those who won our independence by revolution were not cowards. They did not fear political change. They did not exalt order at the cost of liberty. To courageous, self-reliant men, with confidence in the power of free and fearless reasoning applied through the process of popular government, no danger flowing from speech can be deemed clear and present, unless the incidence of the evil apprehended is so imminent that it may befall before there is opportunity for full discussion. If there be time to expose through discussion the falsehood and fallacies, to avert the evil by the processes of education, the remedy to be applied is more speech, not enforced silence. Only an emergency can justify repression. Such must be the rule if authority is to be reconciled with freedom. Such, in my opinion, is the command of the Constitution. It is therefore always open to Americans to challenge a law abridging free speech and assembly by showing that there was no emergency justifying it.

Moreover, even imminent danger cannot justify resort to prohibition of these functions essential to effective democracy, unless the evil apprehended is relatively serious. Prohibition of free speech and assembly is a measure so stringent that it would be inappropriate as the means for averting a relatively trivial harm to society. A police measure may be unconstitutional merely because the remedy, although effective as means of protection, is unduly harsh or oppressive. . . . The fact that speech is likely to result in some violence or in destruction of property is not enough to justify its suppression. There must be the probability of serious injury to the State. Among free men, the deterrents ordinarily to be applied to prevent crime are education and punishment for violations of the law, not abridgment of the rights of free speech and assembly.

Whether in 1919, when Miss Whitney did the things complained of, there was in California such clear and present danger of serious evil, might have been made the important issue in this case. She might have required that the issue be determined either by the court or by the jury. She claimed below that the statute as applied to her violated the federal Constitution; but she did not claim that it was void because there was no clear and present danger of serious evil, nor did she request that the existence of these conditions of a valid measure thus restricting the rights of free speech and assembly be passed upon by the court or a jury. On the other hand, there was evidence on which the court or jury might have found that such danger existed. I am unable to assent to the suggestion in the opinion of the court that assembling with a political party, formed to advocate the desirability of a proletarian revolution by mass action at some date necessarily far in the future, is not a right within the protection of the Fourteenth Amendment. In the present case, however, there was other testimony which tended to establish the existence of a conspiracy, on the part of members of the International Workers of the World, to commit present serious crimes, and likewise to show that such a conspiracy would be furthered by the activity of the society of which

Miss Whitney was a member. Under these circumstances the judgment of the State court cannot be disturbed. . . .

MR. JUSTICE HOLMES joins in this opinion.

Dennis v. *United States*
341 U.S. 494, 71 S.Ct 857, 95 L.Ed. 1137 (1951)

The Dennis case represents the last stage of the 1949 trial of the 11 leaders of the Communist Party of the United States for violations of the Smith Act of 1940. The Supreme Court granted certiorari, limited to a review of whether Sections 2 or 3 of the Smith Act, inherently or as construed and applied, violated the First or Fifth Amendments.

MR. CHIEF JUSTICE VINSON announced the judgment of the court and an opinion in which MR. JUSTICE REED, MR. JUSTICE BURTON, and MR. JUSTICE MINTON join. . . .

Sections 2 and 3 of the Smith Act, provide as follows:

Sec. 2

(a) It shall be unlawful for any person—

(1) to knowingly or willfully advocate, abet, advise, or teach the duty, necessity, desirability, or propriety of overthrowing or destroying any government in the United States by force or violence, or by the assassination of any officer of such government;

(2) with the intent to cause the overthrow or destruction of any government in the United States, to print, publish, edit, issue, circulate, sell, distribute, or publicly display any written or printed matter advocating, advising, or teaching the duty, necessity, desirability, or propriety of overthrowing or destroying any government in the United States by force or violence;

(3) to organize or help to organize any society, group, or assembly of persons who teach, advocate, or encourage the overthrow or destruction of any government in the United States by force or violence; or to be or become a member of, or af-

filiate with, any such society, group, or assembly of persons, knowing the purposes thereof.

(b) For the purposes of this section, the term "government in the United States" means the Government of the United States, the government of any State, Territory, or possession of the United States, the government of the District of Columbia, or the government of any political subdivison of any of them.

Sec. 3. It shall be unlawful for any person to attempt to commit, or to conspire to commit, any of the acts prohibited by the provisions of . . . this title. . . .

The obvious purpose of the statute is to protect existing Government, not from change by peaceable, lawful and constitutional means, but from change by violence, revolution and terrorism. That it is within the *power* of Congress to protect the Government of the United States from armed rebellion is a proposition which requires little discussion. Whatever theoretical merit there may be to the argument that there is a "right" to rebellion against dictatorial governments is without force where the existing structure of the government provides for peaceful and orderly change. We reject any principle of governmental helplessness in the face of preparation for revolution, which principle, carried to its logical conclusion, must lead to anarchy. No one could conceive that it is not within the power of Congress to prohibit acts intended to overthrow the Government by force and violence. The question with which we are concerned here is not whether Congress has such *power,* but whether the *means* which it has employed conflict with the First and Fifth Amendments to the Constitution.

One of the bases for the contention that the means which Congress has employed are invalid takes the form of an attack on the face of the statute on the grounds that by its terms it prohibits academic discussion of the merits of Marxism-Leninism, that it stifles ideas and is contrary to all concepts of a free speech and a free press. . . .

The very language of the Smith Act negates the interpretation which petitioners would have us impose on that Act. It is directed at advocacy, not discussion. Thus, the trial judge properly charged the jury that they could not convict if they found that petitioners did "no more than pursue peaceful studies and discussions or teaching and advocacy in the realm of ideas." He further charged that it was not unlawful "to conduct in an American college or university a course explaining the philosophical theories set forth in the books which have been placed in evidence." Such a charge is in strict accord with the statutory language, and illustrates the meaning to be placed on those words. Congress did not intend to eradicate the free discussion of political theories, to destroy the traditional rights of Americans to discuss and evaluate ideas without fear of governmental sanction. Rather Congress was concerned with the very kind of activity in which the evidence showed these petitioners engaged. . . .

. . . The basis of the First Amendment is the hypothesis that speech can rebut speech, propaganda will answer propaganda, free debate of ideas will result in the wisest governmental policies. It is for this reason that this Court has recognized the inherent value of free discourse. An analysis of the leading cases in this Court which have involved direct limitations on speech, however, will demonstrate that both the majority of the Court and dissenters in particular cases have recognized that this is not an unlimited, unqualified right, but that the societal value of speech must, on occasion, be subordinated to other values and considerations. . . .

[The Court here discussed several post–World War I cases.]

The rule we deduce from these cases is that where an offense is specified by a statute in nonspeech or nonpress terms, a conviction relying upon speech or press as evidence of violation may be sustained only when the speech or publication created a "clear and present danger" of attempting or accomplishing the prohibited crime, e.g., interference with enlistment. The dissents, we repeat, in emphasizing the value of speech, were addressed to the argument of the sufficiency of the evidence. . . .

[The Court next discussed *Gitlow* and *Whitney.*]

Although no case subsequent to *Whitney* and *Gitlow* has expressly overruled the majority opinions in those cases, there is little doubt that subsequent opinions have inclined toward the Holmes-Brandeis rationale. . . . In this case we are squarely presented with the application of the "clear and present danger" test, and must decide what that phrase imports. We first note that many of the cases in which this Court has reversed convictions by use of this or similar tests have been based on the fact that the interest which the State was attempting to protect was itself too insubstantial to warrant restriction of speech. . . . Overthrow of the Government by force and violence is certainly a substantial enough interest for the Government to limit speech. Indeed, this is the ultimate value of any society, for if a society cannot protect its very structure from armed internal attack, it must follow that no subordinate value can be protected. If, then, this interest may be protected, the literal problem which is presented is what has been meant by the use of the phrase "clear and present danger" of the utterances bringing about the evil within the power of Congress to punish.

different from —

Obviously, the words cannot mean that before the Government may act, it must wait until the putsch is about to be executed, the plans have been laid and the signal is awaited. If Government is aware that a group aiming at its overthrow is attempting to indoctrinate its members and to commit them to a course whereby they will strike when the leaders feel the circumstances permit, action by the Government is required. The argument that there is no need for Government to concern itself, for Government is strong, it possesses ample powers to put down a rebellion, it may defeat the revolution with ease needs no answer. For that is not the question. Certainly an attempt to overthrow the Government by force, even though doomed from the outset because of inadequate numbers or power of the revolutionists, is a sufficient evil for Congress to prevent. The damage which such attempts create both physically and politically to a nation makes it impossible to measure the validity in terms of the probability of success, or the immediacy of a successful attempt. In the instant case the trial judge charged the jury that they could not convict unless they found that petitioners intended to overthrow the Government "as speedily as circumstances would permit." This does not mean, and could not properly mean, that they would not strike until there was certainty of success. What was meant was that the revolutionists would strike when they thought the time was ripe. We must therefore reject the contention that success or probability of success is the criterion.

The situation with which Justices Holmes and Brandeis were concerned in Gitlow was a comparatively isolated event, bearing little relation in their minds to any substantial threat to the safety of the community. . . . They were not confronted with any situation comparable to the instant one—the development of an apparatus designed and dedicated to the overthrow of the Government, in the context of world crisis after crisis.

Chief Judge Learned Hand, writing for the majority below, interpreted the phrase as follows: "In each case [courts] must ask whether the gravity of the 'evil,' discounted by its improbability, justifies such invasion of free speech as is necessary to avoid the danger." . . . We adopt this statement of the rule. As articulated by Chief Judge Hand, it is as succinct and inclusive as any other we might devise at this time. It takes into consideration those factors which we deem relevant, and relates their significances. More we cannot expect from words.

Likewise, we are in accord with the court below, which affirmed the trial court's finding that the requisite danger existed. The mere fact that from the period 1945 to 1948 petitioners' activities did not result in an attempt to overthrow the Government by force and violence is of course no answer to the fact that there was a group that was ready to make the attempt. The formation by petitioners of such a highly organized conspiracy, with rigidly disciplined members subject to call when the leaders, these petitioners, felt that the time had come for action, coupled with the inflammable nature of world conditions, similar uprisings in other countries, and the touch-and-go nature of our relations with countries with whom petitioners were in the very least ideologically attuned, convince us that their convictions were justified on this score. And this analysis disposes of the contention that a conspiracy to advocate, as distinguished from the advocacy itself, cannot be constitutionally restrained, because it comprises only the preparation. It is the existence of the conspiracy which creates the danger. . . . If the ingredients of the reaction are present, we cannot bind the government to wait until the catalyst is added. . . .

When facts are found that establish the violation of a statute the protection against conviction afforded by the First Amendment is a matter of law. The doctrine that there must be a clear and present danger of a substantive evil that Congress has a right to prevent is a judicial rule to be applied as a matter of law by the courts. The guilt is established by proof of facts. Whether the First Amendment protects the activity which constitutes the violation of the statute must depend upon a judicial determina-

Scientific analysis

tion of the scope of the First Amendment applied to the circumstances of the case. . . .

We agree that the standard as defined is not a neat, mathematical formulary. Like all verbalizations it is subject to criticism on the score of indefiniteness. But petitioners themselves contend that the verbalization, "clear and present danger" is the proper standard. We see no difference from the standpoint of vagueness, whether the standard of "clear and present danger" is one contained in haec verba within the statute, or whether it is the judicial measure of constitutional applicability. We have shown the indeterminate standard the phrase necessarily connotes. We do not think we have rendered that standard any more indefinite by our attempt to sum up the factors which are included within its scope. We think it well serves to indicate to those who would advocate constitutionally prohibited conduct that there is a line beyond which they may not go—a line, which they, in full knowledge of what they intend and the circumstances in which their activity takes place, will well appreciate and understand. . . .

Affirmed.

MR. JUSTICE CLARK took no part in the consideration or decision of this case.

MR. JUSTICE FRANKFURTER, concurring in affirmance of the judgment. . . .

The language of the First Amendment is to be read not as barren words found in a dictionary but as symbols of historic experience illumined by the presuppositions of those who employed them. Not what words did Madison and Hamilton use, but what was it in their minds which they conveyed? Free speech is subject to prohibition of those abuses of expression which a civilized society may forbid. As in the case of every other provision of the Constitution that is not crystallized by the nature of its technical concepts, the fact that the First Amendment is not self-defining and self-enforcing neither impairs its usefulness nor compels its paralysis as a living instrument. . . .

. . . The demands of free speech in a democratic society as well as the interest in national security are better served by candid and informed weighing of the competing interests, within the confines of the judicial process, than by announcing dogmas too inflexible for the non-Euclidian problems to be solved.

But how are competing interests to be assessed? Since they are not subject to quantitative ascertainment, the issue necessarily resolves itself into asking, who is to make the adjustment?—who is to balance the relevant factors and ascertain which interest is in the circumstances to prevail? Full responsibility for the choice cannot be given to the courts. Courts are not representative bodies. They are not designed to be a good reflex of a democratic society. Their judgment is best informed, and therefore most dependable, within narrow limits. Their essential quality is detachment, founded on independence. History teaches that the independence of the judiciary is jeopardized when courts become embroiled in the passions of the day and assume primary responsibility in choosing between competing political, economic and social pressures.

Primary responsibility for adjusting the interests which compete in the situation before us of necessity belongs to the Congress. The nature of the power to be exercised by this Court has been delineated in decisions not charged with the emotional appeal of situations such as that now before us. . . .

Throughout our decisions there has recurred a distinction between the statement of an idea which may prompt its hearers to take unlawful action, and advocacy that such action be taken. . . .

It is true that there is no divining rod by which we may locate "advocacy." Exposition of ideas readily merges into advocacy. The same Justice who gave currency to application of the incitement doctrine in this field dissented four times from what he thought was its misapplication. As he said in the Gitlow dissent, "Every idea is an incitement." . . . Even though advocacy of overthrow deserves little protection, we should hesitate to prohibit it if we thereby inhibit the interchange of rational ideas so essential to representative government and free society.

But there is underlying validity in the distinction between advocacy and the interchange of ideas, and we do not discard a useful tool because it may be misused. That such a distinction could be used unreasonably by those in power against hostile or unorthodox views does not negate the fact that it may be used reasonably against an organization wielding the power of the centrally controlled international Communist movement. The object of the conspiracy before us is clear enough that the chance of error in saying that the defendants conspired to advocate rather than to express ideas is slight. Mr. Justice Douglas quite properly points out that the conspiracy before us is not a conspiracy to overthrow the Government. But it would be equally wrong to treat it as a seminar in political theory. . . .

It is not for us to decide how we would adjust the clash of interests which this case presents were the primary responsibility for reconciling it ours. Congress has determined that the danger created by advocacy of overthrow justifies the ensuing restriction on freedom of speech. The determination was made after due deliberation, and the seriousness of the congressional purpose is attested by the volume of legislation passed to effectuate the same ends.

Can we then say that the judgment Congress exercised was denied it by the Constitution? Can we establish a constitutional doctrine which forbids the elected representatives of the people to make this choice? Can we hold that the First Amendment deprives Congress of what it deemed necessary for the Government's protection?

To make validity of legislation depend on judicial reading of events still in the womb of time—a forecast, that is, of the outcome of forces at best appreciated only with knowledge of the topmost secrets of nations—is to charge the judiciary with duties beyond its equipment. We do not expect courts to pronounce historic verdicts on bygone events. Even historians have conflicting views to this day on the origin and conduct of the French Revolution. It is as absurd to be confident that we can measure the present clash of forces and their outcome as to ask us to read history still enveloped in clouds of controversy. . . .

Civil liberties draw at best only limited strength from legal guaranties. Preoccupation by our people with the constitutionality, instead of with the wisdom of legislation or of executive action, is preoccupation with a false value. Even those who would most freely use the judicial brake on the democratic process by invalidating legislation that goes deeply against their grain, acknowledge, at least by paying lip service, that constitutionality does not exact a sense of proportion or the sanity of humor or an absence of fear. Focusing attention on constitutionality tends to make constitutionality synonymous with wisdom. When legislation touches freedom of thought and freedom of speech, such a tendency is a formidable enemy of the free spirit. Much that should be rejected as illiberal, because repressive and envenoming, may well be not unconstitutional. The ultimate reliance for the deepest needs of civilization must be found outside their vindication in courts of law; apart from all else, judges, howsoever they may conscientiously seek to discipline themselves against it, unconsciously are too apt to be moved by the deep undercurrents of public feeling. A persistent, positive translation of the liberating faith into the feelings and thoughts and actions of men and women is the real protection against attempts to strait-jacket the human mind. Such temptations will have their way, if fear and hatred are not exorcised. The mark of a truly civilized man is confidence in the strength and security derived from the inquiring mind. We may be grateful for such honest comforts as it supports, but we must be unafraid of its uncertitudes. Without open minds there can be no open society. And if society be not open the spirit of man is mutilated and becomes enslaved. . . .

MR. JUSTICE JACKSON, concurring. . . .

The law of conspiracy has been the chief means at the Government's disposal to deal with the growing problems created by such organizations. I happen to think it is an awkward and inept remedy, but I find no constitutional authority for taking this weapon from the Government. There is no constitutional right to "gang up" on the Government.

While I think there was power in Congress to enact this statute and that, as applied in this case, it cannot be held unconstitutional, I add that I have little faith in the long-range effectiveness of this conviction to stop the rise of the Communist movement. Communism will not go to jail with these Communists. No decision by this Court can forestall revolution whenever the existing government fails to command the respect and loyalty of the people and sufficient distress and discontent is allowed to grow up among the masses. Many failures by fallen governments attest that no government can long prevent revolution by outlawry. Corruption, ineptitude, inflation, oppressive taxation, militarization, injustice, and loss of leadership capable of intellectual initiative in domestic or foreign affairs are allies on which the Communists count to bring opportunity knocking to their door. Sometimes I think they may be mistaken. But the Communists are not building just for today—the rest of us might profit by their example.

MR. JUSTICE BLACK, dissenting. . . .

At the outset I want to emphasize what the crime involved in this case is, and what it is not. These petitioners were not charged with an attempt to overthrow the Government. They were not charged with overt acts of any kind designed to overthrow the Government. They were not even charged with saying anything or writing anything designed to overthrow the Government. The charge was that they agreed to assemble and to talk and publish certain ideas at a later date: The indictment is that they conspired to organize the Communist Party and to use speech or newspapers and other publications in the future to teach and advocate the forcible overthrow of the Government. No matter how it is worded, this is a virulent form of prior censorship of speech and press, which I believe the First Amendment forbids. I would hold § 3 of the Smith Act authorizing this prior restraint unconstitutional on its face and as applied. . . .

So long as this Court exercises the power of judicial review of legislation, I cannot agree that the First Amendment permits us to sustain laws suppressing freedom of speech and press on the basis of Congress's or our own notions of mere "reasonableness." Such a doctrine waters down the First Amendment so that it amounts to little more than an admonition to Congress. The Amendment as so construed is not likely to protect any but those "safe" or orthodox views which rarely need its protection. . . .

Public opinion being what it now is, few will protest the conviction of these Communist petitioners. There is hope, however, that in calmer times, when present pressures, passions and fears subside, this or some later Court will restore the First Amendment liberties to the high preferred place where they belong in a free society.

MR. JUSTICE DOUGLAS, dissenting. . . .

If this were a case where those who claimed protection under the First Amendment were teaching the techniques of sabotage, the assassination of the President, the filching of documents from public files, the planting of bombs, the art of street warfare, and the like, I would have no doubts. The freedom to speak is not absolute; the teaching of methods of terror and other seditious conduct should be beyond the pale along with obscenity and immorality. This case was argued as if those were the facts. The argument imported much seditious conduct into the record. That is easy and it has popular appeal, for the activities of Communists in plotting and scheming against the free world are common knowledge. But the fact is that no such evidence was introduced at the trial. There is a statute which makes a seditious conspiracy unlawful. Petitioners, however, were not charged with a "conspiracy to overthrow" the Government. They were charged with a conspiracy to form a party and groups and assemblies of people who teach and advocate the overthrow of our Government by force or violence and with a conspiracy to advocate and teach its overthrow by force and violence. It may well be that indoctrination in the techniques of terror to destroy the Government would be indictable under either statute. But the teaching which is condemned here is of a different character. . . .

The vice of treating speech as the equivalent of overt acts of a treasonable or seditious character is emphasized by a concurring opinion, which by invoking the law of conspiracy makes speech do service for deeds which are dangerous to society. The doctrine of conspiracy has served divers and oppressive purposes and in its broad reach can be made to do great evil. But never until today has anyone seriously thought that the ancient law of conspiracy could constitutionally be used to turn speech into seditious conduct. Yet that is precisely what is suggested. I repeat that we deal here with speech alone, not with speech *plus* acts of sabotage or unlawful conduct. Not a single seditious act is charged in the indictment. To make a lawful speech unlawful because two men conceive it is to raise the law of conspiracy to appalling proportions. That course is to make a radical break with the past and to violate one of the cardinal principles of our constitutional scheme. . . .

There comes a time when even speech loses its constitutional immunity. Speech innocuous one year may at another time fan such destructive flames that it must be halted in the interests of the safety of the Republic. That is the meaning of the clear and present danger test. When conditions are so critical that there will be no time to avoid the evil that the speech threatens, it is time to call a halt. Otherwise, free speech which is the strength of the Nation will be the cause of its destruction.

Yet free speech is the rule, not the exception. The restraint to be constitutional must be based on more than fear, on more than passionate opposition against the speech, on more than a revolted dislike for its contents. There must be some immediate injury to society that is likely if speech is allowed. . . .

The First Amendment provides that "Congress shall make no law . . . abridging the freedom of speech." The Constitution provides no exception. This does not mean, however, that the Nation need hold its hand until it is in such weakened condition that there is no time to protect itself from incitement to revolution. Seditious conduct can always be punished. But the command of the First Amendment is so clear that we should not allow Congress to call a halt to free speech except in the extreme case of peril from the speech itself. The First Amendment makes confidence in the common sense of our people and in their maturity of judgment the great postulate of our democracy. Its philosophy is that violence is rarely, if ever, stopped by denying civil liberties to those advocating resort to force. The First Amendment reflects the philosophy of Jefferson "that it is time enough for the rightful purposes of civil government for its officers to interfere when principles break out into overt acts against peace and good order." The political censor has no place in our public debates. Unless and until extreme and necessitous circumstances are shown our aim should be to keep speech unfettered and to allow the processes of law to be invoked only when the provocateurs among us move from speech to action.

Vishinsky wrote in 1948 in *The Law of the Soviet State,* "In our state, naturally there can be no place for freedom of speech, press, and so on for the foes of socialism."

Our concern should be that we accept no such standard for the United States. Our faith should be that our people will never give support to these advocates of revolution, so long as we remain loyal to the purposes for which our Nation was founded.

Yates v. United States
354 U.S. 298, 77 S.Ct. 1604, 1 L.Ed. 2d 1356 (1957)

In the years following the Dennis decision the United States began prosecutions of lesser figures in the Communist party. The 14 petitioners in *Yates* were convicted by a federal district court in California of conspiring, first, to advocate and teach the duty and necessity of overthrowing the Government of the United States by force and violence and, second, to organize, as the Communist Party of the United States, a society of persons to advocate and teach subversion. A portion of the opinion construing narrowly the term "organize" so as to exclude evidence of actions involving the "organizing" of the Party in 1945 and earlier, because of the three-year statute of limitations, has been omitted.

MR. JUSTICE HARLAN delivered the opinion of the Court.

We brought these cases here to consider certain questions arising under the Smith Act which have not heretofore been passed upon by this Court, and otherwise to review the convictions of these petitioners for conspiracy to violate that Act. Among other things, the convictions are claimed to rest upon an application of the Smith Act which is hostile to the principles upon which its constitutionality was upheld in *Dennis* v. *United States*, 341 U.S. 494.

. . . The conspiracy is alleged to have originated in 1940 and continued down to the date of the indictment in 1951. The indictment charged that in carrying out the conspiracy the defendants and their co-conspirators would (a) become members and officers of the Communist Party, with knowledge of its unlawful purposes, and assume leadership in carrying out its policies and activities; (b) cause to be organized units of the Party in California and elsewhere; (c) write and publish, in the "Daily Worker" and other Party organs, articles on the proscribed advocacy and teaching; (d) conduct schools for the indoctrination of Party members in such advocacy and teaching, and (e) recruit new Party members, particularly from among persons employed in the key industries of the nation. Twenty-three overt acts in furtherance of the conspiracy were alleged. . . . [After a detailed analysis of the term "organize," the

opinion continued.] We conclude . . . that since the Communist Party came into being in 1945, and indictment was not returned until 1951, the three-year statute of limitations had run on the "organizing" charge, and required the withdrawal of that part of the indictment from the jury's consideration. . . .

Petitioners contend that the instructions to the jury were fatally defective in that the trial court refused to charge that, in order to convict, the jury must find that the advocacy which the defendants conspired to promote was of a kind calculated to incite persons to action for the forcible overthrow of the Government. It is argued that advocacy of forcible overthrow as mere *abstract doctrine* is within the free speech protection of the First Amendment; that the Smith Act, consistently with that constitutional provision, must be taken as proscribing only the sort of advocacy which incites to illegal *action;* and that the trial court's charge, by permitting conviction for mere advocacy, unrelated to its tendency to produce forcible action, resulted in an unconstitutional application of the Smith Act. The Government, which at the trial also requested the court to charge in terms of "incitement," now takes the position, however, that the true constitutional dividing line is not between inciting and abstract advocacy of forcible overthrow, but rather between advocacy as such, irrespective of its inciting qualities, and the mere discussion or exposition of violent overthrow as an abstract theory.

. . . We are faced with the question whether the Smith Act prohibits advocacy and teaching of forcible overthrow as an abstract principle, divorced from any effort to instigate action to that end, so long as such advocacy or teaching is engaged in with evil intent. We hold that it does not.

The distinction between advocacy of abstract doctrine and advocacy directed at promoting unlawful action is one that has been consistently recognized in the opinions of this Court. . . . This distinction was heavily underscored in *Gitlow* v. *New York,* 268 U.S. 652, . . . in which the statute involved was nearly identical with the one now before us.

. . . The legislative history of the Smith Act and related bills shows beyond all question that Congress was aware of the distinction between the advocacy or teaching of abstract doctrine and the advocacy or teaching of action, and that it did not intend to disregard it. The statute was aimed at the advocacy and teaching of concrete action for the forcible overthrow of the Government, and not of principles divorced from action. . . .

In failing to distinguish between advocacy of forcible overthrow as an abstract doctrine and advocacy of action to that end, the District Court appears to have been led astray by the holding in *Dennis* that advocacy of violent action to be taken at some future time was enough. It seems to have considered that, since "inciting" speech is usually thought of as calculated to induce immediate action, and since *Dennis* held advocacy of action for future overthrow sufficient, this meant that advocacy, irrespective of its tendency to generate action, is punishable, provided only that it is uttered with a specific intent to accomplish overthrow. In other words, the District Court apparently thought that *Dennis* obliterated the traditional dividing line between advocacy of abstract doctrine and advocacy of action.

As one of the concurring opinions in *Dennis* put it: "Throughout our decisions there has recurred a distinction between the statement of an idea which may prompt its hearers to take unlawful action, and advocacy that such action

be taken." *Id.* 341 U.S at 545. There is nothing in *Dennis* which makes that historic distinction obsolete. . . .

On this basis we have concluded that the evidence against [5] petitioners . . . is so clearly insufficient that their acquittal should be ordered. . . .

As to [them] we find no adequate evidence in the record which would permit a jury to find that they were members of such a conspiracy. For all purposes relevant here, the sole evidence as to them was that they had long been members, officers or functionaries of the Communist Party of California. . . . So far as this record shows, none of them has engaged in or been associated with any but what appear to have been wholly lawful activities, or has ever made a single remark or been present when someone else made a remark which would tend to prove the charges against them. . . .

Moreover, apart from the inadequacy of the evidence to show, at best, more than the abstract advocacy and teaching of forcible overthrow by the Party, it is difficult to perceive how the requisite specific intent to accomplish such overthrow could be deemed proved by a showing of mere membership or the holding of office in the Communist Party. We therefore think that as to these petitioners the evidence was entirely too meagre to justify putting them to a new trial, and that their acquittal should be ordered. . . .

For the foregoing reasons we think that the way must be left open for a new trial to the extent indicated. . . .

[MR. JUSTICE BURTON concurred in the result.]

MR. JUSTICE BRENNAN and MR. JUSTICE WHITTAKER took no part in the consideration or decision of this case.

MR. JUSTICE BLACK, with whom MR. JUSTICE DOUGLAS joins, concurring in part and dissenting in part.

I would reverse every one of these convictions and direct that all the defendants be acquitted. In my judgment the statutory provisions on which these prosecutions are based abridge freedom of speech, press and assembly in violation of the First Amendment to the United States Constitution. . . .

In essence, petitioners were tried upon the charge that they believe in and want to foist upon this country a different and to us a despicable form of authoritarian government in which voices criticizing the existing order are summarily silenced. I fear that the present type of prosecutions are more in line with the philosophy of authoritarian government than with that expressed by our First Amendment.

Doubtlessly, dictators have to stamp out causes and beliefs which they deem subversive to their evil regimes. But governmental suppression of causes and beliefs seems to me to be the very antithesis of what our Constitution stands for. The choice expressed in the First Amendment in favor of free expression was made against a turbulent background by men such as Jefferson, Madison, and Mason—men who believed that loyalty to the provisions of this Amendment was the best way to assure a long life for this new nation and its Government. Unless there is complete freedom for expression of all ideas, whether we like them or not, concerning the way government should be run and who shall run it, I doubt if any views in the long run can be secured against the censor. The First Amendment provides the only kind of security system that can preserve a free government—one that leaves the way wide open for people to favor, discuss, advocate, or incite causes and doctrines however obnoxious and antagonistic such views may be to the rest of us.

MR. JUSTICE CLARK, dissenting. . . .

National Association for the Advancement of Colored People v. Alabama
357 U.S. 449, 78 S.Ct. 1163, 2 L.Ed. 2d 1488 (1958)

Issues involving civil liberties have commonly been treated as though only individual interests were affected. Increasingly it is recognized that, to be effective, individuals seeking to protect or advance particular interests must act in groups or through associations. This case arose from the efforts of Alabama to enjoin the National Association for the Advancement of Colored People, a nonprofit, membership corporation, chartered in New York State, from conducting further activities within Alabama, and to oust the association from the state. It was claimed that the association did not qualify to do business within the state by failing to comply with the statute requiring foreign corporations to file their corporate charters with the Secretary of State and designate a place of business and an agent to receive service of process. The state circuit court restrained the association from engaging in further activities within the state or taking any steps to qualify itself to do business therein, and required the association to produce records and papers, including the names and addresses of all the association's Alabama members and agents. The association ultimately produced all the data called for by the production order, except its membership lists, as to which it contended that the state could not constitutionally compel disclosure. The state circuit court held the association in contempt of the production order and imposed a fine. The association's petitions for certiorari to review the contempt judgment were dismissed, on two occasions, by the Supreme Court of Alabama.

MR. JUSTICE HARLAN delivered the opinion of the Court.

. . . The question presented is whether Alabama, consistently with the Due Process Clause of the Fourteenth Amendment, can compel petitioner to reveal to the State's Attorney General the names and addresses of all its Alabama members and agents, without regard to their positions or functions in the Association. . . .

[The portion of the opinion rejecting Alabama's contention that the Court lacked jurisdiction because the denial of certiorari by the Supreme Court of Alabama rests on an independent nonfederal ground, is omitted.]

The Association both urges that it is constitutionally entitled to resist official inquiry into its membership lists, and that it may assert, on behalf of its members, a right personal to them to be protected from compelled disclosure by the State of their affiliation with the Association as revealed by the membership lists. . . .

If petitioner's rank-and-file members are constitutionally entitled to withhold their connection with the Association despite the production order, it is manifest that this right is properly assertable by the Association. To require that it be claimed by the members themselves would result in nullification of the right at the very moment of its assertion. Petitioner is the appropriate party to assert these rights, because it and its members are in every practical sense identical. The Association, which provides in its constitution that "[a]ny person who is in accordance with [its] principles and policies . . ." may become a member, is but the medium through which its individual members seek to make more effective the expression of their own views. The reasonable likelihood that the Association itself through diminished financial support and membership may be adversely affected if production is compelled is a further factor pointing towards our holding that petitioner has standing to complain of the production order on behalf of its members. . . .

We . . . reach petitioner's claim that the production order in the state litigation trespasses upon fundamental freedoms protected by the Due Process Clause of the Fourteenth Amendment. Petitioner argues that in view of the facts and circumstances shown in the record, the effect of compelled disclosure of the membership lists will be to abridge the rights of its rank-and-file members to engage in lawful association in support of their common beliefs. It contends that governmental action which, although not directly suppressing association, nevertheless carries this consequence, can be justified only upon some overriding valid interest of the State.

Effective advocacy of both public and private points of view, particularly controversial ones, is undeniably enhanced by group association, as this Court has more than once recognized by remarking upon the close nexus between the freedoms of speech and assembly. . . . It is beyond debate that freedom to engage in association for the advancement of beliefs and ideas is an inseparable aspect of the "liberty" assured by the Due Process Clause of the Fourteenth Amendment, which embraces freedom of speech. . . . Of course, it is immaterial whether the beliefs sought to be advanced by association pertain to political, economic, religious or cultural matters, and state action which may have the effect of curtailing the freedom to associate is subject to the closest scrutiny. . . .

It is hardly a novel perception that compelled disclosure of affiliation with groups engaged in advocacy may constitute as effective a restraint on freedom of association as the forms of governmental action in the cases above were thought likely to produce upon the particular constitutional rights there involved. This Court has recognized the vital relationship between freedom to associate and privacy in one's associations. . . .

We think that the production order, in the respects here drawn in question, must be regarded as entailing the likelihood of a substantial restraint upon the exercise by petitioner's members of their right to freedom of association. Petitioner has made an uncontroverted showing that on past occasions revelation of the identity of its rank-and-file members has exposed these members to economic reprisal, loss of employment, threat of physical coercion, and other manifestations of public hostility. Under these circumstances, we think it apparent that compelled disclosure of petitioner's Alabama membership is likely to affect adversely the ability of petitioner and its members to pursue their collective effort to foster beliefs which they admittedly have the right to advocate, in that it may induce members to withdraw from the Association and dissuade others from joining it because of fear of exposure of their beliefs shown through their associations and of the consequences of this exposure.

It is not sufficient to answer, as the State does here, that whatever repressive effect compulsory disclosure of names of petitioner's members may have upon participation by Alabama citizens in the petitioner's activities follows not from *State* action but from *private* community pressures. The crucial factor is the interplay of governmental and private action, for it is only after the initial exertion of state power represented by the production order that private action takes hold.

We turn to the final question whether Alabama has demonstrated an interest in obtaining the disclosures it seeks from petitioner which is sufficient to justify the deterrent effect which we have concluded these disclosures may well have on the free exercise by petitioner's members of their constitutionally protected right of association. . . . It is not of moment that the State has here acted solely through its judicial branch, for whether legislative or judicial, it is still the application of state power which we are asked to scrutinize.

It is important to bear in mind that petitioner asserts no right to absolute immunity from state investigation, and no right to disregard Alabama's laws. As shown by its substantial compliance with the production order, petitioner does not deny Alabama's right to obtain from it such information as the State desires concerning the purposes of the Association and its activities within the State. Petitioner has not objected to divulging the identity of its members who are employed by or hold official positions with it. It has urged the rights solely of its ordinary rank-and-file members. This is therefore not analogous to a case involving the interests of a State in protecting its citizens in their dealings with paid solicitors or agents of foreign corporations by requiring identification. . . .

We hold that the immunity from state scrutiny of membership lists which the Association claims on behalf of its members is here so related to the right of the members to pursue their lawful private interest privately and to associate freely with others in so doing as to come within the protection of the Fourteenth Amendment. And we conclude that Alabama has fallen short of showing a controlling justification for the deterrent effect on the free enjoyment of the right to associate which disclosure of membership lists is likely to have. Accordingly, the judgment of civil contempt and the $100,000 fine which resulted from petitioner's refusal to comply with the production order in this respect must fall. . . .

Reversed.

III. Protest and Symbolic Speech

feiner &
edwards

Terminiello v. *Chicago*
337 U.S. 1, 69 S.Ct. 894, 93 L.Ed. 1131 (1949)

Terminiello, a speaker at an auditorium meeting, was convicted of violating a Chicago "breach of the peace" ordinance, on the ground that the riot that followed the meeting was the result of his speech. The Illinois Supreme Court affirmed his conviction, and the Supreme Court granted certiorari. Further facts are contained in the excerpts that follow.

MR. JUSTICE DOUGLAS delivered the opinion of the Court.

Petitioner after jury trial was found guilty of disorderly conduct in violation of a city ordinance of Chicago and fined. The case grew out of an address he delivered in an auditorium in Chicago under the auspices of the Christian Veterans of America. The meeting commanded considerable public attention. The auditorium was filled to capacity with over eight hundred persons present. Others were turned away. Outside of the auditorium a crowd of about one thousand persons gathered to protest against the meeting. A cordon of policemen was assigned to the meeting to maintain order; but they were not able to prevent several disturbances. The crowd outside was angry and turbulent.

Petitioner in his speech condemned the conduct of the crowd outside and vigorously, if not viciously, criticized various political and racial groups whose activities he denounced as inimical to the nation's welfare.

The trial court charged that "breach of peace" consists of any "misbehavior which violates the public peace and decorum"; and that the "misbehavior may constitute a breach of the peace if it stirs the public to anger, invites dispute, brings about a condition of unrest, or creates a disturbance, or if it molests the inhabitants in the enjoyment of peace and quiet by arousing alarm." Petitioner did not take exception to the instruction. But he maintained at all times that the ordinance as applied to his conduct violated his right of free speech under the Federal Constitution. . . .

The argument here has been focused on the issue of whether the content of petitioner's speech was composed of derisive, fighting words, which carried it outside the scope of the constitutional guarantees. . . . We do not reach that question, for there is a preliminary question that is dispositive of the case.

As we have noted, the statutory words "breach of the peace" were defined in instructions to the jury to include speech which "stirs the public to anger, invites dispute, brings about a condition of unrest, or creates a disturbance. . . ." That construction of the ordinance is a ruling on a question of state law that is as binding on us as though the precise words had been written into the ordinance. . . .

The vitality of civil and political institutions in our society depends on free discussion. . . .

Accordingly a function of free speech under our system of government is to invite dispute. It may indeed best serve its high purpose when it induces a condition of unrest, creates dissatisfaction with conditions as they are, or even stirs people to anger. Speech is often provocative and challenging. It may strike at prejudices and preconceptions and have profound unsettling effects as it presses for acceptance of an idea. That is why freedom of speech, though not absolute, . . . is nevertheless protected against censorship or punishment, unless shown likely to produce a clear and present danger of a serious substantive evil that rises far above public inconvenience, annoyance, or unrest. . . . There is no room under our Constitution for a more restrictive view. For the alternative would lead to standardization of ideas either by legislatures, courts, or dominant political or community groups.

The ordinance as construed by the trial court seriously invaded this province. It permitted conviction of petitioner if his speech stirred people to anger, invited public dispute, or brought about a condition of unrest. A conviction resting on any of those grounds may not stand. . . .

But it is said that throughout the appellate proceedings the Illinois courts assumed that the only conduct punishable and punished under the ordinance was conduct constituting ''fighting words.'' That emphasizes, however, the importance of the rule of the Stromberg case. Petitioner was not convicted under a statute so narrowly construed. For all anyone knows he was convicted under the parts of the ordinance (as construed) which, for example, make it an offense merely to invite dispute or to bring about a condition of unrest. We cannot avoid that issue by saying that all Illinois did was to measure petitioner's conduct, not the ordinance, against the Constitution. Petitioner raised both points—that his speech was protected by the Constitution; that the inclusion of his speech within the ordinance was a violation of the Constitution. We would, therefore, strain at technicalities to conclude that the constitutionality of the ordinance as construed and applied to petitioner was not before the Illinois courts. The record makes clear that petitioner at all times challenged the constitutionality of the ordinance as construed and applied to him.

Reversed.

[MR. CHIEF JUSTICE VINSON submitted a dissenting opinion.]

MR. JUSTICE FRANKFURTER, dissenting.

For the first time in the course of the 130 years in which State prosecutions have come here for review, this Court is today reversing a sentence imposed by a State court on a ground that was urged neither here nor below and that was explicitly disclaimed on behalf of the petitioner at the bar of this Court.

The impropriety of that part of the charge which is now made the basis of reversal was not raised at the trial nor before the Appellate Court of Illinois. The fact that counsel for Terminiello wholly ignored it is emphasized by the objections that he did make in relation to the instructions given and not given. On appeal to the Supreme Court of Illinois, counsel still failed to claim as error that which this Court on its own motion now finds violative of the Constitution. It was not mentioned by the Illinois Supreme Court in its careful opinion disposing of other claims and it was not included in the elaborate petition for rehearing in that court. Thus an objection, not raised by counsel in the Illinois courts, not made the basis of the petition for certiorari here—not included in the ''Questions Presented,'' nor in the ''Reasons Relied On for the Allowance of the Writ''—and explicitly disavowed at the bar of this Court, is used to upset a conviction which has been sustained by three courts of Illinois. . . .

Only the uninformed will deride as a merely technical point objection to what the Court is doing in this case. The matter touches the very basis of this Court's authority in reviewing the judgments of State courts. We have no authority to meddle with such a judgment unless some claim under the Constitution or the laws of the United States has been made before the State court whose judgment we are reviewing and unless the claim has been denied by that court. How could there have been a denial of a federal claim by the Illinois courts, *i.e.,* that the trial judge offended the Constitution of the United States in what he told the jury, when no such claim was made? The relation of the United States and the courts of the United States to the States and the courts of the States is a very delicate matter. It is too delicate to permit silence when a judgment of a State court is reversed in disregard of the duty of this Court to leave untouched an adjudication of a State unless that adjudication is based upon a claim of a federal right which the State has had an opportunity to meet and to recognize. If such a federal claim was neither before the State court nor presented to this Court, this Court unwarrantably strays from its province in looking through the record to find some federal claim that might have been brought to the attention of the State court, and, if so brought, fronted [sic], and that might have been, but was not, urged here. This is a court of review, not a tribunal unbounded by rules. We do not sit like a kadi under a tree dispensing justice according to considerations of individual expediency.

Freedom of speech undoubtedly means freedom to express views that challenge deep-seated, sacred beliefs and to utter sentiments that may provoke resentment. But those indulging in such stuff as that to which this proceeding gave rise are hardly so deserving as to lead this Court to single them out as beneficiaries of the first departure from the restrictions that bind this Court in reviewing judgments of State courts. . . .

MR. JUSTICE JACKSON and MR. JUSTICE BURTON join this dissent.

MR. JUSTICE JACKSON, dissenting.

The Court reverses this conviction by re-iterating generalized approbations of freedom of speech with which, in the abstract, no one will disagree. Doubts as to their applicability are lulled by avoidance of more than passing reference to the circumstances of Terminiello's speech and judging it as if he had spoken to persons as dispassionate as empty benches, or like a modern Demosthenes practicing his Philippics on a lonely seashore.

But the local court that tried Terminiello was not indulging in theory. It was dealing with a riot and with a speech that provoked a hostile mob and incited a friendly one, and threatened violence between the two. When the trial judge instructed the jury that it might find Terminiello guilty of inducing a breach of the peace if his behavior stirred the public to anger, invited dispute, brought about unrest, created a disturbance or molested peace and quiet by arousing alarm, he was not speaking of these as harmless or abstract conditions. He was addressing his words to the concrete behavior and specific consequences disclosed by the evidence. He was saying to the jury, in effect, that if this particular speech added fuel to the situation already so inflamed as to threaten to get beyond police control, it could be punished as inducing a breach of peace. When the light of the evidence not recited by the Court is thrown upon the Court's opinion, it discloses that underneath a little issue of Terminiello and his hundred-dollar fine lurk some of the most far-reaching constitutional questions that can confront a people who value both liberty and order. This Court seems to regard these as enemies of each other and to be of the view that we must forego order to achieve liberty. So it fixes its eyes on a conception of freedom of speech so rigid as to tolerate no concession to society's need for public order. . . .

[The content of Terminiello's inflammatory speech is then reviewed in detail.]

Such was the speech. Evidence showed that it stirred the audience not only to cheer and applaud but to expressions of immediate anger, unrest and alarm. One called the speaker a "God damned liar" and was taken out by the police. Another said that "Jews, niggers and Catholics would have to be gotten rid of." One response was, "Yes, the Jews are all killers, murderers. If we don't kill them first, they will kill us." The anti-Jewish stories elicited exclamations of "Oh!" and "Isn't that terrible!" and shouts of "Yes, send the Jews back to Russia," "Kill the Jews," "Dirty kikes," and much more of ugly tenor. This is the specific and concrete kind of anger, unrest and alarm, coupled with that of the mob outside, that the trial court charged the jury might find to be a breach of peace induced by Terminiello. It is difficult to believe that this Court is speaking of the same occasion, but it is the only one involved in this litigation. . . .

As this case declares a nation-wide rule that disables local and state authorities from punishing conduct which produces conflicts of this kind, it is unrealistic not to take account of the nature, methods and objectives of the forces involved. This was not an isolated, spontaneous and unintended collision of political, racial or ideological adversaries. It was a local manifestation of a world-wide and standing conflict between two organized groups of revolutionary fanatics, each of which has imported to this country the strong-arm technique developed in the struggle by which their kind has devastated Europe. Increasingly, American cities have to cope with it. One faction organizes a mass meeting, the other organizes pickets; parade is met with counterparade. Each of these mass demonstrations has the potentiality, and more than a few the purpose, of disorder and violence. This technique appeals not to reason but to fears and mob spirit; each is a show of force designed to bully adversaries and to overawe the indifferent. We need not resort to speculation as to the purposes for which these tactics are calculated nor as to their consequences. Recent European history demonstrates both. . . .

This drive by totalitarian groups to undermine the prestige and effectiveness of local democratic governments is advanced whenever either of them can win from this Court a ruling which paralyzes the power of these officials. This is such a case. The group of which Terminiello is a part claims that his behavior, because it involved a speech, is above the reach of local authorities. If the mild action those authorities have taken is forbidden, it is plain that hereafter there is nothing effective left that they can do. If they can do nothing as to him, they are equally powerless as to rival totalitarian groups. Terminiello's victory today certainly fulfills the most extravagant hopes of both right and left totalitarian groups, who want nothing so much as to paralyze and discredit the only democratic authority that can curb them in their battle for the streets. . . .

In considering abuse of freedom by provocative utterances it is necessary to observe that the law is more tolerant of discussion than are most individuals or communities. Law is so indifferent to subjects of talk that I think of none that it should close to discussion. Religious, social and political topics that in other times or countries have not been open to lawful debate may be freely discussed here.

Because a subject is legally arguable, however, does not mean that public sentiment will be patient of its advocacy at all times and in all manners. So it happens that, while peaceful advocacy of communism or fascism is tolerated by the law, both of these doctrines arouse passionate reactions. A great number of people do not agree that introduction to America of communism or fascism is even debatable. Hence many speeches, such as that of Terminiello, may be legally permissible but may nevertheless in some surroundings be a menace to peace and order. When conditions show the speaker that this is the case, as it did here, there certainly comes a point beyond which he cannot indulge in provocations to violence without being answerable to society.

Determination of such an issue involves a heavy responsibility. Courts must beware lest they become mere organs of popular intolerance. Not every show of opposition can justify treating a speech as a breach of peace. Neither speakers nor courts are obliged always and in all circumstances to yield to prevailing opinion and feeling. As a people grow in capacity for civilization and liberty their tolerance will grow, and they will endure, if not welcome, discussion even on topics as to which they are committed. They regard convictions as tentative and know that time and events will make their own terms with theories, by whomever and by whatever majorities they are held, and many will be proved wrong. But on our way to this idealistic state of tolerance the police have to deal with men as they are. . . .

When the right of society to freedom from probable violence should prevail over the right of an individual to defy opposing opinion, presents a problem that always tests wisdom and often calls for immediate and vigorous action to preserve public order and safety. . . .

This Court has gone far toward accepting the doctrine that civil liberty means the removal of all restraints from these crowds and that all local attempts to maintain order are impairments of the liberty of the citizen. The choice is not between order and liberty. It is between liberty with order and anarchy without either. There is danger that, if the Court does not temper its doctrinaire logic with a little practical wisdom, it will convert the constitutional Bill of Rights into a suicide pact.

I would affirm the conviction.

MR. JUSTICE BURTON joins in this opinion.

This case arose from convictions under a Louisiana breach of peace statute. The highest court of Louisiana refused to review the convictions and the Supreme Court granted certiorari. A detailed statement of the facts appears in the excerpts below.

MR. JUSTICE FORTAS announced the judgment of the Court and an opinion in which the CHIEF JUSTICE and MR. JUSTICE DOUGLAS join. . . .

. . . The locus of the events was the Audubon Regional Library in the town of Clinton, Louisiana, Parish of East Feliciana. . . . It has three branches and two bookmobiles. The bookmobiles served 33 schools, both white and Negro, as well as "individuals." One of the bookmobiles was red, the other blue. The red bookmobile served only white persons. The blue bookmobile served only Negroes. It is a permissible inference that no Negroes used the branch libraries.

The registration cards issued to Negroes were stamped with the word "Negro." A Negro in possession of such a card was entitled to borrow books, but only from the blue bookmobile. A white person could not receive service from the blue bookmobile. He would have to wait until the red bookmobile came around, or would have to go to a branch library.

This tidy plan was challenged on Saturday, March 7, 1964, at about 11:30 A.M. Five young Negro males, all residents of East or West Feliciana Parishes, went into the adult reading or service room of the Audubon Regional Library at Clinton. The Branch Assistant, Mrs. Katie Reeves, was alone in the room. She met the men "between the tables" and asked if she "could help." Petitioner Brown requested a book, "The Story of the Negro" by Arna Bontemps. Mrs. Reeves checked the card catalogue, ascertained that the Branch did not have the book, so advised Mr. Brown, and told him that she would request the book from the State Library, that he would be notified upon its receipt and "he could either pick it up or it would be mailed to him." She told him that "his point of service was a bookmobile or it could be mailed to him."

Mrs. Reeves testified that she expected that the men would then leave; they did not, and she asked them to leave. They did not. Petitioner Brown sat down and the others stood near him. They said nothing; there was no noise or boisterous talking. Mrs. Reeves called Mrs. Perkins, the regional librarian, who was in another room. Mrs. Perkins asked the men to leave. They remained.

Neither Mrs. Reeves nor Mrs. Perkins had called the sheriff, but in "10 to 15 minutes" from the time of the arrival of the men at the library, the sheriff and deputies arrived. The sheriff asked the Negroes to leave. They said they would not. The sheriff then arrested them. The sheriff had been notified that morning that members of the Congress of Racial Equality "were going to sit-in" at the library. Ordinarily, the sheriff testified, CORE tells him when they are going to demonstrate or picket. The sheriff was standing at his "place of business" when he saw "these 5 colored males coming down the street." He saw them enter the library. He called the jail to notify his deputies, and he reached the library immediately after the deputies got there. When the sheriff arrived, there was no noise, no disturbance. He testified that he arrested them "for not leaving a public building when asked to do so by an officer."

The library obtained the requested book and mailed it to Mr. Brown on March 29, 1964. The accompanying card said, "You may return the book either by mail or to the Blue Bookmobile." The reference to the color of the vehicle was obviously not designed to facilitate identification of the library vehicle. The blue bookmobile is for Negroes and for Negroes only. . . .

We are here dealing with an aspect of a basic constitutional right—the right under the First and Fourteenth Amendments guaranteeing freedom of speech and of assembly, and freedom to petition the Government for a redress of grievances. The Constitution of the State of Louisiana reiterates these guaranties. As this Court has repeatedly stated, these rights are not confined to verbal expression. They embrace appropriate types of action which certainly include the right in a peaceable and orderly manner to protest by silent and reproachful presence, in a place where the protestant has every right to be, the unconstitutional segregation of public facilities. Accordingly, even if the accused action were within the scope of the statutory instrument, we would be required to assess the constitutional impact of its application, and we would have to hold that the statute cannot constitutionally be applied to punish petitioners' actions in the circumstances of this case. . . .

It is an unhappy circumstance that the locus of these events was a public library—a place dedicated to quiet, to knowledge, and to beauty. It is a sad commentary that this hallowed place in the parishes of East and West Feliciana bore the ugly stamp of racism. It is sad, too, that it was a public library which, reasonably enough in the circumstances, was the stage for a confrontation between those discriminated against and the representatives of the offending parishes. Fortunately, the circumstances here were such that no claim can be made that use of the library by others was disturbed by the demonstration. Perhaps the time and method were carefully chosen with this in mind. Were it otherwise, a factor not present in this case would have to be considered. Here, there was no disturbance of others, no disruption of library activities, and no violation of any library regulations.

A State or its instrumentality may, of course, regulate the use of its libraries or other public facilities. But it must do so in a reasonable and nondiscriminatory manner, equally applicable to all and administered with equality to all. It may not do so as to some and not as to all. It may not provide certain facilities for whites and others for Negroes. And it may not invoke

regulations as to use—whether they are ad hoc or general—as a pretext for pursuing those engaged in lawful, constitutionally protected exercise of their fundamental rights. . . .

The decision below is

Reversed.

The separate opinions of MR. JUSTICE BRENNAN and MR. JUSTICE WHITE concurring in the judgment, are omitted.

MR. JUSTICE BLACK, with whom MR. JUSTICE CLARK, MR. JUSTICE HARLAN, and MR. JUSTICE STEWART join, dissenting.

I do not believe that any provision of the United States Constitution forbids any one of the 50 States of the Union, including Louisiana, to make it unlawful to stage ''sit-ins'' or ''stand-ups'' in their public libraries for the purpose of advertising objections to the State's public policies. That, however, is precisely what the Court or at least a majority of the Court here holds that all the States are forbidden to do by our Constitution. I dissent. . . .

These petitioners were treated with every courtesy and granted every consideration to which they were entitled in the Audubon Library. They asked for a book, perhaps as the prevailing opinion suggests more as a ritualistic ceremonial than anything else. The lady in charge nevertheless hunted for the book, found she did not have it, sent for it, and later obtained it from the state library for petitioners' use. No petitioner asked for any other book, none indicated that he wanted to read any other book, and none attempted to read any other book or any other printed matter. As a matter of fact the record shows, and the prevailing opinion admits, that the five petitioners stayed in the library not to use it for learning but as ''monuments of protest'' to voice their disapproval of what they thought was a policy of the State. . . .

. . . The argument seems to be that without a blatant, loud manifestation of aggressive hostility or an exceedingly long ''sit-in'' or ''sojourn'' in a public library, there are no circumstances which could foreseeably occasion a breach of the peace. . . . Disturbers of the peace do not always rattle swords or shout invectives. It is high time to challenge the assumption in which too many people have too long acquiesced, that groups that think they have been mistreated or that have actually been mistreated have a constitutional right to use the public's streets, buildings, and property to protest whatever, wherever, whenever they want, without regard to whom it may disturb. . . .

I think that the evidence in this case established every element in the offense charged against petitioners. . . .

. . . There is simply no evidence in the record at all that petitioners were arrested because they were exercising the "right to protest." It is nevertheless said that this was the *sole* reason for the arrests. Moreover, the conclusion that the statute was unconstitutionally applied because it interfered with the petitioners' so-called protest establishes a completely new constitutional doctrine. In this case this new constitutional principle means that even though these petitioners did not want to use the Louisiana public library for library purposes, they had a constitutional right nevertheless to stay there over the protest of the librarian who had lawful authority to keep the library orderly for the use of people who wanted to use its books, its magazines, and its papers. But the principle espoused also has a far broader meaning. It means that the Constitution, the First and the Fourteenth Amendments, requires the custodians and supervisors of the public libraries in this country to stand helplessly by while protesting groups advocating one cause or another, stage "sit-ins" or "stand-ups" to dramatize their particular views on particular issues. And it should be remembered that if one group can take over libraries for one cause, other groups will assert the right to do it for causes which, while wholly legal, may not be so appealing to this Court. The States are thus paralyzed with reference to control of their libraries for library purposes, and I suppose that inevitably the next step will be to paralyze the schools. Efforts to this effect have already been made all over the country. . . .

The constitutional doctrine that actually prevails in this Court today for the first time in its history rests at least in great part on the Court's interpretation of the First Amendment as carried into the States by the Fourteenth. This is the First Amendment which, as I have said in the past, is to me the very heart of our free government without which liberty and equality cannot exist. But I have never thought and do not now think that the First Amendment can sustain the startling doctrine the prevailing opinion here creates. The First Amendment, I think, protects speech, writings, and expression of views in any manner in which they can be legitimately and validly communicated. But I have never believed that it gives any person or group of persons the constitutional right to go wherever they want, whenever they please, without regard to the rights of private or public property or to state law. . . . Though the First Amendment guarantees the right of assembly and the right of petition along with the rights of speech, press, and religion, it does not guarantee to any person the right to use someone else's property, even that owned by government and dedicated to other purposes, as a stage to express dissident ideas. The novel constitutional doctrine of the prevailing opinion nevertheless exalts the power of private nongovernmental groups to determine what use shall be made of governmental property over the power of the elected governmental officials of the States and the Nation. . . .

The prevailing opinion laments the fact that the place where these events took place was "a public library—a place dedicated to quiet, to knowledge, and to beauty." I too lament this fact, and for this reason I am deeply troubled with the fear that powerful private groups throughout the Nation will read the Court's action, as I do—that is, as granting them a license to invade the tranquility and beauty of our libraries whenever they have quarrel with some state policy which may or may not exist. It is an unhappy circumstance in my judgment that the group, which more than any other has needed a government of equal laws and equal justice, is now encouraged to believe that the best way for it to advance its cause, which is a worthy one, is by taking the law into its own hands from place to place and from time to time. Governments like ours were formed to substitute the rule of law for the rule of force. Illustrations may be given where crowds have gathered together peaceably by reason of extraordinarily good discipline reinforced by vigilant officers. "Demonstrations" have taken place without any manifestations of force at the time. But I say once more that the crowd moved by noble ideals today can become the mob ruled by hate and passion and greed and violence tomorrow. If we ever doubted that, we know it now. The peaceful songs of love can become as stirring and provocative as the Marseillaise did in the days when a noble revolution gave way to rule by successive mobs until chaos set in. The holding in this case today makes it more necessary than ever that we stop and look more closely at where we are going.

I would affirm.

IV. Freedom of the Press

New York Times Company v. *Sullivan*
376 U.S. 254, 84 S.Ct. 710, 11 L.Ed. 2d 686 (1964)

Action for libel was brought in the Circuit Court of Montgomery County, Alabama, by a city commissioner of public affairs, whose duties included the supervision of the police department, against the *New York Times* for publication of a paid advertisement describing maltreatment in the city of black students protesting segregation, and against four individuals whose names, among others, appeared in the advertisement. The jury awarded plaintiff damages of $500,000 against all defendants, and the judgment on the verdict was affirmed by the Supreme Court of Alabama on the grounds that the statements in the advertisement were libelous per se, false, and not privileged, and that the evidence showed malice on the part of the newspaper. The defendants' constitutional objections were rejected on the ground that the First Amendment does not protect libelous publications. The Supreme Court granted certiorari.

MR. JUSTICE BRENNAN delivered the opinion of the Court.

We are required for the first time in this case to determine the extent to which the constitutional protections for speech and press limit a State's power to award damages in a libel action brought by a public official against critics of his official conduct. . . .

Respondent's complaint alleged that he had been libeled by statements in a full-page advertisement that was carried in the New York Times on March 29, 1960. Entitled "Heed Their Rising Voices," the advertisement began by stating that "As the whole world knows by now, thousands of Southern Negro students are engaged in widespread non-violent demonstrations in positive affirmation of the right to live in human dignity as guaranteed by the U.S. Constitution and the Bill of Rights." It went on to charge that "in their efforts to uphold these guarantees, they are being met by an unprecedented wave of terror by those who would deny and negate that document which the whole world looks upon as setting the pattern for modern freedom. . . ."

Of the 10 paragraphs of text in the advertisement, the third and a portion of the sixth were the basis of respondent's claim of libel. They read as follows:

Third paragraph:

In Montgomery, Alabama, after students sang "My Country 'Tis of Thee" on the State Capitol steps, their leaders were expelled from school, and truckloads of police armed with shotguns and tear-gas ringed the Alabama State College Campus. When the entire student body protested to state authorities by refusing to re-register, their dining hall was padlocked in an attempt to starve them into submission. . . .

Although neither of these statements mentions respondent by name, he contended that the word "police" in the third paragraph referred to him as the Montgomery Commissioner who supervised the Police Department, so that he was being accused of "ringing" the campus with police. He further claimed that the paragraph would be read as imputing to the police, and hence to him, the padlocking of the dining hall in order to starve the students into submission. As to the sixth paragraph, he contended that since arrests are ordinarily made by the police, the statement "They have arrested [Dr. King] seven times" would be read as referring to him; he further contended that the "they" who did the arresting would be equated with the "they" who committed the other described acts and with the "Southern violators." . . .

We hold that the rule of law applied by the Alabama courts is constitutionally deficient for failure to provide the safeguards for freedom of speech and of the press that are required by the First and Fourteenth Amendments in a libel action brought by a public official against critics of his official conduct. We further hold that under the proper safeguards the evidence presented in this case is constitutionally insufficient to support the judgment for respondent. . . .

The publication here was not a "commercial" advertisement. It communicated information, expressed opinion, recited grievances, protested claimed abuses, and sought financial support on behalf of a movement whose existence and objectives are matters of the highest public interest and concern. . . . That the Times was paid for publishing the advertisement is as immaterial in this connection as is the fact that the newspapers and books are sold. . . .

Any other conclusion would discourage newspapers from carrying "editorial advertisements" of this type, and so might shut off an important outlet for the promulgation of information and ideas by persons who do not themselves have access to publishing facilities—who wish to exercise their freedom of speech even though they are not members of the press. . . . The effect would be to shackle the First Amendment in its attempt to secure "the widest possible dissemination of information from diverse and antagonistic sources." . . . To avoid placing such a handicap upon the freedoms of expression, we hold that if the allegedly libelous statements would otherwise be constitutionally protected from the present judgment, they do not forfeit that protection because they were published in the form of a paid advertisement. . . .

Respondent relies heavily, as did the Alabama courts, on statements of this Court to the effect that the Constitution does not protect libelous publications. Those statements do not foreclose our inquiry here. None of the cases sustained the use of libel laws to impose sanctions upon expression critical of the official conduct of public officials. . . . In the only previous case that did present the question of constitutional limitations upon the power to award damages for libel of a public official, the Court was equally divided and the question was not decided. . . . In deciding the question now, we are compelled by neither precedent nor policy to give any more weight to the epithet "libel" than we have to other "mere labels" of state law. . . . Like "insurrection," contempt, advocacy of unlawful acts, breach of the peace, obscenity, solicitation of legal business, and the various other formulae for the repression of expression that have been challenged in this Court, libel can claim no talismanic immunity from constitutional limitations. It must be measured by standards that satisfy the First Amendment.

The general proposition that freedom of expression upon public questions is secured by the First Amendment has long been settled by our decisions. . . .

Thus we consider this case against the

background of a profound national commitment to the principle that debate on public issues should be uninhibited, robust, and wide-open, and that it may well include vehement, caustic, and sometimes unpleasantly sharp attacks on government and public officials.... The present advertisement, as an expression of grievance and protest on one of the major public issues of our time, would seem clearly to qualify for the constitutional protection. The question is whether it forfeits that protection by the falsity of some of its factual statements and by its alleged defamation of respondent....

Authoritative interpretations of the First Amendment guarantees have consistently refused to recognize an exception for any test of truth, whether administered by judges, juries, or administrative officials—and especially not one that puts the burden of proving truth on the speaker.... The constitutional protection does not turn upon "the truth, popularity, or social utility of the ideas and beliefs which are offered."... As Madison said, "Some degree of abuse is inseparable from the proper use of every thing; and in no instance is this more true than in that of the press." 4 Elliot's Debates on the Federal Constitution (1876), p. 571....

That erroneous statement is inevitable in free debate, and that it must be protected if the freedoms of expression are to have the "breathing space" that they "need . . . to survive" . . . [have been recognized].

Just as factual error affords no warrant for repressing speech that would otherwise be free, the same is true of injury to official reputation. Where judicial officers are involved, this Court has held that concern for the dignity and reputation of the courts does not justify the punishment as criminal contempt of criticism of the judge or his decision.... This is true even though the utterance contains "half-truths" and "misinformation."... Such repression can be justified, if at all, only by a clear and present danger of the obstruction of justice. If judges are to be treated as "men of fortitude, able to thrive in a hardy climate," ... surely the same must be true of other government officials, such as elected city commissioners. Criticism of their official conduct does not lose its constitutional protection merely because it is effective criticism and hence diminishes their official reputations.

If neither factual error nor defamatory content suffices to remove the constitutional shield from criticism of official conduct, the combination of the two elements is no less inadequate....

A rule compelling the critic of official conduct to guarantee the truth of all his factual assertions—and to do so on pain of libel judgments virtually unlimited in amount—leads to a comparable "self-censorship." Allowance of the defense of truth, with the burden of proving it on the defendant, does not mean that only false speech will be deterred. Even courts accepting this defense as an adequate safeguard have recognized the difficulties of adducing legal proofs that the alleged libel was true in all its factual particulars....

Under such a rule would-be critics of official conduct may be deterred from voicing their criticism, even though it is believed to be true and even though it is in fact true, because of doubt whether it can be proved in court or fear of the expense of having to do so. They tend to make only statements which "steer far wider of the unlawful zone." ... The rule thus dampens the vigor and limits the variety of public debate. It is inconsistent with the First and Fourteenth Amendments.

The constitutional guarantees require, we think, a federal rule that prohibits a public official from recovering damages for a defamatory falsehood relating to his official conduct unless he proves that the statement was made with "actual malice"—that is, with knowledge that it was false or with reckless disregard of whether it was false or not....

We hold today that the Constitution delimits a State's power to award damages for libel in actions brought by public officials against critics of their official conduct. Since this is such an action, the rule requiring proof of actual malice is applicable. While Alabama law apparently requires proof of actual malice for an award of punitive damages, where general damages are concerned malice is "presumed." Such a presumption is inconsistent with the federal rule. "The power to create presumptions is not a means of escape from unconstitutional restrictions," . . . "the showing of malice required for the forfeiture of the privilege is not presumed but is a matter for proof by the plaintiff. . . ." Since the trial judge did not instruct the jury to differentiate between general and punitive damages, it may be that the verdict was wholly an award of one or the other. But it is impossible to know, in view of the general verdict returned. Because of this uncertainty, the judgment must be reversed and the case remanded.

This Court's duty is not limited to the elaboration of constitutional principles; we must also in proper cases review the evidence to make certain that those principles have been constitutionally applied. This is such a case, particularly since the question is one of alleged trespass across "the line between speech unconditionally guaranteed and speech which may legitimately be regulated." . . . In cases where that line must be drawn, the rule is that we "examine for ourselves the statements in issue and the circumstances under which they were made to see . . . whether they are of a character which the principles of the First Amendment, as adopted by the Due Process Clause of the Fourteenth Amendment protect." . . . We must "make an independent examination of the whole record," . . . so as to assure ourselves that the judgment does not constitute a forbidden intrusion on the field of free expression.

Applying these standards, we consider that the proof presented to show actual malice lacks the convincing clarity which the constitutional standard demands, and hence that it would not constitutionally sustain the judgment for respondent under the proper rule of law. The case of the individual petitioners requires little discussion. Even assuming that they could constitutionally be found to have authorized the use of their names on the advertisement, there was no evidence whatever that they were aware of any erroneous statements or were in any way reckless in that regard. The judgment against them is thus without constitutional support.

As to the Times, we similarly conclude that the facts do not support a finding of actual malice. . . . We think the evidence against the Times supports at most a finding of negligence in failing to discover the misstatements, and is constitutionally insufficient to show the recklessness that is required for a finding of actual malice. . . .

Reversed and remanded.

MR. JUSTICE BLACK, with whom MR. JUSTICE DOUGLAS joins, concurring.

I base my vote to reverse on the belief that the First and Fourteenth Amendments not merely "delimit" a State's power to award damages to "a public official against critics of his official conduct" but completely prohibit a State from exercising such a power. . . .

We would, I think, more faithfully interpret the First Amendment by holding that at the very least it leaves the people and the press free to criticize officials and discuss public affairs with impunity. This Nation of ours elects many of its important officials; so do the States, the municipalities, the counties, and even many precincts. These officials are responsible to the people for the way they perform their duties. While our Court has held that some kinds of speech and writings, such as "obscenity," *Roth* v. *United States,* . . . and "fighting words," *Chaplinsky* v. *New Hampshire,* . . . are not expression within the protection of the First Amendment, freedom to discuss public affairs and public officials is unquestionably, as the Court today holds, the kind of speech the First Amendment was primarily designed to keep within the area of free discussion. To punish the exercise of this right to discuss public affairs or to penalize it through libel judgments is to abridge or shut off discussion of the very kind most needed. This Nation, I suspect, can live in peace without libel suits based on public discussion of public affairs and public officials. But I doubt that a country can live in freedom where its people can be made to suffer physically or financially for criticizing their government, its actions, or its officials. "For a representative democracy ceases to exist the moment that the public functionaries are by any means absolved from their responsibility to their constituents; and this happens whenever the constituent can be restrained in any manner from speaking, writing, or publishing his opinions upon any public measure, or upon the conduct of those who may advise or execute it." An unconditional right to say what one pleases about public affairs is what I consider to be the minimum guarantee of the First Amendment.

MR. JUSTICE GOLDBERG, with whom MR. JUSTICE DOUGLAS joins, concurring in the result.

. . . In my view, the First and Fourteenth Amendments to the Constitution afford to the citizen and to the press an absolute, unconditional privilege to criticize official conduct despite the harm which may flow from excesses and abuses. The prized American right "to speak one's mind" . . . about public officials and affairs needs "breathing space to survive." . . . The right should not depend upon a probing by the jury of the motivation of the citizen or press. The theory of our Constitution is that every citizen may speak his mind and every newspaper express its views on matters of public concern and may not be barred from speaking or publishing because those in control of government think that what is said or written is unwise, unfair, false, or malicious. In a democratic society, one who assumes to act for the citizens in an executive, legislative or judicial capacity must expect that his official acts will be commented upon and criticized. Such criticism cannot, in my opinion, be muzzled or deterred by the courts at the instance of public officials under the label of libel. . . .

This is not to say that the Constitution protects defamatory statements directed against the private conduct of a public official or private citizen. Freedom of press and of speech insure that government will respond to the will of the people and that changes may be obtained by peaceful means. Purely private defamation has little to do with the political ends of a self-governing society. The imposition of liability for private defamation does not abridge the freedom of public speech. This, of course, cannot be said "where public officials are concerned or where public matters are involved. . . . [O]ne main function of the First Amendment is to ensure ample opportunity for the people to determine and resolve public issues. Where public matters are involved, the doubts should be resolved in favor of freedom of expression rather than against it." Douglas, The Right of the People (1958), p. 41.

New York Times Company v. United States
403 U.S. 713, 91 S.Ct. 2140, 29 L.Ed. 2d 822 (1971)

The *New York Times* and the *Washington Post* acquired copies of a multivolume classified study of the evolution of the nation's Vietnam policy. Two federal district courts refused to enjoin publication. One decision was affirmed, one reversed by courts of appeals. The Supreme Court granted certiorari. The format of opinions is unusual—per curiam, with each Justice delivering a separate opinion. (This case is equally appropriate to the discussion of the powers of President, Congress, and the Court in Chapter 3.)

PER CURIAM.

We granted certiorari in these cases in which the United States seeks to enjoin the New York Times and the Washington Post from publishing the contents of a classified study entitled "History of U.S. Decision-Making Process on Viet Nam Policy." . . .

"Any system of prior restraints of expression comes to this Court bearing a heavy presumption against its constitutional validity." . . .

The Government "thus carries a heavy burden of showing justification for the enforcement of such a restraint." . . . The District Court for the Southern District of New York in the *New York Times* case and the District Court for the District of Columbia and the Court of Appeals for the District of Columbia Circuit in the *Washington Post* case held that the Government had not met that burden. We agree. . . .

MR. JUSTICE BLACK, with whom MR. JUSTICE DOUGLAS joins, concurring.

I adhere to the view that the Government's case against the Washington Post should have been dismissed and that the injunction against the New York Times should have been vacated without oral argument when the cases were first presented to this Court. I believe that every moment's continuance of the injunctions against these newspapers amounts to a flagrant, indefensible, and continuing violation of the First Amendment. . . . In my view it is unfortunate that some of my Brethren are apparently willing to hold that the publication of news may sometimes be enjoined. Such a holding would make a shambles of the First Amendment.

Our Government was launched in 1789 with the adoption of the Constitution. The Bill of Rights, including the First Amendment, followed in 1791. Now, for the first time in the 182 years since the founding of the Republic, the federal courts are asked to hold that the First Amendment does not mean what it says, but rather means that Government can halt the publication of current news of vital importance to the people of this country.

In seeking injunctions against these newspapers and in its presentation to the Court, the Executive Branch seems to have forgotten the essential purpose and history of the First Amendment. When the Constitution was adopted, many people strongly opposed it because the document contained no Bill of Rights to safeguard certain basic freedoms. They especially feared that the new powers granted to a central government might be interpreted to permit the government to curtail freedom of religion, press, assembly, and speech. In response to an overwhelming public clamor,

James Madison offered a series of amendments to satisfy citizens that these great liberties would remain safe and beyond the power of government to abridge. . . . The amendments were offered to *curtail* and *restrict* the general powers granted to the Executive, Legislative, and Judicial Branches two years before in the original Constitution. The Bill of Rights changed the original Constitution into a new charter under which no branch of government could abridge the people's freedoms of press, speech, religion, and assembly. Yet the Solicitor General argues and some members of the Court appear to agree that the general powers of the Government adopted in the original Constitution should be interpreted to limit and restrict the specific and emphatic guarantees of the Bill of Rights adopted later. I can imagine no greater perversion of history. . . .

In the First Amendment the Founding Fathers gave the free press the protection it must have to fulfill its essential role in our democracy. The press was to serve the governed, not the governors. The Government's power to censor the press was abolished so that the press would remain forever free to censure the Government. The press was protected so that it could bare the secrets of government and inform the people. Only a free and unrestrained press can effectively expose deception in government. And paramount among the responsibilities of a free press is the duty to prevent any part of the government from deceiving the people and sending them off to distant lands to die of foreign fevers and foreign shot and shell. In my view, far from deserving condemnation for their courageous reporting, the New York Times, the Washington Post, and other newspapers should be commended for serving the purpose that the Founding Fathers saw so clearly. In revealing the workings of government that led to the Viet Nam war, the newspapers nobly did precisely that which the Founders hoped and trusted they would do. . . .

[W]e are asked to hold that despite the First Amendment's emphatic command, the Executive Branch, the Congress, and the Judiciary can make laws enjoining publication of current news and abridging freedom of the press in the name of "national security." The Government does not even attempt to rely on any act of Congress. Instead it makes the bold and dangerously far-reaching contention that the courts should take it upon themselves to "make" a law abridging freedom of the press in the name of equity, presidential power and national security, even when the representatives of the people in Congress have adhered to the command of the First Amendment and refused to make such a law. . . .

The word "security" is a broad, vague generality whose contours should not be invoked to abrogate the fundamental law embodied in the First Amendment. The guarding of military and diplomatic secrets at the expense of informed representative government provides no real security for our Republic. The Framers of the First Amendment, fully aware of both the need to defend a new nation and the abuses of the English and Colonial governments, sought to give this new society strength and security by providing that freedom of speech, press, religion, and assembly should not be abridged. This thought was eloquently expressed in 1937 by Mr. Chief Justice Hughes— great man and great Chief Justice that he was—when the Court held a man could not be punished for attending a meeting run by Communists.

> The greater the importance of safeguarding the community from incitements to the overthrow of our institutions by force and violence, the more imperative is the need to preserve inviolate the constitutional rights of free speech, free press and free assembly in order to maintain the opportunity for free political discussion, to the end that government may be responsive to the will of the people and that changes, if desired, may be obtained by peaceful means. Therein lies the security of the Republic, the very foundation of constitutional government.

MR. JUSTICE DOUGLAS with whom MR. JUSTICE BLACK joins, concurring. . . .

The dominant purpose of the First Amendment was to prohibit the widespread practice of governmental suppression of embarrassing information. It is common knowledge that the First Amendment was adopted against the widespread use of the common law of seditious libel to punish the dissemination of material that is embarrassing to the powers-that-be. . . . The present cases will, I think, go down in history as the most dramatic illustration of that principle. A debate of large proportions goes on in the Nation over our posture in Vietnam. That debate antedated the disclosure of the contents of the present documents. The latter are highly relevant to the debate in progress.

Secrecy in government is fundamentally anti-democratic, perpetuating bureaucratic errors. Open debate and discussion of public issues are vital to our national health. On public questions there should be "open and robust debate." . . .

MR. JUSTICE BRENNAN, concurring. . . .

So far as I can determine, never before has the United States sought to enjoin a newspaper from publishing information in its possession. The relative novelty of the questions presented, the necessary haste with which decisions were reached, the magnitude of the interests asserted, and the fact that all the parties have concentrated their arguments upon the question whether permanent restraints were proper may have justified at least some of the restraints heretofore imposed in these cases. Certainly it is difficult to fault the several courts below for seeking to assure that the issues here involved were preserved for ultimate review by this Court. But even if it be assumed that some of the interim restraints were proper in the two cases before us, that assumption has no bearing upon the propriety of similar judicial action in the future. To begin with, there has now been ample time for reflection and judgment; whatever values there may be in the preservation of novel questions for appellate review may not support any restraints in the future. More important, the First Amendment stands as an absolute bar to the imposition of judicial restraints in circumstances of the kind presented by these cases.

The error which has pervaded these cases from the outset was the granting of any injunctive relief whatsoever, interim or otherwise. The entire thrust of the Government's claim throughout these cases has been that publication of the material sought to be enjoined "could," or "might," or "may" prejudice the national interest in various ways. But the First Amendment tolerates absolutely no prior judicial restraints of the press predicated upon surmise or conjecture that untoward consequences may result. . . .

Only governmental allegation and proof that publication must inevitably, directly and immediately cause the occurrence of an event kindred to imperiling the safety of a transport already at sea can support even the issuance of an interim restraining order. . . .

MR. JUSTICE STEWART, with whom MR. JUSTICE WHITE joins, concurring.

In the governmental structure created by our Constitution, the Executive is endowed with enormous power in the two related areas of national defense and international relations. This power, largely unchecked by the Legislative and Judicial branches, has been pressed to the very hilt since the advent of the nuclear missile age. For better or for worse, the simple fact is that a President of the United States possesses vastly greater constitutional independence in these two vital areas of power than does, say, a prime minister of a country with a parliamentary form of government.

In the absence of the governmental checks and balances present in other areas of our national life, the only effective restraint upon executive policy and power in the areas of national defense and international affairs may lie in an enlightened citizenry—in an informed and critical public opinion which alone can here protect the values of democratic government. For this reason, it is perhaps here that a press that is alert, aware, and free most vitally serves the basic purpose of the First Amendment. For without an informed and free press there cannot be an enlightened people.

Yet it is elementary that the successful conduct of international diplomacy and the maintenance of an effective national defense require both confidentiality and secrecy. Other nations can hardly deal with this Nation in an atmosphere of mutual trust unless they can be assured that their confidences will be kept. And within our own executive departments, the development of considered and intelligent international policies would be impossible if those charged with their formulation could not communicate with each other freely, frankly, and in confidence. In the area of basic national defense the frequent need for absolute secrecy is, of course, self-evident.

I think there can be but one answer to this dilemma, if dilemma it be. The responsibility must be where the power is. If the Constitution gives the Executive a large degree of unshared power in the conduct of foreign affairs and the maintenance of our national defense, then under the Constitution the Executive must have the largely unshared duty to determine and preserve the degree of internal security necessary to exercise that power successfully. It is an awesome responsibility, requiring judgment and wisdom of a high order. I should suppose that moral, political, and practical considerations would dictate that a very first principle of that wisdom would be an insistence upon avoiding secrecy for its own sake. For when everything is classified, then nothing is classified, and the system becomes one to be disregarded by the cynical or the careless, and to be manipulated by those intent on self-protection or self-promotion. . . . [I]t is clear to me that it is the constitutional duty of the Executive—as a matter of sovereign prerogative and not as a matter of law as the courts know law—through the promulgation and enforcement of executive regulations, to protect the confidentiality necessary to carry out its responsibilities in the fields of international relations and national defense.

This is not to say that Congress and the courts have no role to play. Undoubtedly Congress has the power to enact specific and appropriate criminal laws to protect government property and preserve government secrets. Congress has passed such laws, and several of them are of very colorable relevance to the apparent circumstances of these cases. And if a criminal prosecution is instituted, it will be the responsibility of the courts to decide the applicability of the criminal law under which the charge is brought. Moreover, if Congress should pass a specific law authorizing civil proceedings in this field, the courts would likewise have the duty to decide the constitutionality of such a law as well as its applicability to the facts proved.

But in the cases before us we are asked neither to construe specific regulations nor to apply specific laws. We are asked, instead, to perform a function that the Constitution gave to the Executive, not the Judiciary. We are asked, quite simply, to prevent the publication by two newspapers of material that the Executive Branch insists should not, in the national interest, be published. I am convinced that the Executive is correct with respect to some of the documents involved. But I cannot say that disclosure of any of them will surely result in direct, immediate, and irreparable damage to our Nation or its people. That being so, there can under the First Amendment be but one judicial resolution of the issues before us. I join the judgments of the Court.

MR. JUSTICE WHITE, with whom MR. JUSTICE STEWART joins, concurring.

I concur in today's judgments, but only because of the concededly extraordinary protection against prior restraints enjoyed by the press under our constitutional system. I do not say that in no circumstances would the First Amendment permit an injunction against publishing information about government plans or operations. Nor, after examining the materials the Government characterizes as the most sensitive and destructive, can I deny that revelation of these documents will do substantial damage to public interests. Indeed, I am confident that their disclosure will have that result. But I nevertheless agree that the United States has not satisfied the very heavy burden which it must meet to warrant an injunction against publication in these cases, at least in the absence of express and appropriately limited congressional

authorization for prior restraints in circumstances such as these. . . .

It is not easy to reject the proposition urged by the United States and to deny relief on its good-faith claims in these cases that publication will work serious damage to the country. But that discomfiture is considerably dispelled by the infrequency of prior restraint cases. Normally, publication will occur and the damage be done before the Government has either opportunity or grounds for suppression. So here, publication has already begun and a substantial part of the threatened damage has already occurred. The fact of a massive breakdown in security is known, access to the documents by many unauthorized people is undeniable and the efficacy of equitable relief against these or other newspapers to avert anticipated damage is doubtful at best.

What is more, terminating the ban on publication of the relatively few sensitive documents the Government now seeks to suppress does not mean that the law either requires or invites newspapers or others to publish them or that they will be immune from criminal action if they do. Prior restraints require an unusually heavy justification under the First Amendment; but failure by the Government to justify prior restraints does not measure its constitutional entitlement to a conviction for criminal publication. That the Government mistakenly chose to proceed by injunction does not mean that it could not successfully proceed in another way. . . .

It is . . . clear that Congress has addressed itself to the problems of protecting the security of the country and the national defense from unauthorized disclosure of potentially damaging information. *Cf. Youngstown Sheet & Tube Co.* v. *Sawyer.* . . . It has not, however, authorized the injunctive remedy against threatened publication. It has apparently been satisfied to rely on criminal sanctions and their deterrent effect on the responsible as well as the irresponsible press. I am not, of course, saying that either of these newspapers has yet committed a crime or that either would commit a crime if they published all the material now in their possession. That matter must await resolution in the context of a criminal proceeding if one is instituted by the United States. In that event, the issue of guilt or innocence would be determined by procedures and standards quite different from those that have purported to govern these injunctive proceedings.

MR. JUSTICE MARSHALL concurring. . . .

The problem here is whether in this particular case the Executive Branch has authority to invoke the equity jurisdiction of the courts to protect what it believes to be the national interest. . . . The Government argues that in addition to the inherent power of any government to protect itself, the President's power to conduct foreign affairs and his position as Commander-in-Chief give him authority to impose censorship on the press to protect his ability to deal effectively with foreign nations and to conduct the military affairs of the country. Of course, it is beyond cavil that the President has broad powers by virtue of his primary responsibility for the conduct of our foreign affairs and his position as Commander-in-Chief. . . . And in some situations it may be that under whatever inherent powers the Government may have, as well as the implicit authority derived from the President's mandate to conduct foreign affairs and to act as Commander-in-Chief there is a basis for the invocation of the equity jurisdiction of this Court as an aid to prevent the publication of material damaging to "national security," however that term may be defined.

It would, however, be utterly inconsistent with the concept of separation of powers for this Court to use its power of contempt to prevent behavior that Congress has specifically declined to prohibit. . . .

In this case we are not faced with a situation where Congress has failed to provide the Executive with broad power to protect the Nation from disclosure of damaging state secrets. Congress has on several occasions given extensive consideration to the problem of protecting the military and strategic secrets of the United States. This consideration has resulted in the enactment of statutes making it a crime to receive, disclose, communicate, withhold, and publish certain documents, photographs, instruments, appliances, and information. . . .

Either the Government has the power under statutory grant to use traditional criminal law to protect the country or, if there is no basis for arguing that Congress has made the activity a crime, it is plain that Congress has specifically refused to grant the authority the Government seeks from this Court. In either case this Court does not have authority to grant the requested relief. It is not for this Court to fling itself into every breach perceived by some Government official nor is it for this Court to take on itself the burden of enacting law, especially law that Congress has refused to pass. . . .

MR. CHIEF JUSTICE BURGER, dissenting.

So clear are the constitutional limitations on prior restraint against expression, that from the time of *Near* v. *Minnesota* . . . until recently in *Organization for a Better Austin* v. *Keefe,* 402 U.S. 415 (1971), we have had little occasion to be concerned with cases involving prior restraints against news reporting on matters of public interest. There is, therefore, little variation among the members of the Court in terms of resistance to prior restraints against publication. Adherence to this basic constitutional principle, however, does not make this case a simple one. In this case, the imperative of a free and unfettered press comes into collision with another imperative, the effective functioning of a complex modern government and specifically the effective exercise of certain constitutional powers of the Executive. Only those who view the First Amendment as an absolute in all circumstances—a view I respect, but reject—can find such a case as this to be simple or easy.

This case is not simple for another and more immediate reason. We do not know the facts of the case. No district Judge knew all the facts. No Court of Appeals judge knew all the facts. No member of this Court knows all the facts.

Why are we in this posture, in which only those judges to whom the First Amendment is absolute and permits of no restraint in any circumstances or for any reason, are really in a position to act?

I suggest we are in this posture because these cases have been conducted in unseemly haste. . . . [P]rompt judicial action does not mean unjudicial haste.

Here, moreover, the frenetic haste is due in large part to the manner in which the *Times* proceeded from the date it obtained the purloined documents. It seems reasonably clear now that the haste precluded reasonable and deliberate judicial treatment of these cases and was not warranted. The precipitous action of this Court aborting a trial not yet completed is not the kind of judicial conduct which ought to attend the disposition of a great issue.

The newspapers make a derivative claim under the First Amendment; they denominate this right as the public "right-to-know"; by implication, the *Times* asserts a sole trusteeship of that right by virtue of its journalistic "scoop." The right is asserted as an absolute. Of course, the First Amendment right itself is not an absolute, as Justice Holmes so long ago pointed out in his aphorism concerning the right to shout fire in a crowded theatre. There are other exceptions, some of which Chief Justice Hughes mentioned by way of example in *Near* v. *Minnesota.* There are no doubt other exceptions no one has had occasion to describe or discuss. Conceivably such exceptions may be lurking in these cases and would have been flushed had they been properly considered in the trial courts, free from unwarranted deadlines and frenetic pressures. A great issue of this kind should be tried in a judicial atmosphere conducive to thoughtful, reflective deliberation, especially when haste, in terms of hours, is unwarranted in light of the long period the *Times,* by its own choice, deferred publication.

It is not disputed that the *Times* has had unauthorized possession of the documents for three to four months, during which it has had its expert analysts studying them, presumably digesting them and preparing the material for publication. During all of this time, the *Times,* presumably in its capacity as trustee of the public's "right to know," has held up publica-

tion for purposes it considered proper and thus public knowledge was delayed. No doubt this was for a good reason; the analysis of 7,000 pages of complex material drawn from a vastly greater volume of material would inevitably take time and the writing of good news stories takes time. But why should the United States Government, from whom this information was illegally acquired by someone, along with all the counsel, trial judges, and appellate judges be placed under needless pressure? After these months of deferral, the alleged "right-to-know" has somehow and suddenly become a right that must be vindicated instanter. . . .

The consequence of all this melancholy series of events is that we literally do not know what we are acting on. . . .

We all crave speedier judicial processes but when judges are pressured as in these cases the result is a parody of the judicial process.

MR. JUSTICE HARLAN, with whom THE CHIEF JUSTICE and MR. JUSTICE BLACKMUN join, dissenting. . . .

With all respect, I consider that the Court has been almost irresponsibly feverish in dealing with these cases. . . .

This frenzied train of events took place in the name of the presumption against prior restraints created by the First Amendment. Due regard for the extraordinarily important and difficult questions involved in these litigations should have led the Court to shun such a precipitate timetable. . . .

Forced as I am to reach the merits of these cases, I dissent from the opinion and judgments of the Court. . . .

It is plain to me that the scope of the judicial function in passing upon the activities of the Executive Branch of the Government in the field of foreign affairs is very narrowly restricted. This view is, I think, dictated by the concept of separation of powers upon which our constitutional system rests. . . .

The power to evaluate the "pernicious influence" of premature disclosure is not, however, lodged in the Executive alone. I agree that, in performance of its duty to protect the values of the First Amendment against political *[handwritten note at top: Court is asked to hold press up + stop the presses — They are being asked to act, not to ... make an act unconstitutional (To make something unconstitutional)]*

pressures, the judiciary must review the initial Executive determination to the point of satisfying itself that the subject matter of the dispute does lie within the proper compass of the President's foreign relations power. Constitutional considerations forbid "a complete abandonment of judicial control." . . . Moreover, the judiciary may properly insist that the determination that disclosure of the subject matter would irreparably impair the national security be made by the head of the Executive Department concerned—here the Secretary of State or the Secretary of Defense—after actual personal consideration by that officer. This safeguard is required in the analogous area of executive claims of privilege for secrets of state. . . .

Even if there is some room for the judiciary to override the executive determination, it is plain that the scope of review must be exceedingly narrow. I can see no indication in the opinions of either the District Court or the Court of Appeals in the *Post* litigation that the conclusions of the Executive were given even the deference owing to an administrative agency, much less that owing to a co-equal branch of the Government operating within the field of its constitutional prerogative. . . .

MR. JUSTICE BLACKMUN.

I join MR. JUSTICE HARLAN in his dissent. I also am in substantial accord with much that MR. JUSTICE WHITE says, by way of admonition, in the latter part of his opinion. . . .

The First Amendment . . . is only one part of an entire Constitution. Article II of the great document vests in the Executive Branch primary power over the conduct of foreign affairs and places in that branch the responsibility for the Nation's safety. Each provision of the Constitu-

tion is important, and I cannot subscribe to a doctrine of unlimited absolutism for the First Amendment at the cost of downgrading other provisions. First Amendment absolutism has never commanded a majority of the Court. . . . What is needed here is a weighing, upon properly developed standards, of the broad right of the press to print and of the very narrow right of the Government to prevent. Such standards are not yet developed. The parties here are in disagreement as to what those standards should be. But even the newspapers concede that there are situations where restraint is in order and is constitutional. Mr. Justice Holmes gave us a suggestion when he said in *Schenck,*

> It is a question of proximity and degree. When a nation is at war many things that might be said in time of peace are such a hindrance to its effort that their utterance will not be endured so long as men fight and that no Court could regard them as protected by any constitutional right. . . .

I therefore would remand these cases to be developed expeditiously, of course, but on a schedule permitting the orderly presentation of evidence from both sides, with the use of discovery, if necessary, as authorized by the rules, and with the preparation of briefs, oral argument and court opinions of a quality better than has been seen to this point. In making this last statement, I criticize no lawyer or judge. I know from past personal experience the agony of time pressure in the preparation of litigation. But these cases and the issues involved and the courts, including this one, deserve better than has been produced thus far. . . .

Branzburg v. Hayes
408 U.S. 665, 92 S.Ct. 2646, 33 L.Ed. 2d 626 (1972)

Branzburg, Pappas, and Caldwell were reporters who were directed by grand juries conducting investigations to reveal the identity of news sources to whom each journalist had promised confidentiality. Branzburg had observed the processing of hashish from marijuana, and Pappas and Caldwell had observed activities of black militants. The Supreme Court combined the three cases for a ruling on a reporter's First Amendment privilege.

Opinion of the Court by MR. JUSTICE WHITE, announced by THE CHIEF JUSTICE. . . .

Petitioners Branzburg and Pappas and respondent Caldwell press First Amendment claims that may be simply put: that to gather news it is often necessary to agree either not to identify the source of information published or to publish only part of the facts revealed, or both; that if the reporter is nevertheless forced to reveal these confidences to a grand jury, the source so identified and other confidential sources of other reporters will be measurably deterred from furnishing publishable information, all to the detriment of the free flow of information protected by the First Amendment. Although the newsmen in these cases do not claim an absolute privilege against official interrogation in all circumstances, they assert that the reporter should not be forced either to appear or to testify before a grand jury or at trial until and unless sufficient grounds are shown for believing that the reporter possesses information relevant to a crime the grand jury is investigating, that the information the reporter has is unavailable from other sources, and that the need for the information is sufficiently compelling to override the claimed invasion of First Amendment interests occasioned by the disclosure. Principally relied upon are prior cases emphasizing the importance of the First Amendment guarantees to individual development and to our system of representative government, decisions requiring that official action with adverse impact on First Amendment rights be justified by a public interest that is "compelling" or "paramount," and those precedents establishing the principle that justifiable

governmental goals may not be achieved by unduly broad means having an unnecessary impact on protected rights of speech, press, or association. The heart of the claim is that the burden on news gathering resulting from compelling reporters to disclose confidential information outweighs any public interest in obtaining the information.

The sole issue before us is the obligation of reporters to respond to grand jury subpoenas as other citizens do and to answer questions relevant to an investigation into the commission of crime. Citizens generally are not constitutionally immune from grand jury subpoenas; and neither the First Amendment nor any other constitutional provision protects the average citizen from disclosing to a grand jury information that he has received in confidence. The claim is, however, that reporters are exempt from these obligations because if forced to respond to subpoenas and identify their sources or disclose other confidences, their informants will refuse or be reluctant to furnish newsworthy information in the future. This asserted burden on news gathering is said to make compelled testimony from newsmen constitutionally suspect and to require a privileged position for them.

It is clear that the First Amendment does not invalidate every incidental burdening of the press that may result from the enforcement of civil or criminal statutes of general applicability. Under prior cases, otherwise valid laws serving substantial public interests may be enforced against the press as against others, despite the possible burden that may be imposed. The Court has emphasized that "[t]he publisher of a newspaper has no special immunity from the application of general laws. He has no special privilege to invade the rights and liberties of others." *Associated Press* v. *NLRB,* 301 U.S. 103, 132–133 (1937). It was there held that the Associated Press, a news-gathering and disseminating organization, was not exempt from the requirements of the National Labor Relations Act. . . .

Despite the fact that news gathering may be hampered, the press is regularly excluded from grand jury proceedings, our own conferences, the meetings of other official bodies gathered in executive session, and the meetings of private organizations. Newsmen have no constitutional right of access to the scenes of crime or disaster when the general public is excluded, and they may be prohibited from attending or publishing information about trials if such restrictions are necessary to assure a defendant a fair trial before an impartial tribunal. In *Sheppard* v. *Maxwell,* . . . for example, the Court reversed a state court conviction where the trial court failed to adopt "stricter rules governing the use of the courtroom by newsmen, as Sheppard's counsel requested," neglected to insulate witnesses from the press, and made no "effort to control the release of leads, information, and gossip to the press by police officers, witnesses, and the counsel for both sides." . . . "[T]he trial court might well have proscribed extrajudicial statements by any lawyer, party, witness, or court official which divulged prejudicial matters." . . .

It is thus not surprising that the great weight of authority is that newsmen are not exempt from the normal duty of appearing before a grand jury and answering questions relevant to a criminal investigation. At common law, courts consistently refused to recognize the existence of any privilege authorizing a newsman to refuse to reveal confidential information to a grand jury. . . .

The preference for anonymity of those confidential informants involved in actual criminal conduct is presumably a product of their desire to escape criminal prosecution, and this preference, while understandable, is hardly deserving of constitutional protection. It would be frivolous to assert—and no one does in these cases—that the First Amendment, in the interest of securing news or otherwise, confers a license on either the reporter or his news sources to violate valid criminal laws. Although stealing documents or private wiretapping could provide newsworthy information, neither reporter nor source is immune from conviction for such conduct, whatever the impact on the flow of news. Neither is immune, on First Amendment grounds, from testifying against the other, before the grand jury or at a criminal trial. . . .

Thus, we cannot seriously entertain the notion that the First Amendment protects a newsman's agreement to conceal the criminal conduct of his source, or evidence thereof, on the theory that it is better to write about crime than to do something about it. Insofar as any reporter in these cases undertook not to reveal or testify about the crime he witnessed, his claim of privilege under the First Amendment presents no substantial question. The crimes of news sources are no less reprehensible and threatening to the public interest when witnessed by a reporter than when they are not.

There remain those situations where a source is not engaged in criminal conduct but has information suggesting illegal conduct by others. Newsmen frequently receive information from such sources pursuant to a tacit or express agreement to withhold the source's name and suppress any information that the source wishes not published. Such informants presumably desire anonymity in order to avoid being entangled as a witness in a criminal trial or grand jury investigation. They may fear that disclosure will threaten their job security or personal safety or that it will simply result in dishonor or embarrassment.

The argument that the flow of news will be diminished by compelling reporters to aid the grand jury in a criminal investigation is not irrational, nor are the records before us silent on the matter. But we remain unclear how often and to what extent informers are actually deterred from furnishing information when newsmen are forced to testify before a grand jury. . . .

The privilege claimed here is conditional, not absolute; given the suggested preliminary showings and compelling need, the reporter would be required to testify. Presumably, such a rule would reduce the instances in which reporters could be required to appear, but predicting in advance when and in what circumstances they could be compelled to do so would be difficult. Such a rule would also have implications for the issuance of compulsory process to reporters at civil and criminal trials and at legislative hearings. If newsmen's confidential sources are as sensitive as they are claimed to be, the prospect of being unmasked whenever a judge determines the situation justifies it is hardly a satisfactory solution to the problem. For them, it would appear that only an absolute privilege would suffice.

We are unwilling to embark the judiciary on a long and difficult journey to such an uncertain destination. The administration of a constitutional newsman's privilege would present practical and conceptual difficulties of a high order. Sooner or later, it would be necessary to define those categories of newsmen who qualified for the privilege, a questionable procedure in light of the traditional doctrine that liberty of the press is the right of the lonely pamphleteer who uses carbon paper or a mimeograph just as much as of the large metropolitan publisher who utilizes the latest photocomposition methods. . . .

In addition, there is much force in the pragmatic view that the press has at its disposal powerful mechanisms of communication and is far from helpless to protect itself from harassment or substantial harm. Furthermore, if what the newsmen urged in these cases is true—that law enforcement cannot hope to gain and may suffer from subpoenaing newsmen before grand juries—prosecuters will be loath to risk so much for so little. . . .

Finally, as we have earlier indicated, news gathering is not without its First Amendment protections, and grand jury investigations if instituted or conducted other than in good faith, would pose wholly different issues for resolution under the First Amendment. Official harassment of the press undertaken not for purposes of law enforcement but to disrupt a reporter's relationship with his news sources would have

no justification. Grand juries are subject to judicial control and subpoenas to motions to quash. We do not expect courts will forget that grand juries must operate within the limits of the First Amendment as well as the Fifth.

MR. JUSTICE POWELL, concurring. . . .

MR. JUSTICE DOUGLAS, dissenting. . . .

MR. JUSTICE STEWART, with whom MR. JUSTICE BRENNAN and MR. JUSTICE MARSHALL join, dissenting.

The Court's crabbed view of the First Amendment reflects a disturbing insensitivity to the critical role of an independent press in our society. The question whether a reporter has a constitutional right to a confidential relationship with his source is of first impression here, but the principles that should guide our decision are as basic as any to be found in the Constitution. While MR. JUSTICE POWELL'S enigmatic concurring opinion gives some hope of a more flexible view in the future, the Court in these cases holds that a newsman has no First Amendment right to protect his sources when called before a grand jury. The Court thus invites state and federal authorities to undermine the historic independence of the press by attempting to annex the journalistic profession as an investigative arm of government. Not only will this decision impair performance of the press's constitutionally protected functions, but it will, I am convinced, in the long run harm rather than help the administration of justice.

I respectfully dissent.

The reporter's constitutional right to a confidential relationship with his source stems from the broad societal interest in a full and free flow of information to the public. It is this basic concern that underlies the Constitution's protection of a free press. . . .

Enlightened choice by an informed citizenry is the basic ideal upon which an open society is premised, and a free press is thus indispensable to a free society. Not only does the press enhance personal self-fulfillment by providing the people with the widest possible range of fact and opinion, but it also is an incontestable precondition of self-government. The press "has been a mighty catalyst in awakening public interest in governmental affairs, exposing corruption among public officers and employees and generally informing the citizenry of public events and occurrences. . . .'' *Estes* v. *Texas*. . .

As private and public aggregations of power burgeon in size and the pressures for conformity necessarily mount, there is obviously a continuing need for an independent press to disseminate a robust variety of information and opinion through reportage, investigation, and criticism, if we are to preserve our constitutional tradition of maximizing freedom of choice by encouraging diversity of expression.

In keeping with this tradition, we have held that the right to publish is central to the First Amendment and basic to the existence of constitutional democracy. . . .

A corollary of the right to publish must be the right to gather news. The full flow of information to the public protected by the free-press guarantee would be severely curtailed if no protection whatever were afforded to the process by which news is assembled and disseminated. . . .

No less important to the news dissemination process is the gathering of information. News must not be unnecessarily cut off at its source, for without freedom to acquire information the right to publish would be impermissibly compromised. Accordingly, a right to gather news, of some dimensions, must exist. . . . As Madison wrote: ''A popular Government, without popular information, or the means of acquiring it, is but a Prologue to a Farce or a Tragedy; or, perhaps both.'' . . .

The right to gather news implies, in turn, a right to a confidential relationship between a reporter and his source. This proposition follows as a matter of simple logic once three factual predicates are recognized: (1) newsmen require informants to gather news; (2) confidentiality—the promise or understanding that names or certain aspects of communications will be kept off the record—is essential to the creation and maintenance of a news-gathering relationship with informants; and (3) an unbridled sub-

poena power—the absence of a constitutional right protecting, in *any* way, a confidential relationship from compulsory process—will either deter sources from divulging information or deter reporters from gathering and publishing information. . . .

After today's decision, the potential informant can never be sure that his identity or off-the-record communications will not subsequently be revealed through the compelled testimony of a newsman. A public-spirited person inside government, who is not implicated in any crime, will now be fearful of revealing corruption or other governmental wrongdoing, because he will now know he can subsequently be identified by use of compulsory process. The potential source must, therefore, choose between risking exposure by giving information or avoiding the risk by remaining silent.

The reporter must speculate about whether contact with a controversial source or publication of controversial material will lead to a subpoena. In the event of a subpoena, under today's decision, the newsman will know that he must choose between being punished for contempt if he refuses to testify, or violating his profession's ethics and impairing his resourcefulness as a reporter if he discloses confidential information. . . .

The impairment of the flow of news cannot, of course, be proved with scientific precision, as the Court seems to demand. Obviously, not every news-gathering relationship requires confidentiality. And it is difficult to pinpoint precisely how many relationships do require a promise or understanding of nondisclosure. But we have never before demanded that First Amendment rights rest on elaborate empirical studies demonstrating beyond any conceivable doubt that deterrent effects exist; we have never before required proof of the exact number of people potentially affected by governmental action, who would actually be dissuaded from engaging in First Amendment activity.

Nebraska Press Association v. Stuart
427 U.S. 539, 96 S.Ct. 2791, 49 L.Ed. 2d 683 (1976)

Following the arrest of a person accused of murdering a family of six in a small Nebraska community, the local judge imposed a ban on publication of certain information, pending trial, in an attempt to avoid prejudicial publicity that might make impossible the impaneling of an impartial jury. The Nebraska Supreme Court narrowed the scope of Judge Stuart's order, and Justice Blackmun, as Circuit Judge, narrowed the order even further. The Supreme Court granted certiorari to examine the First Amendment issue the case raised. The parts of the opinions reprinted below stress most directly the problems posed by "prior restraints."

MR. CHIEF JUSTICE BURGER delivered the opinion of the Court. . . .

The First Amendment provides that "Congress shall make no law . . . abridging the freedom . . . of the press," and it is "no longer open to doubt that the liberty of the press, and of speech, is within the liberty safeguarded by the due process clause of the Fourteenth Amendment from invasion by state action." *Near* v. *Minnesota ex rel. Olson*, 283 U.S. 697, 707 (1931). . . . The Court has interpreted these guarantees to afford special protection against orders that prohibit the publication or broadcast of particular information or commentary— orders that impose a "previous" or "prior" restraint on speech. None of our decided cases on prior restraint involved restrictive orders entered to protect a defendant's right to a fair and impartial jury, but the opinions on prior restraint have a common thread relevant to this case.

In *Near* v. *Minnesota* . . . the Court held invalid a Minnesota statute providing for the abatement as a public nuisance of any "malicious, scandalous and defamatory newspaper, magazine or other periodical." Near had published an occasional weekly newspaper described by the County Attorney's complaint as "largely devoted to malicious, scandalous and defamatory articles" concerning political and other public figures. . . . Publication was enjoined pursuant to the statute. Excerpts from Near's paper, set out in the dissenting opinion of Mr. Justice Butler, show beyond question that one of its principal characteristics was blatant anti-Semitism. . . .

More recently in *New York Times Co.* v. *United States*, . . . the Government sought to enjoin the publication of excerpts from a massive, classified study of this Nation's involvement in the Vietnam conflict, going back to the end of the Second World War. The dispositive opinion of the Court simply concluded that the Government had not met its heavy burden of showing justification for the prior restraint. Each of the six concurring Justices and the three dissenting Justices expressed his views separately, but "every member of the Court, tacitly or explicitly, accepted the *Near* . . . condemnation of prior restraint as presumptively unconstitutional." . . .

The thread running through all these cases is that prior restraints on speech and publication are the most serious and the least tolerable infringement on First Amendment rights. A criminal penalty or a judgment in a defamation case is subject to the whole panoply of protections afforded by deferring the impact of the judgment until all avenues of appellate review have been exhausted. Only after judgment has become final, correct or otherwise, does the law's sanction become fully operative.

A prior restraint, by contrast and by definition, has an immediate and irreversible sanction. If it can be said that a threat of criminal or civil sanctions after publication "chills" speech, prior restraint "freezes" it at least for the time.

548

The damage can be particularly great when the prior restraint falls upon the communication of news and commentary on current events. Truthful reports of public judicial proceedings have been afforded special protection against subsequent punishment. . . . For the same reasons the protection against prior restraint should have particular force as applied to reporting of criminal proceedings, whether the crime in question is a single isolated act or a pattern of criminal conduct. . . .

The authors of the Bill of Rights did not undertake to assign priorities as between First Amendment and Sixth Amendment rights, ranking one as superior to the other. In this case, the petitioners would have us declare the right of an accused subordinate to their right to publish in all circumstances. But if the authors of these guarantees, fully aware of the potential conflicts between them, were unwilling or unable to resolve the issue by assigning to one priority over the other, it is not for us to rewrite the Constitution by undertaking what they declined to do. It is unnecessary, after nearly two centuries, to establish a priority applicable in all circumstances. Yet it is nonetheless clear that the barriers to prior restraint remain high unless we are to abandon what the Court has said for nearly a quarter of our national existence and implied throughout all of it. The history of even wartime suspension of categorical guarantees, such as habeas corpus or the right to trial by civilian courts, see *Ex parte Milligan*, . . . cautions against suspending explicit guarantees. . . .

The record demonstrates, as the Nebraska courts held, that there was indeed a risk that pretrial news accounts, true or false, would have some adverse impact on the attitudes of those who might be called as jurors. But on the record now before us it is not clear that further publicity, unchecked, would so distort the views of potential jurors that 12 could not be found who would, under proper instructions, fulfill their sworn duty to render a just verdict exclusively on the evidence presented in open court. We cannot say on this record that alternatives to a prior restraint on petitioners would not have suffi-

ciently mitigated the adverse effects of pretrial publicity so as to make prior restraint unnecessary. Nor can we conclude that the restraining order actually entered would serve its intended purpose. Reasonable minds can have few doubts about the gravity of the evil pretrial publicity can work, but the probability that it would do so here was not demonstrated with the degree of certainty our cases on prior restraint require.

Of necessity our holding is confined to the record before us. But our conclusion is not simply a result of assessing the adequacy of the showing made in this case; it results in part from the problems inherent in meeting the heavy burden of demonstrating, in advance of trial, that without prior restraint a fair trial will be denied. The practical problems of managing and enforcing restrictive orders will always be present. In this sense, the record now before us is illustrative rather than exceptional. It is significant that when this Court has reversed a state conviction because of prejudicial publicity, it has carefully noted that some course of action short of prior restraint would have made a critical difference. See *Sheppard* v. *Maxwell* . . . . However difficult it may be, we need not rule out the possibility of showing the kind of threat to fair trial rights that would possess the requisite degree of certainty to justify restraint. This Court has frequently denied that First Amendment rights are absolute and has consistently rejected the proposition that a prior restraint can never be employed. . . .

Our analysis ends as it began, with a confrontation between prior restraint imposed to protect one vital constitutional guarantee and the explicit command of another that the freedom to speak and publish shall not be abridged. We reaffirm that the guarantees of freedom of expression are not an absolute prohibition under all circumstances, but the barriers to prior restraint remain high and the presumption against its use continues intact. We hold that, with respect to the order entered in this case prohibiting reporting or commentary on judicial proceedings held in public, the barriers have not been overcome; to the extent that this order restrained publication of such material, it is clearly invalid. To the extent that it prohibited publication based on information gained from other sources, we conclude that the heavy burden imposed as a condition to securing a prior restraint was not met and the judgment of the Nebraska Supreme Court is therefore

Reversed.

Mr. Justice White, concurring. . . .

Mr. Justice Powell, concurring. . . .

Mr. Justice Brennan, with whom Mr. Justice Stewart and Mr. Justice Marshall join, concurring in the judgment. . . .

Settled case law concerning the impropriety and constitutional invalidity of prior restraints on the press compels the conclusion that there can be no prohibition on the publication by the press of any information pertaining to pending judicial proceedings or the operation of the criminal justice system, no matter how shabby the means by which the information is obtained. This does not imply, however, any subordination of Sixth Amendment rights, for an accused's right to a fair trial may be adequately assured through methods that do not infringe First Amendment values. . . .

I unreservedly agree with Mr. Justice Black that "free speech and fair trials are two of the most cherished policies of our civilization, and it would be a trying task to choose between them." *Bridges* v. *California*, 314 U.S., at 260. But I would reject the notion that a choice is necessary, that there is an inherent conflict that cannot be resolved without essentially abrogating one right or the other. To hold that courts cannot impose any prior restraints on the reporting of or commentary upon information revealed in open court proceedings, disclosed in public documents, or divulged by other sources with respect to the criminal justice system is not, I must emphasize, to countenance the sacrifice of precious Sixth Amendment rights on the altar of the First Amendment. For although there may in some instances be tension between uninhibited and robust reporting by the press

and fair trials for criminal defendants, judges possess adequate tools short of injunctions against reporting for relieving that tension. To be sure, these alternatives may require greater sensitivity and effort on the part of judges conducting criminal trials than would the stifling of publicity through the simple expedient of issuing a restrictive order on the press; but that sensitivity and effort is [*sic*] required in order to ensure the full enjoyment and proper accommodation of both First and Sixth Amendment rights.

There is, beyond peradventure, a clear and substantial damage to freedom of the press whenever even a temporary restraint is imposed on reporting of material concerning the operations of the criminal justice system, an institution of such pervasive influence in our constitutional scheme. And the necessary impact of reporting even confessions can never be so direct, immediate, and irreparable that I would give credence to any notion that prior restraints may be imposed on that rationale. It may be that such incriminating material would be of such slight news value or so inflammatory in particular cases that responsible organs of the media, in an exercise of self-restraint, would choose not to publicize that material, and not make the judicial task of safeguarding precious rights of criminal defendants more difficult. Voluntary codes such as the Nebraska Bar-Press Guidelines are a commendable acknowledgment by the media that constitutional prerogatives bring enormous responsibilities, and I would encourage continuation of such voluntary cooperative efforts between the bar and the media. However, the press may be arrogant, tyrannical, abusive, and sensationalist, just as it may be incisive, probing, and informative. But at least in the context of prior restraints on publication, the decision of what, when, and how to publish is for editors, not judges. . . .

Mr. Justice Stevens, concurring in the judgment. . . .

V. Obscenity

Miller v. *California*
413 U.S. 5, 93 S.Ct. 2607, 37 L.Ed. 2d 419 (1973)

After a jury trial in a California state court, the defendant, who had mailed unsolicited advertising brochures containing pictures and drawings explicitly depicting sexual activities, was convicted of violating a California statute making it a misdemeanor knowingly to distribute obscene matter.

On appeal, the Superior Court of California, County of Orange, affirmed. The United States Supreme Court vacated and remanded.

Chief Justice Burger, joined by Justices Blackmun, Powell, Rehnquist, and White, delivered the majority opinion.

This is one of a group of "obscenity-pornography" cases being reviewed by the Court in a reexamination of standards enunciated in earlier cases involving what Mr. Justice Harlan called "the intractable obscenity problem."

The brochures advertise four books entitled "Intercourse," "Man-Woman," "Sex Orgies Illustrated," and "An Illustrated History of Pornography," and a film entitled "Marital Intercourse." While the brochures contain some descriptive printed material, primarily they consist of pictures and drawings very explicitly depicting men and women in groups of two or more engaging in a variety of sexual activities, with genitals often prominently displayed. . . .

This case involves the application of a State's criminal obscenity statute to a situation in which sexually explicit materials have been thrust by aggressive sales action upon unwilling recipients who had in no way indicated any desire to receive such materials. This Court has recognized that the States have a legitimate interest in prohibiting dissemination or exhibition of obscene material when the mode of dissemination carries with it a significant danger of offending the sensibilities of unwilling recipients or of exposure to juveniles. . . .

It is in this context that we are called on to define the standards which must be used to identify obscene material that a State may regulate without infringing the First Amendment as applicable to the States through the Fourteenth Amendment. . . .

The dissent of Mr. Justice Brennan reviews the background of the obscenity problem, but since the Court now undertakes to formulate standards more concrete than those in the past, it is useful for us to focus on two of the landmark cases in the somewhat tortured history of the Court's obscenity decisions. In *Roth* v. *United States,* 354 U.S. 476 (1957), the Court sustained a conviction under a federal statute punishing the mailing of "obscene, lewd, lascivious or filthy . . ." materials. The key to that holding was the Court's rejection of the claim that obscene materials were protected by the First Amendment. Five Justices joined in the opinion stating,

All ideas having even the slightest redeeming social importance—unorthodox ideas, controversial ideas, even ideas hateful to the prevailing climate of opinion—have the full protection of the [First Amendment] guaranties, unless excludable because they encroach upon the limited area of more important interests. But implicit in the history of the First Amendment is the rejection of obscenity as utterly without redeeming social importance. . . .

Nine years later, in *Memoirs* v. *Massachusetts,* 383 U.S. 413 (1966), the Court veered sharply away from the Roth concept and, with only three Justices in the plurality opinion, articulated a new test of obscenity. The plurality held that under the Roth definition

. . . as elaborated in subsequent cases, three elements must coalesce: it must be established that (a) the dominant theme of the material taken as a whole appeals to a prurient interest in sex; (b) the material is patently offensive because it affronts contemporary community standards relating to the description or representation of sexual matters; and (c) the material is utterly without redeeming social value. . . .

Apart from the initial formulation in the Roth case, no majority of the Court has at any given time been able to agree on a standard to determine what constitutes obscene, pornographic material subject to regulation under the States' police power. . . . We have seen a "variety of views among the members of the Court unmatched in any other course of constitutional adjudication." . . . This is not remarkable, for in the area of freedom of speech and press the courts must always remain sensitive to any infringement on genuinely serious literary, artistic, political, or scientific expression. This is an area in which there are few eternal verities. . . .

This much has been categorically settled by the Court, that obscene material is unprotected by the First Amendment. . . .

The basic guidelines for the trier of fact must be: (a) whether "the average person, applying contemporary community standards" would find that the work, taken as a whole appeals to the prurient interest, (b) whether the work depicts or describes, in a patently offensive way, sexual conduct specifically defined by the applicable state law, and (c) whether the work, taken as a whole, lacks serious literary, artistic, political, or scientific value. We do not adopt as a constitutional standard the "*utterly* without redeeming social value" test. . . . That concept has never commanded the adherence of more than three Justices at one time. . . . If a state law that regulates obscene material is thus limited,

as written or construed, the First Amendment values applicable to the States through the Fourteenth Amendment are adequately protected by the ultimate power of appellate courts to conduct an independent review of constitutional claims when necessary. . . .

. . . We emphasize that it is not our function to propose regulatory schemes for the States. That must await their concrete legislative efforts. It is possible, however, to give a few plain examples of what a state statute could define for regulation:

(a) Patently offensive representations or descriptions of ultimate sexual acts, normal or perverted, actual or simulated.

(b) Patently offensive representations or descriptions of masturbation, excretory functions, and lewd exhibition of the genitals.

Sex and nudity may not be exploited without limit by films or pictures exhibited or sold in places of public accommodation any more than live sex and nudity can be exhibited or sold without limit in such public places. At a minimum, prurient, patently offensive depiction or description of sexual conduct must have serious literary, artistic, political, or scientific value to merit First Amendment protection. . . . For example, medical books for the education of physicians and related personnel necessarily use graphic illustrations and descriptions of human anatomy. In resolving the inevitably sensitive questions of fact and law, we must continue to rely on the jury system, accompanied by the safeguards that judges, rules of evidence, presumption of innocence and other protective features provide, as we do with rape, murder and a host of other offenses against society and its individual members. . . .

Under the holdings announced today, no one will be subject to prosecution for the sale or exposure of obscene materials unless these materials depict or describe patently offensive "hard core" sexual conduct specifically defined by the regulating state law, as written or construed. We are satisfied that these specific prerequisites will provide fair notice to a dealer in such materials that his public and commercial activities may bring prosecution. . . . If the inability to define regulated materials with ultimate, god-like precision altogether removes the power of the States or the Congress to regulate, then "hard core" pornography may be exposed without limit to the juvenile, the passerby, and the consenting adult alike, as, indeed, Mr. Justice Douglas contends . . . In this belief, however, Mr. Justice Douglas now stands alone. . . .

It is certainly true that the absence, since Roth, of a single majority view of this Court as to proper standards for testing obscenity has placed a strain on both state and federal courts. But today, for the first time since Roth was decided in 1957, a majority of this Court has agreed on concrete guidelines to isolate "hard core" pornography from expression protected by the First Amendment. . . .

This may not be an easy road, free from difficulty. But no amount of "fatigue" should lead us to adopt a convenient "institutional" rationale—an absolutist, "anything goes" view of the First Amendment—because it will lighten our burdens. "Such an abnegation of judicial supervision in this field would be inconsistent with our duty to uphold the constitutional guarantees." . . . Nor should we remedy "tension between state and federal courts" by arbitrarily depriving the States of a power reserved to them under the Constitution, a power which they have enjoyed and exercised continuously from before the adoption of the First Amendment to this day. . . .

Under a national Constitution, fundamental First Amendment limitations on the powers of the States do not vary from community to community, but this does not mean that there are, or should or can be, fixed, uniform national standards of precisely what appeals to the "prurient interest" or is "patently offensive." These are essentially questions of fact, and our nation is simply too big and too diverse for this Court to reasonably expect that such standards could be articulated for all 50 States in a single formulation, even assuming the prerequisite consensus exists. When triers of fact are asked to decide whether "the average person, applying contemporary community standards" would

consider certain materials "prurient," it would be unrealistic to require that the answer be based on some abstract formulation. The adversary system, with lay jurors as the usual ultimate factfinders in criminal prosecutions, has historically permitted triers-of-fact to draw on the standards of their community, guided always by limiting instructions on the law. To require a State to structure obscenity proceedings around evidence of a *national* "community standard" would be an exercise in futility. . . .

This, a "national" standard of First Amendment protection enumerated by a plurality of this Court, was correctly regarded at the time of trial as limiting state prosecution under the controlling case law. The jury, however, was explicitly instructed that, in determining whether the "dominant theme of the material as a whole . . . appeals to the prurient interest" and in determining whether the material "goes substantially beyond customary limits of candor and affronts contemporary community standards of decency" it was to apply "contemporary community standards of the State of California." . . .

We conclude that neither the State's alleged failure to offer evidence of "national standards," nor the trial court's charge that the jury consider state community standards, were constitutional errors. Nothing in the First Amendment requires that a jury must consider hypothetical and unascertainable "national standards" when attempting to determine whether certain materials are obscene as a matter of fact. Chief Justice Warren pointedly commented in his dissent in *Jacobellis* v. *Ohio,* 378 U.S., at 200,

It is my belief that when the Court said in Roth that obscenity is to be defined by reference to "community standards," it meant community standards—not a national standard, as is sometimes argued. I believe that there is no provable "national standard" . . . At all events, this Court has not been able to enunciate one, and it would be unreasonable to expect local courts to divine one.

It is neither realistic nor constitutionally sound to read the First Amendment as requiring that the people of Maine or Mississippi accept public depiction of conduct found tolerable in Las Vegas, or New York City. . . . People in different States vary in their tastes and attitudes, and this diversity is not to be strangled by the absolutism of imposed uniformity. . . .

The dissenting Justices sound the alarm of repression. But, in our view, to equate the free and robust exchange of ideas and political debate with commercial exploitation of obscene material demeans the grand conception of the First Amendment and its high purposes in the historic struggle for freedom. It is a "misuse of the great guarantees of free speech and free press. . . ." The First Amendment protects works which, taken as a whole, have serious literary, artistic, political or scientific value, regardless of whether the government or a majority of the people approve of the ideas these works represent. "The protection given speech and press was fashioned to assure unfettered interchange of *ideas* for the bringing about of political and social changes desired by the people." *Roth* v. *United States,* 354 U.S., at 484. . . . But the public portrayal of hard core sexual conduct for its own sake, and for the ensuing commercial gain, is a different matter.

There is no evidence, empirical or historical, that the stern 19th century American censorship of public distribution and display of material relating to sex, . . . anyway limited or affected expression of serious literary, artistic, political, or scientific ideas. On the contrary, it is beyond any question that the era following Thomas Jefferson to Theodore Roosevelt was an "extraordinarily vigorous period" not just in economics and politics, but in belles lettres and in "the outlying fields of social and political philosophies."

We do not see the harsh hand of censorship of ideas—good or bad, sound or unsound—and "repression" of political liberty lurking in every state regulation of commercial exploitation of human interest in sex. . . .

In sum we (a) reaffirm the Roth holding that obscene material is not protected by the First Amendment, (b) hold that such material can be regulated by the States, subject to the specific safeguards enunciated above, without a showing that the material is "*utterly* without redeeming social value," and (c) hold that obscenity is to be determined by applying "contemporary community standards," . . . not "national standards." The judgment of the Appellate Department of the Superior Court, Orange County, California, is vacated and the case remanded to that court for further proceedings not inconsistent with the First Amendment standards established by this opinion.

Mr. Justice Douglas, dissenting.

Today we leave open the way for California to send a man to prison for distributing brochures that advertise books and a movie under freshly written standards defining obscenity which until today's decision were never the part of any law. . . .

Today the Court retreats from the earlier formulations of the constitutional test and undertakes to make new definitions. This effort, like the earlier ones, is earnest and well-intentioned. The difficulty is that we do not deal with constitutional terms, since "obscenity" is not mentioned in the Constitution or Bill of Rights. And the First Amendment makes no such exception from the "the press" which it undertakes to protect nor, as I have said on other occasions, is an exception necessarily implied, for there was no recognized exception to the free press at the time the Bill of Rights was adopted which treated "obscene" publications differently from other types of papers, magazines, and books. So there are no constitutional guidelines for deciding what is and what is not "obscene." The Court is at large because we deal with tastes and standards of literature. What shocks me may be sustenance for my neighbor. What causes one person to boil up in rage over one pamphlet or movie may reflect only his neurosis, not shared by others. We deal here with problems of censorship which, if adopted, should be done by constitutional amendment after full debate by the people.

Obscenity cases usually generate tremendous emotional outbursts. They have no business being in the courts. If a constitutional amendment authorized censorship, the censor would probably be an administrative agency. Then criminal prosecutions could follow as, if and when publishers defied the censor and sold their literature. Under that regime a publisher would know when he was on dangerous ground. Under the present regime—whether the old standards or the new ones are used—the criminal law becomes a trap. A brand new test would put a publisher behind bars under a new law improvised by the Court after the publication. . . .

While the right to know is the corollary of the right to speak or publish, no one can be forced by government to listen to disclosure that he finds offensive. . . . There is no "captive audience" problem in these obscenity cases. No one is being compelled to look or to listen. Those who enter news stands or bookstalls may be offended by what they see. But they are not compelled by the State to frequent those places; and it is only state or governmental action against which the First Amendment, applicable to the States by virtue of the Fourteenth, raises a ban.

The idea that the First Amendment permits government to ban publications that are "offensive" to some people puts an ominous gloss on freedom of the press. That test would make it possible to ban any paper or any journal or magazine in some benighted place. The First Amendment was designed "to invite dispute," to induce "a condition of unrest," to "create dissatisfactions with conditions as they are," and even to stir "people to anger." . . .

If there are to be restraints on what is obscene, then a constitutional amendment should be the way of achieving the end. There are societies where religion and mathematics are the only free segments. It would be a dark day for America if that were our destiny. But the people can make it such if they choose to write obscenity into the Constitution and define it.

We deal with highly emotional, not rational, questions. To many the Song of Solomon is obscene. I do not think we, the judges, were ever given the constitutional power to make definitions of obscenity. If it is to be defined, let the people debate and decide by a constitutional amendment what they want to ban as obscene and what standards they want the legislatures and the courts to apply. Perhaps the people will decide that the path towards a mature, integrated society requires that all ideas competing for acceptance must have no censor. Perhaps they will decide otherwise. Whatever the choice, the courts will have some guidelines. Now we have none except our own predilections.

MR. JUSTICE BRENNAN, with whom MR. JUSTICE STEWART and MR. JUSTICE MARSHALL join, dissenting. . . . (The following is taken from Brennan's dissent in the companion case to *Miller* v. *California, Paris Adult Theatre I* v. *Slaton*, 413 U.S. 49: 1973).

Our experience with the Roth approach has certainly taught us that the outright suppression of obscenity cannot be reconciled with the fundamental principles of the First and Fourteenth Amendments. For we have failed to formulate a standard that sharply distinguishes protected from unprotected speech, and out of necessity, we have resorted to the Redrup approach, which resolves cases as between the parties, but offers only the most obscure guidance to legislation, adjudication by other courts, and primary conduct. By disposing of cases through summary reversal or denial of certiorari we have deliberately and effectively obscured the rationale underlying the decisions. It comes as no surprise that judicial attempts to follow our lead conscientiously have often ended in hopeless confusion.

Of course, the vagueness problem would be largely of our own creation if it stemmed primarily from our failure to reach a consensus on any one standard. But after 16 years of experimentation and debate I am reluctantly forced to the conclusion that none of the available formulas, including the one announced today, can reduce the vagueness to a tolerable level while at the same time striking an acceptable balance between the protections of the First and Fourteenth Amendments, on the one hand, and on the other the asserted state interest in regulating the dissemination of certain sexually oriented materials. . . .

The vagueness of the standards in the obscenity area produces a number of separate problems, and any improvement must rest on an understanding that the problems are to some extent distinct. First, a vague statute fails to provide adequate notice to persons who are engaged in the type of conduct that the statute could be thought to proscribe. The Due Process Clause of the Fourteenth Amendment requires that all criminal laws provide fair notice of "what the State commands or forbids." . . .

In addition to problems that arise when any criminal statute fails to afford fair notice of what it forbids, a vague statute in the areas of speech and press creates a second level of difficulty. We have indicated that "stricter standards of permissible statutory vagueness may be applied to a statute having a potentially inhibiting effect on speech; a man may the less be required to act at his peril here, because the free dissemination of ideas may be the loser." . . .

As a result of our failure to define standards with predictable application to any given piece of material, there is no probability of regularity in obscenity decisions by state and lower federal courts. That is not to say that these courts have performed badly in this area or paid insufficient attention to the principles we have established. The problem is, rather, that one cannot say with certainty that material is obscene until at least five members of this Court, applying inevitably obscure standards, have pronounced it so. The number of obscenity cases on our docket gives ample testimony to the burden that has been placed upon this Court.

But the sheer number of the cases does not define the full extent of the institutional problem. For, quite apart from the number of cases involved and the need to make a fresh constitutional determination in each case, we are tied to the "absurd business of perusing and viewing the miserable stuff that pours into the Court. . . ." While the material may have varying degrees of social importance, it is hardly a source of edification to the members of the Court who are compelled to view it before passing on its obscenity. . . .

More important, . . . the practice effectively censors protected expression by leaving lower court determinations of obscenity intact even though the status of the allegedly obscene material is entirely unsettled until final review here. In addition, the uncertainty of the standards creates a continuing source of tension between state and federal courts, since the need for an independent determination by this Court seems to render superfluous even the most conscientious analysis by state tribunals. And our inability to justify our decisions with a persuasive rationale—or indeed, any rationale at all—necessarily creates the impression that we are merely second-guessing state court judges.

The severe problems arising from the lack of fair notice, from the chill on protected expression, and from the stress imposed on the state and federal judicial machinery persuade me that a significant change in direction is urgently required. . . .

In short, while I cannot say that the interests of the State—apart from the question of juveniles and unconsenting adults—are trivial or nonexistent, I am compelled to conclude that these interests cannot justify the substantial damage to constitutional rights and to this Nation's judicial machinery that inevitably results from state efforts to bar the distribution even of unprotected material to consenting adults. . . . I would hold, therefore, that at least in the absence of distribution to juveniles or obtrusive exposure to unconsenting adults, the First and Fourteenth Amendments prohibit the State and Federal Governments from attempting wholly to suppress sexually oriented materials on the basis of their allegedly "obscene" contents.

VI. Religious Freedom

Minersville School District v. *Gobitis*
310 U.S. 586, 60 S.Ct. 1010, 84 L.Ed. 1375 (1940)
West Virginia State Board of Education v. *Barnette*
319 U.S. 624, 63 S.Ct. 1178, 87 L.Ed. 1628 (1943)

One of the most dramatic reversals of a Court decision occurred in 1943 when a precedent of only three years' standing was overruled. Both cases presented the same issue: Could schoolchildren, members of the sect known as Jehovah's Witnesses, be required to salute the flag, a practice forbidden by their religious tenets? In the earlier case, the Court in an 8-to-1 decision upheld the action of a Pennsylvania school board expelling a recalcitrant pupil; but in the later case the Court by a 6-to-3 vote held a similar action unconstitutional. Excerpts from both cases are included below. It should be noted that this about-face was the result partly of personnel changes (which brought *Justices Jackson* and *Rutledge* to the bench) and partly of the change of viewpoint of *Justices Black, Douglas,* and *Murphy.*

Minersville School District v. *Gobitis* (1940)

MR. JUSTICE FRANKFURTER delivered the opinion of the court.

A grave responsibility confronts this Court whenever in course of litigation it must reconcile the conflicting claims of liberty and authority. But when the liberty invoked is liberty of conscience, and the authority is authority to safeguard the nation's fellowship, judicial conscience is put to its severest test. Of such a nature is the present controversy.

Lillian Gobitis, aged twelve, and her brother William, aged ten, were expelled from the public schools of Minersville, Pennsylvania, for refusing to salute the national flag as part of a daily school exercise. . . .

The Gobitis children were of an age for which Pennsylvania makes school attendance compulsory. Thus they were denied a free education, and their parents had to put them into private schools. To be relieved of the financial burden thereby entailed, their father, on behalf of the children and in his own behalf, brought this suit. He sought to enjoin the authorities from continuing to exact participation in the flag-salute ceremony as a condition of his children's attendance at the Minersville school. . . .

We must decide whether the requirement of participation in such a ceremony, exacted from a child who refuses upon sincere religious grounds, infringes without due process of law the liberty guaranteed by the Fourteenth Amendment.

Centuries of strife over the erection of particular dogmas as exclusive or all-comprehending faiths led to the inclusion of a guarantee for religious freedom in the Bill of Rights. The First Amendment, and the Fourteenth through its absorption of the First, sought to guard against repetition of those bitter religious struggles by prohibiting the establishment of a state religion and by securing to every sect the free exercise of its faith. So pervasive is the acceptance of this precious right that its scope is brought into question, as here, only when the conscience of individuals collides with the felt necessities of society.

557

Certainly the affirmative pursuit of one's convictions about the ultimate mystery of the universe and man's relation to it is placed beyond the reach of law. Government may not interfere with organized or individual expression of belief or disbelief. Propagation of belief—or even of disbelief in the supernatural—is protected, whether in church or chapel, mosque or synagogue, tabernacle or meetinghouse. . . .

But the manifold character of man's relations may bring his conception of religious duty into conflict with the secular interests of his fellowmen. When does the constitutional guarantee compel exemption from doing what society thinks necessary for the promotion of some great common end, or from a penalty for conduct which appears dangerous to the general good? To state the problem is to recall the truth that no single principle can answer all of life's complexities. The right to freedom of religious belief, however dissident and however obnoxious to the cherished beliefs of others—even of a majority—is itself the denial of an absolute. But to affirm that the freedom to follow conscience has itself no limits in the life of a society would deny that very plurality of principles which, as a matter of history, underlies protection of religious toleration. . . . Our present task then, as so often the case with courts, is to reconcile two rights in order to prevent either from destroying the other. But, because in safeguarding conscience we are dealing with interests so subtle and so dear, every possible leeway should be given to the claims of religious faith. . . .

The religious liberty which the Constitution protects has never excluded legislation of general scope not directed against doctrinal loyalties of particular sects. Judicial nullification of legislation cannot be justified by attributing to the framers of the Bill of Rights views for which there is no historic warrant. Conscientious scruples have not, in the course of the long struggle for religious toleration, relieved the individual from obedience to a general law not aimed at the promotion or restriction of religious beliefs. The mere possession of religious convictions which contradict the relevant concerns of a political society does not relieve the citizen from the discharge of political responsibilities. The necessity for this adjustment has again and again been recognized. In a number of situations the exertion of political authority has been sustained, while basic considerations of religious freedom have been left inviolate.

. . . Nor does the freedom of speech assured by Due Process move in a more absolute circle of immunity than that enjoyed by religious freedom. Even if it were assumed that freedom of speech goes beyond the historic concept of full opportunity to utter and to disseminate views, however heretical or offensive to dominant opinion, and includes freedom from conveying what may be deemed an implied but rejected affirmation, the question remains whether school children, like the Gobitis children, must be excused from conduct required of all the other children in the promotion of national cohesion. We are dealing with an interest inferior to none in the hierarchy of legal values. National unity is the basis of national security. To deny the legislature the right to select appropriate means for its attainment presents a totally different order of problem from that of the propriety of subordinating the possible ugliness of littered streets to the free expression of opinion through distribution of handbills. . . .

Situations like the present are phases of the profoundest problems confronting a democracy—the problem which Lincoln cast in memorable dilemma: "Must a government of necessity be too *strong* for the liberties of its people, or too *weak* to maintain its own existence?" No mere textual reading or logical talisman can solve the dilemma. And when the issue demands judicial determination, it is not the personal notion of judges of what wise adjustment requires which must prevail.

Unlike the instances we have cited, the case before us is not concerned with an exertion of legislative power for the promotion of some specific need or interest of secular society—the protection of the family, the promotion of health, the common defense, the raising of public revenues to defray the cost of government. But all these specific activities of government presuppose the existence of an organized political society. The ultimate foundation of a free society is the binding ties of cohesive sentiment. Such a sentiment is fostered by all those agencies of the mind and spirit which may serve to gather up the traditions of a people, transmit them from generation to generation, and thereby create that continuity of a treasured common life which constitutes a civilization. ''We live by symbols.'' The flag is the symbol of our national unity, transcending all internal differences, however large, within the framework of the Constitution. . . .

The precise issue, then, for us to decide is whether the legislatures of the various states and the authorities in a thousand counties and school districts of this country are barred from determining the appropriateness of various means to evoke that unifying sentiment without which there can ultimately be no liberties, civil or religious. To stigmatize legislative judgment in providing for this universal gesture of respect for the symbol of our national life in the setting of the common school as a lawless inroad on that freedom of conscience which the Constitution protects, would amount to no less than the pronouncement of pedagogical and psychological dogma in a field where courts possess no marked and certainly no controlling competence. The influences which help toward a common feeling for the common country are manifold. Some may seem harsh and others no doubt are foolish. Surely, however, the end is legitimate. And the effective means for its attainment are still so uncertain and so unauthenticated by science as to preclude us from putting the widely prevalent belief in flag-saluting beyond the pale of legislative power. It mocks reason and denies our whole history to find in the allowance of a requirement to salute our flag on fitting occasions the seeds of sanction for obeisance to a leader.

The wisdom of training children in patriotic impulses by those compulsions which necessarily pervade so much of the educational process is not for our independent judgment. Even were we convinced of the folly of such a measure, such belief would be no proof of its unconstitutionality. For ourselves, we might be tempted to say that the deepest patriotism is best engendered by giving unfettered scope to the most crotchety beliefs. Perhaps it is best, even from the standpoint of those interests which ordinances like the one under review seek to promote, to give to the least popular sect leave from conformities like those here in issue. But the courtroom is not the arena for debating issues of educational policy. It is not our province to choose among competing considerations in the subtle process of securing effective loyalty to the traditional ideals of democracy, while respecting at the same time individual idiosyncracies among a people so diversified in racial origins and religious allegiances. So to hold would in effect make us the school board for the country. That authority has not been given to this Court, nor should we assume it. . . .

Judicial review, itself a limitation on popular government, is a fundamental part of our constitutional scheme. But to the legislature no less than to courts is committed the guardianship of deeply cherished liberties. . . . Where all the effective means of inducing political changes are left free from interference, education in the abandonment of foolish legislation is itself a training in liberty. To fight out the wise use of legislative authority in the forum of public opinion and before legislative assemblies rather than to transfer such a contest to the judicial arena, serves to vindicate the self-confidence of a free people.

Reversed.

MR. JUSTICE MCREYNOLDS concurs in the result.

MR. JUSTICE STONE, dissenting: . . .

Concededly the constitutional guaranties of personal liberty are not always absolutes. Government has a right to survive and powers conferred upon it are not necessarily set at naught by the express prohibitions of the Bill of Rights. . . . But it is a long step, and one which I am

The idea that the legislature is more important than B.O.R. seems absurd

unable to take, to the position that government may, as a supposed educational measure and as a means of disciplining the young, compel public affirmations which violate their religious conscience. . . .

The guaranties of civil liberty are but guaranties of freedom of the human mind and spirit and of reasonable freedom and opportunity to express them. They presuppose the right of the individual to hold such opinions as he will and to give them reasonably free expression, and his freedom, and that of the state as well, to teach and persuade others by the communication of ideas. The very essence of the liberty which they guarantee is the freedom of the individual from compulsion as to what he shall think and what he shall say, at least where the compulsion is to bear false witness to his religion. If these guaranties are to have any meaning they must, I think, be deemed to withhold from the state any authority to compel belief or the expression of it where that expression violates religious convictions, whatever may be the legislative view of the desirability of such compulsion.

History teaches us that there have been but few infringements of personal liberty by the state which have not been justified, as they are here, in the name of righteousness and the public good, and few which have not been directed, as they are now, at politically helpless minorities. The framers were not unaware that under the system which they created most governmental curtailments of personal liberty would have the support of a legislative judgment that the public interest would be better served by its curtailment than by its constitutional protection. I cannot conceive that in prescribing, as limitations upon the powers of government, the freedom of the mind and spirit secured by the explicit guaranties of freedom of speech and religion, they intended or rightly could have left any latitude for a legislative judgment that the compulsory expression of belief which violates religious convictions would better serve the public interest than their protection. The Constitution may well elicit expressions of loyalty to it and to the government which it created, but it does not command such expressions or otherwise give any indication that compulsory expressions of loyalty play any such part in our scheme of government as to override the constitutional protection of freedom of speech and religion. And while such expressions of loyalty, when voluntarily given, may promote national unity, it is quite another matter to say that their compulsory expression by children in violation of their own and their parents' religious convictions can be regarded as playing so important a part in our national unity as to leave school boards free to exact it despite the constitutional guarantee of freedom of religion. The very terms of the Bill of Rights preclude, it seems to me, any reconciliation of such compulsions with the constitutional guaranties by a legislative declaration that they are more important to the public welfare than the Bill of Rights.

But even if this view be rejected and it is considered that there is some scope for the determination by legislatures whether the citizen shall be compelled to give public expression of such sentiments contrary to his religion, I am not persuaded that we should refrain from passing upon the legislative judgment "as long as the remedial channels of the democratic process remain open and unobstructed." This seems to me no more than the surrender of the constitutional protection of the liberty of small minorities to the popular will. We have previously pointed to the importance of a searching judicial inquiry into the legislative judgment in situations where prejudice against discrete and insular minorities may tend to curtail the operation of those political processes ordinarily to be relied on to protect minorities. See *United States* v. *Carolene Products Co.,* 304 U.S. 144, 152, note 4. And until now we have not hesitated similarly to scrutinize legislation restricting the civil liberty of racial and religious minorities although no political process was affected.

. . . Here we have such a small minority entertaining in good faith a religious belief, which is such a departure from the usual course of human conduct, that most persons are disposed to regard it with little toleration or con-

a question of protecting a minority view.

cern. In such circumstances careful scrutiny of legislative efforts to secure conformity of belief and opinion by a compulsory affirmation of the desired belief, is especially needful if civil rights are to receive any protection. Tested by this standard, I am not prepared to say that the right of this small and helpless minority, including children having a strong religious conviction, whether they understand its nature or not, to refrain from an expression obnoxious to their religion, is to be overborne by the interest of the state in maintaining discipline in the schools.

The Constitution expresses more than the conviction of the people that democratic processes must be preserved at all costs. It is also an expression of faith and a command that freedom of mind and spirit must be preserved, which government must obey, if it is to adhere to that justice and moderation without which no free government can exist. For this reason it would seem that legislation which operates to repress the religious freedom of small minorities, which is admittedly within the scope of the protection of the Bill of Rights, must at least be subject to the same judicial scrutiny as legislation which we have recently held to infringe the constitutional liberty of religious and racial minorities.

With such scrutiny I cannot say that the inconveniences which may attend some sensible adjustment of school discipline in order that the religious convictions of these children may be spared, presents a problem so momentous or pressing as to outweigh the freedom from compulsory violation of religious faith which has been thought worthy of constitutional protection.

Justice Frankfurter to Justice Stone, May 27, 1940:
A *Qualified* Plea for Judicial Self-Restraint

Students of constitutional interpretation have wondered why it took Black and Douglas, two of the sharpest minds on the Court, both ardent liberals, so long to discover their error in joining Frankfurter's well-nigh unanimous opinion in the first Flag Salute case. A clue may be found in the letter Frankfurter wrote Stone in trying to win his vote: "What weighs with me strongly in this case is my anxiety that, while we lean in the direction of the libertarian aspect, we do not exercise our judicial power unduly, and as though we ourselves were legislators by holding with too tight a rein the organs of popular government. . . . For time and circumstances are surely not irrelevant considerations in resolving the conflicts that we do have to resolve in this particular case. . . . [I]t is relevant to make the adjustment that we have to make within the framework of present circumstances and those that are clearly ahead of us."

decide with realm of present circumstances

Hitler's armies were then on the march, threatening to envelop Europe. In this struggle America could not escape involvement.

Taking Frankfurter's opinion as the prime example, Richard Danzig has described how the Justice's constitutional jurisprudence was shaped by preconceived answers arrived at by questions judiciously chosen. (See Danzig, "How Questions Begot Answers in Felix Frankfurter's First Flag Salute Opinion," 1977 *Supreme Court Review* 257.)

CHAMBERS
OF JUSTICE FELIX FRANKFURTER

May 27, 1940

Dear Stone:

Were No. 690 an ordinary case, I should let the opinion speak for itself. But that you should entertain doubts has naturally stirred me to an anxious re-examination of my own views, even though I can assure you that nothing has weighed as much on my conscience, since I have come on this Court, as has this case. Your doubts have stirred me to a reconsideration of the whole matter, because I am not happy that you should entertain doubts that I cannot share or meet in a domain where constitutional power is on one side and my private notions of liberty and toleration and good sense are on the other. After all, the vulgar intrusion of law in the domain of conscience is for me a very sensitive area. For various reasons—I suspect the most dominant one is the old colored man's explanation that Moses was just raised that way—a good part of my mature life has thrown whatever weight it has had against foolish and harsh manifestations of coercion and for the amplest expression of dissident views, however absurd or offensive these may have been to my own notions of rationality and decency. I say this merely to indicate that all my bias and predisposition are in favor of giving the fullest elbow room to every variety of religious, political, and economic view.

But no one has more clearly in his mind than you, that even when it comes to these ultimate civil liberties, insofar as they are protected by the Constitution, we are not in the domain of absolutes. Here, also, we have an illustration of what the Greeks thousands of years ago recognized as a tragic issue, namely, the clash of rights, not the clash of wrongs. For resolving such clash we have no calculus. But there is for me, and I know also for you, a great makeweight for dealing with this problem, namely, that we are not the primary resolvers of the clash. We are not exercising an independent judgment; we are sitting in judgment upon the judgment of the legislature. I am aware of the important distinction which you so skillfully adumbrated in your footnote 4 (particularly the second paragraph of it) in the *Carolene Products Co.* case. I agree with that distinction; I regard it as basic. I have taken over that distinction in its central aspect, however inadequately, in the present opinion by insisting on the importance of keeping open all those channels of free expression by which undesirable legislation may be removed, and keeping unobstructed all forms of protest against what are deemed invasions of conscience, however much the invasion may be justified on the score of the deepest interests of national well-being.

What weighs with me strongly in this case is my anxiety that, while we lean in the direction of the libertarian aspect, we do not exercise our judicial power unduly, and as though we ourselves were legislators by holding with too tight a rein the organs of popular government. In other words, I want to avoid the mistake comparable to that made by those whom we criticized when dealing with the control of property. I hope I am aware of the different interests that are compendiously summarized by opposing ''liberty'' to ''property.'' But I also know that the generalizations implied in these summaries are also inaccurate and hardly correspond to the complicated realities of an advanced society. I cannot rid myself of the notion that it is not fantastic, although I think foolish and perhaps worse, for school authorities to believe—as the record in this case explicitly shows the school authorities to have believed—that to allow exemption to some of the children goes far towards disrupting the whole patriotic exercise. And since certainly we must admit the general right of the school authorities to have such flag-saluting exercises, it seems to me that we do not trench on an undebatable territory of libertarian immunity to permit the school authorities a judgment as to the effect of this exemption in the particular setting of our time and circumstances.

For time and circumstances are surely not irrelevant considerations in resolving the conflicts that we do have to resolve in this particular case. Contingencies that may determine the fate of the constitutionality of a rent act (*Chastleton Corp.* v. *Sinclair,* 264 U.S. 543) may also be operative in the adjustment between legislatively allowable pursuit of national security and the right to stand on individual idiosyncracies. You may have noticed that in my opinion I did not rely on the prior adjudications by this Court of this question. I dealt with the matter as I believe it should have been dealt with, as though it were a new question. But certainly it is relevant to make the adjustment that we have to make within the framework of present circumstances and those that are clearly ahead of us. I had many talks with Holmes about his espionage opinions and he always recognized that he had a right to take into account the things that he did take into account when he wrote Debs and the others, and the different emphasis he gave the matter in the Abrams case. After all, despite some of the jurisprudential ''realists,'' a decision decides not merely the particular case. Just as *Adkins* v. *Children's Hospital* had consequences not merely as to the minimum wage laws but in its radiations and in its psychological effects, so this case would have a tail of implications as to legislative power that is certainly debatable and might easily be invoked far beyond the size of the immediate kite, were it to deny the very minimum exaction, however foolish as to the Gobitis children, of an expression of faith in the heritage and purposes of our country.

For my intention—and I hope my execution did not lag too far behind—was to use this opinion as a vehicle for preaching the true democratic faith of not relying on the Court for the impossible task of assuring a vigorous, mature, self-protecting and tolerant democracy by bringing the responsibility for a combination of firmness and toleration directly home where it belongs—to the people and their representatives themselves.

I have tried in this opinion really to act on what will, as a matter of history, be a lodestar for due regard between legislative and judicial powers, to wit, your dissent in the Butler case. For please bear in mind how very little this case authorizes and how wholly free it leaves us for the future. This is not a case where confinement either of children or of parents is the consequence of non-conformity. It is not a case where conformity is exacted for something that you and I regard as foolish—namely, a gesture of respect for the symbol of our national being—even though we deem it foolish to exact it from Jehovah's Witnesses. It is not a case, for instance, of compelling children to partake in a school dance or other scholastic exercise that may run counter to this or that faith. And, above all, it is not a case where the slightest restriction is involved against the fullest opportunity to disavow—either on the part of the children or their parents—the meaning that ordinary people attach to the gesture of respect. The duty of compulsion being as minimal as it is for an act, the normal legislative authorization of which certainly cannot be denied, and all channels of affirmative free expression being open to both children and parents, I cannot resist the conviction that we ought to let the legislative judgment stand and put the responsibility for its exercise where it belongs. In any event, I hope you will be good enough to give me the benefit of what you think should be omitted or added to the opinion.

Faithfully yours
s/Felix Frankfurter

Mr. Justice Stone.

West Virginia State Board of Education v. Barnette (1943)

MR. JUSTICE JACKSON delivered the opinion of the Court: . . .

This case calls upon us to reconsider a precedent decision, as the Court throughout its history often has been required to do. Before turning to the Gobitis case, however, it is desirable to notice certain characteristics by which this controversy is distinguished.

The freedom asserted by these appellees does not bring them into collision with rights asserted by any other individual. It is such conflicts which most frequently require intervention of the State to determine where the rights of one end and those of another begin. But the refusal of these persons to participate in the ceremony does not interfere with or deny rights of others to do so. Nor is there any question in this case that their behavior is peaceable and orderly. The sole conflict is between authority and rights of the individual. The State asserts power to condition access to public education on making a prescribed sign and profession and at the same time to coerce attendance by punishing both parent and child. The latter stand on a right of self-determination in matters that touch individual opinion and personal attitude. . . .

There is no doubt that, in connection with the pledges, the flag salute is a form of utterance. Symbolism is a primitive but effective way of communicating ideas. . . .

It is also to be noted that the compulsory flag salute and pledge requires [sic] affirmation of a belief and an attitude of mind. It is not clear whether the regulation contemplates that pupils forego any contrary convictions of their own and become unwilling converts to the prescribed ceremony or whether it will be acceptable if they simulate assent by words without belief and by a gesture barren of meaning. It is now a commonplace that censorship or suppression of expression of opinion is tolerated by our Constitution only when the expression presents a clear and present danger of action of a kind the State is empowered to prevent and punish. It would seem that involuntary affirmation could be commanded only on even more immediate and urgent grounds than silence. But here the power of compulsion is invoked without any allegation that remaining passive during a flag salute ritual creates a clear and present danger that would justify an effort even to muffle expression. To sustain the compulsory flag salute we are required to say that a Bill of Rights which guards the individual's right to speak his own mind, left it open to public authorities to compel him to utter what is not in his mind.

Whether the First Amendment to the Constitution will permit officials to order observance of ritual of this nature does not depend upon whether as a voluntary exercise we would think it to be good, bad or merely innocuous. . . .

Nor does the issue as we see it turn on one's possession of particular religious views or the sincerity with which they are held. While religion supplies appellees' motive for enduring the discomforts of making the issue in this case, many citizens who do not share these religious views hold such a compulsory rite to infringe constitutional liberty of the individual. It is not

Should flag-salute be a legal duty?

Is Flag salute a valid general rule?

necessary to inquire whether nonconformist beliefs will exempt from the duty to salute unless we first find power to make the salute a legal duty.

The Gobitis decision, however, *assumed,* as did the argument in that case and in this, that power exists in the State to impose the flag salute discipline upon school children in general. The Court only examined and rejected a claim based on religious beliefs of immunity from an unquestioned general rule. The question which underlies the flag salute controversy is whether such a ceremony so touching matters of opinion and political attitude may be imposed upon the individual by official authority under powers committed to any political organization under our Constitution. . . .

In weighing arguments of the parties it is important to distinguish between the due process clause of the Fourteenth Amendment as an instrument for transmitting the principles of the First Amendment and those cases in which it is applied for its own sake. The test of legislation which collides with the Fourteenth Amendment because it also collides with the principles of the First, is much more definite than the test when only the Fourteenth is involved. Much of the vagueness of the due process clause disappears when the specific prohibitions of the First become its standard. The right of a State to regulate, for example, a public utility may well include, so far as the due process test is concerned, power to impose all of the restrictions which a legislature may have a ''rational basis'' for adopting. But freedoms of speech and of press, of assembly, and of worship may not be infringed on such slender grounds. They are susceptible of restriction only to prevent grave and immediate danger to interests which the State may lawfully protect. It is important to note that while it is the Fourteenth Amendment which bears directly upon the State it is the more specific limiting principles of the First Amendment that finally govern this case. → *1st general applies*

Nor does our duty to apply the Bill of Rights to assertions of official authority depend upon our possession of marked competence in the field where the invasion of rights occurs. True, *clear & present danger?*

the task of translating the majestic generalities of the Bill of Rights, conceived as part of the pattern of liberal government in the eighteenth century, into concrete restraints on officials dealing with the problems of the twentieth century, is one to disturb self-confidence. These principles grew in soil which also produced a philosophy that the individual was the center of society, that his liberty was attainable through mere absence of governmental restraints, and that government should be entrusted with few controls and only the mildest supervision over men's affairs. We must transplant these rights to a soil in which the *laissez-faire* concept or principle of non-interference has withered at least as to economic affairs, and social advancements are increasingly sought through closer integration of society and through expanded and strengthened governmental controls. These changed conditions often deprive precedents of reliability and cast us more than we would choose upon our own judgment. But we act in these matters not by authority of our competence but by force of our commissions. We cannot, because of modest estimates of our competence in such specialties as public education, withhold the judgment that history authenticates as the function of this Court when liberty is infringed. . . .

The case is made difficult not because the principles of its decision are obscure but because the flag involved is our own. Nevertheless, we apply the limitations of the Constitution with no fear that freedom to be intellectually and spiritually diverse or even contrary will disintegrate the social organization. To believe that patriotism will not flourish if patriotic ceremonies are voluntary and spontaneous instead of a compulsory routine is to make an unflattering estimate of the appeal of our institutions to free minds. We can have intellectual individualism and the rich cultural diversities that we owe to exceptional minds only at the price of occasional eccentricity and abnormal attitudes. When they are so harmless to others or to the State as those we deal with here, the price is not too great. But freedom to differ is not limited to things that do not matter much.

Need confidence in our Freedom

That would be a mere shadow of freedom. The test of its substance is the right to differ as to things that touch the heart of the existing order.

If there is any fixed star in our constitutional constellation, it is that no official, high or petty, can prescribe what shall be orthodox in politics, nationalism, religion, or other matters of opinion or force citizens to confess by word or act their faith therein. If there are any circum-stances which permit an exception, they do not now occur to us.

We think the action of the local authorities in compelling the flag salute and pledge transcends constitutional limitations on their power and invades the sphere of intellect and spirit which is the purpose of the First Amendment to our Constitution to reserve from all official control. . . .

compulsory Flag salure invades spirit of 1st amend.

McCollum v. Board of Education
333 U.S. 203, 68 S.Ct. 461, 92 L.Ed. 648 (1948)

The McCollum case involved the validity of the Champaign, Illinois, "released time" program of religious instruction for public school students. The details of the pro-gram are given in the Court's opinion. The parent of a student sought unsuccess-fully in the Illinois courts to obtain a writ of mandamus prohibiting use of school facilities for religious instruction, and appealed.

MR. JUSTICE BLACK delivered the opinion of the Court.

Does "release Time" religious Class violate est. clause

This case relates to the power of a state to utilize its tax-supported public school system in aid of religious instruction insofar as that power may be restricted by the First and Fourteenth Amendments to the Federal Constitution. . . .

Appellant's petition for mandamus alleged that religious teachers, employed by private religious groups, were permitted to come weekly into the school buildings during the regular hours set apart for secular teaching, and then and there for a period of thirty minutes substitute their religious teaching for the secular education provided under the compulsory edu-cation law. . . .

Although there are disputes between the parties as to various inferences that may or may not properly be drawn from the evidence con-cerning the religious program, the following facts are shown by the record without dispute. In 1940 interested members of the Jewish, Roman Catholic, and a few of the Protestant faiths formed a voluntary association called the Champaign Council on Religious Education. They obtained permission from the Board of Education to offer classes in religious instruction to public school pupils in grades four to nine in-clusive. Classes were made up of pupils whose parents signed printed cards requesting that their children be permitted to attend; they were held weekly, thirty minutes for the lower grades, forty-five minutes for the higher. The council employed the religious teachers at no ex-pense to the school authorities, but the instruc-tors were subject to the approval and supervision of the superintendent of schools. The classes were taught in three separate religious groups by Protestant teachers, Catholic priests, and a Jewish rabbi, although for the past several years there have apparently been no classes instructed in the Jewish religion. Classes were conducted in the regular classrooms of the school building. Students who did not choose to take the religious instruction were not released from public school duties; they were required to leave their classrooms and go to some other place in the school building for pursuit of their secular studies. On the other hand, students who were released from secular study for the religious instructions were required to be present at the religious classes. Reports of their presence or absence were to be made to their secular teachers.

The foregoing facts, without reference to others that appear in the record, show the use of tax-supported property for religious instruction and the close cooperation between the school authorities and the religious council in promoting religious education. The operation of the State's compulsory education system thus assists and is integrated with the program of religious instruction carried on by separate religious sects. Pupils compelled by law to go to school for secular education are released in part from their legal duty upon the condition that they attend the religious classes. This is beyond all question a utilization of the tax-established and tax-supported public school system to aid religious groups to spread their faith. And it falls squarely under the ban of the First Amendment (made applicable to the States by the Fourteenth) as we interpreted it in *Everson* v. *Board of Education,* 330 U.S.1. There we said: ''Neither a state nor the Federal Government can set up a church. Neither can pass laws which aid one religion, aid all religions, or prefer one religion over another. Neither can force or influence a person to go or to remain away from church against his will or force him to profess a belief or disbelief in any religion. No person can be punished for entertaining or professing religious beliefs or disbeliefs, for church attendance or nonattendance. No tax in any amount, large or small, can be levied to support any religious activities or institutions, whatever they may be called, or whatever form they may adopt to teach or practice religion. Neither a state nor the Federal Government can, openly or secretly, participate in the affairs of any religious organizations or groups and vice-versa. In the

words of Jefferson, the clause against establishment of religion by law was intended to erect 'a wall of separation between church and State.''''...

To hold that a state cannot consistently with the First and Fourteenth Amendments utilize its public school system to aid any or all religious faiths or sects in the dissemination of their doctrines and ideals does not, as counsel urge, manifest a government hostility to religion or religious teachings. A manifestation of such hostility would be at war with our national tradition as embodied in the First Amendment's guaranty of the free exercise of religion. For the First Amendment rests upon the premise that both religion and government can best work to achieve their lofty aims if each is left free from the other within its respective sphere. Or, as we said in the Everson case, the First Amendment has erected a wall between Church and State which must be kept high and impregnable.

Here not only are the State's tax-supported public school buildings used for the dissemination of religious doctrines. The State also affords sectarian groups an invaluable aid in that it helps to provide pupils for their religious classes through use of the State's compulsory public school machinery. This is not separation of Church and State.

The cause is reversed and remanded to the State Supreme Court for proceedings not inconsistent with this opinion.

Reversed and remanded.

MR. JUSTICE FRANKFURTER delivered the following opinion, in which MR. JUSTICE JACKSON, MR. JUSTICE RUTLEDGE and MR. JUSTICE BURTON join....

...Zealous watchfulness against fusion of secular and religious activities by Government itself, through any of its instruments but especially through its education agencies, was the democratic response of the American community to the particular needs of a young and growing nation, unique in the composition of its people. A totally different situation elsewhere, as illustrated for instance by the English provisions for religious education in State-maintained schools, only serves to illustrate that free societies are not cast in one mould. . . . Different institutions evolve from different historic circumstances. . . .

. . . If it were merely a question of enabling a child to obtain religious instruction with a receptive mind, the thirty or forty-five minutes could readily be found on Saturday or Sunday. If that were all, Champaign might have drawn upon the French system, known in its American manifestation as "dismissed time," whereby one school day is shortened to allow all children to go where they please, leaving those who so desire to go to a religious school. The momentum of the whole school atmosphere and school planning is presumably put behind religious instruction, as given in Champaign, precisely in order to secure for the religious instruction such momentum and planning. To speak of "released time" as being only half or three quarters of an hour is to draw a thread from a fabric. . . .

Separation means separation, not something less. Jefferson's metaphor in describing the relation between Church and State speaks of a "wall of separation," not of a fine line easily overstepped. The public school is at once the symbol of our democracy and the most pervasive means for promoting our common destiny. In no activity of the State is it more vital to keep out divisive forces that in its schools, to avoid confusing, not to say fusing, what the Constitution sought to keep strictly apart. "The great American principle of eternal separation"— Elihu Root's phrase bears repetition—is one of the vital reliances of our Constitutional system for assuring unities among our people stronger than our diversities. It is the Court's duty to enforce this principle in its full integrity. . . .

[MR. JUSTICE JACKSON wrote a separate concurring opinion.]

MR. JUSTICE REED, dissenting. . . .

The phrase "an establishment of religion" may have been intended by Congress to be aimed only at a state church. When the First Amendment was pending in Congress in substantially its present form, "Mr. Madison said, he apprehended the meaning of the words to be, that Congress should not establish a religion, and enforce the legal observation of it by law, nor compel men to worship God in any manner contrary to their conscience." Passing years, however, have brought about acceptance of a broader meaning, although never until today, I believe, has this Court widened its interpretation to any such degree as holding that recognition of the interest of our nation in religion, through the granting, to qualified representatives of the principal faiths, of opportunity to present religion as an optional, extracurricular subject during released school time in public school buildings, was equivalent to an establishment of religion. A reading of the general statements of eminent statesmen of former days, referred to in the opinions in this case and in *Everson* v. *Board of Education* . . . will show that circumstances such as those in this case were far from the minds of the authors. The words and spirit of those statements may be wholeheartedly accepted without in the least impugning the judgment of the State of Illinois. . . .

It seems clear to me that the "aid" referred to by the Court in the Everson case could not have been those incidental advantages that religious bodies, with other groups similarly situated, obtain as a by-product of organized society. This explains the well-known fact that all churches receive "aid" from government in the form of freedom from taxation. The Everson decision itself justified the transportation of children to church schools by New Jersey for safety reasons. It accords with *Cochran* v. *Louisiana State Board of Education*, 281 U.S. 370, where this Court upheld a free textbook statute of Louisiana against a charge that it aided private schools on the ground that the books were for the education of the children, not to aid religious schools. Likewise the National School Lunch Act aids all school children attending tax-exempt schools. In *Bradfield* v. *Roberts*, 175 U.S. 291, this Court held proper the payment of money by the Federal Government to build an addition to a hospital, chartered by individuals who were members of a Roman Catholic sisterhood, and operated under the auspices of the

Roman Catholic Church. This was done over the objection that it aided the establishment of religion. While obviously in these instances the respective churches, in a certain sense, were aided, this Court has never held that such "aid" was in violation of the First or Fourteenth Amendment. . . .

The practices of the federal government offer many examples of this kind of "aid" by the state to religion. The Congress of the United States has a chaplain for each House who daily invokes divine blessings and guidance for the proceedings. The armed forces have commissioned chaplains from early days. They conduct the public services in accordance with the liturgical requirements of their respective faiths, ashore and afloat, employing for the purpose property belonging to the United States and dedicated to the services of religion. Under the Servicemen's Readjustment Act of 1944, eligible veterans may receive training at government expense for the ministry in denominational schools. The schools of the District of Columbia have opening exercises which "include a reading from the Bible without note or comment, and Lord's prayer."

In the United States Naval Academy and the United States Military Academy, schools wholly supported and completely controlled by the federal government, there are a number of religious activities. Chaplains are attached to both schools. Attendance at church services on Sunday is compulsory at both the Military and Naval Academies. At West Point the Protestant Services are held in the Cadet Chapel, the Catholic in the Catholic Chapel, and the Jewish in the Old Cadet Chapel; at Annapolis only the Protestant services are held on the reservation, midshipmen of other religious persuasions attend the churches of the city of Annapolis. These facts indicate that both schools since their earliest beginnings have maintained and enforced a pattern of participation in formal worship.

With the general statements in the opinions concerning the constitutional requirement that the nation and the states, by virtue of the First and Fourteenth Amendments, may "make no law respecting an establishment of religion," I am in agreement. But, in the light of the meaning given to those words by the precedents, customs, and practices which I have detailed above, I cannot agree with the Court's conclusion that when pupils compelled by law to go to school for secular education are released from school so as to attend the religious classes, churches are unconstitutionally aided. . . . The prohibition of enactments respecting the establishment of religion do not bar every friendly gesture between church and state. It is not an absolute prohibition against every conceivable situation where the two may work together, any more than the other provisions of the First Amendment—free speech, free press—are absolutes. . . . This Court cannot be too cautious in upsetting practices embedded in our society by many years of experience. A state is entitled to have great leeway in its legislation when dealing with the important social problems of its population. A definite violation of legislative limits must be established. The Constitution should not be stretched to forbid national customs in the way courts act to reach arrangements to avoid federal taxation. Devotion to the great principle of religious liberty should not lead us into a rigid interpretation of the constitutional guarantee that conflicts with accepted habits of our people. This is an instance where, for me, the history of past practices is determinative of the meaning of a constitutional clause, not a decorous introduction to the study of its text. The judgment should be affirmed.

School District of Abington Township (Pa.) v. Schempp
Murray v. Curlett (Md.)
374 U.S. 203, 83 S.Ct. 1560, 10 L.Ed. 2d 844 (1963)

In a 1962 decision, *Engel* v. *Vitale,* the Court outlawed a New York State nonsectarian prayer prescribed for opening daily public school sessions, a ruling that set off the most violent attacks on the Court since the celebrated 1954 desegregation case. In 1963 the Court was confronted with an issue of broader significance: Does the Constitution forbid a state requirement of the recitation of the Lord's Prayer or reading of passages from the Bible in public schools? A three-judge federal district court held invalid a Pennsylvania statute containing such a requirement, while the Maryland courts refused to hold a similar Baltimore school board rule unconstitutional. The Supreme Court granted appeal and certiorari to review the two decisions.

MR. JUSTICE CLARK delivered the opinion of the Court.

Once again we are called upon to consider the scope of the provision of the First Amendment to the United States Constitution which declares that "Congress shall make no law respecting an establishment of religion or prohibiting the free exercise thereof. . . ." These companion cases present the issues in the context of state action requiring that schools begin each day with readings from the Bible. While raising the basic questions under slightly different factual situations, the cases permit of joint treatment. In light of the history of the First Amendment and of our cases interpreting and applying its requirements, we hold that the practices at issue and the laws requiring them are unconstitutional under the Establishment Clause, as applied to the states through the Fourteenth Amendment. . . .

The fact that the Founding Fathers believed devotedly that there was a God and that the unalienable rights of man were rooted in Him is clearly evidenced in their writings, from the Mayflower Compact to the Constitution itself. This background is evidenced today in our public life through the continuance in our oaths of office from the Presidency to the Alderman of the final supplication, "So help me God." Likewise each House of Congress provides

through its Chaplain an opening prayer, and the sessions of this Court are declared open by the crier in a short ceremony, the final phrase of which invokes the grace of God. Again, there are such manifestations in our military forces, where those of our citizens who are under the restrictions of military service wish to engage in voluntary worship. Indeed, only last year an official survey of the country indicated that 64% of our people have church membership. . . . It can be truly said, therefore, that today, as in the beginning, our national life reflects a religious people who, in the words of Madison, are "earnestly praying, as . . . in duty bound, that the Supreme Lawgiver of the Universe . . . guide them into every measure which may be worthy of his . . . blessing. . . ."

. . . This is not to say, however, that religion has been so identified with our history and government that religious freedom is not likewise as strongly imbedded in our public and private life. . . . This freedom to worship was indispensable in a country whose people came from the four quarters of the earth and brought with them a diversity of religious opinion. Today authorities list 83 separate religious bodies, each with memberships exceeding 50,000, existing among our people, as well as innumerable smaller groups. . . .

Almost a hundred years ago in *Minor* v.

Board of Education of Cincinnati, Judge Alphonso Taft, father of the revered Chief Justice, in an unpublished opinion stated the ideal of our people as to religious freedom as one of "absolute equality before the law of all religious opinion and sects. . . ."

"The government is neutral, and while protecting all, it prefers none, and it disparages none."

. . . Finally, these principles were so universally recognized that the court without the citation of a single case and over the sole dissent of Mr. Justice Stewart reaffirmed them. The Court found the 22-word prayer used in "New York's program of daily classroom invocation of God's blessings as prescribed in the Regent's prayer . . . *to be* a religious activity." . . . It held that "it is no part of the business of government to compose official prayer for any group of the American people to recite as a part of a religious program carried on by the government." . . .

The wholesome "neutrality" of which this Court's cases speak thus stems from a recognition of the teachings of history that powerful sects or groups might bring about a fusion of governmental and religious functions or a concert or dependency of one upon the other to the end that official support of the State or Federal Government would be placed behind the tenets of one or of all orthodoxies. This the Establishment Clause prohibits. And a further reason for neutrality is found in the Free Exercise Clause, which recognized the value of religious training, teaching and observance and, more particularly, the right of every person to freely choose his own course with reference thereto, free of any compulsion from the state. This the Free Exercise Clause guarantees. Thus, as we have seen, the two clauses may overlap.

Applying the Establishment Clause principles to the cases at bar we find that the States are requiring the selection and reading at the opening of the school day of verses from the Holy Bible and the recitation of the Lord's Prayer by the students in unison. These exercises are prescribed as part of the curricular activities of students who are required by law to attend

school. They are held in the school buildings under the supervision and with the participation of teachers employed in those schools. . . . The trial court . . . has found that such an opening exercise is a religious ceremony and was intended by the State to be so. We agree with the trial court's finding as to the religious character of the exercises. Given that finding, the exercises and the law requiring them are in violation of the Establishment Clause.

. . . The conclusion follows that in both cases the laws require religious exercises and such exercises are being conducted in direct violation of the rights of the appellees and petitioners. Nor are these required exercises mitigated by the fact that individual students may absent themselves upon parental request, for that fact furnishes no defense to a claim of unconstitutionality under the Establishment Clause. . . . Further, it is no defense to urge that the religious practices here may be relatively minor encroachments on the First Amendment. The breach of neutrality that is today a trickling stream may all too soon become a raging torrent and, in the words of Madison, "It is proper to take alarm at the first experiment on our liberties." . . .

It is insisted that unless these religious exercises are permitted a "religion of secularism" is established in the schools. We agree of course that the State may not establish a "religion of secularism" in the sense of affirmatively opposing or showing hostility to religion, thus "preferring those who believe in no religion over those who do believe." *Zorach* v. *Clauson.* . . . We do not agree, however, that this decision in any sense has that effect. In addition, it might well be said that one's education is not complete without a study of comparative religion or the history of religion and its relationship to the advancement of civilization. It certainly may be said that the Bible is worthy of study for its literary and historic qualities. Nothing we have said here indicates that such study of the Bible or of religion, when presented objectively as part of a secular program of education, may not be effected consistent with the First Amendment. But the exercises here do not fall into those categories. They are religious exercises, required by the States in violation of the command of the First Amendment that the Government maintain strict neutrality, neither aiding nor opposing religion.

. . . The place of religion in our society is an exalted one, achieved through a long tradition of reliance on the home, the church and the inviolable citadel of the individual heart and mind. We have come to recognize through bitter experience that it is not within the power of government to invade that citadel, whether its purpose or effect be to aid or oppose, to advance or retard. In the relationship between man and religion, the State is firmly committed to a position of neutrality. Though the application of that rule requires interpretation of a delicate sort, the rule itself is clearly and concisely stated in the words of the First Amendment. . . .

MR. JUSTICE BRENNAN, concurring. . . .

It is true that the Framers' immediate concern was to prevent the setting up of an official federal church of the kind which England and some of the Colonies had long supported. But nothing in the text of the Establishment Clause supports the view that the prevention of the setting up of an official church was meant to be the full extent of the prohibitions against official involvements in religion. . . .

But an awareness of history and an appreciation of the aims of the Founding Fathers do not always resolve concrete problems. The specific question before us has, for example, aroused vigorous dispute whether the architects of the First Amendment—James Madison and Thomas Jefferson particularly—understood the prohibition against any "law respecting an establishment of religion" to reach devotional exercises in the public schools. It may be that Jefferson and Madison would have held such exercises to be permissible—although even in Jefferson's case serious doubt is suggested by his admonition against "putting the Bible and Testament into the hands of the children at an age when their judgments are not sufficiently matured for religious inquiries. . . ." But I doubt that their view, even if perfectly clear one

way or the other, would supply a dispositive answer to the question presented by these cases. A more fruitful inquiry, it seems to me, is whether the practices here challenged threaten those consequences which the Framers deeply feared; whether, in short, they tend to promote that type of interdependence between religion and state which the First Amendment was designed to prevent. Our task is to translate "the majestic generalities of the Bill of Rights, conceived as part of the pattern of liberal government in the eighteenth century, into concrete restraints on officials dealing with the problems of the twentieth century. . . ." *West Virginia State Board of Education* v. *Barnette*. . . .

A too literal quest for the advice of the Founding Fathers upon the issues of these cases seems to me futile and misdirected for several reasons: First, on our precise problem the historical record is at best ambiguous, and statements can readily be found to support either side of the proposition. The ambiguity of history is understandable if we recall the nature of the problems uppermost in the thinking of the statesmen who fashioned the religious guarantees; they were concerned with far more flagrant intrusions of government into the realm of religion than any that our century has witnessed. While it is clear to me that the Framers meant the Establishment Clause to prohibit more than the creation of an established federal church such as existed in England, I have no doubt that, in their preoccupation with the imminent question of established churches, they gave no distinct consideration to the particular question whether the clause also forbade devotional exercises in public institutions.

Second, the structure of American education has greatly changed since the First Amendment was adopted. In the context of our modern emphasis upon public education available to all citizens, any views of the eighteenth century as to whether the exercises at bar are an "establishment" offer little aid to decision. Education, as the Framers knew it, was in the main confined to private schools more often than not under strictly sectarian supervision. Only gradually did control of education pass largely to public officials. It would, therefore, hardly be significant if the fact was that the nearly universal devotional exercises in the schools of the young Republic did not provoke criticism; even today religious ceremonies in church-supported private schools are constitutionally unobjectionable.

Third, our religious composition makes us a vastly more diverse people than were our forefathers. They knew differences chiefly among Protestant sects. Today the Nation is far more heterogeneous religiously, including as it does substantial minorities not only of Catholics and Jews but as well as those who worship according to no version of the Bible and those who worship no God at all. In the face of such profound changes, practices which may have been objectionable to no one in the time of Jefferson and Madison may today be highly offensive to many persons, the deeply devout and the nonbelievers alike. . . .

It is "*a constitution* we are expounding," and our interpretation of the First Amendment must necessarily be responsive to the much more highly charged nature of religious questions in contemporary society. . . .

MR. JUSTICE GOLDBERG, with whom MR. JUSTICE HARLAN joins, concurring. . . .

MR. JUSTICE STEWART, dissenting. . . .

The First Amendment declares that "Congress shall make no law respecting an establishment of religion, or prohibiting the free exercise thereof. . . ." It is, I think, a fallacious oversimplification to regard these two provisions as establishing a single constitutional standard of "separation of church and state," which can be mechanically applied in every case to delineate the required boundaries between government and religion. We err in the first place if we do not recognize, as a matter of history and as a matter of the imperatives of our free society, that religion and government must necessarily interact in countless ways. Secondly, the fact is that while in many contexts the Establishment Clause and the Free Exercise Clause fully complement each other, there are areas in which a doctrinaire reading of the Establishment Clause leads to irreconcilable conflict with the Free Exercise Clause.

A single obvious example should suffice to make the point. Spending federal funds to employ chaplains for the armed forces might be said to violate the Establishment Clause. Yet a lone soldier stationed at some faraway outpost could surely complain that a government which did *not* provide him the opportunity for pastoral guidance was affirmatively prohibiting the free exercise of his religion. And such examples could readily be multiplied. The short of the matter is simply that the two relevant clauses of the First Amendment cannot accurately be reflected in a sterile metaphor which by its very nature may distort rather than illumine the problems involved in a particular case. . . .

That the central value embodied in the First Amendment—and, more particularly, in the guarantee of "liberty" contained in the Fourteenth—is the safeguarding of an individual's right to free exercise of his religion has been consistently recognized. . . .

It is this concept of constitutional protection embodied in our decisions which makes the cases before us such difficult ones for me. For there is involved in these cases a substantial free exercise claim on the part of those who affirmatively desire to have their children's school day open with the reading of passages from the Bible. . . .

What seems to me to be of paramount importance, then, is recognition of the fact that the claim advanced here in favor of Bible reading is sufficiently substantial to make simple reference to the constitutional phrase "establishment of religion" as inadequate an analysis of the cases before us as the ritualistic invocation of the nonconstitutional phrase "separation of church and state." What these cases compel, rather, is an analysis of just what the "neutrality" is which is required by the interplay of the Establishment and Free Exercise Clauses of the First Amendment, as imbedded in the Fourteenth.

. . . The dangers both to government and to religion inherent in official support of instruction in the tenets of various religious sects are absent in the present cases, which involve only a reading from the Bible unaccompanied by comments which might otherwise constitute instruction. Indeed, since, from all that appears in either record, any teacher who does not wish to do so is free not to participate, it cannot even be contended that some infinitesimal part of the salaries paid by the State are made contingent upon the performance of a religious function. . . .

To be specific, it seems to me clear that certain types of exercises would present situations in which no possibility of coercion on the part of secular officials could be claimed to exist. Thus, if such exercises were held either before or after the official school day, or if the school schedule were such that participation were merely one among a number of desirable alternatives, it could hardly be contended that the exercises did anything more than to provide an opportunity for the voluntary expression of religious belief. On the other hand, a law which provided for religious exercises during the school day and which contained no excusal provision would obviously be unconstitutionally coercive upon those who did not wish to participate. And even under a law containing an excusal provision, if the exercises were held during the school day, and no equally desirable alternative were provided by the school authorities, the likelihood that children might be under at least some psychological compulsion to participate would be great. In a case such as the latter, however, I think we would err if we *assumed* such coercion in the absence of any evidence.

. . . What our Constitution indispensably protects is the freedom of each of us, be he Jew or Agnostic, Christian or Atheist, Buddhist or Freethinker, to believe or disbelieve, to worship or not worship, to pray or keep silent, according to his own conscience, uncoerced and unrestrained by government. It is conceivable that these school boards, or even all school boards, might eventually find it impossible to administer a system of religious exercises during school hours in such a way as to meet this constitutional standard—in such a way as completely to free from any kind of official coercion those who do not affirmatively want to participate. But I think we must not assume that school boards so lack the qualities of inventiveness and good will as to make impossible the achievement of that goal.

I would remand both cases for further hearings.

Sherbert v. Verner
374 U.S. 398, 83 S.Ct. 1790, 10 L.Ed. 2d 965 (1963)

Adell Sherbert was a member of the Seventh-day Adventist Church who was discharged by her employer in South Carolina because she would not work on Saturday, the Sabbath Day of her religion. After looking for other work and finding none because of her strictures against Saturday work, she filed a claim for unemployment compensation under South Carolina law. Her claim was denied because she failed to accept "suitable work when offered . . . by the employment office or the employer. . . ." This ruling of the Employment Security Commission was sustained by the Court of Common Pleas of Spartanburg County. The South Carolina Supreme Court affirmed.

MR. JUSTICE BRENNAN delivered the opinion of the Court. . . .

We turn first to the question whether the disqualification for benefits imposes any burden on the free exercise of appellant's religion. We think it is clear that it does. In a sense the consequences of such a disqualification to religious principles and practices may be only an indirect result of welfare legislation within the State's general competence to enact; it is true that no criminal sanctions directly compel appellant to work a six-day week. But this is only the beginning, not the end, of our inquiry. For "[i]f the purpose or effect of a law is to impede the observance of one or all religions or is to discriminate invidiously between religions, that law is constitutionally invalid even though the burden may be characterized as being only indirect." *Braunfeld* v. *Brown.* . . . Here not only is it apparent that appellant's declared ineligibility for benefits derives solely from the practice of her religion, but the pressure upon her to forgo that practice is unmistakable. The ruling forces her to choose between following the precepts of her religion and forfeiting benefits, on the one hand, and abandoning one of the precepts of her religion in order to accept work, on the other hand. Governmental imposition of such a choice puts the same kind of burden upon the free exercise of religion as would a fine imposed against appellant for her Saturday worship. . . .

We must next consider whether some compelling state interest enforced in the eligibility provisions of the South Carolina statute justifies the substantial infringement of appellant's First Amendment right. . . . No such abuse or danger has been advanced in the present case. The appellees suggest no more than a possibility that the filing of fraudulent claims by unscrupulous claimants feigning religious objections to Saturday work might not only dilute the unemployment compensation fund but also hinder the scheduling by employers of necessary Saturday work. But that possibility is not apposite here because no such objection appears to have been made before the South Carolina Supreme Court, and we are unwilling to assess the importance of an asserted state interest without the views of the state court. Nor, if the contention had been made below, would the record appear to sustain it; there is no proof whatever to warrant such fears of malingering or deceit as those which the respondents now advance. . . .

In these respects, then, the state interest asserted in the present case is wholly dissimilar to the interests which were found to justify the less direct burden upon religious practices in *Braunfeld* v. *Brown,* supra. The Court recognized that the Sunday closing law which that decision sustained undoubtedly served "to make the practice of [the Orthodox Jewish merchants'] . . . religious beliefs more expensive," . . . . But the statute was nevertheless saved by a countervailing factor which finds no equivalent in the instant case—a strong state interest in providing one uniform day of rest for all workers. . . .

In holding as we do, plainly we are not fostering the "establishment" of the Seventh-day Adventist religion in South Carolina, for the extension of unemployment benefits to Sabbatarians in common with Sunday worshippers reflects nothing more than the governmental obligation of neutrality in the face of religious differences, and does not represent that involvement of religious with secular institutions which it is the object of the Establishment Clause to forestall. . . .

The judgment of the South Carolina Supreme Court is reversed and the case is remanded for further proceedings not inconsistent with this opinion.

It is so ordered.

MR. JUSTICE DOUGLAS, concurring. . . .

MR. JUSTICE STEWART, concurring in the result.

Although fully agreeing with the result which the Court reaches in this case, I cannot join the Court's opinion. . . .

I am convinced that no liberty is more essential to the continued vitality of the free society which our Constitution guarantees than is the religious liberty protected by the Free Exercise Clause explicit in the First Amendment and imbedded in the Fourteenth. And I regret that on occasion, and specifically in *Braunfeld* v. *Brown*, . . . the Court has shown what has seemed to me a distressing insensitivity to the appropriate demands of this constitutional guarantee. By contrast I think that the Court's approach to the Establishment Clause has on occasion, and specifically in *Engel, Schempp*, and *Murray*, been not only insensitive, but positively wooden, and that the Court has accorded to the Establishment Clause a meaning which neither the words, the history, nor the intention of the authors of that specific constitutional provision even remotely suggests.

But my views as to the correctness of the Court's decisions in these cases are beside the point here. The point is that the decisions are on the books. And the result is that there are many situations where legitimate claims under the Free Exercise Clause will run into head-on collision with the Court's insensitive and sterile construction of the Establishment Clause. The controversy now before us is clearly such a case.

Because the appellant refuses to accept available jobs which would require her to work on Saturdays, South Carolina has declined to pay unemployment compensation benefits to her. Her refusal to work on Saturdays is based on the tenets of her religious faith. The Court says that South Carolina cannot under these circumstances declare her to be not "available for work" within the meaning of its statute because to do so would violate her constitutional right to the free exercise of her religion.

Yet what this Court has said about the Establishment Clause must inevitably lead to a diametrically opposite result. If the appellant's refusal to work on Saturdays were based on indolence, or on a compulsive desire to watch the Saturday television programs, no one would say that South Carolina could not hold that she was not "available for work" within the meaning of its statute. That being so, the Establishment Clause as construed by this Court not only *permits* but affirmatively *requires* South Carolina equally to deny the appellant's claim for unemployment compensation when her refusal to work on Saturdays is based upon her religious creed. . . .

My second difference with the Court's opinion is that I cannot agree that today's decision can stand consistently with *Braunfeld* v. *Brown*. . . . The Court says that there was a "less direct burden upon religious practices" in that case than in this. With all respect, I think the Court is mistaken, simply as a matter of fact. The Braunfeld Case involved a state *criminal* statute. . . .

The impact upon the appellant's religious freedom in the present case is considerably less onerous. We deal here not with a criminal statute, but with the particularized administration of South Carolina's Unemployment Compensation Act. Even upon the unlikely assumption that the appellant could not find suitable non-Saturday employment, the appellant at the worst would be denied a maximum of 22 weeks of compensation payments. I agree with the Court that the possibility of that denial is enough to infringe upon the appellant's constitutional right to the free exercise of her religion. But it is clear to me that in order to reach this conclusion the Court must explicitly reject the reasoning of *Braunfeld* v. *Brown*. I think the Braunfeld Case was wrongly decided and should be overruled, and accordingly I concur in the result reached by the Court in the case before us.

MR. JUSTICE HARLAN, whom MR. JUSTICE WHITE joins, dissenting.

Today's decision is disturbing both in its rejection of existing precedent and in its implications for the future. The significance of the decision can best be understood after an examination of the state law applied in this case. . . .

The South Carolina Supreme Court has uniformly applied this law in conformity with its clearly expressed purpose. It has consistently held that one is not "available for work" if his unemployment has resulted not from the inability of industry to provide a job but rather from personal circumstances, no matter how compelling. . . .

Thus in no proper sense can it be said that the State discriminated against the appellant on the basis of her religious beliefs or that she was denied benefits *because* she was a Seventh-day Adventist. She was denied benefits just as any other claimant would be denied benefits who was not "available for work" for personal reasons.

With this background, this Court's decision comes into clearer focus. What the Court is holding is that if the State chooses to condition unemployment compensation on the applicant's availability for work, it is constitutionally compelled to *carve out an exception*—and to provide benefits—for those whose unavailability is due to their religious convictions. Such a holding has particular significance in two respects.

First, despite the Court's protestations to the contrary, the decision necessarily overrules *Braunfeld* v. *Brown*....

Second, the implications of the present decision are far more troublesome than its apparently narrow dimensions would indicate at first glance. The State ... must *single out* for financial assistance those whose behavior is religiously motivated, even though it denies such assistance to others whose identical behavior (in this case, inability to work on Saturdays) is not religiously motivated....

... My own view is that at least under the circumstances of this case it would be a permissible accommodation of religion for the State, if it *chose* to do so, to create an exception to its eligibility requirements for persons like the appellant. The constitutional obligation of "neutrality," see *School Dist. of Abington Township* v. *Schempp*, ... is not so narrow a channel that the slightest deviation from an absolutely straight course leads to condemnation....

Wisconsin v. *Yoder*
406 U.S. 205, 92 S.Ct. 1526, 32 L.Ed. 2d 15 (1972)

Wisconsin's compulsory school attendance law required parents to send their children to school until the age of 16. James Yoder and other members of the Old Order Amish religion and the Conservative Amish Mennonite Church refused to send their children, aged 14 and 15, to public school after completion of the eight grades offered by church schools. The Amish provide only informal vocational education for their children in place of a formal high school education. The parents were convicted of violating the Wisconsin attendance law. The state supreme court set the conviction aside as violating the Free Exercise Clause of the First Amendment. The United States Supreme Court granted certiorari. The concurring opinions of Justices Stewart and White and the separate opinion of Justice Douglas, dissenting in part, are not included below. Burger makes reference in the opinion of the Court to the objection raised by Douglas. The case was argued before Justices Powell and Rehnquist took their seats on the bench, so they took no part in the decision.

MR. CHIEF JUSTICE BURGER delivered the opinion of the Court.

There is no doubt as to the power of a State, having a high responsibility for education of its citizens, to impose reasonable regulations for the control and duration of basic education. See, e.g., *Pierce* v. *Society of Sisters*, 268 U.S. 510 (1925). Providing public schools ranks at the very apex of the function of a State. Yet even this paramount responsibility was, in *Pierce*, made to yield to the right of parents to provide an equivalent education in a privately operated system. There the Court held that Oregon's statute compelling attendance in a public school from age eight to age 16 unreasonably interfered with the interest of parents in directing the rearing of their offspring, including their education in church-operated schools. As that case suggests, the values of parental direction of the religious upbringing and education of their children in their early and formative years have a high place in our society. . . . Thus, a State's interest in universal education, however highly we rank it, is not totally free from a balancing process when it impinges on fundamental rights and interests, such as those specifically protected by the Free Exercise Clause of the First Amendment, and the traditional interest of parents with respect to the religious upbringing of their children so long as they, in the words of Pierce, "prepare [them] for additional obligations." . . .

It follows that in order for Wisconsin to compel school attendance beyond the eighth grade against a claim that such attendance interferes with the practice of a legitimate religious belief, it must appear either that the State does not deny the free exercise of religious belief by its requirement, or that there is a state interest of sufficient magnitude to override the interest claiming protection under the Free Exercise Clause. . . .

The essence of all that has been said and written on the subject is that only those interests of the highest order and those not otherwise served can overbalance legitimate claims to the free exercise of religion. We can accept it as settled, therefore, that, however strong the State's interest in universal compulsory education, it is by no means absolute to the exclusion or subordination of all other interests. . . .

We come then to the quality of the claims of the respondents concerning the alleged encroachment of Wisconsin's compulsory school-attendance statute on their rights and the rights of their children to the free exercise of the religious beliefs they and their forebears have adhered to for almost three centuries. In evaluating those claims we must be careful to determine whether the Amish religious faith and their mode of life are, as they claim, inseparable and interdependent. A way of life, however virtuous and admirable, may not be interposed as a barrier to reasonable state regulation of education if it is based on purely secular considerations; to have the protection of the Religion Clauses, the claims must be rooted in religious belief. Although a determination of what is a "religious" belief or practice entitled to constitutional protection may present a most delicate question, the very concept of ordered liberty precludes allowing every person to make his own standards on matters of conduct in which society as a whole has important interests. Thus, if the Amish asserted their claims because of their subjective evaluation and rejection of the contemporary secular values accepted by the majority, much as Thoreau rejected the social values of his time and isolated himself at Walden Pond, their claims would not rest on a religious basis. Thoreau's choice was philosophical and personal rather than religious, and such belief does not rise to the demands of the Religion Clauses.

Giving no weight to such secular considerations, however, we see that the record in this case abundantly supports the claim that the traditional way of life of the Amish is not merely a matter of personal preference, but one of deep religious conviction, shared by an organized group, and intimately related to daily living. That the Old Order Amish daily life and religious practice stem from their faith is shown by the fact that it is in response to their literal interpretation of the Biblical injunction from the Epistle of Paul to the Romans, "be not conformed to this world. . . ." This command is fundamental to the Amish faith. . . .

As the society around the Amish has become more populous, urban, industrialized, and complex, particularly in this century, government regulation of human affairs has correspondingly become more detailed and pervasive. The Amish mode of life has thus come into conflict increasingly with requirements of contemporary society exerting a hydraulic insistence on conformity to majoritarian standards. So long as compulsory education laws were confined to eight grades of elementary basic education imparted in a nearby rural schoolhouse, with a large proportion of students of the Amish faith, the Old Order Amish had little basis to fear that school attendance would expose their children to the worldly influence they reject. But modern compulsory secondary education in rural areas is now largely carried on in a consolidated school, often remote from the student's home and alien to his daily home life. As the record so strongly shows, the values and programs of the modern secondary school are in sharp conflict with the fundamental mode of life mandated by the Amish religion. . . .

The impact of the compulsory-attendance law on respondents' practice of the Amish religion is not only severe, but inescapable, for the Wisconsin law affirmatively compels them, under threat of criminal sanction, to perform acts undeniably at odds with fundamental tenets of their religious beliefs. . . . Nor is the impact of the compulsory-attendance law confined to grave interference with important Amish religious tenets from a subjective point of view. It carries with it precisely the kind of objective danger to the free exercise of religion that the First Amendment was designed to prevent. As the record shows, compulsory school attendance to age 16 for Amish children carries with it a very real threat of undermining the Amish community and religious practice as they exist today; they must either abandon belief and be assimilated into society at large, or be forced to migrate to some other and more tolerant region. . . .

Wisconsin concedes that under the Religion Clauses religious beliefs are absolutely free from the State's control, but it argues that "actions," even though religiously grounded, are outside the protection of the First Amendment. But our decisions have rejected the idea that religiously grounded conduct is always outside the protection of the Free Exercise Clause. . . .

Nor can this case be disposed of on the grounds that Wisconsin's requirement for school attendance to age 16 applies uniformly to all citizens of the State and does not, on its face, discriminate against religions or a particular religion, or that it is motivated by legitimate secular concerns. A regulation neutral on its face may, in its application, nonetheless offend the constitutional requirement for governmental neutrality if it unduly burdens the free exercise of religion. . . . The Court must not ignore the danger that an exception from a general obligation of citizenship on religious grounds may run afoul of the Establishment Clause, but that danger cannot be allowed to prevent any exception no matter how vital it may be to the protection of values promoted by the right of free exercise. By preserving doctrinal flexibility and recognizing the need for a sensible and realistic application of the Religion Clauses "we have been able to chart a course that preserved the autonomy and freedom of religious bodies while avoiding any semblance of established religion. This is a 'tight rope' and one we have successfully traversed." *Walz* v. *Tax Commission*. . . .

This case, of course, is not one in which any harm to the physical or mental health of the child or to the public safety, peace, order, or welfare has been demonstrated or may be properly inferred. The record is to the contrary, and any reliance on that theory would find no support in the evidence.

Contrary to the suggestion of the dissenting opinion of Mr. Justice Douglas, our holding today in no degree depends on the assertion of the religious interest of the child as contrasted with that of the parents. It is the parents who are subject to prosecution here for failing to cause their children to attend school, and it is their right of free exercise, not that of their children, that must determine Wisconsin's power to impose criminal penalties on the parent. The dissent argues that a child who expresses a desire to attend public high school in conflict with the wishes of his parents should not be prevented from doing so. There is no reason for the Court to consider that point since it is not an issue in the case. The children are not parties to this litigation. The State has at no point tried this case on the theory that respondents were preventing their children from attending school against their expressed desires, and indeed the record is to the contrary. . . .

For the reasons stated we hold, with the Supreme Court of Wisconsin, that the First and Fourteenth Amendments prevent the State from compelling respondents to cause their children to attend formal high school to age 16. Our disposition of this case, however, in no way alters our recognition of the obvious fact that courts are not school boards or legislatures, and are ill-equipped to determine the "necessity" of discrete aspects of a State's program of compulsory education. . . . It cannot be overemphasized that we are not dealing with a way of life and mode of education by a group claiming to have recently discovered some "progressive" or more enlightened process for rearing children for modern life.

Aided by a history of three centuries as an identifiable religious sect and a long history as a successful and self-sufficient segment of American society, the Amish in this case have convincingly demonstrated the sincerity of their religious beliefs, the interrelationship of belief with their mode of life, the vital role that belief and daily conduct play in the continued survival of Old Order Amish communities and their religious organization, and the hazards presented by the State's enforcement of a statute generally valid as to others. Beyond this, they have carried the even more difficult burden of demonstrating the adequacy of their alternative mode of continuing informal vocational education in terms of precisely those overall interests that the State advances in support of its program of compulsory high school education. . . .

Affirmed.

Roemer v. *Board of Public Works of Maryland*
426 U.S. 736, 96 S.Ct. 2337, 49 L.Ed. 2d 179 (1976)

Certain organizations consisting of Maryland citizens and taxpayers instituted action in the United States District Court of Maryland against state officials and private religiously affiliated colleges that had received state aid. The plaintiffs sought declaratory and injunctive relief on the ground that Maryland's statute for aid to private colleges violated the First Amendment's "establishment of religion" clause. The district court upheld the statute. The Supreme Court affirmed.

Justice Blackmun, joined by Chief Justice Burger and Justice Powell, announced the judgment of the Court. Justices Rehnquist and White concurred, and Justices Brennan, Stewart and Stevens each issued a separate dissent.

MR. JUSTICE BLACKMUN:

We are asked once again to police the constitutional boundary between church and state. Maryland, this time, is the alleged trespasser. It has enacted a statute which, as amended, provides for annual noncategorical grants to private colleges, among them religiously affiliated institutions, subject only to the restrictions that the funds not be used for "sectarian purposes." . . .

A system of government that makes itself felt as pervasively as ours could hardly be expected never to cross paths with the church. In fact, our State and Federal Governments impose certain burdens upon, and impart certain benefits to, virtually all our activities, and religious activity is not an exception. The Court has enforced a scrupulous neutrality by the State, as among religions, and also as between religious and other activities, but a hermetic separation of the two is an impossibility it has never required. It long has been established, for example, that the State may send a cleric, indeed even a clerical order, to perform a wholly secular task. . . .

. . . The Court upheld the extension of public aid to a corporation which, although composed entirely of members of a Roman Catholic sisterhood acting "under the auspices of said church," was limited by its corporate charter to the secular purpose of operating a charitable hospital.

And religious institutions need not be quarantined from public benefits that are neutrally available to all. The Court has permitted the State to supply transportation for children to and from church-related as well as public schools. *Everson* v. *Board of Education,* 330 U.S. 1. . . . It has done the same with respect to secular textbooks loaned by the State on equal terms to students attending both public and church-related elementary schools. . . . The State was merely "extending the benefits of state laws to all citizens." . . . *Everson* put to rest any argument that the State may never act in such a way that has the incidental effect of facilitating religious activity. The Court has not been blind to the fact that in aiding a religious institution to perform a secular task, the State frees the institution's resources to be put to sectarian ends. If this were impermissible, however, a church could not be protected by the police and fire departments, or have its public sidewalk kept in repair. The Court never has held that religious activities must be discriminated against in this way.

Neutrality is what is required. The State must confine itself to secular objectives, and neither advance nor impede religious activity. Of course, that principle is more easily stated than applied. The Court has taken the view that a secular purpose and a facial neutrality may not be enough, if in fact the State is lending direct support to a religious activity. The State may not, for example, pay for what is actually a religious education, even though it purports to be paying for a secular one, and even though it makes its aid available to secular and religious institutions alike. The Court also has taken the view that the State's efforts to perform a secular task, and at the same time avoid aiding in the performance of a religious one, may not lead it into such an intimate relationship with religious authority that it appears either to be sponsoring or to be excessively interfering with that authority. . . . The Court distilled these concerns into a three-prong test, resting in part on prior case law, for the constitutionality of statutes affording state aid to church-related schools.

First, the statute must have a secular legislative purpose; second, its principal or primary effect must be one that neither advances nor inhibits religion. . . ; finally, the statute must not foster an excessive government entanglement with religion. . .

(1) First is the character of the aided institutions. . . . As the District Court found, the colleges perform "essentially secular educational functions" that are distinct and separable from religious activity. This finding, which is a prerequisite under the "pervasive sectarianism" test to any state aid at all, is also important for purposes of the entanglement test because it means that secular activities, for the most, can be taken at face value. There is no danger, or at least only a substantially reduced danger, that an ostensibly secular activity—the study of biology, the learning of a foreign language, an athletic event—will actually be infused with religious content or significance. The need for close surveillance of purportedly secular activities is correspondingly reduced. Thus the District Court found that in this case "there is no necessity for state officials to investigate the conduct of particular classes of educational programs to determine whether a school is attempting to indoctrinate its students under the guise of secular education." We cannot say the District Court erred in this judgment or gave it undue significance.

(2) As for the form of aid, . . . no particular use of state funds is before us in this case. The *process* by which aid is disbursed, and a use for it chosen, are before us. . . .

(3). . . The funding process is an annual one. The subsidies are paid out each year, and they can be put to annually varying uses. . . . We

agree with the District Court that ''excessive entanglement'' does not necessarily result from
the fact that the subsidy is an annual one.

There is no exact science in gauging the entanglement of church and state. The wording of
the test, which speaks of ''*excessive* entanglement,'' itself makes that clear. . . . They may
cut different ways, as certainly they do here. In
reaching the conclusion that it did, the District
Court gave dominant importance to the character of the aided institutions and to its finding
that they are capable of separating secular and
religious functions. . . . We cannot say that the
emphasis was misplaced, or the finding erroneous.

MR. JUSTICE BRENNAN, with whom MR.
JUSTICE MARSHALL joins, dissenting.

. . . ''The Act is simply a blunderbuss discharge of public funds to a church-affiliated
or church-related college.'' . . . In other words,
the Act provides for payment of general subsidies to religious institutions from public
funds, and I have heretofore expressed my view
that ''[g]eneral subsidies of religious activities
would, of course, constitute impermissible state
involvement. . . .''

MR. JUSTICE STEVENS, dissenting.

My views are substantially those expressed by
Mr. Justice Brennan. However, I would add emphasis to the pernicious tendency of a state subsidy to tempt religious schools to compromise
their religious mission without wholly abandoning it. The disease of entanglement may infect a
law discouraging wholesome religious activity as
well as a law encouraging the propagation of a
given faith.

VII. Privacy

Meyer v. Nebraska
262 U.S. 390, 43 S.Ct. 625, 67 L.Ed. 1042 (1923)

A Nebraska statute of 1919 prohibited the teaching of subjects in any language
other than English, and forbade the teaching of foreign languages to any pupil who
had not passed the eighth grade. The law applied to private, parochial, and
denominational as well as public school teaching. Meyer, a teacher in a parochial
school, was tried and convicted of violating the statute by teaching the German
language to a boy of ten who had not passed the eighth grade.

MR. JUSTICE MCREYNOLDS delivered the opinion of the court. . . .

The problem for our determination is
whether the statute as construed and applied
unreasonably infringes the liberty guaranteed
to the plaintiff in error by the Fourteenth
Amendment. ''No State shall . . . deprive any
person of life, liberty, or property, without due
process of law.''

While this Court has not attempted to define
with exactness the liberty thus guaranteed, the
term has received much consideration and some
of the included things have been definitely
stated. Without doubt, it denotes not merely
freedom from bodily restraint but also the right
of any individual to contract, to engage in any of
the common occupations of life, to acquire
useful knowledge, to marry, establish a home
and bring up children, to worship God according to the dictates of his own conscience, and
generally to enjoy those privileges long
recognized at common law as essential to the
orderly pursuit of happiness by free men. . . .
The established doctrine is that this liberty may

not be interfered with, under the guise of protecting the public interest, by legislative action which is arbitrary or without reasonable relation to some purpose within the competency of the State to effect. Determination by the legislature of what constitutes proper exercise of police power is not final or conclusive but is subject to supervision by the courts. . . .

Practically, education of the young is only possible in schools conducted by especially qualified persons who devote themselves thereto. The calling always has been regarded as useful and honorable, essential, indeed, to the public welfare. Mere knowledge of the German language cannot reasonably be regarded as harmful. Heretofore it has been commonly looked upon as helpful and desirable. Plaintiff in error taught this language in school as part of his occupation. His right thus to teach and the right of parents to engage him so to instruct their children, we think, are within the liberty of the Amendment.

The challenged statute forbids the teaching in schools of any subject except in English; also the teaching of any other language until the pupil has attained and successfully passed the eighth grade, which is not usually accomplished before the age of twelve. The Supreme Court of the State has held that "the so-called ancient or dead languages" are not "within the spirit or the purpose of the act." . . . Latin, Greek, Hebrew are not proscribed; but German, French, Spanish, Italian and every other alien speech are within the ban. Evidently the legislature has attempted materially to interfere with the calling of modern language teachers, with the opportunities of pupils to acquire knowledge, and with the power of parents to control the education of their own. . . .

That the State may do much, go very far, indeed, in order to improve the quality of its citizens, physically, mentally and morally, is clear; but the individual has certain fundamental rights which must be respected. The protection of the Constitution extends to all, to those who speak other languages as well as to those born with English on the tongue. Perhaps it would be highly advantageous if all had ready

understanding of our ordinary speech, but this cannot be coerced by methods which conflict with the Constitution—a desirable end cannot be promoted by prohibited means. . . .

The desire of the legislature to foster a homogeneous people with American ideals prepared readily to understand current discussions of civic matters is easy to appreciate. Unfortunate experiences during the late war and aversion toward every characteristic of truculent adversaries were certainly enough to quicken that aspiration. But the means adopted, we think, exceed the limitations upon the power of the State and conflict with rights assured to plaintiff in error. The interference is plain enough and no adequate reason therefore in time of peace and domestic tranquillity has been shown.

The power of the State to compel attendance at some school and to make reasonable regulations for all schools, including a requirement that they shall give instruction in English, is not questioned. Nor has challenge been made of the State's power to prescribe a curriculum for institutions which it supports. Those matters are not within the present controversy. Our concern is with the prohibition approved by the Supreme Court. . . . No emergency has arisen which renders knowledge by a child of some language other than English so clearly harmful as to justify its inhibition with the consequent infringement of rights long freely enjoyed. We are constrained to conclude that the statute as applied is arbitrary and without reasonable relation to any end within the competency of the State.

As the statute undertakes to interfere only with teaching which involves a modern language, leaving complete freedom as to other matters, there seems no adequate foundation for the suggestion that the purpose was to protect the child's health by limiting his mental activities. It is well known that proficiency in a foreign language seldom comes to one not instructed at an early age, and experience shows that this is not injurious to the health, morals or understanding of the ordinary child.

The judgment of the court below must be

reversed and the cause remanded for further proceedings not inconsistent with this opinion.

Reversed.

MR. JUSTICE HOLMES, dissenting.

We all agree, I take it, that it is desirable that all citizens of the United States should speak a common tongue, and therefore that the end aimed at by the statute is a lawful and proper one. The only question is whether the means adopted deprive teachers of the liberty secured to them by the Fourteenth Amendment. It is with hesitation and unwillingness that I differ from my brethren with regard to a law like this but I cannot bring my mind to believe that in some circumstances, and circumstances existing it is said in Nebraska, the statute might not be regarded as a reasonable or even necessary method of reaching the desired result. The part of the act with which we are concerned deals with the teaching of young children. Youth is the time when familiarity with a language is established and if there are sections in the State where a child would hear only Polish or French or German spoken at home I am not prepared to say that it is unreasonable to provide that in his early years he shall hear and speak only English at school. But if it is reasonable it is not an undue restriction of the liberty either of teacher or scholar. No one would doubt that a teacher might be forbidden to teach many things, and the only criterion of his liberty under the Constitution that I can think of is "whether, considering the end in view, the statute passes the bounds of reason and assumes the character of a merely arbitrary fiat." ... I think I appreciate the objection to the law but it appears to me to present a question upon which men reasonably might differ and therefore I am unable to say that the Constitution of the United States prevents the experiment being tried. . . .

MR. JUSTICE SUTHERLAND concurs in this opinion.

Griswold v. *Connecticut*
381 U.S. 479, 85 S.Ct. 1678, 14 L.Ed. 2d 510 (1965)

A Connecticut statute made the use of contraceptives a criminal offense. Griswold, executive director of the Planned Parenthood League of Connecticut, was convicted on a charge of having violated the statute as an accessory by giving information, instruction, and advice to married persons as a means of preventing conception. A professor at the Yale Medical School, serving as Medical Director for the League, was a codefendant. The Appellate Division of the Circuit Court and the Supreme Court of Errors of Connecticut affirmed the conviction. The defendants appealed to the Supreme Court.

MR. JUSTICE DOUGLAS delivered the opinion of the Court.

. . . We think that appellants have standing to raise the constitutional rights of the married people with whom they had a professional relationship. . . . Certainly the accessory should have standing to assert that the offense which he is charged with assisting is not, or cannot constitutionally be, a crime. . . .

Coming to the merits, we are met with a wide range of questions that implicate the Due Process Clause of the Fourteenth Amendment. Overtones of some arguments suggest that *Lochner* v. *New York*, . . . should be our guide.

But we decline that invitation as we did in *West Coast Hotel Co.* v. *Parrish,* 300 U.S. 379. . . . We do not sit as a super-legislature to determine the wisdom, need, and propriety of laws that touch economic problems, business affairs, or social conditions. This law, however, operates directly on an intimate relation of husband and wife and their physician's role in one aspect of that relation. . . .

We protected the "freedom to associate and privacy in one's association," noting that freedom of association was a peripheral First Amendment right. Disclosure of membership lists of a constitutionally valid association, we held, was invalid "as entailing the likelihood of a substantial restraint upon the exercise by petitioner's members of their right to freedom of association." In other words, the First Amendment has a penumbra where privacy is protected from governmental intrusion. . . .

The foregoing cases suggest that specific guarantees in the Bill of Rights have penumbras, formed by emanations from those guarantees that help give them life and substance. . . . Various guarantees create zones of privacy. The right of association contained in the penumbra of the First Amendment is one. . . . The Third Amendment in its prohibition against the quartering of soldiers "in any house" in time of peace without the consent of the owner is another facet of that privacy. The Fourth Amendment explicitly affirms the "right of the people to be secure in their persons, houses, papers, and effects against unreasonable searches and seizures." The Fifth Amendment in its Self-Incrimination Clause enables the citizen to create a zone of privacy which government may not force him to surrender to his detriment. The Ninth Amendment provides: "The enumeration in the Constitution, of certain rights, shall not be construed to deny or disparage others retained by the people." . . .

We recently referred in *Mapp* v. *Ohio,* . . . to the Fourth Amendment as creating a "right of privacy, no less important than any other right carefully and particularly reserved to the people." . . .

The present case, then, concerns a relationship lying within the zone of privacy created by several fundamental constitutional guarantees. And it concerns a law which, in forbidding the *use* of contraceptives rather than regulating their manufacture or sale, seeks to achieve its goals by means having a maximum destructive impact upon that relationship. Such a law cannot stand in light of the familiar principle, so often applied by this Court, that a "governmental purpose to control or prevent activities constitutionally subject to state regulation may not be achieved by means which sweep unnecessarily broadly and thereby invade the area of protected freedom." *NAACP* v. *Alabama,* . . . Would we allow the police to search the sacred precincts of marital bedrooms for telltale signs of the use of contraceptives? The very idea is repulsive to the notions of privacy surrounding the marriage relationship.

We deal with a right of privacy older than the Bill of Rights—older than our political parties, older than our school system. Marriage is a coming together for better or for worse, hopefully enduring, and intimate to the degree of being sacred. It is an association that promotes a way of life, not causes; a harmony in living, not political faiths; a bilateral loyalty, not commercial or social projects. Yet it is an association for as noble a purpose as any involved in our prior decisions.

Reversed.

MR. JUSTICE GOLDBERG, whom the CHIEF JUSTICE and MR. JUSTICE BRENNAN join, concurring.

I agree with the Court that Connecticut's birth control law unconstitutionally intrudes upon the right of marital privacy, and I join in its opinion and judgment. . . .

While this Court has had little occasion to interpret the Ninth Amendment, "[i]t cannot be presumed that any clause in the Constitution is intended to be without effect." . . . *Marbury* v. *Madison,* . . . The Ninth Amendment to the Constitution may be regarded by some as a recent discovery and may be forgotten by others, but since 1791 it has been a basic part of the Constitution which we are sworn to uphold. To hold that a right so basic and fundamental and so deep-rooted in our society as the right of privacy in marriage may be infringed because that right is not guaranteed in so many words by the first eight amendments to the Constitution is to ignore the Ninth Amendment and to give it no effect whatsoever. . . .

Nor am I turning somersaults with history in arguing that the Ninth Amendment is relevant in a case dealing with a *State's* infringement of a fundamental right. While the Ninth Amendment—and indeed the entire Bill of Rights—originally concerned restrictions upon *federal* power, the subsequently enacted Fourteenth Amendment prohibits the States as well from abridging fundamental personal liberties. And, the Ninth Amendment, in indicating that not all such liberties are specifically mentioned in the first eight amendments, is surely relevant in showing the existence of other fundamental personal rights, now protected from state, as well as federal, infringement. In sum, the Ninth Amendment simply lends strong support to the view that the "liberty" protected by the Fifth and Fourteenth Amendments from infringement by the Federal Government or the States is not restricted to rights specifically mentioned in the first eight amendments. . . .

MR. JUSTICE HARLAN, concurring in the judgment.

I fully agree with the judgment of reversal, but find myself unable to join the Court's opinion. The reason is that it seems to me to evince an approach to this case very much like that taken by my Brothers Black and Stewart in dissent, namely: the Due Process Clause of the Fourteenth Amendment does not touch this Connecticut statute unless the enactment is found to violate some right assured by the letter or penumbra of the Bill of Rights.

In other words, what I find implicit in the Court's opinion is that the "incorporation" doctrine may be used to *restrict* the reach of Fourteenth Amendment Due Process. For me this is just as unacceptable constitutional doctrine as is the use of the "incorporation" approach to *impose* upon the States all the requirements of the Bill of Rights as found in the provision of the first eight amendments and in the decisions of this Court interpreting them. . . .

In my view, the proper constitutional inquiry in this case is whether this Connecticut statute infringes the Due Process Clause of the Fourteenth Amendment because the enactment violates basic values "implicit in the concept of ordered liberty." . . .

Judicial self-restraint will not, I suggest, be brought about in the "due process" area by the historically unfounded incorporation formula long advanced by my Brother Black, and now in part espoused by my Brother Stewart. It will be achieved in this area, as in other constitutional areas, only by continual insistence upon respect for the teachings of history, solid recognition of the basic values that underlie our society, and wise appreciation of the great roles that the doctrines of federalism and separation of powers have played in establishing and preserving American freedoms.

MR. JUSTICE BLACK, with whom MR. JUSTICE STEWART joins, dissenting. . . .

The Court talks about a constitutional "right of privacy" as though there is some constitutional provision or provisions forbidding any law ever to be passed which might abridge the "privacy" of individuals. But there is not. There are, of course, guarantees in certain specific constitutional provisions which are designed in part to protect privacy at certain times and places with respect to certain activities. Such, for example, is the Fourth Amendment's guarantee against "unreasonable searches and seizures." But I think it belittles that Amendment to talk about it as though it protects nothing but "privacy." To treat it that way is to give it a niggardly interpretation, not the kind of liberal reading I think any Bill of Rights provision should be given. The average man would very likely not have his feelings soothed any more by having his property seized openly than by having it seized privately and by stealth. He simply wants his property left alone. And a person can be just as much, if not more, irritated, annoyed and injured by an unceremonious public arrest by a policeman as he is by a seizure in the privacy of his office or home.

One of the most effective ways of diluting or

expanding a constitutionally guaranteed right is to substitute for the crucial word or words of a constitutional guarantee another word, more or less flexible and more or less restricted in its meaning. This fact is well illustrated by the use of the term "right of privacy" as a comprehensive substitute for the Fourth Amendment's guarantee against "unreasonable searches and seizures." "Privacy" is a broad, abstract and ambiguous concept which can easily be shrunken in meaning but which can also, on the other hand, easily be interpreted as a constitutional ban against many things other than searches and seizures. . . . For these reasons I get nowhere in this case by talk about a constitutional "right of privacy" as an emanation from one or more constitutional provisions.[1] I like my privacy as well as the next one, but I am nevertheless compelled to admit that government has a right to invade it unless prohibited by some specific constitutional provision. For these reasons I cannot agree with the Court's judgment and the reasons it gives for holding this Connecticut law unconstitutional. . . .

I think that if properly construed neither the Due Process Clause nor the Ninth Amendment,

nor both together, could under any circumstances be a proper basis for invalidating the Connecticut law. I discuss the due process and Ninth Amendment arguments together because on analysis they turn out to be the same thing—merely using different words to claim for this Court and the federal judiciary power to invalidate any legislative act which the judges find irrational, unreasonable or offensive.

The due process argument which my Brothers Harlan and White adopt here is based, as their opinions indicate, on the premise that this Court is vested with power to invalidate all state laws that it considers to be arbitrary, capricious, unreasonable, or oppressive, or because of this Court's belief that a particular state law under scrutiny has no "rational or justifying purpose," or is offensive to a "sense of fairness and justice." If these formulas based on "natural justice," or others which mean the same thing, are to prevail, they require judges to determine what is or is not constitutional on the basis of their own appraisal of what laws are unwise or unnecessary. The power to make such decisions is of course that of a legislative body. Surely it has to be admitted that no provision of the Constitution specifically gives such blanket power to courts to exercise such a supervisory veto over the wisdom and value of legislative policies and to hold unconstitutional those laws which they believe unwise or dangerous. I readily admit that no legislative body, state or national, should pass laws that can justly be given any of the invidious labels invoked as constitutional excuses to strike down state laws. But perhaps it is not too much to say that no legislative body ever does pass laws without believing that they will accomplish a sane, rational, wise and justifiable purpose. While I completely subscribe to the holding of *Marbury* v. *Madison,* . . . and subsequent cases, that our Court has constitutional power to strike down statutes, state or federal, that violate commands of the Federal Constitution, I do not believe that we are granted power by the Due Process Clause or any other constitutional provision or provisions to measure constitutionality by our belief that legislation is arbitrary, capricious or unreasonable, or accomplishes no justifiable

[1] The phrase "right to privacy" appears first to have gained currency from an article written by Messrs. Warren and (later Mr. Justice) Brandeis in 1890 which urged that States should give some form of tort relief to persons whose private affairs were exploited by others. *The Right to Privacy,* 4 Harv. L. Rev. 193. Largely as a result of this article, some States have passed statutes creating such a cause of action, and in other States courts have done the same thing by exercising their powers as courts of common law. See generally 41 Am. Jur. 926–927. Thus the Supreme Court of Georgia, in granting a cause of action for damages to a man whose picture had been used in a newspaper advertisement without his consent, said that "A right to privacy in matters purely private is . . . derived from natural law" and that "The conclusion reached by us seems to be . . . thoroughly in accord with natural justice, with the principles of the law of every civilized nation, and especially with the elastic principles of the common law. . . .'" *Pavesich* v. *New England Life Ins. Co.* 122 Ga. 190, 194, 218, 50 S.E. 68, 70, 80. Observing that "the right of privacy . . . presses for recognition here," today this Court, which I did not understand to have power to sit as a court of common law, now appears to be exalting a phrase which Warren and Brandeis used in discussing grounds for tort relief, to the level of a constitutional rule which prevents state legislatures from passing any law deemed by this Court to interfere with "privacy."

purpose, or is offensive to our own notions of "civilized standards of conduct." Such an appraisal of the wisdom of legislation is an attribute of the power to make laws, not of the power to interpret them. The use by federal courts of such a formula or doctrine or whatnot to veto federal or state laws simply takes away from Congress and States the power to make laws based on their own judgment of fairness and wisdom and transfers that power to this Court for ultimate determination—a power which was specifically denied to federal courts by the convention that framed the Constitution.[2] . . .

[2] This Court held in *Marbury* v. *Madison* . . . that this court has power to invalidate laws on the ground that they exceed the constitutional power of Congress or violate some specific prohibition of the Constitution. See also *Fletcher* v. *Peck,* 6 Cranch 87, 3 L.Ed. 162. But the Constitutional Convention did on at least two occasions reject proposals which would have given the federal judiciary a part in recommending laws or in vetoing as bad or unwise the legislation passed by the Congress. Edmund Randolph of Virginia proposed that the President "and a convenient number of the National Judiciary, ought to compose a council of revision with the authority to examine every act of the National Legislature before it shall operate, & every act of a particular Legislature before a Negative thereon shall be final; and that the dissent of the said Council shall amount to a rejection, unless the Act of the National Legislature be again passed, or that of a particular Legislature be again negatived by [3] of the members of each branch." 1 The Records of the Federal Convention of 1787 (Farrand ed. 1911) 21.

In support of a plan of this kind James Wilson of Pennsylvania argued that:

"It had been said that the Judges, as expositors of the Laws would have an opportunity of defending their constitutional rights. There was weight in this observation; but this power of the Judges did not go far enough. Laws may be unjust, may be unwise, may be dangerous, may be destructive; and yet not be so unconstitutional as to justify the Judges in refusing to give them effect. Let them have a share in the Revisionary power, and they will have an opportunity of taking notice of these characters of a law, and of counteracting, by the weight of their opinions the improper views of the Legislature." 2 *Id.,* at 73.

Nathaniel Gorham of Massachusetts "did not see the advantage of employing the Judges in this way. As Judges they are not to be presumed to possess any peculiar knowledge of the mere policy of public measures." *Ibid.*

Elbridge Gerry of Massachusetts likewise opposed the proposal for a council of revision:

"He relied for his part on the Representatives of the people as the guardians of their Rights & interests. It [the pro-

My Brother Goldberg has adopted the recent discovery that the Ninth Amendment as well as the Due Process Clause can be used by this Court as authority to strike down all state legislation which this Court thinks violates "fundamental principles of liberty and justice," or is contrary to the "traditions and collective conscience of our people." He also states, without proof satisfactory to me, that in making decisions on this basis judges will not consider "their personal and private notions." One may ask how they can avoid considering them. Our Court certainly has no machinery with which to take a Gallup Poll. And the scientific miracles of this age have not yet produced a gadget which the Court can use to determine what traditions are rooted in the "collective conscience of our people." Moreover, one would certainly have to look far beyond the language of the Ninth Amendment to find that the Framers vested in this Court any such awesome veto powers over lawmaking, either by the States or by the Congress. . . . If any broad, unlimited power to hold laws unconstitutional because they offend what this Court conceives to be "the collective conscience of our people" is vested in this Court by the Ninth Amendment, or any other provision of the Constitution, it was not given by the Framers, but rather has been bestowed on the Court by the Court. . . .

posal] was making the Expositors of the Laws, the Legislators which ought never to be done." *Id.,* at 75. And at another point:

"Mr. Gerry doubts whether the Judiciary ought to form a part of it [the proposed council of revision], as they will have a sufficient check agst. encroachments on their own department by their exposition of the laws, which involved a power of deciding on their Constitutionality. . . . It was quite foreign from the nature of ye. office to make them judges of the policy of public measures." 1 *Id.,* at 97–98.

Madison supported the proposal on the ground that "a Check [on the legislature] is necessary." *Id.,* at 108. John Dickinson of Delaware opposed it on the ground that "the Judges must interpret the Laws; they ought not to be legislators." *Ibid.* The proposal for a council of revision was defeated.

Roe v. Wade
410 U.S. 113, 93 S.Ct. 705, 35 L.Ed. 2d 147 (1973)

An unmarried pregnant woman who wished to terminate her pregnancy by abortion instituted an action in the United States District Court for the Northern District of Texas, seeking a declaratory judgment that the Texas criminal abortion statutes, which prohibited abortions except with respect to those procured or attempted by medical advice for the purpose of saving the life of the mother, were unconstitutional. She also sought an injunction against their continued enforcement. A physician, who alleged that he had been previously arrested for violations of the Texas statutes and that two prosecutions were presently pending against him in the state courts, sought and was granted permission to intervene. A separate action, similar to that filed by the unmarried, pregnant woman, was filed by a married, childless couple, who alleged that should the wife become pregnant at some future date, they would wish to terminate the pregnancy by abortion. The two actions were consolidated and heard together by a three-judge district court, which held that the Texas criminal abortion statutes were void on their face, because they were unconstitutionally vague and overbroad. All parties took protective appeals to the United States Court of Appeals for the Fifth Circuit, which court ordered the appeals held in abeyance pending decision on the appeal taken by all parties to the United States Supreme Court.

MR. JUSTICE BLACKMUN delivered the opinion of the Court.

. . . We forthwith acknowledge our awareness of the sensitive and emotional nature of the abortion controversy, of the vigorous opposing views, even among physicians, and of the deep and seemingly absolute convictions that the subject inspires. One's philosophy, one's experiences, one's exposure to the raw edges of human existence, one's religious training, one's attitudes toward life and family and their values, and the moral standards one establishes and seeks to observe, are all likely to influence and to color one's thinking and conclusions about abortion.

In addition, population growth, pollution, poverty, and racial overtones tend to complicate and not to simplify the problem.

Our task, of course, is to resolve the issue by constitutional measurement free of emotion and of predilections. We seek earnestly to do this, and, because we do, we have inquired into, and in this opinion place some emphasis upon, medical and medical-legal history and what that history reveals about man's attitudes toward the abortive procedure over the centuries. We bear in mind, too, Mr. Justice Holmes's admonition in his now vindicated dissent in *Lochner* v. *New York.* . . .

It [the Constitution] is made for people of fundamentally differing views, and the accident of our finding certain opinions natural and familiar or novel and even shocking ought not to conclude our judgment upon the question whether statutes embodying them conflict with the Constitution of the United States.

The Texas statutes that concern us here . . . make it a crime to "procure an abortion," as therein defined, or to attempt one, except with respect to "an abortion procured or attempted by medical advice for the purpose of saving the life of the mother." Similar statutes are in existence in a majority of the States. . . .

The principal thrust of appellant's attack on the Texas statutes is that they improperly invade a right, said to be possessed by the pregnant woman, to choose to terminate her pregnancy. Appellant would discover this right in the concept of personal ''liberty'' embodied in the Fourteenth Amendment's Due Process Clause; or in personal, marital, familial, and sexual privacy said to be protected by the Bill of Rights or its penumbras. . . . Before addressing this claim, we feel it desirable briefly to survey, in several aspects, the history of abortion, for such insight as that history may afford us, and then to examine the state purposes and interests behind the criminal abortion laws.

It perhaps is not generally appreciated that the restrictive criminal abortion laws in effect in a majority of States today are of relatively recent vintage. Those laws, generally proscribing abortion or its attempt at any time during pregnancy except when necessary to preserve the pregnant woman's life, are not of ancient or even of common law origin. Instead, they derive from statutory changes effected, for the most part, in the latter half of the 19th century. . . .

It is thus apparent that at common law, at the time of the adoption of our Constitution, and throughout the major portion of the 19th century, abortion was viewed with less disfavor than under most American statutes currently in effect. Phrasing it another way, a woman enjoyed a substantially broader right to terminate a pregnancy than she does in most States today. At least with respect to the early stage of pregnancy, and very possibly without such a limitation, the opportunity to make this choice was present in this country well into the 19th century. Even later, the law continued for some time to treat less punitively an abortion procured in early pregnancy. . . .

Three reasons have been advanced to explain historically the enactment of criminal abortion laws in the 19th century and to justify their continued existence.

It has been argued occasionally that these laws were the product of a Victorian social concern to discourage illicit sexual conduct. Texas, however, does not advance this justification in the present case, and it appears that no court or commentator has taken the argument seriously. The appellants and amici contend, moreover,

that this is not a proper state purpose at all and suggest that, if it were, the Texas statutes are overbroad in protecting it since the law fails to distinguish between married and unwed mothers.

A second reason is concerned with abortion as a medical procedure. When most criminal abortion laws were first enacted, the procedure was a hazardous one for the woman. This was particularly true prior to the development of antisepsis. Antiseptic techniques, of course, were based on discoveries by Lister, Pasteur, and others first announced in 1867, but were not generally accepted and employed until about the turn of the century. Abortion mortality was high. Even after 1900, and perhaps until as late as the development of antibiotics in the 1940s, standard modern techniques such as dilation and currettage were not nearly so safe as they are today. Thus it has been argued that a State's real concern in enacting a criminal abortion law was to protect the pregnant woman, that is, to restrain her from submitting to a procedure that placed her life in serious jeopardy.

Modern medical techniques have altered this situation. Appellants and various amici refer to medical data indicating that abortion in early pregnancy, that is, prior to the end of first trimester, although not without its risk, is now relatively safe. Mortality rates for women undergoing early abortions, where the procedure is legal, appear to be as low or lower than the rates for normal childbirth. Consequently, any interest of the State in protecting the woman from an inherently hazardous procedure, except when it would be equally dangerous for her to forgo it, has largely disappeared. Of course, important state interests in the area of health and medical standards do remain. The State has a legitimate interest in seeing to it that abortion, like any other medical procedure, is performed under circumstances that insure maximum safety for the patient. This interest obviously extends at least to the performing physician and his staff, to the facilities involved, to the availability of aftercare, and to adequate provision for any complication or emergency that might arise. The prevalence of high mortality rates at illegal "abortion mills" strengthens, rather than weakens, the State's interest in regulating the conditions under which abortions are performed. Moreover, the risk to the woman increases as her pregnancy continues. Thus the State retains a definite interest in protecting the woman's own health and safety when an abortion is proposed at a late stage of pregnancy.

The third reason is the State's interest—some phrase it in terms of duty—in protecting prenatal life. Some of the argument for this justification rests on the theory that a new human life is present from the moment of conception. The State's interest and general obligation to protect life then extends, it is argued, to prenatal life. Only when the life of the pregnant mother herself is at stake, balanced against the life she carries within her, should the interest of the embryo or fetus not prevail. Logically, of course, a legitimate state interest in this area need not stand or fall on acceptance of the belief that life begins at conception or at some other point prior to live birth. In assessing the State's interest, recognition may be given to the less rigid claim that as long as at least *potential* life is involved, the State may assert interests beyond the protection of the pregnant woman alone.

Parties challenging state abortion laws have sharply disputed in some courts the contention that a purpose of these laws, when enacted, was to protect prenatal life. Pointing to the absence of legislative history to support the contention, they claim that most state laws were designed soley to protect the woman. Because medical advances have lessened this concern, at least with respect to abortion in early pregnancy, they argue that with respect to such abortions the laws can no longer be justified by any state interest. There is some scholarly support for this view of original purpose. The few state courts called upon to interpret their laws in the late 19th and early 20th centuries did focus on the State's interest in protecting the woman's health rather than in preserving the embryo and fetus. Proponents of this view point out that in many States, including Texas, by statute or judicial interpretation, the pregnant woman herself could not be prosecuted for self-abortion or for cooperating in an abortion performed upon her by another. They claim that adoption of the "quickening" distinction through received common law and state statutes tacitly recognizes the greater health hazards inherent in late abortion and impliedly repudiates the theory that life begins at conception.

It is with these interests, and the weight to be attached to them, that this case is concerned.

The Constitution does not explicitly mention any right of privacy. In a line of decisions, however, going back perhaps as far as *Union Pacific R. Co.* v. *Botsford,* 141 U.S. 250 . . . (1891), the Court has recognized that a right of personal privacy, or a guarantee of certain areas or zones of privacy, does exist under the Constitution. In varying contexts the Court or individual Justices have indeed found at least the roots of that right in the First Amendment; . . . in the Fourth and Fifth Amendments; . . . in the penumbras of the Bill of Rights; . . . in the Ninth Amendment; . . . or in the concept of liberty guaranteed by the first section of the Fourteenth Amendment. . . . These decisions make it clear that only personal rights that can be deemed "fundamental" or "implicit in the concept of ordered liberty" . . . are included in this guarantee of personal privacy. They also make it clear that the right has some extension to activities relating to marriage, . . . procreation, contraception, family relationships, and child rearing and education.

This right of privacy, whether it be founded in the Fourteenth Amendment's concept of personal liberty and restrictions upon state action, as we feel it is, or, as the District Court determined, in the Ninth Amendment's reservation of rights to the people, is broad enough to encompass a woman's decision whether or not to terminate her pregnancy. The detriment that the State would impose upon the pregnant woman by denying this choice altogether is apparent. Specific and direct harm medically diagnosable even in early pregnancy may be involved. Maternity, or additional offspring, may force upon the woman a distressful life and future. Psychological harm may be imminent.

Mental and physical health may be taxed by child care. There is also the distress, for all concerned, associated with the unwanted child, and there is the problem of bringing a child into a family already unable, psychologically and otherwise, to care for it. In other cases, as in this one, the additional difficulties and continuing stigma of unwed motherhood may be involved. All these are factors the woman and her responsible physician necessarily will consider in consultation.

On the basis of elements such as these, appellants and some amici argue that the woman's right is absolute and that she is entitled to terminate her pregnancy at whatever time, in whatever way, and for whatever reason she alone chooses. With this we do not agree. Appellants' arguments that Texas either has no valid interest at all in regulating the abortion decision, or no interest strong enough to support any limitation upon the woman's sole determination, is unpersuasive. The Court's decisions recognizing a right of privacy also acknowledge that some state regulation in areas protected by that right is appropriate. As noted above, a state may properly assert important interests in safeguarding health, in maintaining medical standards, and in protecting potential life. At some point in pregnancy, these respective interests become sufficiently compelling to sustain regulation of the factors that govern the abortion decision. The privacy right involved, therefore, cannot be said to be absolute. In fact, it is not clear to us that the claim asserted by some amici that one has an unlimited right to do with one's body as one pleases bears a close relationship to the right of privacy previously articulated in the Court's decisions. The Court has refused to recognize an unlimited right of this kind in the past. . . .

We therefore conclude that the right of personal privacy includes the abortion decision, but that this right is not unqualified and must be considered against important state interests in regulation. . . .

The appellee and certain amici argue that the fetus is a "person" within the language and meaning of the Fourteenth Amendment. In support of this they outline at length and in detail the well-known facts of fetal development. If this suggestion of personhood is established, the appellant's case, of course, collapses, for the fetus's right to life is then guaranteed specifically by the Amendment. The appellant conceded as much on reargument. On the other hand, the appellee conceded on reargument that no case could be cited that holds a fetus is a person within the meaning of the Fourteenth Amendment.

The Constitution does not define "person" in so many words. Section 1 of the Fourteenth Amendment contains three references to "person." The first, in defining "citizens," speaks of "persons born or naturalized in the United States." The word also appears both in the Due Process Clause and in the Equal Protection Clause. "Person" is used in other places in the Constitution. . . . But in nearly all these instances, the use of the word is such that it has application only postnatally. None indicates, with any assurance, that it has any possible prenatal application. . . .

Texas urges that, apart from the Fourteenth Amendment, life begins at conception and is present throughout pregnancy, and that, therefore, the State has a compelling interest in protecting that life from and after conception. We need not resolve the difficult question of when life begins. When those trained in the respective disciplines of medicine, philosophy, and theology are unable to arrive at any consensus, the judiciary, at this point in the development of man's knowledge, is not in a position to speculate as to the answer.

It should be sufficient to note briefly the wide divergence of thinking on this most sensitive and difficult question. There has always been strong support for the view that life does not begin until live birth. This was the belief of the Stoics. It appears to be the predominant, though not the unanimous, attitude of the Jewish faith. It may be taken to represent also the position of a large segment of the Protestant community, insofar as that can be ascertained; organized groups that have taken a formal position on the abortion issue have generally regarded abortion as a matter for the conscience of the individual and her family. As we have noted, the common law found greater significance in quickening. Physicians and their scientific colleagues have regarded that event with less interest and have tended to focus either upon conception or upon live birth or upon the interim point at which the fetus becomes "viable," that is, potentially able to live outside the mother's womb, albeit with artificial aid. Viability is usually placed at about seven months (28 weeks) but may occur earlier, even at 24 weeks. . . . Substantial problems for precise definition . . . are posed, however, by new embryological data that purport to indicate that conception is a "process" over time, rather than an event, and by new medical techniques such as menstrual extraction, the "morning-after" pill, implantation of embryos, artificial insemination, and even artificial wombs.

. . . We do not agree that, by adopting one theory of life, Texas may override the rights of the pregnant woman that are at stake. We repeat, however, that the State does have an important and legitimate interest in preserving and protecting the health of the pregnant woman, whether she be a resident of the State or a nonresident who seeks medical consultation and treatment there, and that it has still *another* important and legitimate interest in protecting the potentiality of human life. These interests are separate and distinct. Each grows in substantiality as the woman approaches term and, at a point during pregnancy, each becomes "compelling."

With respect to the State's important and legitimate interest in the health of the mother, the "compelling" point, in the light of present medical knowledge, is at approximately the end of the first trimester. This is so because of the now established medical fact, . . . that until the end of the first trimester mortality in abortion is less than mortality in normal childbirth. It follows that, from and after this point, a State may regulate the abortion procedure to the extent that the regulation reasonably relates to the preservation and protection of maternal health. Examples of permissible state regulation in this area are requirements as to the qualifications of

the person who is to perform the abortion; as to the licensure of that person; as to the facility in which the procedure is to be performed, that is, whether it must be a hospital or may be a clinic or some other place of less-than-hospital status; as to the licensing of the facility; and the like.

This means, on the other hand, that, for the period of pregnancy prior to this "compelling" point, the attending physician, in consultation with his patient, is free to determine, without regulation by the State, that in his medical judgment the patient's pregnancy should be terminated. If that decision is reached, the judgment may be effectuated by an abortion free of interference by the State. . . .

With respect to the State's important and legitimate interest in potential life, the "compelling" point is at viability. This is so because the fetus then presumably has the capability of meaningful life outside the mother's womb. State regulation protective of fetal life after viability thus has both logical and biological justifications. If the State is interested in protecting fetal life after viability, it may go so far as to proscribe abortion during that period except when it is necessary to preserve the life or health of the mother.

Measured against these standards, . . . Texas, in restricting legal abortion to those "procured or attempted by medical advice for the purpose of saving the life of the mother," sweeps too broadly. The statute makes no distinction between abortions performed early in pregnancy and those performed later, and it limits to a single reason, "saving" the mother's life, the legal justification for the procedure. The statute, therefore, cannot survive the constitutional attack made upon it here. . . .

MR. JUSTICE WHITE, with whom MR. JUSTICE REHNQUIST joins, dissenting . . . .

With all due respect, I dissent. I find nothing in the language or history of the Constitution to support the Court's judgment. The Court simply fashions and announces a new constitutional right for pregnant mothers and, with scarcely any reason or authority for its action, invests that right with sufficient substance to override most existing state abortion statutes. . . . As an exercise of raw judicial power, the Court perhaps has authority to do what it does today; but in my view its judgment is an improvident and extravagant exercise of the power of judicial review which the Constitution extends to this Court. . . .

MR. JUSTICE REHNQUIST, dissenting.

. . . I would reach a conclusion opposite to that reached by the Court. I have difficulty in concluding, as the Court does, that the right of "privacy" is involved in this case. Texas by the statute here challenged bars the performance of a medical abortion by a licensed physician on a plaintiff such as Roe. A transaction resulting in an operation such as this is not "private" in the ordinary usage of that word. Nor is the "privacy" which the Court finds here even a distant relative of the freedom from searches and seizures protected by the Fourth Amendment to the Constitution which the Court has referred to as embodying a right to privacy. . . .

If the Court means by the term "privacy" no more than that the claim of a person to be free from unwanted state regulation of consensual transactions may be a form of "liberty" protected by the Fourteenth Amendment, there is no doubt that similar claims have been upheld in our earlier decisions on the basis of that liberty. I agree with the statement of Mr. Justice Stewart in his concurring opinion that the "liberty," against deprivation of which without due process the Fourteenth Amendment protects, embraces more than the rights found in the Bill of Rights. But that liberty is not guaranteed absolutely against deprivation, but only against deprivation without due process of law. The test traditionally applied in the area of social and economic legislation is whether or not a law such as that challenged has a rational relation to a valid state objective. . . . But the Court's sweeping invalidation of any restrictions on abortion during the first trimester is impossible to justify under that standard, and the conscious weighing of competing factors which the Court's opinion apparently substitutes for the established test is far more appropriate to a legislative judgment than to a judicial one.

The Court eschews the history of the Four-

teenth Amendment in its reliance on the "compelling state interest" test. . . . But the Court adds a new wrinkle to this test by transposing it from the legal considerations associated with the Equal Protection Clause of the Fourteenth Amendment to this case arising under the Due Process Clause of the Fourteenth Amendment. Unless I misapprehend the consequences of this transplanting of the "compelling state interest test," the Court's opinion will accomplish the seemingly impossible feat of leaving this area of the law more confused than it found it.

While the Court's opinion quotes from the dissent of Mr. Justice Holmes in *Lochner* v. *New York,* . . . the result it reaches is more closely attuned to the majority opinion of Mr. Justice Peckham in that case. As in *Lochner* and similar cases applying substantive due process standards to economic and social welfare legislation, the adoption of the compelling state interest standard will inevitably require this Court to examine the legislative policies and pass on the wisdom of these policies in the very process of deciding whether a particular state interest put forward may or may not be "compelling." The decision here to break the term of pregnancy into three distinct terms and to outline the permissible restrictions the State may impose in each one, for example, partakes more of judicial legislation than it does of a determination of the intent of the drafters of the Fourteenth Amendment.

The fact that a majority of the States, reflecting after all the majority sentiment in those States, have had restrictions on abortions for at least a century seems to me as strong an indication there is that the asserted right to an abortion is not "so rooted in the traditions and conscience of our people as to be ranked as fundamental." . . . Even today, when society's views on abortion are changing, the very existence of the debate is evidence that the "right" to an abortion is not so universally accepted as the appellants would have us believe.

To reach its result the Court necessarily has had to find within the scope of the Fourteenth Amendment a right that was apparently completely unknown to the drafters of the Amendment. As early as 1821, the first state law dealing directly with abortion was enacted by the Connecticut legislature. . . . By the time of the adoption of the Fourteenth Amendment in 1868 there were at least 36 laws enacted by state or territorial legislatures limiting abortion. While many States have amended or updated their laws, 21 of the laws on the books in 1868 remain in effect today. Indeed, the Texas statute struck down today was, as the majority notes, first enacted in 1857 and "has remained substantially unchanged to the present time." . . .

There apparently was no question concerning the validity of this provision or of any of the other state statutes when the Fourteenth Amendment was adopted. The only conclusion possible from this history is that the drafters did not intend to have the Fourteenth Amendment withdraw from the States the power to legislate with respect to this matter. . . .

For all of the foregoing reasons, I respectfully dissent.

Court actively amends by state to invade

ELEVEN

Equal Protection of the Laws

The Founding Fathers, Madison in particular, were wedded to the notion that unequal distribution of wealth is the natural result in a society where individuals of differing capacities are free. Accordingly, any affirmative government action on behalf of those less fortunate, ignoring merit, was suspect. For whatever reason, a conspicuous omission from the original document, as well as the Bill of Rights, is a provision guarding against a denial of equal protection of the laws. This provision now so conspicuous in a wide range of Supreme Court decisions dates only from 1868, when it was made part of the Fourteenth Amendment, along with two other provisions designed to safeguard individual rights against encroachment by the states.

Ironically, when the Fourteenth Amendment was first subjected to judicial scrutiny in the Slaughterhouse Cases, its clauses were reduced to what dissenting Justice Field described as a ''vain and idle'' enactment. The Court's spokesman, Justice Miller, reduced the equal protection clause to even narrower limits, suggesting that it was doubtful whether ''this sweeping injunction would ever be invoked against any state action'' not directed by way of discrimination against Negroes as a class. ''It is,'' he wrote, ''so clearly a provision for that race and that emergency, that a strong case would be necessary for its application to any other.''

But when in 1883 the Court was confronted with congressional legislation guaranteeing equal protection of the laws to blacks (Civil Rights Cases), it balked at giving the clause positive meaning. By reading the first and fifth sections of the Fourteenth Amendment to mean merely that Congress could pass legislation to supersede discriminatory state legislation and official acts (a power similar to that of judicial review), it preserved the existing federal system at the expense of implementing the principle of equal protection of laws. Bradley's opinion for the Court rather naïvely assumed that the then existing laws of all states required innkeepers and public carriers to furnish accommodations to all unobjectionable persons who applied for them, and further, that anyone refused accommodations had an adequate remedy under state law. Harlan, dissenting, treated the right to such accommodations as "legal," rather than "social," and argued realistically that this decision meant in practice the continuation of discrimination under the tolerant eyes of the state.

Again, when the equal protection clause was invoked on behalf of the Negro in *Plessy* v. *Ferguson,* the Court refused to allow the provision to serve even the limited purpose which Justice Miller had earlier acknowledged. Deploring this emasculation, dissenting Justice Harlan observed: "Our Constitution is color-blind, and neither knows nor tolerates classes among citizens. In respect of civil rights all citizens are equal before the law." Denouncing the separate-but-equal formula put forth by the majority in *Plessy,* Harlan predicted that "the judgment this day rendered will in time prove to be quite as pernicious as the decision made by this tribunal in the *Dred Scott* case."

His prophecy, though sound, was not fulfilled until half a century later in the *Brown* case. By that time, the equal protection clause had become a handy constitutional tool, not only on behalf of blacks but also many other disadvantaged persons. This drastic change in the standards of equal protection—from constitutional omission, to constitutional nullity, to constitutional prominence—carries within it a fascinating story.

"SEPARATE BUT EQUAL"

It was essential for the states to have an acceptable legal principle to support the policy of holding blacks in their former status. The answer was soon found in laws requiring segregation of the white and colored races under the formula "separate but equal." An early decision had invalidated a state statute forbidding segregation on steamboats and other common carriers on the ground that interstate commerce required a uniform rule (*Hall* v. *DeCuir,* 95 U.S. 485: 1878). But the Court now accepted laws requiring segregation within a state on the theory that they regulated purely intrastate commerce and did not burden interstate commerce unreasonably (*Louisville N. O. & T. R. Co.* v. *Mississippi,* 133 U.S. 587: 1890). Justice Harlan dissented, contending that *Hall* v. *DeCuir* made such segregation on carriers invalid. "Separate but equal" received the Supreme Court's formal approval in *Plessy* v. *Ferguson.*

Moreover, in spite of its willingness, expressed ten years earlier in *Yick Wo* v. *Hopkins* (118 U.S. 356: 1886), to look behind a law and examine its practical administration, the Supreme Court was unwilling or unprepared to go behind lower federal or state court findings that separate facilities for blacks were in fact "equal."

It was not until the late 1930s that the Court began to give serious attention to the "equality" requirement. In 1938 the Court invalidated a law under which Gaines, a black applicant, was refused admission to the School of Law of the State University of Missouri (*Missouri ex rel. Gaines* v. *Canada,* 305 U.S. 337: 1938). Missouri made funds available to Gaines and other qualified black applicants to finance their legal education in schools of adjacent states that offered unsegregated educational facilities, and argued that by this action it was meeting the "separate but equal" requirement. Chief Justice Hughes, for the majority of seven, disposed of the state's contention emphatically.

The basic consideration is not as to what sort of opportunities other States provide, or whether they are as good as those in Missouri, but as to what opportunities Missouri itself furnishes to white students and denies to negroes solely upon the ground of color. The admissibility of laws separating the races in the enjoyment of privileges afforded by the State rests wholly upon the equality of the privileges which the laws give to the separated groups within the State. The question here is not of a duty of the State to supply legal training, or of the quality of the training which it does supply, but of its duty when it provides such training to furnish it to the residents of the State upon the basis of an equality of right. By the operation of the laws of Missouri a privilege has been created for white law students which is denied to negroes by reason of their race. The white resident is afforded legal education within the State; the negro resident having the same qualifications is refused it there and must go outside the State to obtain it. That is a denial of equality of legal right to the enjoyment of the privilege which the State has set up, and the provision for the payment of tuition fees in another State does not remove the discrimination. . . .

A cluster of cases between 1948 and 1950 indicated that the "separate but equal" doctrine would in the future be more difficult to apply in practice. *Sipuel* v. *University of Oklahoma* (332 U.S. 631: 1948) held that qualified Negroes must be admitted to a state law school or be furnished equivalent professional education within the state. *McLaurin* v. *Oklahoma State Regents* (339 U.S. 637: 1950) nullified state efforts to segregate the scholastic activities of a black student who had been admitted to the graduate school of the University of Oklahoma pursuant to a federal court order. Finally, a direct challenge to segregated education was presented in *Sweatt* v. *Painter,* (339 U.S. 629: 1950), where an applicant who had been denied admission to the University of Texas Law School solely on the basis of color claimed that the instruction available in the newly established state law school for blacks was markedly inferior to the instruction at the University, and that equal protection of laws was thus denied. In a unanimous decision the Supreme Court ordered his admission to the white school, indicating that it was virtually impossible in practice, at least in professional education, for a state to comply with the separate-but-equal formula. Taking into account professional and psychological considerations, thus anticipating the thrust of Chief Justice Warren's opinion in *Brown,* Chief Justice Vinson of Kentucky left that judicial creation hanging by a hair.

Whether the University of Texas Law School is compared with the original or the new law school for Negroes, we cannot find substantial equality in the educational opportunities offered white and Negro law students by the State. In terms of number of the faculty, variety of courses and opportunity for specialization, size of the student body, scope of the library, availability of law review and similar activities, the University of Texas Law School is superior. What is more important, the University of Texas Law School possesses to a far greater degree those qualities which are incapable of objective measurement but which make for greatness in a law school. Such qualities, to name but a few, include reputation of the faculty, experience of the administration, position and influence of the alumni, standing in the community, traditions and prestige. It is difficult to believe that one who had a free choice between these law schools would consider the question close.

Moreover, although the law is a highly learned profession, we are well aware that it is an intensely practical one. The law school, the proving ground for legal learning and practice, cannot be effective in isolation from the individuals and institutions with which the law interacts. Few students and no one who has practiced law would choose to study in an academic vacuum, removed from the interplay of ideas and the exchange of views with which the law is concerned. The law school to which Texas is willing to admit petitioner excludes from its student body members of the racial groups which number 85% of the population of the State and include most of the lawyers, witnesses, jurors, judges and other officials with whom petitioner will inevitably be dealing when he becomes a member of the Texas Bar. With such a substantial and significant segment of society excluded, we cannot conclude that the education offered petitioner is substantially equal to that which he would receive if admitted to the University of Texas Law School.

Following the decision in the Sweatt case the National Association for the Advancement of Colored People and other organizations pressed the fight against segregation in public schools. Would the Court retract the principle of "separate but equal," or, alternatively, would it construe the requirement of "equality" so strictly that segregation in practice would be constitutionally impossible? After hearing argument in a group of public school segregation cases presented at the 1952 term, the justices were unable to reach a decision. In setting the cases for reargument during the 1953 term, the Court took the unusual step of requesting counsel to provide answers to a long list of questions, some seeking information concerning the intention of the Congress that proposed, and the states that ratified, the Fourteenth Amendment, and others requesting advice as to the kind of orders that the Court should issue if it were to hold segregated school arrangements unconstitutional.

The Court's caution, though unusual, was understandable. Its decision would affect the school systems of 17 states and the District of Columbia where segregation was required by law, and four states where segregation was permitted by local option. The pattern of education for more than 8 million white children and $2\frac{1}{2}$ million black children would be drastically changed if segregation practices were found unconstitutional. Even greater issues were involved: if segregation in public schools were deemed a denial of equal protection of the laws, it would be difficult, if not impossible, to defend segregation in other sectors of public life. The legal underpinnings of the social structure of a great part of the nation were under attack.

Eminent counsel, headed by John W. Davis, appeared for the states, and argued that the "separate-but-equal" doctrine embodied a rule that was no longer open to question. Historical data were cited to show that segregated school systems were in existence when the Fourteenth Amendment was adopted, and that advocates of the Amendment had not questioned their constitutionality.

Thurgood Marshall, the noted black spokesman, urged the Supreme Court to meet "separate but equal" squarely, and reject it as "a faulty conception of an era dominated by provincialism." Marshall, now Justice, and his co-counsel also produced historical evidence of the intentions of the proponents of the Fourteenth Amendment, evidence from which they drew conclusions diametrically opposed to those of the states' supporters.

On May 17, 1954, the Court handed down its decision. Speaking for a unanimous Court, Chief Justice Warren declared in *Brown* v. *Board of Education* that "in the field of public education the doctrine of 'separate but equal' has no place. Separate educational facilities are inherently unequal." The opinion is remarkable not only for its brevity, but also for its references to sociological and psychological factors. Reduced to a footnote, these were gratuitous. Earlier decisions had eroded the constitutional foundations of the "separate-but-equal" formula to the vanishing point. Nor did the historical evidence, furnished at the Court's request, and available to it in briefs of counsel, influence the decision. "In approaching this problem," said the Chief Justice, "we cannot turn the clock back to 1868, when the Amendment was adopted, or even to 1896, when *Plessy* v. *Ferguson* was written. We must consider public education in the light of its full development and its present place in American life throughout the nation."

In the District of Columbia case, the Court came to a similar conclusion, using the due process clause of the Fifth Amendment. "Segregation in public education," said the Court, ". . . imposes on Negro children of the District of Columbia a burden that constitutes an arbitrary deprivation of their liberty in violation of the Due Process Clause." Having achieved unanimity on this difficult issue, the Court postponed formulation of a decree until the 1954–55 term, and called for additional argument.

In the following term the Court handed down its decree in the second Brown case, expressing the conclusion that desegregation in public education would necessarily take place at varying speeds and in different ways, depending on local conditions. Federal district court judges, employing the flexible principles of equity court, were given the task of determining when and how desegregation should take place. In a historic pronouncement, the Court said: "The judgments below . . . are remanded to the district courts to take such proceedings and enter such orders and decrees consistent with this opinion as are necessary and proper to admit to public schools on a racially nondiscriminatory basis *with all deliberate speed*" the parties to these cases (Italics added).

Although the Border States showed a disposition to comply with the Supreme Court's mandate, states in the deep South began a campaign of active and passive resistance. Several legislatures passed resolutions declaring the desegregation decisions "unlawful." State sovereignty was "interposed" against this alleged encroachment upon their reserved powers. Almost all Southern senators and representatives joined in 1956 in issuing a "Declaration of Constitutional Principles," and advocated resistance to legally compelled desegregation by "all lawful means."

Realizing that forcible opposition to the Court's requirement of desegregated schools would fail, certain states adopted various legal tactics and devices which gave promise of delaying and forestalling the implementation of *Brown* v. *Board of Education*. Since the recalcitrant states and communities refused to take any steps to desegregate, it was necessary for black citizens to bring individual suits in each school district asking the federal court to compel the school authorities to take steps toward desegregated schools. Interminable hearings followed, with local officials asking for delay because of local conditions which in their view were unfavorable to prompt action. After several years, a plan for one-grade-a-year desegregation might be proposed and accepted by a court, but in many communities no plan had gone into operation by 1963—nine years after the original decision.

Recognizing that delaying tactics would no longer be of avail with many of the federal district judges, certain states enacted "pupil placement" and "transfer privilege" laws. These laws were designed to achieve token integration by permitting black pupils to apply for admission to normally all-white schools or in other situations to permit parents to request transfer of their children to a school other than the assigned one. In any event, these and other devices were for a time successful in maintaining mostly segregated educational facilities. An Alabama school placement statute was held unconstitutional on its face in 1958 (*Shuttlesworth* v. *Birmingham Board of Education*, 358 U.S. 101), and a transfer scheme fell in *Goss* v. *Board of Education of Knoxville* (373 U.S. 683: 1963). Still, even with heightened judicial scrutiny, a multiplicity of suits attacking each administrative decision was required if more than a handful of blacks were to gain admission to white schools.

The Supreme Court staunchly upheld lower federal court decisions ordering steps toward desegregated schools, either by denying certiorari or by per curiam decisions. The executive branch, which took an essentially neutral position in the 1950s, took strong steps in 1958 to support the orders of a federal court in Arkansas, in actions which were upheld by a powerful decision of the Supreme Court (*Cooper* v. *Aaron*, 358 U.S. 1: 1958). In 1962 Mississippi troops were used to meet resistance to the desegregation order.

The pace of integration quickened after 1965, when the combination of two congressional enactments brought both administrative and financial pressure to bear on school districts. The mid-1960s witnessed the first mass infusion of federal funds into local school coffers, and the Civil Rights Act of 1964 in several ways made continued receipt of Washington largess conditional on integrated education. Where litigation often took years to effect even small changes in the schools, bureaucrats with their hands on the federal faucet could accomplish substantial changes in months. Their efforts were reinforced by the Court. Political observers, who thought that President Nixon's new Court appointees after 1969 would take positions supportive of his so-called "Southern Strategy," were poor prophets.

The 1969–70 term had hardly begun when Chief Justice Burger faced the issue of racial segregation (*Alexander* v. *Holmes County Board of Education*, 396 U.S. 19). The Nixon administration had equivocated; the Burger Court acted promptly and decisively. "School Integration Is Ordered by the Supreme Court; Nixon Bid for Delay Rejected," *New York Times* headlines blared. Citing *Griffin* v. *County School Board* (337 U.S. 218: 1964) and *Green* v. *School Board of New Kent County* (391 U.S. 430: 1968), the Court issued a unanimous per curiam holding that the standard of "all deliberate speed" set in 1955 apparently on the insistence of Justice Frankfurter, was no longer constitutionally permissible. (For the origins of this expression see Eugene Gerhart, *Quote It!*, pp. 589–90). Appearing on CBS Television, December 3, 1968, Justice Black said for the first time publicly that it might have been better if the Warren Court had not written this controversial formula into the 1955 opinion.

Even more dramatic evidence that the Burger Court was not willing to turn back the clock came in a pair of 1971 decisions, after Justice Blackmun joined the Court. In one, the Court invalidated a state statute prohibiting assignment or busing of students on the basis of race or for the purpose of creating racial balance (*North Carolina State Board of Education* v. *Swann*, 402 U.S. 43: 1971). At the same time, the Court held valid a desegregation plan which involved busing (*Swann* v. *Charlotte-Mecklenburg Board of Education*, 402 U.S. 1: 1971). Thus, even on the busing issue, a subject that inspired President Nixon to numerous negative pronouncements, the Court continued to act in the spirit of *Brown* v. *Board of Education*.

Decisions in the school segregation cases not only invalidated the concept of "separate but equal" in education but also set forth a rationale that made the local continuance of other segregated public facilities and services doubtful. Segregation was outlawed in intrastate buses (*Gayle* v. *Browder*, 352 U.S. 903: 1956); in public housing (*Detroit Housing Commission* v. *Lewis*, 226 F. 2d. 180: 1955); in public recreation facilities (*Baltimore* v. *Dawson*, 350 U.S. 877: 1955; *Holmes* v. *Atlanta*, 350 U.S. 879: 1955). One of the last forms of state imposed segregation laws—that prohibiting interracial marriages—fell in *Loving* v. *Virginia* (388 U.S. 1: 1967).

In 1973 the Court's attention was drawn to the problem of school segregation in the North. *Keyes* v. *School District* (413 U.S. 189: 1973) did not involve statutes or other obvious official actions to create segregated schools. One section of Denver, Colorado, contained a heavy concentration of black school children, and the wrongdoing of the school officials consisted largely of various administrative decisions in the 1960s that were found by the federal district court to constitute a deliberate plan to maintain segregated schools in that part of the city. The Supreme Court agreed, and ruled that where one part of a school system was segregated, the remedy could take the form of a decree involving busing of students to and from districts where no discriminatory policies had previously existed. While continuing to insist, over the protests of Justice Powell, that a distinction must be made between *de facto* and *de jure* segregation, the former being lawful, the latter unconstitutional, the Court signaled Northern communities that federal district courts would give close scrutiny to all official decisions affecting the racial composition of schools, and that absence of statutory provisions requiring segregation would not prevent judicial action. In other words, the Justices were enlarging the concept of *de jure* segregation in *Keyes,* and correspondingly shrinking what they considered *de facto* segregation.

Southern Justice Powell pointed out a much larger percentage of Negro pupils attended desegregated schools in the South than in the North. As the flight of whites to the suburbs accelerated and blacks and other racial minorities became the dominant population, the question of how to achieve racially integrated schools became acute. More and more the argument was made that the state governments should bear ultimate responsibility for achieving desegregation. By a vote of 5 to 4 the Supreme Court in *Milliken* v. *Bradley* rejected a multidistrict remedy for a single-district segregation problem. This holding should be viewed in the light of the 1975 decision in *Hills* v. *Gautreaux* (425 U.S. 284), allowing a court remedy to extend beyond the Chicago City boundaries, where federal officials were found to have discriminated against blacks in the selection of public housing sites. The distinction between *Milliken* and *Gautreaux,* as Justice Stewart explained, was that HUD officials had violated the Constitution while school officials of the districts which were to be joined with Detroit in the Milliken situation were free of wrongdoing.

Establishing racially discriminatory intent continues to be as important in housing cases as in other Fourteenth Amendment areas. In *Village of Arlington Heights* v. *Metropolitan Housing Development Corporation* (429 U.S. 252: 1977), a nonprofit development corporation desired to build racially-integrated, multifamily housing on a plot zoned for single-family units. The village denied the request for rezoning, and the housing corporation brought suit. After a defeat in district court, the Court of Appeals for the Seventh Circuit reversed, citing the racially discriminatory *effects* of the refusal to rezone. The Supreme Court held otherwise. ''Our decision last Term in *Washington* v. *Davis* . . . ,'' wrote Justice Powell for the majority, ''made it clear that official action will not be held unconstitutional solely because it results in a racially discriminatory impact. . . . Proof of racially discriminatory intent or purpose is required to show a violation of the Equal Protection Clause.'' History and current circumstances might be helpful guides in divining intent, Powell suggested.

For a large majority of the Court, establishing racially discriminatory intent remains far easier in school segregation cases. Building on the logic in the 1973 Denver decision, the Court in 1979 approved judicially-ordered integration on a massive scale in the public school systems of Dayton and Columbus, Ohio (*Columbus Board of Education* v. *Penick,* 443 U.S. 449; *Dayton Board of Education* v. *Brinkman,* 443 U.S. 526). Where schools in a district were largely segregated by race in 1954—not necessarily by law or even by school-board policy such as in the way attendance zones were drawn—and where racially segregated schools persist, the presumption now is that the schools are segregated intentionally. The burden of proof shifts to the school board to explain that it is not responsible for the existing segregation. To be avoided are ''racially identifiable schools''—schools heavily of one race and not reflective of the racial composition of the district. For single school districts, therefore, *Penick* and *Brinkman* almost entirely erase the distinction between *de jure* and *de facto.*

Justice Powell—long ago a member of the school board in Richmond, Virginia—penned a harsh dissent. The Court, he concluded, had gone too far in imposing its ideas of the socially desirable on the nation.

There are unintegrated schools in every major urban area in the country that contains a substantial minority population. This condition results primarily from familiar segregated housing patterns, which—in turn—are caused by social, economic, and demographic forces for which no school board is responsible. . . .

Holding the school boards of these two cities responsible for *all* of the segregation in the Dayton and Columbus systems and prescribing fixed racial ratios in every school as the constitutionally required remedy necessarily implies a belief that the same school boards—under court supervision—will be capable of bringing about and maintaining the desired racial balance in each of these schools. The experience in city after city demonstrates that this is an illusion. The progress of resegregation, stimulated by resentment against judicial coercion and concern as to the effect of court supervision of education, will follow today's decisions as surely as it has in other cities subjected to similar sweeping decrees. . . .

Nor will this resegregation be the only negative effect of court-coerced integration on minority children. Public schools depend on community support for their effectiveness. When substantial elements of the community are driven to abandon these schools, their quality tends to decline, sometimes markedly. Members of minority groups, who have relied especially on education as a means of advancing themselves, also are likely to react to this decline in quality by removing their children from public schools. As a result, public school enrollment increasingly will become limited to children from families that either lack the resources to choose alternatives or are indifferent to the quality of education. The net effect is an overall deterioration in public education. . . .

The time has come for a thoughtful re-examination of the proper limits of the role of courts in confronting the intractable problems of public education in our complex society. . . .

Courts are the branch least competent to provide long-range solutions acceptable to the public and most conducive to achieving both diversity in the classroom and quality education. . . .

May a state simply abandon a formerly segregated function or activity, rather than comply with judicial orders eliminating discrimination? In a 1964 case, *Griffin* v. *School Board* (377 U.S. 218), the Supreme Court said "no," invalidating the closing of public schools by a Virginia county, and stressing the continuing state involvement in the "private" institutions for whites only that replaced the public schools. Here the ban on segregation was circumvented by grants of $100 per child and property tax credits to parents contributing to the "private" schools. In 1971, however, the Burger Court, speaking through Justice Black, rejected the argument that closing public swimming pools to avoid desegregation violated equal protection (*Palmer* v. *Thompson,* 403 U.S. 217: 1971). The motives of the Jackson, Mississippi, city council were not subject to scrutiny, according to the majority, and the city's explanation that money would be saved and conflicts avoided by the pool closings was plausible.

Long before the "separate but equal" formula was invented, discrimination against blacks took other forms. Where a state law expressly excluded blacks from jury service, the law was, of course, invalid (*Strauder* v. *West Virginia,* 100 U.S. 303: 1880). Realizing that a less flagrant method had to be employed, state officials began to exclude blacks from jury service by the simple step of refraining from placing their names on the list from which jurors were selected. After many years had elapsed, the Supreme Court adopted the policy of allowing defendants in state criminal trials to prove that discriminatory administration of jury laws explained the absence of black jurors (*Norris* v. *Alabama*, 294 U.S. 587: 1935; *Patterson* v. *Alabama*, 294 U.S. 600: 1935).

Yet, in *Swain* v. *Alabama* (380 U.S. 202: 1965), the fact that no blacks had served on a trial jury in over a decade was deemed insufficient to prove discrimination. The availability of numerous peremptory challenges under the Alabama system allowed prosecution and defense counsel to eliminate those blacks whose names were on the jury list. And the Justices took a similar position in another ruling involving discrimination in the selection of juries.

Carter v. *Jury Commission of Greene County* (396 U.S. 320: 1970) held 7 to 1 that although Alabama's jury selection law allowed few blacks to sit on grand juries, the statute was not invalid on its face, nor was there a showing of discrimination by juries composed solely of whites. In *Turner* v. *Fouche* (396 U.S. 346: 1970), however, the Court ruled unanimously that where an overwhelming percentage of blacks was disqualified for jury duty as not "upright" and "intelligent," a prima facie case of discrimination was established.

More involved is discrimination in voting. After the Civil War, national legislation implementing the Fourteenth Amendment was invoked successfully to protect black efforts to vote in congressional elections (*United States* v. *Cruikshank*, 92 U.S. 542: 1876; *Ex parte Yarbrough*, 110 U.S. 651: 1884). In *Guinn* v. *United States* (238 U.S. 347: 1915) the Court invalidated state efforts to use a "grandfather clause," exempting from a literacy test for voting all persons and their lineal descendants who had voted on or before January 1, 1866. These decisions were not, however, disastrous to states intent on disfranchising blacks. For one thing, the Supreme Court held in *Newberry* v. *United States* (256 U.S. 232: 1921) that primaries were not "elections" in the constitutional sense; clearly if blacks could be excluded from participation in primaries in one-party states, their political influence would be destroyed. Nevertheless, the equal protection clause was successfully invoked both against a state law forbidding black participation in the Texas Democratic Party primary (*Nixon* v. *Herndon*, 273 U.S. 536: 1927) and against a similar resolution by the Democratic State Executive Committee acting under authority of statute (*Nixon* v. *Condon*, 286 U.S. 73: 1932). But in *Grovey* v. *Townsend* (295 U.S. 45: 1935) a resolution forbidding black participation adopted by the state convention of the Democratic Party was held to be private action, and therefore not within the protective range of "equal protection."

The story was not, however, to end on this note. In 1941 the Court held that the right to vote in a primary election in a one-party state, in this instance Louisiana, where the primary was a step in the election of members of Congress, was a right or privilege secured by the Constitution, since the actions at the primary were officially accepted by the state. Hence, the failure of state officials, acting under "color" of state law, to count ballots properly was held a violation of the provision of the United States Criminal Code that prohibited such "state" action (*United States* v. *Classic*, 313 U.S. 299). In *Smith* v. *Allwright* the Court overruled *Grovey* v. *Townsend* and held that the right to vote guaranteed by the Fifteenth Amendment applied to primaries as well as general elections. Later efforts by Texas to evade the principle of that case by accepting the candidates of the Jaybird party, a Democratic political organization that conducted an unofficial primary in which blacks could not vote, were also held invalid (*Terry* v. *Adams*, 345 U.S. 461: 1953).

Yet the hearings and reports of the United States Commission on Civil Rights, established by the Civil Rights Act of 1957, showed that voting laws in several states were still administered to prevent blacks from voting. Where an applicant for registration was required to demonstrate his understanding of the Constitution of the United States and of the state, blacks were given difficult questions, the answers to which were rarely considered satisfactory. Technical mistakes in filling out forms brought about rejection of black applications. Peculiar working hours of registrars and excruciating slowness in handling applications were other characteristic ways, apart from violence or the threat of violence, of preventing black voting. The Civil Rights Act of 1960, like that of 1957, was designed to protect the right to vote, and authorized the attorney general to initiate actions against local officials who interfered with voting rights. But many of those same factors that thwarted school desegregation operated to limit black voting, and discriminatory administrative practices at the state level showed no signs of abating under continued community opposition.

Black organizations and their white allies became increasingly aware of the hitherto undeveloped potentialities of the black vote in the South. In 1961 only one in four eligible voters was registered. Further measures were therefore sought to achieve a dramatic increase in electoral strength. Adoption of the Twenty-fourth Amendment (1964) prohibiting use of a poll tax in federal elections was a notable success. The poll tax as a requirement in state elections was invalidated in *Harper* v. *Virginia Board of Elections* (383 U.S. 663: 1966). The Court emphasized the economic discrimination in the $1.50 tax requisite for voting, not racial discrimination. "To introduce wealth or payment of a fee," Justice Douglas wrote for the majority, "as a measure of a voter's qualifications is to introduce a capricious or irrelevant factor. The degree of discrimination is irrelevant." Almost 30 years earlier the Court had upheld the tax against constitutional attack (*Breedlove* v. *Suttles,* 302 U.S. 277: 1937).

Of great significance in increasing voter registration and participation was the Voting Rights Act of 1965. It barred literacy and other tests for voting, created new penalties for acts that prevented voting, and directed the Department of Justice to begin suits challenging state poll taxes. By so doing, this act sought to prevent a recurrence of the 1964 presidential election debacle, when less than 50 percent of potentially eligible voters had actually voted. In 1966 about half of the eligible blacks in the southern states were registered, an increase of 1,200,000 since 1960.

The 1965 act was unsuccessfully challenged in *South Carolina* v. *Katzenbach* (383 U.S. 301: 1966). Justice Black, dissenting in part, objected to the provision requiring the submission to the Attorney General of the United States or the Federal District Court for the District of Columbia of any state constitutional amendment or statutory enactment pertaining to voting. Federal courts should accept only justiciable controversies, Black argued, and the alternative appeal to the Attorney General violated established federal principles.

In *White* v. *Regester* (412 U.S. 755: 1973), the Court sustained a claim that multimember legislative districts unconstitutionally diluted the voting strength of a discrete group. In this case from Texas, Mexican-Americans argued successfully that the processes leading to nomination and election were "not equally open to participation." *Connor* v. *Johnson* (402 U.S. 690: 1971) had already stated the Justices' preference for single-member districts. But the path to set aside local political practice is steep, for in *Mobile* v. *Bolden* (446 U.S. 55: 1980) a badly divided majority of six overturned district and appeals court judgments that an at-large voting scheme in Mobile, Alabama, discriminated against blacks in violation of the Fourteenth and Fifteenth Amendments. A majority of the Justices seemed to coalesce around the position that plaintiffs bore the burden of demonstrating how a particular plan—in this case a three-member city commission—was the product of racially discriminatory intent. Division occurred too on the weight to be given racially disparate *impact* as a factor in determining *intent*. Eschewing "motivational analysis," Justice Marshall argued in dissent that proving discriminatory intent was not even necessary. "Our vote-dilution decisions . . . recognize a substantive constitutional right to participate on an equal basis in the electoral process that cannot be denied or diminished for any reason, racial or otherwise, lacking quite substantial justification. . . . The vote-dilution doctrine can logically apply only to groups whose electoral discreteness and insularity allow dominant political factions to ignore them."

However, where litigation is begun under the Voting Rights Act of 1965, six members of the Court, led by Justice Marshall, have ruled that a racially discriminatory effect, without reference to intent, is within the reach of Congress to outlaw (*City of Rome* v. *United States,* 446 U.S. 156: 1980).

Just as laws restricting the right to vote are readily challenged, so are laws whose import is to prohibit persons from residing in certain areas because of race or color (*Buchanan* v. *Warley,* 245 U.S. 60: 1917). The way around this difficulty was to rely on widespread use of restrictive covenants in property deeds by which several owners promised not to sell to nonwhites, with subsequent purchasers similarly bound by the restrictive provision. In 1948, after several decades of use of these covenants, the Supreme Court in *Shelley* v. *Kraemer* severely weakened their legal importance by holding that state courts could not issue orders enforcing such covenants against a property owner who decided not to be bound by the agreement. State court action was "state action" of a kind prohibited by the equal protection clause.

[margin note: As long as states don't act]

Nonetheless, it was assumed that one of the parties to a restrictive covenant agreement might sue another party who had breached the contract and recover damages, as in the case of other broken contracts. In a potentially far-reaching decision, the Supreme Court held that a white man who had sold restricted property to a black man could defend his action by citing the discrimination against black purchasers and by claiming that a state court judgment for damages would constitute state action in the same legal sense as an order for specific enforcement of a restrictive covenant (*Barrows* v. *Jackson,* 346 U.S. 249: 1953). As in the Shelley case, the Court made it clear that private property owners were free to sign and adhere voluntarily to restrictive covenants. But when they sought to use state courts to implement these contracts, "state action" of a nature forbidden by the Fourteenth Amendment was involved.

A 1961 case, *Burton* v. *Wilmington Parking Authority* (365 U.S. 715), shows how a particular relationship between the state and a private party may render the latter's discriminatory policies "state action" of a kind forbidden by the equal protection clause. Burton, a black, was denied service in a privately owned coffee shop that leased space in a building operated by the Wilmington, Delaware, Parking Authority, a state agency. The Supreme Court upheld Burton's claim of discrimination, emphasizing the conditions of the lease, which made operation of the restaurant an integral part of the state-owned facility. There were three dissents and one concurrence on a wholly different ground, thus limiting somewhat the value of the decision as precedent.

Although the nexus between state and private action was clear in *Burton,* a series of cases arising from the inception of more militant civil rights action posed more difficult questions. Beginning in early 1960, nonviolent "sit-ins" and various other "ins" took place in privately owned stores, lunch counters, movies and other enterprises, as well as in public places. When private property was the target, the owners would demand arrest for breach of peace, trespass, or similar offense, or local officials would make the arrests on their own initiative. The constitutional questions posed by these demonstrations against refusal of admission or of service were twofold: (1) Was state discriminatory action involved to such a degree as to allow invocation of the equal protection clause? (2) If private actions were clearly divorced from state action (apart from the arrest and trial), did state action supportive of discrimination in the specific private enterprise deny equal protection? At no time was it seriously urged that an arrest and prosecution resulting from decisions of homeowners or private clubs and associations to exclude individuals on racial grounds constituted discriminatory state action, though clearly, such action might conceivably be so construed.

The first set of cases, *Garner* v. *Louisiana* (368 U.S. 157: 1961), involved defendants who "sat in" segregated lunch counters after being refused service and were arrested for "disturbing the peace." The Court avoided the broader constitutional issue by holding that there was no evidentiary support for the convictions under the Louisiana statute since the defendants had been peaceful and orderly. Justice Douglas, concurring, thought that since the privately owned eating establishments operated under public licenses their facilities were public, and hence, their discriminatory action, enforced by state action, denied equal protection.

Several other sit-in cases involving criminal trespass convictions were decided in 1963. In one, a city ordinance required separation of the races in restaurants (*Peterson* v. *Greenville*, 373 U.S. 244: 1963). In another, announcements by the New Orleans Superintendent of Police and Mayor forbidding sit-ins or efforts to obtain desegregated service were treated as the equivalent of a city ordinance (*Lombard* v. *Louisiana*, 373 U.S. 267: 1963). *Bell* v. *Maryland* (378 U.S. 226: 1964) presented the issue of whether a restaurant owner's policy of not serving blacks, in the apparent absence of state policy, justified arrests and convictions of sit-in defendants. The Court was "saved" by the fortuitous enactment of city and state public accommodations laws shortly thereafter, which afforded a ground for remanding the case to the state court. Six members of the court chose, however, to go on record on the merits of the case. Justices Goldberg, Douglas, and Chief Justice Warren affirmed the proposition that the Civil War Amendments by their own force guaranteed equal access to places of public accommodation. In a separate opinion, Justice Douglas reiterated his thesis that in law a place of public accommodation is not "private" in the same sense as a private residence. In a strong dissent, Justice Black, joined by Justices Harlan and White, asserted that the Constitution itself did not bar a discriminatory policy in a privately owned restaurant. The Court's decision in *Shelley* v. *Kraemer* was distinguished by citing federal statutes of post-Civil War vintage which made the right to buy and sell land a federal right. In the absence of congressional legislation, Black argued, the states might use their criminal trespass laws to protect a private entrepreneur's decision to operate a segregated business.

Having moved close to a final resolution of the private-state action issue in 1963, the Court would certainly have been confronted with a sit-in case devoid of distracting features within the next term or two, had not Congress intervened. The Civil Rights Act of 1964 in Public Accommodations Title II outlawed discrimination in hotels, restaurants, theaters, gas stations, and other public accommodations affecting interstate commerce. The statutory coverage was intended to be pervasive since "affect commerce" was defined to include both establishments serving interstate travelers and those serving or selling products that had "moved" in interstate commerce. Though Congress had also invoked its powers to enforce the Fourteenth and Fifteenth Amendments as justification for this and other provisions of the 1964 Act, the Supreme Court relied on the power to regulate interstate commerce in upholding the application of the Public Accommodations Title II to a Georgia motel that catered to interstate travelers (*Heart of Atlanta Motel* v. *United States*) and to a Birmingham, Alabama, restaurant which annually used about $70,000 worth of food which had moved in interstate commerce (*Katzenbach* v. *McClung*). In view of this extended statutory coverage, discrimination in public accommodations became clearly unlawful, and neither public officials nor owners of affected enterprises can justify discrimination based on race or color. By a 5-to-4 vote the Court decided that state sit-in convictions that occurred before enactment of the 1964 Civil Rights Act were abrogated (*Hamm* v. *City of Rock Hill*, 379 U.S. 306: 1964).

In 1968, Congress enacted a "Fair Housing" title, part of a broad Civil Rights Act, outlawing discrimination in the sale or rental of federally owned or assisted housing, but excluding single-family dwellings sold by an owner. In the same year, the Supreme Court discovered an alternative way of barring private discrimination in housing, based on an act of 1866. The crucial section of that act read: "All citizens of the United States shall have the same right, in every State and Territory, as is enjoyed by white citizens thereof to inherit, purchase, lease, sell, hold and convey real and personal property." In *Jones* v. *Mayer* (392 U.S. 409) the Court upheld the right of a black complainant to sue a white housing development company for refusing to sell him a house. The lower federal courts had assumed that the 1866 statute, like those based on the Fourteenth Amendment, outlawed only state-required or authorized discrimination, but the Supreme Court, relying on the Thirteenth Amendment, found it applicable to all forms of discrimination in housing, public or private.

For a majority of six (Harlan and White dissenting), Justice Stewart ruled: "The Thirteenth Amendment includes freedom to buy whatever a white man can buy, the right to live wherever a white man can live."

The potency of the Thirteenth Amendment, which does not present a state action problem, was shown by a 1976 decision, *Runyan* v. *McCrary* (427 U.S. 160). Here *Jones* v. *Mayer,* upholding the right to purchase property free from discrimination, was the precedent for protecting the contractual rights of black parents against commercially operated, nonsectarian private schools that refused admission to black applicants solely on grounds of race. Justice Stewart for the Court rejected arguments based on the right of association, parental rights, and the right to privacy and upheld congressional power to enforce the Thirteenth Amendment.

"The majority's belated discovery of a congressional purpose," dissenting Justice White observed somewhat derisively, "which escaped this Court only a decade after the statute was passed and which escaped all other federal courts for almost a hundred years is singularly unpersuasive."

The holding in *Jones* was extended in *Sullivan* v. *Little Hunting Park* (396 U.S. 229: 1969), in which the Court ruled that suburban swimming clubs must admit blacks who had rented residences whose occupants were supposed to have club privileges. Though the judicial tendency has been to resolve doubts against racial barriers of clubs, social clubs are still free to close their doors to anyone, for reasons of race, religion, or otherwise. In time, however, even social organizations may run afoul of the Fourteenth Amendment's injunction against the state's denial of equal protection—that is, against discrimination on racial, religious, or other invidious grounds.

During the last 25 years, the Court has expanded the state action principle so that if a state becomes so "entwined" with private affairs that the action of private citizens becomes tantamount to "state action," the provisions of the Fourteenth Amendment then become applicable. The issue in all these cases involves conflict between two constitutionally recognized values—the right of privacy and of equal protection of the law. *Moose Lodge* v. *Irvis* asked the Justices to consider this aspect of the problem. Did the Loyal Order of Moose forfeit its liquor license when it refused to admit K. Leroy Irvis, black majority leader of the Pennsylvania House of Representatives, as a guest of one of its members? Irvis conceded that Moose members have a constitutional right of privacy and association, permitting them to exclude him from their club. But, he argued, their club cannot hold a liquor license if they do. Allowing the club to do so would amount to state licensing of racial discrimination, in violation of the Fourteenth Amendment. In this 1972 ruling, Rehnquist expressed the views of six Justices; Brennan, Douglas, and Marshall dissented.

Moose Lodge v. *Irvis* is important, less for the result than as a portent of the kind of arguments that may be made in the future, against private organizations that possess state-granted privileges and choose to follow racially discriminatory policies.

Perhaps the high-water mark in thwarting state action in support of private discrimination was *Reitman* v. *Mulkey* (387 U.S. 369: 1967). Following a number of California legislative enactments prohibiting discrimination in the sale or rental of private property, Proposition 14, forbidding the state to deny the right of any person to sell or rent his property to anyone at his absolute discretion, was adopted by a two-to-one majority of the voters. Agreeing with the California Supreme Court, a five-man majority speaking through Justice White concluded that Proposition 14 was "intended to authorize, and does authorize, racial discrimination in the housing market." To the dissenters, California, like many other states, had simply adopted a stance which allowed private discrimination.

PROTECTION OF ALIENS

Broad construction of the equal protection clause, so as to include "any person," was evident in *Truax* v. *Raich* (239 U.S. 33: 1915), in which the Court invalidated, as a denial of equal protection, an Arizona law that discriminated against aliens in employment by requiring that at least 80 percent of any firm's employees be United States citizens. A similar result was obtained in *Yick Wo* v. *Hopkins*, where Chinese laundrymen were the victims of discriminatory administration of a local ordinance requiring permits for all wooden buildings used for laundry purposes. However, the Supreme Court has often upheld state laws denying to aliens the privilege of fishing (*Bayside Fish Flour Co.* v. *Gentry*, 297 U.S. 422: 1936), hunting (*Patsone* v. *Pennsylvania*, 232 U.S. 138: 1914), or owning land within state boundaries (*Terrace* v. *Thompson*, 263 U.S. 197: 1923). These decisions rest primarily on the proprietary relationship between the state and all forms of real property and natural life within its jurisdiction. They may be distinguished from the Raich case, where the "right to employment" was considered fundamental. The same distinction may be used to explain *Takahashi* v. *Fish and Game Commission* (334 U.S. 410: 1948), where the Court held that anyone admitted to this country, even though ineligible for citizenship, could not be denied a commercial fishing license because of such ineligibility. Equal protection, said the Court, required that anyone admitted to a state must have the right to work.

It may well be that the Court is prepared to take a less generous attitude toward state laws discriminating against aliens, even where the state has claimed to act in its capacity as sovereign. *Oyama* v. *California* (332 U.S. 633: 1948), invalidated a provision of the California Alien Land Law that made payment by an alien as a consideration for the transfer of land to a third person *prima facie* evidence of intent to evade the statute. Four Justices held the Alien Land Law unconstitutional.

It appears that the absence of the equal protection clause in the Bill of Rights was helpful to the United States government in defending the World War II Japanese exclusion order. "The Fifth Amendment," Chief Justice Stone commented in *Hirabayashi* v. *United States* (320 U.S. 81: 1943), "contains no equal protection clause and it restrains only such discriminatory legislation by Congress as amounts to a denial of due process." In contrast, *Bolling* v. *Sharpe* (347 U.S. 497: 1954), the school segregation case from the District of Columbia, shifted much of the equal protection clause from the Fourteenth Amendment into the due process clause of the Fifth. Wrote Chief Justice Warren: "In view of our decision that the Constitution prohibits the states from maintaining racially segregated public schools, it would be unthinkable that the same Constitution would impose a lesser duty on the Federal Government."

As the Supreme Court began to shape the so-called "new" equal protection, alienage became a suspect category, placing on the state the burden of showing a "compelling interest" to justify the classification. In the 1971 case of *Graham* v. *Richardson* (403 U.S. 365) the Court held that welfare benefits could not be denied resident aliens. The concentration of funds for the benefit of citizens was held insufficient, in light of the Fourteenth Amendment's protection of "persons," which had previously been held to include resident aliens. (*Yick Wo* v. *Hopkins*)

In the same vein, *Sugarman* v. *Dougall* (413 U.S. 634: 1973) invalidated a New York law barring aliens from jobs in the competitive Civil Service. *Examining Board* v. *Flores* (426 U.S. 572: 1976) held invalid a Puerto Rican law permitting only American citizens to practice as civil engineers. Although indicating that Congress might, if it clearly so provided, prefer United States citizens for certain governmental jobs, it had not done so and in *Hampton* v. *Mow Sun Wong* (426 U.S. 88: 1976) the Court rejected a United States Civil Service regulation barring resident aliens from employment in the federal competitive Civil Service. A Connecticut law requiring United States citizenship for admission to the practice of law was held invalid in *In re Griffiths* (413 U.S. 717: 1973). Justice Powell stressed that alienage was a suspect classification subject to "close judicial scrutiny." Chief Justice Burger and Justice Rehnquist dissented, insisting that there was a rational basis for restricting the practice of law to citizens, and attacking the concept that alienage was a suspect classification for all purposes. By contrast, *Foley* v. *Connelie* (435 U.S. 291: 1978), with three dissenting votes, upheld against an equal protection challenge the New York statute limiting appointment of members of the state police force to United States citizens. The standard was that citizenship may be a relevant qualification for fulfilling "important nonelective executive, legislative, and judicial positions held by officers who participate directly in the formulation, execution, or review of broad public policy." Five Justices the following term were persuaded that *Foley* was controlling with respect to teachers in public schools (*Ambach* v. *Norwick*, 441 U.S. 68: 1979). Justice Powell admitted in *Ambach* that "decisions of this Court regarding the permissibility of statutory classifications involving aliens have not formed an unwavering line over the years."

Since virtually all legislation involves classification, it is not surprising that the equal protection clause should be invoked frequently by those challenging state acts under the police power. For a long time the Court rather generously deferred to the legislative judgment on classification. What was needed was a "rational basis" or at least a basis which seemed rational to the Justices. To be avoided was any classification that seemed "arbitrary." Even a statute that provided for sterilization of mental defectives was upheld (*Buck* v. *Bell*, 274 U.S. 200: 1927). Similar treatment of those convicted three times of offenses involving "moral turpitude" was invalidated, however, because the Court considered classification of such offenses as plainly arbitrary (*Skinner* v. *Oklahoma*, 316 U.S. 535: 1942).

In the late 1960s "equal protection" became a far-reaching tool for judicial protection of "fundamental" rights not specified in the Constitution. To indicate the change many writers refer to the "old" and "new" equal protection.

The "new" equal protection can be seen in numerous decisions. In *Levy* v. *Louisiana* (391 U.S. 68: 1968) the Court invalidated a state court decision which had denied illegitimate children recovery of damages for the wrongful death of their mother. The state court had dismissed the suit, holding that "child" under the statute involved meant "legitimate child," the denial to illegitimate children of the right to recover being "based on morals and general welfare because it discourages bringing children into the world out of wedlock." Justice Douglas, writing for the majority, conceded that "In applying the Equal Protection Clause to social and economic legislation, we give great latitude to the Legislature in making classifications." However, he continued, "The rights asserted here involve the intimate, familial relationship between a child and his own mother. When the child's claim of damage for loss of his mother is in issue, why, in terms of 'equal protection,' should the wrongdoers go free merely because the child is illegitimate?" Here, as in many other cases, Justice Harlan protested against a decision, inspired, as he saw it, by political theory—equalitarianism—cutting "deeply into the fabric of our federalism." But in *Labine* v. *Vincent* (401 U.S. 532: 1971), Justice Black led a majority of five in sustaining a Louisiana statutory scheme for intestate succession which barred an illegitimate child from sharing in her father's estate.

Deference to the state was also reflected in *Dandridge* v. *Williams* (397 U.S. 471: 1970), with the Court ruling 5 to 3 that Maryland's administrative regulation placing a $250 a month limit on AFDC grants, regardless of family size, did not violate the Fourteenth Amendment's equal protection clause. For the Court, Justice Stewart ruled that since Maryland's classification of welfare recipients has some reasonable basis, it does not offend the Constitution for want of mathematical nicety and results in some inequalities. Chief Justice Burger joined the majority. Justices Black, Brennan, and Marshall dissented. Marshall deplored "the Court's sweeping refusal to accord the Equal Protection clause any role in this entire area of the law"—that relating to the rights of the poor.

But in *Dunn* v. *Blumstein* (405 U.S. 330: 1972) the Court invalidated durational residence requirements for voting. Although the one-year state residence, three-months county residence provision was consistent with other state rules on this subject, the law curtailed fundamental rights. Voting and travel were restricted by the law, and thus, the state must demonstrate a compelling state interest. In addition, the Court held unanimously (*Williams* v. *Illinois*, 399 U.S. 235: 1970) that a state may not imprison an indigent person beyond the maximum sentence imposed by statute solely because of his inability to pay a fine or court costs. And in 1971 the Court set aside imprisonment of an indigent for non-payment of fines for traffic violations (*Tate* v. *Short,* 401 U.S. 395).

Even more illustrative of the "new" equal protection is the Court's decision in *Shapiro* v. *Thompson* (394 U.S. 618: 1969). Held invalid were the states' one-year residence requirements imposed on all persons seeking welfare assistance. Justice Brennan for the majority spoke of the "right" of freedom to travel throughout the states: "Thus, the purpose of deterring the in-migration of indigents cannot serve as justification for the classification created by the one-year waiting period, since that purpose is constitutionally impermissible. Because the classification here touches on the fundamental right of interstate movement, its constitutionality must be judged by the stricter standard—whether it promotes a compelling state interest. Under this standard, the waiting period requirement clearly violates the Equal Protection Clause."

In dissent, Justice Harlan blasted the "new" equal protection. While concluding that in this instance a "fundamental" right was involved, he could not agree that "the burden imposed by residence requirements upon ability to travel outweighs the governmental interests in their continued employment. . . . Today's decision, it seems to me, reflects to an unusual degree the current notion that this Court possesses a peculiar wisdom all its own whose capacity to lead this Nation out of its present troubles is contained only by the limits of judicial ingenuity in contriving new constitutional principles to meet each problem as it arises."

In *San Antonio Independent School District* v. *Rodriguez* (411 U.S. 1: 1972) Justice Powell spelled out the criteria of the new equal protection. When government action creates a class based on suspect categories—race, nationality, alienage—or abridges a fundamental right, as in *Shapiro,* the regulation is subject to "strict scrutiny," placing on government the burden of demonstrating a "compelling state interest." Education, the Court ruled, is "not among the rights afforded explicit protection under our Constitution." It does not fall within any of the categories calling for strict judicial scrutiny. Accordingly, the Texas local property tax funding law for public schools does not deny equal protection to school children residing in districts with a low property tax base. The majority agreed that the tax system needed reform, but this "must come from the law makers and from the pressures of those who elect them." The "wisdom of traditional limitations on this Court's functions" was recognized and applauded.

In *Rodriguez* the Court might have held that education is a fundamental right and poverty a suspect classification. Either finding would have placed a burden on the state to show a compelling interest. Instead, the Court rejected both possible grounds in upholding the Texas scheme for financing public schools which, admittedly, permitted substantial disparities in expenditures per pupil between districts.

Four Justices—Brennan, Douglas, Marshall, and White—dissented. Justice Marshall deplored Justice Powell's "two neat categories which dictate the appropriate standard of judicial strict scrutiny or mere rationality." For Justice Marshall the necessary effect of the Texas local property tax was "to favor property rich districts, and to disfavor property poor ones." Nor did the dissenters take seriously the Court's elevated self-restraint pose: "One would think that the majority would heed its own fervent affirmation of judicial self-restraint before undertaking the complex task of determining at large what level of education is constitutionally feasible."

Under the "old" equal protection the court scrutinized statutory classifications and imposed a minimal burden of showing "a rational basis" to justify legislation. "New" equal protection, in contrast, imposes a heavy burden on the state when a fundamental right or suspect category is involved. And when the Court chose to invoke this test, which requires the state to show "compelling state interest," it led to invalidation of the legislation under attack.

Justice Marshall's dissent in *Massachusetts Board of Retirement* v. *Murgia* is instructive in explaining application of the equal protection clause and the difficulties various kinds of scrutiny present. In this case, the Court examined a Massachusetts law which forced retirement of state policemen at age 50. A three-judge federal district court set the act aside as lacking "a rational basis in furthering any substantial state interest," but in a *per curiam* opinion the Supreme Court held otherwise (427 U.S. 307: 1976).

> Although the Court outwardly adheres to the two-tier model, it has apparently lost interest in recognizing further "fundamental" rights and "suspect" classes. . . . In my view, this result is the natural consequence of the limitations of the Court's traditional equal protection analysis. If a statute invades a "fundamental" right or discriminates against a "suspect" class, it is subject to strict scrutiny. If a statute is subject to strict scrutiny, the statute always, or nearly always. . . . is struck down. Quite obviously, the only critical decision is whether strict scrutiny should be invoked at all. It should be no surprise, then, that the Court is hesitant to expand the number of categories of rights and classes subject to strict scrutiny, when each expansion involves the invalidation of virtually every classification bearing upon a newly covered category.
>
> But however understandable the Court's hesitancy to invoke strict scrutiny, all remaining legislation should not drop into the bottom tier, and be measured by the mere rationality test. For that test, too, when applied as articulated, leaves little doubt about the outcome; the challenged legislation is always upheld. . . . It cannot be gainsaid that there remain rights, not now classified as "fundamental," that remain vital to the flourishing of a free society, and classes, not now classified as "suspect," that are unfairly burdened by invidious discrimination unrelated to the individual worth of their members. Whatever we call these rights and classes, we simply cannot forgo all judicial protection against discriminatory legislation bearing upon them, but for the rare instances when the legislative choice can be termed "wholly irrelevant" to the legislative goal. . . .
>
> Of course, the Court is quite right in suggesting that distinctions exist between the elderly and traditional suspect classes such as Negroes, and between the elderly and "quasisuspect" classes such as women or illegitimates. . . . The advantage of a flexible equal protection standard, however, is that it can readily accommodate such variables. The elderly are undoubtedly discriminated against, and when legislation denies them an important benefit— employment—I conclude that to sustain the legislation appellants must show a reasonably substantial interest and a scheme reasonably closely tailored to achieving that interest. . . .
>
> [Marshall, J., dissenting.]

In effect Marshall is calling for closer judicial study of almost all classifications in the face of the reluctance exhibited by the current majority to expand on the list of suspect categories.

Equal protection cases involving women have yielded an intermediate form of review, as Marshall's dissent in *Murgia* suggests. In *Reed* v. *Reed* (404 U.S. 71: 1971), while refusing to find sex a suspect classification, the Court unanimously invalidated an Idaho law preferring men to women in the court selection of an administrator of a decedent's estate. In fact the kind of analysis Marshall proposed in *Murgia* is not very different from the analysis Burger undertook in *Reed*. Only the labels are different. In 1973, in *Frontiero* v. *Richardson* (411 U.S. 677), only four justices considered sex a suspect category. Nevertheless, concurring Justices, invoking "rationality" of the statute, as in *Reed*, reached the same result.

Justice Brennan's opinion in *Craig* v. *Boren* (429 U.S. 190: 1976) spelled out the level of scrutiny the Court may in fact be giving sex-based distinctions. In this case, an Oklahoma statute prohibiting the sale of 3.2 percent beer to males under 21 and to females under 18 was found to fall short constitutionally. "[T]o withstand constitutional challenge, previous cases establish that classifications by gender must serve important governmental objectives and must be substantially related to achievement of those objectives." In other words, the purpose of the statute must be valid, and the Justices must be convinced that another law treating the sexes equally would not do as well.

These heightened concerns with the rationality of classification, a more rigorous examination than the old equal protection but less restrictive of the states than the "new," is capable of cutting both ways. Some state laws have fallen. *Taylor* v. *Louisiana* (419 U.S. 522: 1975) held invalid a state jury selection system under which a woman would not be called for jury duty unless she chose to register. In *Weinberger* v. *Wiesenfeld* (420 U.S. 636: 1975) the Justices set aside a provision of the Social Security Act that gave greater benefits to the survivors of a man than to survivors of a woman. Finally, in *Stanton* v. *Stanton* (421 U.S. 7: 1975) a Utah child support provision that differentiated between the ages for male and female children requiring support, was held defective "under any test— compelling state interest, or rational basis or something in between. . . ."

Yet the Court rejected an attack by a male naval officer of a promotion system which allowed women a longer tenure when passed over for promotion (*Schlesinger* v. *Ballard*, 419 U.S. 498: 1975). *Geduldig* v. *Aiello* (417 U.S. 484: 1974) upheld a California state disability benefits insurance plan excluding benefits for normal pregnancy and childbirth. But *City of Los Angeles* v. *Manhart* (435 U.S. 702: 1978) struck down a requirement that females pay 15 percent more each month into a pension fund because of longer life expectancy as a group. Citing *Craig*, a bare majority voided a New York statute which allowed an unwed mother, but not an unwed father, to block their child's adoption by withholding consent (*Caban* v. *Mohammed*, 441 U.S. 380: 1979). Similarly, eight Justices decided that Missouri's workers' compensation law could not make claiming benefits more difficult for widowers than for widows (*Wengler* v. *Druggists Mutual Insurance Co.*, 446 U.S. 142: 1980).

Most recently, a majority of the Court has relied on the fact that sometimes the sexes are not "similarly situated," a term which appeared at least as early as *Reed* v. *Reed*. This conclusion seems to have been partly the basis for *Michael M.* v. *Superior Court of Sonoma County* (49 LW 4273: 1981), which upheld California's statutory rape law against an equal protection attack. Males alone were made criminally liable. Since only the female can become pregnant, the state constitutionally could elect to punish the party to sexual intercourse on whom fewer natural burdens would fall should a pregnancy result. Reliance on the same principle was even more pronounced and important in *Rostker* v. *Goldberg*, reprinted in this chapter. In this case, six Justices expressed considerable deference to Congress and sustained the constitutionality of the Military Selective Service Act, which authorizes the President to require draft registration for males but not females. As Justice Rehnquist maintained for the Court,

The reason women are exempt from registration is not because military needs can be met by drafting men. This is not a case of Congress arbitrarily choosing to burden one of two similarly situated groups, such as would be the case with an all-black or all-white, or an all-Catholic or all-Lutheran, or an all-Republican or all-Democratic registration. Men and women, because of the combat restrictions on women, are simply not similarly situated for purposes of a draft or registration for a draft.

It remains to be seen how this approach will be applied in later cases. Clearly, the Burger Court has adopted a flexible position which allows it to pick and choose freely between claims based on equal protection. Without rejecting the "new" equal protection, it has shaped different tools that leave greater judicial latitude in this rapidly developing area of the law.

AFFIRMATIVE ACTION

As parts of this chapter illustrate, much litigation under the equal protection clause has been aimed at halting segregative practices and other actions deemed harmful to racial minorities. Some of it, especially the school busing cases, has involved remedial steps courts require localities to take in an effort to right past wrongs. The focus in these cases has nonetheless been on what the Constitution *prohibits*.

In a parallel development, various institutions—themselves not necessarily guilty of racial discrimination—have voluntarily established remedial programs. Their efforts are broadly aimed at correcting "societal discrimination." This affirmative action (also termed "reverse discrimination" or "preferential treatment") has been hauled into court as itself being a violation of the Constitution's ban on racial discrimination. So the question becomes one of what the Constitution *permits*. For instance, if a state university makes a special effort to recruit and to admit members of certain racial groups and to apply different criteria in assessing their qualifications, has the equal protection clause been compromised? Opponents of affirmative action argue that such programs are certainly not in the spirit of keeping the Constitution "color-blind." Proponents reply that a cessation of discrimination is not enough. Positive measures are needed, they say, to overcome the residual effects of generations of discrimination. The catch is that jobs, seats in medical school classes, and government contracts are all finite. To give to one means to withhold from someone else. It may also be the case that those "nonminority" individuals who claim to be hurt by affirmative action are in many situations those least able to bear the burden. They are probably also those who have benefited least from the effects of invidious discrimination which do remain. Given the extent of the controversy, it is not surprising that affirmative action has reached the Supreme Court.

By and large, the Court has not spoken unequivocally on this subject. This may be both wise and expected, in view of the divisiveness and complexity of the issue. The outcomes of a series of cases, however, have been generally favorable to affirmative action. A majority of the Justices have found most attempts to aid racial minorities compatible with the Constitution. Those opposed to these policies have yet to be the clear victors in a single case before the Supreme Court.

Two judicial opinions on affirmative action—one in favor and one in opposition—are reprinted in this chapter. They come from two of the cases which have bedeviled the Justices.

In *DeFunis* v. *Odegaard* (416 U.S. 312: 1974), the Court confronted an admissions policy at the University of Washington School of Law which gave special consideration to applicants from certain minority groups even though these applicants as a group did not rate as highly on the standard criteria used for nonminority applicants. DeFunis, the would-be law student, won his case in the trial court which ordered his admission, but lost in the state supreme court. In the United States Supreme Court five Justices ruled that the case was moot since DeFunis was by then in his last year of law school and would be allowed to finish regardless of the outcome of his suit. Justice Douglas, who as Circuit Justice had stayed the decision of the Washington Supreme Court and therefore had kept DeFunis enrolled, thought otherwise. Three others agreed with him on this point. Douglas for himself went on to address the merits of DeFunis's case in a dissent which is reprinted in this chapter.

Mootness was not a factor in Allan Bakke's effort to gain admission to the medical school at the University of California at Davis (*Regents of the University of California* v. *Bakke*, 438 U.S. 265: 1978). Like DeFunis, Bakke faced an explicit use of race as a criterion for some students for admission. The Davis medical school in fact set aside at least 16 of its 100 seats in the entering class for qualifying minority students. Unlike DeFunis, Bakke had won his case before his state's supreme court. Also unlike DeFunis, Bakke and the professional school received an answer from the United States Supreme Court on the merits of the dispute. For those hoping for a clear, forthright, thunderbolt pronouncement, the decision in *Bakke* was a disappointment. Bakke won (and so gained admission to medical school) but so did advocates of affirmative action. These seemingly conflicting results came about because the Court divided into three camps.

Justices Brennan, White, Marshall, and Blackmun found no constitutional violation in the admissions program at Davis. Neither did they see it in conflict with Title VI of the Civil Rights Act of 1964, which outlaws racial discrimination in programs receiving federal funding. The opinion by Justice Marshall is reprinted in this chapter. Four other Justices (Stevens, Burger, Stewart, and Rehnquist) considered the Davis plan a violation of Title VI, and so did not decide the constitutional question. Left was Justice Powell. The Davis plan was flawed, he thought, because race was used in effect as an exclusionary factor. Race, however, could be taken into account, he acknowledged, as an informing factor, especially to achieve racial diversity in the student body for educational reasons. So, combining Powell's conclusion with that of the Brennan group, one finds that race can constitutionally be used in evaluating applications for admission. Combining Powell's view with the position put forth by the Stevens group, the particular plan in question at Davis was unlawful. Significantly, Powell noted the absence in this case "of judicial, legislative, or administrative findings of constitutional or statutory violations. . . . After such findings have been made, the governmental interest in preferring members of the injured groups at the expense of others is substantial, since the legal rights of the victims must be vindicated."

A legislative determination was present in *Fullilove* v. *Klutznick* (448 U.S. 448: 1980), where six Justices found constitutional a statutory requirement that "absent an administrative waiver, 10 percent of the federal funds granted for local public works projects must be used by the state or local grantee to procure services or supplies from businesses owned and controlled by members of statutorily identified minority groups." Finding ample constitutional authority under the spending and commerce powers and the enforcement provision (section 5) of the Fourteenth Amendment, Chief Justice Burger for a plurality was "satisfied that Congress had abundant historical basis from which it could conclude that traditional procurement practices, when applied to minority businesses, could perpetuate the effects of prior discrimination."

It is fundamental that in no organ of government, state or federal, does there repose a more comprehensive remedial power than in the Congress, expressly charged by the Constitution with competence and authority to enforce equal protection guarantees. Congress not only may induce voluntary action to assure compliance with existing federal statutory or constitutional antidiscrimination provisions, but also, where Congress has authority to declare certain conduct unlawful, it may, as here, authorize and induce state action to avoid such conduct.

In a dissenting opinion joined by Justice Rehnquist, Justice Stewart recalled the first Justice Harlan's contention that the Constitution was supposed to be "color-blind." Stewart was sternly critical. "I think today's decision is wrong for the same reason that *Plessy* v. *Ferguson* was wrong. . . ."

Yet Stewart the previous term had been part of a six-Justice majority in *United Steelworkers of America* v. *Weber* (443 U.S. 193: 1979), which upheld the legality of an affirmative-action plan agreed to by a union and a corporation. *Weber* shows that even if the Supreme Court someday were to lose its power of judicial review, statutory interpretation would nonetheless allow the Justices considerable influence on the course of public policy. In this case, the union and a plant in Gramercy, Louisiana, operated by the Kaiser Aluminum & Chemical Corporation entered into a collective bargaining agreement, part of which was designed to increase the number of blacks in craft jobs. While no solid evidence of intentional discrimination in hiring or in admission to craft apprenticeships was part of the record, the Office of Federal Contract Compliance, acting under executive order, had encouraged the union and the company to develop a plan. At stake were federal contracts and therefore jobs and profits. In operation, the plan meant choosing blacks with less seniority over white workers with more. One of the latter was Brian Weber, who thought the plan violated Title VII of the 1964 Civil Rights Act. In part the statute declares: "It shall be an unlawful employment practice for any employer [or] labor organization . . . to discriminate against any individual because of his race, color, religion, sex, or national origin in admission to, or employment in, any program established to provide apprenticeship or other training" (78 Stat. 256).

For the majority of five (neither Powell nor Stevens participated), Justice Brennan reviewed the legislative history of the act. It did not speak precisely to this question, for the simple reason that discrimination against blacks and other minorities was uppermost in the minds of members of Congress when the law was passed fifteen years before. Since the statute was enacted for the purpose of helping minorities, "the natural inference is that Congress chose not to forbid all voluntary race-conscious affirmative action," Brennan concluded.

In a dissent joined by Chief Justice Burger, which was almost three times longer than the majority opinion, Justice Rehnquist took the brethren to task for their supposed misreading of congressional intent and legislative history. "[B]y a *tour de force* reminiscent not of jurists such as Hale, Holmes, and Hughes, but of escape artists such as Houdini, the Court eludes clear statutory language. . . ." While agreeing that "the reality of employment discrimination against Negroes provided the primary impetus for passage of Title VII . . . ," Rehnquist doubted that "Congress intended to leave employers free to discriminate against white persons."

Affirmative action cases will undoubtedly continue to trouble the Court. As the record demonstrates, the Justices do not speak with a single voice. Changes in the personnel of the Court may also work to keep these questions in flux. Yet, the power of precedent is now on the side of those favoring substantial remedial measures.

SELECTED READINGS

DIXON, ROBERT G., "The New Substantive Due Process and the Democratic Ethic: A Prolegomenon," 1976 *Brigham Young University Law Review* 43 (1976).

DORSEN, NORMAN, *Discrimination and Civil Rights.* Boston: Little Brown, 1969.

ELY, JOHN HART, "The Constitutionality of Reverse Discrimination," 41 *University of Chicago Law Review* 723 (1974).

FISS, O. M. "Groups and the Equal Protection Clause," 5 *Philosophy and Public Affairs* 107 (1976)

FRANK, JOHN P., and ROBERT F. MUNRO, "The Original Understanding of Equal Protection of the Laws," 50 *Columbia Law Review* 131 (1950).

GLAZER, NATHAN, *Affirmative Discrimination: Ethnic Inequality in Public Policy.* New York: Basic Books, 1975.

GRAGLIA, L. A., *Disaster by Decree: The Supreme Court Decisions on Race and Schools.* Ithaca: Cornell University Press, 1976.

GUNTHER, GERALD, "In Search of Evolving Doctrine on a Changing Court: A Model for a Newer Equal Protection," 86 *Harvard Law Review* 1 (1972).

HARRIS, ROBERT J., *The Quest for Equality.* Baton Rouge: Louisiana State University Press, 1960.

KARST, KENNETH, "Invidious Discrimination: Justice Douglas and the Return of the Natural Law—Due Process Formula," 16 *UCLA Law Review* 716 (1969).

KITCH, EDMUND W., "The Return of Color-Consciousness to the Constitution: Weber, Dayton and Columbus," 1979 *Supreme Court Review* 1.

KLUGER, RICHARD F. *Simple Justice: The History of Brown v. Board of Education and Black America's Struggle for Equality.* New York: Knopf, 1976.

KONVITZ, MILTON R., *A Century of Civil Rights.* New York: Columbia University Press, 1961.

MICHELMAN, FRANK I., "On Protecting the Poor Through the Fourteenth Amendment," 83 *Harvard Law Review* 71 (1969).

PELTASON, J. W., *Fifty-Eight Lonely Men.* New York: Harcourt, Brace and World, 1961.

RINGLER, SUSAN M., "Sexual Equality: Not for Women Only," 29 *Catholic University Law Review* 427 (1980).

ROSSUM, R. A., "Ameliorative Racial Preference and the Fourteenth Amendment: Some Constitutional Problems," 38 *Journal of Politics* 346 (1976).

STEPHENSON, D. GRIER, JR., "Weber, Affirmative Action, and Restorative Justice," 108 *USA Today* 48 (May 1980).

VOSE, CLEMENT E., *Caucasians Only; The Supreme Court, the NAACP, and the Restrictive Covenant Cases.* Berkeley: University of California Press, 1959.

Civil Rights Cases
109 U.S. 3, 3 S.Ct. 18, 27 L.Ed. 835 (1883)

Five cases involving the Civil Rights Act passed by Congress in 1875 were settled by this decision. The Act, which was intended to implement the Thirteenth and Fourteenth Amendments, made it a misdemeanor to deny any person equal rights and privileges in inns, theaters and amusement places, and transportation facilities, regardless of color or previous conditions of servitude. Penalties for violations were provided.

MR. JUSTICE BRADLEY delivered the opinion of the court. . . .

The essence of the law is, not to declare broadly that all persons shall be entitled to the full and equal enjoyment of the accommodations, advantages, facilities, and privileges of inns, public conveyances, and theatres; but that such enjoyment shall not be subject to any conditions applicable only to citizens of a particular race or color, or who had been in a previous condition of servitude. . . .

Has congress constitutional power to make such a law? Of course, no one will contend that the power to pass it was contained in the Constitution before the adoption of the last three amendments. The power is sought, first, in the Fourteenth Amendment, and the views and arguments of distinguished senators, advanced while the law was under consideration, claiming authority to pass it by virtue of that amendment, are the principal arguments adduced in favor of the power. We have carefully considered those arguments, as was due to the eminent ability of those who put them forward, and have felt, in all its force, the weight of authority which always invests a law that congress deems itself competent to pass. But the responsibility of an independent judgment is now thrown upon this court; and we are bound to exercise it according to the best lights we have.

The first section of the Fourteenth Amendment (which is the one relied on), after declaring who shall be citizens of the United States, and of the several States, is prohibitory in its character, and prohibitory upon the States. It declares that

No state shall make or enforce any law which shall abridge the privileges or immunities of citizens of the United States; nor shall any State deprive any person of life, liberty, or property without due process of law; nor deny to any person within its jurisdiction the equal protection of the laws.

It is State action of a particular character that is prohibited. Individual invasion of individual rights is not the subject matter of the amendment. It has a deeper and broader scope. It nullifies and makes void all State legislation, and State action of every kind, which impairs the privileges and immunities of citizens of the United States, or which injures them in life, liberty or property without due process of law, or which denies to any of them the equal protection of the laws. It not only does this, but, in order that the national will, thus declared, may not be a mere *brutum fulmen,* the last section of the amendment invests Congress with power to enforce it by appropriate legislation. To enforce what? To enforce the prohibition. To adopt appropriate legislation for correcting the effects of such prohibited State laws and State acts, and thus to render them effectually null, void, and innocuous. This is the legislative power conferred upon Congress, and this is the whole of it. It does not invest Congress with power to legislate upon subjects which are within the domain of State legislation; but to provide modes of relief against State legislation, or State action, of the kind referred to. It does not authorize Congress to create a code of municipal law for the regulation of private rights; but to provide modes of redress against the operation of State laws, and the action of State officers, executive or judicial, when these are subversive of the fundamental rights specified in the amendment. Positive rights and privileges are undoubtedly secured by the Fourteenth Amendment; but they are secured by way of prohibition against State laws and State proceedings affecting those rights and privileges, and by power given to Congress to legislate for the purpose of carrying such prohibition into effect: and such legislation must necessarily be predicated upon such supposed State laws or State proceedings, and be directed to the correction of their operation and effect. . . .

. . . Until some State law has been passed, or some State action through its officers or agents has been taken, adverse to the rights of citizens sought to be protected by the Fourteenth Amendment, no legislation of the United States under said amendment nor any proceeding under such legislation, can be called into activity: for the prohibitions of the amendment are against State laws and acts done under State authority. Of course, legislation may, and should be, provided in advance to meet the exigency when it arises; but it should be adapted to the mischief and wrong which the amendment was intended to provide against; and that is, State laws, or State action of some kind, adverse to the rights of the citizen secured by the amendment. Such legislation cannot properly cover the whole domain of rights appertaining to life, liberty and property, defining them and providing for their vindication. That would be to establish a code of municipal law regulative of all private rights between man and man in society. It would be to make Congress take the place of the State legislatures and to supersede them. It is absurd to affirm that, because the rights of life, liberty and property (which include all civil rights that men have), are by the amendment sought to be protected against invasion on the part of the State without due process of law, Congress may therefore provide due process of law for their vindication in every case; and that, because the denial by a State to any persons, of the equal protection of the laws, is prohibited by the amendment, therefore Congress may establish laws for their equal protection. In fine, the legislation which Congress is authorized to adopt in this behalf is not general legislation upon the rights of the citizen, but corrective legislation, that is, such as may be necessary and proper for counteracting such laws as the States may adopt or enforce, and which, by the amendment, they are prohibited from making or enforcing, or such acts and proceedings as the States may commit or take, and which, by the amendment, they are prohibited from committing or taking. It is not necessary for us to state, if we could, what legislation would be proper for Congress to adopt. It is sufficient for us to examine whether the law in question is of that character.

An inspection of the law shows that it makes no reference whatever to any supposed or apprehended violation of the Fourteenth Amendment on the part of the States. It is not predicated on any such view. It proceeds *ex directo* to declare that certain acts committed by individuals shall be deemed offenses, and shall be prosecuted and punished by proceedings in the courts of the United States. It does not profess to be corrective of any constitutional wrong committed by the States; it does not make its operation to depend upon any such wrong committed. It applies equally to cases arising in States which have the justest laws respecting the personal rights of citizens, and whose authorities are ever ready to enforce such laws, as to those which arise in States that may have violated the prohibition of the amendment. In other words, it steps into the domain of local jurisprudence, and lays down rules for the conduct of individuals in society towards each other, and imposes sanctions for the enforcement of those rules, without referring in any manner to any supposed action of the State or its authorities.

If this legislation is appropriate for enforcing the prohibitions of the amendment, it is difficult to see where it is to stop. Why may not Congress with equal show of authority enact a code of laws for the enforcement and vindication of all rights of life, liberty, and property? If it is supposable that the States may deprive persons of life, liberty, and property without due process of law (and the amendment itself does not suppose this), why should not Congress proceed at once to prescribe due process of law for the protection of every one of these fundamental rights, in every possible case, as well as to prescribe equal privileges in inns, public conveyances, and theatres? The truth is, that the implication of a power to legislate in this manner is based upon the assumption that if the States are forbidden to legislate or act in a particular way on a particular subject, and power is conferred upon Congress to enforce the prohibition, this gives Congress power to legislate generally upon that subject, and not merely power to provide modes of redress against such State legislation or action. The assumption is certainly unsound. It is repugnant to the Tenth Amendment of the Constitution, which declares that powers not delegated to the United States by the Constitution, nor prohibited by it to the States, are reserved to the States respectively or to the people. . . .

In this connection it is proper to state that civil rights, such as are guaranteed by the Constitution against State aggression, cannot be impaired by the wrongful acts of individuals, unsupported by State authority in the shape of laws, customs, or judicial or executive proceedings. The wrongful act of an individual, unsupported by any such authority, is simply a private wrong, or a crime of that individual; an invasion of the rights of the injured party, it is true, whether they affect his person, his property, or his reputation; but if not sanctioned in some way by the State, or not done under State authority, his rights remain in full force, and may presumably be vindicated by resort to the laws of the State for redress. An individual cannot deprive a man of his right to vote, to hold property, to buy and sell, to sue in the courts, or to be a witness or a juror; he may, by force or fraud, interfere with the enjoyment of the right in a particular case; he may commit an assault against the person, or commit murder, or use ruffian violence at the polls, or slander the good name of a fellow-citizen; but, unless protected in these wrongful acts by some shield of State law or State authority, he cannot destroy or injure the right; he will only render himself amenable to satisfaction or punishment; and amenable therefore to the laws of the State where the wrongful acts are committed. Hence, in all those cases where the Constitution seeks to protect the rights of the citizen against discriminative and unjust laws of the State by prohibiting such laws, it is not individual offenses, but abrogation and denial of rights, which it denounces, and for which it clothes the Congress with power to provide a remedy. This abrogation and denial of rights, for which the States alone were or could be responsible, was the great seminal and fundamental wrong which was intended to be remedied. And the remedy to be provided must necessarily be predicated upon that wrong. It must assume that in the cases provided for, the evil or wrong actually committed rests upon some State law or State authority for its excuse and perpetration. . . .

We have discussed the question presented by the law on the assumption that a right to enjoy equal accommodation and privileges in all inns, public conveyances, and places of public amusement, is one of the essential rights of the citizen which no State can abridge or interfere with. Whether it is such a right, or not, is a different question which, in the view we have taken of the validity of the law on the ground already stated, it is not necessary to examine. . . .

But the power of Congress to adopt direct and primary, as distinguished from corrective legislation, on the subject in hand, is sought, in the second place, from the Thirteenth Amendment, which abolishes slavery. This amendment declares "that neither slavery, nor involuntary servitude, except as a punishment for crime, whereof the party shall have been duly convicted, shall exist within the United States, or any place subject to their jurisdiction"; and it gives Congress power to enforce the amendment by appropriate legislation. . . .

When a man has emerged from slavery, and by the aid of beneficent legislation has shaken off the inseparable concomitants of that state, there must be some stage in the progress of his elevation when he takes the rank of a mere citizen, and ceases to be the special favorite of the laws, and when his rights as a citizen, or a man, are to be protected in the ordinary modes by which other men's rights are protected. There were thousands of free colored people in this country before the abolition of slavery, enjoying all the essential rights of life, liberty and property the same as white citizens; yet no one, at that time, thought that it was any invasion of his personal status as a freeman because he was not admitted to all the privileges enjoyed by white citizens, or because he was subjected to discriminations in the enjoyment of accommodations in inns, public conveyances and places of amusement. Mere discriminations on account of race or color were not regarded as badges of slavery. If, since that time, the enjoyment of equal rights in all these respects has become established by constitutional enactment, it is not by force of the Thirteenth Amendment (which merely abolishes slavery), but by force of the Fourteenth and Fifteenth Amendments. . . .

MR. JUSTICE HARLAN dissenting. . . .

There seems to be no substantial difference between my brethren and myself as to the purpose of Congress; for, they say that the essence of the law is, not to declare broadly that all persons shall be entitled to the full and equal enjoyment of the accommodations, advantages, facilities, and privileges of inns, public conveyances, and theatres; but that such enjoyment shall not be subject to conditions applicable only to citizens of a particular race or color, or who had been in a previous condition of servitude. The effect of the statute, the court says, is, that colored citizens, whether formerly slaves or not, and citizens of other races, shall have the same accommodations and privileges in all inns, public conveyances, and places of amusement as are enjoyed by white persons; and vice versa.

The court adjudges, I think erroneously, that Congress is without power, under either the Thirteenth or Fourteenth Amendment, to establish such regulations, and that the first and second sections of the statute are, in all their parts, unconstitutional and void. . . .

Congress has not, in these matters, entered the domain of State control and supervision. It does not, as I have said, assume to prescribe the general conditions and limitations under which inns, public conveyances, and places of public amusement, shall be conducted or managed. It simply declares, in effect, that since the nation has established universal freedom in this country, for all time, there shall be no discrimination, based merely upon race or color, in respect of the accommodations and advantages of public conveyances, inns, and places of public amusement.

I am of the opinion that such discrimination practiced by corporations and individuals in the exercise of their public or quasi public functions is a badge of servitude the imposition of which Congress may prevent under its power, by appropriate legislation, to enforce the Thirteenth Amendment; and, consequently, without reference to its enlarged power under the Fourteenth Amendment, the act of March 1, 1875, is not, in my judgment, repugnant to the Constitution. . . . The assumption that this amendment [the Fourteenth] consists wholly of prohibitions upon State laws and State proceedings in hostility to its provisions, is unauthorized by its language. [Its] first clause . . . ''All persons born or naturalized in the United States, and subject to the jurisdiction thereof, are citizens of the United States, and of the State wherein they reside''—is of a distinctly affirmative character. In its application to the colored race, . . . it created and granted, as well as citizenship of the United States, citizenship of the State in which they respectively resided. It introduced all of that race, whose ancestors had been imported and sold as slaves, at once, into the political community known as the ''People of the United States.'' They became, instantly, citizens of the United States, and of their respective States. Further, they were brought, by this supreme act of the nation, within the direct operation of that provision of the Constitution which declares that ''the citizens of each State shall be entitled to all privileges and immunities of citizens in the several States.'' Art. 4, § 2.

The citizenship thus acquired by that race, in

virtue of an affirmative grant from the nation, may be protected, not alone by the judicial branch of the government, but by congressional legislation of a primary direct character; this, because the power of Congress is not restricted to the enforcement of prohibitions upon State laws or State action. It is, in terms distinct and positive, to enforce "the *provisions of this article*" of amendment; not simply those of a prohibitive character, but the provisions—*all* of the provisions—affirmative and prohibitive, of the amendment. It is, therefore, a grave misconception to suppose that the fifth section of the amendment has reference exclusively to express prohibitions upon State laws or State action. If any right was created by that amendment, the grant of power, through appropriate legislation, to enforce its provisions, authorizes Congress, by means of legislation, operating throughout the entire Union, to guard, secure, and protect that right. . . .

It is said that any interpretation of the Fourteenth Amendment different from that adopted by the majority of the court, would imply that Congress had authority to enact a municipal code for all the States, covering every matter affecting the life, liberty, and property of the citizens of the several States. Not so. Prior to the adoption of that amendment the constitutions of the several States, without perhaps an exception, secured all *persons* against deprivation of life, liberty, or property, otherwise than by the due process of law, and, in some form, recognized the right of all *persons* to the equal protection of the laws. Those rights therefore, existed before that amendment was proposed or adopted, and were not created by it. If, by reason of that fact, it be assumed that protection in these rights of persons still rests primarily with the States, and that Congress may not interfere except to enforce, by means of corrective legislation, the prohibitions upon State laws or State proceedings inconsistent with those rights, it does not at all follow, that privileges which have been granted *by the nation,* may not be protected by primary legislation upon the part of Congress. The personal rights and immunities recognized in the prohibitive clauses of the amendment were, prior to its adoption, under the protection, primarily, of the States, while rights, created by or derived from the United States, have always been, and, in the nature of things, should always be, primarily, under the protection of the general government. Exemption from race discrimination in respect of the civil rights which are fundamental in *citizenship* in a republican government, is, as we have seen, a new right, created by the nation, with express power in Congress, by legislation, to enforce the constitutional provision from which it is derived. If, in some sense, such race discrimination is, within the letter of the last clause of the first section, a denial of that equal protection of the laws which is secured against State denial to all persons, whether citizens or not, it cannot be possible that a mere prohibition upon such State denial, or a prohibition upon State laws abridging the privileges and immunities of citizens of the United States, takes from the nation the power which it has uniformly exercised of protecting, by direct primary legislation, those privileges and immunities which existed under the Constitution before the adoption of the Fourteenth Amendment, or have been created by that amendment in behalf of those thereby made *citizens* of their respective States. . . .

But the court says that Congress did not, in the act of 1875, assume, under the authority given by the Thirteenth Amendment, to adjust what may be called the social rights of men and races in the community. I agree that government has nothing to do with social, as distinguished from technically legal, rights of individuals. No government ever has brought, or ever can bring, its people into social intercourse against their wishes. Whether one person will permit or maintain social relations with another is a matter with which government has no concern. I agree that if one citizen chooses not to hold social intercourse with another, he is not and cannot be made amenable to the law for his conduct in that regard; for even upon grounds of race, no legal right of a citizen is violated by the refusal of others to maintain merely social relations with him. What I affirm is that no State, nor the officers of any State, nor any corporation or individual wielding power under State authority for the public benefit or the public convenience, can, consistently either with the freedom established by the fundamental law, or with that equality of civil rights which now belongs to every citizen, discriminate against freemen or citizens, in those rights, because of their race, or because they once labored under the disabilities of slavery imposed upon them as a race. The rights which Congress, by the act of 1875, endeavored to secure and protect are legal, not social rights. The right, for instance, of a colored citizen to use the accommodations of a public highway, upon the same terms as are permitted to white citizens, is no more a social right than his right, under the law, to use the public streets of a city or a town, or a turnpike road, or a public market, or a post office, or his right to sit in a public building with others, of whatever race, for the purpose of hearing the political questions of the day discussed. Scarcely a day passes without our seeing in this court-room citizens of the white and black races sitting side by side, watching the progress of our business. It would never occur to any one that the presence of a colored citizen in a courthouse, or court-room, was an invasion of the social rights of white persons who may frequent such places. And yet, such a suggestion would be quite as sound in law—I say it with all respect—as is the suggestion that the claim of a colored citizen to use, upon the same terms as are permitted to white citizens, the accommodation of public inns, or places of public amusement, established under the license of the law, is an invasion of the social rights of the white race. . . .

Plessy v. Ferguson
163 U.S. 537, 16 S.Ct. 1138, 41 L.Ed. 256 (1896)

A Louisiana statute of 1890 required railroad companies carrying passengers within the state to provide "equal but separate" accommodations for white and colored persons, empowered train officials to enforce the law, and provided penalties for those who refused to obey segregation orders. The statute was upheld by the Supreme Court of Louisiana, and Plessy, a black passenger who had been punished for violating the act, brought the case to the Supreme Court on a writ of error.

MR. JUSTICE BROWN . . . delivered the opinion of the court. . . .

The constitutionality of this act is attacked upon the ground that it conflicts both with the Thirteenth Amendment of the Constitution, abolishing slavery, and the Fourteenth Amendment, which prohibits certain restrictive legislation on the part of the States.

1. That it does not conflict with the Thirteenth Amendment, which abolished slavery and involuntary servitude, except as a punishment for crime, is too clear for argument. . . .

A statute which implies merely a legal distinction between the white and colored races —a distinction which is founded in the color of the two races, and which must always exist so long as white men are distinguished from the other race by color—has no tendency to destroy the legal equality of the two races, or reestablish a state of involuntary servitude. Indeed, we do not understand that the Thirteenth Amendment is strenuously relied upon by the plaintiff in error in this connection.

2. By the Fourteenth Amendment, all per-

sons born or naturalized in the United States, and subject to the jurisdiction thereof, are made citizens of the United States and of the State wherein they reside; and the States are forbidden from making or enforcing any law which shall abridge the privileges or immunities of citizens of the United States, or shall deprive any person of life, liberty, or property without due process of law, or deny to any person within their jurisdiction the equal protection of the laws. . . .

The object of the amendment was undoubtedly to enforce the absolute equality of the two races before the law, but in the nature of things it could not have been intended to abolish distinctions based upon color, or to enforce social, as distinguished from political equality, or a commingling of the two races upon terms unsatisfactory to either. Laws permitting, and even requiring, their separation in places where they are liable to be brought into contact do not necessarily imply the inferiority of either race to the other, and have been generally, if not universally, recognized as within the competency of the state legislatures in the exercise of their police power. The most common instance of this is connected with the establishment of separate schools for white and colored children, which has been held to be a valid exercise of the legislative power even by courts of States where the political rights of the colored race have been longest and most earnestly enforced.

One of the earliest of these cases is that of *Roberts* v. *City of Boston,* 5 Cush. 198 [1849], in which the Supreme Judicial Court of Massachusetts held that the general school committee of Boston had power to make provision for the instruction of colored children in separate schools established exclusively for them, and to prohibit their attendance upon the other schools. "The great principle," said Chief Justice Shaw, p. 206, "advanced by the plaintiff" (Mr. Charles Sumner), "is, that by the constitution and laws of Massachusetts, all persons without distinction of age or sex, birth or color, origin or condition, are equal before the law. . . . But, when this great principle comes to

be applied to the actual and various conditions of persons in society, it will not warrant the assertion, that men and women are legally clothed with the same civil and political powers, and that children and adults are legally to have the same functions and be subject to the same treatment; but only that the rights of all, as they are settled and regulated by law, are equally entitled to the paternal consideration and protection of the law for their maintenance and security." It was held that the powers of the committee extended to the establishment of separate schools for children of different ages, sexes and colors, and that they might also establish special schools for poor and neglected children, who have become too old to attend the primary school, and yet have not acquired the rudiments of learning, to enable them to enter ordinary schools. Similar laws have been enacted by Congress under its general power of legislation over the District of Columbia . . . as well as by the legislatures of many of the States, and have been generally, if not uniformly, sustained by the courts. . . .

The distinction between laws interfering with the political equality of the negro and those requiring the separation of the two races in schools, theatres, and railway carriages has been frequently drawn by this court. Thus in *Strauder* v. *West Virginia,* 100 U.S. 303, it was held that a law of West Virginia limiting to white male persons, 21 years of age and citizens of the State, the right to sit upon juries, was a discrimination which implied a legal inferiority in civil society, which lessened the security of the right of the colored race, and was a step toward reducing them to a condition of servility. Indeed, the right of a colored man that, in the selection of jurors to pass upon his life, liberty and property, there shall be no exclusion of his race, and no discrimination against them because of color, has been asserted in a number of cases. . . .

". . . No question arises under this section, as to the power of the State to separate in different compartments interstate passengers, or affect, in any manner, the privileges and rights of such passengers. All that we can consider is, whether the State has the power to require that railroad trains within her limits shall have separate accommodations for the two races; that affecting only commerce within the State is no invasion of the power given to Congress by the commerce clause.''...

It is claimed by the plaintiff in error that, in any mixed community, the reputation of belonging to the dominant race, in this instance the white race, is property, in the same sense that a right of action, or of inheritance, is property. Conceding this to be so, for the purposes of this case, we are unable to see how this statute deprives him of, or in any way affects his right to, such property. If he be a white man and assigned to a colored coach, he may have his action for damages against the company for being deprived of his so-called property. Upon the other hand, if he be a colored man and be so assigned, he has been deprived of no property, since he is not lawfully entitled to the reputation of being a white man.

In this connection, it is also suggested by the learned counsel for the plaintiff in error that the same argument that will justify the State legislature in requiring railways to provide separate accommodations for the two races will also authorize them to require separate cars to be provided for people whose hair is of a certain color, or who are aliens, or to enact laws requiring colored people to walk upon one side of the street, and white people upon the other, or requiring white men's houses to be painted white, and colored men's black, or their vehicles or business signs to be of different colors, upon the theory that one side of the street is as good as the other, or that a house or vehicle of one color is as good as one of another color. The reply to all this is that every exercise of the police power must be reasonable, and extend only to such laws as are enacted in good faith for the promotion of the public good, and not for the annoyance or oppression of a particular class....

So far, then, as a conflict with the Fourteenth Amendment is concerned the case reduces itself to the question whether the statute of Louisiana is a reasonable regulation, and with respect to this there must necessarily be a large discretion on the part of the legislature. In determining the question of reasonableness it is at liberty to act with reference to the established usages, customs and traditions of the people, and with a view to the promotion of their comfort, and the preservation of the public peace and good order. Gauged by this standard, we cannot say that a law which authorizes or even requires the separation of the two races in public conveyances is unreasonable, or more obnoxious to the Fourteenth Amendment than the acts of Congress requiring separate schools for colored children in the District of Columbia, the constitutionality of which does not seem to have been questioned, or the corresponding acts of state legislatures.

We consider the underlying fallacy of the plaintiff's argument to consist in the assumption that the enforced separation of the two races stamps the colored race with a badge of inferiority. If this be so, it is not by reason of anything found in the act, but solely because the colored race chooses to put that construction upon it. The argument necessarily assumes that if, as has been more than once the case, and is not unlikely to be so again, the colored race should become the dominant power in the state legislature, and should enact a law in precisely similar terms, it would thereby relegate the white race to an inferior position. We imagine that the white race, at least, would not acquiesce in this assumption. The argument also assumes, that social prejudices may be overcome by legislation, and that equal rights cannot be secured to the negro except by an enforced commingling of the two races. We cannot accept this proposition. If the two races are to meet upon terms of social equality, it must be the result of natural affinities, a mutual appreciation of each other's merits and a voluntary consent of individuals. As was said by the Court of Appeals of New York in People v. Gallagher, 93 N.Y. 438, 448, ''this end can neither be accomplished nor promoted by laws which conflict with the general sentiment of the community upon whom they are designed to operate. When the government, therefore, has secured to each of its citizens equal rights before the law and equal opportunities for improvement and progress, it has accomplished the end for which it was organized and performed all of the functions respecting social advantages with which it is endowed.'' Legislation is powerless to eradicate racial instincts or to abolish distinctions based upon physical differences, and the attempt to do so can only result in accentuating the differences of the present situation. If the civil and political rights of both races be equal one cannot be inferior to the other civilly or politically. If one race be inferior to the other socially, the Constitution of the United States cannot put them upon the same plane. . . .

The judgment of the court below is, therefore,

Affirmed.

MR. JUSTICE HARLAN, dissenting. . . .

The white race deems itself to be the dominant race in this country. And so it is, in prestige, in achievements, in education, in wealth and in power. So, I doubt not, it will continue to be for all times, if it remains true to its great heritage and holds fast to the principles of constitutional liberty. But in view of the Constitution, in the eye of the law, there is in this country no superior, dominant, ruling class of citizens. There is no caste here. Our Constitution is color-blind, and neither knows nor tolerates classes among citizens. In respect of civil rights, all citizens are equal before the law. The humblest is the peer of the most powerful. The law regards man as man, and takes no account of his surroundings or of his color when his civil rights as guaranteed by the supreme law of the land are involved. It is, therefore, to be regretted that this high tribunal, the final expositor of the fundamental law of the land, has reached the conclusion that it is competent for a state to regulate the enjoyment by citizens of their civil rights solely upon the basis of race. . . .

The sure guarantee of the peace and security of each race is the clear, distinct, unconditional recognition by our governments, National and State, of every right that inheres in civil freedom, and of the equality before the law of all citizens of the United States without regard to race. State enactments, regulating the enjoyment of civil rights, upon the basis of race, and cunningly devised to defeat legitimate results of the war, under the pretense of recognizing equality of rights, can have no other result than to render permanent peace impossible, and to keep alive a conflict of races, the continuance of which must do harm to all concerned. . . .

The arbitrary separation of citizens on the basis of race, while they are on a public highway, is a badge of servitude wholly inconsistent with the civil freedom and the equality before the law established by the Constitution. It cannot be justified upon any legal grounds.

If evils will result from the commingling of the two races upon public highways established for the benefit of all, they will be infinitely less than those that will surely come from state legislation regulating the enjoyment of civil rights upon the basis of race. We boast of the freedom enjoyed by our people above all other people. But it is difficult to reconcile that boast with a state of the law which, practically, puts the brand of servitude and degradation upon a large class of our fellow-citizens, our equals before the law. The thin disguise of ''equal'' accommodations for passengers in railroad coaches will not mislead any one, nor atone for the wrong this day done. . . .

I do not deem it necessary to review the decisions of state courts to which reference was made in argument. Some, and the most important, of them are wholly inapplicable, because rendered prior to the adoption of the last amendments of the Constitution, when colored people had very few rights which the dominant race felt obliged to respect. Others were made at a time when public opinion, in many localities, was dominated by the institution of slavery; when it would not have been safe to do justice to the black man; and when, so far as the rights of blacks were concerned, race prejudice was, practically, the supreme law of the land. Those decisions cannot be guides in the era introduced by the recent amendments of the supreme law, which established universal civil freedom, gave citizenship to all born or naturalized in the United States and residing here, obliterated the race line from our systems of governments, National and State, and placed our free institutions upon the broad and sure foundation of the equality of all men before the law. . . .

For the reasons stated, I am constrained to withhold my assent from the opinion and judgment of the majority.

MR. JUSTICE BREWER did not hear the argument or participate in the decision of this case.

Smith v. *Allwright*
321 U.S. 649, 64 S.Ct. 757, 88 L.Ed. 987 (1944)

Smith, a black citizen of Texas, sought to obtain a ballot in the Democratic party primary election of 1940, in which candidates for state and national offices were to be selected. Allwright, a precinct election judge, denied Smith's request on the ground that a resolution of the Democratic party convention of 1932 had restricted the privilege of party membership to white persons. Smith then sued for damages in the federal district court, claiming that Allwright had caused him to be deprived of a right and privilege of voting under the Constitution, contrary to §§ 31 and 43 of Title 8, United States Code. Smith obtained certiorari to review judgments for the defendant in the lower federal courts.

MR. JUSTICE REED delivered the opinion of the Court. . . .

The State of Texas by its Constitution and statutes provides that every person, if certain other requirements are met which are not here in issue, qualified by residence in the district or county "shall be deemed a qualified elector." . . . Primary elections for United States Senators, Congressmen and state officers are provided for by Chapters Twelve and Thirteen of the statutes. Under these chapters, the Democratic party was required to hold the primary which was the occasion of the alleged wrong to petitioner. . . . These nominations are to be made by the qualified voters of the party.

The Democratic party of Texas is held by the Supreme Court of that State to be a "voluntary association," free from interference by the State except that:

"In the interest of fair methods and a fair expression by their members of their preferences

in the selection of their nominees, the State may regulate such elections by proper laws."

That court stated further:

"Since the right to organize and maintain a political party is one guaranteed by the Bill of Rights of this State, it necessarily follows that every privilege essential or reasonably appropriate to the exercise of that right is likewise guaranteed—including, of course, the privilege of determining the policies of the party and its membership. Without the privilege of determining the policy of a political association and its membership, the right to organize such an association would be a mere mockery. We think these rights—that is, the right to determine the membership of a political party and to determine its policies, of necessity are to be exercised by the state convention of such party, and cannot, under any circumstances, be conferred upon a state or governmental agency." . . .

Texas is free to conduct her elections and

limit her electorate as she may deem wise, save only as her action may be affected by the prohibitions of the United States Constitution or in conflict with powers delegated to and exercised by the National Government. The Fourteenth Amendment forbids a State from making or enforcing any law which abridges the privileges or immunities of citizens of the United States and the Fifteenth Amendment specifically interdicts any denial or abridgement by a State of the right of citizens to vote on account of color. . . .

Since *Grovey* v. *Townsend* and prior to the present suit, no case from Texas involving primary elections has been before this Court. We did decide, however, *United States* v. *Classic*. . . . We there held that § 4 of Article I of the Constitution authorized Congress to regulate primary as well as general elections, "where the primary is by law made an integral part of the election machinery." Consequently, in the Classic case, we upheld the applicability to frauds in a Louisiana primary of §§ 19 and 20 of the Criminal Code. . . . Classic bears upon *Grovey* v. *Townsend* not because exclusion of Negroes from primaries is any more or less state action by reason of the unitary character of the electoral process but because the recognition of the place of the primary in the electoral scheme makes clear that state delegation to a party of the power to fix the qualifications of primary elections is delegation of a state function that may make the party's action the action of the State. When *Grovey* v. *Townsend* was written, the Court looked upon the denial of a vote in a primary as a mere refusal by a party of party membership. As the Louisiana statutes for holding primaries are similar to those of Texas, our ruling in Classic as to the unitary character of the electoral process calls for a reexamination as to whether or not the exclusion of Negroes from a Texas party primary was state action. . . .

It may now be taken as a postulate that the right to vote in such a primary for the nomination of candidates without discrimination by the State, like the right to vote in a general election, is a right secured by the Constitution. . . . By the terms of the Fifteenth Amendment that right

may not be abridged by any State on account of race. Under our Constitution the great privilege of the ballot may not be denied a man by the State because of his color.

We are thus brought to an examination of the qualifications for Democratic primary electors in Texas, to determine whether state action or private action has excluded Negroes from participation. Despite Texas's decision that the exclusion is produced by private or party action . . . federal courts must for themselves appraise the facts leading to that conclusion. It is only by the performance of this obligation that a final and uniform interpretation can be given to the Constitution, the "supreme Law of the Land." . . .

Primary elections are conducted by the party under state statutory authority. The county executive committee selects precinct election officials and the county, district or state executive committees, respectively, canvass the returns. These party committees or the state convention certify the party's candidates to the appropriate officers for inclusion on the official ballot for the general election. No name which has not been so certified may appear upon the ballot for the general election as a candidate of a political party. No other name may be printed on the ballot which has not been placed in nomination by qualified voters who must take oath that they did not participate in a primary for the selection of a candidate for the office for which the nomination is made.

The state courts are given exclusive original jurisdiction of contested elections and of mandamus proceedings to compel party officers to perform their statutory duties.

We think that this statutory system for the selection of party nominees for inclusion on the general election ballot makes the party which is required to follow these legislative directions an agency of the State in so far as it determines the participants in a primary election. . . . When primaries become a part of the machinery for choosing officials, state and national, as they have here, the same tests to determine the character of discrimination or abridgement should be applied to the primary as are applied to the general election. If the State requires a certain electoral procedure, prescribes a general election ballot made up of party nominees so chosen and limits the choice of the electorate in general elections for state offices, practically speaking, to those whose names appear on such a ballot, it endorses, adopts and enforces the discrimination against Negroes, practiced by a party entrusted by Texas law with the determination of the qualifications of participants in the primary. This is state action within the meaning of the Fifteenth Amendment. . . .

The United States is a constitutional democracy. Its organic law grants to all citizens a right to participate in the choice of elected officials without restriction by any State because of race. This grant to the people of the opportunity for choice is not to be nullified by a State through casting its electoral process in a form which permits a private organization to practice racial discrimination in the election. Constitutional rights would be of little value if they could be thus indirectly denied. . . .

. . . In reaching this conclusion we are not unmindful of the desirability of continuity of decision in constitutional questions. However, when convinced of former error, this Court has never felt constrained to follow precedent. In constitutional questions, where correction depends upon amendment and not upon legislative action this Court throughout its history has freely exercised its power to reexamine the basis of its constitutional decisions. This has long been accepted practice, and this practice has continued to this day. This is particularly true when the decision believed erroneous is the application of a constitutional principle rather than an interpretation of the Constitution to extract the principle itself. Here we are applying, contrary to the recent decision in *Grovey* v. *Townsend,* the well-established principle of the Fifteenth Amendment, forbidding the abridgement by a State of a citizen's right to vote. *Grovey* v. *Townsend* is overruled.

Judgment reversed.

Mr. Justice Frankfurter concurs in the result.

Mr. Justice Roberts:

In *Mahnich* v. *Southern Steamship Co.,* 321 U.S. 96, 105, I have expressed my views with respect to the present policy of the court freely to disregard and to overrule considered decisions and the rules of law announced in them. This tendency, it seems to me, indicates an intolerance for what those who have composed this court in the past have conscientiously and deliberately concluded, and involves an assumption that knowledge and wisdom reside in us which was denied to our predecessors. I shall not repeat what I there said for I consider it fully applicable to the instant decision, which but points the moral anew. . . .

The reason for my concern is that the instant decision, overruling that announced about nine years ago, tends to bring adjudications of this tribunal into the same class as a restricted railroad ticket, good for this day and train only. I have no assurance, in view of current decisions, that the opinion announced today may not shortly be repudiated and overruled by justices who deem they have new light on the subject. In the present term the court has overruled three cases.

In the present case, as in *Mahnich* v. *Southern S. S. Co.,* . . . the court below relied, as it was bound to, upon our previous decision. As that court points out, the statutes of Texas have not been altered since *Grovey* v. *Townsend* was decided. The same resolution is involved as was drawn in question in *Grovey* v. *Townsend.* Not a fact differentiates that case from this except the names of the parties.

It is suggested that *Grovey* v. *Townsend* was overruled *sub silentio* in *United States* v. *Classic.* . . . If so, the situation is even worse than that exhibited by the outright repudiation of an earlier decision, for it is the fact that, in the Classic case, *Grovey* v. *Townsend* was distinguished in brief and argument by the Government without suggestion that it was wrongly decided, and was relied on by the appellees, not as a controlling decision, but by way of analogy. The case is not mentioned in either of the opinions in the Classic case. Again and again it is said in the opinion of the court in that case that the voter who was denied the right to vote was a fully qualified voter. In other words, there was no question of his being a person entitled under state law to vote in the primary. The offense charged was the fraudulent denial of his conceded right by an election officer because of his race. Here the question is altogether different. It is whether, in a Democratic primary, he who tendered his vote was a member of the Democratic party. . . .

It is regrettable that in an era marked by doubt and confusion, an era whose greatest need is steadfastness of thought and purpose, this court, which has been looked to as exhibiting consistency in adjudication, and a steadiness which would hold the balance even in the face of temporary ebbs and flows of opinion, should now itself become the breeder of fresh doubt and confusion in the public mind as to the stability of our institutions.

Shelley v. Kraemer
334 U.S. 1, 68 S.Ct. 836, 92 L.Ed. 1161 (1948)

The Supreme Courts of Michigan and Missouri upheld the validity of restrictive covenants, which were provisions in contracts between private parties declaring that they, and those to whom they might sell, would not permit the acquisition or use of their property by non-Caucasians for a stated period of time. The United States Supreme Court granted certiorari to both state courts.

MR. CHIEF JUSTICE VINSON delivered the opinion of the Court. . . .

It should be observed that these covenants do not seek to proscribe any particular use of the affected properties. Use of the properties for residential occupancy, as such, is not forbidden. The restrictions of these agreements, rather, are directed toward a designated class of persons and seek to determine who may and who may not own or make use of the properties for residential purposes. The excluded class is defined wholly in terms of race or color: "simply that and nothing more."

It cannot be doubted that among the civil rights intended to be protected from discriminatory state action by the Fourteenth Amendment are the rights to acquire, enjoy, own and dispose of property. Equality in the enjoyment of property rights was regarded by the framers of that Amendment as an essential precondition to the realization of other basic civil rights and liberties which the Amendment was intended to guarantee. . . .

It is likewise clear that restrictions on the right of occupancy of the sort sought to be created by the private agreements in these cases could not be squared with the requirements of the Fourteenth Amendment if imposed by state statute or local ordinance. . . .

But the present cases, unlike those just discussed, do not involve action by state legislatures or city councils. Here the particular patterns of discrimination and the areas in which the restrictions are to operate, are determined, in the first instance, by the terms of agreements among private individuals. Participation of the State consists in the enforcement of the restrictions so defined. The crucial issue with which we are here confronted is whether this distinction removes these cases from the operation of the prohibitory provisions of the Fourteenth Amendment.

Since the decision of this Court in the *Civil Rights Cases,* 109 U.S. 3, the principle has become firmly imbedded in our constitutional law that the action inhibited by the first section of the Fourteenth Amendment is only such action as may fairly be said to be that of the States. That Amendment erects no shield against merely private conduct, however discriminatory or wrongful.

We conclude, therefore, that the restrictive agreements standing alone cannot be regarded as violative of any rights guaranteed to petitioners by the Fourteenth Amendment. So long as the purposes of those agreements are effectuated by voluntary adherence to their terms, it would appear clear that there has been no action by the State and the provisions of the amendment have not been violated. . . .

But here there was more. These are cases in which the purposes of the agreements were secured only by judicial enforcement by state courts of the restrictive terms of the agreements. The respondents urge that judicial enforcement of private agreement does not amount to state action; or, in any event, the participation of the States is so attenuated in character as not to amount to state action within the meaning of the Fourteenth Amendment. . . .

That the action of state courts and of judicial officers in their official capacities is to be regarded as action of the State within the meaning of the Fourteenth Amendment, is a proposition which has long been established by decisions of this Court. . . .

. . . The examples of state judicial action which have been held by this Court to violate the Amendment's commands are not restricted to situations in which the judicial proceedings were found in some manner to be procedurally unfair. It has been recognized that the action of state courts in enforcing a substantive common-law rule formulated by those courts, may result in the denial of rights guaranteed by the Fourteenth Amendment, even though the judicial proceedings in such cases may have been in complete accord with the most rigorous conceptions of procedural due process. . . .

The short of the matter is that from the time of the adoption of the Fourteenth Amendment until the present, it has been the consistent ruling of this Court that the action of the States to which the Amendment has reference, includes action of state courts and state judicial officials. Although, in construing the terms of the Fourteenth Amendment, differences have from time to time been expressed as to whether particular types of state action may be said to offend the Amendment's prohibitory provisions, it has never been suggested that state court action is immunized from the operation of those provisions simply because the act is that of the judicial branch of the state government.

Against this background of judicial construction, extending over a period of some three-quarters of a century, we are called upon to consider whether enforcement by state courts of the restrictive agreements in these cases may be deemed to be the acts of those States; and, if so, whether that action has denied these petitioners the equal protection of the laws which the Amendment was intended to insure.

We have no doubt that there has been state action in these cases in the full and complete sense of the phrase. The undisputed facts disclose that petitioners were willing purchasers of properties upon which they desired to establish homes. The owners of the properties were willing sellers; and contracts of sale were accordingly consummated. It is clear that but for the active intervention of the state courts, supported by the full panoply of state power, petitioners would have been free to occupy the properties in question without restraint.

These are not cases, as has been suggested, in which the States have merely abstained from action, leaving private individuals free to impose such discriminations as they see fit. Rather, these are cases in which the States have made available to such individuals the full coercive power of government to deny to petitioners, on the grounds of race or color, the enjoyment of property rights in premises which petitioners are willing and financially able to acquire and which the grantors are willing to sell. The difference between judicial enforcement and non-enforcement of the restrictive covenants is the difference to petitioners between being denied rights of property available to other members of the community and being accorded full enjoyment of those rights on an equal footing. . . .

We hold that in granting judicial enforcement of the restrictive agreements in these cases, the States have denied petitioners the equal protection of the laws and that, therefore, the action of the state courts cannot stand. . . .

. . . The rights created by the first section of the Fourteenth Amendment are, by its terms, guaranteed to the individual. The rights established are personal rights. It is, therefore, no answer to these petitioners to say that the courts may also be induced to deny white persons rights of ownership and occupancy on grounds of race or color. Equal protection of the laws is not achieved through indiscriminate imposition of inequalities. . . .

The historical context in which the Four-teenth Amendment became a part of the Constitution should not be forgotten. Whatever else the framers sought to achieve, it is clear that the matter of primary concern was the establishment of equality in the enjoyment of basic civil and political rights and the preservation of those rights from discriminatory action on the part of the States based on considerations of race or color. Seventy-five years ago this Court announced that the provisions of the Amendment are to be construed with this fundamental purpose in mind. Upon full consideration, we have concluded that in these cases the States have acted to deny petitioners the equal protection of the laws guaranteed by the Fourteenth Amendment. . . .

Reversed.

MR. JUSTICE REED, MR. JUSTICE JACKSON, and MR. JUSTICE RUTLEDGE took no part in the consideration or decision of these cases.

Brown v. Board of Education (First Case)
347 U.S. 483, 74 S.Ct. 686, 98 L.Ed. 873 (1954)

On May 17, 1954, the Supreme Court handed down its long-awaited decision in the public school segregation cases. Although the cases directly involved only South Carolina, Virginia, Delaware, Kansas, and the District of Columbia, the answer to the question of whether segregation of races was permissible under the Constitution affected a total of 17 states and the District of Columbia that required segregation in public schools and four states that permitted segregation at the option of local communities. It should be noted that the Chief Justice spoke for a unanimous Court, and that the Court postponed issuing a decree until the October 1954 term.

MR. CHIEF JUSTICE WARREN delivered the opinion of the court.

THE FOUR STATES

These cases come to us from the States of Kansas, South Carolina, Virginia, and Delaware. They are premised on different facts and dif-ferent local conditions, but a common legal question justifies their consideration together in this consolidated opinion.

In each of the cases, minors of the Negro race, through their legal representatives, seek the aid of the courts in obtaining admission to the public schools of their community on a non-segregated basis. In each instance, they had been denied admission to schools attended by white children under laws requiring or permitting segregation according to race.

This segregation was alleged to deprive the plaintiffs of the equal protection of the laws under the Fourteenth Amendment. In each of the cases other than the Delaware case, a three-judge Federal District Court denied relief to the plaintiffs on the so-called "separate but equal" doctrine, announced by this court in *Plessy* v. *Ferguson*. . . .

Under that doctrine, equality of treatment is accorded when the races are provided substantially equal facilities, even though these facilities be separate. In the Delaware case, the Supreme Court of Delaware adhered to that doctrine, but ordered that the plaintiffs be admitted to the white schools because of their superiority to the Negro schools.

The plaintiffs contend that segregated public schools are not "equal" and cannot be made "equal," and that, hence, they are deprived of the equal protection of the laws. Because of the obvious importance of the question presented, the Court took jurisdiction. Argument was heard in the 1952 term, and reargument was heard this term on certain questions propounded by the Court.

Reargument was largely devoted to the circumstances surrounding the adoption of the Fourteenth Amendment in 1868. It covered, exhaustively, consideration of the Amendment in Congress, ratification by the states, then existing practices in racial segregation, and the views of proponents and opponents of the Amendment.

This discussion and our own investigation convince us that, although these sources cast some light, it is not enough to resolve the problem with which we are faced.

At best, they are inconclusive. The most avid proponents of the postwar Amendments undoubtedly intended them to remove all legal distinctions among "all persons born or naturalized in the United States."

Their opponents, just as certainly, were antagonistic to both the letter and the spirit of the Amendments and wished them to have the most limited effect. What others in Congress and the State legislatures had in mind cannot be determined with any degree of certainty.

An additional reason for the illusive nature of the Amendment's history, with respect to segregated schools, is the status of public education at that time. In the South, the movement toward free common schools, supported by general taxation, had not yet taken hold. Education of white children was largely in the hands of private groups. Education of Negroes was almost nonexistent, and practically all of the race was illiterate. In fact, any education of Negroes was forbidden by law in some states.

Today, in contrast, many Negroes have achieved outstanding success in the arts and sciences as well as in the business and professional world. It is true that public school education at the time of the Amendment had advanced further in the North, but the effect of the Amendment on Northern States was generally ignored by the Congressional debates.

Even in the North, the conditions of public education did not approximate those existing today. The curriculum was usually rudimentary; ungraded schools were common in rural areas, the school term was but three months a year in many states; and compulsory school attendance was virtually unknown.

As a consequence, it is not surprising that there should be so little in the history of the Fourteenth Amendment relating to its intended effect on public education.

In the first cases in this court, construing the Fourteenth Amendment, decided shortly after its adoption, the court interpreted it as proscribing all state-imposed discriminations against the Negro race.

The doctrine of "separate but equal" did not make its appearance in this court until 1896 in the case of *Plessy* v. *Ferguson* . . . involving not education but transportation.

[A footnote explains that "the doctrine apparently originated in *Roberts* v. *City of Boston*, 59 Mass. 198, 206 (1849) upholding school segregation against attack as being violative of a state constitutional guarantee of equality. Segregation in Boston public schools was eliminated in 1855. . . . But elsewhere in the north segregation in public education has persisted until recent years.''].

American courts have since labored with the doctrine for over half a century. In this court, there have been six cases involving the ''separate but equal'' doctrine in the field of public education.

In *Cumming* v. *County Board of Education,* 175 U.S. 528, and *Gong Lum* v. *Rice,* 275 U.S. 78, the validity of the doctrine itself was not challenged. In most recent cases, all on the graduate school level, inequality was found in that specific benefits enjoyed by white students were denied to Negro students of the same educational qualifications. *Missouri ex rel. Gaines* v. *Canada,* 305 U.S. 337; *Sipuel* v. *Oklahoma,* 332 U.S. 631; *Sweatt* v. *Painter,* 339 U.S. 629; *McLaurin* v. *Oklahoma State Regents,* 339 U.S. 637.

In none of these cases was it necessary to re-examine the doctrine to grant relief to the Negro plaintiff. And in *Sweatt* v. *Painter* . . . the court expressly reserved decision on the question whether *Plessy* v. *Ferguson* should be held inapplicable to public education.

In the instant cases, that question is directly presented. Here, unlike *Sweatt* v. *Painter,* there are findings below that the Negro and white schools involved have been equalized, or are being equalized, with respect to buildings, curricula, qualifications and salaries of teachers, and other ''tangible'' factors.

Our decision, therefore, cannot turn on merely a comparison of these tangible factors in the Negro and white schools involved in each of the cases. We must look instead to the effect of segregation itself on public education.

In approaching this problem, we cannot turn the clock back to 1868, when the Amendment was adopted, or even to 1896, when *Plessy* v. *Ferguson* was written. We must consider public education in the light of its full development and its present place in American life throughout the nation. Only in this way can it be determined if segregation in public schools deprives these plaintiffs of the equal protection of the laws.

Today, education is perhaps the most important function of state and local governments. Compulsory school attendance laws and the great expenditures for education both demonstrate our recognition of the importance of education to our democratic society. It is required in the performance of our most basic public responsibilities, even service in the armed forces. It is the very foundation of good citizenship.

Today, it is a principal instrument in awakening the child to cultural values, in preparing him for later professional training, and in helping him to adjust normally to his environment.

In these days, it is doubtful that any child may reasonably be expected to succeed in life if he is denied the opportunity of an education. Such an opportunity, where the state has undertaken to provide it, is a right which must be made available to all on equal terms.

We come then to the question presented: Does segregation of children in public schools solely on the basis of race, even though the physical facilities and other ''tangible'' factors may be equal, deprive the children of the minority group of equal educational opportunities? We believe that it does.

In *Sweatt* v. *Painter* . . . in finding that a segregated law school for Negroes could not provide them equal educational opportunities, this court relied in large part on ''those qualities which are incapable of objective measurement but which make for greatness in a law school.''

In *McLaurin* v. *Oklahoma State Regents* . . . the court, in requiring that a Negro admitted to a white graduate school be treated like all other students, again resorted to intangible considerations: ''. . . his ability to study, engage in discussions and exchange views with other students, and, in general, to learn his profession.''

Such considerations apply with added force to children in grade and high schools. To separate them from others of similar age and qualifications solely because of their race generates a feeling of inferiority as to their status in the community that may affect their hearts and minds in a way unlikely ever to be undone.

The effect of this separation on their educational opportunities was well stated by a finding in the Kansas case by a court which nevertheless felt compelled to rule against the Negro plaintiffs:

> Segregation of white and colored children in public schools has a detrimental effect upon the colored children. The impact is greater when it has the sanction of the law; for the policy of separating the races is usually interpreted as denoting the inferiority of the Negro group.
>
> A sense of inferiority affects the motivation of a child to learn. Segregation with the sanction of law, therefore, has a tendency to [retard] the educational and mental development of Negro children and to deprive them of some of the benefits they would receive in a racial[ly] integrated school system.

Whatever may have been the extent of psychological knowledge at the time of *Plessy* v. *Ferguson,* this finding is amply supported by modern authority.*

. . . Any language in *Plessy* v. *Ferguson* contrary to this finding is rejected.

We conclude that in the field of public education the doctrine of "separate but equal" has no place. Separate educational facilities are inherently unequal. Therefore, we hold that the plaintiffs and others similarly situated for whom the actions have been brought are, by reason of the segregation complained of, deprived of the equal protection of the laws guaranteed by the Fourteenth Amendment. This disposition makes unnecessary any discussion whether such segregation also violates the Due Process Clause of the Fourteenth Amendment.

---

* Citing: K. B. Clark, *Effect of Prejudice and Discrimination on Personality Development* (Mid-century White House Conference); Witmer and Kotinsky, *Personality in the Making* (1952), ch. VI; Deutscher and Chein, "The Psychological Effects of Enforced Segregation: A Survey of Social Science Opinion," 26 *J. Psychol.* 259 (1948); Chein, "What Are the Psychological Effects of Segregation Under Conditions of Equal Facilities?," 3 *Int. J. Opinion and Attitude Res.* 229 (1949); Brameld, "Educational Costs," in *Discrimination and National Welfare* (MacIver, ed., 1949), 44–48; Frazier, *The Negro in the United States* (1949), 674–681. And see generally Myrdal, *An American Dilemma* (1944).

Because these are class actions, because of the wide applicability of this decision, and because of the great variety of local conditions, the formulation of decrees in these cases presents problems of considerable complexity. On reargument, the consideration of appropriate relief was necessarily subordinated to the primary question—the constitutionality of segregation in public education.

We have now announced that such segregation is a denial of the equal protection of the laws. In order that we may have the full assistance of the parties in formulating decrees the cases will be restored to the docket, and the parties are requested to present further argument on Questions 4 and 5 previously propounded by the court for the reargument this Term. [These pertained to the form of decree to be issued if segregated schools were outlawed.]

The Attorney General of the United States is again invited to participate. The Attorneys General of the states requiring or permitting segregation in public education will also be permitted to appear as amici curiae upon request to do so by Sept. 15, 1954, and submission of briefs by Oct. 1, 1954.

It is so ordered.

DISTRICT OF COLUMBIA

This case challenges the validity of segregation in the public schools of the District of Columbia. The petitioners, minors of the Negro race, allege that such segregation deprives them of due process of law under the Fifth Amendment. They were refused admission to a public school attended by white children solely because of their race.

They sought the aid of the District Court for the District of Columbia in obtaining admission. That court dismissed their complaint. The Court granted a writ of certiorari before judgment in the Court of Appeals because of the importance of the constitutional question presented. 344 U.S. 873.

We have this day held that the equal protection clause of the Fourteenth Amendment prohibits the states from maintaining racially segregated public schools.

The legal problem in the District of Columbia is somewhat different, however. The Fifth Amendment, which is applicable in the District of Columbia, does not contain an equal protection clause as does the Fourteenth Amendment which applies only to the states.

But the concepts of equal protection and due process, both stemming from our American ideal of fairness, are not mutually exclusive. The "equal protection of the laws" is a more explicit safeguard of prohibited unfairness than "due process of law," and, therefore, we do not imply that the two are always interchangeable phrases.

But, as this court has recognized, discrimination may be so unjustifiable as to be violative of due process. Classifications based solely upon race must be scrutinized with particular care, since they are contrary to our traditions and hence constitutionally suspect.

As long ago as 1896, this court declared the principle "that the Constitution of the United States, in its present form, forbids, so far as civil and political rights are concerned, discrimination by the general government, or by the states, against any citizen because of his race."

And in *Buchanan* v. *Warley*, 245 U.S. 60, the court held that a statute which limited the right of a property owner to convey his property to a person of another race was, as an unreasonable discrimination, a denial of due process of law.

Although the court has not assumed to define "liberty" with any great precision, that term is not confined to mere freedom from bodily restraint. Liberty under law extends to the full range of conduct which the individual is free to pursue, and it cannot be restricted except for a proper governmental objective.

Segregation in public education is not reasonably related to any proper governmental objective, and thus it imposes on Negro children of the District of Columbia a burden that constitutes an arbitrary deprivation of their liberty in violation of the Due Process Clause.

In view of our decision that the Constitution prohibits the states from maintaining racially segregated public schools, it would be unthinkable that the same Constitution would impose a lesser duty on the Federal Government. We hold that racial segregation in the public schools of the District of Columbia is a denial of the Due Process of Law guaranteed by the Fifth Amendment to the Constitution.

For the reasons set out in *Brown* v. *Board of Education*, this case will be restored to the docket for reargument on Questions 4 and 5 previously propounded by the court. . . .

It is so ordered.

Brown v. Board of Education
(Second Case)
349 U.S. 294, 75 S.Ct. 753, 99 L.Ed. 1083 (1955)

In the term following the decision in *Brown v. Board of Education,* 347 U.S. 483 (1954), the Court handed down its decree to guide lower courts in future litigation involving desegregation. In reaching the views expressed below, representatives of the black parties, the states concerned, and the United States were heard.

MR. CHIEF JUSTICE WARREN delivered the opinion of the Court.

These cases were decided on May 17, 1954. The opinions of that date, declaring the fundamental principle that racial discrimination in public education is unconstitutional, are incorporated herein by reference. All provisions of federal, state, or local law requiring or permitting such discrimination must yield to this principle. There remains for consideration the manner in which relief is to be accorded. . . .

Full implementation of these constitutional principles may require solution of varied local school problems. School authorities have the primary responsibility for elucidating, assessing, and solving these problems; courts will have to consider whether the action of school authorities constitutes good faith implementation of the governing constitutional principles. Because of their proximity to local conditions and the possible need for further hearings, the courts which originally heard these cases can best perform this judicial appraisal. Accordingly, we believe it appropriate to remand the cases to those courts.

In fashioning and effectuating the decrees, the courts will be guided by equitable principles. Traditionally, equity has been characterized by a practical flexibility in shaping its remedies and by a facility for adjusting and reconciling public and private needs. These cases call for the exercise of these traditional attributes of equity power. At stake is the personal interest of the plaintiffs in admission to public schools as soon as practicable on a nondiscriminatory basis. To effectuate this interest may call for elimination of a variety of obstacles in making the transition to school systems operated in accordance with the constitutional principles set forth in our May 17, 1954, decision. Courts of equity may properly take into account the public interest in the elimination of such obstacles in a systematic and effective manner. But it should go without saying that the vitality of these constitutional principles cannot be allowed to yield simply because of disagreement with them.

While giving weight to these public and private considerations, the courts will require that the defendants make a prompt and reasonable start toward full compliance with our May 17, 1954, ruling. Once such a start has been made, the courts may find that additional time is necessary to carry out the ruling in an effective manner. The burden rests upon the defendants to establish that such time is necessary in the public interest and is consistent with good faith compliance at the earliest practicable date. To that end, the courts may consider problems related to administration, arising from the physical condition of the school plant, the school transportation system, personnel, revision of school districts and attendance areas into compact units to achieve a system of determining admission to the public schools on a nonracial basis, and revision of local laws and regulations which may be necessary in solving the foregoing problems. They will also consider the adequacy of any plans the defendants may propose to meet these problems and to effectuate a transition to a racially nondiscriminatory school system. During this period of transition, the courts will retain jurisdiction of these cases. The judgments below . . . are accordingly reversed and the cases are remanded to the District Courts to take such proceedings and enter such orders and decrees consistent with this opinion as are necessary and proper to admit to public schools on a racially nondiscriminatory basis with all deliberate speed the parties to these cases. . . .

It is so ordered.

Milliken v. *Bradley*
418 U.S. 717, 94 S.Ct. 3112, 41 L.Ed. 2d 1069 (1974)

This case represents a class action instituted in the U.S. District Court, Eastern District of Michigan, against certain state officials and the Board of Education, Detroit, seeking desegregation of Detroit's public schools. The district court ordered submission of desegregation plans for the city proper, as well as for the three-county metropolitan area, even though the suburban school districts were not parties to the action and there was no claim that they had committed any constitutional violations. The U.S. Court of Appeals, Sixth Circuit, affirmed findings of de jure segregation in the greater Detroit area. On certiorari, the U.S. Supreme Court reversed and remanded for formulation of a decree restricted to the city of Detroit.

Expressing the views of five members of the Court, Chief Justice Burger wrote the opinion. Justices Brennan, Douglas, Marshall, and White dissented.

MR. CHIEF JUSTICE BURGER: . . .

We granted certiorari in these consolidated cases to determine whether a federal court may impose a multi-district, areawide remedy to a single district de jure segregation problem absent any finding that the other included school districts have failed to operate unitary school systems within their districts, absent any claim or finding that the boundary lines of any affected school district were established with the purpose of fostering racial segregation in public schools, absent any finding that the included districts committed acts which effected segregation within the other districts, and absent a meaningful opportunity for the included neighboring school districts to present evidence or be heard on the propriety of a multi-district remedy or on the question of constitutional violations by those neighboring districts.

Ever since *Brown* v. *Board of Education*, judicial consideration of school desegregation cases has begun with the standard that:

[I]n the field of public education the doctrine of 'separate but equal' has no place. Separate educational facilities are inherently unequal.

This has been reaffirmed time and again as the meaning of the Constitution and the controlling rule of law.

The target of the *Brown* holding was clear and forthright: the elimination of state mandated or deliberately maintained dual school systems with certain schools for Negro pupils and others for white pupils. This duality in racial segregation was held to violate the Constitution in the cases subsequent to 1954. . . .

The Swann case (402 U.S. 1: 1971) of course, dealt

with the problem of defining in more precise terms than heretofore the scope of the duty of school authorities and district courts in implementing Brown I and the mandate to eliminate dual systems and establish unitary systems at once.

In *Brown* v. *Board of Education* . . . (Brown II), the Court's first encounter with the problem of remedies in school desegregation cases, the Court noted that:

In fashioning and effectuating the decrees, the courts will be guided by equitable principles. Traditionally, equity has been characterized by a practical flexibility in shaping its remedies and by a facility for adjusting and reconciling public and private needs. . . .

In further refining the remedial process, *Swann* held, the task is to correct, by a balancing of the individual and collective interests, "the condition that offends the Constitution." A federal remedial power may be exercised "only on the basis of a constitutional violation" and, "[a]s with any equity case, the nature of the violation determines the scope of the remedy." . . .

Proceeding from these basic principles, we first note that in the District Court the complainants sought a remedy aimed at the *condition* alleged to offend the Constitution—the segregation within the Detroit City school district. The court acted on this theory of the case and in its initial ruling on the "Desegregation Area" stated:

The task before this court, therefore, is now, and . . . has always been, how to desegregate the Detroit public schools.

Thereafter, however, the District Court abruptly rejected the proposed Detroit-only plans on the ground that "while it would provide a racial mix more in keeping with the Black-White proportions of the student population, [it] would accentuate the racial identifiability of the [Detroit] district as a Black school system, and would not accomplish desegregation." . . . "[T]he racial composition of the student body is such," said the court, "that the plan's implementation would clearly make the entire Detroit public school system racially identifiable," . . . "leav[ing] many of its schools 75 to 90 percent Black." . . . Consequently, the court reasoned, it was imperative to "look beyond the limits of the Detroit school district for a solution to the problem of segregation in the Detroit schools . . ." since "school district lines are simply matters of political convenience and may not be used to deny constitutional rights." . . . Accordingly, the District Court proceeded to redefine the relevant area to include areas of predominantly white pupil population in order to ensure that "upon implementation, no school, grade or classroom [would be] substantially disproportionate to the overall racial composition" of the entire metropolitan area.

While specifically acknowledging that the District Court's findings of a condition of segregation were limited to Detroit, the Court of Appeals approved the use of a metropolitan remedy largely on the grounds that it is

. . . impossible to declare "clearly erroneous" the District Judge's conclusion that any Detroit-only segregation plan will lead directly to a single segregated Detroit school district overwhelmingly black in all of its schools, surrounded by a ring of suburbs and suburban school districts overwhelmingly white in composition in a state in which the racial composition is 87 percent white and 13 percent black.

Viewing the record as a whole, it seems clear that the District Court and the Court of Appeals shifted the primary focus from a Detroit remedy to the metropolitan area only because of their conclusion that total desegregation of Detroit would not produce the racial balance which they perceived as desirable. Both courts proceeded on an assumption that the Detroit schools could not be truly desegregated—in their view of what constituted desegregation—unless the racial composition of the student body of each school substantially reflected the racial composition of the population of the metropolitan area as a whole. The metropolitan area was then defined as Detroit plus 53 of the outlying school districts. That this was the approach the District Court expressly and frankly employed is shown by the order which expressed the court's view of the constitutional standard.

> Within the limitations of reasonable travel time and distance factors, pupil reassignments shall be effected within the clusters described in Exhibit P. M. 12 so as to achieve the greatest degree of actual desegregation to the end that, upon implementation, *no school, grade or classroom* [will be] substantially disproportionate to the overall pupil racial composition. . . .

In *Swann*, which arose in the context of a single independent school district, the Court held:

> If we were to read the holding of the District Court to require as a matter of substantive constitutional right, any particular degree of racial balance or mixing, that approach would be disapproved and we would be obliged to reverse. . . .

The clear import of this language from *Swann* is that desegregation, in the sense of dismantling a dual school system, does not require any particular racial balance in each "school, grade or classroom." . . .

Here the District Court's approach to what constituted "actual desegregation" raises the fundamental question, not presented in *Swann*, as to the circumstances in which a federal court may order desegregation relief that embraces more than a single school district. The court's analytical starting point was its conclusion that school district lines are no more than arbitrary lines on a map "drawn for political convenience." Boundary lines may be bridged where there has been a constitutional violation calling for inter-district relief, but, the notion that school district lines may be casually ignored or treated as a mere administrative convenience is contrary to the history of public education in our country. No single tradition in public education is more deeply rooted than local control over the operation of schools; local autonomy has long been thought essential both to the maintenance of community concern and support for public schools and to quality of the educational process. . . . Thus, in *San Antonio School District* v. *Rodriguez*, 411 U.S. 1, 50, . . . we observed that local control over the educational process affords citizens an opportunity to participate in decision making, permits the structuring of school programs to fit local needs, and encourages "experimentation, innovation and a healthy competition for educational excellence."

The Michigan educational structure involved in this case, in common with most States, provides for a large measure of local control and a review of the scope and character of these local powers indicates the extent to which the inter-district remedy approved by the two courts could disrupt and alter the structure of public education in Michigan. The metropolitan remedy would require, in effect, consolidation of 54 independent school districts historically administered as separate units into a vast new super school district. . . . Entirely apart from the logistical and other serious problems attending large-scale transportation of students, the consolidation would give rise to an array of other problems in financing and operating this new school system. Some of the more obvious questions would be: What would be the status and authority of the present popularly elected school boards? Would the children of Detroit be within the jurisdiction and operating control of a school board elected by the parents and residents of other districts? What board or boards would levy taxes for school operations in these 54 districts constituting the consolidated metropolitan area? What provisions could be made for assuring substantial equality in tax levies among the 54 districts, if this were deemed requisite? What provisions would be made for financing? Would the validity of long-term bonds be jeopardized unless approved by all of the component districts as well as the State? What body would determine that portion of the curricula now left to the discretion of local school boards? Who would establish attendance zones, purchase school equipment, locate and construct new schools, and indeed attend to all the myriad day-to-day decisions that are necessary to school operations affecting potentially more than three quarters of a million pupils? . . .

Of course, no state law is above the Constitution. School district lines and the present laws with respect to local control, are not sacrosanct and if they conflict with the Fourteenth Amendment, federal courts have a duty to prescribe appropriate remedies. . . .

But our prior holdings have been confined to violations and remedies within a single school district. We therefore turn to address, for the first time, the validity of a remedy mandating cross-district or inter-district consolidation to remedy a condition of segregation found to exist in only one district.

The controlling principle consistently expounded in our holdings is that the scope of the remedy is determined by the nature and extent of the constitutional violation. . . . Before the boundaries of separate and autonomous school districts may be set aside by consolidating the separate units for remedial purposes or by imposing a cross-district remedy, it must first be shown that there has been a constitutional violation within one district that produces a significant segregative effect in another district. Specifically it must be shown that racially discriminatory acts of the state or local school districts, or of a single school district have been a substantial cause of inter-district segregation. Thus an inter-district remedy might be in order where the racially discriminatory acts of one or more school districts caused racial segregation in an adjacent district, or where district lines have been deliberately drawn on the basis of race. In such circumstances an inter-district remedy would be appropriate to eliminate the inter-district segregation directly caused by the constitutional violation. Conversely, without an inter-district violation and inter-district effect, there is no constitutional wrong calling for an inter-district remedy. . . .

The constitutional right of the Negro respondents residing in Detroit is to attend a unitary school system in that district. Unless petitioners drew the district lines in a discriminatory fashion, or arranged for white students residing in the Detroit district to attend schools in Oakland and Macomb Counties, they were under no constitutional duty to make provisions for Negro students to do so. The view of the dissenters, that the existence of a dual system *in Detroit* can be made the basis for a decree requiring cross-district transportation of pupils cannot be supported on the grounds that it represents merely the devising of a suitably flexible remedy for the violation of rights already established by our prior decisions. It can be supported only by drastic expansion of the constitutional right itself, an expansion without any support in either constitutional principle or precedent. . . .

Petitioners have urged that they were denied due process by the manner in which the District Court limited their participation after intervention was allowed thus precluding adequate opportunity to present evidence that they had committed no acts having a segregative effect in Detroit. In light of our holding that absent an inter-district violation there is no basis for an interdistrict remedy, we need not reach these claims. It is clear, however, that the District Court, with the approval of the Court of Appeals, has provided an inter-district remedy in the face of a record which shows no constitutional violations that would call for equitable relief except within the city of Detroit. In these circumstances there was no occasion for the parties to address, or for the District Court to consider whether there were racially discriminatory acts for which any of the 53 outlying districts were responsible and which had direct and significant segregative effect on schools of more than one district.

We conclude that the relief ordered by the District Court and affirmed by the Court of Appeals was based upon an erroneous standard and was unsupported by record evidence that acts of the outlying districts affected the discrimination found to exist in the schools of Detroit. Accordingly, the judgment of the Court of Appeals is reversed and the case is remanded for further proceedings consistent with this opinion leading to prompt formulation of a decree directed to eliminating the segregation found to exist in Detroit city schools, a remedy which has been delayed since 1970.

Reversed and remanded.

MR. JUSTICE DOUGLAS, dissenting.

The Court of Appeals has acted responsibly in these cases and we should affirm its judgment. This was the fourth time the case was before it over a span of less than three years. The Court of Appeals affirmed the District Court on the issue of segregation and on the "Detroit-only" plans of desegregation. The Court of Appeals also approved in principle the use of a metropolitan area plan, vacating and remanding only to allow the other affected school districts to be brought in as parties and in other minor respects.

We have before us today no plan for integration. The only orders entered so far are interlocutory. No new principles of law are presented here. Metropolitan treatment of metropolitan problems is commonplace. If this were a sewage problem or a water problem, or an energy problem, there can be no doubt that Michigan would stay well within federal constitutional bounds if she sought a metropolitan remedy. . . . Here the Michigan educational system is unitary, heading up in the legislature under which is the State Board of Education. The State controls the boundaries of school districts. The State supervised school site selection. The construction was done through municipal bonds approved by several state agencies. Education in Michigan is a state project with very little completely local control, except that the schools are financed locally, not on a statewide basis. Indeed the proposal to put school funding in Michigan on a statewide basis was defeated at the polls in November 1972. Yet the school districts by state law are agencies of the State. State action is indeed challenged as violating the Equal Protection Clause. Whatever the reach of that claim may be, it certainly is aimed at discrimination based on race.

Therefore as the Court of Appeals held, there can be no doubt that as a matter of Michigan law the State herself has the final say as to where and how school district lines should be drawn.

When we rule against the metropolitan area remedy we take a step that will likely put the problems of the blacks and our society back to the period that antedated the "separate but equal" regime of *Plessy* v. *Ferguson,* . . . The reason is simple.

The inner core of Detroit is now rather solidly black; and the blacks, we know, in many instances are likely to be poorer, just as were the Chicanos in *San Antonio Independent School District* v. *Rodriguez,* . . . By that decision the poorer school districts must pay their own way. It is therefore a foregone conclusion that we have now given the States a formula whereby the poor must pay their own way.

Today's decision given Rodriguez means that there is no violation of the Equal Protection Clause though the schools are segregated by race and though the black schools are not only "separate" but "inferior."

So far as equal protection is concerned we are now in a dramatic retreat from the 8-to-1 decision in 1896 that blacks could be segregated in public facilities provided they received equal treatment. . . .

MR. JUSTICE MARSHALL, with MR. JUSTICE DOUGLAS, MR. JUSTICE BRENNAN, and MR. JUSTICE WHITE join, dissenting.

In *Brown* v. *Board of Education,* . . . this Court held that segregation of children in public schools on the basis of race deprives minority group children of equal educational opportunities and therefore denies them the equal protection of the laws under the Fourteenth Amendment. This Court recognized then that remedying decades of segregation in public education would not be an easy task. Subsequent events, unfortunately, have seen that prediction bear bitter fruit. But however imbedded old ways, however ingrained old prejudices, this Court has not been diverted from its appointed task of making "a living truth" of our constitutional idea of equal justice under law. . . .

After 20 years of small, often difficult steps

toward that great end, the Court today takes a giant step backwards. Notwithstanding a record showing widespread and pervasive racial segregation in the educational system provided by the State of Michigan for children in Detroit, this Court holds that the District Court was powerless to require the State to remedy its constitutional violation in any meaningful fashion. Ironically purporting to base its result on the principle that the scope of the remedy in a desegregation case should be determined by the nature and the extent of the constitutional violation, the Court's answer is to provide no remedy at all for the violation proved in this case, thereby guaranteeing that Negro children in Detroit will receive the same separate and inherently unequal education in the future as they have been unconstitutionally afforded in the past.

I cannot subscribe to this emasculation of our constitutional guarantee of equal protection of the laws and must respectfully dissent. Our precedents, in my view, firmly establish that where, as here, state-imposed segregation has been demonstrated, it becomes the duty of the State to eliminate root and branch all vestiges of racial discrimination and to achieve the greatest possible degree of actual desegregation. I agree with both the District Court and the Court of Appeals that, under the facts of this case, this duty cannot be fulfilled unless the State of Michigan involves outlying metropolitan area school districts in its desegregation remedy. Furthermore, I perceive no basis either in law or in the practicalities of the situation justifying the State's interposition of school district boundaries as absolute barriers to the implementation of an effective desegregation remedy. Under established and frequently used Michigan procedures, school district lines are both flexible and permeable for a wide variety of purposes, and there is no reason why they must now stand in the way of meaningful desegregation relief.

The rights at issue in the case are too fundamental to be abridged on grounds as superficial as those relied on by the majority today. We deal here with the right of all our children, whatever their race, to an equal start in life and to an equal

opportunity to reach their full potential as citizens. Those children who have been denied that right in the past deserve better than to see fences thrown up to deny them that right in the future. Our Nation, I fear, will be ill-served by the Court's refusal to remedy separate and unequal education, for unless our children begin to learn together, there is little hope that our people will ever learn to live together.

The great irony of the Court's opinion and, in my view, its most serious analytical flaw may be gleaned from its concluding sentence, in which the Court remands for "prompt formulation of a decree directed to eliminating the segregation found to exist in Detroit city schools, a remedy which has been delayed since 1970." . . . The majority, however, seems to have forgotten the District Court's explicit finding that a Detroit-only decree, the only remedy permitted under today's decision, "would not accomplish desegregation." . . .

Some disruption, of course, is the inevitable product of any desegregation decree, whether it operates within one district or on an inter-district basis. As we said in *Swann*, however,

Absent a constitutional violation there would be no basis for judicially ordering assignment of students on a racial basis. All things being equal, with no history of discrimination, it might well be desirable to assign pupils to schools nearest their homes. But all things are not equal in a system that has been deliberately constructed and maintained to enforce racial segregation. The remedy for such segregation may be administratively awkward, inconvenient, and even bizarre in some situations and may impose burdens on some; but all awkwardness and inconvenience cannot be avoided. . . .

Desegregation is not and was never expected to be an easy task. Racial attitudes ingrained in our nation's childhood and adolescence are not quickly thrown aside in its middle years. But just as the inconvenience of some cannot be allowed to stand in the way of the rights of others, so public opposition, no matter how strident, cannot be permitted to divert this Court from the enforcement of the constitutional principles at issue in this case. Today's holding, I fear, is more a reflection of a perceived public mood that we have gone far enough in enforcing the Constitution's guarantee of equal justice than it is the product of neutral principles of law. In the short run, it may seem to be the easier course to allow our great metropolitan areas to be divided up each into two cities—one white, the other black—but it is a course, I predict, our people will ultimately regret. I dissent.

Moose Lodge v. Irvis
407 U.S. 163, 92 S.Ct. 1965, 32 L.Ed. 2d 627 (1972)

A Caucasian member of the national organization of Moose took a Negro as his guest to the dining room of the local lodge and requested food and beverage. Service was refused to his guest, Irvis, solely because he was a Negro. The lodge is a private club which holds meetings in its own building, receives no public funds, and permits only members and their guests to frequent the club house. Irvis brought action under the Civil Rights Act of 1871, giving every person deprived of any civil right under color of a state statute, ordinance, regulation, custom, or usage the right of appeal on the theory that refusal of service to him was "state action" in violation of the Fourteenth Amendment's equal protection clause. Significantly, the Pennsylvania Liquor Control Board had granted the lodge a license with the requirement that it "adhere to the provisions of its own constitution and bylaws." Irvis sought injunctive relief in the United States district court, which would have required the state liquor board to revoke the lodge's license so long as it continued its discriminatory practices. Relief was granted. Following the district court's decision, the national organization altered its bylaws, making applicable to guests the same racial restrictions as those placed upon members. On appeal, the U.S. Supreme Court reversed and remanded. Justice Rehnquist expressed the views of six members. Justices Brennan, Douglas, and Marshall dissented.

Moose Lodge is a private club in the ordinary meaning of that term. It is a local chapter of a national fraternal organization having well defined requirements for membership. It conducts all of its activities in a building that is owned by it. It is not publicly funded. Only members and guests are permitted in any lodge of the order; one may become a guest only by invitation of a member or upon invitation of the house committee.

Appellee, while conceding the right of private clubs to choose members upon a discriminatory basis, asserts that the licensing of Moose Lodge to serve liquor by the Pennsylvania Liquor Control Board amounts to such State involvement with the club's activities as to make its discriminatory practices forbidden by the Equal Protection Clause of the Fourteenth Amendment. The relief sought and obtained by appellee in the District Court was an injunction forbidding the licensing by the liquor authority of Moose Lodge until it ceased its discriminatory practices. We conclude that Moose Lodge's refusal to serve food and beverages to a guest by reason of the fact that he was a Negro does not, under the circumstances here presented, violate the Fourteenth Amendment.

In 1883, this Court in The Civil Rights Cases, . . . set forth the essential dichotomy between discriminatory action by the State, which is prohibited by the Equal Protection clause, and private conduct, "however discriminatory or wrongful," against which that clause "erects no shield." . . .

While the principle is easily stated, the question of whether particular discriminatory conduct is private, on the one hand, or amounts to "State action," on the other hand, frequently admits of no easy answer. "Only by sifting facts and weighing circumstances can the nonobvious involvement of the State in private conduct be attributed its true significance." . . .

Our cases make clear that the impetus for the forbidden discrimination need not originate with the State if it is state action that enforces privately originated discrimination. . . . The Court held in Burton v. Wilmington Parking Authority . . . that a private restaurant owner who refused service because of a customer's race violated the Fourteenth Amendment, where the restaurant was located in a building owned by a state-created parking authority and leased from the authority. The Court, after a comprehensive review of the relationship between the lessee and the parking authority concluded that the latter had "so far insinuated itself into a position of interdependence with Eagle [the restaurant owner] that it must be recognized as a joint participant in the challenged activity, which, on that account, cannot be considered to have been so 'purely private' as to fall without the scope of the Fourteenth Amendment." . . .

The Court has never held, of course, that discrimination by an otherwise private entity would be violative of the Equal Protection Clause if the private entity receives any sort of benefit or service at all from the State, or if it is subject to state regulation in any degree whatever. Since state-furnished services include such necessities of life as electricity, water, and police and fire protection, such a holding would utterly emasculate the distinction between private

as distinguished from State conduct set forth in The Civil Rights Cases, . . . and adhered to in subsequent decisions. Our holdings indicate that where the impetus for the discrimination is private, the State must have "significantly involved itself with invidious discriminations" . . . in order for the discriminatory action to fall within the ambit of the constitutional prohibition.

Our prior decisions dealing with discriminatory refusal of service in public eating places are significantly different factually from the case now before us. . . . Peterson v. Greenville, 373 U.S. 244, dealt with trespass prosecution of persons who "sat in" at a restaurant to protest its refusal of service to Negroes. There the Court held that although the ostensible initiative for the trespass prosecution came from the proprietor, the existence of a local ordinance requiring segregation of races in such places was tantamount to the State having "commanded a particular result." . . . With one exception, . . . there is no suggestion in this record that the Pennsylvania statutes and regulations governing the sale of liquor are intended either overtly or covertly to encourage discrimination.

In Burton, the Court's full discussion of the facts in its opinion indicates the significant differences between that case and this:

"The land and building were publicly owned. As an entity, the building was dedicated to 'public uses' in performance of the Authority's 'essential governmental functions.' . . . The costs of land acquisition, construction, and maintenance are defrayed entirely from donations by the City of Wilmington, from loans and revenue bonds and from the proceeds of rentals and parking services out of which the loans and bonds were payable. Assuming that the distinction would be significant, the commercially leased areas were not surplus state property, but constituted a physically and financially integral and, indeed, indispensable part of the State's plan to operate its project as a self-sustaining unit. Upkeep and maintenance of the building, including necessary repairs, were responsibilities of the Authority and were payable out of public funds. It cannot be doubted that the peculiar relationship of the restaurant to the parking facility in which it is located confers in each an incidental variety of mutual benefits. Guests of the restaurant are afforded a convenient place to park their automobiles, even if they cannot enter the restaurant directly from the parking area. Similarly, its convenience for diners may well provide additional demand for the Authority's parking facilities. Should any improvements effected in the leasehold by Eagle become part of the realty, there is no possibility of increased taxes being passed on to it since the fee is held by a tax exempt government agency. Neither can it be ignored, especially in view of Eagle's affirmative allegation that for it to serve Negroes would injure its business, that profits earned by discrimination not only contribute to, but also are indispensable elements in, the financial success of a government agency.'' . . .

Here there is nothing approaching the symbiotic relationship between lessor and lessee that was present in Burton, where the private lessee obtained the benefit of locating in a building owned by the state-created parking authority, and the parking authority was enabled to carry out its primary public purpose of furnishing parking space by advantageously leasing portions of the building constructed for that purpose to commercial lessees such as the owner of the Eagle Restaurant. Unlike Burton, the Moose Lodge building is located on land owned by it, not by any public authority. Far from apparently holding itself out as a place of public accommodation, Moose Lodge quite ostentatiously proclaims the fact that it is not open to the public at large. Nor is it located and operated in such surroundings that although private in name, it discharges a function or performs a service that would otherwise in all likelihood be performed by the State. In short, while Eagle was a public restaurant in a public building, Moose Lodge is a private social club in a private building.

. . . The only effect that the state licensing of Moose Lodge to serve liquor can be said to have on the right of any other Pennsylvanian to buy or be served liquor on premises other than those

of Moose Lodge is that for some purposes club licenses are counted in the maximum number of licenses which may be issued in a given municipality. Basically each municipality has a quota of one retail license for each 1,500 inhabitants. Licenses issued to hotels, municipal golf courses and airport restaurants are not counted in this quota, nor are club licenses, until the maximum number of retail licenses is reached. Beyond that point, neither additional retail licenses nor additional club licenses may be issued so long as the number of issued and outstanding retail licenses remains above the statutory maximum. . . .

However detailed this type of regulation may be in some particulars, it cannot be said to in any way foster or encourage racial discrimination. Nor can it be said to make the State in any realistic sense a partner or even a joint venturer in the club's enterprise. The limited effect of the prohibition against obtaining additional club licenses when the maximum number of retail licenses allotted to a municipality has been issued, when considered together with the availability of liquor from hotel, restaurant, and retail licensees, falls far short of conferring upon club licensees a monopoly in the dispensing of liquor in any given municipality or in the State as a whole. We therefore hold that, with the exception hereafter noted, the operation of the regulatory scheme enforced by the Pennsylvania Liquor Control Board does not sufficiently implicate the State in the discriminatory guest policies of Moose Lodge so as to make the latter ''State action'' within the ambit of the Equal Protection Clause of the Fourteenth Amendment.

The District Court found that the regulations of the Liquor Control Board adopted pursuant to the statute affirmatively require that ''every club licensee shall adhere to all the provisions of its constitution and bylaws.'' . . .

The effect of this particular regulation on Moose Lodge under the provisions of the constitution placed in the record in the court below would be to place State sanctions behind its discriminatory membership rules, but not behind its guest practices, which were not embodied in the constitution of the lodge. Had there been no change in the relevant circumstances since the making of the record in the District Court, our holding . . . that appellee has standing to challenge only the guest practices of Moose Lodge would have a bearing on our disposition of this issue. Appellee stated upon oral argument, though, and Moose Lodge conceded in its Brief that the bylaws of the Supreme Lodge have been altered since the lower court decision to make applicable to guests the same sort of racial restrictions as are presently applicable to members.

Even though the Liquor Control Board regulation in question is neutral in its terms, the result of its application in a case where the constitution and bylaws of a club required racial discrimination would be to invoke the sanctions of the State to enforce a concededly discriminatory private rule. State action, for purposes of the Equal Protection Clause, may emanate from rulings of administrative and regulatory agencies as well as from legislative or judicial action. . . . *Shelley* v. *Kraemer* . . . makes it clear that the application of state sanctions to enforce such a rule would violate the Fourteenth Amendment. Although the record before us is not as clear as one would like, appellant has not persuaded us that the District Court should have denied any and all relief. . . .

Reversed and remanded.

MR. JUSTICE DOUGLAS, with whom MR. JUSTICE MARSHALL joins, dissenting.

My view of the First Amendment and the related guarantees of the Bill of Rights is that they create a zone of privacy which precludes government from interfering with private clubs or groups. The associational rights which our system honors permit all white, all black, all brown, and all yellow clubs to be formed. They also permit all Catholic, all Jewish, or all agnostic clubs to be established. Government may not tell a man or woman who his or her associates must be. The individual can be as selective as he desires. So the fact that the Moose Lodge allows only Caucasians to join or come as guests is constitutionally irrelevant, as is the decision of the Black Muslims to admit to their services only members of their race.

The problem is different, however, where the public domain is concerned. . . . Where restaurants or other facilities serving the public are concerned and licenses are obtained from the State for operating the business, the "public" may not be defined by the proprietor to include only people of his choice; nor may a State or municipal service be granted only to some. . . .

Those cases are not precisely apposite, however, for a private club, by definition, is not in the public domain. And the fact that a private club gets some kind of permit from the State or municipality does not make it ipso facto a public enterprise or undertaking, any more than the grant to a householder of a permit to operate an incinerator puts the householder in the public domain. We must therefore examine whether there are special circumstances involved in the Pennsylvania scheme which differentiate the liquor license possessed by Moose Lodge from the incinerator permit.

Pennsylvania has a state store system of alcohol distribution. Resale is permitted by hotels, restaurants, and private clubs which all must obtain licenses from the Liquor Control Board. The scheme of regulation is complete and pervasive; and the state courts have sustained many restrictions on the licensees. . . . Among these requirements is regulation No. 113.09 which says "Every club licensee shall adhere to all the provisions of its Constitution and By-laws." This regulation means, as applied to Moose Lodge, that it must adhere to the racially discriminatory provision of the Constitution of its Supreme Lodge that "The membership of the lodge shall be composed of male persons of the Caucasian or White race above the age of twenty-one years, and not married to someone other than the Caucasian or White race, who are of good moral character, physically and mentally normal who shall profess a belief in a Supreme Being."

It is argued that this regulation only aims at the prevention of subterfuge and at enforcing Pennsylvania's differentiation between places of public accommodation and bona fide private clubs. It is also argued that the regulation only gives effect to the constitutionally protected rights of privacy and of association. But I cannot so read the regulation. . . .

Were this regulation the only infirmity in Pennsylvania's licensing scheme, I would perhaps agree with the majority that the appropriate relief would be a decree enjoining its enforcement. But there is another flaw in the scheme not so easily cured. Liquor licenses in Pennsylvania, unlike driver's licenses, or marriage licenses, are not freely available to those who meet racially neutral qualifications. . . . What the majority neglects to say is that the Harrisburg quota, where Moose Lodge No. 107 is located, has been full for many years. No more club licenses may be issued in that city.

This state-enforced scarcity of licenses restricts the ability of blacks to obtain liquor, for liquor is commercially available *only* at private clubs for a significant portion of each week. Access by blacks to places that serve liquor is further limited by the fact that the state quota is filled. A group desiring to form a non-discriminatory club which would serve blacks must purchase a license held by an existing club, which can exact a monopoly price for the transfer. The availability of such a license is speculative at best, however, for, as Moose Lodge itself concedes, without a liquor license a fraternal organization would be hard-pressed to survive.

Thus, the State of Pennsylvania is putting the weight of its liquor license, concededly a valued and important adjunct to a private club, behind racial discrimination. . . .

As the first Justice Harlan, dissenting in the Civil Rights Cases, . . . said:

"I agree that government has nothing to do with social, as distinguished from technically legal, rights of individuals. No government ever has brought, or ever can bring, its people into social intercourse against their wishes. Whether one person will permit and maintain social relations with another is a matter with which government has no concern. . . . What I affirm is that no State, nor the officers of any State, nor any corporation or individual wielding power under State authority for the public benefit or the public convenience can, consistently . . . with the freedom established by the fundamental law . . . discriminate against freemen or citizens, in those rights, because of their race. . . .''

The regulation governing this liquor license has in it that precise infirmity.

Craig v. Boren
429 U.S. 190, 97 S.Ct. 451, 50 L.Ed. 2d 397 (1976)

Two sections (241 and 245) of an Oklahoma statute combined to prohibit the sale of 3.2 percent beer to males under the age of 21 and to females under the age of 18. Craig (a male between 18 and 21 years of age) and Whitener (a licensed vendor of 3.2 percent beer) sought injunctive relief against the statute in the United States District Court for the Western District of Oklahoma. They contended that the gender-based differential constituted an invidious discrimination against males 18–20 years old, in violation of the equal protection clause of the Fourteenth Amendment. The three-judge panel upheld the classification and dismissed the action. The Supreme Court noted probable jurisdiction. Justice Brennan's opinion for the Court begins with reference to *Reed* v. *Reed* (404 U.S. 71: 1971), where a unanimous bench voided an Idaho statutory probate scheme giving a mandatory preference for appointment as administrator to male applicants over equally qualified female applicants. In *Reed,* Chief Justice Burger's opinion for the Court held that the Fourteenth Amendment denies "to States the power to legislate that different treatment be accorded to persons placed by a statute into different classes on the basis of criteria wholly unrelated to the objective of that statute."

MR. JUSTICE BRENNAN delivered the opinion of the Court. . . .

Analysis may appropriately begin with the reminder that Reed emphasized that statutory classifications that distinguish between males and females are "subject to scrutiny under the Equal Protection Clause." . . . To withstand constitutional challenge, previous cases establish that classifications by gender must serve important governmental objectives and must be substantially related to achievement of those objectives. Thus, in Reed, the objectives of "reducing the workload on probate courts," . . . and "avoiding intrafamily controversy," . . . were deemed of insufficient importance to sustain use of an overt gender criterion in the appointment of administrators of intestate decedents' estates. Decisions following Reed similarly have rejected administrative ease and convenience as sufficiently important objectives to justify gender-based classifications. . . .

We accept for purposes of discussion the District Court's identification of the objective underlying §§ 241 and 245 as the enhancement of traffic safety. Clearly, the protection of public health and safety represents an important function of state and local governments. However, appellees' statistics in our view cannot support the conclusion that the gender-based distinction closely serves to achieve that objective and therefore the distinction cannot under Reed withstand equal protection challenge.

The appellees introduced a variety of statistical surveys. . . .

Even were this statistical evidence accepted as accurate, it nevertheless offers only a weak answer to the equal protection question presented here. The most focused and relevant of the statistical surveys, arrests of 18–20-year-olds for alcohol-related driving offenses, exemplifies the ultimate unpersuasiveness of this evidentiary record. Viewed in terms of the correlation between sex and the actual activity that Oklahoma seeks to regulate—driving while

under the influence of alcohol—the statistics broadly establish that .18 percent of females and 2 percent of males in that age group were arrested for that offense. While such a disparity is not trivial in a statistical sense, it hardly can form the basis for employment of a gender line as a classifying device. Certainly if maleness is to serve as a proxy for drinking and driving, a correlation of 2% must be considered an unduly tenuous "fit." . . .

There is no reason to belabor this line of analysis. It is unrealistic to expect either members of the judiciary or state officials to be well versed in the rigors of experimental or statistical technique. But this merely illustrates that proving broad sociological propositions by statistics is a dubious business, and one that inevitably is in tension with the normative philosophy that underlies the Equal Protection Clause. Suffice to say that the showing offered by the appellees does not satisfy us that sex represents a legitimate, accurate proxy for the regulation of drinking and driving. In fact, when it is further recognized that Oklahoma's statute prohibits only the selling of 3.2% beer to young males and not their drinking the beverage once acquired (even after purchase by their 18–20-year-old female companions), the relationship between gender and traffic safety becomes far too tenuous to satisfy Reed's requirement that the gender-based difference be substantially related to achievement of the statutory objective.

We hold, therefore, that under Reed, Oklahoma's 3.2% beer statute invidiously discriminates against males 18–20 years of age. . . .

MR. JUSTICE POWELL, concurring. . . .

MR. JUSTICE STEVENS, concurring. . . .

MR. JUSTICE BLACKMUN, concurring in part. . . .

MR. JUSTICE STEWART, concurring in the judgment. . . .

MR. CHIEF JUSTICE BURGER, dissenting. . . .

MR. JUSTICE REHNQUIST, dissenting.

The Court's disposition of this case is objectionable on two grounds. First is its conclusion that *men* challenging a gender-based statute which treats them less favorably than women may invoke a more stringent standard of judicial review than pertains to most other types of classifications. Second is the Court's enunciation of this standard, without citation to any source, as being that "classifications by gender must serve *important* governmental objectives and must be *substantially* related to achievement of those objectives." ... The only redeeming feature of the Court's opinion, to my mind, is that it apparently signals a retreat by those who joined the plurality opinion in *Frontiero* v. *Richardson* ... from their view that sex is a "suspect" classification for purposes of equal protection analysis. I think the Oklahoma statute challenged here need pass only the "rational basis" equal protection analysis ... and I believe that it is constitutional under that analysis.

In *Frontiero* v. *Richardson*, ... the opinion for the plurality sets forth the reasons of four Justices for concluding that sex should be regarded as a suspect classification for purposes of equal protection analysis. These reasons center on our Nation's "long and unfortunate history of sex discrimination," ... which has been reflected in a whole range of restrictions on the legal rights of women, not the least of which have concerned the ownership of property and participation in the electoral process. Noting that the pervasive and persistent nature of the discrimination experienced by women is in part the result of their ready identifiability, the plurality rested its invocation of strict scrutiny largely upon the fact that "statutory distinctions between the sexes often have the effect of invidiously relegating the entire class of females to inferior legal status without regard to the actual capabilities of its individual members." ...

Subsequent to Frontiero, the Court has declined to hold that sex is a suspect class, ... and no such holding is imported by the Court's resolution of this case. However, the Court's application here of an elevated or "intermediate" level scrutiny, like that invoked in cases dealing with discrimination against females, raises the question of why the statute here should be treated any differently from countless legislative classifications unrelated to sex which have been upheld under a minimum rationality standard. ...

Most obviously unavailable to support any kind of special scrutiny in this case, is a history or pattern of past discrimination, such as was relied on by the plurality in Frontiero to support its invocation of strict scrutiny. There is no suggestion in the Court's opinion that males in this age group are in any way peculiarly disadvantaged, subject to systematic discriminatory treatment, or otherwise in need of special solicitude from the courts. ...

The Court's conclusion that a law which treats males less favorably than females "must serve important governmental objectives and must be substantially related to achievement of those objectives" apparently comes out of thin air. The Equal Protection Clause contains no such language, and none of our previous cases adopt that standard. I would think we have had enough difficulty with the two standards of review which our cases have recognized—the norm of "rational basis," and the "compelling state interest" required where a "suspect classification" is involved—so as to counsel weightily against the insertion of still another "standard" between those two. How is this Court to divine what objectives are important? How is it to determine whether a particular law is "substantially" related to the achievement of such objective, rather than related in some other way to its achievement? Both of the phrases used are so diaphanous and elastic as to invite subjective judicial preferences or prejudices relating to particular types of legislation, masquerading as judgments whether such legislation is directed at "important" objectives or, whether the relationship to those objectives is "substantial" enough.

I would have thought that if this Court were to leave anything to decision by the popularly elected branches of the Government, where no constitutional claim other than that of equal protection is invoked, it would be the decision as to what governmental objectives to be achieved by law are "important," and which are not. As for the second part of the Court's new test, the Judicial Branch is probably in no worse position than the Legislative or Executive Branches to determine if there is *any* rational relationship between a classification and the purpose which it might be thought to serve. But the introduction of the adverb "substantially" requires courts to make subjective judgments as to operational effects, for which neither their expertise nor their access to data fits them. And even if we manage to avoid both confusion and the mirroring of our own preferences in the development of this new doctrine, the thousands of judges in other courts who must interpret the Equal Protection Clause may not be so fortunate. . . .

Rostker v. *Goldberg*
49 LW 4798 (1981)

The Military Selective Service Act (referred to in the opinions below as the MSSA) authorizes the President to require draft registration for males but not females. Actual conscription was ended in 1973, and a presidential proclamation discontinued registration in 1975. As a result of the invasion of Afghanistan by the Soviet Union, President Carter decided in early 1980 to reinstate draft registration as a national display of strength. In seeking funds from Congress for registration, Carter requested that the statute be amended to permit registration of women as well. In the appropriation, however, Congress provided only enough money to register males, and expressly declined to amend the statute to permit the registration of women. On July 2, 1980, President Carter by proclamation ordered the registration of certain groups of young men, a process to begin on July 21. Carter's action "breathed new life" into an old lawsuit, dating from 1971, against a gender-based draft. On July 18, the District Court for the Eastern District of Pennsylvania invalidated the draft statute under the due process clause of the Fifth Amendment and permanently enjoined the government from conducting registration under the act. On July 19, at the government's request, Justice Brennan, as circuit justice, stayed the district court's order. The full Court noted probable jurisdiction for the government's appeal on December 1, 1980.

JUSTICE REHNQUIST delivered the opinion of the Court.

The question presented is whether the Military Selective Service Act, 50 U. S. C. App. § 451 *et seq.*, violates the Fifth Amendment to the United States Constitution in authorizing the President to require the registration of males and not females. . . .

Whenever called upon to judge the constitu-tionality of an Act of Congress—"the gravest and most delicate duty that this Court is called upon to perform," *Blodgett* v. *Holden*, 275 U.S. 142, 148 (1927) (Holmes, J.)—the Court accords "great weight to the decisions of Congress." *CBS, Inc.* v. *Democratic National Committee*, 412 U.S. 94, 102 (1973). The Congress is a coequal branch of government whose members take the same oath we do to uphold the Constitution of the United States. As Justice Frankfurter noted in *Joint Anti-Fascist Refugee Committee* v. *McGrath*, 341 U.S. 123, 164 (1951) (concurring opinion), we must have "due regard to the fact that this Court is not exercising a primary judgment but is sitting in judgment upon those who also have taken the oath to observe the Constitution and who have the responsibility for carrying on government." The customary deference accorded the judgments of Congress is certainly appropriate when, as here, Congress specifically considered the question of the Act's constitutionality. . . .

This is not, however, merely a case involving the customary deference accorded congressional decisions. The case arises in the context of Congress's authority over national defense and military affairs, and perhaps in no other area has the Court accorded Congress greater deference. . . . This Court has consistently recognized Congress's "broad constitutional power" to raise and regulate armies and navies, *Schlesinger* v. *Ballard*, 419 U.S. 498, 510 (1975). As the Court noted in considering a challenge to the selective service laws, "The constitutional power of Congress to raise and support armies and to make all laws necessary and proper to that end is broad and sweeping." *United States* v. *O'Brien*, 391 U.S. 367, 377 (1968). . . .

Not only is the scope of Congress's constitutional power in this area broad, but the lack of competence on the part of the courts is marked. In *Gilligan* v. *Morgan*, 413 U.S. 1, 10 (1973), the Court noted:

It is difficult to conceive of an area of governmental activity in which the courts have less competence. The complex, subtle, and professional decisions as to the composition, training, equipping, and control of a military force are essentially professional military judgments, subject always to civilian control of the Legislative and Executive branches.

None of this is to say that Congress is free to disregard the Constitution when it acts in the area of military affairs. In that area as any other Congress remains subject to the limitations of the Due Process Clause . . . but the tests and limitations to be applied may differ because of the military context. We of course do not abdicate our ultimate responsibility to decide the constitutional question, but simply recognize that the Constitution itself requires such deference to congressional choice. In deciding the question before us we must be particularly careful not to substitute our judgment of what is desirable for that of Congress, or our own evaluation of evidence for a reasonable evaluation by the Legislative Branch. . . .

No one could deny that under the test of *Craig* v. *Boren*, . . . the Government's interest in raising and supporting armies is an "important governmental interest." Congress and its committees carefully considered and debated two alternative means of furthering that interest: the first was to register only males for potential conscription, and the other was to register both sexes. Congress chose the former alternative. When that decision is challenged on equal protection grounds, the question a court must decide is not which alternative it would have chosen, had it been the primary decision-maker, but whether that chosen by Congress denies equal protection of the laws.

Nor can it be denied that the imposing number of cases from this Court previously cited suggest that judicial deference to such congressional exercise of authority is at its apogee when legislative action under the congressional authority to raise and support armies and make rules and regulations for their governance is challenged. . . .

The foregoing clearly establishes that the decision to exempt women from registration was not the "accidental by-product of a traditional way of thinking about women." . . . In *Michael M.*, . . . we rejected a similar argument because of action by the California Legislature considering and rejecting proposals to make a statute challenged on discrimination grounds gender-neutral. The cause for rejecting the argument is considerably stronger here. The issue was considered at great length, and Congress clearly expressed its purpose and intent. . . .

Congress determined that any future draft,

which would be facilitated by the registration scheme, would be characterized by a need for combat troops. The Senate Report explained, in a specific finding later adopted by both Houses, that "if mobilization were to be ordered in a wartime scenario, the primary manpower need would be for combat replacements." . . .

Women as a group, however, unlike men as a group, are not eligible for combat. The restrictions on the participation of women in combat in the Navy and Air Force are statutory. Under 10 U. S. C. § 6015 "women may not be assigned to duty on vessels or in aircraft that are engaged in combat missions," and under 10 U. S. C. § 8549 female members of the Air Force "may not be assigned to duty in aircraft engaged in combat missions." The Army and Marine Corps preclude the use of women in combat as a matter of established policy. Congress specifically recognized and endorsed the exclusion of women from combat in exempting women from registration. . . .

The reason women are exempt from registration is not because military needs can be met by drafting men. This is not a case of Congress arbitrarily choosing to burden one of two similarly situated groups, such as would be the case with an all-black or all-white, or an all-Catholic or all-Lutheran, or an all-Republican or all-Democratic registration. Men and women, because of the combat restrictions on women, are simply not similarly situated for purposes of a draft or registration for a draft.

Congress's decision to authorize the registration of only men, therefore, does not violate the Due Process Clause. The exemption of women from registration is not only sufficiently but closely related to Congress's purpose in authorizing registration. See *Michael M., . . . Craig* v. *Boren, Reed* v. *Reed.* . . . The fact that Congress and the Executive have decided that women should not serve in combat fully justifies Congress in not authorizing their registration, since the purpose of registration is to develop a pool of potential combat troops. As was the case in *Schlesinger* v. *Ballard* . . . "the gender classification is not invidious, but rather realistically reflects the fact that the sexes are not similarly

situated" in this case. . . . The Constitution requires that Congress treat similarly situated persons similarly, not that it engage in gestures of superficial equality. . . .

Most significantly, Congress determined that staffing noncombat positions with women during a mobilization would be positively detrimental to the important goal of military flexibility. . . . The District Court was quite wrong in undertaking an independent evaluation of this evidence, rather than adopting an appropriately deferential examination of *Congress's* evaluation of that evidence.

In light of the foregoing, we conclude that Congress acted well within its constitutional authority when it authorized the registration of men, and not women, under the Military Selective Service Act. The decision of the District Court holding otherwise is accordingly

Reversed.

JUSTICE WHITE, with whom JUSTICE BRENNAN joins, dissenting. . . .

JUSTICE MARSHALL, with whom JUSTICE BRENNAN joins, dissenting.

The Court today places its imprimatur on one of the most potent remaining public expressions of "ancient canards about the proper role of women," *Phillips* v. *Martin Marietta Corp.,* 400 U.S. 542, 545 (1971). . . . It upholds a statute that requires males but not females to register for the draft, and which thereby categorically excludes women from a fundamental civic obligation. Because I believe the Court's decision is inconsistent with the Constitution's guarantee of equal protection of the laws, I dissent. . . .

By now it should be clear that statutes like the MSSA, which discriminate on the basis of gender, must be examined under the "heightened" scrutiny mandated by *Craig* v. *Boren.* . . . Under this test, a gender-based classification cannot withstand constitutional challenge unless the classification is substantially related to the achievement of an important governmental objective. . . . The party defending the challenged classification carries the burden of demonstrating both the importance of the governmental objective it serves and the substantial relationship between the discriminatory means and the asserted end. . . .

In the first place, although the Court purports to apply the *Craig* v. *Boren* test, the "similarly situated" analysis the Court employs is in fact significantly different from the *Craig* v. *Boren* approach. . . . The Court essentially reasons that the gender classification employed by the MSSA is constitutionally permissible because nondiscrimination is not necessary to achieve the purpose of registration to prepare for a draft of combat troops. In other words, the majority concludes that women may be excluded from registration because they will not be needed in the event of a draft.

This analysis, however, focuses on the wrong question. The relevant inquiry under the *Craig* v. *Boren* test is not whether a *gender-neutral* classification would substantially advance important governmental interests. Rather, the question is whether the gender-based classification is itself substantially related to the achievement of the asserted governmental interest. Thus, the Government's task in this case is to demonstrate that excluding women from registration substantially furthers the goal of preparing for a draft of combat troops. Or to put it another way, the Government must show that registering women would substantially impede its efforts to prepare for such a draft. Under our precedents, the Government cannot meet this burden without showing that a gender neutral statute would be a less effective means of attaining this end. . . . In this case, the Government makes no claim that preparing for a draft of combat troops cannot be accomplished just as effectively by *registering* both men and women but *drafting* only men if only men turn out to be needed. . . .

The fact that registering women in no way obstructs the governmental interest in preparing for a draft of combat troops points up a second flaw in the Court's analysis. The Court essentially reduces the question of the constitutionality of male-only *registration* to the validity of a hypothetical program for *conscripting* only men. The Court posits a draft in which *all* conscripts are either assigned to those specific combat posts presently closed to women or must be available for rotation into such positions. . . .

But even addressing the Court's reasoning on its own terms, its analysis is flawed because the entire argument rests on a premise that is demonstrably false. As noted, the majority simply assumes that registration prepares for a draft in which *every* draftee must be available for assignment to combat. But the majority's draft scenario finds no support in either the testimony before Congress, or more importantly, in the findings of the Senate Report. Indeed, the scenario appears to exist only in the Court's imagination, for even the Government represents only that "in the event of mobilization, *approximately two-thirds* of the demand on the induction system would be for *combat skills.*" . . . For my part, rather than join the Court in imagining hypothetical drafts, I prefer to examine the findings in the Senate Report and the testimony presented to Congress. . . .

This review of the findings contained in the Senate Report and the testimony presented at the congressional hearings demonstrates that there is no basis for the Court's representation that women are ineligible for *all* the positions that would need to be filled in the event of a draft.

After reviewing the discussion and findings contained in the Senate Report, the most I am able to say of the Report is that it demonstrates that drafting *very large numbers* of women would frustrate the achievement of a number of important governmental objectives that relate to the ultimate goal of maintaining "an adequate armed strength . . . to insure the security of this Nation." . . . Or to put it another way, the Senate Report establishes that induction of a large number of men but only a limited number of women, as determined by the military's personnel requirements, would be substantially related to important governmental interests. But the discussion and findings in the Senate Report do not enable the Government to carry its burden of demonstrating that *completely* excluding women from the draft by excluding them from registration substantially furthers important governmental objectives.

In concluding that the Government has carried its burden in this case, the Court adopts "an appropriately deferential examination of *Congress*'s evaluation of [the] evidence," . . . The majority then proceeds to supplement Congress's actual findings with those the Court apparently believes Congress could (and should) have made. Beyond that, the Court substitutes hollow shibboleths about "deference to legislative decisions" for constitutional analysis. It is as if the majority has lost sight of the fact that "it is the responsibility of this Court to act as the ultimate interpreter of the Constitution." . . . Congressional enactments in the area of military affairs must, like all other laws, be *judged* by the standards of the Constitution. For the Constitution is the supreme law of the land and *all* legislation must conform to the principles it lays down. As the Court has pointed out, "the phrase 'war power' cannot be invoked as a talismanic incantation to support any exercise of congressional power which can be brought within its ambit." *United States* v. *Robel.* . . .

Furthermore, "[w]hen it appears that an Act of Congress conflicts with [a constitutional] provisio[n], we have no choice but to enforce the paramount commands of the Constitution. We are sworn to do no less. We cannot push back the limits of the Constitution merely to accommodate challenged legislation." *Trop* v. *Dulles*. . . (plurality opinion). In some 106 instances since this Court was established it has determined that congressional action exceeded the bounds of the Constitution. I believe the same is true of this statute. In an attempt to avoid its constitutional obligation, the Court today "pushes back the limits of the Constitution" to accommodate an Act of Congress.

I would affirm the judgment of the District Court.

AFFIRMATIVE ACTION DEBATES

The judicial opinions reprinted in part below come from two cases decided by the United States Supreme Court. Each presents a point of view on affirmative action. Justice Marshall speaks for, and Justice Douglas speaks against, racially preferential treatment. Details of the litigation are provided in the essay preceding the cases in this chapter. In the first (*DeFunis* v. *Odegaard*), faced with the use of race in law school admissions at the University of Washington, five Justices ruled that the case was moot. Justice Douglas thought otherwise and reached the merits in his dissent. In the second (*Regents of the University of California* v. *Bakke*), the Court scrutinized an admissions plan at the Davis medical school in which race was an important criterion. Justice Marshall was among the four Justices who found no constitutional or statutory objection to the plan.

MR. JUSTICE DOUGLAS, dissenting in *DeFunis* v. *Odegaard,* 416 U.S. 312 (1974).

The Equal Protection Clause did not enact a requirement that Law Schools employ as the sole criterion for admissions a formula based upon the LSAT and undergraduate grades, nor does it prohibit law schools from evaluating an applicant's prior achievements in light of the barriers that he had to overcome. A black applicant who pulled himself out of the ghetto into a junior college may thereby demonstrate a level of motivation, perseverance and ability that would lead a fairminded admissions committee to conclude that he shows more promise for law study than the son of a rich alumnus who achieved better grades at Harvard. That applicant would not be offered admission because he is black, but because as an individual he has shown he has the potential, while the Harvard man may have taken less advantage of the vastly superior opportunities offered him. . . .

The difference between such a policy and the one presented by this case is that the Committee would be making decisions on the basis of individual attributes, rather than according a preference solely on the basis of race. . . .

There is no constitutional right for any race to be preferred. The years of slavery did more than retard the progress of blacks. Even a greater wrong was done the whites by creating arrogance instead of humility and by encouraging the growth of the fiction of a superior race. There is no superior person by constitutional standards. A DeFunis who is white is entitled to no advantage by reason of that fact; nor is he subject to any disability, no matter what his race or color. Whatever his race, he had a constitutional right to have his application considered on its individual merits in a racially neutral manner. . . .

The argument is that a "compelling" state interest can easily justify the racial discrimination that is practiced here. To many, "compelling" would give members of one race even more than pro rata representation. The public payrolls might then be deluged say with Chicanos because they are as a group the poorest of the poor and need work more than others, leaving desperately poor individual blacks and whites without employment. By the same token large quotas of blacks or browns could be added to the Bar, waiving examinations required of other groups, so that it would be better racially balanced. The State, however, may not proceed by racial classification to force strict population equivalencies for every group in every occupation, overriding individual preferences. The Equal Protection Clause commands the elimination of racial barriers, not their creation in order to satisfy our theory as to how society ought to be organized. The purpose of the University of Washington cannot be to produce black lawyers for blacks, Polish lawyers for Poles, Jewish lawyers for Jews, Irish lawyers for Irish. It should be to produce good lawyers for Americans and not to place First Amendment barriers against anyone. That is the point at the heart of all our school desegregation cases. . . .

If discrimination based on race is constitutionally permissible when those who hold the reins can come up with "compelling" reasons to justify it, then constitutional guarantees acquire an accordionlike quality. . . .

MR. JUSTICE MARSHALL, in *Regents* v. *Bakke*, 438 U.S. 265 (1978).

I agree with the judgment of the Court only insofar as it permits a university to consider the race of an applicant in making admissions decisions. I do not agree that petitioner's admissions program violates the Constitution. For it must be remembered that, during most of the past 200 years, the Constitution as interpreted by this Court did not prohibit the most ingenious and pervasive forms of discrimination against the Negro. Now, when a State acts to remedy the effects of that legacy of discrimination, I cannot believe that this same Constitution stands as a barrier.

Three hundred and fifty years ago, the Negro was dragged to this country in chains to be sold into slavery. Uprooted from his homeland and thrust into bondage for forced labor, the slave was deprived of all legal rights. It was unlawful to teach him to read; he could be sold away from his family and friends at the whim of his master; and killing or maiming him was not a crime. The system of slavery brutalized and dehumanized both master and slave. . . .

The status of the Negro as property was officially erased by his emancipation at the end of the Civil War. But the long-awaited emancipation, while freeing the Negro from slavery, did not bring him citizenship or equality in any meaningful way. . . .

The position of the Negro today in America is the tragic but inevitable consequence of centuries of unequal treatment. Measured by any benchmark of comfort or achievement, meaningful equality remains a distant dream for the Negro. . . .

I do not believe that the Fourteenth Amendment requires us to accept that fate. Neither its history nor our past cases lend any support to the conclusion that a university may not remedy the cumulative effects of society's discrimination by giving consideration to race in an effort to increase the number and percentage of Negro doctors. . . .

It is unnecessary in 20th century America to have individual Negroes demonstrate that they have been victims of racial discrimination; the racism of our society has been so pervasive that none, regardless of wealth or position, has managed to escape its impact. The experience of Negroes in America has been different in kind, not just in degree, from that of other ethnic groups. It is not merely the history of slavery alone but also that a whole people were marked as inferior by the law. And that mark has endured. The dream of America as the great melting pot has not been realized for the Negro; because of his skin color he never even made it into the pot. . . .

I fear that we have come full circle. After the Civil War our Government started several "affirmative action" programs. This Court in the Civil Rights Cases and *Plessy* v. *Ferguson* destroyed the movement toward complete equality. For almost a century no action was taken, and this nonaction was with the tacit approval of the courts. Then we had *Brown* v. *Board of Education* and the Civil Rights Acts of Congress, followed by numerous affirmative action programs. *Now,* we have this Court again stepping in, this time to stop affirmative action programs of the type used by the University of California. . . .

APPENDIX

The Constitution
of the United States of America

We the people of the United States, in order to form a more perfect Union, establish Justice, insure domestic Tranquility, provide for the common defence, promote the general Welfare, and secure the Blessings of Liberty to ourselves and our Posterity, do ordain and establish this CONSTITUTION for the United States of America.

Article I

SECTION 1

All legislative Powers herein granted shall be vested in a Congress of the United States, which shall consist of a Senate and House of Representatives.

SECTION 2

The House of Representatives shall be composed of Members chosen every second Year by the People of the several States, and the Electors in each State shall have the Qualifications requisite for Electors of the most numerous Branch of the State Legislature.

No Person shall be a Representative who shall not have attained to the Age of twenty-five Years, and been seven Years a Citizen of the United States, and who shall not, when elected, be an Inhabitant of that State in which he shall be chosen.

[Representatives and direct Taxes shall be apportioned among the several States which may be included within this Union, according to their respective Numbers, which shall be determined by adding to the whole Number of free Persons, including those bound to Service for a Term of Years, and excluding Indians not taxed, three fifths of all other persons.][1] The actual Enumeration shall be made within three Years after the first Meeting of the Congress of the United States, and within every subsequent Term of ten Years, in such Manner as they shall by Law direct. The Number of Representatives shall not exceed one for every thirty thousand, but each State shall have at least one Representative; and until such enumeration shall be made, the State of New Hampshire shall be entitled to chuse three, Massachusetts eight, Rhode Island and Providence Plantations one, Connecticut five, New York six, New Jersey four, Pennsylvania eight, Delaware one, Maryland six, Virginia ten, North Carolina five, South Carolina five, and Georgia three.

When vacancies happen in the Representation from any State, the Executive Authority thereof shall issue Writs of Election to fill such Vacancies.

The House of Representatives shall chuse their

[1] This provision was modified by the Sixteenth Amendment. The three-fifths reference to slaves was rendered obsolete by the Thirteenth and Fourteenth Amendments.

Speaker and other Officers; and shall have the sole Power of Impeachment.

SECTION 3

The Senate of the United States shall be composed of two Senators from each State, chosen by the Legislature thereof,[2] for six Years; and each Senator shall have one Vote.

Immediately after they shall be assembled in Consequence of the first Election, they shall be divided as equally as may be into three Classes. The Seats of the Senators of the first Class shall be vacated at the Expiration of the second Year, of the Second Class at the Expiration of the fourth Year, and the third Class at the Expiration of the sixth Year, so that one-third may be chosen every second Year; and if Vacancies happen by Resignation, or otherwise, during the Recess of the Legislature of any State, the Executive thereof may make temporary Appointments until the next Meeting of the Legislature, which shall then fill such Vacancies.

No Person shall be a Senator who shall not have attained to the Age of thirty Years, and been nine Years a Citizen of the United States, and who shall not, when elected, be an Inhabitant of that State for which he shall be chosen.

The Vice President of the United States shall be President of the Senate, but shall have no Vote, unless they be equally divided.

The Senate shall chuse their other Officers, and also a President pro tempore, in the absence of the Vice President, or when he shall exercise the Office of President of the United States.

The Senate shall have the sole Power to try all Impeachments. When sitting for that Purpose, they shall be on Oath or Affirmation. When the President of the United States is tried, the Chief Justice shall preside; And no Person shall be convicted without the Concurrence of two thirds of the Members present.

Judgment in Cases of Impeachment shall not extend further than to removal from Office, and disqualification to hold and enjoy any Office of honor, Trust or Profit under the United States; but the Party convicted shall nevertheless be liable and subject to Indictment, Trial, Judgment, and Punishment, according to Law.

SECTION 4

The Times, Places and Manner of holding Elections for Senators and Representatives, shall be prescribed in each State by the Legislature thereof; but the Congress may at any time by Law make or alter such Regulations, except as to the Places of chusing Senators.

The Congress shall assemble at least once in every Year, and such Meeting shall be on the first Monday in December, unless they shall by Law appoint a different Day.[3]

SECTION 5

Each House shall be the Judge of the Elections, Returns and Qualifications of its own Members, and a Majority of each shall constitute a Quorum to do Business; but a smaller Number may adjourn from day to day, and may be authorized to compel the Attendance of absent Members, in such Manner, and under such Penalties as each House may provide.

Each House may determine the Rules of its Proceedings, punish its Members for disorderly Behavior, and, with the Concurrence of two thirds, expel a Member.

Each House shall keep a Journal of its Proceedings and from time to time publish the same, excepting such Parts as may in their Judgment require Secrecy; and the Yeas and Nays of the Members of either House on any question shall, at the Desire of one fifth of those Present, be entered on the Journal.

Neither House, during the Session of Congress, shall without the Consent of the other, adjourn for more than three days, nor to any other Place than that in which the two Houses shall be sitting.

SECTION 6

The Senators and Representatives shall receive a Compensation for their Services, to be ascertained by Law, and paid out of the Treasury of the United States. They shall in all Cases, except Treason, Felony, and Breach of the peace, be privileged from Arrest during their Attendance at the Session of their respective Houses, and in going to and returning from the same; and for any Speech or Debate in either House, they shall not be questioned in any other Place.

[2] See the Seventeenth Amendment.

[3] See the Twentieth Amendment.

No Senator or Representative shall, during the Time for which he was elected, be appointed to any civil Office under the Authority of the United States, which shall have been created, or the Emoluments whereof shall have been encreased during such time; and no Person holding any Office under the United States, shall be a Member of either House during his continuance in Office.

SECTION 7

All Bills for raising Revenue shall originate in the House of Representatives; but the Senate may propose or concur with Amendments as on other Bills.

Every Bill which shall have passed the House of Representatives and the Senate, shall, before it become a Law, be presented to the President of the United States; if he approve he shall sign it, but if not he shall return it, with his Objections to that House in which it shall have originated, who shall enter the Objections at large on their Journal, and proceed to reconsider it. If after such Reconsideration two thirds of that House shall agree to pass the Bill it shall be sent, together with the Objections, to the other House, by which it shall likewise be reconsidered, and if approved by two thirds of that House, it shall become a Law. But in all such Cases the Votes of both Houses shall be determined by Yeas and Nays, and the Names of the Persons voting for and against the Bill shall be entered on the Journal of each House respectively. If any Bill shall not be returned by the President within ten Days (Sundays excepted) after it shall have been presented to him, the Same shall be a Law, in like Manner as if he had signed it, unless the Congress by their Adjournment prevent its Return, in which Case it shall not be a Law.

Every Order, Resolution, or Vote to which the Concurrence of the Senate and House of Representatives may be necessary (except on a question of Adjournment) shall be presented to the President of the United States; and before the Same shall take Effect, shall be approved by him, or being disapproved by him, shall be repassed by two thirds of the Senate and House of Representatives, according to the Rules and Limitations prescribed in the Case of a Bill.

SECTION 8

The Congress shall have Power To lay and collect Taxes, Duties, Imposts and Excises, to pay the Debts and provide for the common Defence and general Welfare of the United States; but all Duties, Imposts and Excises shall be uniform throughout the United States;

To borrow money on the Credit of the United States;

To regulate Commerce with foreign Nations, and among the several States, and with the Indian Tribes;

To establish an uniform Rule of Naturalization, and uniform Laws on the subject of Bankruptcies throughout the United States;

To coin Money, regulate the Value thereof, and of foreign Coin, and fix the Standard of Weights and Measures;

To provide for the Punishment of counterfeiting the Securities and current Coin of the United States;

To Establish Post Offices and Post Roads;

To promote the Progress of Science and useful Arts, by securing for limited Times to Authors and Inventors the exclusive Right to their respective Writings and Discoveries;

To constitute Tribunals inferior to the supreme Court;

To define and punish Piracies and Felonies committed on the high Seas, and Offenses against the Law of Nations;

To declare War, grant Letters of Marque and Reprisal, and make Rules concerning Captures on Land and Water;

To raise and support Armies, but no Appropriation of Money to that Use shall be for a longer Term than two Years;

To provide and maintain a Navy;

To make Rules for the Government and Regulation of the land and naval Forces;

To provide for calling forth the Militia to execute the Laws of the Union, suppress Insurrections and repel Invasions;

To provide for organizing, arming, and disciplining the Militia, and for governing such Part of them as may be employed in the Service of the United States, reserving to the States respectively, the Appointment of the Officers, and the Authority of training the Militia according to the discipline prescribed by Congress;

To exercise exclusive Legislation in all Cases whatsoever, over such District (not exceeding ten Miles square) as may, by Cession of particular States, and the acceptance of Congress, become the Seat of the Government of the United States, and to exercise like Authority over all Places purchased by the Consent of the Legislature of the State in which the Same shall be, for the Erection of Forts, Magazines, Arsenals, dock-Yards, and other needful Buildings;—And

To make all Laws which shall be necessary and proper for carrying into Execution the foregoing Powers, and all other Powers vested by this Constitution in the Government of the United States, or in any Department or Officer thereof.

SECTION 9

The Migration or Importation of such Persons as any of the States now existing shall think proper to admit, shall not be prohibited by the Congress prior to the Year one thousand eight hundred and eight, but a tax or duty may be imposed on such Importation, not exceeding ten dollars for each person.

The privilege of the Writ of Habeas Corpus shall not be suspended, unless when in Cases of Rebellion or Invasion the public Safety may require it.

No Bill of Attainder or ex post facto Law shall be passed.

No capitation, or other direct Tax shall be laid, unless in Proportion to the Census or Enumeration herein before directed to be taken.[4]

No Tax or Duty shall be laid on Articles exported from any State.

No Preference shall be given by any Regulation of Commerce or Revenue to the Ports of one State over those of another: nor shall Vessels bound to, or from one State, be obliged to enter, clear, or pay Duties in another.

No Money shall be drawn from the Treasury, but in Consequence of Appropriations made by Law; and a regular Statement and Account of the Receipts and Expenditures of all public Money shall be published from time to time.

No Title of Nobility shall be granted by the United States:—And no Person holding any Office of Profit or Trust under them, shall, without the Consent of the Congress, accept of any present, Emolument, Office, or Title, of any kind whatever, from any King, Prince or foreign State.

[4] See the Sixteenth Amendment.

SECTION 10

No State shall enter into any Treaty, Alliance, or Confederation; grant Letters of Marque and Reprisal; coin Money; emit Bills of Credit; make any Thing but gold and silver Coin a Tender in Payment of Debts; pass any Bill of Attainder, ex post facto Law, or Law impairing the Obligation of Contracts, or grant any Title of Nobility.

No State shall, without the Consent of the Congress, lay any Imposts or Duties on Imports or Exports, except what may be absolutely necessary for executing its inspection Laws: and the net Product of all Duties and Imposts, laid by any State on Imports or Exports, shall be for the Use of the Treasury of the United States and all such Laws shall be subject to the Revision and Controul of the Congress.

No State shall, without the Consent of Congress, lay any duty of Tonnage, keep Troops, or Ships of War in time of Peace, enter into any Agreement or Compact with another State, or with a foreign Power, or engage in War, unless actually invaded, or in such imminent Danger as will not admit of delay.

Article II

SECTION 1

The executive Power shall be vested in a President of the United States of America. He shall hold his Office during the Term of four Years, and, together with the Vice-President, chosen for the same Term, be elected, as follows.

Each State shall appoint, in such Manner as the Legislature thereof may direct, a Number of Electors, equal to the whole number of Senators and Representatives to which the State may be entitled in the Congress; but no Senator or Representative, or Person holding an Office of Trust or Profit under the United States, shall be appointed an Elector.

The Electors shall meet in their respective States, and vote by Ballot for two persons, of whom one at least shall not be an Inhabitant of the same State with themselves. And they shall make a List of all the Persons voted for, and of the Number of Votes for each; which List they shall sign and certify, and transmit sealed to the Seat of the Government of the United States, directed to the President of the Senate. The President of the Senate shall, in the Presence of the Senate and House of Representatives, open all the Certificates, and the Votes shall then be counted. The Person having the greatest Number of Votes shall be the President, if such Number be a Majority of the whole Number of Electors appointed; and if there be more than one who have such Majority, and have an Equal Number of Votes, then the House of Representatives shall immediately chuse by Ballot one of them for President; and if no Person have a Majority, then from the five highest on the List the said House shall in like Manner chuse the President, but in chusing the President, the Votes shall be taken by States, the Representation from each State having one Vote; a quorum for this Purpose shall consist of a Member or Members from two-thirds of the States, and a Majority of all the States shall be necessary to a Choice. In every Case, after the Choice of the President, the Person having the greatest Number of Votes of the Electors shall be the Vice-President. But if there should remain two or more who have equal Votes, the Senate shall chuse from them by Ballot the Vice-President.[5]

The Congress may determine the Time of chusing the Electors, and the Day on which they shall give their Vote; which Day shall be the same throughout the United States.

No person except a natural born Citizen, or a Citizen of the United States, at the time of the Adoption of this Constitution, shall be eligible to the Office of President; neither shall any Person be eligible to that Office who shall not have attained to the Age of thirty-five Years, and been fourteen Years a Resident within the United States.

In Case of the Removal of the President from Office, or of his Death, Resignation, or Inability to discharge the Powers and Duties of the said office, the same shall devolve on the Vice-President, and the Congress may by Law provide for the Case of Removal, Death, Resignation or Inability, both of the President and Vice-President, declaring what Officer shall then act as President, and such Officer shall act accordingly, until the Disability be removed, or a President shall be elected.

The President shall, at stated Times, receive for his Services, a Compensation, which shall neither be en-

---

[5] This paragraph was superseded by the Twelfth Amendment.

creased nor diminished during the Period for which he shall have been elected, and he shall not receive within that Period any other Emolument from the United States, or any of them.

Before he enters on the Execution of his Office, he shall take the following Oath or Affirmation:—"I do solemnly swear (or affirm) that I will faithfully execute the Office of President of the United States, and will to the best of my Ability, preserve, protect and defend the Constitution of the United States.''

SECTION 2

The President shall be Commander in Chief of the Army and Navy of the United States, and of the Militia of the several States, when called into the actual Service of the United States; he may require the Opinion in writing, of the principal Officer in each of the executive Departments, upon any subject relating to the Duties of their respective Offices, and he shall have Power to grant Reprieves and Pardons for Offenses against the United States, except in Cases of Impeachment.

He shall have Power, by and with the Advice and Consent of the Senate, to make Treaties, provided two-thirds of the Senators present concur; and he shall nominate, and by and with the Advice and Consent of the Senate, shall appoint Ambassadors, other public Ministers and Consuls, Judges of the supreme Court, and all other Officers of the United States, whose Appointments are not herein otherwise provided for, and which shall be established by Law: but the Congress may by Law vest the Appointment of such inferior Offices, as they think proper, in the President alone, in the Courts of Law, or in the Heads of Departments.

The President shall have Power to fill up all Vacancies that may happen during the Recess of the Senate, by granting Commissions which shall expire at the End of their next Session.

SECTION 3

He shall from time to time give to the Congress Information of the State of the Union, and recommend to their Consideration such Measures as he shall judge necessary and expedient; he may, on extraordinary Occasions, convene both Houses, or either of them, and in Cases of Disagreement between them, with Respect to the Time of Adjournment, he may adjourn them to such Time as he shall think proper; he shall receive Ambassadors and other public Ministers; he shall take Care that the Laws be faithfully executed, and shall Commission all the Officers of the United States.

SECTION 4

The President, Vice-President and all civil Officers of the United States, shall be removed from Office on Impeachment for, and Conviction of, Treason, Bribery, or other high Crimes and Misdemeanors.

Article III

SECTION 1

The judicial Power of the United States shall be vested in one supreme Court, and in such inferior Courts as the Congress may from time to time ordain and establish. The Judges, both of the supreme and inferior Courts, shall hold their offices during good Behaviour, and shall, at stated Times, receive for their Services a Compensation which shall not be diminished during their Continuance in Office.

SECTION 2

The judicial Power shall extend to all Cases, in Law and Equity, arising under this Constitution, the Laws of the United States and Treaties made, or which shall be made, under their Authority;—to all Cases affecting Ambassadors, other public Ministers and Consuls;—to all Cases of admiralty and maritime Jurisdiction;—to Controversies to which the United States shall be a Party;—to Controversies between two or more States;—between a State and Citizens of another State;[6]—Between Citizens of different States;—between Citizens of the same State claiming Lands under Grants of different States, and between a State, or the Citizens thereof, and foreign States, Citizens or Subjects.

[6] See the Eleventh Amendment.

In all Cases affecting Ambassadors, other public Ministers and Consuls, and those in which a State shall be a Party, the supreme Court shall have original Jurisdiction. In all the other Cases before mentioned, the supreme Court shall have appellate Jurisdiction, both as to Law and Fact, with such Exceptions, and under such Regulations as the Congress shall make.

The trial of all Crimes, except in Cases of Impeachment, shall be by Jury, and such Trial shall be held in the State where the said Crimes shall have been committed; but when not committed within any State, the Trial shall be at such Place or Places as the Congress may by Law have directed.

SECTION 3

Treason against the United States, shall consist only in levying War against them, or, in adhering to their Enemies, giving them Aid and Comfort. No Person shall be convicted of Treason unless on the Testimony of two Witnesses to the same overt Act, or on Confession in open Court.

The Congress shall have Power to declare the Punishment of Treason, but no Attainder of Treason shall work Corruption of Blood, or Forfeiture except during the Life of the Person attained.

Article IV

SECTION 1

Full Faith and Credit shall be given in each State to the public acts, Records, and judicial Proceedings of every other State. And the Congress may by general Laws prescribe the Manner in which such Acts, Records and Proceedings shall be proved, and the Effect thereof.

SECTION 2

The Citizens of each State shall be entitled to all Privileges and Immunities of Citizens in the several States.

A Person charged in any State with Treason, Felony, or other Crime, who shall flee from Justice, and be found in another State, shall on demand of the executive Authority of the State from which he fled, be delivered up, to be removed to the State having Jurisdiction of the Crime.

No Person held to Service or Labour in one State, under the Laws thereof, escaping into another, shall in Consequence of any Law or Regulation therein, be discharged from such Service or Labour, but shall be delivered up on Claim of the Party to whom such Service or Labour may be due.[7]

SECTION 3

New States may be admitted by the Congress into this Union; but no new States shall be formed or erected within the Jurisdiction of any other State; nor any State be formed by the Junction of two or more States, or parts of States, without the Consent of the Legislatures of the States concerned as well as of the Congress.

The Congress shall have Power to dispose of and make all needful Rules and Regulations respecting the Territory or other Property belonging to the United States; and nothing in this Constitution shall be so constructed as to Prejudice any Claims of the United States, or of any particular State.

SECTION 4

The United States shall guarantee to every State in this Union a Republican Form of Government, and shall protect each of them against Invasion; and on Application of the Legislature, or of the Executive (when the Legislature cannot be convened) against domestic Violence.

Article V

The Congress, whenever two-thirds of both Houses shall deem it necessary, shall propose Amendments to this Constitution, or, on the Application of the Legislatures of two-thirds of the several States, shall call a Convention for proposing Amendments, which, in either Case, shall be valid to all Intents and Purposes, as part of this Constitution, when ratified by the Legislatures of three-fourths of the several States, or by Conventions in three-fourths thereof, as

[7] Obsolete. See the Thirteenth Amendment.

the one or the other Mode of Ratification may be proposed by the Congress; Provided that no Amendment which may be made prior to the Year One thousand eight hundred and eight shall in any Manner affect the first and fourth Clauses in the Ninth Section of the first Article; and that no State, without its Consent, shall be deprived of its equal Suffrage in the Senate.

Article VI

All Debts contracted and Engagements entered into, before the Adoption of this Constitution, shall be as valid against the United States under this Constitution, as under the Confederation.

This Constitution, and the Laws of the United States which shall be made in Pursuance thereof; and all Treaties made, or which shall be made, under the Authority of the United States, shall be the supreme Law of the Land; and the Judges in every State shall be bound thereby, any Thing in the Constitution or Laws of any State to the Contrary notwithstanding.

The Senators and Representatives before mentioned, and the Members of the several State Legislatures, and all executive and judicial Officers, both of the United States and of the several States, shall be bound by Oath or Affirmation, to support this Constitution; but no religious Test shall ever be required as a Qualification to any Office or public Trust under the United States.

Article VII

The Ratification of the Conventions of nine States shall be sufficient for the Establishment of this Constitution between the States so ratifying the Same.

Done in Convention by the Unanimous Consent of the States Present the Seventeenth Day of September in the Year of our Lord one thousand seven hundred and eighty-seven and of the Independence of the United States of America the Twelfth. In Witness whereof We have hereunto subscribed our Names.

Geo. WASHINGTON
Presid't and Deputy from Virginia

Delaware
Geo: Read
John Dickinson
Jaco: Broom
Gunning Bedford jun
Richard Bassett

Maryland
James McHenry
Danl Carroll
Dan: of St. Thos. Jenifer

South Carolina
J. Rutledge
Charles Pinckney
Charles Cotesworth Pinckney
Pierce Butler

Georgia
William Few
Abr Baldwin

New York
Alexander Hamilton

New Jersey
Wil: Livingston
David Brearley
Wm. Paterson
Jona: Dayton

New Hampshire
John Langdon
Nicholas Gilman

Massachusetts
Nathaniel Gorham
Rufus King

Connecticut
Wm Saml Johnson
Roger Sherman

Virginia
John Blair
James Madison, Jr.

North Carolina
Wm Blount
Hu Williamson
Richd Dobbs Spaight

Pennsylvania
B. Franklin
Robt. Morris
Thos. Fitzsimons
James Wilson
Thomas Mifflin
Geo. Clymer
Jared Ingersoll
Gouv Morris

Attest:
WILLIAM JACKSON, Secretary

AMENDMENTS[8]

Amendment I

Congress shall make no law respecting an establish-ment of religion, or prohibiting the free exercise thereof; or abridging the freedom of speech, or of the press; or the right of the people peaceably to assem-ble, and to petition the Government for a redress of grievances.

[8] The first 10 Amendments were adopted in 1791.

Amendment II

A well regulated Militia, being necessary to the secur-ity of a free State, the right of the people to keep and bear Arms, shall not be infringed.

Amendment III

No Soldier shall, in time of peace be quartered in any house, without the consent of the Owner, nor in time of war, but in a manner to be prescribed by law.

Amendment IV

The right of the people to be secure in their persons, houses, papers, and effects, against unreasonable searches and seizures, shall not be violated, and no Warrants shall issue, but upon probable cause, supported by Oath or affirmation, and particularly describing the place to be searched, and the persons or things to be seized.

Amendment V

No person shall be held to answer for a capital, or otherwise infamous crime, unless on a presentment or indictment of a Grand Jury, except in cases arising in the land or naval forces, or in the Militia, when in actual service in time of War or public danger; nor shall any person be subject for the same offense to be twice put in jeopardy of life or limb, nor shall be compelled in any criminal case to be a witness against himself, nor be deprived of life, liberty, or property, without due process of law; nor shall private property be taken for public use, without just compensation.

Amendment VI

In all criminal prosecutions, the accused shall enjoy the right to a speedy and public trial, by an impartial jury of the State and district wherein the crime shall have been committed, which district shall have been previously ascertained by law, and to be informed of the nature and cause of the accusation; to be confronted with the witnesses against him; to have compulsory process for obtaining witnesses in his favor, and to have the Assistance of Counsel for his defence.

Amendment VII

In suits at common law, where the value in controversy shall exceed twenty dollars, the right of trial by jury shall be preserved, and no fact tried by jury, shall be otherwise reexamined in any Court of the United States, than according to the rules of the common law.

Amendment VIII

Excessive bail shall not be required, nor excessive fines imposed, nor cruel and unusual punishments inflicted.

Amendment IX

The enumeration in the Constitution, of certain rights shall not be construed to deny or disparage others retained by the people.

Amendment X

The powers not delegated to the United States by the Constitution, nor prohibited by it to the States, are reserved to the States respectively, or to the people.

Amendment XI[9]

The Judicial power of the United States shall not be construed to extend to any suit in law or equity, commenced or prosecuted against one of the United States by Citizens of another State, or by Citizens or Subjects of any Foreign States.

Amendment XII[10]

The Electors shall meet in their respective states and vote by ballot for President and Vice-President, one of whom, at least, shall not be an inhabitant of the same state with themselves; they shall name in their ballots the person voted for as president and in distinct ballots the person voted for as Vice-President, and they shall make distinct lists of all persons voted for as President, and all persons voted for as Vice-President, and of the number of votes for each, which lists they shall sign and certify, and transmit sealed to the seat of the government of the United States, directed to the President of the Senate;—The President of the Senate shall, in the presence of the Senate and House of Representatives, open all the certificates and the votes shall then be counted;—The person having the greatest number of votes for President, shall be the President, if such number be a majority of the whole number of Electors appointed; and if no person have such majority, then from the persons having the highest numbers not exceeding three on the list of those voted for as President, the House of Representatives shall choose immediately, by ballot, the President. But in choosing the President, the votes shall be taken by states, the representation

[9] Adopted in 1798.
[10] Adopted in 1804.

from each state having one vote; a quorum for this purpose shall consist of a member or members from two-thirds of the states, and a majority of all the states shall be necessary to a choice. And if the House of Representatives shall not choose a President whenever the right of choice shall devolve upon them, before the fourth day of March next following, then the Vice-President shall act as President, as in the case of the death or other constitutional disability of the President.—The person having the greatest number of votes as Vice-President, shall be the Vice-President, if such a number be a majority of the whole number of Electors appointed, and if no person have a majority, then from the two highest numbers on the list, the Senate shall choose the Vice-President; a quorum for the purpose shall consist of two-thirds of the whole number of Senators, and a majority of the whole number shall be necessary to a choice. But no person constitutionally ineligible to the office of President shall be eligible to that of Vice-President of the United States.

Amendment XIII[11]

SECTION 1

Neither slavery nor involuntary servitude, except as a punishment for crime whereof the party shall have been duly convicted, shall exist within the United States, or any place subject to their jurisdiction.

SECTION 2

Congress shall have power to enforce this article by appropriate legislation.

Amendment XIV[12]

SECTION 1

All persons born or naturalized in the United States and subject to the jurisdiction thereof, are citizens of the United States and of the State wherein they reside. No State shall make or enforce any law which shall abridge the privileges or immunities of citizens of the United States; nor shall any State deprive any person of life, liberty, or property, without due pro-

[11] Adopted in 1865.
[12] Adopted in 1868.

cess of law; nor deny to any person within its jurisdiction the equal protection of the laws.

SECTION 2

Representatives shall be apportioned among the several States according to their respective numbers, counting the whole number of persons in each State, excluding Indians not taxed. But when the right to vote at any election for the choice of electors for President and Vice-President of the United States, Representatives in Congress, the Executive and Judicial Officers of a State, or the members of the Legislature thereof, is denied to any of the male inhabitants of such State, being twenty-one years of age, and citizens of the United States, or in any way abridged, except for participation in rebellion, or other crime, the basis of representation therein shall be reduced in the proportion which the number of such male citizens shall bear to the whole number of male citizens twenty-one years of age in such State.

SECTION 3

No person shall be a Senator or Representative in Congress, or elector of President and Vice-President, or hold any office, civil or military, under the United States, or under any State, who, having previously taken an oath, as a member of Congress, or as an officer of the United States, or as a member of any State legislature, or as an executive or judicial officer of any State, to support the Constitution of the United States, shall have engaged in insurrection or rebellion against the same, or given aid or comfort to the enemies thereof. But Congress may by a vote of two-thirds of each House, remove such disability.

SECTION 4

The validity of the public debt of the United States, authorized by law, including debts incurred for payment of pensions and bounties for services in suppressing insurrection or rebellion, shall not be questioned. But neither the United States nor any State shall assume to pay any debt or obligation incurred in aid of insurrection or rebellion against the United States, or any claim for the loss or emancipation of any slave; but all such debts, obligations and claims shall be held illegal and void.

SECTION 5

The Congress shall have power to enforce, by appropriate legislation, the provisions of this article.

Amendment XV[13]

SECTION 1

The right of citizens of the United States to vote shall not be denied or abridged by the United States or by any State on account of race, color, or previous condition of servitude.

SECTION 2

The Congress shall have power to enforce this article by appropriate legislation.

Amendment XVI[14]

The Congress shall have power to lay and collect taxes on incomes, from whatever source derived, without apportionment among the several States, and without regard to any census or enumeration.

Amendment XVII[15]

The Senate of the United States shall be composed of two Senators from each State, elected by the people thereof, for six years, and each Senator shall have one vote. The electors in each State shall have the qualifications requisite for electors of the most numerous branch of the State legislatures.

When vacancies happen in the representation of any State in the Senate, the executive authority of such State shall issue writs of election to fill such vacancies: *Provided,* That the legislature of any State may empower the executive thereof to make temporary appointments until the people fill the vacancies by election as the legislature may direct.

This amendment shall not be so construed as to affect the election or term of any Senator chosen before it becomes valid as part of the Constitution.

Amendment XVIII[16]

SECTION 1

After one year from the ratification of this article the manufacture, sale, or transportation of intoxicating liquors within, the importation thereof into, or the exportation thereof from the United States and all territory subject to the jurisdiction thereof for beverage purposes is hereby prohibited.

SECTION 2

The Congress and the several States shall have concurrent power to enforce this article by appropriate legislation.

SECTION 3

This article shall be inoperative unless it shall have been ratified as an amendment to the Constitution by the legislatures of the several States, as provided in the Constitution, within seven years from the date of the submission hereof to the States by the Congress.

Amendment XIX[17]

The right of citizens of the United States to vote shall not be denied or abridged by the United States or by any State on account of sex.

Congress shall have power to enforce this article by appropriate legislation.

Amendment XX[18]

SECTION 1

The terms of the President and Vice-President shall end at noon on the 20th day of January, and the terms of Senators and Representatives at noon on the 3d day of January, of the years in which such terms would have ended if this article had not been ratified; and the terms of their successors shall then begin.

SECTION 2

The Congress shall assemble at least once in every year, and such meeting shall begin at noon on the 3d

[13] Adopted in 1870.
[14] Adopted in 1913.
[15] Adopted in 1913.

[16] Adopted in 1919. Repealed by the Twenty-first Amendment.
[17] Adopted in 1920.
[18] Adopted in 1933.

day of January, unless they shall by law appoint a different day.

SECTION 3

If, at the time fixed for the beginning of the term of the President, the President elect shall have died, the Vice-President elect shall become President. If a President shall not have been chosen before the time fixed for the beginning of his term, or if the President elect shall have failed to qualify, then the Vice-President elect shall act as President until a President shall have qualified; and the Congress may by law provide for the case wherein neither a President elect nor a Vice-President elect shall have qualified, declaring who shall then act as President, or the manner in which one who is to act shall be selected, and such person shall act accordingly until a President or Vice-President shall have qualified.

SECTION 4

The Congress may by law provide for the case of the death of any of the persons from whom the House of Representatives may choose a President whenever the right of choice shall have devolved upon them, and for the case of the death of any of the persons from whom the Senate may choose a Vice-President whenever the right of choice shall have devolved upon them.

SECTION 5

Sections 1 and 2 shall take effect on the 15th day of October following the ratification of this article.

SECTION 6

This article shall be inoperative unless it shall have been ratified as an amendment to the Constitution by the legislatures of three-fourths of the several States within seven years from the date of its submission.

Amendment XXI[19]

SECTION 1

The eighteenth article of amendment to the Constitution of the United States is hereby repealed.

[19] Adopted in 1933.

SECTION 2

The transportation or importation into any State, Territory, or possession of the United States for delivery or use of intoxicating liquors, in violation of the laws thereof, is hereby prohibited.

SECTION 3

This article shall be inoperative unless it shall have been ratified as an amendment to the Constitution by conventions in the several States, as provided in the Constitution, within seven years from the date of the submission hereof to the States by the Congress.

Amendment XXII[20]

SECTION 1

No person shall be elected to the office of the President more than twice, and no person who has held the office of President, or acted as President, for more than two years of a term to which some other person was elected President shall be elected to the office of President more than once. But this Article shall not apply to any person holding the office of President when this Article was proposed by the Congress, and shall not prevent any person who may be holding the office of President, or acting as President, during the term within which this Article becomes operative from holding the office of President, or acting as President during the remainder of such term.

SECTION 2

This article shall be inoperative unless it shall have been ratified as an amendment to the Constitution by the legislatures of three-fourths of the several States within seven years from the date of its submission to the States by the Congress.

Amendment XXIII[21]

SECTION 1

The District constituting the seat of Government of the United States shall appoint in such manner as the Congress may direct:

A number of electors of President and Vice-President equal to the whole number of Senators and Representatives in Congress to which the District would be entitled if it were a State, but in no event

[20] Adopted in 1951.
[21] Adopted in 1961.

more than the least populous State; they shall be in addition to those appointed by the States, but they shall be considered, for the purposes of the election of President and Vice-President, to be electors appointed by a state; and they shall meet in the District and perform such duties as provided by the twelfth article of amendment.

SECTION 2

The Congress shall have power to enforce this article by appropriate legislation.

Amendment XXIV[22]

SECTION 1

The right of citizens of the United States to vote in any primary or other election for President or Vice-President, for electors for President or Vice-President, or for Senator or Representative in Congress, shall not be denied or abridged by the United States or any State by reason of failure to pay any poll tax or other tax.

SECTION 2

The Congress shall have power to enforce this article by appropriate legislation.

Amendment XXV[23]

SECTION 1

In case of the removal of the President from office or his death or resignation, the Vice-President shall become President.

SECTION 2

Whenever there is a vacancy in the office of the Vice-President, the President shall nominate a Vice-President who shall take office upon confirmation by a majority vote of both houses of Congress.

SECTION 3

Whenever the President transmits to the President pro tempore of the Senate and the Speaker of the House of Representatives his written declaration that he is unable to discharge the powers and duties of his office, and until he transmits to them a written declaration to the contrary, such powers and duties

shall be discharged by the Vice-President as Acting President.

SECTION 4

Whenever the Vice-President and a majority of either the principal officers of the executive departments or of such other body as Congress may by law provide, transmit to the President pro tempore of the Senate and the Speaker of the House of Representatives their written declaration that the President is unable to discharge the powers and duties of his office, the Vice-President shall immediately assume the powers and duties of the office as Acting President.

Thereafter, when the President transmits to the President pro tempore of the Senate and the Speaker of the House of Representatives his written declaration that no inability exists, he shall resume the powers and duties of his office unless the Vice-President and a majority of either the principal officers of the executive department or of such other body as Congress may by law provide, transmit within four days to the President pro tempore of the Senate and the Speaker of the House of Representatives their written declaration that the President is unable to discharge the powers and duties of his office. Thereupon Congress shall decide the issue, assembling within 48 hours for that purpose if not in session. If the Congress, within 21 days after receipt of the latter written declaration, or, if Congress is not in session, within 21 days after Congress is required to assemble, determines by two-thirds vote of both houses that the President is unable to discharge the powers and duties of his office, the Vice-President shall continue to discharge the same as Acting President; otherwise, the President shall resume the powers and duties of his office.

Amendment XXVI[24]

SECTION 1

The Right of Citizens of the United States, who are eighteen years of age or older, to vote shall not be denied or abridged by the United States or any State on account of age.

SECTION 2

The Congress shall have power to enforce this article by appropriate legislation.

[22] Adopted in 1964.
[23] Adopted in 1967.

[24] Adopted in 1971.

JUSTICES OF THE SUPREME COURT: 1789–1981

1789	Jay	Rutledge, J.	Cushing	Wilson	Blair					
1790–91	Jay	Rutledge, J.	Cushing	Wilson	Blair	Iredell				
1792	Jay	Johnson, T.	Cushing	Wilson	Blair	Iredell				
1793–94	Jay	Paterson	Cushing	Wilson	Blair	Iredell				
1795	Rutledge, J.	Paterson	Cushing	Wilson	Blair	Iredell				
1796–97	Ellsworth	Paterson	Cushing	Wilson	Chase, S.	Iredell				
1798–99	Ellsworth	Paterson	Cushing	Washington	Chase, S.	Iredell				
1800	Ellsworth	Paterson	Cushing	Washington	Chase, S.	Moore				
1801–03	Marshall, J.	Paterson	Cushing	Washington	Chase, S.	Moore				
1804–05	Marshall, J.	Paterson	Cushing	Washington	Chase, S.	Johnson, W.				
1806	Marshall, J.	Livingston	Cushing	Washington	Chase, S.	Johnson, W.				
1807–10	Marshall, J.	Livingston	Cushing	Washington	Chase, S.	Johnson, W.	Todd			
1811–22	Marshall, J.	Livingston	Story	Washington	Duvall	Johnson, W.	Todd			
1823–25	Marshall, J.	Thompson	Story	Washington	Duvall	Johnson, W.	Todd			
1826–28	Marshall, J.	Thompson	Story	Washington	Duvall	Johnson, W.	Trimble			
1829	Marshall, J.	Thompson	Story	Washington	Duvall	Johnson, W.	McLean			
1830–34	Marshall, J.	Thompson	Story	Baldwin	Duvall	Johnson, W.	McLean			
1835	Marshall, J.	Thompson	Story	Baldwin	Duvall	Wayne	McLean			
1836	Taney	Thompson	Story	Baldwin	Barbour	Wayne	McLean			
1837–40	Taney	Thompson	Story	Baldwin	Barbour	Wayne	McLean	Catron	McKinley	
1841–44	Taney	Thompson	Story	Baldwin	Daniel	Wayne	McLean	Catron	McKinley	
1845	Taney	Nelson	Woodbury		Daniel	Wayne	McLean	Catron	McKinley	
1846–50	Taney	Nelson	Woodbury	Grier	Daniel	Wayne	McLean	Catron	McKinley	
1851–52	Taney	Nelson	Curtis	Grier	Daniel	Wayne	McLean	Catron	McKinley	
1853–57	Taney	Nelson	Curtis	Grier	Daniel	Wayne	McLean	Catron	Campbell	
1858–60	Taney	Nelson	Clifford	Grier	Daniel	Wayne	McLean	Catron	Campbell	
1861	Taney	Nelson	Clifford	Grier		Wayne	McLean	Catron	Campbell	
1862	Taney	Nelson	Clifford	Grier	Miller	Wayne	Swayne	Catron	Davis	
1863	Taney	Nelson	Clifford	Grier	Miller	Wayne	Swayne	Catron	Davis	Field
1864–65	Chase, S. P.	Nelson	Clifford	Grier	Miller	Wayne	Swayne	Catron	Davis	Field
1866–67	Chase, S. P.	Nelson	Clifford	Grier	Miller	Wayne	Swayne		Davis	Field
1868–69	Chase, S. P.	Nelson	Clifford	Grier	Miller		Swayne		Davis	Field
1870–71	Chase, S. P.	Nelson	Clifford	Strong	Miller	Bradley	Swayne		Davis	Field
1872–73	Chase, S. P.	Hunt	Clifford	Strong	Miller	Bradley	Swayne		Davis	Field
1874–76	Waite	Hunt	Clifford	Strong	Miller	Bradley	Swayne		Davis	Field
1877–79	Waite	Hunt	Clifford	Strong	Miller	Bradley	Swayne		Harlan	Field
1880	Waite	Hunt	Clifford	Woods	Miller	Bradley	Swayne		Harlan	Field
1881	Waite	Hunt	Clifford	Woods	Miller	Bradley	Matthews		Harlan	Field
1882–87	Waite	Blatchford	Gray	Woods	Miller	Bradley	Matthews		Harlan	Field
1888	Fuller	Blatchford	Gray	Lamar, L.	Miller	Bradley	Matthews		Harlan	Field
1889	Fuller	Blatchford	Gray	Lamar, L.	Miller	Bradley	Brewer		Harlan	Field

1890–91	Fuller	Blatchford	Gray	Lamar, L.	Brown	Bradley	Brewer	Harlan	Field
1892	Fuller	Blatchford	Gray	Lamar, L.	Brown	Shiras	Brewer	Harlan	Field
1893	Fuller	Blatchford	Gray	Jackson, H.	Brown	Shiras	Brewer	Harlan	Field
1894	Fuller	White, E.	Gray	Jackson, H.	Brown	Shiras	Brewer	Harlan	Field
1895–97	Fuller	White, E.	Gray	Peckham	Brown	Shiras	Brewer	Harlan	Field
1898–1901	Fuller	White, E.	Gray	Peckham	Brown	Shiras	Brewer	Harlan	McKenna
1902	Fuller	White, E.	Holmes	Peckham	Brown	Shiras	Brewer	Harlan	McKenna
1903–05	Fuller	White, E.	Holmes	Peckham	Brown	Day	Brewer	Harlan	McKenna
1906–08	Fuller	White, E.	Holmes	Peckham	Moody	Day	Brewer	Harlan	McKenna
1909	Fuller	White, E.	Holmes	Peckham	Moody	Day	Brewer	Harlan	McKenna
1910–11	White, E.	Van Devanter	Holmes	Lurton	Lamar, J.	Day	Hughes	Harlan	McKenna
1912–13	White, E.	Van Devanter	Holmes	Lurton	Lamar, J.	Day	Hughes	Pitney	McKenna
1914–15	White, E.	Van Devanter	Holmes	McReynolds	Lamar, J.	Day	Hughes	Pitney	McKenna
1916–20	White, E.	Van Devanter	Holmes	McReynolds	Brandeis	Day	Clarke	Pitney	McKenna
1921	Taft	Van Devanter	Holmes	McReynolds	Brandeis	Day	Clarke	Pitney	McKenna
1922	Taft	Van Devanter	Holmes	McReynolds	Brandeis	Day	Sutherland	Pitney	McKenna
1923–24	Taft	Van Devanter	Holmes	McReynolds	Brandeis	Butler	Sutherland	Sanford	McKenna
1925–29	Taft	Van Devanter	Holmes	McReynolds	Brandeis	Butler	Sutherland	Sanford	Stone
1930–31	Hughes	Van Devanter	Holmes	McReynolds	Brandeis	Butler	Sutherland	Roberts	Stone
1932–36	Hughes	Van Devanter	Cardozo	McReynolds	Brandeis	Butler	Sutherland	Roberts	Stone
1937	Hughes	Black	Cardozo	McReynolds	Brandeis	Butler	Sutherland	Roberts	Stone
1938	Hughes	Black	Cardozo	McReynolds	Brandeis	Butler	Reed	Roberts	Stone
1939	Hughes	Black	Frankfurter	McReynolds	Douglas	Butler	Reed	Roberts	Stone
1940	Hughes	Black	Frankfurter	McReynolds	Douglas	Murphy	Reed	Roberts	Stone
1941–42	Stone	Black	Frankfurter	Byrnes	Douglas	Murphy	Reed	Roberts	Jackson, R.
1943–44	Stone	Black	Frankfurter	Rutledge, W.	Douglas	Murphy	Reed	Roberts	Jackson, R.
1945	Stone	Black	Frankfurter	Rutledge, W.	Douglas	Murphy	Reed	Burton	Jackson, R.
1946–48	Vinson	Black	Frankfurter	Rutledge, W.	Douglas	Murphy	Reed	Burton	Jackson, R.
1949–52	Vinson	Black	Frankfurter	Minton	Douglas	Clark	Reed	Burton	Jackson, R.
1953–54	Warren	Black	Frankfurter	Minton	Douglas	Clark	Reed	Burton	Jackson, R.
1955	Warren	Black	Frankfurter	Minton	Douglas	Clark	Reed	Burton	Harlan
1956	Warren	Black	Frankfurter	Brennan	Douglas	Clark	Reed	Burton	Harlan
1957	Warren	Black	Frankfurter	Brennan	Douglas	Clark	Whittaker	Burton	Harlan
1958–61	Warren	Black	Frankfurter	Brennan	Douglas	Clark	Whittaker	Stewart	Harlan
1962–65	Warren	Black	Goldberg	Brennan	Douglas	Clark	White, B.	Stewart	Harlan
1965–67	Warren	Black	Fortas	Brennan	Douglas	Clark	White, B.	Stewart	Harlan
1967–69	Warren	Black	Fortas	Brennan	Douglas	Marshall, T.	White, B.	Stewart	Harlan
1969	Burger	Black	Fortas	Brennan	Douglas	Marshall, T.	White, B.	Stewart	Harlan
1969–70	Burger	Black	Blackmun	Brennan	Douglas	Marshall, T.	White, B.	Stewart	Harlan
1970–71	Burger	Black	Blackmun	Brennan	Douglas	Marshall, T.	White, B.	Stewart	Harlan
1971–75	Burger	Powell	Blackmun	Brennan	Douglas	Marshall, T.	White, B.	Stewart	Rehnquist
1975–81	Burger	Powell	Blackmun	Brennan	Stevens	Marshall, T.	White, B.	Stewart	Rehnquist
1981–	Burger	Powell	Blackmun	Brennan	Stevens	Marshall, T.	White, B.	O'Connor	Rehnquist

Index of Cases *

* Boldface type indicates opinions included in this volume. Lightface italic type is used for case citations in the essays.